11. Format for Bank Reconciliation:

Cash balance according to bank statement .... $xxx
Add: Additions by depositor not on bank
       statement .... $xx
       Bank errors xx   xx
                                       $xxx

Deduct: Deductions by depositor not on bank
       statement .... $xx
       Bank errors xx   xx
Adjusted balance .... $xxx

Cash balance according to depositor's records .... $xxx
Add: Additions by bank not recorded by depositor.. $xx
       Depositor errors................................... xx   xx
                                         $xxx

Deduct: Deductions by bank not recorded
       by depositor .... $xx
       Depositor errors................................... xx   xx
Adjusted balance .... $xxx

12. Inventory Costing Methods:

1. First-in, First-out (fifo)
2. Last-in, First-out (lifo)
3. Average Cost

13. Interest Computations:

Interest = Face Amount (or Principal) × Rate × Time

14. Methods of Determining Annual Depreciation:

STRAIGHT-LINE: $\dfrac{\text{Cost} - \text{Estimated Residual Value}}{\text{Estimated Life}}$

DECLINING-BALANCE: Rate* × Book Value at Beginning of Period

*Rate is commonly twice the straight-line rate (1 ÷ Estimated Life).

15. Cash Provided by Operations on Statement of Cash Flows (indirect method):

Net income, per income statement .... $xx
Add: Depreciation of fixed assets .... $xx
       Amortization of bond payable discount
       and intangible assets xx
       Decreases in current assets (receivables,
       inventories, prepaid expenses)................. xx
       Increases in current liabilities (accounts
       and notes payable, accrued liabilities) xx
       Losses on disposal of assets and retirement
       of debt xx   xx
Deduct: Amortization of bond payable premium...... $xx
       Increases in current assets (receivables,
       inventories, prepaid expenses)................. xx
       Decreases in current liabilities (accounts
       and notes payable, accrued liabilities) xx
       Gains on disposal of assets and retirement
       of debt xx   xx
Net cash flow from operating activities.................... $xx

16. Contribution Margin Ratio $= \dfrac{\text{Sales} - \text{Variable Costs}}{\text{Sales}}$

17. Break-Even Sales (Units) $= \dfrac{\text{Fixed Costs}}{\text{Unit Contribution Margin}}$

18. Sales (Units) $= \dfrac{\text{Fixed Costs} + \text{Target Profit}}{\text{Unit Contribution Margin}}$

19. Margin of Safety $= \dfrac{\text{Sales} - \text{Sales at Break-Even Point}}{\text{Sales}}$

20. Operating Leverage $= \dfrac{\text{Contribution Margin}}{\text{Income from Operations}}$

21. Variances

$\dfrac{\text{Direct Materials}}{\text{Price Variance}} = \dfrac{\text{Actual Price per Unit} -}{\text{Standard Price}} \times \dfrac{\text{Actual Quantity}}{\text{Used}}$

$\dfrac{\text{Direct Materials}}{\text{Quantity Variance}} = \dfrac{\text{Actual Quantity Used} -}{\text{Standard Quantity}} \times \dfrac{\text{Standard Price}}{\text{per Unit}}$

$\dfrac{\text{Direct Labor}}{\text{Rate Variance}} = \dfrac{\text{Actual Rate per Hour} -}{\text{Standard Rate}} \times \dfrac{\text{Actual Hours}}{\text{Worked}}$

$\dfrac{\text{Direct Labor}}{\text{Time Variance}} = \dfrac{\text{Actual Hours Worked} -}{\text{Standard Hours}} \times \dfrac{\text{Standard Rate}}{\text{per Hour}}$

$\dfrac{\text{Variable Factory}}{\text{Overhead Controllable}} = \dfrac{\text{Actual}}{\text{Factory}} - \dfrac{\text{Budgeted Factory}}{\text{Overhead for}}$
Variance   Overhead   Amount Produced

$\dfrac{\text{Fixed Factory}}{\text{Overhead Volume}} = \dfrac{\text{Budgeted Factory}}{\text{Overhead for}} - \dfrac{\text{Applied}}{\text{Factory}}$
Variance   Amount Produced   Overhead

22. Rate of Return on Investment (ROI) $= \dfrac{\text{Income from Operations}}{\text{Invested Assets}}$

Alternative ROI Computation:

$\text{ROI} = \dfrac{\text{Income from Operations}}{\text{Sales}} \times \dfrac{\text{Sales}}{\text{Invested Assets}}$

23. Capital Investment Analysis Methods:

1. Methods That Ignore Present Values:
   A. Average Rate of Return Method
   B. Cash Payback Method
2. Methods That Use Present Values:
   A. Net Present Value Method
   B. Internal Rate of Return Method

24. Average Rate of Return $= \dfrac{\text{Estimated Average Annual Income}}{\text{Average Investment}}$

25. Present Value Index $= \dfrac{\text{Total Present Value of Net Cash Flow}}{\text{Amount to Be Invested}}$

26. Present Value Factor for an Annuity of \$1 $= \dfrac{\text{Amount to Be Invested}}{\text{Equal Annual Net Cash Flows}}$

FINANCIAL & MANAGERIAL ACCOUNTING 8e

CARL S. WARREN
Professor Emeritus of Accounting
University of Georgia, Athens

JAMES M. REEVE
Professor of Accounting
University of Tennessee, Knoxville

PHILIP E. FESS
Professor Emeritus of Accounting
University of Illinois, Champaign-Urbana

THOMSON
SOUTH-WESTERN

Australia · Canada · Mexico · Singapore · Spain · United Kingdom · United States

THOMSON

SOUTH-WESTERN

Financial & Managerial Accounting 8e

Carl S. Warren, James M. Reeve, Philip E. Fess

VP/Editorial Director:
Jack W. Calhoun

VP/Editor-in-Chief:
George Werthman

Publisher:
Rob Dewey

Executive Editor:
Sharon Oblinger

Sr. Developmental Editor:
Ken Martin

Marketing Manager:
Keith Chassé

Sr. Production Editor:
Deanna Quinn

Media Technology Editor:
Jim Rice

Media Developmental Editor:
Sally Nieman

Media Production Editors:
Robin Browning, Kelly Reid

Manufacturing Coordinator:
Doug Wilke

Production House:
Litten Editing and Production, Inc.

Compositor:
GGS Information Services, Inc.

Printer:
Quebecor World
Versailles, KY

Sr. Design Project Manager:
Michael H. Stratton

Internal and Cover Designer:
Michael H. Stratton

Cover Illustration:
Matsu

Preface Designer:
Kathy Heming

Photography Manager:
Deanna Ettinger

Photo Researcher:
Terri Miller

For permission to use material from this
text or product, submit a request online at
http://www.thomsonrights.com.

For more information
contact South-Western,
5191 Natorp Boulevard,
Mason, Ohio 45040.
Or you can visit our Internet site at:
http://www.swlearning.com

Library of Congress
Control Number:
2003115981

Carl S. Warren

Dr. Carl S. Warren is Professor Emeritus of Accounting at the University of Georgia, Athens. He has also taught at the University of Iowa, Michigan State University, and the University of Chicago. He received his doctorate degree (Ph.D.) from Michigan State University and his undergraduate (B.B.A.) and masters (M.A.) degrees from the University of Iowa. Dr. Warren's primary teaching focus is on principles of accounting and auditing. He enjoys interacting and learning from colleagues on how to improve student learning and understanding of accounting. His outside interests include writing short stories, novels, oil painting, handball, golf, skiing, backpacking, and fly-fishing.

James M. Reeve

Dr. James M. Reeve is the William and Sara Clark Professor of Accounting and Business at the University of Tennessee, Knoxville. He teaches and coordinates the Principles of Accounting course at the University of Tennessee. Dr. Reeve received his Ph.D. from Oklahoma State University in 1980. In addition to his teaching experience, he brings to this text a wealth of experience consulting on managerial accounting issues with numerous companies, including Procter & Gamble, Hershey Foods, Coca-Cola, Sony, and Boeing. Dr. Reeve's interests outside the classroom and business world revolve around reading and issues of faith.

Philip E. Fess—40 Years Of Contributions

The 21st edition marks the 40th year of Phil Fess' contribution to this family of texts. Phil first co-authored the 9th edition of Accounting Principles with Rollie Niswonger, his mentor when he was a student at Miami University. Phil and Rollie worked closely together on six editions as they continued to improve accounting education through listening carefully to users of the texts and authoring thoughtfully. During his tenure as the Arthur Andersen & Co. Alumni Professor of Accountancy at the University of Illinois, Champaign-Urbana, Phil's creativity, innovative ideas, and clear, concise writing style enabled *Accounting* to retain its position as the leading accounting principles textbook of all time. This new edition still reflects Phil's attention to detail and his unique ability to make textbooks user-friendly. Phil's continuing legacy is the millions of students who, through using the texts, have gained a strong understanding of and appreciation for accounting and its usefulness.

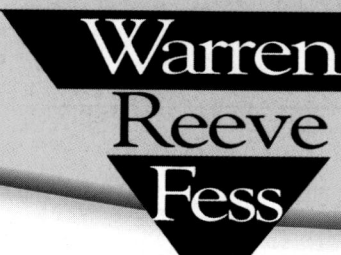

Warren Reeve Fess

Prepare for Tomorrow Today

Even as the undisputed leaders in accounting textbook innovation, we faced a daunting challenge with the 8th edition. Yet once again, we are proud to present the world's best tool for teaching accounting, designed and engineered based on the solid foundation of our past success.

Financial & Managerial Accounting, 8e presents, as always, the most comprehensive content in the market with strikingly clear organization and breakthrough pedagogy. Together with this solid textbook foundation, our leading-edge technology will guide your students toward success in the business world yet to unfold.

We invite you to experience this superior package of text and technology and see how well they perform together.

Tomorrow
takes the WHEEL

Having reached more than 11.5 million students, it would be easy for one of the most widely used textbooks for accounting principles to coast on the momentum of its success. But being number one doesn't come from just coasting. It comes from continuing our long history of innovation with the 8th edition.

To our many colleagues who contributed their valuable assistance, we extend our gratitude. As users of the 7th edition, they shared their personal insights by providing classroom feedback, participating in focus groups, and filling out questionnaires. In addition, dozens of distinguished reviewers have kept us on track during the revision of this edition. We took all comments very seriously, and *Financial & Managerial Accounting, 8e* is more robust than its predecessors because of the wide variety of advice we've incorporated.

Financial & Managerial Accounting, 8e will remain the text of choice for other reasons as well. The companies we profile in the text have grown and changed over time, and so has our coverage of them. We've integrated our work with some of the most powerful and effective technology on the market today. A long list of distinguished authors, editors, and reviewers has guided *Financial & Managerial Accounting* through the better part of the past quarter century. We are proud to take our part in the evolution of this great tradition.

Back in 1929, author James McKinsey could not have imagined the success and influence this family of texts has enjoyed or that his original vision would remain intact. As the current authors, we appreciate the responsibility of protecting this vision, while continuing to refine it to meet the changing needs of students and instructors. We sincerely thank our many colleagues who have helped to make it happen.

Carl S. Warren

James M. Reeve

Philip E. Fess

> **"T**he teaching of accounting is no longer designed to train professional accountants only. With the growing complexity of business and the constantly increasing difficulty of the problems of management, it has become essential that everyone who aspires to a position of responsibility should have a knowledge of the fundamental principles of accounting.**"**
>
> **— James O. McKinsey, Author, first edition, 1929**

CCOUNTING POWERED BY

Based squarely on the success of yesterday, *Financial & Managerial Accounting, 8e* boldly leads the way into the accounting challenges of tomorrow with innovative learning systems that bring accounting principles and practices to life. Reflecting more realistically than ever the way business operates today, this edition integrates learning options designed to extend the classroom beyond its walls into the unlimited world of the Internet.

You are the best judge of which supplements will best suit your class. For this reason, we've engineered the following content-rich and pedagogically sound course-management technologies so that you can tailor them to meet the needs of your curriculum or a particular class.

These breakthrough technologies serve two important purposes: First, they help make sure your students receive the pedagogical benefits that come with completing homework assignments. Second, they give you more time to devote to other classroom activities.

WebTutor™ Advantage on WebCT™ with Personal Trainer 3.0
WebTutor™ Advantage on Blackboard™ with Personal Trainer 3.0

WebTutor Advantage provides you with the most robust and pedagogically advanced content for either the WebCT or Blackboard course management platform. Now you can enliven your course with interactive reinforcement for students as well as powerful instructor tools. With this newest version, the students' content comprehension is assessed after which they are referred to specific content features in WebTutor Advantage or the text to address areas in which they need additional help. Elements of WebTutor Advantage include:

NEW Video Cases
Students get a taste of accounting in action by viewing these lively two- to five-minute segments. Each video covers a key accounting concept as it is played out in a real-world company or situation. Accompanying pedagogy includes a summary of each video, a short description about what the student should look for when watching, and some suggested critical-thinking questions for them to answer at the end.

Chapter Introductory Videos
Students begin each chapter with a brief but engaging Flash introduction to the chapter objectives.

TOMORROW'S TECHNOLOGY

e-Lectures

Because reinforcement is essential to concept retention, each chapter includes two or three Flash presentations that review the chapter's major topics. The presentations are in a visual lecture format with audio that covers one or two key chapter concepts.

Illustrative Problems

These step-by-step Flash presentations review the Illustrative Problems and their solutions from each chapter.

Accounting Cycle Review

With this tool, students get a firm grasp on the key concepts of the accounting cycle by applying what they've learned to realistic situations and problems. Found only in Chapter 4.

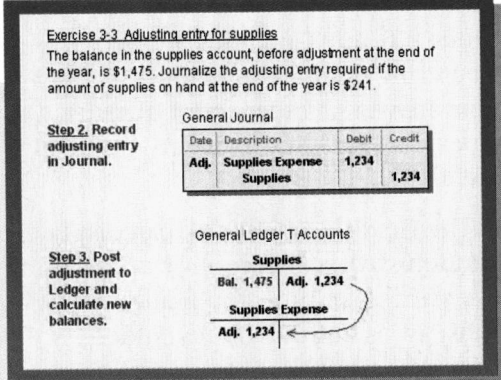

NEW Exercise Demos

These demos allow students to review explanations of two to three representative exercises from each chapter in a step-by-step visual format with audio.

Quizzes

Students make great strides with continuous reinforcement. Now they can select from a variety of intriguing options:

- **RE-ACT Quiz** Ten to fifteen multiple-choice and true-false questions cover key concepts in the chapter. Students are directed to specific resources for additional study related to their incorrect answers.

- **Achievement Tests** Similar to those found in the test bank, these tests provide additional opportunities for students to study and quiz themselves in multiple choice, true-false, and matching test formats.

- **Multiple-Choice, True-False, and Matching Quizzes** These quizzes are comprised of the questions provided in the study guide. Using WebTutor Advantage, students can answer them, have them graded, and submit the results directly to their instructor.

QuizBowl

Popular with students, this engaging game allows them to review key accounting concepts.

Crossword Puzzles

This captivating and rewarding option encourages students to go over key chapter terms.

Spanish Dictionary

This timely resource defines common accounting terms in Spanish.

ACCOUNTING POWERED BY

Personal Trainer 3.0

Specifically designed to ease the time-consuming task of grading homework, Personal Trainer lets students complete their assigned homework from the text or practice on unassigned homework online. The results are instantaneously entered into a gradebook.

With annotated spreadsheets and full-blown gradebook functionality, the greatly enhanced Personal Trainer 3.0 provides an unprecedented real-time, guided, self-correcting, learning reinforcement system outside the classroom. Use this resource as an integrated solution for your distance learning or traditional course.

- **Enhanced Questions** Personal Trainer 3.0 now includes all exercises and problems. Students can get help entering their answers in the proper format and run a spell check on their answers. On selected questions, they can call up additional, similar questions for extra practice. Optional algorithmic questions will also be included.

- **Enhanced Instructor Capabilities** The flexible gradebook can display and download any combination of student work, chapters, or activities. Capture grades on demand or set a particular time for grades to be automatically captured. Tag questions as "required" or "excluded," so students can only access the questions you want them to complete.

- **Enhanced Hints** Students can get up to three hints per activity. These hints can be PowerPoint slides, video clips, images, and more. And instructors can add a hint of their own!

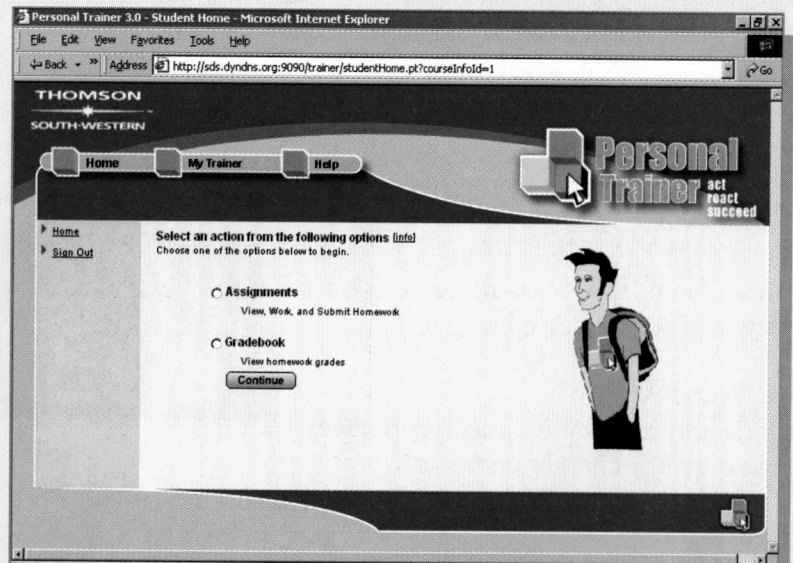

- **Enhanced Look-and-Feel** Fast, reliable, dependable, and even easier to use, Personal Trainer 3.0 sports a fresh, new graphic design.

Personal Trainer is included in WebTutor Advantage, or it can be purchased separately online.

TOMORROW'S TECHNOLOGY

Xtra!

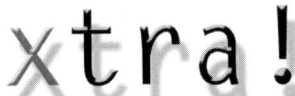

Available as an optional, free bundle with every new textbook, Xtra! gives students FREE access to the following online learning tools:

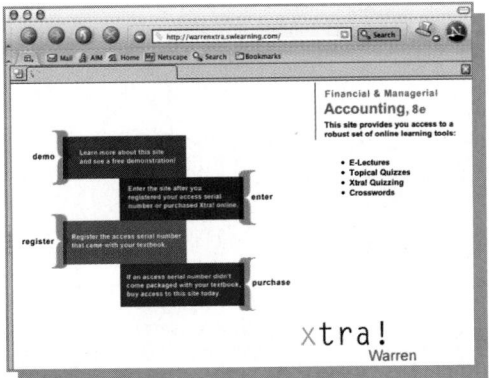

- **e-Lectures** Brief e-Lectures review more difficult concepts from the chapter.

- **Topical Quizzes** Quizzes measure a student's "test readiness" on the concepts in the chapter.

- **Multiple Choice Quizzes** Additional quizzes help students review chapter concepts and prepare for exams. Feedback on their answers gives page references so they know where to look up the questions they've missed!

- **Crosswords** The Crossword Puzzles are a fun way students can review their understanding of key terms and concepts.

P.A.S.S.

Our best-selling computerized accounting software, by Dale Klooster and Warren Allen, **P**ower **A**ccounting **S**ystem **S**oftware *(formerly General Ledger Software)* shows students the effects that accounting entries have on financial statements. Solving end-of-chapter problems, the continuing problem, comprehensive problems, and practice sets with P.A.S.S. helps make learning relevant and interesting.

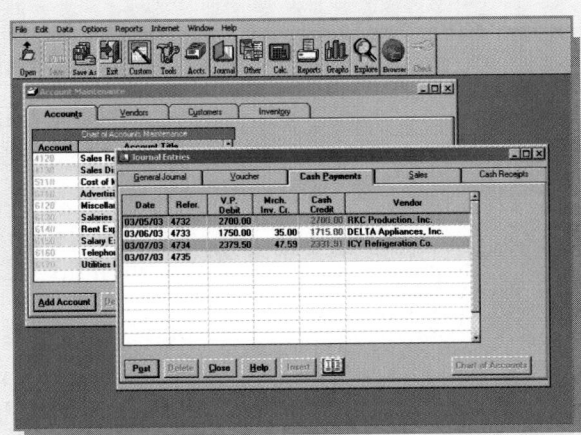

- **Problem Checker** This feature enables students to see if their entries are correct.

- **Real Business Forms** This feature provides students with experience creating invoices and doing payroll.

- **Charts, Graphs, and Ratios** Allows students to analyze financial data, including expense distribution, top customers, sales, budgets, most profitable items, and relevant ratios.

Each problem that can be completed with P.A.S.S. is marked with this icon in the text.

P.A.S.S.

FREE WEB SITE

Product Support Web Site — http://warren.swlearning.com

The Warren/Reeve/Fess Web site provides a variety of free instructor and student resources. There you'll find text-specific content and other related resources organized by chapter and topic.

The free Product Support Web site includes the highly stimulating Interactive Study Center, which provides students with a wide variety of materials for extra studying and review.

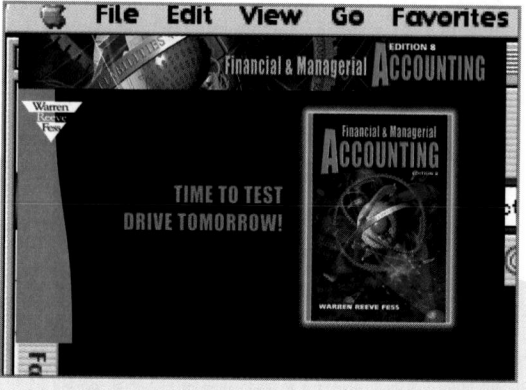

- **Key Points** All key points are pulled from the end of each chapter in the text so that students can review them online.

- **e-Lectures** Because reinforcement is essential to concept retention, each chapter includes a Flash presentation that reviews each chapter's major topics.

- **Review Problem** The Illustrative Problems found in each chapter are presented in a step-by-step fashion, helping students understand how the solutions to each were reached.

- **FAQs** Students can review these Frequently Asked Questions in accounting and learn more about many of the key topics in each chapter.

- **Internet Applications** These activities from the text allow students to apply chapter concepts and improve their online research skills.

- **Quizzes** Interactive quizzes in both True-False and Multiple Choice formats provide students with immediate feedback after they submit their answers.

Instructor Resources available to download from the secure instructor's area include the Instructor's Manual, Solutions Manual, PowerPoint Presentations, Spreadsheet Template Solutions, Instructor's Guide to Online Resources, and Technology Demos.

UNIQUE CONTINUING PROBLEM

Dancin Music Continuing Problem

Here's a great opportunity for students to practice what they've learned as they study each step of the accounting cycle. Dancin' Music, an imaginary and entrepreneurial company, provides a contemporary example of keen interest to students. As they follow Dancin' Music, they examine its transactions and see the effect of those transactions on its financial statements. They can use the P.A.S.S. software with this problem as well.

In **Chapter 1**, students **analyze the effects of Dancin Music's first month's transactions on the accounting equation.**

In **Chapter 2**, students **review debits and credits** by journalizing Dancin Music's second month's transactions.

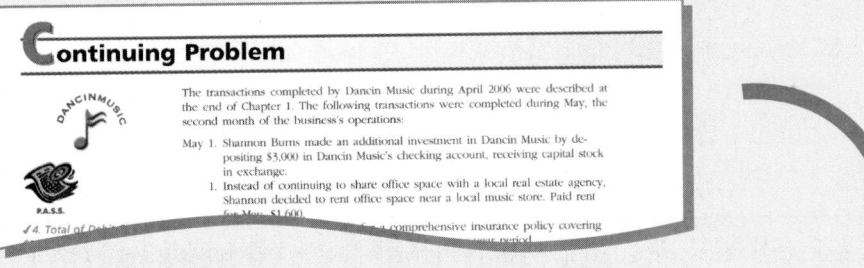

In **Chapter 3**, students **review the adjusting process** for Dancin Music.

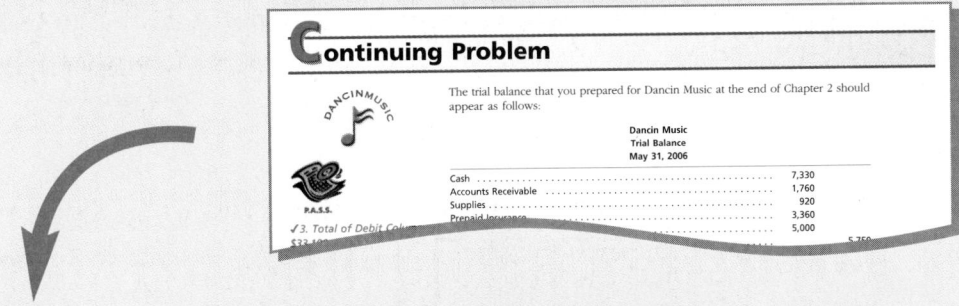

In **Chapter 4**, building on what they've learned in Chapters 1, 2, and 3, students **complete the accounting cycle** for Dancin Music, including **preparing the financial statements**.

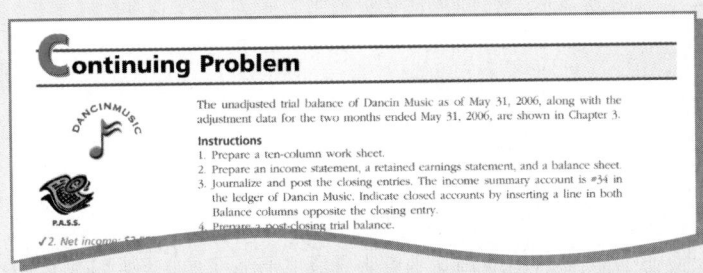

ENHANCEMENTS TO

Financial & Managerial Accounting, 8e speaks to anyone in an introductory accounting course, because 80% of those students will not be accounting majors. For this reason, *Financial & Managerial Accounting, 8e* concentrates intentionally on the business of business—how accounting contributes to effective management while emphasizing the most important accounting procedures.

Chapter 1

Opens with a section that defines "business" and describes common types of businesses and their strategies, value chains, and stakeholders. It also includes a section on business ethics.

Chapter 1 – Introduction to Accounting and Business

Chapter 2 – Analyzing Transactions

Chapter 4

Begins with a discussion of the accounting cycle. Then it introduces the worksheet as an optional tool for collecting accounting data from a company's records. Some of the end-of-chapter materials identify the worksheet as an optional requirement.

Chapter 3 – The Matching Concept and the Adjusting Process

Chapter 4 – Completing the Accounting Cycle

Chapter 5

Introduces merchandising with an income statement that shows the effects of purchases on the cost of goods sold. Sales transactions are illustrated next, followed by purchases transactions and the special topics of transportation costs, sales taxes, and trade discounts.

Chapter 5 – Accounting for Merchandising Businesses

Chapter 6 – Accounting Systems, Internal Controls, and Cash

Chapter 8

Introduces the concept of inventory cost flows without reference to the perpetual or periodic systems. The journal entries in a perpetual system are presented alongside the inventory subsidiary ledger to illustrate the FIFO and LIFO flow of costs.

Chapter 7 – Receivables

Chapter 8 – Inventories

Chapter 9

Includes a discussion of classifying the costs of fixed assets and accounting for donated assets. It continues with sections on stages of acquiring fixed assets and the impairment of goodwill.

Chapter 9 – Fixed Assets and Intangible Assets

Chapter 10
Includes a section on reporting the current portion of long-term debt and an expanded discussion of 401K plans.

Chapter 11
Discusses organization costs as expenses. The chapter also includes a comprehensive illustration of reporting stockholders' equity.

Chapter 12
Includes the reporting of fixed asset impairments and restructuring charges. The section on comprehensive income examines a statement of comprehensive income and an illustration of reporting accumulated other comprehensive income in the stockholders' equity section of the balance sheet.

Chapter 17
An appendix at the end of the chapter describes and illustrates the average cost method in a process costing system.

Chapter 21
Includes a new section on the computation of factory overhead variances as they relate to the factory overhead account.

FOCUS ON SKILLS

Critical Thinking and Analysis

As you'd expect from the leader in pedagogical innovation, the colorful and dynamic *Financial & Managerial Accounting, 8e* text visually highlights conceptual segments designed to help students make the connection between accounting and business. In addition, new box features found in each chapter make the content come to life.

- **Financial Analysis and Interpretation** To help students understand the information in financial statements and how that information is used, this feature describes an important element of financial analysis at the end of each financial chapter.

- **Special Activities** Students need to develop analytical abilities, not just memorize rules. These end-of-chapter activities focus on understanding and solving pertinent business and ethical issues. Some are presented as conversations in which students can "observe" and "participate" when they respond to the issue being discussed.

WHAT DO YOU THINK?

- **"What Do You Think?"** These exercises and activities encourage students to speculate about the real-world effects of newly learned material.

WHAT'S WRONG WITH THIS?

- **"What's Wrong With This?"** These innovative exercises challenge students to analyze and discover problems or errors in a financial statement, report, or management decision.

INTERNET

- **Technology-Assisted Learning System** Combined with WebTutor Advantage elements such as illustrative problems, quizzes, and Accounting Cycle Review, students continue to hone and reinforce their critical-thinking skills.

Use of Technology

Internet Activities
These activities acquaint students with the ever-expanding accounting-related areas of the Web.

Web References
Real World Notes and end-of-chapter activities encourage students to engage in real business research.

Technology-Assisted Learning
Teaching and learning solutions are provided in an interactive learning environment. The learning system consists of three elements: WebTutor™ Advantage (on WebCT™ and Blackboard®), Personal Trainer 3.0, and the product Web site.

FOR TOMORROW'S SUCCESS

Real World Applications

NEW Who Am I?

Presenting a set of intriguing clues about a real company, from The Motley Fool®, this intriguing feature challenges students to identify the company. They can check their decision against the answer provided later in the chapter.

I have 30,000 restaurants in 121 countries, with about 13,000 in the United States. I serve more than 45 million people each day and employ 1.5 million. Moscow's Pushkin Square sports one of my busiest stores. Fortune Magazine named me No. 1 for social responsibility. I'm busy cutting fat from my offerings. I use more than three million pounds of potatoes per day. My New Tastes Menu is Made for You. My spokesman's shoes are size 14½ and he helps sick kids. More

NEW Integrity in Business

Real-life business situations provide students with an opportunity to consider ethical issues that they may encounter in the business world.

---

10   Chapter 1 • Introduction to Accounting and Business

INTEGRITY IN BUSINESS

DOING THE RIGHT THING

Time Magazine named three women as "Persons of the Year 2002." Each of these not-so-ordinary women had the courage, determination, and integrity to do the right thing. Each risked their personal careers to expose shortcomings in their organizations. Sherron Watkins, an Enron vice-president, wrote a letter to Enron's chairman, Kenneth Lay... countant, informed **WorldCom**'s Board of Directors of phony accounting that allowed WorldCom to cover up over $3 billion in losses and forced WorldCom into bankruptcy. Coleen Rowley, an FBI staff attorney, wrote a memo to FBI Director Robert Mueller, exposing how the Bureau brushed off her pleas to investigate Zacarias Moussaoui, who was indicted as a co-conspirator in the...

NEW Spotlight on Strategy boxes

These stimulating, real-business scenarios introduce students to the effects and importance of strategic thinking and its impact on accounting.

SPOTLIGHT ON STRATEGY

WHAT'S NEXT FOR AMAZON?

Amazon.com built its online business strategy on offering books at significant discounts that traditional chains couldn't match. Over the years, Amazon has expanded its online offerings to include DVDs, toys, electronics, and even kitchen appliances. But can its low-cost, discount strategy continue to work across a variety of products? Some have their doubts. The electronics business has lower margins and more competition than books. For example, **Dell Computers** is also... tive of their prices and have refused to make Amazon.com an authorized dealer. As Lauren Levitan, a noted financial analyst, recently said, "It's hard to be the low-cost retailer. You have to execute flawlessly on a very consistent basis. Most people who try a low-price strategy fail." This risk of failing at the low-cost strategy was validated by **Kmart**'s filing for bankruptcy protection in 2002 because of its inability to compete with **Wal-Mart**'s low prices.

Source: "A Profitable Amazon Looks to Do an Encore..."

FINANCIAL REPORTING AND DISCLOSURE

UNEARNED REVENUE

Microsoft Corporation develops, manufactures, licenses, and supports a wide range of computer software products, including Windows XP®, Windows NT®, Word®, Excel®, and the Xbox®. When Microsoft sells its products, it incurs an obligation to support its software with technical support and periodic updates. As a result, not all the revenue from selling software is earned on the date of sale. Instead, some of the revenue is unearned. That is, the portion of... passes and the support services are provided to customers. Thus, it is necessary to make an adjusting entry each year to transfer unearned revenue to revenue.

The excerpts below from Microsoft's 2002 financial statements describe its accounting for unearned revenue. Microsoft further indicated that, of the $7,743 million of unearned revenue at June 30, 2002, it expected to recognize $5,917 million during the next year and $1,826 million in future years.

NEW Financial Reporting and Disclosure or Managerial Disclosure and Analysis

These boxes that feature actual companies take students through the rigors of the reporting and analysis skills they will need in business.

Real World Notes

With these notes, students get a close-up look at how accounting operates in the marketplace. The following companies are among those highlighted in the margin of the text.

- AT&T
- Campbell Soup Co.
- Mercedes-Benz
- UPS
- Gillette
- Coca-Cola Enterprises Inc.

- J.C. Penney Co.
- Hewlett Packard
- Delta Air Lines
- General Electric
- Ford Motor Co.

REAL WORLD

Sears, Roebuck and Co. sells extended warranty contracts with terms between 12 and 36 months. The receipts from sales of these contracts are reported as unearned revenue (deferred revenue) on Sears' balance sheet. Revenue is recorded as the contracts expire.

FOCUS ON SKILLS

Points of Interest
These attention-getting margin notes offer insight into subjects of high interest to students, such as careers and current events, which helps keep accounting concepts relevant.

POINT OF INTEREST

The tuition you pay at the beginning of each term is an example of a deferred expense to you, as a student.

Real World Exercises
Selected exercises and most special activities are based on real-world data to provide students with practice in working with real company data.

Understand and Review

Questions & Answers
Students check whether they understand what they've just read, using these activities in the margin of the text.

If NetSolutions' adjustment for unearned rent had incorrectly been made for $180 instead of $120, what would have been the effect on the financial statements?

Revenues would have been over-

Assume that you have been hired by a pizza restaurant to deliver pizzas, using your own car. You will be paid $6.00 per hour plus $0.30 per mile plus tips. What is the best way for you to determine how many miles you have driven each day in delivering pizzas?

One method would be to record the odometer mileage before work and then at quitting time. The difference would be the miles driven. For example, if the odometer read 56,743 at the start of work and 56,889 at the end of work, you would have driven 146 miles. This method is subject to error, however, if you copy down the wrong reading or make a math error.

In the sam   ed information about the status of the busi
                                    eful for analyzing the

Relevant Chapter Openers
The beginning of each chapter connects the student's own experiences to the chapter's topic. This tangible link is a great motivator.

New Design
A lively, colorful, and interesting design invites students to read the text. Colorful, clear, and relevant infographics help clarify difficult concepts in a visual presentation.

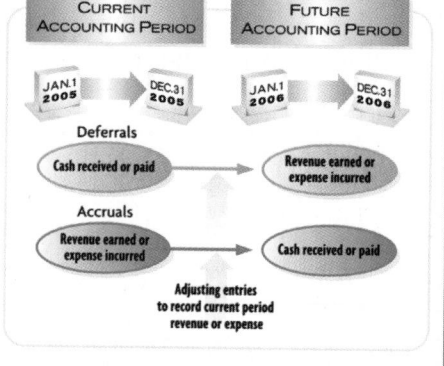

•**Exhibit 1** Deferrals and Accruals

FOR TOMORROW'S SUCCESS

Continuing Case Study

A fictitious dot.com company, NetSolutions, is followed throughout Chapters 1–5 as the example company to demonstrate a variety of transactions.

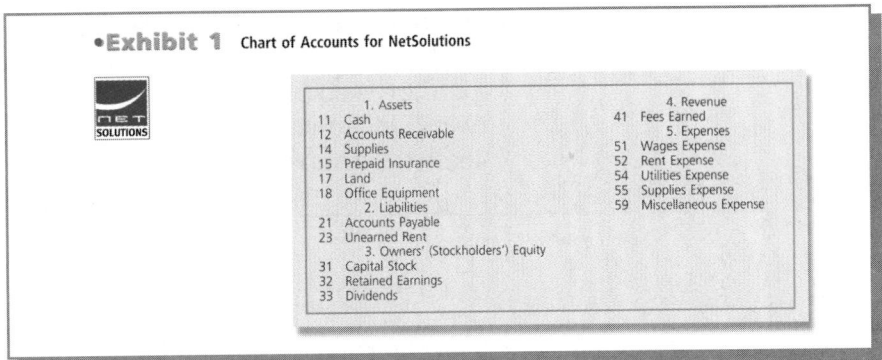

•**Exhibit 1** Chart of Accounts for NetSolutions

	1. Assets		4. Revenue
11	Cash	41	Fees Earned
12	Accounts Receivable		5. Expenses
14	Supplies	51	Wages Expense
15	Prepaid Insurance	52	Rent Expense
17	Land	54	Utilities Expense
18	Office Equipment	55	Supplies Expense
	2. Liabilities	59	Miscellaneous Expense
21	Accounts Payable		
23	Unearned Rent		
	3. Owners' (Stockholders') Equity		
31	Capital Stock		
32	Retained Earnings		
33	Dividends		

20	Miscellaneous Expense	2 7 5 00		20
21	Cash		3 6 5 0 00	21
22	Paid expenses.			22

> **The sum of the debits must always equal the sum of the credits.**

Regardless of the number of accounts, the sum of the debits is always equal to the sum of the credits in a journal entry. This equality of debits and credits for each transaction is built into the accounting equation: Assets = Liabilities + Owners' (Stockholders') Equity. It is also because of this double equality that the system is known as *double-entry accounting*.

On November 30, NetSolutions recorded the amount of supplies used in the operations during the month (transaction g). This transaction increases an

Summaries

Within each chapter, these synopses draw special attention to important points and help clarify difficult concepts.

Business Transactions

In Chapters 1 and 2, students are introduced to the dynamics of business transactions through non-business events to which they can easily relate.

> **Transaction f** When you pay your monthly credit card bill, you decrease the cash in your checking account and also decrease the amount you owe to the credit card company. Likewise, when NetSolutions pays $950 to creditors during the month, it reduces both assets and liabilities, as shown below.
>
> Assets = Liabilities + Owners' Equity
>
> Capital Retained

Self-Examination Questions

Five multiple-choice questions, with answers at the end of the chapter, help students review and retain chapter concepts.

OCUS ON SKILLS

Understand and Review (continued)

Illustrative Problem and Solution

A solved problem models one or more of the chapter's assignment problems, so that students can apply the modeled procedures to end-of-chapter materials.

- **Illustrative Problem on WebTutor Advantage** The illustrative problem from the text is also available in a lively electronic version as part of WebTutor Advantage. In addition, several other features of WebTutor Advantage provide review and reinforce understanding: e-lectures, exercise demos, Accounting Cycle Review, games, quizzes, and more!

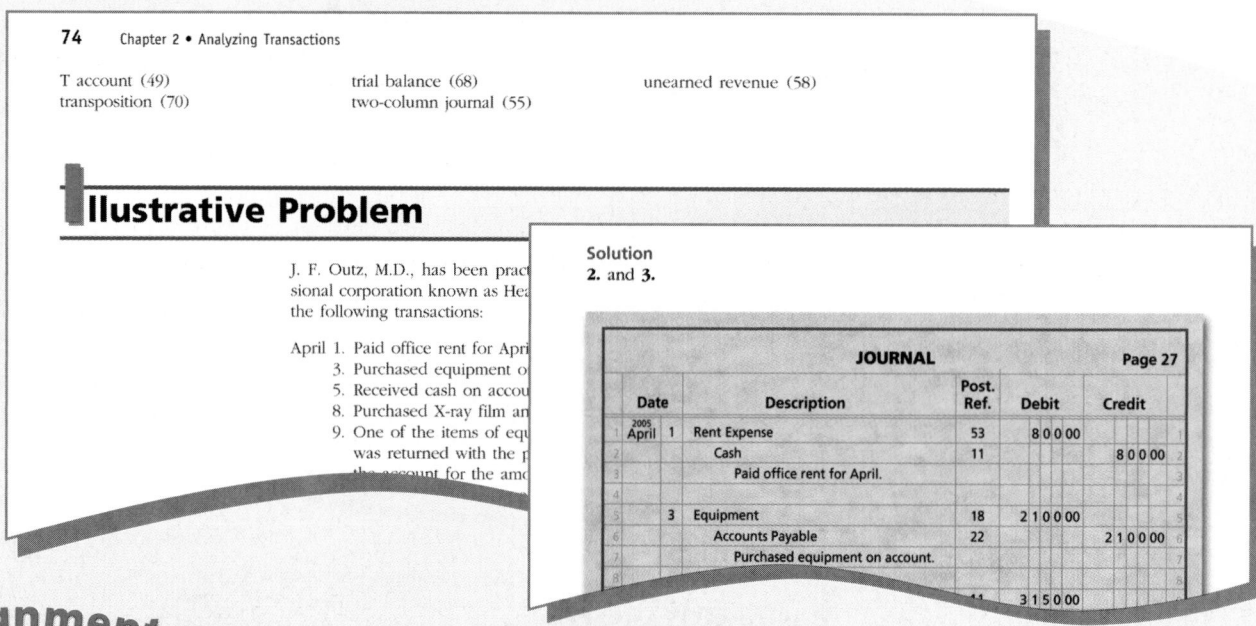

Assignment Materials that Reinforce Learning and Thinking

Students need to practice accounting in order to understand and use it. To give your students the greatest possible advantages in the real world, *Financial & Managerial Accounting, 8e* goes beyond presenting theory and procedure with the following end-of-chapter features.

- Discussion Questions
- Exercises
- Problems Series A
- Problems Series B
- Special Activities
- Continuing Problem, Chapters 1–4
- Comprehensive Problems

Each chapter's Discussion Questions and Exercises can be assigned or used as examples in the classroom. An average of 25 exercises per chapter are included—more than any other text on the market! In addition, the two full sets of problems can be used as classroom illustrations, assignments, alternate assignments, or for independent study. And the Comprehensive Problems at the end of Chapters 4, 5, 10, and 13 integrate and summarize chapter concepts and test students' comprehension.

b. ____ What conclusions concerning the company's ability to meets its financial obligations can you draw from these data?

• **Communication Items** These activities help students develop communication skills that will be essential on the job, regardless of the fields they pursue.

• **Team Building** Group Learning Activities let students learn accounting and business concepts while building teamwork skills.

ACTIVITY 4-4
Compare balance sheets

GROUP ACTIVITY   INTERNET

In groups of three or four, compare the balance sheets of two different companies, and present to the class a summary of the similarities and differences of the two companies. You may obtain the balance sheets you need from one of the following sources:

1. Your school or local library.
2. The investor relations department of each company.
3. The company's Web site on the Internet.
4. EDGAR (Electronic Data Gathering, Analysis, and Retrieval), the electronic archives of financial statements filed with the Securities and Exchange Commission.

SEC documents can be retrieved using the EdgarScan™ service from Pricewater-houseCoopers at **http://edgarscan.pwcglobal.com**. To obtain annual report information, key in a company name in the appropriate space. EdgarScan will list the company you've selected. Select the most recent an-

• **Complete homework online and receive immediate feedback!** Using Personal Trainer 3.0, students can complete all of the end-of-chapter assignment material, utilize hints and tips, and receive scoring feedback. These scores are then recorded into a gradebook for the instructor. Doing homework has never been so easy and fun!

• **Use P.A.S.S. to complete selected end-of-chapter problems** where several sequential activities need to be recorded and an understanding of their effects on the financial statements is required.

P.A.S.S.

REINFORCEMENT TOOLS

Financial & Managerial Accounting, 8e isn't the only "best in the business." Its supplements are top-notch too—a result of taking instructor and student comments to heart over the years and creating products based on those needs.

Supplements for Students*

By offering a broad range of supplements—available both as print material and easy-to-use technologies—*Financial & Managerial Accounting, 8e* not only helps students succeed in the course...but in the business world of tomorrow. Here's a look:

- **Personal Trainer** Specifically designed to ease the time-consuming task of grading homework, Personal Trainer 3.0 lets students complete online their assigned homework from the text or practice on unassigned homework. The results are instantaneously entered into a gradebook. With annotated spreadsheets and full-blown gradebook functionality, the greatly enhanced Personal Trainer 3.0 provides an unprecedented real-time, guided, self-correcting, learning reinforcement system outside the classroom. Use this resource as an integrated solution for your distance learning or traditional course.
Personal Trainer 0-324-20513-9

- **Xtra!** Available as an optional, free bundle with every new textbook, Xtra! gives students FREE access to the following online learning tools:

  — **e-Lectures** briefly review more difficult concepts from the chapter.

  — **Topical Quizzes** measure a student's "test readiness" on the concepts in the chapter.

  — **Multiple Choice Quizzes** help students review chapter concepts and prepare for exams. Feedback on their answers gives page references so they know where to look up the questions they've missed!

  — **Crossword Puzzles** are a fun way for students to review their understanding of key terms and concepts.
Xtra! 0-324-20502-3

- **Product Support Web Site at** http://warren.swlearning.com This site provides students with a wealth of introductory accounting resources, including limited quizzing, Internet application questions, e-lectures, spreadsheet applications software, review problems, and more.

Contact your local sales representative about package options.

- **Study Guides**

  The Study Guides include quiz and test tips, multiple choice, fill-in-the-blank, and true-false questions with solutions. They are designed to assist students in comprehending the concepts and principles presented in the text.

  Study Guide Chapters 1–15. 0-324-20500-7
  Study Guide Chapters 16–26 0-324-20501-5

- **P.A.S.S. (Power Accounting System Software)**

  (formerly General Ledger Software)

  Prepared by Dale Klooster and Warren Allen, this best-selling educational general ledger package makes solving end-of-chapter problems, the Continuing Problem, Comprehensive Problems, and practice sets as easy as clicking a mouse. It allows students to see the difference between manual and computerized accounting systems firsthand. It is enhanced with a problem checker that enables students to determine if their entries are correct and emulates commercial general ledger packages more closely than other educational packages. Problems that can be used with P.A.S.S. are highlighted by an icon. The benefits of using P.A.S.S. are that:
  — Errors are more easily corrected than in commercial software.
  — The Inspector Disk allows instructors to grade students' work.
  — A free Network Version is available to schools whose students purchase P.A.S.S.

  P.A.S.S.. 0-324-20510-4
  P.A.S.S. Network Version 0-324-22329-3

- **Spreadsheet Applications Software**

  SPREADSHEET

  This set of electronic worksheets helps students solve selected exercises and problems that are identified in the text with an icon. These spreadsheets give students the opportunity to solve dozens of problems using Microsoft Excel®. The spreadsheets are available, free, for students to download from the Student Resources section of the product support site.

- **Working Papers for Exercises and Problems**

  The traditional Working Papers include problem-specific forms for preparing solutions for Exercises, A and B Problems, the Continuing Problem, and the Comprehensive Problems from the text. These forms, with preprinted headings, provide a structure for the problems, which helps students get started and saves them time. Additional blank forms are included.

  Working Papers for Exercises and Problems Chapters 1–15 . . 0-324-20496-5
  Working Papers for Exercises and Problems Chapters 16–26 . 0-324-20497-3

REINFORCEMENT TOOLS

- **Working Papers Plus for Selected Exercises and Problems**

  This alternative to traditional working papers integrates selected exercise and problem information into the forms needed to complete the activities. These working papers are invaluable homework aids, and they include learning objectives from the chapter and check figures for selected problems.

  Working Papers Plus for Selected Exercises and Problems
  Chapters 1–15 0-324-20498-1
  Working Papers Plus for Selected Exercises and Problems
  Chapters 16–26 . . . . 0-324-20499-X

- **Blank Working Papers**

  These Working Papers are available for completing exercises and problems from the text or instructor-prepared problems. They have no preprinted headings. A guide at the front of the Working Papers tells students which form they will need for each problem.

  Blank Working Papers. 0-324-20370-5

Practice Sets

- **Tom's Asphalt** This set is a service business operated as a proprietorship. It includes a narrative of transactions and instructions for an optional solution with no debits and credits. This set can be solved manually or with the P.A.S.S. software in 5–7 hours.

  Tom's Asphalt with P.A.S.S. 0-324-20520-1
  Tom's Asphalt Key with Inspector CD 0-324-20522-8

- **Specialty Sports** Formerly published as "The Snow Shop," this set is a merchandising business operated as a proprietorship. It includes business documents, and it can be solved manually or with the P.A.S.S. software in 12–15 hours.

  Specialty Sports with P.A.S.S. 0-324-20525-2
  Specialty Sports Key with Inspector CD 0-324-20526-0

- **Groom and Board** This completely revised set was formerly published as "The Coddled Canine" and includes payroll transactions for a merchandising business operated as a proprietorship. It includes business documents, and it can be solved manually or with the P.A.S.S. software in 12–15 hours.

  Groom and Board with P.A.S.S. 0-324-20531-7
  Groom and Board Key with Inspector CD 0-324-20532-5

- **Coddled Canine with Peachtree® Accounting Software** Completely revised with current Peachtree software. New Instructor CD provides solutions to the Practice Set as well as helpful hints for incorporating the set into the classroom and tips on tailoring the set to fit the specific needs of each classroom. This set can be solved with the Peachtree software in 10–12 hours.

  Coddled Canine with Peachtree Software. 0-324-20588-0
  Coddled Canine Instructor CD 0-324-23230-6

- **Nina's Decorating House** This set is a service and merchandising business operated as a corporation. It includes narrative for six months of transactions, which are to be recorded in a general journal. The set can be solved manually or with the P.A.S.S. software in 10–12 hours.

  Nina's Decorating House with P.A.S.S. 0-324-20519-8
  Nina's Decorating House Key with Inspector CD. 0-324-20549-X

- **First Designs, Inc.** This set is a departmentalized merchandising business operated as a corporation. It includes a narrative of transactions, which are to be recorded in special journals. The set can be solved manually or with the P.A.S.S. software in 12–15 hours.

  First Designs with P.A.S.S. 0-324-20528-7
  First Designs Key with Inspector CD 0-324-20530-9

- **Dynamic Designs, Inc.** This set, formerly published as "Sunblaze Inc.," is a manufacturing business operated as a corporation that uses a job order cost system. The set can be solved manually or with the P.A.S.S. software in 12–15 hours.

  Dynamic Designs, Inc. with P.A.S.S. 0-324-20523-6
  Dynamic Designs, Inc. Key with Inspector CD 0-324-20524-4

TEACHING RESOURCES

From traditional printed materials to the latest integrated classroom technology, the proven *Financial & Managerial Accounting, 8e* is supported by the most extensive instructor resource package on the market. Just take a look.

Supplements for Instructors

- **WebTutor™ Advantage on WebCT™ and WebTutor Advantage on Blackboard®** are platform-driven systems for complete Web-based course management and delivery. More than just an interactive study guide, WebTutor Advantage provides lecture replacement and concept review, in addition to reinforcement, in the forms of quizzing, video cases, and much more. Powerful instructor tools are also provided to assist communication and collaboration between students and faculty. When students purchase this product they also get automatic access to Personal Trainer.

  Webtutor Advantage on WebCT 0-324-20511-2
  Webtutor Advantage on Blackboard 0-324-20512-0

- **WebTutor™ Toolbox.** WebTutor Toolbox on WebCT or Blackboard provides free limited content for your WebCT or Blackboard course.

  Webtutor Toolbox on WebCT 0-324-22359-5
  Webtutor Toolbox on Blackboard 0-324-22360-9

- **An Instructor's Guide to Online Resources** This imaginative resource helps you connect your classroom with *Financial & Managerial Accounting, 8e* and its dynamic spectrum of digital teaching and learning resources. This supplement is available not only in print form but also on the Instructor's Resource CD-ROM and for download from the Product Support Web site.

  An Instructor's Guide to Online Resources 0-324-20459-1

- **Instructor's Resource CD-ROM** This convenient resource includes the PowerPoint® Presentations, Instructor's Manual, Solutions Manual, Test Bank, ExamView®, An Instructor's Guide to Online Resources, and Excel Application Solutions. Lively demonstrations of support technology, including WebTutor Advantage, Personal Trainer 3.0, and P.A.S.S. are also included. All the basic material an instructor would need is available in one place on this IRCD.

  Instructor's Resource CD-ROM 0-324-20577-5

- **Instructor's Manuals** These resources are organized around the chapter learning objectives and offer a comprehensive guide to teaching from the text. The teaching suggestions emulate many of the teaching initiatives being stressed in higher education today, including active learning, collaborative learning, critical thinking, and writing across the curriculum.

  — Demonstration problems can be used in the classroom to illustrate accounting practices. Working through an accounting problem gives the instructor an opportunity to point out pitfalls that students should avoid.

  — Group learning activities provide another opportunity to actively involve students in the learning process. These activities ask students to apply accounting topics by completing an assigned task in small groups of three to five students. Small group work is an excellent way to introduce variety into the accounting classroom and creates a more productive learning environment if top students are mixed with average and poor students.

  — Writing exercises provide an opportunity for students to develop good written communication skills essential to any business person. These exercises probe students' knowledge of conceptual issues related to accounting.

  — Three to five Accounting Scenarios can be used as handouts.

  — The Teaching Transparency Masters can be made into acetate transparencies or can be duplicated and used as handouts.

  Instructor's Manual Chapters 1–15. 0-324-20573-2
  Instructor's Manual Chapters 16–26. 0-324-20574-0

- **Solutions Manuals** The Solutions Manuals provide the answers for all the end-of-chapter materials in the text. Solutions Transparencies are also available (see below).

  Solutions Manual Chapters 1–15 . . . . 0-324-20240-X
  Solutions Manual Chapters 16–26 0-324-20441-8

- **Solutions Transparencies** These acetate transparencies are available for all exercise and problem solutions.

  Solutions Transparencies Chapters 1–15
     A Problems and Exercises. 0-324-20536-8
  Solutions Transparencies Chapters 16–26
     A Problems and Exercises 0-324-20537-6
  Solutions Transparencies Chapters 1–15   B Problems. 0-324-20538-4
  Solutions Transparencies Chapters 16–26 B Problems 0-324-20539-2

TEACHING RESOURCES

- **Test Banks** The Test Banks offer a variety of testing materials designed to test students' comprehension of the materials presented in the text. The relevant chapter learning objective and the level of difficulty of each question are included. Approximately 2,800 true-false questions, multiple choice questions, fill-in-the-blank questions, and problems are available. The Test Banks are in two volumes and are available printed and bound as well as in a computerized version using the ExamView software found on the IRCD. Multi-chapter Achievement Tests assessing students' understanding of terms, calculations, and transaction recording are included in the printed Test Bank volumes.

  Test Bank Chapters 1–15 0-324-20575-9
  Test Bank Chapters 16–26 0-324-20576-7

- **ExamView® Pro Testing Software** is easy-to-use software that allows you to customize exams, practice tests, and tutorials and deliver them over  a network, on the Web, or in printed form. Test banks can also easily be uploaded to your WebCT or Blackboard course. The ExamView software is included on the IRCD.

- **PowerPoint® Presentations** Each presentation, which is included on the IRCD and on the product support site, enhances lectures and simplifies class preparation. Using this popular software package, you can also add your own custom slides. The dynamic Flash version for students is available online.

- **Presentation Transparencies** are acetates of the PowerPoint presentation slides found on the IRCD.

  Presentation Transparencies Chapters 1–15 0-324-20540-6
  Presentation Transparencies Chapters 16–26 0-324-20541-4

- **Instructor Spreadsheet Templates** show the instructor the completed solutions for the exercises and problems marked with an icon in the text. These are available on the IRCD and for download at the product support site.

- **Tutorial Videos** Completely revised and remastered, the tutorial videos provide twenty-six hours of video instruction. Each chapter is presented in two half-hour, interactive, media-intensive segments that reinforce the concepts presented in the text. These videos are free to adopters and are now available in two formats, DVD and VHS.

  Tutorial Videos on DVD Chapters 1–15 0-324-20542-2
  Tutorial Videos on DVD Chapters 16–26 0-324-20572-4

  Tutorial Videos on VHS Chapters 1–15 0-324-20744-1
  Tutorial Videos on VHS Chapters 16–26 . . . . 0-324-20745-X

- **Telecourse Videos** These videos are designed for distributed learning courses and are based on the Tutorial Videos but are of high broadcast quality. The videos are made on demand, and orders must be placed directly with South-Western. Each license is sold for either a one-year or three-year time period.

  Telecourse Videos Chapters 1–26, Three-Year License 0-324-20517-1
  Telecourse Videos Chapters 1–26, One-Year License 0-324-20535-X

- **Product Support Web Site at** http://warren.swlearning.com
  A variety of instructor resources are available through South-Western's password-protected Web site. Downloadable instructor supplement files are available for the Instructor's Manuals, Solutions Manuals, Test Banks, ExamView, PowerPoint, and Spreadsheet Template Solutions, each organized by chapter. An Instructor's Guide to Online Resources can also be downloaded. Many of these resources are available on the Instructor's Resource CD-ROM.

ACKNOWLEDGING THE

Because the textbook plays an important supporting role in the teaching/learning environment, our collaboration with instructors is invaluable. We thank them for their contribution to making *Financial & Managerial Accounting, 8e* and its supplements unsurpassed in quality.

The following instructors created content for the supplements that accompany the text:

Peggy Hussey
Colorado Technical College
Spreadsheet Applications Software

Gary Bower
Community College of Rhode Island
Personal Trainer

Deb Kiss
Davenport University
WebTutor Advantage

Terri Lukshaitis
Davenport University
WebTutor Advantage

Mike Gough
De Anza College
Tutorial Videos

John Wanlass
De Anza College
Working Papers Plus for
  Selected Exercises and Problems
Tutorial Videos
WebTutor Advantage

Kevin McFarlane
Front Range Community College
WebTutor Advantage

Christine Jonick
Gainesville College
Personal Trainer

Cheryl Fries
Guilford Technical Community College
Personal Trainer

Leah O'Goley
Holyoke Community College
WebTutor Advantage

Don Lucy
Indian River Community College
Groom and Board Practice Set
Dynamic Designs, Inc., Practice Set

Ana Cruz
Miami-Dade Community College
Nina's Decorating House Practice Set

Edward Krohn
Miami-Dade Community College
First Designs Practice Set

Blanca Ortega
Miami-Dade Community College
Nina's Decorating House Practice Set

Janice Stoudemire
Midlands Technical College
An Instructor's Guide to Online Resources

L. L. Price
Pierce College
Tom's Asphalt Practice Set
Test Banks

Doug Cloud
Pepperdine University
PowerPoint Presentations

Robin Turner
Rowan-Cabarrus Community College
Personal Trainer

Donna Chadwick
Sinclair Community College
Instructor's Manuals

Jim Shimko
Sinclair Community College
Personal Trainer

John Godfrey
Springfield Tech Community College
Test Banks

Diane Glowacki
Tarrant County College – Northeast Campus
Coddled Canine with Peachtree®
Software Practice Set

Brenda Hester
Volunteer State Community College
Specialty Sports Practice Set

The instructors listed below, along with Fernando Rodriguez, a graduate of Miami-Dade Community College, provided invaluable verification of text and supplement content:

Gary Bower
Community College of Rhode Island
Groom & Board Practice Set
Dynamic Designs Practice Set
Specialty Sports Practice Set
Coddled Canine with Peachtree Practice Set
Nina's Decorating House Practice Set

Patty Holmes
Des Moines Area Community College
Solutions Manuals

Alice Sineath
Forsyth Technical Community College
Solutions Manuals

Jeff Ritter
St. Norbert College
Test Banks

James Emig
Villanova University
Study Guides
Test Banks
WebTutor Advantage Quizzes

TEAM OF LEADERS

The following instructors participated in the reviewing process:

Brenda Fowler
Alamance Community College

Tom Branton
Alvin Community College

Sanithia Boyd
Arkansas State University

Lenny Long
Bay State Junior College

Cathy Peck
Belhaven College

Stuart Brown
Carol Garand
Bristol Community College

Colin Battle
Broward Community College

Luther Ross
Central Piedmont Community College

John Illig
Linda Mallory
Central Virginia Community College

Joan Ryan
Clackamas Community College

Lyle Hicks
Danville Area Community College

Deb Kiss
Davenport University

Bill Parrish
Delgado Community College

Cynthia McCall
Mike Prindle
Brad Smith
Des Moines Area Community College

Nino Gonzalez
El Paso Community College

William Hall
Fayetteville Technical Community College

Teresa Cook
Ferris State University

Alice Sineath
Forsyth Technical Community College

Karen Brayden
Front Range Community College – Fort Collins

Joy Bruce
Gaston College

Cheryl Fries
Guilford Technical Community College

Linda Tarrago
Hillsborough Community College

Jack Klett
Don Lucy
Indian River Community College

Bob Urell
Irvine Valley College

Amy Haas
Kingsborough Community College

Tony Cioffi
Lorain County Community College

Paul Morgan
Mississippi Gulf Coast Community College

Gil Crain
Montana State University

Judy Parker
North Idaho College

Jim Weglin
North Seattle Community College

Karen Mozingo
Pitt Community College

Johnnie Atkins
Rio Hondo College

Fred Blake
Maria Davis
N. MaiLai Eng
San Antonio College

Margaret Black
San Jacinto College – North

Curt Gustafson
South Dakota State University

Bernie Hill
Spokane Falls Community College

Brian Nash
John Teter
St. Petersburg College

Ken O'Brien
SUNY – Farmingdale

Julie Dailey
Tidewater Community College – Virginia Beach

Paul Jensen
University of Central Arkansas

Connie Cooper
University of Cincinnati

Joanie Sompayrac
University of Tennessee – Chattanooga

Mark Henry
Victoria College

Brenda Hester
Volunteer State Community College

Dan Biagi
Walla Walla Community College

Lynette Teal
Western Wisconsin Technical College

Jean Meyer
Xavier University

ACKNOWLEDGING THE

The instructors listed below provided weekly feedback on their experience with the text:

Mary Schaffler
College of the Redwoods

Karen Brayden
Front Range Community College

Joy Bruce
Gaston College

Cheryl Honore
Riverside Community College

Julie Billiris
St. Petersburg Junior College

Dawn Grimm
William Rainey Harper College

The following instructors participated in focus groups:

Julie Derrick
Brevard Community College – Cocoa

Pete Ciolfi
Margaret Cox
Randy Glover
Brevard Community College – Melbourne

Connie Culbreth
Brevard Community College – Palm Bay

J Pat Fuller
Bill Rushing
Brevard Community College – Titusville

Clarice McCoy
Camilla Richardson
Brookhaven College

Mark Fronke
Cerritos College

Elden Price
Coastal Bend College

Robert Carpenter
Eastfield College

Leah O'Goley
Holyoke Community College

Larry Allen
Panola College

Carol Wennagel
San Jacinto College South

Ann Gregory
South Plains College

Meg Bellucci
John Godfrey
William Herd
Pat McClure
Michael Tenerowicz
Springfield Technical College

George Katz
Wallace Satchell
St. Philip's College

Mark Henry
Victoria College

The instructors listed below provided useful feedback by participating in a Web survey:

Nick Lefakis
Asnuntuck Community College

Ronny Marchman
Augusta Technical Institute

Ann Henderson
Austin Peay State University

Rick Kwan
Baker College

William Parks
Barber-Scotia College

John Barden
Binghamton University

Bob Schweikle
Blackburn College

Michael Blue
Mike Shapeero
Anita Singer
Bloomsburg University

Roger Young
Bluffton College

Raymond Gaines
Bossier Parish Community College

Connie Culbreth
Brevard Community College

David Bland
Vickie Campbell
Robert Porter
Cape Fear Community College

Cynthia Thompson
Carl Sandburg College

Norma Montague
Central Carolina Community College

David Stone
Central Carolina Technical College

Michael Farina
Cerritos Community College

Janet Grange
Chicago State University

Nancy Burns
Chipola Junior College

Julie Miller
Brenda Thalacker
Chippewa Valley Technical College

Anthony Woods
City College of San Francisco

Cynthia Ewing
Clarendon College

Teri Zuccaro
Clarke College

Deborah Carter
Coahoma Community College

Jeanene Jones
Coastal Bend College

Mike Wirth
College of Alameda

Barry Stephens
College of the Souhwest

Karen Brayden
Colorado Community College

Stacey Stewart
Colorado Northwestern Community College

Joanne Green
Charles Miller
Columbia State Community College

Wanda Michaels
Corinthian Colleges

Evelyn Koonce
Craven Community College

Mike LaGrone
Cumberland

Dave Weaver
Dallas County Community College

Donna Larner
Davenport University

Mia Tipton
De Anza College

Patricia Holmes
Cynthia McCall
Mike Prindle
Des Moines Area Community College

Joan DiSalvio
Drew University

Terry Mullins
Dyersburg State Community College

Edwin Goldberg
Florida Memorial College

John Stancil
Florida Southern College

Alice Sineath
Forsyth Technical Community College

Jamie Payton
Gadsden State Community College

Mai-Ying Woo
Golden West College

Marlene Murphy
Governors State University

Sushila Kedia
Grambling State University

Lamar Creager
Hagerstown Community College

Susan Carbon
Heritage College

Jonathan Bradshaw
Houghton College

Joanne Avery
Husson College

John Eubanks
Independence Community College

Dale Fowler
Indiana Wesleyan University

Suzanne McKee
Jackson Community College

AJ Chase
Sabrina Segal
Keiser College

Joseph Kuvshinikov
Kent State University

Rose Garvey
Sueann Hely
Kentucky Comm and Tech

Carolyn Bottjer
Lehigh Carbon Community College

Kirk Canzano
Long Beach City College

Lou Wolff
Los Angeles Harbor College

Bradford Nash
Los Medanos College

Mary Dugan
Mansfield University

Ben Powell
The Master's College

Rod Boydstun
Sandra Lang
Kelly Witsberger
McKendree College

Martha Vidmar
*Mesabi Range Technical and
Community College*

Peg Johnson
Idalene Williams
Metropolitan Community College

Jesse Calvin Nipper
Middle Georgia College

Karen McGuire
Mid-Michigan Community College

James Joyce
Miles Community College

Bob Mahan
Milligan College

Mary Holloway
Mississippi Delta Community College

Amy Chataginer
Paul Morgan
Terry Thompson
Mississippi Gulf Coast Community College

Judy Olsen
Molloy College

Carl Essig
Michael Lunday
Montgomery County Community College

Abby Fapetu
Montreat College

Ron Bowman
Mt. San Jacinto College

Tim Miller
Murray State University

Ruth Goran
Myung Yoon
Northeastern Illinois College

Dawn Stevens
Northwest Mississippi Community College

Von Plessner
Northwest State Community College

Jeff James
Northwest Shoals Community College

Dick Van Holland
Northwestern College

Larry Allen
Panola College

Nancy Schrumpf
Gregory Thom
Parkland College

Vaun Day
Thomas Joyce
Jeff Winter
Pasadena City College

Karen Barr
Penn State University

Clarence Duncan
Teresa Walker
Piedmont College

Peggy Newsome
Howard Roberts
Pikeville College

Mary Jo Mettler
Pine Technical College

John Daugherty
Pitt Community College

Linda Beuning
Rasmussen Community College

Larry Waugh
Rio Hondo Community College

Joe Reddick
Karen Williamson
Rochester Community College

Sue Cunningham
Rowan-Cabarrus Community College

Teri Bernstein
Pat Halliday
Ira Landis
Santa Monica College

Donna Chadwick
William Hoover
Robert Reas
Sinclair Community College

David Laurel
South Texas Community College

Daniel Holt
Southeastern Illinois College

J. Rendall Garrett
Southern Nazarene University

Glenn Brooks
Southern Polytechnic State University

Robert Consalvo
Southern Vermont College

Patricia McClure
Springfield Tech Community College

Kevin Leeds
St. Peters College

Joe Shambley
Sullivan County Community College

Philip Dunning
Cora Newcomb
Technical College of the Lowcountry

Mark Freeman
Tuskegee University

Rea Waldon
Union Institute and University

Larry Huus
University of Minnesota

Carol Collinsworth
Dennis Ortiz
Mary Sauceda
University of Texas, Brownsville

Mary Stevens
University of Texas, El Paso

Kathleen Fitzpatrick
University of Toledo

Henry Carbone
Richard Larson
Bernice Murphy
University of Maine

Pam Ondeck
University of Pittsburgh

Ed Shannon
Ursinus College

Brenda Hester
Volunteer State Community College

John Haugen
Wartburg College

Clifford Bellers
Washtenaw Community College

Peggy Helms
Wayne Community College

Jeannette Eberle
John Logsdon
Robert Nagoda
Webber International University

Lynette Teal
Western Wisconsin Technical College

Rick Stevens
Wheaton College

Paul LoRusso
Wilson Technical Community College

Sharon Vetsch
Wisconsin Indianhead Technical College

Barbara Powers
Wytheville Community College

Annette Fisher
Yavapai College

brief contents

contents

Practice Set: Tom's Asphalt
This set is a service business operated as a proprietorship. It includes a narrative of transactions and instructions for an optional solution with no debits and credits. This set can be solved manually or with the P.A.S.S. software.

Practice Set: Specialty Sports
This set is a merchandising business operated as a proprietorship. It includes business documents, and it can be solved manually or with the P.A.S.S. software.

Practice Set: Groom and Board
This set includes payroll transactions for a merchandising business operated as a proprietorship. It includes business documents, and it can be solved manually or with the P.A.S.S. software.

Practice Set: Dynamic Designs, Inc.
This set is a manufacturing business operated as a corporation that uses a job order cost system. The set can be solved manually or with the P.A.S.S. software.

1

INTRODUCTION TO ACCOUNTING AND BUSINESS

objectives

After studying this chapter, you should be able to:

1 Describe the nature of a business.

2 Describe the role of accounting in business.

3 Describe the importance of business ethics and the basic principles of proper ethical conduct.

4 Describe the profession of accounting.

5 Summarize the development of accounting principles and relate them to practice.

6 State the accounting equation and define each element of the equation.

7 Explain how business transactions can be stated in terms of the resulting changes in the basic elements of the accounting equation.

8 Describe the financial statements of a corporation and explain how they interrelate.

9 Use the ratio of liabilities to stockholders' equity to analyze the ability of a business to withstand poor business conditions.

Do you use accounting? Yes, we all use accounting information in one form or another. For example, when you think about buying a car, you use accounting-type information to determine whether you can afford it and whether to lease or buy. Similarly, when you decided to attend college, you considered the costs (the tuition, textbooks, and so on). Most likely, you also considered the benefits (the ability to obtain a higher-paying job or a more desirable job).

Is accounting important to you? Yes, accounting is important in your personal life as well as your career, even though you may not become an accountant. For example, assume that you are the owner/manager of a small Mexican restaurant and are considering opening another restaurant in a neighboring town. Accounting information about the restaurant will be a major factor in your deciding whether to open the new restaurant and the bank's deciding whether to finance the expansion.

Our primary objective in this text is to illustrate basic accounting concepts that will help you to make good personal and business decisions. We begin by discussing what a business is, how it operates, and the role that accounting plays.

Nature of a Business

objective 1

Describe the nature of a business.

You can probably list some examples of companies with which you have recently done business. Your examples might be large companies, such as **Coca-Cola**, **Dell Computer**, or **Amazon.com**. They might be local companies, such as gas stations or grocery stores, or perhaps employers. They might be restaurants, law firms, or medical offices. What do all these examples have in common that identify them as businesses?

In general, a ***business*** is an organization in which basic resources (inputs), such as materials and labor, are assembled and processed to provide goods or services (outputs) to customers.[1] Businesses come in all sizes, from a local coffee house to a **DaimlerChrysler**, which sells several billion dollars worth of cars and trucks each year. A business's customers are individuals or other businesses who purchase goods or services in exchange for money or other items of value. In contrast, a church is not a business because those who receive its services are not obligated to pay for them.

The objective of most businesses is to maximize profits. **Profit** is the difference between the amounts received from customers for goods or services provided and the amounts paid for the inputs used to provide the goods or services. Some businesses operate with an objective other than to maximize profits. The objective of such nonprofit businesses is to provide some benefit to society, such as medical research or conservation of natural resources. In other cases, governmental units such as cities operate water works or sewage treatment plants on a nonprofit basis. We will focus in this text on businesses operating to earn a profit. Keep in mind, though, that many of the same concepts and principles apply to nonprofit businesses as well.

Types of Businesses

There are three different types of businesses that are operated for profit: manufacturing, merchandising, and service businesses. Each type of business has unique characteristics.

Manufacturing businesses change basic inputs into products that are sold to individual customers. Examples of manufacturing businesses and some of their products are as follows.

---
[1]A complete glossary of terms appears at the end of the text.

Manufacturing Business	Product
General Motors	Cars, trucks, vans
Intel	Computer chips
Boeing	Jet aircraft
Nike	Athletic shoes and apparel
Coca-Cola	Beverages
Sony	Stereos and televisions

Merchandising businesses also sell products to customers. However, rather than making the products, they purchase them from other businesses (such as manufacturers). In this sense, merchandisers bring products and customers together. Examples of merchandising businesses and some of the products they sell are shown below.

Merchandising Business	Product
Wal-Mart	General merchandise
Toys "R" Us	Toys
Circuit City	Consumer electronics
Lands' End	Apparel
Amazon.com	Internet books, music, video retailer

Service businesses provide services rather than products to customers. Examples of service businesses and the types of services they offer are shown below.

Service Business	Service
Disney	Entertainment
Delta Air Lines	Transportation
Marriott Hotels	Hospitality and lodging
Merrill Lynch	Financial advice
Sprint	Telecommunications

REAL WORLD

Roughly eight out of every ten workers in the United States are service providers.

Types of Business Organizations

The common forms of business organization are proprietorship, partnership, corporation, or limited liability corporation. In the following paragraphs, we briefly describe each form and discuss its advantages and disadvantages.

A *proprietorship* is owned by one individual. More than 70% of the businesses in the United States are organized as proprietorships. The popularity of this form is due to the ease and the low cost of organizing. The primary disadvantage of proprietorships is that the financial resources available to the business are limited to the individual owner's resources. Small local businesses such as hardware stores, repair shops, laundries, restaurants, and maid services are often organized as proprietorships.

As a business grows and more financial and managerial resources are needed, it may become a partnership. A *partnership* is owned by two or more individuals. Like proprietorships, small local businesses such as automotive repair shops, music stores, beauty salons, and clothing stores may be organized as partnerships. Currently, about 10% of the businesses in the United States are organized as partnerships.

A *corporation* is organized under state or federal statutes as a separate legal taxable entity. The ownership of a corporation is divided into shares of stock. A corporation issues the stock to individuals or other businesses, who then become owners or stockholders of the corporation.

A primary advantage of the corporate form is the ability to obtain large amounts of resources by issuing stock. For this reason, most companies that require large investments in equipment and facilities are organized as corporations. For example, **Toys "R" Us** has raised over $400 million by issuing shares of common stock to finance its operations. Other examples of corporations include **General Motors**, **Ford**, **International Business Machines (IBM)**, **Coca-Cola**, and **General Electric**.

About 20% of the businesses in the United States are organized as corporations. Given that most large companies are organized as corporations, over 90% of the total dollars of business receipts are received by corporations. Thus, corporations have a major influence on the economy.

> **Manufacturing, merchandising, and service businesses are commonly organized as either proprietorships, partnerships, corporations, or limited liability corporations.**

A ***limited liability corporation*** combines attributes of a partnership and a corporation in that it is organized as a corporation, but it can elect to be taxed as a partnership. Thus, its owners' (or members') liability is limited to their investment in the business, and its income is taxed when the owners report it on their individual tax returns.

The three types of businesses we discussed earlier—manufacturing, merchandising, and service—may be either proprietorships, partnerships, corporations, or limited liability corporations. However, because of the large amount of resources required to operate a manufacturing business, most manufacturing businesses are corporations. Likewise, most large retailers such as **Wal-Mart**, **Sears**, and **J. C. Penney** are corporations.

Business Strategies

How does a business decide which products or services to offer its customers? For example, should **Best Buy** offer warranty and repair services to its customers? Many factors influence this decision, but ultimately the decision is made on the basis of whether it is consistent with the overall business strategy of the company.

 A ***business strategy*** is an integrated set of plans and actions designed to enable the business to gain an advantage over its competitors, and in doing so, to maximize its profits. The two basic strategies a business may use are a low-cost strategy or a differentiation strategy.

Under a ***low-cost strategy***, a business designs and produces products or services of acceptable quality at a cost lower than that of its competitors. **Wal-Mart** and **Southwest Airlines** are examples of businesses with a low-cost strategy. Such businesses often sell no-frills, standardized products to the most typical customer in the industry. Following this strategy, businesses must continually focus on lowering costs.

Businesses may try to achieve lower costs in a variety of ways. For example, a business may employ strict budgetary controls, use sophisticated training programs, implement simple manufacturing technologies, or enter into cost-saving supplier relationships. Such supplier relationships may involve linking the supplier's production process directly to the client's production processes to minimize inventory costs, variations in raw materials, and record keeping costs.

A primary concern of a business using a low-cost strategy is that a competitor may achieve even lower costs by replicating the low costs or developing technological advances. Another concern is that competitors may differentiate their products in such a way that customers no longer desire a standardized, no-frills product. For example, local pharmacies most often try to compete with **Wal-Mart** on the basis of personalized service rather than cost.

Under a ***differentiation strategy***, a business designs and produces products or services that possess unique attributes or characteristics for which customers are willing to pay a premium price. For the differentiation strategy to be successful, a product or service must be truly unique or perceived as unique in quality, reliability, image, or design. To illustrate, **Maytag** attempts to differentiate its appliances on the basis of reliability, while **Tommy Hilfiger** differentiates its clothing on the basis of image.

Businesses using a differentiation strategy often use information systems to capture and analyze customer buying habits and preferences. For example, many grocery stores such as **Kroger** and **Safeway** issue magnetic cards to preferred customers that allow the consumer to receive special discounts on purchases. In addition to establishing brand loyalty, the cards allow the stores to track consumer preferences and buying habits for use in purchasing and advertising campaigns.

Companies may enhance differentiation by investing in manufacturing and service technologies, such as flexible manufacturing methods that allow timely product design and delivery. Some companies use marketing and sales efforts to promote product differences. Other companies use unique credit-granting arrangements, emphasize personal relationships with customers, or offer extensive training and after-sales service programs for customers.

A business using a differentiation strategy wants customers to pay a premium price for the differentiated features of its products. However, a business may provide features that exceed the customers' needs. In this case, competitors may be able to offer customers less differentiated products at lower costs. Also, customers' perceptions of the differentiated features may change. As a result, customers may not be willing to continue to pay a premium price for the products. For example, as **Tommy Hilfiger** clothing becomes more commonplace, customers may be unwilling to pay a premium price for Hilfiger clothing. Over time, customers may also become better educated about the products and the value of the differentiated features. For example, **IBM** personal computers were once viewed as being differentiated on quality. However, as consumers have become better educated and more experienced with personal computers, **Dell** computers have also become perceived as being of high quality.

A business may attempt to implement a ***combination strategy*** that includes elements of both the low-cost and differentiation strategies. That is, a business may attempt to develop a differentiated product at competitive, low-cost prices. For example, **Andersen Windows** allows customers to design their own windows through the use of its proprietary manufacturing software. By using flexible manufacturing, Andersen Windows can produce a variety of windows in small quantities with a low or moderate cost. Thus, Andersen windows sell at a higher price than standard low-cost windows but at a lower price than fully customized windows built on site.

Exhibit 1 summarizes the characteristics of the low-cost, differentiation, and combination strategies. In addition, some common examples of businesses that employ each strategy are also listed.

I have 30,000 restaurants in 121 countries, with about 13,000 in the United States. I serve more than 45 million people each day and employ 1.5 million. Moscow's Pushkin Square sports one of my busiest stores. Fortune Magazine named me No. 1 for social responsibility. I'm busy cutting fat from my offerings. I use more than three million pounds of potatoes per day. My New Tastes Menu is Made for You. My spokesman's shoes are size 14½ and he helps sick kids. More than 37 percent of my American owner/operators are women and minorities. Who am I? (Go to page 28 for answer.)

•Exhibit 1 Business Strategies and Industries

Business Strategy	Industry					
	Airline	Freight	Automotive	Retail	Financial Services	Hotel
Low-cost	Southwest	Union Pacific	Saturn	Sam's Clubs	Schwab	Super 8
Differentiated	Virgin Atlantic	Federal Express	BMW	Talbot's	Morgan Stanley	Four Seasons
Combination	Delta	United Postal Service	Ford	Target	Merrill Lynch	Marriott

As you might expect, a danger of a business using a combination strategy is that its products might not adequately satisfy either end of the market. That is, because its products are differentiated, it cannot establish itself as the low-cost leader, and at the same time, its products may not be differentiated enough that customers are willing to pay a premium price. In other words, the business may become "stuck in the middle." For example, **J. C. Penney** has difficulty competing as a low-cost leader against **Wal-Mart**, **Kmart**, **Goody's Family Clothing**, **Fashion USA**, and **T.J. Maxx**. At the same time, J.C.Penney cannot adequately differentiate its stores and merchandise from such competitors as **The Gap**, **Old Navy**, **Eddie Bauer**, and **Talbot's** so that it can charge higher prices.

A business may also attempt to implement different strategies for different markets. For example, **Toyota** segments the market for automobiles by offering the Lexus to image- and quality-conscious buyers. To reinforce this image, Toyota developed a separate dealer network. At the same time, Toyota offers a low-cost automobile, the Echo, to price-sensitive buyers.

Value Chain of a Business

Once a business has chosen a strategy, it must implement the strategy in its value chain. A ***value chain*** is the way a business adds value for its customers by processing inputs into a product or service, as shown in Exhibit 2.

•Exhibit 2   **The Value Chain**

Inputs → Business Processes → Products or Services → Customer Value

To illustrate, **Delta Air Lines'** value chain consists of taking inputs, such as people, aircraft, and equipment, and processing these inputs into a service of transporting goods and passengers throughout the world. The extent to which customers value Delta's passenger service is reflected by the air fares Delta is able to charge as well as passenger load factors (percentage of seats occupied). For example, the extent to which Delta can, on average, charge higher fares than discount airlines, such as **AirTran**, implies that passengers value Delta's services more than AirTran's. These services may include newer, more comfortable aircraft, the ability to earn frequent flyer miles, more convenient passenger schedules, passenger lounges for frequent flyers, and international connections.

A business's value chain can be divided into primary and supporting processes. Primary processes are those that are directly involved in creating value for customers. Examples of primary processes include manufacturing, selling, and customer service. Supporting processes are those that facilitate the primary processes. Examples of support processes include purchasing and personnel.[2] For Delta Air Lines, primary processes would include aircraft maintenance, baggage handling, ticketing, and flight operations. Secondary processes for Delta Air Lines would include the accounting and finance functions, contracting for fuel deliveries, and investor relations.

Business Stakeholders

A ***business stakeholder*** is a person or entity having an interest in the economic performance of the business. These stakeholders normally include the owners, managers, employees, customers, creditors, and the government.

The **owners** who have invested resources in the business clearly have an interest in how well the business performs. Most owners want to get the most economic value for their investments. To the extent that the business is profitable, owners will expect to share in the business profits. Since owners may eventually decide to sell their business, they also have an interest in the total economic worth of the business. This economic worth may reflect results of past profits as well as prospects for future profits.

The **managers** are those individuals who the owners have authorized to operate the business. Managers are primarily evaluated on the economic performance of the business. The managers of poor-performing businesses are often fired by the owners. Thus, managers have an incentive to maximize the economic value of the

---

[2]The value chain is described and illustrated in most management textbooks.

business. Owners may offer managers salary contracts that are tied directly to how well the business performs. For example, a manager might receive a percent of the profits or a percent of the increase in profits. Such contracts are often referred to as profit-sharing plans.

The **employees** provide services to the business in exchange for a paycheck. The employees have an interest in the economic performance of the business because their jobs depend upon it. During business downturns, it is not unusual for a business to lay off workers for extended periods of time. Whenever a business fails, the employees lose their jobs permanently. Employee labor unions often use the good economic performance of a business to argue for wage increases. In contrast, businesses often cite poor economic performance as a reason for decreasing wages or denying raises.

The **customers** may also have an interest in the continued success of a business. For example, if **Apple Computer** were to fail, customers might not be able to get hardware and software for their computers. Likewise, customers who purchase advance tickets on **Southwest Airlines** have an interest in whether Southwest will continue in business. Frequent flyers on **Eastern Airlines** lost their accumulated frequent-flyer points when Eastern went out of business.

Like the owners, the **creditors** invest resources in the business by extending credit, such as a loan. They, too, have an interest in how well the business performs. In order for the creditors to recover their investment, the business must generate enough cash to pay them back. In addition, creditors view the business as their customer and thus have a stake in the continued success of the business.

Various **governments** have an interest in the economic performance of businesses. City, county, state, and federal governments collect taxes from businesses within their jurisdictions. The better a business does, the more taxes the government can collect. In addition, workers are taxed on their wages. In contrast, workers who are laid off and are unemployed can file claims for unemployment compensation, which results in a financial burden for the government. City and state governments often provide incentives for businesses to locate in their jurisdictions.

REAL WORLD

The state of Alabama offered **DaimlerChrysler** millions of dollars in incentives to locate a Mercedes plant in Alabama.

SUCCESSFUL ENTREPRENEURS

What are the characteristics of entrepreneurs who successfully start and manage a new business?

It goes without saying that an entrepreneur must have a thorough technical knowledge of the business. For example, a successful computer consultant must have a thorough knowledge of computers. Entrepreneurs must also have basic management skills, such as the ability to organize and interact with others. Terms that are often used to describe entrepreneurs are listed below.

Terms

Vision	Spirit of adventure
Perseverance	Need for achievement
Independent	Self-starter
Self-confident	Sense of commitment
Risk taker	Willingness to make
High energy level	personal sacrifices
Motivated	Communication skills
Personal drive	

Examples of some well-known entrepreneurs and their companies are listed below.

Entrepreneur	Company
Jeffrey Yang	Yahoo!
Henry Ford	Ford Motor Company
George Eastman	Kodak
King C. Gillette	Gillette Company
Steven Jobs	Apple Computer
Bill Gates	Microsoft
Frederick Smith	Federal Express
Sam Walton	Wal-Mart

Examples of entrepreneurs also include the owners of many small businesses in your community, from local restaurants to video rental stores.

The Role of Accounting in Business

What is the role of accounting in business? The simplest answer to this question is that accounting provides information for managers to use in operating the business. In addition, accounting provides information to other stakeholders to use in assessing the economic performance and condition of the business.

In a general sense, **accounting** can be defined as an information system that provides reports to stakeholders about the economic activities and condition of a business. As we indicated earlier in this chapter, we will focus our discussions on accounting and its role in business. However, many of the concepts in this text apply also to individuals, governments, and other types of organizations. For example, individuals must account for activities such as hours worked, checks written, and bills due. Stakeholders for individuals include creditors, dependents, and the government. A main interest of the government is making sure that individuals pay the proper taxes.

> **Accounting is an information system that provides reports to stakeholders about the economic activities and condition of a business.**

You may think of accounting as the "language of business." This is because accounting is the means by which business information is communicated to the stakeholders. For example, accounting reports summarizing the profitability of a new product help **Coca-Cola**'s management decide whether to continue selling the product. Likewise, financial analysts use accounting reports in deciding whether to recommend the purchase of Coca-Cola's stock. Banks use accounting reports in determining the amount of credit to extend to Coca-Cola. Suppliers use accounting reports in deciding whether to offer credit for Coca-Cola's purchases of supplies and raw materials. State and federal governments use accounting reports as a basis for assessing taxes on Coca-Cola.

The process by which accounting provides information to business stakeholders is illustrated in Exhibit 3. A business must first identify its stakeholders. It must then assess the various informational needs of those stakeholders and design its accounting system to meet those needs. Finally, the accounting system records the economic data about business activities and events, which the business reports to the stakeholders according to their informational needs.

Stakeholders use accounting reports as a primary source of information on which they base their decisions. They use other information as well. For example, in deciding whether to extend credit to an appliance store, a banker might use economic forecasts to assess the future demand for the store's products. During periods of economic downturn, the demand for consumer appliances normally declines. The banker might inquire about the ability and reputation of the managers of the business. For small corporations, bankers may require major stockholders to personally guarantee the loans of the business. Finally, bankers might consult industry publications that rank similar businesses as to their quality of products, customer satisfaction, and future prospects for growth.

Business Ethics

Individuals may have different views about what is "right" and "wrong" in a given situation. For example, you may believe it is wrong to copy another student's homework and hand it in as your own. Other students may feel that it is acceptable to copy homework if the instructor has no stated rule against it. Unfortunately, business managers sometimes find themselves in situations where they feel pressure to violate personal ethics. For example, managers of **Sears** automotive service departments were accused of recommending unnecessary repairs and overcharging customers for actual repairs in order to meet company goals and earn bonuses.

•Exhibit 3   **Accounting Information and the Stakeholders of a Business**

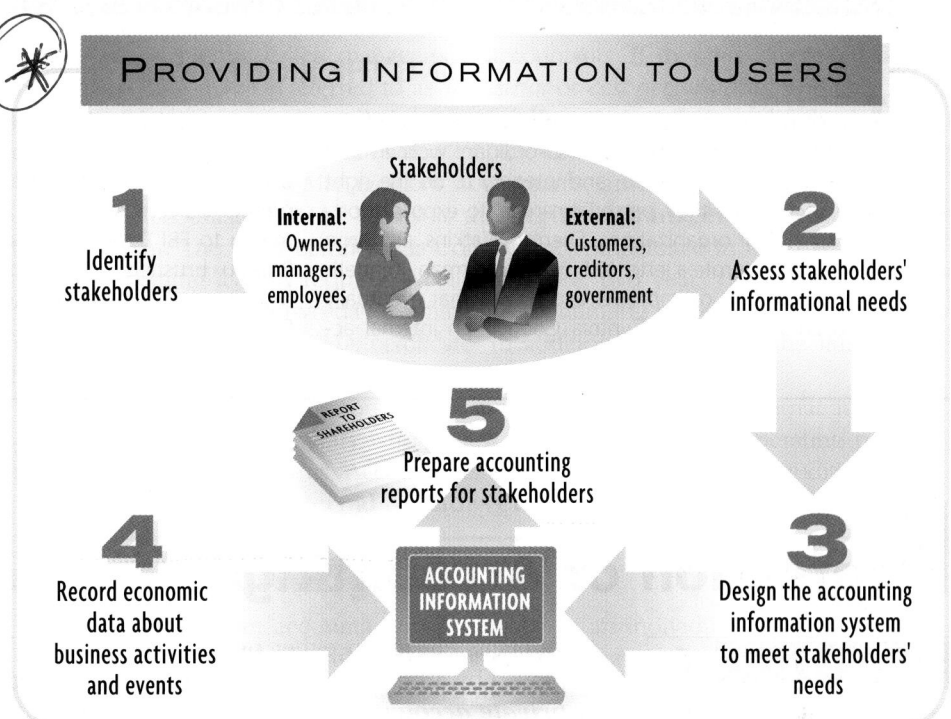

PROVIDING INFORMATION TO USERS

Stakeholders

1 Identify stakeholders

Internal: Owners, managers, employees

External: Customers, creditors, government

2 Assess stakeholders' informational needs

5 Prepare accounting reports for stakeholders

ACCOUNTING INFORMATION SYSTEM

4 Record economic data about business activities and events

3 Design the accounting information system to meet stakeholders' needs

POINT OF INTEREST

Most colleges and universities publish a Student Code of Conduct that sets forth the ethical conduct expected of students.

REAL WORLD

Stanley James Cardiges, the former top U.S. sales representative for **American Honda**, admitted to receiving $2 million to $5 million in illegal kickbacks from dealers. After being sentenced to five years in prison, he admitted to falling into a pattern of unethical behavior early in his career.

The moral principles that guide the conduct of individuals are called ***ethics***. Regardless of differences among individuals, proper ethical conduct implies a behavior that considers the impact of one's actions on society and others. In other words, proper ethical conduct implies that you not only consider what's in your best interest but also what's in the best interests of others.

Ethical conduct is good business. For example, an automobile manufacturer that fails to correct a safety defect to save costs may later lose sales due to lack of consumer confidence. Likewise, a business that pollutes the environment may find itself the target of lawsuits and customer boycotts.

Businesspeople should work within an ethical framework.[3] Although an ethical framework is based on individual experiences and training, there are a number of sound principles that form the foundation for ethical behavior:

1. *Avoid small ethical lapses.* Small ethical lapses may appear harmless in and of themselves. Unfortunately, such lapses can compromise your work. Small ethical lapses can build up and lead to larger consequences later.
2. *Focus on your long-term reputation.* One characteristic of an ethical dilemma is that it places you under severe short-term pressure. The ethical dilemma is created by the stated or unstated threat that failure to "go along" may result in undesirable consequences. You should respond to ethical dilemmas by minimizing the short-term pressures and focusing on long-term reputation instead. Your reputation is very valuable. You will lose your effectiveness if your reputation becomes tarnished.
3. *You may suffer adverse personal consequences for holding to an ethical position.* In some unethical organizations, managers have endured career setbacks for not budging from their ethical positions. Some managers have resigned because they were unable to support management in what they perceived as unethical behavior. Thus, in the short term, ethical behavior can sometimes adversely affect your career.

---

[3]"Integrity in Business" items and end-of-chapter ethics discussion cases are provided throughout this text to focus attention on the importance of proper ethical conduct in business.

accounting, tax accounting, accounting systems, international accounting, not-for-profit accounting, and social accounting.

Financial accounting is primarily concerned with the recording and reporting of economic data and activities for a business. Although such reports provide useful information for managers, they are the primary reports for owners, creditors, governmental agencies, and the public. For example, if you wanted to buy some stock in **PepsiCo**, **American Airlines**, or **McDonald's**, how would you know in which company to invest? One way is to review financial reports and compare the financial performance and condition of each company. The purpose of financial accounting is to provide such reports.

Managerial accounting, or **management accounting**, uses both financial accounting and estimated data to aid management in running day-to-day operations and in planning future operations. Management accountants gather and report information that is relevant and timely to the decision-making needs of management. For example, management might need information on alternative ways to finance the construction of a new building. Alternatively, management might need information on whether to expand its operations into a new product line. Thus, reports to management can differ widely in form and content.

Generally Accepted Accounting Principles

objective 5

Summarize the development of accounting principles and relate them to practice.

REAL WORLD

The FASB is also developing a broad conceptual framework for financial accounting. Seven Statements of *Financial Accounting Concepts* have been published to date.

If the management of a company could record and report financial data as it saw fit, comparisons among companies would be difficult, if not impossible. Thus, financial accountants follow *generally accepted accounting principles (GAAP)* in preparing reports. These reports allow investors and other stakeholders to compare one company to another.

To illustrate the importance of generally accepted accounting principles, assume that each sports conference in college football used different rules for counting touchdowns. For example, assume that the Pacific Athletic Conference (PAC 10) counted a touchdown as six points and the Atlantic Coast Conference (ACC) counted a touchdown as two points. It would be difficult to evaluate the teams under such different scoring systems. A standard set of rules and a standard scoring system help fans compare teams across conferences. Likewise, a standard set of generally accepted accounting principles allows for the comparison of financial performance and condition across companies.

Accounting principles and concepts develop from research, accepted accounting practices, and pronouncements of authoritative bodies. Currently, the *Financial Accounting Standards Board (FASB)* is the authoritative body having the primary responsibility for developing accounting principles. The FASB publishes *Statements of Financial Accounting Standards* and *Interpretations* to these Standards.

Because generally accepted accounting principles impact how companies report and what they report, all stakeholders are interested in the setting of these principles. For example, the setting of accounting standards for stock-based compensation or stock options has been especially controversial. Even the United States Senate has been involved in the debate. Many managers opposed an initial proposal by the FASB that would record the value of such options as a reduction of profits because doing so would negatively impact their financial results. The FASB issued a revised proposal, but investors, analysts, and other stakeholders criticized manager stock options in light of the poor financial performances of many companies and the financial failures of **Enron**, **Tyco**, and **WorldCom**. As the debate continues, some companies are voluntarily treating stock options as a reduction of profits.

In this chapter and throughout this text, we emphasize accounting principles and concepts. It is through this emphasis on the "why" of accounting as well as the "how" that you will gain an understanding of the full significance of accounting. In the following paragraphs, we discuss the business entity concept and the cost concept.

Business Entity Concept

The individual business unit is the business entity for which economic data are needed. This entity could be an automobile dealer, a department store, or a grocery store. The business entity must be identified, so that the accountant can determine which economic data should be analyzed, recorded, and summarized in reports.

The ***business entity concept*** is important because it limits the economic data in the accounting system to data related directly to the activities of the business. In other words, the business is viewed as an entity separate from its owners, creditors, or other stakeholders. For example, the accountant for a business with one owner (a proprietorship) would record the activities of the business only, not the personal activities, property, or debts of the owner.

> **Under the business entity concept, the activities of a business are recorded separately from the activities of the stakeholders.**

The Cost Concept

If a building is bought for $150,000, that amount should be entered into the buyer's accounting records. The seller may have been asking $170,000 for the building up to the time of the sale. The buyer may have initially offered $130,000 for the building. The building may have been assessed at $125,000 for property tax purposes. The buyer may have received an offer of $175,000 for the building the day after it was acquired. These latter amounts have no effect on the accounting records because they did not result in an exchange of the building from the seller to the buyer. The **cost concept** is the basis for entering the *exchange price, or cost, of $150,000* into the accounting records for the building.

Continuing the illustration, the $175,000 offer received by the buyer the day after the building was acquired indicates that it was a bargain purchase at $150,000. To use $175,000 in the accounting records, however, would record an illusory or unrealized profit. If, after buying the building, the buyer accepts the offer and sells the building for $175,000, a profit of $25,000 is then realized and recorded. The new owner would record $175,000 as the cost of the building.

Using the cost concept involves two other important accounting concepts—objectivity and the unit of measure. The **objectivity concept** requires that the accounting records and reports be based upon objective evidence. In exchanges between a buyer and a seller, both try to get the best price. Only the final agreed-upon amount is objective enough for accounting purposes. If the amounts at which properties were recorded were constantly being revised upward and downward based on offers, appraisals, and opinions, accounting reports could soon become unstable and unreliable.

The ***unit of measure concept*** requires that economic data be recorded in dollars. Money is a common unit of measurement for reporting uniform financial data and reports.

Assets, Liabilities, and Owner's Equity

objective	6

State the accounting equation and define each element of the equation.

The resources owned by a business are its ***assets***. Examples of assets include cash, land, buildings, and equipment. The rights or claims to the properties are normally divided into two principal types: (1) the rights of creditors and (2) the rights of owners. The rights of creditors represent debts of the business and are called ***liabilities***. The rights of the owners are called ***owners' equity***. The relationship between the two may be stated in the form of an equation, as follows:

$$\text{Assets} = \text{Liabilities} + \text{Owners' Equity}$$

This equation is known as the ***accounting equation***. It is usual to place liabilities before owners' equity in the accounting equation because creditors have first

If a company's assets increase by $20,000 and its liabilities decrease by $5,000, how much did the owners' equity increase or decrease?

Change in Assets	=	Change in Liabilities	+	Change in Owners' Equity
+$20,000	=	−$5,000	+	X
+$25,000	=			X

rights to the assets. The claim of the owners is sometimes given greater emphasis by transposing liabilities to the other side of the equation, which yields:

$$\text{Assets} - \text{Liabilities} = \text{Owners' Equity}$$

To illustrate, if the assets owned by a business amount to $100,000 and the liabilities amount to $30,000, the owners' equity is equal to $70,000, as shown below.

Assets	− Liabilities	= Owners' Equity
$100,000	− $30,000	= $70,000

FINANCIAL REPORTING AND DISCLOSURE

THE ACCOUNTING EQUATION

The accounting equation provides a basic framework for recording the effects of transactions on companies of all sizes and types. This basic framework serves as the foundation for accounting systems from the smallest business, such as a local convenience store, to the largest businesses. Some examples taken from recent financial reports of well-known companies are shown below.

Company	Assets*	= Liabilities	+ Owners' Equity
Coca-Cola	$22,417	= $11,051	+ $11,366
Circuit City	3,815	= 1,436	+ 2,379
Dell Computer	13,435	= 7,813	+ 5,622
eBay	1,182	= 168	+ 1,014
Hilton Hotels	9,140	= 7,498	+ 1,642
McDonald's	22,535	= 13,047	+ 9,488
Microsoft	59,257	= 11,968	+ 47,289
Southwest Airlines	8,997	= 4,983	+ 4,014
Wal-Mart	78,130	= 46,787	+ 31,343

*Amounts are shown in millions of dollars.

Business Transactions and the Accounting Equation

objective 7

Explain how business transactions can be stated in terms of the resulting changes in the basic elements of the accounting equation.

Paying a monthly telephone bill of $168 affects a business's financial condition because it now has less cash on hand. Such an economic event or condition that directly changes an entity's financial condition or directly affects its results of operations is a ***business transaction***. For example, purchasing land for $50,000 is a business transaction. In contrast, a change in a business's credit rating does not directly affect cash or any other element of its financial condition.

All business transactions can be stated in terms of changes in the elements of the accounting equation. You will see how business transactions affect the accounting equation by studying some typical transactions. As a basis for illustration, we will use a business organized by Chris Clark.

Assume that on November 1, 2005, Chris Clark organizes a corporation that will be known as NetSolutions. The first phase of Chris's business plan is to operate Net-

All business transactions can be stated in terms of changes in the elements of the accounting equation.

Solutions as a service business that provides assistance to individuals and small businesses in developing Web pages and in configuring and installing application software. Chris expects this initial phase of the business to last one to two years. During this period, Chris will gather information on the software and hardware needs of customers. During the second phase of the business plan, Chris plans to expand NetSolutions into a personalized retailer of software and hardware for individuals and small businesses.

Each transaction or group of similar transactions during NetSolutions' first month of operations is described in the following paragraphs. The effect of each transaction on the accounting equation is then shown.

Transaction a   Chris Clark deposits $25,000 in a bank account in the name of Net-Solutions in return for shares of stock in the corporation. Stock issued to owners (stockholders), such as Chris Clark, is referred to as ***capital stock***. The effect of this transaction is to increase the asset (cash), on the left side of the equation, by $25,000. To balance the equation, the owners' equity (capital stock), on the right side of the equation, is increased by the same amount. The effect of this transaction on NetSolutions' accounting equation is shown below.

	Assets	=	Owners' Equity	
	Cash	=	**Capital Stock**	
a.	25,000		25,000	Investment by stockholder

Note that the accounting equation shown above relates only to the business, NetSolutions. Under the business entity concept, Chris Clark's personal assets, such as a home or personal bank account, and personal liabilities are excluded from the equation.

Transaction b   If you purchased this textbook by paying cash, you entered into a transaction in which you exchanged one asset for another. That is, you exchanged cash for the textbook. Businesses often enter into similar transactions. Net-Solutions, for example, exchanged $20,000 cash for land. The land is located in a new business park with convenient access to transportation facilities. Chris Clark plans to rent office space and equipment during the first phase of the business plan. During the second phase, Chris plans to build an office and warehouse on the land.

The purchase of the land changes the makeup of the assets but does not change the total assets. The items in the equation prior to this transaction and the effect of the transaction are shown next, as well as the new amounts, or *balances*, of the items.

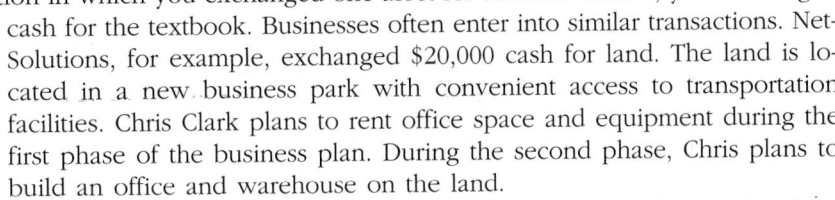

If NetSolutions had purchased a van for $28,000, paying $8,000 cash and signing a loan agreement (note payable) for $20,000, how would the transaction be recorded using the accounting equation?

Cash	+	Van	=	Notes Payable
−8,000	+	28,000		+20,000

	Assets			=	Owners' Equity
	Cash	+	Land	=	Capital Stock
Bal.	25,000				25,000
b.	−20,000		+20,000		
Bal.	5,000		20,000		25,000

Transaction c   You have probably used a credit card at one time or another to buy clothing or other merchandise. In this type of transaction, you received clothing for a promise to pay your credit card bill in the future. That is, you received an asset and incurred a liability to pay a future bill. During the month, NetSolutions entered into a similar transaction, buying supplies for $1,350 and agreeing to pay the supplier in the near future. This type of transaction is called a purchase *on account*. The liability created is called an ***account payable***. Items such as supplies that will be used in the business in the future are called ***prepaid expenses***, which are assets. The effect of this transaction is to increase assets and liabilities by $1,350, as follows:

Other examples of common prepaid expenses include insurance and rent. Businesses usually report these assets together as a single item, prepaid expenses.

Assets			=	Liabilities + Owners' Equity	
Cash +	Supplies +	Land		Accounts Payable +	Capital Stock
Bal. 5,000		20,000			25,000
c.	+1,350			+1,350	
Bal. 5,000	1,350	20,000		1,350	25,000

Transaction d You may have earned money by painting houses. If so, you received money for rendering services to a customer. Likewise, a business earns money by selling goods or services to its customers. This amount is called *revenue*.

During its first month of operations, NetSolutions provided services to customers, earning fees of $7,500 and receiving the amount in cash. This transaction increased cash and the owners' equity by $7,500, as shown here.

Assets			=	Liabilities +	Owners' Equity		
Cash +	Supplies +	Land		Accounts Payable +	Capital Stock +	Retained Earnings	
Bal. 5,000	1,350	20,000		1,350	25,000		
d. +7,500						+7,500	Fees earned
Bal. 12,500	1,350	20,000		1,350	25,000	7,500	

You should note that the increase in owners' equity from earning revenue is listed in the equation under "Retained Earnings." **Retained earnings** is the owners' equity created by the business operations (revenues less expenses). Transactions affecting earnings are kept separate from transactions related to owners' investments (capital stock). This is useful in preparing reports to owners and creditors and in satisfying legal requirements that we will discuss later in the text.

Special terms may be used to describe certain kinds of revenue, such as **sales** for the sale of merchandise. Revenue from providing services is called **fees earned**. For example, a physician would record fees earned for services to patients. Other examples include **rent revenue** (money received for rent) and **interest revenue** (money received for interest).

Instead of requiring the payment of cash at the time services are provided or goods are sold, a business may accept payment at a later date. Such revenues are called *fees on account* or *sales on account*. In such cases, the firm has an **account receivable**, which is a claim against the customer. An account receivable is an asset, and the revenue is earned as if cash had been received. When customers pay their accounts, there is an exchange of one asset for another. Cash increases, while accounts receivable decreases.

Transaction e If you painted houses to earn money, you probably used your own ladders and brushes. NetSolutions also spent cash or used up other assets in earning revenue. The amounts used in this process of earning revenue are called **expenses**. Expenses include supplies used, wages of employees, and other assets and services used in operating the business.

For NetSolutions, the expenses paid during the month were as follows: wages, $2,125; rent, $800; utilities, $450; and miscellaneous, $275. Miscellaneous expenses include small amounts paid for such items as postage, coffee, and magazine subscriptions. The effect of this group of transactions is the opposite of the effect of revenues. These transactions reduce cash and owners' equity, as shown here.

Assets			=	Liabilities +	Owners' Equity		
Cash +	Supplies +	Land		Accounts Payable +	Capital Stock +	Retained Earnings	
Bal. 12,500	1,350	20,000		1,350	25,000	7,500	
e. +3,650						−2,125	Wages expense
						− 800	Rent expense
						− 450	Utilities expense
						− 275	Misc. expense
8,850	1,350	20,000		1,350	25,000	3,850	

Businesses usually record each revenue and expense transaction separately as it occurs. However, to simplify this illustration, we have summarized NetSolutions' revenues and expenses for the month in transactions (d) and (e).

Transaction f   When you pay your monthly credit card bill, you decrease the cash in your checking account and also decrease the amount you owe to the credit card company. Likewise, when NetSolutions pays $950 to creditors during the month, it reduces both assets and liabilities, as shown below.

	Assets			=	Liabilities +		Owners' Equity	
					Accounts	Capital	Retained	
	Cash +	Supplies +	Land		Payable +	Stock +	Earnings	
Bal.	8,850	1,350	20,000		1,350	25,000	3,850	
f.	−950				−950			
Bal.	7,900	1,350	20,000		400	25,000	3,850	

If supplies of $2,500 were purchased during the month and supplies of $350 are on hand at the end of the month, how much is supplies expense for the month?

$2,150 ($2,500 supplies purchased − $350 on hand)

You should note that paying an amount on account is different from paying an amount for an expense. The payment of an expense reduces owners' equity, as illustrated in transaction (e). Paying an amount on account reduces the amount owed on a liability.

Transaction g   At the end of the month, the cost of the supplies on hand (not yet used) is $550. The remainder of the supplies ($1,350 − $550) was used in the operations of the business and is treated as an expense. This decrease of $800 in supplies and owners' equity is shown as follows:

	Assets			=	Liabilities +		Owners' Equity	
					Accounts	Capital	Retained	
	Cash +	Supplies +	Land		Payable +	Stock +	Earnings	
Bal.	7,900	1,350	20,000		400	25,000	3,850	
g.		−800					− 800	Supplies expense
Bal.	7,900	550	20,000		400	25,000	3,050	

Transaction h   At the end of the month, NetSolutions pays $2,000 to stockholders (Chris Clark) as dividends. *Dividends* are distributions of earnings to stockholders. The payment of the dividends reduces both cash and owners' equity. The effect of this transaction is shown as follows:

	Assets			=	Liabilities +		Owners' Equity	
					Accounts	Capital	Retained	
	Cash +	Supplies +	Land		Payable +	Stock +	Earnings	
Bal.	7,900	550	20,000		400	25,000	3,050	
h.	−2,000						−2,000	Dividends
Bal.	5,900	550	20,000		400	25,000	1,050	

You should be careful not to confuse dividends with expenses. Dividends *do not* represent assets or services used in the process of earning revenues. The owners' equity decrease from dividends is listed in the equation under Retained Earnings. This is because dividends are considered a distribution of earnings to stockholders.

Summary   The transactions of NetSolutions are summarized as follows. They are identified by letter, and the balance of each item is shown after each transaction.

	Cash	+ Supplies +	Land	= Accounts Payable +	Capital Stock +	Retained Earnings	
a.	+25,000				+25,000		Investment by stockholder
b.	−20,000		+20,000				
Bal.	5,000		20,000		25,000		
c.		+1,350		+1,350			
Bal.	5,000	1,350	20,000	1,350	25,000		
d.	+ 7,500					+ 7,500	Fees earned
Bal.	12,500	1,350	20,000	1,350	25,000	7,500	
e.	− 3,650					− 2,125	Wages expense
						− 800	Rent expense
						− 450	Utilities expense
						− 275	Misc. expense
Bal.	8,850	1,350	20,000	1,350	25,000	3,850	
f.	− 950			− 950			
Bal.	7,900	1,350	20,000	400		3,850	
g.		− 800				− 800	Supplies expense
Bal.	7,900	550	20,000	400	25,000	3,050	
h.	− 2,000					− 2,000	Dividends
Bal.	5,900	550	20,000	400	25,000	1,050	

In reviewing the preceding summary, you should note the following, which apply to all types of businesses:

1. The effect of every transaction is *an increase or a decrease in one or more of the accounting equation elements.*
2. The two sides of the accounting equation are *always equal.*
3. The owners' equity is *increased by amounts invested by stockholders (capital stock)* and is *decreased by dividends to stockholders (retained earnings).* In addition, the owners' equity (retained earnings) is *increased by revenues* and is *decreased by expenses.* The effects of these four types of transactions on owners' equity are illustrated in Exhibit 5.

•Exhibit 5   Effects of Transactions on Owners' Equity

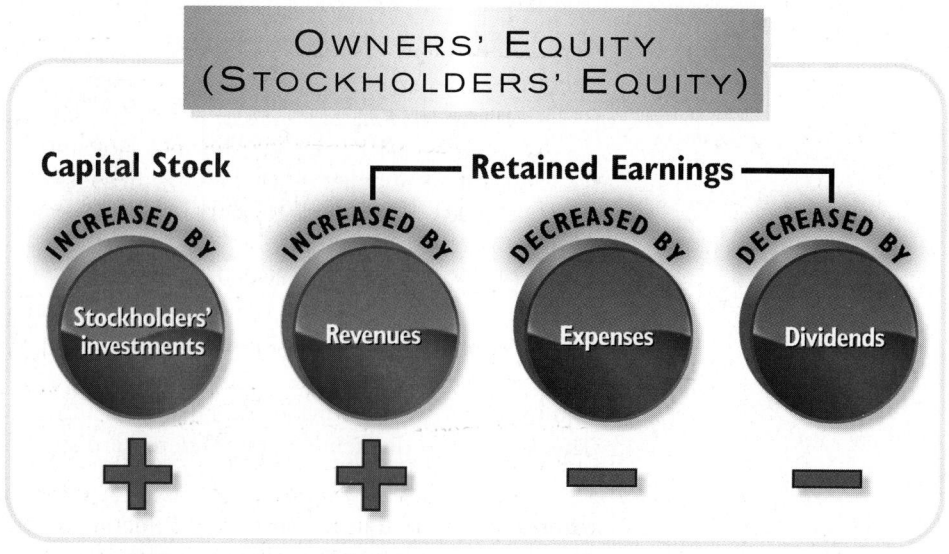

Financial Statements

objective   **8**

Describe the financial statements of a corporation and explain how they interrelate.

After transactions have been recorded and summarized, reports are prepared for users. The accounting reports that provide this information are called ***financial statements***. The principal financial statements of a corporation are the income statement, the retained earnings statement, the balance sheet, and the statement of cash flows. The order in which the statements are normally prepared and the nature of the data presented in each statement are as follows:

- ***Income statement***—A summary of the revenue and expenses *for a specific period of time*, such as a month or a year.
- ***Retained earnings statement***—A summary of the changes in the earnings retained in the corporation for *a specific period of time*, such as a month or a year.
- ***Balance sheet***—A list of the assets, liabilities, and owners' (stockholders') equity *as of a specific date*, usually at the close of the last day of a month or a year.
- ***Statement of cash flows***—A summary of the cash receipts and cash payments *for a specific period of time*, such as a month or a year.

The basic features of the four statements and their interrelationships are illustrated in Exhibit 6. The data for the statements were taken from the summary of transactions of NetSolutions.

All financial statements should be identified by the name of the business, the title of the statement, and the *date* or *period of time*. The data presented in the income statement, the retained earnings statement, and the statement of cash flows are for a period of time. The data presented in the balance sheet are for a specific date.

You should note the use of indents, captions, dollar signs, and rulings in the financial statements. They aid the reader by emphasizing the sections of the statements.

Income Statement

REAL WORLD

When you buy something at a store, you may *match* the cash register total with the amount you paid the cashier and with the amount of change, if any, you received.

The income statement reports the revenues and expenses for a period of time, based on the ***matching concept***. This concept is applied by *matching* the expenses with the revenue generated during a period by those expenses. The income statement also reports the excess of the revenue over the expenses incurred. This excess of the revenue over the expenses is called ***net income*** or **net profit**. If the expenses exceed the revenue, the excess is a ***net loss***.

The effects of revenue earned and expenses incurred during the month for Net-Solutions were shown in the equation as increases and decreases in owners' equity (retained earnings). Net income for a period has the effect of increasing owners' equity (retained earnings) for the period, whereas a net loss has the effect of decreasing owners' equity (retained earnings) for the period.

Net income—the excess of revenue over expenses—increases owners' equity.

The revenue, expenses, and the net income of $3,050 for NetSolutions are reported in the income statement in Exhibit 6. The order in which the expenses are listed in the income statement varies among businesses. One method is to list them in order of size, beginning with the larger items. Miscellaneous expense is usually shown as the last item, regardless of the amount.

Retained Earnings Statement

The primary statement for analyzing changes in the owners' equity of a corporation is the retained earnings statement. The retained earnings statement is a connecting link between the income statement and the balance sheet.

Two types of transactions affect the retained earnings during the month: (1) the revenues and expenses that resulted in net income of $3,050 for the month and (2) dividends of $2,000 paid to stockholders. These transactions are summarized in the retained earnings statement for NetSolutions shown in Exhibit 6.

•Exhibit 6

Financial Statements

NetSolutions
Income Statement
For the Month Ended November 30, 2005

Fees earned		$7 5 0 0 00
Operating expenses:		
Wages expense	$2 1 2 5 00	
Rent expense	8 0 0 00	
Supplies expense	8 0 0 00	
Utilities expense	4 5 0 00	
Miscellaneous expense	2 7 5 00	
Total operating expenses		4 4 5 0 00
Net income		$3 0 5 0 00

NetSolutions
Retained Earnings Statement
For the Month Ended November 30, 2005

Retained earnings, November 1, 2005		$ 0
Net income for November		3 0 5 0 00
Less dividends		2 0 0 0 00
Retained earnings, November 30, 2005		$1 0 5 0 00

NetSolutions
Balance Sheet
November 30, 2005

Assets		Liabilities	
Cash	$ 5 9 0 0 00	Accounts payable	$ 4 0 0 00
Supplies	5 5 0 00	**Stockholders' Equity**	
Land	20 0 0 0 00	Capital stock $25,000	
		Retained earnings 1,050	26 0 5 0 00
		Total liabilities and	
Total assets	$26 4 5 0 00	Stockholders' equity	$26 4 5 0 00

NetSolutions
Statement of Cash Flows
For the Month Ended November 30, 2005

Cash flows from operating activities:		
Cash received from customers	$ 7 5 0 0 00	
Deduct cash payments for expenses and		
payments to creditors	4 6 0 0 00	
Net cash flow from operating activities		$ 2 9 0 0 00
Cash flows from investing activities:		
Cash payments for acquisition of land		
Cash flows from financing activities:		(20 0 0 0 00)
Cash received from sale of stock	$25 0 0 0 00	
Deduct cash dividends	2 0 0 0 00	
Net cash flow from financing activities		23 0 0 0 00
Net cash flow and November 30, 2005 cash balance		$ 5 9 0 0 00

Financial statements are used to evaluate the current financial condition of a business and to predict its future operating results and cash flows. For example, bank loan officers use a business's financial statements in deciding whether to grant a loan to the business. Once the loan is granted, the borrower may be required to maintain a certain level of assets in excess of liabilities. The business's financial statements are used to monitor this level.

Since NetSolutions has been in operation for only one month, it has no retained earnings at the beginning of November. For December, however, there is a beginning balance—the balance at the end of November. This balance of $1,050 is reported on the retained earnings statement. To illustrate, assume that NetSolutions earned net income of $4,155 and paid dividends of $2,000 during December. The retained earnings statement for NetSolutions for December is shown here.

NetSolutions Retained Earnings Statement For the Month Ended December 31, 2005		
Retained earnings, December 1, 2005		$1 0 5 0 00
Net income for the month	$4 1 5 5 00	
Less dividends	2 0 0 0 00	
Increase in retained earnings		2 1 5 5 00
Retained earnings, December 31, 2005		$3 2 0 5 00

Balance Sheet

The balance sheet in Exhibit 6 reports the amounts of NetSolutions' assets, liabilities, and owners' (stockholders') equity at the end of November. These amounts are taken from the last line of the summary of transactions presented earlier. The form of balance sheet shown in Exhibit 6 is called the **account form** because it resembles the basic format of the accounting equation, with assets on the left side and the liabilities and stockholders' equity sections on the right side. We illustrate an alternative form of balance sheet called the **report form** in a later chapter. It presents the liabilities and stockholders' equity sections below the assets section.

The assets section of the balance sheet normally presents assets in the order that they will be converted into cash or used in operations. Cash is presented first, followed by receivables, supplies, prepaid insurance, and other assets. The assets of a more permanent nature are shown next, such as land, buildings, and equipment.

In the liabilities section of the balance sheet in Exhibit 6, accounts payable is the only liability. When there are two or more categories of liabilities, each should be listed and the total amount of liabilities presented as follows.

Liabilities		
Accounts payable	$12,900	
Wages payable	2,570	
Total liabilities		$15,470

Statement of Cash Flows

The statement of cash flows consists of three sections, as we see in Exhibit 6: (1) operating activities, (2) investing activities, and (3) financing activities. Each of these sections is briefly described below.

Cash Flows from Operating Activities

This section reports a summary of cash receipts and cash payments from operations. The net cash flow from operating activities ($2,900 in Exhibit 6) will normally differ from the amount of net income for the period ($3,050 in Exhibit 6). This difference occurs because revenues and expenses may not be recorded at the same time that cash is received from customers or paid to creditors.

Cash Flows from Investing Activities

This section reports the cash transactions for the acquisition and sale of relatively permanent assets.

Cash Flows from Financing Activities

This section reports the cash transactions related to cash investments by the stockholders, borrowings, and cash dividends.

Preparing the statement of cash flows requires an understanding of concepts that we have not discussed in this chapter. Therefore, we will illustrate the preparation of the statement of cash flows in a later chapter.

Financial Analysis and Interpretation

objective 9

Use the ratio of liabilities to stockholders' equity to analyze the ability of a business to withstand poor business conditions.

As we discussed earlier in this chapter, financial statements are useful to bankers, creditors, owners, and other stakeholders in analyzing and interpreting the financial performance and condition of a business. Throughout this text, we will discuss various tools that are often used in practice to analyze and interpret the financial performance and condition of a business. The first such tool we will introduce is especially useful in analyzing the ability of a business to pay its creditors.

The relationship between liabilities and stockholders' equity, expressed as a ratio, is calculated as follows:

$$\text{Ratio of liabilities to stockholders' equity} = \frac{\text{Total liabilities}}{\text{Total stockholders' equity}}$$

To illustrate, NetSolutions' ratio of liabilities to stockholders' equity at the end of November is 0.015, as calculated below.

$$\text{Ratio of liabilities to stockholders' equity} = \frac{\$400}{\$26,050} = 0.015$$

The rights of creditors to a business's assets take precedence over the rights of stockholders. Thus, the lower the ratio of liabilities to stockholders' equity, the better able the business is to withstand poor business conditions and still fully meet its obligations to creditors.

To illustrate, a ratio of 1 indicates that the liabilities and stockholders' equity are equal. In other words, if the business suffers a loss equal to the total liabilities, the amount of total assets available to creditors will not drop below their claims on the assets. If this were to happen, the creditors could collect their claims and the stockholders would be left with nothing.

SPOTLIGHT ON STRATEGY

IT'S ALL IN THE NAME

Intel develops and produces microprocessors for use in electronic equipment, including personal computers and organizers. Beginning with the 8086 processor and continuing with the 286, 386, and 486 processors, Intel's processors were widely used in personal computers during the 1980s and 1990s. Intel's competitors, however, also developed and sold 386 and 486 processors. In doing so, its competitors were able to erode Intel's market share. In responding, Intel named its next microprocessor the "Pentium," rather than the 586, and registered "Pentium" as a trademark. By doing so, Intel prevented its competitors from selling their products as "Pentiums." Thus, Intel developed a "differentiated" brand name that its competitors were unable to duplicate. Intel's newest processor is called the "Pentium M."

Key Points

1 Describe the nature of a business.

A business is an organization in which basic resources (inputs), such as materials and labor, are assembled and processed to provide goods or services (outputs) to customers. The objective of most businesses is to maximize profits.

There are three different types of businesses that are operated for profit: manufacturing, merchandising, and service businesses. A business is normally organized in one of the following forms: proprietorship, partnership, corporation, or limited liability corporation. A business stakeholder is a person or entity (such as an owner, manager, employee, customer, creditor, or the government) who has an interest in the economic performance of the business.

2 Describe the role of accounting in business.

Accounting is an information system that provides reports to stakeholders about the economic activities and condition of a business. Accounting is the "language of business."

3 Describe the importance of business ethics and the basic principles of proper ethical conduct.

Ethics are moral principles that guide the conduct of individuals. Proper ethical conduct implies a behavior that considers the impact of one's actions on society and others. Sound ethical principles include (1) avoiding small ethical lapses, (2) focusing on your long-term reputation, and (3) being willing to suffer adverse personal consequences for holding to an ethical position.

4 Describe the profession of accounting.

Accountants are engaged in either private accounting or public accounting. The two most common specialized fields of accounting are financial accounting and managerial accounting. Other fields include cost accounting, environmental accounting, tax accounting, accounting systems, international accounting, not-for-profit accounting, and social accounting.

5 Summarize the development of accounting principles and relate them to practice.

Financial accountants follow generally accepted accounting principles (GAAP) in preparing reports so that stakeholders can compare one company to another. Accounting principles and concepts develop from research, accepted accounting practices, and pronouncements of authoritative bodies. Currently, the Financial Accounting Standards Board (FASB) is the authoritative body having the primary responsibility for developing accounting principles.

The business entity concept views the business as an entity separate from its owners, creditors, or other stakeholders. The business entity limits the economic data in the accounting system to that related directly to the activities of the business. The cost concept requires that properties and services bought by a business be recorded in terms of actual cost. The objectivity concept requires that the accounting records and reports be based upon objective evidence. The unit of measure concept requires that economic data be recorded in dollars.

6 State the accounting equation and define each element of the equation.

The resources owned by a business and the rights or claims to these resources may be stated in the form of an equation, as follows:

Assets = Liabilities + Owners' Equity

7 Explain how business transactions can be stated in terms of the resulting changes in the basic elements of the accounting equation.

All business transactions can be stated in terms of the change in one or more of the three elements of the accounting equation. That is, the effect of every transaction can be stated in terms of increases or decreases in one or more of these elements, while maintaining the equality between the two sides of the equation.

8 Describe the financial statements of a corporation and explain how they interrelate.

The principal financial statements of a corporation are the income statement, the retained earnings statement, the balance sheet, and the statement of cash flows. The income statement reports a period's net income or net loss, which also appears on the retained earnings statement. The ending retained earnings reported on the retained earnings statement is also reported on the balance sheet. The ending cash balance is reported on the balance sheet and the statement of cash flows.

9 Use the ratio of liabilities to stockholders' equity to analyze the ability of a business to withstand poor business conditions.

The ratio of liabilities to stockholders' equity is useful in analyzing the ability of a business to pay its creditors. The lower the ratio, the better able the business is to withstand poor business conditions and still fully meet its obligations to creditors.

Key Terms

account form (21)
account payable (15)
account receivable (16)
accounting (8)
accounting equation (13)
assets (13)
balance sheet (19)
business (2)
business entity concept (13)
business stakeholder (6)
business strategy (4)
business transaction (14)
capital stock (15)
Certified Public Accountant (CPA) (11)
combination strategy (5)
corporation (3)

differentiation strategy (4)
dividends (17)
ethics (9)
expenses (16)
financial accounting (12)
Financial Accounting Standards Board (FASB) (12)
financial statements (19)
generally accepted accounting principles (GAAP) (12)
income statement (19)
liabilities (13)
limited liability corporation (4)
low-cost strategy (4)
managerial accounting (12)
manufacturing businesses (2)
matching concept (19)

merchandising businesses (3)
net income (19)
net loss (19)
owners' equity (13)
partnership (3)
prepaid expenses (15)
private accounting (10)
proprietorship (3)
public accounting (10)
report form (21)
retained earnings (16)
retained earnings statement (19)
revenue (16)
service businesses (3)
statement of cash flows (19)
unit of measure concept (13)
value chain (6)

Illustrative Problem

Cecil Jameson, Attorney-at-Law, P.C., is organized as a professional corporation owned and operated by Cecil Jameson. On July 1, 2005, Cecil Jameson, Attorney-at-Law, P.C., has the following assets and liabilities: cash, $1,000; accounts receivable, $3,200; supplies, $850; land, $10,000; accounts payable, $1,530; capital stock, $10,000. Office space and office equipment are currently being rented, pending the construction of an office complex on land purchased last year. Business transactions during July are summarized as follows:

a. Received cash from clients for services, $3,928.
b. Paid creditors on account, $1,055.
c. Received cash from Cecil Jameson as an additional investment and issued capital stock, $3,700.
d. Paid office rent for the month, $1,200.
e. Charged clients for legal services on account, $2,025.
f. Purchased office supplies on account, $245.
g. Received cash from clients on account, $3,000.
h. Received invoice for paralegal services from Legal Aid Inc. for July (to be paid on August 10), $1,635.
i. Paid the following: wages expense, $850; answering service expense, $250; utilities expense, $325; and miscellaneous expense, $75.
j. Determined that the cost of office supplies on hand was $980; therefore, the cost of supplies used during the month was $115.
k. Paid dividends of $1,000.

Instructions

1. Determine the amount of retained earnings as of July 1, 2005.
2. State the assets, liabilities, and owners' equity as of July 1 in equation form similar to that shown in this chapter. In tabular form below the equation, indicate the increases and decreases resulting from each transaction and the new balances

after each transaction. Explain the nature of each increase and decrease in owners' equity by an appropriate notation at the right of the amount.

3. Prepare an income statement for July, a retained earnings statement for July, and a balance sheet as of July 31, 2005.

Solution

1. Assets − Liabilities = Owners' Equity

$15,050 − $1,530 = Capital Stock + Retained Earnings

$13,520 = $10,000 + Retained Earnings

$3,250 = Retained Earnings

2.

			Assets			= Liabilities +		Owners' Equity	
	Cash	+ Accounts Receivable	+ Supplies	+ Land	=	Accounts Payable	+ Capital Stock	+ Retained Earnings	
Bal.	1,000	3,200	850	10,000		1,530	10,000	3,520	
a.	+3,928							+3,928	Fees earned
Bal.	4,928	3,200	850	10,000		1,530	10,000	7,448	
b.	−1,055					−1,055			
Bal.	3,873	3,200	850	10,000		475	10,000	7,448	
c.	+3,700						+3,700		Investment
Bal.	7,573	3,200	850	10,000		475	13,700	7,448	
d.	−1,200							−1,200	Rent expense
Bal.	6,373	3,200	850	10,000		475	13,700	6,248	
e.		+2,025						+2,025	Fees earned
Bal.	6,373	5,225	850	10,000		475	13,700	8,273	
f.			+ 245			+ 245			
Bal.	6,373	5,225	1,095	10,000		720	13,700	8,273	
g.	+3,000	−3,000							
Bal.	9,373	2,225	1,095	10,000		720	13,700	8,273	
h.						+1,635		−1,635	Paralegal exp.
Bal.	9,373	2,225	1,095	10,000		2,355	13,700	6,638	
i.	−1,500							− 850	Wages exp.
								− 250	Answ. svc. exp.
								− 325	Utilities exp.
								− 75	Misc. exp.
Bal.	7,873	2,225	1,095	10,000		2,355	13,700	5,138	
j.			− 115					− 115	Supplies exp.
Bal.	7,873	2,225	980	10,000		2,355	13,700	5,023	
k.	−1,000							−1,000	Dividends
	6,873	2,225	980	10,000		2,355	13,700	4,023	

3.

Cecil Jameson, Attorney-at-Law, P.C.
Income Statement
For the Month Ended July 31, 2005

Fees earned			$5 9 5 3 00
Operating expenses:			
Paralegal expense	$1 6 3 5 00		
Rent expense	1 2 0 0 00		
Wages expense	8 5 0 00		
Utilities expense	3 2 5 00		
Answering service expense	2 5 0 00		
Supplies expense	1 1 5 00		
Miscellaneous expense	7 5 00		
Total operating expenses		4 4 5 0 00	
Net income		$1 5 0 3 00	

(continued)

Cecil Jameson, Attorney-at-Law, P.C.
Retained Earnings Statement
For the Month Ended July 31, 2005

Retained earnings, July 1, 2005		$3 5 2 0 00
Net income for the month	$1 5 0 3 00	
Less dividends	1 0 0 0 00	
Increase in retained earnings		5 0 3 00
Retained earnings, July 31, 2005		$4 0 2 3 00

Cecil Jameson, Attorney-at-Law, P.C.
Balance Sheet
July 31, 2005

Assets		Liabilities	
Cash	$ 6 8 7 3 00	Accounts payable	$ 2 3 5 5 00
Accounts receivable	2 2 2 5 00	**Stockholders' Equity**	
Supplies	9 8 0 00	Capital stock $13,700	
Land	10 0 0 0 00	Retained earnings 4,023	17 7 2 3 00
		Total liabilities and	
Total assets	$20 0 7 8 00	stockholders' equity	$20 0 7 8 00

Self-Examination Questions (Answers at End of Chapter)

1. A profit-making business operating as a separate legal entity and in which ownership is divided into shares of stock is known as a:
   A. proprietorship.   C. partnership.
   B. service business.   D. corporation.

2. The resources owned by a business are called:
   A. assets.
   B. liabilities.
   C. the accounting equation.
   D. owners' equity.

3. A listing of a business entity's assets, liabilities, and owners' equity as of a specific date is:
   A. a balance sheet.
   B. an income statement.

C. a retained earnings statement.
D. a statement of cash flows.

4. If total assets increased $20,000 during a period and total liabilities increased $12,000 during the same period, the amount and direction (increase or decrease) of the change in owners' equity for that period is:
   A. a $32,000 increase.   C. an $8,000 increase.
   B. a $32,000 decrease.   D. an $8,000 decrease.

5. If revenue was $45,000, expenses were $37,500, and dividends were $10,000, the amount of net income or net loss would be:
   A. $45,000 net income. C. $37,500 net loss.
   B. $7,500 net income.   D. $2,500 net loss.

Class Discussion Questions

1. What is the objective of most businesses?
2. What is the difference between a manufacturing business and a service business? Is a restaurant a manufacturing business, a service business, or both?
3. Why are most large companies like **Microsoft**, **Pepsi**, **Caterpillar**, and **AutoZone** organized as corporations?
4. Both **KIA** and **Porche** produce and sell automobiles. Describe and contrast the business strategies of KIA and Porche.
5. Assume that a friend of yours operates a family-owned pharmacy. A **Super Wal-Mart** is scheduled to open in the next several months that will also offer pharmacy services. What business strategy would your friend use to compete with the Super Wal-Mart pharmacy?
6. How does **eBay** offer value to its customers?
7. Who are normally included as the stakeholders of a business?
8. What is the role of accounting in business?
9. Deana Moran is the owner of First Delivery Service. Recently, Deana paid interest of $3,600 on a personal loan of $60,000 that she used to begin the business. Should First Delivery Service record the interest payment? Explain.
10. On July 10, Elrod Repair Service extended an offer of $100,000 for land that had been priced for sale at $120,000. On July 25, Elrod Repair Service accepted the seller's counteroffer of $112,000. Describe how Elrod Repair Service should record the land.
11. a. Land with an assessed value of $300,000 for property tax purposes is acquired by a business for $500,000. Seven years later, the plot of land has an assessed value of $400,000 and the business receives an offer of $600,000 for it. Should the monetary amount assigned to the land in the business records now be increased?
    b. Assuming that the land acquired in (a) was sold for $600,000, how would the various elements of the accounting equation be affected?
12. Describe the difference between an account receivable and an account payable.
13. A business had revenues of $280,000 and operating expenses of $315,000. Did the business (a) incur a net loss or (b) realize net income?
14. A business had revenues of $750,000 and operating expenses of $670,000. Did the business (a) incur a net loss or (b) realize net income?
15. What particular item of financial or operating data appears on both the income statement and the retained earnings statement? What item appears on both the balance sheet and the retained earnings statement? What item appears on both the balance sheet and statement of cash flows?

WebTutor Advantage on WebCT or Blackboard with Personal Trainer 3.0

Get the most robust interactive study materials available on the Web! Includes:

- Automatic and immediate feedback from Pre-Tests, Achievement Tests, Multiple-Choice and True-False Quizzes, and Quiz Bowl.
- Exercise Demos and Illustrative Problems in Flash presentations that review and reinforce what you've learned.
- Video cases that cover key concepts in the context of a real company.
- A Flash introduction with audio for each chapter.
- E-lectures that provide Flash lecture presentations with audio to help you review one or two key concepts in each chapter.
- Crossword Puzzles to test your knowledge of the glossary.

Xtreme!
0-324-20503-1

This hybrid CD-ROM and Internet-based product provides you with the same media-rich content from WebTutor Advantage, but without the WebCT or Blackboard platforms.

Xtra!
0-324-20502-3

This CD-ROM provides lecture replacement resources and access to interactive quizzes to test your understanding of the content of the text.

Personal Trainer
0-324-20514-7

This product helps you complete the end-of-chapter exercises and problems from the text using:

- Concept warm-ups.
- Helpful hints.
- Immediate feedback.
- A personal gradebook.

P.A.S.S. Software (formerly General Ledger Software)
0-324-20510-4

- This software package teaches you the basics of a computerized accounting system in an easy-to-use environment.
- You will get hints and tips for completing end-of-chapter problems.
- You will get immediate feedback to determine if you have done the problems correctly.

Study Guide
Corporate
Financial   0-324-20500-7
Managerial   0-324-20501-5

- This guide will give you quiz and test hints.
- You can practice chapter concepts, learn through numerous multiple choice, fill-in-the-blank, true-false questions, and exercises, and check your answers against the provided solutions.

Working Papers for Exercises and Problems
Corporate
Financial   0-324-20496-5
Managerial   0-324-20497-3

This supplement contains forms that help you organize your solutions.

Working Papers Plus for Selected Exercises and Problems
Corporate
Financial   0-324-20498-1
Managerial   0-324-20499-X

This supplement includes selected exercises and problems from the text, along with the forms for your use in solving them.

Exercises

EXERCISE 1-1
Types of businesses
Objective 1

Indicate whether each of the following companies is primarily a service, merchandise, or manufacturing business. If you are unfamiliar with the company, you may use the Internet to locate the company's home page or use the finance Web site of **Yahoo.com**.

1. Ford Motor
2. Citigroup
3. Sears Roebuck
4. AT&T
5. H&R Block Inc.
6. Boeing
7. First Union Corporation
8. Alcoa
9. CVS
10. Caterpillar
11. FedEx
12. Dow Chemical
13. Gap
14. Hilton Hotels
15. Procter & Gamble

EXERCISE 1-2
Business strategy
Objective 1

Identify the primary business strategy of each of the following companies as (a) a low-cost strategy, (b) a differentiation strategy, or (c) a combination strategy. If you are unfamiliar with the company, you may use the Internet to locate the company's home page or use the finance Web site of **Yahoo.com**.

1. Southwest Airlines
2. Home Depot
3. BMW
4. Coca-Cola
5. Target
6. Goldman Sachs Group
7. Sara Lee
8. Delta Air Lines
9. Circuit City Stores
10. Maytag
11. Office Depot
12. Nike
13. Charles Schwab
14. Dollar General
15. General Motors

EXERCISE 1-3
Professional ethics
Objective 3

ETHICS

A fertilizer manufacturing company wants to relocate to Collier County. A 13-year-old report from a fired researcher at the company says the company's product is releasing toxic by-products. The company has suppressed that report. A second report commissioned by the company shows there is no problem with the fertilizer.
⬛▭▷ Should the company's chief executive officer reveal the context of the unfavorable report in discussions with Collier County representatives? Discuss.

EXERCISE 1-4
Business entity concept
Objective 5

Bechler Sports sells hunting and fishing equipment and provides guided hunting and fishing trips. Bechler Sports is owned and operated by Lefty Wisman, a well-known sports enthusiast and hunter. Lefty's wife, Betsy, owns and operates Eagle Boutique, a women's clothing store. Lefty and Betsy have established a trust fund to finance their children's college education. The trust fund is maintained by First Montana Bank in the name of the children, Jeff and Steph.

For each of the following transactions, identify which of the entities listed should record the transaction in its records.

Entities	
B	Bechler Sports
F	First Montana Bank
E	Eagle Boutique
X	None of the above

1. Lefty paid a local doctor for his annual physical, which was required by the workmen's compensation insurance policy carried by Bechler Sports.

(continued)

2. Lefty received a cash advance from customers for a guided hunting trip.
3. Betsy purchased two dozen spring dresses from a Billings (MT) designer for a special spring sale.
4. Betsy deposited a $2,000 personal check in the trust fund at First Montana Bank.
5. Lefty paid for an advertisement in a hunters' magazine.
6. Betsy purchased mutual fund shares as an investment for the children's trust.
7. Lefty paid for dinner and a movie to celebrate their twentieth wedding anniversary.
8. Betsy donated several dresses from inventory for a local charity auction for the benefit of a women's abuse shelter.
9. Betsy paid her dues to the YWCA.
10. Lefty paid a breeder's fee for an English springer spaniel to be used as a hunting guide dog.

EXERCISE 1-5
Accounting equation
Objective 6

REAL WORLD

✓ *Coca-Cola, $11,800*

The total assets and total liabilities of **Coca-Cola** and **PepsiCo** are shown below.

	Coca-Cola (in millions)	PepsiCo (in millions)
Assets	$24,501	$23,474
Liabilities	12,701	14,183

Determine the owners' (stockholders') equity of each company.

EXERCISE 1-6
Accounting equation
Objective 6

✓ *Toys "R" Us, $4,030*

The total assets and total liabilities of **Toys "R" Us Inc.** and **Estée Lauder Companies Inc.** are shown below.

	Toys "R" Us (in millions)	Estée Lauder Companies (in millions)
Assets	$9,397	$3,417
Liabilities	5,367	1,955

Determine the owners' (stockholders') equity of each company.

EXERCISE 1-7
Accounting equation
Objective 6

✓ *a. $96,500*

Determine the missing amount for each of the following:

	Assets	=	Liabilities	+	Owners' Equity
a.	X	=	$25,000	+	$71,500
b.	$82,750	=	X	+	15,000
c.	37,000	=	17,500	+	X

EXERCISE 1-8
Accounting equation
Objectives 6, 8

✓ *b. $310,000*

Chris Lund is the sole stockholder and operator of Saluki, a motivational consulting business. At the end of its accounting period, December 31, 2005, Saluki has assets of $475,000 and liabilities of $200,000. Using the accounting equation and considering each case independently, determine the following amounts:

a. Owners' equity, as of December 31, 2005.
b. Owners' equity, as of December 31, 2006, assuming that assets increased by $75,000 and liabilities increased by $40,000 during 2006.
c. Owners' equity, as of December 31, 2006, assuming that assets decreased by $15,000 and liabilities increased by $27,000 during 2006.
d. Owners' equity, as of December 31, 2006, assuming that assets increased by $125,000 and liabilities decreased by $65,000 during 2006.
e. Net income (or net loss) during 2006, assuming that as of December 31, 2006, assets were $425,000, liabilities were $105,000, and there were no dividends and no additional capital stock was issued.

EXERCISE 1-9
Asset, liability, owners' equity items
Objective 7

Indicate whether each of the following is identified with (1) an asset, (2) a liability, or (3) owners' equity:

a. wages expense   d. land
b. accounts payable   e. fees earned
c. cash   f. supplies

EXERCISE 1-10
Effect of transactions on accounting equation
Objective 7

Describe how the following business transactions affect the three elements of the accounting equation.

a. Received cash for services performed.
b. Invested cash in business.
c. Paid for utilities used in the business.
d. Purchased supplies on account.
e. Purchased supplies for cash.

EXERCISE 1-11
Effect of transactions on accounting equation
Objective 7

✓ (a)(1) increase $80,000

a. A vacant lot acquired for $50,000 is sold for $130,000 in cash. What is the effect of the sale on the total amount of the seller's (1) assets, (2) liabilities, and (3) owners' equity?
b. Assume that the seller owes $30,000 on a loan for the land. After receiving the $130,000 cash in (a), the seller pays the $30,000 owed. What is the effect of the payment on the total amount of the seller's (1) assets, (2) liabilities, and (3) owners' equity?

EXERCISE 1-12
Effect of transactions on owners' equity
Objective 7

Indicate whether each of the following types of transactions will (a) increase owners' (stockholders') equity or (b) decrease owners' (stockholders') equity:

1. revenues   3. issuance of capital stock
2. expenses   4. cash dividends

EXERCISE 1-13
Transactions
Objective 7

The following selected transactions were completed by Salvo Delivery Service during February:

1. Received cash from issuance of capital stock, $35,000.
2. Received cash for providing delivery services, $15,000.
3. Paid creditors on account, $1,800.
4. Billed customers for delivery services on account, $11,250.
5. Paid advertising expense, $750.
6. Purchased supplies for cash, $800.
7. Paid rent for February, $2,000.
8. Received cash from customers on account, $6,740.
9. Determined that the cost of supplies on hand was $135; therefore, $665 of supplies had been used during the month.
10. Paid dividends, $1,000.

Indicate the effect of each transaction on the accounting equation by listing the numbers identifying the transactions, (1) through (10), in a vertical column, and inserting at the right of each number the appropriate letter from the following list:

a. Increase in an asset, decrease in another asset.
b. Increase in an asset, increase in a liability.
c. Increase in an asset, increase in owners' equity.
d. Decrease in an asset, decrease in a liability.
e. Decrease in an asset, decrease in owners' equity.

EXERCISE 1-14
Nature of transactions
Objective 7

✓ d. $7,600

Mike Renner operates his own catering service. Summary financial data for March are presented in equation form as follows. Each line designated by a number indicates the effect of a transaction on the equation. Each increase and decrease in owners' equity, except transaction (5), affects net income.

	Cash	+ Supplies +	Land	= Liabilities +	Capital Stock +	Retained Earnings
Bal.	18,000	1,500	54,000	15,000	10,000	48,500
1.	+25,000					+25,000
2.	−10,000		+10,000			
3.	−16,000					−16,000
4.		+ 800		+ 800		
5.	− 2,000					− 2,000
6.	−10,600			−10,600		
7.		−1,400				− 1,400
Bal.	4,400	900	64,000	5,200	10,000	54,100

a. Describe each transaction.
b. What is the amount of net decrease in cash during the month?
c. What is the amount of net increase in retained earnings during the month?
d. What is the amount of the net income for the month?
e. How much of the net income for the month was retained in the business?

EXERCISE 1-15
Net income and dividends
Objective 8

The income statement of a corporation for the month of October indicates a net income of $158,250. During the same period, $180,000 in cash dividends were paid.

Would it be correct to say that the business incurred a net loss of $21,750 during the month? Discuss.

EXERCISE 1-16
Net income and owners' equity for four businesses
Objective 8

✓ *Company O: Net loss, ($50,000)*

Four different corporations, M, N, O, and P, show the same balance sheet data at the beginning and end of a year. These data, exclusive of the amount of owners' equity, are summarized as follows:

	Total Assets	Total Liabilities
Beginning of the year	$750,000	$300,000
End of the year	$1,200,000	$650,000

On the basis of the above data and the following additional information for the year, determine the net income (or loss) of each company for the year. (*Hint:* First determine the amount of increase or decrease in owners' (stockholders') equity during the year.)

Company M: No additional capital stock was issued and no dividends were paid.
Company N: No additional capital stock was issued but dividends of $60,000 were paid.
Company O: Additional capital stock of $150,000 was issued but no dividends were paid.
Company P: Additional capital stock of $150,000 was issued and dividends of $60,000 were paid.

EXERCISE 1-17
Balance sheet items
Objective 8

From the following list of selected items taken from the records of Ishmael Appliance Service as of a specific date, identify those that would appear on the balance sheet:

1. Supplies
2. Wages Expense
3. Cash
4. Land
5. Utilities Expense
6. Fees Earned
7. Supplies Expense
8. Accounts Payable
9. Capital Stock
10. Wages Payable

EXERCISE 1-18
Income statement items
Objective 8

Based on the data presented in Exercise 1-17, identify those items that would appear on the income statement.

EXERCISE 1-19
Retained earnings statement

Objective 8

SPREADSHEET

✓*Retained earnings, April 30, 2006: $358,200*

Financial information related to Madras Company, for the month ended April 30, 2006, is as follows:

Net income for April	$ 73,000
Dividends during April	12,000
Retained earnings, April 1, 2006	297,200

Prepare a retained earnings statement for the month ended April 30, 2006.

EXERCISE 1-20
Income statement

Objective 8

SPREADSHEET

✓*Net income: $89,320*

Hercules Services was organized on November 1, 2006. A summary of the revenue and expense transactions for November follows:

Fees earned	$232,120
Wages expense	100,100
Miscellaneous expense	3,150
Rent expense	35,000
Supplies expense	4,550

Prepare an income statement for the month ended November 30.

EXERCISE 1-21
Missing amounts from balance sheet and income statement data

Objective 8

✓*(a) $156,300*

One item is omitted in each of the following summaries of balance sheet and income statement data for four different corporations, A, B, C, and D.

	A	B	C	D
Beginning of the year:				
Assets	$720,000	$125,000	$160,000	(d)
Liabilities	432,000	65,000	121,600	$150,000
End of the year:				
Assets	894,000	175,000	144,000	310,000
Liabilities	390,000	55,000	128,000	170,000
During the year:				
Additional issue of				
capital stock	(a)	25,000	16,000	50,000
Dividends	48,000	8,000	(c)	75,000
Revenue	237,300	(b)	184,000	140,000
Expenses	129,600	32,000	196,000	160,000

Determine the missing amounts, identifying them by letter. [*Hint:* First determine the amount of increase or decrease in owners' (stockholders') equity during the year.]

EXERCISE 1-22
Balance sheets, net income

Objective 8

SPREADSHEET

✓*b. $36,340*

Financial information related to Derby Interiors for October and November 2006 is as follows:

	October 31, 2006	November 30, 2006
Accounts payable	$12,320	$13,280
Accounts receivable	27,200	31,300
Capital stock	15,000	15,000
Retained earnings	?	?
Cash	48,000	81,600
Supplies	2,400	2,000

a. Prepare balance sheets for Derby Interiors as of October 31 and as of November 30, 2006.
b. Determine the amount of net income for November, assuming that no additional capital stock was issued and no dividends were paid during the month.
c. Determine the amount of net income for November, assuming that no additional capital stock was issued but dividends of $10,000 were paid during the month.

EXERCISE 1-23
Financial statements
Objective 8

REAL WORLD

Each of the following items is shown in the financial statements of **Exxon Mobil Corporation**. Identify the financial statement (balance sheet or income statement) in which each item would appear.

a. Operating expenses **I.S.**
b. Crude oil inventory
c. Income taxes payable
d. Sales
e. Investments
f. Marketable securities
g. Exploration expenses
h. Notes and loans payable

i. Cash equivalents
j. Long-term debt
k. Selling expenses
l. Notes receivable
m. Equipment
n. Accounts payable
o. Prepaid taxes

EXERCISE 1-24
Statement of cash flows
Objective 8

Indicate whether each of the following activities would be reported on the statement of cash flows as (a) an operating activity, (b) an investing activity, or (c) a financing activity:

1. Cash paid for land
2. Cash received from fees earned
3. Cash received as investment from stockholders
4. Cash paid for expenses

EXERCISE 1-25
Financial statements
Objective 8

WHAT'S WRONG
WITH THIS?

✓ *Correct Amount of Total Assets is $19,600*

Caddis Realty, organized June 1, 2006, is owned and operated by Jerry Maris. How many errors can you find in the following financial statements for Caddis Realty, prepared after its second month of operations?

Caddis Realty
Income Statement
July 31, 2006

Sales commissions		$51,900
Operating expenses:		
Office salaries expense	$32,400	
Rent expense	11,000	
Automobile expense	2,500	
Miscellaneous expense	800	
Supplies expense	300	
Total operating expenses		47,000
Net income		$14,900

Jerry Maris
Retained Earnings Statement
July 31, 2005

Retained earnings, July 1, 2006	$ 7,900
Less dividends during July	2,000
	$ 5,900
Net income for the month	14,900
Retained earnings, July 31, 2006	$20,800

Balance Sheet
For the Month Ended July 31, 2006

Assets		Liabilities	
Cash	$3,300	Accounts receivable	$14,300
Accounts payable	3,800	Supplies	2,000
		Stockholders' Equity	
		Capital stock	5,000
		Retained earnings	20,800
Total assets	$7,100	Total liabilities and stockholders' equity	$42,100

EXERCISE 1-26
Ratio of liabilities to stockholders' equity

Objective 9

REAL WORLD

The Home Depot, Inc., is the world's largest home improvement retailer and one of the largest retailers in the United States based on net sales volume. The Home Depot operates over 1,100 Home Depot® stores that sell a wide assortment of building materials and home improvement and lawn and garden products. The Home Depot also operates over 25 EXPO Design Center stores that offer interior design products, such as kitchen and bathroom cabinetry, tiles, flooring, and lighting fixtures, and installation services.

For the years ending February 2, 2003, and February 3, 2002, The Home Depot reported the following balance sheet data (in millions):

	2003	2002
Total assets	$30,011	$26,394
Total stockholders' equity	19,802	18,082

a. Determine the total liabilities as of February 2, 2003, and February 3, 2002.
b. Determine the ratio of liabilities to stockholders' equity for 2003 and 2002. Round to two decimal places.
c. What conclusions regarding the margin of protection to the creditors can you draw from (b)?

EXERCISE 1-27
Ratio of liabilities to stockholders' equity

Objective 9

REAL WORLD

Lowe's, a major competitor of The Home Depot in the home improvement business, operates over 700 stores. For the years ending January 31, 2003, and February 1, 2002, Lowe's reported the following balance sheet data (in millions):

	2003	2002
Total assets	$16,109	$13,736
Total liabilities	8,302	7,062

a. Determine the total stockholders' equity as of January 31, 2003, and February 1, 2002.
b. Determine the ratio of liabilities to stockholders' equity for 2003 and 2002. Round to two decimal places.
c. What conclusions regarding the margin of protection to the creditors can you draw from (b)?
d. How does the ratio of liabilities to stockholders' equity of Lowe's compare to that of The Home Depot?

Problems Series A

PROBLEM 1-1A
Transactions

Objective 7

✓ *Cash bal. at end of July:*
$16,000

Duane Mays established an insurance agency on July 1 of the current year and completed the following transactions during July:

a. Opened a business bank account with a deposit of $18,000 in exchange for capital stock.
b. Purchased supplies on account, $950.
c. Paid creditors on account, $575.
d. Received cash from fees earned on insurance commissions, $4,250.
e. Paid rent on office and equipment for the month, $1,200.
f. Paid automobile expenses for month, $600, and miscellaneous expenses, $375.
g. Paid office salaries, $1,500.
h. Billed insurance companies for sales commissions earned, $6,350.
i. Determined that the cost of supplies on hand was $225; therefore, the cost of supplies used was $725.
j. Paid dividends of $2,000.

Instructions

1. Indicate the effect of each transaction and the balances after each transaction, using the following tabular headings:

Assets			=	Liabilities	+	Owners' Equity		

Cash + Accounts Receivable + Supplies = Accounts Payable + Capital Stock + Retained Earnings

Explain the nature of each increase and decrease in owners' equity by an appropriate notation at the right of the amount.

2. ▬▬▶ Briefly explain why the stockholders' investment and revenues increased owners' equity, while dividends and expenses decreased owners' equity.

PROBLEM 1-2A
Financial statements

Objective 8

SPREADSHEET

✓ *Net income: $55,550*

The amounts of the assets and liabilities of Chickadee Travel Service at April 30, 2006, the end of the current year, and its revenue and expenses for the year are listed below. The retained earnings were $35,000, and the capital stock was $15,000 at May 1, 2005, the beginning of the current year. Dividends of $30,000 were paid during the current year.

Accounts payable	$ 12,200	Supplies	$ 3,350
Accounts receivable	31,350	Supplies expense	7,100
Cash	53,050	Taxes expense	5,600
Fees earned	263,200	Utilities expense	22,500
Miscellaneous expense	2,950	Wages expense	131,700
Rent expense	37,800		

Instructions

1. Prepare an income statement for the current year ended April 30, 2006.
2. Prepare a retained earnings statement for the current year ended April 30, 2006.
3. Prepare a balance sheet as of April 30, 2006.

PROBLEM 1-3A
Financial statements

Objective 8

SPREADSHEET

✓ *Net income: $5,950*

Jeanine Sykes established Linchpin Computer Services on August 1, 2006. The effect of each transaction and the balances after each transaction for August are as follows:

	Assets			= Liabilities +	Owners' Equity		
	Cash	Accounts + Receivable	+ Supplies =	Accounts Payable +	Capital Stock +	Retained Earnings	
a.	+10,000				+10,000		Investment
b.			+1,440	+1,440			
Bal.	10,000		1,440	1,440	10,000		
c.	+ 9,000					+ 9,000	Fees earned
Bal.	19,000		1,440	1,440	10,000	9,000	
d.	− 3,600					− 3,600	Rent expense
Bal.	15,400		1,440	1,440	10,000	5,400	
e.	− 500			− 500			
Bal.	14,900		1,440	940	10,000	5,400	
f.		+7,500				+ 7,500	Fees earned
Bal.	14,900	7,500	1,440	940	10,000	12,900	
g.	− 2,300					− 1,550	Auto expense
						− 750	Misc. expense
Bal.	12,600	7,500	1,440	940	10,000	10,600	
h.	− 4,000					− 4,000	Salaries expense
Bal.	8,600	7,500	1,440	940	10,000	6,600	
i.			− 650			− 650	Supplies expense
Bal.	8,600	7,500	790	940	10,000	5,950	
j.	− 2,000					− 2,000	Dividends
Bal.	6,600	7,500	790	940	10,000	3,950	

Instructions

1. Prepare an income statement for the month ended August 31, 2006.
2. Prepare a retained earnings statement for the month ended August 31, 2006.
3. Prepare a balance sheet as of August 31, 2006.

PROBLEM 1-4A
Transactions; financial statements

Objectives 7, 8

SPREADSHEET

✓*Net income: $9,545*

On August 1, 2006, Shad Menard established Centillion Realty. Shad completed the following transactions during the month of August:

a. Opened a business bank account with a deposit of $15,000 in exchange for capital stock. → owns 100% of company. → cash. asset.
b. Paid rent on office and equipment for the month, $2,400.
c. Paid automobile expenses (including rental charge) for month, $750, and miscellaneous expenses, $380.
d. Purchased supplies (pens, file folders, and copy paper) on account, $950.
e. Earned sales commissions, receiving cash, $17,350.
f. Paid creditor on account, $580.
g. Paid office salaries, $3,600.
h. Paid dividends of $1,500.
i. Determined that the cost of supplies on hand was $275; therefore, the cost of supplies used was $675.

Instructions

1. Indicate the effect of each transaction and the balances after each transaction, using the following tabular headings:

Assets	=	Liabilities	+	Owners' Equity

Cash + Supplies = Accounts Payable + Capital Stock + Retained Earnings

Explain the nature of each increase and decrease in owners' equity by an appropriate notation at the right of the amount.

2. Prepare an income statement for August, a retained earnings statement for August, and a balance sheet as of August 31.

PROBLEM 1-5A
Transactions; financial statements

Objectives 7, 8

SPREADSHEET
P.A.S.S.

✓*Net income: $7,850*

Eureka Dry Cleaners is owned and operated by Vince Fry. A building and equipment are currently being rented, pending expansion to new facilities. The actual work of dry cleaning is done by another company at wholesale rates. The assets, liabilities, and capital stock of the business on June 1, 2006, are as follows: Cash, $8,600; Accounts Receivable, $9,500; Supplies, $1,875; Land, $15,000; Accounts Payable, $4,100; Capital Stock, $5,000. Business transactions during June are summarized as follows:

a. Paid rent for the month, $4,000.
b. Charged customers for dry cleaning sales on account, $8,150.
c. Paid creditors on account, $2,680.
d. Purchased supplies on account, $1,500.
e. Received cash from cash customers for dry cleaning sales, $17,600.
f. Received cash from customers on account, $8,450.
g. Received monthly invoice for dry cleaning expense for June (to be paid on July 10), $7,400.
h. Paid the following: wages expense, $2,800; truck expense, $825; utilities expense, $710; miscellaneous expense, $390.
i. Determined that the cost of supplies on hand was $1,600; therefore, the cost of supplies used during the month was $1,775.
j. Paid dividends of $3,500.

Instructions

1. Determine the amount of retained earnings as of June 1.
2. State the assets, liabilities, and owners' equity as of June 1 in equation form similar to that shown in this chapter. In tabular form below the equation, indicate increases and decreases resulting from each transaction and the new balances after each transaction. Explain the nature of each increase and decrease in owners' equity by an appropriate notation at the right of the amount.
3. Prepare an income statement for June, a retained earnings statement for June, and a balance sheet as of June 30.

PROBLEM 1-6A
Missing amounts from financial statements

The financial statements at the end of Ameba Realty's first month of operations are shown on the next page.

Objective 8

SPREADSHEET

✓ j. $40,440

Ameba Realty
Income Statement
For the Month Ended June 30, 2006

Fees earned		$18 8 0 0 00
Operating expenses:		
Wages expense	$ (a)	
Rent expense	1 9 2 0 00	
Supplies expense	1 6 0 0 00	
Utilities expense	1 0 8 0 00	
Miscellaneous expense	6 6 0 00	
Total operating expenses		9 5 6 0 00
Net income		(b)

Ameba Realty
Retained Earnings Statement
For the Month Ended June 30, 2006

Net income for June	(c)	
Less dividends	(d)	
Retained earnings, June 30, 2006		(e)

Ameba Realty
Balance Sheet
June 30, 2006

Assets		Liabilities	
Cash	$11 8 0 0 00	Accounts payable	$ 9 6 0 00
Supplies	8 0 0 00	**Stockholders' Equity**	
Land	(f)	Capital stock (h)	
		Retained earnings (i)	(j)
		Total liabilities and	
Total assets	(g)	stockholders' equity	(k)

Ameba Realty
Statement of Cash Flows
For the Month Ended June 30, 2006

Cash flows from operating activities:		
Cash received from customers	$ (l)	
Deduct cash payments for expenses and		
payments to creditors	9 4 0 0 00	
Net cash flow from operating activities		$ (m)
Cash flows from investing activities:		
Cash payments for acquisition of land		28 8 0 0 00
Cash flows from financing activities:		
Cash received from issuing capital stock	$36 0 0 0 00	
Deduct dividends	4 8 0 0 00	
Net cash flow from financing activities		(n)
Net cash flow and June 30, 2006 cash balance		(o)

Instructions

By analyzing the interrelationships among the four financial statements, determine the proper amounts for (a) through (o).

Problems Series B

PROBLEM 1-1B
Transactions
Objective 7

✓ *Cash bal. at end of Sept.:*
$14,275

On September 1 of the current year, Pamela Larsen established a business to manage rental property. She completed the following transactions during September:

a. Opened a business bank account with a deposit of $15,000 in exchange for capital stock.
b. Purchased supplies (pens, file folders, and copy paper) on account, $1,350.
c. Received cash from fees earned for managing rental property, $6,500.
d. Paid rent on office and equipment for the month, $2,500.
e. Paid creditors on account, $700.
f. Billed customers for fees earned for managing rental property, $1,250.
g. Paid automobile expenses (including rental charges) for month, $550, and miscellaneous expenses, $675.
h. Paid office salaries, $1,800.
i. Determined that the cost of supplies on hand was $380; therefore, the cost of supplies used was $970.
j. Paid dividends of $1,000.

Instructions

1. Indicate the effect of each transaction and the balances after each transaction, using the following tabular headings:

Assets	=	Liabilities	+	Owners' Equity

Cash + Accounts Receivable + Supplies = Accounts Payable + Capital Stock + Retained Earnings

Explain the nature of each increase and decrease in owners' equity by an appropriate notation at the right of the amount.
2. ▬▬▶ Briefly explain why the stockholders' investment and revenues increased owners' equity, while dividends and expenses decreased owners' equity.

PROBLEM 1-2B
Financial statements
Objective 8

SPREADSHEET

✓ *Net income: $71,400*

Following are the amounts of the assets and liabilities of Greco Travel Agency at December 31, 2006, the end of the current year, and its revenue and expenses for the year. The retained earnings were $8,700 and the capital stock was $7,500 on January 1, 2006, the beginning of the current year. During the current year, dividends of $47,000 were paid.

Accounts payable	$ 5,120	Rent expense	$36,000
Accounts receivable	31,200	Supplies	3,000
Cash	11,520	Supplies expense	4,500
Fees earned → Revenue.	188,000	Utilities expense	16,500
Miscellaneous expense	2,800	Wages expense	56,800

Instructions

1. Prepare an income statement for the current year ended December 31, 2006.
2. Prepare a retained earnings statement for the current year ended December 31, 2006.
3. Prepare a balance sheet as of December 31, 2006.

PROBLEM 1-3B
Financial statements
Objective 8

Lynn Rosberg established Jack-in-the-Pulpit Financial Services on January 1, 2006. Jack-in-the-Pulpit Financial Services offers financial planning advice to its clients. The effect of each transaction and the balances after each transaction for January are as follows:

SPREADSHEET

✓ Net income: $14,080

		Assets			= Liabilities +	Owners' Equity		
		Cash	+ Accounts Receivable	+ Supplies =	Accounts Payable +	Capital Stock +	Retained Earnings	
a.		+30,000				+30,000		Investment
b.				+3,180	+3,180			
Bal.		30,000		3,180	3,180	30,000		
c.		− 2,000			−2,000			
Bal.		28,000		3,180	1,180	30,000		
d.		+21,000					+21,000	Fees earned
Bal.		49,000		3,180	1,180	30,000	21,000	
e.		− 6,000					− 6,000	Rent expense
Bal.		43,000		3,180	1,180	30,000	15,000	
f.		− 3,800					− 3,000	Auto expense
							− 800	Misc. expense
Bal.		39,200		3,180	1,180	30,000	11,200	
g.		− 5,000					− 5,000	Salaries expense
Bal.		34,200		3,180	1,180	30,000	6,200	
h.				−2,520			− 2,520	Supplies expense
Bal.		34,200		660	1,180	30,000	3,680	
i.			+10,400				+10,400	Fees earned
Bal.		34,200	10,400	660	1,180	30,000	14,080	
j.		− 7,000					− 7,000	Dividends
Bal.		27,200	10,400	660	1,180	30,000	7,080	

Instructions

1. Prepare an income statement for the month ended January 31, 2006.
2. Prepare a retained earnings statement for the month ended January 31, 2006.
3. Prepare a balance sheet as of January 31, 2006.

PROBLEM 1-4B
Transactions; financial statements
Objectives 7, 8

SPREADSHEET

✓ Net income: $6,700

On July 1, 2006, Beth Nesbit established Patriotic Realty. Nesbit completed the following transactions during the month of July:

a. Opened a business bank account with a deposit of $18,000 in exchange for capital stock.
b. Purchased supplies (pens, file folders, fax paper, etc.) on account, $1,650.
c. Paid creditor on account, $1,100.
d. Earned sales commissions, receiving cash, $25,200.
e. Paid rent on office and equipment for the month, $7,200.
f. Paid dividends of $4,000.
g. Paid automobile expenses (including rental charge) for month, $1,500, and miscellaneous expenses, $750.
h. Paid office salaries, $8,000.
i. Determined that the cost of supplies on hand was $600; therefore, the cost of supplies used was $1,050.

Instructions

1. Indicate the effect of each transaction and the balances after each transaction, using the following tabular headings:

Assets	=	Liabilities	+	Owners' Equity
Cash + Supplies	=	Accounts Payable	+	Capital Stock + Retained Earnings

Explain the nature of each increase and decrease in owners' equity by an appropriate notation at the right of the amount.
2. Prepare an income statement for July, a retained earnings statement for July, and a balance sheet as of July 31.

PROBLEM 1-5B
Transactions; financial statements
Objectives 7, 8

Daisy Dry Cleaners is owned and operated by Gloria Carson. A building and equipment are currently being rented, pending expansion to new facilities. The actual work of dry cleaning is done by another company at wholesale rates. The assets, liabilities, and capital stock of the business on March 1, 2006, are as follows: Cash, $7,150; Ac-

SPREADSHEET
P.A.S.S.

✓ *Net income: $12,330*

counts Receivable, $12,880; Supplies, $3,400; Land, $20,000; Accounts Payable, $6,360; Capital Stock, $10,000. Business transactions during March are summarized as follows:

a. Received cash from cash customers for dry cleaning sales, $22,000.
b. Paid rent for the month, $3,500.
c. Purchased supplies on account, $2,100.
d. Paid creditors on account, $4,800.
e. Charged customers for dry cleaning sales on account, $11,700.
f. Received monthly invoice for dry cleaning expense for March (to be paid on April 10), $8,400.
g. Paid the following: wages expense, $3,400; truck expense, $1,580; utilities expense, $960; miscellaneous expense, $630.
h. Received cash from customers on account, $10,100.
i. Determined that the cost of supplies on hand was $2,600; therefore, the cost of supplies used during the month was $2,900.
j. Paid dividends of $6,000.

Instructions

1. Determine the amount of retained earnings as of March 1 of the current year.
2. State the assets, liabilities, and owners' equity as of March 1 in equation form similar to that shown in this chapter. In tabular form below the equation, indicate increases and decreases resulting from each transaction and the new balances after each transaction. Explain the nature of each increase and decrease in owners' equity by an appropriate notation at the right of the amount.
3. Prepare an income statement for March, a retained earnings statement for March, and a balance sheet as of March 31.

PROBLEM 1-6B
Missing amounts from financial statements

Objective 8

SPREADSHEET

✓ *j. $30,000*

The financial statements at the end of Zeppelin Realty's first month of operations are shown below and on the next page.

Zeppelin Realty Income Statement For the Month Ended November 30, 2006			
Fees earned		$	(a)
Operating expenses:			
Wages expense	$8 5 0 0 00		
Rent expense	3 2 0 0 00		
Supplies expense	(b)		
Utilities expense	1 8 0 0 00		
Miscellaneous expense	1 1 0 0 00		
Total operating expenses		17 6 0 0 00	
Net income		$12 4 0 0 00	

Zeppelin Realty Retained Earnings Statement For the Month Ended November 30, 2006		
Net income for November		(c)
Less dividends	6 0 0 0 00	
Retained earnings, November 30, 2006		(d)

Zeppelin Realty
Balance Sheet
November 30, 2006

Assets			Liabilities		
Cash	$ 5 8 0 0 00		Accounts payable	$ 1 6 0 0 00	
Supplies	2 2 0 0 00		**Stockholders' Equity**		
Land	40 0 0 0 00		Capital stock (f)		
			Retained earnings (g)		(h)
Total assets		(e)	Total liabilities and		
			stockholders' equity		(i)

Zeppelin Realty
Statement of Cash Flows
For the Month Ended November 30, 2006

Cash flows from operating activities:			
Cash received from customers	$	(j)	
Deduct cash payments for expenses and			
payments to creditors	18 2 0 0 00		
Net cash flow from operating activities		$	(k)
Cash flows from investing activities:			
Cash payments for acquisition of land			(l)
Cash flows from financing activities:			
Cash received from issuing capital stock	(m)		
Deduct cash dividends	(n)		
Net cash flow from financing activities			(o)
Net cash flow and November 30, 2006 cash balance			(p)

Instructions

By analyzing the interrelationships among the four financial statements, determine the proper amounts for (a) through (p).

Continuing Problem

P.A.S.S.

✓2. Net income: $530

Shannon Burns enjoys listening to all types of music and owns countless CDs and tapes. Over the years, Shannon has gained a local reputation for knowledge of music from classical to rap and the ability to put together sets of recordings that appeal to all ages.

During the last several months, Shannon served as a guest disc jockey on a local radio station. In addition, Shannon has entertained at several friends' parties as the host deejay.

On April 1, 2006, Shannon established a corporation known as Dancin Music. Using an extensive collection of CDs and tapes, Shannon will serve as a disc jockey on a fee basis for weddings, college parties, and other events. During April, Shannon entered into the following transactions:

April 1. Deposited $7,000 in a checking account in the name of Dancin Music in exchange for capital stock.

　　2. Received $2,000 from a local radio station for serving as the guest disc jockey for April.

April 2. Agreed to share office space with a local real estate agency, Folsom Realty. Dancin Music will pay one-fourth of the rent. In addition, Dancin Music agreed to pay a portion of the salary of the receptionist and to pay one-fourth of the utilities. Paid $1,000 for the rent of the office.

4. Purchased supplies (blank cassette tapes, poster board, extension cords, etc.) from Rockne Office Supply Co. for $350. Agreed to pay $100 within 10 days and the remainder by May 3, 2006.

6. Paid $600 to a local radio station to advertise the services of Dancin Music twice daily for two weeks.

8. Paid $650 to a local electronics store for renting digital recording equipment.

12. Paid $200 (music expense) to Rocket Music for the use of its current music demos to make various music sets.

13. Paid Rockne Office Supply Co. $100 on account.

16. Received $150 from a dentist for providing two music sets for the dentist to play for her patients.

22. Served as disc jockey for a wedding party. The father of the bride agreed to pay $1,200 the 1st of May.

25. Received $500 from a friend for serving as the disc jockey for a cancer charity ball hosted by the local hospital.

29. Paid $240 (music expense) to Score Music for the use of its library of music demos.

30. Received $900 for serving as disc jockey for a local club's monthly dance.

30. Paid Folsom Realty $400 for Dancin Music's share of the receptionist's salary for April.

30. Paid Folsom Realty $300 for Dancin Music's share of the utilities for April.

30. Determined that the cost of supplies on hand is $170. Therefore, the cost of supplies used during the month was $180.

30. Paid for miscellaneous expenses, $150.

30. Paid $500 royalties (music expense) to Federated Clearing for use of various artists' music during the month.

30. Paid dividends of $250.

Instructions

1. Indicate the effect of each transaction and the balances after each transaction, using the following tabular headings:

Assets	=	Liabilities	+	Owners' Equity

Cash + Accounts Receivable + Supplies = Accounts Payable + Capital Stock + Retained Earnings

Explain the nature of each increase and decrease in owners' equity by an appropriate notation at the right of the amount.

2. Prepare an income statement for Dancin Music for the month ended April 30, 2006.

3. Prepare a retained earnings statement for Dancin Music for the month ended April 30, 2006.

4. Prepare a balance sheet for Dancin Music as of April 30, 2006.

Special Activities

ACTIVITY 1-1
Ethics and professional conduct in business

Sue Alejandro, president of Tobago Enterprises, applied for a $300,000 loan from First National Bank. The bank requested financial statements from Tobago Enterprises as a basis for granting the loan. Sue has told her accountant to provide the bank with a balance sheet. Sue has decided to omit the other financial statements because there was a net loss during the past year.

In groups of three or four, discuss the following questions:

1. Is Sue behaving in a professional manner by omitting some of the financial statements?
2. a. What types of information about their businesses would managers be willing to provide bankers? What types of information would managers not be willing to provide?
   b. What types of information about a business would bankers want before extending a loan?
   c. What common interests are shared by bankers and business managers?

ACTIVITY 1-2
Business strategy

Assume that you are the chief executive officer for Gold Kist Inc., a national poultry producer. The company's operations include hatching chickens through the use of breeder stock and feeding, raising, and processing the mature chicks into finished products. The finished products include breaded chicken nuggets and patties and deboned, skinless, and marinated chicken. Gold Kist sells its products to schools, military services, fast food chains, and grocery stores.

In groups of four or five, discuss the following business strategy and risk issues:

1. In a commodity business like poultry production, what do you think is the dominant business strategy? What are the implications in this dominant strategy for how you would run Gold Kist?
2. Identify at least two major business risks for operating Gold Kist.
3. How could Gold Kist try to differentiate its products?

ACTIVITY 1-3
Net income

On January 3, 2005, Dr. Rosa Smith established First Opinion, a medical practice organized as a professional corporation. The following conversation occurred the following August between Dr. Smith and a former medical school classmate, Dr. Brett Wommack, at an American Medical Association convention in Nassau.

Dr. Wommack: Rosa, good to see you again. Why didn't you call when you were in Las Vegas? We could have had dinner together.

Dr. Smith: Actually, I never made it to Las Vegas this year. My husband and kids went up to our Lake Tahoe condo twice, but I got stuck in New York. I opened a new consulting practice this January and haven't had any time for myself since.

Dr. Wommack: I heard about it . . . First . . . something . . . right?

Dr. Smith: Yes, First Opinion. My husband chose the name.

Dr. Wommack: I've thought about doing something like that. Are you making any money? I mean, is it worth your time?

Dr. Smith: You wouldn't believe it. I started by opening a bank account with $60,000, and my July bank statement has a balance of $240,000. Not bad for seven months—all pure profit.

Dr. Wommack: Maybe I'll try it in Las Vegas. Let's have breakfast together tomorrow and you can fill me in on the details.

Comment on Dr. Smith's statement that the difference between the opening bank balance ($60,000) and the July statement balance ($240,000) is pure profit.

ACTIVITY 1-4
Transactions and financial statements

Dawn Ivy, a junior in college, has been seeking ways to earn extra spending money. As an active sports enthusiast, Dawn plays tennis regularly at the Racquet Club, where her family has a membership. The president of the club recently approached Dawn with the proposal that she manage the club's tennis courts. Dawn's primary duty would be to supervise the operation of the club's four indoor and six outdoor courts, including court reservations.

In return for her services, the club would pay Dawn $150 per week, plus Dawn could keep whatever she earned from lessons and the fees from the use of the ball machine. The club and Dawn agreed to a one-month trial, after which both would consider an arrangement for the remaining two years of Dawn's college career. On this basis, Dawn organized Deuce as a proprietorship. During June 2005, Dawn managed the tennis courts and entered into the following transactions:

a. Opened a business account by depositing $1,000.
b. Paid $320 for tennis supplies (practice tennis balls, etc.).
c. Paid $160 for the rental of videotape equipment to be used in offering lessons during June.
d. Arranged for the rental of two ball machines during September for $200. Paid $140 in advance, with the remaining $60 due July 1.
e. Received $1,600 for lessons given during June.
f. Received $300 in fees from the use of the ball machines during June.
g. Paid $600 for salaries of part-time employees who answered the telephone and took reservations while Dawn was giving lessons.
h. Paid $150 for miscellaneous expenses.
i. Received $600 from the club for managing the tennis courts during June.
j. Determined that the cost of supplies on hand at the end of the month totaled $150; therefore, the cost of supplies used was $170.
k. Withdrew $800 for personal use on June 30.

As a friend and accounting student, you have been asked by Dawn to aid her in assessing the venture.

1. Small businesses such as Deuce are often organized as proprietorships. The accounting for proprietorships is similar to that for a corporation, except for owner's equity. Instead of Capital Stock and Retained Earnings, an item entitled Dawn Ivy, Capital, is used to indicate owner's equity in the accounting equation. Withdrawals for personal use are handled similarly to dividends. Indicate the effect of each transaction, using the following tabular headings:

Assets	=	Liabilities	+	Owner's Equity
Cash + Supplies	=	Accounts Payable	+	Dawn Ivy, Capital

Explain the nature of each increase and decrease in owner's equity by an appropriate notation at the right of the amount.

2. Prepare an income statement for June.

3. a. Assume that Dawn Ivy could earn $8 per hour working 30 hours as a waitress. Evaluate which of the two alternatives, working as a waitress or operating Deuce, would provide Dawn with the most income per month.

   b. ▬➤ Discuss any other factors that you believe Dawn should consider before discussing a long-term arrangement with the Racquet Club.

ACTIVITY 1-5
Certification requirements for accountants

INTERNET

By satisfying certain specific requirements, accountants may become certified as public accountants (CPAs), management accountants (CMAs), or internal auditors (CIAs). Find the certification requirements for one of these accounting groups by accessing the appropriate Internet site listed below.

Site	Description
http://www.ais-cpa.com	This site lists the address and/or Internet link for each state's board of accountancy. Find your state's requirements.
http://www.imanet.org	This site lists the requirements for becoming a CMA.
http://www.theiia.org	This site lists the requirements for becoming a CIA.

ACTIVITY 1-6
Cash flows

REAL WORLD

Amazon.com, an Internet retailer, was incorporated in July 1994, and opened its virtual doors on the Web in July 1995. On the statement of cash flows, would you expect Amazon.com's net cash flows from operating, investing, and financing activities to be positive or negative for each year, 1996, 1997, and 1998? Use the following format for your answers, and briefly explain your logic.

	1998	1997	1996
Net cash flows from operating activities	positive		
Net cash flows from investing activities			
Net cash flows from financing activities			

ACTIVITY 1-7
Financial analysis of Enron Corporation

REAL WORLD   INTERNET

The now defunct **Enron Corporation**, headquartered in Houston, Texas, provided products and services for natural gas, electricity, and communications to wholesale and retail customers. Enron's operations were conducted through a variety of subsidiaries and affiliates that involved transporting gas through pipelines, transmitting electricity, and managing energy commodities. The following data were taken from Enron's December 31, 2000 financial statements.

	In millions
Total revenues	$100,789
Total costs and expenses	98,836
Operating income	1,953
Net income	979
Total assets	65,503
Total liabilities	54,033
Total stockholders' equity	11,470
Net cash flows from operating activities	4,779
Net cash flows from investing activities	(4,264)
Net cash flows from financing activities	571
Net increase in cash	1,086

At the end of 2000, the market price of Enron's stock was approximately $83 per share. By March 15, 2002, Enron's stock was selling for $0.22 per share.

 Review the preceding financial statement data and search the Internet for articles on Enron Corporation. Briefly explain why Enron's stock dropped so dramatically in such a short time.

Answers to Self-Examination Questions

1. **D** A corporation, organized in accordance with state or federal statutes, is a separate legal entity in which ownership is divided into shares of stock (answer D). A proprietorship (answer A) is an unincorporated business owned by one individual. A service business (answer B) provides services to its customers. It can be organized as a proprietorship, partnership, corporation, or limited liability corporation. A partnership (answer C) is an unincorporated business owned by two or more individuals.

2. **A** The resources owned by a business are called assets (answer A). The debts of the business are called liabilities (answer B), and the equity of the owners is called owners' equity (answer D). The relationship between assets, liabilities, and owners' equity is expressed as the accounting equation (answer C).

3. **A** The balance sheet is a listing of the assets, liabilities, and owners' equity of a business at a specific date (answer A). The income statement (answer B) is a summary of the revenue and expenses of a business for a specific period of time. The retained earnings statement (answer C) summarizes the changes in retained earnings for a cor-

poration during a specific period of time. The statement of cash flows (answer D) summarizes the cash receipts and cash payments for a specific period of time.

4. **C** The accounting equation is:

Assets = Liabilities + Owners' Equity

Therefore, if assets increased by $20,000 and liabilities increased by $12,000, owners' equity must have increased by $8,000 (answer C), as indicated in the following computation:

Assets	= Liabilities + Owners' Equity
+$20,000	= +$12,000 + Owners' Equity
+$20,000 − $12,000 =	Owners' Equity
+$8,000	= Owners' Equity

5. **B** Net income is the excess of revenue over expenses, or $7,500 (answer B). If expenses exceed revenue, the difference is a net loss. Dividends are the opposite of the stockholders' investing in the business and do not affect the amount of net income or net loss.

ANALYZING TRANSACTIONS

objectives

After studying this chapter, you should be able to:

1 Explain why accounts are used to record and summarize the effects of transactions on financial statements.

2 Describe the characteristics of an account.

3 List the rules of debit and credit and the normal balances of accounts.

4 Analyze and summarize the financial statement effects of transactions.

5 Prepare a trial balance and explain how it can be used to discover errors.

6 Discover errors in recording transactions and correct them.

7 Use horizontal analysis to compare financial statements from different periods.

Assume that you have been hired by a pizza restaurant to deliver pizzas, using your own car. You will be paid $6.00 per hour plus $0.30 per mile plus tips. What is the best way for you to determine how many miles you have driven each day in delivering pizzas?

One method would be to record the odometer mileage before work and then at quitting time. The difference would be the miles driven. For example, if the odometer read 56,743 at the start of work and 56,889 at the end of work, you would have driven 146 miles. This method is subject to error, however, if you copy down the wrong reading or make a math error.

In the same way, business managers need information about the status of the business at different points in time. Such information is useful for analyzing the effects of transactions on the business and for making decisions. For example, the manager of your neighborhood dry cleaners needs to know how much cash is available, how much has been spent, and what services have been provided.

In Chapter 1, we analyzed and recorded this kind of information by using the accounting equation, Assets = Liabilities + Owners' Equity. Since such a format is not practical for most businesses, in Chapter 2 we will study more efficient methods of recording transactions. We will conclude this chapter by discussing how accounting errors may occur and how they may be detected by the accounting process.

Usefulness of an Account

objective 1

Explain why accounts are used to record and summarize the effects of transactions on financial statements.

Before making a major cash purchase, such as buying a digital camera, you need to know the balance of your bank account. Likewise, managers need timely, useful information in order to make good decisions about their businesses.

How are accounting systems designed to provide this information? We illustrated a very simple design in Chapter 1, where transactions were recorded and summarized in the accounting equation format. However, this format is difficult to use when thousands of transactions must be recorded daily. Thus, accounting systems are designed to show the increases and decreases in each financial statement item in a separate record. This record is called an **account**. For example, since cash appears on the balance sheet, a separate record is kept of the increases and decreases in cash. Likewise, a separate record is kept of the increases and decreases for supplies, land, accounts payable, and the other balance sheet items. Similar records would be kept for income statement items, such as fees earned, wages expense, and rent expense.

A group of accounts for a business entity is called a **ledger**. A list of the accounts in the ledger is called a **chart of accounts**. The accounts are normally listed in the order in which they appear in the financial statements. The balance sheet accounts are usually listed first, in the order of assets, liabilities, and owners' equity. The income statement accounts are then listed in the order of revenues and expenses. Each of these major account classifications is briefly described below.

Assets are resources owned by the business entity. These resources can be physical items, such as cash and supplies, or intangibles that have value, such as patent rights. Some other examples of assets include accounts receivable, prepaid expenses (such as insurance), buildings, equipment, and land.

Liabilities are debts owed to outsiders (creditors). Liabilities are often identified on the balance sheet by titles that include the word *payable*. Examples of liabilities include accounts payable, notes payable, and wages payable. Cash received before services are delivered creates a liability to perform the services. These future service commitments are often called *unearned revenues*. Examples of unearned revenues are magazine subscriptions received by a publisher and tuition received by a college at the beginning of a term.

Owners' equity is the owners' right to the assets of the business. For a corporation, the owners' equity on the balance sheet is called **stockholders' equity** and

> **The increases and decreases in each financial statement item are shown in an account.**

is represented by the balance of the capital stock and retained earnings accounts. A ***dividends*** account represents distributions of earnings to stockholders.

Revenues are increases in owners' equity as a result of selling services or products to customers. Examples of revenues include fees earned, fares earned, commissions revenue, and rent revenue.

The using up of assets or consuming services in the process of generating revenues results in ***expenses***. Examples of typical expenses include wages expense, rent expense, utilities expense, supplies expense, and miscellaneous expense.

A chart of accounts is designed to meet the information needs of a company's managers and other users of its financial statements. The accounts within the chart of accounts are numbered for use as references. A flexible numbering system is normally used, so that new accounts can be added without affecting other account numbers.

Exhibit 1 is NetSolutions' chart of accounts that we will be using in this chapter. Additional accounts will be introduced in later chapters. In Exhibit 1, each account number has two digits. The first digit indicates the major classification of the ledger in which the account is located. Accounts beginning with 1 represent assets; 2, liabilities; 3, stockholders' equity; 4, revenue; and 5, expenses. The second digit indicates the location of the account within its class.

REAL WORLD

Procter & Gamble's account numbers have over 30 digits to reflect P&G's many different operations and regions.

•Exhibit 1   Chart of Accounts for NetSolutions

1. Assets		4. Revenue	
11	Cash	41	Fees Earned
12	Accounts Receivable		5. Expenses
14	Supplies	51	Wages Expense
15	Prepaid Insurance	52	Rent Expense
17	Land	54	Utilities Expense
18	Office Equipment	55	Supplies Expense
	2. Liabilities	59	Miscellaneous Expense
21	Accounts Payable		
23	Unearned Rent		
	3. Owners' (Stockholders') Equity		
31	Capital Stock		
32	Retained Earnings		
33	Dividends		

Characteristics of an Account

objective 2

Describe the characteristics of an account.

An account, in its simplest form, has three parts. First, each account has a title, which is the name of the item recorded in the account. Second, each account has a space for recording increases in the amount of the item. Third, each account has a space for recording decreases in the amount of the item. The account form presented below is called a ***T account*** because it resembles the letter T. The left side of the account is called the *debit* side, and the right side is called the *credit* side.[1]

Title	
Left side *debit*	Right side *credit*

Amounts entered on the left side of an account, regardless of the account title, are called ***debits*** to the account. When debits are entered in an account, the account is said to be *debited* (or charged). Amounts entered on the right side of an account

---

[1]The terms *debit* and *credit* are derived from the Latin *debere* and *credere*.

POINT OF INTEREST

Many times when accountants analyze complex transactions, they use T accounts to simplify the thought process. In the same way, you will find T accounts a useful device in this and later accounting courses.

Amounts entered on the left side of an account are debits, and amounts entered on the right side of an account are credits.

are called **credits**, and the account is said to be *credited*. Debits and credits are sometimes abbreviated as *Dr.* and *Cr.*

In the cash account that follows, transactions involving receipts of cash are listed on the debit side of the account. The transactions involving cash payments are listed on the credit side. If at any time the total of the cash receipts is needed, the entries on the debit side of the account may be added and the total ($10,950) inserted below the last debit.[2] The total of the cash payments, $6,850 in the example, may be inserted on the credit side in a similar manner. Subtracting the smaller sum from the larger, $10,950 − $6,850, identifies the amount of cash on hand, $4,100. This amount is called the **balance of the account**. It may be inserted in the account, next to the total of the debit column. In this way, the balance is identified as a **debit balance**. If a balance sheet were to be prepared at this time, cash of $4,100 would be reported.

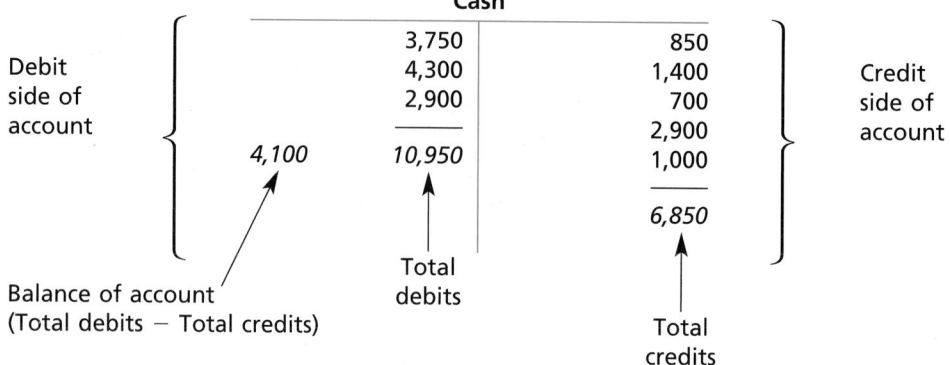

Analyzing and Summarizing Transactions in Accounts

objective 3

List the rules of debit and credit and the normal balances of accounts.

Every business transaction affects at least two accounts. To illustrate how transactions are analyzed and summarized in accounts, we will use the NetSolutions transactions from Chapter 1, with dates added. First, we illustrate how transactions (a), (b), (c), and (f) are analyzed and summarized in balance sheet accounts (assets, liabilities, and stockholders' equity). Next, we illustrate how transactions (d), (e), and (g) are analyzed and summarized in income statement accounts (revenues and expenses). Finally, we illustrate how the payment of dividends, transaction (h), is analyzed and summarized in the accounts.

Balance Sheet Accounts

Chris Clark's first transaction, (a), was to deposit $25,000 in a bank account in the name of NetSolutions in exchange for capital stock. The effect of this November 1 transaction on the balance sheet is to increase assets and stockholders' equity, as shown below.

Every transaction affects at least two accounts.

NetSolutions Balance Sheet November 1, 2005				
Assets			**Stockholders' Equity**	
Cash	$25 0 0 0 00		Capital Stock	$25 0 0 0 00

---

[2]This amount, called a *memorandum balance*, should be written in small figures or identified in some other way to avoid mistaking the amount for an additional debit.

This transaction is initially entered in a record called a *journal*. The title of the account to be debited is listed first, followed by the amount to be debited. The title of the account to be credited is listed below and to the right of the debit, followed by the amount to be credited. This process of recording a transaction in the journal is called *journalizing*. This form of recording a transaction is called a *journal entry*. The journal entry for transaction (a) is shown below.

Entry A

	JOURNAL				Page 1
Date	Description	Post. Ref.	Debit	Credit	
2005 Nov. 1	Cash		25 000 00		1
	Capital Stock			25 000 00	2
	Issued capital stock for cash.				3

The increase in the asset (Cash), which is reported on the left side of the balance sheet, is debited to the cash account. The increase in stockholders' equity (capital stock), which is reported on the right side of the balance sheet, is credited to the capital stock account. As other assets are acquired, the increases are also recorded as debits to asset accounts. Likewise, other increases in stockholders' equity will be recorded as credits to stockholders' equity accounts.

The effects of this transaction are shown in the accounts by transferring the amount and date of the journal entry to the left (debit) side of Cash and to the right (credit) side, Capital Stock, as follows:

Cash		Capital Stock	
Nov. 1 25,000			Nov. 1 25,000

On November 5 (transaction b), NetSolutions bought land for $20,000, paying cash. This transaction increases one asset account and decreases another. It is entered in the journal as a $20,000 increase (debit) to Land and a $20,000 decrease (credit) to Cash, as shown below.

Entry B

					4
5	Land		20 000 00		5
	Cash			20 000 00	6
	Purchased land for building site.				7

The effect of this entry is shown in the accounts of NetSolutions as follows:

Cash		Land		Capital Stock	
Nov. 1 25,000	Nov. 5 20,000	Nov. 5 20,000			Nov. 1 25,000

On November 10 (transaction c), NetSolutions purchased supplies on account for $1,350. This transaction increases an asset account and increases a liability account. It is entered in the journal as a $1,350 increase (debit) to Supplies and a $1,350 increase (credit) to Accounts Payable, as shown below. To simplify the illustration, the effect of entry (c) and the remaining journal entries for NetSolutions will be shown in the accounts later.

Entry C

					8
10	Supplies		1 350 00		9
	Accounts Payable			1 350 00	10
	Purchased supplies on account.				11

On November 30 (transaction f), NetSolutions paid creditors on account, $950. This transaction decreases a liability account and decreases an asset account. It is entered in the journal as a $950 decrease (debit) to Accounts Payable and a $950 decrease (credit) to Cash, as shown below.

Entry F

23					23
24	30	Accounts Payable	9 5 0 00		24
25		Cash		9 5 0 00	25
26		Paid creditors on account.			26

> **The left side of all accounts is the debit side, and the right side is the credit side.**

In the preceding examples, you should observe that the left side of asset accounts is used for recording increases and the right side is used for recording decreases. Also, the right side of liability and owners' (stockholders') equity accounts is used to record increases, and the left side of such accounts is used to record decreases. The left side of all accounts, whether asset, liability, or owners' equity, is the debit side, and the right side is the credit side. Thus, a debit may be either an increase or a decrease, depending on the account affected. Likewise, a credit may be either an increase or a decrease, depending on the account. The general rules of debit and credit for balance sheet accounts may be thus stated as follows:

	Debit	Credit
Asset accounts	Increase (+)	Decrease (−)
Liability accounts	Decrease (−)	Increase (+)
Owners' (stockholders') equity accounts	Decrease (−)	Increase (+)

The rules of debit and credit for balance sheet accounts may also be stated in relationship to the accounting equation, as shown below.

Balance Sheet Accounts

ASSETS		LIABILITIES	
Asset Accounts		Liability Accounts	
Debit for increases (+)	Credit for decreases (−)	Debit for decreases (−)	Credit for increases (+)

OWNERS' EQUITY	
Stockholders' Equity Accounts	
Debit for decreases (−)	Credit for increases (+)

Income Statement Accounts

The analysis of revenue and expense transactions focuses on how each transaction affects stockholders' equity (retained earnings). Just as increases in capital stock are recorded as credits, so, too, are increases in retained earnings. Because revenue transactions increase retained earnings, increases in revenues are recorded as credits. Similarly, because expense transactions decrease retained earnings, increases in expenses are recorded as debits.

We will use NetSolutions' transactions (d), (e), and (g) to illustrate the analysis of transactions and the rules of debit and credit for revenue and expense accounts. On November 18 (transaction d), NetSolutions received fees of $7,500 from customers for services provided. This transaction increases an asset account and in-

FINANCIAL REPORTING AND DISCLOSURE

THE HIJACKING RECEIVABLE

A company's chart of accounts should reflect the basic nature of its operations. Occasionally, however, transactions take place that give rise to unusual accounts. The following is a story of one such account.

During the early 1970s, before strict airport security was implemented across the United States, several airlines experienced hijacking incidents. One such incident occurred on November 10, 1972, when a Southern Airways DC-9 en route from Memphis to Miami was hijacked during a stopover in Birmingham, Alabama. The three hijackers boarded the plane in Birmingham armed with handguns and hand grenades. At gunpoint, the hijackers took the plane, the plane's crew of four, and 27 passengers to nine American cities, Toronto, and eventually to Havana, Cuba.

During the long flight, the hijackers threatened to crash the plane into the Oak Ridge, Tennessee, nuclear facilities, insisted on talking with President Nixon, and demanded a ransom of $10 million. **Southern Airways**, however, was only able to come up with $2 million. Eventually, the pilot talked the hijackers into settling for the $2 million when the plane landed in Chattanooga for refueling.

Upon landing in Havana, the Cuban authorities arrested the hijackers and, after a brief delay, sent the plane, passengers, and crew back to the United States. The hijackers and $2 million stayed in Cuba.

How did Southern Airways account for and report the hijacking payment in its subsequent financial statements? As you might have analyzed, the initial entry credited Cash for $2 million. The debit was to an account entitled "Hijacking Payment." This account was reported as a type of receivable under "other assets" on Southern's balance sheet. The company maintained that it would be able to collect the cash from the Cuban government and that, therefore, a receivable existed. In fact, in August 1975, Southern Airways was repaid $2 million by the Cuban government, which was, at that time, attempting to improve relations with the United States.

creases a revenue account. It is entered in the journal as a $7,500 increase (debit) to Cash and a $7,500 increase (credit) to Fees Earned, as shown below.

Entry D

12						12
13	18	Cash	7 5 0 0 00		13
14		Fees Earned		7 5 0 0 00	14
15		Received fees from customers.			15

Throughout the month, NetSolutions incurred the following expenses: wages, $2,125; rent, $800; utilities, $450; and miscellaneous, $275. To simplify the illustration, the entry to journalize the payment of these expenses is recorded on November 30 (transaction e), as shown below. This transaction increases various expense accounts and decreases an asset account.

Entry E

17	30	Wages Expense	2 1 2 5 00		17
18		Rent Expense	8 0 0 00		18
19		Utilities Expense	4 5 0 00		19
20		Miscellaneous Expense	2 7 5 00		20
21		Cash		3 6 5 0 00	21
22		Paid expenses.			22

The sum of the debits must always equal the sum of the credits.

Regardless of the number of accounts, the sum of the debits is always equal to the sum of the credits in a journal entry. This equality of debits and credits for each transaction is built into the accounting equation: Assets = Liabilities + Owners' (Stockholders') Equity. It is also because of this double equality that the system is known as *double-entry accounting*.

On November 30, NetSolutions recorded the amount of supplies used in the operations during the month (transaction g). This transaction increases an expense account and decreases an asset account. The journal entry for transaction (g) is shown below.

Entry G

28		30	Supplies Expense		8 0 0 00		28
29			Supplies			8 0 0 00	29
30			Supplies used during November.				30

POINT OF INTEREST

In 1494, Luca Pacioli, a Franciscan monk, invented the double-entry accounting system that is still used today.

The general rules of debit and credit for analyzing transactions affecting income statement accounts are stated as follows:

	Debit	Credit
Revenue accounts	Decrease (−)	Increase (+)
Expense accounts	Increase (+)	Decrease (−)

The rules of debit and credit for income statement accounts may also be summarized in relationship to the owners' (stockholders') equity in the accounting equation, as shown below.

Income Statement Accounts

Expense Accounts		Revenue Accounts	
Debit for increases (+)	Credit for decreases (−)	Debit for decreases (−)	Credit for increases (+)

Dividends Account

Dividends are the distribution of earnings to stockholders. Since earnings (revenues minus expenses) increase retained earnings, the distribution of these earnings to stockholders decreases retained earnings. Because dividend transactions decrease retained earnings, increases in dividends are recorded as debits.

On November 30 (transaction h), NetSolutions paid dividends of $2,000. This transaction increases the dividends account and decreases the cash account. The journal entry for transaction (h) is shown below.

Entry H

1	2005 Nov.	30	Dividends		2 0 0 0 00		1
2			Cash			2 0 0 0 00	2
3			Paid dividends to stockholders.				3

INTEGRITY IN BUSINESS

WILL JOURNALIZING PREVENT FRAUD?

While journalizing transactions reduces the possibility of fraud, it by no means eliminates it. For example, embezzlement can be hidden within the double-entry bookkeeping system by creating fictitious suppliers to whom checks are issued.

Normal Balances of Accounts

The sum of the increases recorded in an account is usually equal to or greater than the sum of the decreases recorded in the account. For this reason, the normal balances of all accounts are positive rather than negative. For example, the total debits (increases) in an asset account will ordinarily be greater than the total credits (decreases). Thus, asset accounts normally have debit balances.

The rules of debit and credit and the normal balances of the various types of accounts are summarized as follows:

A debit balance in which of the following accounts—Cash, Dividends, Wages Expense, Supplies, Fees Earned—would indicate that an error has occurred?

Fees Earned

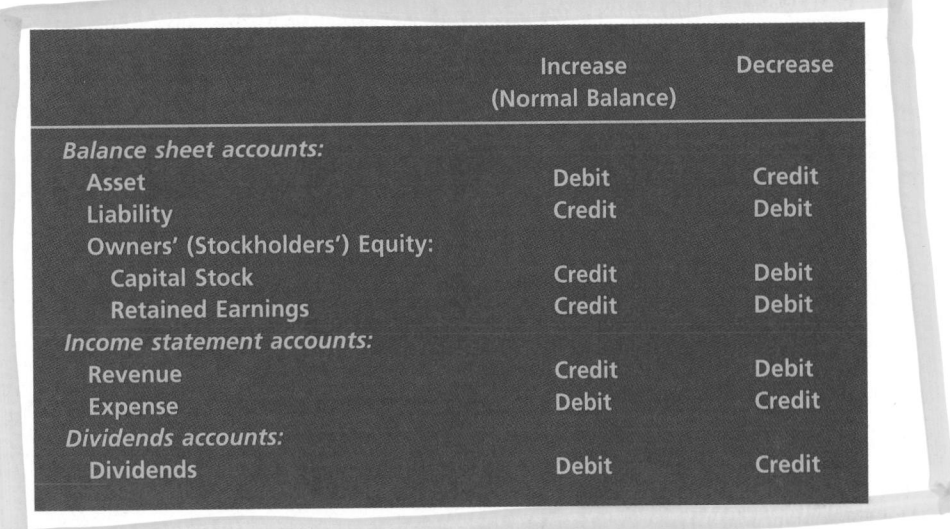

	Increase (Normal Balance)	Decrease
Balance sheet accounts:		
Asset	Debit	Credit
Liability	Credit	Debit
Owners' (Stockholders') Equity:		
Capital Stock	Credit	Debit
Retained Earnings	Credit	Debit
Income statement accounts:		
Revenue	Credit	Debit
Expense	Debit	Credit
Dividends accounts:		
Dividends	Debit	Credit

When an account normally having a debit balance actually has a credit balance, or vice versa, an error may have occurred or an unusual situation may exist. For example, a credit balance in the office equipment account could result only from an error. On the other hand, a debit balance in an accounts payable account could result from an overpayment.

Illustration of Analyzing and Summarizing Transactions

objective **4**

Analyze and summarize the financial statement effects of transactions.

POINT OF INTEREST

In computerized accounting systems, some transactions may be automatically authorized and recorded when certain events occur. For example, the salaries of managers may be paid automatically at the end of each pay period.

How does a transaction take place in a business? First, a manager or other employee authorizes the transaction. The transaction then takes place. The businesses involved in the transaction usually prepare documents that give details of the transaction. These documents then become the basis for analyzing and recording the transaction. For example, Chris Clark might authorize the purchase of supplies for NetSolutions by telling an employee to buy computer paper at the local office supply store. The employee purchases the supplies for cash and receives a sales slip from the office supply store listing the supplies bought. The employee then gives the sales slip to Chris Clark, who verifies and records the transaction.

As we discussed in the preceding section, a transaction is first recorded in a journal. Thus, the journal is a history of transactions by date. Periodically, the journal entries are transferred to the accounts in the ledger. The ledger is a history of transactions by account. The process of transferring the debits and credits from the journal entries to the accounts is called ***posting***. The flow of a transaction from its authorization to its posting in the accounts is shown in Exhibit 2.

In practice, businesses use a variety of formats for recording journal entries. A business may use one all-purpose journal, sometimes called a ***two-column journal***, or it

•**Exhibit 2**

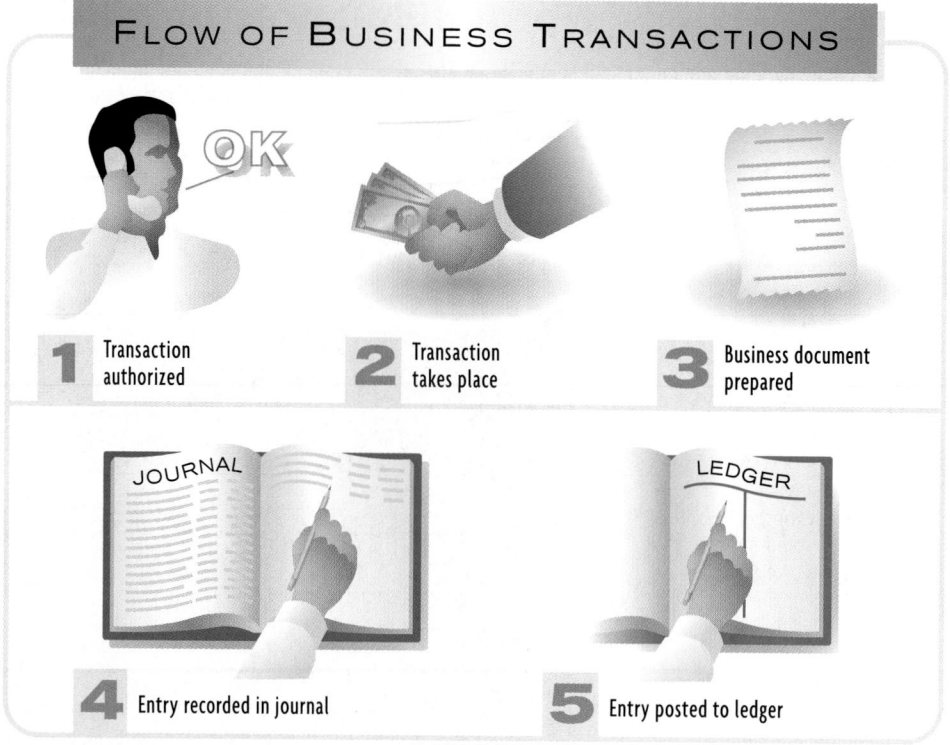

FLOW OF BUSINESS TRANSACTIONS

1 Transaction authorized

2 Transaction takes place

3 Business document prepared

4 Entry recorded in journal

5 Entry posted to ledger

I was founded in 1866, when a pharmacist tried to develop an economical alternative to breast milk for mothers who couldn't nurse their babies. Today I'm Switzerland's largest industrial company and the world's largest food company, employing nearly a quarter of a million people. My brands are available in almost every nation, and include Taster's Choice, Carnation, Libby's, PowerBar, Maggi, Buitoni, Stouffer's, KitKat, Smarties, After Eight, Baby Ruth, Butterfinger, Friskies, Fancy Feast, Alpo, and Mighty Dog. I also hold a major interest in L'Oréal. Sales of my instant coffee more than doubled during World War II. Who am I? (Go to page 81 for answer.)

may use several journals. In the latter case, each journal is used to record different types of transactions, such as cash receipts or cash payments. The journals may be part of either a manual accounting system or a computerized accounting system.

The double-entry accounting system is a very powerful tool in analyzing the effects of transactions. Using this system to analyze transactions is summarized as follows:

1. Determine whether an asset, a liability, capital stock, retained earnings, revenue, expense, or dividends account is affected by the transaction.
2. For each account affected by the transaction, determine whether the account increases or decreases.
3. Determine whether each increase or decrease should be recorded as a debit or a credit.

To illustrate recording a transaction in an all-purpose journal and posting in a manual accounting system, we will use the December transactions of NetSolutions. The first transaction in December occurred on December 1.

Dec. 1. NetSolutions paid a premium of $2,400 for a comprehensive insurance policy covering liability, theft, and fire. The policy covers a two-year period.

Analysis   When you purchased insurance for your automobile, you may have been required to pay the insurance premium in advance. In this case, your transaction was similar to NetSolutions. Advance payments of expenses such as insurance are prepaid expenses, which are assets. For NetSolutions, the asset acquired for the cash payment is insurance protection for 24 months. The asset Prepaid Insurance increases and is debited for $2,400. The asset Cash decreases and is credited for $2,400. The recording and posting of this transaction is shown in Exhibit 3.

Note where the date of the transaction is recorded in the journal. Also note that the entry is explained as the payment of an insurance premium. Such explanations should be brief. For unusual and complex transactions, such as a long-term rental

•Exhibit 3   **Diagram of the Recording and Posting of a Debit and a Credit**

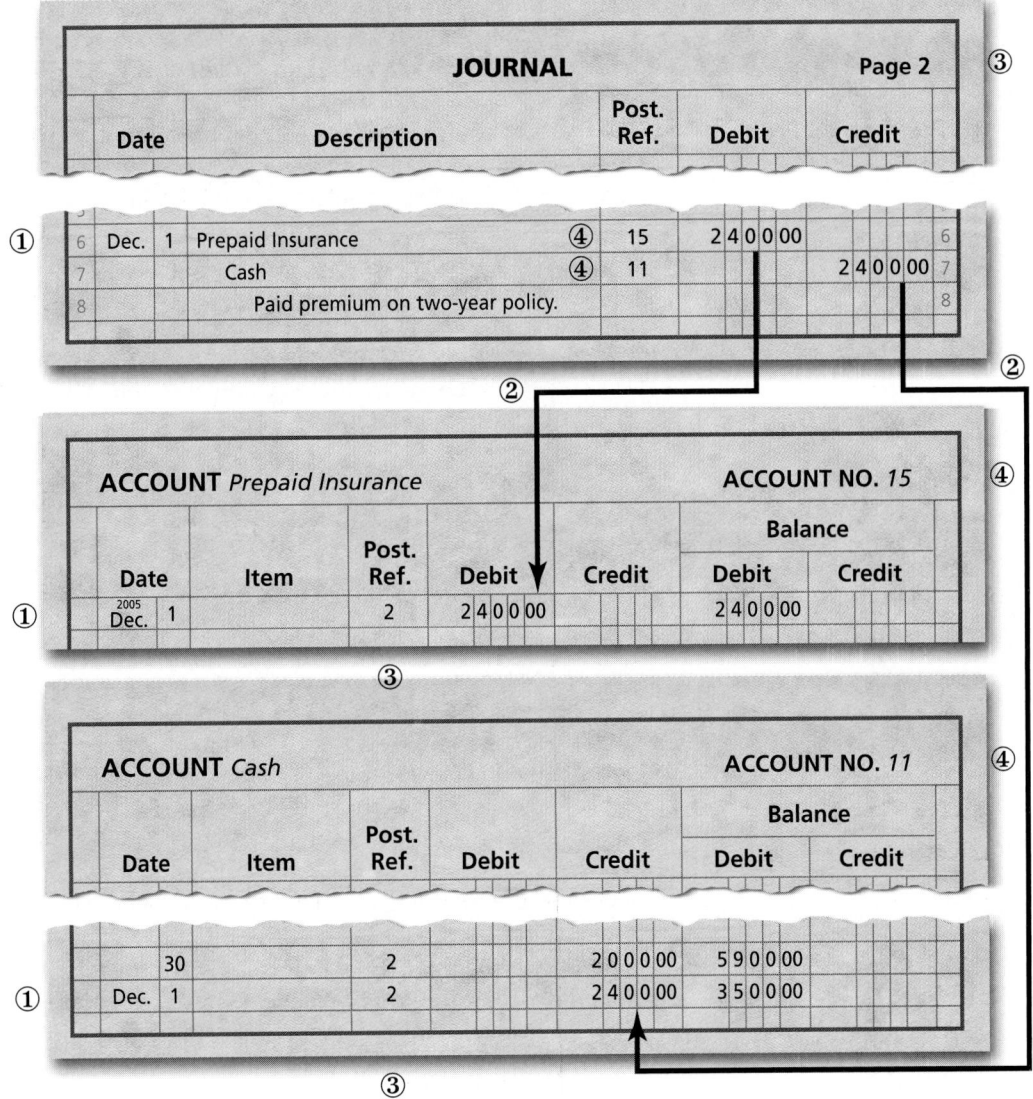

arrangement, the journal entry explanation may include a reference to the rental agreement or other business document.

You will note that the T account form is not used in this illustration. Although the T account clearly separates debit and credit entries, it is inefficient for summarizing a large quantity of transactions. In practice, the T account is usually replaced with the standard form shown in Exhibit 3.

The debits and credits for each journal entry are posted to the accounts in the order in which they occur in the journal. In posting to the standard account, (1) the date is entered, and (2) the amount of the entry is entered. For future reference, (3) the journal page number is inserted in the Posting Reference column of the account, and (4) the account number is inserted in the Posting Reference column of the journal.

The remaining December transactions for NetSolutions are analyzed in the following paragraphs. These transactions are posted to the ledger in Exhibit 4, shown later. To simplify and reduce repetition, some of the December transactions are stated in summary form. For example, cash received for services is normally recorded on a daily basis. In this example, however, only summary totals are recorded at the middle and end of the month. Likewise, all fees earned on account during December are recorded at the middle and end of the month. In practice, each fee earned is recorded separately.

Dec. 1. NetSolutions paid rent for December, $800. The company from which Net-Solutions is renting its store space now requires the payment of rent on the 1st of each month, rather than at the end of the month.

Analysis You may pay monthly rent on an apartment on the first of each month. Your rent transaction is similar to NetSolutions. The advance payment of rent is an asset, much like the advance payment of the insurance premium in the preceding transaction. However, unlike the insurance premium, this prepaid rent will expire in one month. When an asset that is purchased will be used up in a short period of time, such as a month, it is normal to debit an expense account initially. This avoids having to transfer the balance from an asset account (Prepaid Rent) to an expense account (Rent Expense) at the end of the month. Thus, when the rent for December is prepaid at the beginning of the month, Rent Expense is debited for $800 and Cash is credited for $800.

10	1	Rent Expense	52	8 0 0 00			10
11		Cash	11		8 0 0 00		11
12		Paid rent for December.					12

Dec. 1. NetSolutions received an offer from a local retailer to rent the land purchased on November 5. The retailer plans to use the land as a parking lot for its employees and customers. NetSolutions agreed to rent the land to the retailer for three months, with the rent payable in advance. NetSolutions received $360 for three months' rent beginning December 1.

Analysis By agreeing to rent the land and accepting the $360, NetSolutions has incurred an obligation (liability) to the retailer. This obligation is to make the land available for use for three months and not to interfere with its use. The liability created by receiving the cash in advance of providing the service is called ***unearned revenue***. Thus, the $360 received is an increase in an asset and is debited to Cash. The liability account Unearned Rent increases and is credited for $360. As time passes, the unearned rent liability will decrease and will become revenue.

14	1	Cash	11	3 6 0 00			14
15		Unearned Rent	23		3 6 0 00		15
16		Received advance payment for					16
17		three months' rent on land.					17

Dec. 4. NetSolutions purchased office equipment on account from Executive Supply Co. for $1,800.

Analysis The asset account Office Equipment increases and is therefore debited for $1,800. The liability account Accounts Payable increases and is credited for $1,800.

19	4	Office Equipment	18	1 8 0 0 00			19
20		Accounts Payable	21		1 8 0 0 00		20
21		Purchased office equipment					21
22		on account.					22

Dec. 6. NetSolutions paid $180 for a newspaper advertisement.

Analysis An expense increases and is debited for $180. The asset Cash decreases and is credited for $180. Expense items that are expected to be minor in amount are normally included as part of the miscellaneous expense. Thus, Miscellaneous Expense is debited for $180.

					Post. Ref.	Debit	Credit	
24		6	Miscellaneous Expense		59	1 8 0 00		24
25			Cash		11		1 8 0 00	25
26			Paid for newspaper ad.					26

Dec. 11. NetSolutions paid creditors $400.

Analysis This payment decreases the liability account Accounts Payable, which is debited for $400. Cash also decreases and is credited for $400.

					Post. Ref.	Debit	Credit	
28		11	Accounts Payable		21	4 0 0 00		28
29			Cash		11		4 0 0 00	29
30			Paid creditors on account.					30

Dec. 13. NetSolutions paid a receptionist and a part-time assistant $950 for two weeks' wages.

Analysis This transaction is similar to the December 6 transaction, where an expense account is increased and Cash is decreased. Thus, Wages Expense is debited for $950, and Cash is credited for $950.

				JOURNAL			Page 3	
	Date		Description		Post. Ref.	Debit	Credit	
1	2005 Dec.	13	Wages Expense		51	9 5 0 00		1
2			Cash		11		9 5 0 00	2
3			Paid two weeks' wages.					3

Dec. 16. NetSolutions received $3,100 from fees earned for the first half of December.

Analysis Cash increases and is debited for $3,100. The revenue account Fees Earned increases and is credited for $3,100.

					Post. Ref.	Debit	Credit	
5		16	Cash		11	3 1 0 0 00		5
6			Fees Earned		41		3 1 0 0 00	6
7			Received fees from customers.					7

Dec. 16. Fees earned on account totaled $1,750 for the first half of December.

Analysis Assume that you have agreed to take care of a neighbor's dog for a week for $100. At the end of the week, you agree to wait until the first of the next month to receive the $100. Like NetSolutions, you have provided services on account and thus have a right to receive the payment from your neighbor. When a business agrees that payment for services provided or goods sold can be accepted at a later date, the firm has an **account receivable**, which is a claim against the customer. The account receivable is an asset, and the revenue is earned even though no cash has been received. Thus, Accounts Receivable increases and is debited for $1,750. The revenue account Fees Earned increases and is credited for $1,750.

9		16	Accounts Receivable	12	1 7 5 0 00		9
10			Fees Earned	41		1 7 5 0 00	10
11			Recorded fees earned on account.				11

Dec. 20. NetSolutions paid $900 to Executive Supply Co. on the $1,800 debt owed from the December 4 transaction.

Analysis   This is similar to the transaction of December 11.

13		20	Accounts Payable	21	9 0 0 00		13
14			Cash	11		9 0 0 00	14
15			Paid part of amount owed to				15
16			Executive Supply Co.				16

Dec. 21. NetSolutions received $650 from customers in payment of their accounts.

Analysis   When customers pay amounts owed for services they have previously received, one asset increases and another asset decreases. Thus, Cash is debited for $650, and Accounts Receivable is credited for $650.

18		21	Cash	11	6 5 0 00		18
19			Accounts Receivable	12		6 5 0 00	19
20			Received cash from customers				20
21			on account.				21

Dec. 23. NetSolutions paid $1,450 for supplies.

Analysis   The asset account Supplies increases and is debited for $1,450. The asset account Cash decreases and is credited for $1,450.

23		23	Supplies	14	1 4 5 0 00		23
24			Cash	11		1 4 5 0 00	24
25			Purchased supplies.				25

Dec. 27. NetSolutions paid the receptionist and the part-time assistant $1,200 for two weeks' wages.

Analysis   This is similar to the transaction of December 13.

27		27	Wages Expense	51	1 2 0 0 00		27
28			Cash	11		1 2 0 0 00	28
29			Paid two weeks' wages.				29

Dec. 31. NetSolutions paid its $310 telephone bill for the month.

Analysis You pay a telephone bill each month. Businesses, such as NetSolutions, also must pay monthly utility bills. Such transactions are similar to the transaction of December 6. The expense account Utilities Expense is debited for $310, and Cash is credited for $310.

				Debit	Credit	
31	31	Utilities Expense	54	3 1 0 00		31
32		Cash	11		3 1 0 00	32
33		Paid telephone bill.				33

Dec. 31. NetSolutions paid its $225 electric bill for the month.

Analysis This is similar to the preceding transaction.

		JOURNAL			Page 4	
	Date	Description	Post. Ref.	Debit	Credit	
1	2005 Dec. 31	Utilities Expense	54	2 2 5 00		1
2		Cash	11		2 2 5 00	2
3		Paid electric bill.				3

Dec. 31. NetSolutions received $2,870 from fees earned for the second half of December.

Analysis This is similar to the transaction of December 16.

				Debit	Credit	
5	31	Cash	11	2 8 7 0 00		5
6		Fees Earned	41		2 8 7 0 00	6
7		Received fees from customers.				7

Dec. 31. Fees earned on account totaled $1,120 for the second half of December.

Analysis This is similar to the transaction of December 16.

				Debit	Credit	
9	31	Accounts Receivable	12	1 1 2 0 00		9
10		Fees Earned	41		1 1 2 0 00	10
11		Recorded fees earned on account.				11

Dec. 31. NetSolutions paid dividends of $2,000 to stockholders.

Analysis This transaction resulted in an increase in the amount of dividends and is recorded by a $2,000 debit to Dividends. The decrease in business cash is recorded by a $2,000 credit to Cash.

				Debit	Credit	
13	31	Dividends	33	2 0 0 0 00		13
14		Cash	11		2 0 0 0 00	14
15		Paid dividends to stockholders.				15

The journal for NetSolutions since it was organized on November 1 is shown in Exhibit 4. Exhibit 4 also shows the ledger after the transactions for both November and December have been posted.

•Exhibit 4 Journal and Ledger—NetSolutions

	Date		Description	Post. Ref.	Debit	Credit	
1	2005 Nov.	1	Cash	11	25 0 0 0 00		1
2			Capital Stock	31		25 0 0 0 00	2
3			Issued capital stock for cash.				3
4							4
5		5	Land	17	20 0 0 0 00		5
6			Cash	11		20 0 0 0 00	6
7			Purchased land for building site.				7
8							8
9		10	Supplies	14	1 3 5 0 00		9
10			Accounts Payable	21		1 3 5 0 00	10
11			Purchased supplies on account.				11
12							12
13		18	Cash	11	7 5 0 0 00		13
14			Fees Earned	41		7 5 0 0 00	14
15			Received fees from customers.				15
16							16
17		30	Wages Expense	51	2 1 2 5 00		17
18			Rent Expense	52	8 0 0 00		18
19			Utilities Expense	54	4 5 0 00		19
20			Miscellaneous Expense	59	2 7 5 00		20
21			Cash	11		3 6 5 0 00	21
22			Paid expenses.				22
23							23
24		30	Accounts Payable	21	9 5 0 00		24
25			Cash	11		9 5 0 00	25
26			Paid creditors on account.				26
27							27
28		30	Supplies Expense	55	8 0 0 00		28
29			Supplies	14		8 0 0 00	29
30			Supplies used during November.				30

JOURNAL — Page 2

	Date		Description	Post. Ref.	Debit	Credit	
1	2005 Nov.	30	Dividends	33	2 0 0 0 00		1
2			Cash	11		2 0 0 0 00	2
3			Paid dividends to stockholders.				3

•Exhibit 4
(continued)

JOURNAL   Page 2

	Date		Description	Post. Ref.	Debit	Credit	
6	2005 Dec.	1	Prepaid Insurance	15	2 4 0 0 00		6
7			Cash	11		2 4 0 0 00	7
8			Paid premium on two-year policy.				8
9							9
10		1	Rent Expense	52	8 0 0 00		10
11			Cash	11		8 0 0 00	11
12			Paid rent for December.				12
13							13
14		1	Cash	11	3 6 0 00		14
15			Unearned Rent	23		3 6 0 00	15
16			Received advance payment for				16
17			three months' rent on land.				17
18							18
19		4	Office Equipment	18	1 8 0 0 00		19
20			Accounts Payable	21		1 8 0 0 00	20
21			Purchased office equipment				21
22			on account.				22
23							23
24		6	Miscellaneous Expense	59	1 8 0 00		24
25			Cash	11		1 8 0 00	25
26			Paid for newspaper ad.				26
27							27
28		11	Accounts Payable	21	4 0 0 00		28
29			Cash	11		4 0 0 00	29
30			Paid creditors on account.				30

JOURNAL   Page 3

	Date		Description	Post. Ref.	Debit	Credit	
1	2005 Dec.	13	Wages Expense	51	9 5 0 00		1
2			Cash	11		9 5 0 00	2
3			Paid two weeks' wages.				3
4							4
5		16	Cash	11	3 1 0 0 00		5
6			Fees Earned	41		3 1 0 0 00	6
7			Received fees from customers.				7
8							8
9		16	Accounts Receivable	12	1 7 5 0 00		9
10			Fees Earned	41		1 7 5 0 00	10
11			Recorded fees earned on account.				11
12							12
13		20	Accounts Payable	21	9 0 0 00		13
14			Cash	11		9 0 0 00	14
15			Paid part of amount owed to				15
16			Executive Supply Co.				16

•**Exhibit 4**
(continued)

	Date		Description	Post. Ref.	Debit	Credit	
	2005 Dec.	21	Cash	11	6 5 0 00		18
19			Accounts Receivable	12		6 5 0 00	19
20			Received cash from customers				20
21			on account.				21
22							22
23		23	Supplies	14	1 4 5 0 00		23
24			Cash	11		1 4 5 0 00	24
25			Purchased supplies.				25
26							26
27		27	Wages Expense	51	1 2 0 0 00		27
28			Cash	11		1 2 0 0 00	28
29			Paid two weeks' wages.				29
30							30
31		31	Utilities Expense	54	3 1 0 00		31
32			Cash	11		3 1 0 00	32
33			Paid telephone bill.				33

JOURNAL — Page 3

	Date		Description	Post. Ref.	Debit	Credit	
1	2005 Dec.	31	Utilities Expense	54	2 2 5 00		1
2			Cash	11		2 2 5 00	2
3			Paid electric bill.				3
4							4
5		31	Cash	11	2 8 7 0 00		5
6			Fees Earned	41		2 8 7 0 00	6
7			Received fees from customers.				7
8							8
9		31	Accounts Receivable	12	1 1 2 0 00		9
10			Fees Earned	41		1 1 2 0 00	10
11			Recorded fees earned on account.				11
12							12
13		31	Dividends	33	2 0 0 0 00		13
14			Cash	11		2 0 0 0 00	14
15			Paid dividends to stockholders.				15

JOURNAL — Page 4

•Exhibit 4
(continued)

LEDGER

ACCOUNT *Cash* — **ACCOUNT NO.** *11*

Date		Item	Post. Ref.	Debit	Credit	Balance Debit	Balance Credit
2005 Nov.	1		1	25 0 0 0 00		25 0 0 0 00	
	5		1		20 0 0 0 00	5 0 0 0 00	
	18		1	7 5 0 0 00		12 5 0 0 00	
	30		1		3 6 5 0 00	8 8 5 0 00	
	30		1		9 5 0 00	7 9 0 0 00	
	30		2		2 0 0 0 00	5 9 0 0 00	
Dec.	1		2		2 4 0 0 00	3 5 0 0 00	
	1		2		8 0 0 00	2 7 0 0 00	
	1		2	3 6 0 00		3 0 6 0 00	
	6		2		1 8 0 00	2 8 8 0 00	
	11		2		4 0 0 00	2 4 8 0 00	
	13		3		9 5 0 00	1 5 3 0 00	
	16		3	3 1 0 0 00		4 6 3 0 00	
	20		3		9 0 0 00	3 7 3 0 00	
	21		3	6 5 0 00		4 3 8 0 00	
	23		3		1 4 5 0 00	2 9 3 0 00	
	27		3		1 2 0 0 00	1 7 3 0 00	
	31		3		3 1 0 00	1 4 2 0 00	
	31		4		2 2 5 00	1 1 9 5 00	
	31		4	2 8 7 0 00		4 0 6 5 00	
	31		4		2 0 0 0 00	2 0 6 5 00	

ACCOUNT *Accounts Receivable* — **ACCOUNT NO.** *12*

Date		Item	Post. Ref.	Debit	Credit	Balance Debit	Balance Credit
2005 Dec.	16		3	1 7 5 0 00		1 7 5 0 00	
	21		3		6 5 0 00	1 1 0 0 00	
	31		4	1 1 2 0 00		2 2 2 0 00	

ACCOUNT *Supplies* — **ACCOUNT NO.** *14*

Date		Item	Post. Ref.	Debit	Credit	Balance Debit	Balance Credit
2005 Nov.	10		1	1 3 5 0 00		1 3 5 0 00	
	30		1		8 0 0 00	5 5 0 00	
Dec.	23		3	1 4 5 0 00		2 0 0 0 00	

•Exhibit 4
(continued)

ACCOUNT *Prepaid Insurance* **ACCOUNT NO.** *15*

Date	Item	Post. Ref.	Debit	Credit	Balance Debit	Balance Credit
2005 Dec. 1		2	2 4 0 0 00		2 4 0 0 00	

ACCOUNT *Land* **ACCOUNT NO.** *17*

Date	Item	Post. Ref.	Debit	Credit	Balance Debit	Balance Credit
2005 Nov. 5		1	20 0 0 0 00		20 0 0 0 00	

ACCOUNT *Office Equipment* **ACCOUNT NO.** *18*

Date	Item	Post. Ref.	Debit	Credit	Balance Debit	Balance Credit
2005 Dec. 4		2	1 8 0 0 00		1 8 0 0 00	

ACCOUNT *Accounts Payable* **ACCOUNT NO.** *21*

Date	Item	Post. Ref.	Debit	Credit	Balance Debit	Balance Credit
2005 Nov. 10		1		1 3 5 0 00		1 3 5 0 00
30		1	9 5 0 00			4 0 0 00
Dec. 4		2		1 8 0 0 00		2 2 0 0 00
11		2	4 0 0 00			1 8 0 0 00
20		3	9 0 0 00			9 0 0 00

ACCOUNT *Unearned Rent* **ACCOUNT NO.** *23*

Date	Item	Post. Ref.	Debit	Credit	Balance Debit	Balance Credit
2005 Dec. 1		2		3 6 0 00		3 6 0 00

•**Exhibit 4**
(continued)

ACCOUNT *Capital Stock*   **ACCOUNT NO.** *31*

Date		Item	Post. Ref.	Debit	Credit	Balance Debit	Balance Credit
2005 Nov.	1		1		25 0 0 0 00		25 0 0 0 00

ACCOUNT *Dividends*   **ACCOUNT NO.** *33*

Date		Item	Post. Ref.	Debit	Credit	Balance Debit	Balance Credit
2005 Nov.	30		2	2 0 0 0 00		2 0 0 0 00	
Dec.	31		4	2 0 0 0 00		4 0 0 0 00	

ACCOUNT *Fees Earned*   **ACCOUNT NO.** *41*

Date		Item	Post. Ref.	Debit	Credit	Balance Debit	Balance Credit
2005 Nov.	18		1		7 5 0 0 00		7 5 0 0 00
Dec.	16		3		3 1 0 0 00		10 6 0 0 00
	16		3		1 7 5 0 00		12 3 5 0 00
	31		4		2 8 7 0 00		15 2 2 0 00
	31		4		1 1 2 0 00		16 3 4 0 00

ACCOUNT *Wages Expense*   **ACCOUNT NO.** *51*

Date		Item	Post. Ref.	Debit	Credit	Balance Debit	Balance Credit
2005 Nov.	30		1	2 1 2 5 00		2 1 2 5 00	
Dec.	13		3	9 5 0 00		3 0 7 5 00	
	27		3	1 2 0 0 00		4 2 7 5 00	

ACCOUNT *Rent Expense*   **ACCOUNT NO.** *52*

Date		Item	Post. Ref.	Debit	Credit	Balance Debit	Balance Credit
2005 Nov.	30		1	8 0 0 00		8 0 0 00	
Dec.	1		2	8 0 0 00		1 6 0 0 00	

•**Exhibit 4**
(concluded)

ACCOUNT *Utilities Expense*					ACCOUNT NO. *54*	
		Post.			Balance	
Date	Item	Ref.	Debit	Credit	Debit	Credit
2005 Nov. 30		1	4 5 0 00		4 5 0 00	
Dec. 31		3	3 1 0 00		7 6 0 00	
31		4	2 2 5 00		9 8 5 00	

ACCOUNT *Supplies Expense*					ACCOUNT NO. *55*	
		Post.			Balance	
Date	Item	Ref.	Debit	Credit	Debit	Credit
2005 Nov. 30		1	8 0 0 00		8 0 0 00	

ACCOUNT *Miscellaneous Expense*					ACCOUNT NO. *59*	
		Post.			Balance	
Date	Item	Ref.	Debit	Credit	Debit	Credit
2005 Nov. 30		1	2 7 5 00		2 7 5 00	
Dec. 6		2	1 8 0 00		4 5 5 00	

Trial Balance

Prepare a trial balance and explain how it can be used to discover errors.

If you incorrectly record $1,000 received on account as a debit to Cash and a credit to Accounts Payable, will the trial balance totals be equal?

Yes.

How can you be sure that you have not made an error in posting the debits and credits to the ledger? One way is to determine the equality of the debits and credits in the ledger. This equal-

POINT OF INTEREST

The proof of the equality of the debit and credit balances is called a trial balance because a "trial" is a process of proving or testing.

ity should be proved at the end of each accounting period, if not more often. Such a proof, called a ***trial balance***, may be in the form of a computer printout or in the form shown in Exhibit 5.

The first step in preparing the trial balance is to determine the balance of each account in the ledger. When the standard account form is used, the balance of each account appears in the balance column on the same line as the last posting to the account.

The trial balance does not provide complete proof of the accuracy of the ledger. It indicates only that the debits and the credits are equal. This proof is of value, however, because errors often affect the equality of debits and credits. If the two totals of a trial balance are not equal, an error has occurred. In the next section of this chapter, we will discuss procedures for discovering and correcting errors.

•Exhibit 5 Trial Balance

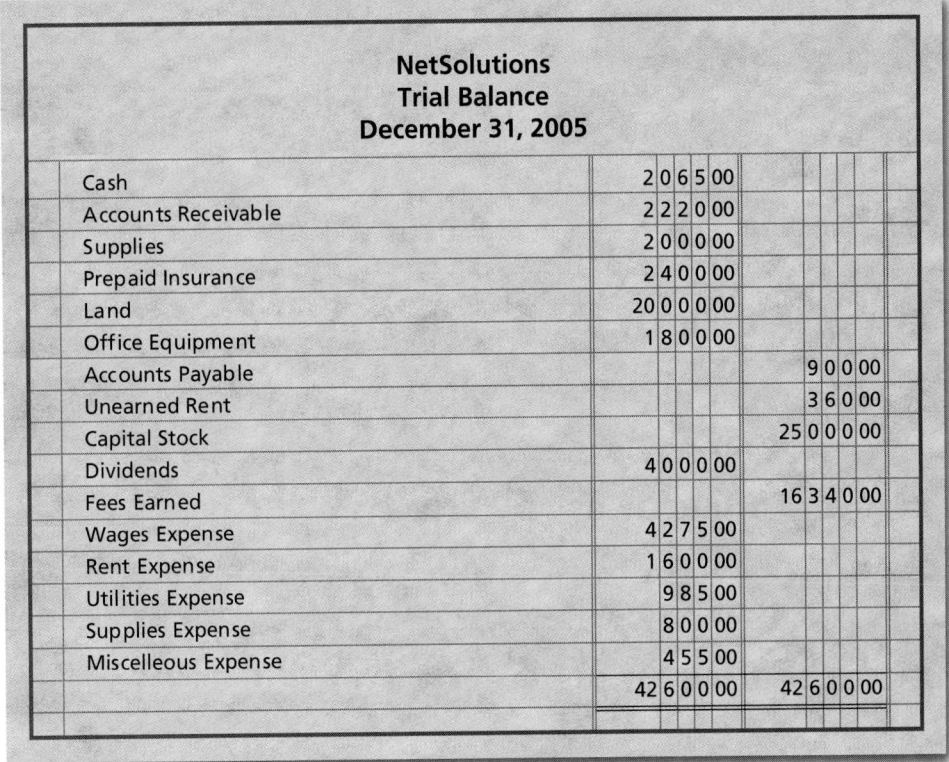

NetSolutions Trial Balance December 31, 2005		
Cash	2 0 6 5 00	
Accounts Receivable	2 2 2 0 00	
Supplies	2 0 0 0 00	
Prepaid Insurance	2 4 0 0 00	
Land	20 0 0 0 00	
Office Equipment	1 8 0 0 00	
Accounts Payable		9 0 0 00
Unearned Rent		3 6 0 00
Capital Stock		25 0 0 0 00
Dividends	4 0 0 0 00	
Fees Earned		16 3 4 0 00
Wages Expense	4 2 7 5 00	
Rent Expense	1 6 0 0 00	
Utilities Expense	9 8 5 00	
Supplies Expense	8 0 0 00	
Miscelleous Expense	4 5 5 00	
	42 6 0 0 00	42 6 0 0 00

Discovery and Correction of Errors

objective 6

Discover errors in recording transactions and correct them.

REAL WORLD

Many large corporations such as **Microsoft** and **Quaker Oats** round the figures in their financial statements to millions of dollars.

Errors will sometimes occur in journalizing and posting transactions. In some cases, however, an error might not be significant enough to affect the decisions of management or others. In such cases, the ***materiality concept*** implies that the error may be treated in the easiest possible way. For example, an error of a few dollars in recording an asset as an expense for a business with millions of dollars in assets would be considered immaterial, and a correction would not be necessary. In the remaining paragraphs, we assume that errors discovered are material and should be corrected.

Discovery of Errors

As mentioned previously, preparing the trial balance is one of the primary ways to discover errors in the ledger. However, it indicates only that the debits and credits are equal. If the two totals of the trial balance are not equal, it is probably due to one or more of the errors described in Exhibit 6.

Among the types of errors that will *not* cause the trial balance totals to be unequal are the following:

1. Failure to record a transaction or to post a transaction.
2. Recording the same erroneous amount for both the debit and the credit parts of a transaction.
3. Recording the same transaction more than once.
4. Posting a part of a transaction correctly as a debit or credit but to the wrong account.

•Exhibit 6   Errors Causing Unequal Trial Balance

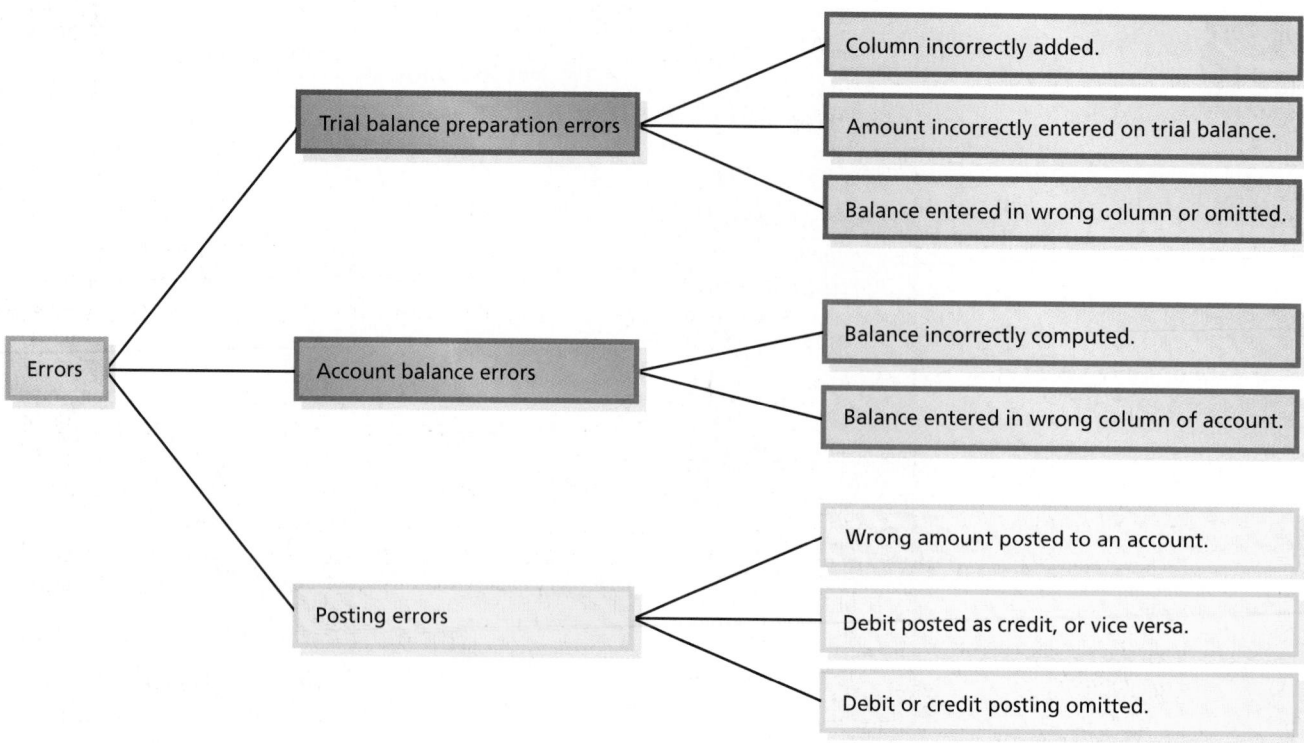

It is obvious that care should be used in recording transactions in the journal and in posting to the accounts. The need for accuracy in determining account balances and reporting them on the trial balance is also evident.

Errors in the accounts may be discovered in various ways: (1) through audit procedures, (2) by looking at the trial balance or (3) by chance. If the two trial balance totals are not equal, the amount of the difference between the totals should be determined before searching for the error.

The amount of the difference between the two totals of a trial balance sometimes gives a clue as to the nature of the error or where it occurred. For example, a difference of 10, 100, or 1,000 between two totals is often the result of an error in addition. A difference between totals can also be due to omitting a debit or a credit posting. If the difference can be evenly divided by 2, the error may be due to the posting of a debit as a credit, or vice versa. For example, if the debit total is $20,640 and the credit total is $20,236, the difference of $404 may indicate that a credit posting of $404 was omitted or that a credit of $202 was incorrectly posted as a debit.

Two other common types of errors are known as transpositions and slides. A ***transposition*** occurs when the order of the digits is changed mistakenly, such as writing $542 as $452 or $524. In a ***slide***, the entire number is mistakenly moved one or more spaces to the right or the left, such as writing $542.00 as $54.20 or $5,420.00. If an error of either type has occurred and there are no other errors, the difference between the two trial balance totals can be evenly divided by 9.

If an error is not revealed by the trial balance, the steps in the accounting process must be retraced, beginning with the last step and working back to the entries in the journal. Usually, errors causing the trial balance totals to be unequal will be discovered before all of the steps are retraced.

Correction of Errors

The procedures used to correct an error in journalizing or posting vary according to the nature of the error and when the error is discovered. These procedures are summarized in Exhibit 7.

What type of error occurs when $14,500 is recorded as $15,400?

A transposition.

•Exhibit 7 Procedures for Correcting Errors

Error	Correction Procedure
1. Journal entry is incorrect but not posted.	Draw a line through the error and insert correct title or amount.
2. Journal entry is correct but posted incorrectly.	Draw a line through the error and post correctly.
3. Journal entry is incorrect and posted.	Journalize and post a correcting entry.

Correcting the first two types of errors shown in Exhibit 7 involves simply drawing a line through the error and inserting the correct title or amount. Usually, the person making corrections initials the correction in case questions arise later.

Correcting the third type of error in Exhibit 7 is more complex. To illustrate, assume that on May 5 a $12,500 purchase of office equipment on account was incorrectly journalized and posted as a debit to Supplies and a credit to Accounts Payable for $12,500. This posting of the incorrect entry is shown in the following T accounts.

	Supplies			Accounts Payable	
Incorrect:	12,500				12,500

Before making a correcting entry, it is best to determine the debit(s) and credit(s) that should have been recorded. These are shown in the following T accounts.

	Office Equipment			Accounts Payable	
Correct:	12,500				12,500

Comparing the two sets of T accounts shows that the incorrect debit to Supplies may be corrected by debiting Office Equipment for $12,500 and crediting Supplies for $12,500. The following correcting entry is then journalized and posted:

Entry to Correct Error:

18	May	31	Office Equipment	18	12 5 0 0 00		18
19			Supplies	14		12 5 0 0 00	19
20			To correct erroneous debit				20
21			to Supplies on May 5. See invoice				21
22			from Bell Office Equipment Co.				22

Financial Analysis and Interpretation

objective 7

Use horizontal analysis to compare financial statements from different periods.

A single item appearing in a financial statement is often useful in interpreting the financial results of a business. However, comparing this item in a current statement with the same item in prior statements often makes the financial information more useful. **Horizontal analysis** is the term used to describe such comparisons.

In horizontal analysis, the amount of each item on the current financial statements is compared with the same item on one or more earlier statements. The increase or decrease in the *amount* of the item is computed, together with the *percent* of increase or decrease. When two statements are being compared, the earlier statement is used as the base for computing the amount and the percent of change.

To illustrate, the horizontal analysis of two income statements for J. Holmes, Attorney-at-Law, organized as a professional corporation, is shown in Exhibit 8. Exhibit 8 indicates both favorable and unfavorable trends affecting the income statement of J. Holmes, Attorney-at-Law. The increase in fees earned is a favorable trend, as is the decrease in supplies expense. Unfavorable trends include the increase in wages expense, utilities expense, and miscellaneous expense. These expenses increased faster than the increase in revenues, with total operating expenses increasing by 30.6%. Overall, net income increased by $15,800, or 19.9%, a favorable trend.

The significance of the various increases and decreases in the revenue and expense items in Exhibit 8 should be investigated to see if operations could be further improved. For example, the increase in utilities expense of 38.9% was the result of renting additional office space for use by a part-time law student in performing paralegal services. This explains the increase in rent expense of 25% and the increase in wages expense of 33.3%. The increase in revenues of 25% reflects the fees generated by the new paralegal.

This example illustrates how horizontal analysis can be useful in interpreting and analyzing financial statements. Horizontal analyses similar to that shown in Exhibit 8 can also be performed for the balance sheet, the retained earnings statement, and the statement of cash flows.

•Exhibit 8 Horizontal Analysis of Income Statement

J. Holmes, Attorney-at-Law
Income Statement
For the Years Ended December 31, 2005 and 2006

	2006	2005	Increase (Decrease) Amount	Increase (Decrease) Percent
Fees earned	$187,500	$150,000	$37,500	25.0%*
Operating expenses:				
Wages expense	$ 60,000	$ 45,000	$15,000	33.3%
Rent expense	15,000	12,000	3,000	25.0%
Utilities expense	12,500	9,000	3,500	38.9%
Supplies expense	2,700	3,000	(300)	(10.0)%
Miscellaneous expense	2,300	1,800	500	27.8%
Total operating expenses	$ 92,500	$ 70,800	$21,700	30.6%
Net income	$ 95,000	$ 79,200	$15,800	19.9%

*$37,500 ÷ $150,000

SPOTLIGHT ON STRATEGY

GOT THE FLU? WHY NOT CHEW SOME GUM?

Facing a slumping market for sugared chewing gum, such as Juicy Fruit and Doublemint, **Wm. J. Wrigley Jr. Company** is reinventing itself with a strategy to expand its product lines and introduce new chewing gum applications. Wrigley's new products include sugarless breath mints and more powerful flavored mint chewing gum, like Extra Polar Ice. In addition, Wrigley is experimenting with health-care applications of chewing gum. Wrigley's Health Care Division has already developed Surpass, an antacid chewing gum to compete with Rolaids and Mylanta. In addition, Wrigley is experimenting with a cold-relief chewing gum and a gum that would provide dental benefits, such as whitening teeth and reducing plaque. Given that the U.S. population is aging, the company figures that people might prefer chewing gum to taking pills for sore throats, colds, or the flu. The effects of these new strategic initiatives will ultimately be reflected in Wrigley's financial statements.

Source: Adapted from "A Young Heir Has New Plans at Old Company," by David Barboza, *The New York Times*, August 28, 2001.

Key Points

1 **Explain why accounts are used to record and summarize the effects of transactions on financial statements.**

The record used for recording individual transactions is an account. A group of accounts is called a ledger. The system of accounts that make up a ledger is called a chart of accounts. The accounts are numbered and listed in the order in which they appear in the balance sheet and the income statement.

2 **Describe the characteristics of an account.**

The simplest form of an account, a T account, has three parts: (1) a title, which is the name of the item recorded in the account; (2) a left side, called the debit side; (3) a right side, called the credit side. Amounts entered on the left side of an account, regardless of the account title, are called debits to the account. Amounts entered on the right side of an account are called credits. Periodically, the debits in an account are added, the credits in the account are added, and the balance of the account is determined.

3 **List the rules of debit and credit and the normal balances of accounts.**

General rules of debit and credit have been established for recording increases or decreases in asset, liability, capital stock, retained earnings, revenue, expense, and dividends accounts. Each transaction is recorded so that the sum of the debits is always equal to the sum of the credits. Transactions are initially entered in a record called a journal.

The sum of the increases recorded in an account is usually equal to or greater than the sum of the decreases recorded in the account. For this reason, the normal balance of an account is indicated by the side of the account (debit or credit) that receives the increases.

The rules of debit and credit and normal account balances are summarized in the following table:

	Increase (Normal Balance)	Decrease
Balance sheet accounts:		
Asset	Debit	Credit
Liability	Credit	Debit
Owners' (Stockholders') Equity:		
Capital Stock	Credit	Debit
Retained Earnings	Credit	Debit
Income statement accounts:		
Revenue	Credit	Debit
Expense	Debit	Credit
Dividends accounts:		
Dividends	Debit	Credit

4 **Analyze and summarize the financial statement effects of transactions.**

Transactions are analyzed by determining whether: (1) an asset, liability, capital stock, retained earnings, revenue, expense, or dividends account is affected, (2) each account affected increases or decreases, and (3) each increase or decrease is recorded as a debit or a credit. A journal is used for recording the transaction initially. The journal entries are periodically posted to the accounts.

5 **Prepare a trial balance and explain how it can be used to discover errors.**

A trial balance is prepared by listing the accounts from the ledger and their balances. If the two totals of the trial balance are not equal, an error has occurred.

6 **Discover errors in recording transactions and correct them.**

Errors may be discovered (1) by audit procedures, (2) by looking at the trial balance or (3) by chance. The procedures for correcting errors are summarized in Exhibit 7.

7 **Use horizontal analysis to compare financial statements from different periods.**

In horizontal analysis, the amount of each item on the current financial statements is compared with the same item on one or more earlier statements. The increase or decrease in the *amount* of the item is computed, together with the *percent* of increase or decrease.

Key Terms

account (48)
assets (48)
balance of the account (50)
chart of accounts (48)
credits (50)
debits (49)
dividends (49)

double-entry accounting (53)
expenses (49)
horizontal analysis (71)
journal (51)
journal entry (51)
journalizing (51)
ledger (48)

liabilities (48)
materiality concept (69)
owners' equity (48)
posting (55)
revenues (49)
slide (70)
stockholders' equity (48)

T account (49)
transposition (70)

trial balance (68)
two-column journal (55)

unearned revenue (58)

Illustrative Problem

J. F. Outz, M.D., has been practicing as a cardiologist for three years in a professional corporation known as Hearts, P.C. During April, 2005, Hearts, P.C. completed the following transactions:

April 1. Paid office rent for April, $800.
   3. Purchased equipment on account, $2,100.
   5. Received cash on account from patients, $3,150.
   8. Purchased X-ray film and other supplies on account, $245.
   9. One of the items of equipment purchased on April 3 was defective. It was returned with the permission of the supplier, who agreed to reduce the account for the amount charged for the item, $325.
   12. Paid cash to creditors on account, $1,250.
   17. Paid cash for renewal of a six-month property insurance policy, $370.
   20. Discovered that the balances of the cash account and the accounts payable account as of April 1 were overstated by $200. A payment of that amount to a creditor in March had not been recorded. Journalize the $200 payment as of April 20.
   24. Paid cash for laboratory analysis, $545.
   27. Paid cash dividends, $1,250.
   30. Recorded the cash received in payment of services (on a cash basis) to patients during April, $1,720.
   30. Paid salaries of receptionist and nurses, $1,725.
   30. Paid various utility expenses, $360.
   30. Recorded fees charged to patients on account for services performed in April, $5,145.
   30. Paid miscellaneous expenses, $132.

Hearts' account titles, numbers, and balances as of April 1 (all normal balances) are listed as follows: Cash, 11, $4,123; Accounts Receivable, 12, $6,725; Supplies, 13, $290; Prepaid Insurance, 14, $465; Equipment, 18, $19,745; Accounts Payable, 22, $765; Capital Stock, 31, $10,000; Retained Earnings, 32, $20,583; Dividends, 33; Professional Fees, 41; Salary Expense, 51; Rent Expense, 53; Laboratory Expense, 55; Utilities Expense, 56; Miscellaneous Expense, 59.

Instructions

1. Open a ledger of standard four-column accounts for Hearts, P.C. as of April 1. Enter the balances in the appropriate balance columns and place a check mark (✓) in the posting reference column. (*Hint:* Verify the equality of the debit and credit balances in the ledger before proceeding with the next instruction.)
2. Journalize each transaction in a two-column journal.
3. Post the journal to the ledger, extending the month-end balances to the appropriate balance columns after each posting.
4. Prepare a trial balance as of April 30.

Solution

2. and **3.**

	Date		Description	Post. Ref.	Debit	Credit	
1	2005 April	1	Rent Expense	53	8 0 0 00		1
2			Cash	11		8 0 0 00	2
3			Paid office rent for April.				3
4							4
5		3	Equipment	18	2 1 0 0 00		5
6			Accounts Payable	22		2 1 0 0 00	6
7			Purchased equipment on account.				7
8							8
9		5	Cash	11	3 1 5 0 00		9
10			Accounts Receivable	12		3 1 5 0 00	10
11			Received cash on account.				11
12							12
13		8	Supplies	13	2 4 5 00		13
14			Accounts Payable	22		2 4 5 00	14
15			Purchased supplies.				15
16							16
17		9	Accounts Payable	22	3 2 5 00		17
18			Equipment	18		3 2 5 00	18
19			Returned defective equipment.				19
20							20
21		12	Accounts Payable	22	1 2 5 0 00		21
22			Cash	11		1 2 5 0 00	22
23			Paid creditors on account.				23
24							24
25		17	Prepaid Insurance	14	3 7 0 00		25
26			Cash	11		3 7 0 00	26
27			Renewed 6-month property policy.				27
28							28
29		20	Accounts Payable	22	2 0 0 00		29
30			Cash	11		2 0 0 00	30
31			Recorded March payment				31
32			to creditor.				32
33							33

JOURNAL — Page 27

	Date		Description	Post. Ref.	Debit	Credit	
1	2005 April	24	Laboratory Expense	55	5 4 5 00		1
2			Cash	11		5 4 5 00	2
3			Paid for laboratory analysis.				3
4							4

JOURNAL — Page 28

JOURNAL   Page 28

	Date		Description	Post. Ref.	Debit	Credit	
5	2005 April	27	Dividends	33	1 2 5 0 00		5
6			Cash	11		1 2 5 0 00	6
7			Paid dividends to stockholders.				7
8							8
9		30	Cash	11	1 7 2 0 00		9
10			Professional Fees	41		1 7 2 0 00	10
11			Received fees from patients.				11
12							12
13		30	Salary Expense	51	1 7 2 5 00		13
14			Cash	11		1 7 2 5 00	14
15			Paid salaries.				15
16							16
17		30	Utilities Expense	56	3 6 0 00		17
18			Cash	11		3 6 0 00	18
19			Paid utilities.				19
20							20
21		30	Accounts Receivable	12	5 1 4 5 00		21
22			Professional Fees	41		5 1 4 5 00	22
23			Recorded fees earned on account.				23
24							24
25		30	Miscellaneous Expense	59	1 3 2 00		25
26			Cash	11		1 3 2 00	26
27			Paid expenses.				27

1. and **3.**

ACCOUNT *Cash*   **ACCOUNT NO.** *11*

Date		Item	Post. Ref.	Debit	Credit	Balance Debit	Balance Credit
2005 April	1	Balance	✓			4 1 2 3 00	
	1		27		8 0 0 00	3 3 2 3 00	
	5		27	3 1 5 0 00		6 4 7 3 00	
	12		27		1 2 5 0 00	5 2 2 3 00	
	17		27		3 7 0 00	4 8 5 3 00	
	20		27		2 0 0 00	4 6 5 3 00	
	24		28		5 4 5 00	4 1 0 8 00	
	27		28		1 2 5 0 00	2 8 5 8 00	
	30		28	1 7 2 0 00		4 5 7 8 00	
	30		28		1 7 2 5 00	2 8 5 3 00	
	30		28		3 6 0 00	2 4 9 3 00	
	30		28		1 3 2 00	2 3 6 1 00	

ACCOUNT *Accounts Receivable*   **ACCOUNT NO.** *12*

Date		Item	Post. Ref.	Debit	Credit	Balance Debit	Balance Credit
2005 April	1	Balance	✓			6 7 2 5 00	
	5		27		3 1 5 0 00	3 5 7 5 00	
	30		28	5 1 4 5 00		8 7 2 0 00	

ACCOUNT *Supplies*   **ACCOUNT NO.** *13*

Date		Item	Post. Ref.	Debit	Credit	Balance Debit	Balance Credit
2005 April	1	Balance	✓			2 9 0 00	
	8		27	2 4 5 00		5 3 5 00	

ACCOUNT *Prepaid Insurance*   **ACCOUNT NO.** *14*

Date		Item	Post. Ref.	Debit	Credit	Balance Debit	Balance Credit
2005 April	1	Balance	✓			4 6 5 00	
	17		27	3 7 0 00		8 3 5 00	

ACCOUNT *Equipment*   **ACCOUNT NO.** *18*

Date		Item	Post. Ref.	Debit	Credit	Balance Debit	Balance Credit
2005 April	1	Balance	✓			19 7 4 5 00	
	3		27	2 1 0 0 00		21 8 4 5 00	
	9		27		3 2 5 00	21 5 2 0 00	

ACCOUNT *Accounts Payable*   **ACCOUNT NO.** *22*

Date		Item	Post. Ref.	Debit	Credit	Balance Debit	Balance Credit
2005 April	1	Balance	✓				7 6 5 00
	3		27		2 1 0 0 00		2 8 6 5 00
	8		27		2 4 5 00		3 1 1 0 00
	9		27	3 2 5 00			2 7 8 5 00
	12		27	1 2 5 0 00			1 5 3 5 00
	20		27	2 0 0 00			1 3 3 5 00

ACCOUNT *Capital Stock*   **ACCOUNT NO.** *31*

Date		Item	Post. Ref.	Debit	Credit	Balance Debit	Balance Credit
2005 April	1	Balance	✓				10 0 0 0 00

ACCOUNT *Retained Earnings*   **ACCOUNT NO.** *32*

Date		Item	Post. Ref.	Debit	Credit	Balance Debit	Balance Credit
2005 April	1	Balance	✓				2 0 5 8 3 00

ACCOUNT *Dividends*   **ACCOUNT NO.** *33*

Date		Item	Post. Ref.	Debit	Credit	Balance Debit	Balance Credit
2005 April	27		28	1 2 5 0 00		1 2 5 0 00	

ACCOUNT *Professional Fees*   **ACCOUNT NO.** *41*

Date		Item	Post. Ref.	Debit	Credit	Balance Debit	Balance Credit
2005 April	30		28		1 7 2 0 00		1 7 2 0 00
	30		28		5 1 4 5 00		6 8 6 5 00

ACCOUNT *Salary Expense*   **ACCOUNT NO.** *51*

Date		Item	Post. Ref.	Debit	Credit	Balance Debit	Balance Credit
2005 April	30		28	1 7 2 5 00		1 7 2 5 00	

ACCOUNT *Rent Expense*   **ACCOUNT NO.** *53*

Date		Item	Post. Ref.	Debit	Credit	Balance Debit	Balance Credit
2005 April	1		27	8 0 0 00		8 0 0 00	

ACCOUNT *Laboratory Expense*   **ACCOUNT NO.** *55*

Date	Item	Post. Ref.	Debit	Credit	Balance Debit	Balance Credit
2005 April 24		28	5 4 5 00		5 4 5 00	

ACCOUNT *Utilities Expense*   **ACCOUNT NO.** *56*

Date	Item	Post. Ref.	Debit	Credit	Balance Debit	Balance Credit
2005 April 30		28	3 6 0 00		3 6 0 00	

ACCOUNT *Miscellaneous Expense*   **ACCOUNT NO.** *59*

Date	Item	Post. Ref.	Debit	Credit	Balance Debit	Balance Credit
2005 April 30		28	1 3 2 00		1 3 2 00	

4.

Hearts, P.C.
Trial Balance
April 30, 2005

	Debit	Credit
Cash	2 3 6 1 00	
Accounts Receivable	8 7 2 0 00	
Supplies	5 3 5 00	
Prepaid Insurance	8 3 5 00	
Equipment	21 5 2 0 00	
Accounts Payable		1 3 3 5 00
Capital Stock		10 0 0 0 00
Retained Earnings		20 5 8 3 00
Dividends	1 2 5 0 00	
Professional Fees		6 8 6 5 00
Salary Expense	1 7 2 5 00	
Rent Expense	8 0 0 00	
Laboratory Expense	5 4 5 00	
Utilities Expense	3 6 0 00	
Miscellaneous Expense	1 3 2 00	
	38 7 8 3 00	38 7 8 3 00

Self-Examination Questions (Answers at End of Chapter)

1. A debit may signify:
   A. an increase in an asset account.
   B. a decrease in an asset account.
   C. an increase in a liability account.
   D. an increase in the capital stock account.

2. The type of account with a normal credit balance is:
   A. an asset.   C. a revenue.
   B. dividends.   D. an expense.

3. A debit balance in which of the following accounts would indicate a likely error?
   A. Accounts Receivable
   B. Cash
   C. Fees Earned
   D. Miscellaneous Expense

4. The receipt of cash from customers in payment of their accounts would be recorded by a:
   A. debit to Cash; credit to Accounts Receivable.
   B. debit to Accounts Receivable; credit to Cash.
   C. debit to Cash; credit to Accounts Payable.
   D. debit to Accounts Payable; credit to Cash.

5. The form listing the titles and balances of the accounts in the ledger on a given date is the:
   A. income statement.
   B. balance sheet.
   C. retained earnings statement.
   D. trial balance.

Class Discussion Questions

1. What is the difference between an account and a ledger?
2. Do the terms *debit* and *credit* signify increase or decrease or can they signify either? Explain.
3. Explain why the rules of debit and credit are the same for liability accounts and stockholders' equity accounts.
4. What is the effect (increase or decrease) of a debit to an expense account (a) in terms of retained earnings and (b) in terms of expense?
5. What is the effect (increase or decrease) of a credit to a revenue account (a) in terms of retained earnings and (b) in terms of revenue?
6. Kemp Company adheres to a policy of depositing all cash receipts in a bank account and making all payments by check. The cash account as of August 31 has a credit balance of $3,000, and there is no undeposited cash on hand. (a) Assuming no errors occurred during journalizing or posting, what caused this unusual balance? (b) Is the $3,000 credit balance in the cash account an asset, a liability, stockholders' equity, a revenue, or an expense?
7. McElwee Company performed services in May for a specific customer for a fee of $7,500. Payment was received the following June. (a) Was the revenue earned in May or June? (b) What accounts should be debited and credited in (1) May and (2) June?
8. What proof is provided by a trial balance?
9. If the two totals of a trial balance are equal, does it mean that there are no errors in the accounting records? Explain.
10. Assume that a trial balance is prepared with an account balance of $18,950 listed as $18,590 and an account balance of $7,200 listed as $720. Identify the transposition and the slide.
11. Assume that when a purchase of supplies of $1,250 for cash was recorded, both the debit and the credit were journalized and posted as $1,520. (a) Would this error cause the trial balance to be out of balance? (b) Would the trial balance be out of balance if the $1,250 entry had been journalized correctly but the credit to Cash had been posted as $1,520?
12. Assume that Margarita Consulting erroneously recorded the payment of $7,500 of dividends as a debit to salary expense. (a) How would this error affect the

equality of the trial balance? (b) How would this error affect the income statement, retained earnings statement, and balance sheet?

13. Assume that Blitzkrieg Realty Co. borrowed $25,000 from First Union Bank and Trust. In recording the transaction, Blitzkrieg erroneously recorded the receipt of $25,000 as a debit to cash, $25,000, and a credit to fees earned, $25,000. (a) How would this error affect the equality of the trial balance? (b) How would this error affect the income statement, retained earnings statement, and balance sheet?

14. In journalizing and posting the entry to record the purchase of supplies on account, the accounts receivable account was credited in error. What is the preferred procedure to correct this error?

15. Banks rely heavily upon customers' deposits as a source of funds. Demand deposits normally pay interest to the customer, who is entitled to withdraw at any time without prior notice to the bank. Checking and NOW (negotiable order of withdrawal) accounts are the most common form of demand deposits for banks. Assume that Kennon Storage has a checking account at Livingston Savings Bank. What type of account (asset, liability, capital stock, retained earnings, revenue, expense, or dividends) does the account balance of $15,600 represent from the viewpoint of (a) Kennon Storage and (b) Livingston Savings Bank?

REAL WORLD

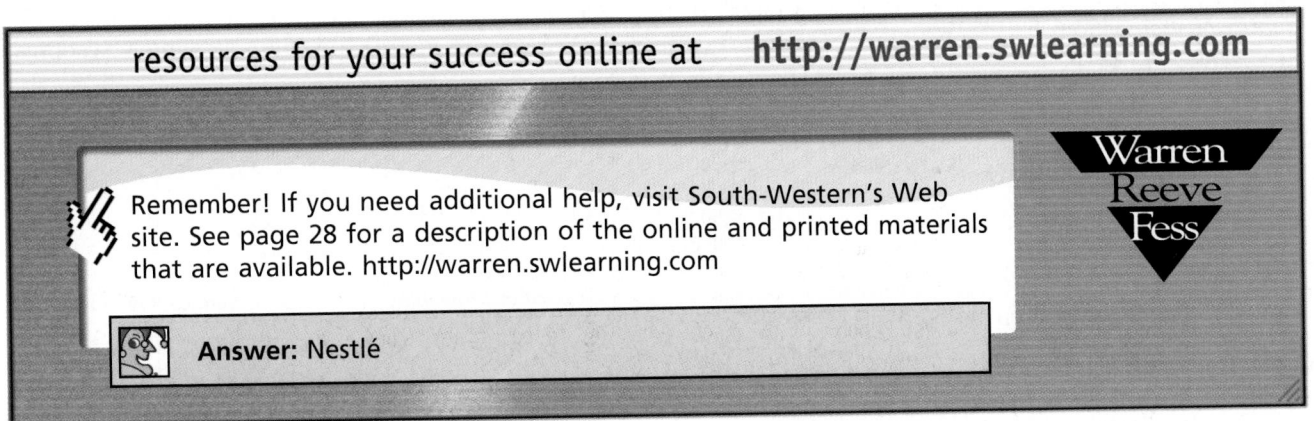

resources for your success online at **http://warren.swlearning.com**

Remember! If you need additional help, visit South-Western's Web site. See page 28 for a description of the online and printed materials that are available. http://warren.swlearning.com

Warren Reeve Fess

Answer: Nestlé

Exercises

EXERCISE 2-1
Chart of accounts
Objective 1

REAL WORLD

The following accounts appeared in recent financial statements of **Continental Airlines**:

Accounts Payable	Flight Equipment
Aircraft Fuel Expense	Landing Fees
Air Traffic Liability	Passenger Revenue
Cargo and Mail Revenue	Purchase Deposits for Flight Equipment
Commissions	Spare Parts and Supplies

Identify each account as either a balance sheet account or an income statement account. For each balance sheet account, identify it as an asset, a liability, or stockholders' equity. For each income statement account, identify it as a revenue or an expense.

EXERCISE 2-2
Chart of accounts
Objective 1

Clarendon Interiors is owned and operated by Corey Krum, an interior decorator. In the ledger of Clarendon Interiors, the first digit of the account number indicates its major account classification (1—assets, 2—liabilities, 3—stockholders' equity, 4—revenues, 5—expenses). The second digit of the account number indicates the specific account within each of the preceding major account classifications.

Match each account number with its most likely account in the following list. The account numbers are 11, 12, 13, 21, 31, 33, 41, 51, 52, and 53.

Accounts:

Accounts Payable	Dividends	Miscellaneous Expense
Accounts Receivable	Fees Earned	Supplies Expense
Capital Stock	Land	Wages Expense
Cash		

EXERCISE 2-3
Chart of accounts
Objective 1

The Inflorescence School is a newly organized business that teaches people how to inspire and influence others. The list of accounts to be opened in the general ledger is as follows:

Accounts Payable	Dividends	Prepaid Insurance	Supplies Expense
Accounts Receivable	Equipment	Rent Expense	Unearned Rent
Capital Stock	Fees Earned	Retained Earnings	Wages Expense
Cash	Miscellaneous Expense	Supplies	

List the accounts in the order in which they should appear in the ledger of The Inflorescence School and assign account numbers. Each account number is to have two digits: the first digit is to indicate the major classification (*1* for assets, etc.), and the second digit is to identify the specific account within each major classification (*11* for Cash, etc.).

EXERCISE 2-4
Identifying transactions
Objectives 2, 3

Malta Co. is a travel agency. The nine transactions recorded by Malta during February 2006, its first month of operations, are indicated in the following T accounts:

Cash			
(1) 40,000	(2)	1,800	
(7) 9,500	(3)	9,000	
	(4)	3,050	
	(6)	7,500	
	(8)	5,000	

Equipment	
(3) 24,000	

Dividends	
(8) 5,000	

Accounts Receivable	
(5) 12,000	(7) 9,500

Accounts Payable	
(6) 7,500	(3) 15,000

Service Revenue	
	(5) 12,000

Supplies	
(2) 1,800	(9) 1,050

Capital Stock	
	(1) 40,000

Operating Expenses	
(4) 3,050	
(9) 1,050	

Indicate for each debit and each credit: (a) whether an asset, liability, capital stock, dividends, revenue, or expense account was affected and (b) whether the account was increased (+) or decreased (−). Present your answers in the following form, with transaction (1) given as an example:

	Account Debited		Account Credited	
Transaction	Type	Effect	Type	Effect
(1)	asset	+	capital stock	+

EXERCISE 2-5
Journal entries
Objectives 3, 4

Based upon the T accounts in Exercise 2-4, prepare the nine journal entries from which the postings were made. Journal entry explanations may be omitted.

EXERCISE 2-6
Trial balance
Objective 5

SPREADSHEET

✓ *Total Debit Column:*
$59,500

Based upon the data presented in Exercise 2-4, prepare a trial balance, listing the accounts in their proper order.

EXERCISE 2-7
Normal entries for accounts
Objective 3

During the month, Orion Labs Co. has a substantial number of transactions affecting each of the following accounts. State for each account whether it is likely to have (a) debit entries only, (b) credit entries only, or (c) both debit and credit entries.

1. Accounts Payable
2. Accounts Receivable
3. Cash
4. Dividends

5. Fees Earned
6. Insurance Expense
7. Supplies Expense

EXERCISE 2-8
Normal balances of accounts
Objective 3

Identify each of the following accounts of Universal Services Co. as asset, liability, stockholders' equity, revenue, or expense, and state in each case whether the normal balance is a debit or a credit.

a. Accounts Payable
b. Accounts Receivable
c. Cash
d. Capital Stock
e. Fees Earned

f. Office Equipment
g. Rent Expense
h. Supplies
i. Wages Expense

EXERCISE 2-9
Rules of debit and credit
Objective 3

The following table summarizes the rules of debit and credit. For each of the items (a) through (l), indicate whether the proper answer is a debit or a credit.

	Increase	Decrease	Normal Balance
Balance sheet accounts:			
Asset	Debit	(a)	Debit
Liability	(b)	(c)	(d)
Stockholders' Equity:			
Capital Stock	Credit	(e)	(f)
Retained Earnings	(g)	Debit	(h)
Income statement accounts:			
Revenue	Credit	(i)	(j)
Expense	(k)	(l)	Debit
Dividends accounts:			
Dividends	(m)	Credit	(n)

EXERCISE 2-10
Capital account balance
Objectives 2, 3

As of January 1, Retained Earnings had a credit balance of $10,500. During the year, dividends totaled $4,000 and the business incurred a net loss of $8,000.

a. Calculate the balance of retained earnings, as of the end of the year.
b. Assuming that there have been no recording errors, will the balance sheet prepared at December 31 balance? Explain.

EXERCISE 2-11
Cash account balance
Objectives 2, 3

During the month, Wembley Co. received $212,500 in cash and paid out $183,750 in cash.

a. Do the data indicate that Wembley Co. earned $28,750 during the month? Explain.
b. If the balance of the cash account is $36,300 at the end of the month, what was the cash balance at the beginning of the month?

EXERCISE 2-12
Account balances
Objectives 2, 3
✓c. $20,800

a. On April 1, the cash account balance was $7,850. During April, cash receipts totaled $41,850 and the April 30 balance was $9,150. Determine the cash payments made during April.
b. On July 1, the accounts receivable account balance was $15,500. During July, $61,000 was collected from customers on account. Assuming the July 31 balance was $17,500, determine the fees billed to customers on account during July.
c. During January, $40,500 was paid to creditors on account and purchases on account were $57,700. Assuming the January 31 balance of Accounts Payable was $38,000, determine the account balance on January 1.

EXERCISE 2-13
Transactions
Objectives 3, 4

The Zuni Co. has the following accounts in its ledger: Cash; Accounts Receivable; Supplies; Office Equipment; Accounts Payable; Capital Stock; Dividends; Fees Earned; Rent Expense; Advertising Expense; Utilities Expense; Miscellaneous Expense.

Journalize the following selected transactions for August 2005 in a two-column journal. Journal entry explanations may be omitted.

August 1. Paid rent for the month, $1,500.
     2. Paid advertising expense, $700.
     4. Paid cash for supplies, $1,050.
     6. Purchased office equipment on account, $7,500.
     8. Received cash from customers on account, $3,600.
    12. Paid creditor on account, $1,150.
    20. Paid dividends, $1,000.
    25. Paid cash for repairs to office equipment, $500.
    30. Paid telephone bill for the month, $195.
    31. Fees earned and billed to customers for the month, $10,150.
    31. Paid electricity bill for the month, $380.

EXERCISE 2-14
Journalizing and posting
Objectives 3, 4

On October 27, 2006, Lintel Co. purchased $1,320 of supplies on account. In Lintel Co.'s chart of accounts, the supplies account is No. 15 and the accounts payable account is No. 21.

a. Journalize the October 27, 2006 transaction on page 43 of Lintel Co.'s two-column journal. Include an explanation of the entry.
b. Prepare a four-column account for Supplies. Enter a debit balance of $585 as of October 1, 2006. Place a check mark (✔) in the posting reference column.
c. Prepare a four-column account for Accounts Payable. Enter a credit balance of $6,150 as of October 1, 2006. Place a check mark (✔) in the posting reference column.
d. Post the October 27, 2006 transaction to the accounts.

EXERCISE 2-15
Transactions and T accounts
Objectives 2, 3, 4

SPREADSHEET

The following selected transactions were completed during May of the current year:

1. Billed customers for fees earned, $12,190. *owe DR accts Receivable.*
2. Purchased supplies on account, $1,250.
3. Received cash from customers on account, $9,150. *DR asset.*
4. Paid creditors on account, $750.

a. Journalize the above transactions in a two-column journal, using the appropriate number to identify the transactions. Journal entry explanations may be omitted.
b. Post the entries prepared in (a) to the following T accounts: Cash, Supplies, Accounts Receivable, Accounts Payable, and Fees Earned. To the left of each amount posted in the accounts, place the appropriate number to identify the transactions.

EXERCISE 2-16
Trial balance
Objective 5

SPREADSHEET

✔ *Total Credit Column: $464,350*

The accounts in the ledger of Haleakala Park Co. as of March 31, 2006, are listed in alphabetical order as follows. All accounts have normal balances. The balance of the cash account has been intentionally omitted.

Accounts Payable	$ 18,710	Notes Payable	$ 40,000
Accounts Receivable	37,500	Prepaid Insurance	3,000
Capital Stock	50,000	Rent Expense	60,000
Cash	?	Retained Earnings	36,640
Dividends	20,000	Supplies	2,100
Fees Earned	310,000	Supplies Expense	7,900
Insurance Expense	6,000	Unearned Rent	9,000
Land	85,000	Utilities Expense	41,500
Miscellaneous Expense	8,900	Wages Expense	175,000

Prepare a trial balance, listing the accounts in their proper order and inserting the missing figure for cash.

EXERCISE 2-17
Effect of errors on trial balance

Objective 5

Indicate which of the following errors, each considered individually, would cause the trial balance totals to be unequal:

a. A payment of $7,000 for equipment purchased was posted as a debit of $700 to Equipment and a credit of $700 to Cash.
b. Payment of a cash dividend of $12,000 was journalized and posted as a debit of $21,000 to Salary Expense and a credit of $12,000 to Cash.
c. A fee of $1,850 earned and due from a client was not debited to Accounts Receivable or credited to a revenue account, because the cash had not been received.
d. A payment of $1,475 to a creditor was posted as a debit of $1,475 to Accounts Payable and a debit of $1,475 to Cash.
e. A receipt of $325 from an account receivable was journalized and posted as a debit of $325 to Cash and a credit of $325 to Fees Earned.

EXERCISE 2-18
Errors in trial balance

Objective 5

✓ *Total of Credit Column: $181,600*

The following preliminary trial balance of Escalade Co., a sports ticket agency, does not balance:

Escalade Co.
Trial Balance
December 31, 2006

Cash	47,350	
Accounts Receivable	22,100	
Prepaid Insurance		8,000
Equipment	57,000	
Accounts Payable		12,980
Unearned Rent		4,520
Capital Stock	25,000	
Retained Earnings	57,420	
Dividends	10,000	
Service Revenue		83,750
Wages Expense		42,000
Advertising Expense	7,200	
Miscellaneous Expense		1,425
	226,070	152,675

When the ledger and other records are reviewed, you discover the following: (1) the debits and credits in the cash account total $47,350 and $33,975, respectively; (2) a billing of $2,500 to a customer on account was not posted to the accounts receivable account; (3) a payment of $1,800 made to a creditor on account was not posted to the accounts payable account; (4) the balance of the unearned rent account is $4,250; (5) the correct balance of the equipment account is $75,000; and (6) each account has a normal balance.

Prepare a corrected trial balance.

EXERCISE 2-19
Effect of errors on trial balance

Objective 5

The following errors occurred in posting from a two-column journal:

1. A debit of $1,250 to Supplies was posted twice.
2. A debit of $3,575 to Wages Expense was posted as $3,557.
3. A credit of $4,175 to Accounts Payable was not posted.
4. A debit of $400 to Accounts Payable was posted as a credit.
5. An entry debiting Accounts Receivable and crediting Fees Earned for $6,000 was not posted.
6. A credit of $350 to Cash was posted as $530.
7. A debit of $1,000 to Cash was posted to Miscellaneous Expense.

Considering each case individually (i.e., assuming that no other errors had occurred), indicate: (a) by "yes" or "no" whether the trial balance would be out of balance; (b) if answer to (a) is "yes," the amount by which the trial balance totals would differ; and (c) whether the debit or credit column of the trial balance would have the larger total. Answers should be presented in the following form, with error (1) given as an example:

(continued)

Error	(a) Out of Balance	(b) Difference	(c) Larger Total
1.	yes	$1,250	debit

EXERCISE 2-20
Errors in trial balance

Objective 5

**WHAT'S WRONG
WITH THIS?**

✓ *Total of Credit Column:*
$125,000

Identify the errors in the following trial balance. All accounts have normal balances.

Dinero Co.
Trial Balance
For the Month Ending January 31, 2006

Cash	7,500	
Accounts Receivable		16,400
Prepaid Insurance	3,600	
Equipment	50,000	
Accounts Payable	1,850	
Salaries Payable		1,250
Capital Stock		5,000
Retained Earnings		38,200
Dividends		6,000
Service Revenue		78,700
Salary Expense	32,810	
Advertising Expense		7,200
Miscellaneous Expense	1,490	
	152,750	152,750

EXERCISE 2-21
Entries to correct errors

Objective 6

The following errors took place in journalizing and posting transactions:

a. Dividends of $15,000 were recorded as a debit to Wages Expense and a credit to Cash.

b. Rent of $4,500 paid for the current month was recorded as a debit to Rent Expense and a credit to Prepaid Rent.

Journalize the entries to correct the errors. Omit explanations.

EXERCISE 2-22
Entries to correct errors

Objective 6

The following errors took place in journalizing and posting transactions:

a. A $550 purchase of supplies on account was recorded as a debit to Miscellaneous Expense and a credit to Prepaid Rent.

b. Cash of $3,750 received on account was recorded as a debit to Accounts Payable and a credit to Cash.

Journalize the entries to correct the errors. Omit explanations.

EXERCISE 2-23
Horizontal analysis of income statement

Objective 7

REAL WORLD

The financial statements for **The Home Depot** are presented in Appendix F at the end of the text.

a. For Home Depot, comparing 2003 with 2002, determine the amount of change in millions and the percent of change for
   1. net sales (revenues) and
   2. total operating expenses.

b. ✏ What conclusions can you draw from your analysis of the net sales and the total operating expenses?

EXERCISE 2-24
Horizontal analysis of income statement

Objective 7

REAL WORLD

The following data were adapted from the financial statements of **Kmart Corporation**, prior to its filing for bankruptcy:

	In millions	
For years ending January 31	**2000**	**1999**
Sales	$37,028	$35,925
Cost of sales (expense)	(29,658)	(28,111)
Selling, general, and administrative expenses	(7,415)	(6,514)
Operating income (loss)	(45)	1,300

a. Prepare a horizontal analysis for the income statement showing the amount and percent of change in each of the following:
   1. Sales
   2. Cost of sales
   3. Selling, general, and administative expenses
   4. Operating income (loss)
b. Comment on the results of your horizontal analysis in (a).

Problems Series A

PROBLEM 2-1A
Entries into T accounts and trial balance
Objectives 2, 3, 4, 5
✓ *3. Total of Debit Column: $39,875*

Shaun Wilcox opened an office on April 1, 2006. During the month, he completed the following transactions connected with his professional corporation, Shawn Wilcox, Architect, P.C.:

a. Transferred cash from a personal bank account to an account to be used for the business in exchange for capital stock, $17,500.
b. Purchased used automobile for $15,300, paying $4,000 cash and giving a note payable for the remainder.
c. Paid April rent for office and workroom, $2,200.
d. Paid cash for supplies, $660.
e. Purchased office and computer equipment on account, $5,200.
f. Paid cash for annual insurance policies on automobile and equipment, $1,200.
g. Received cash from a client for plans delivered, $3,725.
h. Paid cash to creditors on account, $1,800.
i. Paid cash for miscellaneous expenses, $235.
j. Received invoice for blueprint service, due in May, $650.
k. Recorded fee earned on plans delivered, payment to be received in May, $3,500.
l. Paid salary of assistant, $1,300.
m. Paid cash for miscellaneous expenses, $105.
n. Paid installment due on note payable, $200.
o. Paid gas, oil, and repairs on automobile for April, $115.

Instructions

1. Record the foregoing transactions directly in the following T accounts without journalizing: Cash; Accounts Receivable; Supplies; Prepaid Insurance; Automobiles; Equipment; Notes Payable; Accounts Payable; Capital Stock; Professional Fees; Rent Expense; Salary Expense; Blueprint Expense; Automobile Expense; Miscellaneous Expense. To the left of each amount entered in the accounts, place the appropriate letter to identify the transaction.
2. Determine the balances of the T accounts having two or more debits or credits. A memorandum balance should be inserted in accounts having both debits and credits, in the manner illustrated in the chapter. For accounts with entries on one side only (such as Professional Fees), there is no need to insert the memorandum balance in the item column. For accounts containing only a single debit and a single credit (such as Notes Payable), the memorandum balance should be inserted in the appropriate item column. Accounts containing a single entry only (such as Prepaid Insurance) do not need a memorandum balance.
3. Prepare a trial balance for Shaun Wilcox, Architect, P.C. as of April 30, 2006.

PROBLEM 2-2A
Journal entries and trial balance
Objectives 2, 3, 4, 5

On March 1, 2006, Tim Cochran established Star Realty, which completed the following transactions during the month:

a. Tim Cochran transferred cash from a personal bank account to an account to be used for the business in exchange for capital stock, $12,000.
b. Purchased supplies on account, $850.

✓ 4. c. $4,920

c. Earned sales commissions, receiving cash, $12,600. *DR. Cash CR Revenue.*
d. Paid rent on office and equipment for the month, $2,000.
e. Paid creditor on account, $450.
f. Paid dividends, $1,500.
g. Paid automobile expenses (including rental charge) for month, $1,700, and miscellaneous expenses, $375.
h. Paid office salaries, $3,000.
i. Determined that the cost of supplies used was $605.

Instructions

1. Journalize entries for transactions (a) through (i), using the following account titles: Cash; Supplies; Accounts Payable; Capital Stock; Dividends; Sales Commissions; Rent Expense; Office Salaries Expense; Automobile Expense; Supplies Expense; Miscellaneous Expense. Journal entry explanations may be omitted.
2. Prepare T accounts, using the account titles in (1). Post the journal entries to these accounts, placing the appropriate letter to the left of each amount to identify the transactions. Determine the account balances, after all posting is complete, for all accounts having two or more debits or credits. A memorandum balance should be inserted in accounts having both debits and credits in the manner illustrated in the chapter. For accounts with entries on one side only, there is no need to insert a memorandum balance in the item column. For accounts containing only a single debit and a single credit, the memorandum balance should be inserted in the appropriate item column.
3. Prepare a trial balance as of March 31, 2006.
4. Determine the following:
   a. Amount of total revenue recorded in the ledger.
   b. Amount of total expenses recorded in the ledger.
   c. Amount of net income for March.

PROBLEM 2-3A
Journal entries and trial balance

Objectives 2, 3, 4, 5

✓ 3. Total of Credit Column:
$40,880

On July 1, 2006, Leon Cruz established an interior decorating business, Ingres Designs. During the remainder of the month, Leon Cruz completed the following transactions related to the business:

July 1. Leon transferred cash from a personal bank account to an account to be used for the business in exchange for capital stock, $18,000.
   5. Paid rent for period of July 5 to end of month, $1,500.
   10. Purchased a truck for $15,000, paying $5,000 cash and giving a note payable for the remainder.
   13. Purchased equipment on account, $4,500.
   14. Purchased supplies for cash, $975.
   Asset - Prepaid Insurance 15. Paid annual premiums on property and casualty insurance, $3,000.
   15. Received cash for job completed, $4,100.
   Accts Pay 21. Paid creditor a portion of the amount owed for equipment purchased on July 13, $2,400.
   Accts Rec 24. Recorded jobs completed on account and sent invoices to customers, $6,100.
   26. Received an invoice for truck expenses, to be paid in August, $580.
   27. Paid utilities expense, $950.
   27. Paid miscellaneous expenses, $315.
   ↓ Accts Rec 29. Received cash from customers on account, $3,420.
   30. Paid wages of employees, $2,500.
   31. Paid dividends, $2,000.

Instructions

1. Journalize each transaction in a two-column journal, referring to the following chart of accounts in selecting the accounts to be debited and credited. (Do not insert the account numbers in the journal at this time.) Journal entry explanations may be omitted.

11	Cash	31	Capital Stock
12	Accounts Receivable	33	Dividends
13	Supplies	41	Fees Earned
14	Prepaid Insurance	51	Wages Expense
16	Equipment	53	Rent Expense
18	Truck	54	Utilities Expense
21	Notes Payable	55	Truck Expense
22	Accounts Payable	59	Miscellaneous Expense

2. Post the journal to a ledger of four-column accounts, inserting appropriate posting references as each item is posted. Extend the balances to the appropriate balance columns after each transaction is posted.

3. Prepare a trial balance for Ingres Designs as of July 31, 2006.

PROBLEM 2-4A
Journal entries and trial balance

Objectives 2, 3, 4, 5

SPREADSHEET

P.A.S.S.

✓ 4. Total of Debit Column: $374,650

Fickle Realty acts as an agent in buying, selling, renting, and managing real estate. The account balances at the end of July 2006 are as follows:

11	Cash	31,200	
12	Accounts Receivable	45,750	
13	Prepaid Insurance	2,800	
14	Office Supplies	1,000	
16	Land	0	
21	Accounts Payable		5,200
22	Unearned Rent		0
23	Notes Payable		0
31	Capital Stock		8,000
32	Retained Earnings		31,700
33	Dividends	16,000	
41	Fees Earned		224,000
51	Salary and Commission Expense	133,000	
52	Rent Expense	17,500	
53	Advertising Expense	14,300	
54	Automobile Expense	6,400	
59	Miscellaneous Expense	950	
		268,900	268,900

The following business transactions were completed by Fickle Realty during August 2006:

Aug. 1. Purchased office supplies on account, $1,760.

2. Paid rent on office for month, $2,500.

3. Received cash from clients on account, $38,720.

5. Paid annual insurance premiums, $3,600.

9. Returned a portion of the office supplies purchased on August 1, receiving full credit for their cost, $240.

17. Paid advertising expense, $3,450.

23. Paid creditors on account, $2,670.

29. Paid miscellaneous expenses, $350.

30. Paid automobile expense (including rental charges for an automobile), $1,360.

31. Discovered an error in computing a commission; received cash from the salesperson for the overpayment, $800.

31. Paid salaries and commissions for the month, $17,400.

31. Recorded revenue earned and billed to clients during the month, $41,900.

31. Purchased land for a future building site for $75,000, paying $10,000 in cash and giving a note payable for the remainder.

31. Paid dividends, $2,500.

31. Rented land purchased on August 31 to local university for use as a parking lot during football season (September, October, and November), received advance payment of $1,500.

Instructions

1. Record the August 1 balance of each account in the appropriate balance column of a four-column account, write *Balance* in the item section, and place a check mark (✓) in the posting reference column. *(continued)*

2. Journalize the transactions for August in a two-column journal. Journal entry explanations may be omitted.
3. Post to the ledger, extending the account balance to the appropriate balance column after each posting.
4. Prepare a trial balance of the ledger as of August 31, 2006.

If the working papers correlating with this textbook are not used, omit Problem 2-5A.

PROBLEM 2-5A
Errors in trial balance
Objectives 5, 6

WHAT'S WRONG WITH THIS?

✓ *7. Total of Credit Column: $43,338.10*

The following records of Cypress TV Repair are presented in the working papers:

- Journal containing entries for the period July 1–31.
- Ledger to which the July entries have been posted.
- Preliminary trial balance as of July 31, which does not balance.

Locate the errors, supply the information requested, and prepare a corrected trial balance according to the following instructions. The balances recorded in the accounts as of July 1 and the entries in the journal are correctly stated. If it is necessary to correct any posted amounts in the ledger, a line should be drawn through the erroneous figure and the correct amount inserted above. Corrections or notations may be inserted on the preliminary trial balance in any manner desired. It is not necessary to complete all of the instructions if equal trial balance totals can be obtained earlier. However, the requirements of instructions (6) and (7) should be completed in any event.

Instructions
1. Verify the totals of the preliminary trial balance, inserting the correct amounts in the schedule provided in the working papers.
2. Compute the difference between the trial balance totals.
3. Compare the listings in the trial balance with the balances appearing in the ledger, and list the errors in the space provided in the working papers.
4. Verify the accuracy of the balance of each account in the ledger, and list the errors in the space provided in the working papers.
5. Trace the postings in the ledger back to the journal, using small check marks to identify items traced. Correct any amounts in the ledger that may be necessitated by errors in posting, and list the errors in the space provided in the working papers.
6. Journalize as of July 31 the payment of $210.00 for gas and electricity. The bill had been paid on July 31 but was inadvertently omitted from the journal. Post to the ledger. (Revise any amounts necessitated by posting this entry.)
7. Prepare a new trial balance.

PROBLEM 2-6A
Corrected trial balance
Objectives 5, 6

SPREADSHEET

✓ *1. Total of Debit Column: $156,000*

Onyx Videography has the following trial balance as of August 31, 2006:

Cash	4,700	
Accounts Receivable	8,450	
Supplies	1,464	
Prepaid Insurance	140	
Equipment	36,000	
Notes Payable		16,500
Accounts Payable		3,470
Capital Stock		1,000
Retained Earnings		18,800
Dividends	7,200	
Fees Earned		118,680
Wages Expense	68,000	
Rent Expense	13,900	
Advertising Expense	630	
Gas, Electricity, and Water Expense	3,780	
	144,264	158,450

The debit and credit totals are not equal as a result of the following errors:

a. The balance of cash was overstated by $3,500.

b. A cash receipt of $2,100 was posted as a credit to Cash of $1,200.

c. A debit of $1,750 to Accounts Receivable was not posted.

d. A return of $115 of defective supplies was erroneously posted as a $151 credit to Supplies.

e. An insurance policy acquired at a cost of $500 was posted as a credit to Prepaid Insurance.

f. The balance of Notes Payable was overstated by $4,500.

g. A credit of $250 in Accounts Payable was overlooked when the balance of the account was determined.

h. A debit of $1,800 for dividends was posted as a debit to Retained Earnings.

i. The balance of $6,300 in Advertising Expense was entered as $630 in the trial balance.

j. Miscellaneous Expense, with a balance of $1,680, was omitted from the trial balance.

Instructions

1. Prepare a corrected trial balance as of August 31 of the current year.

2. ▄▄▄▄▶ Does the fact that the trial balance in (1) is balanced mean that there are no errors in the accounts? Explain.

Problems Series B

PROBLEM 2-1B
Entries into T accounts and trial balance

Objectives 2, 3, 4, 5

 3. Total of Debit Column: $43,475

Christina Kiff opened an office on July 1, 2006. During the month, she completed the following transactions connected with her professional corporation, Christina Kiff, Architect, P.C.:

a. Transferred cash from a personal bank account to an account to be used for the business, in exchange for capital stock, $18,000.

b. Paid July rent for office and workroom, $1,500.

c. Purchased used automobile for $16,500, paying $1,500 cash and giving a note payable for the remainder.

d. Purchased office and computer equipment on account, $6,500.

e. Paid cash for supplies, $1,050.

f. Paid cash for annual insurance policies, $1,200.

g. Received cash from client for plans delivered, $2,750.

h. Paid cash for miscellaneous expenses, $140.

i. Paid cash to creditors on account, $3,000.

j. Paid installment due on note payable, $450.

k. Received invoice for blueprint service, due in August, $525.

l. Recorded fee earned on plans delivered, payment to be received in August, $4,150.

m. Paid salary of assistant, $1,000.

n. Paid gas, oil, and repairs on automobile for July, $130.

Instructions

1. Record the foregoing transactions directly in the following T accounts without journalizing: Cash; Accounts Receivable; Supplies; Prepaid Insurance; Automobiles; Equipment; Notes Payable; Accounts Payable; Capital Stock; Professional Fees; Rent Expense; Salary Expense; Automobile Expense; Blueprint Expense; Miscellaneous Expense. To the left of the amount entered in the accounts, place the appropriate letter to identify the transaction.

2. Determine the balances of the T accounts having two or more debits or credits. A memorandum balance should be inserted in accounts having both debits and credits in the manner illustrated in the chapter. For accounts with entries on one side only (such as Professional Fees), there is no need to insert the memorandum balance in the item column. For accounts containing only a single debit and

a single credit (such as Notes Payable), the memorandum balance should be inserted in the appropriate item column. Accounts containing a single entry only (such as Prepaid Insurance) do not need a memorandum balance.

3. Prepare a trial balance for Christina Kiff, Architect, P.C., as of July 31, 2006.

PROBLEM 2-2B
Journal entries and trial balance

Objectives 2, 3, 4, 5

SPREADSHEET
P.A.S.S.

✓ *4. c. $3,795*

On January 2, 2006, Lela Peterson established Acadia Realty, which completed the following transactions during the month:

a. Lela Peterson transferred cash from a personal bank account to an account to be used for the business in exchange for capital stock, $9,000.
b. Paid rent on office and equipment for the month, $2,000.
c. Purchased supplies on account, $700.
d. Paid creditor on account, $290.
e. Earned sales commissions, receiving cash, $10,750.
f. Paid automobile expenses (including rental charge) for month, $1,400, and miscellaneous expenses, $480.
g. Paid office salaries, $2,500.
h. Determined that the cost of supplies used was $575.
i. Paid dividends, $1,000.

Instructions

1. Journalize entries for transactions (a) through (i), using the following account titles: Cash; Supplies; Accounts Payable; Capital Stock; Dividends; Sales Commissions; Office Salaries Expense; Rent Expense; Automobile Expense; Supplies Expense; Miscellaneous Expense. Explanations may be omitted.
2. Prepare T accounts, using the account titles in (1). Post the journal entries to these accounts, placing the appropriate letter to the left of each amount to identify the transactions. Determine the account balances, after all posting is complete, for all accounts having two or more debits or credits. A memorandum balance should also be inserted in accounts having both debits and credits, in the manner illustrated in the chapter. For accounts with entries on one side only, there is no need to insert a memorandum balance in the item column. For accounts containing only a single debit and a single credit, the memorandum balance should be inserted in the appropriate item column.
3. Prepare a trial balance as of January 31, 2006.
4. Determine the following:
   a. Amount of total revenue recorded in the ledger.
   b. Amount of total expenses recorded in the ledger.
   c. Amount of net income for January.

PROBLEM 2-3B
Journal entries and trial balance

Objectives 2, 3, 4, 5

SPREADSHEET
P.A.S.S.

✓ *3. Total of Credit Column: $41,425*

On November 2, 2006, Nicole Oliver established an interior decorating business, Devon Designs. During the remainder of the month, Nicole completed the following transactions related to the business:

Nov. 2. Nicole transferred cash from a personal bank account to an account to be used for the business in exchange for capital stock, $15,000.
    5. Paid rent for period of November 5 to end of month, $1,750.
    6. Purchased office equipment on account, $8,500.
    8. Purchased a used truck for $18,000, paying $10,000 cash and giving a note payable for the remainder.
   10. Purchased supplies for cash, $1,115.
   12. Received cash for job completed, $7,500.
   15. Paid annual premiums on property and casualty insurance, $2,400.
   23. Recorded jobs completed on account and sent invoices to customers, $3,950.
   24. Received an invoice for truck expenses, to be paid in December, $600.
   29. Paid utilities expense, $750.
   29. Paid miscellaneous expenses, $310.
   30. Received cash from customers on account, $2,200.
   30. Paid wages of employees, $2,700.

Nov. 30. Paid creditor a portion of the amount owed for equipment purchased on November 6, $2,125.

30. Paid dividends, $1,400.

Instructions

1. Journalize each transaction in a two-column journal, referring to the following chart of accounts in selecting the accounts to be debited and credited. (Do not insert the account numbers in the journal at this time.) Explanations may be omitted.

11	Cash	31	Capital Stock
12	Accounts Receivable	33	Dividends
13	Supplies	41	Fees Earned
14	Prepaid Insurance	51	Wages Expense
16	Equipment	53	Rent Expense
18	Truck	54	Utilities Expense
21	Notes Payable	55	Truck Expense
22	Accounts Payable	59	Miscellaneous Expense

2. Post the journal to a ledger of four-column accounts, inserting appropriate posting references as each item is posted. Extend the balances to the appropriate balance columns after each transaction is posted.

3. Prepare a trial balance for Devon Designs as of November 30, 2006.

PROBLEM 2-4B
Journal entries and trial balance

Objectives 2, 3, 4, 5

SPREADSHEET

P.A.S.S.

✓ *4. Total of Debit Column:*
$465,275

Boomerang Realty acts as an agent in buying, selling, renting, and managing real estate. The account balances at the end of October 2006 are as follows:

11	Cash	36,300	
12	Accounts Receivable	97,500	
13	Prepaid Insurance	2,200	
14	Office Supplies	2,100	
16	Land	0	
21	Accounts Payable		23,020
22	Unearned Rent		0
23	Notes Payable		0
31	Capital Stock		20,000
32	Retained Earnings		48,680
33	Dividends	2,000	
41	Fees Earned		253,000
51	Salary and Commission Expense	148,200	
52	Rent Expense	30,000	
53	Advertising Expense	17,800	
54	Automobile Expense	5,500	
59	Miscellaneous Expense	3,100	
		344,700	344,700

The following business transactions were completed by Boomerang Realty during November 2006:

Nov. 1. Paid rent on office for month, $7,000.

2. Purchased office supplies on account, $1,675.

5. Paid annual insurance premiums, $4,800.

10. Received cash from clients on account, $52,000.

15. Purchased land for a future building site for $90,000, paying $10,000 in cash and giving a note payable for the remainder.

17. Paid creditors on account, $9,100.

20. Returned a portion of the office supplies purchased on November 2, receiving full credit for their cost, $400.

23. Paid advertising expense, $2,050.

27. Discovered an error in computing a commission; received cash from the salesperson for the overpayment, $700.

28. Paid automobile expense (including rental charges for an automobile), $1,100.

29. Paid miscellaneous expenses, $390.

30. Recorded revenue earned and billed to clients during the month, $48,400.

Nov. 30. Paid salaries and commissions for the month, $24,000.
  30. Paid dividends, $7,500.
  30. Rented land purchased on November 15 to local merchants association for use as a parking lot in December and January, during a street rebuilding program; received advance payment of $2,000.

Instructions

1. Record the November 1, 2006 balance of each account in the appropriate balance column of a four-column account, write *Balance* in the item section, and place a check mark (✔) in the posting reference column.
2. Journalize the transactions for November in a two-column journal. Journal entry explanations may be omitted.
3. Post to the ledger, extending the account balance to the appropriate balance column after each posting.
4. Prepare a trial balance of the ledger as of November 30, 2006.

If the working papers correlating with this textbook are not used, omit Problem 2-5B.

PROBLEM 2-5B
Errors in trial balance
Objectives 5, 6

WHAT'S WRONG WITH THIS?

✔ *7. Total of Debit Column: $43,338.10*

The following records of Cypress TV Repair are presented in the working papers:

* Journal containing entries for the period July 1–31.
* Ledger to which the July entries have been posted.
* Preliminary trial balance as of July 31, which does not balance.

Locate the errors, supply the information requested, and prepare a corrected trial balance according to the following instructions. The balances recorded in the accounts as of July 1 and the entries in the journal are correctly stated. If it is necessary to correct any posted amounts in the ledger, a line should be drawn through the erroneous figure and the correct amount inserted above. Corrections or notations may be inserted on the preliminary trial balance in any manner desired. It is not necessary to complete all of the instructions if equal trial balance totals can be obtained earlier. However, the requirements of instructions (6) and (7) should be completed in any event.

Instructions

1. Verify the totals of the preliminary trial balance, inserting the correct amounts in the schedule provided in the working papers.
2. Compute the difference between the trial balance totals.
3. Compare the listings in the trial balance with the balances appearing in the ledger, and list the errors in the space provided in the working papers.
4. Verify the accuracy of the balance of each account in the ledger, and list the errors in the space provided in the working papers.
5. Trace the postings in the ledger back to the journal, using small check marks to identify items traced. Correct any amounts in the ledger that may be necessitated by errors in posting, and list the errors in the space provided in the working papers.
6. Journalize as of July 31 the payment of $175 for advertising expense. The bill had been paid on July 31 but was inadvertently omitted from the journal. Post to the ledger. (Revise any amounts necessitated by posting this entry.)
7. Prepare a new trial balance.

PROBLEM 2-6B
Corrected trial balance
Objectives 5, 6

SPREADSHEET

✔ *1. Total of Debit Column: $125,000*

Montero Carpet's trial balance as of October 31, 2006, is shown at the top of the next page. The debit and credit totals are not equal as a result of the following errors:

a. The balance of cash was understated by $1,500.
b. A cash receipt of $2,500 was posted as a debit to Cash of $5,200.
c. A debit of $2,000 for a dividend was posted as a credit to Retained Earnings.
d. The balance of $4,480 in Advertising Expense was entered as $448 in the trial balance.
e. A debit of $750 to Accounts Receivable was not posted.
f. A return of $125 of defective supplies was erroneously posted as a $215 credit to Supplies.

Cash	5,200	
Accounts Receivable	7,825	
Supplies	1,450	
Prepaid Insurance	370	
Equipment	35,000	
Notes Payable		26,000
Accounts Payable		4,850
Capital Stock		6,000
Retained Earnings		17,825
Dividends	9,200	
Fees Earned		76,700
Wages Expense	43,540	
Rent Expense	10,400	
Advertising Expense	448	
Miscellaneous Expense	1,095	
	114,528	131,375

g. The balance of Notes Payable was overstated by $5,000.

h. An insurance policy acquired at a cost of $200 was posted as a credit to Prepaid Insurance.

i. Gas, Electricity, and Water Expense, with a balance of $4,400, was omitted from the trial balance.

j. A credit of $625 in Accounts Payable was overlooked when determining the balance of the account.

Instructions

1. Prepare a corrected trial balance as of October 31, 2006.
2. ▰▰▰▰➤ Does the fact that the trial balance in (1) is balanced mean that there are no errors in the accounts? Explain.

Continuing Problem

P.A.S.S.

✓ *4. Total of Debit Column: $31,760*

The transactions completed by Dancin Music during April 2006 were described at the end of Chapter 1. The following transactions were completed during May, the second month of the business's operations:

May 1. Shannon Burns made an additional investment in Dancin Music by depositing $3,000 in Dancin Music's checking account, receiving capital stock in exchange.

1. Instead of continuing to share office space with a local real estate agency, Shannon decided to rent office space near a local music store. Paid rent for May, $1,600.

1. Paid a premium of $3,360 for a comprehensive insurance policy covering liability, theft, and fire. The policy covers a two-year period.

2. Received $1,200 on account.

3. On behalf of Dancin Music, Shannon signed a contract with a local radio station, KPRG, to provide guest spots for the next three months. The contract requires Dancin Music to provide a guest disc jockey for 80 hours per month for a monthly fee of $2,400. Any additional hours beyond 80 will be billed to KPRG at $40 per hour. In accordance with the contract, Shannon received $4,800 from KPRG as an advance payment for the first two months.

3. Paid $250 on account.

4. Paid an attorney $150 for reviewing the May 3rd contract with KPRG. (Record as Miscellaneous Expense.)

5. Purchased office equipment on account from One-Stop Office Mart, $5,000.

8. Paid for a newspaper advertisement, $200.

May 11. Received $600 for serving as a disc jockey for a college fraternity party.
    13. Paid $500 to a local audio electronics store for rental of digital recording equipment.
    14. Paid wages of $1,200 to receptionist and part-time assistant.
    16. Received $1,100 for serving as a disc jockey for a wedding reception.
    18. Purchased supplies on account, $750.
    21. Paid $240 to Rocket Music for use of its current music demos in making various music sets.
    22. Paid $500 to a local radio station to advertise the services of Dancin Music twice daily for the remainder of May.
    23. Served as disc jockey for a party for $1,560. Received $400, with the remainder due June 4, 2006.
    27. Paid electric bill, $560.
    28. Paid wages of $1,200 to receptionist and part-time assistant.
    29. Paid miscellaneous expenses, $170.
    30. Served as a disc jockey for a charity ball for $1,200. Received $600, with the remainder due on June 9, 2006.
    31. Received $2,000 for serving as a disc jockey for a party.
    31. Paid $600 royalties (music expense) to Federated Clearing for use of various artists' music during May.
    31. Paid dividends, $2,000.

Dancin Music's chart of accounts and the balance of accounts as of May 1, 2006 (all normal balances), are as follows:

11	Cash	$6,160		41	Fees Earned	$4,750
12	Accounts Receivable	1,200		50	Wages Expense	400
14	Supplies	170		51	Office Rent Expense	1,000
15	Prepaid Insurance	—		52	Equipment Rent Expense	650
17	Office Equipment	—		53	Utilities Expense	300
21	Accounts Payable	250		54	Music Expense	940
23	Unearned Revenue	—		55	Advertising Expense	600
31	Capital Stock	7,000		56	Supplies Expense	180
33	Dividends	250		59	Miscellaneous Expense	150

Instructions

1. Enter the May 1, 2006 account balances in the appropriate balance column of a four-column account. Write *Balance* in the Item column, and place a check mark (✔) in the Posting Reference column. (*Hint:* Verify the equality of the debit and credit balances in the ledger before proceeding with the next instruction.)
2. Analyze and journalize each transaction in a two-column journal, omitting journal entry explanations.
3. Post the journal to the ledger, extending the account balance to the appropriate balance column after each posting.
4. Prepare a trial balance as of May 31, 2006.

Special Activities

ACTIVITY 2-1
Ethics and professional conduct in business

ETHICS

At the end of the current month, Ross Heimlich prepared a trial balance for Main Street Motor Co. The credit side of the trial balance exceeds the debit side by a significant amount. Ross has decided to add the difference to the balance of the miscellaneous expense account in order to complete the preparation of the current month's financial statements by a 5 o'clock deadline. Ross will look for the difference next week when he has more time.

→ Discuss whether Ross is behaving in a professional manner.

ACTIVITY 2-2
Account for revenue

WHAT DO YOU THINK?

Krypton College requires students to pay tuition each term before classes begin. Students who have not paid their tuition are not allowed to enroll or to attend classes.

What journal entry do you think Krypton College would use to record the receipt of the students' tuition payments? Describe the nature of each account in the entry.

ACTIVITY 2-3
Record transactions

The following discussion took place between Heather Sims, the office manager of Sedgemoor Data Company, and a new accountant, Ed Hahn.

Ed: I've been thinking about our method of recording entries. It seems that it's inefficient.

Heather: In what way?

Ed: Well—correct me if I'm wrong—it seems like we have unnecessary steps in the process. We could easily develop a trial balance by posting our transactions directly into the ledger and bypassing the journal altogether. In this way we could combine the recording and posting process into one step and save ourselves a lot of time. What do you think?

Heather: We need to have a talk.

What should Heather say to Ed?

ACTIVITY 2-4
Debits and credits

GROUP ACTIVITY

The following excerpt is from a conversation between Peter Kaiser, the president and chief operating officer of Sprocket Construction Co., and his neighbor, Doris Nesmith.

Doris: Peter, I'm taking a course in night school, "Intro to Accounting." I was wondering—could you answer a couple of questions for me?

Peter: Well, I will if I can.

Doris: Okay, our instructor says that it's critical we understand the basic concepts of accounting, or we'll never get beyond the first test. My problem is with those rules of debit and credit . . . you know, assets increase with debits, decrease with credits, etc.

Peter: Yes, pretty basic stuff. You just have to memorize the rules. It shouldn't be too difficult.

Doris: Sure, I can memorize the rules, but my problem is I want to be sure I understand the basic concepts behind the rules.

For example, why can't assets be increased with credits and decreased with debits like revenue? As long as everyone did it that way, why not? It would seem easier if we had the same rules for all increases and decreases in accounts.

Also, why is the left side of an account called the debit side? Why couldn't it be called something simple . . . like the "LE" for Left Entry? The right side could be called just "RE" for Right Entry.

Finally, why are there just two sides to an entry? Why can't there be three or four sides to an entry?

In a group of four or five, select one person to play the role of Peter and one person to play the role of Doris.

1. After listening to the conversation between Peter and Doris, help Peter answer Doris's questions.
2. What information (other than just debit and credit journal entries) could the accounting system gather that might be useful to Peter in managing Sprocket Construction Co.?

ACTIVITY 2-5
Transactions and income statement

Kercy Hepner is planning to manage and operate Eagle Caddy Service at Helena Golf and Country Club during June through August 2006. Kercy will rent a small maintenance building from the country club for $300 per month and will offer cad' services, including cart rentals, to golfers. Kercy has had no formal training in record keeping.

Kercy keeps notes of all receipts and expenses in a shoe box. An examination of Kercy's shoe box records for June revealed the following:

June 1. Withdrew $2,250 from personal bank account to be used to operate the caddy service.
   1. Paid rent to Helena Golf and Country Club, $300.
   2. Paid for golf supplies (practice balls, etc.), $225.
   3. Arranged for the rental of forty regular (pulling) golf carts and ten gasoline-driven carts for $1,500 per month. Paid $1,125 in advance, with the remaining $375 due June 20.
   7. Purchased supplies, including gasoline, for the golf carts on account, $270. Helena Golf and Country Club has agreed to allow Kercy to store the gasoline in one of its fuel tanks at no cost.
  15. Received cash for services from June 1–15, $1,680.
  17. Paid cash to creditors on account, $270.
  20. Paid remaining rental on golf carts, $375.
  22. Purchased supplies, including gasoline, on account, $255.
  25. Accepted IOUs from customers on account, $570.
  28. Paid miscellaneous expenses, $180.
  30. Received cash for services from June 16-30, $2,200.
  30. Paid telephone and electricity (utilities) expenses, $160.
  30. Paid wages of part-time employees, $390.
  30. Received cash in payment of IOUs on account, $270.
  30. Determined the amount of supplies on hand at the end of June, $140.

Kercy has asked you several questions concerning her financial affairs to date, and she has asked you to assist with her record keeping and reporting of financial data.

a. To assist Kercy with her record keeping, prepare a chart of accounts that would be appropriate for Eagle Caddy Service. *Note:* Small businesses such as Eagle Caddy Services are often organized as proprietorships. The accounting for proprietorships is similar to that for a corporation, except that the owner's equity accounts differ. Specifically, instead of the account for Capital Stock, a capital account entitled Kercy Hepner, Capital is used to record investments in the business. In addition, instead of a dividends account, withdrawals from the business are debited to Kercy Hepner, Drawing. A proprietorship has no retained earnings account.
b. Prepare an income statement for June in order to help Kercy assess the profitability of Eagle Caddy Service. For this purpose, the use of T accounts may be helpful in analyzing the effects of each June transaction.
c. Based on Kercy's records of receipts and payments, calculate the amount of cash on hand on June 30. For this purpose, a T account for cash may be useful.
d. ▬▬▶ A count of the cash on hand on June 30 totaled $3,180. Briefly discuss the possible causes of the difference between the amount of cash computed in (c) and the actual amount of cash on hand.

ACTIVITY 2-6
Business strategy

GROUP ACTIVITY

Assume that you are considering developing a nationwide chain of women's clothing stores. You have contacted a Houston-based firm that specializes in financing new business ventures and enterprises. Such firms, called venture capital firms, finance new businesses in exchange for a percentage of the ownership.

1. In groups of four or five, discuss the different business strategies that you might use in your venture.
2. For each strategy you listed in (1), provide an example of a real world business using the same strategy.
3. What percentage of the ownership would you be willing to give the venture capital firm in exchange for its financing?

ACTIVITY 2-7
Opportunities for accountants

INTERNET

The increasing complexity of the current business and regulatory environment has created an increased demand for accountants who can analyze business transactions and interpret their effects on the financial statements. In addition, a basic ability to analyze the effects of transactions is necessary to be successful in all fields of business as well as in other disciplines, such as law. To better understand the importance of accounting in today's environment, search the Internet or your local newspaper for job opportunities. One possible Internet site is **http://www.jobweb .com**. Then do one of the following:

1. Print a listing of at least two ads for accounting jobs. Alternatively, bring to class at least two newspaper ads for accounting jobs.
2. Print a listing of at least two ads for nonaccounting jobs for which some knowledge of accounting is preferred or necessary. Alternatively, bring to class at least two newspaper ads for such jobs.

Answers to Self-Examination Questions

1. **A** A debit may signify an increase in an asset account (answer A) or a decrease in a liability or capital stock account. A credit may signify a decrease in an asset account (answer B) or an increase in a liability or capital stock account (answers C and D).
2. **C** Liability, capital stock, retained earnings, and revenue (answer C) accounts have normal credit balances. Asset (answer A), dividends (answer B), and expense (answer D) accounts have normal debit balances.
3. **C** Accounts Receivable (answer A), Cash (answer B), and Miscellaneous Expense (answer D) would all normally have debit balances. Fees Earned should normally have a credit balance. Hence, a debit balance in Fees Earned (answer C) would indicate a likely error in the recording process.
4. **A** The receipt of cash from customers on account increases the asset Cash and decreases the asset

Accounts Receivable, as indicated by answer A. Answer B has the debit and credit reversed, and answers C and D involve transactions with creditors (accounts payable) and not customers (accounts receivable).
5. **D** The trial balance (answer D) is a listing of the balances and the titles of the accounts in the ledger on a given date, so that the equality of the debits and credits in the ledger can be verified. The income statement (answer A) is a summary of revenue and expenses for a period of time. The balance sheet (answer B) is a presentation of the assets, liabilities, and owners' equity on a given date. The retained earnings statement (answer C) is a summary of the changes in retained earnings for a period of time.

THE MATCHING CONCEPT AND THE ADJUSTING PROCESS

objectives

After studying this chapter, you should be able to:

1 Explain how the matching concept relates to the accrual basis of accounting.

2 Explain why adjustments are necessary and list the characteristics of adjusting entries.

3 Journalize entries for accounts requiring adjustment.

4 Summarize the adjustment process and prepare an adjusted trial balance.

5 Use vertical analysis to compare financial statement items with each other and with industry averages.

Assume that you rented an apartment last month and signed a nine-month lease. When you signed the lease agreement, you were required to pay the final month's rent of $500. This amount is not returnable to you.

You are now applying for a student loan at a local bank. The loan application requires a listing of all your assets. Should you list the $500 deposit as an asset?

The answer to this question is "yes." The deposit is an asset to you until you receive the use of the apartment in the ninth month.

A business faces similar accounting problems at the end of a period. A business must determine what assets, liabilities, and owners' equity should be reported on its balance sheet. It must also determine what revenues and expenses should be reported on its income statement.

As we illustrated in previous chapters, transactions are normally recorded as they take place. Periodically, financial statements are prepared, summarizing the effects of the transactions on the financial position and operations of the business.

At any one point in time, however, the accounting records may not reflect all transactions. For example, most businesses do not record the daily use of supplies. Likewise, revenue may have been earned from providing services to customers, yet the customers have not been billed by the time the accounting period ends. Thus, at the end of the period, the revenue and receivable accounts must be updated.

In this chapter, we describe and illustrate this updating process. We will focus on accounts that normally require updating and the journal entries that update them.

The Matching Concept

objective 1

Explain how the matching concept relates to the accrual basis of accounting.

REAL WORLD

American Airlines uses the accrual basis of accounting. Revenues are recognized when passengers take flights, not when the passenger makes the reservation or pays for the ticket.

When accountants prepare financial statements, they assume that the economic life of the business can be divided into time periods. Using this ***accounting period concept***, accountants must determine in which period the revenues and expenses of the business should be reported. To determine the appropriate period, accountants will use either (1) the cash basis of accounting or (2) the accrual basis of accounting.

REAL WORLD

A bank loan officer requires an individual, who normally keeps records on a cash basis, to list assets (automobiles, homes, investments, etc.) on an application for a loan or a line of credit. In addition, the application often asks for an estimate of the individual's liabilities, such as outstanding credit card amounts and automobile loan balances. In a sense, the loan application converts the individual's cash-basis accounting system to an estimated accrual basis. The loan officer uses this information to assess the individual's ability to repay the loan.

Under the ***cash basis***, revenues and expenses are reported in the income statement in the period in which cash is received or paid. For example, fees are recorded when cash is received from clients, and wages are recorded when cash is paid to employees. The net income (or net loss) is the difference between the cash receipts (revenues) and the cash payments (expenses).

Under the ***accrual basis***, revenues are reported in the income statement in the period in which they are earned. For example, revenue is reported when the services are provided to customers. Cash may or may not be received from customers during this period. The concept that supports this reporting of revenues is called the ***revenue recognition concept***.

Under the accrual basis, expenses are reported in the same period as the revenues to which they relate. For example, employee wages are reported as an expense in the period in which the employees provided services to customers, and not necessarily when the wages are paid.

The accounting concept that supports reporting revenues and related expenses in the same period is called the ***matching concept***, or **matching principle**. Under this concept, an income statement will report the resulting income or loss for the period.

Generally accepted accounting principles require the use of the accrual basis. However, small service businesses may use the cash basis because they have few receivables and payables. For example, attorneys, physicians, and real estate agents often use the cash basis. For them, the cash basis will yield financial statements similar to those prepared under the accrual basis.

For most large businesses, the cash basis will not provide accurate financial statements for user needs. For this reason, we will emphasize the accrual basis in this text. The accrual basis and its related matching concept require an analysis and updating of some accounts when financial statements are prepared. In the following paragraphs, we will describe and illustrate this process, called the ***adjusting process***.

> **The matching concept supports reporting revenues and related expenses in the same period.**

Nature of the Adjusting Process

> **objective 2**
>
> Explain why adjustments are necessary and list the characteristics of adjusting entries.

At the end of an accounting period, many of the balances of accounts in the ledger can be reported, without change, in the financial statements. For example, the balance of the cash account is normally the amount reported on the balance sheet.

Some accounts in the ledger, however, require updating. For example, the balances listed for prepaid expenses are normally overstated because the use of these assets is not recorded on a day-to-day basis. The balance of the supplies account usually represents the cost of supplies at the beginning of the period plus the cost of supplies acquired during the period. To record the daily use of supplies would require many entries with small amounts. In addition, the total amount of supplies is small relative to other assets, and managers usually do not require day-to-day information about supplies.

The journal entries that bring the accounts up to date at the end of the accounting period are called ***adjusting entries***. All adjusting entries affect at least one income statement account and one balance sheet account. Thus, an adjusting entry will *always* involve a revenue or an expense account *and* an asset or a liability account.

> **All adjusting entries affect at least one income statement account and one balance sheet account.**

Is there an easy way to know when an adjusting entry is needed? Yes, four basic items require adjusting entries. The first two items are ***deferrals***. Deferrals are created by recording a transaction in a way that *delays* or *defers* the recognition of an expense or a revenue, as described below.

- ***Deferred expenses***, or ***prepaid expenses***, are items that have been initially recorded as assets but are expected to become expenses over time or through the normal operations of the business. Supplies and prepaid insurance are two examples of prepaid expenses that may require adjustment at the end of an accounting period. Other examples include prepaid advertising and prepaid interest.
- ***Deferred revenues***, or ***unearned revenues***, are items that have been initially recorded as liabilities but are expected to become revenues over time or through the normal operations of the business. An example of deferred revenue is unearned rent. Other examples include tuition received in advance by a school, an annual retainer fee received by an attorney, premiums received in advance by an insurance company, and magazine subscriptions received in advance by a publisher.

The second two items that require adjusting entries are accruals. ***Accruals*** are created by an unrecorded expense that has been incurred or an unrecorded revenue that has been earned, as described below.

- ***Accrued expenses***, or ***accrued liabilities***, are expenses that have been incurred *but have not been recorded* in the accounts. An example of an accrued expense is accrued wages owed to employees at the end of a period. Other examples include accrued interest on notes payable and accrued taxes.

• *Accrued revenues*, or *accrued assets*, are revenues that have been earned *but have not been recorded* in the accounts. An example of an accrued revenue is fees for services that an attorney has provided but hasn't billed to the client at the end of the period. Other examples include unbilled commissions by a travel agent, accrued interest on notes receivable, and accrued rent on property rented to others.

How do you tell the difference between deferrals and accruals? Determine when cash is received or paid, as shown in Exhibit 1. If cash is received (for revenue) or paid (for expense) in the *current* period, but the revenue or expense relates to a future period, the revenue or expense is a deferred item. If cash will not be received or paid until a *future* period, but the revenue or expense relates to the current period, the revenue or expense is an accrued item.

•Exhibit 1   Deferrals and Accruals

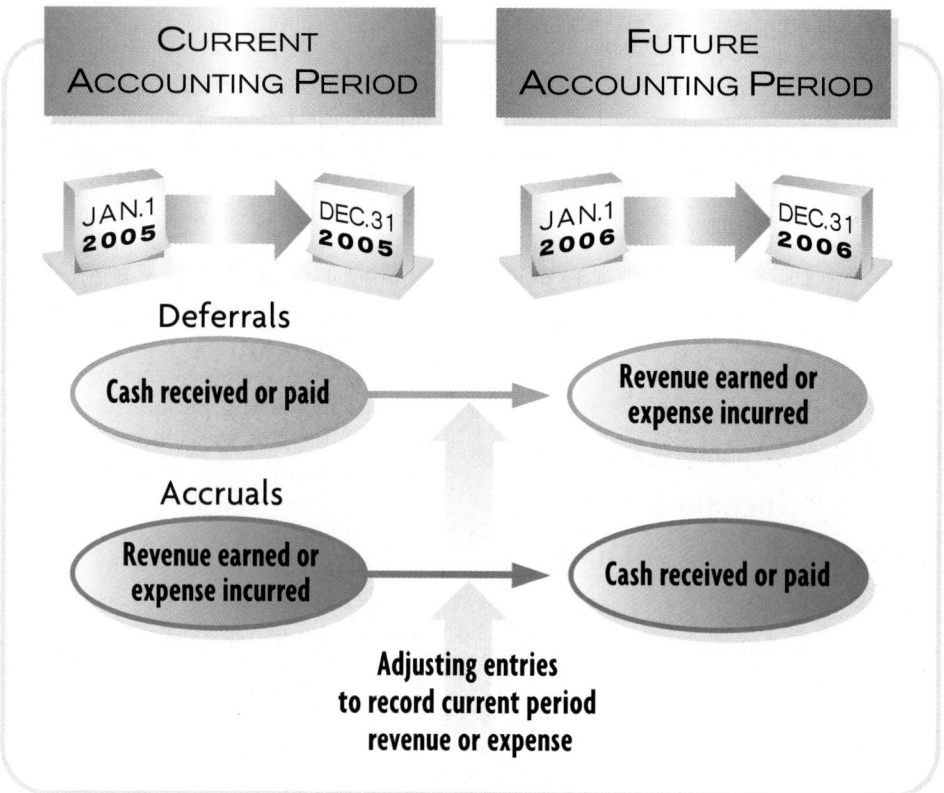

Recording Adjusting Entries

objective **3**

Journalize entries for accounts requiring adjustment.

The examples of adjusting entries in the following paragraphs are based on the ledger of NetSolutions as reported in the December 31, 2005 trial balance in Exhibit 2. The adjusting entries are shown in color in T accounts to separate them from other transactions. An expanded chart of accounts for NetSolutions is shown in Exhibit 3. The additional accounts that will be used in this chapter are shown in color.

•**Exhibit 2**   Unadjusted Trial Balance for NetSolutions

NetSolutions Trial Balance December 31, 2005		
Cash	2 0 6 5 00	
Accounts Receivable	2 2 2 0 00	
Supplies	2 0 0 0 00	
Prepaid Insurance	2 4 0 0 00	
Land	20 0 0 0 00	
Office Equipment	1 8 0 0 00	
Accounts Payable		9 0 0 00
Unearned Rent		3 6 0 00
Capital Stock		25 0 0 0 00
Dividends	4 0 0 0 00	
Fees Earned		16 3 4 0 00
Wages Expense	4 2 7 5 00	
Rent Expense	1 6 0 0 00	
Utilities Expense	9 8 5 00	
Supplies Expense	8 0 0 00	
Miscelleous Expense	4 5 5 00	
	42 6 0 0 00	42 6 0 0 00

•**Exhibit 3**   Expanded Chart of Accounts for NetSolutions

1. Assets		4. Revenue	
11	Cash	41	Fees Earned
12	Accounts Receivable	42	Rent Revenue
14	Supplies		5. Expenses
15	Prepaid Insurance	51	Wages Expense
17	Land	52	Rent Expense
18	Office Equipment	53	Depreciation Expense
19	Accumulated Depreciation	54	Utilities Expense
	2. Liabilities	55	Supplies Expense
21	Accounts Payable	56	Insurance Expense
22	Wages Payable	59	Miscellaneous Expense
23	Unearned Rent		
	3. Owners' (Stockholders') Equity		
31	Capital Stock		
32	Retained Earnings		
33	Dividends		

Deferred Expenses (Prepaid Expenses)

The concept of adjusting the accounting records was introduced in Chapters 1 and 2 in the illustration for NetSolutions. In that illustration, supplies were purchased on November 10 (transaction c). The supplies used during November were recorded on November 30 (transaction g).

The balance in NetSolutions' **supplies** account on December 31 is $2,000. Some of these supplies (computer diskettes, paper, envelopes, etc.) were used during December, and some are still on hand (not used). If either amount is known, the other can be determined. It is normally easier to determine the cost of the supplies on hand at the end of the month than it is to keep a daily record of those used. Assuming that on December 31 the amount of supplies on hand is $760, the amount to be transferred from the asset account to the expense account is $1,240, computed as follows:

Supplies available during December (balance of account)	$2,000
Supplies on hand, December 31	760
Supplies used (amount of adjustment)	$1,240

As we discussed in Chapter 2, increases in expense accounts are recorded as debits and decreases in asset accounts are recorded as credits. Hence, at the end of December, the supplies expense account should be debited for $1,240, and the supplies account should be credited for $1,240 to record the supplies used during December. The adjusting journal entry and T accounts for Supplies and Supplies Expense are as follows:

2	2005 Dec.	31	Supplies Expense	55	1 2 4 0 00	2
3			Supplies	14		1 2 4 0 00 3

Supplies				Supplies Expense		
Bal.	2,000	Dec. 31	1,240	Bal.	800	
760				Dec. 31	1,240	
					2,040	

After the adjustment has been recorded and posted, the supplies account has a debit balance of $760. This balance represents an asset that will become an expense in a future period.

The debit balance of $2,400 in NetSolutions' **prepaid insurance** account represents a December 1 prepayment of insurance for 24 months. At the end of December, the insurance expense account should be increased (debited), and the prepaid insurance account should be decreased (credited) by $100, the insurance for one month. The adjusting journal entry and T accounts for Prepaid Insurance and Insurance Expense are as follows:

> **The balance of a prepaid (deferred) expense is an asset that will become an expense in a future period.**

5		31	Insurance Expense	56	1 0 0 00	5
6			Prepaid Insurance	15		1 0 0 00 6

Prepaid Insurance				Insurance Expense		
Bal.	2,400	Dec. 31	100	Dec. 31	100	
2,300						

POINT OF INTEREST

The tuition you pay at the beginning of each term is an example of a deferred expense to you, as a student.

After the adjustment has been recorded and posted, the prepaid insurance account has a debit balance of $2,300. This balance represents an asset that will become an expense in future periods. The insurance expense account has a debit balance of $100, which is an expense of the current period.

What is the effect of omitting adjusting entries? If the preceding adjustments for supplies ($1,240) and insurance ($100) are not recorded, the financial statements prepared as of December 31 will be misstated. On the income statement, Supplies Expense and Insurance Expense will be understated by a total of $1,340, and net income will be overstated by $1,340. On the balance sheet, Supplies and Prepaid Insurance will be overstated by a total of $1,340. Since net income increases stockholders' equity (retained earnings), stockholders' equity will also be overstated by $1,340 on the balance sheet. The effects of omitting these adjusting entries on the income statement and balance sheet are shown below.

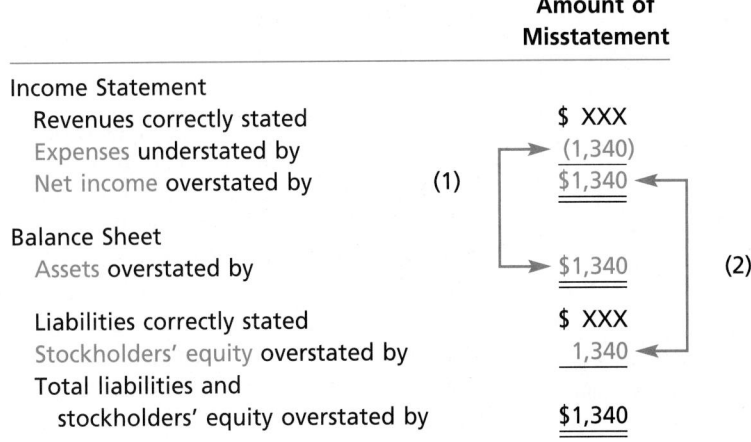

		Amount of Misstatement
Income Statement		
Revenues correctly stated		$ XXX
Expenses understated by		(1,340)
Net income overstated by	(1)	$1,340
Balance Sheet		
Assets overstated by		$1,340 (2)
Liabilities correctly stated		$ XXX
Stockholders' equity overstated by		1,340
Total liabilities and stockholders' equity overstated by		$1,340

Arrow (1) indicates the effect of the understated expenses on assets. Arrow (2) indicates the effect of the overstated net income on stockholders' equity.

Prepayments of expenses are sometimes made at the beginning of the period in which they will be *entirely consumed*. On December 1, for example, NetSolutions paid rent of $800 for the month. On December 1, the rent payment represents the asset prepaid rent. The prepaid rent expires daily, and at the end of December, the entire amount has become an expense (rent expense). In cases such as this, the initial payment is recorded as an expense rather than as an asset. Thus, if the payment is recorded as a debit to Rent Expense, no adjusting entry is needed at the end of the period.[1]

Supplies of $1,250 were on hand at the beginning of the period, supplies of $3,800 were purchased during the period, and supplies of $1,000 were on hand at the end of the period. What is the supplies expense for the period?

$4,050 ($1,250 + $3,800 − $1,000)

INTEGRITY IN BUSINESS

FREE ISSUE

Office supplies are often available to employees on a "free issue" basis. This means employees do not have to "sign" for the release of office supplies but merely obtain the necessary supplies from a local storage area as needed.

Just because supplies are easily available, however, doesn't mean they can be taken for personal use. There are many instances when employees have been terminated for taking supplies home for personal use.

Deferred Revenue (Unearned Revenue)

According to NetSolutions' trial balance on December 31, the balance in the **unearned rent** account is $360. This balance represents the receipt of three months' rent on December 1 for December, January, and February. At the end of December, the unearned rent account should be decreased (debited) by $120, and the rent

---

[1]This alternative treatment of recording the cost of supplies, rent, and other prepayments of expenses is discussed in Appendix B.

revenue account should be increased (credited) by $120. The $120 represents the rental revenue for one month ($360/3). The adjusting journal entry and T accounts are shown below.

| 8 | 31 | Unearned Rent | 23 | 1 2 0 00 | | 8 |
| 9 | | Rent Revenue | 42 | | 1 2 0 00 | 9 |

Unearned Rent					Rent Revenue	
Dec. 31	120	Bal.	360		Dec. 31	120
		240				

After the adjustment has been recorded and posted, the unearned rent account, which is a liability, has a credit balance of $240. This amount represents a deferral that will become revenue in a future period. The rent revenue account has a balance of $120, which is revenue of the current period.[2]

If the preceding adjustment of unearned rent and rent revenue is not recorded, the financial statements prepared on December 31 will be misstated. On the income statement, Rent Revenue and the net income will be understated by $120. On the balance sheet, Unearned Rent will be overstated by $120, and stockholders' equity (retained earnings) will be understated by $120. The effects of omitting this adjusting entry are shown below.

If NetSolutions' adjustment for unearned rent had incorrectly been made for $180 instead of $120, what would have been the effect on the financial statements?

Revenues would have been overstated by $60; net income would have been overstated by $60; liabilities would have been understated by $60; and stockholders' equity would have been overstated by $60.

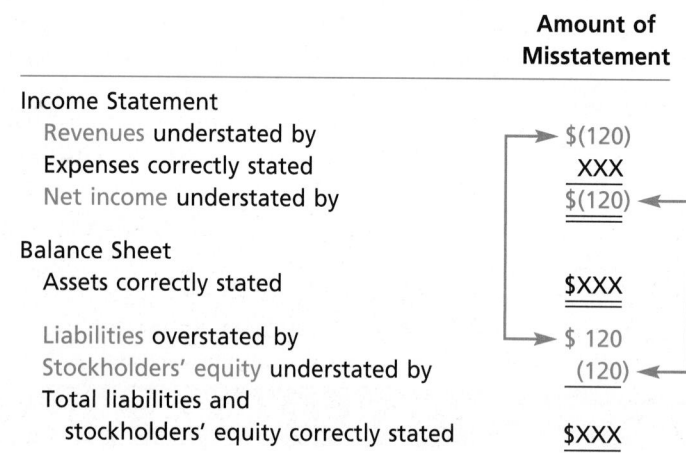

	Amount of Misstatement
Income Statement	
Revenues understated by	$(120)
Expenses correctly stated	XXX
Net income understated by	$(120)
Balance Sheet	
Assets correctly stated	$XXX
Liabilities overstated by	$ 120
Stockholders' equity understated by	(120)
Total liabilities and	
stockholders' equity correctly stated	$XXX

Accrued Expenses (Accrued Liabilities)

Some types of services, such as insurance, are normally paid for *before* they are used. These prepayments are deferrals. Other types of services are paid for *after* the service has been performed. For example, wages expense accumulates or *accrues* hour by hour and day by day, but payment may be made only weekly, biweekly, or monthly. The amount of such an accrued but unpaid item at the end of the accounting period is both an expense and a liability. In the case of wages expense, if the last day of a pay period is not the last day of the accounting period, the accrued wages expense and the related liability must be recorded in the accounts by an adjusting entry. This adjusting entry is necessary so that expenses are properly matched to the period in which they were incurred.

At the end of December, accrued wages for NetSolutions were $250. This amount is an additional expense of December and is debited to the **wages expense** account. It is also a liability as of December 31 and is credited to Wages Payable. The adjusting journal entry and T accounts are as follows.

---

[2] An alternative treatment of recording revenues received in advance of their being earned is discussed in Appendix B.

	31	Wages Expense	51	2 5 0 00		
		Wages Payable	22		2 5 0 00	

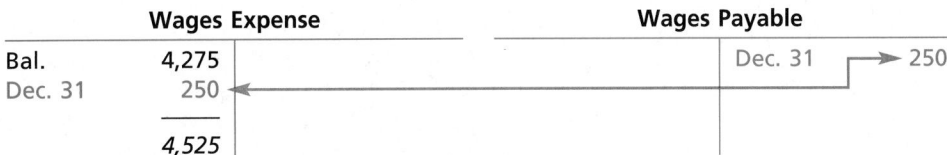

	Wages Expense				Wages Payable	
Bal.	4,275				Dec. 31	250
Dec. 31	250					
	4,525					

FINANCIAL REPORTING AND DISCLOSURE

UNEARNED REVENUE

Microsoft Corporation develops, manufactures, licenses, and supports a wide range of computer software products, including Windows XP®, Windows NT®, Word®, Excel®, and the Xbox®. When Microsoft sells its products, it incurs an obligation to support its software with technical support and periodic updates. As a result, not all the revenue from selling software is earned on the date of sale. Instead, some of the revenue is unearned. That is, the portion of revenue related to support services, such as updates and technical support, is earned only as time passes and the support services are provided to customers. Thus, it is necessary to make an adjusting entry each year to transfer unearned revenue to revenue.

The excerpts below from Microsoft's 2002 financial statements describe its accounting for unearned revenue. Microsoft further indicated that, of the $7,743 million of unearned revenue at June 30, 2002, it expected to recognize $5,917 million during the next year and $1,826 million in future years.

UNEARNED REVENUE

. . . Revenue attributable [to] technical support and Internet browser technologies . . . is recognized ratably . . . over the product's life cycle. The percentage of revenue recognized ratably . . . ranges from approximately 20% to 25% for Windows XP Home, approximately 10% to 15% for Windows XP Professional, and approximately 10% to 15% for desktop applications . . . Product life cycles are currently estimated at three years for Windows operating systems and 18 months for desktop applications. The unearned revenue as of June 30, 2002, was as follows:

	In Millions	
June 30	**2001**	**2002**
Unearned revenue	$5,614	$7,743

Unearned revenue by product was as follows:

	In Millions	
June 30	**2001**	**2002**
Desktop applications	$2,189	$3,489
Desktop platforms	2,586	3,198
Enterprise software and services	391	791
Desktop and enterprise software and services	5,166	7,478
Consumer software, services, and devices, and other	448	265
Unearned revenue	$5,614	$7,743

I'm 165 years old and came to life as a small family-run soap and candle company in Cincinnati. My celestial logo dates back to the 1850s. I recorded $1 million in annual sales in 1859 and take in around $40 billion annually now. I sell more than 250 items in 130 nations to more than five billion consumers. My Cheer-y and Joyous customers shout Olay! They've a Zest for my Bounty, which Cascades over their Head and Shoulders and Pampers them. It's no Secret that they Sure have a Gleam in their eyes and a Bounce in their step, Always. Who am I? (Go to page 123 for answer.)

After the adjustment has been recorded and posted, the debit balance of the wages expense account is $4,525, which is the wages expense for the two months, November and December. The credit balance of $250 in Wages Payable is the amount of the liability for wages owed as of December 31.

The accrual of the wages expense for NetSolutions is summarized in Exhibit 4. Note that NetSolutions paid wages of $950 on December 13 and $1,200 on December 27. These payments covered the biweekly pay periods that ended on those days. The wages of $250 incurred for Monday and Tuesday, December 30 and 31, are accrued at December 31. The wages paid on January 10 totaled $1,275, which included the $250 accrued wages of December 31.

•Exhibit 4   Accrued Wages

1. Wages are paid on the second and fourth Fridays for the two-week periods ending on those Fridays. The payments were $950 on December 13 and $1,200 on December 27.

2. The wages accrued for Monday and Tuesday, December 30 and 31, are $250.

3. Wages paid on Friday, January 10, total $1,275.

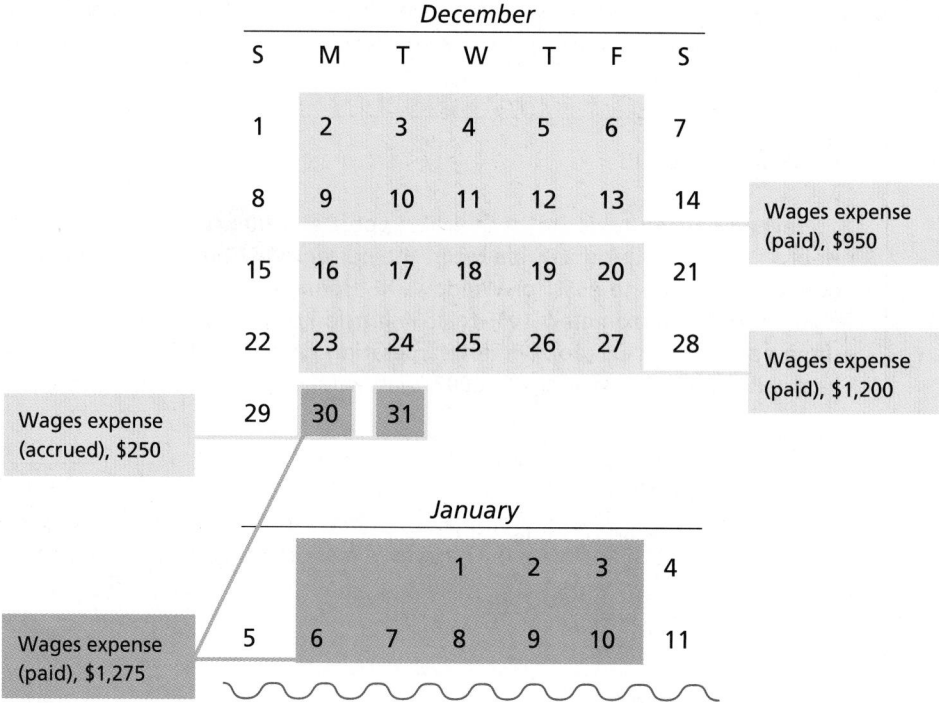

What would be the effect on the financial statements if the adjustment for wages ($250) is not recorded? On the income statement, Wages Expense will be understated by $250, and the net income will be overstated by $250. On the balance sheet, Wages Payable will be understated by $250, and stockholders' equity (retained earnings) will be overstated by $250. The effects of omitting this adjusting entry are shown as follows.

Assume that weekly wages of $1,500 are paid on Fridays. If wages are incurred evenly throughout the week, what is the accrued wages payable if the accounting period ends on a Tuesday?

$600 ($1,500/5 × 2 days)

REAL WORLD

Radio Shack Corporation is engaged in consumer electronics retailing. Radio Shack accrues revenue (accrued receivables) for finance charges, late charges, and returned check fees related to its credit operations.

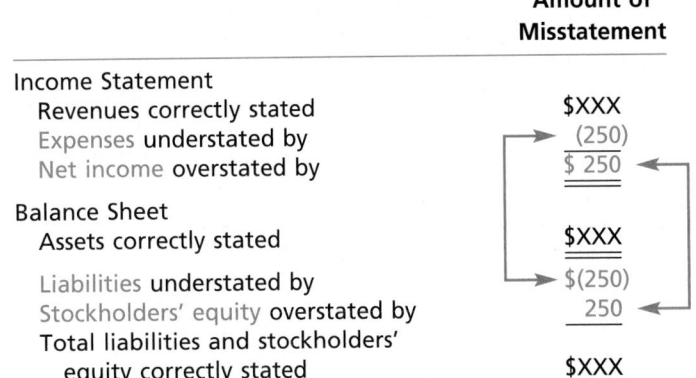

	Amount of Misstatement
Income Statement	
Revenues correctly stated	$XXX
Expenses understated by	(250)
Net income overstated by	$ 250
Balance Sheet	
Assets correctly stated	$XXX
Liabilities understated by	$(250)
Stockholders' equity overstated by	250
Total liabilities and stockholders' equity correctly stated	$XXX

Accrued Revenues (Accrued Assets)

During an accounting period, some revenues are recorded only when cash is received. Thus, at the end of an accounting period, there may be items of revenue that have been earned *but have not been recorded*. In such cases, the amount of the revenue should be recorded by debiting an asset account and crediting a revenue account.

To illustrate, assume that NetSolutions signed an agreement with Dankner Co. on December 15. The agreement provides that NetSolutions will be on call to answer computer questions and render assistance to Dankner Co.'s employees. The services provided will be billed to Dankner Co. on the fifteenth of each month at a rate of $20 per hour. As of December 31, NetSolutions had provided 25 hours of assistance to Dankner Co. Although the revenue of $500 (25 hours × $20) will be billed and collected in January, NetSolutions earned the revenue in December. The adjusting journal entry and T accounts to record the claim against the customer (an account receivable) and the **fees earned** in December are shown below.

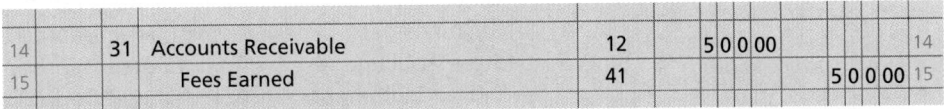

| 14 | 31 | Accounts Receivable | 12 | 5 0 0 00 | | 14 |
| 15 | | Fees Earned | 41 | | 5 0 0 00 | 15 |

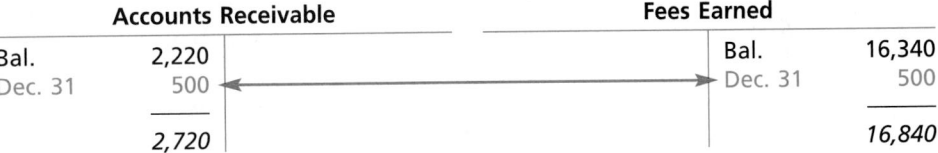

Accounts Receivable			Fees Earned	
Bal.	2,220		Bal.	16,340
Dec. 31	500		Dec. 31	500
	2,720			16,840

If the adjustment for the accrued asset ($500) is not recorded, Fees Earned and the net income will be understated by $500 on the income statement. On the balance sheet, Accounts Receivable and stockholders' equity (retained earnings) will be understated by $500. The effects of omitting this adjusting entry are shown below.

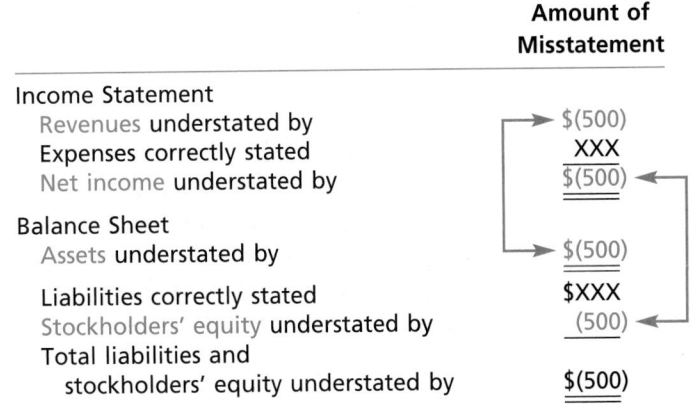

	Amount of Misstatement
Income Statement	
Revenues understated by	$(500)
Expenses correctly stated	XXX
Net income understated by	$(500)
Balance Sheet	
Assets understated by	$(500)
Liabilities correctly stated	$XXX
Stockholders' equity understated by	(500)
Total liabilities and stockholders' equity understated by	$(500)

Fixed Assets

Physical resources that are owned and used by a business and are permanent or have a long life are called *fixed assets*, or **plant assets**. In a sense, fixed assets are a type of long-term deferred expense. However, because of their nature and long life, they are discussed separately from other deferred expenses, such as supplies and prepaid insurance.

NetSolutions' fixed assets include office equipment that is used much like supplies are used to generate revenue. Unlike supplies, however, there is no visible reduction in the quantity of the equipment. Instead, as time passes, the equipment loses its ability to provide useful services. This decrease in usefulness is called *depreciation*.

All fixed assets, except land, lose their usefulness. Decreases in the usefulness of assets that are used in generating revenue are recorded as expenses. However, such decreases for fixed assets are difficult to measure. For this reason, a portion of the cost of a fixed asset is recorded as an expense each year of its useful life. This periodic expense is called *depreciation expense*. Methods of computing depreciation expense are discussed and illustrated in a later chapter.

The adjusting entry to record depreciation is similar to the adjusting entry for supplies used. The account debited is a depreciation expense account. However, the asset account Office Equipment is not credited because both the original cost of a fixed asset and the amount of depreciation recorded since its purchase are normally reported on the balance sheet. The account credited is an *accumulated depreciation* account. Accumulated depreciation accounts are called *contra accounts*, or **contra asset accounts** because they are deducted from the related asset accounts on the balance sheet.

Normal titles for fixed asset accounts and their related contra asset accounts are as follows:

Fixed Asset	Contra Asset
Land	None—Land is not depreciated.
Buildings	Accumulated Depreciation—Buildings
Store Equipment	Accumulated Depreciation—Store Equipment
Office Equipment	Accumulated Depreciation—Office Equipment

The adjusting entry to record depreciation for December for NetSolutions is illustrated in the following journal entry and T accounts. The estimated amount of depreciation for the month is assumed to be $50.

17	31	Depreciation Expense	53	50 00	17
18		Accumulated Depreciation—			18
19		Office Equipment	19	50 00	19

	Office Equipment		Accumulated Depreciation
Bal.	1,800		Dec. 31 50

Depreciation Expense
Dec. 31 50

The $50 increase in the accumulated depreciation account is subtracted from the $1,800 cost recorded in the related fixed asset account. The difference between the two balances is the $1,750 cost that has not yet been depreciated. This amount ($1,750) is called the *book value of the asset* (or **net book value**), which may be presented on the balance sheet in the following manner:

Office equipment	$1,800	
Less accumulated depreciation	50	$1,750

If equipment cost $5,000 and the related accumulated depreciation is $3,000, what is the book value?

$2,000 ($5,000 − $3,000)

You should note that the market value of a fixed asset usually differs from its book value. This is because depreciation is an *allocation* method, not a *valuation* method. That is, depreciation allocates the cost of a fixed asset to expense over its estimated life. Depreciation does not attempt to measure changes in market values, which may vary significantly from year to year.

If the previous adjustment for depreciation ($50) is not recorded, Depreciation Expense on the income statement will be understated by $50, and the net income will be overstated by $50. On the balance sheet, the book value of Office Equipment and stockholders' equity (retained earnings) will be overstated by $50. The effects of omitting the adjustment for depreciation are shown below.

	Amount of Misstatement
Income Statement	
Revenues correctly stated	$XX
Expenses understated by	(50)
Net income overstated by	$ 50
Balance Sheet	
Assets overstated by	$ 50
Liabilities correctly stated	$XX
Stockholders' equity overstated by	50
Total liabilities and stockholders' equity overstated by	$ 50

Summary of Adjustment Process

objective **4**

Summarize the adjustment process and prepare an adjusted trial balance.

We have described and illustrated the basic types of adjusting entries in the preceding section. A summary of these basic adjustments, including the type of adjustment, the adjusting entry, and the effect of omitting an adjustment on the financial statements, is shown in Exhibit 5.

The adjusting entries for NetSolutions that we illustrated in this chapter are shown in Exhibit 6. The adjusting entries are dated as of the last day of the period. However, because some time may be needed for collecting the adjustment information, the entries are usually recorded at a later date. Each entry may be supported by an explanation, but a caption above the first adjusting entry is acceptable.

Which of the accounts—Fees Earned, Miscellaneous Expense, Cash, Wages Expense, Supplies, Accounts Receivable, Dividends, Equipment, Accumulated Depreciation—would normally require an adjusting entry?

Fees Earned; Wages Expense; Supplies; Accounts Receivable; Accumulated Depreciation.

These adjusting entries have been posted to the ledger for Net-Solutions, and are shown in color in Exhibit 7 on pages 115–116. You should note that in the posting process the Post. Ref. column of the journal indicates the account number to which the entry was posted. The corresponding Post. Ref. column of the account indicates the journal page from which the entry was posted.

One way for an accountant to check whether all adjustments have been made is to compare the current period's adjustments with those of the prior period.

POINT OF INTEREST

After all the adjusting entries have been posted, another trial balance, called the **adjusted trial balance**, is prepared. The purpose of the adjusted trial balance is to verify the equality of the total debit balances and total credit balances before we prepare the financial statements. If the adjusted trial balance does not balance, an error has occurred. However, as we discussed in Chapter 2, errors may have occurred even though the adjusted trial balance totals agree. For example, the adjusted trial balance totals would agree if an adjusting entry has been omitted.

•Exhibit 5 Summary of Basic Adjustments

Type of Adjustment	Adjusting Entry	Effect of Omitting Adjusting Entry on the Balance Sheet and Income Statement
Deferred expense	Dr. Expense Cr. Asset	Expenses Understated and Net Income Overstated Assets Overstated and Stockholders' Equity Overstated
Deferred revenue	Dr. Liability Cr. Revenue	Liabilities Overstated and Stockholders' Equity Understated Revenues Understated and Net Income Understated
Accrued expense	Dr. Expense Cr. Liability	Expenses Understated and Net Income Overstated Liabilities Understated and Stockholders' Equity Overstated
Accrued revenue	Dr. Asset Cr. Revenue	Assets Understated and Stockholders' Equity Understated Revenues Understated and Net Income Understated
Fixed assets	Dr. Expense Cr. Contra Asset	Expenses Understated and Net Income Overstated Assets Overstated and Stockholders' Equity Overstated

•Exhibit 6 Adjusting Entries—NetSolutions

		JOURNAL				Page 5
	Date	Description	Post. Ref.	Debit	Credit	
1		Adjusting Entries				1
2	2005 Dec. 31	Supplies Expense	55	1 2 4 0 00		2
3		Supplies	14		1 2 4 0 00	3
4						4
5	31	Insurance Expense	56	1 0 0 00		5
6		Prepaid Insurance	15		1 0 0 00	6
7						7
8	31	Unearned Rent	23	1 2 0 00		8
9		Rent Revenue	42		1 2 0 00	9
10						10
11	31	Wages Expense	51	2 5 0 00		11
12		Wages Payable	22		2 5 0 00	12
13						13
14	31	Accounts Receivable	12	5 0 0 00		14
15		Fees Earned	41		5 0 0 00	15
16						16
17	31	Depreciation Expense	53	5 0 00		17
18		Accumulated Depreciation—				18
19		Office Equipment	19		5 0 00	19

•Exhibit 7 Ledger with Adjusting Entries—NetSolutions

ACCOUNT Cash — ACCOUNT NO. 11

Date	Item	Post. Ref.	Debit	Credit	Balance Debit	Balance Credit
2005 Nov. 1		1	25,000		25,000	
5		1		20,000	5,000	
18		1	7,500		12,500	
30		1		3,650	8,850	
30		1		950	7,900	
30		2		2,000	5,900	
Dec. 1		2		2,400	3,500	
1		2		800	2,700	
1		2	360		3,060	
6		2		180	2,880	
11		2		400	2,480	
13		3		950	1,530	
16		3	3,100		4,630	
20		3		900	3,730	
21		3	650		4,380	
23		3		1,450	2,930	
27		3		1,200	1,730	
31		3		310	1,420	
31		4		225	1,195	
31		4	2,870		4,065	
31		4		2,000	2,065	

ACCOUNT Accounts Receivable — ACCOUNT NO. 12

Date	Item	Post. Ref.	Debit	Credit	Balance Debit	Balance Credit
2005 Dec. 16		3	1,750		1,750	
21		3		650	1,100	
31		4	1,120		2,220	
31	Adjusting	5	500		2,720	

ACCOUNT Supplies — ACCOUNT NO. 14

Date	Item	Post. Ref.	Debit	Credit	Balance Debit	Balance Credit
2005 Nov. 10		1	1,350		1,350	
30		1		800	550	
Dec. 23		3	1,450		2,000	
31	Adjusting	5		1,240	760	

ACCOUNT Prepaid Insurance — ACCOUNT NO. 15

Date	Item	Post. Ref.	Debit	Credit	Balance Debit	Balance Credit
2005 Dec. 1		2	2,400		2,400	
31	Adjusting	5		100	2,300	

ACCOUNT Land — ACCOUNT NO. 17

Date	Item	Post. Ref.	Debit	Credit	Balance Debit	Balance Credit
2005 Nov. 5		1	20,000		20,000	

ACCOUNT Office Equipment — ACCOUNT NO. 18

Date	Item	Post. Ref.	Debit	Credit	Balance Debit	Balance Credit
2005 Dec. 4		2	1,800		1,800	

ACCOUNT Accumulated Depreciation — ACCOUNT NO. 19

Date	Item	Post. Ref.	Debit	Credit	Balance Debit	Balance Credit
2005 Dec. 31	Adjusting	5		50		50

ACCOUNT Accounts Payable — ACCOUNT NO. 21

Date	Item	Post. Ref.	Debit	Credit	Balance Debit	Balance Credit
2005 Nov. 10		1		1,350		1,350
30		1	950			400
Dec. 4		2		1,800		2,200
11		2	400			1,800
20		3	900			900

ACCOUNT Wages Payable — ACCOUNT NO. 22

Date	Item	Post. Ref.	Debit	Credit	Balance Debit	Balance Credit
2005 Dec. 31	Adjusting	5		250		250

ACCOUNT Unearned Rent — ACCOUNT NO. 23

Date	Item	Post. Ref.	Debit	Credit	Balance Debit	Balance Credit
2005 Dec. 1		2		360		360
31	Adjusting	5	120			240

ACCOUNT Capital Stock — ACCOUNT NO. 31

Date	Item	Post. Ref.	Debit	Credit	Balance Debit	Balance Credit
2005 Nov. 1		1		25,000		25,000

ACCOUNT Dividends — ACCOUNT NO. 33

Date	Item	Post. Ref.	Debit	Credit	Balance Debit	Balance Credit
2005 Nov. 30		2	2,000		2,000	
Dec. 31		4	2,000		4,000	

•**Exhibit 7** (concluded)

ACCOUNT *Fees Earned*   **ACCOUNT NO. 41**

Date	Item	Post. Ref.	Debit	Credit	Balance Debit	Balance Credit
2005 Nov. 18		1		7,500		7,500
Dec. 16		3		3,100		10,600
16		3		1,750		12,350
31		4		2,870		15,220
31		4		1,120		16,340
31	Adjusting	5		500		16,840

ACCOUNT *Rent Revenue*   **ACCOUNT NO. 42**

Date	Item	Post. Ref.	Debit	Credit	Balance Debit	Balance Credit
2005 Dec. 31	Adjusting	5		120		120

ACCOUNT *Wages Expense*   **ACCOUNT NO. 51**

Date	Item	Post. Ref.	Debit	Credit	Balance Debit	Balance Credit
2005 Nov. 30		1	2,125		2,125	
Dec. 13		3	950		3,075	
27		3	1,200		4,275	
31	Adjusting	5	250		4,525	

ACCOUNT *Rent Expense*   **ACCOUNT NO. 52**

Date	Item	Post. Ref.	Debit	Credit	Balance Debit	Balance Credit
2005 Nov. 30		1	800		800	
Dec. 1		2	800		1,600	

ACCOUNT *Depreciation Expense*   **ACCOUNT NO. 53**

Date	Item	Post. Ref.	Debit	Credit	Balance Debit	Balance Credit
2005 Dec. 31	Adjusting	5	50		50	

ACCOUNT *Utilities Expense*   **ACCOUNT NO. 54**

Date	Item	Post. Ref.	Debit	Credit	Balance Debit	Balance Credit
2005 Nov. 30		1	450		450	
Dec. 31		3	310		760	
31		4	225		985	

ACCOUNT *Supplies Expense*   **ACCOUNT NO. 55**

Date	Item	Post. Ref.	Debit	Credit	Balance Debit	Balance Credit
2005 Nov. 30		1	800		800	
Dec. 31	Adjusting	5	1,240		2,040	

ACCOUNT *Insurance Expense*   **ACCOUNT NO. 56**

Date	Item	Post. Ref.	Debit	Credit	Balance Debit	Balance Credit
2005 Dec. 31	Adjusting	5	100		100	

ACCOUNT *Miscellaneous Expense*   **ACCOUNT NO. 59**

Date	Item	Post. Ref.	Debit	Credit	Balance Debit	Balance Credit
2005 Nov. 30		1	275		275	
Dec. 6		2	180		455	

To highlight the effect of the adjustments on the accounts, Exhibit 8 shows the unadjusted trial balance, the accounts affected by the adjustments, and the adjusted trial balance. In Chapter 4, we discuss how financial statements, including a classified balance sheet, can be prepared from an adjusted trial balance. We also discuss the use of a work sheet as an aid to summarize the data for preparing adjusting entries and financial statements.

•Exhibit 8   Trial Balances

	NetSolutions Unadjusted Trial Balance December 31, 2005				Effect of Adjusting Entry			NetSolutions Adjusted Trial Balance December 31, 2005			
1	Cash	2,065		1		1	Cash	2,065		1
2	Accounts Receivable	2,220		2	+ 500	2	Accounts Receivable	2,720		2
3	Supplies	2,000		3	−1,240	3	Supplies	760		3
4	Prepaid Insurance	2,400		4	− 100	4	Prepaid Insurance	2,300		4
5	Land	20,000		5		5	Land	20,000		5
6	Office Equipment	1,800		6		6	Office Equipment	1,800		6
7	Accumulated Depreciation			7	+ 50	7	Accumulated Depreciation		50	7
8	Accounts Payable		900	8		8	Accounts Payable		900	8
9	Wages Payable			9	+ 250	9	Wages Payable		250	9
10	Unearned Rent		360	10	− 120	10	Unearned Rent		240	10
11	Capital Stock		25,000	11		11	Capital Stock		25,000	11
12	Dividends	4,000		12		12	Dividends	4,000		12
13	Fees Earned		16,340	13	+ 500	13	Fees Earned		16,840	13
14	Rent Revenue			14	+ 120	14	Rent Revenue		120	14
15	Wages Expense	4,275		15	+ 250	15	Wages Expense	4,525		15
16	Rent Expense	1,600		16		16	Rent Expense	1,600		16
17	Depreciation Expense			17	+ 50	17	Depreciation Expense	50		17
18	Utilities Expense	985		18		18	Utilities Expense	985		18
19	Supplies Expense	800		19	+1,240	19	Supplies Expense	2,040		19
20	Insurance Expense			20	+ 100	20	Insurance Expense	100		20
21	Miscellaneous Expense	455		21		21	Miscellaneous Expense	455		21
22		42,600	42,600	22		22		43,400	43,400	22

Financial Analysis and Interpretation

Use vertical analysis to compare financial statement items with each other and with industry averages.

Comparing each item in a current statement with a total amount within that same statement can be useful in highlighting significant relationships within a financial statement. **Vertical analysis** is the term used to describe such comparisons.

In vertical analysis of a balance sheet, each asset item is stated as a percent of the total assets. Each liability and stockholders' equity item is stated as a percent of the total liabilities and stockholders' equity. In vertical analysis of an income statement, each item is stated as a percent of revenues or fees earned.

Vertical analysis may also be prepared for several periods to highlight changes in relationships over time. Vertical analysis of two years of income statements for J. Holmes, Attorney-at-Law, P.C., is shown in Exhibit 9. This exhibit indicates both favorable and unfavorable trends affecting the income statement of J. Holmes, Attorney-at-Law, P.C. The increase in wages expense of 2% (32% − 30%) is an unfavorable trend, as is the increase in utilities expense of 0.7% (6.7% − 6.0%). A favorable trend is the decrease in supplies expense of 0.6% (2.0% − 1.4%). Rent expense and miscellaneous expense as a percent of fees earned were constant. The net result of these trends was that net income decreased as a percent of fees earned from 52.8% to 50.7%.

The analysis of the various percentages shown for J. Holmes, Attorney-at-Law, P.C., can be enhanced by comparisons with industry averages published by trade associations and financial information services. Any major differences between industry averages should be investigated.

•Exhibit 9   Vertical Analysis of Income Statements

J. Holmes, Attorney-at-Law
Income Statements
For the Years Ended December 31, 2005 and 2006

	2006		2005	
	Amount	**Percent**	**Amount**	**Percent**
Fees earned	$187,500	100.0%	$150,000	100.0%
Operating expenses:				
Wages expense	$ 60,000	32.0%	$ 45,000	30.0%*
Rent expense	15,000	8.0%	12,000	8.0%
Utilities expense	12,500	6.7%	9,000	6.0%
Supplies expense	2,700	1.4%	3,000	2.0%
Miscellaneous expense	2,300	1.2%	1,800	1.2%
Total operating expenses ..	$ 92,500	49.3%	$ 70,800	47.2%
Net income	$ 95,000	50.7%	$ 79,200	52.8%

*$45,000 ÷ $150,000

SPOTLIGHT ON STRATEGY

NOT CUTTING CORNERS

Have you ever ordered a hamburger from **Wendy's** and noticed that the meat patty is square? The square meat patty reflects a business strategy instilled in Wendy's by its founder, Dave Thomas. Mr. Thomas's strategy was to offer high-quality products at a fair price in a friendly atmosphere, without "cutting corners"; hence, the square meat patty. In the highly competitive fast-food industry, Dave Thomas's strategy enabled Wendy's to grow to be the third largest fast-food restaurant in the world, with annual sales of over $7 billion.

Source: "Dave Thomas, 69, Wendy's Founder, Dies," by Douglas Martin, *The New York Times*, January 9, 2002.

Key Points

1 Explain how the matching concept relates to the accrual basis of accounting.

The accrual basis of accounting requires the use of an adjusting process at the end of the accounting period to match revenues and expenses properly. Revenues are reported in the period in which they are earned, and expenses are matched with the revenues they generate.

2 Explain why adjustments are necessary and list the characteristics of adjusting entries.

At the end of an accounting period, some of the amounts listed on the trial balance are not necessarily current balances. For example, amounts listed for prepaid expenses are normally overstated because the use of these assets has not been recorded on a daily basis. A delay in recognizing an expense already paid or a revenue already received is called a deferral.

Some revenues and expenses related to a period may not be recorded at the end of the period, since these items are normally recorded only when cash has been received or paid. A revenue or expense that has not been paid or recorded is called an accrual.

The entries required at the end of an accounting period to bring accounts up to date and to ensure the proper matching of revenues and expenses are called adjusting entries. Adjusting entries require a debit or a credit to a revenue or an expense account and an offsetting debit or credit to an asset or a liability account.

Adjusting entries affect amounts reported in the income statement and the balance sheet. Thus, if an adjusting entry is not recorded, these financial statements will be incorrect (misstated).

3 Journalize entries for accounts requiring adjustment.

Adjusting entries illustrated in this chapter include deferred (prepaid) expenses, deferred (unearned) revenues, accrued expenses (accrued liabilities), and accrued revenues (accrued assets). In addition, the adjusting entry necessary to record depreciation on fixed assets was illustrated.

4 Summarize the adjustment process and prepare an adjusted trial balance.

A summary of adjustments, including the type of adjustment, the adjusting entry, and the effect of omitting an adjustment on the financial statements, is shown in Exhibit 5. After all the adjusting entries have been posted, the equality of the total debit balances and total credit balances is verified by an adjusted trial balance.

5 Use vertical analysis to compare financial statement items with each other and with industry averages.

Comparing each item in a current statement with a total amount within the same statement is called vertical analysis. In vertical analysis of a balance sheet, each asset item is stated as a percent of the total assets. Each liability and stockholders' equity item is stated as a percent of the total liabilities and stockholders' equity. In vertical analysis of an income statement, each item is stated as a percent of revenues or fees earned.

Key Terms

accounting period concept (102)
accrual basis (102)
accruals (103)
accrued assets (104)
accrued expenses (103)
accrued liabilities (103)
accrued revenues (104)
accumulated depreciation (112)
adjusted trial balance (113)

adjusting entries (103)
adjusting process (103)
book value of the asset (112)
cash basis (102)
contra account (112)
deferrals (103)
deferred expenses (103)
deferred revenues (103)
depreciation (112)

depreciation expense (112)
fixed assets (112)
matching concept (102)
prepaid expenses (103)
revenue recognition concept (102)
unearned revenues (103)
vertical analysis (117)

Illustrative Problem

Three years ago, T. Roderick organized Harbor Realty Inc. At July 31, 2006, the end of the current year, the unadjusted trial balance of Harbor Realty appears as shown at the top of the following page. The data needed to determine year-end adjustments are as follows:

a. Supplies on hand at July 31, 2006, 380.
b. Insurance premiums expired during the year, $315.
c. Depreciation of equipment during the year, $4,950.
d. Wages accrued but not paid at July 31, 2006, $440.
e. Accrued fees earned but not recorded at July 31, 2006, $1,000.
f. Unearned fees on July 31, 2006, $750.

Instructions

1. Prepare the necessary adjusting journal entries.
2. Determine the balance of the accounts affected by the adjusting entries and prepare an adjusted trial balance.

Harbor Realty Inc.
Trial Balance
July 31, 2006

	Debit	Credit
Cash	3 4 2 5 00	
Accounts Receivable	7 0 0 0 00	
Supplies	1 2 7 0 00	
Prepaid Insurance	6 2 0 00	
Office Equipment	51 6 5 0 00	
Accumulated Depreciation		9 7 0 0 00
Accounts Payance		9 2 5 00
Wages Payable		0 00
Unearned Fees		1 2 5 0 00
Capital Stock		5 0 0 0 00
Retained Earnings		24 0 0 0 00
Dividends	5 2 0 0 00	
Fees Earned		59 1 2 5 00
Wages Expense	22 4 1 5 00	
Depreciation Expense	0 00	
Rent Expense	4 2 0 0 00	
Utilities Expense	2 7 1 5 00	
Supplies Expense	0 00	
Insurance Expense	0 00	
Miscellaneous Expense	1 5 0 5 00	
	100 0 0 0 00	100 0 0 0 00

Solution

1.

JOURNAL

	Date		Description	Post. Ref.	Debit	Credit	
1	2006 July	31	Supplies Expense		8 9 0 00		1
2			Supplies			8 9 0 00	2
3							3
4		31	Insurance Expense		3 1 5 00		4
5			Prepaid Insurance			3 1 5 00	5
6							6
7		31	Depreciation Expense		4 9 5 0 00		7
8			Accumulated Depreciation			4 9 5 0 00	8
9							9
10		31	Wages Expense		4 4 0 00		10
11			Wages Payable			4 4 0 00	11
12							12
13		31	Accounts Receivable		1 0 0 0 00		13
14			Fees Earned			1 0 0 0 00	14
15							15
16		31	Unearned Fees		5 0 0 00		16
17			Fees Earned			5 0 0 00	17

2.

Harbor Realty Inc.
Trial Balance
July 31, 2006

Cash	3 4 2 5 00	
Accounts Receivable	8 0 0 0 00	
Supplies	3 8 0 00	
Prepaid Insurance	3 0 5 00	
Office Equipment	51 6 5 0 00	
Accumulated Depreciation		14 6 5 0 00
Accounts Payable		9 2 5 00
Wages Payable		4 4 0 00
Unearned Fees		7 5 0 00
Capital Stock		5 0 0 0 00
Retained Earnings		24 0 0 0 00
Dividends	5 2 0 0 00	
Fees Earned		60 6 2 5 00
Wages Expense	22 8 5 5 00	
Depreciation Expense	4 9 5 0 00	
Rent Expense	4 2 0 0 00	
Utilities Expense	2 7 1 5 00	
Supplies Expense	8 9 0 00	
Insurance Expense	3 1 5 00	
Miscellaneous Expense	1 5 0 5 00	
	106 3 9 0 00	106 3 9 0 00

Self-Examination Questions (Answers at End of Chapter)

1. Which of the following items represents a deferral?
   A. Prepaid insurance
   B. Wages payable
   C. Fees earned
   D. Accumulated depreciation

2. If the supplies account, before adjustment on May 31, indicated a balance of $2,250, and supplies on hand at May 31 totaled $950, the adjusting entry would be:
   A. debit Supplies, $950; credit Supplies Expense, $950.
   B. debit Supplies, $1,300; credit Supplies Expense, $1,300.
   C. debit Supplies Expense, $950; credit Supplies, $950.
   D. debit Supplies Expense, $1,300; credit Supplies, $1,300.

3. The balance in the unearned rent account for Jones Co. as of December 31 is $1,200. If Jones Co. failed to record the adjusting entry for $600 of rent earned during December, the effect on the balance sheet and income statement for December is:
   A. assets understated $600; net income overstated $600.
   B. liabilities understated $600; net income understated $600.
   C. liabilities overstated $600; net income understated $600.
   D. liabilities overstated $600; net income overstated $600.

4. If the estimated amount of depreciation on equipment for a period is $2,000, the adjusting entry to record depreciation would be:
   A. debit Depreciation Expense, $2,000; credit Equipment, $2,000.
   B. debit Equipment, $2,000; credit Depreciation Expense, $2,000.
   C. debit Depreciation Expense, $2,000; credit Accumulated Depreciation, $2,000.
   D. debit Accumulated Depreciation, $2,000; credit Depreciation Expense, $2,000.

5. If the equipment account has a balance of $22,500 and its accumulated depreciation account has a balance of $14,000, the book value of the equipment is:

   A. $36,500.   C. $14,000.
   B. $22,500.   D. $8,500.

Class Discussion Questions

1. How are revenues and expenses reported on the income statement under (a) the cash basis of accounting and (b) the accrual basis of accounting?
2. Fees for services provided are billed to a customer during 2005. The customer remits the amount owed in 2006. During which year would the revenues be reported on the income statement under (a) the cash basis? (b) the accrual basis?
3. Employees performed services in 2005, but the wages were not paid until 2006. During which year would the wages expense be reported on the income statement under (a) the cash basis? (b) the accrual basis?
4. Is the matching concept related to (a) the cash basis of accounting or (b) the accrual basis of accounting?
5. Is the balance listed for cash on the trial balance, before the accounts have been adjusted, the amount that should normally be reported on the balance sheet? Explain.
6. Is the balance listed for supplies on the trial balance, before the accounts have been adjusted, the amount that should normally be reported on the balance sheet? Explain.
7. Why are adjusting entries needed at the end of an accounting period?
8. What is the difference between *adjusting entries* and *correcting entries*?
9. Identify the five different categories of adjusting entries frequently required at the end of an accounting period.
10. If the effect of the credit portion of an adjusting entry is to increase the balance of a liability account, which of the following statements describes the effect of the debit portion of the entry?
   a. Increases the balance of a revenue account.
   b. Increases the balance of an expense account.
   c. Increases the balance of an asset account.
11. If the effect of the debit portion of an adjusting entry is to increase the balance of an asset account, which of the following statements describes the effect of the credit portion of the entry?
   a. Increases the balance of a revenue account.
   b. Increases the balance of an expense account.
   c. Increases the balance of a liability account.
12. Does every adjusting entry have an effect on determining the amount of net income for a period? Explain.
13. What is the nature of the balance in the prepaid insurance account at the end of the accounting period (a) before adjustment? (b) after adjustment?
14. On August 1 of the current year, a business paid the August rent on the building that it occupies. (a) Do the rights acquired at August 1 represent an asset or an expense? (b) What is the justification for debiting Rent Expense at the time of payment?
15. (a) Explain the purpose of the two accounts: Depreciation Expense and Accumulated Depreciation. (b) What is the normal balance of each account? (c) Is it customary for the balances of the two accounts to be equal in amount? (d) In what financial statements, if any, will each account appear?

Exercises

EXERCISE 3-1
Classify accruals and deferrals
Objectives 2, 3

Classify the following items as (a) deferred expense (prepaid expense), (b) deferred revenue (unearned revenue), (c) accrued expense (accrued liability), or (d) accrued revenue (accrued asset).

1. Salary owed but not yet paid.
2. Supplies on hand.
3. Fees received but not yet earned.
4. Fees earned but not yet received.
5. Taxes owed but payable in the following period.
6. Utilities owed but not yet paid.
7. A two-year premium paid on a fire insurance policy.
8. Subscriptions received in advance by a magazine publisher.

EXERCISE 3-2
Classify adjusting entries
Objectives 2, 3

The following accounts were taken from the unadjusted trial balance of Dobro Co., a congressional lobbying firm. Indicate whether or not each account would normally require an adjusting entry. If the account normally requires an adjusting entry, use the following notation to indicate the type of adjustment:

AE—Accrued Expense
AR—Accrued Revenue
DR—Deferred Revenue
DE—Deferred Expense

To illustrate, the answers for the first two accounts are shown below.

Account	Answer
Dividends	Does not normally require adjustment.
Accounts Receivable	Normally requires adjustment (AR).
Accumulated Depreciation	
Cash	
Interest Payable	
Interest Receivable	
Land	
Office Equipment	
Prepaid Rent	
Supplies Expense	
Unearned Fees	
Wages Expense	

EXERCISE 3-3
Adjusting entry for supplies
Objective 3

The balance in the supplies account, before adjustment at the end of the year, is $1,175. Journalize the adjusting entry required if the amount of supplies on hand at the end of the year is $374.

EXERCISE 3-4
Determine supplies purchased
Objective 3

The supplies and supplies expense accounts at December 31, after adjusting entries have been posted at the end of the first year of operations, are shown in the following T accounts:

Supplies		Supplies Expense	
Bal.	118	Bal.	949

Determine the amount of supplies purchased during the year.

EXERCISE 3-5
Effect of omitting adjusting entry
Objective 3

At December 31, the end of the first month of operations, the usual adjusting entry transferring prepaid insurance expired to an expense account is omitted. Which items will be incorrectly stated, because of the error, on (a) the income statement for December and (b) the balance sheet as of December 31? Also indicate whether the items in error will be overstated or understated.

EXERCISE 3-6
Adjusting entries for prepaid insurance
Objective 3

The balance in the prepaid insurance account, before adjustment at the end of the year, is $2,475. Journalize the adjusting entry required under each of the following *alternatives* for determining the amount of the adjustment: (a) the amount of insurance expired during the year is $1,215; (b) the amount of unexpired insurance applicable to future periods is $1,260.

EXERCISE 3-7
Adjusting entries for prepaid insurance
Objective 3

The prepaid insurance account had a balance of $5,600 at the beginning of the year. The account was debited for $1,800 for premiums on policies purchased during the year. Journalize the adjusting entry required at the end of the year for each of the following situations: (a) the amount of unexpired insurance applicable to future periods is $3,680; (b) the amount of insurance expired during the year is $3,720.

EXERCISE 3-8
Adjusting entries for unearned fees
Objective 3
✓*Amount of entry: $9,570*

The balance in the unearned fees account, before adjustment at the end of the year, is $21,880. Journalize the adjusting entry required if the amount of unearned fees at the end of the year is $12,310.

EXERCISE 3-9
Effect of omitting adjusting entry
Objective 3

At the end of July, the first month of the business year, the usual adjusting entry transferring rent earned to a revenue account from the unearned rent account was omitted. Indicate which items will be incorrectly stated, because of the error, on (a) the income statement for July and (b) the balance sheet as of July 31. Also indicate whether the items in error will be overstated or understated.

EXERCISE 3-10
Adjusting entries for accrued salaries
Objective 3
✓*a. Amount of entry: $9,360*

Xenon Realty Co. pays weekly salaries of $15,600 on Friday for a five-day week ending on that day. Journalize the necessary adjusting entry at the end of the accounting period, assuming that the period ends (a) on Wednesday, (b) on Thursday.

EXERCISE 3-11
Determine wages paid
Objective 3

The wages payable and wages expense accounts at August 31, after adjusting entries have been posted at the end of the first month of operations, are shown in the following T accounts:

Wages Payable		Wages Expense	
	Bal.	3,150	Bal.	63,000

Determine the amount of wages paid during the month.

EXERCISE 3-12
Effect of omitting adjusting entry
Objective 3

Accrued salaries of $1,590 owed to employees for December 30 and 31 are not considered in preparing the financial statements for the year ended December 31. Indicate which items will be erroneously stated, because of the error, on (a) the income statement for the year and (b) the balance sheet as of December 31. Also indicate whether the items in error will be overstated or understated.

EXERCISE 3-13
Effect of omitting adjusting entry
Objective 3

Assume that the error in Exercise 3-12 was not corrected and that the $1,590 of accrued salaries was included in the first salary payment in January. Indicate which items will be erroneously stated, because of failure to correct the initial error, on (a) the income statement for the month of January and (b) the balance sheet as of January 31.

EXERCISE 3-14
Adjusting entries for prepaid and accrued taxes
Objective 3
✓ b. $9,695

Titanium Financial Services was organized on April 1 of the current year. On April 2, Titanium prepaid $1,260 to the city for taxes (license fees) for the *next* 12 months and debited the prepaid taxes account. Titanium is also required to pay in January an annual tax (on property) for the *previous* calendar year. The estimated amount of the property tax for the current year (April 1 to December 31) is $8,750. (a) Journalize the two adjusting entries required to bring the accounts affected by the two taxes up to date as of December 31, the end of the current year. (b) What is the amount of tax expense for the current year?

EXERCISE 3-15
Effects of errors on financial statements
Objective 3

REAL WORLD

For a recent period, **Circuit City Stores** reported accrued expenses and other current liabilities of $128,776,000. For the same period, Circuit City reported earnings of $67,040,000 before income taxes. If accrued expenses and other current liabilities had not been recorded, what would have been the earnings (loss) before income taxes?

EXERCISE 3-16
Effects of errors on financial statements
Objective 3

REAL WORLD

The balance sheet for **The Campbell Soup Co.** as of July 31, 2002, includes accrued liabilities of $503,000,000. The income before taxes for The Campbell Soup Co. for the year ended July 28, 2002, was $798,000,000. (a) If the accruals had not been recorded at July 28, 2002, by how much would income before taxes have been misstated for the fiscal year ended July 28, 2002? (b) What is the percentage of the misstatement in (a) to the reported income of $798,000,000?

EXERCISE 3-17
Effects of errors on financial statements
Objective 3
✓ 1. a. Revenue understated, $6,900

The accountant for Glacier Medical Co., a medical services consulting firm, mistakenly omitted adjusting entries for (a) unearned revenue earned during the year ($6,900) and (b) accrued wages ($3,740). Indicate the effect of each error, considered individually, on the income statement for the current year ended December 31. Also indicate the effect of each error on the December 31 balance sheet. Set up a table similar to the following, and record your answers by inserting the dollar amount in the appropriate spaces. Insert a zero if the error does not affect the item.

	Error (a)		Error (b)	
	Over-stated	Under-stated	Over-stated	Under-stated
1. Revenue for the year would be	$	$	$	$
2. Expenses for the year would be	$	$	$	$
3. Net income for the year would be	$	$	$	$

(continued)

	Error (a)		Error (b)	
	Over-stated	Under-stated	Over-stated	Under-stated
4. Assets at December 31 would be	$	$	$	$
5. Liabilities at December 31 would be	$	$	$	$
6. Stockholders' equity at December 31 would be	$	$	$	$

EXERCISE 3-18
Effects of errors on financial statements
Objective 3

If the net income for the current year had been $172,680 in Exercise 3-17, what would be the correct net income if the proper adjusting entries had been made?

EXERCISE 3-19
Adjusting entry for accrued fees
Objective 3

At the end of the current year, $11,500 of fees have been earned but have not been billed to clients.

a. Journalize the adjusting entry to record the accrued fees.
b. If the cash basis rather than the accrual basis had been used, would an adjusting entry have been necessary? Explain.

EXERCISE 3-20
Adjusting entries for unearned and accrued fees
Objective 3

The balance in the unearned fees account, before adjustment at the end of the year, is $27,600. Of these fees, $8,100 have been earned. In addition, $6,450 of fees have been earned but have not been billed. Journalize the adjusting entries (a) to adjust the unearned fees account and (b) to record the accrued fees.

EXERCISE 3-21
Effect on financial statements of omitting adjusting entry
Objective 3

The adjusting entry for accrued fees was omitted at December 31, the end of the current year. Indicate which items will be in error, because of the omission, on (a) the income statement for the current year and (b) the balance sheet as of December 31. Also indicate whether the items in error will be overstated or understated.

EXERCISE 3-22
Adjustment for depreciation
Objective 3

The estimated amount of depreciation on equipment for the current year is $5,200. Journalize the adjusting entry to record the depreciation.

EXERCISE 3-23
Determine fixed asset's book value
Objective 3

The balance in the equipment account is $318,500, and the balance in the accumulated depreciation—equipment account is $113,900.

a. What is the book value of the equipment?
b. Does the balance in the accumulated depreciation account mean that the equipment's loss of value is $113,900? Explain.

EXERCISE 3-24
Book value of fixed assets
Objective 3

REAL WORLD

Microsoft Corporation reported *Property, Plant, and Equipment* of $5,891 million and *Accumulated Depreciation* of $3,623 million at June 30, 2002.

a. What was the book value of the fixed assets at June 30, 2002?
b. Would the book value of Microsoft Corporation's fixed assets normally approximate their fair market values?

EXERCISE 3-25
Adjusting entries for depreciation; effect of error
Objective 3

On December 31, a business estimates depreciation on equipment used during the first year of operations to be $7,500. (a) Journalize the adjusting entry required as of December 31. (b) If the adjusting entry in (a) were omitted, which items would be erroneously stated on (1) the income statement for the year and (2) the balance sheet as of December 31?

EXERCISE 3-26
Adjusting entries from trial balances

Objectives 3, 4

The unadjusted and adjusted trial balances for Aleutian Services Co. on December 31, 2006, are shown below.

Aleutian Services Co.
Trial Balance
December 31, 2006

	Unadjusted		Adjusted	
Cash	16		16	
Accounts Receivable	38		42	
Supplies	12		9	
Prepaid Insurance	20		12	
Land	26		26	
Equipment	40		40	
Accumulated Depreciation—Equipment		8		13
Accounts Payable		26		26
Wages Payable		0		1
Capital Stock		40		40
Retained Earnings		52		52
Dividends	8		8	
Fees Earned		74		78
Wages Expense	24		25	
Rent Expense	8		8	
Insurance Expense	0		8	
Utilities Expense	4		4	
Depreciation Expense	0		5	
Supplies Expense	0		3	
Miscellaneous Expense	4		4	
Totals	200	200	210	210

Journalize the five entries that adjusted the accounts at December 31, 2006. None of the accounts were affected by more than one adjusting entry.

EXERCISE 3-27
Adjusting entries from trial balances

Objectives 3, 4

WHAT'S WRONG WITH THIS?

✓ *Corrected trial balance totals, $168,450*

The accountant for Minaret Laundry prepared the following unadjusted and adjusted trial balances. Assume that all balances in the unadjusted trial balance and the amounts of the adjustments are correct. Identify the errors in the accountant's adjusting entries.

Minaret Laundry
Trial Balance
May 31, 2006

	Unadjusted		Adjusted	
Cash	2,500		2,500	
Accounts Receivable	7,500		9,500	
Laundry Supplies	1,750		2,850	
Prepaid Insurance*	2,825		1,125	
Laundry Equipment	85,600		80,000	
Accumulated Depreciation		55,700		55,700
Accounts Payable		4,950		4,950
Wages Payable				850
Capital Stock		18,000		18,000
Retained Earnings		14,450		14,450
Dividends	10,000		10,000	
Laundry Revenue		66,900		66,900
Wages Expense	24,500		24,500	
Rent Expense	15,575		15,575	
Utilities Expense	8,500		8,500	
Depreciation Expense			5,600	
Laundry Supplies Expense			1,100	
Insurance Expense			700	
Miscellaneous Expense	1,250		1,250	
	160,000	160,000	163,200	160,850

*$1,700 of insurance expired during the year.

EXERCISE 3-28
Vertical analysis of income statement
Objective 5

REAL WORLD

The financial statements for **The Home Depot** are presented in Appendix F at the end of the text.

a. Determine for Home Depot:
    1. The amount of the change (in millions) and percent of change in net earnings (net income) for the year ended February 2, 2003.
    2. The percentage relationship between net earnings (net income) and net sales (net earnings divided by net sales) for the years ended February 2, 2003 and February 3, 2002.

b. What conclusions can you draw from your analysis?

EXERCISE 3-29
Vertical analysis of income statement
Objective 5

REAL WORLD

The following income statement data (in thousands) for **Dell Computer Corporation** and **Gateway Inc.** were taken from their recent annual reports:

	Dell	Gateway
Net sales	$35,404,000	$ 4,171,325
Cost of goods sold (expense)	(29,055,000)	(3,605,120)
Operating expenses	(3,505,000)	(1,077,447)
Operating income (loss)	$ 2,844,000	$ (511,242)

a. Prepare a vertical analysis of the income statement for Dell.
b. Prepare a vertical analysis of the income statement for Gateway.
c. Based upon (a) and (b), how does Dell compare to Gateway?

Problems Series A

PROBLEM 3-1A
Adjusting entries
Objective 3

On August 31, 2006, the following data were accumulated to assist the accountant in preparing the adjusting entries for Osage Realty:

a. Fees accrued but unbilled at August 31 are $7,100.
b. The supplies account balance on August 31 is $3,010. The supplies on hand at August 31 are $1,150.
c. Wages accrued but not paid at August 31 are $1,380.
d. The unearned rent account balance at August 31 is $4,950, representing the receipt of an advance payment on August 1 of three months' rent from tenants.
e. Depreciation of office equipment is $1,120.

Instructions
1. Journalize the adjusting entries required at August 31, 2006.
2. Briefly explain the difference between adjusting entries and entries that would be made to correct errors.

PROBLEM 3-2A
Adjusting entries
Objective 3

Selected account balances before adjustment for Flanders Realty at March 31, 2006, the end of the current year, are as follows:

	Debits	Credits		Debits	Credits
Accounts Receivable	$28,250		Unearned Fees		$ 4,800
Supplies	1,770		Fees Earned		170,850
Prepaid Rent	15,500		Wages Expense	$69,750	
Equipment	80,500		Rent Expense	—	
Accumulated Depreciation		$16,900	Depreciation Expense	—	
Wages Payable	—		Supplies Expense	—	

Data needed for year-end adjustments are as follows:

a. Supplies on hand at March 31, $350.
b. Depreciation of equipment during year, $1,450.
c. Rent expired during year, $9,500.
d. Wages accrued but not paid at March 31, $1,050.
e. Unearned fees at March 31, $1,200.
f. Unbilled fees at March 31, $7,100.

Instructions
Journalize the six adjusting entries required at March 31, based upon the data presented.

PROBLEM 3-3A
Adjusting entries
Objective 3

P.A.S.S.

Wild Trout Co., an outfitter store for fishing treks, prepared the following trial balance at the end of its first year of operations:

Wild Trout Co.
Trial Balance
November 30, 2006

Cash	1,610	
Accounts Receivable	11,900	
Supplies	1,820	
Equipment	27,860	
Accounts Payable		1,050
Unearned Fees		2,800
Capital Stock		10,000
Retained Earnings		27,800
Dividends	1,400	
Fees Earned		51,450
Wages Expense	28,210	
Rent Expense	13,790	
Utilities Expense	5,250	
Miscellaneous Expense	1,260	
	93,100	93,100

For preparing the adjusting entries, the following data were assembled:

a. Supplies on hand on November 30 were $315.
b. Fees earned but unbilled on November 30 were $1,750.
c. Depreciation of equipment was estimated to be $1,600 for the year.
d. Unpaid wages accrued on November 30 were $380.
e. The balance in unearned fees represented the November 1 receipt in advance for services to be provided. Only $700 of the services were provided between November 1 and November 30.

Instructions
Journalize the adjusting entries necessary on November 30.

PROBLEM 3-4A
Adjusting entries
Objectives 3, 4

P.A.S.S.

Dynamo Company specializes in the maintenance and repair of signs, such as billboards. On March 31, 2006, the accountant for Dynamo Company prepared the trial balances shown at the top of the next page.

Instructions
Journalize the seven entries that adjusted the accounts at March 31. None of the accounts were affected by more than one adjusting entry.

(continued)

Dynamo Company
Trial Balance
March 31, 2006

	Unadjusted		Adjusted	
Cash	4,750		4,750	
Accounts Receivable	17,400		17,400	
Supplies	3,880		1,175	
Prepaid Insurance	4,800		3,200	
Land	47,500		47,500	
Buildings	111,590		111,590	
Accumulated Depreciation—Buildings		56,600		60,700
Trucks	73,000		73,000	
Accumulated Depreciation—Trucks		11,800		20,300
Accounts Payable		6,920		7,435
Salaries Payable		—		1,080
Unearned Service Fees		6,400		4,750
Capital Stock		25,000		25,000
Retained Earnings		100,600		100,600
Dividends	5,000		5,000	
Service Fees Earned		152,680		154,330
Salary Expense	73,600		74,680	
Depreciation Expense—Trucks	—		8,500	
Rent Expense	9,600		9,600	
Supplies Expense	—		2,705	
Utilities Expense	6,200		6,715	
Depreciation Expense—Buildings	—		4,100	
Taxes Expense	1,720		1,720	
Insurance Expense	—		1,600	
Miscellaneous Expense	960		960	
	360,000	360,000	374,195	374,195

PROBLEM 3-5A
Adjusting entries and adjusted trial balances
Objectives 3, 4

SPREADSHEET
P.A.S.S.

✓ *2. Total of Debit Column:*
$552,520

Greco Service Co., which specializes in appliance repair services, is owned and operated by Curtis Loomis. Greco Service Co.'s accounting clerk prepared the following trial balance at December 31, 2006:

Greco Service Co.
Trial Balance
December 31, 2006

Cash	4,200	
Accounts Receivable	20,600	
Prepaid Insurance	6,000	
Supplies	1,450	
Land	100,000	
Building	161,500	
Accumulated Depreciation—Building		75,700
Equipment	80,100	
Accumulated Depreciation—Equipment		35,300
Accounts Payable		7,500
Unearned Rent		7,200
Capital Stock		35,000
Retained Earnings		122,100
Dividends	5,000	
Fees Earned		257,200
Salaries and Wages Expense	101,800	
Utilities Expense	28,200	
Advertising Expense	15,000	
Repairs Expense	12,100	
Miscellaneous Expense	4,050	
	540,000	540,000

The data needed to determine year-end adjustments are as follows:

a. Depreciation of building for the year, $3,600.

7200
−2800
4400
1450
375
1075

b. Depreciation of equipment for the year, $2,400.
c. Accrued salaries and wages at December 31, $2,170.
d. Unexpired insurance at December 31, $3,500. *—left* *6000*
3500
2500
e. Fees earned but unbilled on December 31, $4,350.
f. Supplies on hand at December 31, $375. *→ 1450*
−375
1075
g. Rent unearned at December 31, $2,800.

Instructions

1. Journalize the adjusting entries. Add additional accounts as needed.
2. Determine the balances of the accounts affected by the adjusting entries and prepare an adjusted trial balance.

PROBLEM 3-6A
Adjusting entries and errors

Objective 3

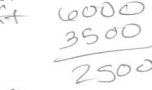

SPREADSHEET

✓ *Corrected Net Income:*
$127,900

At the end of July, the first month of operations, the following selected data were taken from the financial statements of Kay Lopez, Attorney-at-Law, P.C.:

Net income for July	$124,350
Total assets at July 31	500,000
Total liabilities at July 31	125,000
Total stockholders' equity at July 31	375,000

In preparing the financial statements, adjustments for the following data were overlooked:

a. Unbilled fees earned at July 31, $9,600.
b. Depreciation of equipment for July, $3,500.
c. Accrued wages at July 31, $1,450.
d. Supplies used during July, $1,100.

Instructions

1. Journalize the entries to record the omitted adjustments.
2. Determine the correct amount of net income for July and the total assets, liabilities, and stockholders' equity at July 31. In addition to indicating the corrected amounts, indicate the effect of each omitted adjustment by setting up and completing a columnar table similar to the following. Adjustment (a) is presented as an example.

	Net Income	Total Assets	Total Liabilities	Total Stockholders' Equity
Reported amounts	$124,350	$500,000	$125,000	$375,000
Corrections:				
Adjustment (a)	+9,600	+9,600	0	+9,600
Adjustment (b)	_____	_____	_____	_____
Adjustment (c)	_____	_____	_____	_____
Adjustment (d)	_____	_____	_____	_____
Corrected amounts	======	======	======	======

Problems Series B

PROBLEM 3-1B
Adjusting entries

Objective 3

On October 31, 2006, the following data were accumulated to assist the accountant in preparing the adjusting entries for Melville Realty:

a. The supplies account balance on October 31 is $1,875. The supplies on hand on October 31 are $310.
b. The unearned rent account balance on October 31 is $4,020, representing the receipt of an advance payment on October 1 of three months' rent from tenants.
c. Wages accrued but not paid at October 31 are $2,150.
d. Fees accrued but unbilled at October 31 are $11,278.
e. Depreciation of office equipment is $1,000.

Instructions

1. Journalize the adjusting entries required at October 31, 2006.
2. Briefly explain the difference between adjusting entries and entries that would be made to correct errors.

PROBLEM 3-2B
Adjusting entries
Objective 3

Selected account balances before adjustment for Maltese Realty at May 31, 2006, the end of the current year, are as follows:

	Debits	Credits		Debits	Credits
Accounts Receivable	$11,250		Unearned Fees		$ 6,500
Supplies	1,750		Fees Earned		117,950
Prepaid Rent	7,500		Wages Expense	$59,400	
Equipment	52,500		Rent Expense	—	
Accumulated Depreciation		$8,900	Depreciation Expense	—	
Wages Payable		—	Supplies Expense	—	

Data needed for year-end adjustments are as follows:

a. Unbilled fees at May 31, $1,150.
b. Supplies on hand at May 31, $360.
c. Rent expired $6,000.
d. Depreciation of equipment during year, $1,650.
e. Unearned fees at May 31, $1,775.
f. Wages accrued but not paid at May 31, $2,180.

Instructions

Journalize the six adjusting entries required at May 31, based upon the data presented.

PROBLEM 3-3B
Adjusting entries
Objective 3

P.A.S.S.

Anguilla Company, an electronics repair store, prepared the following trial balance at the end of its first year of operations:

Anguilla Company
Trial Balance
April 30, 2006

Cash	2,300	
Accounts Receivable	15,000	
Supplies	3,600	
Equipment	75,800	
Accounts Payable		3,500
Unearned Fees		4,000
Capital Stock		20,000
Retained Earnings		32,000
Dividends	3,000	
Fees Earned		90,500
Wages Expense	21,000	
Rent Expense	16,000	
Utilities Expense	11,500	
Miscellaneous Expense	1,800	
	150,000	150,000

For preparing the adjusting entries, the following data were assembled:

a. Fees earned but unbilled on April 30 were $3,200.
b. Supplies on hand on April 30 were $1,010.
c. Depreciation of equipment was estimated to be $3,850 for the year.
d. The balance in unearned fees represented the April 1 receipt in advance for services to be provided. Only $1,000 of the services was provided between April 1 and April 30.
e. Unpaid wages accrued on April 30 were $820.

Instructions

Journalize the adjusting entries necessary on April 30, 2006.

PROBLEM 3-4B
Adjusting entries
Objectives 3, 4

P.A.S.S.

Expose′ Company specializes in the repair of music equipment and is owned and operated by Gavin Staub. On June 30, 2006, the end of the current year, the accountant for Expose′ Company prepared the following trial balances:

Expose′ Company
Trial Balance
June 30, 2006

	Unadjusted		Adjusted	
Cash	8,315		8,315	
Accounts Receivable	30,500		30,500	
Supplies	3,750		1,080	
Prepaid Insurance	4,750		2,200	
Equipment	92,150		92,150	
Accumulated Depreciation—Equipment		33,480		40,500
Automobiles	36,500		36,500	
Accumulated Depreciation—Automobiles		18,250		21,900
Accounts Payable		8,310		8,730
Salaries Payable		—		1,560
Unearned Service Fees		6,000		4,000
Capital Stock		10,000		10,000
Retained Earnings		59,360		59,360
Dividends	5,000		5,000	
Service Fees Earned		244,600		246,600
Salary Expense	172,300		173,860	
Rent Expense	18,000		18,000	
Supplies Expense	—		2,670	
Depreciation Expense—Equipment	—		7,020	
Depreciation Expense—Automobiles	—		3,650	
Utilities Expense	4,300		4,720	
Taxes Expense	2,725		2,725	
Insurance Expense	—		2,550	
Miscellaneous Expense	1,710		1,710	
	380,000	380,000	392,650	392,650

Instructions
Journalize the seven entries that adjusted the accounts at June 30. None of the accounts were affected by more than one adjusting entry.

PROBLEM 3-5B
Adjusting entries and adjusted trial balances
Objectives 3, 4

SPREADSHEET
P.A.S.S.

✓2. Total of Debit Column: $510,380

Berserk Company is a small editorial services company owned and operated by Ethel Pringle. On December 31, 2006, the end of the current year, Berserk Company's accounting clerk prepared the trial balance shown at the top of the next page.
    The data needed to determine year-end adjustments are as follows:

a. Unexpired insurance at December 31, $1,600.
b. Supplies on hand at December 31, $280.
c. Depreciation of building for the year, $1,320.
d. Depreciation of equipment for the year, $4,100.
e. Rent unearned at December 31, $1,500.
f. Accrued salaries and wages at December 31, $1,760.
g. Fees earned but unbilled on December 31, $3,200.

Instructions
1. Journalize the adjusting entries. Add additional accounts as needed.
2. Determine the balances of the accounts affected by the adjusting entries and prepare an adjusted trial balance.

(continued)

Berserk Company
Trial Balance
December 31, 2006

Cash	3,700	
Accounts Receivable	18,900	
Prepaid Insurance	4,800	
Supplies	1,320	
Land	75,000	
Building	141,500	
Accumulated Depreciation—Building		91,700
Equipment	90,200	
Accumulated Depreciation—Equipment		65,300
Accounts Payable		8,100
Unearned Rent		4,500
Capital Stock		60,000
Retained Earnings		74,000
Dividends	10,000	
Fees Earned		196,400
Salaries and Wages Expense	95,580	
Utilities Expense	28,250	
Advertising Expense	15,200	
Repairs Expense	11,500	
Miscellaneous Expense	4,050	
	500,000	500,000

PROBLEM 3-6B
Adjusting entries and errors
Objective 3

SPREADSHEET

✓ *Corrected Net Income:*
$209,745

At the end of November, the first month of operations, the following selected data were taken from the financial statements of Jaime McCune, Attorney-at-Law, P.C.:

Net income for November	$207,320
Total assets at November 30	440,960
Total liabilities at November 30	29,720
Total stockholders' equity at November 30	411,240

In preparing the financial statements, adjustments for the following data were overlooked:

a. Supplies used during November, $1,025.
b. Unbilled fees earned at November 30, $7,650.
c. Depreciation of equipment for November, $3,100.
d. Accrued wages at November 30, $1,100.

Instructions

1. Journalize the entries to record the omitted adjustments.
2. Determine the correct amount of net income for November and the total assets, liabilities, and stockholders' equity at November 30. In addition to indicating the corrected amounts, indicate the effect of each omitted adjustment by setting up and completing a columnar table similar to the following. Adjustment (a) is presented as an example.

	Net Income	Total Assets	Total Liabilities	Total Stockholders' Equity
Reported amounts	$207,320	$440,960	$29,720	$411,240
Corrections:				
Adjustment (a)	−1,025	−1,025	0	−1,025
Adjustment (b)				
Adjustment (c)				
Adjustment (d)				
Corrected amounts				

Continuing Problem

P.A.S.S.

✓ *3. Total of Debit Column:*
$33,190

The trial balance that you prepared for Dancin Music at the end of Chapter 2 should appear as follows:

Dancin Music
Trial Balance
May 31, 2006

Cash	7,330	
Accounts Receivable	1,760	
Supplies	920	
Prepaid Insurance	3,360	
Office Equipment	5,000	
Accounts Payable		5,750
Unearned Revenue		4,800
Capital Stock		10,000
Dividends	2,250	
Fees Earned		11,210
Wages Expense	2,800	
Office Rent Expense	2,600	
Equipment Rent Expense	1,150	
Utilities Expense	860	
Music Expense	1,780	
Advertising Expense	1,300	
Supplies Expense	180	
Miscellaneous Expense	470	
	31,760	31,760

The data needed to determine adjustments for the two-month period ending May 31, 2006, are as follows:

a. During May, Dancin Music provided guest disc jockeys for KPRG for a total of 110 hours. For information on the amount of the accrued revenue to be billed to KPRG, see the contract described in the May 3, 2006 transaction at the end of Chapter 2.
b. Supplies on hand at May 31, $170.
c. The balance of the prepaid insurance account relates to the May 1, 2006 transaction at the end of Chapter 2.
d. Depreciation of the office equipment is $100.
e. The balance of the unearned revenue account relates to the contract between Dancin Music and KPRG, described in the May 3, 2006 transaction at the end of Chapter 2.
f. Accrued wages as of May 31, 2006, were $130.

Instructions
1. Prepare adjusting journal entries. You will need the following additional accounts:

   18 Accumulated Depreciation—Office Equipment
   22 Wages Payable
   57 Insurance Expense
   58 Depreciation Expense

2. Post the adjusting entries, inserting balances in the accounts affected.
3. Prepare an adjusted trial balance.

Special Activities

ACTIVITY 3-1
Ethics and professional conduct in business

ETHICS

Ruth Harbin opened Macaw Real Estate Co. on January 1, 2005. At the end of the first year, the business needed additional capital. On behalf of Macaw Real Estate, Ruth applied to First City Bank for a loan of $120,000. Based on Macaw Real Estate's financial statements, which had been prepared on a cash basis, the First City Bank loan officer rejected the loan as too risky.

After receiving the rejection notice, Ruth instructed her accountant to prepare the financial statements on an accrual basis. These statements included $41,500 in accounts receivable and $13,200 in accounts payable. Ruth then instructed her accountant to record an additional $12,500 of accounts receivable for commissions on property for which a contract had been signed on December 28, 2005, but which would not be formally "closed" and the title transferred until January 20, 2006.

Ruth then applied for a $120,000 loan from Second National Bank, using the revised financial statements. On this application, Ruth indicated that she had not previously been rejected for credit.

Discuss the ethical and professional conduct of Ruth Harbin in applying for the loan from Second National Bank.

ACTIVITY 3-2
Accrued expense

REAL WORLD

On December 30, 2006, you buy a Ford Expedition. It comes with a three-year, 36,000-mile warranty. On January 18, 2007, you return the Expedition to the dealership for some basic repairs covered under the warranty. The cost of the repairs to the dealership is $725. In what year, 2006 or 2007, should **Ford Motor Co.** recognize the cost of the warranty repairs as an expense?

ACTIVITY 3-3
Accrued revenue

REAL WORLD   WHAT DO YOU THINK?

The following is an excerpt from a conversation between Nathan Cisneros and Sonya Lucas just before they boarded a flight to Paris on **American Airlines**. They are going to Paris to attend their company's annual sales conference.

Nathan: Sonya, aren't you taking an introductory accounting course at college?

Sonya: Yes, I decided it's about time I learned something about accounting. You know, our annual bonuses are based upon the sales figures that come from the accounting department.

Nathan: I guess I never really thought about it.

Sonya: You should think about it! Last year, I placed a $300,000 order on December 27. But when I got my bonus, the $300,000 sale wasn't included. They said it hadn't been shipped until January 5, so it would have to count in next year's bonus.

Nathan: A real bummer!

Sonya: Right! I was counting on that bonus including the $300,000 sale.

Nathan: Did you complain?

Sonya: Yes, but it didn't do any good. Beth, the head accountant, said something about matching revenues and expenses. Also, something about not recording revenues until the sale is final. I figure I'd take the accounting course and find out whether she's just jerking me around.

Nathan: I never really thought about it. When do you think American Airlines will record its revenues from this flight?

Sonya: Mmm . . . I guess it could record the revenue when it sells the ticket . . . or . . . when the boarding passes are taken at the door . . . or . . . when we get off the plane . . . or when our company pays for the tickets . . . or . . . I don't know. I'll ask my accounting instructor.

Discuss when American Airlines should recognize the revenue from ticket sales to properly match revenues and expenses.

ACTIVITY 3-4
Adjustments and financial statements

Several years ago, your brother opened Chestnut Television Repair. He made a small initial investment and added money from his personal bank account as needed. He withdrew money for living expenses at irregular intervals. As the business grew, he hired an assistant. He is now considering adding more employees, purchasing additional service trucks, and purchasing the building he now rents. To secure funds for the expansion, your brother submitted a loan application to the bank and included the most recent financial statements (shown below) prepared from accounts maintained by a part-time bookkeeper.

Chestnut Television Repair
Income Statement
For the Year Ended August 31, 2006

Service revenue		$83,280
Less: Rent paid	$20,000	
Wages paid	18,500	
Supplies paid	5,100	
Utilities paid	3,175	
Insurance paid	2,400	
Miscellaneous payments	2,150	51,325
Net income		$31,955

Chestnut Television Repair
Balance Sheet
August 31, 2006

Assets	
Cash	$11,150
Amounts due from customers	6,100
Truck	30,000
Total assets	$47,250

Equities	
Stockholders' equity	$47,250

After reviewing the financial statements, the loan officer at the bank asked your brother if he used the accrual basis of accounting for revenues and expenses. Your brother responded that he did and that is why he included an account for "Amounts Due from Customers." The loan officer then asked whether or not the accounts were adjusted prior to the preparation of the statements. Your brother answered that they had not been adjusted.

a. Why do you think the loan officer suspected that the accounts had not been adjusted prior to the preparation of the statements?
b. Indicate possible accounts that might need to be adjusted before an accurate set of financial statements could be prepared.

ACTIVITY 3-5
Codes of ethics

GROUP ACTIVITY   **ETHICS**

Obtain a copy of your college or university's student code of conduct. In groups of three or four, answer the following questions.

1. Compare this code of conduct with the accountant's Codes of Professional Conduct, which is linked to the text Web site at http://warren.swlearning.com. What are the similarities and differences between the two codes of conduct?
2. One of your classmates asks you for permission to copy your homework, which your instructor will be collecting and grading for part of your overall term grade. Although your instructor has not stated whether one student may or may not copy another student's homework, is it ethical for you to allow your classmate to copy your homework? Is it ethical for your classmate to copy your homework?

ACTIVITY 3-6
Business strategy

GROUP ACTIVITY

Assume that you and two friends are debating whether to open an automotive and service retail chain that will be called Auto-Mart. Initially, Auto-Mart will open three stores locally, but the business plan anticipates going nationwide within five years.

Currently, you and your future business partners are debating whether to focus Auto-Mart on a "do-it-yourself" or "do-it-for-me" business strategy. A "do-it-yourself" business strategy emphasizes the sale of retail auto parts that customers will use themselves to repair and service their cars. A "do-it-for-me" business strategy emphasizes the offering of maintenance and service for customers.

1. In groups of three or four, discuss whether to implement a "do-it-yourself" or "do-it-for-me" business strategy. List the advantages of each strategy and arrive at a conclusion as to which strategy to implement.
2. Provide examples of real world businesses that use "do-it-yourself" or "do-it-for-me" business strategies.

Answers to Self-Examination Questions

1. **A**   A deferral is the delay in recording an expense already paid, such as prepaid insurance (answer A). Wages payable (answer B) is considered an accrued expense or accrued liability. Fees earned (answer C) is a revenue item. Accumulated depreciation (answer D) is a contra account to a fixed asset.

2. **D**   The balance in the supplies account, before adjustment, represents the amount of supplies available. From this amount ($2,250) is subtracted the amount of supplies on hand ($950) to determine the supplies used ($1,300). Since increases in expense accounts are recorded by debits and decreases in asset accounts are recorded by credits, answer D is the correct entry.

3. **C**   The failure to record the adjusting entry debiting unearned rent, $600, and crediting rent revenue, $600, would have the effect of overstating liabilities by $600 and understating net income by $600 (answer C).

4. **C**   Since increases in expense accounts (such as depreciation expense) are recorded by debits and it is customary to record the decreases in usefulness of fixed assets as credits to accumulated depreciation accounts, answer C is the correct entry.

5. **D**   The book value of a fixed asset is the difference between the balance in the asset account and the balance in the related accumulated depreciation account, or $22,500 − $14,000, as indicated by answer D ($8,500).

COMPLETING THE ACCOUNTING CYCLE

objectives

After studying this chapter, you should be able to:

1 Review the seven basic steps of the accounting cycle.

2 Prepare a work sheet.

3 Prepare financial statements from a work sheet.

4 Prepare the adjusting and closing entries from a work sheet.

5 Explain what is meant by the fiscal year and the natural business year.

6 Analyze and interpret the financial solvency of a business by computing working capital and the current ratio.

Most of us have had to file a personal tax return. At the beginning of the year, you estimate your upcoming income and decide whether you need to increase your payroll tax withholdings or perhaps pay estimated taxes. During the year, you earn income, make investments, and enter into other tax-related transactions, such as making charitable contributions. At the end of the year, your employer sends you a tax withholding information form (W-2 form), and you collect the tax records needed for completing your yearly tax forms. If any tax is owed, you pay it; if you overpaid your taxes, you file for a refund. As the next year begins, you start the cycle all over again.

Businesses also go through a cycle of activities. At the beginning of the cycle, management plans where it wants the business to go and begins the necessary actions to achieve its operating goals. Throughout the cycle, which is normally one year, the accountant records the operating activities (transactions) of the business. At the end of the cycle, the accountant prepares financial statements that summarize the operating activities for the year. The accountant then prepares the accounts for recording the operating activities in the next cycle.

As we saw in Chapter 1, the initial cycle for NetSolutions began with Chris Clark's investment in the business on November 1, 2005. The cycle continued with recording NetSolutions' transactions for November and December, as we discussed in Chapters 1 and 2. In Chapter 3, the cycle continued and we recorded the adjusting entries for the two months ending December 31, 2005. Now, in this chapter, we discuss the flow of the adjustment data into the accounts and into the financial statements.

Accounting Cycle

<table>
<tr><td>objective 1</td></tr>
</table>

Review the seven basic steps of the accounting cycle.

REAL WORLD

In a computerized accounting system, the software automatically records and posts transactions. The ledger and supporting records are maintained in computerized master files. In addition, a work sheet is normally not prepared.

The accounting process that begins with analyzing and journalizing transactions and ends with summarizing and reporting these transactions is called the **accounting cycle**. The most important output of this cycle is the financial statements.

The basic steps of the accounting cycle are shown, by number, in the flowchart in Exhibit 1.

In earlier chapters, we described and illustrated the analysis and recording of transactions, posting to the ledger, preparing a trial balance, analyzing adjustment data, preparing adjusting entries, and preparing financial statements. In this chapter, we complete our discussion of the accounting cycle by describing how work sheets may be used as an aid in preparing the financial statements. We also describe and illustrate how closing entries and a post-closing trial balance are used in preparing the accounting records for the next period.

Work Sheet

<table>
<tr><td>objective 2</td></tr>
</table>

Prepare a work sheet.

REAL WORLD

Common spreadsheet programs used in business include Microsoft Excel® and Lotus 1-2-3®.

Accountants often use **working papers** for collecting and summarizing data they need for preparing various analyses and reports. Such working papers are useful tools, but they are not considered a part of the formal accounting records. This is in contrast to the chart of accounts, the journal, and the ledger, which are essential parts of the accounting system. Working papers are usually prepared by using a spreadsheet program on a computer.

The **work sheet** is a working paper that accountants can use to summarize adjusting entries and the account balances for the financial statements. In small companies with few accounts and adjustments, a work sheet may not be necessary. For example, the financial statements for NetSolutions can be prepared directly from the adjusted trial balance illustrated in Chapter 3. In a computerized accounting system,

•Exhibit 1   Accounting Cycle

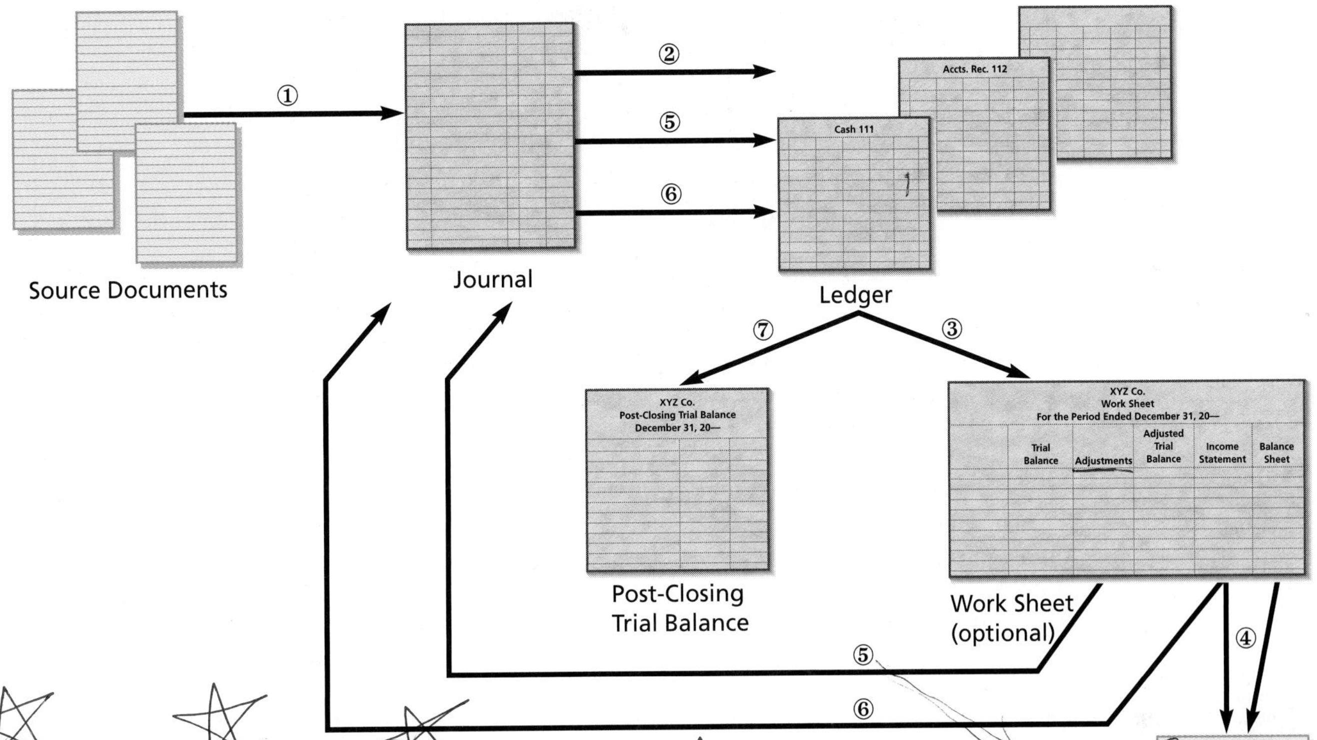

Source Documents → ① → Journal → ② ⑤ ⑥ → Ledger

Cash 111 · Accts. Rec. 112

Ledger → ⑦ → Post-Closing Trial Balance (XYZ Co. Post-Closing Trial Balance December 31, 20—)

Ledger → ③ → Work Sheet (optional) (XYZ Co. Work Sheet For the Period Ended December 31, 20— / Trial Balance · Adjustments · Adjusted Trial Balance · Income Statement · Balance Sheet)

④ → Financial Statements (Income Statement, Retained Earnings Statement, Balance Sheet)

① Transactions are analyzed and recorded in the journal.
② Transactions are posted to the ledger.
③ A trial balance is prepared, adjustment data are assembled, and an optional work sheet is completed.
④ Financial statements are prepared.
⑤ Adjusting entries are journalized and posted to the ledger.
⑥ Closing entries are journalized and posted to the ledger.
⑦ A post-closing trial balance is prepared.

a work sheet may not be necessary because the software program automatically posts entries to the accounts and prepares financial statements.

The work sheet (Exhibits 2 through 5 on pages 142–146) is a useful device for understanding the flow of the accounting data from the unadjusted trial balance to the financial statements (Exhibit 6). This flow of data is the same in either a manual or a computerized accounting system.

> **The work sheet is a useful device for understanding the flow of the accounting data from the unadjusted trial balance to the financial statements.**

Unadjusted Trial Balance Columns

To begin the work sheet, list at the top the name of the business, the type of working paper (work sheet), and the period of time, as shown in Exhibit 2. Next, enter the unadjusted trial balance directly on the work sheet. The work sheet in Exhibit 2 shows the unadjusted trial balance for NetSolutions at December 31, 2005.

•Exhibit 2   Work Sheet with Unadjusted Trial Balance Entered

NetSolutions
Work Sheet
For the Two Months Ended December 31, 2005

	Trial Balance		Adjustments		Adjusted Trial Balance		Income Statement		Balance Sheet	
Account Title	Dr.	Cr.	Dr.	Cr.	Dr.	Cr.	Dr.	Cr.	Dr.	Cr.
1 Cash	2,065									
2 Accounts Receivable	2,220									
3 Supplies	2,000									
4 Prepaid Insurance	2,400									
5 Land	20,000									
6 Office Equipment	1,800									
7 Accounts Payable		900								
8 Unearned Rent		360								
9 Capital Stock		25,000								
10 Dividends	4,000									
11 Fees Earned		16,340								
12 Wages Expense	4,275									
13 Rent Expense	1,600									
14 Utilities Expense	985									
15 Supplies Expense	800									
16 Miscellaneous Expense	455									
17	42,600	42,600								
18										

> The work sheet is used for summarizing the effects of adjusting entries. It also aids in preparing financial statements.

Adjustments Columns

The adjustments that we explained and illustrated for NetSolutions in Chapter 3 are entered in the Adjustments columns, as shown in Exhibit 3. Cross-referencing (by letters) the debit and credit of each adjustment is useful in reviewing the work sheet. It is also helpful for identifying the adjusting entries that need to be recorded in the journal.

The order in which the adjustments are entered on the work sheet is not important. Most accountants enter the adjustments in the order in which the data are assembled. If the titles of some of the accounts to be adjusted do not appear in the trial balance, they should be inserted in the Account Title column, below the trial balance totals, as needed.

To review, the entries in the Adjustments columns of the work sheet are:

(a) **Supplies.** The supplies account has a debit balance of $2,000. The cost of the supplies on hand at the end of the period is $760. Therefore, the supplies expense for December is the difference between the two amounts, or $1,240. Enter the adjustment by writing (1) $1,240 in the Adjustments Debit column on the same line as Supplies Expense and (2) $1,240 in the Adjustments Credit column on the same line as Supplies.

(b) **Prepaid Insurance.** The prepaid insurance account has a debit balance of $2,400, which represents the prepayment of insurance for 24 months beginning December 1. Thus, the insurance expense for December is $100 ($2,400/24). Enter the adjustment by writing (1) $100 in the Adjustments Debit column on the same line as Insurance Expense and (2) $100 in the Adjustments Credit column on the same line as Prepaid Insurance.

(c) **Unearned Rent.** The unearned rent account has a credit balance of $360, which represents the receipt of three months' rent, beginning with December. Thus, the rent revenue for December is $120. Enter the adjustment by writing (1) $120 in the Adjustments Debit column on the same line as Unearned Rent and (2) $120 in the Adjustments Credit column on the same line as Rent Revenue.

(d) **Wages.** Wages accrued but not paid at the end of December total $250. This amount is an increase in expenses and an increase in liabilities. Enter the adjustment by writing (1) $250 in the Adjustments Debit column on the same line as Wages Expense and (2) $250 in the Adjustments Credit column on the same line as Wages Payable.

(e) **Accrued Fees.** Fees accrued at the end of December but not recorded total $500. This amount is an increase in an asset and an increase in revenue. Enter the adjustment by writing (1) $500 in the Adjustments Debit column on the same line as Accounts Receivable and (2) $500 in the Adjustments Credit column on the same line as Fees Earned.

(f) **Depreciation.** Depreciation of the office equipment is $50 for December. Enter the adjustment by writing (1) $50 in the Adjustments Debit column on the same line as Depreciation Expense and (2) $50 in the Adjustments Credit column on the same line as Accumulated Depreciation.

Total the Adjustments columns to verify the mathematical accuracy of the adjustment data. The total of the Debit column must equal the total of the Credit column.

Adjusted Trial Balance Columns

The adjustment data are added to or subtracted from the amounts in the unadjusted Trial Balance columns. The adjusted amounts are then extended to (placed in) the Adjusted Trial Balance columns, as shown in Exhibit 3. For example, the cash amount of $2,065 is extended to the Adjusted Trial Balance Debit column, since no adjustments affected Cash. Accounts Receivable has an initial balance of $2,220 and a debit adjustment (increase) of $500. The amount to write in the Adjusted Trial Balance Debit column is the debit balance of $2,720. The same procedure continues until all account balances are extended to the Adjusted Trial Balance columns. Total the columns of the Adjusted Trial Balance to verify the equality of debits and credits.

Income Statement and Balance Sheet Columns

The work sheet is completed by extending the adjusted trial balance amounts to the Income Statement and Balance Sheet columns. The amounts for revenues and expenses are extended to the Income Statement columns. The amounts for assets, liabilities, owner's capital, and drawing are extended to the Balance Sheet columns.[1]

In the NetSolutions work sheet, the first account listed is Cash, and the balance appearing in the Adjusted Trial Balance Debit column is $2,065. Cash is an asset, is listed on the balance sheet, and has a debit balance. Therefore, $2,065 is extended to the Balance Sheet Debit column. The Fees Earned balance of $16,840 is extended to the Income Statement Credit column. The same procedure continues until all account balances have been extended to the proper columns, as shown in Exhibit 4 (page 145).

After all of the balances have been extended to the four statement columns, total each of these columns, as shown in Exhibit 5. The difference between the two

---

[1] The balances of the retained earnings and dividends accounts are also extended to the Balance Sheet columns because this work sheet does not provide for separate Retained Earnings Statement columns.

•Exhibit 3 Work Sheet with Unadjusted Trial Balance, Adjustments, and Adjusted Trial Balance Entered

NetSolutions
Work Sheet
For the Two Months Ended December 31, 2005

	Account Title	Trial Balance Dr.	Trial Balance Cr.	Adjustments Dr.	Adjustments Cr.	Adjusted Trial Balance Dr.	Adjusted Trial Balance Cr.	Income Statement Dr.	Income Statement Cr.	Balance Sheet Dr.	Balance Sheet Cr.	
1	Cash	2,065				2,065						1
2	Accounts Receivable	2,220		(e) 500		2,720						2
3	Supplies	2,000			(a)1,240	760						3
4	Prepaid Insurance	2,400			(b) 100	2,300						4
5	Land	20,000				20,000						5
6	Office Equipment	1,800				1,800						6
7	Accounts Payable		900				900					7
8	Unearned Rent		360	(c) 120			240					8
9	Capital Stock		25,000				25,000					9
10	Dividends	4,000				4,000						10
11	Fees Earned		16,340		(e) 500		16,840					11
12	Wages Expense	4,275		(d) 250		4,525						12
13	Rent Expense	1,600				1,600						13
14	Utilities Expense	985				985						14
15	Supplies Expense	800		(a)1,240		2,040						15
16	Miscellaneous Expense	455				455						16
17		42,600	42,600									17
18	Insurance Expense			(b) 100		100						18
19	Rent Revenue				(c) 120		120					19
20	Wages Payable				(d) 250		250					20
21	Depreciation Expense			(f) 50		50						21
22	Accumulated Depreciation				(f) 50		50					22
23				2,260	2,260	43,400	43,400					23
24												24
25												25

> The adjustments on the work sheet are used in preparing the adjusting journal entries.

> The adjusted trial balance amounts are determined by adding the adjustments to or subtracting the adjustments from the trial balance amounts. For example, the Wages Expense debit of $4,525 is the trial balance amount of $4,275 plus the $250 adjustment debit.

> Accounts are added, as needed, to complete the adjustments.

Income Statement column totals is the amount of the net income or the net loss for the period. Likewise, the difference between the two Balance Sheet column totals is also the amount of the net income or net loss for the period.

If the Income Statement Credit column total (representing total revenue) is greater than the Income Statement Debit column total (representing total expenses), the difference is the net income. If the Income Statement Debit column total is greater than the Income Statement Credit column total, the difference is a net loss. For Net-Solutions, the computation of net income is as follows:

Total of Credit column (revenues)	$16,960
Total of Debit column (expenses)	9,755
Net income (excess of revenues over expenses)	$ 7,205

As shown in Exhibit 5 (page 146), write the amount of the net income, $7,205, in the Income Statement Debit column and the Balance Sheet Credit column. Write

•Exhibit 4   Work Sheet with Amounts Extended to Income Statement and Balance Sheet Columns

NetSolutions
Work Sheet
For the Two Months Ended December 31, 2005

	Trial Balance Dr.	Trial Balance Cr.	Adjustments Dr.	Adjustments Cr.	Adjusted Trial Balance Dr.	Adjusted Trial Balance Cr.	Income Statement Dr.	Income Statement Cr.	Balance Sheet Dr.	Balance Sheet Cr.	
1 Cash	2,065				2,065				2,065		1
2 Accounts Receivable	2,220		(e) 500		2,720				2,720		2
3 Supplies	2,000			(a)1,240	760				760		3
4 Prepaid Insurance	2,400			(b) 100	2,300				2,300		4
5 Land	20,000				20,000				20,000		5
6 Office Equipment	1,800				1,800				1,800		6
7 Accounts Payable		900				900				900	7
8 Unearned Rent		360	(c) 120			240				240	8
9 Capital Stock		25,000				25,000				25,000	9
10 Dividends	4,000				4,000				4,000		10
11 Fees Earned		16,340		(e) 500		16,840		16,840			11
12 Wages Expense	4,275		(d) 250		4,525		4,525				12
13 Rent Expense	1,600				1,600		1,600				13
14 Utilities Expense	985				985		985				14
15 Supplies Expense	800		(a)1,240		2,040		2,040				15
16 Miscellaneous Expense	455				455		455				16
17	42,600	42,600									17
18 Insurance Expense			(b) 100		100		100				18
19 Rent Revenue				(c) 120		120		120			19
20 Wages Payable				(d) 250		250				250	20
21 Depreciation Expense			(f) 50		50		50				21
22 Accumulated Depreciation				(f) 50		50				50	22
23			2,260	2,260	43,400	43,400					23
24											24
25											25

The revenue and expense amounts are extended to (placed in) the Income Statement columns.

The asset, liability, capital stock, and dividends amounts are extended to (placed in) the Balance Sheet columns.

If the total of the Balance Sheet Debit column of the work sheet is $350,000 and the total of the Balance Sheet Credit column is $400,000, what is the net income or net loss?

$50,000 net loss ($350,000 − $400,000)

•Exhibit 5 Completed Work Sheet with Net Income Shown

NetSolutions
Work Sheet
For the Two Months Ended December 31, 2005

	Account Title	Trial Balance Dr.	Trial Balance Cr.	Adjustments Dr.	Adjustments Cr.	Adjusted Trial Balance Dr.	Adjusted Trial Balance Cr.	Income Statement Dr.	Income Statement Cr.	Balance Sheet Dr.	Balance Sheet Cr.	
1	Cash	2,065				2,065				2,065		1
2	Accounts Receivable	2,220		(e) 500		2,720				2,720		2
3	Supplies	2,000			(a)1,240	760				760		3
4	Prepaid Insurance	2,400			(b) 100	2,300				2,300		4
5	Land	20,000				20,000				20,000		5
6	Office Equipment	1,800				1,800				1,800		6
7	Accounts Payable		900				900				900	7
8	Unearned Rent		360	(c) 120			240				240	8
9	Capital Stock		25,000				25,000				25,000	9
10	Dividends	4,000				4,000				4,000		10
11	Fees Earned		16,340		(e) 500		16,840		16,840			11
12	Wages Expense	4,275		(d) 250		4,525		4,525				12
13	Rent Expense	1,600				1,600		1,600				13
14	Utilities Expense	985				985		985				14
15	Supplies Expense	800		(a)1,240		2,040		2,040				15
16	Miscellaneous Expense	455				455		455				16
17		42,600	42,600									17
18	Insurance Expense			(b) 100		100		100				18
19	Rent Revenue				(c) 120		120		120			19
20	Wages Payable				(d) 250		250				250	20
21	Depreciation Expense			(f) 50		50		50				21
22	Accumulated Depreciation				(f) 50		50				50	22
23				2,260	2,260	43,400	43,400	9,755	16,960	33,645	26,440	23
24	Net income							7,205			7,205	24
25								16,960	16,960	33,645	33,645	25

The difference between the Income Statement column totals is the net income (or net loss) for the period. The difference between the Balance Sheet column totals is also the net income (or net loss) for the period.

Financial Statements

objective 3

Prepare financial statements from a work sheet.

The work sheet is an aid in preparing the income statement, the retained earnings statement, and the balance sheet, which are presented in Exhibit 6. In the following paragraphs, we discuss these financial statements for NetSolutions, prepared from the completed work sheet in Exhibit 5. The statements are similar in form to those presented in Chapter 1.

•Exhibit 6

Financial Statements Prepared from Work Sheet

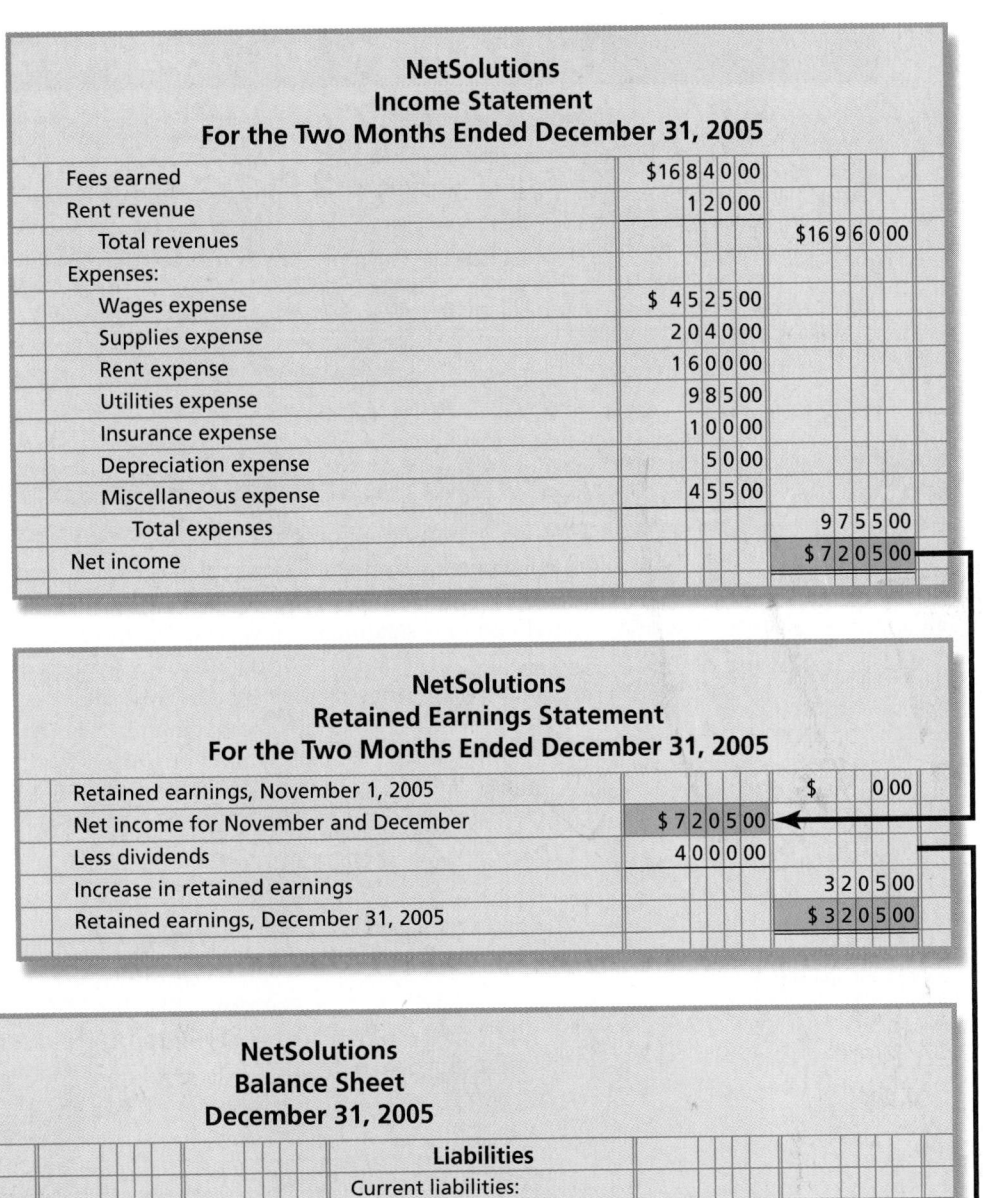

Income Statement

The income statement is normally prepared directly from the work sheet. However, the order of the expenses may be changed. As we did in Chapter 1, we list the expenses in the income statement in Exhibit 6 in order of size, beginning with the larger items. Miscellaneous expense is the last item, regardless of its amount.

INTEGRITY IN BUSINESS

THE ROUND TRIP

A common type of fraud involves artificially inflating revenue. One fraudulent method of inflating revenue is called "round tripping." Under this scheme, a selling company (S) "lends" money to a customer company (C). The money is then used by C to purchase a product from S. Thus, S sells product to C and is paid with the money just loaned to C! This looks like a sale in the accounting records, but in reality, S is shipping free product. The fraud is exposed when it is determined that there was no intent to repay the original loan.

 I'm one of the world's largest hotel operating companies, with names such as these under my roof: Sheraton, Westin, St. Regis, W, Ciga, Luxury Collection and Four Points. Some of my better known units include the St. Regis in New York; the Phoenician in Scottsdale, Ariz.; the Hotel Danieli in Venice; and the Palace Hotel in Madrid. My Westin division recently bought nine legendary luxury hotels in Europe. I own, lease, manage or franchise more than 700 hotels with more than 217,000 rooms in some 80 countries. I aim to increase earnings per share by 15 percent annually. Who am I? (Go to page 169 for answer.)

Retained Earnings Statement

The first item normally presented on the retained earnings statement is the balance of the retained earnings account at the beginning of the period. Since NetSolutions began operations on November 1, this balance is zero in Exhibit 5. Then, the retained earnings statement shows the net income for the two months ended December 31, 2005. The amount of dividends is deducted from the net income to arrive at the retained earnings as of December 31, 2005.

For the following period, the beginning balance of retained earnings for NetSolutions is the ending balance that was reported for the previous period. For example, assume that during 2006, NetSolutions earned net income of $59,595 and paid dividends of $24,000. The retained earnings statement for the year ending December 31, 2006, for NetSolutions is as follows:

NetSolutions Retained Earnings Statement For the Year Ended December 31, 2006		
Retained earnings, January 1, 2006		$ 3 2 0 5 00
Net income for the year	$59 5 9 5 00	
Less dividends	24 0 0 0 00	
Increase in retained earnings		35 5 9 5 00
Retained earnings, December 31, 2006		$38 8 0 0 00

For NetSolutions, the amount of dividends was less than the net income. If the dividends had exceeded the net income, the order of the net income and the dividends could have been reversed. The difference between the two items would then be deducted from the beginning Retained Earnings balance. Other factors, such as a net loss, may also require some change in the form of the retained earnings statement, as shown in the following example:

Retained earnings, January 1, 20—		$45,000
Net loss for the year	$5,600	
Dividends	9,500	
Decrease in retained earnings		15,100
Retained earnings, December 31, 20—		$29,900

Some accountants prefer to debit dividends directly to Retained Earnings. When you are preparing a retained earnings statement and there is no dividends account in the ledger, you will need to refer to the retained earnings account to determine the beginning balance of Retained Earnings and the amount of the dividends paid during the period.

Balance Sheet

The balance sheet in Exhibit 6 was expanded by adding subsections for current assets; property, plant, and equipment; and current liabilities. Such a balance sheet is a *classified* balance sheet. In the following paragraphs, we describe some of the sections and subsections that may be used in a balance sheet. We will introduce additional sections in later chapters.

Assets

Assets are commonly divided into classes for presentation on the balance sheet. Two of these classes are (1) current assets and (2) property, plant, and equipment.

> Two common classes of assets are current assets and property, plant, and equipment.

Current Assets   Cash and other assets that are expected to be converted to cash or sold or used up usually within one year or less, through the normal operations of the business, are called **current assets**. In addition to cash, the current assets usually owned by a service business are notes receivable, accounts receivable, supplies, and other prepaid expenses.

Notes receivable are amounts customers owe. They are written promises to pay the amount of the note and possibly interest at an agreed-upon rate. Accounts receivable are also amounts customers owe, but they are less formal than notes and do not provide for interest. Accounts receivable normally result from providing services or selling merchandise on account. Notes receivable and accounts receivable are current assets because they will usually be converted to cash within one year or less.

Property, Plant, and Equipment   The **property, plant, and equipment** section may also be described as **fixed assets** or **plant assets**. These assets include equipment, machinery, buildings, and land. With the exception of land, as we discussed in Chapter 3, fixed assets depreciate over a period of time. The cost, accumulated depreciation, and book value of each major type of fixed asset is normally reported on the balance sheet or in accompanying notes.

Liabilities

Liabilities are the amounts the business owes to creditors. The two most common classes of liabilities are (1) current liabilities and (2) long-term liabilities.

> Two common classes of liabilities are current liabilities and long-term liabilities.

Current Liabilities   Liabilities that will be due within a short time (usually one year or less) and that are to be paid out of current assets are called **current liabilities**. The most common liabilities in this group are notes payable and accounts payable. Other current liability accounts commonly found in the ledger are Wages Payable, Interest Payable, Taxes Payable, and Unearned Fees.

Long-Term Liabilities   Liabilities that will not be due for a long time (usually more than one year) are called **long-term liabilities**. If NetSolutions had long-term liabilities, they would be reported below the current liabilities. As long-term liabilities come due and are to be paid within one year, they are classified as current liabilities. If they are to be renewed rather than paid, they would continue to be classified as long-term. When an asset is pledged as security for a liability, the obligation may be called a *mortgage note payable* or a *mortgage payable*.

Stockholders' Equity

The stockholders' right to the assets of the business is presented on the balance sheet below the liabilities section. The stockholders' equity is added to the total liabilities, and this total must be equal to the total assets.

Adjusting and Closing Entries

objective **4**

Prepare the adjusting and closing entries from a work sheet.

As we discussed in Chapter 3, the adjusting entries are recorded in the journal at the end of the accounting period. If a work sheet has been prepared, the data for these entries are in the Adjustments columns. For NetSolutions, the adjusting entries prepared from the work sheet are shown in Exhibit 7.

After the adjusting entries have been posted to NetSolutions' ledger, shown in Exhibit 11 (on pages 153–157), the ledger is in agreement with the data reported on the financial statements. The balances of the accounts reported on the balance sheet are carried forward from year to year. Because they are relatively permanent, these accounts are called **real accounts**. The balances of the accounts reported on the income statement are *not* carried forward from year to year. Likewise, the balance of the dividends account, which is reported on the retained earnings statement, is not carried forward. Because these accounts report amounts for only one period, they are called **temporary accounts** or **nominal accounts**.

•Exhibit 7

Adjusting Entries for NetSolutions

	Date		Description	Post. Ref.	Debit	Credit	
JOURNAL						Page 5	
1			Adjusting Entries				1
2	2005 Dec.	31	Supplies Expense	55	1 2 4 0 00		2
3			Supplies	14		1 2 4 0 00	3
4							4
5		31	Insurance Expense	56	1 0 0 00		5
6			Prepaid Insurance	15		1 0 0 00	6
7							7
8		31	Unearned Rent	23	1 2 0 00		8
9			Rent Revenue	42		1 2 0 00	9
10							10
11		31	Wages Expense	51	2 5 0 00		11
12			Wages Payable	22		2 5 0 00	12
13							13
14		31	Accounts Receivable	12	5 0 0 00		14
15			Fees Earned	41		5 0 0 00	15
16							16
17		31	Depreciation Expense	53	5 0 00		17
18			Accumulated Depreciation—				18
19			Office Equipment	19		5 0 00	19

Closing entries transfer the balances of temporary accounts to the retained earnings account.

To report amounts for only one period, temporary accounts should have zero balances at the beginning of a period. How are these balances converted to zero? The revenue and expense account balances are transferred to an account called **Income Summary**. The balance of Income Summary is then transferred to the retained earnings account. The balance of the dividends account is also transferred to the retained earnings account. The entries that transfer these balances are called **closing entries**. The transfer process is called the **closing process**. Exhibit 8 is a diagram of this process.

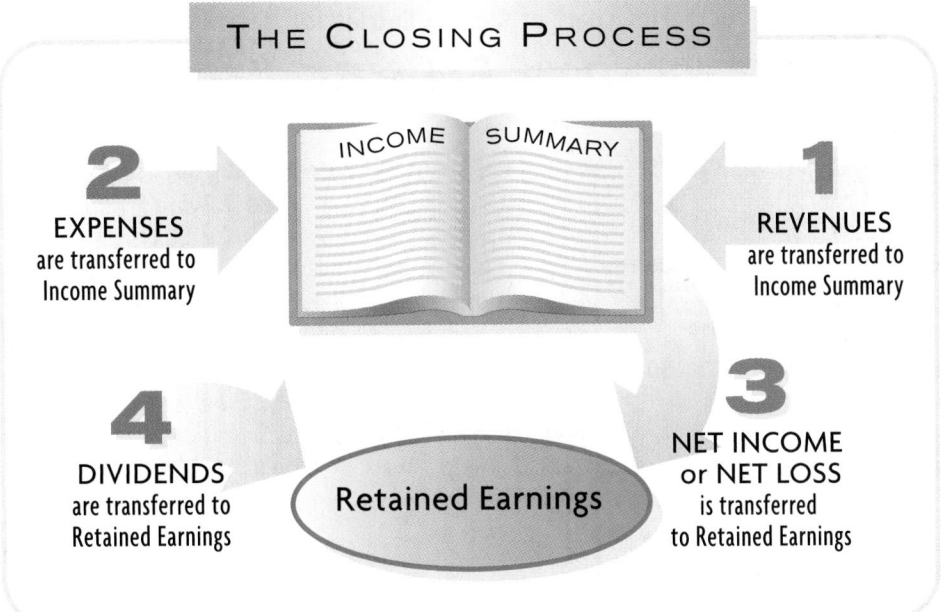

•Exhibit 8

THE CLOSING PROCESS

2 EXPENSES are transferred to Income Summary

1 REVENUES are transferred to Income Summary

INCOME SUMMARY

4 DIVIDENDS are transferred to Retained Earnings

Retained Earnings

3 NET INCOME or NET LOSS is transferred to Retained Earnings

> **The income summary account does <u>not</u> appear on the financial statements.**

You should note that Income Summary is used only at the end of the period. At the beginning of the closing process, Income Summary has no balance. During the closing process, Income Summary will be debited and credited for various amounts. At the end of the closing process, Income Summary will again have no balance. Because Income Summary has the effect of clearing the revenue and expense accounts of their balances, it is sometimes called a **_clearing account_**.

Other titles used for this account include Revenue and Expense Summary, Profit and Loss Summary, and Income and Expense Summary.

It is possible to close the temporary revenue and expense accounts without using a clearing account such as Income Summary. In this case, the balances of the revenue and expense accounts are closed directly to the retained earnings account. This process is automatic in a computerized accounting system. In a manual system, the use of an income summary account aids in detecting and correcting errors.

Journalizing and Posting Closing Entries

Four closing entries are required at the end of an accounting period, as outlined in Exhibit 8. The account titles and balances needed in preparing these entries may be obtained from the work sheet, the income statement and the retained earnings statement, or the ledger. If a work sheet is used, the data for the first two entries appear in the Income Statement columns. The amount for the third entry is the net income or net loss appearing at the bottom of the work sheet. The amount for the fourth entry is the dividends account balance that appears in the Balance Sheet Debit column of the work sheet.

A flowchart of the closing entries for NetSolutions is shown in Exhibit 9. The balances in the accounts are those shown in the Adjusted Trial Balance columns of the work sheet in Exhibit 3.

The closing entries for NetSolutions are shown in Exhibit 10. After the closing entries have been posted to the ledger, as shown in Exhibit 11 (on pages 153–157), the balance in the retained earnings account will agree with the amount reported on the retained earnings statement and the balance sheet. In addition, the revenue, expense, and dividend accounts will have zero balances.

After the entry to close an account has been posted, a line should be inserted in both balance columns opposite the final entry. The next period's transactions for the revenue, expense, and dividends accounts will be posted directly below the closing entry.

If total revenues are $600,000, total expenses are $525,000, and dividends are $50,000, what is the balance of the income summary account that is closed to retained earnings?

$75,000 ($600,000 − $525,000). The dividends account balance is closed directly to retained earnings, rather than to Income Summary.

•Exhibit 9   Flowchart of Closing Entries for NetSolutions

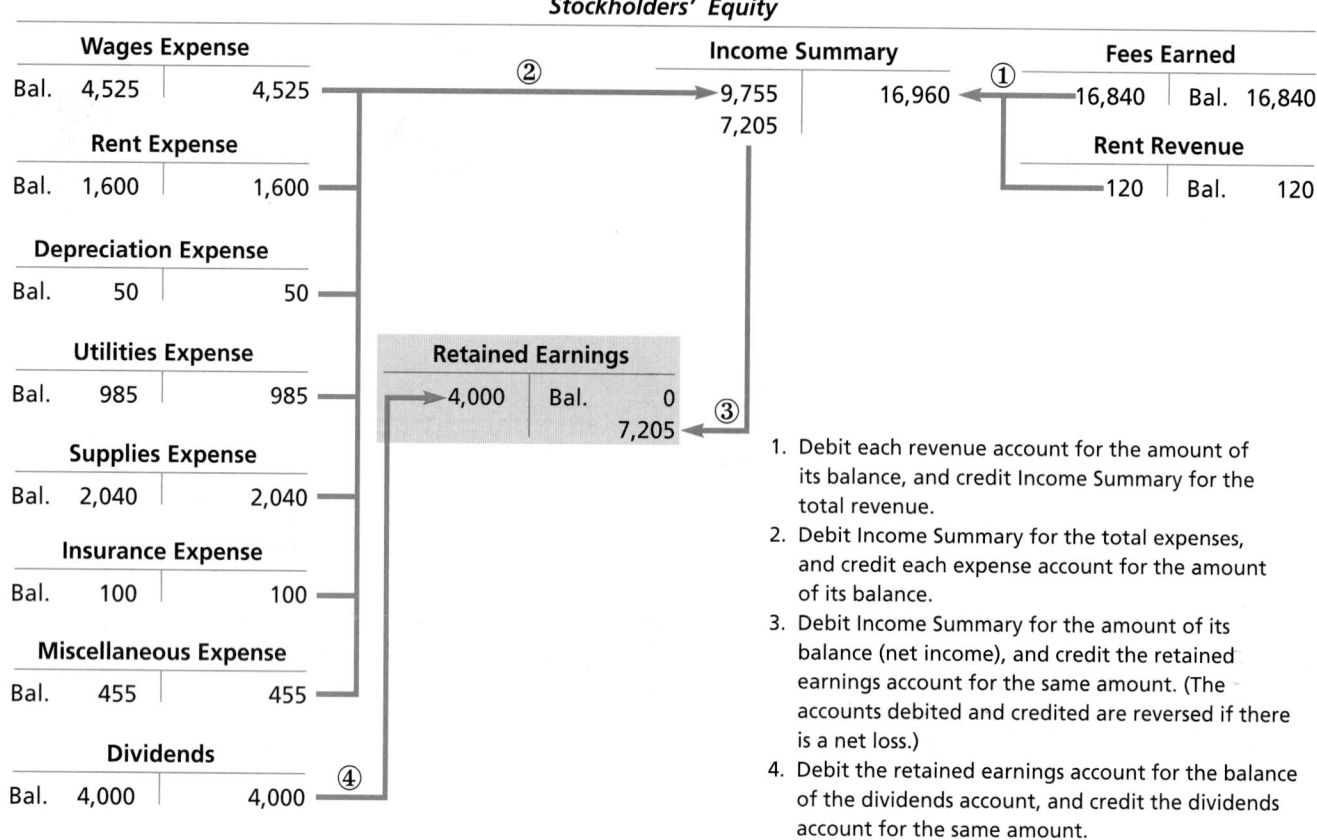

Stockholders' Equity

Wages Expense
Bal. 4,525 | 4,525

Rent Expense
Bal. 1,600 | 1,600

Depreciation Expense
Bal. 50 | 50

Utilities Expense
Bal. 985 | 985

Supplies Expense
Bal. 2,040 | 2,040

Insurance Expense
Bal. 100 | 100

Miscellaneous Expense
Bal. 455 | 455

Dividends
Bal. 4,000 | 4,000

Income Summary
② | 9,755 | 16,960 ← ①
7,205

Fees Earned
16,840 | Bal. 16,840

Rent Revenue
120 | Bal. 120

Retained Earnings
4,000 | Bal. 0
③ 7,205

1. Debit each revenue account for the amount of its balance, and credit Income Summary for the total revenue.
2. Debit Income Summary for the total expenses, and credit each expense account for the amount of its balance.
3. Debit Income Summary for the amount of its balance (net income), and credit the retained earnings account for the same amount. (The accounts debited and credited are reversed if there is a net loss.)
4. Debit the retained earnings account for the balance of the dividends account, and credit the dividends account for the same amount.

•Exhibit 10   Closing Entries for NetSolutions

	JOURNAL				Page 6
Date	Description	Post. Ref.	Debit	Credit	
1	Closing Entries				1
2005 Dec. 31	Fees Earned	41	16 84 0 00		2
	Rent Revenue	42	1 20 00		3
	Income Summary	34		16 96 0 00	4
					5
31	Income Summary	34	9 75 5 00		6
	Wages Expense	51		4 52 5 00	7
	Rent Expense	52		1 60 0 00	8
	Depreciation Expense	53		5 0 00	9
	Utilities Expense	54		9 85 00	10
	Supplies Expense	55		2 04 0 00	11
	Insurance Expense	56		1 00 00	12
	Miscellaneous Expense	59		4 55 00	13
					14
31	Income Summary	34	7 20 5 00		15
	Retained Earnings	32		7 20 5 00	16
					17
31	Retained Earnings	32	4 00 0 00		18
	Dividends	33		4 00 0 00	19

•Exhibit 11   Ledger for NetSolutions

LEDGER

ACCOUNT *Cash*   **ACCOUNT NO. 11**

Date		Item	Post. Ref.	Debit	Credit	Balance Debit	Balance Credit
2005 Nov.	1		1	25 00 0 00		25 00 0 00	
	5		1		20 00 0 00	5 00 0 00	
	18		1	7 50 0 00		12 50 0 00	
	30		1		3 65 0 00	8 85 0 00	
	30		1		9 50 00	7 90 0 00	
	30		2		2 00 0 00	5 90 0 00	
Dec.	1		2		2 40 0 00	3 50 0 00	
	1		2		8 00 00	2 70 0 00	
	1		2	3 60 00		3 06 0 00	
	6		2		1 80 00	2 88 0 00	
	11		2		4 00 00	2 48 0 00	
	13		3		9 50 00	1 53 0 00	
	16		3	3 10 0 00		4 63 0 00	
	20		3		9 00 00	3 73 0 00	
	21		3	6 50 00		4 38 0 00	
	23		3		1 45 0 00	2 93 0 00	
	27		3		1 20 0 00	1 73 0 00	
	31		3		3 10 00	1 42 0 00	
	31		4		2 25 00	1 19 5 00	
	31		4	2 87 0 00		4 06 5 00	
	31		4		2 00 0 00	2 06 5 00	

ACCOUNT *Accounts Receivable*   **ACCOUNT NO. 12**

Date		Item	Post. Ref.	Debit	Credit	Balance Debit	Balance Credit
2005 Dec.	16		3	1 75 0 00		1 75 0 00	
	21		3		6 50 00	1 10 0 00	
	31		4	1 12 0 00		2 22 0 00	
	31	Adjusting	5	5 00 00		2 72 0 00	

ACCOUNT *Supplies*   **ACCOUNT NO. 14**

Date		Item	Post. Ref.	Debit	Credit	Balance Debit	Balance Credit
2005 Nov.	10		1	1 35 0 00		1 35 0 00	
	30		1		8 00 00	5 50 00	
	23		3	1 45 0 00		2 00 0 00	
Dec.	31	Adjusting	5		1 24 0 00	7 60 00	

b. Enter the adjusting entries into the work sheet, based upon the adjustment data.
c. Add the Debit and Credit columns of the unadjusted Trial Balance columns of the work sheet to verify that the totals are equal.
d. Enter the amount of net income or net loss for the period in the proper Income Statement column and Balance Sheet column.
e. Add the Debit and Credit columns of the Balance Sheet and Income Statement columns of the work sheet to verify that the totals are equal.
f. Enter the unadjusted account balances from the general ledger into the unadjusted Trial Balance columns of the work sheet.
g. Add or deduct adjusting entry data to trial balance amounts and extend amounts to the Adjusted Trial Balance columns.
h. Add the Debit and Credit columns of the Adjustments columns of the work sheet to verify that the totals are equal.
i. Add the Debit and Credit columns of the Balance Sheet and Income Statement columns of the work sheet to determine the amount of net income or net loss for the period.
j. Add the Debit and Credit columns of the Adjusted Trial Balance columns of the work sheet to verify that the totals are equal.

Indicate the order in which the preceding steps would be performed in preparing and completing a work sheet.

EXERCISE 4-5
Adjustment data on work sheet

Objective 2

SPREADSHEET

✓ *Total debits of Adjustments column: $24*

Ithaca Services Co. offers cleaning services to business clients. The trial balance for Ithaca Services Co. has been prepared on the work sheet for the year ended January 31, 2006, shown below.

Ithaca Services Co.
Work Sheet
For the Year Ended January 31, 2006

Account Title	Trial Balance Dr.	Trial Balance Cr.	Adjustments Dr.	Adjustments Cr.	Adjusted Trial Balance Dr.	Adjusted Trial Balance Cr.
Cash	8					
Accounts Receivable	50					
Supplies	8					
Prepaid Insurance	12					
Land	50					
Equipment	32					
Accumulated Depr.—Equip.		2				
Accounts Payable		26				
Wages Payable		0				
Capital Stock		20				
Retained Earnings		92				
Dividends	8					
Fees Earned		60				
Wages Expense	16					
Rent Expense	8					
Insurance Expense	0					
Utilities Expense	6					
Depreciation Expense	0					
Supplies Expense	0					
Miscellaneous Expense	2					
Totals	200	200				

The data for year-end adjustments are as follows:

a. Fees earned, but not yet billed, $7.
b. Supplies on hand, $3.
c. Insurance premiums expired, $6.
d. Depreciation expense, $5.
e. Wages accrued, but not paid, $1.

Enter the adjustment data, and place the balances in the Adjusted Trial Balance columns.

EXERCISE 4-6
Complete a work sheet
Objective 2

SPREADSHEET

✓*Net income: $18*

Ithaca Services Co. offers cleaning services to business clients. Complete the following work sheet for Ithaca Services Co.

Ithaca Services Co.
Work Sheet
For the Year Ended January 31, 2006

Account Title	Adjusted Trial Balance Dr.	Adjusted Trial Balance Cr.	Income Statement Dr.	Income Statement Cr.	Balance Sheet Dr.	Balance Sheet Cr.
Cash	8					
Accounts Receivable	57					
Supplies	3					
Prepaid Insurance	6					
Land	50					
Equipment	32					
Accumulated Depr.—Equip.		7				
Accounts Payable		26				
Wages Payable		1				
Capital Stock		20				
Retained Earnings		92				
Dividends	8					
Fees Earned		67				
Wages Expense	17					
Rent Expense	8					
Insurance Expense	6					
Utilities Expense	6					
Depreciation Expense	5					
Supplies Expense	5					
Miscellaneous Expense	2					
Totals	213	213				
Net income (loss)						

EXERCISE 4-7
Financial statements
Objective 3

SPREADSHEET

✓*Retained earnings, Jan. 31, 2006: $102*

Based upon the data in Exercise 4-6, prepare an income statement, retained earnings statement, and balance sheet for Ithaca Services Co.

EXERCISE 4-8
Adjusting entries
Objective 4

Based upon the data in Exercise 4-5, prepare the adjusting entries for Ithaca Services Co.

EXERCISE 4-9
Closing entries
Objective 4

Based upon the data in Exercise 4-6, prepare the closing entries for Ithaca Services Co.

EXERCISE 4-10
Income statement
Objective 3

The following account balances were taken from the Adjusted Trial Balance columns of the work sheet for Larynx Messenger Service, a delivery service firm, for the current fiscal year ended June 30, 2006:

SPREADSHEET

Fees Earned	$273,700	Supplies Expense	$2,750
Salaries Expense	77,100	Miscellaneous Expense	1,350
Rent Expense	22,500	Insurance Expense	1,500
Utilities Expense	6,500	Depreciation Expense	5,200

Prepare an income statement.

EXERCISE 4-11
Income statement; net loss
Objective 3

SPREADSHEET

The following revenue and expense account balances were taken from the ledger of Sirocco Services Co. after the accounts had been adjusted on March 31, 2006, the end of the current fiscal year:

Depreciation Expense	$ 8,000	Service Revenue	$103,850
Insurance Expense	4,100	Supplies Expense	3,100
Miscellaneous Expense	2,250	Utilities Expense	11,500
Rent Expense	21,270	Wages Expense	56,800

Prepare an income statement.

EXERCISE 4-12
Income statement
Objective 3

REAL WORLD   INTERNET

SPREADSHEET

✓ *a. Net income: $443*

FedEx Corporation had the following revenue and expense account balances (in millions) at its fiscal year-end of May 31, 2002:

Rentals and Landing Fees	$1,524	Depreciation and Amortization	$ 806
Maintenance and Repairs	980	Interest Expense	56
Purchased Transportation	562	Revenues	15,327
Fuel	1,009	Provision for Income Taxes	260
Salaries and Employee Benefits	6,467	Other Expenses	52
Other Operating Expenses	3,168		

a. Prepare an income statement.
b.  Compare your income statement with the 2002 income statement that is available at the FedEx Corporation Web site, which is linked to the text's Web site at **http://warren.swlearning.com**. What similarities and differences do you see?

EXERCISE 4-13
Retained earnings statement
Objective 3

SPREADSHEET

✓ *Retained earnings, Oct. 31, 2006: $206,000*

Synthesis Systems Co. offers its services to residents in the Dillon City area. Selected accounts from the ledger of Synthesis Systems Co. for the current fiscal year ended October 31, 2006, are as follows:

Retained Earnings				Dividends			
Oct. 31	12,000	Nov. 1 (2005)	173,750	Jan. 31	3,000	Oct. 31	12,000
		Oct. 31	44,250	Apr. 30	3,000		
				July 31	3,000		
				Oct. 31	3,000		

Income Summary			
Oct. 31	277,150	Oct. 31	321,400
31	44,250		

Prepare a retained earnings statement for the year.

EXERCISE 4-14
Retained earnings statement; net loss
Objective 3

SPREADSHEET

Selected accounts from the ledger of Bobcat Sports for the current fiscal year ended August 31, 2006, are as follows:

Retained Earnings				Dividends			
Aug. 31	16,000	Sep. 1 (2005)	210,300	Nov. 30	4,000	Aug. 31	16,000
31	49,650			Feb. 28	4,000		
				May 31	4,000		
				Aug. 31	4,000		

Income Summary

Aug. 31	224,900	Aug. 31	175,250
		31	49,650

✓ *Retained earnings, Aug. 31, 2006: $144,650*

Prepare a retained earnings statement for the year.

EXERCISE 4-15
Classify assets
Objective 3

Identify each of the following as (a) a current asset or (b) property, plant, and equipment:

1. Cash
2. Equipment
3. Accounts receivable
4. Building
5. Prepaid insurance
6. Supplies

EXERCISE 4-16
Balance sheet classification
Objective 3

At the balance sheet date, a business owes a mortgage note payable of $500,000, the terms of which provide for monthly payments of $13,750.

Explain how the liability should be classified on the balance sheet.

EXERCISE 4-17
Balance sheet
Objective 3

SPREADSHEET

✓ *Total assets: $126,650*

Tudor Co. offers personal weight reduction consulting services to individuals. After all the accounts have been closed on April 30, 2006, the end of the current fiscal year, the balances of selected accounts from the ledger of Tudor Co. are as follows:

Accounts Payable	$ 9,500	Prepaid Insurance	$ 7,200
Accounts Receivable	21,850	Prepaid Rent	4,800
Accumulated Depreciation—		Retained Earnings	74,200
Equipment	21,100	Salaries Payable	1,750
Capital Stock	40,000	Supplies	1,800
Cash	?	Unearned Fees	1,200
Equipment	80,600		

Prepare a classified balance sheet that includes the correct balance for Cash.

EXERCISE 4-18
Balance sheet
Objective 3

SPREADSHEET   WHAT'S WRONG WITH THIS?

✓ *Corrected balance sheet, total assets: $140,500*

List the errors you find in the following balance sheet. Prepare a corrected balance sheet.

Warburg Services Co.
Balance Sheet
For the Year Ended May 31, 2006

Assets			Liabilities		
Current assets:			Current liabilities:		
Cash	$ 4,170		Accounts receivable	$ 12,500	
Accounts payable	7,250		Accum. depr.—building	23,000	
Supplies	1,650		Accum. depr.—equipment	16,000	
Prepaid insurance	2,400		Net loss	10,000	
Land	75,000		Total liabilities	$ 61,500	
Total current assets		$ 90,470			
Property, plant,			**Stockholders' Equity**		
and equipment:			Wages payable	$ 1,500	
Building	$ 55,500		Capital stock	35,000	
Equipment	28,280		Retained earnings	96,750	
Total property, plant,			Total stockholders' equity	$133,250	
and equipment		$104,280	Total liabilities and		
Total assets		$194,750	stockholders' equity	$194,750	

EXERCISE 4-19
Adjusting entries from work sheet
Objective 4

Green Earth Co. is a consulting firm specializing in pollution control. The entries in the Adjustments columns of the work sheet for Green Earth Co. are as follows.

	Adjustments	
	Dr.	**Cr.**
Accounts Receivable	4,100	
Supplies		1,300
Prepaid Insurance		2,000
Accumulated Depreciation—Equipment		2,800
Wages Payable		1,000
Unearned Rent	2,500	
Fees Earned		4,100
Wages Expense	1,000	
Supplies Expense	1,300	
Rent Revenue		2,500
Insurance Expense	2,000	
Depreciation Expense	2,800	

Prepare the adjusting journal entries.

EXERCISE 4-20
Identify accounts to be closed
Objective 4

From the following list, identify the accounts that should be closed to Income Summary at the end of the fiscal year:

a. Accounts Payable
b. Accumulated Depreciation—
    Equipment
c. Capital Stock
d. Depreciation Expense—Equipment
e. Dividends
f. Equipment
g. Fees Earned
h. Land
i. Salaries Expense
j. Salaries Payable
k. Supplies
l. Supplies Expense

EXERCISE 4-21
Closing entries
Objective 4

Prior to its closing, Income Summary had total debits of $450,750 and total credits of $712,500.

➤ Briefly explain the purpose served by the income summary account and the nature of the entries that resulted in the $450,750 and the $712,500.

EXERCISE 4-22
Closing entries with net income
Objective 4
✓ b. $284,900

After all revenue and expense accounts have been closed at the end of the fiscal year, Income Summary has a debit of $312,600 and a credit of $480,150. At the same date, Retained Earnings has a credit balance of $142,350, and Dividends has a balance of $25,000. (a) Journalize the entries required to complete the closing of the accounts. (b) Determine the amount of Retained Earnings at the end of the period.

EXERCISE 4-23
Closing entries with net loss
Objective 4

Edessa Services Co. offers its services to individuals desiring to improve their personal images. After the accounts have been adjusted at March 31, the end of the fiscal year, the following balances were taken from the ledger of Edessa Services Co.

Retained Earnings	$225,750
Dividends	50,000
Fees Earned	180,700
Wages Expense	180,000
Rent Expense	75,000
Supplies Expense	24,000
Miscellaneous Expense	6,200

Journalize the four entries required to close the accounts.

EXERCISE 4-24
Identify permanent accounts
Objective 4

Which of the following accounts will usually appear in the post-closing trial balance?

a. Accounts Receivable
b. Accumulated Depreciation
c. Capital Stock
d. Cash
e. Depreciation Expense
f. Dividends
g. Equipment
h. Fees Earned
i. Retained Earnings
j. Supplies
k. Wages Expense
l. Wages Payable

EXERCISE 4-25
Post-closing trial balance

Objective 4

SPREADSHEET   WHAT'S WRONG
WITH THIS?

✓ *Correct column totals,
$107,505*

An accountant prepared the following post-closing trial balance:

Rhombic Repairs Co.
Post-Closing Trial Balance
March 31, 2006

Cash	9,225	
Accounts Receivable	33,300	
Supplies		1,980
Equipment		63,000
Accumulated Depreciation—Equipment	19,980	
Accounts Payable	11,250	
Salaries Payable		2,700
Unearned Rent	5,400	
Capital Stock	18,000	
Retained Earnings	50,175	
	147,330	67,680

Prepare a corrected post-closing trial balance. Assume that all accounts have normal balances and that the amounts shown are correct.

EXERCISE 4-26
*Working capital and
current ratio*

Objective 6

REAL WORLD

The financial statements for **The Home Depot** are presented in Appendix F at the end of the text.

a. Determine the working capital (in millions) and the current ratio for Home Depot as of February 2, 2003 and February 3, 2002.

b. ➤ What conclusions concerning the company's ability to meets its financial obligations can you draw from these data?

EXERCISE 4-27
*Working capital and
current ratio*

Objective 6

The following data (in thousands) were taken from recent financial statements of **7 Eleven, Inc.**, a convenience store chain:

	December 31	
	2002	**2001**
Current assets	$624,176	$632,247
Current liabilities	767,210	791,700

a. Compute the working capital and the current ratio as of December 31, 2002 and 2001. Round to two decimal places.

b. What conclusions concerning the company's ability to meet its financial obligations can you draw from (a)?

**APPENDIX
EXERCISE 4-28**
*Adjusting and reversing
entries*

On the basis of the following data, (a) journalize the adjusting entries at December 31, the end of the current fiscal year, and (b) journalize the reversing entries on January 1, the first day of the following year.

1. Sales salaries are uniformly $16,200 for a five-day workweek, ending on Friday. The last payday of the year was Friday, December 27.
2. Accrued fees earned but not recorded at December 31, $10,250.

**APPENDIX
EXERCISE 4-29**
*Entries posted to the wages
expense account*

Portions of the wages expense account of a business are shown at the top of the following page.

a. Indicate the nature of the entry (payment, adjusting, closing, reversing) from which each numbered posting was made.

b. Journalize the complete entry from which each numbered posting was made.

ACCOUNT	Wages Expense				ACCOUNT NO. 53		
		Post.				Balance	
Date	Item	Ref.	Dr.	Cr.	Dr.	Cr.
2006						
Dec. 26	(1)	91	45,000		1,102,800	
31	(2)	92	18,000		1,120,800	
31	(3)	93		1,120,800	—	—
2007						
Jan. 1	(4)	94		18,000		18,000
2	(5)	95	43,000		25,000	

Problems Series A

PROBLEM 4-1A
Work sheet and related items

Objectives 2, 3, 4

SPREADSHEET

P.A.S.S.

✓ 2. Net income: $25,100

The trial balance of Dynamite Laundry at July 31, 2006, the end of the current fiscal year, and the data needed to determine year-end adjustments are as follows:

Dynamite Laundry
Trial Balance
July 31, 2006

Cash	2,900	
Laundry Supplies	7,500	
Prepaid Insurance	4,800	
Laundry Equipment	109,050	
Accumulated Depreciation		41,100
Accounts Payable		6,100
Capital Stock		10,000
Retained Earnings		27,800
Dividends	2,000	
Laundry Revenue		165,000
Wages Expense	71,400	
Rent Expense	36,000	
Utilities Expense	13,650	
Miscellaneous Expense	2,700	
	250,000	250,000

a. Wages accrued but not paid at July 31 are $1,200.
b. Depreciation of equipment during the year is $6,800.
c. Laundry supplies on hand at July 31 are $1,750.
d. Insurance premiums expired during the year are $2,400.

Instructions
1. Enter the trial balance on a ten-column work sheet and complete the work sheet. Add accounts as needed.
2. Prepare an income statement, a retained earnings statement, and a balance sheet.
3. On the basis of the adjustment data in the work sheet, journalize the adjusting entries.
4. On the basis of the data in the work sheet, journalize the closing entries.

PROBLEM 4-2A
Adjusting and closing entries; retained earnings statement

Objectives 3, 4

The Xavier Company is a financial planning services firm owned and operated by Kim Bosworth. As of August 31, 2006, the end of the current fiscal year, the accountant for The Xavier Company prepared a work sheet, part of which is shown on the following page.

✓ *2. Retained earnings,*
Aug. 31: $149,000

The Xavier Company
Work Sheet (Partial)
August 31, 2006

	Income Statement		Balance Sheet	
Cash			4,650	
Accounts Receivable			13,960	
Supplies			2,800	
Prepaid Insurance			2,500	
Land			60,000	
Buildings			120,000	
Accumulated Depreciation—Buildings				72,400
Equipment			86,090	
Accumulated Depreciation—Equipment				40,900
Accounts Payable				7,100
Salaries Payable				1,100
Taxes Payable				4,000
Unearned Rent				500
Capital Stock				15,000
Retained Earnings				98,500
Dividends			10,000	
Service Fees Earned		175,000		
Rent Revenue		1,500		
Salary Expense	73,000			
Depreciation Expense—Equipment	9,500			
Rent Expense	8,500			
Supplies Expense	7,650			
Utilities Expense	5,300			
Depreciation Expense—Buildings	5,200			
Taxes Expense	4,150			
Insurance Expense	1,000			
Miscellaneous Expense	1,700			
	116,000	176,500	300,000	239,500
Net income	60,500			60,500
	176,500	176,500	300,000	300,000

Instructions

1. Journalize the entries that were required to close the accounts at August 31.
2. Prepare a retained earnings statement for the fiscal year ended August 31.
3. If the balance of Retained Earnings decreased $15,000 after the closing entries were posted, and the dividends remained the same, what was the amount of net income or net loss?

If the working papers correlating with this textbook are not used, omit Problem 4-3A.

PROBLEM 4-3A
Ledger accounts and work sheet, and related items
Objectives 2, 3, 4

✓ *2. Net income: $18,017*

The ledger and trial balance of Lithium Services Co. as of March 31, 2006, the end of the first month of its current fiscal year, are presented in the working papers.

Instructions

1. Complete the ten-column work sheet. Data needed to determine the necessary adjusting entries are as follows:
    a. Service revenue accrued at March 31 is $1,500.
    b. Supplies on hand at March 31 are $300.
    c. Insurance premiums expired during March are $150.
    d. Depreciation of the building during March is $625.
    e. Depreciation of equipment during March is $200.
    f. Unearned rent at March 31 is $2,100.
    g. Wages accrued but not paid at March 31 are $501.
2. Prepare an income statement, a retained earnings statement, and a balance sheet.
3. Journalize and post the adjusting entries, inserting balances in the accounts affected.

(continued)

4. Journalize and post the closing entries. Indicate closed accounts by inserting a line in both Balance columns opposite the closing entry.

5. Prepare a post-closing trial balance.

PROBLEM 4-4A
Optional work sheet and financial statements

Objectives 2, 3, 4

SPREADSHEET

P.A.S.S.

✓ *4. Net loss: $6,720*

Heritage Company offers legal consulting advice to death-row inmates. Heritage Company prepared the following trial balance at April 30, 2006, the end of the current fiscal year:

Heritage Company
Trial Balance
April 30, 2006

Cash	3,200	
Accounts Receivable	10,500	
Prepaid Insurance	1,800	
Supplies	1,350	
Land	50,000	
Building	136,500	
Accumulated Depreciation—Building		50,700
Equipment	92,700	
Accumulated Depreciation—Equipment		36,300
Accounts Payable		6,500
Unearned Rent		3,000
Capital Stock		50,000
Retained Earnings		162,500
Dividends	10,000	
Fees Revenue		191,000
Salaries and Wages Expense	96,200	
Advertising Expense	63,200	
Utilities Expense	18,000	
Repairs Expense	12,500	
Miscellaneous Expense	4,050	
	500,000	500,000

The data needed to determine year-end adjustments are as follows:

a. Accrued fees revenue at April 30 are $2,800.
b. Insurance expired during the year is $450.
c. Supplies on hand at April 30 are $650.
d. Depreciation of building for the year is $1,620.
e. Depreciation of equipment for the year is $3,500.
f. Accrued salaries and wages at April 30 are $1,800.
g. Unearned rent at April 30 is $1,500.

Instructions

1. **Optional:** Enter the trial balance on a ten-column work sheet and complete the work sheet. Add accounts as needed.
2. Journalize the adjusting entires, adding accounts as needed.
3. Prepare an adjusted trial balance of April 30, 2006.
4. Prepare an income statement for the year ended April 30.
5. Prepare a retained earnings statement for the year ended April 30.
6. Prepare a balance sheet as of April 30.
7. Compute the percent of total revenue to total assets for the year.

PROBLEM 4-5A
Ledger accounts, optional work sheet, and related items

Objectives 2, 3, 4

The trial balance of Pablo Repairs at December 31, 2006, the end of the current year, is shown at the top of the following page.

✓ 2. Net income: $16,245

Pablo Repairs
Trial Balance
December 31, 2006

11	Cash	2,825	
13	Supplies	5,820	
14	Prepaid Insurance	2,500	
16	Equipment	44,200	
17	Accumulated Depreciation—Equipment		12,050
18	Trucks	45,000	
19	Accumulated Depreciation—Trucks		27,100
21	Accounts Payable		2,015
31	Capital Stock		12,000
32	Retained Earnings		20,885
33	Dividends	5,000	
41	Service Revenue		75,950
51	Wages Expense	28,010	
53	Rent Expense	8,100	
55	Truck Expense	6,350	
59	Miscellaneous Expense	2,195	
		150,000	150,000

The data needed to determine year-end adjustments are as follows:

a. Supplies on hand at December 31 are $1,250.
b. Insurance premiums expired during year are $1,000.
c. Depreciation of equipment during year is $5,080.
d. Depreciation of trucks during year is $3,500.
e. Wages accrued but not paid at December 31 are $900.

Instructions

1. For each account listed in the trial balance, enter the balance in the appropriate Balance column of a four-column account and place a check mark (✓) in the Posting Reference column.
2. **Optional:** Enter the trial balance on a ten-column work sheet and complete the work sheet. Add accounts as needed.
3. Journalize and post the adjusting entries, inserting balances in the accounts affected. The following additional accounts from Pablo's chart of accounts should be used: Wages Payable, 22; Supplies Expense, 52; Depreciation Expense—Equipment, 54; Depreciation Expense—Trucks, 56; Insurance Expense, 57.
4. Prepare an adjusted trial balance.
5. Prepare an income statement, a retained earnings statement, and a balance sheet.
6. Journalize and post the closing entries. (Income Summary is account #34 in the chart of accounts.) Indicate closed accounts by inserting a line in both Balance columns opposite the closing entry.
7. Prepare a post-closing trial balance.

Problems Series B

PROBLEM 4-1B
Work sheet and related items

Objectives 2, 3, 4

The trial balance of The Utopia Laundromat at October 31, 2006, the end of the current fiscal year, is shown at the top of the next page.

The data needed to determine year-end adjustments are as follows:

a. Laundry supplies on hand at October 31 are $1,250.
b. Insurance premiums expired during the year are $1,800.
c. Depreciation of equipment during the year is $5,500.
d. Wages accrued but not paid at October 31 are $2,160.

✓ 2. Net income: $10,240

The Utopia Laundromat
Trial Balance
October 31, 2006

Cash	4,600	
Laundry Supplies	7,850	
Prepaid Insurance	3,600	
Laundry Equipment	120,000	
Accumulated Depreciation		62,700
Accounts Payable		4,100
Capital Stock		18,000
Retained Earnings		28,450
Dividends	3,500	
Laundry Revenue		96,750
Wages Expense	43,400	
Rent Expense	16,400	
Utilities Expense	8,500	
Miscellaneous Expense	2,150	
	210,000	210,000

Instructions

1. Enter the trial balance on a ten-column work sheet and complete the work sheet. Add accounts as needed.
2. Prepare an income statement, a retained earnings statement, and a balance sheet.
3. On the basis of the adjustment data in the work sheet, journalize the adjusting entries.
4. On the basis of the data in the work sheet, journalize the closing entries.

PROBLEM 4-2B
Adjusting and closing entries; retained earnings statement

Objectives 3, 4

✓ 2. Retained earnings, June 30: $56,910

The Alligator Company is an investigative services firm that is owned and operated by Bruce Driskell. On June 30, 2006, the end of the current fiscal year, the accountant for The Alligator Company prepared a work sheet, a part of which is shown here.

The Alligator Company
Work Sheet (Partial)
June 30, 2006

	Income Statement		Balance Sheet	
Cash			4,500	
Accounts Receivable			18,600	
Supplies			1,750	
Prepaid Insurance			2,400	
Equipment			84,750	
Accumulated Depreciation—Equipment				26,100
Accounts Payable				5,230
Salaries Payable				1,260
Taxes Payable				1,500
Unearned Rent				1,000
Capital Stock				20,000
Retained Earnings				51,410
Dividends			8,000	
Service Fees Earned		180,000		
Rent Revenue		3,000		
Salary Expense	133,500			
Rent Expense	18,000			
Supplies Expense	4,000			
Depreciation Expense—Equipment	3,500			
Utilities Expense	3,200			
Taxes Expense	3,100			
Insurance Expense	2,400			
Miscellaneous Expense	1,800			
	169,500	183,000	120,000	106,500
Net income	13,500			13,500
	183,000	183,000	120,000	120,000

Instructions
1. Journalize the entries that were required to close the accounts at June 30.
2. Prepare a retained earnings statement for the fiscal year ended June 30, 2006.
3. If Retained Earnings decreased $30,000 after the closing entries were posted, and the dividends remained the same, what was the amount of net income or net loss?

If the working papers correlating with this textbook are not used, omit Problem 4-3B.

PROBLEM 4-3B
Ledger accounts, work sheet, and related items

Objectives 2, 3, 4

✓ *2. Net income: $18,042*

The ledger and trial balance of Lithium Services Co. as of March 31, 2006, the end of the first month of its current fiscal year, are presented in the working papers.

Instructions
1. Complete the ten-column work sheet. Data needed to determine the necessary adjusting entries are as follows:
   a. Service revenue accrued at March 31 is $1,250.
   b. Supplies on hand at March 31 are $400.
   c. Insurance premiums expired during March are $150.
   d. Depreciation of the building during March is $500.
   e. Depreciation of equipment during March is $150.
   f. Unearned rent at March 31 is $2,000.
   g. Wages accrued at March 31 are $601.
2. Prepare an income statement, a retained earnings statement, and a balance sheet.
3. Journalize and post the adjusting entries, inserting balances in the accounts affected.
4. Journalize and post the closing entries. Indicate closed accounts by inserting a line in both Balance columns opposite the closing entry.
5. Prepare a post-closing trial balance.

PROBLEM 4-4B
Optional worksheet and financial statements

Objectives 2, 3, 4

SPREADSHEET
P.A.S.S.

✓ *4. Net income: $69,470*

Flamingo Company maintains and repairs warning lights, such as those found on radio towers and lighthouses. Flamingo Company prepared the following trial balance at July 31, 2006, the end of the current fiscal year:

Flamingo Company
Trial Balance
July 31, 2006

Cash	4,500	
Accounts Receivable	13,500	
Prepaid Insurance	3,000	
Supplies	1,950	
Land	70,000	
Building	100,500	
Accumulated Depreciation—Building		71,700
Equipment	71,400	
Accumulated Depreciation—Equipment		60,800
Accounts Payable		4,100
Unearned Rent		1,500
Capital Stock		5,000
Retained Earnings		50,700
Dividends	4,000	
Fees Revenue		181,200
Salaries and Wages Expense	73,200	
Advertising Expense	15,500	
Utilities Expense	8,100	
Repairs Expense	6,300	
Miscellaneous Expense	3,050	
	375,000	375,000

The data needed to determine year-end adjustments are as follows:

a. Fees revenue accrued at July 31 is $3,500.
b. Insurance expired during the year is $2,000.
c. Supplies on hand at July 31 are $350.
d. Depreciation of building for the year is $1,520.
e. Depreciation of equipment for the year is $2,160.
f. Accrued salaries and wages at July 31 are $2,800.
g. Unearned rent at July 31 is $500.

Instructions

1. **Optional:** Enter the trial balance on a ten-column work sheet and complete the work sheet. Add accounts as needed.
2. Journalize the adjusting entries, adding accounts as needed.
3. Prepare an adjusted trial balance as of July 31, 2006.
4. Prepare an income statement for the year ended July 31.
5. Prepare a retained earnings statement for the year ended July 31.
6. Prepare a balance sheet as of July 31.
7. Compute the percent of net income to total revenue for the year.

PROBLEM 4-5B
Ledger accounts, optional work sheet, and related items

Objectives 2, 3, 4

SPREADSHEET
P.A.S.S.

✓ 5. Net income: $30,080

The trial balance of Gesundheit Repairs at October 31, 2006, the end of the current year, is shown below.

Gesundheit Repairs
Trial Balance
October 31, 2006

11	Cash	3,950	
13	Supplies	6,295	
14	Prepaid Insurance	2,735	
16	Equipment	50,650	
17	Accumulated Depreciation—Equipment		11,209
18	Trucks	36,300	
19	Accumulated Depreciation—Trucks		7,400
21	Accounts Payable		4,015
31	Capital Stock		9,000
32	Retained Earnings		28,426
33	Dividends	6,000	
41	Service Revenue		89,950
51	Wages Expense	26,925	
53	Rent Expense	9,600	
55	Truck Expense	5,350	
59	Miscellaneous Expense	2,195	
		150,000	150,000

The data needed to determine year-end adjustments are as follows:

a. Supplies on hand at October 31 are $1,150.
b. Insurance premiums expired during year are $1,800.
c. Depreciation of equipment during year is $3,380.
d. Depreciation of trucks during year is $4,400.
e. Wages accrued but not paid at October 31 are $1,075.

Instructions

1. For each account listed in the trial balance, enter the balance in the appropriate Balance column of a four-column account and place a check mark (✔) in the Posting Reference column.
2. **Optional:** Enter the trial balance on a ten-column work sheet and complete the work sheet. Add accounts as needed.
3. Journalize and post the adjusting entries, inserting balances in the accounts affected. The following additional accounts from Gesundheit's chart of accounts should be used: Wages Payable, 22; Supplies Expense, 52; Depreciation Expense—Equipment, 54; Depreciation Expense—Trucks, 56; Insurance Expense, 57.

4. Prepare an adjusted trial balance.
5. Prepare an income statement, a retained earnings statement, and a balance sheet.
6. Journalize and post the closing entries. (Income Summary is account #34 in the chart of accounts.) Indicate closed accounts by inserting a line in both Balance columns opposite the closing entry.
7. Prepare a post-closing trial balance.

ontinuing Problem

P.A.S.S.

✓ 2. Net income: $2,550

The unadjusted trial balance of Dancin Music as of May 31, 2006, along with the adjustment data for the two months ended May 31, 2006, are shown in Chapter 3.

Instructions
1. Prepare a ten-column work sheet.
2. Prepare an income statement, a retained earnings statement, and a balance sheet.
3. Journalize and post the closing entries. The income summary account is #34 in the ledger of Dancin Music. Indicate closed accounts by inserting a line in both Balance columns opposite the closing entry.
4. Prepare a post-closing trial balance.

omprehensive Problem 1

P.A.S.S.

✓ 4. Net income: $17,930

For the past several years, Kelly Pitney has operated a part-time consulting business from her home. As of April 1, 2006, Kelly decided to move to rented quarters and to operate the business, which was to be known as Hippocrates Consulting, on a full-time basis. Hippocrates Consulting entered into the following transactions during April:

April 1. The following assets were received from Kelly Pitney in exchange for capital stock: cash, $13,100; accounts receivable, $3,000; supplies, $1,400; and office equipment, $12,500. There were no liabilities received.
1. Paid three months' rent on a lease rental contract, $4,800.
2. Paid the premiums on property and casualty insurance policies, $1,800.
4. Received cash from clients as an advance payment for services to be provided and recorded it as unearned fees, $5,000.
5. Purchased additional office equipment on account from Office Station Co., $2,000.
6. Received cash from clients on account, $1,800.
10. Paid cash for a newspaper advertisement, $120.
12. Paid Office Station Co. for part of the debt incurred on April 5, $1,200.
12. Recorded services provided on account for the period April 1–12, $4,200.
14. Paid part-time receptionist for two weeks' salary, $750.
17. Recorded cash from cash clients for fees earned during the period April 1–16, $6,250.
18. Paid cash for supplies, $800.
20. Recorded services provided on account for the period April 13–20, $2,100.
24. Recorded cash from cash clients for fees earned for the period April 17–24, $3,850.
26. Received cash from clients on account, $5,600.
27. Paid part-time receptionist for two weeks' salary, $750.
29. Paid telephone bill for April, $130.
30. Paid electricity bill for April, $200.

April 30. Recorded cash from cash clients for fees earned for the period April 25–30, $3,050.

    30. Recorded services provided on account for the remainder of April, $1,500.

    30. Paid dividends, $6,000.

Instructions

1. Journalize each transaction in a two-column journal, referring to the following chart of accounts in selecting the accounts to be debited and credited. (Do not insert the account numbers in the journal at this time.)

11	Cash	31	Capital Stock
12	Accounts Receivable	32	Retained Earnings
14	Supplies	33	Dividends
15	Prepaid Rent	41	Fees Earned
16	Prepaid Insurance	51	Salary Expense
18	Office Equipment	52	Rent Expense
19	Accumulated Depreciation	53	Supplies Expense
21	Accounts Payable	54	Depreciation Expense
22	Salaries Payable	55	Insurance Expense
23	Unearned Fees	59	Miscellaneous Expense

2. Post the journal to a ledger of four-column accounts.
3. Prepare a trial balance as of April 30, 2006, on a ten-column work sheet, listing all the accounts in the order given in the ledger. Complete the work sheet, using the following adjustment data:
   a. Insurance expired during April is $300.
   b. Supplies on hand on April 30 are $1,350.
   c. Depreciation of office equipment for April is $700.
   d. Accrued receptionist salary on April 30 is $120.
   e. Rent expired during April is $1,600.
   f. Unearned fees on April 30 are $2,500.
4. Prepare an income statement, a retained earnings statement, and a balance sheet.
5. Journalize and post the adjusting entries.
6. Journalize and post the closing entries. (Income Summary is account #34 in the chart of accounts.) Indicate closed accounts by inserting a line in both Balance columns opposite the closing entry.
7. Prepare a post-closing trial balance.

Alternative Instructions for P.A.S.S.

Complete the above instructions in the following order: 1, 2, 5 (using the adjustment data in 3), and 4.

Special Activities

ACTIVITY 4-1
Ethics and professional conduct in business

ETHICS

Lighthouse Co. is a graphics arts design consulting firm. Robin Dover, its treasurer and vice president of finance, has prepared a classified balance sheet as of July 31, 2006, the end of its fiscal year. This balance sheet will be submitted with Lighthouse's loan application to Central Trust & Savings Bank.

In the Current Assets section of the balance sheet, Robin reported an $80,000 receivable from Ron Knoll, the president of Lighthouse, as a trade account receivable. Ron borrowed the money from Lighthouse in February 2005 for a down payment on a new home. He has orally assured Robin that he will pay off the account receivable within the next year. Robin reported the $80,000 in the same manner on the preceding year's balance sheet.

Evaluate whether it is acceptable for Robin Dover to prepare the July 31, 2006 balance sheet in the manner indicated above.

ACTIVITY 4-2
Financial statements

The following is an excerpt from a telephone conversation between Pedro Mendoza, president of Goliath Supplies Co., and Natalie Welch, owner of Flint Employment Co.

Pedro: Natalie, you're going to have to do a better job of finding me a new computer programmer. That last guy was great at programming, but he didn't have any common sense.

Natalie: What do you mean? The guy had a master's degree with straight A's.

Pedro: Yes, well, last month he developed a new financial reporting system. He said we could do away with manually preparing a work sheet and financial statements. The computer would automatically generate our financial statements with "a push of a button."

Natalie: So what's the big deal? Sounds to me like it would save you time and effort.

Pedro: Right! The balance sheet showed a minus for supplies!

Natalie: Minus supplies? How can that be?

Pedro: That's what I asked.

Natalie: So, what did he say?

Pedro: Well, after he checked the program, he said that it must be right. The minuses were greater than the pluses . . .

Natalie: Didn't he know that supplies can't have a credit balance—it must have a debit balance?

Pedro: He asked me what a debit and credit were.

Natalie: I see your point.

1. ▬▬▶ Comment on (a) the desirability of computerizing Goliath Supplies Co.'s financial reporting system, (b) the elimination of the work sheet in a computerized accounting system, and (c) the computer programmer's lack of accounting knowledge.

2. ▬▬▶ Explain to the programmer why supplies could not have a credit balance.

ACTIVITY 4-3
Financial statements

Assume that you recently accepted a position with the Bozeman National Bank as an assistant loan officer. As one of your first duties, you have been assigned the responsibility of evaluating a loan request for $150,000 from Sasquatch.com, a small proprietorship. In support of the loan application, Samantha Joyner, owner, submitted a "Statement of Accounts" (trial balance) for the first year of operations ended December 31, 2006.

1. ▬▬▶ Explain to Samantha Joyner why a set of financial statements (income statement, retained earnings statement, and balance sheet) would be useful to you in evaluating the loan request.

2. In discussing the "Statement of Accounts" with Samantha Joyner, you discovered that the accounts had not been adjusted at December 31. Analyze the "Statement of Accounts" (shown below) and indicate possible adjusting entries that might be necessary before an accurate set of financial statements could be prepared.

Sasquatch.com
Statement of Accounts
December 31, 2006

Cash	4,100	
Billings Due from Others	30,150	
Supplies (chemicals, etc.)	14,950	
Trucks	52,750	
Equipment	16,150	
Amounts Owed to Others		5,700
Investment in Business		47,000
Service Revenue		147,300
Wages Expense	60,100	
Utilities Expense	14,660	
Rent Expense	4,800	
Insurance Expense	1,400	
Other Expenses	940	
	200,000	200,000

(continued)

3. ▭▶ Assuming that an accurate set of financial statements will be submitted by Samantha Joyner in a few days, what other considerations or information would you require before making a decision on the loan request?

ACTIVITY 4-4
Compare balance sheets

GROUP ACTIVITY   INTERNET

In groups of three or four, compare the balance sheets of two different companies, and present to the class a summary of the similarities and differences of the two companies. You may obtain the balance sheets you need from one of the following sources:

1. Your school or local library.
2. The investor relations department of each company.
3. The company's Web site on the Internet.
4. EDGAR (Electronic Data Gathering, Analysis, and Retrieval), the electronic archives of financial statements filed with the Securities and Exchange Commission.

SEC documents can be retrieved using the EdgarScan™ service from **Pricewater-houseCoopers** at **http://edgarscan.pwcglobal.com**. To obtain annual report information, key in a company name in the appropriate space. EdgarScan will list the reports available to you for the company you've selected. Select the most recent annual report filing, identified as a 10-K or 10-K405. EdgarScan provides an outline of the report, including the separate financial statements, which can also be selected in an Excel® spreadsheet.

ACTIVITY 4-5
Business strategy

REAL WORLD   INTERNET

Mohawk Industries is a leading distributor of carpets and rugs in the United States. The company sells its carpets and rugs to locally-owned, independent carpet retailers, home centers such as **Home Depot** and **Lowe's**, and department stores such as **Sears**. Mohawk's carpets are marked under the brand names that include "Aladdin, Mohawk Home, Bigelow, Custom Weave, Durkan, Karastan, and Townhouse."

1. ▭▶ List some factors that increase the demand for carpet.
2. ▭▶ From a strategic viewpoint, do you think Mohawk should view itself as a carpet or floorcovering manufacturer? Discuss the advantages and disadvantages of Mohawk viewing itself as a floorcovering manufacturer rather than just a carpet manufacturer.
3. ▭▶ Read Mohawk's latest 10-K filing with the **Securities and Exchange Commission** by using EdgarScan (**http://edgarscan.pwcglobal.com**). Does Mohawk view itself as a carpet manufacturer or as a floorcovering manufacturer? Explain.

Answers to Self-Examination Questions

1. **C** The dividends account (answer C), would be extended to the Balance Sheet columns of the work sheet. Utilities Expense (answer A), Rent Revenue (answer B), and Miscellaneous Expense (answer D) would all be extended to the Income Statement columns of the work sheet.

2. **D** Cash or other assets that are expected to be converted to cash or sold or used up within one year or less, through the normal operations of the business, are classified as current assets on the balance sheet. Accounts Receivable (answer D) is a current asset, since it will normally be converted to cash within one year. Office Equipment (answer A), Land (answer B), and Accumulated Depreciation (answer C) are all reported in the property, plant, and equipment section of the balance sheet.

3. **B** The entry to close the dividends account is to debit the retained earnings account and credit the dividends account (answer B).

4. **D** Since all revenue and expense accounts are closed at the end of the period, Fees Earned (answer A), Wages Expense (answer B), and Rent Expense (answer C) would all be closed to Income Summary. Accumulated Depreciation (answer D) is a contra asset account that is not closed.

5. **B** Since the post-closing trial balance includes only balance sheet accounts (all of the revenue, expense, and dividends accounts are closed), Cash (answer A), Accumulated Depreciation (answer C), and Capital Stock (answer D) would appear on the post-closing trial balance. Fees Earned (answer B) is a temporary account that is closed prior to preparing the post-closing trial balance.

increases, the ledger becomes unwieldy when a separate account for each supplier is included. Thus, individual accounts payable to suppliers may be placed in a separate ledger, called a ***subsidiary ledger***. Similarly, individual accounts receivable from customers may be placed in a subsidiary ledger. Each subsidiary ledger is represented in the primary ledger (now called the ***general ledger***) by a summarizing account, called a ***controlling account***. The balance of this controlling account must equal the sum of the balances of the individual accounts in the subsidiary ledger. For example, the accounts payable controlling account must equal the sum of the balances of the accounts in the accounts payable subsidiary ledger.[1]

In the remainder of this chapter, we illustrate merchandiser financial statements and transactions that affect the income statement (sales, cost of merchandise sold, and gross profit) and the balance sheet (merchandise inventory).

THE OPERATING CYCLE

The operations of a manufacturing business involve the purchase of raw materials (purchasing activity), the conversion of the raw materials into a product through the use of labor and machinery (production activity), the sale and distribution of the products to customers (sales activity), and the receipt of cash from customers (collection activity). This overall process is referred to as the *operating cycle*. Thus, the operating cycle begins with spending cash and it ends with receiving cash from customers. The operating cycle for a manufacturing business is shown below.

Operating cycles differ, depending upon the nature of the business and its operations. For example, the operating cycles for tobacco, distillery, and lumber industries are much longer than the operating cycles of the automobile, consumer electronics, and home furnishings industries. Likewise, the operating cycles for retailers are usually shorter than for manufacturers because retailers purchase goods in a form ready for sale to the customer. Of course, some retailers will have shorter operating cycles than others because of the nature of their products. For example, a jewelry store or an automobile dealer normally has a longer operating cycle than a consumer electronics store or a grocery store.

Businesses with longer operating cycles normally have higher profit margins on their products than businesses with shorter operating cycles. For example, it is not unusual for jewelry stores to price their jewelry at 30%–50% above cost. In contrast, grocery stores operate on very small profit margins, often below 5%. Grocery stores make up the difference by selling their products more quickly.

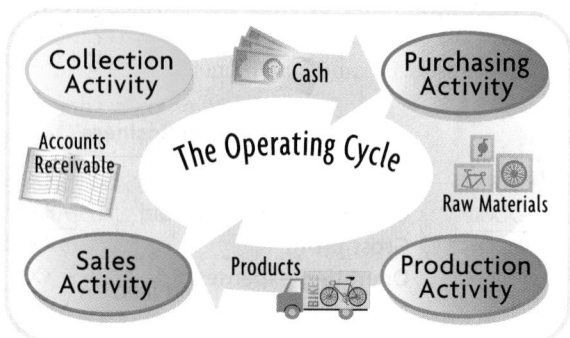

Financial Statements for a Merchandising Business

objective **2**

Describe and illustrate the financial statements of a merchandising business.

In this section, we illustrate the financial statements for NetSolutions after it becomes a retailer of computer hardware and software. During 2005, we assume that Chris Clark implemented the second phase of NetSolutions' business plan. Accordingly, Chris notified clients that beginning July 1, 2006, NetSolutions would be terminating its consulting services. Instead, it would become a personalized retailer.

NetSolutions' business strategy is to focus on offering personalized service to individuals and small businesses who are upgrading or purchasing new computer sys-

---

[1]Subsidiary ledgers are further described and illustrated in Appendix C.

tems. NetSolutions' personal service before the sale will include a no-obligation, on-site assessment of the customer's computer needs. By providing tailor-made solutions, personalized service, and follow-up, Chris feels that NetSolutions can compete effectively against larger retailers, such as **Best Buy** or **Office Depot**.

Multiple-Step Income Statement

The 2007 income statement for NetSolutions is shown in Exhibit 1.[2] This form of income statement, called a ***multiple-step income statement***, contains several sections, subsections, and subtotals.

Sales is the total amount charged customers for merchandise sold, including cash sales and sales on account. Both sales returns and allowances and sales discounts are subtracted in arriving at net sales.

Sales returns and allowances are granted by the seller to customers for damaged or defective merchandise. For example, rather than have a buyer return merchandise, a seller may offer a $500 allowance to the customer as compensation for damaged merchandise. Sales returns and allowances are recorded when the merchandise is returned or when the allowance is granted by the seller.

•Exhibit 1

Multiple-Step Income Statement

NetSolutions					
Income Statement					
For the Year Ended December 31, 2007					
Revenue from sales:					
Sales			$720 1 8 5 00		
Less: Sales returns and allowances	$ 6 1 4 0 00				
Sales discounts	5 7 9 0 00		11 9 3 0 00		
Net sales				$708 2 5 5 00	
Cost of merchandise sold				525 3 0 5 00	
Gross profit				$182 9 5 0 00	
Operating expenses:					
Selling expenses:					
Sales salaries expense	$56 2 3 0 00				
Advertising expense	10 8 6 0 00				
Depr. expense—store equipment	3 1 0 0 00				
Miscellaneous selling expense	6 3 0 00				
Total selling expenses			$ 70 8 2 0 00		
Administrative expenses:					
Office salaries expense	$21 0 2 0 00				
Rent expense	8 1 0 0 00				
Depr. expense—office equipment	2 4 9 0 00				
Insurance expense	1 9 1 0 00				
Office supplies expense	6 1 0 00				
Misc. administrative expense	7 6 0 00				
Total administrative expenses			34 8 9 0 00		
Total operating expenses				105 7 1 0 00	
Income from operations				$ 77 2 4 0 00	
Other income and expense:					
Rent revenue			$ 6 0 0 00		
Interest expense			(2 4 4 0 00)	(1 8 4 0 00)	
Net income				$ 75 4 0 0 00	

---

[2]We use the NetSolutions income statement for 2007 as a basis for illustration because, as will be shown, it allows us to better illustrate the computation of the cost of merchandise sold.

Sales discounts are granted by the seller to customers for early payment of amounts owed. For example, a seller may offer a customer a 2% discount on a sale of $10,000 if the customer pays within ten days. If the customer pays within the ten-day period, the seller receives cash of $9,800 and the buyer receives a discount of $200 ($10,000 × 2%). Sales discounts are recorded when the customer pays the bill.

Net sales is determined by subtracting sales returns and allowances and sales discounts from sales. Rather than reporting sales, sales returns and allowances, and sales discounts as shown in Exhibit 1, many companies report only net sales.

Cost of merchandise sold is the cost of the merchandise sold to customers. To illustrate the determination of the cost of merchandise sold, assume that NetSolutions purchased $340,000 of merchandise during the last half of 2006. If the inventory at December 31, 2006, the end of the year, is $59,700, the cost of the merchandise sold during 2006 is $280,300, as shown below.

Purchases	$340,000
Less merchandise inventory, December 31, 2006	59,700
Cost of merchandise sold	$280,300

As we discussed in the preceding paragraphs, sellers may offer customers sales discounts for early payment of their bills. Such discounts are referred to as ***purchases discounts*** by the buyer. Purchase discounts reduce the cost of merchandise. A buyer may return merchandise to the seller (a ***purchase return***), or the buyer may receive a reduction in the initial price at which the merchandise was purchased (a ***purchase allowance***). Like purchase discounts, purchases returns and allowances reduce the cost of merchandise purchased during a period. In addition, transportation costs paid by the buyer for merchandise also increase the cost of merchandise purchased.

To continue the illustration, assume that during 2007 NetSolutions purchased additional merchandise of $521,980. It received credit for purchases returns and allowances of $9,100, took purchases discounts of $2,525, and paid transportation costs of $17,400. The purchases returns and allowances and the purchases discounts are deducted from the total purchases to yield the *net purchases*. The transportation costs, termed **transportation in**, are added to the net purchases to yield the *cost of merchandise purchased* of $527,755, as shown below.

Purchases		$521,980
Less: Purchases returns and allowances	$9,100	
Purchases discounts	2,525	11,625
Net purchases		$510,355
Add transportation in		17,400
Cost of merchandise purchased		$527,755

The ending inventory of NetSolutions on December 31, 2006, $59,700, becomes the beginning inventory for 2007. This beginning inventory is added to the cost of merchandise purchased to yield **merchandise available for sale**. The ending inventory, which is assumed to be $62,150, is then subtracted from the merchandise available for sale to yield the cost of merchandise sold of $525,305, as shown in Exhibit 2.

The cost of merchandise sold was determined by deducting the merchandise on hand at the end of the period from the merchandise available for sale during the period. The merchandise on hand at the end of the period is determined by taking a physical count of inventory on hand. This method of determining the cost of merchandise sold and the amount of merchandise on hand is called the ***periodic method*** of accounting for merchandise inventory. Under the periodic method, the inventory records do not show the amount available for sale or the amount sold during the period. In contrast, under the ***perpetual method*** of accounting for merchandise inventory, each purchase and sale of merchandise is recorded in the inventory and the cost of merchandise sold accounts. As a result, the amount of

•Exhibit 2

Cost of Merchandise Sold

Merchandise inventory, January 1, 2007		$ 59,700
Purchases	$521,980	
Less: Purchases returns and allowances $9,100		
Purchases discounts 2,525	11,625	
Net purchases	$510,355	
Add transportation in	17,400	
Cost of merchandise purchased		527,755
Merchandise available for sale		$587,455
Less merchandise inventory, December 31, 2007 . .		62,150
Cost of merchandise sold		$525,305

REAL WORLD

Retailers, such as **Best Buy**, **Sears**, and **Wal-Mart**, and grocery store chains, such as **Winn-Dixie** and **Kroger**, use bar codes and optical scanners as part of their computerized inventory systems.

merchandise available for sale and the amount sold are continuously (perpetually) disclosed in the inventory records.

Most large retailers and many small merchandising businesses use computerized perpetual inventory systems. Such systems normally use bar codes, such as the one on the back of this textbook. An optical scanner reads the bar code to record merchandise purchased and sold. Merchandise businesses using a perpetual inventory system report the cost of merchandise sold as a single line on the income statement, as shown in Exhibit 1 for NetSolutions. Merchandise businesses using the periodic inventory method report the cost of merchandise sold by using the format shown in Exhibit 2. Because of its wide use, we will use the perpetual inventory method throughout the remainder of this chapter.

Gross profit is determined by subtracting the cost of merchandise sold from net sales. Exhibit 1 shows that NetSolutions reported gross profit of $182,950 in 2007. *Operating income*, sometimes called ***income from operations***, is determined by subtracting operating expenses from gross profit. Most merchandising businesses classify operating expenses as either selling expenses or administrative expenses.

FINANCIAL REPORTING AND DISCLOSURE

H&R BLOCK VERSUS HOME DEPOT

H&R Block is a service business that primarily offers tax planning and preparation to its customers. **Home Depot** is the world's largest home improvement retailer and the second largest merchandise business in the United States. The differences in the operations of a service and merchandise business are illustrated in their income statements, as shown below.

As will be discussed in a later chapter, corporations are subject to income taxes. Thus, the income statements of H&R Block and Home Depot report "income taxes" as a deduction from "income before income taxes" in arriving at net income.

H&R Block Inc.
Condensed Income Statement
For the Year Ending April 30, 2003
(in millions)

Revenue	$3,780
Operating expenses	2,800
Operating income	$ 980
Other income	7
Income before taxes	$ 987
Income taxes	407
Net income	$ 580

Home Depot Inc.
Condensed Income Statement
For the Year Ending February 2, 2003
(in millions)

Net sales	$58,247
Cost of merchandise sold	40,139
Gross profit	$18,108
Operating expenses	12,278
Operating income	$ 5,830
Other income	42
Income before taxes	$ 5,872
Income taxes	2,208
Net income	$ 3,664

I was founded in 1966 in St. Paul, Minn., as an audio component systems retailer called "Sound of Music." I'm now the largest volume specialty retailer of consumer electronics, personal computers, entertainment software, and appliances. I call myself a "bricks and clicks" retailer because along with a vibrant Web site, I also have more than 500 retail stores in 47 states. In 1989, I began keeping all my inventory on the sales floor, to be sold by non-commissioned product specialists. I bought the Musicland, Magnolia Hi-Fi, and Future Shop chains and am expanding into Canada. Who am I? (Go to page 218 for answer.)

Expenses that are incurred directly in the selling of merchandise are **selling expenses**. They include such expenses as salespersons' salaries, store supplies used, depreciation of store equipment, and advertising. Expenses incurred in the administration or general operations of the business are **administrative expenses** or general expenses. Examples of these expenses are office salaries, depreciation of office equipment, and office supplies used. Credit card expense is also normally classified as an administrative expense. Although selling and administrative expenses may be reported separately, many companies report operating expenses as a single item.

Other income and expense is reported on NetSolutions' income statement in Exhibit 1. Revenue from sources other than the primary operating activity of a business is classified as **other income**. In a merchandising business, these items include income from interest, rent, and gains resulting from the sale of fixed assets.

Expenses that cannot be traced directly to operations are identified as **other expense**. Interest expense that results from financing activities and losses incurred in the disposal of fixed assets are examples of these items.

Other income and other expense are offset against each other on the income statement, as shown in Exhibit 1. If the total of other income exceeds the total of other expense, the difference is added to income from operations to determine net income. If the reverse is true, the difference is subtracted from income from operations.

Single-Step Income Statement

An alternate form of income statement is the **single-step income statement**. As shown in Exhibit 3, the income statement for NetSolutions deducts the total of all expenses *in one step* from the total of all revenues.

•Exhibit 3

Single-Step Income Statement

NetSolutions Income Statement For the Year Ended December 31, 2007		
Revenues:		
Net sales		$708 255 00
Rent revenue		6 00 00
Total revenues		$708 855 00
Expenses:		
Cost of merchandise sold	$525 305 00	
Selling expenses	70 820 00	
Administrative expenses	34 890 00	
Interest expense	2 440 00	
Total expenses		633 455 00
Net income		$ 75 400 00

The single-step form emphasizes total revenues and total expenses as the factors that determine net income. A criticism of the single-step form is that such amounts as gross profit and income from operations are not readily available for analysis.

Retained Earnings Statement

The retained earnings statement for NetSolutions is shown in Exhibit 4. This statement is prepared in the same manner that we described previously for a service business.

Balance Sheet

As we discussed and illustrated in previous chapters, the balance sheet may be presented with assets on the left-hand side and the liabilities and stockholders' equity

•Exhibit 4

Retained Earnings
Statement for
Merchandising Business

NetSolutions Retained Earnings Statement For the Year Ended December 31, 2007		
Retained earnings, January 1, 2007		$128 800 00
Net income for year	$75 400 00	
Less dividends	18 000 00	
Increase in retained earnings		57 400 00
Retained earnings, December 31, 2007		$186 200 00

on the right-hand side. This form of the balance sheet is called the **account form**. The balance sheet may also be presented in a downward sequence in three sections. This form of balance sheet is called the **report form**. The report form of balance sheet for NetSolutions is shown in Exhibit 5. In this balance sheet, note that merchandise inventory at the end of the period is reported as a current asset and that the current portion of the note payable is $5,000.

•Exhibit 5

Report Form of Balance
Sheet

NetSolutions Balance Sheet December 31, 2007			
Assets			
Current assets:			
Cash		$ 52 950 00	
Accounts receivable		91 080 00	
Merchandise inventory		62 150 00	
Office supplies		4 80 00	
Prepaid insurance		2 650 00	
Total current assets			$209 310 00
Property, plant, and equipment:			
Land		$ 20 000 00	
Store equipment	$27 100 00		
Less accumulated depreciation	5 700 00	21 400 00	
Office equipment	$15 570 00		
Less accumulated depreciation	4 720 00	10 850 00	
Total property, plant, and equipment			52 250 00
Total assets			$261 560 00
Liabilities			
Current liabilities:			
Accounts payable		$22 420 00	
Note payable (current portion)		5 000 00	
Salaries payable		1 140 00	
Unearned rent		1 800 00	
Total current liabilities			$ 30 360 00
Long-term liabilities:			
Note payable (final payment due 2017)			20 000 00
Total liabilities			$ 50 360 00
Stockholders' Equity			
Capital stock		$ 25 000 00	
Retained earnings		186 200 00	211 200 00
Total liabilities and stockholders' equity			$261 560 00

Sales Transactions

In the remainder of this chapter, we illustrate transactions that affect the financial statements of a merchandising business. These transactions affect the reporting of net sales, cost of merchandise sold, gross profit, and merchandise inventory.

Cash Sales

A business may sell merchandise for cash. Cash sales are normally rung up (entered) on a cash register and recorded in the accounts. To illustrate, assume that on January 3, NetSolutions sells merchandise for $1,800. These cash sales can be recorded as follows:

		JOURNAL			Page 25
Date		**Description**	**Post. Ref.**	**Debit**	**Credit**
2007 Jan.	3	Cash		1 8 0 0 00	
		Sales			1 8 0 0 00
		To record cash sales.			

Under the perpetual inventory system, the cost of merchandise sold and the reduction in merchandise inventory should also be recorded. In this way, the merchandise inventory account will indicate the amount of merchandise on hand (not sold). To illustrate, assume that the cost of merchandise sold on January 3 was $1,200. The entry to record the cost of merchandise sold and the reduction in the merchandise inventory is as follows:

Jan.	3	Cost of Merchandise Sold		1 2 0 0 00	
		Merchandise Inventory			1 2 0 0 00
		To record the cost of merchandise sold.			

Sales made to customers using credit cards issued by banks, such as **MasterCard** or **VISA**, are treated as *cash sales*. The record of the sale is electronically sent to a clearing house for credit card transactions. The clearing house processes the sale by contacting the bank that issued the credit card. Within one or two days, the seller's bank account is credited for the amount of the sale.

Retailers are charged service fees for credit card sales. The seller debits these service fees to an expense account. An entry at the end of a month to record the payment of service charges on bank credit card sales is shown below.

Jan.	31	Credit Card Expense		4 8 00	
		Cash			4 8 00
		To record service charges on credit card sales for the month.			

Sales on Account

A business may sell merchandise on account. The seller records such sales as a debit to Accounts Receivable and a credit to Sales. An example of an entry for a NetSolutions sale on account of $510 follows. The cost of merchandise sold was $280.

Jan.	12	Accounts Receivable—Sims Co.	5 1 0 00	
		Sales		5 1 0 00
		Invoice No. 7172.		
	12	Cost of Merchandise Sold	2 8 0 00	
		Merchandise Inventory		2 8 0 00
		Cost of merchandise sold on Invoice		
		No. 7172.		

REAL WORLD

A retailer may accept **MasterCard** or **VISA** but not **American Express**. Why? The service fees that credit card companies charge retailers is the primary reason that some businesses do not accept all credit cards. For example, American Express Co.'s service fees are normally higher than MasterCard's or VISA's. As a result, some retailers choose not to accept American Express cards. The disadvantage of this practice is that the retailer may lose customers to competitors who do accept American Express cards.

Sales may also be made to customers using nonbank credit cards. An example of a nonbank credit card is the **American Express** card. Nonbank credit card sales may first be reported to the card company before cash is received. Therefore, such sales create a *receivable* with the card company. Before the card company pays cash, it normally deducts a service fee. For example, assume that American Express card sales of $1,000 are made by NetSolutions and reported to the card company on January 20. The cost of the merchandise sold was $550. On January 27, the card company deducts a service fee of $50 and sends $950 to NetSolutions. These transactions are recorded by NetSolutions as follows:

Jan.	20	Accounts Receivable—American Express	1 0 0 0 00	
		Sales		1 0 0 0 00
		American Express (nonbank) credit		
		card sales.		
	20	Cost of Merchandise Sold	5 5 0 00	
		Merchandise Inventory		5 5 0 00
		Cost of merchandise sold on		
		American Express credit card sales.		
	27	Cash	9 5 0 00	
		Credit Card Expense	5 0 00	
		Accounts Receivable—American Express		1 0 0 0 00
		Received cash from American Express		
		for sales reported on January 20.		

Sales Discounts

The terms of a sale are normally indicated on the ***invoice*** or bill that the seller sends to the buyer. An example of a sales invoice for NetSolutions is shown in Exhibit 6.

The terms for when payments for merchandise are to be made, agreed on by the buyer and the seller, are called the **credit terms**. If payment is required on delivery, the terms are *cash* or *net cash*. Otherwise, the buyer is allowed an amount of time, known as the **credit period**, in which to pay.

The credit period usually begins with the date of the sale as shown on the invoice. If payment is due within a stated number of days after the date of the invoice,

If an invoice dated August 13 has terms n/30, what is the due date of the invoice?

September 12 [30 days = 18 days in August (31 days − 13 days) + 12 days in September]

•Exhibit 6   Invoice

net SOLUTIONS Invoice

106-8

5101 Washington Ave.
Cincinnati, OH 45227-5101

Made in U.S.A.

SOLD TO Omega Technologies 1000 Matrix Blvd. San Jose, CA. 95116–1000	**CUSTOMER'S ORDER NO. & DATE** 412 Jan. 10, 2007

DATE SHIPPED Jan. 12, 2007	**HOW SHIPPED AND ROUTE** US Express Trucking Co.	**TERMS** 2/10, n/30	**INVOICE DATE** Jan. 12, 2007
FROM Cincinnati	**F.O.B.** Cincinnati		

QUANTITY 10	**DESCRIPTION** 3COM Megahertz 10/100 Lan PC Card	**UNIT PRICE** 150.00	**AMOUNT** 1,500.00

such as 30 days, the terms are *net 30 days*. These terms may be written as *n/30*.[3] If payment is due by the end of the month in which the sale was made, the terms are written as *n/eom*.

As a means of encouraging the buyer to pay before the end of the credit period, the seller may offer a discount. For example, a seller may offer a 2% discount if the buyer pays within 10 days of the invoice date. If the buyer does not take the discount, the total amount is due within 30 days. These terms are expressed as *2/10, n/30* and are read as *2% discount if paid within 10 days, net amount due within 30 days*. The credit terms of 2/10, n/30 are summarized in Exhibit 7, using the information from the invoice in Exhibit 6.

•Exhibit 7   Credit Terms

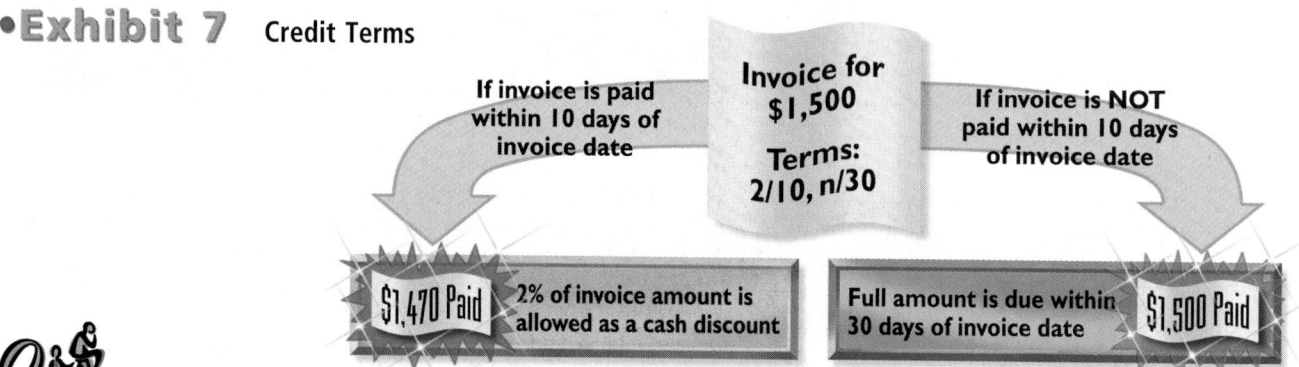

If an invoice dated November 22 has credit terms 2/10, n/30, what is (a) the last day the invoice may be paid within the discount period and (b) the last day of the credit period if the discount is not taken?

(a) December 2 [10 days = 8 days in November (30 days − 22 days) + 2 days in December]; (b) December 22 [30 days = 8 days in November (30 days − 22 days) + 22 days in December]

Discounts taken by the buyer for early payment are recorded as sales discounts by the seller. Since managers may want to know the amount of the sales discounts for a period, the seller normally records the sales discounts in a separate account. The sales discounts account is a *contra* (or *offsetting*) account to Sales. To illustrate, assume that cash is received within the discount period (10 days) from the credit sale of $1,500, shown on the invoice in Exhibit 6. NetSolutions would record the receipt of the cash as follows:

----

[3]The word *net* as used here does not have the usual meaning of a number after deductions have been subtracted, as in *net income*.

Jan.	22	Cash		1 4 7 0 00						
		Sales Discounts		3 0 00						
		Accounts Receivable—Omega								
		Technologies				1 5 0 0 00				
		Collection on Invoice No. 106-8, less								
		2% discount.								

Sales Returns and Allowances

Merchandise sold may be returned to the seller (**sales return**). In addition, because of defects or for other reasons, the seller may reduce the initial price at which the goods were sold (**sales allowance**). If the return or allowance is for a sale on account, the seller usually issues the buyer a ***credit memorandum***. This memorandum shows the amount of and the reason for the seller's credit to an account receivable. A credit memorandum issued by NetSolutions is illustrated in Exhibit 8.

•**Exhibit 8** **Credit Memorandum**

Like sales discounts, sales returns and allowances reduce sales revenue. They also result in additional shipping and other expenses. Since managers often want to know the amount of returns and allowances for a period, the seller records sales returns and allowances in a separate account. Sales Returns and Allowances is a *contra* (or *offsetting*) account to Sales.

The seller debits Sales Returns and Allowances for the amount of the return or allowance. If the original sale was on account, the seller credits Accounts Receivable. Since the merchandise inventory is kept up to date in a perpetual system, the seller adds the cost of the returned merchandise to the merchandise inventory account. The seller must also credit the cost of returned merchandise to the cost of merchandise sold account, since this account was debited when the original sale was recorded. To illustrate, assume that the cost of the merchandise returned in Exhibit 8 was $140. NetSolutions records the credit memo in Exhibit 8 as follows:

REAL WORLD

Book publishers often experience large returns if a book is not immediately successful. For example, 35% of adult hardcover books shipped to retailers are returned to publishers, according to the Association of American Publishers.

Jan.	13	Sales Returns and Allowances		2 2 5 00						
		Accounts Receivable—Krier Company				2 2 5 00				
		Credit Memo No. 32.								

Jan.	13	Merchandise Inventory		1 4 0 00		
		Cost of Merchandise Sold			1 4 0 00	
		Cost of merchandise returned, Credit				
		Memo No. 32.				

What if the buyer pays for the merchandise and the merchandise is later returned? In this case, the seller may issue a credit and apply it against other accounts receivable owed by the buyer, or the cash may be refunded. If the credit is applied against the buyer's other receivables, the seller records entries similar to those preceding. If cash is refunded for merchandise returned or for an allowance, the seller debits Sales Returns and Allowances and credits Cash.

INTEGRITY IN BUSINESS

THE CASE OF THE FRAUDULENT PRICE TAGS

One of the challenges for a retailer is policing its sales return policy. There are many ways in which customers can unethically or illegally abuse such policies. In one case, a couple was accused of attaching **Marshall's** store price tags to cheaper merchandise bought or obtained elsewhere. The couple then returned the cheaper goods and received the substantially higher refund amount. Company security officials discovered the fraud and had the couple arrested after they had allegedly bilked the company for over $1 million.

Purchase Transactions

objective 4

Describe the accounting for the purchase of merchandise.

As we indicated earlier in this chapter, most large retailers and many small merchandising businesses use computerized perpetual inventory systems. Under the perpetual inventory system, cash purchases of merchandise are recorded as follows:

JOURNAL						Page 24	
Date		Description	Post. Ref.	Debit		Credit	
2007 Jan.	3	Merchandise Inventory		2 5 1 0 00			
		Cash				2 5 1 0 00	
		Purchased inventory from Bowen Co.					

Purchases of merchandise on account are recorded as follows:

Jan.	4	Merchandise Inventory		9 2 5 0 00		
		Accounts Payable—Thomas Corporation			9 2 5 0 00	
		Purchased inventory on account.				

Purchases Discounts

Purchases discounts taken by the buyer for early payment of an invoice reduce the cost of the merchandise purchased. Most businesses design their accounting systems

so that all available discounts are taken. Even if the buyer has to borrow to make the payment within a discount period, it is normally to the buyer's advantage to do so. To illustrate, assume that Alpha Technologies issues an invoice for $3,000 to Net-Solutions, dated March 12, with terms 2/10, n/30. The last day of the discount period in which the $60 discount can be taken is March 22. Assume that in order to pay the invoice on March 22, NetSolutions borrows the money for the remaining 20 days of the credit period. If we assume an annual interest rate of 6% and a 360-day year, the interest on the loan of $2,940 ($3,000 − $60) is $9.80 ($2,940 × 6% × 20/360). The net savings to NetSolutions is $50.20, computed as follows:

Discount of 2% on $3,000	$60.00
Interest for 20 days at rate of 6% on $2,940	−9.80
Savings from borrowing	$50.20

The savings can also be seen by comparing the interest rate on the money *saved* by taking the discount and the interest rate on the money *borrowed* to take the discount. For NetSolutions, the interest rate on the money saved in this example is estimated by converting 2% for 20 days to a yearly rate, as follows:

$$2\% \times \frac{360 \text{ days}}{20 \text{ days}} = 2\% \times 18 = 36\%$$

If NetSolutions borrows the money to take the discount, it *pays* interest of 6%. If NetSolutions does not take the discount, it *pays* estimated interest of 36% for using the $60 for an additional 20 days.

Under the perpetual inventory system, the buyer initially debits the merchandise inventory account for the amount of the invoice. When paying the invoice, the buyer credits the merchandise inventory account for the amount of the discount. In this way, the merchandise inventory shows the *net* cost to the buyer. For example, Net-Solutions would record the Alpha Technologies invoice and its payment at the end of the discount period as follows:

Mar.	12	Merchandise Inventory	3 0 0 0 00	
		Accounts Payable—Alpha Technologies		3 0 0 0 00
	22	Accounts Payable—Alpha Technologies	3 0 0 0 00	
		Cash		2 9 4 0 00
		Merchandise Inventory		6 0 00

If NetSolutions does not take the discount because it does not pay the invoice until April 11, it would record the payment as follows:

Apr.	11	Accounts Payable—Alpha Technologies	3 0 0 0 00	
		Cash		3 0 0 0 00

Purchases Returns and Allowances

When merchandise is returned (**purchases return**) or a price adjustment is requested (**purchases allowance**), the buyer (debtor) usually sends the seller a letter or a debit memorandum. A ***debit memorandum***, shown in Exhibit 9, informs the seller of the amount the buyer proposes to *debit* to the account payable due the seller. It also states the reasons for the return or the request for a price reduction.

•Exhibit 9 Debit Memorandum

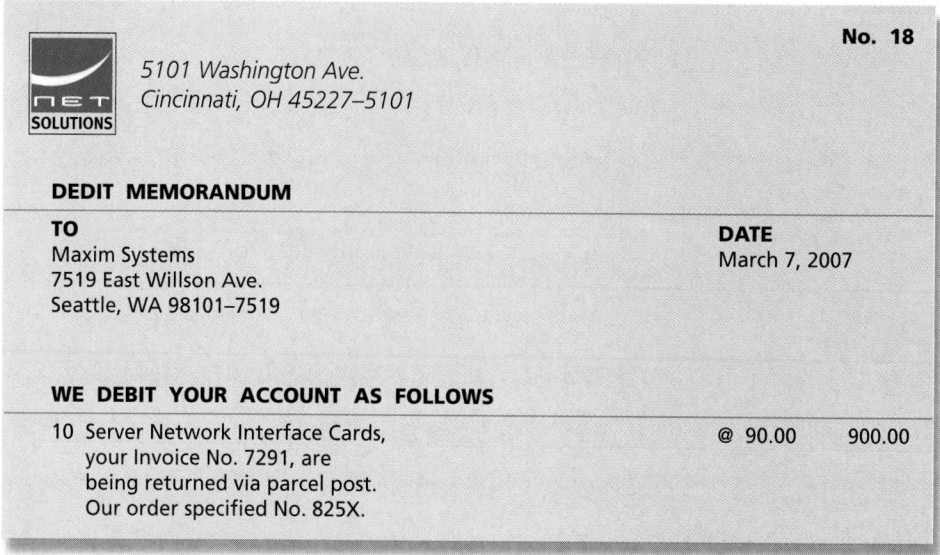

The buyer may use a copy of the debit memorandum as the basis for recording the return or allowance or wait for approval from the seller (creditor). In either case, the buyer must debit Accounts Payable and credit Merchandise Inventory. To illustrate, NetSolutions records the return of the merchandise indicated in the debit memo in Exhibit 9 as follows:

Ennis Co. purchases merchandise of $8,000 on terms 2/10, n/30. Ennis pays the original invoice, less a return of $2,500, within the discount period. How much did Ennis Co. pay?

$5,390 [($8,000 − $2,500) × 2% = $110 discount; $8,000 − $2,500 − $110 = $5,390]

Mar.	7	Accounts Payable—Maxim Systems		9 0 0 00	
		Merchandise Inventory			9 0 0 00
		Debit Memo No. 18.			

When a buyer returns merchandise or has been granted an allowance prior to paying the invoice, the amount of the debit memorandum is deducted from the invoice amount. The amount is deducted before the purchase discount is computed. For example, assume that on May 2, NetSolutions purchases $5,000 of merchandise from Delta Data Link, subject to terms 2/10, n/30. On May 4, NetSolutions returns $3,000 of the merchandise, and on May 12, NetSolutions pays the original invoice less the return. NetSolutions would record these transactions as follows:

May	2	Merchandise Inventory		5 0 0 0 00	
		Accounts Payable—Delta Data Link			5 0 0 0 00
		Purchased merchandise.			
	4	Accounts Payable—Delta Data Link		3 0 0 0 00	
		Merchandise Inventory			3 0 0 0 00
		Returned portion of merchandise			
		purchased.			
	12	Accounts Payable—Delta Data Link		2 0 0 0 00	
		Cash			1 9 6 0 00
		Merchandise Inventory			4 0 00
		Paid invoice [($5,000 − $3,000) × 2%			
		= $40; $2,000 − $40 = $1,960].			

Transportation Costs, Sales Taxes, and Trade Discounts

In the preceding two sections, we described and illustrated merchandise transactions involving sales and purchases. In this section, we discuss merchandise transactions involving transportation costs, sales taxes, and trade discounts.

Transportation Costs

The terms of a sale should indicate when the ownership (title) of the merchandise passes to the buyer. This point determines which party, the buyer or the seller, must pay the transportation costs.[4]

The ownership of the merchandise may pass to the buyer when the seller delivers the merchandise to the transportation company or freight carrier. For example, **DaimlerChrysler** records the sale and the transfer of ownership of its vehicles to dealers when the vehicles are shipped from the factory. In this case, the terms are said to be ***FOB (free on board) shipping point***. This term means that the dealer pays the transportation costs from the shipping point (factory) to the final destination. Such costs are part of the dealer's total cost of purchasing inventory and should be added to the cost of the inventory by debiting Merchandise Inventory.

> **The buyer bears the transportation costs if the shipping terms are FOB shipping point.**

To illustrate, assume that on June 10, NetSolutions buys merchandise from Magna Data on account, $900, terms FOB shipping point, and pays the transportation cost of $50. NetSolutions records these two transactions as follows:

June	10	Merchandise Inventory		9 0 0 00	
		Accounts Payable—Magna Data			9 0 0 00
		Purchased merchandise, terms FOB			
		shipping point.			
	10	Merchandise Inventory		5 0 00	
		Cash			5 0 00
		Paid shipping cost on merchandise			
		purchased.			

Sometimes FOB shipping point and FOB destination are expressed in terms of the location at which the title to the merchandise passes to the buyer. For example, if **Toyota Motor Co.**'s assembly plant in Osaka, Japan, sells automobiles to a dealer in Chicago, FOB shipping point could be expressed as FOB Osaka. Likewise, FOB destination could be expressed as FOB Chicago.

The ownership of the merchandise may pass to the buyer when the buyer receives the merchandise. In this case, the terms are said to be ***FOB (free on board) destination***. This term means that the seller delivers the merchandise to the buyer's final destination, free of transportation charges to the buyer. The seller thus pays the transportation costs to the final destination. The seller debits Transportation Out or Delivery Expense, which is reported on the seller's income statement as an expense.

> **The seller bears the transportation costs if the shipping terms are FOB destination.**

To illustrate, assume that on June 15, NetSolutions sells merchandise to Kranz Company on account, $700, terms FOB destination. The cost of the merchandise sold is $480, and NetSolutions pays the transportation cost of $40. NetSolutions records the sale, the cost of the sale, and the transportation cost as follows:

---

[4]The passage of title also determines whether the buyer or seller must pay other costs, such as the cost of insurance, while the merchandise is in transit.

June	15	Accounts Receivable—Kranz Company	7 0 0 00	
		Sales		7 0 0 00
		Sold merchandise, terms FOB		
		destination.		
	15	Cost of Merchandise Sold	4 8 0 00	
		Merchandise Inventory		4 8 0 00
		Recorded cost of merchandise sold to		
		Kranz Company.		
	15	Transportation Out	4 0 00	
		Cash		4 0 00
		Paid shipping cost on merchandise		
		sold.		

Martin Co. sells $4,000 of merchandise to Oblinger Co. on account on terms 2/10, n/30, FOB shipping point. As a convenience to Oblinger, Martin Co. pays transportation costs of $250 and adds those costs to the invoice. (a) How much will Martin Co. bill Oblinger? (b) If Oblinger Co. pays within the discount period, what amount will Oblinger pay Martin?

(a) $4,250 ($4,000 + $250); (b) $4,170 [$4,000 − ($4,000 × 2%) + $250]

As a convenience to the buyer, the seller may prepay the transportation costs, even though the terms are FOB shipping point. The seller will then add the transportation costs to the invoice. The buyer will debit Merchandise Inventory for the total amount of the invoice, including the transportation costs. Any discount terms would not apply to the prepaid transportation costs.

To illustrate, assume that on June 20, NetSolutions sells merchandise to Planter Company on account, $800, terms FOB shipping point. NetSolutions pays the transportation cost of $45 and adds it to the invoice. The cost of the merchandise sold is $360. NetSolutions records these transactions as follows:

June	20	Accounts Receivable—Planter Company	8 0 0 00	
		Sales		8 0 0 00
		Sold merchandise, terms FOB shipping		
		point.		
	20	Cost of Merchandise Sold	3 6 0 00	
		Merchandise Inventory		3 6 0 00
		Recorded cost of merchandise sold to		
		Planter Company.		
	20	Accounts Receivable—Planter Company	4 5 00	
		Cash		4 5 00
		Prepaid shipping cost on merchandise		
		sold.		

Shipping terms, the passage of title, and whether the buyer or seller is to pay the transportation costs are summarized in Exhibit 10.

Sales Taxes

The five states with the highest sales tax are Illinois, Minnesota, Nevada, Texas, and Washington. Some states have no sales tax, including Alaska, Delaware, Montana, New Hampshire, and Oregon.

Almost all states and many other taxing units levy a tax on sales of merchandise.[5] The liability for the sales tax is incurred when the sale is made.

At the time of a cash sale, the seller collects the sales tax. When a sale is made on account, the seller charges the tax to the buyer by debiting Accounts Receivable.

[5]Businesses that purchase merchandise for resale to others are normally exempt from paying sales taxes on their purchases. Only final buyers of merchandise normally pay sales taxes.

•Exhibit 10   Transportation Terms

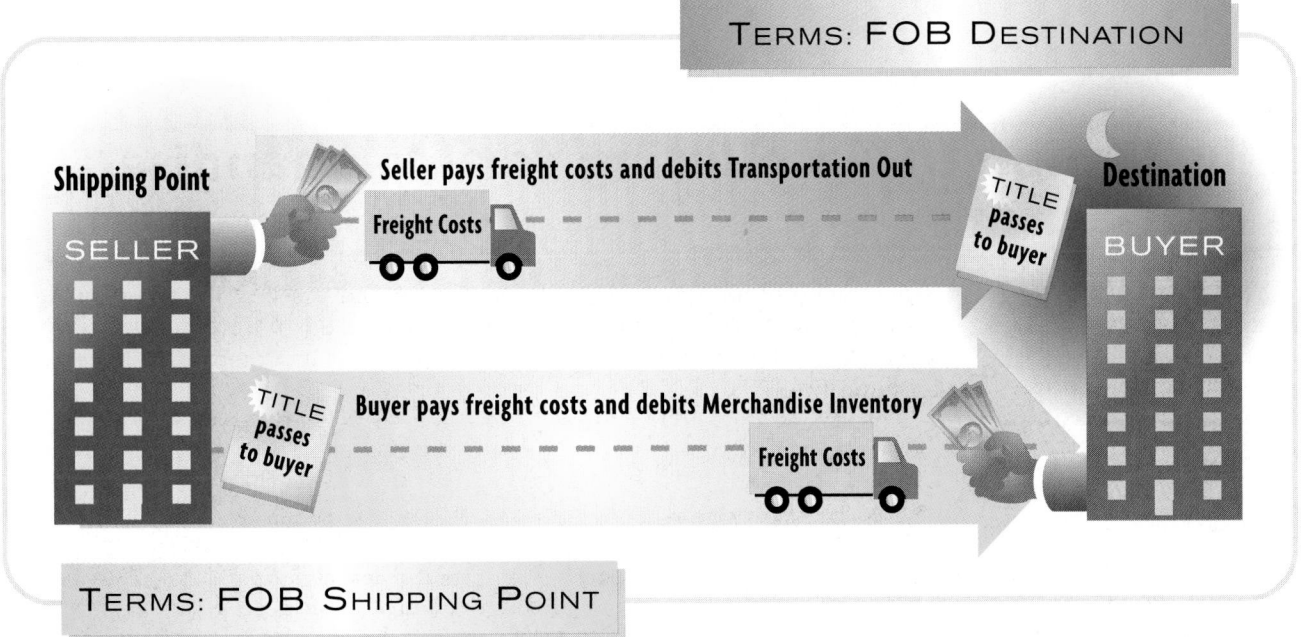

The seller credits the sales account for the amount of the sale and credits the tax to Sales Tax Payable. For example, the seller would record a sale of $100 on account, subject to a tax of 6%, as follows:

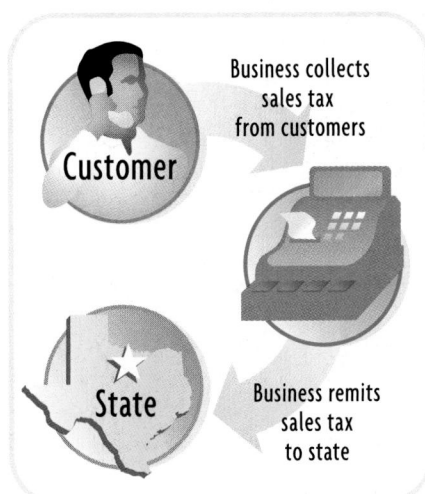

Aug.	12	Accounts Receivable—Lemon Co.	1 0 6 00		
		Sales		1 0 0 00	
		Sales Tax Payable		6 00	
		Invoice No. 339.			

Normally on a regular basis, the seller pays to the taxing unit the amount of the sales tax collected. The seller records such a payment as follows:

Sept.	15	Sales Tax Payable	2 9 0 0 00		
		Cash		2 9 0 0 00	
		Payment for sales taxes collected			
		during August.			

Trade Discounts

Wholesalers are businesses that sell merchandise to other businesses rather than to the general public. Many wholesalers publish catalogs. Rather than updating their catalogs frequently, wholesalers often publish price updates, which may involve large discounts from the list prices in their catalogs. In addition, wholesalers may offer special discounts to certain classes of buyers, such as government agencies or businesses that order large quantities. Such discounts are called ***trade discounts***.

Sellers and buyers do not normally record the list prices of merchandise and the related trade discounts in their accounts. For example, assume that an item has a

A seller offered a 30% trade discount on an item listed in its catalog for $2,400. At what amount would the seller record the sale?

$1,680 [$2,400 − ($2,400 × 30%), or $2,400 × 70%]

list price of $1,000 and a 40% trade discount. The seller records the sale of the item at $600 [$1,000 less the trade discount of $400 ($1,000 × 40%)]. Likewise, the buyer records the purchase at $600.

Illustration of Accounting for Merchandise Transactions

objective 6

Illustrate the dual nature of merchandising transactions.

Each merchandising transaction affects a buyer and a seller. In the following illustration, we show how the same transactions would be recorded by both the seller and the buyer. In this example, the seller is Scully Company and the buyer is Burton Co.

Transaction	Scully Company (Seller)			Burton Co. (Buyer)		
July 1. Scully Company sold merchandise on account to Burton Co., $7,500, terms FOB shipping point, n/45. The cost of the merchandise sold was $4,500.	Accounts Receivable—Burton Co. Sales	7,500	7,500	Merchandise Inventory Accounts Payable—Scully Co.	7,500	7,500
	Cost of Merchandise Sold Merchandise Inventory	4,500	4,500			
July 2. Burton Co. paid transportation charges of $150 on July 1 purchase from Scully Company.	No entry.			Merchandise Inventory Cash	150	150
July 5. Scully Company sold merchandise on account to Burton Co., $5,000, terms FOB destination, n/30. The cost of the merchandise sold was $3,500.	Accounts Receivable—Burton Co. Sales	5,000	5,000	Merchandise Inventory Accounts Payable—Scully Co.	5,000	5,000
	Cost of Merchandise Sold Merchandise Inventory	3,500	3,500			
July 7. Scully Company paid transportation costs of $250 for delivery of merchandise sold to Burton Co. on July 5.	Transportation Out Cash	250	250	No entry.		
July 13. Scully Company issued Burton Co. a credit memorandum for merchandise returned, $1,000. The merchandise had been purchased by Burton Co. on account on July 5. The cost of the merchandise returned was $700.	Sales Returns & Allowances Accounts Receivable—Burton Co.	1,000	1,000	Accounts Payable—Scully Co. Merchandise Inventory	1,000	1,000
	Merchandise Inventory Cost of Merchandise Sold	700	700			
July 15. Scully Company received payment from Burton Co. for purchase of July 5.	Cash Accounts Receivable—Burton Co.	4,000	4,000	Accounts Payable—Scully Co. Cash	4,000	4,000

Transaction	Scully Company (Seller)		Burton Co. (Buyer)	

July 18. Scully Company sold merchandise on account to Burton Co., $12,000, terms FOB shipping point, 2/10, n/eom. Scully Company prepaid transportation costs of $500, which were added to the invoice. The cost of the merchandise sold was $7,200.	Accounts Receivable—Burton Co.
	   Sales
		12,000
		
		12,000
			Merchandise Inventory
			   Accounts Payable—Scully Co.
				12,500
				
				12,500

	Accounts Receivable—Burton Co. Cash	500 500		
	Cost of Merchandise Sold Merchandise Inventory	7,200 7,200		

July 28. Scully Company received payment from Burton Co. for purchase of July 18, less discount (2% × $12,000).	Cash
	Sales Discounts
	   Accounts Receivable—Burton Co.
		12,260
		240
		
		12,500
			Accounts Payable—Scully Co.
			   Merchandise Inventory
			   Cash
				12,500
				
				240
				12,260

Chart of Accounts for a Merchandising Business

objective 7

Prepare a chart of accounts for a merchandising business.

The chart of accounts for a merchandising business should reflect the types of merchandising transactions we have described in this chapter. As a basis for illustration, we use NetSolutions.

On July 1, 2006, when NetSolutions began its operations as a personalized retailer of software and hardware, its chart of accounts changed from that of a service business to that of a merchandiser. The new chart of accounts is shown in Exhibit 11. The accounts related to merchandising transactions are shown in color.

•Exhibit 11

Chart of Accounts for NetSolutions, Merchandising Business

Balance Sheet Accounts		Income Statement Accounts	
	100 Assets		400 Revenues
110	Cash	410	Sales
112	Accounts Receivable	411	Sales Returns and Allowances
115	Merchandise Inventory	412	Sales Discounts
116	Office Supplies		
117	Prepaid Insurance		500 Costs and Expenses
120	Land	510	Cost of Merchandise Sold
123	Store Equipment	520	Sales Salaries Expense
124	Accumulated Depreciation— Store Equipment	521	Advertising Expense
		522	Depreciation Expense—Store Equipment
125	Office Equipment	523	Transportation Out
126	Accumulated Depreciation— Office Equipment	529	Miscellaneous Selling Expense
		530	Office Salaries Expense
	200 Liabilities	531	Rent Expense
210	Accounts Payable	532	Depreciation Expense—Office Equipment
211	Salaries Payable	533	Insurance Expense
212	Unearned Rent	534	Office Supplies Expense
215	Notes Payable	539	Misc. Administrative Expense
	300 Stockholders' Equity		600 Other Income
310	Capital Stock	610	Rent Revenue
311	Retained Earnings		
312	Dividends		700 Other Expense
313	Income Summary	710	Interest Expense

NetSolutions is now using three-digit account numbers, which permits it to add new accounts as they are needed. The first digit indicates the major financial statement classification (1 for assets, 2 for liabilities, and so on). The second digit indicates the subclassification (e.g., 11 for current assets, 12 for noncurrent assets). The third digit identifies the specific account (e.g., 110 for Cash, 123 for Store Equipment).

NetSolutions is using a more complex numbering system because it has a greater variety of transactions. In addition, its growth creates a need for more detailed information for use in managing it. For example, a wages expense account was adequate for NetSolutions when it was a small service business with few employees. However, as a merchandising business, NetSolutions now uses two payroll accounts, one for Sales Salaries Expense and one for Office Salaries Expense.

The Accounting Cycle for a Merchandising Business

objective **8**

Describe the accounting cycle for a merchandising business.

We have described and illustrated the chart of accounts and the analysis and recording of transactions for a merchandising business. We have also illustrated the preparation of financial statements for a merchandiser, NetSolutions, at the end of an accounting cycle. In the remainder of this chapter, we describe the other elements of the accounting cycle for a merchandising business. In this discussion, we will focus primarily on the elements of this cycle that are likely to differ from those of a service business.

Merchandise Inventory Shrinkage

> $62,150
> Actual
> Inventory Per
> Physical Count
>
> $1,800
> Shrinkage
>
> $63,950
> Available
> For Sale
> Per Records

Under the perpetual inventory system, a separate merchandise inventory account is maintained in the ledger. During the accounting period, this account shows the amount of merchandise for sale at any time. However, merchandising businesses may experience some loss of inventory due to shoplifting, employee theft, or errors in recording or counting inventory. As a result, the physical inventory taken at the end of the accounting period may differ from the amount of inventory shown in the inventory records. Normally, the amount of merchandise for sale, as indicated by the balance of the merchandise inventory account, is larger than the total amount of merchandise counted during the physical inventory. For this reason, the difference is often called *inventory shrinkage* or *inventory shortage*.

To illustrate, NetSolutions' inventory records indicate that $63,950 of merchandise should be available for sale on December 31, 2007. The physical inventory taken on December 31, 2007, however, indicates that only $62,150 of merchandise is actually available. Thus, the inventory shrinkage for the year ending December 31, 2007, is $1,800 ($63,950 − $62,150), as shown at the left. This amount is recorded by the following adjusting entry:

		Adjusting Entry		
Dec.	31	Cost of Merchandise Sold	1 8 0 0 00	
		Merchandise Inventory		1 8 0 0 00

After this entry has been recorded, the accounting records agree with the actual physical inventory at the end of the period. Since no system of procedures and safeguards can totally eliminate it, inventory shrinkage is often considered a normal cost of operations. If the amount of the shrinkage is abnormally large, it may be disclosed separately on the income statement. In such cases, the shrinkage may be recorded in a separate account, such as Loss from Merchandise Inventory Shrinkage.

Work Sheet

Merchandising businesses that use a perpetual inventory system are also likely to use a computerized accounting system. In a computerized system, the adjusting entries are recorded and financial statements prepared without using a work sheet. For this reason, we illustrate the work sheet and the adjusting entries for NetSolutions in the appendix at the end of this chapter.

Closing Entries

The closing entries for a merchandising business are similar to those for a service business. The first entry closes the temporary accounts with credit balances, such as Sales, to the income summary account. The second entry closes the temporary accounts with debit balances, including Sales Returns and Allowances, Sales Discounts, and Cost of Merchandise Sold, to the income summary account. The third entry closes the balance of the income summary account to the retained earnings account. The fourth entry closes the dividends account to the retained earnings account.

In a computerized accounting system, the closing entries are prepared automatically. For this reason, we illustrate the closing entries for NetSolutions in the appendix at the end of this chapter.

REAL WORLD

Retailers lose an estimated $30 billion to inventory shrinkage. The primary causes of the shrinkage are employee theft and shoplifting.

If the inventory account has a balance of $280,000 and the physical inventory indicates merchandise on hand of $265,000, what is the amount of inventory shrinkage?

$15,000 ($280,000 − $265,000)

INTEGRITY IN BUSINESS

THE COST OF EMPLOYEE THEFT

One survey reported that the 30 largest retail store chains have lost over $5 billion to shoplifting and employee theft. Of this amount only 3.45% of the losses resulted in any recovery. The stores apprehended over 600,000 shoplifters and 78,000 dishonest employees. Approximately one out of every 27 employees was apprehended for theft from his or her employer. Each dishonest employee stole approximately 8 times the amount stolen by shoplifters ($900 vs. $114).

Source: Jack L. Hayes International, *Fourteenth Annual Retail Theft Survey*, 2001.

Financial Analysis and Interpretation

Compute the ratio of net sales to assets as a measure of how effectively a business is using its assets.

The ratio of net sales to assets measures how effectively a business is using its assets to generate sales. A high ratio indicates an effective use of assets. The assets used in computing the ratio may be the total assets at the end of the year, the average of the total assets at the beginning and end of the year, or the average of the monthly assets. For our purposes, we will use the average of the total assets at the beginning and end of the year. The ratio is computed as follows:

$$\text{Ratio of net sales to assets} = \frac{\text{Net sales}}{\text{Average total assets}}$$

To illustrate the use of this ratio, the following data are taken from annual reports of **Sears** and **J.C.Penney**:

	Sears	J.C.Penney
Net sales (in millions)	$41,366	$31,846
Total assets (in millions):		
Beginning of year	50,409	19,742
End of year	44,317	20,908

The ratio of net sales to assets for each company is as follows:

	Sears	J.C.Penney
Ratio of net sales to assets	0.87*	1.57**

*$41,366/[($50,409 + $44,317)/2]
**$31,846/[($19,742 + $20,908)/2]

Based on these ratios, J.C.Penney appears better than Sears in utilizing its assets to generate sales. Comparing this ratio over time for both Sears and J.C.Penney, as well as comparing it with industry averages, would provide a better basis for interpreting the financial performance of each company.

SPOTLIGHT ON STRATEGY

UNDER ONE ROOF AT J.C.PENNEY

Most businesses cannot be all things to all people. Businesses must seek a position in the marketplace to serve a unique customer need. Companies that are unable to do this can be squeezed out of the marketplace. The mall-based department store has been under pressure from both ends of the retail spectrum. At the discount store end of the market, **Wal-Mart** has been a formidable competitor. At the high end, specialty retailers have established strong presence in identifiable niches, such as electronics and apparel. Over a decade ago, **J.C.Penney** abandoned its "hard goods," such as electronics and sporting goods, in favor of providing "soft goods" because of the emerging strength of specialty retailers in the hard goods segments. J.C.Penney is positioning itself against these forces by "exceeding the fashion, quality, selection, and service components of the discounter, equaling the merchandise intensity of the specialty store, and providing the selection and 'under one roof' shopping convenience of the department store." J.C.Penney merchandise strategy is focused toward customers it terms the "modern spender" and "starting outs." It views these segments as most likely to value its higher-end merchandise offered under the convenience of "one roof."

Appendix Work Sheet and Adjusting and Closing Entries for a Merchandising Business

A merchandising business that does not use a computerized accounting system may use a work sheet in assembling the data for preparing financial statements and adjusting and closing entries. In this appendix, we illustrate such a work sheet, along with the adjusting and closing entries for a merchandising business.

The work sheet in Exhibit 12 is for NetSolutions on December 31, 2007, the end of its second year of operations as a merchandiser. In this work sheet, we list all of the accounts, including the accounts that have no balances, in the order that they appear in NetSolutions' ledger.

•Exhibit 12   Work Sheet for Merchandising Business

NetSolutions
Work Sheet
For the Year Ended December 31, 2007

	Account Title	Trial Balance Dr.	Trial Balance Cr.	Adjustments Dr.	Adjustments Cr.	Adjusted Trial Balance Dr.	Adjusted Trial Balance Cr.	Income Statement Dr.	Income Statement Cr.	Balance Sheet Dr.	Balance Sheet Cr.	
1	Cash	52,950				52,950				52,950		1
2	Accounts Receivable	91,080				91,080				91,080		2
3	Merchandise Inventory	63,950			(a)1,800	62,150				62,150		3
4	Office Supplies	1,090			(b) 610	480				480		4
5	Prepaid Insurance	4,560			(c)1,910	2,650				2,650		5
6	Land	20,000				20,000				20,000		6
7	Store Equipment	27,100				27,100				27,100		7
8	Accum. Depr.—Store Equipment		2,600		(d)3,100		5,700				5,700	8
9	Office Equipment	15,570				15,570				15,570		9
10	Accum. Depr.—Office Equipment		2,230		(e)2,490		4,720				4,720	10
11	Accounts Payable		22,420				22,420				22,420	11
12	Salaries Payable				(f)1,140		1,140				1,140	12
13	Unearned Rent		2,400	(g) 600			1,800				1,800	13
14	Notes Payable											14
15	(final payment due 2017)		25,000				25,000				25,000	15
16	Capital Stock		25,000				25,000				25,000	16
17	Retained Earnings		128,800				128,800				128,800	17
18	Dividends	18,000				18,000				18,000		18
19	Sales		720,185				720,185		720,185			19
20	Sales Returns and Allowances	6,140				6,140		6,140				20
21	Sales Discounts	5,790				5,790		5,790				21
22	Cost of Merchandise Sold	523,505		(a)1,800		525,305		525,305				22
23	Sales Salaries Expense	55,450		(f) 780		56,230		56,230				23
24	Advertising Expense	10,860				10,860		10,860				24
25	Depr. Exp.—Store Equipment			(d)3,100		3,100		3,100				25
26	Miscellaneous Selling Expense	630				630		630				26
27	Office Salaries Expense	20,660		(f) 360		21,020		21,020				27
28	Rent Expense	8,100				8,100		8,100				28
29	Depr. Exp.—Office Equipment			(e)2,490		2,490		2,490				29
30	Insurance Expense			(c)1,910		1,910		1,910				30
31	Office Supplies Expense			(b) 610		610		610				31
32	Misc. Administrative Expense	760				760		760				32
33	Rent Revenue				(g) 600		600		600			33
34	Interest Expense	2,440				2,440		2,440				34
35		928,635	928,635	11,650	11,650	935,365	935,365	645,385	720,785	289,980	214,580	35
36	Net income							75,400			75,400	36
37								720,785	720,785	289,980	289,980	37

(a) Merchandise inventory shrinkage for period, $1,800 ($63,950 − $62,150).

(b) Office supplies used, $610 ($1,090 − $480).

(c) Insurance expired, $1,910.

(d) Depreciation of store equipment, $3,100.

(e) Depreciation of office equipment, $2,490.

(f) Salaries accrued but not paid (sales salaries, $780; office salaries, $360), $1,140.

(g) Rent earned from amount received in advance, $600.

The data needed for adjusting the accounts of NetSolutions are as follows:

Physical merchandise inventory on December 31, 2007	$62,150
Office supplies on hand on December 31, 2007	480
Insurance expired during 2007	1,910
Depreciation during 2007 on: Store equipment	3,100
Office equipment	2,490
Salaries accrued on December 31, 2007: Sales salaries $780	
Office salaries 360	1,140
Rent earned during 2007	600

There is no specific order in which to analyze the accounts in the work sheet, assemble the adjustment data, and make the adjusting entries. However, you can normally save time by selecting the accounts in the order in which they appear on the trial balance. Using this approach, the adjustment for merchandise inventory shrinkage is listed first {entry (a) on the work sheet}, followed by the adjustment for office supplies used {entry (b) on the work sheet}, and so on.

After all the adjustments have been entered on the work sheet, the Adjustments columns are totaled to prove the equality of debits and credits. As we illustrated in a previous chapter, the adjusted amounts of the balances in the Trial Balance columns are extended to the Adjusted Trial Balance columns.[6] The Adjusted Trial Balance columns are then totaled to prove the equality of debits and credits.

The balances, as adjusted, are then extended to the statement columns. The four statement columns are totaled, and the net income or net loss is determined. For Net-Solutions, the difference between the credit and debit columns of the Income Statement section is $75,400, the amount of the net income. The difference between the debit and credit columns of the Balance Sheet section is also $75,400, which is the increase in retained earnings as a result of the net income. Agreement between the two balancing amounts is evidence of debit-credit equality and mathematical accuracy.

The income statement, retained earnings statement, and balance sheet are prepared from the work sheet in a manner similar to that of a service business. These financial statements are shown in Exhibits 3, 4, and 5. The Adjustments columns in the work sheet provide the data for journalizing the adjusting entries. NetSolutions' adjusting entries at the end of 2007 are as follows:

JOURNAL					Page 28
Date	Description	Post. Ref.	Debit	Credit	
	Adjusting Entries				1
2007 Dec. 31	Cost of Merchandise Sold	510	1 8 0 0 00		2
	Merchandise Inventory	115		1 8 0 0 00	3
					4
31	Office Supplies Expense	534	6 1 0 00		5
	Office Supplies	116		6 1 0 00	6
					7
31	Insurance Expense	533	1 9 1 0 00		8
	Prepaid Insurance	117		1 9 1 0 00	9
					10
31	Depreciation Expense—				11
	Store Equipment	522	3 1 0 0 00		12
	Accumulated Depreciation—				13
	Store Equipment	124		3 1 0 0 00	14

	Date		Item	Post. Ref.	Debit	Credit	
16	2007 Dec.	31	Depreciation Expense—				16
17			Office Equipment	532	2 4 9 0 00		17
18			Accumulated Depreciation—				18
19			Office Equipment	126		2 4 9 0 00	19
20							20
21		31	Sales Salaries Expense	520	7 8 0 00		21
22			Office Salaries Expense	530	3 6 0 00		22
23			Salaries Payable	211		1 1 4 0 00	23
24							24
25		31	Unearned Rent	212	6 0 0 00		25
26			Rent Revenue	610		6 0 0 00	26

The Income Statement columns of the work sheet provide the data for preparing the closing entries. The closing entries for NetSolutions at the end of 2007 are as follows:

			JOURNAL			Page 29	
	Date		Item	Post. Ref.	Debit	Credit	
1			Closing Entries				1
2	2007 Dec.	31	Sales	410	720 1 8 5 00		2
3			Rent Revenue	610	6 0 0 00		3
4			Income Summary	313		720 7 8 5 00	4
5							5
6		31	Income Summary	313	645 3 8 5 00		6
7			Sales Returns and Allowances	411		6 1 4 0 00	7
8			Sales Discounts	412		5 7 9 0 00	8
9			Cost of Merchandise Sold	510		525 3 0 5 00	9
10			Sales Salaries Expense	520		56 2 3 0 00	10
11			Advertising Expense	521		10 8 6 0 00	11
12			Depr. Expense—Store Equipment	522		3 1 0 0 00	12
13			Miscellaneous Selling Expense	529		6 3 0 00	13
14			Office Salaries Expense	530		21 0 2 0 00	14
15			Rent Expense	531		8 1 0 0 00	15
16			Depr. Expense—Office Equipment	532		2 4 9 0 00	16
17			Insurance Expense	533		1 9 1 0 00	17
18			Office Supplies Expense	534		6 1 0 00	18
19			Misc. Administrative Expense	539		7 6 0 00	19
20			Interest Expense	710		2 4 4 0 00	20
21							21
22		31	Income Summary	313	75 4 0 0 00		22
23			Retained Earnings	311		75 4 0 0 00	23
24							24
25		31	Retained Earnings	311	18 0 0 0 00		25
26			Dividends	312		18 0 0 0 00	26

The balance of Income Summary, after the first two closing entries have been posted, is the net income or net loss for the period. The third closing entry transfers this balance to the retained earnings account. NetSolutions' income summary account after the closing entries have been posted is as follows:

ACCOUNT *Income Summary*   **ACCOUNT NO.** *313*

Date	Item	Post. Ref.	Debit	Credit	Balance Debit	Balance Credit
2007 Dec. 31	Revenues	29		720 785 00		720 785 00
31	Expenses	29	645 385 00			75 400 00
31	Net income	29	75 400 00		—	—

After the closing entries have been prepared and posted to the accounts, a post-closing trial balance may be prepared to verify the debit-credit equality. The only accounts that should appear on the post-closing trial balance are the asset, contra asset, liability, and stockholders' equity accounts with balances. These are the same accounts that appear on the end-of-period balance sheet.

Key Points

1 Distinguish the activities of a service business from those of a merchandising business.

The primary differences between a service business and a merchandising business relate to revenue activities. Merchandising businesses purchase merchandise for selling to customers.

On a merchandising business's income statement, revenue from selling merchandise is reported as sales. The cost of the merchandise sold is subtracted from sales to arrive at gross profit. The operating expenses are subtracted from gross profit to arrive at net income.

Merchandise inventory, which is merchandise not sold, is reported as a current asset on the balance sheet.

2 Describe and illustrate the financial statements of a merchandising business.

The multiple-step income statement of a merchandiser reports sales, sales returns and allowances, sales discounts, and net sales. The cost of the merchandise sold is subtracted from net sales to determine the gross profit. The cost of merchandise sold is determined by using either the periodic or perpetual method. Operating in-

come is determined by subtracting operating expenses from gross profit. Operating expenses are normally classified as selling or administrative expenses. Net income is determined by adding or subtracting the net of other income and expense. The income statement may also be reported in a single-step form. The retained earnings statement is similar to that for a service business. The balance sheet reports merchandise inventory at the end of the period as a current asset.

3 Describe the accounting for the sale of merchandise.

Sales of merchandise for cash or on account are recorded by crediting Sales. The cost of merchandise sold and the reduction in merchandise inventory are also recorded for the sale. For sales of merchandise on account, the credit terms may allow discounts for early payment. Such discounts are recorded by the seller as a debit to Sales Discounts. Sales discounts are reported as a deduction from the amount initially recorded in Sales. Likewise, when merchandise is returned or a price adjustment is granted, the seller debits Sales Returns and Allowances.

For sales on account, a subsidiary ledger is maintained for individual customer accounts receivable.

Under the perpetual inventory system, the cost of merchandise sold and the reduction of merchandise inventory on hand are recorded at the time of sale. In this way, the merchandise inventory account indicates the amount of merchandise on hand at all times. Likewise, any returned merchandise is recorded in the merchandise inventory account, with a related reduction in the cost of merchandise sold.

4 Describe the accounting for the purchase of merchandise.

Purchases of merchandise for cash or on account are recorded by debiting Merchandise Inventory. For purchases of merchandise on account, the credit terms may allow cash discounts for early payment. Such purchases discounts are viewed as a reduction in the cost of the merchandise purchased. When merchandise is returned or a price adjustment is granted, the buyer credits Merchandise Inventory.

5 Describe the accounting for transportation costs, sales taxes, and trade discounts.

EXERCISE 5-27
Normal balances of merchandise accounts
Objectives 3, 4, 5

What is the normal balance of the following accounts: (a) Cost of Merchandise Sold, (b) Merchandise Inventory, (c) Sales, (d) Sales Discounts, (e) Sales Returns and Allowances, (f) Transportation Out?

EXERCISE 5-28
Chart of accounts
Objective 7

Igloo Co. is a newly organized business with the following list of accounts, arranged in alphabetical order:

Accounts Payable	Notes Payable (short-term)
Accounts Receivable	Office Equipment
Accumulated Depreciation—Office Equipment	Office Salaries Expense
Accumulated Depreciation—Store Equipment	Office Supplies
Advertising Expense	Office Supplies Expense
Capital Stock	Prepaid Insurance
Cash	Rent Expense
Cost of Merchandise Sold	Retained Earnings
Depreciation Expense—Office Equipment	Salaries Payable
Depreciation Expense—Store Equipment	Sales
Dividends	Sales Discounts
Income Summary	Sales Returns and Allowances
Insurance Expense	Sales Salaries Expense
Interest Expense	Store Equipment
Land	Store Supplies
Merchandise Inventory	Store Supplies Expense
Miscellaneous Administrative Expense	Transportation Out
Miscellaneous Selling Expense	

Construct a chart of accounts, assigning account numbers and arranging the accounts in balance sheet and income statement order, as illustrated in Exhibit 11. Each account number is three digits: the first digit is to indicate the major classification ("1" for assets, and so on); the second digit is to indicate the subclassification ("11" for current assets, and so on); and the third digit is to identify the specific account ("110" for Cash, and so on).

EXERCISE 5-29
Adjusting entry for merchandise inventory shrinkage
Objective 8

Pulmonary Inc.'s perpetual inventory records indicate that $382,800 of merchandise should be on hand on March 31, 2006. The physical inventory indicates that $371,250 of merchandise is actually on hand. Journalize the adjusting entry for the inventory shrinkage for Pulmonary Inc. for the year ended March 31, 2006.

EXERCISE 5-30
Closing the accounts of a merchandiser
Objective 8

From the following list, identify the accounts that should be closed to Income Summary at the end of the fiscal year: (a) Accounts Receivable, (b) Cost of Merchandise Sold, (c) Merchandise Inventory, (d) Sales, (e) Sales Discounts, (f) Sales Returns and Allowances, (g) Salaries Expense, (h) Salaries Payable, (i) Supplies, (j) Supplies Expense.

EXERCISE 5-31
Ratio of net sales to total assets
Objective 9

REAL WORLD

The financial statements for **Home Depot** are presented in Appendix F at the end of the text.

a. Determine the ratio of net sales to average total assets for Home Depot for the years ended February 2, 2003, and February 3, 2002.
b. What conclusions can be drawn from these ratios concerning the trend in the ability of Home Depot to effectively use its assets to generate sales?

Note: Home Depot's total assets on January 28, 2001, were $21,385,000,000.

EXERCISE 5-32
Ratio of net sales to total assets

Objective 9

REAL WORLD

Winn-Dixie Stores reported the following data in its financial statements for 2002:

Net sales and revenues	$12,334,353,000
Total assets at end of 2002	2,937,578,000
Total assets at end of 2001	3,041,670,000

a. Compute the ratio of net sales to assets for 2002. Round to two decimal places.
b. ▰▰▰▶ Would you expect the ratio of net sales to assets for Winn-Dixie to be similar to or different from that of **Zales Corp.**? Zales is the largest North American retailer of jewelry, with a ratio of net sales to assets of 1.53.

APPENDIX EXERCISE 5-33
Closing entries

Based on the data presented in Exercise 5-11, journalize the closing entries.

Problems Series A

PROBLEM 5-1A
Multiple-step income statement and report form of balance sheet

Objective 2

SPREADSHEET
P.A.S.S.

✓ 1. Net income: $81,600

The following selected accounts and their current balances appear in the ledger of Sombrero Co. for the fiscal year ended November 30, 2006:

Cash	$ 91,800	Sales	$1,802,400
Accounts Receivable	74,400	Sales Returns and Allowances	25,200
Merchandise Inventory	120,000	Sales Discounts	13,200
Office Supplies	3,120	Cost of Merchandise Sold	1,284,000
Prepaid Insurance	8,160	Sales Salaries Expense	252,000
Office Equipment	76,800	Advertising Expense	33,960
Accumulated Depreciation—		Depreciation Expense—	
Office Equipment	12,960	Store Equipment	5,520
Store Equipment	141,000	Miscellaneous Selling Expense	1,320
Accumulated Depreciation—		Office Salaries Expense	49,200
Store Equipment	58,320	Rent Expense	26,580
Accounts Payable	32,400	Insurance Expense	15,300
Salaries Payable	2,400	Depreciation Expense—	
Note Payable		Office Equipment	10,800
(final payment due 2016)	36,000	Office Supplies Expense	1,080
Capital Stock	60,000	Miscellaneous Administrative	
Retained Earnings	261,600	Expense	1,440
Dividends	30,000	Interest Expense	1,200

Instructions

1. Prepare a multiple-step income statement.
2. Prepare a retained earnings statement.
3. Prepare a report form of balance sheet, assuming that the current portion of the note payable is $3,000.
4. Briefly explain (a) how multiple-step and single-step income statements differ and (b) how report-form and account-form balance sheets differ.

PROBLEM 5-2A
Single-step income statement and account form of balance sheet

Objective 2

SPREADSHEET

✓ 3. Total assets: $444,000

Selected accounts and related amounts for Sombrero Co. for the fiscal year ended November 30, 2006, are presented in Problem 5-1A.

Instructions

1. Prepare a single-step income statement in the format shown in Exhibit 3.
2. Prepare a retained earnings statement.
3. Prepare an account form of balance sheet, assuming that the current portion of the note payable is $3,000.

PROBLEM 5-3A
Sales-related transactions

Objectives 3, 5

P.A.S.S.

The following selected transactions were completed by Interstate Supplies Co., which sells irrigation supplies primarily to wholesalers and occasionally to retail customers.

Mar. 1. Sold merchandise on account to Babcock Co., $7,500, terms FOB shipping point, n/eom. The cost of merchandise sold was $4,500.

2. Sold merchandise for $8,000 plus 6% sales tax to cash customers. The cost of merchandise sold was $4,750.

5. Sold merchandise on account to North Star Company, $16,000, terms FOB destination, 1/10, n/30. The cost of merchandise sold was $10,500.

8. Sold merchandise for $6,150 plus 6% sales tax to customers who used VISA cards. Deposited credit card receipts into the bank. The cost of merchandise sold was $3,700.

13. Sold merchandise to customers who used American Express cards, $6,500. The cost of merchandise sold was $3,600.

14. Sold merchandise on account to Blech Co., $7,500, terms FOB shipping point, 1/10, n/30. The cost of merchandise sold was $4,000.

15. Received check for amount due from North Star Company for sale on March 5.

16. Issued credit memorandum for $800 to Blech Co. for merchandise returned from sale on March 14. The cost of the merchandise returned was $360.

18. Sold merchandise on account to Westech Company, $6,850, terms FOB shipping point, 2/10, n/30. Paid $210 for transportation costs and added them to the invoice. The cost of merchandise sold was $4,100.

24. Received check for amount due from Blech Co. for sale on March 14 less credit memorandum of May 16 and discount.

27. Received $7,680 from American Express for $8,000 of sales reported during the week of May 1–12.

28. Received check for amount due from Westech Company for sale of March 18.

31. Paid Downtown Delivery Service $1,275 for merchandise delivered during March to customers under shipping terms of FOB destination.

31. Received check for amount due from Babcock Co. for sale of March 1.

April 3. Paid First National Bank $725 for service fees for handling MasterCard sales during March.

10. Paid $2,800 to state sales tax division for taxes owed on March sales.

Instructions

Journalize the entries to record the transactions of Interstate Supplies Co.

PROBLEM 5-4A
Purchase-related transactions

Objectives 4, 5

P.A.S.S.

The following selected transactions were completed by Petunia Co. during August of the current year:

Aug. 1. Purchased merchandise from Fisher Co., $8,500, terms FOB shipping point, 2/10, n/eom. Prepaid transportation costs of $250 were added to the invoice.

5. Purchased merchandise from Byrd Co., $10,400, terms FOB destination, n/30.

10. Paid Fisher Co. for invoice of August 1, less discount.

13. Purchased merchandise from Mickle Co., $7,500, terms FOB destination, 1/10, n/30.

14. Issued debit memorandum to Mickle Co. for $2,500 of merchandise returned from purchase on August 13.

18. Purchased merchandise from Lanning Company, $10,000, terms FOB shipping point, n/eom.

18. Paid transportation charges of $150 on August 18 purchase from Lanning Company.

19. Purchased merchandise from Hatcher Co., $7,500, terms FOB destination, 2/10, n/30.

23. Paid Mickle Co. for invoice of August 13, less debit memorandum of August 14 and discount.

Aug. 29. Paid Hatcher Co. for invoice of August 19, less discount.
   31. Paid Lanning Company for invoice of August 18.
   31. Paid Byrd Co. for invoice of August 5.

Instructions
Journalize the entries to record the transactions of Petunia Co. for August.

PROBLEM 5-5A
Sales-related and purchase-related transactions

Objectives 3, 4, 5

P.A.S.S.

The following were selected from among the transactions completed by Ingress Company during January of the current year:

Jan. 3. Purchased merchandise on account from Pynn Co., list price $16,000, trade discount 35%, terms FOB shipping point, 2/10, n/30, with prepaid transportation costs of $320 added to the invoice.
   5. Purchased merchandise on account from Wilhelm Co., $8,000, terms FOB destination, 1/10, n/30.
   6. Sold merchandise on account to Sievert Co., list price $12,500, trade discount 40%, terms 2/10, n/30. The cost of the merchandise sold was $4,500.
   7. Returned $1,800 of merchandise purchased on January 5 from Wilhelm Co.
  13. Paid Pynn Co. on account for purchase of January 3, less discount.
  15. Paid Wilhelm Co. on account for purchase of January 5, less return of January 7 and discount.
  16. Received cash on account from sale of January 6 to Sievert Co., less discount.
  19. Sold merchandise on nonbank credit cards and reported accounts to the card company, American Express, $6,450. The cost of the merchandise sold was $3,950.
  22. Sold merchandise on account to Elk River Co., $3,480, terms 2/10, n/30. The cost of the merchandise sold was $1,400.
  23. Sold merchandise for cash, $9,350. The cost of the merchandise sold was $5,750.
  25. Received merchandise returned by Elk River Co. from sale on January 22, $1,480. The cost of the returned merchandise was $600.
  31. Received cash from American Express for nonbank credit card sales of January 19, less $225 service fee.

Instructions
Journalize the transactions.

PROBLEM 5-6A
Sales-related and purchase-related transactions for seller and buyer

Objective 6

The following selected transactions were completed during June between Schnaps Company and Brandy Company:

June 2. Schnaps Company sold merchandise on account to Brandy Company, $14,000, terms FOB shipping point, 2/10, n/30. Schnaps Company paid transportation costs of $350, which were added to the invoice. The cost of the merchandise sold was $8,000.
   8. Schnaps Company sold merchandise on account to Brandy Company, $12,500, terms FOB destination, 1/15, n/eom. The cost of the merchandise sold was $7,500.
   8. Schnaps Company paid transportation costs of $550 for delivery of merchandise sold to Brandy Company on June 8.
  12. Brandy Company returned $3,000 of merchandise purchased on account on June 8 from Schnaps Company. The cost of the merchandise returned was $1,800.
  12. Brandy Company paid Schnaps Company for purchase of June 2, less discount.
  23. Brandy Company paid Schnaps Company for purchase of June 8, less discount and less return of June 12.
  24. Schnaps Company sold merchandise on account to Brandy Company, $10,000, terms FOB shipping point, n/eom. The cost of the merchandise sold was $6,000.

June 26. Brandy Company paid transportation charges of $310 on June 24 purchase from Schnaps Company.

30. Brandy Company paid Schnaps Company on account for purchase of June 24.

Instructions

Journalize the June transactions for (1) Schnaps Company and (2) Brandy Company.

APPENDIX PROBLEM 5-7A
Work sheet, financial statements, and adjusting and closing entries

SPREADSHEET

✓ *2. Net income: $73,665*

The accounts and their balances in the ledger of Glycol Co. on December 31, 2006, are as follows:

Cash	$ 11,165	Sales	$847,500
Accounts Receivable	86,100	Sales Returns and Allowances	15,500
Merchandise Inventory	235,000	Sales Discounts	6,000
Prepaid Insurance	10,600	Cost of Merchandise Sold	501,200
Store Supplies	3,750	Sales Salaries Expense	86,400
Office Supplies	1,700	Advertising Expense	29,450
Store Equipment	225,000	Depreciation Expense—	
Accumulated Depreciation—		Store Equipment	—
Store Equipment	40,300	Store Supplies Expense	—
Office Equipment	72,000	Miscellaneous Selling Expense	1,885
Accumulated Depreciation—		Office Salaries Expense	60,000
Office Equipment	17,200	Rent Expense	30,000
Accounts Payable	56,700	Insurance Expense	—
Salaries Payable	—	Depreciation Expense—	
Unearned Rent	1,200	Office Equipment	—
Note Payable		Office Supplies Expense	—
(final payment due 2016)	185,000	Miscellaneous Administrative	
Capital Stock	80,000	Expense	1,650
Retained Earnings	202,100	Rent Revenue	—
Dividends	40,000	Interest Expense	12,600
Income Summary	—		

The data needed for year-end adjustments on December 31 are as follows:

Physical merchandise inventory on December 31		$228,600
Insurance expired during the year		5,000
Supplies on hand on December 31:		
Store supplies		1,200
Office supplies		900
Depreciation for the year:		
Store equipment		8,500
Office equipment		4,500
Salaries payable on December 31:		
Sales salaries	$1,450	
Office salaries	750	2,200
Unearned rent on December 31		400

Instructions

1. Prepare a work sheet for the fiscal year ended December 31, 2006. List all accounts in the order given.
2. Prepare a multiple-step income statement.
3. Prepare a retained earnings statement.
4. Prepare a report form of balance sheet, assuming that the current portion of the note payable is $25,000.
5. Journalize the adjusting entries.
6. Journalize the closing entries.

Problems Series B

PROBLEM 5-1B
Multiple-step income statement and report form of balance sheet

Objective 2

SPREADSHEET
P.A.S.S.

√1. Net income: $80,000

The following selected accounts and their current balances appear in the ledger of Sciatic Co. for the fiscal year ended July 31, 2006:

Cash	$123,000	Sales	$1,028,000
Accounts Receivable	96,800	Sales Returns and Allowances	18,480
Merchandise Inventory	140,000	Sales Discounts	17,520
Office Supplies	4,480	Cost of Merchandise Sold	620,000
Prepaid Insurance	2,720	Sales Salaries Expense	138,560
Office Equipment	68,000	Advertising Expense	35,040
Accumulated Depreciation—		Depreciation Expense—	
Office Equipment	10,240	Store Equipment	5,120
Store Equipment	122,400	Miscellaneous Selling Expense	1,280
Accumulated Depreciation—		Office Salaries Expense	67,320
Store Equipment	27,360	Rent Expense	25,080
Accounts Payable	44,480	Depreciation Expense—	
Salaries Payable	1,920	Office Equipment	10,160
Note Payable		Insurance Expense	3,120
(final payment due 2016)	44,800	Office Supplies Expense	1,040
Capital Stock	75,000	Miscellaneous Administrative	
Retained Earnings	301,600	Expense	1,280
Dividends	28,000	Interest Expense	4,000

Instructions
1. Prepare a multiple-step income statement.
2. Prepare a retained earnings statement.
3. Prepare a report form of balance sheet, assuming that the current portion of the note payable is $6,000.
4. Briefly explain (a) how multiple-step and single-step income statements differ and (b) how report-form and account-form balance sheets differ.

PROBLEM 5-2B
Single-step income statement and account form of balance sheet

Objective 2

SPREADSHEET

√3. Total assets: $519,800

Selected accounts and related amounts for Sciatic Co. for the fiscal year ended July 31, 2006, are presented in Problem 5-1B.

Instructions
1. Prepare a single-step income statement in the format shown in Exhibit 3.
2. Prepare a retained earnings statement.
3. Prepare an account form of balance sheet, assuming that the current portion of the note payable is $6,000.

PROBLEM 5-3B
Sales-related transactions

Objectives 3, 5

P.A.S.S.

The following selected transactions were completed by Holistic Supply Co., which sells office supplies primarily to wholesalers and occasionally to retail customers.

Aug. 2. Sold merchandise on account to Runyan Co., $12,800, terms FOB destination, 2/10, n/30. The cost of the merchandise sold was $7,600.
3. Sold merchandise for $5,000 plus 7% sales tax to cash customers. The cost of merchandise sold was $3,000.
4. Sold merchandise on account to McNutt Co., $2,800, terms FOB shipping point, n/eom. The cost of merchandise sold was $1,800.
5. Sold merchandise for $4,400 plus 7% sales tax to customers who used MasterCard. Deposited credit card receipts into the bank. The cost of merchandise sold was $2,500.
12. Received check for amount due from Runyan Co. for sale on August 2.

Aug. 14. Sold merchandise to customers who used American Express cards, $15,000. The cost of merchandise sold was $9,200.

16. Sold merchandise on account to Westpark Co., $12,000, terms FOB shipping point, 1/10, n/30. The cost of merchandise sold was $7,200.

18. Issued credit memorandum for $3,000 to Westpark Co. for merchandise returned from sale on August 16. The cost of the merchandise returned was $1,800.

19. Sold merchandise on account to DeGroot Co., $9,500, terms FOB shipping point, 1/10, n/30. Added $200 to the invoice for transportation costs prepaid. The cost of merchandise sold was $5,700.

26. Received check for amount due from Westpark Co. for sale on August 16 less credit memorandum of August 18 and discount.

27. Received $7,680 from American Express for $8,000 of sales reported August 1–12.

28. Received check for amount due from DeGroot Co. for sale of August 19.

31. Received check for amount due from McNutt Co. for sale of August 4.

31. Paid Fast Delivery Service $1,050 for merchandise delivered during August to customers under shipping terms of FOB destination.

Sept. 3. Paid First City Bank $850 for service fees for handling MasterCard sales during August.

15. Paid $4,100 to state sales tax division for taxes owed on August sales.

Instructions

Journalize the entries to record the transactions of Holistic Supply Co.

PROBLEM 5-4B
Purchase-related transactions

Objectives 4, 5

P.A.S.S.

The following selected transactions were completed by Daffodil Company during March of the current year:

Mar. 1. Purchased merchandise from Fastow Co., $16,000, terms FOB destination, n/30.

3. Purchased merchandise from Moss Co., $9,000, terms FOB shipping point, 2/10, n/eom. Prepaid transportation costs of $150 were added to the invoice.

4. Purchased merchandise from Picadilly Co., $7,500, terms FOB destination, 2/10, n/30.

6. Issued debit memorandum to Picadilly Co. for $1,000 of merchandise returned from purchase on March 4.

13. Paid Moss Co. for invoice of March 3, less discount.

14. Paid Picadilly Co. for invoice of March 4, less debit memorandum of March 6 and discount.

19. Purchased merchandise from Reardon Co., $12,000, terms FOB shipping point, n/eom.

19. Paid transportation charges of $500 on March 19 purchase from Reardon Co.

20. Purchased merchandise from Hatcher Co., $8,000, terms FOB destination, 1/10, n/30.

30. Paid Hatcher Co. for invoice of March 20, less discount.

31. Paid Fastow Co. for invoice of March 1.

31. Paid Reardon Co. for invoice of March 19.

Instructions

Journalize the entries to record the transactions of Daffodil Company for March.

PROBLEM 5-5B
Sales-related and purchase-related transactions

Objectives 3, 4, 5

P.A.S.S.

The following were selected from among the transactions completed by Girder Company during November of the current year:

Nov. 3. Purchased merchandise on account from Whiting Co., list price $25,000, trade discount 20%, terms FOB destination, 2/10, n/30.

4. Sold merchandise for cash, $7,100. The cost of the merchandise sold was $4,150.

(continued)

Nov. 5. Purchased merchandise on account from Alamosa Co., $10,500, terms FOB shipping point, 2/10, n/30, with prepaid transportation costs of $300 added to the invoice.

6. Returned $5,000 of merchandise purchased on November 3 from Whiting Co.

11. Sold merchandise on account to Bowles Co., list price $2,250, trade discount 20%, terms 1/10, n/30. The cost of the merchandise sold was $1,050.

13. Paid Whiting Co. on account for purchase of November 3, less return of November 6 and discount.

14. Sold merchandise on nonbank credit cards and reported accounts to the card company, American Express, $9,850. The cost of the merchandise sold was $5,900.

15. Paid Alamosa Co. on account for purchase of November 5, less discount.

21. Received cash on account from sale of November 11 to Bowles Co., less discount.

24. Sold merchandise on account to Kapinos Co., $4,200, terms 1/10, n/30. The cost of the merchandise sold was $1,850.

28. Received cash from American Express for nonbank credit card sales of November 14, less $440 service fee.

30. Received merchandise returned by Kapinos Co. from sale on November 24, $1,100. The cost of the returned merchandise was $600.

Instructions
Journalize the transactions.

PROBLEM 5-6B
Sales-related and purchase-related transactions for seller and buyer

Objective 6

The following selected transactions were completed during March between Snyder Company and Brooks Co.:

Mar. 1. Snyder Company sold merchandise on account to Brooks Co., $12,750, terms FOB destination, 2/15, n/eom. The cost of the merchandise sold was $6,000.

2. Snyder Company paid transportation costs of $150 for delivery of merchandise sold to Brooks Co. on March 1.

5. Snyder Company sold merchandise on account to Brooks Co., $18,500, terms FOB shipping point, n/eom. The cost of the merchandise sold was $11,000.

6. Brooks Co. returned $2,000 of merchandise purchased on account on March 1 from Snyder Company. The cost of the merchandise returned was $1,200.

9. Brooks Co. paid transportation charges of $180 on March 5 purchase from Snyder Company.

15. Snyder Company sold merchandise on account to Brooks Co., $20,000, terms FOB shipping point, 1/10, n/30. Snyder Company paid transportation costs of $1,750, which were added to the invoice. The cost of the merchandise sold was $12,000.

16. Brooks Co. paid Snyder Company for purchase of March 1, less discount and less return of March 6.

25. Brooks Co. paid Snyder Company on account for purchase of March 15, less discount.

31. Brooks Co. paid Snyder Company on account for purchase of March 5.

Instructions
Journalize the March transactions for (1) Snyder Company and (2) Brooks Co.

APPENDIX PROBLEM 5-7B
Work sheet, financial statements, and adjusting and closing entries

The accounts and their balances in the ledger of Viaduct Co. on December 31, 2006, are as follows:

✓ *2. Net income: $127,250*

Cash	$ 18,000	Sales	$815,000
Accounts Receivable	82,500	Sales Returns and Allowances	11,900
Merchandise Inventory	165,000	Sales Discounts	7,100
Prepaid Insurance	9,700	Cost of Merchandise Sold	476,200
Store Supplies	4,250	Sales Salaries Expense	76,400
Office Supplies	2,100	Advertising Expense	25,000
Store Equipment	157,000	Depreciation Expense—	
Accumulated Depreciation—		Store Equipment	—
Store Equipment	40,300	Store Supplies Expense	—
Office Equipment	50,000	Miscellaneous Selling Expense	1,600
Accumulated Depreciation—		Office Salaries Expense	34,000
Office Equipment	17,200	Rent Expense	16,000
Accounts Payable	66,700	Insurance Expense	—
Salaries Payable	—	Depreciation Expense—	
Unearned Rent	1,200	Office Equipment	—
Note Payable		Office Supplies Expense —	
(final payment due 2016)	105,000	Miscellaneous Administrative	
Capital Stock	50,000	Expense	1,650
Retained Earnings	84,600	Rent Revenue	—
Dividends	30,000	Interest Expense	11,600
Income Summary	—		

The data needed for year-end adjustments on December 31 are as follows:

Physical merchandise inventory on December 31		$157,500
Insurance expired during the year		4,000
Supplies on hand on December 31:		
Store supplies		1,100
Office supplies		600
Depreciation for the year:		
Store equipment		4,500
Office equipment		2,800
Salaries payable on December 31:		
Sales salaries	$2,850	
Office salaries	800	3,650
Unearned rent on December 31		400

Instructions

1. Prepare a work sheet for the fiscal year ended December 31, 2006. List all accounts in the order given.
2. Prepare a multiple-step income statement.
3. Prepare a retained earnings statement.
4. Prepare a report form of balance sheet, assuming that the current portion of the note payable is $15,000.
5. Journalize the adjusting entries.
6. Journalize the closing entries.

Comprehensive Problem 2

✓ *5. Net income: $163,105*

Lyre Co. is a merchandising business. The account balances for Lyre Co. as of August 1, 2006 (unless otherwise indicated), are as follows:

110	Cash	$ 14,160
112	Accounts Receivable	34,220
115	Merchandise Inventory	133,900
116	Prepaid Insurance	3,750
117	Store Supplies	2,550

(continued)

123	Store Equipment	$104,300
124	Accumulated Depreciation—Store Equipment	12,600
210	Accounts Payable	21,450
211	Salaries Payable	—
310	Capital Stock	40,000
311	Retained Earnings, September 1, 2005	63,280
312	Dividends	10,000
313	Income Summary	—
410	Sales	715,800
411	Sales Returns and Allowances	20,600
412	Sales Discounts	13,200
510	Cost of Merchandise Sold	360,500
520	Sales Salaries Expense	74,400
521	Advertising Expense	18,000
522	Depreciation Expense	—
523	Store Supplies Expense	—
529	Miscellaneous Selling Expense	2,800
530	Office Salaries Expense	40,500
531	Rent Expense	18,600
532	Insurance Expense	—
539	Miscellaneous Administrative Expense	1,650

During August, the last month of the fiscal year, the following transactions were completed:

Aug. 1. Paid rent for August, $1,600.
   3. Purchased merchandise on account from Biathlon Co., terms 2/10, n/30, FOB shipping point, $15,000.
   4. Paid transportation charges on purchase of August 3, $400.
   6. Sold merchandise on account to Hillcrest Co., terms 2/10, n/30, FOB shipping point, $8,500. The cost of the merchandise sold was $5,000.
   7. Received $7,500 cash from Aaberg Co. on account, no discount.
   10. Sold merchandise for cash, $18,300. The cost of the merchandise sold was $11,000.
   13. Paid for merchandise purchased on August 3, less discount.
   14. Received merchandise returned on sale of August 6, $1,500. The cost of the merchandise returned was $900.
   15. Paid advertising expense for last half of August, $1,500.
   16. Received cash from sale of August 6, less return of August 14 and discount.
   19. Purchased merchandise for cash, $8,100.
   19. Paid $6,100 to Ramler Co. on account, no discount.
   20. Sold merchandise on account to Petroski Co., terms 1/10, n/30, FOB shipping point, $16,000. The cost of the merchandise sold was $9,600.
   21. For the convenience of the customer, paid shipping charges on sale of August 20, $600.
   21. Received $11,750 cash from Phillips Co. on account, no discount.
   21. Purchased merchandise on account from Walden Co., terms 1/10, n/30, FOB destination, $15,000.
   24. Returned $3,500 of damaged merchandise purchased on August 21, receiving credit from the seller.
   26. Refunded cash on sales made for cash, $720. The cost of the merchandise returned was $380.
   28. Paid sales salaries of $1,750 and office salaries of $950.
   29. Purchased store supplies for cash, $550.
   30. Sold merchandise on account to Whitetail Co., terms 2/10, n/30, FOB shipping point, $18,750. The cost of the merchandise sold was $11,250.
   30. Received cash from sale of August 20, less discount, plus transportation paid on August 21.
   31. Paid for purchase of August 21, less return of August 24 and discount.

Instructions

(*Note:* If the work sheet described in the appendix is used, follow the alternative instructions.)

1. Enter the balances of each of the accounts in the appropriate balance column of a four-column account. Write *Balance* in the item section, and place a check mark (✔) in the Posting Reference column.
2. Journalize the transactions for August.
3. Post the journal to the general ledger, extending the month-end balances to the appropriate balance columns after all posting is completed. In this problem, you are not required to update or post to the accounts receivable and accounts payable subsidiary ledgers.
4. Journalize and post the adjusting entries, using the following adjustment data:

a.	Merchandise inventory on August 31	$124,115
b.	Insurance expired during the year	1,250
c.	Store supplies on hand on August 31	975
d.	Depreciation for the current year	7,400
e.	Accrued salaries on August 31:	
	Sales salaries	$350
	Office salaries	180 530

5. Prepare a multiple-step income statement, a retained earnings statement, and a report form of balance sheet.
6. Journalize and post the closing entries. Indicate closed accounts by inserting a line in both balance columns opposite the closing entry. Insert the new balance in the retained earnings account.
7. Prepare a post-closing trial balance.

Alternative Instructions

1. Enter the balances of each of the accounts in the appropriate balance column of a four-column account. Write *Balance* in the item section, and place a check mark (✔) in the Posting Reference column.
2. Journalize the transactions for August.
3. Post the journal to the general ledger, extending the month-end balances to the appropriate balance columns after all posting is completed. In this problem, you are not required to update or post to the accounts receivable and accounts payable subsidiary ledgers.
4. Prepare a trial balance as of August 31 on a ten-column work sheet, listing all accounts in the order given in the ledger. Complete the work sheet for the fiscal year ended August 31, using the following adjustment data:

a.	Merchandise inventory on August 31	$124,115
b.	Insurance expired during the year	1,250
c.	Store supplies on hand on August 31	975
d.	Depreciation for the current year	7,400
e.	Accrued salaries on August 31:	
	Sales salaries	$350
	Office salaries	180 530

5. Prepare a multiple-step income statement, a retained earnings statement, and a report form of balance sheet.
6. Journalize and post the adjusting entries.
7. Journalize and post the closing entries. Indicate closed accounts by inserting a line in both balance columns opposite the closing entry. Insert the new balance in the retained earnings account.
8. Prepare a post-closing trial balance.

Special Activities

ACTIVITY 5-1
Ethics and professional conduct in business

ETHICS

On December 1, 2006, Cardinal Company, a garden retailer, purchased $20,000 of corn seed, terms 2/10, n/30, from Iowa Farm Co. Even though the discount period had expired, Sandi Kurtz subtracted the discount of $400 when she processed the documents for payment on December 15, 2006.

Discuss whether Sandi Kurtz behaved in a professional manner by subtracting the discount, even though the discount period had expired.

ACTIVITY 5-2
Purchases discounts and accounts payable

The Video Store Co. is owned and operated by Todd Shovic. The following is an excerpt from a conversation between Todd Shovic and Susan Mastin, the chief accountant for The Video Store.

Todd: Susan, I've got a question about this recent balance sheet.
Susan: Sure, what's your question?
Todd: Well, as you know, I'm applying for a bank loan to finance our new store in Three Forks, and I noticed that the accounts payable are listed as $110,000.
Susan: That's right. Approximately $90,000 of that represents amounts due our suppliers, and the remainder is miscellaneous payables to creditors for utilities, office equipment, supplies, etc.
Todd: That's what I thought. But as you know, we normally receive a 2% discount from our suppliers for earlier payment, and we always try to take the discount.
Susan: That's right. I can't remember the last time we missed a discount.
Todd: Well, in that case, it seems to me the accounts payable should be listed minus the 2% discount. Let's list the accounts payable due suppliers as $88,200, rather than $90,000. Every little bit helps. You never know. It might make the difference between getting the loan and not.

How would you respond to Todd Shovic's request?

ACTIVITY 5-3
Determining cost of purchase

The following is an excerpt from a conversation between Brad Hass and Terry Fauck. Brad is debating whether to buy a stereo system from Radiant Sound, a locally owned electronics store, or Audio Pro Electronics, a mail-order electronics company.

Brad: Terry, I don't know what to do about buying my new stereo.
Terry: What's the problem?
Brad: Well, I can buy it locally at Radiant Sound for $395.00. However, Audio Pro Electronics has the same system listed for $399.99.
Terry: So what's the big deal? Buy it from Radiant Sound.
Brad: It's not quite that simple. Audio Pro said something about not having to pay sales tax, since I was out-of-state.
Terry: Yes, that's a good point. If you buy it at Radiant Sound, they'll charge you 6% sales tax.
Brad: But Audio Pro Electronics charges $12.50 for shipping and handling. If I have them send it next-day air, it'll cost $25 for shipping and handling.
Terry: I guess it is a little confusing.
Brad: That's not all. Radiant Sound will give an additional 1% discount if I pay cash. Otherwise, they will let me use my MasterCard, or I can pay it off in three monthly installments.
Terry: Anything else???
Brad: Well . . . Audio Pro says I have to charge it on my MasterCard. They don't accept checks.
Terry: I am not surprised. Many mail-order houses don't accept checks.
Brad: I give up. What would you do?

1. Assuming that Audio Pro Electronics doesn't charge sales tax on the sale to Brad, which company is offering the best buy?
2. ➤ What might be some considerations other than price that might influence Brad's decision on where to buy the stereo system?

ACTIVITY 5-4
Sales discounts

Your sister operates Callender Parts Company, a mail-order boat parts distributorship that is in its third year of operation. The following income statement was recently prepared for the year ended March 31, 2006:

Callender Parts Company
Income Statement
For the Year Ended March 31, 2006

Revenues:		
Net sales		$960,000
Interest revenue		8,000
Total revenues		$968,000
Expenses:		
Cost of merchandise sold	$672,000	
Selling expenses	105,600	
Administrative expenses	54,400	
Interest expense	16,000	
Total expenses		848,000
Net income		$120,000

Your sister is considering a proposal to increase net income by offering sales discounts of 2/15, n/30, and by shipping all merchandise FOB shipping point. Currently, no sales discounts are allowed and merchandise is shipped FOB destination. It is estimated that these credit terms will increase net sales by 10%. The ratio of the cost of merchandise sold to net sales is expected to be 70%. All selling and administrative expenses are expected to remain unchanged, except for store supplies, miscellaneous selling, office supplies, and miscellaneous administrative expenses, which are expected to increase proportionately with increased net sales. The amounts of these preceding items for the year ended March 31, 2006, were as follows:

Store supplies expense	$8,000
Miscellaneous selling expense	3,200
Office supplies expense	1,600
Miscellaneous administrative expense	2,880

The other income and other expense items will remain unchanged. The shipment of all merchandise FOB shipping point will eliminate all transportation-out expenses, which for the year ended March 31, 2006, were $32,240.

1. Prepare a projected single-step income statement for the year ending March 31, 2007, based on the proposal. Assume all sales are collected within the discount period.
2. a. ➤ Based on the projected income statement in (1), would you recommend the implementation of the proposed changes?
   b. Describe any possible concerns you may have related to the proposed changes described in (1).

ACTIVITY 5-5
Shopping for a television

REAL WORLD

Assume that you are planning to purchase a 50-inch Plasma television. In groups of three or four, determine the lowest cost for the television, considering the available alternatives and the advantages and disadvantages of each alternative. For example, you could purchase locally, through mail order, or through an Internet shopping service. Consider such factors as delivery charges, interest-free financing, discounts, coupons, and availability of warranty services. Prepare a report for presentation to the class.

# nswers to Self-Examination Questions

1. **A** A debit memorandum (answer A), issued by the buyer, indicates the amount the buyer proposes to debit to the accounts payable account. A credit memorandum (answer B), issued by the seller, indicates the amount the seller proposes to credit to the accounts receivable account. An invoice (answer C) or a bill (answer D), issued by the seller, indicates the amount and terms of the sale.

2. **C** The amount of discount for early payment is $10 (answer C), or 1% of $1,000. Although the $50 of transportation costs paid by the seller is debited to the customer's account, the customer is not entitled to a discount on that amount.

3. **B** The single-step form of income statement (answer B) is so named because the total of all expenses is deducted in one step from the total of all revenues. The multiple-step form (answer A) includes numerous sections and subsections with several subtotals. The account form (answer C) and the report form (answer D) are two common forms of the balance sheet.

4. **C** Gross profit (answer C) is the excess of net sales over the cost of merchandise sold. Operating income (answer A) or income from operations (answer B) is the excess of gross profit over operating expenses. Net income (answer D) is the final figure on the income statement after all revenues and expenses have been reported.

5. **D** Expenses such as interest expense (answer D) that cannot be associated directly with operations are identified as *Other expense* or *Nonoperating expense*. Depreciation expense—office equipment (answer A) is an administrative expense. Sales salaries expense (answer B) is a selling expense. Insurance expense (answer C) is a mixed expense with elements of both selling expense and administrative expense. For small businesses, insurance expense is usually reported as an administrative expense.

6

ACCOUNTING SYSTEMS, INTERNAL CONTROLS, AND CASH

objectives

After studying this chapter, you should be able to:

1 Define an accounting system and describe its implementation.

2 List the three objectives of internal control, and define and give examples of the five elements of internal control.

3 Describe the nature of cash and the importance of internal control over cash.

4 Summarize basic procedures for achieving internal control over cash receipts.

5 Summarize basic procedures for achieving internal control over cash payments, including the use of a voucher system.

6 Describe the nature of a bank account and its use in controlling cash.

7 Prepare a bank reconciliation and journalize any necessary entries.

8 Account for small cash transactions using a petty cash fund.

9 Summarize how cash is presented on the balance sheet.

10 Compute and interpret the ratio of cash to current liabilities.

Controls are a part of your everyday life. At one extreme, laws are used to govern your behavior. For example, the speed limit is a control on your driving, designed for traffic safety. In addition, you are also affected by many nonlegal controls. For example, you can keep credit card receipts in order to compare your transactions to the monthly credit card statement. Comparing receipts to the monthly statement is a control designed to catch mistakes made by the credit card company. Likewise, recording checks in your checkbook is a control that you can use at the end of the month to verify the accuracy of your bank statement. In addition, banks give you a personal identification number (PIN) as a control against unauthorized access to your cash if you lose your automated teller machine (ATM) card. Dairies use freshness dating on their milk containers as a control to prevent the purchase or sale of soured milk. As you can see, you use and encounter controls every day.

Just as there are many examples of controls throughout society, businesses must also implement controls to help guide the behavior of their employees toward business objectives. For example, some businesses require you to punch a time card when you enter and leave the workplace. This is a control used to verify that you get paid for the actual hours you worked.

In the previous chapters, we discussed completing the accounting cycle and preparing financial statements for NetSolutions. In this chapter, we will discuss accounting systems, which are the source of the financial statements. We also discuss controls that can provide assurance that these statements are reliable. As a basis for illustration, we apply these concepts to the control of cash receipts and cash payments. We illustrate how businesses reconcile their monthly bank statements as a means of accounting for and controlling cash. You may want to use this illustration as a guide for reconciling your own bank statement to your checking account.

Basic Accounting Systems

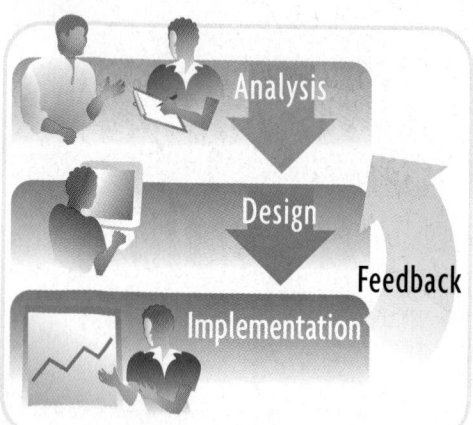

In the previous chapters, we developed an accounting system for NetSolutions. An *accounting system* is the methods and procedures for collecting, classifying, summarizing, and reporting a business's financial and operating information. The accounting system for most businesses, however, is more complex than NetSolutions'. Accounting systems for large businesses must be able to collect, accumulate, and report many types of transactions. For example, **American Airlines**' accounting system collects and maintains information on ticket reservations, credit card collections, aircraft maintenance, employee hours, frequent-flier mileage balances, fuel consumption, and travel agent commissions, just to name a few. As you might expect, American Airlines' accounting system has evolved as the company has grown.

Accounting systems evolve through a three-step process as a business grows and changes. The first step in this process is **analysis**, which consists of (1) identifying the needs of those who use the business's financial information and (2) determining how the system should provide this information. For NetSolutions, we determined that Chris Clark would need financial statements for the new business. In the second step, the system is **designed** so that it will meet the users' needs. For NetSolutions, a very basic manual system was designed. This system included a chart of accounts, a two-column journal, and a general ledger. Finally, the system is **implemented** and used. For NetSolutions, the system was used to record transactions and prepare financial statements.

Once a system has been implemented, **feedback**, or input, from the users of the information can be used to analyze and improve the system. For example, in later chapters we will see that NetSolutions will expand its chart of accounts as it becomes a more complex business.

Hershey Foods learned the hard way about the importance of careful analysis and design prior to implementing a complex information system. Hershey implemented a $112 million computer system by using a "big-bang" start-up, rather than using a gradual implementation strategy. When the switch was thrown, the company ran into immediate problems shipping orders to customers. As a result, profits were cut by 20%, and product shipments during the all-important Halloween selling season were delayed.

Internal controls and information processing methods are essential in an accounting system. ***Internal controls*** are the policies and procedures that protect assets from misuse, ensure that business information is accurate, and ensure that laws and regulations are being followed. **Processing methods** are the means by which the system collects, summarizes, and reports accounting information. These methods may be either *manual* or *computerized*.

In the preceding chapters, we described and illustrated manual accounting systems. In many cases, a modified manual accounting system may be adequate to meet the needs of a business.[1] Understanding manual systems helps you understand how computerized systems function. Computerized accounting systems use electronic technology and media to perform more rapidly the same processing functions as manual accounting systems.

Internal Control

List the three objectives of internal control, and define and give examples of the five elements of internal control.

Businesses use internal controls to guide their operations, safeguard assets, and prevent abuses of their systems. For example, assume that you own and manage a lawn care service. Your business uses several employee teams, and you provide each team with a vehicle and lawn equipment. What are some of the issues you would face as a manager in controlling the operations of this business? Below are some examples.

- Lawn care must be provided on time.
- The quality of lawn care services must meet customer expectations.
- Employees must provide work for the hours they are paid.
- Lawn care equipment should be used for business purposes only.
- Vehicles should be used for business purposes only.
- Customers must be billed and bills collected for services rendered.

How would you address these issues? You could, for example, develop a schedule at the beginning of each day and then inspect the work at the end of the day to verify that it was completed according to quality standards. You could have "surprise" inspections by arriving on site at random times to verify that the teams are working according to schedule. You could require employees to "clock in" at the beginning of the day and "clock out" at the end of the day to make sure that they are paid for hours worked. You could require the work teams to return the vehicles and equipment to a central location to prevent unauthorized use. You could keep a log of odometer readings at the end of each day to verify that the vehicle has not been used for "joy riding." You could bill customers after you have inspected the work and then monitor the collection of all receivables. All of these are examples of internal control.

Objectives of Internal Control

The objectives of internal control are to provide reasonable assurance that:

1. assets are safeguarded and used for business purposes.
2. business information is accurate.
3. employees comply with laws and regulations.

The Association of Certified Fraud Examiners has estimated that businesses will lose over $600 billion, or around 6% of revenue, to employee fraud. The study also showed that falsifying financial statements is the costliest form of fraud, with a median loss of $4.25 million per event.

Source: *2002 Report to the Nation: Occupational Fraud and Abuse*, Association of Certified Fraud Examiners.

Internal control can safeguard assets by preventing theft, fraud, misuse, or misplacement. One of the most serious breaches of internal control is employee fraud. ***Employee fraud*** is the intentional act of deceiving an employer for personal gain. Such deception may range from purposely overstating expenses on a travel expense report in order to receive a higher reimbursement to embezzling millions of dollars through complex schemes.

---

[1]One means by which manual systems can be modified is to use special journals. In each special journal, selected kinds of transactions are recorded. The basic features of special journals are presented in Appendix C.

Accurate business information is necessary for operating a business successfully. The safeguarding of assets and accurate information often go hand-in-hand. The reason is that employees attempting to defraud a business will also need to adjust the accounting records in order to hide the fraud.

Businesses must comply with applicable laws, regulations, and financial reporting standards. Examples of such standards and laws include environmental regulations, contract terms, safety regulations, and generally accepted accounting principles (GAAP).

Elements of Internal Control

How does management achieve its internal control objectives? Management is responsible for designing and applying five **elements of internal control** to meet the three internal control objectives. These elements are:[2]

1. the control environment
2. risk assessment
3. control procedures
4. monitoring
5. information and communication

The elements of internal control are illustrated in Exhibit 1. In this exhibit, the elements of internal control form an umbrella over the business to protect it from control threats. The business's control environment is represented by the size of the umbrella. Risk assessment, control procedures, and monitoring are the fabric that keeps the umbrella from leaking. Information and communication links the umbrella to management. In the following paragraphs, we discuss each of these elements.

•Exhibit 1

Control Environment

A business's control environment is the overall attitude of management and employees about the importance of controls. One of the factors that influences the control environment is *management's philosophy and operating style*. A management that overemphasizes operating goals and deviates from control policies may indi-

[2]*Internal Control—Integrated Framework* by the *Committee of Sponsoring Organizations* of the Treadway Commission (COSO), pp. 12–14. This document provides a professionally sponsored framework for internal control.

Over $700,000 of child support money disappeared over seven years due to the alleged falsification of checks by an accountant in Indiana's Family and Social Services Administration. The fraud could have been discovered, according to the State Examiner, if the agency reconciled its books, controlled access to blank checks, and used receipts.

rectly encourage employees to ignore controls. For example, the pressure to achieve revenue targets may encourage employees to fraudulently record sham sales. On the other hand, a management that emphasizes the importance of controls and encourages adherence to control policies will create an effective control environment.

The business's *organizational structure*, which is the framework for planning and controlling operations, also influences the control environment. For example, a department store chain might organize each of its stores as separate business units. Each store manager has full authority over pricing and other operating activities. In such a structure, each store manager has the responsibility for establishing an effective control environment.

Personnel policies also affect the control environment. Personnel policies involve the hiring, training, evaluation, compensation, and promotion of employees. In addition, job descriptions, employee codes of ethics, and conflict-of-interest policies are part of the personnel policies. Such policies and procedures can enhance the internal control environment if they provide reasonable assurance that only competent, honest employees are hired and retained.

Risk Assessment

All organizations face risks. Examples of risk include changes in customer requirements, competitive threats, regulatory changes, changes in economic factors such as interest rates, and employee violations of company policies and procedures. Management should assess these risks and take necessary actions to control them, so that the objectives of internal control can be achieved.

Once risks are identified, they can be analyzed to estimate their significance, to assess their likelihood of occurring, and to determine actions that will minimize them. For example, the manager of a warehouse operation may analyze the risk of employee back injuries, which might give rise to lawsuits. If the manager determines that the risk is significant, the company may take action by purchasing back support braces for its warehouse employees and requiring them to wear the braces.

Control Procedures

Control procedures are established to provide reasonable assurance that business goals will be achieved, including the prevention of fraud. In the following paragraphs, we will briefly discuss control procedures that can be integrated throughout the accounting system. These procedures are listed in Exhibit 2.

•Exhibit 2

INTERNAL CONTROL PROCEDURES

CONTROL THREATS

CONTROL PROCEDURES:
Competent personnel, rotating duties, and mandatory vacations
Separating responsibilities for related operations
Separating operations, custody of assets, and accounting
Proofs and securities measures

Information and Communication

Management

An accounting clerk for the Grant County (Washington) Alcoholism Program was in charge of collecting money, making deposits, and keeping the records. While the clerk was away on maternity leave, the replacement clerk discovered a fraud: $17,800 in fees had been collected but had been hidden for personal gain.

Competent Personnel, Rotating Duties, and Mandatory Vacations   The successful operation of an accounting system requires procedures to ensure that people are able to perform the duties to which they are assigned. Hence, it is necessary that all accounting employees be adequately trained and supervised in performing their jobs. It may also be advisable to rotate duties of clerical personnel and mandate vacations for nonclerical personnel. These policies encourage employees to adhere to prescribed procedures. In addition, existing errors or fraud may be detected.

Separating Responsibilities for Related Operations   To decrease the possibility of inefficiency, errors, and fraud, the responsibility for related operations should be divided among two or more persons. For example, the responsibilities for purchasing, receiving, and paying for computer supplies should be divided among three persons or departments. If the same person orders supplies, verifies the receipt of the supplies, and pays the supplier, the following abuses are possible:

1. Orders may be placed on the basis of friendship with a supplier, rather than on price, quality, and other objective factors.
2. The quantity and quality of supplies received may not be verified, thus causing payment for supplies not received or poor-quality supplies.
3. Supplies may be stolen by the employee.
4. The validity and accuracy of invoices may be verified carelessly, thus causing the payment of false or inaccurate invoices.

The "checks and balances" provided by dividing responsibilities among various departments requires no duplication of effort. The business documents prepared by one department are designed to coordinate with and support those prepared by other departments.

Separating Operations, Custody of Assets, and Accounting   Control policies should establish the responsibilities for various business activities. To reduce the possibility of errors and fraud, the responsibilities for operations, custody of assets, and accounting should be separated. The accounting records then serve as an independent check on the individuals who have custody of the assets and who engage in the business operations. For example, the employees entrusted with handling cash receipts from credit customers should not record cash receipts in the accounting records. To do so would allow employees to borrow or steal cash and hide the theft in the records. Likewise, if those engaged in operating activities also record the results of operations, they could distort the accounting reports to show favorable results. For example, a store manager whose year-end bonus is based upon operating profits might be tempted to record fictitious sales in order to receive a larger bonus.

Why is separation of duties considered a control procedure?

Internal control is enhanced by separating the control of a transaction from the record-keeping function. Fraud is more easily committed when a single individual controls both the transaction and the accounting for the transaction.

Proofs and Security Measures   Proofs and security measures should be used to safeguard assets and ensure reliable accounting data. This control procedure applies to many different techniques, such as authorization, approval, and reconciliation procedures. For example, employees who travel on company business may be required to obtain a department manager's approval on a travel request form.

Other examples of control procedures include the use of bank accounts and other measures to ensure the safety of cash and valuable documents. A cash register that displays the amount recorded for each sale and provides the customer a printed receipt can be an effective part of the internal control structure. An all-night convenience store could use the following security measures to deter robberies:

1. Locate the cash register near the door, so that it is fully visible from outside the store; have two employees work late hours; employ a security guard.
2. Deposit cash in the bank daily, before 5 p.m.

3. Keep only small amounts of cash on hand after 5 p.m. by depositing excess cash in a store safe that can't be opened by employees on duty.
4. Install cameras and alarm systems.

INTEGRITY IN BUSINESS

FRAUDULENT AID

In one of the largest frauds ever committed against a university, a former financial aid officer for **New York University** was charged with stealing $4.1 million from the state of New York. The aid officer allegedly falsified over a thousand tuition assistance checks to students who were not entitled to receive aid and who did not know about the checks. The aid officer deposited the bogus checks for personal use. The initial evidence of the fraud was the officer's spending of $785,000 on expensive jewelry.

Monitoring

Monitoring the internal control system locates weaknesses and improves control effectiveness. The internal control system can be monitored through either ongoing efforts by management or by separate evaluations. Ongoing monitoring efforts may include observing both employee behavior and warning signs from the accounting system. The indicators shown in Exhibit 3 may be clues to internal control problems.[3]

•Exhibit 3

CLUES TO POTENTIAL PROBLEMS

Warning signs with regard to people

1. Abrupt change in lifestyle (without winning the lottery).
2. Close social relationships with suppliers.
3. Refusing to take a vacation.
4. Frequent borrowing from other employees.
5. Excessive use of alcohol or drugs.

Warning signs from the accounting system

1. Missing documents or gaps in transaction numbers (could mean documents are being used for fraudulent transactions).
2. An unusual increase in customer refunds (refunds may be phony).
3. Differences between daily cash receipts and bank deposits (could mean receipts are being pocketed before being deposited).
4. Sudden increase in slow payments (employee may be pocketing the payment).
5. Backlog in recording transactions (possibly an attempt to delay detection of fraud).

---

[3]Edwin C. Bliss, "Employee Theft," *Boardroom Reports*, July 15, 1994, pp. 5–6.

How do companies discover fraud? Most fraud is discovered from tips by employees, customers, suppliers, or anonymous sources. Coming in second place is fraud discovered by accident.

Source: *2002 Report to the Nation: Occupational Fraud and Abuse,* Association of Certified Fraud Examiners.

Separate monitoring evaluations are generally performed when there are major changes in strategy, senior management, business structure, or operations. In large businesses, internal auditors who are independent of operations normally are responsible for monitoring the internal control system. Internal auditors can report issues and concerns to an audit committee of the board of directors, who are independent of management. In addition, external auditors also evaluate internal control as a normal part of their annual financial statement audit.

Information and Communication

Information and communication are essential elements of internal control. Information about the control environment, risk assessment, control procedures, and monitoring are needed by management to guide operations and ensure compliance with reporting, legal, and regulatory requirements.

Management can also use external information to assess events and conditions that impact decision making and external reporting. For example, management uses information from the Financial Accounting Standards Board (FASB) to assess the impact of possible changes in reporting standards.

FINANCIAL REPORTING AND DISCLOSURE

INTERNAL CONTROL REPORT OF MANAGEMENT

The financial statements of public companies are required, under the recently legislated Sarbanes-Oxley Act, to report on management's conclusions about the effectiveness of the company's internal controls and procedures, including any material weaknesses in internal controls. An example of such a report for **Bank of America** follows:

Report of Management

. . . The Corporation maintains a system of internal accounting controls to provide reasonable assurance that assets are safeguarded and that transactions are executed in accordance with management's authorization and recorded properly to permit the preparation of consolidated financial statements in accordance with accounting principles generally accepted in the United States of America. Management recognizes that even a highly effective internal control system has inherent risks, including the possibility of human error and the circumvention or overriding of controls, and that the effectiveness of an internal control system can change with circumstances. However, management believes that the internal control system provides reasonable assurance that errors or irregularities that could be material to the consolidated financial statements are prevented or would be detected on a timely basis and corrected through the normal course of business. As of December 31, 2001, management believes that the internal controls are in place and operating effectively.

*The **Internal Audit Division** of the Corporation reviews, evaluates, monitors and makes recommendations on both administrative and accounting control and acts as an integral, but independent, part of the system of internal controls.*

*The **independent accountants** were engaged to perform an independent audit of the consolidated financial statements. In determining the nature and extent of their auditing procedures, they have evaluated the Corporation's accounting policies and procedures and the effectiveness of the related internal control system. . . .*

*The Board of Directors discharges its responsibility for the Corporation's . . . financial statements through its **Audit Committee**. The Audit Committee meets periodically with the independent accountants, internal auditors and management. Both the independent accountants and internal auditors have direct access to the Audit Committee to discuss the scope and results of their work, the adequacy of internal accounting controls and the quality of financial reporting. . . .*

As can be seen, internal auditors, independent accountants, and the Audit Committee of the Board of Directors oversee Bank of America's internal control system. Even so, management recognizes these will not guarantee the elimination of fraud.

Nature of Cash and the Importance of Controls Over Cash

objective 3

Describe the nature of cash and the importance of internal control over cash.

POINT OF INTEREST

The Internet has given rise to a form of cash called "cybercash."

Cash includes coins, currency (paper money), checks, money orders, and money on deposit that is available for unrestricted withdrawal from banks and other financial institutions. Normally, you can think of cash as anything that a bank would accept for deposit in your account. For example, a check made payable to you could normally be deposited in a bank and thus is considered cash.

We will assume in this chapter that a business maintains only *one* bank account, represented in the ledger as *Cash*. In practice, however, a business may have several bank accounts, such as one for general cash payments and another for payroll. For each of its bank accounts, the business will maintain a ledger account, one of which may be called *Cash in Bank—First Bank*, for example. It will also maintain separate ledger accounts for cash that it does not keep in the bank, such as cash for small payments, and cash used for special purposes, such as travel reimbursements. We will introduce some of these other cash accounts in the chapter.

Because of the ease with which money can be transferred, cash is the asset most likely to be diverted and used improperly by employees. In addition, many transactions either directly or indirectly affect the receipt or the payment of cash. Businesses must therefore design and use controls that safeguard cash and control the authorization of cash transactions. In the following paragraphs, we will discuss these controls.

Control of Cash Receipts

objective 4

Summarize basic procedures for achieving internal control over cash receipts.

REAL WORLD

Fast-food restaurants, such as **McDonald's**, **Wendy's**, and **Burger King**, receive cash primarily from over-the-counter sales to customers. Mail-order and Internet retailers, such as **Lands' End**, **Orvis**, **L.L. Bean**, and **Amazon.com**, receive cash primarily through the mail and from credit card companies.

To protect cash from theft and misuse, a business must control cash from the time it is received until it is deposited in a bank. Such procedures are called **preventive controls**. Procedures that are designed to detect theft or misuse of cash are called **detective controls**. In a sense, detective controls are also preventive in nature, since employees are less likely to steal or misuse cash if they know there is a good chance they will be discovered.

Retail businesses normally receive cash from two main sources: (1) cash receipts from customers and (2) mail receipts from customers making payments on account. These two sources of cash are shown in Exhibit 4.

Controlling Cash Received from Cash Sales

Regardless of the source of cash receipts, every business must properly safeguard and record its cash receipts. One of the most important controls to protect cash received in over-the-counter sales is a cash register. You may have noticed that when a clerk (cashier) enters the amount of a sale, the cash register normally displays the amount. This is a control to ensure that the clerk has charged you the correct amount. You also receive a receipt to verify the accuracy of the amount.

At the beginning of a work shift, each cash register clerk is given a cash drawer that contains a predetermined amount of cash for making change for customers. The amount in each drawer is sometimes called a **change fund**. At the end of the work shift, each clerk and the supervisor count the cash in the clerk's cash drawer. The amount of cash in each drawer should equal the beginning amount of cash plus the cash sales for the day. However, errors in recording cash sales or errors in making change cause the amount of actual cash on hand to differ from this amount. Such differences are recorded in a **cash short and over account**. For example,

•Exhibit 4

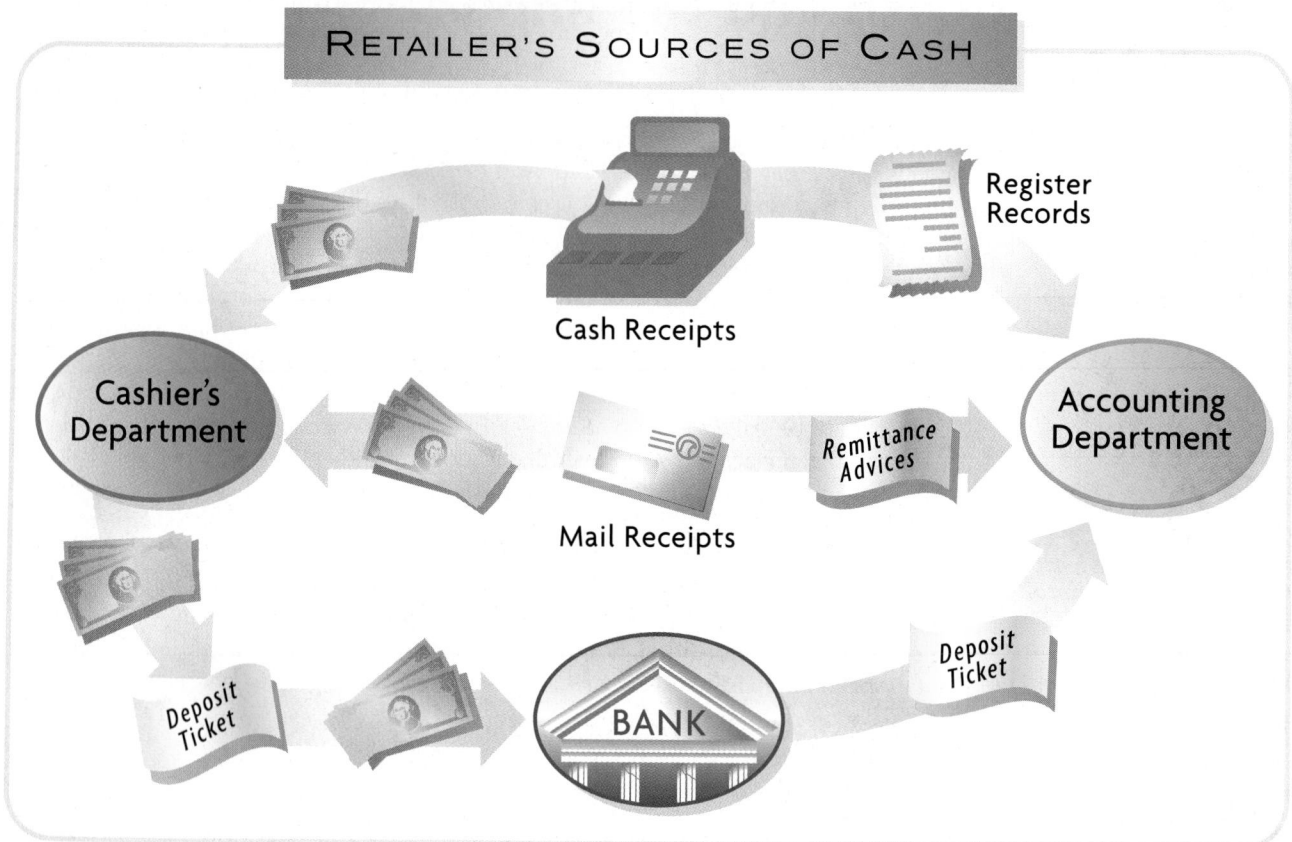

RETAILER'S SOURCES OF CASH

Register Records

Cash Receipts

Cashier's Department

Remittance Advices

Accounting Department

Mail Receipts

Deposit Ticket

BANK

Deposit Ticket

the following entry records a clerk's cash sales of $3,150 when the actual cash on hand is $3,142:

	Cash		3 1 4 2 00			
	Cash Short and Over		8 00			
	Sales				3 1 5 0 00	
	To record cash sales and actual cash					
	on hand.					

I rake in more than $4 billion per year as the world's largest athletic footwear and apparel retailer, with more than 5,900 stores around the globe. I think I've "turned the sport of sneaker shopping into a theatrical and entertainment experience." My brand names include Champs Sports, direct marketer Eastbay, and San Francisco Music Box gift stores. Online I offer 10,000 footwear and apparel products and 150 brands. I serve ladies and kids, too, and have the ultimate ticker symbol. I used to be Venator Group, and before that, Woolworth. Who am I? (Go to page 262 for answer.)

At the end of the accounting period, a debit balance in the cash short and over account is included in Miscellaneous Administrative Expense in the income statement. A credit balance is included in the Other Income section. If a clerk consistently has significant cash short and over amounts, the supervisor may require the clerk to take additional training.

After a cash register clerk's cash has been counted and recorded on a memorandum form, the cash is then placed in a store safe in the Cashier's Department until it can be deposited in the bank. The supervisor forwards the clerk's cash register records to the Accounting Department, where they become the basis for recording the transactions for the day.

Controlling Cash Received in the Mail

Cash is received in the mail when customers pay their bills. This cash is usually in the form of checks and money orders. Most companies' invoices are designed so that customers return a portion of the invoice, called a **remittance advice**, with their payment. The employee who opens the incoming mail should initially compare the amount of cash received with the amount shown on the remittance advice. If a customer does not return a remittance advice, an employee prepares one. Like the cash register, the remittance advice serves as a record of cash initially received. It also helps ensure that the posting to the customer's account is accurate. Finally, as a preventive control, the employee opening the mail normally also stamps checks and money orders "For Deposit Only" in the bank account of the business.

All cash received in the mail is sent to the Cashier's Department. An employee there combines it with the receipts from cash sales and prepares a bank deposit ticket. The remittance advices and their summary totals are delivered to the Accounting Department. An accounting clerk then prepares the records of the transactions and posts them to the customer accounts.

When cash is deposited in the bank, the bank normally stamps a duplicate copy of the deposit ticket with the amount received. This bank receipt is returned to the Accounting Department, where a clerk then compares the receipt with the total amount that should have been deposited. This control helps ensure that all the cash is deposited and that no cash is lost or stolen on the way to the bank. Any shortages are thus promptly detected.

The separation of the duties of the Cashier's Department, which handles cash, and the Accounting Department, which records cash, is a preventive control. If Accounting Department employees both handled and recorded cash, an employee could steal cash and change the accounting records to hide the theft.

Internal Control of Cash Payments

Internal control of cash payments should provide reasonable assurance that payments are made for only authorized transactions. In addition, controls should ensure that cash is used efficiently. For example, controls should ensure that all available discounts, such as purchase and trade discounts, are taken.

In a small business, an owner/manager may sign all checks, based upon personal knowledge of goods and services purchased. In a large business, however, checks are often prepared by employees who do not have such a complete knowledge of the transactions. In a large business, for example, the duties of purchasing goods, inspecting the goods received, and verifying the invoices are usually performed by different employees. These duties must be coordinated to ensure that checks for proper amounts are issued to creditors. One system used for this purpose is the voucher system.

Basic Features of the Voucher System

A *voucher system* is a set of procedures for authorizing and recording liabilities and cash payments. A voucher system normally uses (1) vouchers, (2) a file for unpaid vouchers, and (3) a file for paid vouchers. Generally, a voucher is any document that serves as proof of authority to pay cash. For example, an invoice properly approved for payment could be considered a voucher. In many businesses, however, a *voucher* is a special form for recording relevant data about a liability and the details of its payment. An example of such a form is shown in Exhibit 5.

Each voucher includes the creditor's invoice number and the amount and terms of the invoice. The accounts used in recording the purchase (or transaction) are listed in the *account distribution*.

A voucher is normally prepared in the Accounting Department, after all necessary supporting documents have been received. For example, when a voucher is prepared for the purchase of goods, the voucher should be supported by the supplier's invoice, a purchase order, and a receiving report. In preparing the voucher, an accounts payable clerk verifies the quantity, price, and mathematical accuracy of the supporting documents. This provides assurance that the payment is for goods that were properly ordered and received.

•Exhibit 5   Voucher

(face)   *(back)*

VOUCHER

① Date July 1, 2007   Voucher No. 451

② Payee Allied Manufacturing Company
         683 Fairmont Road
         Chicago, IL 60630-3168

Date	Details	Amount
③ June 28, 2007	Invoice No. 4693-C, $1,500.00, FOB Chicago, 2/10, n/30	1,500.00

Attach Supporting Documents

④ **ACCOUNT DISTRIBUTION**

DEBIT	AMOUNT	
MERCHANDISE INVENTORY	1500	00
SUPPLIES		
ADVERTISING EXPENSE		
DELIVERY EXPENSE		
MISC. SELLING EXPENSE		
MISC. ADMIN. EXPENSE		
CREDIT ACCOUNTS PAYABLE	1500	00

DISTRIBUTION APPROVED   *L. Donnelly*

NO. 451
DATE 7/1/07   DUE 7/8/07

PAYEE
Allied Manufacturing Company
683 Fairmont Road
Chicago, IL 60630-3168

VOUCHER SUMMARY

AMOUNT	1500	00
ADJUSTMENT		
DISCOUNT	30	00
NET	1470	00

APPROVED M.C. Leshen CONTROLLER
RECORDED W.B.

⑤ **PAYMENT SUMMARY**

DATE	7/8/07
AMOUNT	1470.00
CHECK NO.	863
APPROVED	Chris Clark
RECORDED	L.K.R. A.S.	⑥

① Date the voucher was prepared
② Name and address of the creditor
③ Description of the supporting documents
④ Accounts used to record the purchase or transaction
⑤ Details of payment
⑥ Spaces for signature or initials of approving employees

INTEGRITY IN BUSINESS

THE THEFT AT PERINI CORPORATION

The financial vice president of **Perini Corporation** received a disturbing call from one of the company's banks. The bank reported that Perini's bank account was substantially overdrawn. Perini, a large construction company based near Boston, had never overdrawn any of its bank accounts in over twenty-five years. Shortly thereafter, another of Perini's banks called and reported that its Perini account was also overdrawn. A review of the recent bank statements, which had been lying around unreconciled for two weeks, revealed canceled checks of more than $1.1 million that had not been recorded.

Perini kept its unused checks in an unlocked room. Perini also kept its supply of coffee cups in the same room, where every clerk and secretary had access to them. A quick review revealed two missing boxes of checks.

Perini used a checkwriting machine that automatically signed the vice president's name. Unfortunately, Perini didn't implement the controls suggested by its accountant. Instead, the machine-processed checks were placed in an unlocked box, there was no reconciliation of the counter on the machine with the number of checks that should have been written, and the keys to lock the machine were not carefully safeguarded. The vice president said that such controls were "too much trouble," even though one purpose of controls is to help ensure integrity in business.

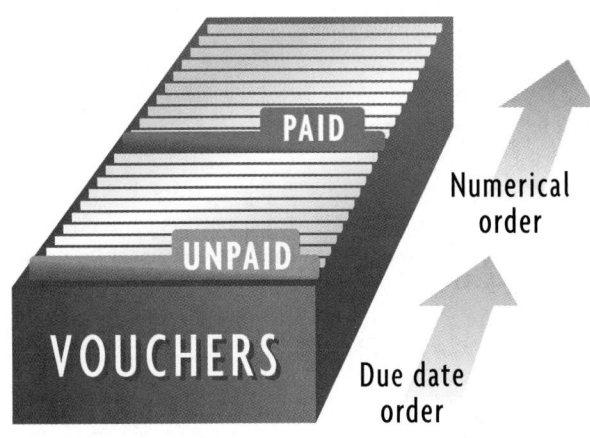

After a voucher is prepared, the voucher and its supporting documents are given to the proper official for approval. After it has been approved, the voucher is returned to the Accounting Department, where it is recorded in the accounts. It is then filed in an unpaid voucher file by its due date so that all available purchase discounts are taken.[4]

On its due date, the voucher is removed from the unpaid voucher file. The date, the number, and the amount of the check written in payment are listed on the back of the voucher. The payment of the voucher is recorded in the same manner as the payment of an account payable.

After payment, vouchers are marked "Paid" and are usually filed in numerical order in a paid voucher file. They are then readily available for examination by employees needing information about past payments.

A voucher system may be either manual or computerized. In a computerized system, properly approved supporting documents (such as purchase orders and receiving reports) would be entered directly into computer files. At the due date, the checks would be automatically generated and mailed to creditors. At that time, the voucher would be automatically transferred to a paid voucher file. In some cases, payments may be made electronically rather than by check.

Electronic Funds Transfer

With rapidly changing technology, new systems are being devised to more efficiently record and transfer cash among companies. Such systems often use *electronic funds transfer (EFT)*. In an EFT system, computers rather than paper (money, checks, etc.) are used to effect cash transactions. For example, a business may pay its employees by means of EFT. Under such a system, employees may authorize the deposit of their payroll checks directly into checking accounts. Each pay period, the business electronically transfers the employees' net pay to their checking accounts through the use of computer systems and telephone lines. Likewise, many companies are using EFT systems to pay their suppliers and other vendors.

Bank Accounts: Their Nature and Use as a Control Over Cash

Describe the nature of a bank account and its use in controlling cash.

Most of you are already familiar with bank accounts. You have a checking account at a local bank, credit union, savings and loan association, or other financial institution. In this section, we discuss the nature of a bank account used by a business. The features of such accounts will be similar to your own bank account. We then discuss the use of bank accounts as an additional control over cash.

Business Bank Accounts

A business often maintains several bank accounts. The forms used with each bank account are a signature card, deposit ticket, check, and record of checks drawn.

When you open a checking account, you sign a **signature card**. This card is used by the bank to verify the signature on checks that are submitted for payment. Also, when you open an account, the bank assigns an identifying number to the account.

---

[4]Occasionally, a purchase discount is missed. Some companies record the amounts of missed discounts in an account titled *Discounts Lost*. Doing so allows managers to monitor the significance of discounts lost. Since most companies design controls to take all purchase discounts, we do not illustrate the use of a discounts lost account.

Many businesses and individuals are now using Internet banking services, which provide for the payment of funds electronically. Also, **TeleCheck Services, Inc.**, the world's leading check acceptance company, offers an online real-time check payment option for purchases made over the Internet. "It is apparent from the rapid growth of online sales that many consumers are as comfortable writing checks for Internet purchases as they are at their local brick-and-mortar store," explains Steve Shaper, chief executive officer of TeleCheck.

The details of a deposit are listed by the depositor on a printed **deposit ticket** supplied by the bank. These forms are often prepared in duplicate. The bank teller stamps or initials a copy of the deposit ticket and gives it to the depositor as a receipt. Other types of receipts may also be used to give the depositor written proof of the date and the total amount of the deposit.

A **check** is a written document signed by the depositor, ordering the bank to pay a sum of money to an individual or entity. There are three parties to a check—the drawer, the drawee, and the payee. The **drawer** is the one who signs the check, ordering payment by the bank. The **drawee** is the bank on which the check is drawn. The **payee** is the party to whom payment is to be made.

Drawer   Payee   Drawee

The name and address of the depositor are usually printed on each check. In addition, checks are prenumbered, so that they can easily be kept track of by both the issuer and the bank. Banks encode their identification number and the depositor's account number in magnetic ink on each check. These numbers make it possible for the bank to sort and post checks automatically. When a check is presented for payment, the amount for which it is drawn is inserted, next to the account number, in magnetic ink. The processed check shown at the beginning of this chapter illustrated these features.

A record of each check should be prepared at the time a check is written. A small booklet called a **transactions register** is often used by both businesses and individuals for this purpose.

The purpose of a check may be written in space provided on the check or on an attachment to the check. Normally, checks issued to a creditor on account are sent with a form that identifies the specific invoice that is being paid. The purpose of this remittance advice is to make sure that proper credit is recorded in the accounts of the creditor. In this way, mistakes are less likely to occur. A check and remittance advice is shown in Exhibit 6.

Before depositing the check, the payee removes the remittance advice. The payee may then use the remittance advice as written proof of the details of the cash receipt.

INTEGRITY IN BUSINESS

CHECK FRAUD

Check fraud involves counterfeiting, altering, or otherwise manipulating the information on checks in order to fraudulently cash a check. According to the **National Check Fraud Center**, check fraud and counterfeiting are among the fastest growing problems affecting the financial system, generating over $10 billion in losses annually.

Criminals perpetrate the fraud by taking blank checks from your checkbook, finding a canceled check in the garbage, or removing a check you have mailed to pay bills. Consumers can prevent check fraud by carefully storing blank checks, placing outgoing mail in postal mailboxes, and shredding canceled checks.

•**Exhibit 6**

Check and Remittance Advice

POWER NETWORKING				363
1000 Belkin Los Angeles, CA 90014-1000			July 07 20 06	9-42 / 720

Pay to the Order of _____ Interface Data Systems _____ $ 921.20

Nine hundred twenty-one 20/100 ----------------------------- Dollars

K.R. Simons   **Treasurer**

VALLEY NATIONAL BANK OF LOS ANGELES

Earl M. Hartman   **Vice President**

LOS ANGELES, CA 90020-4283   (310) 851-5151   MEMBER FDIC

⑈07 20004 23⑈   16 27042   363⑈

DETACH THIS PORTION BEFORE CASHING

Date	Description	Gross Amount	Deductions	Net Amount
07/07/06	Invoice No. 529482	940.00	18.80	921.20

POWER NETWORKING

Bank Statement

Banks usually maintain a record of all checking account transactions. A summary of all transactions, called a **statement of account**, is mailed to the depositor, usually each month. Like any account with a customer or a creditor, the bank statement shows the beginning balance, additions, deductions, and the balance at the end of the period. A typical bank statement is shown in Exhibit 7.

The depositor's checks received by the bank during the period may accompany the bank statement, arranged in the order of payment. The paid checks are stamped "Paid," together with the date of payment. Other entries that the bank has made in the depositor's account may be described in debit or credit memorandums enclosed with the statement.

You should note that a depositor's checking account balance *in the bank's records* is a liability with a credit balance. Debit memorandums issued by the bank on a depositor's account therefore decrease the depositor's balance. Likewise, credit memorandums increase the depositor's balance. A bank issues a debit memorandum to charge (decrease) a depositor's account for service charges or for deposited checks returned because of insufficient funds. Likewise, a bank issues a credit memorandum when it increases the depositor's account for collecting a note receivable for the depositor, making a loan to the depositor, receiving a wire deposit, or adding interest to the depositor's account.[5]

Bank Accounts as a Control Over Cash

A bank account is one of the primary tools a business uses to control cash. For example, businesses often require that all cash receipts be initially deposited in a bank

---

[5]Although interest-bearing checking accounts are common for individuals, Federal Reserve Regulation Q prohibits the paying of interest on corporate checking accounts.

•Exhibit 7

Bank Statement

MEMBER FDIC				PAGE	1

VALLEY NATIONAL BANK OF LOS ANGELES

LOS ANGELES, CA 90020-4253   (310)851-5151

	ACCOUNT NUMBER	1627042
	FROM 6/30/06	TO 7/31/06
	BALANCE	4,218.60
22 DEPOSITS		13,749.75
52 WITHDRAWALS		14,698.57
3 OTHER DEBITS AND CREDITS		90.00CR
	NEW BALANCE	3,359.78

POWER NETWORKING
1000 Belkin Street
Los Angeles, CA 90014-1000

* – CHECKS AND OTHER DEBITS – – – * – – – DEPOSITS – – * – – DATE – – * – – BALANCE – *				
819.40	122.54		585.75	07/01	3,862.41
369.50	732.26	20.15	421.53	07/02	3,162.03
600.00	190.70	52.50	781.30	07/03	3,100.13
25.93	160.00		662.50	07/05	3,576.70
921.20	NSF 300.00		503.18	07/07	2,858.68
32.26	535.09		932.00	07/29	3,404.40
21.10	126.20		705.21	07/30	3,962.31
	SC 18.00		MS 408.00	07/30	4,352.31
26.12	1,615.13		648.72	07/31	3,359.78

EC—ERROR CORRECTION   OD—OVERDRAFT
MS—MISCELLANEOUS   PS—PAYMENT STOPPED
NSF—NOT SUFFICENT FUNDS   SC—SERVICE CHARGE

* * *   * * *   * * *

THE RECONCILEMENT OF THIS STATEMENT WITH YOUR RECORDS IS ESSENTIAL.
ANY ERROR OR EXCEPTION SHOULD BE REPORTED IMMEDIATELY.

A bank account and a business's records provide a double record of cash transactions.

account. Likewise, businesses usually use checks to make all cash payments, except for very small amounts. When such a system is used, there is a double record of cash transactions—one by the business and the other by the bank.

A business can use a bank statement to compare the cash transactions recorded in its accounting records to those recorded by the bank. The cash balance shown by a bank statement is usually different from the cash balance shown in the accounting records of the business, as shown in Exhibit 8.

This difference may be the result of a delay by either party in recording transactions. For example, there is a time lag of one day or more between the date a check is written and the date that it is presented to the bank for payment. If the depositor mails deposits to the bank or uses the night depository, a time lag between the date of the deposit and the date that it is recorded by the bank is also probable. The bank may also debit or credit the depositor's account for transactions about which the depositor will not be informed until later.

The difference may be the result of errors made by either the business or the bank in recording transactions. For example, the business may incorrectly post to Cash a check written for $4,500 as $450. Likewise, a bank may incorrectly record the amount of a check.

•Exhibit 8

Power Networking's Records and Bank Statement

Bank Statement			Power Networking Records	
Beginning Balance		$ 4,218.60	Beginning Balance	$ 4,227.60
Additions:				
Deposits		13,749.75	Deposits	14,565.95
Miscellaneous		408.00		
Deductions:				
Checks		14,698.57	Checks	16,243.56
NSF Check	$300			
Service Charge	18	318.00		
Ending Balance		$ 3,359.78	Ending Balance	$ 2,549.99

Power Networking should determine the reason for the difference in these two amounts.

Bank Reconciliation

For effective control, the reasons for the difference between the cash balance on the bank statement and the cash balance in the accounting records should be determined by preparing a bank reconciliation. A **bank reconciliation** is a listing of the items and amounts that cause the cash balance reported in the bank statement to differ from the balance of the cash account in the ledger.

A bank reconciliation is usually divided into two sections. The first section begins with the cash balance according to the bank statement and ends with the adjusted balance. The second section begins with the cash balance according to the depositor's records and ends with the adjusted balance. The two amounts designated as the adjusted balance must be equal. The content of the bank reconciliation is shown below.

Cash balance according to bank statement . . .		$XXX	Cash balance according to depositor's records		$XXX
Add: Additions by depositor not on			Add: Additions by bank not recorded by		
bank statement	$XX		depositor	$XX	
Bank errors	XX	XX	Depositor errors	XX	XX
		$XXX			$XXX
Deduct: Deductions by depositor not on			Deduct: Deductions by bank not recorded		
bank statement	$XX		by depositor	$XX	
Bank errors	XX	XX	Depositor errors	XX	XX
Adjusted balance		$XXX	Adjusted balance		$XXX

must be equal

The following steps are useful in finding the reconciling items and determining the adjusted balance of Cash:

1. Compare each deposit listed on the bank statement with unrecorded deposits appearing in the preceding period's reconciliation and with deposit receipts or other records of deposits. *Add deposits not recorded by the bank to the balance according to the bank statement.*

2. Compare paid checks with outstanding checks appearing on the preceding period's reconciliation and with recorded checks. *Deduct checks outstanding that have not been paid by the bank from the balance according to the bank statement.*

3. Compare bank credit memorandums to entries in the journal. For example, a bank would issue a credit memorandum for a note receivable and interest that it collected for a depositor. *Add credit memorandums that have not been recorded to the balance according to the depositor's records.*

4. Compare bank debit memorandums to entries recording cash payments. For example, a bank normally issues debit memorandums for service charges and check printing charges. A bank also issues debit memorandums for not-sufficient-funds checks. A *not-sufficient-funds (NSF) check* is a customer's check that was recorded and deposited but was not paid when it was presented to the customer's bank for payment. NSF checks are normally charged back to the customer as an account receivable. *Deduct debit memorandums that have not been recorded from the balance according to the depositor's records.*

5. List any errors discovered during the preceding steps. For example, if an amount has been recorded incorrectly by the depositor, the amount of the error should be added to or deducted from the cash balance according to the depositor's records. Similarly, errors by the bank should be added to or deducted from the cash balance according to the bank statement.

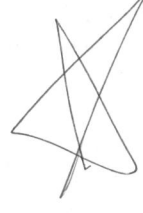

Assume that the bank recorded a deposit of $4,100 as $1,400. How would this bank error be shown on the bank reconciliation?

The error of $2,700 would be added to the cash balance according to the bank statement.

To illustrate a bank reconciliation, we will use the bank statement for Power Networking in Exhibit 7. This bank statement shows a balance of $3,359.78 as of July 31. The cash balance in Power Networking's ledger as of the same date is $2,549.99. The following reconciling items are revealed by using the steps outlined above:

Deposit of July 31, not recorded on bank statement	$ 816.20
Checks outstanding: No. 812, $1,061.00; No. 878, $435.39; No. 883, $48.60 . . .	1,544.99
Note plus interest of $8 collected by bank (credit memorandum), not recorded in the journal	408.00
Check from customer (Thomas Ivey) returned by bank because of insufficient funds (NSF)	300.00
Bank service charges (debit memorandum), not recorded in the journal	18.00
Check No. 879 for $732.26 to Taylor Co. on account, recorded in the journal as $723.26	9.00

•Exhibit 9

Bank Reconciliation for Power Networking

The bank reconciliation based on the bank statement and the reconciling items is shown in Exhibit 9.

Power Networking
Bank Reconciliation
July 31, 2006

Cash balance according to bank statement			Cash balance according to depositor's records		
		$3 3 5 9 78			$2 5 4 9 99
Add deposit of July 31, not recorded by bank		8 1 6 20	Add note and interest collected by bank		4 0 8 00
		$4 1 7 5 98			$2 9 5 7 99
			Deduct: Check returned because of insufficient funds	$ 3 0 0 00	
Deduct outstanding checks:					
No. 812	$1 0 6 1 00		Bank service charges	1 8 00	
No. 878	4 3 5 39		Error in recording		
No. 883	4 8 60	1 5 4 4 99	Check No. 879	9 00	3 2 7 00
Adjusted balance		$2 6 3 0 99	Adjusted balance		$2 6 3 0 99

No entries are necessary on the depositor's records as a result of the information included in the first section of the bank reconciliation. This section begins with the

Entries must be made in the depositor's accounts for any items that affect the business's record of cash.

cash balance according to the bank statement. However, the bank should be notified of any errors that need to be corrected on its records.

Any items in the second section of the bank reconciliation must be recorded in the depositor's accounts. This section begins with the cash balance according to the depositor's records. For example, journal entries should be made for any unrecorded bank memorandums and any depositor's errors.

The journal entries for Power Networking, based on the preceding bank reconciliation, are as follows:

July	31	Cash	4 0 8 00		
		Notes Receivable		4 0 0 00	
		Interest Revenue		8 00	
		Note collected by bank.			
	31	Accounts Receivable—Thomas Ivey	3 0 0 00		
		Miscellaneous Administrative Expense	1 8 00		
		Accounts Payable—Taylor Co.	9 00		
		Cash		3 2 7 00	
		NSF check, bank service charges, and error			
		in recording Check No. 879.			

POINT OF INTEREST

If you reconcile your bank account each month, you first scan your bank statement for any bank entries that you have not yet recorded. Examples of such entries include service charges (a debit entry) and interest earned (a credit entry). You then enter these amounts in your checkbook (register) and determine the balance of your account. If you stop at this point, you are assuming that the bank hasn't made any errors.

If you fully reconcile your account, you should also scan your checkbook for items that the bank has not yet recorded: (1) deposits in transit and (2) outstanding checks. Deposits in transit should be added to the bank balance, and outstanding checks should be subtracted from the bank balance. The result is an adjusted bank balance, which should agree with the balance of your checkbook. If the two are not equal, either you or the bank has made an error.

After these entries have been posted, the cash account will have a debit balance of $2,630.99. This balance agrees with the adjusted cash balance shown on the bank reconciliation. This is the amount of cash available as of July 31 and the amount that would be reported on Power Networking's July 31 balance sheet.

Although businesses may reconcile their bank accounts in a slightly different format from what we described above, the objective is the same: to control cash by reconciling the company's records to the records of an independent outside source, the bank. In doing so, any errors or misuse of cash may be detected.

For effective control, the bank reconciliation should be prepared by an employee who does not take part in or record cash transactions. When these duties are not properly separated, mistakes are likely to occur, and it is more likely that cash will be stolen or otherwise misapplied. For example, an employee who takes part in all of these duties could prepare and cash an unauthorized check, omit it from the accounts, and omit it from the reconciliation.

Petty Cash

objective 8

Account for small cash transactions using a petty cash fund.

As in your own day-to-day life, it is usually not practical for a business to write checks to pay small amounts, such as postage. Yet, these small payments may occur often enough to add up to a significant total amount. Thus, it is desirable to control such payments. For this purpose, a special cash fund, called a ***petty cash fund***, is used.

A petty cash fund is established by first estimating the amount of cash needed for payments from the fund during a period, such as a week or a month. After necessary approvals, a check is written and cashed for this amount. The money obtained from cashing the check is then given to an employee, called the petty cash custodian, who is authorized to disburse monies from the fund. For control purposes, the

REAL WORLD

Businesses often use other cash funds to meet their special needs, such as travel expenses for salespersons. For example, each salesperson might be given $200 for travel-related expenses. Periodically, the salesperson submits a detailed expense report and the travel funds are replenished.

company may place restrictions on the maximum amount and the types of payments that can be made from the fund.

Each time monies are paid from petty cash, the custodian records the details of the payment on a petty cash receipt form. A typical petty cash receipt is illustrated in Exhibit 10.

The petty cash fund is normally replenished at periodic intervals or when it is depleted or reaches a minimum amount. When a petty cash fund is replenished, the accounts debited are determined by summarizing the petty cash receipts. A check is then written for this amount, payable to the petty cash custodian.

•Exhibit 10

Petty Cash Receipt

PETTY CASH RECEIPT

No. _____121_____   Date __August 1, 2006__

Paid to _____Metropolitan Times_____   **Amount**

             3 | 00

For _____Daily newspaper_____

Charge to __Miscellaneous Administrative Expense__

Payment received:

_____S.O. Hall_____   **Approved by** __N.E.R.__

To illustrate normal petty cash fund entries, assume that a petty cash fund of $100 is established on August 1. The entry to record this transaction is as follows:

Aug.	1	Petty Cash	1 0 0 00	
		Cash		1 0 0 00
		Established petty cash fund.		

If the petty cash account has a balance of $200, the cash in the fund totals $20, and the petty cash receipts total $180 at the end of a period, what account is credited and what is the amount of the credit in the entry to replenish the fund?

Cash is credited for $180.

At the end of August, the petty cash receipts indicate expenditures for the following items: office supplies, $28; postage (office supplies), $22; store supplies, $35; and daily newspapers (miscellaneous administrative expense), $3. The entry to replenish the petty cash fund on August 31 is as follows:

Aug.	31	Office Supplies	5 0 00	
		Store Supplies	3 5 00	
		Miscellaneous Administrative Expense	3 00	
		Cash		8 8 00
		Replenished petty cash fund.		

Petty Cash is debited only when the fund is set up or the amount of the fund is increased.

Replenishing the petty cash fund restores it to its original amount of $100. You should note that there is no entry in Petty Cash when the fund is replenished. Petty Cash is debited only when the fund is initially set up or when the amount of the fund is increased at a later time. Petty Cash is credited if it is being decreased.

Presentation of Cash on the Balance Sheet

The following note discloses compensating balance requirements for **Kmart Corporation**: . . . *In support of lines of credit, it is expected that compensating balances will be maintained on deposit with the banks, which will average 10% of the line to the extent that it is not in use and an additional 10% on the portion in use. . . .*

REAL WORLD

Cash is the most liquid asset, and therefore it is listed as the first asset in the Current Assets section of the balance sheet. Most companies present only a single cash amount on the balance sheet by combining all their bank and cash fund accounts.

A company may have cash in excess of its operating needs. In such cases, the company normally invests in highly liquid investments in order to earn interest. These investments are called ***cash equivalents***.[6] Examples of cash equivalents include U.S. Treasury Bills, notes issued by major corporations (referred to as commercial paper), and money market funds. Companies that have invested excess cash in cash equivalents usually report *Cash and cash equivalents* as one amount on the balance sheet.

Banks may require depositors to maintain minimum cash balances in their bank accounts. Such a balance is called a **compensating**

FINANCIAL REPORTING AND DISCLOSURE

MICROSOFT CORPORATION

Microsoft Corporation develops, manufactures, licenses, and supports software products for computing devices. Microsoft software products include computer operating systems, such as Windows, and application software, such as Microsoft Word™ and Excel.™ Microsoft is actively involved in the video game market through its Xbox and is also involved in online products and services.

Microsoft is known for its strong cash position. Microsoft's June 30, 2002 balance sheet reported over $38 billion of cash and short-term investments, as shown below.

Balance Sheet
June 30, 2002
(In millions)
Assets

Current assets:	
Cash and equivalents	$ 3,016
Short-term investments	35,636
Total cash and short-term investments	$38,652

The cash and cash equivalents of $3 billion are further described in the notes to the financial statements, as shown below.

The short-term investments are invested in short-term securities so that they can easily be converted to cash for operating or strategic cash needs, such as possible mergers or acquisitions.

Cash and equivalents:	
Cash	$1,114
Commercial paper	260
Certificates of deposit	31
Money market mutual funds	714
Corporate notes and bonds	560
Municipal securities	337
Total cash and equivalents	$3,016

---

[6]To be classified as a cash equivalent, according to *FASB Statement 95*, the investment is expected to be converted to cash within 90 days.

balance. This requirement is often imposed by the bank as a part of a loan agreement or line of credit. A *line of credit* is a preapproved amount the bank is willing to lend to a customer upon request. Compensating balance requirements should be disclosed in notes to the financial statements.

Financial Analysis and Interpretation

objective 10

Compute and interpret the ratio of cash to current liabilities.

In an earlier chapter, we discussed the use of working capital and the current ratio in evaluating a company's ability to pay its current liabilities (short-term solvency). Both of these measures assume that the noncash current assets will be converted to cash in time to pay the current liabilities. For most companies, these measures are useful for assessing short-term solvency. However, a company that is in financial distress may have difficulty converting its receivables, inventory, and prepaid assets to cash on a timely basis. In these cases, the ratio of cash to current liabilities may be useful in assessing the ability of creditors to collect what they are owed. Because this ratio is most relevant for companies in financial distress, it is called the **doomsday ratio**.[7] Its name comes from the worst case assumption that the business ceases to exist and only the cash on hand is available to meet creditor obligations.

In computing the ratio of cash to current liabilities, cash and cash equivalents are used in the numerator, as shown below.

$$\text{Doomsday ratio} = \frac{\text{Cash and cash equivalents}}{\text{Current liabilities}}$$

To illustrate, assume the following data for Laettner Co. and Oakley Co. for the current year:

	Laettner Co.	Oakley Co.
Cash and cash equivalents	$100,000	$ 120,000
Current liabilities	400,000	1,500,000

The doomsday ratio for each company is computed as follows. In this case, Oakley Co. is more risky to creditors than is Laettner.

	Doomsday Ratio	
Laettner Co.	0.25	($100,000/$400,000)
Oakley Co.	0.08	($120,000/$1,500,000)

Because most businesses maintain cash and cash equivalents at amounts substantially less than their current liabilities, the doomsday ratio is almost always less than one. For example, the doomsday ratio for **Radio Shack Corporation** is 0.18. For **La-Z-Boy Chair Company**, it is 0.25.

Differences among companies will occur because of differences in management philosophy and operating styles. Nevertheless, a comparison over time that indicates a decreasing ratio generally indicates more risk for creditors.

---

[7]This ratio is discussed more fully in *101 Business Ratios* by Sheldon Gates, McLane Publications, Scottsdale, Arizona, 1993.

SPOTLIGHT ON STRATEGY

TURN OFF THE LIGHT?

Kmart recently filed for bankruptcy. What happened? What went wrong?

Most analysts blame Kmart's problems on a strategy that relied heavily upon advertising circulars to get customers into its stores. Such circulars, which are expensive to produce, accounted for 10.6% of Kmart's operating expenses, as compared to 2.2% for **Target** and 0.4% for **Wal-Mart**. In addition, Kmart continued to use its "blue-light specials," in which merchandise prices would be reduced at periodic intervals for customers who were shopping within its stores. These specials created inventory shortages as merchandise sold out and suppliers could not accurately predict customer needs. As a result, suppliers increased Kmart's prices, which in turn were passed on to customers. In contrast, Wal-Mart employs an "always

low price" strategy for getting customers into its stores. Kmart reacted by promoting a "Blue-Light Always" program, developing a Bluelight.com Web site, and reducing its use of ad circulars. Unfortunately, Kmart's traditional customers who were used to the circulars stopped shopping at Kmart. In addition, Kmart couldn't compete with Wal-Mart's efficiency and low costs. Thus, Kmart filed for bankruptcy, eventually reorganizing and hoping once again to become competitive and profitable.

Sources: Amy Merrick, "Expensive Ad Circulars Precipitate Kmart President's Departure," *The Wall Street Journal*, January 18, 2002; Michael Levy and Dhruv Grewal, "So Long, Kmart Shoppers," *The Wall Street Journal*, January 28, 2002; and "Blue Light Blues," *The Economist*, January 18, 2002.

Key Points

1 Define an accounting system and describe its implementation.

An accounting system is the methods and procedures for collecting, classifying, summarizing, and reporting a business's financial information. The three steps through which an accounting system evolves are (1) analysis of information needs, (2) design of the system, and (3) implementation of the system's design.

2 List the three objectives of internal control, and define and give examples of the five elements of internal control.

Internal control provides reasonable assurance that (1) assets are safeguarded and used for business purposes, (2) business information is accurate, and (3) laws and regulations are complied with. The five elements of internal control are the control environment, risk assessment, control procedures, monitoring, and information and communication.

3 Describe the nature of cash and the importance of internal control over cash.

Cash includes coins, currency (paper money), checks, money orders, and money on deposit that is available for unrestricted withdrawal from banks and other financial institutions. Because of the ease with which money can be transferred, businesses should design and use controls that safeguard cash and authorize cash transactions.

4 Summarize basic procedures for achieving internal control over cash receipts.

One of the most important controls to protect cash received in over-the-counter sales is a cash register. A remittance advice is a preventive control for cash received through the mail. Separating the duties of handling cash and recording cash is also a preventive control.

5 Summarize basic procedures for achieving internal control over cash payments, including the use of a voucher system.

A voucher system is a set of procedures for authorizing and recording liabilities and cash payments. A

voucher system uses vouchers, a file for unpaid vouchers, and a file for paid vouchers.

6 Describe the nature of a bank account and its use in controlling cash.

The forms used with bank accounts are a signature card, deposit ticket, check, and record of checks drawn. Each month, the bank usually sends a bank statement to the depositor, summarizing all of the transactions for the month. The bank statement allows a business to compare the cash transactions recorded in the accounting records to those recorded by the bank.

7 Prepare a bank reconciliation and journalize any necessary entries.

The first section of the bank reconciliation begins with the cash balance according to the bank statement. This balance is adjusted for the depositor's changes in cash that do not appear on the bank statement and for any bank errors. The second section begins with the cash balance according to the depositor's records. This balance is adjusted for the bank's changes in cash that do not appear on the depositor's records and for any depositor errors. The adjusted balances for the two sections must be equal.

No entries are necessary on the depositor's records as a result of the information included in the first section of the bank reconciliation. However, the items in the second section must be journalized on the depositor's records.

8 Account for small cash transactions using a petty cash fund.

A petty cash fund may be used by a business to make small payments that occur frequently. The money in a petty cash fund is placed in the custody of a specific employee, who authorizes payments from the fund. Periodically or when the amount of money in the fund is depleted or reduced to a minimum amount, the fund is replenished.

9 Summarize how cash is presented on the balance sheet.

Cash is listed as the first asset in the Current Assets section of the balance sheet. Companies that have invested excess cash in highly liquid invest-

ments usually report *Cash and cash equivalents* on the balance sheet.

10 Compute and interpret the ratio of cash to current liabilities.

A company that is in financial distress may have difficulty converting its receivables, inventory, and prepaid assets to cash on a timely basis. In these cases, the ratio of cash to current liabilities, called the doomsday ratio, may be useful in assessing the ability of creditors to collect what they are owed.

Key Terms

accounting system (238)
bank reconciliation (253)
cash (245)
cash equivalents (257)
cash short and over account (245)

doomsday ratio (258)
electronic funds transfer (EFT) (249)
elements of internal control (240)
employee fraud (239)
internal controls (239)

petty cash fund (255)
voucher (247)
voucher system (247)

Illustrative Problem

The bank statement for Urethane Company for June 30, 2006, indicates a balance of $9,143.11. All cash receipts are deposited each evening in a night depository, after banking hours. The accounting records indicate the following summary data for cash receipts and payments for June:

Cash balance as of June 1	$ 3,943.50
Total cash receipts for June	28,971.60
Total amount of checks issued in June	28,388.85

Comparing the bank statement and the accompanying canceled checks and memorandums with the records reveals the following reconciling items:

a. The bank had collected for Urethane Company $1,030 on a note left for collection. The face of the note was $1,000.
b. A deposit of $1,852.21, representing receipts of June 30, had been made too late to appear on the bank statement.
c. Checks outstanding totaled $5,265.27.
d. A check drawn for $139 had been incorrectly charged by the bank as $157.
e. A check for $30 returned with the statement had been recorded in the depositor's records as $240. The check was for the payment of an obligation to Avery Equipment Company for the purchase of office supplies on account.
f. Bank service charges for June amounted to $18.20.

Instructions

1. Prepare a bank reconciliation for June.
2. Journalize the entries that should be made by Urethane Company.

Solution

1.

Urethane Company
Bank Reconciliation
June 30, 2006

Cash balance according to bank statement		$ 9,143.11
Add: Deposit of June 30 not recorded by bank	$1,852.21	
Bank error in charging check as $157 instead of $139	18.00	1,870.21
		$11,013.32
Deduct: Outstanding checks		5,265.27
Adjusted balance		$ 5,748.05
Cash balance according to depositor's records		$ 4,526.25*
Add: Proceeds of note collected by bank, including $30 interest	$1,030.00	
Error in recording check	210.00	1,240.00
		$ 5,766.25
Deduct: Bank service charges		18.20
Adjusted balance		$ 5,748.05

*$3,943.50 + $28,971.60 − $28,388.85

2. Cash 1,240.00
    Notes Receivable 1,000.00
    Interest Revenue 30.00
    Accounts Payable—Avery Equipment 210.00

    Miscellaneous Administrative Expense 18.20
    Cash 18.20

Self-Examination Questions (Answers at End of Chapter)

1. The initial step in the process of developing an accounting system is called:
   A. analysis
   B. design
   C. implementation
   D. feedback

2. The policies and procedures used by management to protect assets from misuse, ensure accurate business information, and ensure compliance with laws and regulations are called:
   A. internal controls
   B. systems analysis
   C. systems design
   D. systems implementation

3. In preparing a bank reconciliation, the amount of checks outstanding would be:
   A. added to the cash balance according to the bank statement.
   B. deducted from the cash balance according to the bank statement.
   C. added to the cash balance according to the depositor's records.

D. deducted from the cash balance according to the depositor's records.

4. Journal entries based on the bank reconciliation are required for:
   A. additions to the cash balance according to the depositor's records.
   B. deductions from the cash balance according to the depositor's records.
   C. both A and B.
   D. neither A nor B.

5. A petty cash fund is:
   A. used to pay relatively small amounts.
   B. established by estimating the amount of cash needed for disbursements of relatively small amounts during a specified period.
   C. reimbursed when the amount of money in the fund is reduced to a predetermined minimum amount.
   D. all of the above.

Class Discussion Questions

1. How does a policy of rotating clerical employees from job to job aid in strengthening the control procedures within the control environment?
2. Why should the employee who handles cash receipts not have the responsibility for maintaining the accounts receivable records?
3. The ticket seller at a movie theater doubles as a ticket taker for a few minutes each day while the ticket taker is on a break. Which control procedure of a business's system of internal control is violated in this situation?
4. Why is cash the asset that often warrants the most attention in the design of an effective internal control structure?
5. The combined cash count of all cash registers at the close of business is $110 less than the cash sales indicated by the cash register records. (a) In what account is the cash shortage recorded? (b) Are cash shortages debited or credited to this account?
6. Before a voucher for the purchase of merchandise is approved for payment, supporting documents should be compared to verify the accuracy of the liability. Name an example of a supporting document for the purchase of merchandise.
7. The accounting clerk pays all obligations by prenumbered checks. What are the strengths and weaknesses in the internal control over cash payments in this situation?
8. In what order are vouchers ordinarily filed (a) in the unpaid voucher file and (b) in the paid voucher file? Give reasons for the answers.
9. The balance of Cash is likely to differ from the bank statement balance. What two factors are likely to be responsible for the difference?
10. What is the purpose of preparing a bank reconciliation?
11. Do items reported on the bank statement as credits represent (a) additions made by the bank to the depositor's balance, or (b) deductions made by the bank from the depositor's balance?
12. What entry should be made if a check received from a customer and deposited is returned by the bank for lack of sufficient funds (an NSF check)?
13. What account or accounts are debited when (a) establishing a petty cash fund and (b) replenishing a petty cash fund?
14. The petty cash account has a debit balance of $800. At the end of the accounting period, there is $110 in the petty cash fund, along with petty cash receipts totaling $690. Should the fund be replenished as of the last day of the period? Discuss.
15. How are cash equivalents and compensating balances reported in the financial statements?

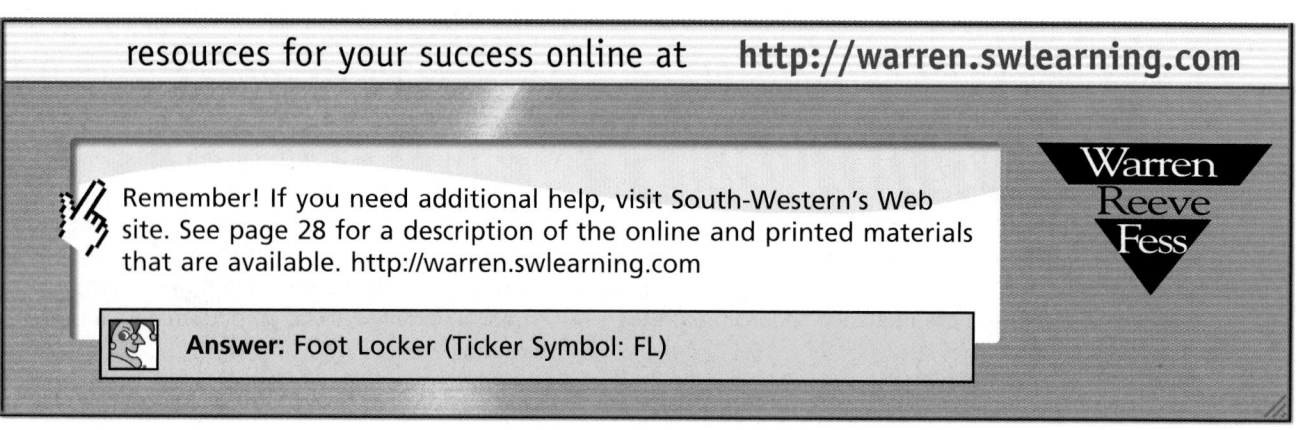

resources for your success online at   **http://warren.swlearning.com**

Remember! If you need additional help, visit South-Western's Web site. See page 28 for a description of the online and printed materials that are available. http://warren.swlearning.com

Warren Reeve Fess

Answer: Foot Locker (Ticker Symbol: FL)

Exercises

EXERCISE 6-1
Internal controls
Objective 2

Barbara Holmes has recently been hired as the manager of Fresh Start Coffee. Fresh Start Coffee is a national chain of franchised coffee shops. During her first month as store manager, Barbara encountered the following internal control situations:

a. Fresh Start Coffee has one cash register. Prior to Barbara's joining the coffee shop, each employee working on a shift would take a customer order, accept payment, and then prepare the order. Barbara made one employee on each shift responsible for taking orders and accepting the customer's payment. Other employees prepare the orders.

b. Since only one employee uses the cash register, that employee is responsible for counting the cash at the end of the shift and verifying that the cash in the drawer matches the amount of cash sales recorded by the cash register. Barbara expects each cashier to balance the drawer to the penny *every* time—no exceptions.

c. Barbara caught an employee putting a box of 100 single-serving tea bags in his car. Not wanting to create a scene, Barbara smiled and said, "I don't think you're putting those tea bags on the right shelf. Don't they belong inside the coffee shop?" The employee returned the tea bags to the stockroom.

State whether you agree or disagree with Barbara's method of handling each situation and explain your answer.

EXERCISE 6-2
Internal controls
Objective 2

Elegance by Elaine is a retail store specializing in women's clothing. The store has established a liberal return policy for the holiday season in order to encourage gift purchases. Any item purchased during November and December may be returned through January 31, with a receipt, for cash or exchange. If the customer does not have a receipt, cash will still be refunded for any item under $50. If the item is more than $50, a check is mailed to the customer.

Whenever an item is returned, a store clerk completes a return slip, which the customer signs. The return slip is placed in a special box. The store manager visits the return counter approximately once every two hours to authorize the return slips. Clerks are instructed to place the returned merchandise on the proper rack on the selling floor as soon as possible.

This year, returns at Elegance by Elaine have reached an all-time high. There are a large number of returns under $50 without receipts.

a. How can sales clerks employed at Elegance by Elaine use the store's return policy to steal money from the cash register?

b. 1. What internal control weaknesses do you see in the return policy that make cash thefts easier?

2. Would issuing a store credit in place of a cash refund for all merchandise returned without a receipt reduce the possibility of theft? List some advantages and disadvantages of issuing a store credit in place of a cash refund.

3. Assume that Elegance by Elaine is committed to the current policy of issuing cash refunds without a receipt. What changes could be made in the store's procedures regarding customer refunds in order to improve internal control?

EXERCISE 6-3
Internal controls for bank lending
Objective 2

First Charter Bank provides loans to businesses in the community through its Commercial Lending Department. Small loans (less than $100,000) may be approved by an individual loan officer, while larger loans (greater than $100,000) must be approved by a board of loan officers. Once a loan is approved, the funds are made available to the loan applicant under agreed-upon terms. The president of First Charter Bank has instituted a policy whereby she has the individual authority to approve loans up to $5,000,000. The president believes that this policy will allow flexibility to approve loans to valued clients much quicker than under the previous policy.

→ As an internal auditor of First Charter Bank, how would you respond to this change in policy?

EXERCISE 6-4
Internal controls
Objective 2

REAL WORLD

One of the largest fraud losses in history involved a securities trader for the Singapore office of **Barings Bank**, a British merchant bank. The trader established an unauthorized account number that was used to hide $1.4 billion in losses. Even after Barings' internal auditors noted that the trader both executed trades and recorded them, management did not take action. As a result, a lone individual in a remote office bankrupted an internationally recognized firm overnight.

→ What general weaknesses in Barings' internal controls contributed to the occurrence and size of the fraud?

EXERCISE 6-5
Internal controls
Objective 2

REAL WORLD

An employee of **JHT Holdings Inc.**, a trucking company, was responsible for resolving roadway accident claims under $25,000. The employee created fake accident claims and wrote settlement checks of between $5,000 and $25,000 to friends or acquaintances acting as phony "victims." One friend recruited subordinates at his place of work to cash some of the checks. Beyond this, the JHT employee also recruited lawyers, who he paid to represent both the trucking company and the fake victims in the bogus accident settlements. When the lawyers cashed the checks, they allegedly split the money with the corrupt JHT employee. This fraud went undetected for two years.

→ Why would it take so long to discover such a fraud?

EXERCISE 6-6
Internal controls
Objective 2

Event Sound Co. discovered a fraud whereby one of its front office administrative employees used company funds to purchase goods, such as computers, digital cameras, compact disk players, and other electronic items for her own use. The fraud was discovered when employees noticed an increase in delivery frequency from vendors and the use of unusual vendors. After some investigation, it was discovered that the employee would alter the description or change the quantity on an invoice in order to explain the cost on the bill.

→ What general internal control weaknesses contributed to this fraud?

EXERCISE 6-7
Financial statement fraud
Objective 2

REAL WORLD

The former chairman, the CFO, and the controller of **Donnkenny**, an apparel company that makes sportswear for Pierre Cardin and Victoria Jones, pleaded guilty to financial statement fraud. These managers used false journal entries to record fictitious sales, hid inventory in public warehouses so that it could be recorded as "sold," and required sales orders to be backdated so that the sale could be moved back to an earlier period. The combined effect of these actions caused $25 million out of $40 million in quarterly sales to be phony.

a. → Why might control procedures listed in this chapter be insufficient in stopping this type of fraud?
b. → How could this type of fraud be stopped?

EXERCISE 6-8
Internal control of cash receipts
Objective 4

The procedures used for over-the-counter receipts are as follows. At the close of each day's business, the sales clerks count the cash in their respective cash drawers, after which they determine the amount recorded by the cash register and prepare the memorandum cash form, noting any discrepancies. An employee from the cashier's office counts the cash, compares the total with the memorandum, and takes the cash to the cashier's office.

a. → Indicate the weak link in internal control.
b. → How can the weakness be corrected?

EXERCISE 6-9
Internal control of cash receipts
Objective 4

Deana Crisman works at the drive-through window of Awesome Burgers. Occasionally, when a drive-through customer orders, Deana fills the order and pockets the customer's money. She does not ring up the order on the cash register.
Identify the internal control weaknesses that exist at Awesome Burgers, and discuss what can be done to prevent this theft.

EXERCISE 6-10
Internal control of cash receipts
Objective 4

The mailroom employees send all remittances and remittance advices to the cashier. The cashier deposits the cash in the bank and forwards the remittance advices and duplicate deposit slips to the Accounting Department.

a. Indicate the weak link in internal control in the handling of cash receipts.
b. How can the weakness be corrected?

EXERCISE 6-11
Entry for cash sales; cash short
Objective 4

The actual cash received from cash sales was $17,572.40, and the amount indicated by the cash register total was $17,589.65. Journalize the entry to record the cash receipts and cash sales.

EXERCISE 6-12
Entry for cash sales; cash over
Objective 4

The actual cash received from cash sales was $6,973.60, and the amount indicated by the cash register total was $6,932.15. Journalize the entry to record the cash receipts and cash sales.

EXERCISE 6-13
Internal control of cash payments
Objective 5

Migraine Co. is a medium-size merchandising company. An investigation revealed that in spite of a sufficient bank balance, a significant amount of available cash discounts had been lost because of failure to make timely payments. In addition, it was discovered that several purchases invoices had been paid twice.
Outline procedures for the payment of vendors' invoices, so that the possibilities of losing available cash discounts and of paying an invoice a second time will be minimized.

EXERCISE 6-14
Internal control of cash payments
Objective 5

Satchell Company, a communications equipment manufacturer, recently fell victim to an embezzlement scheme masterminded by one of its employees. To understand the scheme, it is necessary to review Satchell's procedures for the purchase of services.

The purchasing agent is responsible for ordering services (such as repairs to a photocopy machine or office cleaning) after receiving a service requisition from an authorized manager. However, since no tangible goods are delivered, a receiving report is not prepared. When the Accounting Department receives an invoice billing Satchell for a service call, the accounts payable clerk calls the manager who requested the service in order to verify that it was performed.

The embezzlement scheme involves Drew Brogan, the manager of plant and facilities. Drew arranged for his uncle's company, Brogan Industrial Supply and Service, to be placed on Satchell's approved vendor list. Drew did not disclose the family relationship.

On several occasions, Drew would submit a requisition for services to be provided by Brogan Industrial Supply and Service. However, the service requested was really not needed, and it was never performed. Brogan would bill Satchell for the service and then split the cash payment with Drew.
Explain what changes should be made to Satchell's procedures for ordering and paying for services in order to prevent such occurrences in the future.

EXERCISE 6-15
Bank reconciliation
Objective 7

Identify each of the following reconciling items as: (a) an addition to the cash balance according to the bank statement, (b) a deduction from the cash balance according to the bank statement, (c) an addition to the cash balance according to the depositor's records, or (d) a deduction from the cash balance according to the depositor's records. (None of the transactions reported by bank debit and credit memorandums have been recorded by the depositor.)

1. Check drawn by depositor for $300 but incorrectly recorded as $3,000.
2. Check of a customer returned by bank to depositor because of insufficient funds, $775.
3. Bank service charges, $35.
4. Check for $129 incorrectly charged by bank as $219.
5. Outstanding checks, $6,137.68.
6. Deposit in transit, $7,500.
7. Note collected by bank, $12,000.

EXERCISE 6-16
Entries based on bank reconciliation
Objective 7

Which of the reconciling items listed in Exercise 6-15 require an entry in the depositor's accounts?

EXERCISE 6-17
Bank reconciliation
Objective 7

SPREADSHEET

✓ *Adjusted balance:*
$7,961.45

The following data were accumulated for use in reconciling the bank account of Kidstock Co. for March:

a. Cash balance according to the depositor's records at March 31, $7,671.45.
b. Cash balance according to the bank statement at March 31, $4,457.25.
c. Checks outstanding, $2,276.20.
d. Deposit in transit, not recorded by bank, $5,780.40.
e. A check for $145 in payment of an account was erroneously recorded in the check register as $451.
f. Bank debit memorandum for service charges, $16.00.

Prepare a bank reconciliation, using the format shown in Exhibit 9.

EXERCISE 6-18
Entries for bank reconciliation
Objective 7

Using the data presented in Exercise 6-17, journalize the entry or entries that should be made by the depositor.

EXERCISE 6-19
Entries for note collected by bank
Objective 7

Accompanying a bank statement for Covershot Company is a credit memorandum for $15,300, representing the principal ($15,000) and interest ($300) on a note that had been collected by the bank. The depositor had been notified by the bank at the time of the collection but had made no entries. Journalize the entry that should be made by the depositor to bring the accounting records up to date.

EXERCISE 6-20
Bank reconciliation
Objective 7

SPREADSHEET

✓ *Adjusted balance:*
$14,452.75

An accounting clerk for Dubitzky Co. prepared the following bank reconciliation:

Dubitzky Co.
Bank Reconciliation
July 31, 2006

Cash balance according to depositor's records		$8,100.75
Add: Outstanding checks	$6,557.12	
Error by Dubitzky Co. in recording Check No. 4217 as $6,315 instead of $3,615	2,700.00	
Note for $3,600 collected by bank, including interest	3,672.00	12,929.12
		$21,029.87
Deduct: Deposit in transit on July 31	$7,150.00	
Bank service charges	20.00	7,170.00
Cash balance according to bank statement		$13,859.87

a. From the data in the above bank reconciliation, prepare a new bank reconciliation for Dubitzky Co., using the format shown in the illustrative problem.
b. If a balance sheet were prepared for Dubitzky Co. on July 31, 2006, what amount should be reported for cash?

EXERCISE 6-21
Bank reconciliation
Objective 7

WHAT'S WRONG WITH THIS?

✓ *Corrected adjusted balance: $8,898.02*

Identify the errors in the following bank reconciliation:

Imaging Services Co.
Bank Reconciliation
For the Month Ended April 30, 2006

Cash balance according to bank statement			$ 9,767.76
Add outstanding checks: (—)			
No. 821		$ 345.95	
839		272.75	
843		759.60	
844		501.50	1,879.80
			$11,647.56
Deduct deposit of April 30, not recorded by bank . . . . (+)			1,010.06
Adjusted balance			$ 9,637.50
Cash balance according to depositor's records			$ 1,118.32
Add: Proceeds of note collected by bank:			
Principal	$8,000.00		
Interest	280.00	$8,280.00	
(—) Service charges		18.00	8,298.00
			$ 9,416.32
Deduct: Check returned because of			
insufficient funds		$ 752.30	
Error in recording April 10			
deposit of $4,850 as $4,580 . . . . (+)		270.00	1,022.30
Adjusted balance			$ 8,394.02

EXERCISE 6-22
Using bank reconciliation to determine cash receipts stolen
Objective 7

SPREADSHEET

Prometheus Co. records all cash receipts on the basis of its cash register tapes. Prometheus Co. discovered during April 2006 that one of its sales clerks had stolen an undetermined amount of cash receipts when she took the daily deposits to the bank. The following data have been gathered for April:

Cash in bank according to the general ledger	$12,573.22
Cash according to the April 30, 2006 bank statement	13,271.14
Outstanding checks as of April 30, 2006	1,750.20
Bank service charge for April	45.10
Note receivable, including interest collected by bank in April	5,200.00

No deposits were in transit on April 30, which fell on a Sunday.

a. Determine the amount of cash receipts stolen by the sales clerk.
b. ▬▬▶ What accounting controls would have prevented or detected this theft?

EXERCISE 6-23
Petty cash fund entries
Objective 8

Journalize the entries to record the following:

a. Check No. 2715 is issued to establish a petty cash fund of $750.
b. The amount of cash in the petty cash fund is now $119.57. Check No. 3120 is issued to replenish the fund, based on the following summary of petty cash receipts: office supplies, $415.83; miscellaneous selling expense, $107.90; miscellaneous administrative expense, $88.10. (Since the amount of the check to replenish the fund plus the balance in the fund do not equal $750, record the discrepancy in the cash short and over account.)

EXERCISE 6-24
Variation in cash balances
Objective 9

For a recent fiscal year, **Circuit City**'s quarterly balances of cash and cash equivalents were as follows:

End of February	$885 million
End of May	$1,176 million
End of August	$847 million
End of November	$438 million

▬▬▶ What would you expect would be the cause of the variation in Circuit City's balances of cash and cash equivalents?

EXERCISE 6-25
Doomsday ratio
Objective 10

The financial statements for **Home Depot** are presented in Appendix F at the end of the text.

a. Compute the doomsday ratio for Home Depot for 2003 and 2002.
b.  What conclusions can be drawn from comparing the ratios for 2003 and 2002?

Problems Series A

PROBLEM 6-1A
Evaluate internal control of cash
Objectives 2, 3, 4, 5

The following procedures were recently installed by The Geodesic Company:

a. All sales are rung up on the cash register, and a receipt is given to the customer. All sales are recorded on a record locked inside the cash register.
b. Vouchers and all supporting documents are perforated with a PAID designation after being paid by the treasurer.
c. Checks received through the mail are given daily to the accounts receivable clerk for recording collections on account and for depositing in the bank.
d. At the end of a shift, each cashier counts the cash in his or her cash register, unlocks the cash register record, and compares the amount of cash with the amount on the record to determine cash shortages and overages.
e. Each cashier is assigned a separate cash register drawer to which no other cashier has access.
f. The bank reconciliation is prepared by the accountant.
g. Disbursements are made from the petty cash fund only after a petty cash receipt has been completed and signed by the payee.

Instructions
Indicate whether each of the procedures of internal control over cash represents (1) a strength or (2) a weakness. For each weakness, indicate why it exists.

PROBLEM 6-2A
Transactions for petty cash, cash short and over
Objectives 4, 8

SPREADSHEET

The Orchid Company completed the following selected transactions during June 2006:

June 1. Established a petty cash fund of $600.
    6. The cash sales for the day, according to the cash register records, totaled $7,998.50. The actual cash received from cash sales was $8,008.15.
  30. Petty cash on hand was $50.75. Replenished the petty cash fund for the following disbursements, each evidenced by a petty cash receipt:
    June 3. Store supplies, $30.75.
        8. Express charges on merchandise purchased, $100.75 (Merchandise Inventory).
      12. Office supplies, $74.30.
      15. Office supplies, $35.20.
      19. Postage stamps, $52.00 (Office Supplies).
      20. Repair to fax, $110.00 (Miscellaneous Administrative Expense).
      21. Repair to printer, $51.50 (Miscellaneous Administrative Expense).
      22. Postage due on special delivery letter, $18.00 (Miscellaneous Administrative Expense).
      27. Express charges on merchandise purchased, $65.50 (Merchandise Inventory).
  30. The cash sales for the day, according to the cash register records, totaled $9,009.50. The actual cash received from cash sales was $8,988.35.
  30. Decreased the petty cash fund by $150.

Instructions
Journalize the transactions.

PROBLEM 6-3A
Bank reconciliation and entries

Objective 7

SPREADSHEET
P.A.S.S.

✓ *1. Adjusted balance: $26,315.40*

The cash account for Showtime Systems at February 28, 2006, indicated a balance of $19,144.15. The bank statement indicated a balance of $31,391.40 on February 28, 2006. Comparing the bank statement and the accompanying canceled checks and memorandums with the records reveals the following reconciling items:

a. Checks outstanding totaled $11,021.50.
b. A deposit of $6,215.50, representing receipts of February 28, had been made too late to appear on the bank statement.
c. The bank had collected $6,300 on a note left for collection. The face of the note was $6,000.
d. A check for $1,275 returned with the statement had been incorrectly recorded by Showtime Systems as $2,175. The check was for the payment of an obligation to Wilson Co. for the purchase of office supplies on account.
e. A check drawn for $855 had been incorrectly charged by the bank as $585.
f. Bank service charges for February amounted to $28.75.

Instructions
1. Prepare a bank reconciliation.
2. Journalize the necessary entries. The accounts have not been closed.

PROBLEM 6-4A
Bank reconciliation and entries

Objective 7

SPREADSHEET
P.A.S.S.

✓ *1. Adjusted balance: $16,821.88*

The cash account for Alpine Sports Co. on April 1, 2006, indicated a balance of $16,911.95. During April, the total cash deposited was $65,500.40, and checks written totaled $68,127.47. The bank statement indicated a balance of $18,880.45 on April 30, 2006. Comparing the bank statement, the canceled checks, and the accompanying memorandums with the records revealed the following reconciling items:

a. Checks outstanding totaled $5,180.27.
b. A deposit of $3,481.70, representing receipts of April 30, had been made too late to appear on the bank statement.
c. A check for $620 had been incorrectly charged by the bank as $260.
d. A check for $479.30 returned with the statement had been recorded by Alpine Sports Co. as $497.30. The check was for the payment of an obligation to Bray & Son on account.
e. The bank had collected for Alpine Sports Co. $3,424 on a note left for collection. The face of the note was $3,200.
f. Bank service charges for April amounted to $25.
g. A check for $880 from Shuler Co. was returned by the bank because of insufficient funds.

Instructions
1. Prepare a bank reconciliation as of April 30.
2. Journalize the necessary entries. The accounts have not been closed.

PROBLEM 6-5A
Bank reconciliation and entries

Objective 7

SPREADSHEET

✓ *1. Adjusted balance: $14,244.09*

Rocky Mountain Interiors deposits all cash receipts each Wednesday and Friday in a night depository after banking hours. The data required to reconcile the bank statement as of May 31 have been taken from various documents and records and are reproduced as follows. The sources of the data are printed in capital letters. All checks were written for payments on account.

BANK RECONCILIATION FOR PRECEDING MONTH (DATED APRIL 30):

Cash balance according to bank statement		$10,422.80
Add deposit of April 30, not recorded by bank		780.80
		$11,203.60
Deduct outstanding checks:		
No. 580	$310.10	
No. 602	85.50	
No. 612	92.50	
No. 613	137.50	625.60
Adjusted balance		$10,578.00
Cash balance according to depositor's records		$10,605.70
Deduct service charges		27.70
Adjusted balance		$10,578.00

CASH ACCOUNT:
Balance as of May 1 $10,578.00

CHECKS WRITTEN:
Number and amount of each check issued in May:

Check No.	Amount	Check No.	Amount	Check No.	Amount
614	$243.50 ✓	621	$309.50	628	$ 837.70
615	350.10	622	Void	629	329.90 ✓
616	279.90	623	Void	630	882.80 ✓
617	395.50	624	707.01 ✓	631	1,081.56 ✓
618	435.40	625	158.63 ✓	632	624.00
619	320.10	626	550.03 ✓	633	310.08
620	238.87	627	318.73	634	303.30

Total amount of checks issued in May $8,676.61

MAY BANK STATEMENT:

MEMBER FDIC   PAGE   1

AMERICAN NATIONAL BANK OF DETROIT

DETROIT, MI 48201-2500   (313)933-8547

ROCKY MOUNTAIN INTERIORS

	ACCOUNT NUMBER	
FROM 5/01/20– TO 5/31/20–		
BALANCE	10,422.80	
9 DEPOSITS	6,086.35	
20 WITHDRAWALS	7,514.11	
4 OTHER DEBITS AND CREDITS	5,150.50CR	
NEW BALANCE	14,145.54	

----- CHECKS AND OTHER DEBITS ----- *- DEPOSITS -* *- DATE -* *- BALANCE-*

				DEPOSITS	DATE	BALANCE
No.580	310.10 ✓	No.612	92.50	780.80	05/01	10,801.00
No.613	137.50 ✓	No.614	243.50 ✓	569.50 ✓	05/03	10,989.50
No.615	350.10 ✓	No.616	279.90	701.80 ✓	05/06	11,061.30
No.617	395.50 ✓	No.618	435.40 ✓	819.24 ✓	05/11	11,049.64
No.619	320.10 ✓	No.620	238.87	580.70 ✓	05/13	11,071.37
No.621	309.50 ✓	No.624	707.01 ✓	MS 5,000.00 ✓	05/14	15,054.86
No.625	158.63 ✓	No.626	550.03 ✓	MS 400.00	05/14	14,746.20
No.627	318.73 ✓	No.629	329.90 ✓	600.10 ✓	05/17	14,697.67
No.630	882.80 ✓	No.631	1,081.56	NSF 225.40	05/20	12,507.91
No.632	62.40 ✓	No.633	310.08 ✓	701.26 ✓	05/21	12,836.69
				731.45 ✓	05/24	13,568.14
		SC	24.10	601.50 ✓	05/28	14,169.64
					05/31	14,145.54

EC — ERROR CORRECTION   OD — OVERDRAFT
MS — MISCELLANEOUS   PS — PAYMENT STOPPED
NSF — NOT SUFFICIENT FUNDS   SC — SERVICE CHARGE

* * *   * * *   * * *

THE RECONCILEMENT OF THIS STATEMENT WITH YOUR RECORDS IS ESSENTIAL.
ANY ERROR OR EXCEPTION SHOULD BE REPORTED IMMEDIATELY.

(handwritten annotations: "these are from last month", "error", "error", "stub")

 CASH RECEIPTS FOR MONTH OF MAY $6,630.60

DUPLICATE DEPOSIT TICKETS:
Date and amount of each deposit in May:

Date	Amount	Date	Amount	Date	Amount
May 2	$569.50 ✓	May 12	$580.70 ✓	May 23	$ 731.45 ✓
5	701.80 ✓	16	600.10 ✓	26	601.50 ✓
9	819.24 ✓	19	701.26 ✓	31	1,325.05

(handwritten: Didn't clear bank → deposit in transit.)

Instructions

1. Prepare a bank reconciliation as of May 31. If errors in recording deposits or checks are discovered, assume that the errors were made by the company. Assume that all deposits are from cash sales. All checks are written to satisfy accounts payable.
2. Journalize the necessary entries. The accounts have not been closed.
3. What is the amount of cash that should appear on the balance sheet as of May 31?
4. ▭▬► Assume that a canceled check for $1,375 has been incorrectly recorded by the bank as $1,735. Briefly explain how the error would be included in a bank reconciliation and how it should be corrected.

Problems Series B

PROBLEM 6-1B
Evaluating internal control of cash
Objectives 2, 3, 4, 5

The following procedures were recently installed by Pancreas Company:

a. At the end of each day, an accounting clerk compares the duplicate copy of the daily cash deposit slip with the deposit receipt obtained from the bank.
b. The bank reconciliation is prepared by the cashier, who works under the supervision of the treasurer.
c. At the end of the day, cash register clerks are required to use their own funds to make up any cash shortages in their registers.
d. Along with petty cash expense receipts for postage, office supplies, etc., several post-dated employee checks are in the petty cash fund.
e. The accounts payable clerk prepares a voucher for each disbursement. The voucher along with the supporting documentation is forwarded to the treasurer's office for approval.
f. All mail is opened by the mail clerk, who forwards all cash remittances to the cashier. The cashier prepares a listing of the cash receipts and forwards a copy of the list to the accounts receivable clerk for recording in the accounts.
g. After necessary approvals have been obtained for the payment of a voucher, the treasurer signs and mails the check. The treasurer then stamps the voucher and supporting documentation as paid and returns the voucher and supporting documentation to the accounts payable clerk for filing.
h. At the end of each day, any deposited cash receipts are placed in the bank's night depository.

Instructions

▭▬► Indicate whether each of the procedures of internal control over cash represents (1) a strength or (2) a weakness. For each weakness, indicate why it exists.

PROBLEM 6-2B
Transactions for petty cash; cash short and over
Objectives 4, 8

Kewpie Company completed the following selected transactions during March 2006:

Mar. 1. Established a petty cash fund of $850.
    18. The cash sales for the day, according to the cash register records, totaled $11,970.60. The actual cash received from cash sales was $12,007.50.

(continued)

SPREADSHEET

Mar. 31. Petty cash on hand was $20.18. Replenished the petty cash fund for the following disbursements, each evidenced by a petty cash receipt:
   Mar. 3. Store supplies, $198.10.
      6. Express charges on merchandise sold, $120 (Transportation Out).
      9. Office supplies, $13.75.
      18. Office supplies, $49.30.
      20. Postage stamps, $74 (Office Supplies).
      21. Repair to office printer, $150.00 (Miscellaneous Administrative Expense).
      22. Postage due on special delivery letter, $40.00 (Miscellaneous Administrative Expense).
      24. Express charges on merchandise sold, $125 (Transportation Out).
      27. Office supplies, $41.15.
   31. The cash sales for the day, according to the cash register records, totaled $9,055.50. The actual cash received from cash sales was $9,010.25.
   31. Increased the petty cash fund by $100.

Instructions

Journalize the transactions.

PROBLEM 6-3B
Bank reconciliation and entries

Objective 7

SPREADSHEET
P.A.S.S.

✓ *1. Adjusted balance: $16,215.95*

The cash account for Pickron Co. at April 30, 2006, indicated a balance of $13,290.95. The bank statement indicated a balance of $18,016.30 on April 30, 2006. Comparing the bank statement and the accompanying canceled checks and memorandums with the records revealed the following reconciling items:

a. Checks outstanding totaled $7,169.75.
b. A deposit of $5,189.40, representing receipts of April 30, had been made too late to appear on the bank statement.
c. The bank had collected $3,240 on a note left for collection. The face of the note was $3,000.
d. A check for $1,960 returned with the statement had been incorrectly recorded by Pickron Co. as $1,690. The check was for the payment of an obligation to Jones Co. for the purchase of office equipment on account.
e. A check drawn for $1,680 had been erroneously charged by the bank as $1,860.
f. Bank service charges for April amounted to $45.00.

Instructions

1. Prepare a bank reconciliation.
2. Journalize the necessary entries. The accounts have not been closed.

PROBLEM 6-4B
Bank reconciliation and entries

Objective 7

SPREADSHEET
P.A.S.S.

✓ *1. Adjusted balance: $5,689.87*

The cash account for Seal-Tek Co. at December 1, 2006, indicated a balance of $3,945.90. During December, the total cash deposited was $31,077.75, and checks written totaled $30,395.78. The bank statement indicated a balance of $5,465.50 on December 31. Comparing the bank statement, the canceled checks, and the accompanying memorandums with the records revealed the following reconciling items:

a. Checks outstanding totaled $3,003.84.
b. A deposit of $2,148.21, representing receipts of December 31, had been made too late to appear on the bank statement.
c. The bank had collected for Seal-Tek Co. $1,908 on a note left for collection. The face of the note was $1,800.
d. A check for $120 returned with the statement had been incorrectly charged by the bank as $1,200.
e. A check for $318 returned with the statement had been recorded by Seal-Tek Co. as $138. The check was for the payment of an obligation to Kenyon Co. on account.
f. Bank service charges for December amounted to $30.
g. A check for $636 from Fontana Co. was returned by the bank because of insufficient funds.

Instructions

1. Prepare a bank reconciliation as of December 31.
2. Journalize the necessary entries. The accounts have not been closed.

PROBLEM 6-5B
Bank reconciliation and entries
Objective 7

SPREADSHEET

✓ *1. Adjusted balance: $10,322.02*

Heritage Furniture Company deposits all cash receipts each Wednesday and Friday in a night depository, after banking hours. The data required to reconcile the bank statement as of November 30 have been taken from various documents and records and are reproduced as follows. The sources of the data are printed in capital letters. All checks were written for payments on account.

NOVEMBER BANK STATEMENT:

						PAGE 1
	MEMBER FDIC		**ACCOUNT NUMBER**			
AMERICAN NATIONAL BANK OF DETROIT			FROM 11/01/20–	TO 11/30/20–		
DETROIT, MI 48201-2500 (313)933-8547			BALANCE	7,447.20		
			9 DEPOSITS	8,691.77		
			20 WITHDRAWALS	7,345.91		
HERITAGE FURNITURE COMPANY			4 OTHER DEBITS AND CREDITS	2,298.70CR		
			NEW BALANCE	11,091.76		

* – – CHECKS AND OTHER DEBITS – – – *		– – DEPOSITS – –	* – DATE – *	– – BALANCE – – *
No.731 162.15	No.738 251.40	690.25	11/01	7,723.90
No.739 60.55	No.740 237.50	1,080.50	11/02	8,506.35
No.741 495.15	No.742 501.90	854.17	11/04	8,363.47
No.743 671.30	No.744 506.88	840.50	11/09	8,025.79
No.745 117.25	No.746 298.66	MS 2,500.00	11/09	10,109.88
No.748 450.90	No.749 640.13	MS 125.00	11/09	9,143.85
No.750 276.77	No.751 299.37	896.61	11/11	9,464.32
No.752 537.01	No.753 380.95	882.95	11/16	9,429.31
No.754 449.75	No.756 113.95	1,606.74	11/18	10,472.35
No.757 407.95	No.760 486.39	897.34	11/23	10,475.35
		942.71	11/25	11,418.06
	NSF 291.90		11/28	11,126.16
	SC 34.40		11/30	11,091.76

EC — ERROR CORRECTION   OD — OVERDRAFT
MS — MISCELLANEOUS   PS — PAYMENT STOPPED
NSF — NOT SUFFICIENT FUNDS   SC — SERVICE CHARGE

* * *   * * *   * * *

THE RECONCILEMENT OF THIS STATEMENT WITH YOUR RECORDS IS ESSENTIAL.
ANY ERROR OR EXCEPTION SHOULD BE REPORTED IMMEDIATELY.

CASH ACCOUNT:
    Balance as of November 1 $7,317.40

CASH RECEIPTS FOR MONTH OF NOVEMBER $8,651.58

DUPLICATE DEPOSIT TICKETS:
    Date and amount of each deposit in November:

Date	Amount	Date	Amount	Date	Amount
Nov. 1	$1,080.50	Nov. 10	$ 896.61	Nov. 22	$ 537.34
3	854.17	15	882.95	24	942.71
8	840.50	17	1,606.74	29	1,010.06

CHECKS WRITTEN:

Number and amount of each check issued in November:

Check No.	Amount	Check No.	Amount	Check No.	Amount
740	$237.50	747	Void	754	$ 449.75
741	495.15	748	$450.90	755	272.75
742	501.90	749	640.13	756	113.95
743	671.30	750	276.77	757	407.95
744	506.88	751	299.37	758	259.60
745	117.25	752	337.01	759	901.50
746	298.66	753	380.95	760	486.39

Total amount of checks issued in November $8,105.66

BANK RECONCILIATION FOR PRECEDING MONTH:

Heritage Furniture Company
Bank Reconciliation
October 31, 20—

Cash balance according to bank statement		$7,447.20
Add deposit for October 31, not recorded by bank		690.25
		$8,137.45
Deduct outstanding checks:		
No. 731	$162.15	
736	345.95	
738	251.40	
739	60.55	820.05
Adjusted balance		$7,317.40
Cash balance according to depositor's records		$7,352.50
Deduct service charges		35.10
Adjusted balance		$7,317.40

Instructions

1. Prepare a bank reconciliation as of November 30. If errors in recording deposits or checks are discovered, assume that the errors were made by the company. Assume that all deposits are from cash sales. All checks are written to satisfy accounts payable.
2. Journalize the necessary entries. The accounts have not been closed.
3. What is the amount of cash that should appear on the balance sheet as of November 30?
4. ▭▬▶ Assume that a canceled check for $580 has been incorrectly recorded by the bank as $850. Briefly explain how the error would be included in a bank reconciliation and how it should be corrected.

Special Activities

ACTIVITY 6-1
Ethics and professional conduct in business

Lee Garrett sells security systems for Guardsman Security Co. Garrett has a monthly sales quota of $40,000. If Garrett exceeds this quota, he is awarded a bonus. In measuring the quota, a sale is credited to the salesperson when a customer signs a contract for installation of a security system. Through the 25th of the current month, Garrett has sold $30,000 in security systems.

Vortex Co., a business rumored to be on the verge of bankruptcy, contacted Garrett on the 26th of the month about having a security system installed. Garrett estimates that the contract would yield about $14,000 worth of business for Guardsman Security Co. In addition, this contract would be large enough to put Garrett "over the top" for a bonus in the current month. However, Garrett is concerned that Vortex Co. will not be able to make the contract payment after the security system is installed. In fact, Garrett has heard rumors that a competing security services company refused to install a system for Vortex Co. because of these concerns.

Upon further consideration, Garrett concluded that his job is to sell security systems and that it's someone else's problem to collect the resulting accounts receivable. Thus, Garrett wrote the contract with Vortex Co. and received a bonus for the month.

a. ▨▶ Discuss whether Lee Garrett was acting in an ethical manner.
b. ▨▶ How might Guardsman Security Co. use internal controls to prevent this scenario from occurring?

ACTIVITY 6-2
*Ethics and financial
statement fraud*

REAL WORLD   ETHICS

WorldCom Corporation, the second largest telecommunications company in the United States, became the largest bankruptcy in history due to financial reporting irregularities and misstatements of nearly $7 billion. WorldCom's controller, director of general accounting, and director of management reporting all pleaded guilty to financial reporting fraud. These employees all stated that they were ordered by superiors to adjust the records to artificially boost the company's profits. Under protest, these employees made the adjustments.

a. ▨▶ Should these employees be held responsible for their actions, since they were "following orders"?
b. ▨▶ How should an employee respond to questionable or unethical requests from superiors?

ACTIVITY 6-3
*Ethics and professional
conduct in business*

ETHICS

During the preparation of the bank reconciliation for The Image Co., Chris Renees, the assistant controller, discovered that Empire National Bank incorrectly recorded a $936 check written by The Image Co. as $396. Chris has decided not to notify the bank but wait for the bank to detect the error. Chris plans to record the $540 error as Other Income if the bank fails to detect the error within the next three months. ▨▶ Discuss whether Chris is behaving in a professional manner.

ACTIVITY 6-4
Internal controls

The following is an excerpt from a conversation between two sales clerks, Carol Dickson and Jill Kesner. Both Carol and Jill are employed by Reboot Electronics, a locally owned and operated computer retail store.

Carol: Did you hear the news?
Jill: What news?
Carol: Candis and Albert were both arrested this morning.
Jill: What? Arrested? You're putting me on!
Carol: No, really! The police arrested them first thing this morning. Put them in handcuffs, read them their rights—the whole works. It was unreal!
Jill: What did they do?
Carol: Well, apparently they were filling out merchandise refund forms for fictitious customers and then taking the cash.
Jill: I guess I never thought of that. How did they catch them?
Carol: The store manager noticed that returns were twice that of last year and seemed to be increasing. When he confronted Candis, she became flustered and admitted to taking the cash, apparently over $2,800 in just three months. They're going over the last six months' transactions to try to determine how much Albert stole. He apparently started stealing first.

▨▶ Suggest appropriate control procedures that would have prevented or detected the theft of cash.

ACTIVITY 6-5
Internal controls

The following is an excerpt from a conversation between the store manager of Piper Grocery Stores, Bill Dowell, and Cary Wynne, president of Piper Grocery Stores.

Cary: Bill, I'm concerned about this new scanning system.
Bill: What's the problem?

Cary: Well, how do we know the clerks are ringing up all the merchandise?

Bill: That's one of the strong points about the system. The scanner automatically rings up each item, based on its bar code. We update the prices daily, so we're sure that the sale is rung up for the right price.

Cary: That's not my concern. What keeps a clerk from pretending to scan items and then simply not charging his friends? If his friends were buying 10–15 items, it would be easy for the clerk to pass through several items with his finger over the bar code or just pass the merchandise through the scanner with the wrong side showing. It would look normal for anyone observing. In the old days, we at least could hear the cash register ringing up each sale.

Bill: I see your point.

▭▶ Suggest ways that Piper Grocery Stores could prevent or detect the theft of merchandise as described.

ACTIVITY 6-6
Ethics and professional conduct in business

ETHICS

Tim Jost and Kerri Stein are both cash register clerks for Frontier Markets. Kathy Rostad is the store manager for Frontier Markets. The following is an excerpt of a conversation between Tim and Kerri:

Tim: Kerri, how long have you been working for Frontier Markets?

Kerri: Almost five years this August. You just started two weeks ago . . . right?

Tim: Yes. Do you mind if I ask you a question?

Kerri: No, go ahead.

Tim: What I want to know is, have they always had this rule that if your cash register is short at the end of the day, you have to make up the shortage out of your own pocket?

Kerri: Yes, as long as I've been working here.

Tim: Well, it's the pits. Last week I had to pay in almost $30.

Kerri: It's not that big a deal. I just make sure that I'm not short at the end of the day.

Tim: How do you do that?

Kerri: I just short-change a few customers early in the day. There are a few jerks that deserve it anyway. Most of the time, their attention is elsewhere and they don't think to check their change.

Tim: What happens if you're over at the end of the day?

Kerri: Rostad lets me keep it as long as it doesn't get to be too large. I've not been short in over a year. I usually clear about $20 to $30 extra per day.

▭▶ Discuss this case from the viewpoint of proper controls and professional behavior.

ACTIVITY 6-7
Bank reconciliation and internal control

The records of Lumberjack Company indicate a July 31 cash balance of $9,806.05, which includes undeposited receipts for July 30 and 31. The cash balance on the bank statement as of July 31 is $6,004.95. This balance includes a note of $4,000 plus $240 interest collected by the bank but not recorded in the journal. Checks outstanding on July 31 were as follows: No. 670, $781.20; No. 679, $610; No. 690, $716.50; No. 1996, $127.40; No. 1997, $520; and No. 1999, $851.50.

On July 3, the cashier resigned, effective at the end of the month. Before leaving on July 31, the cashier prepared the following bank reconciliation:

Cash balance per books, July 31		$ 9,806.05
Add outstanding checks:		
No. 1996	$127.40	
1997	520.00	
1999	851.50	1,198.90
		$11,004.95
Less undeposited receipts		5,000.00
Cash balance per bank, July 31		$ 6,004.95
Deduct unrecorded note with interest		4,240.00
True cash, July 31		$ 1,764.95

> *Calculator Tape of Outstanding Checks:*
> 0.00 *
> 127.40 +
> 520.00 +
> 851.50 +
> 1,198.90 *

Subsequently, the owner of Lumberjack Company discovered that the cashier had stolen an unknown amount of undeposited receipts, leaving only $5,000 to be deposited on July 31. The owner, a close family friend, has asked your help in determining the amount that the former cashier has stolen.

1. Determine the amount the cashier stole from Lumberjack Company. Show your computations in good form.
2. How did the cashier attempt to conceal the theft?
3. a. Identify two major weaknesses in internal controls, which allowed the cashier to steal the undeposited cash receipts.
   b. ➡ Recommend improvements in internal controls, so that similar types of thefts of undeposited cash receipts can be prevented.

ACTIVITY 6-8
Observe internal controls over cash

GROUP ACTIVITY

Select a business in your community and observe its internal controls over cash receipts and cash payments. The business could be a bank or a bookstore, restaurant, department store, or other retailer. In groups of three or four, identify and discuss the similarities and differences in each business's cash internal controls.

ACTIVITY 6-9
Invest excess cash

INTERNET

Assume that you have just received a $100,000 check! Go to the Web site of (or visit) a local bank and collect information about the savings and checking options that are available. Identify the option that is best for you and why it is best.

Answers to Self-Examination Questions

1. **A**   Analysis (answer A) is the initial step of determining the informational needs and how the system provides this information. Design (answer B) is the step in which proposals for changes are developed. Implementation (answer C) is the final step involving carrying out or implementing the proposals for changes. Feedback (answer D) is not a separate step but is considered part of the systems implementation.

2. **A**   The policies and procedures that are established to safeguard assets, ensure accurate business information, and ensure compliance with laws and regulations are called internal controls (answer A). The

three steps in setting up an accounting system are (1) analysis (answer B), (2) design (answer C), and (3) implementation (answer D).

3. **B**   On any specific date, the cash account in a depositor's ledger may not agree with the account in the bank's ledger because of delays and/or errors by either party in recording transactions. The purpose of a bank reconciliation, therefore, is to determine the reasons for any differences between the two account balances. All errors should then be corrected by the depositor or the bank, as appropriate. In arriving at the adjusted (correct) cash balance according to the bank statement, outstanding

checks must be deducted (answer B) to adjust for checks that have been written by the depositor but that have not yet been presented to the bank for payment.

4. **C** All reconciling items that are added to and deducted from the cash balance according to the depositor's records on the bank reconciliation (answer C) require that journal entries be made by the depositor to correct errors made in recording transactions or to bring the cash account up to date for delays in recording transactions.

5. **D** To avoid the delay, annoyance, and expense that is associated with paying all obligations by check, relatively small amounts (answer A) are paid from a petty cash fund. The fund is established by estimating the amount of cash needed to pay these small amounts during a specified period (answer B), and it is then reimbursed when the amount of money in the fund is reduced to a predetermined minimum amount (answer C).

7

RECEIVABLES

objectives

After studying this chapter, you should be able to:

1 List the common classifications of receivables.

2 Summarize and provide examples of internal control procedures that apply to receivables.

3 Describe the nature of and the accounting for uncollectible receivables.

4 Journalize the entries for the allowance method of accounting for uncollectibles, and estimate uncollectible receivables based on sales and on an analysis of receivables.

5 Journalize the entries for the direct write-off of uncollectible receivables.

6 Describe the nature and characteristics of promissory notes.

7 Journalize the entries for notes receivable transactions.

8 Prepare the Current Assets presentation of receivables on the balance sheet.

9 Compute and interpret the accounts receivable turnover and the number of days' sales in receivables.

Assume that you have decided to sell your car to a neighbor for $7,500. Your neighbor agrees to pay you $1,500 immediately and the remaining $6,000 in a year. How much should you charge your neighbor for interest?

You could determine an appropriate interest rate by asking some financial institutions what they currently charge their customers. Using this information as a starting point, you could then negotiate with your neighbor and agree upon a rate. Assuming that the agreed-upon rate is 8%, you will receive interest totaling $480 for the one-year loan.

In this chapter, we will describe and illustrate how interest is computed. In addition, we will discuss the accounting for receivables, including uncollectible receivables. Most of these receivables result from a business providing services or selling merchandise on account.

Classification of Receivables

objective 1

List the common classifications of receivables.

REAL WORLD

An annual report of **La-Z-Boy Chair Company** reported that receivables made up over 60% of La-Z-Boy's current assets.

POINT OF INTEREST

If you have purchased an automobile on credit, you probably signed a note. From your viewpoint, the note is a note payable. From the creditor's viewpoint, the note is a note receivable.

Many companies sell on credit in order to sell more services or products. The receivables that result from such sales are normally classified as accounts receivable or notes receivable. The term ***receivables*** includes all money claims against other entities, including people, business firms, and other organizations. These receivables are usually a significant portion of the total current assets.

Accounts Receivable

The most common transaction creating a receivable is selling merchandise or services on credit. The receivable is recorded as a debit to the accounts receivable account. Such ***accounts receivable*** are normally expected to be collected within a relatively short period, such as 30 or 60 days. They are classified on the balance sheet as a current asset.

Notes Receivable

Notes receivable are amounts that customers owe, for which a formal, written instrument of credit has been issued. As long as notes receivable are expected to be collected within a year, they are normally classified on the balance sheet as a current asset.

Notes are often used for credit periods of more than sixty days. For example, a dealer in automobiles or furniture may require a down payment at the time of sale and accept a note or a series of notes for the remainder. Such arrangements usually provide for monthly payments.

Notes may be used to settle a customer's account receivable. Notes and accounts receivable that result from sales transactions are sometimes called **trade receivables**. Unless we indicate otherwise, we will assume that all notes and accounts receivable in this chapter are from sales transactions.

Other Receivables

Other receivables are normally listed separately on the balance sheet. If they are expected to be collected within one year, they are classified as current assets. If collection is expected beyond one year, they are classified as noncurrent assets and reported under the caption *Investments*. **Other receivables** include interest receivable, taxes receivable, and receivables from officers or employees.

Internal Control of Receivables

objective 2

Summarize and provide examples of internal control procedures that apply to receivables.

The principles of internal control that we discussed in prior chapters can be used to establish controls to safeguard receivables. For example, the four functions of credit approval, sales, accounting, and collections should be separated, as shown in Exhibit 1.

The individuals responsible for sales should be separate from the individuals accounting for the receivables and approving credit. By doing so, the accounting and credit approval functions serve as independent checks on sales. The employee who handles the accounting for receivables should not be involved with collecting receivables. Separating these functions reduces the possibility of errors and misuse of funds.

•Exhibit 1

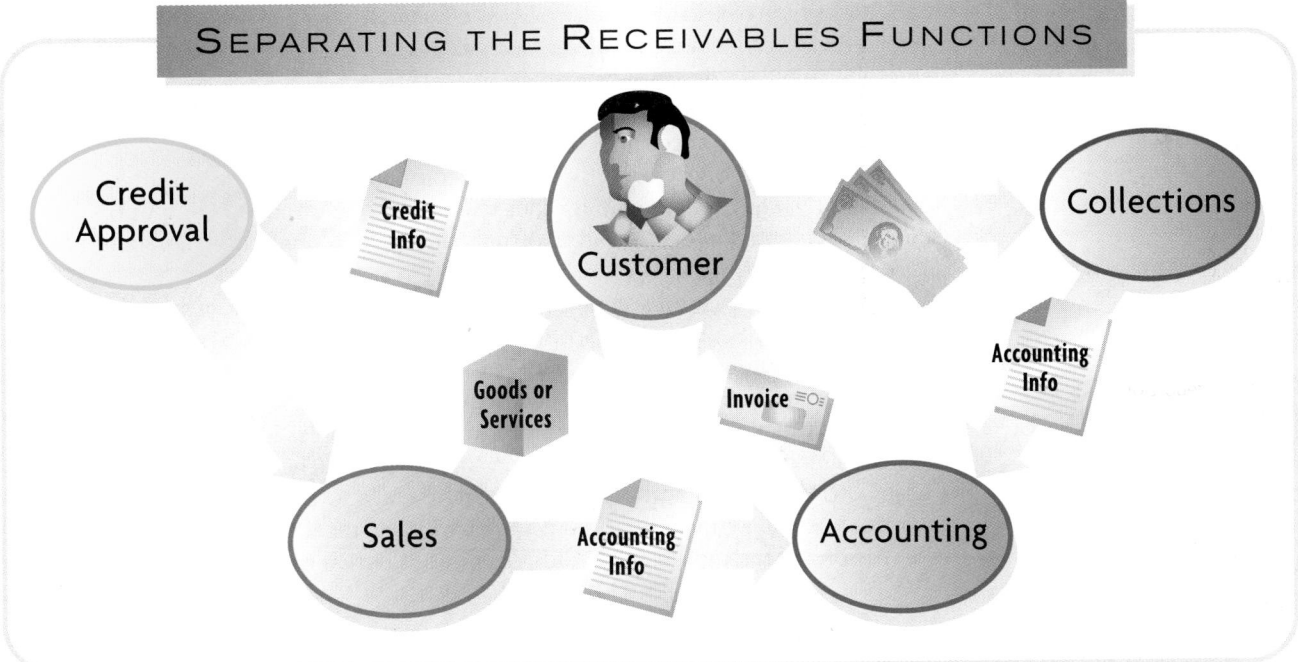

SEPARATING THE RECEIVABLES FUNCTIONS

 I was founded in 1886 when a railroad station agent began selling watches. I competed effectively against high-priced rural stores via railroads and mail delivery. By 1895 I had a 532-page catalog and my annual sales topped $750,000. Henry Ford reportedly studied my assembly-line process. I opened my first retail store in 1925 in Chicago, where I tower today. In 1931 retail sales topped mail-order sales, and I created Allstate Insurance Co. I launched the Discover Card in 1985 and bought Lands' End in 2002. Today I operate more than 2,000 retail locations and rake in more than $40 billion annually. Who am I? (Go to page 299 for answer.)

To illustrate the need to separate functions, assume that the accounts receivable billing clerk has access to cash receipts from customer collections. The clerk can steal a customer's cash payment and then alter the customer's monthly statement to indicate that the payment was received. The customer would not complain and the theft could go undetected.

To further illustrate the need for internal control of receivables, assume that salespersons have authority to approve credit. If the salespersons are paid commissions, say 10% of sales, they can increase their commissions by approving poor credit risks. Thus, the credit approval function is normally assigned to individuals outside the sales area.

Uncollectible Receivables

Describe the nature of and the accounting for uncollectible receivables.

REAL WORLD

In addition to their own credit departments, many businesses use external credit agencies, such as **Dun and Bradstreet**, to evaluate credit customers.

In prior chapters, we described and illustrated the accounting for transactions involving sales of merchandise or services on credit. A major issue that we have not yet discussed is uncollectible receivables from these transactions.

Businesses attempt to limit the number and amount of uncollectible receivables by using various controls. The primary controls in this area involve the credit-granting function. These controls normally involve investigating customer creditworthiness, using references and background checks. For example, most of us have completed credit application forms requiring such information. Companies may also impose credit limits on new customers. For example, you may have been limited to a maximum of $500 or $1,000 when your credit card was first issued to you.

Once a receivable is past due, companies should use procedures to maximize the collection of an account. After repeated attempts at collection, such procedures may include turning an account over to a collection agency.

Retail businesses often attempt to shift the risk of uncollectible receivables to other companies. For example, some retailers do not accept sales on account but will only accept cash or credit cards. Such policies effectively shift the risk to the credit card companies. Other retailers, however, such as **Macy's**, **Sears**, and **J.C.Penney's**, have issued their own credit cards.

Companies often sell their receivables to other companies. This transaction is called **factoring** the receivables, and the buyer of the receivables is called a **factor**. An advantage of factoring is that the company selling its receivables receives immediate cash for operating and other needs. In addition, depending upon the factoring agreement, some of the risk of uncollectible accounts may be shifted to the factor.[1]

Regardless of the care used in granting credit and the collection procedures used, a part of the credit sales will not be collectible. The operating expense incurred because of the failure to collect receivables is called **uncollectible accounts expense**, **bad debts expense**, or **doubtful accounts expense**.[2]

When does an account or a note become uncollectible? There is no general rule for determining when an account becomes uncollectible. The fact that a debtor fails to pay an account according to a sales contract or fails to pay a note on the due date does not necessarily mean that the account will be uncollectible. The debtor's bankruptcy is one of the most significant indications of partial or complete uncollectibility.

INTEGRITY IN BUSINESS

SELLER BEWARE

A company in financial distress will still try to purchase goods and services on account. In these cases, rather than "buyer beware," it is more like "seller beware." Sellers must be careful in advancing credit to such companies, because trade creditors have low priority for cash payments in the event of bankruptcy. To help suppliers, third-party services specialize in evaluating financially distressed customers. These services analyze credit risk for these firms by evaluating recent management payment decisions (who is getting paid and when), court actions (if in bankruptcy), and other supplier credit tightening or suspension actions. Such information helps a supplier monitor and tune trade credit amounts and terms with the financially distressed customer.

---

[1] The accounting for the factoring of accounts receivable is discussed in advanced accounting texts.
[2] If both notes and accounts are involved, both may be included in the expense account title, as in Uncollectible Notes and Accounts Expense, or Uncollectible Receivables Expense.

Other indications include the closing of the customer's business and the failure of repeated attempts to collect.

There are two methods of accounting for receivables that appear to be uncollectible. The **allowance method** provides an expense for uncollectible receivables in advance of their write-off.[3] The other procedure, called the **direct write-off method**, recognizes the expense only when accounts are judged to be worthless. We will discuss each of these methods next.

Allowance Method of Accounting for Uncollectibles

Most large businesses use the allowance method to estimate the uncollectible portion of their trade receivables. To illustrate this method, we will use assumed data for Richards Company. This new business began in August and chose to use the calendar year as its fiscal year. The accounts receivable account has a balance of $105,000 at the end of December.

The customer accounts making up the $105,000 balance in Accounts Receivable include some that are past due. However, Richards doesn't know which specific accounts will be uncollectible at this time. It is likely that some accounts will be collected only in part and that others will become worthless. Based on a careful study, Richards estimates that a total of $4,000 will eventually be uncollectible. The following adjusting entry at the end of the fiscal period records this estimate:

		Adjusting Entry			
Dec.	31	Uncollectible Accounts Expense	4 0 0 0 00	
		Allowance for Doubtful Accounts		4 0 0 0 00

Because the $4,000 reduction in accounts receivable is an estimate, it cannot be credited to specific customer accounts or to the accounts receivable controlling account. Instead, a **contra asset** account entitled *Allowance for Doubtful Accounts* is credited.

As with all periodic adjustments, the entry above serves two purposes. First, it reduces the value of the receivables to the amount of cash expected to be realized in the future. This amount, which is $101,000 ($105,000 − $4,000), is called the **net realizable value** of the receivables. Second, the adjusting entry matches the $4,000 expense of uncollectible accounts with the related revenues of the period.

> **The adjusting entry reduces receivables to their net realizable value and matches the uncollectible expense with revenues.**

After the adjusting entry has been posted, as shown in the following T accounts, Accounts Receivable still has a debit balance of $105,000. This balance is the amount of the total claims against customers on account. The credit balance of $4,000 in Allowance for Doubtful Accounts is the amount to be deducted from Accounts Receivable to determine the net realizable value. The balance of the Uncollectible Accounts Expense is reported in the current period income statement, normally as an administrative expense. This classification is used because the credit-granting and collection duties are the responsibilities of departments within the administrative area.

If the balance of accounts receivable is $380,000 and the balance of the allowance for doubtful accounts is $56,000, what is the net realizable value of the receivables?

- -

$324,000 ($380,000 − $56,000)

---

[3]The allowance method is not acceptable for determining the federal income tax of most taxpayers.

Accounts Receivable				
Aug. 31	20,000	Sept. 30	15,000	
Sept. 30	25,000	Oct. 31	25,000	
Oct. 31	40,000	Nov. 30	23,000	
Nov. 30	38,000	Dec. 31	30,000	
Dec. 31	75,000			
			93,000	
Bal. 105,000	198,000			

Allowance for Doubtful Accounts	
Dec. 31 Adj.	4,000

Uncollectible Accounts Expense	
Dec. 31 Adj. 4,000	

Write-Offs to the Allowance Account

When a customer's account is identified as uncollectible, it is written off against the allowance account as follows:

Jan.	21	Allowance for Doubtful Accounts	6 1 0 00	
		Accounts Receivable—John Parker		6 1 0 00
		To write off the uncollectible		
		account.		

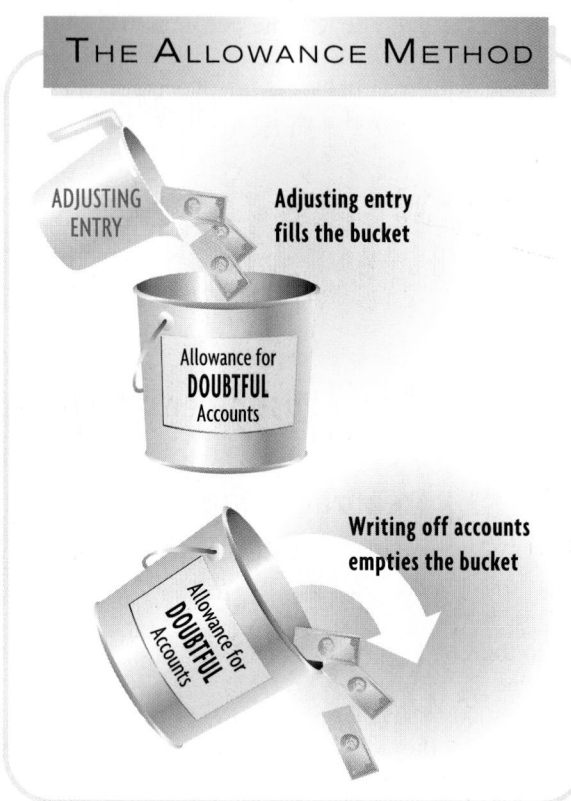

THE ALLOWANCE METHOD

ADJUSTING ENTRY

Adjusting entry fills the bucket

Allowance for **DOUBTFUL** Accounts

Writing off accounts empties the bucket

Allowance for **DOUBTFUL** Accounts

The authorization to support this entry should come from a designated manager. It should normally be in writing.

The total amount written off against the allowance account during a period will rarely be equal to the amount in the account at the beginning of the period. The allowance account will have a credit balance at the end of the period if the write-offs during the period are less than the beginning balance. It will have a debit balance if the write-offs exceed the beginning balance. However, after the year-end adjusting entry is recorded, the allowance account should have a credit balance. The flow into and out of the allowance account can be shown as in the illustration at the left.

An account receivable that has been written off against the allowance account may later be collected. In such cases, the account should be reinstated by an entry that reverses the write-off entry. The cash received in payment should then be recorded as a receipt on account. For example, assume that the account of $610 written off in the preceding entry is later collected on June 10. The entry to reinstate the account and the entry to record its collection are as follows:

June	10	Accounts Receivable—John Parker	6 1 0 00	
		Allowance for Doubtful Accounts		6 1 0 00
		To reinstate account written off		
		earlier in the year.		
	10	Cash	6 1 0 00	
		Accounts Receivable—John Parker		6 1 0 00
		To record collection on account.		

The percentage of uncollectible accounts will vary across companies and industries. For example, in their annual reports, **J.C.Penney** reported 1.7% of its receivables as uncollectible, **Deere & Company** (manufacturer of John Deere tractors, etc.) reported only 1.0% of its dealer receivables as uncollectible, and **HCA, Inc.**, a hospital management company, reported 42% of its receivables as uncollectible.

The two preceding entries can be combined. However, recording two separate entries in the customer's account, with proper notation of the write-off and reinstatement, provides useful credit information.

Estimating Uncollectibles

How is the amount of uncollectible accounts estimated? The estimate of uncollectibles at the end of a fiscal period is based on past experience and forecasts of the future. When the general economy is doing well, the amount of uncollectible expense is normally less than it would be when the economy is doing poorly. The estimate of uncollectibles is usually based on either (1) the amount of sales, as shown on the income statement for the period, or (2) the amount of the receivables, as shown on the balance sheet at the end of the period, and the age of the receivable accounts.

Estimate Based on Sales

Accounts receivable are created by credit sales. The amount of credit sales during the period may therefore be used to estimate the amount of uncollectible accounts expense. The amount of this estimate is added to whatever balance exists in Allowance for Doubtful Accounts. For example, assume that the allowance account has a credit balance of $700 before adjustment. It is estimated from past experience that 1% of credit sales will be uncollectible. If credit sales for the period are $300,000, the adjusting entry for uncollectible accounts at the end of the period is as follows:

> **The estimate based on sales is <u>added</u> to any balance in Allowance for Doubtful Accounts.**

		Adjusting Entry		
Dec.	31	Uncollectible Accounts Expense	3 0 0 0 00	
		Allowance for Doubtful Accounts		3 0 0 0 00

FINANCIAL REPORTING AND DISCLOSURE

DELTA AIR LINES

Delta Air Lines is a major air carrier that services over 200 cities in 45 states within the United States and 46 cities in 31 countries throughout the world. Delta is the second largest airline in terms of passengers carried and the third largest in operating revenues and revenue passenger miles flown. In its operations, Delta generates accounts receivable as reported in the following note to its financial statements:

Our accounts receivable are generated largely from the sale of passenger airline tickets and cargo transportation services to customers. The majority of these sales are processed through major credit card companies, resulting in accounts receivable which are generally short-term in duration. We also have receivables from the sale of mileage credits to partners, such as credit card companies, hotels and car rental agencies, that participate in our SkyMiles program. We believe that the credit risk associated with these receivables is minimal and that the allowance for bad debts that we have provided is sufficient.

In its December 31, 2002 balance sheet, Delta reported the following accounts receivable (in millions):

	2002	2001
Current Assets:		
· · ·		
Accounts receivable, net of an allowance for uncollectible accounts of $43 at 12/31/01 and $33 at 12/31/02	292	368

Finally, Delta also reported that it took a separate nonrecurring charge of $9 million in accounts receivable write-offs due to the September 11 terrorist attacks, as follows:

It (nonrecurring charge) also includes $9 million related to the write-off of certain receivables that we believe we will not be able to realize as a result of the September 11 terrorist attacks.

Before the year-end adjustment, Allowance for Doubtful Accounts has a credit balance of $45,000. Uncollectible accounts are estimated as 2% of credit sales of $1,200,000. The accounts receivable balance before adjustment is $290,000. What are (1) the uncollectible expense for the period, (2) the balance of Allowance for Doubtful Accounts after adjustment, and (3) the net realizable value of the receivables after adjustment?

---

(1) $24,000 (2% × $1,200,000); (2) $69,000 ($24,000 + $45,000); and (3) $221,000 ($290,000 − $69,000)

The Commercial Collection Agency Section of the Commercial Law League of America reported the following collection rates by number of months past due:

REAL WORLD

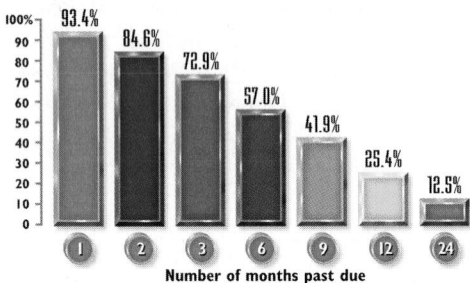

Number of months past due

The estimate based on receivables is compared to the balance in the allowance account to determine the amount of the adjusting entry.

After the adjusting entry has been posted, the balance of the allowance account is $3,700. If there had been a debit balance of $200 in the allowance account before the year-end adjustment, the amount of the adjustment would still have been $3,000. The balance in the allowance account would have been $2,800 ($3,000 − $200).

The estimate-based-on-sales method *emphasizes the matching of uncollectible accounts expense with the related sales of the period*. Thus, this method places more emphasis on the income statement than on the balance sheet.

Estimate Based on Analysis of Receivables

The longer an account receivable remains outstanding, the less likely that it will be collected. Thus, we can base the estimate of uncollectible accounts on how long the accounts have been outstanding. For this purpose, we can use a process called **aging the receivables**.

In aging the receivables, an aging schedule is prepared by classifying each receivable by its due date. The number of days an account is past due is determined from the due date of the account to the date the aging schedule is prepared. To illustrate, assume that Rodriguez Company is preparing an aging schedule as of August 31. Its account receivable for Saxon Woods Company was due on May 29. As of August 31, Saxon's account is 94 days past due, as shown below.

Number of days past due in May	2 days (31–29)
Number of days past due in June	30 days
Number of days past due in July	31 days
Number of days past due in August	31 days
Total number of days past due	94 days

After the number of days past due has been determined for each account, an aging schedule is prepared similar to the one shown in Exhibit 2.

The aging schedule is completed by adding the columns to determine the total amount of receivables in each age class. A sliding scale of percentages, based on industry or company experience, is used to estimate the amount of uncollectibles in each age class, as shown in Exhibit 3.

•Exhibit 2 Aging of Accounts Receivable

Customer	Balance	Not Past Due	Days Past Due					
			1–30	31–60	61–90	91–180	181–365	over 365
Ashby & Co.	$ 150			$ 150				
B.T. Barr	610					$ 350	$260	
Brock Co.	470	$ 470						
Saxon Woods Co.	160					160		
Total	$86,300	$75,000	$4,000	$3,100	$1,900	$1,200	$800	$300

•Exhibit 3   Estimate of Uncollectible Accounts

Age Interval	Balance	Estimated Uncollectible Accounts	
		Percent	Amount
Not past due	$75,000	2%	$1,500
1–30 days past due	4,000	5	200
31–60 days past due	3,100	10	310
61–90 days past due	1,900	20	380
91–180 days past due	1,200	30	360
181–365 days past due	800	50	400
Over 365 days past due	300	80	240
Total	$86,300		$3,390

Before the year-end adjustment, Allowance for Doubtful Accounts has a debit balance of $3,000. Using the aging-of-receivables method, the desired balance of the allowance for doubtful accounts is estimated as $55,000. The accounts receivable balance before adjustment is $290,000. What are (1) the uncollectible expense for the period, (2) the balance of Allowance for Doubtful Accounts after adjustment, and (3) the net realizable value of the receivables after adjustment?

----

(1) $58,000 ($3,000 + $55,000); (2) $55,000; and (3) $235,000 ($290,000 − $55,000)

Based on Exhibit 3, the desired balance for the Allowance for Doubtful Accounts is estimated as $3,390. Comparing this estimate with the unadjusted balance of the allowance account determines the amount of the adjusting entry for Uncollectible Accounts Expense. For example, assume that the unadjusted balance of the allowance account is a credit balance of $510. The amount to be added to this balance is therefore $2,880 ($3,390 − $510). The adjusting entry is as follows:

		Adjusting Entry			
Aug.	31	Uncollectible Accounts Expense	2 8 8 0 00	
		Allowance for Doubtful Accounts		2 8 8 0 00

After the adjusting entry has been posted, the credit balance in the allowance account is $3,390, the desired amount. The net realizable value of the receivables is $82,910 ($86,300 − $3,390). If the unadjusted balance of the allowance account had been a debit balance of $300, the amount of the adjustment would have been $3,690 ($3,390 + $300).

Estimates of the uncollectible accounts expense based on the analysis of receivables *emphasizes the current net realizable value of the receivables*. Thus, this method places more emphasis on the balance sheet than on the income statement.

Direct Write-Off Method of Accounting for Uncollectibles

objective   5

Journalize the entries for the direct write-off of uncollectible receivables.

The allowance method emphasizes reporting uncollectible accounts expense in the period in which the related sales occur. This emphasis on matching expenses with related revenue is the preferred method of accounting for uncollectible receivables.

There are situations, however, where it is impossible to estimate, with reasonable accuracy, the uncollectibles at the end of the period. Also, if a business sells most of its goods or services on a cash basis, the amount of its expense from uncollectible accounts is usually small. In such cases, the amount of receivables is also likely to represent a small part of the current assets. Examples of such a business are a restaurant, an attorney's office, and a small retail store such as a hardware store. In such cases, the direct write-off method of recording uncollectible expense may be used.

Under the direct write-off method, uncollectible accounts expense is not recorded until an account has been determined to be worthless. Thus, an allowance account and an adjusting entry are not needed at the end of the period. The entry to write off an account that has been determined to be uncollectible is as follows:

May	10	Uncollectible Accounts Expense	4 2 0 00		
		Accounts Receivable—D. L. Ross			4 2 0 00
		To write off uncollectible account.			

What if a customer later pays on an account that has been written off? If this happens, the account should be reinstated. The account is reinstated by reversing the earlier write-off entry. For example, assume that the account written off in the May 10 entry is collected in November of the same fiscal year.[4] The entry to reinstate the account is as follows:

Nov.	21	Accounts Receivable—D. L. Ross	4 2 0 00		
		Uncollectible Accounts Expense			4 2 0 00
		To reinstate account written off			
		earlier in the year.			

Cash received in payment of the reinstated amount is recorded in the usual manner. That is, Cash is debited and Accounts Receivable is credited for $420.

INTEGRITY IN BUSINESS

SALES AND COLLECTION FRAUD

A sales transaction may involve "sales fraud" or "collection fraud." Sales fraud occurs when money is received in advance of the sale and the goods are either not delivered or are not what was promised. This type of fraud has occurred in **eBay** auctions where buyers must pay for the goods prior to receiving them. eBay's seller ratings help reduce the incidence of fraudulent sellers. In collection fraud, the goods are delivered to a customer that does not intend to pay for them. This type of fraud is common among customers of small businesses that fail to screen such customers by using credit reports and analyses.

Characteristics of Notes Receivable

objective **6**

Describe the nature and characteristics of promissory notes.

A claim supported by a note has some advantages over a claim in the form of an account receivable. By signing a note, the debtor recognizes the debt and agrees to pay it according to the terms listed. A note is therefore a stronger legal claim if there is a court action.

A **promissory note** is a written promise to pay a sum of money on demand or at a definite time. It is payable to the order of a person or firm or to the bearer or holder of the note. It is signed by the person or firm that makes the promise. The

---

[4]As a practical matter, the entries to record the collection on an account previously written off are the same, regardless of whether the collection occurs in the current period or in a later fiscal period.

one to whose order the note is payable is called the **payee**, and the one making the promise is called the **maker**. In the example in Exhibit 4, Judson Company is the payee and Willard Company is the maker.

•Exhibit 4   Promissory Note

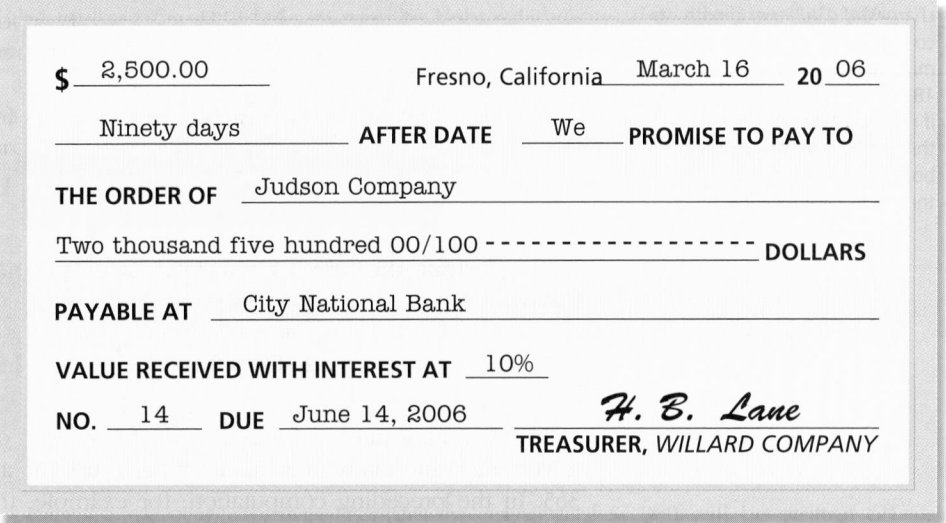

Notes have several characteristics that affect how they are recorded and reported in the financial statements. We describe these characteristics next.

What is the due date of a 120-day note receivable dated September 9?

January 7 [21 days in September (30 days − 9 days) + 31 days in October + 30 days in November + 31 days in December + 7 days in January = 120 days]

Due Date

The date a note is to be paid is called the **due date** or **maturity date**. The period of time between the issuance date and the due date of a short-term note may be stated in either days or months. When the term of a note is stated in days, the due date is the specified number of days after its issuance. To illustrate, the due date of the 90-day note in Exhibit 4 is determined as follows:

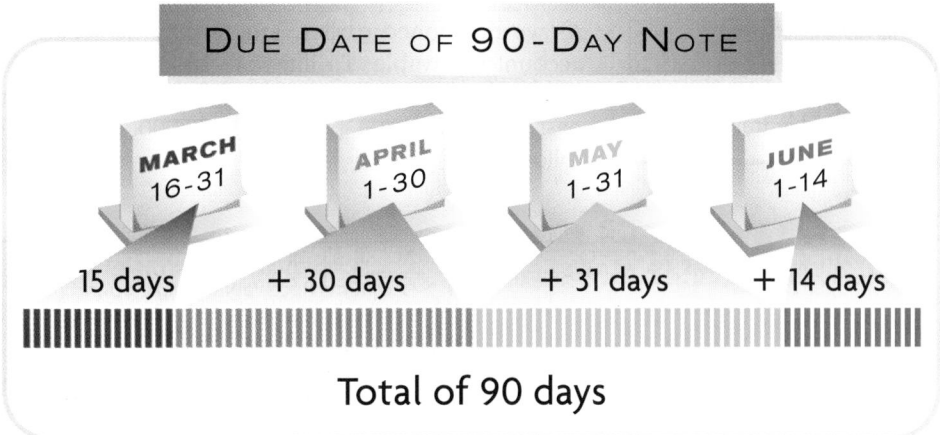

The term of a note may be stated as a certain number of months after the issuance date. In such cases, the due date is determined by counting the number of months from the issuance date. For example, a three-month note dated June 5 would be due on September 5. A two-month note dated July 31 would be due on September 30.

EXERCISE 7-8
Entry for uncollectible accounts
Objective 4

Using the data in Exercise 7-7, assume that the allowance for doubtful accounts for Kubota Co. had a debit balance of $1,575 as of December 31, 2006.

Journalize the adjusting entry for uncollectible accounts as of December 31, 2006.

EXERCISE 7-9
Providing for doubtful accounts
Objective 4

✓ a. $17,875
✓ b. $13,600

At the end of the current year, the accounts receivable account has a debit balance of $840,000, and net sales for the year total $7,150,000. Determine the amount of the adjusting entry to provide for doubtful accounts under each of the following assumptions:

a. The allowance account before adjustment has a credit balance of $1,780. Uncollectible accounts expense is estimated at 1/4 of 1% of net sales.
b. The allowance account before adjustment has a credit balance of $2,750. An aging of the accounts in the customer's ledger indicates estimated doubtful accounts of $16,350.
c. The allowance account before adjustment has a debit balance of $3,050. Uncollectible accounts expense is estimated at 1/2 of 1% of net sales.
d. The allowance account before adjustment has a debit balance of $3,050. An aging of the accounts in the customer's ledger indicates estimated doubtful accounts of $38,400.

EXERCISE 7-10
Entries to write off accounts receivable
Objectives 4, 5

Anchor.com, a computer consulting firm, has decided to write off the $7,130 balance of an account owed by a customer. Journalize the entry to record the write-off, (a) assuming that the allowance method is used, and (b) assuming that the direct write-off method is used.

EXERCISE 7-11
Entries for uncollectible receivables, using allowance method
Objective 4

Journalize the following transactions in the accounts of Linden Company, a restaurant supply company that uses the allowance method of accounting for uncollectible receivables:

Feb. 20. Sold merchandise on account to Darlene Brogan, $12,100. The cost of the merchandise sold was $7,260.
May 30. Received $6,000 from Darlene Brogan and wrote off the remainder owed on the sale of February 20 as uncollectible.
Aug. 3. Reinstated the account of Darlene Brogan that had been written off on May 30 and received $6,100 cash in full payment.

EXERCISE 7-12
Entries for uncollectible accounts, using direct write-off method
Objective 5

Journalize the following transactions in the accounts of Graybeal Co., a hospital supply company that uses the direct write-off method of accounting for uncollectible receivables:

July   6. Sold merchandise on account to Dr. Jerry Jagers, $18,500. The cost of the merchandise sold was $11,100.
Sept. 12. Received $9,000 from Dr. Jerry Jagers and wrote off the remainder owed on the sale of July 6 as uncollectible.
Dec. 20. Reinstated the account of Dr. Jerry Jagers that had been written off on September 12 and received $9,500 cash in full payment.

EXERCISE 7-13
Effect of doubtful accounts on net income
Objectives 4, 5

During its first year of operations, O'Hara Automotive Supply Co. had net sales of $4,050,000, wrote off $112,350 of accounts as uncollectible using the direct write-off method, and reported net income of $212,800. If the allowance method of accounting for uncollectibles had been used, 2½% of net sales would have been estimated as uncollectible. Determine what the net income would have been if the allowance method had been used.

EXERCISE 7-14
Effect of doubtful accounts on net income
Objectives 4, 5

Using the data in Exercise 7-13, assume that during the second year of operations O'Hara Automotive Supply Co. had net sales of $4,800,000, wrote off $114,800 of accounts as uncollectible using the direct write-off method, and reported net income of $262,300.

a. Determine what net income would have been in the second year if the allowance method (using 2½% of net sales) had been used in both the first and second years.
b. Determine what the balance of the allowance for doubtful accounts would have been at the end of the second year if the allowance method had been used in both the first and second years.

EXERCISE 7-15
Determine due date and interest on notes
Objective 6

SPREADSHEET

✓ a. August 31, $120

Determine the due date and the amount of interest due at maturity on the following notes:

	Date of Note	Face Amount	Term of Note	Interest Rate
a.	June 2	$ 8,000	90 days	6%
b.	August 30	18,000	120 days	8%
c.	October 1	12,500	60 days	12%
d.	March 6	10,000	60 days	9%
e.	May 20	6,000	60 days	10%

EXERCISE 7-16
Entries for notes receivable
Objectives 6, 7

✓ b. $24,480

Magpie Interior Decorators issued a 120-day, 6% note for $24,000, dated April 10, to Peel's Furniture Company on account.

a. Determine the due date of the note.
b. Determine the maturity value of the note.
c. Journalize the entries to record the following: (1) receipt of the note by the payee, and (2) receipt by the payee of payment of the note at maturity.

EXERCISE 7-17
Entries for notes receivable
Objective 7

The series of seven transactions recorded in the following T accounts were related to a sale to a customer on account and the receipt of the amount owed. Briefly describe each transaction.

Cash			Notes Receivable		
(7)	21,777		(5)	21,000	(6) 21,000

Accounts Receivable				Merchandise Inventory		
(1)	24,000	(3)	3,000	(4) 1,800	(2)	15,000
(6)	21,420	(5)	21,000			
		(7)	21,420			

Sales			Sales Returns and Allowances		
		(1)	24,000	(3) 3,000	

Cost of Merchandise Sold			Interest Revenue		
(2)	15,000	(4)	1,800	(6)	420
				(7)	357

EXERCISE 7-18
Entries for notes receivable, including year-end entries
Objective 7

The following selected transactions were completed by Cassidy Co., a supplier of elastic bands for clothing:

2005
Dec. 13. Received from Visage Co., on account, a $25,000, 120-day, 6% note dated December 13.

Dec. 31. Recorded an adjusting entry for accrued interest on the note of December 13.

31. Closed the interest revenue account. The only entry in this account originated from the December 31 adjustment.

2006

Apr. 12. Received payment of note and interest from Visage Co.

Journalize the transactions.

EXERCISE 7-19
Entries for receipt and dishonor of note receivable

Objective 7

Journalize the following transactions of Prairie Theater Productions:

July 8. Received a $30,000, 90-day, 8% note dated July 8 from Pennington Company on account.

Oct. 6. The note is dishonored by Pennington Company.

Nov. 5. Received the amount due on the dishonored note plus interest for 30 days at 10% on the total amount charged to Pennington Company on October 6.

EXERCISE 7-20
Entries for receipt and dishonor of notes receivable

Objectives 4, 7

Journalize the following transactions in the accounts of Blue Sky Co., which operates a riverboat casino:

Mar. 1. Received a $15,000, 60-day, 5% note dated March 1 from Absaroka Co. on account.

18. Received a $12,000, 90-day, 9% note dated March 18 from Sturgis Co. on account.

Apr. 30. The note dated March 1 from Absaroka Co. is dishonored, and the customer's account is charged for the note, including interest.

June 16. The note dated March 18 from Sturgis Co. is dishonored, and the customer's account is charged for the note, including interest.

July 11. Cash is received for the amount due on the dishonored note dated March 1 plus interest for 72 days at 8% on the total amount debited to Absaroka Co. on April 30.

Oct. 12. Wrote off against the allowance account the amount charged to Sturgis Co. on June 16 for the dishonored note dated March 18.

EXERCISE 7-21
Receivables in the balance sheet

Objective 8

WHAT'S WRONG WITH THIS?

List any errors you can find in the following partial balance sheet.

Pembroke Company
Balance Sheet
July 31, 2006

Assets		
Current assets:		
Cash		$ 43,750
Notes receivable	$300,000	
Less interest receivable	18,000	282,000
Accounts receivable	$576,180	
Plus allowance for doubtful accounts	71,200	647,380

EXERCISE 7-22
Accounts receivable turnover

Objective 9

REAL WORLD

✓ a. 2002: 19.5

Circuit City Stores, Inc. is a national retailer of brand-name consumer electronics including televisions, DVD players, compact disc players, personal computers, printers, video games, DVD movies, and music. For the fiscal years 2003 and 2002, Circuit City reported the following (in thousands):

	Year Ending February 28,	
	2003	**2002**
Net sales	$9,953,530	$9,518,231
Accounts Receivable	216,200	159,477

Assume that the accounts receivable (in thousands) were $265,515 at March 1, 2001.

a. Compute the accounts receivable turnover for 2003 and 2002. Round to one decimal place.
b. What conclusions can be drawn from these analyses regarding Circuit City's efficiency in collecting receivables?

EXERCISE 7-23
Days' sales in receivables
Objective 9

REAL WORLD

✓ *a. 2002: 20.7 days*

Use the Circuit City data in Exercise 7-22 to analyze days' sales in receivables.

a. Compute the days' sales in receivables at the end of 2002 and 2001. Round to one decimal place.
b. What conclusions can be drawn from these analyses regarding Circuit City's efficiency in collecting receivables?

EXERCISE 7-24
Accounts receivable turnover and days' sales in receivables
Objective 9

REAL WORLD

✓ *a. 2002: 108.2*

The **Limited Inc.** sells women's and men's clothing through specialty retail stores, including **Structure, Limited, Express, Lane Bryant**, and **Lerner New York**. The Limited sells women's intimate apparel and personal care products through **Victoria Secret** and **Bath & Body Works** stores. For the fiscal years 2002 and 2001, The Limited reported the following (in thousands):

	Year Ending February 2,	
	2002	**2001**
Net sales	$9,363,000	$10,105,000
Accounts Receivable	79,000	94,000

Assume that the accounts receivable (in thousands) were $109,000 at the beginning of the 2001 fiscal year.

a. Compute the accounts receivable turnover for 2002 and 2001. Round to one decimal place.
b. Compute the days' sales in receivables at the end of 2002 and 2001. Round to one decimal place.
c. What conclusions can be drawn from these analyses regarding The Limited's efficiency in collecting receivables?

APPENDIX EXERCISE 7-25
Discounting notes receivable

✓ *a. $20,300*

Theisen Co., a building construction company, holds a 90-day, 6% note for $20,000, dated March 15, which was received from a customer on account. On April 14, the note is discounted at the bank at the rate of 8%.

a. Determine the maturity value of the note.
b. Determine the number of days in the discount period.
c. Determine the amount of the discount. Round to the nearest dollar.
d. Determine the amount of the proceeds.
e. Journalize the entry to record the discounting of the note on April 14.

APPENDIX EXERCISE 7-26
Entries for receipt and discounting of note receivable and dishonored notes

Journalize the following transactions in the accounts of Allied Theater Productions:

June   1. Received a $60,000, 60-day, 8% note dated June 1 from Rhodes Company on account.
July   1. Discounted the note at City Bank at 9%.
       31. The note is dishonored by Rhodes Company; paid the bank the amount due on the note, plus a protest fee of $200.
Aug. 30. Received the amount due on the dishonored note plus interest for 30 days at 12% on the total amount charged to Rhodes Company on July 31.

Problems Series A

PROBLEM 7-1A
Entries related to uncollectible accounts

Objective 4

P.A.S.S.

✓ 3. $522,050

The following transactions, adjusting entries, and closing entries were completed by Elko Contractors Co. during the year ended December 31, 2006:

Mar. 15. Received 60% of the $18,500 balance owed by Bimba Co., a bankrupt business, and wrote off the remainder as uncollectible.

Apr. 16. Reinstated the account of Tom Miner, which had been written off in the preceding year as uncollectible. Journalized the receipt of $5,782 cash in full payment of Miner's account.

July 20. Wrote off the $5,500 balance owed by Martz Co., which has no assets.

Oct. 31. Reinstated the account of Two Bit Saloon Co., which had been written off in the preceding year as uncollectible. Journalized the receipt of $6,100 cash in full payment of the account.

Dec. 31. Wrote off the following accounts as uncollectible (compound entry): Asche Co., $950; Dorsch Co., $4,600; Krebs Distributors, $2,500; J. J. Levi, $1,200.

31. Based on an analysis of the $535,750 of accounts receivable, it was estimated that $13,700 will be uncollectible. Journalized the adjusting entry.

31. Journalized the entry to close the appropriate account to Income Summary.

Instructions

1. Post the January 1 credit balance of $12,050 to Allowance for Doubtful Accounts.
2. Journalize the transactions and the adjusting and closing entries. Post each entry that affects the following three selected accounts and determine the new balances:

115	Allowance for Doubtful Accounts
313	Income Summary
718	Uncollectible Accounts Expense

3. Determine the expected net realizable value of the accounts receivable as of December 31.
4. Assuming that instead of basing the provision for uncollectible accounts on an analysis of receivables, the adjusting entry on December 31 had been based on an estimated expense of 1/2 of 1% of the net sales of $3,100,000 for the year, determine the following:
   a. Uncollectible accounts expense for the year.
   b. Balance in the allowance account after the adjustment of December 31.
   c. Expected net realizable value of the accounts receivable as of December 31.

PROBLEM 7-2A
Aging of receivables; estimating allowance for doubtful accounts

Objective 4

SPREADSHEET

✓ 3. $65,212

Blue Ribbon Flies Company supplies flies and fishing gear to sporting goods stores and outfitters throughout the western United States. The accounts receivable clerk for Blue Ribbon Flies prepared the partially completed aging-of-receivables schedule as of the end of business on December 31, 2006, shown at the top of the following page.

The following accounts were unintentionally omitted from the aging schedule.

Customer	Due Date	Balance
Able Sports & Flies	June 15, 2006	3,500
Red Tag Sporting Goods	July 28, 2006	4,000
Highlite Flies	Sept. 11, 2006	2,500
Midge Co.	Sept. 30, 2006	3,100
Snake River Outfitters	Oct. 7, 2006	4,500
Pheasant Tail Sports	Oct. 27, 2006	1,600
Big Sky Sports	Oct. 30, 2006	2,000
Ross Sports	Nov. 18, 2006	500
Sawyer's Pheasant Tail	Nov. 26, 2006	2,800
Tent Caddis Outfitters	Nov. 29, 2006	3,500
Wulff Company	Dec. 10, 2006	1,000
Zug Bug Sports	Jan. 6, 2007	6,200

Customer	Balance	Not Past Due	Days Past Due					
			1–30	31–60	61–90	91–120	Over 120
Alpha Fishery	5,000	5,000					
Brown Trout Sports	6,400			6,400			
Zinger Sports	2,900		2,900				
Subtotals	580,000	248,600	147,250	98,750	33,300	29,950	22,150

Blue Ribbon Flies Company has a past history of uncollectible accounts by age category, as follows:

Age Class	Percentage Uncollectible
Not past due	1%
1–30 days past due	4
31–60 days past due	8
61–90 days past due	25
91–120 days past due	40
Over 120 days past due	80

Instructions

1. Determine the number of days past due for each of the preceding accounts.
2. Complete the aging-of-receivables schedule.
3. Estimate the allowance for doubtful accounts, based on the aging-of-receivables schedule.
4. Assume that the allowance for doubtful accounts for Blue Ribbon Flies Company has a debit balance of $2,800 before adjustment on December 31, 2006. Journalize the adjusting entry for uncollectible accounts.

PROBLEM 7-3A
Compare two methods of accounting for uncollectible receivables

Objectives 4, 5

SPREADSHEET

✓ 1. Year 4: Balance of allowance account, end of year, $14,625.

Kiohertz Company, a telephone service and supply company, has just completed its fourth year of operations. The direct write-off method of recording uncollectible accounts expense has been used during the entire period. Because of substantial increases in sales volume and amount of uncollectible accounts, the firm is considering changing to the allowance method. Information is requested as to the effect that an annual provision of 3/4% of sales would have had on the amount of uncollectible accounts expense reported for each of the past four years. It is also considered desirable to know what the balance of Allowance for Doubtful Accounts would have been at the end of each year. The following data have been obtained from the accounts:

Year	Sales	Uncollectible Accounts Written Off	Year of Origin of Accounts Receivable Written Off as Uncollectible			
			1st	2nd	3rd	4th
1st	$ 850,000	$3,500	$3,500			
2nd	960,000	3,250	1,900	$1,350		
3rd	1,200,000	6,300	800	4,500	$1,000	
4th	1,800,000	8,400		1,800	2,550	$4,050

Instructions

1. Assemble the desired data, using the following column headings:

	Uncollectible Accounts Expense			Balance of Allowance Account, End of Year
Year	Expense Actually Reported	Expense Based on Estimate	Increase (Decrease) in Amount of Expense	

2. ▬▬▶ Experience during the first four years of operations indicated that the receivables were either collected within two years or had to be written off as uncollectible. Does the estimate of 3/4% of sales appear to be reasonably close to the actual experience with uncollectible accounts originating during the first two years? Explain.

PROBLEM 7-4A
Details of notes receivable and related entries

Objectives 6, 7

SPREADSHEET

✓ *1. Note 2: Due date, July 18; Interest due at maturity, $126.*

Matrix Co. wholesales bathroom fixtures. During the current fiscal year, Matrix Co. received the following notes.

	Date	Face Amount	Term	Interest Rate
1.	March 7	$24,000	60 days	6%
2.	June 18	16,800	30 days	9%
3.	Aug. 30	10,200	120 days	6%
4.	Oct. 31	27,000	60 days	9%
5.	Nov. 19	12,000	60 days	6%
6.	Dec. 23	16,000	30 days	9%

Instructions

1. Determine for each note (a) the due date and (b) the amount of interest due at maturity, identifying each note by number.
2. Journalize the entry to record the dishonor of Note (3) on its due date.
3. Journalize the adjusting entry to record the accrued interest on Notes (5) and (6) on December 31.
4. Journalize the entries to record the receipt of the amounts due on Notes (5) and (6) in January.

PROBLEM 7-5A
Notes receivable entries

Objective 7

The following data relate to notes receivable and interest for Clyde Park Optic Co., a cable manufacturer and supplier. (All notes are dated as of the day they are received.)

June 4. Received an $18,800, 9%, 60-day note on account.
July 15. Received a $27,000, 10%, 120-day note on account.
Aug. 3. Received $19,082 on note of June 4.
Sept. 1. Received a $24,000, 9%, 60-day note on account.
Oct. 31. Received $24,360 on note of September 1.
Nov. 5. Received a $9,600, 7%, 30-day note on account.
     12. Received $27,900 on note of July 15.
     30. Received a $15,000, 10%, 30-day note on account.
Dec. 5. Received $9,656 on note of November 5.
     30. Received $15,125 on note of November 30.

Instructions

Journalize entries to record the transactions.

PROBLEM 7-6A
Sales and notes receivable transactions

Objective 7

The following were selected from among the transactions completed by Rimrock Co. during the current year. Rimrock Co. sells and installs home and business security systems.

Jan. 10. Loaned $12,000 cash to Brenda Norby, receiving a 90-day, 8% note.
Feb. 4. Sold merchandise on account to Emerson and Son, $24,000. The cost of the merchandise sold was $14,400.

Feb. 12. Sold merchandise on account to Gwyn Co., $25,000. The cost of merchandise sold was $15,000.

Mar. 6. Accepted a 60-day, 6% note for $24,000 from Emerson and Son on account.

14. Accepted a 60-day, 12% note for $25,000 from Gwyn Co. on account.

Apr. 10. Received the interest due from Brenda Norby and a new 90-day, 9% note as a renewal of the loan of January 10. (Record both the debit and the credit to the notes receivable account.)

May 5. Received from Emerson and Son the amount due on the note of March 6.

13. Gwyn Co. dishonored its note dated March 14.

June 12. Received from Gwyn Co. the amount owed on the dishonored note, plus interest for 30 days at 12% computed on the maturity value of the note.

July 9. Received from Brenda Norby the amount due on her note of April 10.

Aug. 24. Sold merchandise on account to Haggerty Co., $10,200. The cost of the merchandise sold was $6,000.

Sept. 3. Received from Haggerty Co. the amount of the invoice of August 24, less 1% discount.

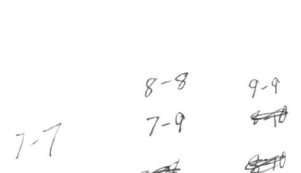

Instructions
Journalize the transactions. Round to the nearest dollar.

Problems Series B

PROBLEM 7-1B
Entries related to uncollectible accounts

Objective 4

✓ *3. $857,050*

The following transactions, adjusting entries, and closing entries were completed by The Eagle Rock Gallery during the year ended December 31, 2006:

Feb. 24. Reinstated the account of Dina Ibis, which had been written off in the preceding year as uncollectible. Journalized the receipt of $1,025 cash in full payment of Ibis's account.

Mar. 29. Wrote off the $7,500 balance owed by Hoxsey Co., which is bankrupt.

July 10. Received 40% of the $12,000 balance owed by Foust Co., a bankrupt business, and wrote off the remainder as uncollectible.

Sept. 8. Reinstated the account of Louis Sabo, which had been written off two years earlier as uncollectible. Recorded the receipt of $1,200 cash in full payment.

Dec. 31. Wrote off the following accounts as uncollectible (compound entry): Emery Co., $8,050; Darigold Co., $6,260; Zheng Furniture, $3,775; Carey Wenzel, $2,820.

31. Based on an analysis of the $887,550 of accounts receivable, it was estimated that $30,500 will be uncollectible. Journalized the adjusting entry.

31. Journalized the entry to close the appropriate account to Income Summary.

Instructions
1. Post the January 1 credit balance of $28,500 to Allowance for Doubtful Accounts.
2. Journalize the transactions and the adjusting and closing entries. Post each entry that affects the following three selected accounts and determine the new balances:

115	Allowance for Doubtful Accounts
313	Income Summary
718	Uncollectible Accounts Expense

3. Determine the expected net realizable value of the accounts receivable as of December 31.
4. Assuming that instead of basing the provision for uncollectible accounts on an analysis of receivables, the adjusting entry on December 31 had been based on

an estimated expense of 1/4 of 1% of the net sales of $12,750,000 for the year, determine the following:

a. Uncollectible accounts expense for the year.

b. Balance in the allowance account after the adjustment of December 31.

c. Expected net realizable value of the accounts receivable as of December 31.

PROBLEM 7-2B
Aging of receivables; estimating allowance for doubtful accounts

Objective 4

SPREADSHEET

✓ 3. $54,473

Vanity Wigs Company supplies wigs and hair care products to beauty salons throughout California and the Pacific Northwest. The accounts receivable clerk for Vanity Wigs prepared the following partially completed aging-of-receivables schedule as of the end of business on December 31, 2006:

Customer	Balance	Not Past Due	Days Past Due				
			1–30	31–60	61–90	91–120	Over 120
Adams Beauty	8,000	8,000					
Barkell Wigs	7,500			7,500			
Zimmer's Beauty	2,900		2,900				
Subtotals	880,000	498,600	197,250	88,750	43,300	29,950	22,150

The following accounts were unintentionally omitted from the aging schedule.

Customer	Due Date	Balance
Allison's Uniquely Yours	July 6, 2006	1,000
Western Designs	Aug. 10, 2006	2,500
Treat's	Sept. 6, 2006	1,800
Nicole's Beauty Store	Sept. 29, 2006	4,000
Ginburg Supreme	Oct. 10, 2006	1,500
Jeremy's Hair Products	Oct. 20, 2006	600
Hairy's Hair Care	Oct. 31, 2006	2,000
Southern Images	Nov. 18, 2006	1,200
Lopez's Blond Bombs	Nov. 23, 2006	1,800
Josset Ritz	Nov. 30, 2006	3,500
Cool Designs	Dec. 4, 2006	1,000
Buttram Images	Jan. 3, 2007	5,200

Vanity Wigs has a past history of uncollectible accounts by age category, as follows:

Age Class	Percentage Uncollectible
Not past due	1%
1–30 days past due	4
31–60 days past due	6
61–90 days past due	15
91–120 days past due	30
Over 120 days past due	70

Instructions

1. Determine the number of days past due for each of the preceding accounts.

2. Complete the aging-of-receivables schedule.

3. Estimate the allowance for doubtful accounts, based on the aging-of-receivables schedule.

4. Assume that the allowance for doubtful accounts for Vanity Wigs has a credit balance of $8,350 before adjustment on December 31, 2006. Journalize the adjusting entry for uncollectible accounts.

PROBLEM 7-3B
Compare two methods of accounting for uncollectible receivables

Objectives 4, 5

SPREADSHEET

✓ 1. Year 4: Balance of allowance account, end of year, $5,350

Blue Goose Company, which operates a chain of 50 electronics supply stores, has just completed its fourth year of operations. The direct write-off method of recording uncollectible accounts expense has been used during the entire period. Because of substantial increases in sales volume and amount of uncollectible accounts, the firm is considering changing to the allowance method. Information is requested as to the effect that an annual provision of 1/2% of sales would have had on the amount of uncollectible accounts expense reported for each of the past four years. It is also considered desirable to know what the balance of Allowance for Doubtful Accounts would have been at the end of each year. The following data have been obtained from the accounts:

Year	Sales	Uncollectible Accounts Written Off	Year of Origin of Accounts Receivable Written Off as Uncollectible			
			1st	2nd	3rd	4th
1st	$ 650,000	$1,000	$1,000			
2nd	920,000	2,650	750	$1,900		
3rd	1,050,000	6,200	1,800	1,400	$3,000	
4th	2,250,000	9,150		1,900	2,950	$4,300

Instructions
1. Assemble the desired data, using the following column headings:

	Uncollectible Accounts Expense			Balance of Allowance Account, End of Year
Year	Expense Actually Reported	Expense Based on Estimate	Increase (Decrease) in Amount of Expense	

2. ▬▬▶ Experience during the first four years of operations indicated that the receivables were either collected within two years or had to be written off as uncollectible. Does the estimate of 1/2% of sales appear to be reasonably close to the actual experience with uncollectible accounts originating during the first two years? Explain.

PROBLEM 7-4B
Details of notes receivable and related entries

Objectives 6, 7

SPREADSHEET

✓ 1. Note 2: Due date, Sept. 8; Interest due at maturity, $300

Incubate Co. produces advertising videos. During the last six months of the current fiscal year, Incubate Co. received the following notes.

	Date	Face Amount	Term	Interest Rate
1.	May 23	$18,000	45 days	8%
2.	July 10	20,000	60 days	9%
3.	Aug. 8	36,000	90 days	6%
4.	Sept. 16	20,000	90 days	7%
5.	Nov. 23	18,000	60 days	9%
6.	Dec. 18	48,000	60 days	12%

Instructions
1. Determine for each note (a) the due date and (b) the amount of interest due at maturity, identifying each note by number.
2. Journalize the entry to record the dishonor of Note (3) on its due date.
3. Journalize the adjusting entry to record the accrued interest on Notes (5) and (6) on December 31.
4. Journalize the entries to record the receipt of the amounts due on Notes (5) and (6) in January and February.

PROBLEM 7-5B
Notes receivable entries

Objective 7

The following data relate to notes receivable and interest for Sciatic Co., a financial services company. (All notes are dated as of the day they are received.)

Controls for safeguarding inventory include developing and using security measures to prevent inventory damage or employee theft. For example, inventory should be stored in a warehouse or other area to which access is restricted to authorized employees. The removal of merchandise from the warehouse should be controlled by using requisition forms, which should be properly authorized. The storage area should also be climate controlled to prevent damage from heat or cold. Further, when the business is not operating or is not open, the storage area should be locked.

When shopping, you may have noticed how retail stores protect inventory from customer theft. Retail stores often use such devices as two-way mirrors, cameras, and security guards. High-priced items are often displayed in locked cabinets. Retail clothing stores often place plastic alarm tags on valuable items such as leather coats. Sensors at the exit doors set off alarms if the tags have not been removed by the clerk. These controls are designed to prevent customers from shoplifting.

Using a perpetual inventory system for merchandise also provides an effective means of control over inventory. The amount of each type of merchandise is always readily available in a subsidiary **inventory ledger**. In addition, the subsidiary ledger can be an aid in maintaining inventory quantities at proper levels. Frequently comparing balances with predetermined minimum and maximum levels allows for timely reordering and prevents ordering excess inventory.

To ensure the accuracy of the amount of inventory reported in the financial statements, a merchandising business should take a *physical inventory* (i.e., count the merchandise). In a perpetual inventory system, the physical inventory is compared to the recorded inventory in order to determine the amount of shrinkage or shortage. If the inventory shrinkage is unusually large, management can investigate further and take any necessary corrective action. Knowledge that a physical inventory will be taken also helps prevent employee thefts or misuses of inventory.

How does a business "take" a physical inventory? The first step in this process is to determine the quantity of each kind of merchandise owned by the business. A common practice is to use teams of two persons. One person determines the quantity, and the other lists the quantity and description on inventory count sheets. Quantities of high-cost items are usually verified by supervisors or a second count team.

What merchandise should be included in inventory? All the merchandise *owned* by the business on the inventory date should be included. For merchandise in transit, the party (the seller or the buyer) who has title to the merchandise on the inventory date is the owner. To determine who has title, it may be necessary to examine purchases and sales invoices of the last few days of the current period and the first few days of the following period.

> **All merchandise <u>owned</u> by a business should be included in the business's inventory.**

As we discussed in an earlier chapter, shipping terms determine when title passes. When goods are purchased or sold **FOB shipping point**, title passes to the buyer when the goods are shipped. When the terms are **FOB destination**, title passes to the buyer when the goods are delivered.

To illustrate, assume that Roper Co. orders $25,000 of merchandise on December 28, 2006. The merchandise is shipped FOB shipping point by the seller on December 30 and arrives at Roper Co.'s warehouse on January 4, 2007. As a result, the merchandise is not counted by the inventory crew on December 31, the end of

Sam's Club and **Wal-Mart** stores use a greeter at the entry of each store to welcome customers. The greeter also serves as a preventive control by asking customers not to bring in packages or other bags, which could be used for shoplifting.

Most companies take their physical inventories when their inventory levels are the lowest. For example, most retailers take their physical inventory in late January or early February, which is after the holiday selling season but before restocking for spring.

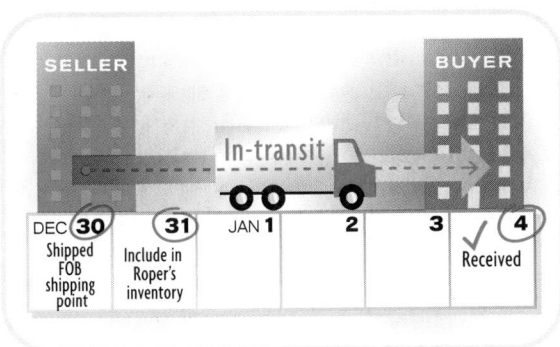

SELLER · BUYER

In-transit

DEC 30	31	JAN 1	2	3	✓ 4
Shipped FOB shipping point	Include in Roper's inventory				Received

Roper Co.'s fiscal year. However, the $25,000 of merchandise should be included in Roper's inventory because title has passed. Roper Co. should record the merchandise in transit on December 31, debiting Merchandise Inventory and crediting Accounts Payable for $25,000.

Manufacturers sometimes ship merchandise to retailers who act as the manufacturer's agent when selling the merchandise. The manufacturer retains title until the goods are sold. Such merchandise is said to be shipped *on consignment* to the retailers. The unsold merchandise is a part of the manufacturer's (consignor's) inventory, even though the merchandise is in the hands of the retailers. The consigned merchandise should not be included in the retailer's (consignee's) inventory.

Effect of Inventory Errors on Financial Statements

objective 2

Describe the effect of inventory errors on the financial statements.

Any errors in the inventory count will affect both the balance sheet and the income statement. For example, an error in the physical inventory will misstate the ending inventory, current assets, and total assets on the balance sheet. This is because the physical inventory is the basis for recording the adjusting entry for inventory shrinkage. Also, an error in taking the physical inventory misstates the cost of goods sold, gross profit, and net income on the income statement. In addition, because net income is closed to retained earnings at the end of the period, total stockholders' equity will also be misstated on the balance sheet. This misstatement of stockholders' equity (retained earnings) will equal the misstatement of the ending inventory, current assets, and total assets.

To illustrate, assume that in taking the physical inventory on December 31, 2006, Sapra Company incorrectly recorded its physical inventory as $115,000 instead of the correct amount of $125,000. As a result, the merchandise inventory, current assets, and total assets reported on the December 31, 2006 balance sheet would be understated by $10,000 ($125,000 − $115,000). Because the ending physical inventory is understated, the inventory shrinkage and the cost of merchandise sold will be overstated by $10,000. Thus, the gross profit and the net income for the year will be understated by $10,000. Since the net income is closed to retained earnings at the end of the period, the total stockholders' equity on the December 31, 2006 balance sheet will also be understated by $10,000. The effects on Sapra Company's financial statements are summarized as follows:

Inventory fraud reared its ugly head during the early 2000s. Officers of **HealthSouth**, one of the largest healthcare providers in the United States, have been indicted for falsifying financial information, including allegedly making false entries in the accounting records to artificially inflate the value of inventory. A former financial officer of **Network Associates**, a supplier of security software for e-businesses, plead guilty to a scheme involving secret fees paid to distributors to hold excess inventory and prevent returns of unsold products. Senior officers of **Rite Aid Corporation**, a drugstore chain, plead guilty to a variety of schemes, including fraudulently taking purchase discounts and allowances on good merchandise claimed as outdated or damaged.

At the end of 2006, the physical ending inventory of Melchor Co. was overstated by $25,000. What is the effect of this error on the financial statements?

- -

On the 2006 balance sheet, the merchandise inventory, current assets, total assets, and total stockholders' equity are overstated by $25,000. On the income statement, the cost of merchandise sold is understated by $25,000, and the gross profit and net income are overstated by $25,000.

	Amount of Misstatement
Balance Sheet:	
Merchandise inventory understated	$(10,000)
Current assets understated	(10,000)
Total assets understated	(10,000)
Total stockholders' equity understated	(10,000)
Income Statement:	
Cost of merchandise sold overstated	$ 10,000
Gross profit understated	(10,000)
Net income understated	(10,000)

Now assume that in the preceding example the physical inventory had been *overstated* on December 31, 2006, by $10,000. That is, Sapra Company erroneously recorded its inventory as $135,000. In this case, the effects on the balance sheet and income statement would be just the *opposite* of those indicated above.

Errors in the physical inventory are normally detected in the period after they occur. In such cases, the financial statements of the prior year must be corrected. We will discuss such corrections in a later chapter.

Inventory Cost Flow Assumptions

objective 3

Describe three inventory cost flow assumptions and how they impact the income statement and balance sheet.

A major accounting issue arises when identical units of merchandise are acquired at different unit costs during a period. In such cases, when an item is sold, it is necessary to determine its unit cost so that the proper accounting entry can be recorded. To illustrate, assume that three identical units of Item X are purchased during May, as shown below.

	Item X	Units	Cost
May 10	Purchase	1	$ 9
18	Purchase	1	13
24	Purchase	1	14
	Total	3	$36
	Average cost per unit		$12

Assume that one unit is sold on May 30 for $20. If this unit can be identified with a specific purchase, the **specific identification method** can be used to determine the cost of the unit sold. For example, if the unit sold was purchased on May 18, the cost assigned to the unit is $13 and the gross profit is $7 ($20 − $13). If, however, the unit sold was purchased on May 10, the cost assigned to the unit is $9 and the gross profit is $11 ($20 − $9).

The specific identification method is not practical unless each unit can be identified accurately. An automobile dealer, for example, may be able to use this method, since each automobile has a unique serial number. For many businesses, however, identical units cannot be separately identified, and a cost flow must be assumed. That is, which units have been sold and which units are still in inventory must be assumed.

There are three common cost flow assumptions used in business. Each of these assumptions is identified with an inventory costing method, as shown below.

REAL WORLD

The specific identification method is normally used by automobile dealerships, jewelry stores, and art galleries.

Cost Flow Assumption	1. Cost flow is in the order in which the costs were incurred.	2. Cost flow is in the reverse order in which the costs were incurred.	3. Cost flow is an average of the costs.
Inventory Costing Method	First-in, first-out (fifo)	Last-in, first-out (lifo)	Average cost

When the ***first-in, first-out (fifo) method*** is used, the ending inventory is made up of the most recent costs. When the ***last-in, first-out (lifo) method*** is used, the ending inventory is made up of the earliest costs. When the ***average cost method*** is used, the cost of the units in inventory is an average of the purchase costs.

To illustrate, we use the preceding example to prepare the income statement for May and the balance sheet as of May 31 for each of the cost flow methods, again assuming that one unit is sold. These financial statements are shown in Exhibit 1.

•Exhibit 1   Effect of Inventory Costing Methods on Financial Statements

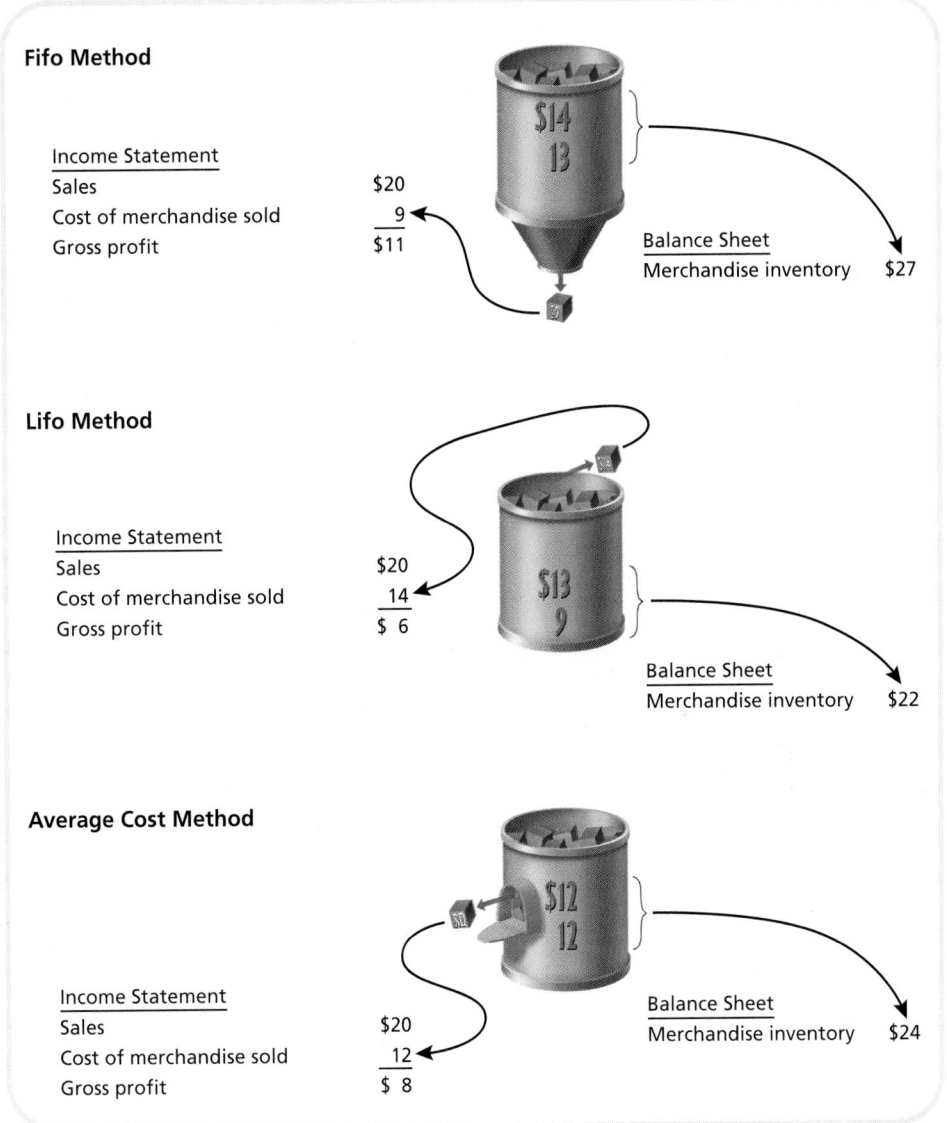

Fifo Method

Income Statement
Sales $20
Cost of merchandise sold   9
Gross profit $11

Balance Sheet
Merchandise inventory $27

Lifo Method

Income Statement
Sales $20
Cost of merchandise sold   14
Gross profit $ 6

Balance Sheet
Merchandise inventory $22

Average Cost Method

Income Statement
Sales $20
Cost of merchandise sold   12
Gross profit $ 8

Balance Sheet
Merchandise inventory $24

My namesake, born in Bavaria in 1829, founded me as a dry-goods store in San Francisco in 1853. I was cranking out copper-riveted "waist overalls" in 1873. In 1912, I introduced "Koveralls," one-piece playsuits for tots. I entered the sportswear business in 1954, with my "denim family" line, and debuted bell-bottoms around 1969 and Dockers in 1986. I went public in 1971, only to become a private entity again later. Always progressive, I've been named one of America's most admired companies and employers. I have been supporting community charities for 148 years. Who am I? (Go to page 339 for answer.)

As you can see, the selection of an inventory costing method can have a significant impact on the financial statements. For this reason, the selection has important implications for managers and others in analyzing and interpreting the financial statements. The chart in Exhibit 2 shows the frequency with which fifo, lifo, and the average methods are used in practice.

•Exhibit 2   Inventory Costing Methods*

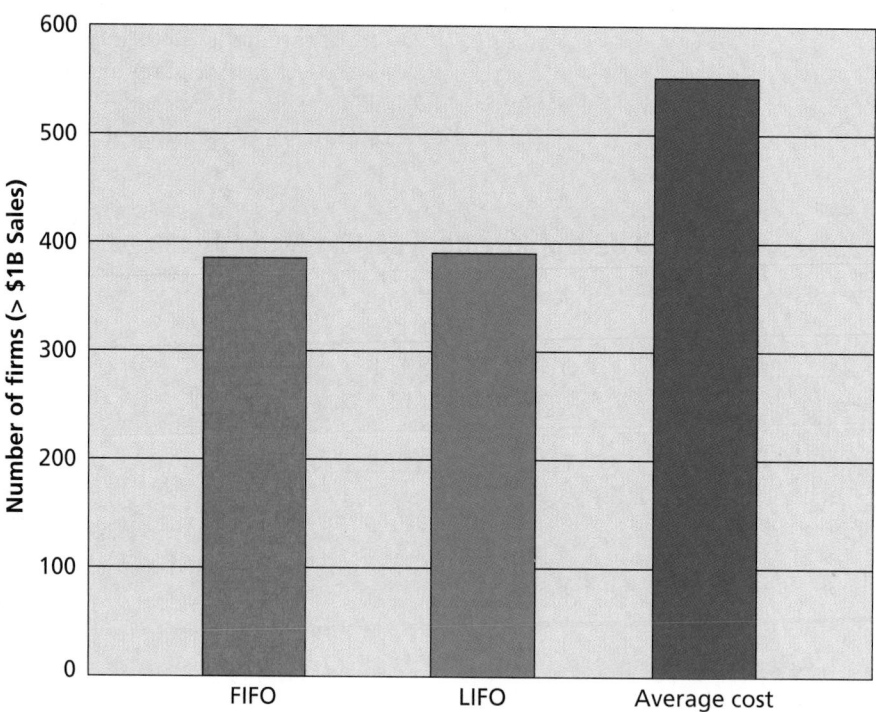

Source: Derived from Disclosure financial database.

*Firms may be counted more than once for using multiple methods.

Inventory Costing Methods Under a Perpetual Inventory System

REAL WORLD

Although e-tailers, such as **eToys**, **Amazon.com**, and **Furniture .com**, don't have retail stores, they still take possession of inventory in warehouses. Thus, they must account for inventory as we are illustrating in this chapter.

objective **4**

Compute the cost of inventory under the perpetual inventory system, using the following costing methods: first-in, first-out; last-in, first-out; and average cost.

In a perpetual inventory system, as we discussed in a previous chapter, all merchandise increases and decreases are recorded in a manner similar to recording increases and decreases in cash. The merchandise inventory account at the beginning of an accounting period indicates the merchandise in stock on that date. Purchases are recorded by debiting *Merchandise Inventory* and crediting *Cash* or *Accounts Payable*. On the date of each sale, the cost of the merchandise sold is recorded by debiting *Cost of Merchandise Sold* and crediting *Merchandise Inventory*.

As we illustrated in the preceding section, when identical units of an item are purchased at different unit costs during a period, a cost flow must be assumed. In such cases, the fifo, lifo, or average cost method is used. We illustrate each of these methods, using the data for Item 127B, shown below.

	Item 127B	Units	Cost
Jan. 1	Inventory	10	$20
4	Sale	7	
10	Purchase	8	21
22	Sale	4	
28	Sale	2	
30	Purchase	10	22

First-In, First-Out Method

Most businesses dispose of goods in the order in which the goods are purchased. This would be especially true of perishables and goods whose styles or models often change. For example, grocery stores shelve their milk products by expiration dates. Likewise, men's and women's clothing stores display clothes by season. At the end of a season, they often have sales to clear their stores of off-season or out-of-style clothing. Thus, the fifo method is often consistent with the *physical flow* or movement of merchandise. To the extent that this is the case, the fifo method provides results that are about the same as those obtained by identifying the specific costs of each item sold and in inventory.

> **Using fifo, costs are included in the merchandise sold in the order in which they were incurred.**

When the fifo method of costing inventory is used, costs are included in the cost of merchandise sold in the order in which they were incurred. To illustrate, Exhibit 3 shows the journal entries for purchases and sales and the inventory subsidiary ledger account for Item 127B. The number of units in inventory after each transaction, together with total costs and unit costs, are shown in the account. We assume that the units are sold for $30 each on account.

•Exhibit 3   Entries and Perpetual Inventory Account (Fifo)

Jan. 4	Accounts Receivable	210	
	Sales		210
4	Cost of Merchandise Sold	140	
	Merchandise Inventory		140
10	Merchandise Inventory	168	
	Accounts Payable		168
22	Accounts Receivable	120	
	Sales		120
22	Cost of Merchandise Sold	81	
	Merchandise Inventory		81
28	Accounts Receivable	60	
	Sales		60
28	Cost of Merchandise Sold	42	
	Merchandise Inventory		42
30	Merchandise Inventory	220	
	Accounts Payable		220

Item 127B

	Purchases			Cost of Merchandise Sold			Inventory		
Date	Quantity	Unit Cost	Total Cost	Quantity	Unit Cost	Total Cost	Quantity	Unit Cost	Total Cost
Jan. 1							10	20	200
4				7	20	140	3	20	60
10	8	21	168				3	20	60
							8	21	168
22				3	20	60			
				1	21	21	7	21	147
28				2	21	42	5	21	105
30	10	22	220				5	21	105
							10	22	220

You should note that after the 7 units were sold on January 4, there was an inventory of 3 units at $20 each. The 8 units purchased on January 10 were acquired at a unit cost of $21, instead of $20. Therefore, the inventory after the January 10 purchase is reported on two lines, 3 units at $20 each and 8 units at $21 each. Next, note that the $81 cost of the 4 units sold on January 22 is made up of the remaining 3 units at $20 each and 1 unit at $21. At this point, 7 units are in inventory at a cost of $21 per unit. The remainder of the illustration is explained in a similar manner.

Last-In, First-Out Method

> **Using lifo, the cost of units sold is the cost of the most recent purchases.**

When the lifo method is used in a perpetual inventory system, the cost of the units sold is the cost of the most recent purchases. To illustrate, Exhibit 4 shows the journal entries for purchases and sales and the subsidiary ledger account for Item 127B, prepared on a lifo basis.

•Exhibit 4   Entries and Perpetual Inventory Account (Lifo)

Jan.	4	Accounts Receivable	210	
		Sales		210
	4	Cost of Merchandise Sold	140	
		Merchandise Inventory		140
	10	Merchandise Inventory	168	
		Accounts Payable		168
	22	Accounts Receivable	120	
		Sales		120
	22	Cost of Merchandise Sold	84	
		Merchandise Inventory		84
	28	Accounts Receivable	60	
		Sales		60
	28	Cost of Merchandise Sold	42	
		Merchandise Inventory		42
	30	Merchandise Inventory	220	
		Accounts Payable		220

Item 127B

Date	Purchases Quantity	Unit Cost	Total Cost	Cost of Merchandise Sold Quantity	Unit Cost	Total Cost	Inventory Quantity	Unit Cost	Total Cost
Jan. 1							10	20	200
4				7	20	140	3	20	60
10	8	21	168				3	20	60
							8	21	168
22				4	21	84	3	20	60
							4	21	84
28				2	21	42	3	20	60
							2	21	42
30	10	22	220				3	20	60
							2	21	42
							10	22	220

If you compare the ledger accounts for the fifo perpetual system and the lifo perpetual system, you should discover that the accounts are the same through the January 10 purchase. Using lifo, however, the cost of the 4 units sold on January 22 is the cost of the units from the January 10 purchase ($21 per unit). The cost of the 7 units in inventory after the sale on January 22 is the cost of the 3 units remaining from the beginning inventory and the cost of the 4 units remaining from the January 10 purchase. The remainder of the lifo illustration is explained in a similar manner.

When the lifo method is used, the inventory ledger is sometimes maintained in units only. The units are converted to dollars when the financial statements are prepared at the end of the period.

The use of the lifo method was originally limited to rare situations in which the units sold were taken from the most recently acquired goods. For tax reasons, which we will discuss later, its use has greatly increased during the past few decades. Lifo is now often used even when it does not represent the physical flow of goods.

Average Cost Method

When the average cost method is used in a perpetual inventory system, an average unit cost for each type of item is computed each time a purchase is made. This unit cost is then used to determine the cost of each sale until another purchase is made and a new average is computed. This averaging technique is called a *moving average*. Since the average cost method is rarely used in a perpetual inventory system, we do not illustrate it in this chapter.

Computerized Perpetual Inventory Systems

The records for a perpetual inventory system may be maintained manually. However, such a system is costly and time consuming for businesses with a large number of inventory items with many purchase and sales transactions. In most cases, the record keeping for perpetual inventory systems is computerized.

An example of using computers in maintaining perpetual inventory records for retail stores follows.

REAL WORLD

The fifo, lifo, and average cost flow assumptions also apply to other areas of business. For example, individuals and businesses often purchase marketable securities at different costs per share. When such investments are sold, the investor must either specifically identify which shares are sold or use the fifo cost flow assumption. To illustrate, assume that a business purchased 100 shares of **Microsoft Corporation** at $25 and 100 shares at $35. If the business later sells 100 shares for $30, which shares did it sell? The business must determine the cost of the shares sold so that it can report either a gain or loss on the sale for tax purposes. In addition, it must report the gain or loss on its income statement.

1. The relevant details for each inventory item, such as a description, quantity, and unit size, are stored in an inventory record. The individual inventory records make up the computerized inventory file, the total of which agrees with the balance of the inventory ledger account.
2. Each time an item is purchased or returned by a customer, the inventory data are entered into the computer's inventory records and files.
3. Each time an item is sold, a salesclerk scans the item's bar code with an optical scanner. The scanner reads the magnetic code and rings up the sale on the cash register. The inventory records and files are then updated for the cost of goods sold.
4. After a physical inventory is taken, the inventory count data are entered into the computer. These data are compared with the current balances, and a listing of the overages and shortages is printed. The inventory balances are then adjusted to the quantities determined by the physical count.

Such systems can be extended to aid managers in controlling and managing inventory quantities. For example, items that are selling fast can be reordered before the stock is depleted. Past sales patterns can be analyzed to determine when to mark down merchandise for sales and when to restock seasonal merchandise. In addition, such systems can provide managers with data for developing and fine-tuning their marketing strategies. For example, such data can be used to evaluate the effectiveness of advertising campaigns and sales promotions.

REAL WORLD

Wal-Mart, Target, Sears, and other retailers use bar code scanners as part of their perpetual inventory systems.

Inventory Costing Methods Under a Periodic Inventory System

objective 5

Compute the cost of inventory under the periodic inventory system, using the following costing methods: first-in, first-out; last-in, first-out; and average cost.

When the periodic inventory system is used, only revenue is recorded each time a sale is made. No entry is made at the time of the sale to record the cost of the merchandise sold. At the end of the accounting period, a physical inventory is taken to determine the cost of the inventory and the cost of the merchandise sold.[1]

Like the perpetual inventory system, a cost flow assumption must be made when identical units are acquired at different unit costs during a period. In such cases, the fifo, lifo, or average cost method is used.

First-In, First-Out Method

To illustrate the use of the fifo method in a periodic inventory system, we assume the following data:

Jan. 1	Inventory:	200 units at	$ 9	$ 1,800
Mar. 10	Purchase:	300 units at	10	3,000
Sept. 21	Purchase:	400 units at	11	4,400
Nov. 18	Purchase:	100 units at	12	1,200
Available for sale during year		1,000		$10,400

The physical count on December 31 shows that 300 units have not been sold. Using the fifo method, the cost of the 700 units sold is determined as follows:

Earliest costs, Jan. 1:	200 units at	$ 9	$1,800
Next earliest costs, Mar. 10:	300 units at	10	3,000
Next earliest costs, Sept. 21:	200 units at	11	2,200
Cost of merchandise sold:	700		$7,000

---

[1]Computing the cost of merchandise sold using the periodic method was illustrated in Chapter 5.

Deducting the cost of merchandise sold of $7,000 from the $10,400 of merchandise available for sale yields $3,400 as the cost of the inventory at December 31. The $3,400 inventory is made up of the most recent costs incurred for this item. Exhibit 5 shows the relationship of the cost of merchandise sold during the year and the inventory at December 31.

•Exhibit 5   First-In, First-Out Flow of Costs

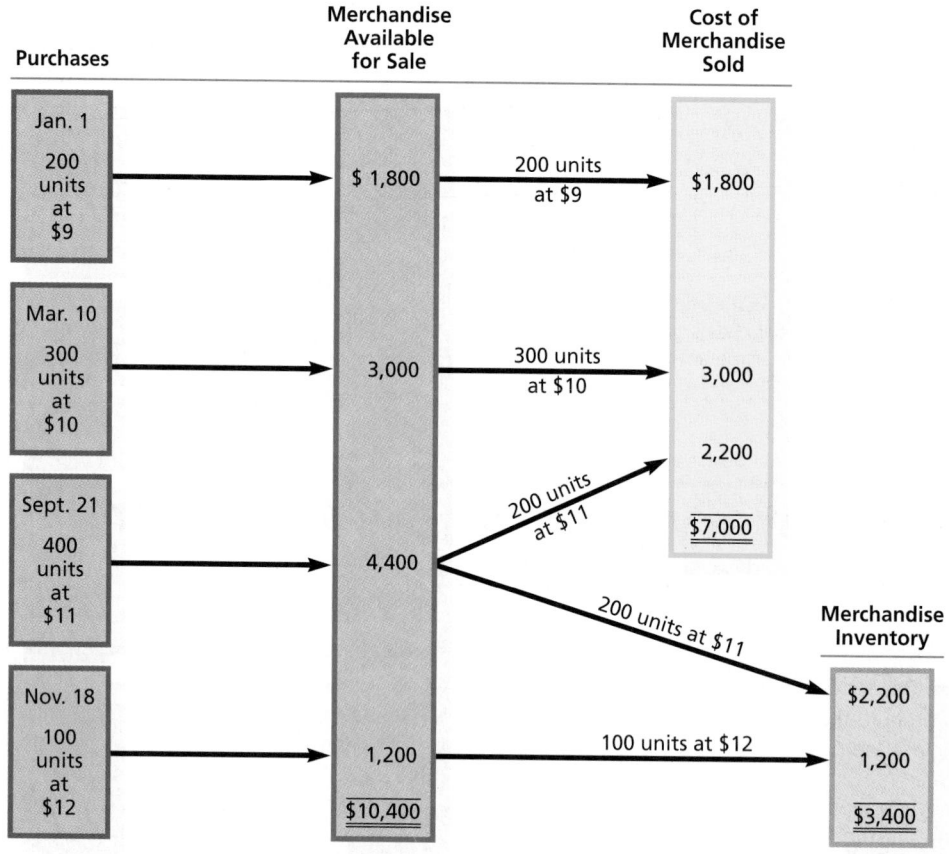

Last-In, First-Out Method

When the lifo method is used, the cost of merchandise sold is made up of the most recent costs. Based on the data in the fifo example, the cost of the 700 units of inventory is determined as follows:

Most recent costs, Nov. 18:	100 units at $12	$1,200
Next most recent costs, Sept. 21:	400 units at 11	4,400
Next most recent costs, Mar. 10:	200 units at 10	2,000
Cost of merchandise sold:	700	$7,600

Deducting the cost of merchandise sold of $7,600 from the $10,400 of merchandise available for sale yields $2,800 as the cost of the inventory at December 31. The $2,800 inventory is made up of the earliest costs incurred for this item. Exhibit 6 shows the relationship of the cost of merchandise sold during the year and the inventory at December 31.

Average Cost Method

The average cost method is sometimes called the **weighted average method**. When this method is used, costs are matched against revenue according to an average of

•Exhibit 6 Last-In, First-Out Flow of Costs

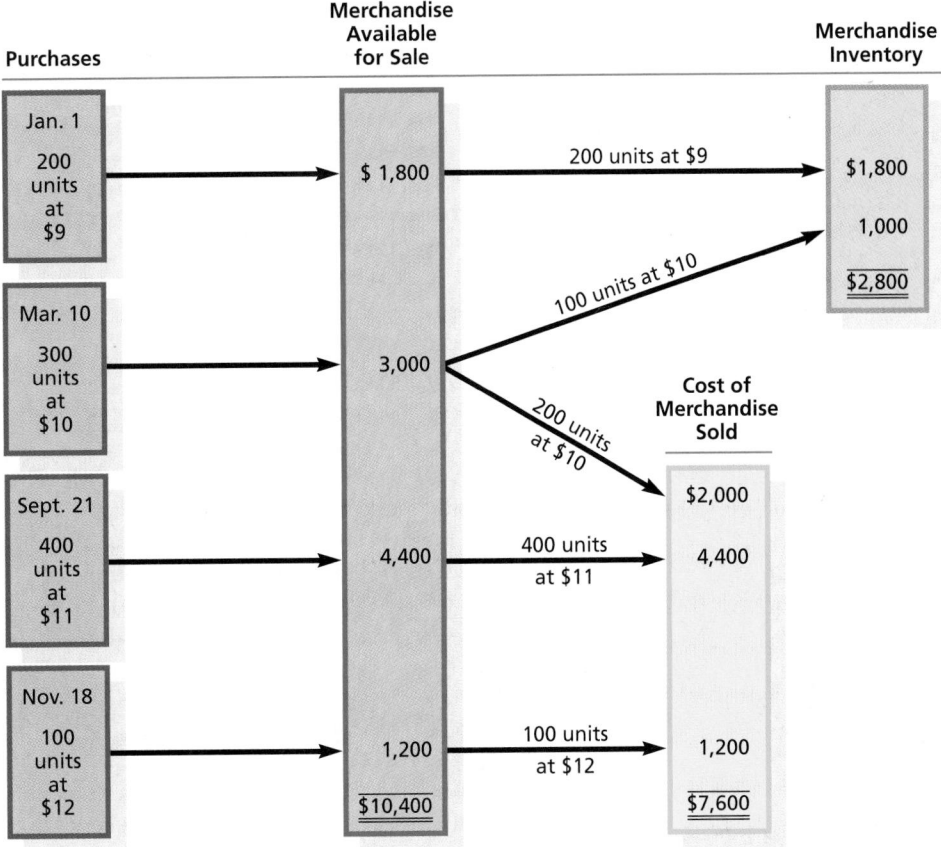

the unit costs of the goods sold. The same weighted average unit costs are used in determining the cost of the merchandise inventory at the end of the period. For businesses in which merchandise sales may be made up of various purchases of identical units, the average method approximates the physical flow of goods.

The weighted average unit cost is determined by dividing the total cost of the units of each item available for sale during the period by the related number of units of that item. Using the same cost data as in the fifo and lifo examples, the average cost of the 1,000 units, $10.40, and the cost of the 700 units, $7,280, are determined as follows:

Average unit cost: $10,400/1,000 units = $10.40
Cost of merchandise sold: 700 units at $10.40 = $7,280

Deducting the cost of merchandise sold of **$7,280** from the **$10,400** of merchandise available for sale yields **$3,120** as the cost of the inventory at December 31.

Comparing Inventory Costing Methods

objective 6

Compare and contrast the use of the three inventory costing methods.

As we have illustrated, a different cost flow is assumed for each of the three alternative methods of costing inventories. You should note that if the cost of units had remained stable, all three methods would have yielded the same results. Since prices do change, however, the three methods will normally yield different amounts for (1) the cost of the merchandise sold for the period, (2) the gross profit (and net income) for the period, and (3) the ending inventory. Using the preceding examples for the periodic inventory system and assuming that net sales were $15,000, the following partial income statements indicate the effects of each method when prices are rising:[2]

Partial Income Statements

	First-In, First-Out		Average Cost		Last-In, First-Out	
Net sales		$15,000		$15,000		$15,000
Cost of merchandise sold:						
Beginning inventory	$ 1,800		$ 1,800		$ 1,800	
Purchases	8,600		8,600		8,600	
Merchandise available for sale	$10,400		$10,400		$10,400	
Less ending inventory	3,400		3,120		2,800	
Cost of merchandise sold		7,000		7,280		7,600
Gross profit		$ 8,000		$ 7,720		$ 7,400

As shown above, the fifo method yielded the lowest amount for the cost of merchandise sold and the highest amount for gross profit (and net income). It also yielded the highest amount for the ending inventory. On the other hand, the lifo method yielded the highest amount for the cost of merchandise sold, the lowest amount for gross profit (and net income), and the lowest amount for ending inventory. The average cost method yielded results that were between those of fifo and lifo.

Use of the First-In, First-Out Method

When the fifo method is used during a period of inflation or rising prices, the earlier unit costs are lower than the more recent unit costs, as shown in the preceding fifo example. Thus, fifo will show a larger gross profit. However, the inventory must be replaced at prices higher than indicated by the cost of merchandise sold. In fact, the balance sheet will report the ending merchandise inventory at an amount that is about the same as its current replacement cost. When the rate of inflation reaches double digits, as it did during the 1970s, the larger gross profits that result from the fifo method are often called *inventory profits* or *illusory profits*. You should note that in a period of deflation or declining prices, the effect is just the opposite.

Use of the Last-In, First-Out Method

When the lifo method is used during a period of inflation or rising prices, the results are opposite those of the other two methods. As shown in the preceding example, the lifo method will yield a higher amount of cost of merchandise sold, a lower amount of gross profit, and a lower amount of inventory at the end of the period than the other two methods. The reason for these effects is that the cost of the most recently acquired units is about the same as the cost of their replacement. In a period of inflation, the more recent unit costs are higher than the earlier unit costs. Thus, it can be argued that the lifo method more nearly matches current costs with current revenues.

During periods of rising prices, using lifo offers an income tax savings. The income tax savings results because lifo reports the lowest amount of net income of the three methods. During the double-digit inflationary period of the 1970s, many businesses changed from fifo to lifo for the tax savings. However, the ending inventory on the balance sheet may be quite different from its current replacement cost. In such cases, the financial statements normally include a note that states the estimated difference between the lifo inventory and the inventory if fifo had been

REAL WORLD

DaimlerChrysler's reason for changing from the fifo method to the lifo method was stated in the following footnote that accompanied its financial statements: *DaimlerChrysler changed its method of accounting from first-in, first-out (fifo) to last-in, first-out (lifo) for substantially all of its domestic productive inventories. The change to lifo was made to more accurately match current costs with current revenues.*

REAL WORLD

In the following note, **Sears, Roebuck and Co.** reported the difference in its inventory if fifo had been used instead of lifo: *Inventories would have been $730 million higher if valued on the first-in, first-out, or FIFO, method.*

---

[2]Similar results would also occur when comparing inventory costing methods under a perpetual inventory system.

used. Again, you should note that in a period of deflation or falling price levels, the effects are just the opposite.

Use of the Average Cost Method

As you might have already reasoned, the average cost method of inventory costing is, in a sense, a compromise between fifo and lifo. The effect of price trends is averaged in determining the cost of merchandise sold and the ending inventory. For a series of purchases, the average cost will be the same, regardless of the direction of price trends. For example, a complete reversal of the sequence of unit costs presented in the preceding illustration would not affect the reported cost of merchandise sold, gross profit, or ending inventory.

INTEGRITY IN BUSINESS

WHERE'S THE BONUS?

Managers are often given bonuses based on reported earnings numbers. This can create a conflict. Lifo can improve the value of the company through lower taxes. However, lifo also produces a lower earnings number and, therefore, lower management bonuses. Ethically, managers should select accounting procedures that will maximize the value of the firm, rather than their own compensation. Compensation specialists can help avoid this ethical dilemma by adjusting the bonus plan for the accounting procedure differences.

Valuation of Inventory at Other than Cost

objective 7

Compute the proper valuation of inventory at other than cost, using the lower-of-cost-or-market and net realizable value concepts.

REAL WORLD

Dell Computer Company recorded over $39.3 million of charges (expenses) in writing down its inventory of notebook computers. The remaining inventories of computers were then sold at significantly reduced prices.

As we indicated earlier, cost is the primary basis for valuing inventories. In some cases, however, inventory is valued at other than cost. Two such cases arise when (1) the cost of replacing items in inventory is below the recorded cost and (2) the inventory is not salable at normal sales prices. This latter case may be due to imperfections, shop wear, style changes, or other causes.

Valuation at Lower of Cost or Market

If the cost of replacing an item in inventory is lower than the original purchase cost, the **lower-of-cost-or-market (LCM) method** is used to value the inventory. *Market*, as used in *lower of cost or market*, is the cost to replace the merchandise on the inventory date. This market value is based on quantities normally purchased from the usual source of supply. In businesses where inflation is the norm, market prices rarely decline. In businesses where technology changes rapidly (e.g., microcomputers and televisions), market declines are common. The primary advantage of the lower-of-cost-or-market method is that gross profit (and net income) is reduced in the period in which the market decline occurred.

In applying the lower-of-cost-or-market method, the cost and replacement cost can be determined in one of three ways. Cost and replacement cost can be determined for (1) each item in the inventory, (2) major classes or categories of inventory, or (3) the inventory as a whole. In practice, the cost and replacement cost of each item are usually determined.

To illustrate, assume that there are 400 identical units of Item A in inventory, acquired at a unit cost of $10.25 each. If at the inventory date the item would cost $10.50 to replace, the cost price of $10.25 would be multiplied by 400 to determine

If the cost of an item is $410, its current replacement cost is $400, and its selling price is $525, at what amount should the item be included in the inventory according to the LCM method?

$400

the inventory value. On the other hand, if the item could be replaced at $9.50 a unit, the replacement cost of $9.50 would be used for valuation purposes.

Exhibit 7 illustrates a method of organizing inventory data and applying the lower-of-cost-or-market method to each inventory item. The amount of the market decline, $450 ($15,520 − $15,070), may be reported as a separate item on the income statement or included in the cost of merchandise sold. Regardless, net income will be reduced by the amount of the market decline.

•Exhibit 7 Determining Inventory at Lower of Cost or Market

Commodity	Inventory Quantity	Unit Cost Price	Unit Market Price	Total Cost	Total Market	Total Lower of C or M
A	400	$10.25	$ 9.50	$ 4,100	$ 3,800	$ 3,800
B	120	22.50	24.10	2,700	2,892	2,700
C	600	8.00	7.75	4,800	4,650	4,650
D	280	14.00	14.75	3,920	4,130	3,920
Total				$15,520	$15,472	$15,070

Valuation at Net Realizable Value

Out-of-date merchandise is a major problem for many types of retailers. For example, you may have noticed the shelf-life dates of grocery products, such as milk, eggs, canned goods, and meat. Grocery stores often mark down the prices of products nearing the end of their shelf life to avoid having to dispose of the products as waste.

REAL WORLD

As you would expect, merchandise that is out of date, spoiled, or damaged or that can be sold only at prices below cost should be written down. Such merchandise should be valued at net realizable value. **Net realizable value** is the estimated selling price less any direct cost of disposal, such as sales commissions. For example, assume that damaged merchandise costing $1,000 can be sold for only $800, and direct selling expenses are estimated to be $150. This inventory should be valued at $650 ($800 − $150), which is its net realizable value.

Presenting Merchandise Inventory on the Balance Sheet

objective 8

Prepare a balance sheet presentation of merchandise inventory.

Merchandise inventory is usually presented in the Current Assets section of the balance sheet, following receivables. Both the method of determining the cost of the inventory (fifo, lifo, or average) and the method of valuing the inventory (cost or the lower of cost or market) should be shown. It is not unusual for large businesses with varied activities to use different costing methods for different segments of their inventories. The details may be disclosed in parentheses on the balance sheet or in a footnote to the financial statements. Exhibit 8 shows how parentheses may be used.

A company may change its inventory costing methods for a valid reason. In such cases, the effect of the change and the reason for the change should be disclosed in the financial statements for the period in which the change occurred.

General Motors Corporation uses the last-in, first-out (lifo) method to account for all U.S. inventories other than those of **Saturn Corporation**. The cost of non-U.S., Saturn inventories is determined by using either first-in, first-out (fifo) or average cost.

REAL WORLD

•**Exhibit 8** Merchandise Inventory on the Balance Sheet

Metro Arts Balance Sheet December 31, 2007			
Assets			
Current assets:			
Cash			$ 19 4 0 0 00
Accounts receivable	$80 0 0 0 00		
Less allowance for doubtful accounts	3 0 0 0 00		77 0 0 0 00
Merchandise inventory—at lower of cost (first-in, first-out method) or market			216 3 0 0 00

FINANCIAL REPORTING AND DISCLOSURE

COSTCO WHOLESALE CORPORATION

Costco Wholesale Corporation operates over three hundred membership warehouses that offer members low prices on a limited selection of nationally branded and selected private label products. Costco's business strategy is to generate high sales volumes and rapid inventory turnover. This enables Costco to operate profitably at significantly lower gross margins than traditional wholesalers, discount retailers, and supermarkets. In addition, Costco's rapid turnover provides it the opportunity to conserve on its cash, as described below.

Because of its high sales volume and rapid inventory turnover, Costco generally has the opportunity to receive cash from the sale of a substantial portion of its inventory at mature warehouse operations before it is required to pay all its merchandise vendors, even though Costco takes advantage of early payment terms to obtain payment discounts. As sales in a given warehouse increase and inventory turnover becomes more rapid, a greater percentage of the inventory is financed through payment terms provided by vendors rather than by working capital (cash).

On its September 1, 2002 balance sheet, Costco reported over $3 billion of inventory, as follows. Costco uses the FIFO method in its foreign operations because some countries do not permit the use of the LIFO method.

Merchandise inventories (in thousands):

United States (LIFO)	$2,552,820
Foreign (FIFO)	574,401
Total	$3,127,221

Merchandise inventories are valued at the lower of cost or market . . . and are stated using the last-in, first-out (LIFO) method for . . . U.S. merchandise inventories. Merchandise inventories for all foreign operations are . . . stated using the first-in, first-out (FIFO) method. The Company believes the LIFO method more fairly presents the results of operations by more closely matching current costs with current revenues.

As with all retailers, Costco experiences inventory shrinkage, as described below.

The Company provides for estimated inventory losses between physical inventory counts on the basis of a standard percentage of sales. This provision is adjusted periodically to reflect the actual shrinkage results of the physical inventory counts . . . .

Estimating Inventory Cost

objective 9

Estimate the cost of inventory, using the retail method and the gross profit method.

It may be necessary for a business to know the amount of inventory when perpetual inventory records are not maintained and it is impractical to take a physical inventory. For example, a business that uses a periodic inventory system may need monthly income statements, but taking a physical inventory each month may be too costly. Moreover, when a disaster such as a fire has destroyed the inventory, the amount of the loss must be determined. In this case, taking a physical inventory is impossible, and even if perpetual inventory records have been kept, the accounting records may also have been destroyed. In such cases, the inventory cost can be estimated by using (1) the retail method or (2) the gross profit method.

Retail Method of Inventory Costing

The ***retail inventory method*** of estimating inventory cost is based on the relationship of the cost of merchandise available for sale to the retail price of the same merchandise. To use this method, the retail prices of all merchandise are maintained and totaled. Next, the inventory at retail is determined by deducting sales for the period from the retail price of the goods that were available for sale during the period. The estimated inventory cost is then computed by multiplying the inventory at retail by the ratio of cost to selling (retail) price for the merchandise available for sale, as illustrated in Exhibit 9.

•Exhibit 9   **Determining Inventory by the Retail Method**

	Cost	Retail
Merchandise inventory, January 1	$19,400	$ 36,000
Purchases in January (net)	42,600	64,000
Merchandise available for sale	$62,000	$100,000
Ratio of cost to retail price: $\dfrac{\$\,62,000}{\$100,000} = 62\%$		
Sales for January (net)		70,000
Merchandise inventory, January 31, at retail		$ 30,000
Merchandise inventory, January 31, at estimated cost ($30,000 × 62%)		$ 18,600

When estimating the percent of cost to selling price, we assume that the mix of the items in the ending inventory is the same as the entire stock of merchandise available for sale. In Exhibit 9, for example, it is unlikely that the retail price of every item was made up of exactly 62% cost and 38% gross profit. We assume, however, that the weighted average of the cost percentages of the merchandise in the inventory ($30,000) is the same as in the merchandise available for sale ($100,000).

When the inventory is made up of different classes of merchandise with very different gross profit rates, the cost percentages and the inventory should be developed for each class of inventory.

One of the major advantages of the retail method is that it provides inventory figures for preparing monthly or quarterly statements when the periodic system is used. Department stores and similar merchandisers like to determine gross profit and operating income each month but may take a physical inventory only once or twice a year. In addition, comparing the estimated ending inventory with the physical ending inventory, both at retail prices, will help identify inventory shortages resulting from shoplifting and other causes. Management can then take appropriate actions.

The retail method may also be used as an aid in taking a physical inventory. In this case, the items counted are recorded on the inventory sheets at their retail (selling) prices instead of their cost prices. The physical inventory at selling price is then converted to cost by applying the ratio of cost to selling (retail) price for the merchandise available for sale.

If the ratio of cost to retail is 70% and the ending inventory at retail is $100,000, what is the estimated ending inventory at cost?

$70,000 (70% × $100,000)

To illustrate, assume that the data in Exhibit 9 are for an entire fiscal year rather than for only January. If the physical inventory taken at the end of the year totaled $29,000, priced at retail, this amount rather than the $30,000 would be converted to cost. Thus, the inventory at cost would be $17,980 ($29,000 × 62%) instead of $18,600 ($30,000 × 62%). The $17,980 would be used for the year-end financial statements and for income tax purposes.

Gross Profit Method of Estimating Inventories

The *gross profit method* uses the estimated gross profit for the period to estimate the inventory at the end of the period. The gross profit is usually estimated from the actual rate for the preceding year, adjusted for any changes made in the cost and sales prices during the current period. By using the gross profit rate, the dollar amount of sales for a period can be divided into its two components: (1) gross profit and (2) cost of merchandise sold. The latter amount may then be deducted from the cost of merchandise available for sale to yield the estimated cost of the inventory.

Exhibit 10 illustrates the gross profit method for estimating a company's inventory on January 31. In this example, the inventory on January 1 is assumed to be $57,000, the net purchases during the month are $180,000, and the net sales during the month are $250,000. In addition, the historical gross profit was 30% of net sales.

•Exhibit 10   **Estimating Inventory by Gross Profit Method**

Merchandise inventory, January 1		$ 57,000
Purchases in January (net)		180,000
Merchandise available for sale		$237,000
Sales in January (net)	$250,000	
Less estimated gross profit ($250,000 × 30%)	75,000	
Estimated cost of merchandise sold		175,000
Estimated merchandise inventory, January 31		$ 62,000

What is the estimated cost of the ending inventory if the merchandise available for sale is $350,000, sales are $500,000, and the gross profit percentage is 40%?

The gross profit method is useful for estimating inventories for monthly or quarterly financial statements in a periodic inventory system. It is also useful in estimating the cost of merchandise destroyed by fire or other disasters.

$50,000 [$350,000 − (60% × $500,000)]

Financial Analysis and Interpretation

objective 10

Compute and interpret the inventory turnover ratio and the number of days' sales in inventory.

A merchandising business should keep enough inventory on hand to meet the needs of its customers. A failure to do so may result in lost sales. At the same time, too much inventory reduces solvency by tying up funds that could be better used to expand or improve operations. In addition, excess inventory increases expenses such as storage, insurance, and property taxes. Finally, excess inventory increases the risk of losses due to price declines, damage, or changes in customers' buying patterns.

As with many types of financial analyses, it is possible to use more than one measure to analyze the efficiency and effectiveness by which a business manages its inventory. Two such measures are the inventory turnover and the number of days' sales in inventory.

Inventory turnover measures the relationship between the volume of goods (merchandise) sold and the amount of inventory carried during the period. It is computed as follows:

$$\text{Inventory turnover} = \frac{\text{Cost of merchandise sold}}{\text{Average inventory}}$$

The average inventory can be computed using weekly, monthly, or yearly figures. To simplify, we determine the average inventory by dividing the sum of the inventories at the beginning and end of the year by 2. As long as the amount of inventory carried throughout the year remains stable, this average will be accurate enough for our analysis.

To illustrate, the following data have been taken from recent annual reports for **SUPERVALU INC.** and **Zale Corporation**:

	SUPERVALU	Zale
Cost of merchandise sold	$16,567,397,000	$1,083,053,000
Inventories:		
Beginning of year	$1,038,050,000	$724,157,000
End of year	$1,049,283,000	$782,316,000
Average	$1,043,666,000	$753,236,000
Inventory turnover	15.9	1.4

The inventory turnover is 15.9 for SUPERVALU and 1.4 for Zale. Generally, the larger the inventory turnover, the more efficient and effective the management of inventory. However, differences in companies and industries are too great to allow specific statements as to what is a good inventory turnover. For example, SUPERVALU is a leading food distributor and the tenth largest food retailer in the United States. Because SUPERVALU's inventory is perishable, we would expect it to have a high inventory turnover. In contrast, Zale Corporation is the largest speciality retailer of fine jewelry in the United States. Thus, we would expect Zale to have a lower inventory turnover than SUPERVALU. As with other financial measures we have discussed, a comparison of a company's inventory turnover over time and with industry averages will provide useful insights into the management of its inventory.

The *number of days' sales in inventory* is a rough measure of the length of time it takes to acquire, sell, and replace the inventory. It is computed as follows:

$$\text{Number of days' sales in inventory} = \frac{\text{Inventory, end of year}}{\text{Average daily cost of merchandise sold}}$$

The average daily cost of merchandise sold is determined by dividing the cost of merchandise sold by 365. The number of days' sales in inventory for SUPERVALU and Zale is computed as shown below.

	SUPERVALU	Zale
Average daily cost of merchandise sold:		
$16,567,397,000/365	$45,370,129	
$1,083,053,000/365		$2,967,268
Ending inventory	$1,049,283,000	$782,316,000
Number of days' sales in inventory	23.1 days	263.6 days

Generally, the lower the number of days' sales in inventory, the better. As with inventory turnover, we should expect differences among industries, such as those for SUPERVALU and Zale.

SPOTLIGHT ON STRATEGY

A BEER RUN?

Adolph Coors Company has an estimated 11 percent market share in the United States, in contrast with **Anheuser-Busch**'s 50 percent and **Miller Brewing**'s 20 percent shares. Because of its smaller size, Coors has difficulty competing domestically with Anheuser-Busch and Miller, who often offer rebates and other incentives to their distributors to sell their beer. Coors recently decided to expand operations outside the United States by purchasing Carling beer from **Interbrew SA** for $1.7 billion. Carling is Britain's best-selling beer. So what is Coors' underlying strategy? In addition to allowing Coors to obtain an immediate international presence in Europe, Carling provides Coors with a beer for possible import into the United States. Carling also provides Coors with another brand to offer its distributors, and thus take advantage of offering as many beers as possible through its distribution channel. However, adding Carling to its product will increase Coors' inventory, thus increasing its related costs of shipping, handling, storing, and financing inventory.

Source: Adapted from "Coors Gets Europe Access in Carling Deal," by Gary McWilliams and Philip Shishkin, *The Wall Street Journal*, December 26, 2001, and "Coors Acquires A Big Brand in Britain," by Suzanne Kapner, *The New York Times*, December 25, 2001.

Key Points

1 Summarize and provide examples of internal control procedures that apply to inventories.
Internal control procedures for inventories include those developed to protect the inventories from damage, employee theft, and customer theft. In addition, a physical inventory count should be taken periodically to detect shortages as well as to deter employee thefts.

2 Describe the effect of inventory errors on the financial statements.
Any errors in reporting inventory based upon the physical inventory will misstate the ending inventory, current assets, total assets, and total stockholders' equity (retained earnings) on the balance sheet. In addition, the cost of goods sold, gross profit, and net income will be misstated on the income statement.

3 Describe three inventory cost flow assumptions and how they impact the income statement and balance sheet.
The three common cost flow assumptions used in business are the (1) first-in, first-out method, (2) last-in, first-out method, and (3) average cost method. Each method normally yields different amounts for the cost of merchandise sold and the ending merchandise inventory. Thus, the choice of a cost flow assumption directly affects the income statement and balance sheet.

4 Compute the cost of inventory under the perpetual inventory system, using the following costing methods: first-in, first-out; last-in, first-out; and average cost.
In a perpetual inventory system, the number of units and the cost of each type of merchandise are recorded in a subsidiary inventory ledger, with a separate account for each type of merchandise. Inventory costs and the amounts charged against revenue are illustrated using the fifo and lifo methods.

5 Compute the cost of inventory under the periodic inventory system, using the following costing methods: first-in, first-out; last-in, first-out; and average cost.
In a periodic inventory system, a physical inventory is taken to determine the cost of the inventory and the cost of merchandise sold. Inventory costs and the amounts charged against revenue are illustrated using fifo, lifo, and average cost methods.

6 Compare and contrast the use of the three inventory costing methods.
The three inventory costing methods will normally yield different amounts for (1) the ending inventory, (2) the cost of the merchandise sold for the period, and (3) the gross profit (and net income) for the period. During periods of inflation, the fifo method yields the lowest amount for the cost of merchandise sold, the highest amount for gross profit (and net income), and the highest amount for the ending inventory. The lifo method yields the opposite results. During periods of deflation, the preceding effects are reversed. The average cost method yields results that are between those of fifo and lifo.

7 Compute the proper valuation of inventory at other than cost, using the lower-of-cost-or-market and net realizable value concepts.
If the market price of an item of inventory is lower than its cost, the lower market price is used to compute the value of the item. Market price is the cost to replace the merchandise on the inventory date. It is possible to apply the lower of cost or market to each item in the inventory,

to major classes or categories, or to the inventory as a whole.

Merchandise that can be sold only at prices below cost should be valued at net realizable value, which is the estimated selling price less any direct cost of disposal.

8 Prepare a balance sheet presentation of merchandise inventory.

Merchandise inventory is usually presented in the Current Assets section of the balance sheet, following receivables. Both the method of determining the cost of the inventory (fifo, lifo, or average) and the method of valuing the inventory (cost or the lower of cost or market) should be shown.

9 Estimate the cost of inventory, using the retail method and the gross profit method.

In using the retail method to estimate inventory, the retail prices of all merchandise acquired are accumulated. The inventory at retail is determined by deducting sales for the period from the retail price of the goods that were available for sale during the period. The inventory at retail is then converted to cost on the basis of the ratio of cost to selling (retail) price for the merchandise available for sale.

In using the gross profit method to estimate inventory, the estimated gross profit is deducted from the sales to determine the estimated cost of merchandise sold. This amount is then deducted from the cost of merchandise available for sale to determine the estimated ending inventory.

10 Compute and interpret the inventory turnover ratio and the number of days' sales in inventory.

The inventory turnover ratio, computed as the cost of merchandise sold divided by the average inventory, measures the relationship between the volume of goods (merchandise) sold and the amount of inventory carried during the period. The number of days' sales in inventory, computed as the ending inventory divided by the average daily cost of merchandise sold, measures the length of time it takes to acquire, sell, and replace the inventory.

Key Terms

average cost method (321)
first-in, first-out (fifo) method (321)
gross profit method (333)
inventory turnover (334)

last-in, first-out (lifo) method (321)
lower-of-cost-or-market (LCM) method (329)
net realizable value (330)

number of days' sales in inventory (334)
physical inventory (318)
retail inventory method (332)

Illustrative Problem

Stewart Co.'s beginning inventory and purchases during the year ended December 31, 2007, were as follows:

		Units	Unit Cost	Total Cost
January 1	Inventory	1,000	$50.00	$ 50,000
March 10	Purchase	1,200	52.50	63,000
June 25	Sold 800 units			
August 30	Purchase	800	55.00	44,000
October 5	Sold 1,500 units			
November 26	Purchase	2,000	56.00	112,000
December 31	Sold 1,000 units			
Total		5,000		$269,000

Instructions

1. Determine the cost of inventory on December 31, 2007, using the perpetual inventory system and each of the following inventory costing methods:
   a. first-in, first-out
   b. last-in, first-out

2. Determine the cost of inventory on December 31, 2007, using the periodic inventory system and each of the following inventory costing methods:
   a. first-in, first-out
   b. last-in, first-out
   c. average cost
3. Assume that during the fiscal year ended December 31, 2007, sales were $290,000 and the estimated gross profit rate was 40%. Estimate the ending inventory at December 31, 2007, using the gross profit method.

Solution

1. a. First-in, first-out method: $95,200

Date	Purchases Quantity	Unit Cost	Total Cost	Cost of Merchandise Sold Quantity	Unit Cost	Total Cost	Inventory Quantity	Unit Cost	Total Cost
2007 Jan. 1							1,000	50.00	50,000
Mar. 10	1,200	52.50	63,000				1,000	50.00	50,000
							1,200	52.50	63,000
June 25				800	50.00	40,000	200	50.00	10,000
							1,200	52.50	63,000
Aug. 30	800	55.00	44,000				200	50.00	10,000
							1,200	52.50	63,000
							800	55.00	44,000
Oct. 5				200	50.00	10,000	700	55.00	38,500
				1,200	52.50	63,000			
				100	55.00	5,500			
Nov. 26	2,000	56.00	112,000				700	55.00	38,500
							2,000	56.00	112,000
Dec. 31				700	55.00	38,500	1,700	56.00	95,200
				300	56.00	16,800			

b. Last-in, first-out method: $91,000 ($35,000 + $56,000)

Date	Purchases Quantity	Unit Cost	Total Cost	Cost of Merchandise Sold Quantity	Unit Cost	Total Cost	Inventory Quantity	Unit Cost	Total Cost
2007 Jan. 1							1,000	50.00	50,000
Mar. 10	1,200	52.50	63,000				1,000	50.00	50,000
							1,200	52.50	63,000
June 25				800	52.50	42,000	1,000	50.00	50,000
							400	52.50	21,000
Aug. 30	800	55.00	44,000				1,000	50.00	50,000
							400	52.50	21,000
							800	55.00	44,000
Oct. 5				800	55.00	44,000	700	50.00	35,000
				400	52.50	21,000			
				300	50.00	15,000			
Nov. 26	2,000	56.00	112,000				700	50.00	35,000
							2,000	56.00	112,000
Dec. 31				1,000	56.00	56,000	700	50.00	35,000
							1,000	56.00	56,000

2. a. First-in, first-out method:
   1,700 units at $56 = $95,200

(continued)

b. Last-in, first-out method:

1,000 units at $50.00	$50,000
700 units at $52.50	36,750
1,700 units	$86,750

c. Average cost method:

Average cost per unit: $269,000 ÷ 5,000 units = $53.80
Inventory, December 31, 2007:   1,700 units at $53.80 = $91,460

3. Merchandise inventory, January 1, 2007 . . . . $ 50,000
Purchases (net)   219,000
Merchandise available for sale $269,000
Sales (net) $290,000
Less estimated gross profit ($290,000 × 40%)   116,000
Estimated cost of merchandise sold   174,000
Estimated merchandise inventory, December 31, 2007 . . . . $ 95,000

Self-Examination Questions (Answers at End of Chapter)

1. If the inventory shrinkage at the end of the year is overstated by $7,500, the error will cause an:
   A. understatement of cost of merchandise sold for the year by $7,500.
   B. overstatement of gross profit for the year by $7,500.
   C. overstatement of merchandise inventory for the year by $7,500.
   D. understatement of net income for the year by $7,500.

2. The inventory costing method that is based on the assumption that costs should be charged against revenue in the order in which they were incurred is:
   A. fifo
   B. lifo
   C. average cost
   D. perpetual inventory

3. The following units of a particular item were purchased and sold during the period:

Beginning inventory	40 units at $20
First purchase	50 units at $21
Second purchase	50 units at $22
First sale	110 units
Third purchase	50 units at $23
Second sale	45 units

What is the cost of the 35 units on hand at the end of the period as determined under the perpetual inventory system by the lifo costing method?
   A. $715
   B. $705
   C. $700
   D. $805

4. The following units of a particular item were available for sale during the period:

Beginning inventory	40 units at $20
First purchase	50 units at $21
Second purchase	50 units at $22
Third purchase	50 units at $23

What is the unit cost of the 35 units on hand at the end of the period as determined under the periodic inventory system by the fifo costing method?
   A. $20
   B. $21
   C. $22
   D. $23

5. If merchandise inventory is being valued at cost and the price level is steadily rising, the method of costing that will yield the highest net income is:
   A. lifo
   B. fifo
   C. average
   D. periodic

Class Discussion Questions

1. What security measures may be used by retailers to protect merchandise inventory from customer theft?

2. Which inventory system provides the more effective means of controlling inventories (perpetual or periodic)? Why?

3. Before inventory purchases are recorded, the receiving report should be reconciled to what documents?

4. What document should be presented by an employee requesting inventory items to be released from the company's warehouse?

5. Why is it important to periodically take a physical inventory if the perpetual system is used?

6. The inventory shrinkage at the end of the year was understated by $18,500. (a) Did the error cause an overstatement or an understatement of the gross profit for the year? (b) Which items on the balance sheet at the end of the year were overstated or understated as a result of the error?

7. Martin Co. sold merchandise to Fess Company on December 31, FOB shipping point. If the merchandise is in transit on December 31, the end of the fiscal year, which company would report it in its financial statements? Explain.

8. A manufacturer shipped merchandise to a retailer on a consignment basis. If the merchandise is unsold at the end of the period, in whose inventory should the merchandise be included?

9. Do the terms *fifo* and *lifo* refer to techniques used in determining quantities of the various classes of merchandise on hand? Explain.

10. Does the term *last-in* in the lifo method mean that the items in the inventory are assumed to be the most recent (last) acquisitions? Explain.

11. If merchandise inventory is being valued at cost and the price level is steadily rising, which of the three methods of costing—fifo, lifo, or average cost—will yield (a) the highest inventory cost, (b) the lowest inventory cost, (c) the highest gross profit, (d) the lowest gross profit?

12. Which of the three methods of inventory costing—fifo, lifo, or average cost—will in general yield an inventory cost most nearly approximating current replacement cost?

13. If inventory is being valued at cost and the price level is steadily rising, which of the three methods of costing—fifo, lifo, or average cost—will yield the lowest annual income tax expense? Explain.

14. Can a company change its method of costing inventory? Explain.

15. Because of imperfections, an item of merchandise cannot be sold at its normal selling price. How should this item be valued for financial statement purposes?

16. How is the method of determining the cost of the inventory and the method of valuing it disclosed in the financial statements?

17. What uses can be made of the estimate of the cost of inventory determined by the gross profit method?

Exercises

EXERCISE 8-1
Internal control of inventories

Objective 1

Onsite Hardware Store currently uses a periodic inventory system. Dana Cogburn, the owner, is considering the purchase of a computer system that would make it feasible to switch to a perpetual inventory system.

Dana is unhappy with the periodic inventory system because it does not provide timely information on inventory levels. Dana has noticed on several occasions that the store runs out of good-selling items, while too many poor-selling items are on hand.

Dana is also concerned about lost sales while a physical inventory is being taken. Onsite Hardware currently takes a physical inventory twice a year. To minimize distractions, the store is closed on the day inventory is taken. Dana believes that closing the store is the only way to get an accurate inventory count.

➤ Will switching to a perpetual inventory system strengthen Onsite Hardware's control over inventory items? Will switching to a perpetual inventory system eliminate the need for a physical inventory count? Explain.

EXERCISE 8-2
Internal control of inventories

Objective 1

Pacific Luggage Shop is a small retail establishment located in a large shopping mall. This shop has implemented the following procedures regarding inventory items:

a. Whenever Pacific receives a shipment of new inventory, the items are taken directly to the stockroom. Pacific's accountant uses the vendor's invoice to record the amount of inventory received.

b. Since the shop carries mostly high-quality, designer luggage, all inventory items are tagged with a control device that activates an alarm if a tagged item is removed from the store.

c. Since the display area of the store is limited, only a sample of each piece of luggage is kept on the selling floor. Whenever a customer selects a piece of luggage, the salesclerk gets the appropriate piece from the store's stockroom. Since all salesclerks need access to the stockroom, it is not locked. The stockroom is adjacent to the break room used by all mall employees.

➤ State whether each of these procedures is appropriate or inappropriate, considering the principles of internal control. If it is inappropriate, state which internal control procedure is violated.

EXERCISE 8-3
Identifying items to be included in inventory

Objective 1

Marcelle's Boutiques, which is located in Iowa City, Iowa, has identified the following items for possible inclusion in its December 31, 2005 year-end inventory.

a. Merchandise Marcelle's shipped to a customer FOB shipping point was picked up by the freight company on December 26, 2005, but had still not arrived at its destination as of December 31, 2005.

b. Marcelle's has in its warehouse $30,500 of merchandise on consignment from Putnam Co.

c. Marcelle's has segregated $6,570 of merchandise ordered by one of its customers for shipment on January 3, 2006.

d. Merchandise Marcelle's shipped FOB shipping point on December 31, 2005, was picked up by the freight company at 11:52 p.m.

e. Marcelle's has sent $78,000 of merchandise to various retailers on a consignment basis.

f. Marcelle's has $18,750 of merchandise on hand, which was sold to customers earlier in the year, but which has been returned by customers to Marcelle's for various warranty repairs.

g. On December 31, 2005, Marcelle's received $17,050 of merchandise that had been returned by customers because the wrong merchandise had been shipped. The replacement order is to be shipped overnight on January 3, 2006.

h. On December 21, 2005, Marcelle's ordered $21,000 of merchandise, FOB Iowa City. The merchandise was shipped from the supplier on December 28, 2005, but had not been received by December 31, 2005.

i. On December 27, 2005, Marcelle's ordered $15,750 of merchandise from a supplier in Davenport. The merchandise was shipped FOB Davenport on December 30, 2005, but had not been received by December 31, 2005.

Indicate which items should be included (I) and which should be excluded (E) from the inventory.

EXERCISE 8-4
Effect of errors in physical inventory
Objective 2

Crazy Rapids Co. sells canoes, kayaks, whitewater rafts, and other boating supplies. During the taking of its physical inventory on December 31, 2006, Crazy Rapids incorrectly counted its inventory as $117,800 instead of the correct amount of $119,750.

a. State the effect of the error on the December 31, 2006 balance sheet of Crazy Rapids.
b. State the effect of the error on the income statement of Crazy Rapids for the year ended December 31, 2006.

EXERCISE 8-5
Effect of errors in physical inventory
Objective 2

Ray's Motorcycle Shop sells motorcycles, jet skis, and other related supplies and accessories. During the taking of its physical inventory on December 31, 2006, Ray's Motorcycle Shop incorrectly counted its inventory as $187,900 instead of the correct amount of $183,750.

a. State the effect of the error on the December 31, 2006 balance sheet of Ray's Motorcycle Shop.
b. State the effect of the error on the income statement of Ray's Motorcycle Shop for the year ended December 31, 2006.

EXERCISE 8-6
Error in inventory shrinkage
Objective 2

WHAT'S WRONG WITH THIS?

During 2006, the accountant discovered that the physical inventory at the end of 2005 had been understated by $12,800. Instead of correcting the error, however, the accountant assumed that a $12,800 overstatement of the physical inventory in 2006 would balance out the error.

➡ Are there any flaws in the accountant's assumption? Explain.

EXERCISE 8-7
Perpetual inventory using fifo
Objectives 3, 4

SPREADSHEET

✔ *Inventory balance, April 30, $802*

Beginning inventory, purchases, and sales data for portable CD players are as follows:

April	1	Inventory	35 units at $50
	5	Sale	26 units
	11	Purchase	15 units at $53
	21	Sale	12 units
	28	Sale	4 units
	30	Purchase	7 units at $54

The business maintains a perpetual inventory system, costing by the first-in, first-out method. Determine the cost of the merchandise sold for each sale and the inventory balance after each sale, presenting the data in the form illustrated in Exhibit 3.

EXERCISE 8-8
Perpetual inventory using lifo
Objectives 3, 4

SPREADSHEET

✔ *Inventory balance, April 30, $778*

Assume that the business in Exercise 8-7 maintains a perpetual inventory system, costing by the last-in, first-out method. Determine the cost of merchandise sold for each sale and the inventory balance after each sale, presenting the data in the form illustrated in Exhibit 4.

EXERCISE 8-9
Perpetual inventory using lifo

Objectives 3, 4

SPREADSHEET

✓*Inventory balance, March 31, $1,295*

Beginning inventory, purchases, and sales data for cell phones for March are as follows:

Inventory		Purchases		Sales	
Mar. 1	25 units at $90	Mar. 5	20 units at $94	Mar. 9	18 units
		21	15 units at $95	13	20 units
				31	8 units

Assuming that the perpetual inventory system is used, costing by the lifo method, determine the cost of merchandise sold for each sale and the inventory balance after each sale, presenting the data in the form illustrated in Exhibit 4.

EXERCISE 8-10
Perpetual inventory using fifo

Objectives 3, 4

SPREADSHEET

✓*Inventory balance, March 31, $1,330*

Assume that the business in Exercise 8-9 maintains a perpetual inventory system, costing by the first-in, first-out method. Determine the cost of merchandise sold for each sale and the inventory balance after each sale, presenting the data in the form illustrated in Exhibit 3.

EXERCISE 8-11
Fifo, lifo costs under perpetual inventory system

Objectives 3, 4

✓*a. $700*

The following units of a particular item were available for sale during the year:

Beginning inventory	20 units at $45
Sale	15 units at $80
First purchase	31 units at $47
Sale	27 units at $80
Second purchase	40 units at $50
Sale	35 units at $80

The firm uses the perpetual inventory system, and there are 14 units of the item on hand at the end of the year. What is the total cost of the ending inventory according to (a) fifo, (b) lifo?

EXERCISE 8-12
Periodic inventory by three methods

Objectives 3, 5

✓*b. $318*

The units of an item available for sale during the year were as follows:

Jan. 1	Inventory	6 units at $28
Feb. 4	Purchase	12 units at $30
July 20	Purchase	14 units at $32
Dec. 30	Purchase	8 units at $33

There are 11 units of the item in the physical inventory at December 31. The periodic inventory system is used. Determine the inventory cost by (a) the first-in, first-out method, (b) the last-in, first-out method, and (c) the average cost method.

EXERCISE 8-13
Periodic inventory by three methods; cost of merchandise sold

Objectives 3, 5

SPREADSHEET

✓*a. Inventory, $5,016*

The units of an item available for sale during the year were as follows:

Jan. 1	Inventory	42 units at $120
Mar. 4	Purchase	58 units at $130
Aug. 7	Purchase	20 units at $136
Nov. 15	Purchase	30 units at $140

There are 36 units of the item in the physical inventory at December 31. The periodic inventory system is used. Determine the inventory cost and the cost of merchandise sold by three methods, presenting your answers in the following form:

	Cost	
Inventory Method	Merchandise Inventory	Merchandise Sold
a. First-in, first-out	$	$
b. Last-in, first-out		
c. Average cost		

EXERCISE 8-14
Comparing inventory methods
Objective 6

Assume that a firm separately determined inventory under fifo and lifo and then compared the results.

1. In each space below, place the correct sign [less than (<), greater than (>), or equal (=)] for each comparison, assuming periods of rising prices.

a. Lifo inventory	_____	Fifo inventory
b. Lifo cost of goods sold	_____	Fifo cost of goods sold
c. Lifo net income	_____	Fifo net income
d. Lifo income tax	_____	Fifo income tax

2. Why would management prefer to use lifo over fifo in periods of rising prices?

EXERCISE 8-15
Lower-of-cost-or-market inventory
Objective 7

SPREADSHEET

✓ LCM: $8,325

On the basis of the following data, determine the value of the inventory at the lower of cost or market. Assemble the data in the form illustrated in Exhibit 7.

Commodity	Inventory Quantity	Unit Cost Price	Unit Market Price
M76	8	$150	$160
T53	20	75	70
A19	10	275	260
J81	15	50	40
K10	25	101	105

EXERCISE 8-16
Merchandise inventory on the balance sheet
Objective 8

Based on the data in Exercise 8-15 and assuming that cost was determined by the fifo method, show how the merchandise inventory would appear on the balance sheet.

EXERCISE 8-17
Retail inventory method
Objective 9

A business using the retail method of inventory costing determines that merchandise inventory at retail is $825,750. If the ratio of cost to retail price is 60%, what is the amount of inventory to be reported on the financial statements?

EXERCISE 8-18
Retail inventory method
Objective 9

SPREADSHEET

✓ Inventory, June 30: $227,500

On the basis of the following data, estimate the cost of the merchandise inventory at June 30 by the retail method:

		Cost	Retail
June 1	Merchandise inventory	$160,000	$ 180,000
June 1–30	Purchases (net)	680,000	1,020,000
June 1–30	Sales (net)		875,000

EXERCISE 8-19
Gross profit inventory method
Objective 9

The merchandise inventory was destroyed by fire on May 17. The following data were obtained from the accounting records:

Jan. 1	Merchandise inventory	$ 180,000
Jan. 1–May 17	Purchases (net)	750,000
	Sales (net)	1,250,000
	Estimated gross profit rate	35%

a. Estimate the cost of the merchandise destroyed.
b. Briefly describe the situations in which the gross profit method is useful.

EXERCISE 8-20
Inventory turnover
Objective 10

The following data were taken from recent annual reports of **Apple Computer, Inc.**, a manufacturer of personal computers and related products, and **American Greetings Corporation**, a manufacturer and distributor of greeting cards and related products:

REAL WORLD

	Apple	American Greetings
Cost of goods sold	$4,139,000,000	$881,771,000
Inventory, end of year	45,000,000	278,807,000
Inventory, beginning of the year	11,000,000	290,804,000

a. Determine the inventory turnover for Apple and American Greetings. Round to two decimal places.

b. Would you expect American Greetings' inventory turnover to be higher or lower than Apple's? Why?

EXERCISE 8-21
Inventory turnover and number of days' sales in inventory

Objective 10

REAL WORLD

✓ *a. Albertson's, 43 days' sales in inventory*

Kroger Co., **Albertson's Inc.**, and **Safeway Inc.** are the three largest grocery chains in the United States. Inventory management is an important aspect of the grocery retail business. Recent balance sheets for these three companies indicated the following merchandise inventory information:

	Merchandise Inventory	
	End of Year **(in millions)**	**Beginning of Year** **(in millions)**
Albertson's	$2,973	$3,196
Kroger	4,175	4,178
Safeway	2,558	2,437

The cost of goods sold for each company were:

	Cost of Goods Sold (in millions)
Albertson's	$25,242
Kroger	37,810
Safeway	22,303

a. Determine the number of days' sales in inventory and inventory turnover for the three companies. Round to the nearest day and one decimal place.

b. Interpret your results in (a).

c. If Albertson's had Kroger's number of days' sales in inventory, how much additional cash flow would have been generated from the hypothetically smaller inventory relative to its actual ending inventory position?

roblems Series A

PROBLEM 8-1A
Fifo perpetual inventory

Objectives 3, 4

SPREADSHEET

✓ *3. $240,100*

The beginning inventory of drift boats at Heritage Float Co. and data on purchases and sales for a three-month period are as follows:

Date		Transaction	Number of Units	Per Unit	Total
August	1	Inventory	22	$2,200	$ 48,400
	8	Purchase	18	2,250	40,500
	11	Sale	12	4,800	57,600
	22	Sale	11	4,800	52,800
September	3	Purchase	16	2,300	36,800
	10	Sale	10	5,000	50,000
	21	Sale	5	5,000	25,000
	30	Purchase	20	2,350	47,000
October	5	Sale	20	5,250	105,000
	13	Sale	12	5,250	63,000
	21	Purchase	30	2,400	72,000
	28	Sale	15	5,400	81,000

Instructions

1. Record the inventory, purchases, and cost of merchandise sold data in a perpetual inventory record similar to the one illustrated in Exhibit 3, using the first-in, first-out method.
2. Determine the total sales and the total cost of drift boats sold for the period. Journalize the entries in the sales and cost of merchandise sold accounts. Assume that all sales were on account.
3. Determine the gross profit from sales of drift boats for the period.
4. Determine the ending inventory cost.

PROBLEM 8-2A
Lifo perpetual inventory
Objectives 3, 4

SPREADSHEET

✓ *2. Gross profit, $238,900*

The beginning inventory of drift boats and data on purchases and sales for a three-month period are shown in Problem 8-1A.

Instructions

1. Record the inventory, purchases, and cost of merchandise sold data in a perpetual inventory record similar to the one illustrated in Exhibit 4, using the last-in, first-out method.
2. Determine the total sales, the total cost of drift boats sold, and the gross profit from sales for the period.
3. Determine the ending inventory cost.

PROBLEM 8-3A
Periodic inventory by three methods
Objectives 3, 5

SPREADSHEET

✓ *1. $12,701*

Henning Appliances uses the periodic inventory system. Details regarding the inventory of appliances at January 1, 2006, purchases invoices during the year, and the inventory count at December 31, 2006, are summarized as follows:

Model	Inventory, January 1	Purchases Invoices 1st	2nd	3rd	Inventory Count, December 31
231T	3 at $208	3 at $212	5 at $213	4 at $225	6
673W	2 at 520	2 at 527	2 at 530	2 at 535	4
193Q	6 at 520	8 at 531	4 at 549	6 at 542	7
144Z	9 at 213	7 at 215	6 at 222	6 at 225	11
160M	6 at 305	3 at 310	3 at 316	4 at 317	5
180X	—	4 at 222	4 at 232	—	2
971K	4 at 140	6 at 144	8 at 148	7 at 156	6

Instructions

1. Determine the cost of the inventory on December 31, 2006, by the first-in, first-out method. Present data in columnar form, using the following headings:

Model	Quantity	Unit Cost	Total Cost

If the inventory of a particular model comprises one entire purchase plus a portion of another purchase acquired at a different unit cost, use a separate line for each purchase.
2. Determine the cost of the inventory on December 31, 2006, by the last-in, first-out method, following the procedures indicated in (1).
3. Determine the cost of the inventory on December 31, 2006, by the average cost method, using the columnar headings indicated in (1).
4. ➤ Discuss which method (fifo or lifo) would be preferred for income tax purposes in periods of (a) rising prices and (b) declining prices.

If the working papers correlating with this textbook are not used, omit Problem 8-4A.

PROBLEM 8-4A
Lower-of-cost-or-market inventory
Objective 7
✓ *Total LCM, $38,238*

Data on the physical inventory of Timberline Co. as of December 31, 2006, are presented in the working papers. The quantity of each commodity on hand has been determined and recorded on the inventory sheet. Unit market prices have also been determined as of December 31 and recorded on the sheet. The inventory is to be determined at cost and also at the lower of cost or market, using the first-in, first-out method. Quantity and cost data from the last purchases invoice of the year and the next-to-the-last purchases invoice are summarized as follows:

Instructions

1. Determine the cost of the inventory on April 30, 2006, by the first-in, first-out method. Present data in columnar form, using the following headings:

Model	Quantity	Unit Cost	Total Cost

   If the inventory of a particular model comprises one entire purchase plus a portion of another purchase acquired at a different unit cost, use a separate line for each purchase.

2. Determine the cost of the inventory on April 30, 2006, by the last-in, first-out method, following the procedures indicated in (1).

3. Determine the cost of the inventory on April 30, 2006, by the average cost method, using the columnar headings indicated in (1).

4. ◖▬▬▶ Discuss which method (fifo or lifo) would be preferred for income tax purposes in periods of (a) rising prices and (b) declining prices.

If the working papers correlating with this textbook are not used, omit Problem 8-4B.

PROBLEM 8-4B
Lower-of-cost-or-market inventory
Objective 7
✓ *Total LCM, $38,585*

Data on the physical inventory of Cinnabar Company as of December 31, 2006, are presented in the working papers. The quantity of each commodity on hand has been determined and recorded on the inventory sheet. Unit market prices have also been determined as of December 31 and recorded on the sheet. The inventory is to be determined at cost and also at the lower of cost or market, using the first-in, first-out method. Quantity and cost data from the last purchases invoice of the year and the next-to-the-last purchases invoice are summarized as follows:

	Last Purchases Invoice		Next-to-the-Last Purchases Invoice	
Description	Quantity Purchased	Unit Cost	Quantity Purchased	Unit Cost
A90	25	$ 59	30	$ 58
C18	35	206	20	205
D41	10	144	25	142
E34	150	25	100	24
F17	10	565	10	560
G68	100	15	100	14
K41	10	385	5	384
Q79	500	6	500	6
R72	80	20	50	18
S60	5	250	4	260
W21	100	20	75	19
Z35	7	701	6	699

Instructions

Record the appropriate unit costs on the inventory sheet, and complete the pricing of the inventory. When there are two different unit costs applicable to an item, proceed as follows:

1. Draw a line through the quantity, and insert the quantity and unit cost of the last purchase.

2. On the following line, insert the quantity and unit cost of the next-to-the-last purchase.

3. Total the cost and market columns and insert the lower of the two totals in the Lower of C or M column. The first item on the inventory sheet has been completed as an example.

PROBLEM 8-5B
Retail method; gross profit method
Objective 9

Selected data on merchandise inventory, purchases, and sales for Avalanche Co. and Bridger Co. are as follows:

✓1. $204,000

	Cost	Retail
Avalanche Co.		
Merchandise inventory, October 1	$ 98,000	$ 140,000
Transactions during October:		
Purchases (net)	813,200	1,200,000
Sales		1,080,000
Sales returns and allowances		40,000
Bridger Co.		
Merchandise inventory, August 1	$ 150,000	
Transactions during August and September:		
Purchases (net)	1,375,000	
Sales	1,800,000	
Sales returns and allowances	100,000	
Estimated gross profit rate	35%	

Instructions

1. Determine the estimated cost of the merchandise inventory of Avalanche Co. on October 31 by the retail method, presenting details of the computations.
2. a. Estimate the cost of the merchandise inventory of Bridger Co. on September 30 by the gross profit method, presenting details of the computations.
   b. Assume that Bridger Co. took a physical inventory on September 30 and discovered that $402,600 of merchandise was on hand. What was the estimated loss of inventory due to theft or damage during August and September?

Special Activities

ACTIVITY 8-1
Ethics and professional conduct in business

ETHICS

Follicle Co. is experiencing a decrease in sales and operating income for the fiscal year ending December 31, 2006. Preston Shipley, controller of Follicle Co., has suggested that all orders received before the end of the fiscal year be shipped by midnight, December 31, 2006, even if the shipping department must work overtime. Since Follicle Co. ships all merchandise FOB shipping point, it would record all such shipments as sales for the year ending December 31, 2006, thereby offsetting some of the decreases in sales and operating income.

▬▬▶ Discuss whether Preston Shipley is behaving in a professional manner.

ACTIVITY 8-2
Fifo vs. lifo

REAL WORLD

The following note was taken from the 2002 financial statements of **Walgreen Co.**:

Inventories are valued on a . . . last-in, first-out (LIFO) cost . . . basis. At August 31, 2002 and 2001, inventories would have been greater by $693,500,000 and $637,600,000 respectively, if they had been valued on a lower of first-in, first-out (FIFO) cost or market basis.

Additional data are as follows:

Earnings before income taxes, 2002	$1,637,300,000
Total lifo inventories, August 31, 2002	3,645,200,000

Based on the preceding data, determine (a) what the total inventories at August 31, 2002, would have been, using the fifo method, and (b) what the earnings before income taxes for the year ended August 31, 2002, would have been if fifo had been used instead of lifo.

ACTIVITY 8-3
Lifo and inventory flow

The following is an excerpt from a conversation between Jaime Noll, the warehouse manager for Baltic Wholesale Co., and its accountant, Tara Stroud. Baltic Wholesale operates a large regional warehouse that supplies produce and other grocery products to grocery stores in smaller communities.

Jaime: Tara, can you explain what's going on here with these monthly statements?

Tara: Sure, Jaime. How can I help you?

Jaime: I don't understand this last-in, first-out inventory procedure. It just doesn't make sense.

Tara: Well, what it means is that we assume that the last goods we receive are the first ones sold. So the inventory is made up of the items we purchased first.

Jaime: Yes, but that's my problem. It doesn't work that way! We always distribute the oldest produce first. Some of that produce is perishable! We can't keep any of it very long or it'll spoil.

Tara: Jaime, you don't understand. We only *assume* that the products we distribute are the last ones received. We don't actually have to distribute the goods in this way.

Jaime: I always thought that accounting was supposed to show what really happened. It all sounds like "make believe" to me! Why not report what really happens?

➤ Respond to Jaime's concerns.

ACTIVITY 8-4
Observe internal controls over inventory

GROUP ACTIVITY

Select a business in your community and observe its internal controls over inventory. In groups of three or four, identify and discuss the similarities and differences in each business's inventory controls. Prepare a written summary of your findings.

ACTIVITY 8-5
Costing inventory

Feedbag Company began operations in 2005 by selling a single product. Data on purchases and sales for the year were as follows:

Purchases:

Date	Units Purchased	Unit Cost	Total Cost
April 3	7,750	$24.40	$ 189,100
May 15	8,250	26.00	214,500
June 6	10,000	26.40	264,000
July 10	10,000	28.00	280,000
August 3	6,800	28.50	193,800
October 5	3,200	29.00	92,800
November 1	2,000	29.90	59,800
December 10	2,000	32.00	64,000
	50,000		$1,358,000

Sales:

April	4,000 units
May	4,000
June	5,000
July	6,000
August	7,000
September	7,000
October	4,500
November	2,500
December	2,000
Total units	42,000
Total sales	$1,300,000

On January 3, 2006, the president of the company, Heather Ola, asked for your advice on costing the 8,000-unit physical inventory that was taken on December 31,

2005. Moreover, since the firm plans to expand its product line, she asked for your advice on the use of a perpetual inventory system in the future.

1. Determine the cost of the December 31, 2005 inventory under the periodic system, using the (a) first-in, first-out method, (b) last-in, first-out method, and (c) average cost method.
2. Determine the gross profit for the year under each of the three methods in (1).
3. a. ▭▬▸ Explain varying viewpoints why each of the three inventory costing methods may best reflect the results of operations for 2005.
   b. ▭▬▸ Which of the three inventory costing methods may best reflect the replacement cost of the inventory on the balance sheet as of December 31, 2005?
   c. ▭▬▸ Which inventory costing method would you choose to use for income tax purposes? Why?
   d. ▭▬▸ Discuss the advantages and disadvantages of using a perpetual inventory system. From the data presented in this case, is there any indication of the adequacy of inventory levels during the year?

ACTIVITY 8-6
SAKS Incorporated inventory note

REAL WORLD

SAKS Incorporated disclosed the following note regarding its merchandise inventories for its February 1, 2003 financial statements:

> *Merchandise inventories are . . . stated at the lower of cost (last-in, first-out ["lifo"]), or market and include freight and certain buying and distribution costs. The company also takes markdowns related to slow moving inventory, ensuring an appropriate inventory valuation. At February 1, 2003 and February 2, 2002, the lifo value of inventories exceeded market value and, as a result, inventory was stated at the lower market amount.*
>
> *Consignment merchandise on hand of $112,435 and $110,567 at February 1, 2003, and February 2, 2002, respectively, is not reflected in the consolidated balance sheets.*

a. Why were inventories recorded at market value?
b. What are consignment inventories and why were they excluded from the balance sheet valuation?

ACTIVITY 8-7
Inventory ratios for Dell and HP

REAL WORLD

Dell Computer Corporation and **Hewlett-Packard Company (HP)** are both manufacturers of computer equipment and peripherals. However, the two companies follow two different strategies. Dell follows a build-to-order strategy, where the consumer orders the computer from a Web page. The order is then manufactured and shipped to the customer within days of the order. In contrast, HP follows a build-to-stock strategy, where the computer is first built for inventory, then sold from inventory to retailers, such as **Best Buy**. The two strategies can be seen in the difference between the inventory turnover and number of days' sales in inventory ratios for the two companies. The following financial statement information is provided for Dell and HP for a recent fiscal year (in millions):

	Dell	HP
Inventory, beginning of period	$ 278	$ 5,204
Inventory, end of period	306	5,797
Cost of goods sold	29,055	34,573

a. Determine the inventory turnover ratio and number of days' sales in inventory ratio for each company.
b. Interpret the difference between the ratios for the two companies.

ACTIVITY 8-8
Compare inventory cost flow assumptions

In groups of three or four, examine the financial statements of a well-known retailing business. You may obtain the financial statements you need from one of the following sources:

GROUP ACTIVITY   INTERNET

1. Your school or local library.
2. The investor relations department of the company.
3. The company's Web site on the Internet.
4. EDGAR (Electronic Data Gathering, Analysis, and Retrieval), the electronic archives of financial statements filed with the Securities and Exchange Commission. SEC documents can be retrieved using the EdgarScan service from **Pricewaterhouse-Coopers** at **http://edgarscan.pwcglobal.com**. To obtain annual report information, type in a company name in the appropriate space. EdgarScan will list the reports available to you for the company you've selected. Select the most recent annual report filing, identified as a 10-K or 10-K405. EdgarScan provides an outline of the report, including the separate financial statements. You can double-click the income statement and balance sheet for the selected company into an Excel spreadsheet for further analysis.

 Determine the cost flow assumption(s) that the company is using for its inventory, and determine whether the company is using the lower-of-cost-or-market rule. Prepare a written summary of your findings.

Answers to Self-Examination Questions

1. **D** The overstatement of inventory shrinkage by $7,500 at the end of the year will cause the cost of merchandise sold for the year to be overstated by $7,500, the gross profit for the year to be understated by $7,500, the merchandise inventory to be understated by $7,500, and the net income for the year to be understated by $7,500 (answer D).

2. **A** The fifo method (answer A) is based on the assumption that costs are charged against revenue in the order in which they were incurred. The lifo method (answer B) charges the most recent costs incurred against revenue, and the average cost method (answer C) charges a weighted average of unit costs of items sold against revenue. The perpetual inventory system (answer D) is a system and not a method of costing.

3. **A** The lifo method of costing is based on the assumption that costs should be charged against revenue in the reverse order in which costs were

incurred. Thus, the oldest costs are assigned to inventory. Thirty of the 35 units would be assigned a unit cost of $20 (since 110 of the beginning inventory units were sold on the first sale), and the remaining 5 units would be assigned a cost of $23, for a total of $715 (answer A).

4. **D** The fifo method of costing is based on the assumption that costs should be charged against revenue in the order in which they were incurred (first-in, first-out). Thus, the most recent costs are assigned to inventory. The 35 units would be assigned a unit cost of $23 (answer D).

5. **B** When the price level is steadily rising, the earlier unit costs are lower than recent unit costs. Under the fifo method (answer B), these earlier costs are matched against revenue to yield the highest possible net income. The periodic inventory system (answer D) is a system and not a method of costing.

9

FIXED ASSETS AND INTANGIBLE ASSETS

objectives

After studying this chapter, you should be able to:

1   Define fixed assets and describe the accounting for their cost.

2   Compute depreciation, using the following methods: straight-line method, units-of-production method, and declining-balance method.

3   Classify fixed asset costs as either capital expenditures or revenue expenditures.

4   Journalize entries for the disposal of fixed assets.

5   Define a lease and summarize the accounting rules related to the leasing of fixed assets.

6   Describe internal controls over fixed assets.

7   Compute depletion and journalize the entry for depletion.

8   Describe the accounting for intangible assets, such as patents, copyrights, and goodwill.

9   Describe how depreciation expense is reported in an income statement, and prepare a balance sheet that includes fixed assets and intangible assets.

10   Compute and interpret the ratio of fixed assets to long-term liabilities.

Assume that you are a certified flight instructor and you would like to earn a little extra money by teaching people how to fly. Since you don't own an airplane, one of the pilots at the local airport is willing to let you use her airplane for a fixed fee per year. You will also have to pay your share of the annual operating costs, based on hours flown. In addition, the owner will consider your request for upgrading the plane's equipment. At the end of the year, the owner has the right to cancel the agreement.

One of your friends is an airplane mechanic. He is familiar with the plane and has indicated that it needs its annual inspection. There is some structural damage on the right aileron. In addition to this repair, you would like to equip the plane with another radio and a better navigation system.

Since you will not have any ownership in the airplane, it is important for you to distinguish between normal operating costs and costs that add future value or worth to the airplane. These latter costs should be the responsibility of the owner. In this case, you should be willing to pay for part of the cost of the annual inspection. The cost of repairing the structural damage and upgrading the navigation system should be the responsibility of the owner.

Businesses also distinguish between the cost of a fixed asset and the cost of operating the asset. In this chapter, we discuss how to determine the portion of a fixed asset's cost that becomes an expense over a period of time. We also discuss accounting for the disposal of fixed assets and accounting for intangible assets, such as patents and copyrights.

Nature of Fixed Assets

objective	**1**

Define fixed assets and describe the accounting for their cost.

Businesses use a variety of fixed assets, such as equipment, furniture, tools, machinery, buildings, and land. **Fixed assets** are long-term or relatively permanent assets. They are **tangible assets** because they exist physically. They are owned and used by the business and are not offered for sale as part of normal operations. Other descriptive titles for these assets are **plant assets** or **property, plant, and equipment**.

The fixed assets of a business can be a significant part of the total assets. Exhibit 1 shows the percent of fixed assets to total assets for some select companies, divided between service, manufacturing, and merchandising firms. As you can see, the fixed

•Exhibit 1   Fixed Assets as a Percent of Total Assets—Selected Companies

	Fixed Assets as a Percentage of Total Assets
Service Firms	
Pacific Gas and Electric Co.	47%
Sprint Corporation	59%
Computer Associates	6%
Manufacturing Firms	
Sun Microsystems Inc.	15%
Boeing Co.	21%
Dupont E I De Nemours & Co.	36%
Merchandising Firms	
Barnes & Noble Inc.	49%
Kroger Company	48%
Wal-Mart Stores Inc.	52%

St. Mary's Hospital maintains an auxiliary generator for use in electrical outages. Such outages are rare, and the generator has not been used for the past two years. Should the generator be reported as a fixed asset on St. Mary's balance sheet?

Yes. Even though the generator has not been used recently, it should be reported as a fixed asset.

assets for most firms comprise a significant proportion of their total assets. In contrast, **Computer Associates** is a consulting firm that relies less on fixed assets to deliver value to customers.

Classifying Costs

Exhibit 2 displays questions that help classify costs. If the purchased item is long-lived, then it should be *capitalized*, which means it should appear on the balance sheet as an asset. Otherwise, the cost should be reported as an expense on the income statement. Capitalized costs are normally expected to last more than a year. If the asset is also used for a productive purpose, which involves a repeated use or benefit, then it should be classified as a fixed asset, such as land, buildings, or equipment. An asset need not actually be used on an ongoing basis or even often. For example, standby equipment for use in the event of a breakdown of regular equipment or for use only during peak periods is included in fixed assets. Fixed assets that have been abandoned or are no longer used should not be classified as a fixed asset.

•Exhibit 2   **Classifying Costs**

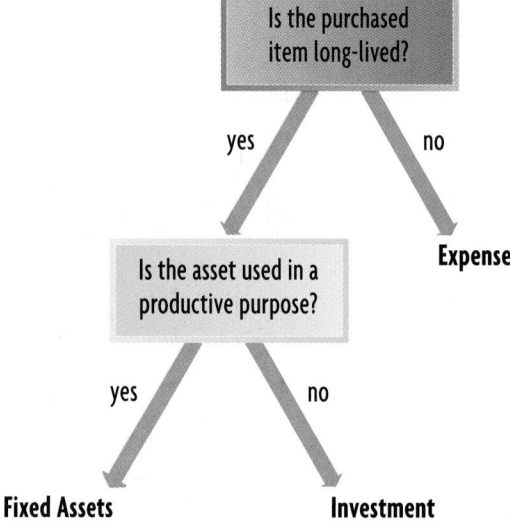

Fixed assets are owned and used by the business and are not offered for resale. Long-lived assets held for resale are not classified as fixed assets, but should be listed on the balance sheet in a section entitled *investments*. For example, undeveloped land acquired as an investment for resale would be classified as an investment, not land.

The Cost of Fixed Assets

The costs of acquiring fixed assets include all amounts spent to get the asset in place and ready for use. For example, freight costs and the costs of installing equipment are included as part of the asset's total cost. The direct costs associated with new construction, such as labor and materials, should be debited to a "construction in progress" asset account. When the construction is complete, the costs should be reclassified by crediting the construction in progress account and debiting the appropriate fixed asset account. For growing companies, construction in progress can be significant. For example, **Intel Corporation** disclosed $2.7 billion of construction in progress, which was over 15 percent of its total fixed assets.

The details of fixed assets are disclosed on the face of the balance sheet or the notes to the financial statements. For example, **Marriott International Inc.** had the following fixed asset disclosures on a recent balance sheet:

	($ in millions)
Land	$ 386
Buildings	547
Furniture and equipment	676
Timeshare properties	1,270
Construction in progress	180
Total	$3,059

These categories are typical for a lodging company. Other types of companies would have categories to fit their particular business.

Exhibit 3 summarizes some of the common costs of acquiring fixed assets. These costs should be recorded by debiting the related fixed asset account, such as Land,[1] Building, Land Improvements, or Machinery and Equipment.

Only costs necessary for preparing a long-lived asset for use should be included as a cost of the asset. Unnecessary costs that do not increase the asset's usefulness are recorded as an expense. For example, the following costs are included as an expense:

- Vandalism
- Mistakes in installation
- Uninsured theft
- Damage during unpacking and installing
- Fines for not obtaining proper permits from governmental agencies

Founded in 1849 in Brooklyn, my first product was an anti-parasitic. By 1900, I mainly sold citric acid, camphor, cream of tartar, borax, and iodine. I began making penicillin during World War II and was soon the world's largest producer of it. My animal products division began in 1952. My portfolio, including Lipitor, Norvasc, Zithromax, Diflucan, Viracept, Zoloft, Aricept, Celebrex, and Zyrtec, features many of the world's top-selling medicines. Eight generate more than $1 billion in sales annually each. To help low-income Americans, I introduced my Share Card program in 2002. My annual sales top $30 billion and I'm buying Pharmacia Corp. Who am I? (Go to page 382 for answer.)

Donated Assets

Civic groups and municipalities sometimes give land or buildings to a corporation as an incentive to locate or remain in a community. In such cases, the corporation debits the assets for their fair market value and credits a revenue account.[2] To illustrate, assume that on April 20 the city of Moraine donates land to Merrick Corporation as an incentive to relocate its headquarters to Moraine. The land was valued at $500,000. Merrick Corporation would record the land as follows:

Apr.	20	Land		500 0 0 0 00	
		Revenue from Donated Land			500 0 0 0 00

Nature of Depreciation

As we have discussed in earlier chapters, land has an unlimited life and therefore can provide unlimited services. On the other hand, other fixed assets such as equipment, buildings, and land improvements lose their ability, over time, to provide services. As a result, the costs of equipment, buildings, and land improvements should be transferred to expense accounts in a systematic manner during their expected useful lives. This periodic transfer of cost to expense is called ***depreciation***.

The adjusting entry to record depreciation is usually made at the end of each month or at the end of the year. This entry debits *Depreciation Expense* and credits a *contra asset* account entitled *Accumulated Depreciation* or *Allowance for Depreciation*. The use of a contra asset account allows the original cost to remain unchanged in the fixed asset account.

> **The adjusting entry to record depreciation debits Depreciation Expense and credits Accumulated Depreciation.**

---

[1]As discussed here, land is assumed to be used only as a location or site and not for its mineral deposits or other natural resources.

[2]*Statement of Financial Accounting Standards No. 116*, "Accounting for Contributions Received and Contributions Made," Financial Accounting Standards Board (Norwalk, Connecticut: 1993).

•Exhibit 3   Costs of Acquiring Fixed Assets

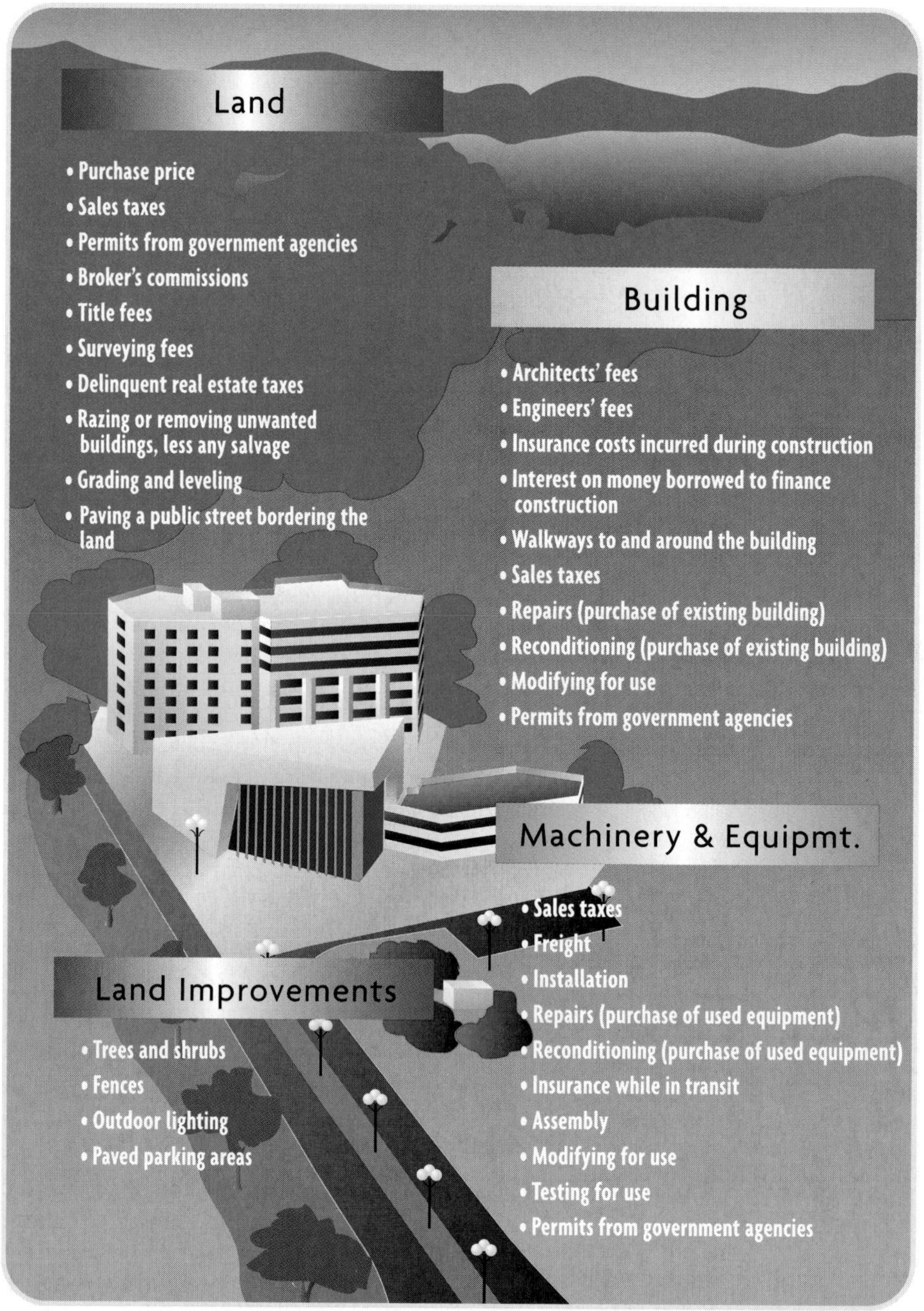

Land

- Purchase price
- Sales taxes
- Permits from government agencies
- Broker's commissions
- Title fees
- Surveying fees
- Delinquent real estate taxes
- Razing or removing unwanted buildings, less any salvage
- Grading and leveling
- Paving a public street bordering the land

Building

- Architects' fees
- Engineers' fees
- Insurance costs incurred during construction
- Interest on money borrowed to finance construction
- Walkways to and around the building
- Sales taxes
- Repairs (purchase of existing building)
- Reconditioning (purchase of existing building)
- Modifying for use
- Permits from government agencies

Machinery & Equipmt.

- Sales taxes
- Freight
- Installation
- Repairs (purchase of used equipment)
- Reconditioning (purchase of used equipment)
- Insurance while in transit
- Assembly
- Modifying for use
- Testing for use
- Permits from government agencies

Land Improvements

- Trees and shrubs
- Fences
- Outdoor lighting
- Paved parking areas

REAL WORLD

Companies often use different useful lives for similar assets. For example, the primary useful life for buildings is 50 years for **J.C.Penney Co.**, while the useful life for buildings for **Radio Shack** varies from 10 to 40 years.

Factors that cause a decline in the ability of a fixed asset to provide services may be identified as physical depreciation or functional depreciation. **Physical depreciation** occurs from wear and tear while in use and from the action of the weather. **Functional depreciation** occurs when a fixed asset is no longer able to provide services at the level for which it was intended. For example, a personal computer made in the 1980s would not be able to provide an Internet connection. Such advances in technology during this century have made functional depreciation an increasingly important cause of depreciation.

The term *depreciation* as used in accounting is often misunderstood because the same term is also used in business to mean a decline in the market value of an asset. However, the amount of a fixed asset's unexpired cost reported in the balance

sheet usually does not agree with the amount that could be realized from its sale. Fixed assets are held for use in a business rather than for sale. It is assumed that the business will continue as a going concern. Thus, a decision to dispose of a fixed asset is based mainly on the usefulness of the asset to the business and not on its market value.

Another common misunderstanding is that accounting for depreciation provides cash needed to replace fixed assets as they wear out. This misunderstanding probably occurs because depreciation, unlike most expenses, does not require an outlay of cash in the period in which it is recorded. The cash account is neither increased nor decreased by the periodic entries that transfer the cost of fixed assets to depreciation expense accounts.

Accounting for Depreciation

objective 2

Compute depreciation, using the following methods: straight-line method, units-of-production method, and declining-balance method.

Three factors are considered in determining the amount of depreciation expense to be recognized each period. These three factors are (a) the fixed asset's initial cost, (b) its expected useful life, and (c) its estimated value at the end of its useful life. This third factor is called the **residual value**, **scrap value**, **salvage value**, or **trade-in value**. Exhibit 4 shows the relationship among the three factors and the periodic depreciation expense.

A fixed asset's ***residual value*** at the end of its expected useful life must be estimated at the time the asset is placed in service. If a fixed asset is expected to have little or no residual value when it is taken out of service, then its initial cost should be spread over its expected useful life as depreciation expense. If, however, a fixed asset is expected to have a significant residual value, the difference between its initial cost and its residual value, called the asset's **depreciable cost**, is the amount that is spread over the asset's useful life as depreciation expense.

•Exhibit 4

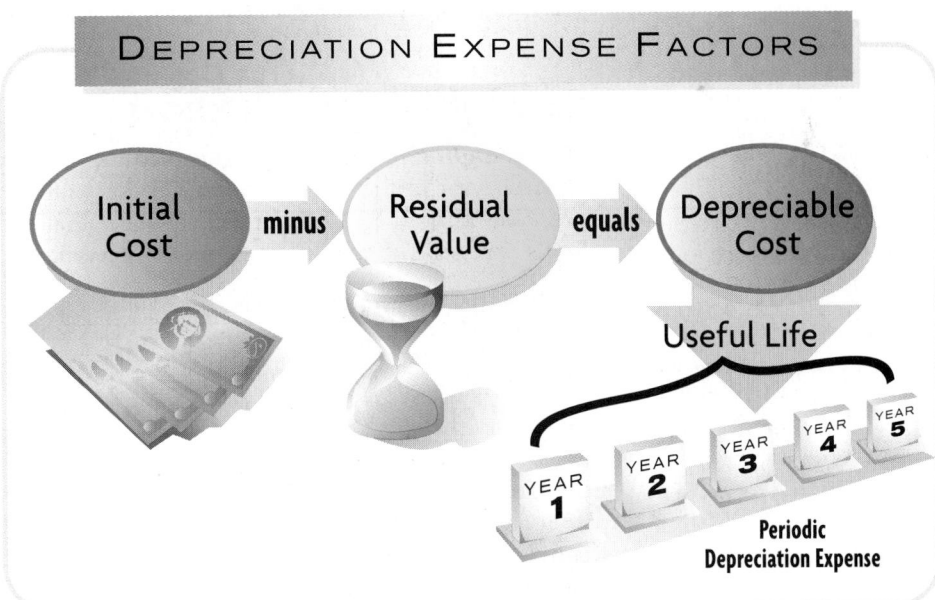

A fixed asset's **expected useful life** must also be estimated at the time the asset is placed in service. Estimates of expected useful lives are available from various trade associations and other publications. For federal income tax purposes, the Internal Revenue Service has established guidelines for useful lives. These guidelines may also be helpful in determining depreciation for financial reporting purposes.

The Internal Revenue Service guideline for the useful life of automobiles and light-duty trucks is 5 years, while the designated life for most machinery and equipment is 7 years.

In practice, many businesses use the guideline that all assets placed in or taken out of service during the first half of a month are treated as if the event occurred on the first day of *that* month. That is, these businesses compute depreciation on these assets for the entire month. Likewise, all fixed asset additions and deductions during the second half of a month are treated as if the event occurred on the first day of the *next* month. We will follow this practice in this chapter.

It is not necessary that a business use a single method of computing depreciation for all its depreciable assets. The methods used in the accounts and financial statements may also differ from the methods used in determining income taxes and property taxes. The three methods used most often are (1) straight-line, (2) units-of-production, and (3) declining-balance.[3] Exhibit 5 shows the extent of the use of these methods in financial statements.

•Exhibit 5   Use of Depreciation Methods

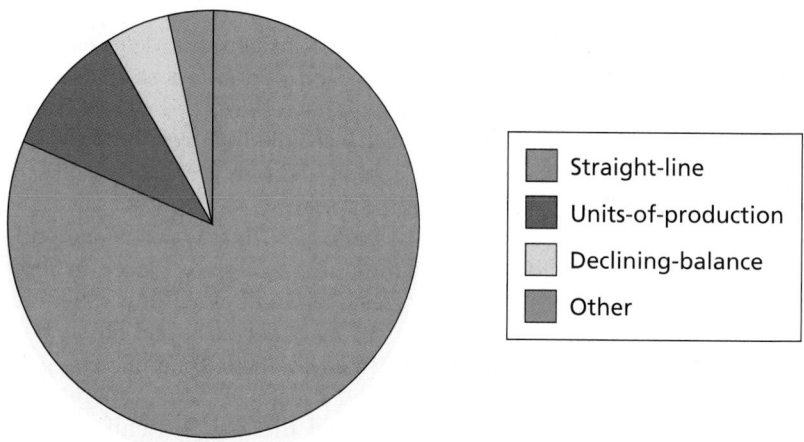

Legend:
- Straight-line
- Units-of-production
- Declining-balance
- Other

Source: *Accounting Trends & Techniques*, 56th ed., American Institute of Certified Public Accountants, New York, 2002.

Straight-Line Method

The ***straight-line method*** provides for the same amount of depreciation expense for each year of the asset's useful life. For example, assume that the cost of a depreciable asset is $24,000, its estimated residual value is $2,000, and its estimated life is 5 years. The annual depreciation is computed as follows:

$$\frac{\$24{,}000 \text{ cost} - \$2{,}000 \text{ estimated residual value}}{5 \text{ years estimated life}} = \$4{,}400 \text{ annual depreciation}$$

When an asset is used for only part of a year, the annual depreciation is prorated. For example, assume that the fiscal year ends on December 31 and that the asset in the above example is placed in service on October 1. The depreciation for the first fiscal year of use would be $1,100 ($4,400 × 3/12).

For ease in applying the straight-line method, the annual depreciation may be converted to a percentage of the depreciable cost. This percentage is determined by dividing 100% by the number of years of useful life. For example, a useful life of 20 years converts to a 5% rate (100%/20), 8 years converts to a 12.5% rate (100%/8), and so on.[4] In the above example, the annual depreciation of $4,400 can be computed by multiplying the depreciable cost of $22,000 by 20% (100%/5).

A truck that cost $35,000 has a residual value of $5,000 and a useful life of 12 years. What are (a) the depreciable cost, (b) the straight-line rate, and (c) the annual straight-line depreciation?

- - - - - - - - - - - - - - - - - - - -

(a) $30,000 ($35,000 − $5,000), (b) 8¹/₃% (¹/₁₂), (c) $2,500 ($30,000 × 8¹/₃%).

---

[3]Another method not often used today, called the *sum-of-the-years-digits method*, is described and illustrated in the appendix at the end of this chapter.

[4]The depreciation rate may also be expressed as a fraction. For example, the annual straight-line rate for an asset with a 3-year useful life is 1/3.

The straight-line method is simple and is widely used. It provides a reasonable transfer of costs to periodic expense when the asset's use and the related revenues from its use are about the same from period to period.

Units-of-Production Method

How would you depreciate a fixed asset when its service is related to use rather than time? When the amount of use of a fixed asset varies from year to year, the units-of-production method is more appropriate than the straight-line method. In such cases, the units-of-production method better matches the depreciation expense with the related revenue.

The ***units-of-production method*** provides for the same amount of depreciation expense for each unit produced or each unit of capacity used by the asset. To apply this method, the useful life of the asset is expressed in terms of units of productive capacity such as hours or miles. The total depreciation expense for each accounting period is then determined by multiplying the unit depreciation by the number of units produced or used during the period. For example, assume that a machine with a cost of $24,000 and an estimated residual value of $2,000 is expected to have an estimated life of 10,000 operating hours. The depreciation for a unit of one hour is computed as follows:

$$\frac{\$24,000 \text{ cost} - \$2,000 \text{ estimated residual value}}{10,000 \text{ estimated hours}} = \$2.20 \text{ hourly depreciation}$$

Assuming that the machine was in operation for 2,100 hours during a year, the depreciation for that year would be $4,620 ($2.20 × 2,100 hours).

Declining-Balance Method

The ***declining-balance method*** provides for a declining periodic expense over the estimated useful life of the asset. To apply this method, the annual straight-line depreciation rate is doubled. For example, the declining-balance rate for an asset with an estimated life of 5 years is 40%, which is double the straight-line rate of 20% (100%/5).

For the first year of use, the cost of the asset is multiplied by the declining-balance rate. After the first year, the declining ***book value*** (cost minus accumulated depreciation) of the asset is multiplied by this rate. To illustrate, the annual declining-balance depreciation for an asset with an estimated 5-year life and a cost of $24,000 is shown below.

Year	Cost	Accum. Depr. at Beginning of Year	Book Value at Beginning of Year		Rate	Depreciation for Year	Book Value at End of Year
1	$24,000		$24,000.00	×	40%	$9,600.00	$14,400.00
2	24,000	$ 9,600.00	14,400.00	×	40%	5,760.00	8,640.00
3	24,000	15,360.00	8,640.00	×	40%	3,456.00	5,184.00
4	24,000	18,816.00	5,184.00	×	40%	2,073.60	3,110.40
5	24,000	20,889.60	3,110.40	—		1,110.40	2,000.00

You should note that when the declining-balance method is used, the estimated residual value is *not* considered in determining the depreciation rate. It is also ignored in computing the periodic depreciation. However, the asset should not be depreciated below its estimated residual value. In the above example, the estimated residual value was $2,000. Therefore, the depreciation for the fifth year is $1,110.40 ($3,110.40 − $2,000.00) instead of $1,244.16 (40% × $3,110.40).

In the example above, we assumed that the first use of the asset occurred at the beginning of the fiscal year. This is normally not the case in practice, however, and depreciation for the first partial year of use must be computed. For example, assume that the asset above was in service at the end of the *third* month of the fiscal year. In this case, only a portion (9/12) of the first full year's depreciation of $9,600 is allocated to the first fiscal year. Thus, depreciation of $7,200 (9/12 × $9,600) is allocated to the first partial year of use. The depreciation for the second fiscal year would then be $6,720 [40% × ($24,000 − $7,200)].

Comparing Depreciation Methods

The straight-line method provides for the same periodic amounts of depreciation expense over the life of the asset. The units-of-production method provides for periodic amounts of depreciation expense that vary, depending upon the amount the asset is used.

The declining-balance method provides for a higher depreciation amount in the first year of the asset's use, followed by a gradually declining amount. For this reason, the declining-balance method is called an ***accelerated depreciation method***. It is most appropriate when the decline in an asset's productivity or earning power is greater in the early years of its use than in later years. Further, using this method is often justified because repairs tend to increase with the age of an asset. The reduced amounts of depreciation in later years are thus offset to some extent by increased repair expenses.

The periodic depreciation amounts for the straight-line method and the declining-balance method are compared in Exhibit 6. This comparison is based on an asset cost of $24,000, an estimated life of 5 years, and an estimated residual value of $2,000.

•Exhibit 6 Comparing Depreciation Methods

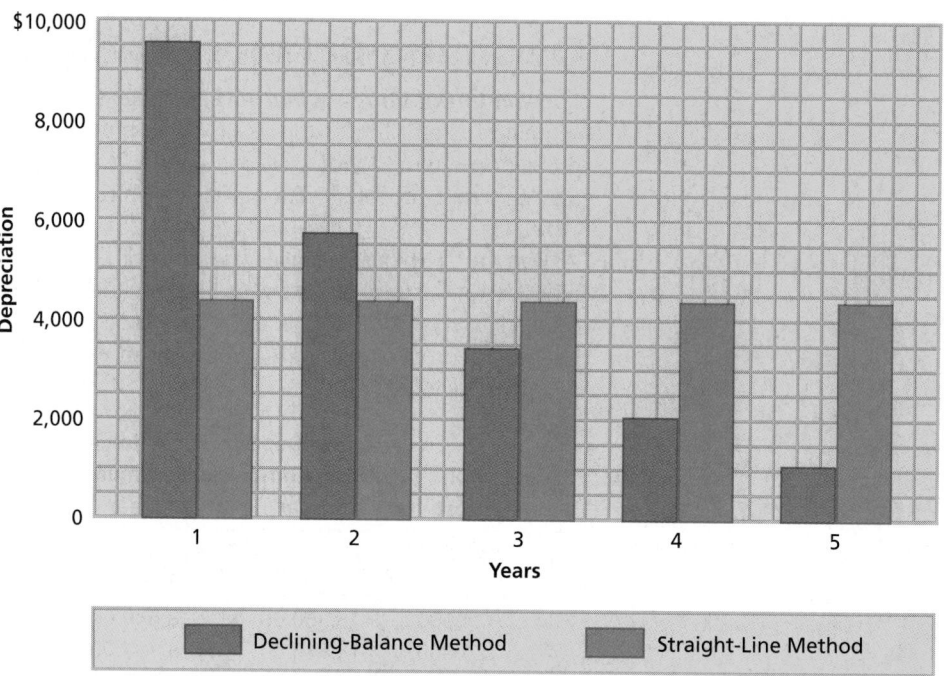

Depreciation for Federal Income Tax

The Internal Revenue Code specifies the *Modified Accelerated Cost Recovery System (MACRS)* for use by businesses in computing depreciation for tax purposes. MACRS specifies eight classes of useful life and depreciation rates for each class. The two most common classes, other than real estate, are the 5-year class and the 7-year class.[5] The 5-year class includes automobiles and light-duty trucks, and the

---

[5]Real estate is in 27½-year classes and 31½-year classes and is depreciated by the straight-line method.

Tax Code Section 179 allows a business to deduct up to $100,000 of the cost of qualified property in the year it is placed in service.

7-year class includes most machinery and equipment. The depreciation deduction for these two classes is similar to that computed using the declining-balance method.

In using the MACRS rates, residual value is ignored, and all fixed assets are assumed to be put in and taken out of service in the middle of the year. For the 5-year-class assets, depreciation is spread over six years, as shown in the following MACRS schedule of depreciation rates:

Year	5-Year-Class Depreciation Rates
1	20.0%
2	32.0
3	19.2
4	11.5
5	11.5
6	5.8
	100.0%

What is the third year's MACRS depreciation for an automobile that cost $26,000 and has a residual value of $6,500?

$4,992 ($26,000 × 19.2%)

To simplify its record keeping, a business will sometimes use the MACRS method for both financial statement and tax purposes. This is acceptable if MACRS does not result in significantly different amounts than would have been reported using one of the three depreciation methods discussed earlier in this chapter.

Using MACRS for both financial statement and tax purposes may, however, hurt a business. In one case, a business that had used MACRS depreciation for its financial statements lost a $1 million order because its fixed assets had low book values. The bank viewed these low book values as inadequate, so it would not loan the business the amount needed to produce the order.

Revising Depreciation Estimates

Revising the estimates of the residual value and the useful life is normal. When these estimates are revised, they are used to determine the depreciation expense in future periods. They do not affect the amounts of depreciation expense recorded in earlier years.

To illustrate, assume that a fixed asset purchased for $130,000 was originally estimated to have a useful life of 30 years and a residual value of $10,000. The asset has been depreciated at $4,000 per year [($130,000 − $10,000) ÷ 30 years] for 10 years by the straight-line method. At the end of ten years, the asset's book value (undepreciated cost) is $90,000, determined as follows:

For the $130,000 asset in the example on this page, assume that after 10 more years (20 years in total) its remaining useful life is estimated at 5 years with no residual value. What is the revised depreciation for the twenty-first year?

$11,200 ($130,000 − $40,000 depreciation for years 1–10 = $90,000; $90,000 − $34,000 depreciation for years 11–20 = $56,000; $56,000 divided by 5 years = $11,200)

Asset cost	$130,000
Less accumulated depreciation ($4,000 per year × 10 years)	40,000
Book value (undepreciated cost), end of tenth year	$ 90,000

During the eleventh year, it is estimated that the remaining useful life is 25 years (instead of 20) and that the residual value is $5,000 (instead of $10,000). The depreciation expense for each of the remaining 25 years is $3,400, computed as follows:

Book value (undepreciated cost), end of tenth year	$90,000
Less revised estimated residual value	5,000
Revised remaining depreciable cost	$85,000
Remaining years	÷ 25
Revised annual depreciation expense	$ 3,400

Apr.	1	Crane		150 0 0 0 00	
		Cash			150 0 0 0 00

Identify each of the items related to a truck as capitalized or expensed: (a) a snowplow attachment that allows the truck to be used for snow removal, (b) a new transmission, (c) a hydraulic hitch to replace a manual hitch, (d) the cost of scheduled maintenance.

(a) capitalize (new component),
(b) capitalize (replaced component),
(c) capitalize (replaced component),
(d) expense (normal repair)

A company can also *replace a component*. Replacements are accounted for in two steps. First, the book value of the replaced component is debited to Depreciation Expense and credited to Accumulated Depreciation. This treatment is consistent with a change of estimate. That is, the fixed asset component is now recognized as being fully depreciated upon replacement. In addition, any costs to remove the old component should be charged to expense. Second, the identifiable direct costs associated with the new component are then capitalized. To illustrate, assume that Boxter removes a warehouse roof on August 1 at a cost of $1,000. As of August 1, the old roof has a remaining book value ($40,000 initial cost less $31,000 accumulated depreciation) of $9,000. On August 5, the new roof is completed at a cost of $60,000 and is estimated to have a 20-year life, which is the remaining life of the building. First, the cost of removing the old roof must be expensed, and the book value of the replaced roof must be completely depreciated, as follows:

Aug.	1	Removal Expenses		1 0 0 0 00	
		Cash			1 0 0 0 00
	1	Depreciation Expense		9 0 0 0 00	
		Accumulated Depreciation—Warehouse			9 0 0 0 00

After the preceding entry, the book value of the old roof is zero ($40,000 cost less $40,000 accumulated depreciation). Since the old roof is being replaced, its cost and related depreciation must now be removed from the accounting records, as shown in the following entry:

		Accumulated Depreciation—Warehouse		40 0 0 0 00	
		Warehouse			40 0 0 0 00

Next, the cost of the new roof must be capitalized as a separate component as follows:

Aug.	5	Warehouse		60 0 0 0 00	
		Cash			60 0 0 0 00

Using the straight-line method, the new roof will be depreciated over 20 years at $3,000 per year ($60,000 ÷ 20 years).

Disposal of Fixed Assets

objective 4

Journalize entries for the disposal of fixed assets.

Fixed assets that are no longer useful may be discarded, sold, or traded for other fixed assets. The details of the entry to record a disposal will vary. In all cases, however, the book value of the asset must be removed from the accounts. The entry for this purpose debits the asset's accumulated depreciation account for its balance on the date of disposal and credits the asset account for the cost of the asset.

> The entry to record the disposal of a fixed asset removes the cost of the asset and its accumulated depreciation from the accounts.

A fixed asset should not be removed from the accounts only because it has been fully depreciated. If the asset is still used by the business, the cost and accumulated depreciation should remain in the ledger. This maintains accountability for the asset in the ledger. If the book value of the asset was removed from the ledger, the accounts would contain no evidence of the continued existence of the asset. In addition, the cost and the accumulated depreciation data on such assets are often needed for property tax and income tax reports.

Discarding Fixed Assets

When fixed assets are no longer useful to the business and have no residual or market value, they are discarded. To illustrate, assume that an item of equipment acquired at a cost of $25,000 is fully depreciated at December 31, the end of the preceding fiscal year. On February 14, the equipment is discarded. The entry to record this is as follows:

Feb.	14	Accumulated Depreciation—Equipment	25 000 00	
		Equipment		25 000 00
		To write off equipment discarded.		

If an asset has not been fully depreciated, depreciation should be recorded prior to removing it from service and from the accounting records. To illustrate, assume that equipment costing $6,000 is depreciated at an annual straight-line rate of 10%. In addition, assume that on December 31 of the preceding fiscal year, the accumulated depreciation balance, after adjusting entries, is $4,750. Finally, assume that the asset is removed from service on the following March 24. The entry to record the depreciation for the three months of the current period prior to the asset's removal from service is as follows:

Mar.	24	Depreciation Expense—Equipment	1 5 0 00	
		Accumulated Depreciation—Equipment		1 5 0 00
		To record current depreciation on		
		equipment discarded ($600 × 3/12).		

The discarding of the equipment is then recorded by the following entry:

Mar.	24	Accumulated Depreciation—Equipment	4 900 00	
		Loss on Disposal of Fixed Assets	1 100 00	
		Equipment		6 000 00
		To write off equipment discarded.		

The loss of $1,100 is recorded because the balance of the accumulated depreciation account ($4,900) is less than the balance in the equipment account ($6,000). Losses on the discarding of fixed assets are nonoperating items and are normally reported in the Other Expense section of the income statement.

Selling Fixed Assets

The entry to record the sale of a fixed asset is similar to the entries illustrated above, except that the cash or other asset received must also be recorded. If the selling price is more than the book value of the asset, the transaction results in a gain. If the selling price is less than the book value, there is a loss.

To illustrate, assume that equipment is acquired at a cost of $10,000 and is depreciated at an annual straight-line rate of 10%. The equipment is sold for cash on October 12 of the eighth year of its use. The balance of the accumulated depreciation account as of the preceding December 31 is $7,000. The entry to update the depreciation for the nine months of the current year is as follows:

Oct.	12	Depreciation Expense—Equipment	7 5 0 00	
		Accumulated Depreciation—Equipment		7 5 0 00
		To record current depreciation on		
		equipment sold ($10,000 × ¾ × 10%).		

After the current depreciation is recorded, the book value of the asset is $2,250 ($10,000 − $7,750). The entries to record the sale, assuming three different selling prices, are as follows:

Sold at book value, for $2,250. No gain or loss.

Oct.	12	Cash	2 2 5 0 00	
		Accumulated Depreciation—Equipment	7 7 5 0 00	
		Equipment		10 0 0 0 00

Sold below book value, for $1,000. Loss of $1,250.

Oct.	12	Cash	1 0 0 0 00	
		Accumulated Depreciation—Equipment	7 7 5 0 00	
		Loss on Disposal of Fixed Assets	1 2 5 0 00	
		Equipment		10 0 0 0 00

Sold above book value, for $2,800. Gain of $550.

Oct.	12	Cash	2 8 0 0 00	
		Accumulated Depreciation—Equipment	7 7 5 0 00	
		Equipment		10 0 0 0 00
		Gain on Disposal of Fixed Assets		5 5 0 00

Exchanging Similar Fixed Assets

Old equipment is often traded in for new equipment having a similar use. In such cases, the seller allows the buyer an amount for the old equipment traded in. This amount, called the **trade-in allowance**, may be either greater or less than the book value of the old equipment. The remaining balance—the amount owed—is either paid in cash or recorded as a liability. It is normally called **boot**, which is its tax name.

REAL WORLD

Gains on exchanges of similar fixed assets are also not recognized for federal income tax purposes.

Gains on Exchanges

Gains on exchanges of similar fixed assets are not recognized for financial reporting purposes.[7] This is based on the theory that revenue occurs from the production and sale of goods produced by fixed assets and not from the exchange of similar fixed assets.

When the trade-in allowance exceeds the book value of an asset traded in and no gain is recognized, the cost recorded for the new asset can be determined in either of two ways:

---

[7]Gains on exchanges of similar fixed assets are recognized if cash (boot) is received. This topic is discussed in advanced accounting texts.

> 1. Cost of new asset = List price of new asset − Unrecognized gain
>
> *or*
>
> 2. Cost of new asset = Cash given (or liability assumed) + Book value of old asset

To illustrate, assume the following exchange:

Similar equipment acquired (new):

List price of new equipment	$5,000
Trade-in allowance on old equipment	1,100
Cash paid at June 19, date of exchange	$3,900

Equipment traded in (old):

Cost of old equipment	$4,000
Accumulated depreciation at date of exchange	3,200
Book value at June 19, date of exchange	$ 800

Recorded cost of new equipment:

Method One:

List price of new equipment		$5,000
Trade-in allowance	$1,100	
Book value of old equipment	800	
Unrecognized gain on exchange		(300)
Cost of new equipment		$4,700

Method Two:

Book value of old equipment	$ 800
Cash paid at date of exchange	3,900
Cost of new equipment	$4,700

The entry to record this exchange and the payment of cash is as follows:

June	19	Accumulated Depreciation—Equipment	3 2 0 0 00		
		Equipment (new equipment)	4 7 0 0 00		
		Equipment (old equipment)		4 0 0 0 00	
		Cash		3 9 0 0 00	
		To record exchange of equipment.			

Equipment with a book value of $14,000 is traded in for similar equipment with a list price of $50,000. A trade-in allowance of $15,000 was allowed on the old equipment. What is the cost of the new equipment to be recorded in the accounts?

$49,000 ($50,000 − $1,000 gain, or $14,000 + $35,000 boot)

Not recognizing the $300 gain ($1,100 trade-in allowance minus $800 book value) at the time of the exchange reduces future depreciation expense. That is, the depreciation expense for the new asset is based on a cost of $4,700 rather than on the list price of $5,000. In effect, the unrecognized gain of $300 reduces the total amount of depreciation taken during the life of the equipment by $300.

Losses on Exchanges

For financial reporting purposes, losses are recognized on exchanges of similar fixed assets if the trade-in allowance is less than the book value of the old equipment. When there is a loss, the cost recorded for the new asset should be the market (list) price. To illustrate, assume the following exchange:

REAL WORLD

Losses on exchanges of similar fixed assets are *not* recognized for federal income tax purposes.

Similar equipment acquired (new):

List price of new equipment	$10,000
Trade-in allowance on old equipment	2,000
Cash paid at September 7, date of exchange	$ 8,000

whether to replace the asset. A company that maintains a computerized subsidiary ledger may use bar-coded tags, similar to the one on the back of this textbook, so that fixed asset data can be directly scanned into computer records.

Fixed assets should be insured against theft, fire, flooding, or other disasters. They should also be safeguarded from theft, misuse, or other damage. For example, fixed assets that are highly open to theft, such as computers, should be locked or otherwise protected when not in use. For computers, safeguarding also includes climate controls and special fire-extinguishing equipment. Procedures should also exist for training employees to properly operate fixed assets such as equipment and machinery.

A physical inventory of fixed assets should be taken periodically in order to verify the accuracy of the accounting records. Such an inventory would detect missing, obsolete, or idle fixed assets. In addition, fixed assets should be inspected periodically in order to determine their condition.

Careful control should also be exercised over the disposal of fixed assets. All disposals should be properly authorized and approved. Fully depreciated assets should be retained in the accounting records until disposal has been authorized and they are removed from service.

Natural Resources

objective 7

Compute depletion and journalize the entry for depletion.

A business purchased mineral rights to 250,000 tons of ore for $1,500,000. If 35,000 tons of ore were mined in the first year, what are (a) the depletion rate per ton and (2) the depletion expense for the first year?

(a) $6 per ton ($1,500,000/ 250,000 tons); (b) $210,000 (35,000 tons × $6)

The fixed assets of some businesses include timber, metal ores, minerals, or other natural resources. As these businesses harvest or mine and then sell these resources, a portion of the cost of acquiring them must be debited to an expense account. This process of transferring the cost of natural resources to an expense account is called *depletion*. The amount of depletion is determined by multiplying the quantity extracted during the period by the depletion rate. This rate is computed by dividing the cost of the mineral deposit by its estimated size.

Computing depletion is similar to computing units-of-production depreciation. To illustrate, assume that a business paid $400,000 for the mining rights to a mineral deposit estimated at 1,000,000 tons of ore. The depletion rate is $0.40 per ton ($400,000/1,000,000 tons). If 90,000 tons are mined during the year, the periodic depletion is $36,000 (90,000 tons × $0.40). The entry to record the depletion is shown below.

		Adjusting Entry		
Dec.	31	Depletion Expense	36 0 0 0 00	
		Accumulated Depletion		36 0 0 0 00

Like the accumulated depreciation account, Accumulated Depletion is a *contra asset* account. It is reported on the balance sheet as a deduction from the cost of the mineral deposit.

Intangible Assets

objective 8

Describe the accounting for intangible assets, such as patents, copyrights, and goodwill.

Patents, copyrights, trademarks, and goodwill are long-lived assets that are useful in the operations of a business and are not held for sale. These assets are called *intangible assets* because they do not exist physically.

The basic principles of accounting for intangible assets are like those described earlier for fixed assets. The major concerns are determining (1) the initial cost and

(2) the *amortization*—the amount of cost to transfer to expense. Amortization results from the passage of time or a decline in the usefulness of the intangible asset.

Patents

Manufacturers may acquire exclusive rights to produce and sell goods with one or more unique features. Such rights are granted by *patents*, which the federal government issues to inventors. These rights continue in effect for 20 years. A business may purchase patent rights from others, or it may obtain patents developed by its own research and development efforts.

The initial cost of a purchased patent, including any related legal fees, is debited to an asset account. This cost is written off, or amortized, over the years of the patent's expected usefulness. This period of time may be less than the remaining legal life of the patent. The estimated useful life of the patent may also change as technology or consumer tastes change.

The straight-line method is normally used to determine the periodic amortization. When the amortization is recorded, it is debited to an expense account and credited directly to the patents account. A separate contra asset account is usually *not* used for intangible assets.

To illustrate, assume that at the beginning of its fiscal year, a business acquires patent rights for $100,000. The patent had been granted 6 years earlier by the Federal Patent Office. Although the patent will not expire for 14 years, its remaining useful life is estimated as 5 years. The adjusting entry to amortize the patent at the end of the fiscal year is as follows:

Dec.	31	Amortization Expense—Patents	20 0 0 0 00	
		Patents		20 0 0 0 00

Rather than purchase patent rights, a business may incur significant costs in developing patents through its own research and development efforts. Such *research and development costs* are usually accounted for as current operating expenses in the period in which they are incurred. Expensing research and development costs is justified because the future benefits from research and development efforts are highly uncertain.

Copyrights and Trademarks

The exclusive right to publish and sell a literary, artistic, or musical composition is granted by a *copyright*. Copyrights are issued by the federal government and extend for 70 years beyond the author's death. The costs of a copyright include all costs of creating the work plus any administrative or legal costs of obtaining the copyright. A copyright that is purchased from another should be recorded at the price paid for it. Copyrights are amortized over their estimated useful lives. For example, **Sony Corporation** states the following amortization policy with respect to its artistic and music intangible assets:

Intangibles, which mainly consist of artist contracts and music catalogs, are being amortized on a straight-line basis principally over 16 years and 21 years, respectively.

A *trademark* is a name, term, or symbol used to identify a business and its products. For example, the distinctive red-and-white **Coca-Cola** logo is an example of a trademark. Most businesses identify their trademarks with ® in their advertisements and on their products. Under federal law, businesses can protect against others using

REAL WORLD

Coke® is one of the world's most recognizable trademarks. As stated in *LIFE*, "Two-thirds of the earth is covered by water; the rest is covered by Coke. If the French are known for wine and the Germans for beer, America achieved global beverage dominance with fizzy water and caramel color."

their trademarks by registering them for 10 years and renewing the registration for 10-year periods thereafter. Like a copyright, the legal costs of registering a trademark with the federal government are recorded as an asset. Thus, even though the Coca-Cola trademarks are extremely valuable, they are not shown on the balance sheet, because the legal costs for establishing these trademarks are immaterial. If, however, a trademark is purchased from another business, the cost of its purchase is recorded as an asset. The cost of a trademark is in most cases considered to have an indefinite useful life. Thus, trademarks are not amortized over a useful life, as are the previously discussed intangible assets. Rather, trademarks should be tested periodically for impaired value. When a trademark is impaired from competitive threats or other circumstances, the trademark should be written down and a loss recognized.

INTEGRITY IN BUSINESS

21st CENTURY PIRATES

Pirated software is a major concern of software companies. For example, during a recent global sweep, **Microsoft** seized nearly five million units of counterfeit Microsoft software with an estimated retail value of $1.7 billion. U.S. copyright laws and practices are sometimes ignored or disputed in other parts of the world.

Businesses must honor the copyrights held by software companies by eliminating pirated software from corporate computers. The **Business Software Alliance (BSA)** represents the largest software companies in campaigns to investigate illegal use of unlicensed software by businesses. The BSA estimates software industry losses of nearly $12 billion annually from software piracy. Employees using pirated software on business assets risk bringing legal penalties to themselves and their employers.

Goodwill

In business, *goodwill* refers to an intangible asset of a business that is created from such favorable factors as location, product quality, reputation, and managerial skill. Goodwill allows a business to earn a rate of return on its investment that is often in excess of the normal rate for other firms in the same business.

Generally accepted accounting principles permit goodwill to be recorded in the accounts only if it is objectively determined by a transaction. An example of such a transaction is the purchase of a business at a price in excess of the net assets (assets − liabilities) of the acquired business. The excess is recorded as goodwill and reported as an intangible asset. Unlike patents and copyrights, goodwill is not amortized. However, a loss should be recorded if the business prospects of the acquired firm become significantly impaired. This loss would normally be disclosed in the Other Expense section of the income statement. To illustrate, **AOL Time Warner** recorded one of the largest losses in corporate history (nearly $54 billion) for the write-down of goodwill associated with the AOL and Time Warner merger. The entry is recorded as:

	Loss from Impaired Goodwill	54 0 0 0 0 0 0 0 0 0 00	
	Goodwill		54 0 0 0 0 0 0 0 0 0 00

Exhibit 10 shows the frequency of intangible asset disclosures for a sample of 600 large firms. As you can see, goodwill is the most frequently reported intangible asset. This is because goodwill arises from merger transactions, which are very common.

•Exhibit 10 Frequency of Intangible Asset Disclosures for 600 Firms

Intangible Asset Category	Number of Firms
Goodwill	490
Trademarks, brand names, and copyrights	120
Patents	73
Customer lists	52
Technology	51
Franchises and licenses	45
Other	102

Source: *Accounting Trends & Techniques*, 56th ed., American Institute of Certified Public Accountants, New York, 2002.
Note: Some firms have multiple disclosures.

FINANCIAL REPORTING AND DISCLOSURE

DELTA AIR LINES

Delta Air Lines, Inc., provides air transportation for passengers and freight throughout the United States and around the world. Delta is the second largest carrier in terms of passengers carried and third largest as measured by operating revenues and revenue passenger miles flown. Delta is the leading U.S. transatlantic airline, offering the most daily flight departures, serving the largest number of nonstop markets, and carrying more passengers than any other U.S. airline.

Delta reported the following financial information on its fixed assets in its financial statements for a recent year.

ASSETS (in millions)
Property and Equipment:

Flight equipment	$19,427
Less: Accumulated depreciation	5,730
Flight equipment, net	$13,697
Flight equipment under capital leases	$ 382
Less: Accumulated amortization	262
Flight equipment under capital leases, net	$ 120
Ground property and equipment	$ 4,412
Less: Accumulated depreciation	2,355
Ground property and equipment, net	$ 2,057
Advance payments for equipment	$ 223
Total property and equipment, net	$16,097

We record our property and equipment at cost and depreciate these assets on a straight-line basis to their estimated residual values over their respective estimated useful life. Residual values for flight equipment range from 5%–40% of cost. The estimated useful lives for major asset classifications are as follows:

Asset Classification	Estimated Useful Life
Owned flight equipment	15–25 years
Flight equipment under capital lease	Lease Term
Ground property and equipment	3–30 years
Leasehold rights and landing slots	Lease Term

. . . We capitalize interest on advance payments for the acquisition of new aircraft and on construction of ground facilities as an additional cost of the related assets. . . . Interest capitalization ends when the equipment or facility is ready for service or its intended use.

. . . We record impairment losses on long-lived assets used in operations, goodwill and other intangible assets when events and circumstances indicate the assets may be impaired . . . .

. . . We record maintenance costs in operating expense as they are incurred.

. . . Future expenditures for aircraft and engines on firm order as of January 31, 2002, are estimated to be $6.0 billion.

. . . [We recorded] a $363 million charge resulting from a decrease in value of certain aircraft. This charge includes . . . $191 million related to our 16 MD-90 and eight owned MD-11 aircraft . . . $83 million related to the accelerated retirement of 40 B-727 aircraft . . . $77 million writedown related to our decision to accelerate the retirement of nine B-737 aircraft in 2002 and a $12 million writedown . . . of 18 L-1011 aircraft which are held for disposal. We recorded $303 million of these charges as a result of the effects of the September 11 terrorist attacks. The remaining $60 million was recorded . . . when we initially decided to accelerate the retirement of the nine B-737 aircraft to more closely align capacity and demand, and to improve scheduling and operating efficiency.

Financial Reporting for Fixed Assets and Intangible Assets

How should fixed assets and intangible assets be reported in the financial statements? The amount of depreciation and amortization expense of a period should be reported separately in the income statement or disclosed in a note. A general description of the method or methods used in computing depreciation should also be reported.

The amount of each major class of fixed assets should be disclosed in the balance sheet or in notes. The related accumulated depreciation should also be disclosed, either by major class or in total. The fixed assets may be shown at their **book value** (cost less accumulated depreciation), which can also be described as their **net** amount. If there are too many classes of fixed assets, a single amount may be presented in the balance sheet, supported by a separate detailed listing. Fixed assets are normally presented under the more descriptive caption of **property, plant, and equipment**.

The cost of mineral rights or ore deposits is normally shown as part of the fixed assets section of the balance sheet. The related accumulated depletion should also be disclosed. In some cases, the mineral rights are shown net of depletion on the face of the balance sheet, accompanied by a note that discloses the amount of the accumulated depletion.

Intangible assets are usually reported in the balance sheet in a separate section immediately following fixed assets. The balance of each major class of intangible assets should be disclosed at an amount net of amortization taken to date. Exhibit 11 is a partial balance sheet that shows the reporting of fixed assets and intangible assets.

Financial Analysis and Interpretation

Long-term liabilities are often secured by fixed assets. The ratio of total fixed assets to long-term liabilities provides a solvency measure that indicates the margin of safety to creditors. It also gives an indication of the potential ability of the business to borrow additional funds on a long-term basis. The **ratio of fixed assets to long-term liabilities** is computed as follows:

$$\text{Ratio of fixed assets to long-term liabilities (debt)} = \frac{\text{Fixed assets (net)}}{\text{Long-term liabilities (debt)}}$$

To illustrate, the following data were taken from the 2002 and 2001 financial statements of **Procter & Gamble**:

	(in millions)	
	2002	**2001**
Property, plant, and equipment (net)	$13,349	$13,095
Long-term debt	11,201	9,792

The ratio of fixed assets to long-term liabilities (debt) is 1.2 ($13,349/$11,201) for 2002 and 1.3 ($13,095/$9,792) for 2001. The decrease in the ratio from 2001 to 2002 indicates less of a margin of safety for creditors. As with other financial measures, the interpretation and analysis is enhanced by comparisons over time and with industry averages.

•Exhibit 11   Fixed Assets and Intangible Assets in the Balance Sheet

Discovery Mining Co.
Balance Sheet
December 31, 2006

Assets

	Cost	Accum. Depr.	Book Value	
Total current assets				$ 462,500
Property, plant, and equipment:	Cost	Accum. Depr.	Book Value	
Land	$ 30,000	—	$ 30,000	
Buildings	110,000	$ 26,000	84,000	
Factory equipment	650,000	192,000	458,000	
Office equipment	120,000	13,000	107,000	
	$ 910,000	$ 231,000		$679,000
Mineral deposits:	Cost	Accum. Depl.	Book Value	
Alaska deposit	$1,200,000	$ 800,000	$ 400,000	
Wyoming deposit	750,000	200,000	550,000	
	$1,950,000	$1,000,000		950,000
Total property, plant, and equipment				1,629,000
Intangible assets:				
Patents			$ 75,000	
Goodwill			50,000	
Total intangible assets				125,000

SPOTLIGHT ON STRATEGY

HUB-AND-SPOKE OR POINT-TO-POINT?

Southwest Airlines uses a simple fare structure, featuring low, unrestricted, unlimited, everyday coach fares. These fares are possible by Southwest's use of a point-to-point, rather than hub-and-spoke, business strategy. **United**, **Delta**, and **American** employ a hub-and-spoke strategy in which an airline establishes major hubs that serve as connecting links to other cities. For example, Delta has established major connecting hubs in Atlanta, Cincinnati, and Salt Lake City. In contrast, Southwest focuses on point-to-point service between selected cities with over 300 one-way, nonstop city pairs with an average length of 500 miles and average flying time of 1.5 hours. As a result, Southwest minimizes connections, delays, and total trip time. Southwest also focuses on serving conveniently located satellite or downtown airports, such as Dallas Love Field, Houston Hobby, and Chicago Midway. Because these airports are normally less congested than hub airports, Southwest is better able to maintain high employee productivity and reliable ontime performance. This operating strategy permits the company to achieve high asset utilization of its fixed assets, such as its 737 aircraft. For example, aircraft are scheduled to spend only 25 minutes at the gate, thereby reducing the number of aircraft and gate facilities that would otherwise be required.

Appendix   Sum-of-the-Years-Digits Depreciation

REAL WORLD

A recent edition of *Accounting Trends & Techniques* reported that only 1%–2% of the surveyed companies now use this method for financial reporting purposes.

At one time, the sum-of-the-years-digits method of depreciation was used by many businesses. However, tax law changes limited its use for tax purposes.

Under the **sum-of-the-years-digits method**, depreciation expense is determined by multiplying the original cost of the asset less its estimated residual value by a smaller fraction each year. Thus, the sum-of-the-years-digits method is similar to the declining-balance method in that the depreciation expense declines each year.

The denominator of the fraction used in determining the depreciation expense is the sum of the digits of the years of the asset's useful life. For example, an asset with a useful life of 5 years would have a denominator of 15 (5 + 4 + 3 + 2 + 1).[8] The numerator of the fraction is the number of years of useful life remaining at the beginning of each year for which depreciation is being computed. Thus, the numerator decreases each year by 1. For a useful life of 5 years, the numerator is 5 the first year, 4 the second year, 3 the third year, and so on.

The following depreciation schedule illustrates the sum-of-the-years-digits method for an asset with a cost of $24,000, an estimated residual value of $2,000, and an estimated useful life of 5 years:

Year	Cost Less Residual Value	Rate	Depreciation for Year	Accum. Depr. at End of Year	Book Value at End of Year
1	$22,000	$5/15$	$7,333.33	$ 7,333.33	$16,666.67
2	22,000	$4/15$	5,866.67	13,200.00	10,800.00
3	22,000	$3/15$	4,400.00	17,600.00	6,400.00
4	22,000	$2/15$	2,933.33	20,533.33	3,466.67
5	22,000	$1/15$	1,466.67	22,000.00	2,000.00

What if the fixed asset is not placed in service at the beginning of the year? When the date an asset is first put into service is not the beginning of a fiscal year, each full year's depreciation must be allocated between the two fiscal years benefited. To illustrate, assume that the asset in the above example was put into service at the beginning of the fourth month of the first fiscal year. The depreciation for that year would be $5,500 (9/12 × 5/15 × $22,000). The depreciation for the second year would be $6,233.33, computed as follows:

$3/12 \times 5/15 \times \$22,000$	$1,833.33
$9/12 \times 4/15 \times \$22,000$	4,400.00
Total depreciation for second fiscal year	$6,233.33

Key Points

1 Define fixed assets and describe the accounting for their cost.

Fixed assets are long-term tangible assets that are owned by the business and are used in the normal operations of the business. Examples of fixed assets are equipment, buildings, and land. The initial cost of a fixed asset includes all amounts spent to get the asset in place and ready for use. For example, sales tax, freight, insurance in transit, and

---

[8]The denominator can also be determined from the following formula: S = N[(N + 1)/2], where S = sum of the digits and N = number of years of estimated life.

installation costs are all included in the cost of a fixed asset. As time passes, all fixed assets except land lose their ability to provide services. As a result, the cost of a fixed asset should be transferred to an expense account, in a systematic manner, during the asset's expected useful life. This periodic transfer of cost to expense is called depreciation.

2 Compute depreciation, using the following methods: straight-line method, units-of-production method, and declining-balance method.

In computing depreciation, three factors need to be considered: (1) the fixed asset's initial cost, (2) the useful life of the asset, and (3) the residual value of the asset.

The straight-line method spreads the initial cost less the residual value equally over the useful life. The units-of-production method spreads the initial cost less the residual value equally over the units expected to be produced by the asset during its useful life. The declining-balance method is applied by multiplying the declining book value of the asset by twice the straight-line rate.

3 Classify fixed asset costs as either capital expenditures or revenue expenditures.

Fixed assets are acquired and used through the following four stages: preliminary, preacquistion, acquisition or construction, and in-service. The costs incurred during the preliminary stage are generally expensed, while the direct costs incurred during the preacquisition and acquisition stages are capitalized. During the in-service stage, ordinary and normal repairs are expensed, while new and replaced components are capitalized.

4 Journalize entries for the disposal of fixed assets.

The journal entries to record disposals of fixed assets will vary. In all cases, however, any depreciation for the current period should be recorded, and the book value of the asset is then removed from the accounts. The entry to remove the book value from the accounts is a debit to the asset's accumulated depreciation account and a credit to the asset account for the cost of the asset. For assets retired from service, a loss may be recorded for any remaining book value of the asset.

When a fixed asset is sold, the book value is removed and the cash or other asset received is also recorded. If the selling price is more than the book value of the asset, the transaction results in a gain. If the selling price is less than the book value, there is a loss.

When a fixed asset is exchanged for another of similar nature, no gain is recognized on the exchange. The acquired asset's cost is adjusted for any gains. A loss on an exchange of similar assets is recorded.

5 Define a lease and summarize the accounting rules related to the leasing of fixed assets.

A lease is a contract for the use of an asset for a period of time. A capital lease is accounted for as if the lessee has purchased the asset. The lease payments under an operating lease are accounted for as rent expense for the lessee.

6 Describe internal controls over fixed assets.

Internal controls over fixed assets should include procedures for authorizing the purchase of assets. Once acquired, fixed assets should be safeguarded from theft, misuse, or damage. A physical inventory of fixed assets should be taken periodically.

7 Compute depletion and journalize the entry for depletion.

The amount of periodic depletion is computed by multiplying the quantity of minerals extracted during the period by a depletion rate. The depletion rate is computed by dividing the cost of the mineral deposit by its estimated size. The entry to record depletion debits a depletion expense account and credits an accumulated depletion account.

8 Describe the accounting for intangible assets, such as patents, copyrights, and goodwill.

Long-term assets that are without physical attributes but are used in the business are classified as intangible assets. Examples of intangible assets are patents, copyrights, trademarks, and goodwill. The initial cost of an intangible asset should be debited to an asset account. For patents and copyrights, this cost should be written off, or amortized, over the years of the asset's expected usefulness by debiting an expense account and crediting the intangible asset account. Trademarks and goodwill are not amortized, but are written down only upon impairment.

9 Describe how depreciation expense is reported in an income statement, and prepare a balance sheet that includes fixed assets and intangible assets.

The amount of depreciation expense and the method or methods used in computing depreciation should be disclosed in the financial statements. In addition, each major class of fixed assets should be disclosed, along with the related accumulated depreciation. Intangible assets are usually presented in the balance sheet in a separate section immediately following fixed assets. Each major class of intangible assets should be disclosed at an amount net of the amortization recorded to date.

10 Compute and interpret the ratio of fixed assets to long-term liabilities.

The ratio of fixed assets to long-term liabilities is a solvency measure that indicates the margin of safety to creditors. It also provides an indication of the ability of a company to borrow additional funds on a long-term basis.

Key Terms

accelerated depreciation method (362)

amortization (373)

book value (361)

boot (368)

capital expenditures (364)

capital lease (370)

component (365)

copyright (373)

declining-balance method (361)

depletion (372)

depreciation (357)

fixed assets (355)

goodwill (374)

intangible assets (372)

operating lease (370)

patents (373)

ratio of fixed assets to long-term liabilities (376)

residual value (359)

revenue expenditures (364)

straight-line method (360)

trade-in allowance (368)

trademark (373)

units-of-production method (361)

Illustrative Problem

McCollum Company, a furniture wholesaler, acquired new equipment at a cost of $150,000 at the beginning of the fiscal year. The equipment has an estimated life of 5 years and an estimated residual value of $12,000. Ellen McCollum, the president, has requested information regarding alternative depreciation methods.

Instructions

1. Determine the annual depreciation for each of the five years of estimated useful life of the equipment, the accumulated depreciation at the end of each year, and the book value of the equipment at the end of each year by (a) the straight-line method and (b) the declining-balance method (at twice the straight-line rate).

2. Assume that the equipment was depreciated under the declining-balance method. In the first week of the fifth year, the equipment was traded in for similar equipment priced at $175,000. The trade-in allowance on the old equipment was $10,000, and cash was paid for the balance. Journalize the entry to record the exchange.

Solution

1.

	Year	Depreciation Expense	Accumulated Depreciation, End of Year	Book Value, End of Year
a.	1	$27,600*	$ 27,600	$122,400
	2	27,600	55,200	94,800
	3	27,600	82,800	67,200
	4	27,600	110,400	39,600
	5	27,600	138,000	12,000

*$27,600 = ($150,000 − $12,000) ÷ 5

	Year	Depreciation Expense	Accumulated Depreciation, End of Year	Book Value, End of Year
b.	1	$60,000**	$ 60,000	$ 90,000
	2	36,000	96,000	54,000
	3	21,600	117,600	32,400
	4	12,960	130,560	19,440
	5	7,440***	138,000	12,000

**$60,000 = $150,000 × 40%

***The asset is not depreciated below the estimated residual value of $12,000.

2.

			Accumulated Depreciation—Equipment	130 5 6 0 00	
			Equipment	175 0 0 0 00	
			Loss on Disposal of Fixed Assets	9 4 4 0 00	
			Equipment		150 0 0 0 00
			Cash		165 0 0 0 00

Self-Examination Questions (Answers at End of Chapter)

1. Which of the following expenditures incurred in connection with acquiring machinery is a proper charge to the asset account?
   A. Freight
   B. Installation costs
   C. Both A and B
   D. Neither A nor B

2. What is the amount of depreciation, using the declining-balance method (twice the straight-line rate) for the second year of use for equipment costing $9,000, with an estimated residual value of $600 and an estimated life of 3 years?
   A. $6,000
   B. $3,000
   C. $2,000
   D. $400

3. An example of an accelerated depreciation method is:
   A. Straight-line
   B. Declining-balance
   C. Units-of-production
   D. Depletion

4. A fixed asset priced at $100,000 is acquired by trading in a similar asset that has a book value of $25,000. Assuming that the trade-in allowance is $30,000 and that $70,000 cash is paid for the new asset, what is the cost of the new asset for financial reporting purposes?
   A. $100,000
   B. $95,000
   C. $70,000
   D. $30,000

5. Which of the following is an example of an intangible asset?
   A. Patents
   B. Goodwill
   C. Copyrights
   D. All of the above

Class Discussion Questions

1. Which of the following qualities are characteristic of fixed assets? (a) tangible, (b) capable of repeated use in the operations of the business, (c) held for sale in the normal course of business, (d) used rarely in the operations of the business, (e) long-lived.

2. Wang Office Equipment Co. has a fleet of automobiles and trucks for use by salespersons and for delivery of office supplies and equipment. Lake City Auto Sales Co. has automobiles and trucks for sale. Under what caption would the automobiles and trucks be reported on the balance sheet of (a) Wang Office Equipment Co., (b) Lake City Auto Sales Co.?

3. Muskegon Co. acquired an adjacent vacant lot with the hope of selling it in the future at a gain. The lot is not intended to be used in Muskegon's business operations. Where should such real estate be listed in the balance sheet?

4. Redding Company solicited bids from several contractors to construct an addition to its office building. The lowest bid received was for $420,000. Redding Company decided to construct the addition itself at a cost of $375,000. What amount should be recorded in the building account?

5. Are the amounts at which fixed assets are reported in the balance sheet their approximate market values as of the balance sheet date? Discuss.

6. a. Does the recognition of depreciation in the accounts provide a special cash fund for the replacement of fixed assets? Explain.

   b. Describe the nature of depreciation as the term is used in accounting.

7. Lowell Company purchased a machine that has a manufacturer's suggested life of 18 years. The company plans to use the machine on a special project that will last 12 years. At the completion of the project, the machine will be sold. Over how many years should the machine be depreciated?

8. Is it necessary for a business to use the same method of computing depreciation (a) for all classes of its depreciable assets, (b) in the financial statements and in determining income taxes?

9. a. Under what conditions is the use of an accelerated depreciation method most appropriate?

   b. Why is an accelerated depreciation method often used for income tax purposes?

   c. What is the Modified Accelerated Cost Recovery System (MACRS), and under what conditions is it used?

10. A company revised the estimated useful lives of its fixed assets, which resulted in an increase in the remaining lives of several assets. Do GAAP permit the company to include, as income of the current period, the cumulative effect of the changes, which reduces the depreciation expense of past periods? Discuss.

11. Differentiate between the accounting for capital expenditures and revenue expenditures.

12. Immediately after a used truck is acquired, a new motor is installed and the tires are replaced at a total cost of $5,750. Is this a capital expenditure or a revenue expenditure?

13. For some of the fixed assets of a business, the balance in Accumulated Depreciation is exactly equal to the cost of the asset. (a) Is it permissible to record additional depreciation on the assets if they are still useful to the business? Explain. (b) When should an entry be made to remove the cost and the accumulated depreciation from the accounts?

14. a. Describe the internal controls for acquiring fixed assets.

   b. Explain why a physical count of fixed assets is desirable.

15. a. Over what period of time should the cost of a patent acquired by purchase be amortized?

   b. In general, what is the required accounting treatment for research and development costs?

   c. How should goodwill be amortized?

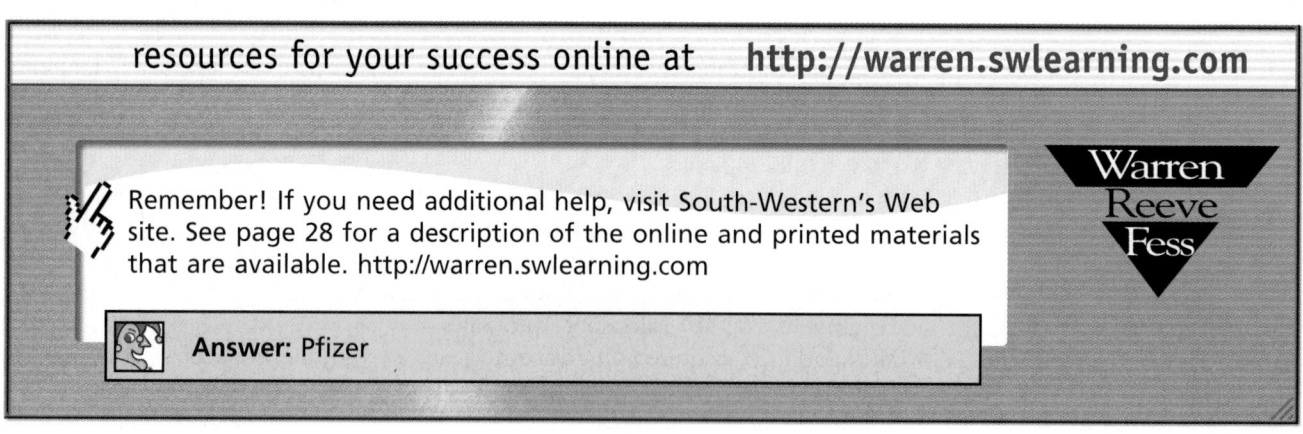

Exercises

EXERCISE 9-1
Costs of acquiring fixed assets
Objective 1

Cristy Fleming owns and operates Quesenberry Print Co. During February, Quesenberry Print Co. incurred the following costs in acquiring two printing presses. One printing press was new, and the other was used by a business that recently filed for bankruptcy.

Costs related to new printing press:

1. Freight
2. Special foundation
3. Sales tax on purchase price
4. Insurance while in transit
5. Fee paid to factory representative for installation
6. New parts to replace those damaged in unloading

Costs related to secondhand printing press:

7. Repair of vandalism during installation
8. Replacement of worn-out parts
9. Freight
10. Installation
11. Repair of damage incurred in reconditioning the press
12. Fees paid to attorney to review purchase agreement

a. Indicate which costs incurred in acquiring the new printing press should be debited to the asset account.
b. Indicate which costs incurred in acquiring the secondhand printing press should be debited to the asset account.

EXERCISE 9-2
Determine cost of land
Objective 1

A company has developed a tract of land into a ski resort. The company has cut the trees, cleared and graded the land and hills, and constructed ski lifts. (a) Should the tree cutting, land clearing, and grading costs of constructing the ski slopes be debited to the land account? (b) If such costs are debited to Land, should they be depreciated?

EXERCISE 9-3
Determine cost of land
Objective 1
✓ *$188,000*

Alligator Delivery Company acquired an adjacent lot to construct a new warehouse, paying $35,000 and giving a short-term note for $125,000. Legal fees paid were $1,100, delinquent taxes assumed were $12,500, and fees paid to remove an old building from the land were $18,000. Materials salvaged from the demolition of the building were sold for $3,600. A contractor was paid $512,500 to construct a new warehouse. Determine the cost of the land to be reported on the balance sheet.

EXERCISE 9-4
Nature of depreciation
Objective 1

Ball-Peen Metal Casting Co. reported $859,600 for equipment and $317,500 for accumulated depreciation—equipment on its balance sheet.
➤ Does this mean (a) that the replacement cost of the equipment is $859,600 and (b) that $317,500 is set aside in a special fund for the replacement of the equipment? Explain.

EXERCISE 9-5
Straight-line depreciation rates
Objective 2
✓ *a. 5%*

Convert each of the following estimates of useful life to a straight-line depreciation rate, stated as a percentage, assuming that the residual value of the fixed asset is to be ignored: (a) 20 years, (b) 25 years, (c) 40 years, (d) 4 years, (e) 5 years, (f) 10 years, (g) 50 years.

EXERCISE 9-6
Straight-line depreciation
Objective 2

✓ *$18,000*

A refrigerator used by a meat processor has a cost of $312,000, an estimated residual value of $42,000, and an estimated useful life of 15 years. What is the amount of the annual depreciation computed by the straight-line method?

EXERCISE 9-7
Depreciation by units-of-production method
Objective 2

✓ *$5,450*

A diesel-powered generator with a cost of $345,000 and estimated residual value of $18,000 is expected to have a useful operating life of 75,000 hours. During July, the generator was operated 1,250 hours. Determine the depreciation for the month.

EXERCISE 9-8
Depreciation by units-of-production method
Objective 2

✓ *a. Truck #1, credit Accumulated Depreciation, $8,000*

Prior to adjustment at the end of the year, the balance in Trucks is $182,600 and the balance in Accumulated Depreciation—Trucks is $75,500. Details of the subsidiary ledger are as follows:

Truck No.	Cost	Estimated Residual Value	Estimated Useful Life	Accumulated Depreciation at Beginning of Year	Miles Operated During Year
1	$68,000	$8,000	300,000 miles	$27,000	40,000 miles
2	48,600	6,600	200,000	39,900	12,000
3	38,000	3,000	200,000	8,050	36,000
4	28,000	4,000	120,000	—	21,000

a. Determine the depreciation rates per mile and the amount to be credited to the accumulated depreciation section of each of the subsidiary accounts for the miles operated during the current year.
b. Journalize the entry to record depreciation for the year.

EXERCISE 9-9
Depreciation by two methods
Objective 2

✓ *a. $7,000*

A backhoe acquired on January 5 at a cost of $84,000 has an estimated useful life of 12 years. Assuming that it will have no residual value, determine the depreciation for each of the first two years (a) by the straight-line method and (b) by the declining-balance method, using twice the straight-line rate. Round to the nearest dollar.

EXERCISE 9-10
Depreciation by two methods
Objective 2

✓ *a. $9,100*

A dairy storage tank acquired at the beginning of the fiscal year at a cost of $98,500 has an estimated residual value of $7,500 and an estimated useful life of 10 years. Determine the following: (a) the amount of annual depreciation by the straight-line method and (b) the amount of depreciation for the first and second year computed by the declining-balance method (at twice the straight-line rate).

EXERCISE 9-11
Partial-year depreciation
Objective 2

✓ *a. First year, $2,700*

Sandblasting equipment acquired at a cost of $54,000 has an estimated residual value of $10,800 and an estimated useful life of 12 years. It was placed in service on April 1 of the current fiscal year, which ends on December 31. Determine the depreciation for the current fiscal year and for the following fiscal year by (a) the straight-line method and (b) the declining-balance method, at twice the straight-line rate.

EXERCISE 9-12
Revision of depreciation
Objective 2

✓ *a. $15,000*

A warehouse with a cost of $800,000 has an estimated residual value of $200,000, an estimated useful life of 40 years, and is depreciated by the straight-line method. (a) What is the amount of the annual depreciation? (b) What is the book value at the end of the twentieth year of use? (c) If at the start of the twenty-first year it is estimated that the remaining life is 25 years and that the residual value is $150,000, what is the depreciation expense for each of the remaining 25 years?

EXERCISE 9-13
Book value of fixed assets
Objective 2

The following data were taken from recent annual reports of **Interstate Bakeries Corporation (IBC)**. Interstate Bakeries produces, distributes, and sells fresh bakery products nationwide through supermarkets, convenience stores, and its 67 bakeries and 1,500 thrift stores.

	Current Year	Preceding Year
Land and buildings	$ 426,322,000	$ 418,928,000
Machinery and equipment	1,051,861,000	1,038,323,000
Accumulated depreciation	633,178,000	582,941,000

a. Compute the book value of the fixed assets for the current year and the preceding year and explain the differences, if any.

b. Would you normally expect the book value of fixed assets to increase or decrease during the year?

EXERCISE 9-14
Capital and revenue expenditures
Objective 3

Hicks Co. incurred the following costs related to trucks and vans used in operating its delivery service:

1. Removed a two-way radio from one of the trucks and installed a new radio with a greater range of communication.
2. Overhauled the engine on one of the trucks that had been purchased three years ago.
3. Changed the oil and greased the joints of all the trucks and vans.
4. Installed security systems on four of the newer trucks.
5. Changed the radiator fluid on a truck that had been in service for the past 4 years.
6. Installed a hydraulic lift to a van.
7. Tinted the back and side windows of one of the vans to discourage theft of contents.
8. Repaired a flat tire on one of the vans.
9. Rebuilt the transmission on one of the vans that had been driven 40,000 miles. The van was no longer under warranty.
10. Replaced the trucks' suspension system with a new suspension system that allows for the delivery of heavier loads.

Classify each of the costs as a capital expenditure or a revenue expenditure. For those costs identified as capital expenditures, classify each as an additional or replacement component.

EXERCISE 9-15
Capital and revenue expenditures
Objective 3

Felix Little owns and operates Big Sky Transport Co. During the past year, Felix incurred the following costs related to his 18-wheel truck.

1. Replaced a headlight that had burned out.
2. Removed the old CB radio and replaced it with a newer model with a greater range.
3. Replaced a shock absorber that had worn out.
4. Installed a television in the sleeping compartment of the truck.
5. Replaced the old radar detector with a newer model that detects the KA frequencies now used by many of the state patrol radar guns. The detector is wired directly into the cab, so that it is partially hidden. In addition, Felix fastened the detector to the truck with a locking device that prevents its removal.
6. Installed fog and cab lights.
7. Installed a wind deflector on top of the cab to increase fuel mileage.
8. Modified the factory-installed turbo charger with a special-order kit designed to add 50 more horsepower to the engine performance.
9. Replaced the hydraulic brake system that had begun to fail during his latest trip through the Rocky Mountains.
10. Overhauled the engine.

Classify each of the costs as a capital expenditure or a revenue expenditure. For those costs identified as capital expenditures, classify each as an additional or replacement component.

EXERCISE 9-16
Fixed asset component replacement

Objectives 2, 3

✓ *c. Depreciation Expense, $2,250*

Jacobs Company replaced carpeting throughout its general offices. The old carpet was removed at a cost of $1,500 on March 15. The book value of the old carpet was $6,000 on March 15 ($18,000 original cost less $12,000 accumulated depreciation). New carpet was purchased and installed during the last two weeks of March for a total cost of $45,000. The carpet is estimated to have a 15-year useful life.

a. Record the cost of removing the old carpet.
b. Prepare the journal entries necessary for recording the replacement of the old carpet with the new carpet.
c. Record the December 31 adjusting entry for the partial-year depreciation expense for the carpet, assuming that Jacobs uses the straight-line method.

EXERCISE 9-17
Fixed asset component replacement

Objectives 2, 3

✓ *b. $29,000*

Dale's Edge, Inc., purchased and installed an alarm system for its retail store on January 1, 1999, at a cost of $50,000. The alarm system was estimated to have a ten-year life with no salvage value. On January 1, 2006, the alarm system was replaced with a system having more advanced technology. The removal of the old alarm system cost $2,000. The new system cost $120,000 and is estimated to have a ten-year life, with no residual value. Dale's Edge uses the straight-line depreciation method.

a. Determine the total depreciation expense for 2006 related to the alarm system.
b. Determine the total expense reported in the income statement in 2006 from these transactions.

EXERCISE 9-18
Entries for sale of fixed asset

Objective 4

Metal recycling equipment acquired on January 3, 2003, at a cost of $240,000, has an estimated useful life of 10 years, an estimated residual value of $15,000, and is depreciated by the straight-line method.

a. What was the book value of the equipment at December 31, 2006, the end of the fiscal year?
b. Assuming that the equipment was sold on July 1, 2007, for $135,000, journalize the entries to record (1) depreciation for the six months until the sale date, and (2) the sale of the equipment.

EXERCISE 9-19
Disposal of fixed asset

Objective 4

✓ *b. $51,000*

Equipment acquired on January 3, 2003, at a cost of $96,000, has an estimated useful life of 6 years and an estimated residual value of $6,000.

a. What was the annual amount of depreciation for the years 2003, 2004, and 2005, using the straight-line method of depreciation?
b. What was the book value of the equipment on January 1, 2006?
c. Assuming that the equipment was sold on January 2, 2006, for $38,000, journalize the entry to record the sale.
d. Assuming that the equipment had been sold on January 2, 2006, for $53,000 instead of $38,000, journalize the entry to record the sale.

EXERCISE 9-20
Asset traded for similar asset

Objective 4

✓ *a. $205,000*

A printing press priced at $315,000 is acquired by trading in a similar press and paying cash for the difference between the trade-in allowance and the price of the new press.

a. Assuming that the trade-in allowance is $110,000, what is the amount of cash given?
b. Assuming that the book value of the press traded in is $98,750, what is the cost of the new press for financial reporting purposes?

EXERCISE 9-21
Asset traded for similar asset

Objective 4

✓ *a. $205,000*

Assume the same facts as in Exercise 9-20, except that the book value of the press traded in is $128,500. (a) What is the amount of cash given? (b) What is the cost of the new press for financial reporting purposes?

EXERCISE 9-22
Entries for trade of fixed asset
Objective 4

On July 1, Jaguar Co., a water distiller, acquired new bottling equipment with a list price of $385,000. Jaguar received a trade-in allowance of $100,000 on the old equipment of a similar type, paid cash of $35,000, and gave a series of five notes payable for the remainder. The following information about the old equipment is obtained from the account in the equipment ledger: cost, $280,000; accumulated depreciation on December 31, the end of the preceding fiscal year, $144,000; annual depreciation, $16,000. Journalize the entries to record (a) the current depreciation of the old equipment to the date of trade-in and (b) the exchange transaction on July 1 for financial reporting purposes.

EXERCISE 9-23
Entries for trade of fixed asset
Objective 4

On April 1, O'Dell Co. acquired a new truck with a list price of $80,000. O'Dell received a trade-in allowance of $29,000 on an old truck of similar type, paid cash of $11,000, and gave a series of five notes payable for the remainder. The following information about the old truck is obtained from the account in the equipment ledger: cost, $62,500; accumulated depreciation on December 31, the end of the preceding fiscal year, $36,000; annual depreciation, $6,000. Journalize the entries to record (a) the current depreciation of the old truck to the date of trade-in and (b) the transaction on April 1 for financial reporting purposes.

EXERCISE 9-24
Depreciable cost of asset acquired by exchange
Objective 4

On the first day of the fiscal year, a delivery truck with a list price of $55,000 was acquired in exchange for an old delivery truck and $30,000 cash. The old truck had a book value of $28,250 at the date of the exchange.

a. Determine the depreciable cost for financial reporting purposes.
b. Assuming that the book value of the old delivery truck was $24,000, determine the depreciable cost for financial reporting purposes.

EXERCISE 9-25
Internal control of fixed assets
Objective 6

MarketNet Co. is a computer software company marketing products in the United States and Canada. While MarketNet Co. has over 90 sales offices, all accounting is handled at the company's headquarters in Phoenix, Arizona.

MarketNet Co. keeps all its fixed asset records on a computerized system. The computer maintains a subsidiary ledger of all fixed assets owned by the company and calculates depreciation automatically. Whenever a manager at one of the 90 sales offices wants to purchase a fixed asset, a purchase request is submitted to headquarters for approval. Upon approval, the fixed asset is purchased and the invoice is sent back to headquarters so that the asset can be entered into the fixed asset system.

A manager who wants to dispose of a fixed asset simply sells or disposes of the asset and notifies headquarters to remove the asset from the system. Company cars and personal computers are frequently purchased by employees when they are disposed of. Most pieces of office equipment are traded in when new assets are acquired.

➤ What internal control weakness exists in the procedures used to acquire and dispose of fixed assets at MarketNet Co.?

EXERCISE 9-26
Depletion entries
Objective 7
✓ *a. $12,400,000*

Discovery Co. acquired mineral rights for $80,000,000. The mineral deposit is estimated at 100,000,000 tons. During the current year, 15,500,000 tons were mined and sold for $16,500,000.

a. Determine the amount of depletion expense for the current year.
b. Journalize the adjusting entry to recognize the depletion expense.

EXERCISE 9-27
Amortization entries
Objective 8
✓ *a. $37,750*

Colmey Company acquired patent rights on January 3, 2003, for $472,500. The patent has a useful life equal to its legal life of 15 years. On January 5, 2006, Colmey successfully defended the patent in a lawsuit at a cost of $75,000.

a. Determine the patent amortization expense for the current year ended December 31, 2006.
b. Journalize the adjusting entry to recognize the amortization.

EXERCISE 9-28
Balance sheet presentation

Objective 9

WHAT'S WRONG WITH THIS?

List the errors you find in the following partial balance sheet:

Kraftmaid Company
Balance Sheet
December 31, 2006

Assets

Total current assets $597,500

	Replacement Cost	Accumulated Depreciation	Book Value
Property, plant, and equipment:			
Land	$ 100,000	$ 20,000	$ 80,000
Buildings	260,000	76,000	184,000
Factory equipment	550,000	292,000	258,000
Office equipment	120,000	80,000	40,000
Patents	80,000	—	80,000
Goodwill	45,000	5,000	40,000
Total property, plant, and equipment	$1,155,000	$473,000	682,000

EXERCISE 9-29
Ratio of fixed assets to long-term liabilities

Objective 10

REAL WORLD

The following data were taken from recent annual reports of **Intuit Inc.**, a developer and distributor of financial planning software:

	Current Year	Preceding Year
Property and equipment (net)	$181,758,000	$174,659,000
Long-term liabilities	14,610,000	12,150,000

a. Compute the ratio of fixed assets to long-term liabilities for the current and preceding year. Round to one decimal place.
b. ➤ What conclusions can you draw?

EXERCISE 9-30
Ratio of fixed assets to long-term liabilities

Objective 10

REAL WORLD

The financial statements of **Home Depot** are presented in Appendix F at the end of the text.

a. Compute the ratio of fixed assets to long-term liabilities for 2002 and 2001.
b. ➤ What conclusions can you draw?

APPENDIX EXERCISE 9-31
Sum-of-the-years-digits depreciation

✓ *First year: $12,923*

Based on the data in Exercise 9-9, determine the depreciation for the backhoe for each of the first two years, using the sum-of-the-years-digits depreciation method. Round to the nearest dollar.

APPENDIX EXERCISE 9-32
Sum-of-the-years-digits depreciation

✓ *First year: $16,545*

Based on the data in Exercise 9-10, determine the depreciation for the dairy storage tank for each of the first two years, using the sum-of-the-years-digits depreciation method. Round to the nearest dollar.

APPENDIX EXERCISE 9-33
Partial-year depreciation

✓ *First year: $4,985*

Based on the data in Exercise 9-11, determine the depreciation for the sandblasting equipment for each of the first two years, using the sum-of-the-years-digits depreciation method. Round to the nearest dollar.

Problems Series A

PROBLEM 9-1A
Allocate payments and receipts to fixed asset accounts

Objective 1

SPREADSHEET

The following payments and receipts are related to land, land improvements, and buildings acquired for use in a wholesale apparel business. The receipts are identified by an asterisk.

a. Finder's fee paid to real estate agency	$ 5,000
b. Cost of real estate acquired as a plant site: Land	100,000
Building	60,000
c. Fee paid to attorney for title search	3,500
d. Delinquent real estate taxes on property, assumed by purchaser . . .	17,500
e. Cost of razing and removing building	16,250
f. Cost of filling and grading land	12,500
g. Proceeds from sale of salvage materials from old building	4,500*
h. Special assessment paid to city for extension of water main to the property	11,000
i. Premium on 1-year insurance policy during construction	7,200
j. Architect's and engineer's fees for plans and supervision	50,000
k. Cost of repairing windstorm damage during construction	2,500
l. Cost of repairing vandalism damage during construction	1,800
m. Cost of trees and shrubbery planted	12,000
n. Cost of paving parking lot to be used by customers	18,500
o. Proceeds from insurance company for windstorm and vandalism damage	4,000*
p. Interest incurred on building loan during construction	65,000
q. Money borrowed to pay building contractor	1,000,000*
r. Payment to building contractor for new building	1,250,000
s. Refund of premium on insurance policy (i) canceled after 10 months	1,200*

Instructions

1. Assign each payment and receipt to Land (unlimited life), Land Improvements (limited life), Building, or Other Accounts. Indicate receipts by an asterisk. Identify each item by letter and list the amounts in columnar form, as follows:

Item	Land	Land Improvements	Building	Other Accounts

2. Determine the amount debited to Land, Land Improvements, and Building.
3. ▬▬▶ The costs assigned to the land, which is used as a plant site, will not be depreciated, while the costs assigned to land improvements will be depreciated. Explain this seemingly contradictory application of the concept of depreciation.

PROBLEM 9-2A
Compare three depreciation methods

Objective 2

Cero Company purchased waterproofing equipment on January 2, 2005, for $214,000. The equipment was expected to have a useful life of 4 years, or 31,250 operating hours, and a residual value of $14,000. The equipment was used for 10,750 hours during 2005, 9,500 hours in 2006, 6,000 hours in 2007, and 5,000 hours in 2008.

Instructions

Determine the amount of depreciation expense for the years ended December 31, 2005, 2006, 2007, and 2008, by (a) the straight-line method, (b) the units-of-production

SPREADSHEET

✓ *a. 2005: straight-line depreciation, $50,000*

method, and (c) the declining-balance method, using twice the straight-line rate. Also determine the total depreciation expense for the four years by each method. The following columnar headings are suggested for recording the depreciation expense amounts:

	Depreciation Expense		
Year	Straight-Line Method	Units-of-Production Method	Declining-Balance Method

PROBLEM 9-3A
Depreciation by three methods; partial years

Objective 2

SPREADSHEET

✓ *a. 2005, $30,600*

Caribou Company purchased tool sharpening equipment on July 1, 2005, for $194,400. The equipment was expected to have a useful life of 3 years, or 22,950 operating hours, and a residual value of $10,800. The equipment was used for 4,650 hours during 2005, 7,500 hours in 2006, 7,350 hours in 2007, and 3,450 hours in 2008.

Instructions
Determine the amount of depreciation expense for the years ended December 31, 2005, 2006, 2007, and 2008, by (a) the straight-line method, (b) the units-of-production method, and (c) the declining-balance method, using twice the straight-line rate.

PROBLEM 9-4A
Depreciation by two methods; trade of fixed asset

Objectives 2, 4

SPREADSHEET

P.A.S.S.

✓ *1. b. Year 1, $80,000 depreciation expense*
✓ *2. $196,000*

New tire retreading equipment, acquired at a cost of $160,000 at the beginning of a fiscal year, has an estimated useful life of 4 years and an estimated residual value of $16,000. The manager requested information regarding the effect of alternative methods on the amount of depreciation expense each year. On the basis of the data presented to the manager, the declining-balance method was selected.

In the first week of the fourth year, the equipment was traded in for similar equipment priced at $200,000. The trade-in allowance on the old equipment was $24,000, cash of $16,000 was paid, and a note payable was issued for the balance.

Instructions
1. Determine the annual depreciation expense for each of the estimated 4 years of use, the accumulated depreciation at the end of each year, and the book value of the equipment at the end of each year by (a) the straight-line method and (b) the declining-balance method (at twice the straight-line rate). The following columnar headings are suggested for each schedule:

Year	Depreciation Expense	Accumulated Depreciation, End of Year	Book Value, End of Year

2. For financial reporting purposes, determine the cost of the new equipment acquired in the exchange.
3. Journalize the entry to record the exchange.
4. Journalize the entry to record the exchange, assuming that the trade-in allowance was $12,800 instead of $24,000.

PROBLEM 9-5A
Transactions for fixed assets, including trade

Objectives 1, 3, 4

P.A.S.S.

The following transactions, adjusting entries, and closing entries were completed by Yellowstone Furniture Co. during a 3-year period. All are related to the use of delivery equipment. The declining-balance method (at twice the straight-line rate) of depreciation is used.

2005
Jan. 2 Purchased a used delivery truck for $37,000, paying cash.
     5 Paid $5,000 to replace the engine. The old engine was estimated to have a value of $2,000. The new engine is expected to have a useful life equal to the remaining life of the truck.
Apr. 7 Paid garage $125 for changing the oil, replacing the oil filter, and tuning the engine on the delivery truck.

2005

Dec. 31 Recorded depreciation on the truck and engine component for the fiscal year. The estimated useful life of the truck and engine is 8 years, with a residual value of $3,000 for the truck.

2006

Jan. 1 Purchased a new truck for $80,000, paying cash.

Mar. 13 Paid garage $180 to tune the engine and make other minor repairs on the truck.

Apr. 30 Sold the used truck for $24,500. (Record depreciation to date in 2006 for the truck.)

Dec. 31 Recorded depreciation on the truck. It has an estimated trade-in value of $4,000 and an estimated life of 10 years.

2007

July 1 Purchased a new truck for $45,000, paying cash.

Oct. 2 Sold the truck purchased Jan. 1, 2006, for $63,075. (Record depreciation for the year.)

Dec. 31 Recorded depreciation on the remaining truck. It has an estimated residual value of $4,500 and an estimated useful life of 10 years.

Instructions

Journalize the transactions and the adjusting entries.

PROBLEM 9-6A
Amortization and depletion entries

Objectives 7, 8

✓ *1. b. $14,100*

Data related to the acquisition of timber rights and intangible assets during the current year ended December 31 are as follows:

a. Goodwill in the amount of $29,500,000 was purchased on January 18.

b. Governmental and legal costs of $225,600 were incurred on July 5 in obtaining a patent with an estimated economic life of 8 years. Amortization is to be for one-half year.

c. Timber rights on a tract of land were purchased for $820,000 on April 10. The stand of timber is estimated at 4,000,000 board feet. During the current year, 550,000 board feet of timber were cut.

Instructions

1. Determine the amount of the amortization or depletion expense for the current year for each of the foregoing items.

2. Journalize the adjusting entries to record the amortization or depletion expense for each item.

Problems Series B

PROBLEM 9-1B
Allocate payments and receipts to fixed asset accounts

Objective 1

SPREADSHEET

The following payments and receipts are related to land, land improvements, and buildings acquired for use in a wholesale ceramic business. The receipts are identified by an asterisk.

a. Fee paid to attorney for title search	$ 2,500
b. Cost of real estate acquired as a plant site: Land	150,000
Building	40,000
c. Delinquent real estate taxes on property, assumed by purchaser	13,750
d. Cost of razing and removing building	4,800
e. Special assessment paid to city for extension of water main to the property	10,200
f. Proceeds from sale of salvage materials from old building	5,000*
g. Cost of filling and grading land	29,700
h. Premium on 1-year insurance policy during construction	6,600
i. Cost of repairing windstorm damage during construction	3,500

(continued)

j. Cost of paving parking lot to be used by customers	$ 12,500
k. Cost of trees and shrubbery planted	7,000
l. Architect's and engineer's fees for plans and supervision	75,000
m. Cost of repairing vandalism damage during construction	1,600
n. Interest incurred on building loan during construction	30,000
o. Cost of floodlights installed on parking lot	8,500
p. Money borrowed to pay building contractor	500,000*
q. Payment to building contractor for new building	750,000
r. Proceeds from insurance company for windstorm and vandalism damage	4,000*
s. Refund of premium on insurance policy (h) canceled after 11 months	550*

Instructions

1. Assign each payment and receipt to Land (unlimited life), Land Improvements (limited life), Building, or Other Accounts. Indicate receipts by an asterisk. Identify each item by letter and list the amounts in columnar form, as follows:

Item	Land	Land Improvements	Building	Other Accounts

2. Determine the amount debited to Land, Land Improvements, and Building.
3. ➡ The costs assigned to the land, which is used as a plant site, will not be depreciated, while the costs assigned to land improvements will be depreciated. Explain this seemingly contradictory application of the concept of depreciation.

PROBLEM 9-2B
Compare three depreciation methods
Objective 2

SPREADSHEET

✓ *a. 2005: straight-line depreciation, $55,800*

Red Tiger Company purchased packaging equipment on January 3, 2005, for $180,000. The equipment was expected to have a useful life of 3 years, or 22,320 operating hours, and a residual value of $12,600. The equipment was used for 12,500 hours during 2005, 6,000 hours in 2006, and 3,820 hours in 2007.

Instructions

Determine the amount of depreciation expense for the years ended December 31, 2005, 2006, and 2007, by (a) the straight-line method, (b) the units-of-production method, and (c) the declining-balance method, using twice the straight-line rate. Also determine the total depreciation expense for the three years by each method. The following columnar headings are suggested for recording the depreciation expense amounts:

	Depreciation Expense		
Year	Straight-Line Method	Units-of-Production Method	Declining-Balance Method

---

PROBLEM 9-3B
Depreciation by three methods; partial years
Objective 2

SPREADSHEET

✓ *a. 2005: $28,050*

Rhymer Company purchased plastic laminating equipment on July 1, 2005, for $174,000. The equipment was expected to have a useful life of 3 years, or 14,025 operating hours, and a residual value of $5,700. The equipment was used for 2,500 hours during 2005, 5,500 hours in 2006, 4,025 hours in 2007, and 2,000 hours in 2008.

Instructions

Determine the amount of depreciation expense for the years ended December 31, 2005, 2006, 2007, and 2008, by (a) the straight-line method, (b) the units-of-production method, and (c) the declining-balance method, using twice the straight-line rate. Round to the nearest dollar.

PROBLEM 9-4B
Depreciation by two methods; trade of fixed asset
Objectives 2, 4

New lithographic equipment, acquired at a cost of $100,000 at the beginning of a fiscal year, has an estimated useful life of 5 years and an estimated residual value of $8,000. The manager requested information regarding the effect of alternative methods on the amount of depreciation expense each year. On the basis of the data presented to the manager, the declining-balance method was selected.

SPREADSHEET

P.A.S.S.

✓ 1. b. Year 1: $40,000 depreciation expense

✓ 2. $116,960

In the first week of the fifth year, the equipment was traded in for similar equipment priced at $120,000. The trade-in allowance on the old equipment was $16,000, cash of $24,000 was paid, and a note payable was issued for the balance.

Instructions

1. Determine the annual depreciation expense for each of the estimated 5 years of use, the accumulated depreciation at the end of each year, and the book value of the equipment at the end of each year by (a) the straight-line method and (b) the declining-balance method (at twice the straight-line rate). The following columnar headings are suggested for each schedule:

Year	Depreciation Expense	Accumulated Depreciation, End of Year	Book Value, End of Year

2. For financial reporting purposes, determine the cost of the new equipment acquired in the exchange.
3. Journalize the entry to record the exchange.
4. Journalize the entry to record the exchange, assuming that the trade-in allowance was $12,000 instead of $16,000.

PROBLEM 9-5B

Transactions for fixed assets, including trade

Objectives 1, 3, 4

P.A.S.S.

The following transactions, adjusting entries, and closing entries were completed by Lodge Pole Pine Furniture Co. during a 3-year period. All are related to the use of delivery equipment. The declining-balance method (at twice the straight-line rate) of depreciation is used.

2005

Jan. 3 Purchased a used delivery truck for $26,500, paying cash.

5 Paid $4,000 for a new transmission for the truck. The old transmission was estimated to have a value of $500. The new transmission is expected to have a useful life equal to the remaining life of the truck.

Aug. 16 Paid garage $285 for miscellaneous repairs to the truck.

Dec. 31 Recorded depreciation on the truck and transmission component for the fiscal year. The estimated useful life of the truck and transmission is 4 years, with a residual value of $6,000 for the truck.

2006

Jan. 1 Purchased a new truck for $65,000, paying cash.

June 30 Sold the used truck for $12,000. (Record depreciation to date in 2006 for the truck.)

Aug. 10 Paid garage $175 for miscellaneous repairs to the truck.

Dec. 31 Recorded depreciation on the truck. It has an estimated residual value of $7,500 and an estimated life of 5 years.

2007

July 1 Purchased a new truck for $84,000, paying cash.

Oct. 1 Sold the truck purchased January 1, 2006, for $26,750. (Record depreciation for the year.)

Dec. 31 Recorded depreciation on the remaining truck. It has an estimated residual value of $5,000 and an estimated useful life of 8 years.

Instructions

Journalize the transactions and the adjusting entries.

PROBLEM 9-6B

Amortization and depletion entries

Objectives 7, 8

✓ 1. a. $192,000

Data related to the acquisition of timber rights and intangible assets during the current year ended December 31 are as follows:

a. Timber rights on a tract of land were purchased for $720,000 on July 11. The stand of timber is estimated at 2,250,000 board feet. During the current year, 600,000 board feet of timber were cut.

b. Goodwill in the amount of $10,000,000 was purchased on January 3.

c. Governmental and legal costs of $420,000 were incurred on October 2 in obtaining a patent with an estimated economic life of 10 years. Amortization is to be for one-fourth year.

Instructions

1. Determine the amount of the amortization or depletion expense for the current year for each of the foregoing items.
2. Journalize the adjusting entries required to record the amortization or depletion for each item.

Special Activities

ACTIVITY 9-1
Ethics and professional conduct in business

Lizzie Paulk, CPA, is an assistant to the controller of Insignia Co. In her spare time, Lizzie also prepares tax returns and performs general accounting services for clients. Frequently, Lizzie performs these services after her normal working hours, using Insignia Co.'s computers and laser printers. Occasionally, Lizzie's clients will call her at the office during regular working hours.

Discuss whether Lizzie is performing in a professional manner.

ACTIVITY 9-2
Financial vs. tax depreciation

The following is an excerpt from a conversation between two employees of Ermine Co., Jody Terpin and Hal Graves. Jody is the accounts payable clerk, and Hal is the cashier.

Jody: Hal, could I get your opinion on something?
Hal: Sure, Jody.
Jody: Do you know Margaret, the fixed assets clerk?
Hal: I know who she is, but I don't know her real well. Why?
Jody: Well, I was talking to her at lunch last Monday about how she liked her job, etc. You know, the usual . . . and she mentioned something about having to keep two sets of books . . . one for taxes and one for the financial statements. That can't be good accounting, can it? What do you think?
Hal: Two sets of books? It doesn't sound right.
Jody: It doesn't seem right to me either. I was always taught that you had to use generally accepted accounting principles. How can there be two sets of books? What can be the difference between the two?

How would you respond to Hal and Jody if you were Margaret?

ACTIVITY 9-3
Effect of depreciation on net income

Five Points Construction Co. specializes in building replicas of historic houses. Sharon Higgs, president of Five Points, is considering the purchase of various items of equipment on July 1, 2004, for $120,000. The equipment would have a useful life of 5 years and no residual value. In the past, all equipment has been leased. For tax purposes, Sharon is considering depreciating the equipment by the straight-line method. She discussed the matter with her CPA and learned that, although the straight-line method could be elected, it was to her advantage to use the modified accelerated cost recovery system (MACRS) for tax purposes. She asked for your advice as to which method to use for tax purposes.

1. Compute depreciation for each of the years (2004, 2005, 2006, 2007, 2008, and 2009) of useful life by (a) the straight-line method and (b) MACRS. In using the straight-line method, one-half year's depreciation should be computed for 2004 and 2009. Use the MACRS rates presented in the chapter.
2. Assuming that income before depreciation and income tax is estimated to be $200,000 uniformly per year and that the income tax rate is 30%, compute the

net income for each of the years 2004, 2005, 2006, 2007, 2008, and 2009, if (a) the straight-line method is used and (b) MACRS is used.

3. ▬▬▶ What factors would you present for Sharon's consideration in the selection of a depreciation method?

ACTIVITY 9-4
Shopping for a delivery truck

GROUP ACTIVITY

You are planning to acquire a delivery truck for use in your business for three years. In groups of three or four, explore a local dealer's purchase and leasing options for the truck. Summarize the costs of purchasing versus leasing, and list other factors that might help you decide whether to buy or lease the truck.

ACTIVITY 9-5
Applying for patents, copyrights, and trademarks

INTERNET

Go to the Internet and review the procedures for applying for a patent, a copyright, and a trademark. One Internet site that is useful for this purpose is **idresearch.com**, which is linked to the text's Web site at **http://warren.swlearning.com**. Prepare a written summary of these procedures.

Answers to Self-Examination Questions

1. **C** All amounts spent to get a fixed asset (such as machinery) in place and ready for use are proper charges to the asset account. In the case of machinery acquired, the freight (answer A) and the installation costs (answer B) are both (answer C) proper charges to the machinery account.

2. **C** The periodic charge for depreciation under the declining-balance method (twice the straight-line rate) for the second year is determined by first computing the depreciation charge for the first year. The depreciation for the first year of $6,000 (answer A) is computed by multiplying the cost of the equipment, $9,000, by 2/3 (the straight-line rate of 1/3 multiplied by 2). The depreciation for the second year of $2,000 (answer C) is then determined by multiplying the book value at the end of the first year, $3,000 (the cost of $9,000 minus the first-year depreciation of $6,000), by 2/3. The third year's depreciation is $400 (answer D). It is determined by multiplying the book value at the end of the second year, $1,000, by 2/3, thus yielding $667. However, the equipment cannot be depreciated

below its residual value of $600; thus, the third-year depreciation is $400 ($1,000 − $600).

3. **B** A depreciation method that provides for a higher depreciation amount in the first year of the use of an asset and a gradually declining periodic amount thereafter is called an accelerated depreciation method. The declining-balance method (answer B) is an example of such a method.

4. **B** The acceptable method of accounting for an exchange of similar assets in which the trade-in allowance ($30,000) exceeds the book value of the old asset ($25,000) requires that the cost of the new asset be determined by adding the amount of cash given ($70,000) to the book value of the old asset ($25,000), which totals $95,000. Alternatively, the unrecognized gain ($5,000) can be subtracted from the list price ($100,000).

5. **D** Long-lived assets that are useful in operations, not held for sale, and without physical qualities are called intangible assets. Patents, goodwill, and copyrights are examples of intangible assets (answer D).

10

CURRENT LIABILITIES

objectives

After studying this chapter, you should be able to:

1 Define and give examples of current liabilities.

2 Prepare journal entries for short-term notes payable and the disclosure for the current portion of long-term debt.

3 Describe the accounting treatment for contingent liabilities and journalize entries for product warranties.

4 Determine employer liabilities for payroll, including liabilities arising from employee earnings and deductions from earnings.

5 Describe payroll accounting systems that use a payroll register, employee earnings records, and a general journal.

6 Journalize entries for employee fringe benefits, including vacation pay and pensions.

7 Use the quick ratio to analyze the ability of a business to pay its current liabilities.

If you are employed, you know that your paycheck is normally less than the total amount you earned because your employer deducted amounts for such items as federal income tax and social security tax. For example, if you worked 20 hours last week at $10 per hour and you are paid weekly, your payroll check could appear as follows:

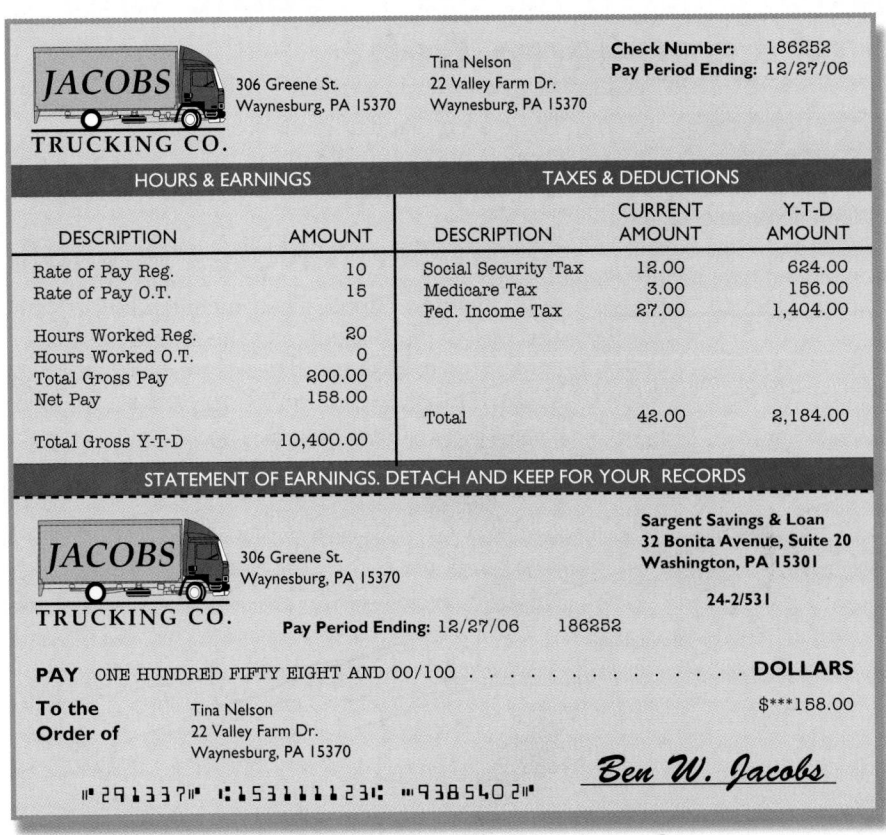

Your employer has a liability to you for your earnings until you are paid. Your employer also has a liability to deposit the taxes withheld. In this chapter, we will discuss liabilities for amounts that must be paid within a short period of time. In addition to liabilities related to payroll and payroll taxes, we will discuss liabilities from notes payable and product warranties.

The Nature of Current Liabilities

objective   1

Define and give examples of current liabilities.

Your credit card balance is probably due within a short time, such as 30 days. Such liabilities that are to be paid out of current assets and are due within a short time, usually within one year, are called **current liabilities**. Most current liabilities arise from two basic transactions:

1. Receiving goods or services prior to making payment.
2. Receiving payment prior to delivering goods or services.

An example of the first type of transaction is **accounts payable** arising from purchases of merchandise for resale. An example of the second type of transaction is **unearned rent** arising from the receipt of rent in advance. Some additional examples of current liabilities that we discussed in previous chapters are:

- Taxes payable—the amount of taxes owed to governmental units
- Interest payable—the amount of interest owed on borrowed funds
- Wages payable—the amount owed to employees

In this chapter, we will introduce some other common current liabilities. These include short-term notes payable, contingencies, payroll liabilities, and employee fringe benefits.

Short-Term Notes Payable and Current Portion of Long-Term Debt

<table>
<tr><td>objective 2</td></tr>
</table>

Prepare journal entries for short-term notes payable and the disclosure for the current portion of long-term debt.

The current liability section of the balance sheet can contain items that are used to finance business operations, such as short-term notes payable and the portion of long-term debt that is due within the coming period.

Short-Term Notes Payable

Notes may be issued when merchandise or other assets are purchased. They may also be issued to creditors to temporarily satisfy an account payable created earlier. For example, assume that a business issues a 90-day, 12% note for $1,000, dated August 1, 2006, to Murray Co. for a $1,000 overdue account. The entry to record the issuance of the note is as follows:

Aug.	1	Accounts Payable—Murray Co.	1 0 0 0 00	
		Notes Payable		1 0 0 0 00
		Issued a 90-day, 12% note on account.		

When the note matures, the entry to record the payment of $1,000 principal plus $30 interest ($1,000 × 12% × 90/360) is as follows:

Oct.	30	Notes Payable	1 0 0 0 00	
		Interest Expense	3 0 00	
		Cash		1 0 3 0 00
		Paid principal and interest due on note.		

The interest expense is reported in the Other Expense section of the income statement for the year ended December 31, 2006. The interest expense account is closed at December 31.

The preceding entries for notes payable are similar to those we discussed in an earlier chapter for notes receivable. Notes payable entries are presented from the viewpoint of the borrower, while notes receivable entries are presented from the viewpoint of the creditor or lender. To illustrate, the following entries are journalized for a borrower (Bowden Co.), who issues a note payable to a creditor (Coker Co.):

	Bowden Co. (Borrower)			Coker Co. (Creditor)		

May 1. Bowden Co. purchased merchandise on account from Coker Co., $10,000, 2/10, n/30. The merchandise cost Coker Co. $7,500.	Merchandise Inventory
	  Accounts Payable
		10,000	10,000	Accounts Receivable
				  Sales
					10,000	10,000

				Cost of Merchandise Sold Merchandise Inventory	7,500	7,500

May 31. Bowden Co. issued a 60-day, 12% note for $10,000 to Coker Co. on account.	Accounts Payable
	  Notes Payable
		10,000	10,000	Notes Receivable
				  Accounts Receivable
					10,000	10,000

July 30. Bowden Co. paid Coker Co. the amount due on the note of May 31. Interest: $10,000 × 12% × 60/360.	Notes Payable
	Interest Expense
	  Cash
		10,000
		200
			10,200	Cash
				  Interest Revenue
				  Notes Receivable
					10,200	200
						10,000

I began as a small store in 1943 in Cleveland, founded by immigrants from Nazi Germany. Today I'm America's premiere fabric and crafts chain, with nearly 1,000 locations and more than 20,000 employees. In 1976, I joined the New York Stock Exchange under the name "Fabri-Centers of America." In 1994, I acquired Clothworld and its 342 stores. I opened my first giant superstore in 1995. In 2002, my superstores generated more than four times the revenue of our traditional stores. The name I go by today reflects the names of two daughters of my founding families. Who am I? (Go to page 423 for answer.)

Notes may also be issued when money is borrowed from banks. Although the terms may vary, many banks would accept from the borrower an interest-bearing note for the amount of the loan. For example, assume that on September 19 a firm borrows $4,000 from First National Bank by giving the bank a 90-day, 15% note. The entry to record the receipt of cash and the issuance of the note is as follows:

Sep.	19	Cash	4 0 0 0 00	
		Notes Payable		4 0 0 0 00
		Issued a 90-day, 15% note to the bank.		

On the due date of the note (December 18), the borrower owes $4,000, the principal of the note, plus interest of $150 ($4,000 × 15% × 90/360). The entry to record the payment of the note is as follows:

Dec.	18	Notes Payable	4 0 0 0 00	
		Interest Expense	1 5 0 00	
		Cash		4 1 5 0 00
		Paid principal and interest due on note.		

REAL WORLD

The U.S. Treasury issues short-term treasury bills to investors at a discount.

Sometimes a borrower will issue to a creditor a discounted note rather than an interest-bearing note. Although such a note does not specify an interest rate, the creditor sets a rate of interest and deducts the interest from the face amount of the note. This interest is called the **discount**. The rate used in computing the discount is called the **discount rate**. The borrower is given the remainder, called the **proceeds**.

To illustrate, assume that on August 10, Cary Company issues a $20,000, 90-day note to Rock Company in exchange for inventory. Rock discounts the note at a rate of 15%. The amount of the discount, $750, is debited to *Interest Expense*. The proceeds, $19,250, are debited to *Merchandise Inventory*. *Notes Payable* is credited for the face amount of the note, which is also its maturity value. This entry is shown below.

Aug.	10	Merchandise Inventory	19 2 5 0 00	
		Interest Expense	7 5 0 00	
		Notes Payable		20 0 0 0 00
		Issued a 90-day note to Rock Co.,		
		discounted at 15%.		

In buying a used delivery truck, a business issues an $8,000, 60-day note dated July 15, which the truck's seller discounts at 12%. What is the cost of the truck (the proceeds)?

- -

$7,840 [$8,000 − ($8,000 × 12% × 60/360)]

When the note is paid, the following entry is recorded:[1]

Nov.	8	Notes Payable	20 0 0 0 00	
		Cash		20 0 0 0 00
		Paid note due.		

Current Portion of Long-Term Debt

Long-term liabilities are often paid back in periodic payments, called **installments**, much like a car loan. Long-term liability installments that are due *within* the coming year must be classified as a current liability. The total amount of the installments due *after* the coming year is classified as a long-term liability. To illustrate, **Starbucks**

---

[1]If the accounting period ends before a discounted note is paid, an adjusting entry should record the prepaid (deferred) interest that is not yet an expense. This deferred interest would be deducted from Notes Payable in the Current Liabilities section of the balance sheet.

Corp. reported the following scheduled debt payments in the notes to its September 30, 2002 annual report to shareholders:

Fiscal year ending

2003	$ 710,000
2004	722,000
2005	735,000
2006	748,000
2007	762,000
Thereafter	2,109,000
Total principal payments	$5,786,000

The debt of $710,000 due in 2003 would be reported as a current liability on the September 30, 2002 balance sheet. The remaining debt of $5,076,000 ($5,786,000 − $710,000) would be reported as a long-term liability on the balance sheet, which we will discuss in a later chapter.

Contingent Liabilities

objective 3

Describe the accounting treatment for contingent liabilities and journalize entries for product warranties.

Some past transactions will result in liabilities if certain events occur in the future. These potential obligations are called **contingent liabilities**. For example, **Ford Motor Company** would have a contingent liability for the estimated costs associated with warranty work on new car sales. The obligation is contingent upon a *future event*, namely, a customer requiring warranty work on a vehicle. The obligation is the result of a *past transaction*, which is the original sale of the vehicle.

If a contingent liability is *probable* and the amount of the liability can be *reasonably estimated*, it should be recorded in the accounts. **Ford Motor Company**'s vehicle warranty costs are an example of a *recordable* contingent liability. The warranty costs are *probable* because it is known that warranty repairs will be required on some vehicles. In addition, the costs can be *estimated* from past warranty experience.

To illustrate, assume that during June a company sells a product for $60,000 on which there is a 36-month warranty for repairing defects. Past experience indicates that the average cost to repair defects is 5% of the sales price over the warranty period. The entry to record the estimated product warranty expense for June is as follows:

June	30	Product Warranty Expense	3 0 0 0 00	
		Product Warranty Payable		3 0 0 0 00
		Warranty expense for June, 5% × $60,000.		

A business sells to a customer $120,000 of commercial audio equipment with a one-year repair and replacement warranty. Historically, the average cost to repair or replace is 2% of sales. How is this contingent liability recorded?

Product Warranty Expense	2,400
Product Warranty Payable	2,400

This transaction matches revenues and expenses properly by recording warranty costs in the same period in which the sale is recorded. When the defective product is repaired, the repair costs are recorded by debiting *Product Warranty Payable* and crediting *Cash*, *Supplies*, or other appropriate accounts. Thus, if a customer required a $200 part replacement on August 16, the entry would be:

Aug.	16	Product Warranty Payable	2 0 0 00	
		Supplies		2 0 0 00
		Replaced defective part under warranty.		

If a contingent liability is probable but cannot be *reasonably estimated* or is only *possible*, then the nature of the contingent liability should be disclosed in the notes to the financial statements. Professional judgment is required in distinguishing between contingent liabilities that are probable versus those that are only possible.

Common examples of contingent liabilities disclosed in notes to the financial statements are litigation, environmental matters, guarantees, and contingencies from the sale of receivables. The following example of a contingency disclosure, related to litigation, was taken from a recent annual report of **eBay Inc.**:

> . . . eBay was served with a lawsuit . . . filed on behalf of a purported class of eBay users who purchased allegedly forged autographed sports memorabilia on eBay. The lawsuit claims eBay was negligent in permitting certain named (and other unnamed) defendants to sell allegedly forged autographed sports memorabilia on eBay. . . . Management believes that the ultimate resolution of these disputes will not have a material adverse impact on eBay's consolidated financial positions, results of operations, or cash flows.

The accounting treatment of contingent liabilities is summarized in Exhibit 1.

•Exhibit 1 Accounting Treatment of Contingent Liabilities

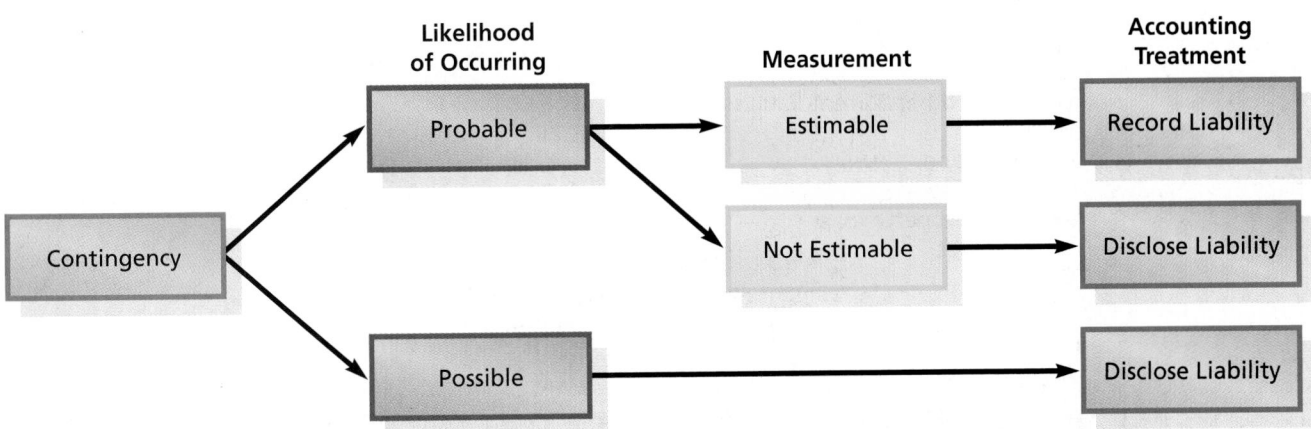

INTEGRITY IN BUSINESS

TODAY'S MISTAKES CAN BE TOMORROW'S LIABILITY

Environmental and public health claims are quickly growing into some of the largest contingent liabilities facing companies. For example, tobacco, asbestos, and environmental cleanup claims have reached billions of dollars and have led to a number of corporate bankruptcies. Managers must be careful that today's decisions do not become tomorrow's nightmare.

Payroll and Payroll Taxes

objective 4

Determine employer liabilities for payroll, including liabilities arising from employee earnings and deductions from earnings.

We are all familiar with the term payroll. In accounting, the term **payroll** refers to the amount paid to employees for the services they provide during a period. A business's payroll is usually significant for several reasons. First, employees are sensitive to payroll errors and irregularities. Maintaining good employee morale requires that the payroll be paid on a timely, accurate basis. Second, the payroll is subject to various federal and state regulations. Finally, the payroll and related payroll taxes have

FINANCIAL REPORTING AND DISCLOSURE

WARRANTY AND CURRENT LIABILITIES

Companies with significant warranty costs disclose the method of *estimating* warranty expense for the period. However, companies are not required to disclose the actual warranty expense or the product warranty payable. The warranty expense is rarely disclosed, while the product warranty payable is disclosed in the notes, if deemed material. The following is the warranty accounting policy for **Dell Computer Corp.**:

Warranty—The Company provides for an estimate of costs that may be incurred under its basic limited warranty at the time product revenue is recognized. These costs primarily include parts and labor associated with service dispatches. Factors that affect the Company's warranty liability include the number of installed units, historical and anticipated rate of warranty claims on those units, and cost per claim to satisfy the Company's warranty obligation. As these factors are impacted by actual experience and future expectations, the Company assesses the adequacy of its recorded warranty liabilities and adjusts the amounts as necessary. Costs associated with service and extended warranty contracts for which the Company is obligated to perform are recognized over the term of the contract.

Dell accounts for warranties the way we described in the chapter. The warranty expense is recognized at the same time revenue from product sales is recognized. The amount of the expense is estimated from the number of installed units, historical and anticipated rate of claim, and the estimated cost per claim. Dell discloses the warranty liability in the notes to its financial statements as follows:

	January 31, 2003	February 1, 2002
Accrued and other current liabilities:		
Warranty	$ 674	$ 444
Compensation	545	384
Deferred income	360	322
Sales and property taxes	239	259
Income taxes	54	5
Other	1,072	1,030
	$2,944	$2,444

As can be seen, the warranty liability is included in the broad category of "accrued and other current liabilities" along with other current liabilities discussed in this chapter, such as salaries payable (compensation), taxes payable (sales, property, and income), and unearned revenue (deferred income).

---

a significant effect on the net income of most businesses. Although the amount of such expenses varies widely, it is not unusual for a business's payroll and payroll-related expenses to equal nearly one-third of its revenue.

Liability for Employee Earnings

Salaries and wages paid to employees are an employer's labor expenses. The term **salary** usually refers to payment for managerial, administrative, or similar services. The rate of salary is normally expressed in terms of a month or a year. The term **wages** usually refers to payment for manual labor, both skilled and unskilled. The rate of wages is normally stated on an hourly or weekly basis. In practice, the terms salary and wages are often used interchangeably.

The basic salary or wage of an employee may be increased by commissions, profit sharing, or cost-of-living adjustments. Many businesses pay managers an annual bonus in addition to a basic salary. The amount of the bonus is often based on some measure of productivity, such as income or profit of the business. Although payment is usually made by check or in cash, it may be in the form of securities, notes, lodging, or other property or services. Generally, the form of payment has no effect on how salaries and wages are treated by either the employer or the employee.

Employee salaries and wages are expenses to an employer.

INTEGRITY IN BUSINESS

$15,000 UMBRELLA STAND

Dennis Kozlowski, ex-CEO of **Tyco International**, was indicted for enterprise corruption and grand larceny for allegedly stealing corporate funds through unauthorized executive compensation. He was accused of taking millions of dollars in excused loans and unauthorized expenses, including a $15,000 dog umbrella stand, $97,000 for flowers, and a $2,200 waste basket.

Source: Tyco Reveals Tens of Millions in Unauthorized Payments, Harry R. Weber, The Associated Press, 09/18/2002, St. Louis Post-Dispatch, C.12.

POINT OF INTEREST

Information on average salaries for a variety of professions can be found at the *Economic Research Institute's* Web site, which is linked to the text's Web site at **http://warren.swlearning.com**.

Salary and wage rates are determined by agreement between the employer and the employees. Businesses engaged in interstate commerce must follow the requirements of the Fair Labor Standards Act. Employers covered by this legislation, which is commonly called the Federal Wage and Hour Law, are required to pay a minimum rate of 1½ times the regular rate for all hours worked in excess of 40 hours per week. Exemptions are provided for executive, administrative, and certain supervisory positions. Premium rates for overtime or for working at night, holidays, or other less desirable times are fairly common, even when not required by law. In some cases, the premium rates may be as much as twice the base rate.

To illustrate computing an employee's earnings, assume that John T. McGrath is a salesperson employed by McDermott Supply Co. at the rate of $34 per hour. Any hours in excess of 40 hours per week are paid at a rate of 1½ times the normal rate, or $51 ($34 + $17) per hour. For the week ended December 27, McGrath's time card indicates that he worked 42 hours. His earnings for that week are computed as follows:

Earnings at base rate (40 × $34)	$1,360
Earnings at overtime rate (2 × $51)	102
Total earnings	$1,462

Deductions from Employee Earnings

REAL WORLD

Professional athletes must pay local taxes in each location in which they play their sport.

The total earnings of an employee for a payroll period, including bonuses and overtime pay, are called **gross pay**. From this amount is subtracted one or more **deductions** to arrive at the net pay. **Net pay** is the amount the employer must pay the employee. The deductions for federal taxes are usually the largest deduction. Deductions may also be required for state or local income taxes. Other deductions may be made for medical insurance, contributions to pensions, and for items authorized by individual employees.

Income Taxes

REAL WORLD

Federal income tax withholding tables are subject to frequent changes and are available from the Internal Revenue Service in Publication 15-A.

Except for certain types of employment, all employers must withhold a portion of employee earnings for payment of the employees' federal income tax. As a basis for determining the amount to be withheld, each employee completes and submits to the employer an "Employee's Withholding Allowance Certificate," often called a W-4. Exhibit 2 is an example of a completed W-4 form.

You may recall filling out a W-4 form. On the W-4, an employee indicates marital status, the number of withholding allowances, and whether any additional withholdings are authorized. A single employee may claim one withholding allowance. A married employee may claim an additional allowance for a spouse. An employee may also claim an allowance for each dependent other than a spouse. Each allowance claimed reduces the amount of federal income tax withheld from the employee's check.

•Exhibit 2   Employee's Withholding Allowance Certificate (W-4 Form)

Form **W-4**	**Employee's Withholding Allowance Certificate**	OMB No. 1545-0010
Department of the Treasury Internal Revenue Service	► For Privacy Act and Paperwork Reduction Act Notice, see page 2.	**2005**

Cut here and give Form W-4 to your employer. Keep the top part for your records.

1 Type or print your first name and middle initial   **John T.**   Last name   **McGrath**   2 Your social security number   **381 : 48 : 9120**

Home address (number and street or rural route)   **1830 4th Street**

3 ☒ Single ☐ Married ☐ Married, but withhold at higher Single rate.
Note: If married, but legally separated, or spouse is a nonresident alien, check the "Single" box.

City or town, state, and ZIP code   **Clinton, Iowa 52732-6142**

4 If your last name differs from that shown on your social security card, check here. You must call 1-800-772-1213 for a new card. ► ☐

5 Total number of allowances you are claiming (from line **H** above **or** from the applicable worksheet on page 2) . . . . . | 5 | **1**

6 Additional amount, if any, you want withheld from each paycheck . . . . | 6 | $

7 I claim exemption from withholding for 2005, and I certify that I meet **both** of the following conditions for exemption:
 • Last year I had a right to a refund of **all** Federal income tax withheld because I had **no** tax liability **and**
 • This year I expect a refund of **all** Federal income tax withheld because I expect to have **no** tax liability.
 If you meet both conditions, write "Exempt" here . . . . ► | 7 |

Under penalties of perjury, I certify that I am entitled to the number of withholding allowances claimed on this certificate, or I am entitled to claim exempt status.

Employee's signature
(Form is not valid unless you sign it.) ► *John T. McGrath*   Date ► June 2, 2005

8 Employer's name and address (Employer: Complete lines 8 and 10 only if sending to the IRS.)   9 Office code (optional)   10 Employer identification number

Cat. No. 10220Q

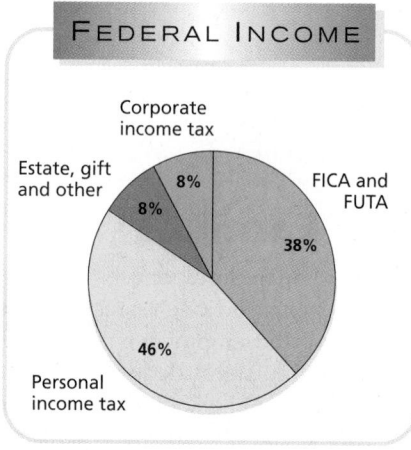

The U.S. Government receives income from various taxes, which are spent on a variety of government services. The relative sizes of these incomes and outlays for a recent fiscal year, as reported by the Internal Revenue Service, are:

REAL WORLD

FEDERAL INCOME

Corporate income tax 8%
Estate, gift and other 8%
FICA and FUTA 38%
Personal income tax 46%

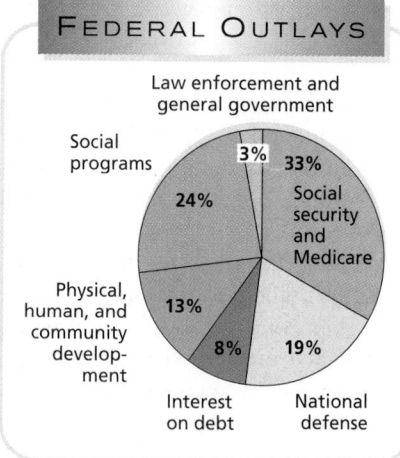

FEDERAL OUTLAYS

Law enforcement and general government 3%
Social programs 24%
Social security and Medicare 33%
Physical, human, and community development 13%
Interest on debt 8%
National defense 19%

The amount that must be withheld for income tax differs, depending upon each employee's gross pay and completed W-4. Most employers use wage bracket withholding tables furnished by the Internal Revenue Service to determine the amount to be withheld.

Exhibit 3 is an example of a wage bracket withholding table. This table is for a single employee who is paid weekly. Other tables are used for employees who are married or who are paid in time periods other than weekly. In using the withholding table, the amount of federal income tax withheld each pay period is determined by the following computational procedure:

1. Identify the appropriate subsection for the number of allowances claimed by the employee.
2. Read across the selected subsection and locate the applicable wage bracket in columns A and B.
3. Subtract the amount shown in column C from the employee's gross wages.[2]
4. Multiply the result by the withholding percentage rate shown in column D to obtain the tax to be withheld.

For example, assume that John T. McGrath, who is single and has declared one withholding allowance, made $1,462 for the week ended December 27. Using the computational procedure and information in Exhibit 3 would yield the following federal income tax withholding:

Amount of wage	$1,462.00
Less: Amount from column C	463.76
Wage, net of deduction	$ 998.24
Multiplier from column D	× 28%
Federal income tax withholding	$ 279.51

[2] The amount subtracted represents the tax benefit of the allowances and lower tax rates applied at lower income thresholds.

•Exhibit 3   Wage Bracket Withholding Table

Wage Bracket Percentage Method Table for Computing Income Tax Withholding From Gross Wages

Weekly Payroll Period

If the number of allowances is—	And gross wages are—		from gross wages		Multiply result by—
	Over	But not over			
	A	**B**	**C**		**D**
0	$0.00	$187.00	subtract	$51.00	10%
	$187.00	$592.00	subtract	$96.33	15%
	$592.00	$1,317.00	subtract	$294.60	25%
	$1,317.00	$2,860.00	subtract	$404.14	28%
	$2,860.00	$6,177.00	subtract	$776.24	33%
	$6,177.00	. . . . . .	subtract	$1,084.86	35%
1	$0.00	$246.62	subtract	$110.62	10%
	$246.62	$651.62	subtract	$155.95	15%
	$651.62	$1,376.62	subtract	$354.22	25%
	$1,376.62	$2,919.62	subtract	$463.76	28%
	$2,919.62	$6,236.62	subtract	$835.86	33%
	$6,236.62	. . . . . .	subtract	$1,144.48	35%
2	$0.00	$306.24	subtract	$170.24	10%
	$306.24	$711.24	subtract	$215.57	15%
	$711.24	$1,436.24	subtract	$413.84	25%
	$1,436.24	$2,979.24	subtract	$523.38	28%
	$2,979.24	$6,296.24	subtract	$895.48	33%
	$6,296.24	. . . . . .	subtract	$1,204.10	35%
3	$0.00	$365.86	subtract	$229.86	10%
	$365.86	$770.86	subtract	$275.19	15%
	$770.86	$1,495.86	subtract	$473.46	25%
	$1,495.86	$3,038.86	subtract	$583.00	28%
	$3,038.86	$6,355.86	subtract	$955.10	33%
	$6,355.86	. . . . . .	subtract	$1,263.72	35%

POINT OF INTEREST

In 1936, the Social Security Board described how the tax was expected to affect a worker's pay, as follows:

The taxes called for in this law will be paid both by your employer and by you. For the next 3 years you will pay maybe 15 cents a week, maybe 25 cents a week, maybe 30 cents or more, according to what you earn. That is to say, during the next 3 years, beginning January 1, 1937, you will pay 1 cent for every dollar you earn, and at the same time your employer will pay 1 cent for every dollar you earn, up to $3,000 a year. . . .

. . . Beginning in 1940 you will pay, and your employer will pay, 1½ cents for each dollar you earn, up to $3,000 a year . . . and then beginning in 1943, you will pay 2 cents, and so will your employer, for every dollar you earn for the next three years. After that, you and your employer will each pay half a cent more for 3 years, and finally, beginning in 1949, . . . you and your employer will each pay 3 cents on each dollar you earn, up to $3,000 a year. That is the most you will ever pay.

The rate on January 1, 2003, was 7.65 cents per dollar earned (7.65%). The social security portion was 6.20% on the first $87,000 of earnings. The Medicare portion was 1.45% on all earnings.

Source: Arthur Lodge, "That Is the Most You Will Ever Pay," *Journal of Accountancy*, October 1985, p. 44.

In addition to the federal income tax, employees may also be required to pay a state income tax and a city income tax. State and city taxes are withheld from employees' earnings and paid to state and city governments.

FICA Tax

Most of us have FICA tax withheld from our payroll checks by our employers. Employers are required by the Federal Insurance Contributions Act (FICA) to withhold a portion of the earnings of each of the employees. The amount of **FICA tax** withheld is the employees' contribution to two federal programs. Tax is withheld separately under each program. The first program, called **social security**, is for old age, survivors, and disability insurance (OASDI). The second program, called **Medicare**, is health insurance for senior citizens.

The amount of tax that employers are required to withhold from each employee is normally based on the amount of earnings paid in the *calendar* year. Although both the schedule of future tax rates and the maximum amount subject to tax are revised often by Congress, such changes have little effect on the basic payroll system. In this text, we will use a social security rate of 6% on the first $100,000 of annual earnings and a Medicare rate of 1.5% on all annual earnings.

To illustrate, assume that John T. McGrath's annual earnings prior to the current payroll period total $99,038. Assume also that the current period earnings are $1,462. The total FICA tax of $79.65 is determined as follows:

If an employee earns $9,000 per month and has been employed since January 1 of the current year, what is the total FICA tax deducted from the employee's December paycheck?

Social security tax	
($1,000* × 6%)	$ 60.00
Medicare tax	
($9,000 × 1.5%)	135.00
Total FICA tax	$195.00

*$100,000 − ($9,000 × 11)

Earnings subject to 6% social security tax		
($100,000 − $99,038)	$ 962	
Social security tax rate	× 6%	
Social security tax		$57.72
Earnings subject to 1.5% Medicare tax	$1,462	
Medicare tax rate	× 1.5%	
Medicare tax		21.93
Total FICA tax		$79.65

Other Deductions

Neither the employer nor the employee has any choice in deducting taxes from gross earnings. However, employees may choose to have additional amounts deducted for other purposes. For example, you as an employee may authorize deductions for retirement savings, for contributions to charitable organizations, or for premiums on employee insurance. A union contract may also require the deduction of union dues.

Computing Employee Net Pay

Gross earnings less payroll deductions equals the amount to be paid to an employee for the payroll period. This amount is the *net pay*, which is often called the *take-home pay*. Assuming that John T. McGrath authorized deductions for retirement savings and for a United Way contribution, the amount to be paid McGrath for the week ended December 27 is $1,077.84, as shown below.

Gross earnings for the week		$1,462.00
Deductions:		
Social security tax	$ 57.72	
Medicare tax	21.93	
Federal income tax	279.51	
Retirement savings	20.00	
United Way	5.00	
Total deductions		384.16
Net pay		$1,077.84

Liability for Employer's Payroll Taxes

So far, we have discussed the payroll taxes that are withheld from the employees' earnings. Most employers are also subject to federal and state payroll taxes based on the amount paid their employees. Such taxes are an operating expense of the business. Exhibit 4 summarizes the responsibility for employee and employer payroll taxes.

FICA Tax

Employers are required to contribute to the social security and Medicare programs for each employee. The employer must match the employee's contribution to each program.

Federal Unemployment Compensation Tax

The Federal Unemployment Tax Act (FUTA) provides for temporary payments to those who become unemployed as a result of layoffs due to economic causes beyond their control. Types of employment subject to this program are similar to those covered by FICA taxes. A tax of 6.2% is levied on employers only, rather than on both employers and employees.[3] It is applied to only the first $7,000 of the earn-

---

[3]This rate may be reduced to 0.8% for credits for state unemployment compensation tax.

•Exhibit 4

ings of each covered employee during a calendar year. Congress often revises the rate and maximum earnings subject to federal unemployment compensation tax. The funds collected by the federal government are not paid directly to the unemployed but are allocated among the states for use in state programs.

State Unemployment Compensation Tax

State Unemployment Tax Acts (SUTA) also provide for payments to unemployed workers. The amounts paid as benefits are obtained, for the most part, from a tax levied upon employers only. A few states require employee contributions also. The rates of tax and the tax bases vary. In most states, employers who provide stable employment for their employees are granted reduced rates. The employment experience and the status of each employer's tax account are reviewed annually, and the tax rates are adjusted accordingly.[4]

INTEGRITY IN BUSINESS

RESUMÉ PADDING

Misrepresenting your accomplishments on your resumé could come back to haunt you. In one case, the Chief Financial Officer (CFO) of **Veritas Software** was forced to resign his position when it was discovered that he had lied about earning an MBA from Stanford University, when in actuality he had earned only an undergraduate degree from Idaho State University.

Source: Reuters News Service, October 4, 2002

---

[4]As of January 1, 2004, the maximum state rate credited against the federal unemployment rate was 5.4% of the first $7,000 of each employee's earnings during a calendar year.

Accounting Systems for Payroll and Payroll Taxes

objective 5

Describe payroll accounting systems that use a payroll register, employee earnings records, and a general journal.

In designing payroll systems, the requirements of various federal, state, and local agencies for payroll data are considered. Payroll data must also be maintained accurately for each payroll period and for each employee. Periodic reports using payroll data must be submitted to government agencies. The payroll data itself must be retained for possible inspection by the various agencies.

Payroll systems must be designed to pay employees on a timely basis. Payroll systems should also be designed to provide useful data for management decision-making needs. Such needs might include settling employee grievances and negotiating retirement or other benefits with employees.

Although payroll systems differ among businesses, the major elements common to most payroll systems are the payroll register, employee's earnings record, and payroll checks. We discuss and illustrate each of these elements next. We have kept the illustrations relatively simple, and they may be modified in practice to meet the needs of each individual business.

Payroll Register

The **payroll register** is a multicolumn report used for summarizing the data for each payroll period. Its design varies according to the number and classes of employees and the extent to which computers are used. Exhibit 5 shows a report suitable for a small number of employees.

The nature of the data appearing in the payroll register is evident from the column headings. The number of hours worked and the earnings and deduction data are inserted in their proper columns. The sum of the deductions for each employee is then subtracted from the total earnings to yield the amount to be paid. The check numbers are recorded in the payroll register as evidence of payment.

The last two columns of the payroll register are used to accumulate the total wages or salaries to be debited to the various expense accounts. This process is usually called **payroll distribution**.

•Exhibit 5 Payroll Register

| | Employee Name | Total Hours | Earnings | | | |
			Regular	Overtime	Total	
1	Abrams, Julie S.	40	500.00		500.00	1
2	Elrod, Fred G.	44	392.00	58.80	450.80	2
3	Gomez, Jose C.	40	840.00		840.00	3
4	McGrath, John T.	42	1,360.00	102.00	1,462.00	4
25	Wilkes, Glenn K.	40	480.00		480.00	25
26	Zumpano, Michael W.	40	600.00		600.00	26
27	Total		13,328.00	574.00	13,902.00	27
28						28

Recording Employees' Earnings

The column totals of the payroll register support the journal entry for payroll. The entry based on the payroll register in Exhibit 5 follows.

Dec.	27	Sales Salaries Expense	11 1 2 2 00		
		Office Salaries Expense	2 7 8 0 00		
		Social Security Tax Payable		6 4 3 07	
		Medicare Tax Payable		2 0 8 53	
		Employees Federal Income Tax Payable		3 3 3 2 00	
		Retirement Savings Deductions Payable		6 8 0 00	
		United Way Deductions Payable		4 7 0 00	
		Accounts Receivable—Fred G. Elrod (emp.)		5 0 00	
		Salaries Payable		8 5 1 8 40	
		Payroll for week ended December 27.			

Recording and Paying Payroll Taxes

The employer's payroll taxes become liabilities when the related payroll is *paid* to employees. In addition, employers are required to compute and report payroll taxes on a *calendar-year* basis, even if a different fiscal year is used for financial reporting and income tax purposes.

To illustrate, assume that Everson Company's fiscal year ends on April 30. Also, assume that Everson Company owes its employees $26,000 of wages on December 31. The following portions of the $26,000 of wages are subject to payroll taxes on December 31:

> **Payroll taxes become a liability to the employer when the payroll is paid.**

	Earnings Subject to Payroll Taxes
Social Security Tax (6.0%)	$18,000
Medicare Tax (1.5%)	26,000
State and Federal Unemployment Compensation Tax	1,000

If the payroll is paid on December 31, the payroll taxes will be based on the preceding amounts. If the payroll is paid on January 2, however, the *entire* $26,000 will be subject to *all* payroll taxes. This is because the maximum earnings limitation for determining social security and unemployment taxes will not be exceeded at the beginning of the calendar year.

•Exhibit 5   (concluded)

	Deductions						Paid		Accounts Debited		
	Social Security Tax	Medicare Tax	Federal Income Tax	Retirement Savings	Misc.	Total	Net Amount	Check No.	Sales Salaries Expense	Office Salaries Expense	
1	30.00	7.50	74.00	20.00	UW 10.00	141.50	358.50	6857	500.00		1
2	27.05	6.76	62.00		AR 50.00	145.81	304.99	6858		450.80	2
3	50.40	12.60	131.00	25.00	UW 10.00	229.00	611.00	6859	840.00		3
4	57.72	21.93	279.51	20.00	UW 5.00	384.16	1,077.84	6860	1,462.00		4
25	28.80	7.20	69.00	10.00		115.00	365.00	6880	480.00		25
26	36.00	9.00	79.00	5.00	UW 2.00	131.00	469.00	6881		600.00	26
27	643.07	208.53	3,332.00	680.00	UW 470.00	5,383.60	8,518.40		11,122.00	2,780.00	27
28					AR 50.00						28

Miscellaneous Deductions: UW—United Way; AR—Accounts Receivable

Social security contributions (both the employees' and employer's amounts) and federal income taxes must be deposited quarterly in a federal depository bank. An "Employer's Quarterly Federal Tax Return" (Form 941) must also be filed. Unemployment compensation tax returns and payments are required annually by the federal government and most state governments.

The payroll register for McDermott Supply Co. in Exhibit 5 indicates that the amount of social security tax withheld is $643.07 and Medicare tax withheld is $208.53. Since the employer must match the employees' FICA contributions, the employer's social security payroll tax will also be $643.07, and the Medicare tax will be $208.53. Further, assume that the earnings subject to state and federal unemployment compensation taxes are $2,710. Multiplying this amount by the state (5.4%) and federal (0.8%) rates yields the unemployment compensation taxes shown in the following payroll tax computation:

Social security tax	$ 643.07
Medicare tax	208.53
State unemployment compensation tax (5.4% × $2,710)	146.34
Federal unemployment compensation tax (0.8% × $2,710)	21.68
Total payroll tax expense	$1,019.62

The entry to journalize the payroll tax expense for the week and the liability for the taxes accrued is shown below.

Date		Description	Debit	Credit
Dec.	27	Payroll Tax Expense	1 0 1 9 62	
		Social Security Tax Payable		6 4 3 07
		Medicare Tax Payable		2 0 8 53
		State Unemployment Tax Payable		1 4 6 34
		Federal Unemployment Tax Payable		2 1 68
		Payroll taxes for week ended		
		December 27.		

Employee's Earnings Record

The amount of each employee's earnings to date must be available at the end of each payroll period. This cumulative amount is required in order to compute each employee's social security and Medicare tax withholding and the employer's payroll taxes. It is essential, therefore, that a detailed payroll record be maintained for each employee. This record is called an ***employee's earnings record***.

Exhibit 6, on pages 412–413, shows a portion of the employee's earnings record for John T. McGrath. The relationship between this record and the payroll register can be seen by tracing the amounts entered on McGrath's earnings record for December 27 back to its source—the fourth line of the payroll register in Exhibit 5.

In addition to spaces for recording data for each payroll period and the cumulative total of earnings, the employee's earnings record has spaces for quarterly totals and the yearly total. These totals are used in various reports for tax, insurance, and other purposes. One such report is the Wage and Tax Statement, commonly called a **Form W-2**. You may recall receiving a W-2 form for use in preparing your individual tax return. This form must be provided annually to each employee as well as to the Social Security Administration. The amounts reported in the Form W-2 shown at the top of the following page were taken from McGrath's employee's earnings record.

Payroll Checks

At the end of each pay period, **payroll checks** are prepared. Each check includes a detachable statement showing the details of how the net pay was computed. Exhibit 7, on page 414, is a payroll check for John T. McGrath.

The amount paid to employees is normally recorded as a single amount, regardless of the number of employees. There is no need to record each payroll check separately in the journal, since all of the details are available in the payroll register.

For paying their payroll, most employers use payroll checks drawn on a special bank account. After the data for the payroll period have been recorded and summarized in the payroll register, a single check for the total amount to be paid is

a Control number		22222	Void ☐	For Official Use Only ▶ OMB No. 1545-0008			
b Employer identification number 61-8436524					1 Wages, tips, other compensation $ 100,500.00	2 Federal income tax withheld $ 21,387.65	
c Employer's name, address, and ZIP code McDermott Supply Co. 415 5th Ave. So. Dubuque, IA 52736-0142					3 Social security wages $ 100,000.00	4 Social security tax withheld $ 6,000.00	
					5 Medicare wages and tips $ 100,500.00	6 Medicare tax withheld $ 1,507.50	
					7 Social security tips $	8 Allocated tips $	
d Employee's social security number 381-48-9120					9 Advance EIC payment $	10 Dependent care benefits $	
e Employee's first name and initial John T.		Last name McGrath			11 Nonqualified plans $	12a See instructions for box 12 $	
					13 Statutory employee ☐ Retirement plan ☐ Third-party sick pay ☐	12b $	
1830 4th St. Clinton, IA 52732-6142					14 Other	12c $	
						12d $	
f Employee's address and ZIP code							
15 State IA	Employer's state ID number	16 State wages, tips, etc. $	17 State income tax $	18 Local wages, tips, etc. $	19 Local income tax $		20 Locality name Dubuque
		$	$	$	$		

Form **W-2** Wage and Tax Statement (99)   **2005**   Department of the Treasury—Internal Revenue Service
Copy A For Social Security Administration—Send this entire page with Form W-3 to the Social Security Administration; photocopies are **not** acceptable.   Cat. No. 10134D   For Privacy Act and Paperwork Reduction Act Notice, see separate instructions.

Do Not Cut, Fold, or Staple Forms on This Page — Do Not Cut, Fold, or Staple Forms on This Page

written on the firm's regular bank account. This check is then deposited in the special payroll bank account. Individual payroll checks are written from the payroll account, and the numbers of the payroll checks are inserted in the payroll register.

An advantage of using a separate payroll bank account is that the task of reconciling the bank statements is simplified. In addition, a payroll bank account establishes control over payroll checks by preventing the theft or misuse of uncashed payroll checks.

Currency may be used to pay payroll. However, many employees have their net pay deposited directly in a bank. In these cases, funds are transferred electronically.

Payroll System Diagram

You may find Exhibit 8, on page 414, useful in following the flow of data within the payroll segment of an accounting system. The diagram indicates the relationships among the primary components of the payroll system we described in this chapter.

Our focus in the preceding discussion has been on the outputs of a payroll system: the payroll register, payroll checks, the employees' earnings records, and tax and other reports. As shown in the diagram in Exhibit 8, the inputs into a payroll system may be classified as either constants or variables.

Constants are data that remain unchanged from payroll to payroll and thus do not need to be entered into the system each pay period. Examples of constants include such data as each employee's name and social security number, marital status, number of income tax withholding allowances, rate of pay, payroll category (office, sales, etc.), and department where employed. The FICA tax rates and various tax tables are also constants that apply to all employees. In a computerized accounting system, constants are stored within a payroll file.

Variables are data that change from payroll to payroll and thus must be entered into the system each pay period. Examples of variables include such data as the number of hours or days worked for each employee during the payroll period, days of sick leave with pay, vacation credits, and cumulative earnings and taxes withheld. If salespersons are paid commissions, the amount of their sales would also vary from period to period.

Internal Controls for Payroll Systems

Payroll processing, as we discussed above, requires the input of a large amount of data, along with numerous and sometimes complex computations. These factors,

•Exhibit 6   Employee's Earnings Record

John T. McGrath
1830 4th Street
Clinton, IA 52732-6142   PHONE: 555-3148

SINGLE	NUMBER OF WITHHOLDING ALLOWANCES: 1	PAY RATE:	$1,360.00 Per Week
OCCUPATION:	Salesperson	EQUIVALENT HOURLY RATE: $34	

	Period Ending	Total Hours	Regular Earnings	Overtime Earnings	Total Earnings	Cumulative Total	
42	SEP. 27	53	1,360.00	663.00	2,023.00	75,565.00	42
43	THIRD QUARTER		17,680.00	7,605.00	25,285.00		43
44	OCT. 4	51	1,360.00	561.00	1,921.00	77,486.00	44
50	NOV. 15	50	1,360.00	510.00	1,870.00	89,382.00	50
51	NOV. 22	53	1,360.00	663.00	2,023.00	91,405.00	51
52	NOV. 29	47	1,360.00	357.00	1,717.00	93,122.00	52
53	DEC. 6	53	1,360.00	663.00	2,023.00	95,145.00	53
54	DEC.13	52	1,360.00	612.00	1,972.00	97,117.00	54
55	DEC. 20	51	1,360.00	561.00	1,921.00	99,038.00	55
56	DEC. 27	42	1,360.00	102.00	1,462.00	100,500.00	56
57	FOURTH QUARTER		17,680.00	7,255.00	24,935.00		57
58	YEARLY TOTAL		70,720.00	29,780.00	100,500.00		58

combined with the large dollar amounts involved, require controls to ensure that payroll payments are timely and accurate. In addition, the system must also provide adequate safeguards against theft or other misuse of funds.

The cash payment controls we discussed in the cash chapter also apply to payrolls. Thus, it is normally desirable to use a system that includes procedures for proper authorization and approval of payroll. When a check-signing machine is used, it is important that blank payroll checks and access to the machine be carefully controlled to prevent the theft or misuse of payroll funds.

It is especially important to authorize and approve in writing employee additions and deletions and changes in pay rates. For example, numerous payroll frauds have involved a supervisor adding fictitious employees to the payroll. The supervisor then cashes the fictitious employees' checks. Similar frauds have occurred where employees have been fired but the Payroll Department is not notified. As a result, payroll checks to the fired employees are prepared and cashed by a supervisor.

To prevent or detect frauds such as those we described above, employees' attendance records should be controlled. For example, you may have used an "In and Out" card on which your time of arrival to and departure from work was recorded when you inserted the card into a time clock. A Payroll Department employee may be stationed near the time clock during normal arrival and departure times in order to verify that employees "clock in" only once and only for themselves. Employee identification cards or badges may also be used to verify that only authorized employees are clocking in and are permitted to enter work areas. When payroll checks

•Exhibit 6 (concluded)

| SOC. SEC. NO.: 381-48-9120 | | | | | | | | EMPLOYEE NO.: 814 | |

DATE OF BIRTH: February 15, 1980

DATE EMPLOYMENT TERMINATED:

| | Deductions | | | | | | Paid | | |
	Social Security Tax	Medicare Tax	Federal Income Tax	Retirement Savings	Other		Total	Net Amount	Check No.	
42	121.38	30.35	436.59	20.00			608.32	1,416.68	6175	42
43	1,517.10	379.28	5,391.71	260.00	UF	40.00	7,588.09	17,696.91		43
44	115.26	28.82	408.03	20.00			572.11	1,348.89	6225	44
50	112.20	28.05	393.75	20.00			554.00	1,316.00	6530	50
51	121.38	30.35	436.59	20.00			608.32	1,414.68	6582	51
52	103.02	25.76	350.91	20.00			499.69	1,217.31	6640	52
53	121.38	30.35	436.59	20.00	UF	5.00	613.32	1,409.68	6688	53
54	118.32	29.58	422.31	20.00			590.21	1,381.79	6743	54
55	115.26	28.82	408.03	20.00			572.11	1,348.89	6801	55
56	57.72	21.93	279.51	20.00	UF	5.00	384.16	1,077.84	6860	56
57	1,466.10	374.03	5,293.71	260.00	UF	15.00	7,408.84	17,526.16		57
58	6,000.00	1,507.50	21,387.65	1,040.00	UF	100.00	30,035.15	70,464.85		58

are distributed, employee identification cards may be used to deter one employee from picking up another's check.

Other controls include verifying and approving all payroll rate changes. In addition, in a computerized system, all program changes should be properly approved and tested by employees who are independent of the payroll system. The use of a special payroll bank account, as we discussed earlier in this chapter, also enhances control over payroll.

INTEGRITY IN BUSINESS

$8 MILLION FOR 18 MINUTES WORK

Computer system controls can be very important in issuing payroll checks. In one case, a Detroit schoolteacher was paid $4,015,625 after deducting $3,884,375 in payroll deductions for 18 minutes of overtime work. The error was caused by a computer glitch when the teacher's employee identification number was substituted incorrectly in the "hourly wage" field and wasn't caught by the payroll software. After six days, the error was discovered and the money was returned. "One of the things that came with (the software) is a fail-safe that prevents that. It doesn't work," a financial officer said. The district has since installed a program to flag any paycheck exceeding $10,000.

Source: Associated Press, September 27, 2002.

	Noble Co.	Hart Co.
Current liabilities:		
Current portion of long-term debt	$ 50,000	$200,000
Accounts payable	75,000	227,000
Wages payable	65,000	120,000
Employees federal income tax payable	18,000	36,000
Social security tax payable	3,025	7,200
Medicare tax payable	975	1,800
Notes payable	8,000	148,000
Total	$220,000	$740,000

We can use this information to evaluate Noble's and Hart's ability to pay their current liabilities within a short period of time, using the **quick ratio** or **acid-test ratio**. The quick ratio is computed as follows:

$$\text{Quick Ratio} = \frac{\text{Quick Assets}}{\text{Current Liabilities}}$$

The quick ratio measures the "instant" debt-paying ability of a company, using quick assets. **Quick assets** are cash, cash equivalents, and receivables that can quickly be converted into cash. It is often considered desirable to have a quick ratio exceeding 1.0. A ratio less than 1 would indicate that current liabilities cannot be covered by cash and "near cash" assets.

To illustrate, the quick ratios for both companies would be,

$$\text{Noble Co:} \frac{\$100,000 + \$47,000 + \$84,000}{\$220,000} = 1.05$$

$$\text{Hart Co:} \frac{\$55,000 + \$65,000 + \$472,000}{\$740,000} = 0.80$$

As you can see, Noble Co. has quick assets in excess of current liabilities, or a quick ratio of 1.05. The ratio exceeds 1, indicating that the quick assets should be sufficient to meet current liabilities. Hart Co., however, has a quick ratio of 0.8. Its quick assets will not be sufficient to cover the current liabilities. Hart could solve this problem by working with a bank to convert its short-term debt of $148,000 into a long-term obligation. This would remove the notes payable from current liabilities. If Hart did this, then its quick ratio would improve to 1 ($592,000 ÷ $592,000), which would be just sufficient for quick assets to cover current liabilities.

DO YOU WANT TO BE A MILLIONAIRE?

A recent survey found that 66% of individuals believe that their standard of living at retirement will be the same or higher than during their current working years. Yet, a third of these respondents don't have a formal savings plan for retirement. One-fourth of these respondents believe that they will need to save only $100,000 in order to maintain their lifestyle in retirement. However, experts believe that today's 25-year-old will need savings of $750,000 to $1 million to support a basic retirement, given increased life expectancies and inflation. How do you save this much money? The two keys to savings success are (1) save regularly, such as monthly or quarterly, even if it's a small amount, and (2) start early. For example, to have the same retirement income as a 25-year-old saving $100 per month, a 30-year-old would need to save $200 per month. Waiting until you are 35 years old would require saving $400 per month. Every five years of delay requires doubling the necessary contribution. This is the power of compound interest. Therefore, the worst strategy is to begin retirement saving at middle age.

So how much would a 25-year-old need to save monthly to reach the $1 million mark? There are many assumptions that go into such a calculation. Let's assume that an individual begins saving $150 per month at the age of 25, earns 8% on these savings, increases the amount contributed by 5% per year (to match salary increases), and retires at the age of 65. Under these assumptions, the individual would accumulate $975,000 by age 65.

Key Points

1 Define and give examples of current liabilities.

Current liabilities are obligations that are to be paid out of current assets and are due within a short time, usually within one year. Current liabilities arise from either (1) receiving goods or services prior to making payment or (2) receiving payment prior to delivering goods or services.

2 Prepare journal entries for short-term notes payable and the disclosure for the current portion of long-term debt.

A note issued to a creditor to temporarily satisfy an account payable is recorded as a debit to *Accounts Payable* and a credit to *Notes Payable*. At the time the note is paid, *Notes Payable* and *Interest Expense* are debited and *Cash* is credited. Notes may also be issued to purchase merchandise or other assets or to borrow money from a bank.

When a discounted note is issued, *Interest Expense* is debited for the interest deduction at the time of issuance, an asset account is debited for the proceeds, and *Notes Payable* is credited for the face value of the note. The face value and the maturity value of a discounted note are equal. In addition, the current portion of an installment note payable should be disclosed as a current liability.

3 Describe the accounting treatment for contingent liabilities and journalize entries for product warranties.

A contingent liability is a potential obligation that results from a past transaction but depends on a future event. If the contingent liability is both probable and estimable, the liability should be recorded. If the contingent liability is reasonably possible or is not estimable, it should be

disclosed in the notes to the financial statements. An example of a recordable contingent liability is product warranties. If a company grants a warranty on a product, an estimated warranty expense and liability should be recorded in the period of the sale. The expense and the liability are recorded by debiting *Product Warranty Expense* and crediting *Product Warranty Payable*.

4 Determine employer liabilities for payroll, including liabilities arising from employee earnings and deductions from earnings.

An employer's liability for payroll is calculated by determining employees' total earnings for a payroll period, including overtime pay. From this amount, employee deductions are subtracted to arrive at the net pay to be paid each employee. The employer's liabilities for employee deductions are recognized at the time the payroll is recorded. Most employers also incur liabilities for payroll taxes, such as social security tax, Medicare tax, federal unemployment compensation tax, and state unemployment compensation tax.

5 **Describe payroll accounting systems that use a payroll register, employee earnings records, and a general journal.**

The payroll register is used in assembling and summarizing the data needed for each payroll period. The data recorded in the payroll register include the number of hours worked and the earnings and deduction data for each employee. The payroll register also includes columns for accumulating total wages or salaries to be debited to the various expense accounts. It is supported by a detailed payroll record for each employee, called an employee's earnings record.

6 **Journalize entries for employee fringe benefits, including vacation pay and pensions.**

Fringe benefits are expenses of the period in which the employees earn the benefits. Fringe benefits are recorded by debiting an expense ac-count and crediting a liability account. For example, the entry to record accrued vacation pay debits *Vacation Pay Expense* and credits *Vacation Pay Payable*.

7 **Use the quick ratio to analyze the ability of a business to pay its current liabilities.**

The quick ratio or acid-test ratio is a measure of a business's ability to pay current liabilities within a short period of time. The quick ratio is quick assets divided by current liabilities. A quick ratio exceeding 1 is usually desirable.

Key Terms

defined benefit plan (416)
defined contribution plan (416)
discount (399)
discount rate (399)
employee's earnings record (410)

FICA tax (405)
fringe benefits (415)
gross pay (403)
net pay (403)
payroll (401)

payroll register (408)
proceeds (399)
quick assets (418)
quick ratio (418)

Illustrative Problem

Selected transactions of Taylor Company, completed during the fiscal year ended December 31, are as follows:

Mar. 1. Purchased merchandise on account from Kelvin Co., $20,000.
Apr. 10. Issued a 60-day, 12% note for $20,000 to Kelvin Co. on account.
June 9. Paid Kelvin Co. the amount owed on the note of April 10.
Aug. 1. Issued a $50,000, 90-day note to Harold Co. in exchange for a building. Harold Co. discounted the note at 15%.
Oct. 30. Paid Harold Co. the amount due on the note of August 1.
Dec. 27. Journalized the entry to record the biweekly payroll. A summary of the payroll record follows:

Salary distribution:		
Sales	$63,400	
Officers	36,600	
Office	10,000	$110,000
Deductions:		
Social security tax	$ 5,050	
Medicare tax	1,650	
Federal income tax withheld	17,600	
State income tax withheld	4,950	
Savings bond deductions	850	
Medical insurance deductions	1,120	31,220
Net amount		$ 78,780

Dec. 30. Issued a check in payment of liabilities for employees' federal income tax of $17,600, social security tax of $10,100, and Medicare tax of $3,300.

31. Issued a check for $9,500 to the pension fund trustee to fully fund the pension cost for December.

31. Journalized an entry to record the employees' accrued vacation pay, $36,100.

31. Journalized an entry to record the estimated accrued product warranty liability, $37,240.

Instructions
Journalize the preceding transactions.

Solution

			Debit	Credit
Mar.	1	Merchandise Inventory	20 0 0 0 00	
		Accounts Payable—Kelvin Co.		20 0 0 0 00
Apr.	10	Accounts Payable—Kelvin Co.	20 0 0 0 00	
		Notes Payable		20 0 0 0 00
June	9	Notes Payable	20 0 0 0 00	
		Interest Expense	4 0 0 00	
		Cash		20 4 0 0 00
Aug.	1	Building	48 1 2 5 00	
		Interest Expense	1 8 7 5 00	
		Notes Payable		50 0 0 0 00
Oct.	30	Notes Payable	50 0 0 0 00	
		Cash		50 0 0 0 00
Dec.	27	Sales Salaries Expense	63 4 0 0 00	
		Officers Salaries Expense	36 6 0 0 00	
		Office Salaries Expense	10 0 0 0 00	
		Social Security Tax Payable		5 0 5 0 00
		Medicare Tax Payable		1 6 5 0 00
		Employees Federal Income Tax Payable		17 6 0 0 00
		Employees State Income Tax Payable		4 9 5 0 00
		Bond Deductions Payable		8 5 0 00
		Medical Insurance Payable		1 1 2 0 00
		Salaries Payable		78 7 8 0 00
	30	Employees Federal Income Tax Payable	17 6 0 0 00	
		Social Security Tax Payable	10 1 0 0 00	
		Medicare Tax Payable	3 3 0 0 00	
		Cash		31 0 0 0 00
	31	Pension Expense	9 5 0 0 00	
		Cash		9 5 0 0 00
	31	Vacation Pay Expense	36 1 0 0 00	
		Vacation Pay Payable		36 1 0 0 00
	31	Product Warranty Expense	37 2 4 0 00	
		Product Warranty Payable		37 2 4 0 00

EXERCISE 10-3
Evaluate alternative notes
Objective 2

A borrower has two alternatives for a loan: (1) issue a $90,000, 90-day, 6% note or (2) issue a $90,000, 90-day note that the creditor discounts at 6%.

a. Calculate the amount of the interest expense for each option.
b. Determine the proceeds received by the borrower in each situation.
c. ▇▇▇▇▷ Which alternative is more favorable to the borrower? Explain.

EXERCISE 10-4
Entries for notes payable
Objective 2

A business issued a 60-day, 5% note for $9,000 to a creditor on account. Journalize the entries to record (a) the issuance of the note and (b) the payment of the note at maturity, including interest.

EXERCISE 10-5
Fixed asset purchases with note
Objective 2

On June 30, Mystic Mountain Game Company purchased land for $250,000 and a building for $730,000, paying $180,000 cash and issuing an 8% note for the balance, secured by a mortgage on the property. The terms of the note provide for 20 semi-annual payments of $40,000 on the principal plus the interest accrued from the date of the preceding payment. Journalize the entry to record (a) the transaction on June 30, (b) the payment of the first installment on December 31, and (c) the payment of the second installment the following June 30.

EXERCISE 10-6
Current portion of long-term debt
Objective 2

REAL WORLD

WD-40 Co., the manufacturer and marketer of WD-40® lubricant, reported the following information about its long-term debt in the notes to a recent financial statement:

Long-term debt is comprised of the following:

	2002	2001
Term loans	$95,000,000	$45,000,000
Bank line of credit	299,000	34,783,000
Total debt	95,299,000	79,783,000
Less current portion	(299,000)	(4,650,000)
Long-term debt	$95,000,000	$75,133,000

Term loans are long-term notes payable, while a bank line of credit is usually due within the current period.

a. How much was disclosed as a current liability on the 2001 balance sheet?
b. ▇▇▇▇▷ What appears to have happened to the 2001 bank credit line during 2002?
c. How much did the total current liabilities change between 2001 and 2002 as a result of the current portion of long-term debt?

EXERCISE 10-7
Accrued product warranty
Objective 3

Crystal Audio Company warrants its products for one year. The estimated product warranty is 2% of sales. Assume that sales were $750,000 for January. In February, a customer received warranty repairs requiring $390 of parts and $570 of labor.

a. Journalize the adjusting entry required at January 31, the end of the first month of the current year, to record the accrued product warranty.
b. Journalize the entry to record the warranty work provided in February.

EXERCISE 10-8
Accrued product warranty
Objective 3

REAL WORLD

Ford Motor Company disclosed estimated product warranty payable for comparative years as follows.

	(in millions)	
	12/31/02	12/31/01
Current estimated product warranty payable	$14,166	$13,605
Noncurrent estimated product warranty payable	9,125	6,805
Total	$23,291	$20,410

Ford's sales were $130,800 million in 2001 and increased to $134,400 million in 2002. Assume that the total cash paid on warranty claims during 2002 was $12,000 million.

a. ▇▇▇▇▷ Why are short- and long-term estimated warranty liabilities separately disclosed?

b. Provide the journal entry for the 2002 product warranty expense.

c. ▭➤ Assuming $12,000 million in warranty claims paid during 2002, explain the $2,881 million increase in the total warranty liability.

EXERCISE 10-9
Contingent liabilities
Objective 3

Several months ago, Satin Cover Paint Company experienced a hazardous materials spill at one of its plants. As a result, the Environmental Protection Agency (EPA) fined the company $390,000. The company is contesting the fine. In addition, an employee is seeking $600,000 damages related to the spill. Lastly, a homeowner has sued the company for $150,000. The homeowner lives 25 miles from the plant, but believes that the incident has reduced the home's resale value by $150,000.

Satin Cover's legal counsel believes that it is probable that the EPA fine will stand. In addition, counsel indicates that an out-of-court settlement of $280,000 has recently been reached with the employee. The final papers will be signed next week. Counsel believes that the homeowner's case is much weaker and will be decided in favor of Satin. Other litigation related to the spill is possible, but the damage amounts are uncertain.

a. Journalize the contingent liabilities associated with the hazardous materials spill.

b. ▭➤ Prepare a note disclosure relating to this incident.

EXERCISE 10-10
Contingent liabilities
Objective 3

REAL WORLD

The following note accompanied recent financial statements for **Goodyear Tire and Rubber Company**:

Goodyear is a defendant in numerous lawsuits involving at December 31, 2002, approximately 62,000 claimants alleging various asbestos related personal injuries purported to result from exposure to asbestos in certain rubber coated products manufactured by Goodyear in the past or in certain Goodyear facilities. . . . In the past, Goodyear has disposed of approximately 23,500 cases by defending and obtaining the dismissal thereof or by entering into a settlement.

At December 31, 2002, Goodyear has recorded liabilities aggregating $229.1 million for potential product liability and other (asbestos) tort claims, including related legal fees expected to be incurred, presently asserted against Goodyear.

The portion of the recorded liabilities for potential product liability and other tort claims relating to asbestos claims is based on pending claims. The amount recorded reflects an estimate of the cost of defending and resolving pending claims, based on available information and our experience in disposing of asbestos claims in the past.

a. Provide a journal entry to record the contingent liability, assuming that all the liabilities for the 62,000 claimants were accrued on December 31, 2002.

b. Assume that $75 million was accrued on December 31, 2001, for the cases settled in 2002. Provide a summary journal entry for the settlements.

c. ▭➤ Why was the contingent liability accrued on December 31, 2002?

EXERCISE 10-11
Calculate payroll
Objective 4
✓*b. Net pay, $730.75*

An employee earns $18 per hour and $1\frac{1}{2}$ times that rate for all hours in excess of 40 hours per week. Assume that the employee worked 50 hours during the week, and that the gross pay prior to the current week totaled $38,540. Assume further that the social security tax rate was 6.0% (on earnings up to $100,000), the Medicare tax rate was 1.5%, and federal income tax to be withheld was $185.

a. Determine the gross pay for the week.

b. Determine the net pay for the week.

EXERCISE 10-12
Calculate payroll
Objective 4

Omega Business Consultants has three employees—a consultant, a computer programmer, and an administrator. The following payroll information is available for each employee:

✓ *Administrator net pay,*
$739.36

	Consultant	Computer Programmer	Administrator
Regular earnings rate	$2,500 per week	$40 per hour	$20 per hour
Overtime earnings rate	Not applicable	1½ times hourly rate	1½ times hourly rate
Gross pay prior to current pay period	$120,000	$98,900	$38,800
Number of withholding allowances	1	0	3

For the current pay period, the computer programmer worked 46 hours and the administrator worked 44 hours. The federal income tax withheld for all three employees, who are single, can be determined from the wage bracket withholding table in Exhibit 3 in the chapter. Assume further that the social security tax rate was 6.0% on the first $100,000 of annual earnings, and the Medicare tax rate was 1.5%.

Determine the gross pay and the net pay for each of the three employees for the current pay period.

EXERCISE 10-13
Summary payroll data
Objectives 4, 5

✓ *a. (3) Total earnings,*
$269,000

In the following summary of data for a payroll period, some amounts have been intentionally omitted:

Earnings:	
1. At regular rate	?
2. At overtime rate	$ 44,200
3. Total earnings	?
Deductions:	
4. Social security tax	15,730
5. Medicare tax	4,035
6. Income tax withheld	47,915
7. Medical insurance	7,860
8. Union dues	?
9. Total deductions	80,000
10. Net amount paid	189,000
Accounts debited:	
11. Factory Wages	135,400
12. Sales Salaries	?
13. Office Salaries	57,800

a. Calculate the amounts omitted in lines (1), (3), (8), and (12).
b. Journalize the entry to record the payroll accrual.
c. Journalize the entry to record the payment of the payroll.
d. ▭▬▸ From the data given in this exercise and your answer to (a), would you conclude that this payroll was paid sometime during the first few weeks of the calendar year? Explain.

EXERCISE 10-14
Payroll internal control procedures
Objective 5

Opry Sounds is a retail store specializing in the sale of country music. The store employs 3 full-time and 10 part-time workers. The store's weekly payroll averages $2,200 for all 13 workers.

Opry Sounds uses a personal computer to assist in preparing paychecks. Each week, the store's accountant collects employee time cards and enters the hours worked into the payroll program. The payroll program calculates each employee's pay and prints a paycheck. The accountant uses a check-signing machine to sign the paychecks. Next, the store's owner authorizes the transfer of funds from the store's regular bank account to the payroll account.

For the week of May 10, the accountant accidentally recorded 400 hours worked instead of 40 hours for one of the full-time employees.

▭▬▸ Does Opry Sounds have internal controls in place to catch this error? If so, how will this error be detected?

EXERCISE 10-15
Internal control procedures
Objective 5

Shop-Aid Tools is a small manufacturer of home workshop power tools. The company employs 30 production workers and 10 administrative persons. The following procedures are used to process the company's weekly payroll:

a. Paychecks are signed by using a check-signing machine. This machine is located in the main office so that it can be easily accessed by anyone needing a check signed.

b. Shop-Aid maintains a separate checking account for payroll checks. Each week, the total net pay for all employees is transferred from the company's regular bank account to the payroll account.

c. Whenever an employee receives a pay raise, the supervisor must fill out a wage adjustment form, which is signed by the company president. This form is used to change the employee's wage rate in the payroll system.

d. Whenever a salaried employee is terminated, Personnel authorizes Payroll to remove the employee from the payroll system. However, this procedure is not required when an hourly worker is terminated. Hourly employees only receive a paycheck if their time cards show hours worked. The computer automatically drops an employee from the payroll system when that employee has six consecutive weeks with no hours worked.

e. All employees are required to record their hours worked by clocking in and out on a time clock. Employees must clock out for lunch break. Due to congestion around the time clock area at lunch time, management has not objected to having one employee clock in and out for an entire department.

State whether each of the procedures is appropriate or inappropriate after considering the principles of internal control. If a procedure is inappropriate, describe the appropriate procedure.

EXERCISE 10-16
Payroll tax entries
Objective 5

According to a summary of the payroll of Glamour Publishing Co., $480,000 was subject to the 6.0% social security tax and $540,000 was subject to the 1.5% Medicare tax. Also, $12,000 was subject to state and federal unemployment taxes.

a. Calculate the employer's payroll taxes, using the following rates: state unemployment, 4.3%; federal unemployment, 0.8%.

b. Journalize the entry to record the accrual of payroll taxes.

EXERCISE 10-17
Payroll procedures
Objective 5

WHAT'S WRONG
WITH THIS?

The fiscal year for Tip Top Stores Inc. ends on June 30. In addition, the company computes and reports payroll taxes on a fiscal-year basis. Thus, it applies social security and FUTA maximum earnings limitations to the fiscal-year payroll.

What is wrong with these procedures for accounting for payroll taxes?

EXERCISE 10-18
Accrued vacation pay
Objective 6

A business provides its employees with varying amounts of vacation per year, depending on the length of employment. The estimated amount of the current year's vacation pay is $165,120. Journalize the adjusting entry required on January 31, the end of the first month of the current year, to record the accrued vacation pay.

EXERCISE 10-19
Pension plan entries
Objective 6

Keepsake Photos Inc. operates a chain of photography stores. The company maintains a defined contribution pension plan for its employees. The plan requires quarterly installments to be paid to the funding agent, Boston Funds, by the fifteenth of the month following the end of each quarter. Assuming that the pension cost is $315,000 for the quarter ended December 31, journalize entries to record (a) the accrued pension liability on December 31 and (b) the payment to the funding agent on January 15.

EXERCISE 10-20
Defined benefit pension plan terms
Objective 6

REAL WORLD

In a recent year's financial statements, **Procter & Gamble Co.** showed an unfunded pension liability of $1,032 million and a periodic pension cost of $151 million.

Explain the meaning of the $1,032 million unfunded pension liability and the $151 million periodic pension cost.

EXERCISE 10-21
Quick ratio
Objective 7

✓ a. 2005: 1.10

The Office-to-Go Furniture Company had the following current assets and liabilities for two comparative years:

	Dec. 31, 2006	Dec. 31, 2005
Current assets:		
Cash	$ 356,000	$ 530,000
Accounts receivable	400,000	350,000
Inventory	800,000	500,000
Total current assets	$1,556,000	$1,380,000
Current liabilities:		
Current portion of long-term debt	$ 150,000	$ 150,000
Accounts payable	570,000	450,000
Accrued expenses payable	180,000	200,000
Total current liabilities	$ 900,000	$ 800,000

a. Determine the quick ratio for December 31, 2006 and 2005.
b. ▶ Interpret the change in the quick ratio between the two balance sheet dates.

EXERCISE 10-22
Quick ratio
Objective 7

REAL WORLD

The current assets and current liabilities for **Apple Computer Inc.** and **Dell Computer Corp.** are shown as follows at the end of a recent fiscal period:

	Apple Computer Inc. (In millions) Sept. 29, 2002	Dell Computer Corp. (In millions) Jan. 31, 2003
Current assets:		
Cash and cash equivalents	$2,252	$4,232
Short-term investments	2,085	406
Accounts receivable	565	2,586
Inventories	45	306
Other current assets*	441	1,394
Total current assets	$5,388	$8,924
Current liabilities:		
Accounts payable	$ 911	$5,989
Accrued and other current liabilities	747	2,944
Total current liabilities	$1,658	$8,933

*These represent deferred tax assets, prepaid expenses, and other nonquick current assets

a. Determine the quick ratio for both companies.
b. ▶ Interpret the quick ratio difference between the two companies.

Problems Series A

PROBLEM 10-1A
Liability transactions
Objectives 2, 3

P.A.S.S.

The following items were selected from among the transactions completed by Made Rite Products Co. during the current year:

Feb. 15. Purchased merchandise on account from Ranier Co., $30,000, terms n/30.
Mar. 17. Issued a 30-day, 5% note for $30,000 to Ranier Co., on account.
Apr. 16. Paid Ranier Co. the amount owed on the note of March 17.
July 15. Borrowed $40,000 from Security Bank, issuing a 90-day, 6% note.
~~Skip~~ 25. Purchased tools by issuing a $45,000, 120-day note to Sun Supply Co., which discounted the note at the rate of 7%.
Oct. 13. Paid Security Bank the interest due on the note of July 15 and renewed the loan by issuing a new 30-day, 9% note for $40,000. (Journalize both the debit and credit to the notes payable account.)
Nov. 12. Paid Security Bank the amount due on the note of October 13.
~~Skip~~ 22. Paid Sun Supply Co. the amount due on the note of July 25.
Dec. 1. Purchased office equipment from Valley Equipment Co. for $80,000, paying $20,000 and issuing a series of ten 8% notes for $6,000 each, coming due at 30-day intervals.
17. Settled a product liability lawsuit with a customer for $41,000, payable in January. Made Rite accrued the loss in a litigation claims payable account.
31. Paid the amount due Valley Equipment Co. on the first note in the series issued on December 1.

Instructions
1. Journalize the transactions.
2. Journalize the adjusting entry for each of the following accrued expenses at the end of the current year: (a) product warranty cost, $15,680; (b) interest on the nine remaining notes owed to Valley Equipment Co.

PROBLEM 10-2A
Entries for payroll and payroll taxes
Objectives 4, 5

P.A.S.S.

✓ 1. (b) Dr. Payroll Taxes
Expense, $22,722

The following information about the payroll for the week ended December 30 was obtained from the records of Capstone Suppy Co.:

Salaries:		Deductions:	
Sales salaries	$185,300	Income tax withheld	$55,440
Warehouse salaries	47,800	Social security tax withheld	17,402
Office salaries	74,900	Medicare tax withheld	4,620
	$308,000	U.S. savings bonds	10,780
		Group insurance	17,556

Tax rates assumed:
  Social security, 6% on first $100,000 of employee annual earnings
  Medicare, 1.5%
  State unemployment (employer only), 4.2%
  Federal unemployment (employer only), 0.8%

Instructions
1. Assuming that the payroll for the last week of the year is to be paid on December 31, journalize the following entries:
   a. December 30, to record the payroll.
   b. December 30, to record the employer's payroll taxes on the payroll to be paid on December 31. Of the total payroll for the last week of the year, $14,000 is subject to unemployment compensation taxes.
2. Assuming that the payroll for the last week of the year is to be paid on January 5 of the following fiscal year, journalize the following entries:
   a. December 30, to record the payroll.
   b. January 5, to record the employer's payroll taxes on the payroll to be paid on January 5.

PROBLEM 10-3A
Wage and tax statement data on employer FICA tax

Objectives 4, 5

SPREADSHEET

✓2. (e) $30,063

Wholesome Dairy Co. began business on January 2, 2005. Salaries were paid to employees on the last day of each month, and social security tax, Medicare tax, and federal income tax were withheld in the required amounts. An employee who is hired in the middle of the month receives half the monthly salary for that month. All required payroll tax reports were filed, and the correct amount of payroll taxes was remitted by the company for the calendar year. Early in 2006, before the Wage and Tax Statements (Form W-2) could be prepared for distribution to employees and for filing with the Social Security Administration, the employees' earnings records were inadvertently destroyed.

None of the employees resigned or were discharged during the year, and there were no changes in salary rates. The social security tax was withheld at the rate of 6.0% on the first $100,000 of salary and Medicare tax at the rate of 1.5% on salary. Data on dates of employment, salary rates, and employees' income taxes withheld, which are summarized as follows, were obtained from personnel records and payroll records.

Employee	Date First Employed	Monthly Salary	Monthly Income Tax Withheld
Alvarez	Jan. 16	$10,800	$2,700
Carver	Nov. 1	3,000	450
Felix	Jan. 2	3,400	544
Lydall	July 16	4,000	700
Porter	Jan. 2	8,500	2,040
Song	May 1	4,500	810
Walker	Feb. 16	5,600	1,064

Instructions

1. Calculate the amounts to be reported on each employee's Wage and Tax Statement (Form W-2) for 2005, arranging the data in the following form:

Employee	Gross Earnings	Federal Income Tax Withheld	Social Security Tax Withheld	Medicare Tax Withheld

2. Calculate the following employer payroll taxes for the year: (a) social security; (b) Medicare; (c) state unemployment compensation at 4.2% on the first $7,000 of each employee's earnings; (d) federal unemployment compensation at 0.8% on the first $7,000 of each employee's earnings; (e) total.

If the working papers correlating with this textbook are not used, omit Problem 10-4A.

PROBLEM 10-4A
Payroll register

Objectives 4, 5

✓3. Dr. Payroll Taxes Expense, $671.91

The payroll register for Scottish Heritage Stores, Inc., for the week ended December 12, 2006, is presented in the working papers.

Instructions

1. Journalize the entry to record the payroll for the week.
2. Journalize the entry to record the issuance of the checks to employees.
3. Journalize the entry to record the employer's payroll taxes for the week. Assume the following tax rates: state unemployment, 3.6%; federal unemployment, 0.8%. Of the earnings, $1,250 is subject to unemployment taxes.
4. Journalize the entry to record a check issued on December 15 to Second National Bank in payment of employees' income taxes, $1,402.06, social security taxes, $987.06, and Medicare taxes, $246.76.

PROBLEM 10-5A
Payroll register

Objectives 4, 5

The following data for Southern Home Products Inc. relate to the payroll for the week ended December 7, 2006:

SPREADSHEET

✓ 1. Total net amount
payable, $7,248.29

Employee	Hours Worked	Hourly Rate	Weekly Salary	Federal Income Tax	U.S. Savings Bonds	Accumulated Earnings, Nov. 30
M	45.00	$28.00		$292.60	$35.00	$ 64,200.00
N	25.00	22.00		82.50		12,600.00
O			$2,350.00	564.00	50.00	112,800.00
P	40.00	18.00		144.00	15.00	35,600.00
Q	40.00	20.00		168.00	10.00	40,500.00
R	46.00	18.50		190.37		38,700.00
S	40.00	16.00		121.60	15.00	30,720.00
T			1,000.00	215.00		48,000.00
U	50.00	36.00		455.40	40.00	82,600.00

Employees O and T are office staff, and all of the other employees are sales personnel. All sales personnel are paid 1½ times the regular rate for all hours in excess of 40 hours per week. The social security tax rate is 6.0% on the first $100,000 of each employee's annual earnings, and Medicare tax is 1.5% of each employee's annual earnings. The next payroll check to be used is No. 818.

Instructions
1. Prepare a payroll register for Southern Home Products Inc. for the week ended December 7, 2006.
2. Journalize the entry to record the payroll for the week.

PROBLEM 10-6A
Payroll accounts and year-end entries

Objectives 4, 5, 6

P.A.S.S.

The following accounts, with the balances indicated, appear in the ledger of Brownie Points Gifts Inc. on December 1 of the current year:

211	Salaries Payable	—	218	Bond Deductions Payable	$ 2,400
212	Social Security Tax Payable	$ 8,276	219	Medical Insurance Payable	9,000
213	Medicare Tax Payable	2,178	611	Operations Salaries Expense	946,000
214	Employees Federal Income Tax Payable	13,431	711	Officers Salaries Expense	404,800
215	Employees State Income Tax Payable	13,068	712	Office Salaries Expense	246,400
216	State Unemployment Tax Payable	1,200	719	Payroll Taxes Expense	123,244
217	Federal Unemployment Tax Payable	300			

The following transactions relating to payroll, payroll deductions, and payroll taxes occurred during December:

Dec. 2. Issued Check No. 728 for $2,400 to First National Bank to purchase U.S. savings bonds for employees.
　3. Issued Check No. 729 to First National Bank for $23,885, in payment of $8,276 of social security tax, $2,178 of Medicare tax, and $13,431 of employees' federal income tax due.
　14. Journalized the entry to record the biweekly payroll. A summary of the payroll record follows:

Salary distribution:		
Operations	$42,500	
Officers	18,500	
Office	11,000	$72,000
Deductions:		
Social security tax	$ 3,960	
Medicare tax	1,080	
Federal income tax withheld	12,816	
State income tax withheld	3,240	
Savings bond deductions	1,200	
Medical insurance deductions	1,500	23,796
Net amount		$48,204

　14. Issued Check No. 738 in payment of the net amount of the biweekly payroll.

(continued)

Dec. 14. Journalized the entry to record payroll taxes on employees' earnings of December 14: social security tax, $3,960; Medicare tax, $1,080; state unemployment tax, $285; federal unemployment tax, $71.

17. Issued Check No. 744 to First National Bank for $22,896, in payment of $7,920 of social security tax, $2,160 of Medicare tax, and $12,816 of employees' federal income tax due.

18. Issued Check No. 750 to Pico Insurance Company for $9,000, in payment of the semiannual premium on the group medical insurance policy.

28. Journalized the entry to record the biweekly payroll. A summary of the payroll record follows:

Salary distribution:		
Operations	$43,200	
Officers	18,200	
Office	11,400	$72,800
Deductions:		
Social security tax	$ 3,931	
Medicare tax	1,092	
Federal income tax withheld	12,958	
State income tax withheld	3,276	
Savings bond deductions	1,200	22,457
Net amount		$50,343

28. Issued Check No. 782 in payment of the net amount of the biweekly payroll.

28. Journalized the entry to record payroll taxes on employees' earnings of December 28: social security tax, $3,931; Medicare tax, $1,092; state unemployment tax, $166; federal unemployment tax, $42.

30. Issued Check No. 791 to First National Bank for $2,400 to purchase U.S. savings bonds for employees.

30. Issued Check No. 792 for $19,584 to First National Bank in payment of employees' state income tax due on December 31.

31. Paid $46,000 to the employee pension plan. The annual pension cost is $50,000. (Record both the payment and unfunded pension liability.)

Instructions
1. Journalize the transactions.
2. Journalize the following adjusting entries on December 31:
   a. Salaries accrued: operations salaries, $4,320; officers salaries, $1,820; office salaries, $1,140. The payroll taxes are immaterial and are not accrued.
   b. Vacation pay, $13,200.

Problems Series B

PROBLEM 10-1B
Liability transactions
Objectives 2, 3

P.A.S.S.

The following items were selected from among the transactions completed by Electronic Universe Stores during the current year:

Apr. 7. Borrowed $20,000 from First Financial Corporation, issuing a 60-day, 6% note for that amount.

May 10. Purchased equipment by issuing a $90,000, 120-day note to Milford Equipment Co., which discounted the note at the rate of 8%.

June 6. Paid First Financial Corporation the interest due on the note of April 7 and renewed the loan by issuing a new 30-day, 9% note for $20,000. (Record both the debit and credit to the notes payable account.)

July 6. Paid First Financial Corporation the amount due on the note of June 6.

Aug. 3. Purchased merchandise on account from Hamilton Co., $18,000, terms, n/30.

Sept. 2. Issued a 60-day, 7.5% note for $18,000 to Hamilton Co., on account.
      ✗—7. Paid Milford Equipment Co. the amount due on the note of May 10.
Nov. 1. Paid Hamilton Co. the amount owed on the note of September 2.
      15. Purchased store equipment from Merchandising Systems, Inc., for
          $100,000, paying $37,000 and issuing a series of seven 6% notes for
          $9,000 each, coming due at 30-day intervals.
Dec. 15. Paid the amount due Merchandising Systems, Inc., on the first note in
          the series issued on November 15.
      21. Settled a personal injury lawsuit with a customer for $45,000, to be paid
          in January. Electronic Universe Stores accrued the loss in a litigation
          claims payable account.

Instructions

1. Journalize the transactions.
2. Journalize the adjusting entry for each of the following accrued expenses at the
   end of the current year:
   a. Product warranty cost, $13,900.
   b. Interest on the six remaining notes owed to Merchandising Systems, Inc.

PROBLEM 10-2B
Entries for payroll and payroll taxes

Objectives 4, 5

P.A.S.S.

✓ 1. (b) Dr. Payroll Taxes
Expense, $51,450

The following information about the payroll for the week ended December 30 was
obtained from the records of Sparta Co.:

Salaries:		Deductions:	
Sales salaries	$436,000	Income tax withheld	$127,440
Warehouse salaries	93,400	Social security tax withheld	40,002
Office salaries	178,600	Medicare tax withheld	10,620
	$708,000	U.S. savings bonds	24,780
		Group insurance	40,356

Tax rates assumed:
  Social security, 6% on first $100,000 of employee annual earnings
  Medicare, 1.5%
  State unemployment (employer only), 3.8%
  Federal unemployment (employer only), 0.8%

Instructions

1. Assuming that the payroll for the last week of the year is to be paid on December 31, journalize the following entries:
   a. December 30, to record the payroll.
   b. December 30, to record the employer's payroll taxes on the payroll to be paid
      on December 31. Of the total payroll for the last week of the year, $18,000 is
      subject to unemployment compensation taxes.
2. Assuming that the payroll for the last week of the year is to be paid on January
   4 of the following fiscal year, journalize the following entries:
   a. December 30, to record the payroll.
   b. January 4, to record the employer's payroll taxes on the payroll to be paid on
      January 4.

PROBLEM 10-3B
Wage and tax statement data and employer FICA tax

Objectives 4, 5

SPREADSHEET

✓ 2. (e) $30,633

Diamond Distribution Company began business on January 2, 2005. Salaries were
paid to employees on the last day of each month, and social security tax, Medicare
tax, and federal income tax were withheld in the required amounts. An employee
who is hired in the middle of the month receives half the monthly salary for that
month. All required payroll tax reports were filed, and the correct amount of payroll taxes was remitted by the company for the calendar year. Early in 2006, before
the Wage and Tax Statements (Form W-2) could be prepared for distribution to employees and for filing with the Social Security Administration, the employees' earnings records were inadvertently destroyed.

None of the employees resigned or were discharged during the year, and there
were no changes in salary rates. The social security tax was withheld at the rate of

Dec. 17. Issued Check No. 744 to First National Bank for $17,045, in payment for $5,896 of social security tax, $1,608 of Medicare tax, and $9,541 of employees' federal income tax due.

28. Journalized the entry to record the biweekly payroll. A summary of the payroll record follows:

Salary distribution:		
Sales	$33,600	
Officers	16,000	
Office	5,200	$54,800
Deductions:		
Social security tax	$ 2,959	
Medicare tax	822	
Federal income tax withheld	9,754	
State income tax withheld	2,466	
Savings bond deductions	750	16,751
Net amount		$38,049

28. Issued Check No. 782 for the net amount of the biweekly payroll.

28. Journalized the entry to record payroll taxes on employees' earnings of December 28: social security tax, $2,959; Medicare tax, $822; state unemployment tax, $160; federal unemployment tax, $40.

30. Issued Check No. 791 for $14,724 to First National Bank, in payment of employees' state income tax due on December 31.

30. Issued Check No. 792 to First National Bank for $1,500 to purchase U.S. savings bonds for employees.

31. Paid $59,500 to the employee pension plan. The annual pension cost is $65,000. (Record both the payment and the unfunded pension liability.)

Instructions

1. Journalize the transactions.
2. Journalize the following adjusting entries on December 31:
   a. Salaries accrued: sales salaries, $3,360; officers salaries, $1,600; office salaries, $520. The payroll taxes are immaterial and are not accrued.
   b. Vacation pay, $13,600.

Comprehensive Problem 3

✓ 5. Total assets, $1,221,890

Selected transactions completed by Calico Interiors, Inc., during its first fiscal year ending December 31 were as follows:

Jan.   2. Issued a check to establish a petty cash fund of $800.

Mar.   1. Replenished the petty cash fund, based on the following summary of petty cash receipts: office supplies, $265; miscellaneous selling expense, $304; miscellaneous administrative expense, $158.

Apr.   5. Purchased $10,000 of merchandise on account, terms 1/10, n/30. The perpetual inventory system is used to account for inventory.

May   5. Paid the invoice of April 5 after the discount period had passed.

10. Received cash from daily cash sales for $8,480. The amount indicated by the cash register was $8,490.

June   2. Received a 60-day, 7.2% note for $50,000 on account.

Aug.   1. Received amount owed on June 2 note, plus interest at the maturity date.

3. Received $1,400 on account and wrote off the remainder owed on a $2,000 accounts receivable balance. (The allowance method is used in accounting for uncollectible receivables.)

28. Reinstated the account written off on August 3 and received $600 cash in full payment.

Sept. 2. Purchased land by issuing a $120,000, 90-day note to Ace Development Co., which discounted it at 6%.

Oct. 2. Traded office equipment for new similar equipment with a list price of $135,000. A trade-in allowance of $66,000 was received on the old equipment that had cost $96,000 and had accumulated depreciation of $35,000 as of October 1. A 120-day, 9% note was issued for the balance owed.

Nov. 30. Journalized the monthly payroll for November, based on the following data:

Salaries		Deductions	
Sales salaries	$42,500	Income tax withheld	$13,650
Office salaries	22,500	Social security tax	
	$65,000	withheld	3,770
		Medicare tax withheld	975

Unemployment tax rates:	
State unemployment	3.8%
Federal unemployment	0.8%
Amount subject to unemployment taxes:	
State unemployment	$1,000
Federal unemployment	1,000

30. Journalized the employer's payroll taxes on the payroll.

Dec. 1. Journalized the payment of the September 2 note at maturity.

30. The pension cost for the year was $65,000, of which $61,300 was paid to the pension plan trustee.

Instructions

1. Journalize the selected transactions.

2. Based on the following data, prepare a bank reconciliation for December of the current year:
   a. Balance according to the bank statement at December 31, $105,700.
   b. Balance according to the ledger at December 31, $93,600.
   c. Checks outstanding at December 31, $22,680.
   d. Deposit in transit, not recorded by bank, $10,400.
   e. Bank debit memorandum for service charges, $80.
   f. A check for $110 in payment of an invoice was incorrectly recorded in the accounts as $10.

3. Based on the bank reconciliation prepared in (2), journalize the entry or entries to be made by Calico Interiors, Inc.

4. Based on the following selected data, journalize the adjusting entries as of December 31 of the current year:
   a. Estimated uncollectible accounts at December 31, $5,980, based on an aging of accounts receivable. The balance of Allowance for Doubtful Accounts at December 31 was $500 (debit).
   b. The physical inventory on December 31 indicated an inventory shrinkage of $1,260.
   c. Prepaid insurance expired during the year, $14,300.
   d. Office supplies used during the year, $5,680.
   e. Depreciation is computed as follows:

Asset	Cost	Residual Value	Acquisition Date	Useful Life in Years	Depreciation Method Used
Buildings	$320,000	$ 0	January 2	50	Straight-line
Office Equip.	130,000	14,000	October 2	5	Straight-line
Store Equip.	42,000	10,000	January 3	8	Declining-balance (at twice the straight-line rate)

   f. A patent costing $42,900 when acquired on January 2 has a remaining legal life of 9 years and is expected to have value for 6 years.   *(continued)*

g. The cost of mineral rights was $105,000. Of the estimated deposit of 42,000 tons of ore, 6,000 tons were mined during the year.

h. Total vacation pay expense for the year, $11,400.

i. A product warranty was granted beginning December 1 and covering a one-year period. The estimated cost is 2.5% of sales, which totaled $568,000 in December.

j. Interest was accrued on the note payable issued on October 2.

5. Based on the following information and the post-closing trial balance shown below, prepare a balance sheet in report form at December 31 of the current year.

Notes receivable is a current asset.

The merchandise inventory is stated at cost by the LIFO method.

The product warranty payable is a current liability.

Vacation pay payable:
Current liability	$10,000
Long-term liability	1,400

The unfunded pension liability is a long-term liability.

Notes payable:
Current liability	$69,000
Long-term liability	26,000

Calico Interiors, Inc.
Post-Closing Trial Balance
December 31, 2006

Petty Cash	800	
Cash	93,420	
Notes Receivable	40,000	
Accounts Receivable	202,300	
Allowance for Doubtful Accounts		5,980
Merchandise Inventory	140,600	
Prepaid Insurance	28,600	
Office Supplies	7,100	
Land	118,200	
Buildings	320,000	
Accumulated Depreciation—Buildings		6,400
Office Equipment	130,000	
Accumulated Depreciation—Office Equipment		5,800
Store Equipment	42,000	
Accumulated Depreciation—Store Equipment		10,500
Mineral Rights	105,000	
Accumulated Depletion		15,000
Patents	35,750	
Social Security Tax Payable		7,772
Medicare Tax Payable		2,010
Employees Federal Income Tax Payable		14,070
State Unemployment Tax Payable		33
Federal Unemployment Tax Payable		6
Salaries Payable		67,000
Accounts Payable		125,300
Interest Payable		1,553
Product Warranty Payable		14,200
Vacation Pay Payable		11,400
Unfunded Pension Liability		3,700
Notes Payable		95,000
Capital Stock		250,000
Retained Earnings		628,046
	1,263,770	1,263,770

6. On February 7 of the following year, the merchandise inventory was destroyed by fire. Based on the following data obtained from the accounting records, estimate the cost of the merchandise destroyed:

Jan. 1 Merchandise inventory	$140,600
Jan. 1–Feb. 7 Purchases (net)	246,720
Jan. 1–Feb. 7 Sales (net)	430,000
Estimated gross profit rate	40%

Special Activities

ACTIVITY 10-1
Ethics and professional conduct in business

ETHICS

Sarah Lindsay is a certified public accountant (CPA) and staff assistant for Kim and Horkin, a local CPA firm. It had been the policy of the firm to provide a holiday bonus equal to two weeks' salary to all employees. The firm's new management team announced on November 25 that a bonus equal to only one week's salary would be made available to employees this year. Sarah thought that this policy was unfair because she and her co-workers planned on the full two-week bonus. The two-week bonus had been given for ten straight years, so it seemed as though the firm had breached an implied commitment. Thus, Sarah decided that she would make up the lost bonus week by working an extra six hours of overtime per week over the next five weeks until the end of the year. Kim and Horkin's policy is to pay overtime at 150% of straight time.

Sarah's supervisor was surprised to see overtime being reported, since there is generally very little additional or unusual client service demands at the end of the calendar year. However, the overtime was not questioned, since firm employees are on the "honor system" in reporting their overtime.

➤ Discuss whether the firm is acting in an ethical manner by changing the bonus. Is Sarah behaving in an ethical manner?

ACTIVITY 10-2
Recognizing pension expense

WHAT DO YOU THINK?

The annual examination of Horizon Company's financial statements by its external public accounting firm (auditors) is nearing completion. The following conversation took place between the controller of Horizon Company (Peter) and the audit manager from the public accounting firm (Connie).

Connie: You know, Peter, we are about to wrap up our audit for this fiscal year. Yet, there is one item still to be resolved.

Peter: What's that?

Connie: Well, as you know, at the beginning of the year, Horizon began a defined benefit pension plan. This plan promises your employees an annual payment when they retire, using a formula based on their salaries at retirement and their years of service. I believe that a pension expense should be recognized this year, equal to the amount of pension earned by your employees.

Peter: Wait a minute. I think you have it all wrong. The company doesn't have a pension expense until it actually pays the pension in cash when the employee retires. After all, some of these employees may not reach retirement, and if they don't, the company doesn't owe them anything.

Connie: You're not really seeing this the right way. The pension is earned by your employees during their working years. You actually make the payment much later—when they retire. It's like one long accrual—much like incurring wages in one period and paying them in the next. Thus, I think that you should recognize the expense in the period the pension is earned by the employees.

Peter: Let me see if I've got this straight. I should recognize an expense this period for something that may or may not be paid to the employees in 20 or 30 years, when they finally retire. How am I supposed to determine what the expense is for the current year? The amount of the final retirement depends on many uncertainties: salary levels, employee longevity, mortality rates, and interest earned on investments to fund the pension. I don't think that an amount can be determined, even if I accepted your arguments.

➤ Evaluate Connie's position. Is she right or is Peter correct?

ACTIVITY 10-3
Executive bonuses and accounting methods

Mark Cary, the owner of Cary Trucking Company, initiated an executive bonus plan for his chief executive officer (CEO). The new plan provides a bonus to the CEO equal to 3% of the income before taxes. Upon learning of the new bonus arrangement, the CEO issued instructions to change the company's accounting for trucks. The CEO has asked the controller to make the following two changes:

a. Change from the double-declining-balance method to the straight-line method of depreciation.
b. Add 50% to the useful lives of all trucks.

Why did the CEO ask for these changes? How would you respond to the CEO's request?

ACTIVITY 10-4
Ethics and professional conduct in business

Carl Mason was discussing summer employment with Kevin Cross, president of Juniper Landscaping Service:

Kevin: I'm glad that you're thinking about joining us for the summer. We could certainly use the help.
Carl: Sounds good. I enjoy outdoor work, and I could use the money to help with next year's school expenses.
Kevin: I've got a plan that can help you out on that. As you know, I'll pay you $10 per hour, but in addition, I'd like to pay you with cash. Since you're only working for the summer, it really doesn't make sense for me to go to the trouble of formally putting you on our payroll system. In fact, I do some jobs for my clients on a strictly cash basis, so it would be easy to just pay you that way.
Carl: Well, that's a bit unusual, but I guess money is money.
Kevin: Yeah, not only that, its tax-free!
Carl: What do you mean?
Kevin: Didn't you know? Any money that you receive in cash is not reported to the IRS on a W-2 form; therefore, the IRS doesn't know about the income—hence, it's the same as tax-free earnings.

a. Why does Kevin Cross want to conduct business transactions using cash (not check or credit card)?
b. How should Carl respond to Kevin's suggestion?

ACTIVITY 10-5
Salary survey

INTERNET

Several Internet services provide career guidance, classified employment ads, placement services, resumé posting, career questionnaires, and salary surveys. Select one of the following Internet sites, which are linked to the text's Web site at **http://warren.swlearning.com**, to determine current average salary levels for one of your career options:

Creative Financial Staffing	Accounting salary information
Spherion®	Links to computer, engineering, finance, marketing, and accounting salary information
Monster®	Online Career Center, with links to salary information
Institute of Management Accountants	Salary survey information (see Career Center)

ACTIVITY 10-6
Payroll forms

GROUP ACTIVITY   INTERNET

Payroll accounting involves the use of government-supplied forms to account for payroll taxes. Three common forms are the W-2, Form 940, and Form 941. Form a team with three of your classmates and retrieve copies of each of these forms. They may be obtained from a local IRS office, a library, or downloaded from the Internet at **http://www.irs.gov** (go to forms and publications).

Briefly describe the purpose of each of the three forms.

# Answers to Self-Examination Questions

1. **C** The maturity value is $5,100, determined as follows:

Face amount of note	$5,000
Plus interest ($5,000 × 12% × 60/360)	100
Maturity value	$5,100

2. **B** The net amount available to a borrower from discounting a note payable is called the proceeds. The proceeds of $4,900 (answer B) is determined as follows:

Face amount of note	$5,000
Less discount ($5,000 × 12% × 60/360)	100
Proceeds	$4,900

3. **B** Employers are usually required to withhold a portion of their employees' earnings for payment of federal income taxes (answer A), Medicare tax (answer C), and state and local income taxes (answer D). Generally, federal unemployment compensation taxes (answer B) are levied against the employer only and thus are not deducted from employee earnings.

4. **D** The amount of net pay of $1,385.50 (answer D) is determined as follows:

Gross pay:			
40 hours at $40		$1,600.00	
5 hours at $60		300.00	$1,900.00
Deductions:			
Federal income tax withheld		$ 450.00	
FICA:			
Social security tax ($600 × 0.06)	$36.00		
Medicare tax ($1,900 × 0.015)	28.50	64.50	514.50
			$1,385.50

5. **D** The employer incurs an expense for social security tax (answer A), federal unemployment compensation tax (answer B), and state unemployment compensation tax (answer C). The employees' federal income tax (answer D) is not an expense of the employer. It is withheld from the employees' earnings.

11

CORPORATIONS: ORGANIZATION, CAPITAL STOCK TRANSACTIONS, AND DIVIDENDS

objectives

After studying this chapter, you should be able to:

1   Describe the nature of the corporate form of organization.

2   List the major sources of paid-in capital, including the various classes of stock.

3   Journalize the entries for issuing stock.

4   Journalize the entries for treasury stock transactions.

5   State the effect of stock splits on corporate financial statements.

6   Journalize the entries for cash dividends and stock dividends.

7   Describe and illustrate the reporting of stockholders' equity.

8   Compute and interpret the dividend yield on common stock.

If you own stock in a corporation, you are interested in how the stock is doing in the market. If you are considering buying stocks, you are interested in your rights as a stockholder and returns that you can expect from the stock. In either case, you should be able to interpret stock market quotations, such as the following:

Ytd % Chg	52 Weeks		Stock	Sym	Div	Yld %	PE	Vol 100s	Close	Net Chg
	Hi	Lo								
4.9	37.70	26.90	Walgreen	WAG	.17f	.6	28	27361	30.63	−0.24
12.2	58.03	43.72	WalMart	WMT	.36	.6	30	89617	56.65	0.12
23.8	43.99	27.80	WashMut	WM	1.20f	2.8	10	37919	42.75	0.70
−1.7	764	516	WashPost B	WPO	5.80	.8	26	74	725.50	−2.00
−7.9	39.98	25.60	WsteConn	WCN	...		18	1260	35.56	0.18
6.8	26.39	19.39	WasteMgt	WMI	.01	...	19	10754	24.48	0.07
8.2	12.58	6.22	WtrPikTch	PIK		...	26	107	7.95	−0.01

Although you may not own any stocks, you probably buy services or products from corporations, and you may work for a corporation. Understanding the corporate form of organization will help you in your role as a stockholder, a consumer, or an employee. In this chapter, we discuss the characteristics of corporations, as well as how corporations account for stocks.

Nature of a Corporation

REAL WORLD

A corporation was defined in the Dartmouth College case of 1819, in which Chief Justice Marshall of the United States Supreme Court stated: "A corporation is an artificial being, invisible, intangible, and existing only in contemplation of the law."

REAL WORLD

The Coca-Cola Corporation is a well-known public corporation. The Mars Candy Company, which is owned by family members, is a well-known private corporation.

In a previous chapter, we mentioned that more than 70% of all businesses are proprietorships and 10% are partnerships. Most of these businesses are small businesses. The remaining 20% of businesses are corporations. Many corporations are large and, as a result, they generate more than 90% of the total business dollars in the United States.

Characteristics of a Corporation

A **corporation** is a legal entity, distinct and separate from the individuals who create and operate it. As a legal entity, a corporation may acquire, own, and dispose of property in its own name. It may also incur liabilities and enter into contracts. Most importantly, it can sell shares of ownership, called **stock**. This characteristic gives corporations the ability to raise large amounts of capital.

The **stockholders** or **shareholders** who own the stock own the corporation. They can buy and sell stock without affecting the corporation's operations or continued existence. Corporations whose shares of stock are traded in public markets are called **public corporations**. Corporations whose shares are not traded publicly are usually owned by a small group of investors and are called **nonpublic** or **private corporations**.

The stockholders of a corporation have **limited liability**. This means that a corporation's creditors usually may not go beyond the assets of the corporation to satisfy their claims. Thus, the financial loss that a stockholder may suffer is limited to the amount invested. This feature has contributed to the rapid growth of the corporate form of business.

The stockholders control a corporation by electing a **board of directors**. This board meets periodically to establish corporate policies. It also selects the chief executive officer (CEO) and other major officers to manage the corporation's day-to-day affairs. Exhibit 1 shows the organizational structure of a corporation.

As a separate entity, a corporation is subject to taxes. For example, corporations must pay federal income taxes on their income.[1] Thus, corporate income that is dis-

---
[1]A majority of states also require corporations to pay income taxes.

•Exhibit 1   **Organizational Structure of a Corporation**

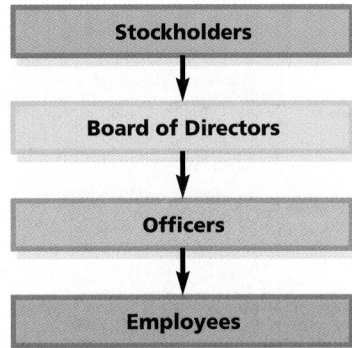

> **Corporations have a separate legal existence, transferable units of ownership, and limited stockholder liability.**

tributed to stockholders in the form of **dividends** has already been taxed. In turn, stockholders must pay income taxes on the dividends they receive. This *double taxation* of corporate earnings is a major disadvantage of the corporate form.[2]

INTEGRITY IN BUSINESS

THE RESPONSIBLE BOARD

Recent corporate failures, such as **Enron**, **WorldCom**, and **Global Crossing**, have highlighted the roles of boards of directors in executing their responsibilities. New standards for corporate governance are being suggested, such as (1) independent directors to oversee management, (2) board member expertise and education, (3) separation of the Board Chairmanship from the CEO position, (4) transparent disclosure of all board activities and transactions with the corporation (insider trades), and (5) an independent audit committee. Indeed, one study

found that "audit committees of companies where financial statement fraud has occurred generally were less independent, less expert, met less often and were less likely to have internal audit support."

Sources: R. Luke, "Inquisitive Directors: Tough Audit Questions Loom Large Since Enron," *Atlanta Journal—Constitution*, March 29, 2002; and *21st Century Governance Principles for U.S. Corporations* (Corporate Governance Center), 2002.

REAL WORLD

Corporations may be organized for nonprofit reasons, such as recreational, educational, charitable, or humanitarian purposes. Such corporations are not required to pay federal taxes. Examples of nonprofit corporations include the **Sierra Club** and the **National Audubon Society**. However, most corporations are organized to earn a profit and a fair rate of return for their stockholders. Examples of for-profit corporations include **PepsiCo**, **General Motors**, and **Microsoft**.

Forming a Corporation

The first step in forming a corporation is to file an **application of incorporation** with the state. State incorporation laws differ, and corporations often organize in those states with the more favorable laws. For this reason, more than half of the largest companies are incorporated in Delaware. Exhibit 2 lists some corporations that you may be familiar with, their states of incorporation, and the location of their headquarters.

After the application of incorporation has been approved, the state grants a **charter** or **articles of incorporation**. The articles of incorporation formally create the corporation.[3] The corporate management and board of directors then prepare a set of **bylaws**, which are the rules and procedures for conducting the corporation's affairs.

---

[2]Dividends presently receive a preferential individual tax rate of 15% to reduce the impact of double taxation.
[3]The articles of incorporation may also restrict a corporation's activities in certain areas, such as owning certain types of real estate, conducting certain types of business activities, or purchasing its own stock.

•Exhibit 2

Examples of Corporations and Their States of Incorporation

Corporation	State of Incorporation	Headquarters
Borden, Inc.	New Jersey	New York, N.Y.
Caterpillar, Inc.	Delaware	Peoria, Ill.
Delta Air Lines, Inc.	Delaware	Atlanta, Ga.
Dow Chemical Company	Delaware	Midland, Mich.
General Electric Company	New York	Fairfield, Conn.
The Home Depot	Delaware	Atlanta, Ga.
Kellogg Company	Delaware	Battle Creek, Mich.
3M	Delaware	St. Paul, Minn.
May Department Stores	New York	St. Louis, Mo.
RJR Nabisco	Delaware	New York, N.Y.
Radio Shack	Delaware	Ft. Worth, Tex.
The Washington Post Company	Delaware	Washington, D.C.
Whirlpool Corporation	Delaware	Benton Harbor, Mich.

Costs may be incurred in organizing a corporation. These costs include legal fees, taxes, state incorporation fees, license fees, and promotional costs. Such costs are debited to an expense account entitled *Organizational Expenses*. To illustrate, the recording of a corporation's organizing costs of $8,500 on January 5 is shown below.

Jan.	5	Organizational Expenses		8 5 0 0 00	
		Cash			8 5 0 0 00
		Paid costs of organizing the corporation.			

Sources of Paid-In Capital

As we discussed and illustrated in earlier chapters, the two main sources of stockholders' equity are paid-in capital (or contributed capital) and retained earnings. The main source of paid-in capital is from issuing stock. In the following paragraphs, we discuss the characteristics of the various classes of stock.

Stock

The number of shares of stock that a corporation is *authorized* to issue is stated in its charter. The term *issued* refers to the shares issued to the stockholders. A corporation may, under circumstances we discuss later in this chapter, reacquire some of the stock that it has issued. The stock remaining in the hands of stockholders is then called **outstanding stock**. The relationship between authorized, issued, and outstanding stock is shown in the graphic at the left.

Shares of stock are often assigned a monetary amount, called **par**. Corporations may issue **stock certificates** to stockholders to document their ownership. Printed on a stock certificate is the par value of the stock, the name of the stockholder, and the number of shares owned. Stock may also be issued without par, in which case it is called **no-par stock**. Some states require the board of directors to assign a *stated value* to no-par stock.

Number of shares authorized, issued, and outstanding

Some corporations have stopped issuing stock certificates except on special request. In these cases, the corporation maintains records of ownership by using electronic media.

FINANCIAL REPORTING AND DISCLOSURE

ADOLPH COORS COMPANY

Adolph Coors Company is a multinational brewer, marketer, and seller of beer and other malt-based beverages. For the year ending December 29, 2002, Coors reported sales of almost $5 billion and net income of $162 million.

Coors is incorporated in Colorado and has its headquarters in Golden, Colorado. Recently, Coors amended its articles of incorporation with the state of Colorado. Some excerpts from its articles of incorporation are shown below.

Pursuant to the provisions of the Colorado Business Corporation Act (the "Act"), the . . . corporation adopts the following . . . Articles of Incorporation.

ARTICLE I
The name of the Corporation is Adolph Coors Company.

ARTICLE II
The Corporation shall have perpetual existence.
. . .

ARTICLE IV
. . . Authorized Capital. The aggregate number of shares of Capital Stock which the Corporation shall have authority to issue is 226,260,000, said shares to consist of the following:

(1) 1,260,000 shares of Class A Common Stock (Voting), without par value ("Class A Stock");

(2) 200,000,000 shares of Class B Common Stock (Non-Voting), without par value ("Class B Stock");

(3) 25,000,000 shares of Preferred Stock, without par value ("Preferred Stock").

. . . Rights of Common Stock. The Class A Stock and Class B Stock shall be identical in all respects, share for share, except with respect to the right to vote. The right to vote for the election of directors and for all other purposes shall be vested exclusively in the holders of Class A Stock. . . . The holders of Class A Stock and the holders of Class B Stock shall

be entitled to receive such dividends as shall be declared from time to time by the Board of Directors (the "Board") out of funds legally available therefor, except that so long as any shares of Class B Stock are outstanding, no dividends shall be declared or paid on any Class A Stock unless at the same time there shall be declared or paid on Class B Stock in an amount per share equal to the amount per share of the dividend declared or paid on the Class A Stock. . . . The Board may declare and distribute dividends to the holders of Class A Stock and the holders of Class B Stock in the form of shares of Common Stock of the Corporation. . . .

. . . Rights of Preferred Stock. The Board is authorized . . . to establish . . . any dividend rights . . . whether such dividends are cumulative . . . whether any of the shares of such series shall be redeemable . . . whether such series shall have a . . . fund for the redemption or purchase of shares . . . the rights of the shares of such series upon the voluntary or involuntary liquidation, dissolution or winding up of the Corporation . . . voting rights of shares, and . . . conversion privileges.
. . .

ARTICLE VIII
. . . Board of Directors. The affairs of the Corporation shall be governed by a Board of not less than three (3) directors. Subject to such limitation, the number of directors and the method by which the directors shall be elected shall be set forth in the Bylaws of the Corporation.
. . .

ARTICLE X
. . . The Board shall be vested with the power to alter, amend, or repeal the Bylaws and to adopt new Bylaws.

 On its balance sheet, a corporation reports the following three numbers related to its common stock: 200,000 shares; 150,000 shares; and 138,000 shares. What is the number of shares authorized, issued, outstanding, and reacquired?

200,000 shares authorized; 150,000 shares issued; 138,000 shares outstanding; 12,000 (150,000 − 138,000) shares reacquired.

Because corporations have limited liability, creditors have no claim against the personal assets of stockholders. However, some state laws require that corporations maintain a minimum stockholder contribution to protect creditors. This minimum amount is called **legal capital**. The amount of required legal capital varies among the states, but it usually includes the amount of par or stated value of the shares of stock issued.

The major rights that accompany ownership of a share of stock are as follows:

1. The right to vote in matters concerning the corporation.
2. The right to share in distributions of earnings.
3. The right to share in assets on liquidation.

The two primary classes of paid-in capital are common stock and preferred stock.

When only one class of stock is issued, it is called **common stock**. In this case, each share of common stock has equal rights. To appeal to a broader investment market, a corporation may issue one or more classes of stock with various preference rights. A common example of such a right is the preference to dividends. Such a stock is generally called a **preferred stock**.

The dividend rights of preferred stock are usually stated in monetary terms or as a percent of par. For example, *$4 preferred stock* has a right to an annual $4 per share dividend. If the par value of the preferred stock were $50, the same right to dividends could be stated as *8% ($4/$50) preferred stock*.

The board of directors of a corporation has the sole authority to distribute dividends to the stockholders. When such action is taken, the directors are said to *declare* a dividend. Since dividends are normally based on earnings, a corporation cannot guarantee dividends even to preferred stockholders. However, because they have first rights to any dividends, the preferred stockholders have a greater chance of receiving regular dividends than do the common stockholders.

Nonparticipating Preferred Stock

Preferred stockholders' dividend rights are usually limited to a certain amount. Such stock is said to be **nonparticipating preferred stock**.[4] To continue our preceding example, assume that a corporation has 1,000 shares of $4 nonparticipating preferred stock and 4,000 shares of common stock outstanding. Also assume that the net income, amount of earnings retained, and the amount of earnings distributed by the board of directors for the first three years of operations are as follows:

	2005	2006	2007
Net income	$20,000	$55,000	$62,000
Amount retained	10,000	20,000	40,000
Amount distributed	$10,000	$35,000	$22,000

Exhibit 3 shows the earnings distributed each year to the preferred stock and the common stock. In this example, the preferred stockholders received an annual dividend of $4 per share, compared to the common stockholders' dividends of $1.50, $7.75, and $4.50 per share. You should note that although preferred stockholders have a greater chance of receiving a regular dividend, common stockholders have a greater chance of receiving larger returns than do the preferred stockholders.

•Exhibit 3   Dividends to Nonparticipating Preferred Stock

	2005	2006	2007
Amount distributed	$10,000	$35,000	$22,000
Preferred dividend (1,000 shares)	4,000	4,000	4,000
Common dividend (4,000 shares)	$ 6,000	$31,000	$18,000
Dividends per share:			
Preferred	$ 4.00	$ 4.00	$ 4.00
Common	$ 1.50	$ 7.75	$ 4.50

---

[4]In some cases, preferred stock may receive additional dividends if certain conditions are met. Such stock is called *participating preferred stock*. It is rarely used in today's financial markets.

Cumulative Preferred Stock

Cumulative preferred stock has a right to receive regular dividends that were not paid (not declared) in prior years before any common stock dividends are paid. Noncumulative preferred stock does not have this right.

Romer Corporation has 50,000 shares of $2 cumulative preferred stock outstanding. Preferred dividends are three years in arrears (not including the current year). What amount of preferred dividends must be paid before any dividends on common shares can be paid?

$400,000 [3 years in arrears (50,000 × $2 × 3) plus the current year's dividend of $100,000]

Dividends that have not been declared in prior years are said to be **in arrears**. Such dividends should be disclosed, normally in a note to the financial statements.

To illustrate how dividends on cumulative preferred stock are calculated, assume that the preferred stock in Exhibit 3 is cumulative, and that no dividends were paid in 2005 and 2006. In 2007, the board of directors declares dividends of $22,000. Exhibit 4 shows how the dividends paid in 2007 are distributed between the preferred and common stockholders.

•Exhibit 4   Dividends to Cumulative Preferred Stock

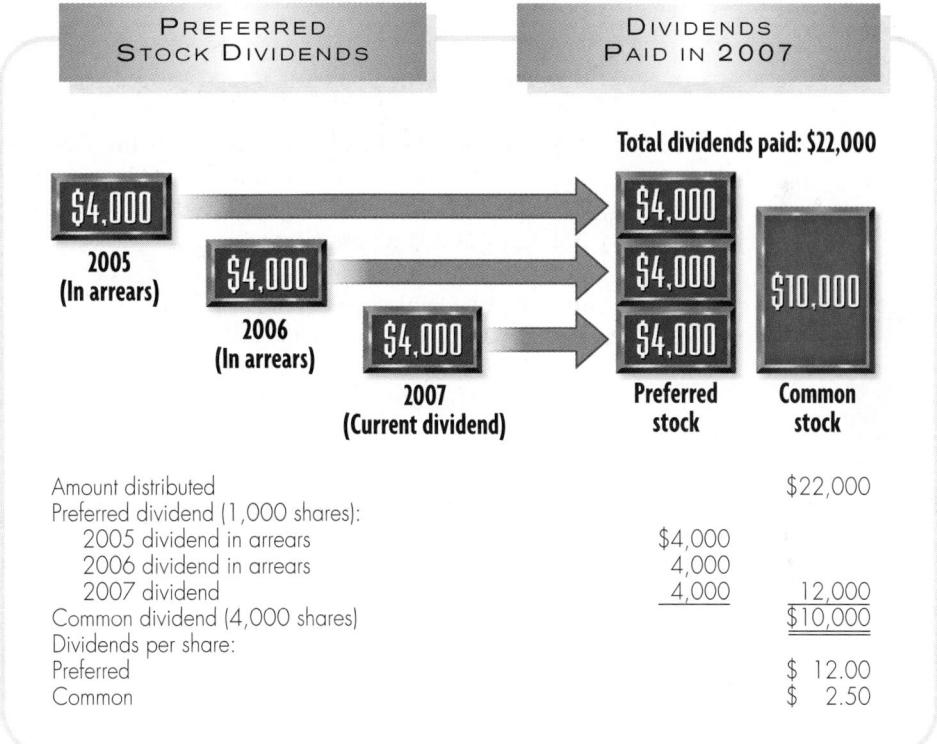

Amount distributed			$22,000
Preferred dividend (1,000 shares):			
2005 dividend in arrears		$4,000	
2006 dividend in arrears		4,000	
2007 dividend		4,000	12,000
Common dividend (4,000 shares)			$10,000
Dividends per share:			
Preferred			$ 12.00
Common			$ 2.50

Other Preferential Rights

In addition to dividend preference, preferred stock may be given preferences to assets if the corporation goes out of business and is liquidated. However, claims of creditors must be satisfied first. Preferred stockholders are next in line to receive any remaining assets, followed by the common stockholders.

Issuing Stock

objective 3

Journalize the entries for issuing stock.

A separate account is used for recording the amount of each class of stock issued to investors in a corporation. For example, assume that a corporation is authorized to issue 10,000 shares of preferred stock, $100 par, and 100,000 shares of common stock, $20 par. One-half of each class of authorized shares is issued at par for cash. The corporation's entry to record the stock issue is as follows:[5]

Cash	1,500 0 0 0 00		
Preferred Stock		500 0 0 0 00
Common Stock		1,000 0 0 0 00
Issued preferred stock and common		
stock at par for cash.		

Stock is often issued by a corporation at a price other than its par. This is because the par value of a stock is simply its legal capital. The price at which stock can be sold by a corporation depends on a variety of factors, such as:

1. The financial condition, earnings record, and dividend record of the corporation.
2. Investor expectations of the corporation's potential earning power.
3. General business and economic conditions and prospects.

When stock is issued for a price that is more than its par, the stock has sold at a **premium**. When stock is issued for a price that is less than its par, the stock has sold at a **discount**. Thus, if stock with a par of $50 is issued for a price of $60, the stock has sold at a premium of $10. If the same stock is issued for a price of $45, the stock has sold at a discount of $5. Many states do not permit stock to be issued at a discount. In others, it may be done only under unusual conditions. Since issuing stock at a discount is rare, we will not illustrate it.

A corporation issuing stock must maintain records of the stockholders in order to issue dividend checks and distribute financial statements and other reports. Large public corporations normally use a financial institution, such as a bank, for this purpose.[6] In such cases, the financial institution is referred to as a *transfer agent* or *registrar*. For example, the transfer agent and registrar for **Coca-Cola Enterprises** is **First Chicago Trust Company of New York**.

REAL WORLD

The following stock quotation for **Wal-Mart Corporation** is taken from *The Wall Street Journal*:

NEW YORK STOCK EXCHANGE

Ytd % Chg	52 Weeks Hi	Lo	Stock	Sym	Div	Yld %	PE	Vol 100s	Close	Net Chg
12.2	58.03	43.72	WalMart	WMT	.36	.6	30	89617	56.65	0.12

The preceding quotation is interpreted as follows:

Ytd % Chg	Stock price percentage change for the year to date
Hi	Highest price during the past 52 weeks
Lo	Lowest price during the past 52 weeks
Stock	Name of the company
Sym	Stock exchange symbol (WMT for Wal-Mart)
Div	Dividends paid per share during the past year
Yld %	Annual dividend yield per share based on the closing price (Wal-Mart's 0.5% yield on common stock is computed as $0.24/$49.06)
PE	Price-earnings ratio on common stock (price ÷ earnings per share)
Vol	The volume of stock traded in 100s
Close	Closing price for the day
Net Chg	The net change in price from the previous day

Premium on Stock

When stock is issued at a premium, Cash or other asset accounts are debited for the amount received. Common Stock or Preferred Stock is then credited for the par amount. The excess of the amount paid over par is a part of the total investment of the stockholders in the corporation. Therefore, such an amount in excess of par should be classified as a part of the paid-in capital. An account entitled *Paid-In Capital in Excess of Par* is usually credited for this amount.

To illustrate, assume that Caldwell Company issues 2,000 shares of $50 par preferred stock for cash at $55. The entry to record this transaction is as follows:

Cash	110 0 0 0 00	
Preferred Stock		100 0 0 0 00
Paid-In Capital in Excess of Par—		
Preferred Stock		10 0 0 0 00
Issued $50 par preferred stock at $55.		

---

[5]The accounting for investments in stocks from the point of view of the investor is discussed in the next chapter.
[6]Small corporations may use a subsidiary ledger, called a *stockholders ledger*. In this case, the stock accounts (Preferred Stock and Common Stock) are controlling accounts for the subsidiary ledger.

When stock is issued in exchange for assets other than cash, such as land, buildings, and equipment, the assets acquired should be recorded at their fair market value. If this value cannot be objectively determined, the fair market price of the stock issued may be used.

To illustrate, assume that a corporation acquired land for which the fair market value cannot be determined. In exchange, the corporation issued 10,000 shares of its $10 par common. Assuming that the stock has a current market price of $12 per share, this transaction is recorded as follows:

Land		120 0 0 0 00	
Common Stock			100 0 0 0 00
Paid-In Capital in Excess of Par			20 0 0 0 00
Issued $10 par common stock, valued			
at $12 per share, for land.			

INTEGRITY IN BUSINESS

WHAT'S THE REAL VALUE?

Stock fraud often involves illegal methods to sell stock or other investments at a price that is higher than its actual value. This can be done through illegally manipulating the stock price, selling stock in nonexistent companies, or using the proceeds of later investors to pay off earlier investors (pyramid scheme). You can avoid these kinds of fraud by following three rules:

1. Don't invest in small new companies that have market prices below $1, based on hot tips from callers in high-pressure "boiler rooms."
2. Don't invest on advice from acquaintances in social or religious groups, without checking the merits yourself.
3. Don't invest in unsolicited "risk-free" and "guaranteed" investments that promise quick profits if you act immediately.

I was born in 1913, when a banker, a bookkeeper, a lawyer, a miner, and a wood and coal purveyor invested $100 each to form the **Electro-Alkaline Co.**, to convert local brine into a liquid cleanser and germicide. My first customers were laundries, breweries, walnut processing sheds, and municipal water companies. I was briefly owned by **Procter & Gamble**. Today I'm a worldwide producer of household grocery, food, and insecticide products, with annual sales totaling $4 billion, and products sold in more than 110 countries. My brands include Glad, Pine-Sol, Hidden Valley, S.O.S., Kingsford, Fresh Step, Black Flag, and STP. Who am I? (Go to page 464 for answer.)

No-Par Stock

In most states, both preferred and common stock may be issued without a par value. When no-par stock is issued, the entire proceeds are credited to the stock account. This is true even though the issue price varies from time to time. For example, assume that a corporation issues 10,000 shares of no-par common stock at $40 a share and at a later date issues 1,000 additional shares at $36. The entries to record the no-par stock are as follows:

Cash		400 0 0 0 00	
Common Stock			400 0 0 0 00
Issued 10,000 shares of no-par			
common at $40.			
Cash		36 0 0 0 00	
Common Stock			36 0 0 0 00
Issued 1,000 shares of no-par			
common at $36.			

Some states require that the entire proceeds from the issue of no-par stock be recorded as legal capital. In this case, the preceding entries would be proper. In other states, no-par stock may be assigned a *stated value per share*. The stated value is recorded like a par value, and the excess of the proceeds over the stated value is recorded as follows:

Cash		400 0 0 0 00		
Common Stock				250 0 0 0 00
Paid-In Capital in Excess of Stated Value				150 0 0 0 00
Issued 10,000 shares of no-par common				
at $40; stated value, $25.				
Cash		36 0 0 0 00		
Common Stock				25 0 0 0 00
Paid-In Capital in Excess of Stated Value				11 0 0 0 00
Issued 1,000 shares of no-par common				
at $36; stated value, $25.				

Treasury Stock Transactions

objective 4

Journalize the entries for treasury stock transactions.

REAL WORLD

The 2002 edition of *Accounting Trends & Techniques* indicated that over 65% of the companies surveyed reported treasury stock.

A corporation may buy its own stock to provide shares for resale to employees, for reissuing as a bonus to employees, or for supporting the market price of the stock. For example, **General Motors** bought back its common stock and stated that two primary uses of this stock would be for incentive compensation plans and employee savings plans. Such stock that a corporation has once issued and then reacquires is called ***treasury stock***.

A commonly used method of accounting for the purchase and resale of treasury stock is the **cost method**.[7] When the stock is purchased by the corporation, paid-in capital is reduced by debiting *Treasury Stock* for its cost (the price paid for it). The par value and the price at which the stock was originally issued are ignored. When the stock is resold, Treasury Stock is credited for its cost, and any difference between the cost and the selling price is normally debited or credited to *Paid-In Capital from Sale of Treasury Stock*.

To illustrate, assume that the paid-in capital of a corporation is as follows:

Common stock, $25 par (20,000 shares authorized and issued)	$500,000	
Excess of issue price over par	150,000	$650,000

The purchase and sale of the treasury stock are recorded as follows:

Treasury Stock		45 0 0 0 00		
Cash				45 0 0 0 00
Purchased 1,000 shares of treasury				
stock at $45.				
Cash		12 0 0 0 00		
Treasury Stock				9 0 0 0 00
Paid-In Capital from Sale of Treasury Stock				3 0 0 0 00
Sold 200 shares of treasury stock at $60.				

(continued)

---

[7] Another method that is infrequently used, called the *par value method*, is discussed in advanced accounting texts.

Cash		8 0 0 0 00	
Paid-In Capital from Sale of Treasury Stock		1 0 0 0 00	
Treasury Stock			9 0 0 0 00
Sold 200 shares of treasury stock at $40.			

As shown above, a sale of treasury stock may result in a decrease in paid-in capital. To the extent that Paid-In Capital from Sale of Treasury Stock has a credit balance, it should be debited for any decrease. Any remaining decrease should then be debited to the retained earnings account.

Stock Splits

REAL WORLD

When **Nature's Sunshine Products Inc.** declared a two-for-one stock split, the company president said:

We believe the split will place our stock price in a range attractive to both individual and institutional investors, broadening the market for the stock.

LTM Corporation announced a 4-for-1 stock split of its $50 par value common stock, which is currently trading for $120 per share. What is the new par value and the estimated market price of the stock after the split?

$12.50 ($50/4) par value; $30 ($120/4) estimated market price.

Corporations sometimes reduce the par or stated value of their common stock and issue a proportionate number of additional shares. When this is done, a corporation is said to have *split* its stock, and the process is called a ***stock split***.

When stock is split, the reduction in par or stated value applies to all shares, including the unissued, issued, and treasury shares. A major objective of a stock split is to reduce the market price per share of the stock. This, in turn, should attract more investors to enter the market for the stock and broaden the types and numbers of stockholders.

To illustrate a stock split, assume that Rojek Corporation has 10,000 shares of $100 par common stock outstanding with a current market price of $150 per share. The board of directors declares a 5-for-1 stock split, reduces the par to $20, and increases the number of shares to 50,000. The amount of common stock outstanding is $1,000,000 both before and after the stock split. Only the number of shares and the par per share are changed. Each Rojek Corporation shareholder owns the same total par amount of stock before and after the stock split. For example, a stockholder who owned 4 shares of $100 par stock before the split (total par of $400) would own 20 shares of $20 par stock after the split (total par of $400).

Since there are more shares outstanding after the stock split, we would expect that the market price of the stock would fall. For example, in the preceding example, there would be 5 times as many shares outstanding after the split. Thus, we would expect the market price of the stock to fall from $150 to approximately $30 ($150/5).

Since a stock split changes only the par or stated value and the number of shares outstanding, it is not recorded by a journal entry. Although the accounts are not affected, the details of stock splits are normally disclosed in the notes to the financial statements.

BEFORE STOCK SPLIT

4 shares, $100 par

$400 total par value

AFTER 5:1 STOCK SPLIT

20 shares, $20 par

$400 total par value

> **A stock split does not change the balance of any corporation accounts.**

Accounting for Dividends

objective 6

Journalize the entries for cash dividends and stock dividends.

When a board of directors declares a cash dividend, it authorizes the distribution of a portion of the corporation's cash to stockholders. When a board of directors declares a stock dividend, it authorizes the distribution of a portion of its stock. In both cases, the declaration of a dividend reduces the retained earnings of the corporation.[8]

Cash Dividends

A cash distribution of earnings by a corporation to its shareholders is called a **cash dividend**. Although dividends may be paid in the form of other assets, cash dividends are the most common form.

There are usually three conditions that a corporation must meet to pay a cash dividend:

1. Sufficient retained earnings
2. Sufficient cash
3. Formal action by the board of directors

A large amount of retained earnings does not always mean that a corporation is able to pay dividends. As we indicated earlier in the chapter, the balances of the cash and retained earnings accounts are often unrelated. Thus, a large retained earnings account does not mean that there is cash available to pay dividends.

A corporation's board of directors is not required by law to declare dividends. This is true even if both retained earnings and cash are large enough to justify a dividend. However, many corporations try to maintain a stable dividend record in order to make their stock attractive to investors. Although dividends may be paid once a year or semiannually, most corporations pay dividends quarterly. In years of high profits, a corporation may declare a *special* or *extra* dividend.

You may have seen announcements of dividend declarations in financial newspapers or investor services. An example of such an announcement is shown below.

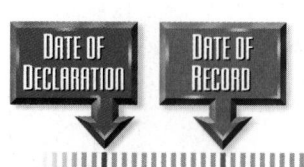

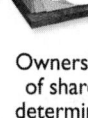

DATE OF DECLARATION

DATE OF RECORD

DATE OF PAYMENT

JUNE 26

JULY 8

JULY 31

Board of Directors takes action to declare dividends.

ENTRY:
Debit *Cash Dividends*

Credit *Cash Dividends Payable*

Ownership of shares determines who receives dividend (no entry required).

Dividend is paid.

ENTRY:
Debit *Cash Dividends Payable*

Credit *Cash*

On June 26, the board of directors of **Campbell Soup Co.** *declared a quarterly cash dividend of $0.225 per common share to stockholders of record as of the close of business on July 8, payable on July 31.*

This announcement includes three important dates: the *date of declaration* (June 26), the *date of record* (July 8), and the *date of payment* (July 31). During the period of time between the record date and the payment date, the stock price is usually quoted as selling *ex-dividends*. This means that since the date of record has passed, a new investor will not receive the dividend.

To illustrate, assume that on *December 1* the board of directors of Hiber Corporation declares the following quarterly cash dividends. The date of record is *December 10*, and the date of payment is *January 2*.

	Dividend per Share	Total Dividends
Preferred stock, $100 par, 5,000 shares outstanding	$2.50	$12,500
Common stock, $10 par, 100,000 shares outstanding	$0.30	30,000
Total		$42,500

---

[8]In rare cases, when a corporation is reducing its operations or going out of business, a dividend may be a distribution of paid-in capital. Such a dividend is called a *liquidating dividend*.

Hiber Corporation records the $42,500 liability for the dividends on December 1, the declaration date, as follows:

Dec.	1	Cash Dividends	42 5 0 0 00		
		Cash Dividends Payable		42 5 0 0 00	
		Declared cash dividend.			

No entry is required on the date of record, December 10, since this date merely determines which stockholders will receive the dividend. On the date of payment, January 2, the corporation records the $42,500 payment of the dividends as follows:

Jan.	2	Cash Dividends Payable	42 5 0 0 00		
		Cash		42 5 0 0 00	
		Paid cash dividend.			

If Hiber Corporation's fiscal year ends December 31, the balance in Cash Dividends will be transferred to Retained Earnings as a part of the closing process by debiting Retained Earnings and crediting Cash Dividends. Cash Dividends Payable will be listed on the December 31 balance sheet as a current liability.

If a corporation that holds treasury stock declares a cash dividend, the dividends are not paid on the treasury shares. To do so would place the corporation in the position of earning income through dealing with itself. For example, if Hiber Corporation in the preceding illustration had held 5,000 shares of its own common stock, the cash dividends on the common stock would have been $28,500 [(100,000 − 5,000) × $0.30] instead of $30,000.

Stock Dividends

A distribution of shares of stock to stockholders is called a ***stock dividend***. Usually, such distributions are in common stock and are issued to holders of common stock. Stock dividends are different from cash dividends in that there is no distribution of cash or other assets to stockholders.

The effect of a stock dividend on the stockholders' equity of the issuing corporation is to transfer retained earnings to paid-in capital. For public corporations, the amount transferred from retained earnings to paid-in capital is normally the *fair value* (market price) of the shares issued in the stock dividend.[9] To illustrate, assume that the stockholders' equity accounts of Hendrix Corporation as of December 15 are as follows:

Common Stock, $20 par (2,000,000 shares issued)	$40,000,000
Paid-In Capital in Excess of Par—Common Stock	9,000,000
Retained Earnings	26,600,000

On December 15, the board of directors declares a stock dividend of 5% or 100,000 shares (2,000,000 shares × 5%) to be issued on January 10 to stockholders of record on December 31. The market price of the stock on the declaration date is $31 a share. The entry to record the declaration is as follows:

Dec.	15	Stock Dividends (100,000 × $31 market price)	3,100 000 00	
		Stock Dividends Distributable		
		(100,000 × $20 Par)		2,000 000 00
		Paid-In Capital in Excess of		
		Par—Common Stock		1,100 000 00
		Declared stock dividend.		

The $3,100,000 balance in Stock Dividends is closed to Retained Earnings on December 31. The stock dividends distributable account is listed in the Paid-In Capital section of the balance sheet. Thus, the effect of the stock dividend is to transfer $3,100,000 of retained earnings to paid-in capital.

On January 10, the number of shares outstanding is increased by 100,000 by the following entry to record the issue of the stock:

Jan.	10	Stock Dividends Distributable	2,000 000 00	
		Common Stock		2,000 000 00
		Issued stock for the stock dividend.		

A stock dividend does not change the assets, liabilities, or total stockholders' equity of the corporation. Likewise, it does not change a stockholder's proportionate interest (equity) in the corporation. For example, if a stockholder owned 1,000 of a corporation's 10,000 shares outstanding, the stockholder owns 10% (1,000/10,000) of the corporation. After declaring a 6% stock dividend, the corporation will issue 600 additional shares (10,000 shares × 6%), and the total shares outstanding will be 10,600. The stockholder of 1,000 shares will receive 60 additional shares and will now own 1,060 shares, which is still a 10% equity interest.

Reporting Stockholders' Equity

objective **7**

Describe and illustrate the reporting of stockholders' equity.

We discussed and illustrated simple stockholders' equity sections of balance sheets in earlier chapters. However, as with other sections of the balance sheet, alternative terms and formats may be used in reporting stockholders' equity. In addition, the significant changes in the sources of stockholders' equity—paid-in capital and retained earnings—may be reported in separate statements or notes that support the balance sheet presentation.

---

[9]The use of fair market value is justified as long as the number of shares issued for the stock dividend is small (less than 25% of the shares outstanding).

Stockholders' Equity in the Balance Sheet

Two alternatives for reporting stockholders' equity in the balance sheet are shown in Exhibit 5. In the first example, each class of stock is listed first, followed by its related paid-in capital accounts. In the second example, the stock accounts are listed first. The other paid-in capital accounts are listed as a single item described as *Additional paid-in capital*. These combined accounts could also be described as *Capital in excess of par (or stated value) of shares* or a similar title.

•Exhibit 5   **Stockholders' Equity Section of a Balance Sheet**

Stockholders' Equity

Paid-in capital:			
Preferred 10% stock, cumulative,			
$50 par (2,000 shares			
authorized and issued)	$100,000		
Excess of issue price over par	10,000	$ 110,000	
Common stock, $20 par			
(50,000 shares authorized,			
45,000 shares issued)	$900,000		
Excess of issue price over par	190,000	1,090,000	
From sale of treasury stock		2,000	
Total paid-in capital			$1,202,000
Retained earnings			350,000
Total			$1,552,000
Deduct treasury stock (600 shares at cost) . . .			27,000
Total stockholders' equity			$1,525,000

Shareholders' Equity

Contributed capital:		
Preferred 10% stock, cumulative,		
$50 par (2,000 shares		
authorized and issued)	$100,000	
Common stock, $20 par		
(50,000 shares authorized,		
45,000 shares issued)	900,000	
Additional paid-in capital	202,000	
Total contributed capital		$1,202,000
Retained earnings		350,000
Total		$1,552,000
Deduct treasury stock (600 shares at cost)		27,000
Total stockholders' equity		$1,525,000

Significant changes in stockholders' equity during a period may be presented either in a ***statement of stockholders' equity*** or in notes to the financial statements. In addition, relevant rights and privileges of the various classes of stock outstanding must be disclosed.[10] Examples of types of information that must be disclosed

---

[10]*Statement of Financial Accounting Standards No. 129*, "Disclosure Information about Capital Structure," Financial Accounting Standards Board (Norwalk, Connecticut: 1997).

include dividend and liquidation preferences, rights to participate in earnings, conversion rights, and redemption rights. Such information may be disclosed on the face of the balance sheet or in the accompanying notes.

When a statement of stockholders' equity is prepared, it often includes a column for each major stockholders' equity classification. Changes in each classification are then described in the left-hand column, as illustrated in Exhibit 6.

•Exhibit 6   Statement of Stockholders' Equity

	Preferred Stock	Common Stock	Paid-In Capital in Excess of Par	Retained Earnings	Treasury Stock	Total
Balance, January 1, 2006	$5,000 0 0 0	$3,000 0 0 0	$10,000 0 0 0	$2,000 0 0 0	$(500 0 0 0)	$19,500 0 0 0
Net income				850 0 0 0		850 0 0 0
Dividends on preferred stock				(250 0 0 0)		(250 0 0 0)
Dividends on common stock				(400 0 0 0)		(400 0 0 0)
Issuance of additional common stock		50 0 0 0	500 0 0 0			550 0 0 0
Purchase of treasury stock					(30 0 0 0)	(30 0 0 0)
Balance, December 31, 2006	$5,000 0 0 0	$3,050 0 0 0	$10,500 0 0 0	$2,200 0 0 0	$(530 0 0 0)	$20,220 0 0 0

Telex Inc.
Statement of Stockholders' Equity
For the Year Ended December 31, 2006

REAL WORLD

The 2002 edition of *Accounting Trends & Techniques* indicated that 1.5% of the companies surveyed presented a separate statement of retained earnings, 1% presented a combined income and retained earnings statement, and 1% presented changes in retained earnings in the notes to the financial statements. The other 96% of the companies presented changes in retained earnings in a statement of stockholders' equity.

Reporting Retained Earnings

A corporation may report changes in retained earnings by preparing a separate retained earnings statement, a combined income and retained earnings statement, or a statement of stockholders' equity.

When a separate **retained earnings statement** is prepared, as illustrated in earlier chapters, the beginning balance of retained earnings is reported. The net income is then added (or net loss is subtracted) and any dividends are subtracted to arrive at the ending retained earnings for the period. An example of a such a statement for Adang Corporation is shown in Exhibit 7.

An alternative format for presenting the retained earnings statement is to combine it with the income statement. An advantage of the combined format is that it emphasizes net income as the connecting link between the income statement and the retained earnings portion of stockholders' equity. Since the combined form is not often used, we do not illustrate it.

Restrictions

The retained earnings available for use as dividends may be limited by action of a corporation's board of directors. These amounts, called **restrictions** or **appropriations**, remain part of the retained earnings. However, they must be disclosed, usually in the notes to the financial statements.

Restrictions may be classified as either legal, contractual, or discretionary. The board of directors may be legally required to restrict retained earnings because of state laws. For example, some state laws require that retained earnings be restricted by the amount of treasury stock purchased, so that legal capital will not be used for dividends. The board may also be required to restrict retained earnings because of contractual requirements. For example, the terms of a bank loan may require restrictions, so that

•Exhibit 7 **Retained Earnings Statement**

Adang Corporation
Retained Earnings Statement
For the Year Ended June 30, 2006

Retained earnings, July 1, 2005		$350,000
Net income	$280,000	
Less dividends declared	75,000	
Increase in retained earnings		205,000
Retained earnings, June 30, 2006		$555,000

money for repaying the loan will not be used for dividends. Finally, the board may restrict retained earnings voluntarily. For example, the board may limit dividend distributions so that more money is available for expanding the business.

Prior Period Adjustments

Material errors in a prior period's net income may arise from mathematical mistakes and from mistakes in applying accounting principles. The effect of material errors that are not discovered within the same fiscal period in which they occurred should not be included in determining net income for the current period. Instead, corrections of such errors, called **prior period adjustments**, are reported in the retained earnings statement. These adjustments are reported as an adjustment to the retained earnings balance at the beginning of the period in which the error is discovered and corrected.[11]

Financial Analysis and Interpretation

objective **8**

Compute and interpret the dividend yield on common stock.

The **dividend yield** indicates the rate of return to stockholders in terms of cash dividend distributions. Although the dividend yield can be computed for both preferred and common stock, it is most often computed for common stock. This is because most preferred stock has a stated dividend rate or amount. In contrast, the amount of common stock dividends normally varies with the profitability of the corporation.

The dividend yield is computed by dividing the annual dividends paid per share of common stock by the market price per share at a specific date, as shown below.

$$\text{Dividend Yield} = \frac{\text{Dividends per Share of Common Stock}}{\text{Market Price per Share of Common Stock}}$$

To illustrate, the market price of **Coca-Cola**'s common stock was $44.28 as of the close of business, July 15, 2003. During the past year, Coca-Cola had paid dividends of $0.88 per share. Thus, the dividend yield of Coca-Cola's common stock is 2.0% ($0.88/$44.28). Because the market price of a corporation's stock will vary from day to day, its dividend yield will also vary from day to day.

The dividend yield on common stock is of special interest to investors whose main objective is to receive a current dividend return on their investment. This is in contrast to investors whose main objective is a rapid increase in the market price of their investments. For example, technology companies often do not pay dividends

---

[11]Prior period adjustments are illustrated in advanced texts.

but reinvest their earnings in research and development. The main attraction of such stocks, such as **Cisco Systems, Inc.**'s common stock, is the expectation of the market price of the stock rising. Since many factors affect stock prices, an investment strategy relying solely on market price increases is more risky than a strategy based on dividend yields.

SPOTLIGHT ON STRATEGY

FASHION BLUES

During the 1990s, **The Gap** became the nation's largest specialty apparel retailer, with sales rising from $1.93 billion in 1990 to $11.64 billion in 1999. The Gap achieved this rapid growth by employing a strategy that emphasized simple, high-quality, casual clothing. Its strategy was aided by the shift in the 1990s to casual attire in the workplace. However, The Gap's same-store sales and profits have plummeted over the past year and a half. Perhaps never before have so many shoppers stopped patronizing a retail chain so quickly. So what happened?

Many former customers blame The Gap's changing fashion mix towards more far-fetched fashions, such as a denim trenchcoat with faux-fur collar, a bleached graphic T shirt, and fuschia-glittered disco jeans. In other words, The Gap became too trendy for its targeted customers, who are between the ages of 20 and 30. In addition, as The Gap expanded its trendy fashions, it curtailed customer choices within its basic apparel. For example, one former customer visited a Gap store in search of Capri pants but wasn't pleased with what she found. "You can't take pink and baby-blue to work, " she said.

Source: Adapted from "Gap's Image Is Wearing Out," by Amy Merrick, *The Wall Street Journal*, December 6, 2001.

Key Points

1 Describe the nature of the corporate form of organization.

Corporations have a separate legal existence, transferable units of stock, and limited stockholders' liability. Corporations may be either public or private corporations, and they are subject to federal income taxes.

The documents included in forming a corporation include an application of incorporation, articles of incorporation, and bylaws. Costs often incurred in organizing a corporation include legal fees, taxes, state incorporation fees, and promotional costs. Such costs are debited to an expense account entitled Organizational Expenses.

2 List the major sources of paid-in capital, including the various classes of stock.

The main source of paid-in capital is from issuing stock. The two primary classes of stock are common stock and preferred stock. Preferred stock is normally nonparticipating and may be cumulative or noncumulative. In addition to the issuance of stock, paid-in capital may arise from treasury stock transactions.

3 Journalize the entries for issuing stock.

When a corporation issues stock at par for cash, the cash account is debited and the class of stock issued is credited for its par amount. When a corporation issues stock at more than par, Paid-In Capital in Excess of Par is credited for the difference between the cash received and the par value of the stock. When stock is issued in exchange for assets other than cash, the assets acquired should be recorded at their fair market value.

When no-par stock is issued, the entire proceeds are credited to the stock account. No-par stock may be assigned a stated value per share, and the excess of the proceeds over the stated value may be credited to Paid-In Capital in Excess of Stated Value.

4 Journalize the entries for treasury stock transactions.

When a corporation buys its own stock, the cost method of accounting is normally used. Treasury Stock is debited for its cost, and Cash is credited. If the stock is resold, Treasury Stock is credited for its cost and any difference between the cost and the selling price is normally debited or credited to Paid-In Capital from Sale of Treasury Stock.

5 State the effect of stock splits on corporate financial statements.

When a corporation reduces the par or stated value of its common stock and issues a proportionate number of additional shares, a stock split has occurred. There are no changes in the balances of any corporation accounts, and no entry is required for a stock split.

6 Journalize the entries for cash dividends and stock dividends.

The entry to record a declaration of cash dividends debits Dividends and credits Dividends Payable for each class of stock. The payment of dividends is recorded in the normal manner. When a stock dividend is declared, Stock Dividends is debited for the fair value of the stock to be issued. Stock Dividends Distributable is credited for the par or stated value of the common stock to be issued. The difference between the fair value of the stock and its par or stated value is credited to Paid-In Capital in Excess of Par—Common Stock.

When the stock is issued on the date of payment, Stock Dividends Distributable is debited and Common Stock is credited for the par or stated value of the stock issued.

7 Describe and illustrate the reporting of stockholders' equity.

Significant changes in the sources of stockholders' equity—paid-in capital and retained earnings—may be reported in separate statements or notes that support the balance sheet presentation. Changes in retained earnings may be reported by preparing a separate retained earnings statement, a combined income and retained earnings statement, or a statement of stockholders' equity. Restrictions to retained earnings must be disclosed,

usually in the notes to the financial statements. Material errors in a prior period's net income, called prior-period adjustments, are reported in the retained earnings statement.

8 Compute and interpret the dividend yield on common stock.

The dividend yield indicates the rate of return to stockholders in terms of cash dividend distributions. It is computed by dividing the annual dividends paid per share of common stock by the market price per share at a specific date. This ratio is of special interest to investors whose main objective is to receive a current dividend return on their investment.

Key Terms

cash dividend (454)
common stock (448)
cumulative preferred stock (449)
discount (450)
dividend yield (459)
nonparticipating preferred stock (448)
outstanding stock (446)

par (446)
preferred stock (448)
premium (450)
prior period adjustments (459)
restrictions (458)
retained earnings statement (458)
stated value (446)

statement of stockholders' equity (457)
stock (444)
stock dividend (455)
stock split (453)
stockholders (444)
treasury stock (452)

Illustrative Problem

Altenburg Inc. is a lighting fixture wholesaler located in Arizona. During its current fiscal year, ended December 31, 2006, Altenburg Inc. completed the following selected transactions:

Feb. 3. Purchased 2,500 shares of its own common stock at $26, recording the stock at cost. (Prior to the purchase, there were 40,000 shares of $20 par common stock outstanding.)

May 1. Declared a semiannual dividend of $1 on the 10,000 shares of preferred stock and a 30¢ dividend on the common stock to stockholders of record on May 31, payable on June 15.

June 15. Paid the cash dividends.

Sept. 23. Sold 1,000 shares of treasury stock at $28, receiving cash.

Nov. 1. Declared semiannual dividends of $1 on the preferred stock and 30¢ on the common stock. In addition, a 5% common stock dividend was declared on the common stock outstanding, to be capitalized at the fair market value of the common stock, which is estimated at $30.

Dec. 1. Paid the cash dividends and issued the certificates for the common stock dividend.

Instructions

Journalize the entries to record the transactions for Altenburg Inc.

Solution

2006					
Feb.	3	Treasury Stock		65 0 0 0 00	
		Cash			65 0 0 0 00
May	1	Cash Dividends		21 2 5 0 00	
		Cash Dividends Payable			21 2 5 0 00 *
		*(10,000 × $1) + [(40,000 − 2,500)			
		× $0.30]			
June	15	Cash Dividends Payable		21 2 5 0 00	
		Cash			21 2 5 0 00
Sept.	23	Cash		28 0 0 0 00	
		Treasury Stock			26 0 0 0 00
		Paid-In Capital from Sale of Treasury Stock			2 0 0 0 00
Nov.	1	Cash Dividends		21 5 5 0 00 *	
		Cash Dividends Payable			21 5 5 0 00
		*(10,000 × $1) + [(40,000 − 1,500)			
		× $0.30]			
	1	Stock Dividends		57 7 5 0 00 *	
		Stock Dividends Distributable			38 5 0 0 00
		Paid-In Capital in Excess of			
		Par—Common Stock			19 2 5 0 00
		*(40,000 − 1,500) × 5% × $30			
Dec.	1	Cash Dividends Payable		21 5 5 0 00	
		Stock Dividends Distributable		38 5 0 0 00	
		Cash			21 5 5 0 00
		Common Stock			38 5 0 0 00

Self-Examination Questions (Answers at End of Chapter)

1. If a corporation has outstanding 1,000 shares of 9% cumulative preferred stock of $100 par and dividends have been passed for the preceding three years, what is the amount of preferred dividends that must be declared in the current year before a dividend can be declared on common stock?
   - A. $ 9,000
   - B. $27,000
   - C. $36,000
   - D. $45,000

2. Paid-in capital for a corporation may arise from which of the following sources?
   - A. Issuing cumulative preferred stock
   - B. Receiving donations of real estate
   - C. Selling the corporation's treasury stock
   - D. All of the above

3. The Stockholders' Equity section of the balance sheet may include:
   - A. Common Stock
   - B. Stock Divdiends Distributable
   - C. Preferred Stock
   - D. All of the above

4. If a corporation reacquires its own stock, the stock is listed on the balance sheet in the:
   - A. Current Assets section.
   - B. Long-Term Liabilities section.
   - C. Stockholders' Equity section.
   - D. Investments section.

5. A corporation has issued 25,000 shares of $100 par common stock and holds 3,000 of these shares as treasury stock. If the corporation declares a $2 per share cash dividend, what amount will be recorded as cash dividends?

A. $22,000	C. $44,000
B. $25,000	D. $50,000

Class Discussion Questions

1. Describe the stockholders' liability to creditors of a corporation.
2. Why are most large businesses organized as corporations?
3. Of two corporations organized at approximately the same time and engaged in competing businesses, one issued $75 par common stock, and the other issued $1 par common stock. Do the par designations provide any indication as to which stock is preferable as an investment? Explain.
4. A stockbroker advises a client to "buy cumulative preferred stock. . . . With that type of stock, . . . [you] will never have to worry about losing the dividends." Is the broker right?
5. What are some of the factors that influence the market price of a corporation's stock?
6. When a corporation issues stock at a premium, is the premium income? Explain.
7. a. In what respect does treasury stock differ from unissued stock?
   b. How should treasury stock be presented on the balance sheet?
8. A corporation reacquires 10,000 shares of its own $25 par common stock for $420,000, recording it at cost. (a) What effect does this transaction have on revenue or expense of the period? (b) What effect does it have on stockholders' equity?
9. The treasury stock in Question 8 is resold for $500,000. (a) What is the effect on the corporation's revenue of the period? (b) What is the effect on stockholders' equity?
10. What is the primary purpose of a stock split?
11. (a) What are the three conditions for the declaration and the payment of a cash dividend? (b) The dates in connection with the declaration of a cash dividend are July 1, August 15, and September 1. Identify each date.
12. A corporation with both cumulative preferred stock and common stock outstanding has a substantial credit balance in its retained earnings account at the beginning of the current fiscal year. Although net income for the current year is sufficient to pay the preferred dividend of $250,000 each quarter and a common dividend of $610,000 each quarter, the board of directors declares dividends only on the preferred stock. Suggest possible reasons for passing the dividends on the common stock.
13. An owner of 150 shares of Morse Company common stock receives a stock dividend of 3 shares. (a) What is the effect of the stock dividend on the stockholder's proportionate interest (equity) in the corporation? (b) How does the total equity of 153 shares compare with the total equity of 150 shares before the stock dividend?
14. a. Where should a declared but unpaid cash dividend be reported on the balance sheet?
    b. Where should a declared but unissued stock dividend be reported on the balance sheet?
15. What is the primary advantage of combining the retained earnings statement with the income statement?
16. What are the three classifications of appropriations and how are appropriations normally reported in the financial statements?
17. Indicate how prior period adjustments would be reported on the financial statements presented only for the current period.

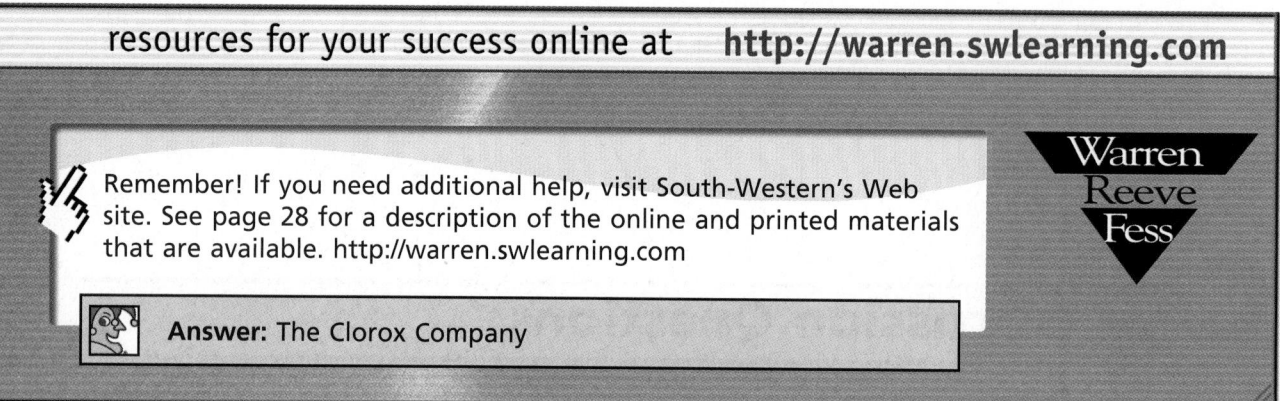

Remember! If you need additional help, visit South-Western's Web site. See page 28 for a description of the online and printed materials that are available. http://warren.swlearning.com

Answer: The Clorox Company

Exercises

EXERCISE 11-1
Dividends per share

Objective 2

✓ *Preferred stock, 3rd year: $1.40*

Fiji Inc., a developer of radiology equipment, has stock outstanding as follows: 25,000 shares of 1% nonparticipating, cumulative preferred stock of $100 par, and 250,000 shares of $50 par common. During its first five years of operations, the following amounts were distributed as dividends: first year, none; second year, $40,000; third year, $80,000; fourth year, $120,000; fifth year, $140,000. Calculate the dividends per share on each class of stock for each of the five years.

EXERCISE 11-2
Dividends per share

Objective 2

✓ *Preferred stock, 3rd year: $0.75*

Infinity.com, a software development firm, has stock outstanding as follows: 100,000 shares of 2% cumulative, nonparticipating preferred stock of $20 par, and 50,000 shares of $100 par common. During its first five years of operations, the following amounts were distributed as dividends: first year, none; second year, $45,000; third year, $110,000; fourth year, $130,000; fifth year, $180,000. Calculate the dividends per share on each class of stock for each of the five years.

EXERCISE 11-3
Entries for issuing par stock

Objective 3

On July 7, Sloth Inc., a marble contractor, issued for cash 40,000 shares of $25 par common stock at $40, and on October 20, it issued for cash 15,000 shares of $100 par preferred stock at $120.

a. Journalize the entries for July 7 and October 20.
b. What is the total amount invested (total paid-in capital) by all stockholders as of October 20?

EXERCISE 11-4
Entries for issuing no-par stock

Objective 3

On February 20, Mudguard Corp., a carpet wholesaler, issued for cash 100,000 shares of no-par common stock (with a stated value of $10) at $15, and on April 30, it issued for cash 4,000 shares of $25 par preferred stock at $30.

a. Journalize the entries for February 20 and April 30, assuming that the common stock is to be credited with the stated value.
b. What is the total amount invested (total paid-in capital) by all stockholders as of April 30?

EXERCISE 11-5
Issuing stock for assets other than cash

Objective 3

On August 29, Welch Corporation, a wholesaler of hydraulic lifts, acquired land in exchange for 10,000 shares of $15 par common stock with a current market price of $28. Journalize the entry to record the transaction.

EXERCISE 11-6
Selected stock transactions
Objective 3

Megaton Corp., an electric guitar retailer, was organized by Bonita Eaves, Helen Brock, and Freida Sager. The charter authorized 400,000 shares of common stock with a par of $10. The following transactions affecting stockholders' equity were completed during the first year of operations:

a. Issued 5,000 shares of stock at par to Brock for cash.
b. Issued 200 shares of stock at par to Eaves for promotional services provided in connection with the organization of the corporation, and issued 1,200 shares of stock at par to Eaves for cash.
c. Purchased land and a building from Sager. The building is mortgaged for $180,000 for 20 years at 6%, and there is accrued interest of $900 on the mortgage note at the time of the purchase. It is agreed that the land is to be priced at $60,000 and the building at $200,000, and that Sagar's equity will be exchanged for stock at par. The corporation agreed to assume responsibility for paying the mortgage note and the accrued interest.

Journalize the entries to record the transactions.

EXERCISE 11-7
Issuing stock
Objective 3

Pearl.com, with an authorization of 50,000 shares of preferred stock and 200,000 shares of common stock, completed several transactions involving its stock on May 1, the first day of operations. The trial balance at the close of the day follows:

Cash	475,000	
Land	45,000	
Buildings	80,000	
Preferred 4% Stock, $50 par		100,000
Paid-In Capital in Excess of Par—Preferred Stock		25,000
Common Stock, $100 par		400,000
Paid-In Capital in Excess of Par—Common Stock		75,000
	600,000	600,000

All shares within each class of stock were sold at the same price. The preferred stock was issued in exchange for the land and buildings.

Journalize the two entries to record the transactions summarized in the trial balance.

EXERCISE 11-8
Issuing stock
Objective 3

Calvert Products Inc., a wholesaler of office products, was organized on January 5 of the current year, with an authorization of 80,000 shares of 2% noncumulative preferred stock, $50 par and 250,000 shares of $100 par common stock. The following selected transactions were completed during the first year of operations:

Jan. 5. Issued 10,000 shares of common stock at par for cash.
      18. Issued 100 shares of common stock at par to an attorney in payment of legal fees for organizing the corporation.
Feb. 13. Issued 4,250 shares of common stock in exchange for land, buildings, and equipment with fair market prices of $50,000, $280,000, and $120,000, respectively.
April 1. Issued 3,500 shares of preferred stock at $52 for cash.

Journalize the transactions.

EXERCISE 11-9
Treasury stock transactions
Objective 4
✓ b. $5,500 credit

Crystal Springs Inc. bottles and distributes spring water. On June 1 of the current year, Crystal reacquired 2,500 shares of its common stock at $60 per share. On July 8, Crystal sold 1,500 of the reacquired shares at $65 per share. The remaining 1,000 shares were sold at $58 per share on November 2.

a. Journalize the transactions of June 1, July 8, and November 2.
b. What is the balance in Paid-In Capital from Sale of Treasury Stock on December 31 of the current year?
c. ▬▬▶ For what reasons might Crystal Springs have purchased the treasury stock?

EXERCISE 11-10
Treasury stock transactions
Objectives 4, 7

✓ b. $50,000 credit

Geyser Inc. develops and produces spraying equipment for lawn maintenance and industrial uses. On March 3 of the current year, Geyser Inc. reacquired 7,500 shares of its common stock at $120 per share. On August 11, 4,000 of the reacquired shares were sold at $130 per share, and on October 3, 2,500 of the reacquired shares were sold at $124.

a. Journalize the transactions of March 3, August 11, and October 3.
b. What is the balance in Paid-In Capital from Sale of Treasury Stock on December 31 of the current year?
c. What is the balance in Treasury Stock on December 31 of the current year?
d. How will the balance in Treasury Stock be reported on the balance sheet?

EXERCISE 11-11
Treasury stock transactions
Objectives 4, 7

✓ b. $1,500 credit

Aspen Inc. bottles and distributes spring water. On August 1 of the current year, Aspen Inc. reacquired 12,000 shares of its common stock at $36 per share. On September 23, Aspen Inc. sold 7,500 of the reacquired shares at $38 per share. The remaining 4,500 shares were sold at $33 per share on December 29.

a. Journalize the transactions of August 1, September 23, and December 29.
b. What is the balance in Paid-In Capital from Sale of Treasury Stock on December 31 of the current year?
c. Where will the balance in Paid-In Capital from Sale of Treasury Stock be reported on the balance sheet?
d. ▭▬▸ For what reasons might Aspen Inc. have purchased the treasury stock?

EXERCISE 11-12
Effect of stock split
Objective 5

Paranormal Corporation wholesales ovens and ranges to restaurants throughout the Midwest. Paranormal Corporation, which had 25,000 shares of common stock outstanding, declared a 5-for-1 stock split (4 additional shares for each share issued).

a. What will be the number of shares outstanding after the split?
b. If the common stock had a market price of $165 per share before the stock split, what would be an approximate market price per share after the split?

EXERCISE 11-13
Effect of cash dividend and stock split
Objectives 5, 6

Indicate whether the following actions would (+) increase, (−) decrease, or (0) not affect Indigo Inc.'s total assets, liabilities, and stockholders' equity:

		Assets	Liabilities	Stockholders' Equity
(1)	Declaring a cash dividend	_____	_____	_____
(2)	Paying the cash dividend declared in (1)	_____	_____	_____
(3)	Authorizing and issuing stock certificates in a stock split	_____	_____	_____
(4)	Declaring a stock dividend	_____	_____	_____
(5)	Issuing stock certificates for the stock dividend declared in (4)	_____	_____	_____

EXERCISE 11-14
Entries for cash dividends
Objective 6

The dates of importance in connection with a cash dividend of $120,000 on a corporation's common stock are February 13, March 15, and April 10. Journalize the entries required on each date.

EXERCISE 11-15
Entries for stock dividends
Objective 6

✓ b. (1) $13,250,000
    (3) $43,828,000

Health Co. is an HMO for twelve businesses in the Chicago area. The following account balances appear on the balance sheet of Health Co.: Common stock (250,000 shares authorized), $100 par, $12,500,000; Paid-in capital in excess of par—common stock, $750,000; and Retained earnings, $30,578,000. The board of directors declared a 2% stock dividend when the market price of the stock was $110 a share. Health Co. reported no income or loss for the current year.

a. Journalize the entries to record (1) the declaration of the dividend, capitalizing an amount equal to market value, and (2) the issuance of the stock certificates.
b. Determine the following amounts before the stock dividend was declared: (1) total paid-in capital, (2) total retained earnings, and (3) total stockholders' equity.

c. Determine the following amounts after the stock dividend was declared and closing entries were recorded at the end of the year: (1) total paid-in capital, (2) total retained earnings, and (3) total stockholders' equity.

EXERCISE 11-16
Selected stock and dividend transactions
Objectives 5, 6

Selected transactions completed by Indy Boating Supply Corporation during the current fiscal year are as follows:

Feb. 9. Split the common stock 3 for 1 and reduced the par from $120 to $40 per share. After the split, there were 900,000 common shares outstanding.

Apr. 10. Declared semiannual dividends of $1 on 12,000 shares of preferred stock and $0.05 on the common stock to stockholders of record on April 20, payable on May 1.

May 1. Paid the cash dividends.

Oct. 12. Declared semiannual dividends of $1 on the preferred stock and $0.15 on the common stock (before the stock dividend). In addition, a 1% common stock dividend was declared on the common stock outstanding. The fair market value of the common stock is estimated at $48.

Nov. 14. Paid the cash dividends and issued the certificates for the common stock dividend.

Journalize the transactions.

EXERCISE 11-17
Reporting paid-in capital
Objective 7

✓ *Total paid-in capital,*
$1,541,250

The following accounts and their balances were selected from the unadjusted trial balance of Sailors Inc., a freight forwarder, at August 31, the end of the current fiscal year:

Preferred 2% Stock, $100 par	$ 750,000
Paid-In Capital in Excess of Par—Preferred Stock	90,000
Common Stock, no par, $5 stated value	562,500
Paid-In Capital in Excess of Stated Value—Common Stock	75,000
Paid-In Capital from Sale of Treasury Stock	63,750
Retained Earnings	1,875,000

Prepare the Paid-In Capital portion of the Stockholders' Equity section of the balance sheet. There are 200,000 shares of common stock authorized and 80,000 shares of preferred stock authorized.

EXERCISE 11-18
Stockholders' equity section of balance sheet
Objective 7

SPREADSHEET

✓ *Total stockholders' equity,*
$2,165,000

The following accounts and their balances appear in the ledger of Dimension Inc. on June 30 of the current year:

Common Stock, $25 par	$ 750,000
Paid-In Capital in Excess of Par	120,000
Paid-In Capital from Sale of Treasury Stock	25,000
Retained Earnings	1,350,000
Treasury Stock	80,000

Prepare the Stockholders' Equity section of the balance sheet as of June 30. Sixty thousand shares of common stock are authorized, and 2,000 shares have been reacquired.

EXERCISE 11-19
Stockholders' equity section of balance sheet
Objective 7

SPREADSHEET

✓ *Total stockholders' equity,*
$5,193,000

Big Boy Toys Inc. retails racing products for BMWs, Porsches, and Ferraris. The following accounts and their balances appear in the ledger of Big Boy Toys Inc. on October 31, the end of the current year:

Common Stock, $4 par	$ 600,000
Paid-In Capital in Excess of Par—Common Stock	210,000
Paid-In Capital in Excess of Par—Preferred Stock	78,000
Paid-In Capital from Sale of Treasury Stock—Common	42,000
Preferred 2% Stock, $100 par	480,000
Retained Earnings	3,903,000
Treasury Stock—Common	120,000

Ten thousand shares of preferred and 250,000 shares of common stock are authorized. There are 12,000 shares of common stock held as treasury stock.

Prepare the Stockholders' Equity section of the balance sheet as of October 31, the end of the current year.

EXERCISE 11-20
Statement of stockholders' equity

Objective 7

SPREADSHEET

✓ *Total stockholders' equity, Dec. 31, $2,285,000*

The stockholders' equity accounts of Tender Heart Greeting Cards Inc. for the current fiscal year ended Decmber 31, 2006, are as follows. Prepare a statement of stockholders' equity for the fiscal year ended December 31, 2006.

ACCOUNT *Common Stock, $2 Par*

Date		Item	Debit	Credit	Balance Debit	Balance Credit
2006 Jan.	1	Balance				500 000 00
Mar.	13	Issued 50,000 shares		100 000 00		600 000 00

ACCOUNT *Paid-In Capital in Excess of Par*

Date		Item	Debit	Credit	Balance Debit	Balance Credit
2006 Jan.	1	Balance				400 000 00
Mar.	13	Issued 50,000 shares		45 000 00		445 000 00

ACCOUNT *Treasury Stock*

Date		Item	Debit	Credit	Balance Debit	Balance Credit
2006 Apr.	30	Purchased 10,000 shares	25 000 00		25 000 00	

ACCOUNT *Retained Earnings*

Date		Item	Debit	Credit	Balance Debit	Balance Credit
2006 Jan.	1	Balance				1,075 000 00
Dec.	31	Income summary		240 000 00		1,315 000 00
	31	Cash dividends	50 000 00			1,265 000 00

ACCOUNT *Cash Dividends*

Date		Item	Debit	Credit	Balance Debit	Balance Credit
2006 June	30		25 000 00		25 000 00	
Dec.	30		25 000 00		50 000 00	
	31	Closing		50 000 00	—	—

EXERCISE 11-21
Retained earnings statement

Objective 7

Bravo Corporation, a manufacturer of industrial pumps, reports the following results for the year ending July 31, 2006:

✓ *Retained earnings, July 31, $2,441,400*

Retained earnings, August 1, 2005	$2,213,400
Net income	558,000
Cash dividends declared	180,000
Stock dividends declared	150,000

Prepare a retained earnings statement for the fiscal year ended July 31, 2006.

EXERCISE 11-22
Stockholders' equity section of balance sheet

Objective 7

WHAT'S WRONG WITH THIS?

✓ *Corrected total stockholders' equity, $3,064,200*

List the errors in the following Stockholders' Equity section of the balance sheet prepared as of the end of the current year.

Stockholders' Equity

Paid-in capital:		
Preferred 2% stock, cumulative, $50 par		
(9,800 shares authorized and issued)	$ 490,000	
Excess of issue price over par	84,000	$ 574,000
Retained earnings		906,000
Treasury stock (5,000 shares at cost)		105,000
Dividends payable		140,000
Total paid-in capital		$1,725,000
Common stock, $20 par (100,000 shares		
authorized, 75,000 shares issued)		1,789,200
Organizing costs		100,000
Total stockholders' equity		$3,614,200

EXERCISE 11-23
Dividend yield

Objective 8

REAL WORLD

eBay developed a Web-based marketplace at **http://www.ebay.com**, in which individuals can buy and sell a variety of items. eBay also developed PayPal, an on-line payments system that allows businesses and individuals to send and receive online payments securely. In a recent annual report, eBay published the following dividend policy:

> *We have never paid cash dividends on our stock, and currently anticipate that we will continue to retain any future earnings to finance the growth of our business.*

Given eBay's dividend policy, why would an investor be attracted to its stock?

EXERCISE 11-24
Dividend yield

Objective 8

REAL WORLD

In 2002, **Hershey Foods Corporation** paid dividends of $1.26 per share to its common stockholders (excluding its Class B Common Stock). The market price of Hershey's common stock on December 31, 2002, was $67.44.

a. Determine Hershey's dividend yield on its common stock as of December 31, 2002.
b. What conclusions can you draw from an analysis of Hershey's dividend yield?

Problems Series A

PROBLEM 11-1A
Dividends on preferred and common stock

Objective 2

SPREADSHEET

Lemonds Corp. manufactures mountain bikes and distributes them through retail outlets in Oregon and Washington. Lemonds Corp. has declared the following annual dividends over a six-year period: 2002, $40,000; 2003, $18,000; 2004, $24,000; 2005, $27,000; 2006, $65,000; and 2007, $54,000. During the entire period, the outstanding stock of the company was composed of 25,000 shares of cumulative, non-participating, 6% preferred stock, $20 par, and 40,000 shares of common stock, $1 par.

✓ *1. Common dividends in 2002: $10,000*

Instructions

1. Calculate the total dividends and the per-share dividends declared on each class of stock for each of the six years. There were no dividends in arrears on January 1, 2002. Summarize the data in tabular form, using the following column headings:

Year	Total Dividends	Preferred Dividends		Common Dividends	
		Total	Per Share	Total	Per Share
2002	$40,000				
2003	18,000				
2004	24,000				
2005	27,000				
2006	65,000				
2007	54,000				

2. Calculate the average annual dividend per share for each class of stock for the six-year period.
3. Assuming that the preferred stock was sold at par and common stock was sold at $8 at the beginning of the six-year period, calculate the average annual percentage return on initial shareholders' investment, based on the average annual dividend per share (a) for preferred stock and (b) for common stock.

PROBLEM 11-2A
Stock transaction for corporate expansion

Objective 3

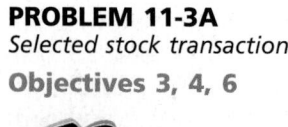

P.A.S.S.

Diamond Optics produces medical lasers for use in hospitals. The following accounts and their balances appear in the ledger of Diamond Optics on September 30 of the current year:

Preferred 5% Stock, $100 par (20,000 shares authorized, 12,000 shares issued)	$1,200,000
Paid-In Capital in Excess of Par—Preferred Stock	180,000
Common Stock, $25 par (100,000 shares authorized, 72,000 shares issued)	1,800,000
Paid-In Capital in Excess of Par—Common Stock	240,000
Retained Earnings	3,572,500

At the annual stockholders' meeting on October 19, the board of directors presented a plan for modernizing and expanding plant operations at a cost of approximately $2,500,000. The plan provided (a) that the corporation borrow $780,000, (b) that 6,000 shares of the unissued preferred stock be issued through an underwriter, and (c) that a building, valued at $900,000, and the land on which it is located, valued at $120,000, be acquired in accordance with preliminary negotiations by the issuance of 24,000 shares of common stock. The plan was approved by the stockholders and accomplished by the following transactions:

Nov. 5. Borrowed $780,000 from Bozeman National Bank, giving a 7% mortgage note.
  20. Issued 6,000 shares of preferred stock, receiving $120 per share in cash from the underwriter.
  23. Issued 24,000 shares of common stock in exchange for land and a building, according to the plan.

No other transactions occurred during November.

Instructions
Journalize the entries to record the foregoing transactions.

PROBLEM 11-3A
Selected stock transactions

Objectives 3, 4, 6

P.A.S.S.

Elk River Corporation sells and services pipe welding equipment in Wyoming. The following selected accounts appear in the ledger of Elk River Corporation on January 1, 2006, the beginning of the current fiscal year:

Preferred 2% Stock, $100 par (80,000 shares authorized,	
18,000 shares issued)	$1,800,000
Paid-In Capital in Excess of Par—Preferred Stock	172,500
Common Stock, $10 par (800,000 shares authorized,	
500,000 shares issued)	5,000,000
Paid-In Capital in Excess of Par—Common Stock	1,236,000
Retained Earnings	6,450,000

During the year, the corporation completed a number of transactions affecting the stockholders' equity. They are summarized as follows:

a. Purchased 60,000 shares of treasury common for $1,080,000.
b. Sold 20,000 shares of treasury common for $420,000.
c. Sold 7,000 shares of preferred 2% stock at $108.
d. Issued 40,000 shares of common stock at $23, receiving cash.
e. Sold 35,000 shares of treasury common for $595,000.
f. Declared cash dividends of $2 per share on preferred stock and $0.16 per share on common stock.
g. Paid the cash dividends.

Instructions
Journalize the entries to record the transactions. Identify each entry by letter.

PROBLEM 11-4A
Entries for selected corporate transactions

Objectives 3, 4, 6, 7

SPREADSHEET
P.A.S.S.

✓ *4. Total stockholders' equity, $1,796,950*

Areotronics Enterprises Inc. produces aeronautical navigation equipment. The stockholders' equity accounts of Areotronics Enterprises Inc., with balances on January 1, 2006, are as follows:

Common Stock, $10 stated value (100,000 shares authorized,	
60,000 shares issued)	$600,000
Paid-In Capital in Excess of Stated Value	150,000
Retained Earnings	497,750
Treasury Stock (7,500 shares, at cost)	120,000

The following selected transactions occurred during the year:

Jan. 19. Paid cash dividends of $0.60 per share on the common stock. The dividend had been properly recorded when declared on December 28 of the preceding fiscal year for $31,500.

Feb. 2. Sold all of the treasury stock for $150,000.

Mar. 15. Issued 20,000 shares of common stock for $480,000.

July 30. Declared a 2% stock dividend on common stock, to be capitalized at the market price of the stock, which is $25 a share.

Aug. 30. Issued the certificates for the dividend declared on July 30.

Oct. 10. Purchased 5,000 shares of treasury stock for $105,000.

Dec. 30. Declared a $0.50-per-share dividend on common stock.

31. Closed the credit balance of the income summary account, $182,500.

31. Closed the two dividends accounts to Retained Earnings.

Instructions
1. Enter the January 1 balances in T accounts for the stockholders' equity accounts listed. Also prepare T accounts for the following: Paid-In Capital from Sale of Treasury Stock; Stock Dividends Distributable; Stock Dividends; Cash Dividends.
2. Journalize the entries to record the transactions, and post to the eight selected accounts.
3. Prepare a retained earnings statement for the year ended December 31, 2006.
4. Prepare the stockholders' equity section of the December 31, 2006 balance sheet.

PROBLEM 11-5A
Entries for selected corporate transactions

Objectives 3, 4, 5, 6

Serra do Mar Corporation manufactures and distributes leisure clothing. Selected transactions completed by Serra do Mar during the current fiscal year are as follows:

Jan. 8. Split the common stock 3 for 1 and reduced the par from $18 to $6 per share. After the split, there were 600,000 common shares outstanding.

Mar. 20. Declared semiannual dividends of $1 on 20,000 shares of preferred stock and $0.14 on the 600,000 shares of $10 par common stock to stockholders of record on March 31, payable on April 20.

Apr. 20. Paid the cash dividends.

May 8. Purchased 50,000 shares of the corporation's own common stock at $48, recording the stock at cost.

Aug. 2. Sold 30,000 shares of treasury stock at $56, receiving cash.

Sept. 15. Declared semiannual dividends of $1 on the preferred stock and $0.07 on the common stock (before the stock dividend). In addition, a 1% common stock dividend was declared on the common stock outstanding, to be capitalized at the fair market value of the common stock, which is estimated at $52.

Oct. 15. Paid the cash dividends and issued the certificates for the common stock dividend.

Instructions

Journalize the transactions.

Problems Series B

PROBLEM 11-1B
Dividends on preferred and common stock

Objective 2

✓ *1. Common dividends in 2004: $22,000*

Da Show Inc. owns and operates movie theaters throughout Texas and California. Da Show has declared the following annual dividends over a six-year period: 2002, $18,000; 2003, $54,000; 2004, $70,000; 2005, $75,000; 2006, $80,000; and 2007, $90,000. During the entire period, the outstanding stock of the company was composed of 20,000 shares of cumulative, nonparticipating, 2% preferred stock, $100 par, and 25,000 shares of common stock, $10 par.

Instructions

1. Calculate the total dividends and the per-share dividends declared on each class of stock for each of the six years. There were no dividends in arrears on January 1, 2002. Summarize the data in tabular form, using the following column headings:

Year	Total Dividends	Preferred Dividends		Common Dividends	
		Total	Per Share	Total	Per Share
2002	$18,000				
2003	54,000				
2004	70,000				
2005	75,000				
2006	80,000				
2007	90,000				

2. Calculate the average annual dividend per share for each class of stock for the six-year period.

3. Assuming that the preferred stock was sold at par and common stock was sold at $39.20 at the beginning of the six-year period, calculate the average annual percentage return on initial shareholders' investment, based on the average annual dividend per share (a) for preferred stock and (b) for common stock.

PROBLEM 11-2B
Stock transactions for corporate expansion

Objective 3

On January 1 of the current year, the following accounts and their balances appear in the ledger of Dahof Corp., a meat processor:

Preferred 4% Stock, $100 par (20,000 shares authorized, 6,000 shares issued)	$ 600,000
Paid-In Capital in Excess of Par—Preferred Stock	120,000
Common Stock, $50 par (100,000 shares authorized, 50,000 shares issued)	2,500,000
Paid-In Capital in Excess of Par—Common Stock	320,000
Retained Earnings	1,675,000

At the annual stockholders' meeting on March 6, the board of directors presented a plan for modernizing and expanding plant operations at a cost of approximately $800,000. The plan provided (a) that a building, valued at $225,000, and the land on which it is located, valued at $45,000, be acquired in accordance with preliminary negotiations by the issuance of 4,800 shares of common stock, (b) that 3,000 shares of the unissued preferred stock be issued through an underwriter, and (c) that the corporation borrow $155,000. The plan was approved by the stockholders and accomplished by the following transactions:

April 3. Issued 4,800 shares of common stock in exchange for land and a building, according to the plan.

18. Issued 3,000 shares of preferred stock, receiving $125 per share in cash from the underwriter.

28. Borrowed $155,000 from Northeast National Bank, giving an 8% mortgage note.

No other transactions occurred during April.

Instructions

Journalize the entries to record the foregoing transactions.

PROBLEM 11-3B
Selected stock transactions
Objectives 3, 4, 6

P.A.S.S.

The following selected accounts appear in the ledger of Kingfisher Environmental Corporation on March 1, 2006, the beginning of the current fiscal year:

Preferred 2% Stock, $75 par (10,000 shares authorized, 8,000 shares issued)	$ 600,000
Paid-In Capital in Excess of Par—Preferred Stock	100,000
Common Stock, $10 par (50,000 shares authorized, 35,000 shares issued)	350,000
Paid-In Capital in Excess of Par—Common Stock	85,000
Retained Earnings	1,050,000

During the year, the corporation completed a number of transactions affecting the stockholders' equity. They are summarized as follows:

a. Issued 7,500 shares of common stock at $24, receiving cash.
b. Sold 800 shares of preferred 2% stock at $81.
c. Purchased 3,000 shares of treasury common for $66,000. *22*
d. Sold 1,800 shares of treasury common for $50,400. *28*
e. Sold 750 shares of treasury common for $14,250. *19*
f. Declared cash dividends of $1.50 per share on preferred stock and $0.40 per share on common stock.
g. Paid the cash dividends.

Instructions

Journalize the entries to record the transactions. Identify each entry by letter.

PROBLEM 11-4B
Entries for selected corporate transactions
Objectives 3, 4, 6, 7

SPREADSHEET
P.A.S.S.

✓ *4. Total stockholders' equity, $2,859,825*

Shoshone Enterprises Inc. manufactures bathroom fixtures. The stockholders' equity accounts of Shoshone Enterprises Inc., with balances on January 1, 2006, are as follows:

Common Stock, $20 stated value (100,000 shares authorized, 75,000 shares issued)	$1,500,000
Paid-In Capital in Excess of Stated Value	180,000
Retained Earnings	725,000
Treasury Stock (5,000 shares, at cost)	140,000

The following selected transactions occurred during the year:

Jan. 28. Paid cash dividends of $0.80 per share on the common stock. The dividend had been properly recorded when declared on December 30 of the preceding fiscal year for $56,000.

Mar. 21. Issued 15,000 shares of common stock for $480,000.

May 10. Sold all of the treasury stock for $165,000.

July 1. Declared a 4% stock dividend on common stock, to be capitalized at the market price of the stock, which is $36 a share.

Aug. 11. Issued the certificates for the dividend declared on July 1.

Oct. 20. Purchased 7,500 shares of treasury stock for $255,000.

Dec. 27. Declared a $0.75-per-share dividend on common stock.

31. Closed the credit balance of the income summary account, $269,400.

31. Closed the two dividends accounts to Retained Earnings.

Instructions

1. Enter the January 1 balances in T accounts for the stockholders' equity accounts listed. Also prepare T accounts for the following: Paid-In Capital from Sale of Treasury Stock; Stock Dividends Distributable; Stock Dividends; Cash Dividends.

2. Journalize the entries to record the transactions, and post to the eight selected accounts.

3. Prepare a retained earnings statement for the year ended December 31, 2006.

4. Prepare the stockholders' equity section of the December 31, 2006 balance sheet.

PROBLEM 11-5B
Entries for selected corporate transactions

Objectives 3, 4, 5, 6

SPREADSHEET
P.A.S.S.

Selected transactions completed by Mead Boating Supply Corporation during the current fiscal year are as follows:

Jan. 20. Split the common stock 5 for 1 and reduced the par from $50 to $10 per share. After the split, there were 500,000 common shares outstanding.

Apr. 1. Purchased 20,000 shares of the corporation's own common stock at $30, recording the stock at cost.

May 1. Declared semiannual dividends of $1.50 on 24,000 shares of preferred stock and $0.15 on the common stock to stockholders of record on May 20, payable on June 1.

June 1. Paid the cash dividends.

Aug. 7. Sold 12,000 shares of treasury stock at $38, receiving cash.

Nov. 15. Declared semiannual dividends of $1.50 on the preferred stock and $0.08 on the common stock (before the stock dividend). In addition, a 2% common stock dividend was declared on the common stock outstanding. The fair market value of the common stock is estimated at $35.

Dec. 15. Paid the cash dividends and issued the certificates for the common stock dividend.

Instructions
Journalize the transactions.

Special Activities

ACTIVITY 11-1
Business strategy

GROUP ACTIVITY   INTERNET

REAL WORLD

7-Eleven operates more than 22,000 convenience food stores worldwide. 7-Eleven stores are normally less than 3,000 square feet and carry a variety of items, including soft drinks, candy and snacks, cigarettes, milk, and t-shirts. Many stores also sell CITGO-brand gasoline. 7-Eleven faces increasing competition from other convenience store chains as well as from grocery and supermarket chains, grocery wholesalers and buying clubs, gasoline/miniconvenience stores, food stores, fast food chains, and variety, drug, and candy stores. In groups of three to four, answer the following questions:

1. Go to the 7-Eleven Web site, which is linked to the text's Web site at **http://warren.swlearning.com**. How did the name 7-Eleven orginate?

2. How many items do you think an average 7-Eleven carries?

3. Excluding gasoline, rank the following "seven" categories of merchandise in the order in which you believe they generate the most sales for 7-Eleven. Rank the merchandise category with the most sales 1, the second most sales 2, and so on.

<u>Merchandise Category</u>
* baked and fresh foods, such as bread and rolls
* beer and wine
* beverages, such as soft drinks and coffee
* candy and snacks
* dairy products
* nonfood products and services, such as automobile oil, toothpaste, coolers, money orders, and lottery tickets
* tobacco products

4. Describe some ways (strategies) that you think 7-Eleven can increase its same-store sales in the face of increasing competition.

ACTIVITY 11-2
Board of directors' actions

REAL WORLD   ETHICS

In early 2002, Bernie Ebbers, the CEO of **WorldCom Group**, a major telecommunications company, was having personal financial troubles. Ebbers pledged a large stake of his Worldcom stock as security for some personal loans. As the price of Worldcom stock sank, Ebbers' bankers threatened to sell his stock in order to protect their loans. To avoid having his stock sold, Ebbers asked the board of directors of Worldcom to loan him nearly $400 million of corporate assets at 2.5% interest to pay off his bankers. The board agreed to lend him the money.

Comment on the decision of the board of directors in this situation.

ACTIVITY 11-3
Ethics and professional conduct in business

ETHICS

Lois Heck and Keith Ryan are organizing Beaufort Unlimited Inc. to undertake a high-risk gold-mining venture in Canada. Lois and Keith tentatively plan to request authorization for 80,000,000 shares of common stock to be sold to the general public. Lois and Keith have decided to establish par of $1 per share in order to appeal to a wide variety of potential investors. Lois and Keith feel that investors would be more willing to invest in the company if they received a large quantity of shares for what might appear to be a "bargain" price.

➡ Discuss whether Lois and Keith are behaving in a professional manner.

ACTIVITY 11-4
Issuing stock

WHAT DO YOU THINK?

Kilimanjaro Inc. began operations on January 6, 2006, with the issuance of 400,000 shares of $50 par common stock. The sole stockholders of Kilimanjaro Inc. are Donna White and Dr. Larry Klein, who organized Kilimanjaro Inc. with the objective of developing a new flu vaccine. Dr. Klein claims that the flu vaccine, which is nearing the final development stage, will protect individuals against 98% of the flu types that have been medically identified. To complete the project, Kilimanjaro Inc. needs $20,000,000 of additional funds. The local banks have been unwilling to loan the funds because of the lack of sufficient collateral and the riskiness of the business.

The following is a conversation between Donna White, the chief executive officer of Kilimanjaro Inc., and Dr. Larry Klein, the leading researcher.

White: What are we going to do? The banks won't loan us any more money, and we've got to have $20 million to complete the project. We are so close! It would be a disaster to quit now. The only thing I can think of is to issue additional stock. Do you have any suggestions?

Klein: I guess you're right. But if the banks won't loan us any more money, how do you think we can find any investors to buy stock?

White: I've been thinking about that. What if we promise the investors that we will pay them 2% of net sales until they have received an amount equal to what they paid for the stock?

Klein: What happens when we pay back the $20 million? Do the investors get to keep the stock? If they do, it'll dilute our ownership.

White: How about, if after we pay back the $20 million, we make them turn in their stock for $100 per share? That's twice what they paid for it, plus they would have already gotten all their money back. That's a $100 profit per share for the investors.

Klein: It could work. We get our money, but don't have to pay any interest, dividends, or the $100 until we start generating net sales. At the same time, the investors could get their money back plus $100 per share.

White: We'll need current financial statements for the new investors. I'll get our accountant working on them and contact our attorney to draw up a legally binding contract for the new investors. Yes, this could work.

In late 2006, the attorney and the various regulatory authorities approved the new stock offering, and 400,000 shares of common stock were privately sold to new investors at the stock's par of $50.

In preparing financial statements for 2006, Donna White and Anita Sparks, the controller for Kilimanjaro Inc., have the following conversation.

Sparks: Donna, I've got a problem.

White: What's that, Anita?

Sparks: Issuing common stock to raise that additional $20 million was a great idea. But . . .

White: But what?

Sparks: I've got to prepare the 2006 annual financial statements, and I am not sure how to classify the common stock.

White: What do you mean? It's common stock.

Sparks: I'm not so sure. I called the auditor and explained how we are contractually obligated to pay the new stockholders 2% of net sales until $50 per share is paid. Then, we may be obligated to pay them $100 per share.

White: So . . .

Sparks: So the auditor thinks that we should classify the additional issuance of $20 million as debt, not stock! And, if we put the $20 million on the balance sheet as debt, we will violate our other loan agreements with the banks. And, if these agreements are violated, the banks may call in all our debt immediately. If they do that, we are in deep trouble. We'll probably have to file for bankruptcy. We just don't have the cash to pay off the banks.

1. ▭▭▭▸ Discuss the arguments for and against classifying the issuance of the $20 million of stock as debt.

2. ▭▭▭▸ What do you think might be a practical solution to this classification problem?

ACTIVITY 11-5
Dividends

Matterhorn Inc. has paid quarterly cash dividends since 1993. These dividends have steadily increased from $0.05 per share to the latest dividend declaration of $0.40 per share. The board of directors would like to continue this trend and is hesitant to suspend or decrease the amount of quarterly dividends. Unfortunately, sales dropped sharply in the fourth quarter of 2006 because of worsening economic conditions and increased competition. As a result, the board is uncertain as to whether it should declare a dividend for the last quarter of 2006.

On November 1, 2006, Matterhorn Inc. borrowed $400,000 from Cheyenne National Bank to use in modernizing its retail stores and to expand its product line in reaction to its competition. The terms of the 10-year, 12% loan require Matterhorn Inc. to:

a. Pay monthly interest on the last day of month.

b. Pay $40,000 of the principal each November 1, beginning in 2007.

c. Maintain a current ratio (current assets ÷ current liabilities) of 2.

d. Maintain a minimum balance (a compensating balance) of $20,000 in its Cheyenne National Bank account.

On December 31, 2006, $100,000 of the $400,000 loan had been disbursed in modernization of the retail stores and in expansion of the product line. Matterhorn Inc.'s balance sheet as of December 31, 2006, is as follows:

Matterhorn Inc.
Balance Sheet
December 31, 2006

Assets

Current assets:			
Cash		$ 32,000	
Marketable securities		300,000	
Accounts receivable	$ 73,200		
Less allowance for doubtful accounts	5,200	68,000	
Merchandise inventory		100,000	
Prepaid expenses		3,600	
Total current assets			$ 503,600
Property, plant, and equipment:			
Land		$120,000	
Buildings	$760,000		
Less accumulated depreciation	172,000	588,000	
Equipment	$368,000		
Less accumulated depreciation	88,000	280,000	
Total property, plant, and equipment			988,000
Total assets			$1,491,600

Liabilities

Current liabilities:			
Accounts payable	$ 57,440		
Notes payable (Cheyenne National Bank)	40,000		
Salaries payable	2,560		
Total current liabilities		$100,000	
Long-term liabilities:			
Notes payable (Cheyenne National Bank)		360,000	
Total liabilities			$ 460,000

Stockholders' Equity

Paid-in capital:			
Common stock, $20 par (50,000 shares authorized, 20,000 shares issued)	$400,000		
Excess of issue price over par	32,000		
Total paid-in capital		$432,000	
Retained earnings		599,600	
Total stockholders' equity			1,031,600
Total liabilities and stockholders' equity			$1,491,600

The board of directors is scheduled to meet January 6, 2007, to discuss the results of operations for 2006 and to consider the declaration of dividends for the fourth quarter of 2006. The chairman of the board has asked for your advice on the declaration of dividends.

1.  What factors should the board consider in deciding whether to declare a cash dividend?
2.  The board is considering the declaration of a stock dividend instead of a cash dividend. Discuss the issuance of a stock dividend from the point of view of (a) a stockholder and (b) the board of directors.

ACTIVITY 11-6
Profiling a corporation

GROUP ACTIVITY   INTERNET

Select a public corporation you are familiar with or which interests you. Using the Internet, your school library, and other sources, develop a short (2 to 5 pages) profile of the corporation. Include in your profile the following information:

1. Name of the corporation.
2. State of incorporation.
3. Nature of its operations.
4. Total assets for the most recent balance sheet.
5. Total revenues for the most recent income statement.
6. Net income for the most recent income statement.

(continued)

7. Classes of stock outstanding.
8. Market price of the stock outstanding.
9. High and low price of the stock for the past year.
10. Dividends paid for each share of stock during the past year.

In groups of three or four, discuss each corporate profile. Select one of the corporations, assuming that your group has $100,000 to invest in its stock. Summarize why your group selected the corporation it did and how financial accounting information may have affected your decision. Keep track of the performance of your corporation's stock for the remainder of the term.

Note: Most major corporations maintain "home pages" on the Internet. This home page provides a variety of information on the corporation and often includes the corporation's financial statements. In addition, the New York Stock Exchange Web site (**http://www.nyse.com**) includes links to the home pages of many listed companies. Financial statements can also be accessed using EDGAR, the electronic archives of financial statements filed with the Securities and Exchange Commission (SEC).

SEC documents can also be retrieved using the EdgarScan™ service from **PricewaterhouseCoopers** at **http://edgarscan.pwcglobal.com**. To obtain annual report information, key in a company name in the appropriate space. EdgarScan will list the reports, available to you for the company you've selected. Select the most recent annual report filing, identified as a 10-K or 10-K405. EdgarScan provides an outline of the report, including the separate financial statements, which can also be selected in an Excel® spreadsheet.

# nswers to Self-Examination Questions

1. **C** If a corporation has cumulative preferred stock outstanding, dividends that have been passed for prior years plus the dividend for the current year must be paid before dividends may be declared on common stock. In this case, dividends of $27,000 ($9,000 × 3) have been passed for the preceding three years, and the current year's dividends are $9,000, making a total of $36,000 (answer C) that must be paid to preferred stockholders before dividends can be declared on common stock.

2. **D** Paid-in capital is one of the two major subdivisions of the stockholders' equity of a corporation. It may result from many sources, including the issuance of cumulative preferred stock (answer A), the receipt of donated real estate (answer B), or the sale of a corporation's treasury stock (answer C).

3. **D** The Stockholders' Equity section of corporate balance sheets is divided into two principal subsections: (1) investments contributed by the stockholders and others and (2) net income retained in the business. Included as part of the investments by stockholders and others is the par of common stock (answer A), stock dividends distributable (answer B), and the par of preferred stock (answer C).

4. **C** Reacquired stock, known as treasury stock, should be listed in the Stockholders' Equity section (answer C) of the balance sheet. The price paid for the treasury stock is deducted from the total of all the stockholders' equity accounts.

5. **C** If a corporation that holds treasury stock declares a cash dividend, the dividends are not paid on the treasury shares. To do so would place the corporation in the position of earning income through dealing with itself. Thus, the corporation will record $44,000 (answer C) as cash dividends [(25,000 shares issued less 3,000 shares held as treasury stock) × $2 per share dividend].

12

INCOME TAXES, UNUSUAL INCOME ITEMS, AND INVESTMENTS IN STOCKS

objectives

After studying this chapter, you should be able to:

1 Journalize the entries for corporate income taxes, including deferred income taxes.

2 Prepare an income statement reporting the following unusual items: fixed asset impairments, restructuring charges, discontinued operations, extraordinary items, and cumulative changes in accounting principles.

3 Prepare an income statement reporting earnings per share data.

4 Describe the concept and the reporting of comprehensive income.

5 Describe the accounting for investments in stocks.

6 Describe alternative methods of combining businesses and how consolidated financial statements are prepared.

7 Compute and interpret the price-earnings ratio.

If you apply for a bank loan, you will be required to list your assets and liabilities on a loan application. In addition, you will be asked to indicate your monthly income. Assume that the day you were filling out the application, you won $4,000 in the state lottery. The $4,000 lottery winnings increase your assets by $4,000. Should you also show your lottery winnings as part of your monthly income?

The answer, of course, is no. Winning the lottery is an unusual event and, for most of us, a nonrecurring event. In determining whether to grant the loan, the bank is interested in your ability to make monthly loan payments. Such payments depend upon your recurring monthly income.

Businesses also experience unusual and nonrecurring events that affect their financial statements. Such events should be clearly disclosed in the financial statements so that stakeholders in the business will not misinterpret the financial effects of the events.

In this chapter, we discuss unusual items that affect income statements and illustrate how such items should be reported. In addition, we discuss other specialized accounting and reporting topics, including accounting for income taxes, investments, and business combinations.

Corporate Income Taxes

objective 1

Journalize the entries for corporate income taxes, including deferred income taxes.

Under the United States tax code, corporations are taxable entities that must pay federal income taxes.[1] Depending upon where it is located, a corporation may also be required to pay state and local income taxes. Although we limit our discussion to federal income taxes, the basic concepts also apply to other income taxes.

Payment of Income Taxes

Most corporations are required to pay estimated federal income taxes in four installments throughout the year. For example, assume that a corporation with a calendar-year accounting period estimates its income tax expense for the year as $84,000. The entry to record the first of the four estimated tax payments of $21,000 (1/4 of $84,000) is as follows:

Apr.	15	Income Tax Expense		21 0 0 0 00	
		Cash			21 0 0 0 00

REAL WORLD

Individuals pay quarterly estimated taxes if the amount of tax withholding is not sufficient to pay their taxes at the end of the year. This usually occurs when a significant portion of an individual's income is from rent, dividends, or interest.

At year-end, the actual taxable income and the related tax are determined.[2] If additional taxes are owed, the additional liability is recorded. If the total estimated tax payments are greater than the tax liability based on actual taxable income, the overpayment should be debited to a receivable account and credited to *Income Tax Expense.*[3]

Income taxes are normally disclosed as a deduction at the bottom of the income statement in determining net income, as shown at the top of the next page, in an excerpt from an income statement for the **Procter & Gamble Company**.

---

[1]Limited liability corporations (LLCs) are not separate taxable entities and thus are not subject to federal (and most state) income taxes. For this reason, the material in this section would not generally apply to an LLC.

[2]A corporation's income tax returns and supporting records are subject to audits by taxing authorities, who may assess additional taxes. Because of this possibility, the liability for income taxes is sometimes described in the balance sheet as *Estimated income tax payable.*

[3]Another common term used for income taxes on the income statement and note disclosures is "provision for income taxes."

Year Ended June 30, 2002	(Amounts in Millions)
Net Sales	**$40,238**
Cost of products sold	20,989
Marketing, research, and administrative expenses	12,571
Income from Operations	**$ 6,678**
Interest expense	(603)
Other income, net	308
Earnings Before Income Taxes	**$ 6,383**
Income taxes	2,031
Net Earnings	**$ 4,352**

The ratio of reported income tax expense to earnings before taxes is shown for selected industries, as follows:

Industry	Percent of Reported Income Tax Expense to Earnings before Taxes
Automobiles	33%
Banking	35
Computers	35
Food	35
Integrated oil	39
Pharmaceuticals	30
Retail	39
Telecommunication	37
Transportation	38

As you can see, the reported income tax expense is normally between 30%–40% of earnings before tax. Therefore, taxes are a significant expense for most companies and must be considered when analyzing a company. Differences in tax rates between industries can be due to tax regulations unique to certain industries.

Allocating Income Taxes

The **taxable income** of a corporation is determined according to the tax laws and is reported to taxing authorities on the corporation's tax return.[4] It is often different from the income before income taxes reported in the income statement according to generally accepted accounting principles. As a result, the *income tax based on taxable income* usually differs from the *income tax based on income before taxes*. This difference may need to be allocated between various financial statement periods, depending on the nature of the items causing the differences.

Some differences between taxable income and income before income taxes are created because items are recognized in one period for tax purposes and in another period for income statement purposes. Such differences, called **temporary differences**, reverse or turn around in later years. Some examples of items that create temporary differences are listed below.

1. *Revenues or gains are taxed **after** they are reported in the income statement.*
   Example: In some cases, companies that make sales under an installment plan

---

[4]Accounting for deferred income taxes is a complex topic that is treated in greater detail in advanced accounting texts. The treatment here provides a general overview and conceptual understanding of the topic.

recognize revenue for financial reporting purposes when a sale is made but defer recognizing revenue for tax purposes until cash is collected.

2. *Expenses or losses are deducted in determining taxable income **after** they are reported in the income statement.* Example: Product warranty expense estimated and reported in the year of the sale for financial statement reporting is deducted for tax reporting when paid.

3. *Revenues or gains are taxed **before** they are reported in the income statement.* Example: Cash received in advance for magazine subscriptions is included in taxable income when received but included in the income statement only when earned in a future period.

4. *Expenses or losses are deducted in determining taxable income **before** they are reported in the income statement.* Example: MACRS depreciation is used for tax purposes, and the straight-line method is used for financial reporting purposes.

Since temporary differences reverse in later years, they do not change or reduce the total amount of taxable income over the life of a business. Exhibit 1 illustrates the reversing nature of temporary differences in which a business uses MACRS depreciation for tax purposes and straight-line depreciation for financial statement purposes. Exhibit 1 assumes that MACRS recognizes more depreciation in the early years and less depreciation in the later years. The total depreciation expense is the same for both methods over the life of the asset.

•Exhibit 1

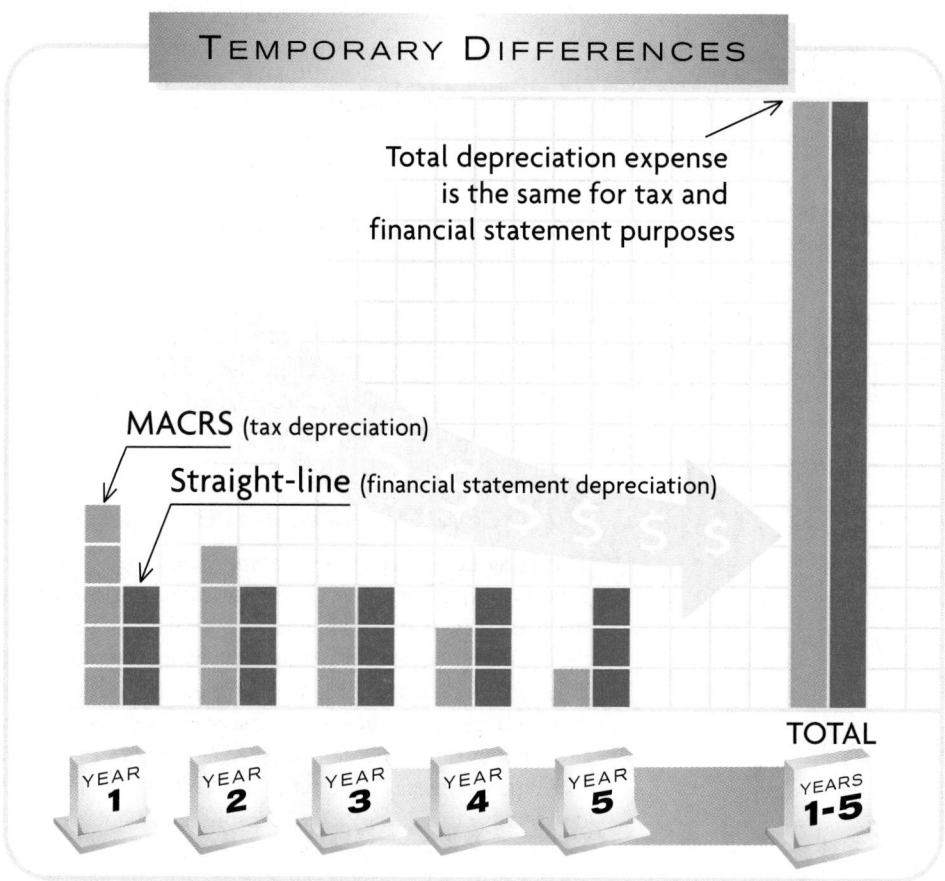

TEMPORARY DIFFERENCES

Total depreciation expense
is the same for tax and
financial statement purposes

MACRS (tax depreciation)
Straight-line (financial statement depreciation)

YEAR 1   YEAR 2   YEAR 3   YEAR 4   YEAR 5   TOTAL YEARS 1-5

As Exhibit 1 illustrates, temporary differences affect only the timing of when revenues and expenses are recognized for tax purposes. As a result, the total amount of taxes paid does not change. Only the timing of the payment of taxes is affected. In most cases, managers use tax-planning techniques so that temporary differences delay or defer the payment of taxes to later years. As a result, at the end of each year the amount of the current tax liability and the postponed (deferred) liability must be recorded.

A corporation has $300,000 income before income taxes, a 40% tax rate, and $130,000 taxable income. What is the amount of deferred income tax?

$68,000 [($300,000 × 40%) − ($130,000 × 40%)]

To illustrate, assume that at the end of the first year of operations a corporation reports $300,000 income before income taxes on its income statement. If we assume an income tax rate of 40%, the income tax expense reported on the income statement is $120,000 ($300,000 × 40%).[5] However, to reduce the amount owed for current income taxes, the corporation uses tax planning to reduce the taxable income to $100,000. Thus, the income tax actually due for the year is only $40,000 ($100,000 × 40%). The $80,000 ($120,000 − $40,000) difference between the two tax amounts is created by timing differences in recognizing revenue. This amount is deferred to future years. The example is summarized below.

Income tax based on $300,000 reported income at 40%	$120,000
Income tax based on $100,000 taxable income at 40%	40,000
Income tax deferred to future years	$ 80,000

To match the current year's expenses (including income tax) against the current year's revenue on the income statement, income tax is allocated between periods, using the following journal entry:

Income Tax Expense		120 000 00	
Income Tax Payable			40 000 00
Deferred Income Tax Payable			80 000 00

The income tax expense reported on the income statement is the total tax, $120,000, expected to be paid on the income for the year. In future years, the $80,000 in *Deferred Income Tax Payable* will be transferred to *Income Tax Payable* as the timing differences reverse and the taxes become due. For example, if $48,000 of the deferred tax reverses and becomes due in the second year, the following journal entry would be made in the second year:

Deferred Income Tax Payable		48 000 00	
Income Tax Payable			48 000 00

Reporting and Analyzing Taxes

The balance of *Deferred Income Tax Payable* at the end of a year is reported as a liability.[6] The amount due within one year is classified as a current liability. The remainder is classified as a long-term liability or reported in a Deferred Credits section following the Long-Term Liabilities section.[7]

Differences between taxable income and income (before taxes) reported on the income statement may also arise because certain revenues are exempt from tax and certain expenses are not deductible in determining taxable income. Such differences, which will not reverse with the passage of time, are sometimes called **permanent differences**. For example, interest income on municipal bonds may be exempt from taxation. Such differences create no special financial reporting problems, since the amount of income tax determined according to the tax laws is the *same* amount reported on the income statement.

POINT OF INTEREST

Interest from investments in municipal bonds is also tax exempt for individual taxpayers.

----

[5]For purposes of illustration, the 40% rate is assumed to include all federal, state, and local income taxes.
[6]In some cases, a deferred tax asset may arise for tax benefits to be received in the future. Such deferred tax assets are reported as either current or long-term assets, depending on when the benefits are expected to be realized.
[7]Additional note disclosures for deferred income taxes are also required. These are discussed in advanced accounting texts.

Unusual Items Affecting the Income Statement

Prepare an income statement reporting the following unusual items: fixed asset impairments, restructuring charges, discontinued operations, extraordinary items, and cumulative changes in accounting principles.

Generally accepted accounting principles require that certain unusual items be reported separately on the income statement. These items can be classified into the following two categories:

1. Those items that are reported in determining income from continuing operations, sometimes called **above-the-line** items.
2. Those items that are reported as deductions from income from continuing operations, sometimes called **below-the-line** items.

In the following paragraphs, we discuss each of these unusual items.

Unusual Items Affecting Income from Continuing Operations

Some unusual items are deducted from gross profit in arriving at income from continuing operations. Unusual above-the-line items consist of fixed asset impairments and restructuring charges.

Fixed Asset Impairments

A *fixed asset impairment* occurs when the fair value of a fixed asset falls below its book value and is not expected to recover.[8] Examples of events that might cause an asset impairment are (1) decreases in the market price of fixed assets, (2) significant changes in the business or regulations related to fixed assets, (3) adverse conditions affecting the use of fixed assets, or (4) expected cash flow losses from using fixed assets.[9] For example, on March 1, assume that Jones Company consolidates operations by closing a factory. As a result of the closing, plant and equipment is impaired by $750,000. The journal entry to record the impairment is as follows:

Mar.	1	Loss on Fixed Asset Impairment	750 0 0 0 00	
		Fixed Assets—Plant and Equipment		750 0 0 0 00

The loss on fixed asset impairment is reported as a separate expense item deducted from gross profit in determining income from continuing operations, as illustrated for Jones Company in Exhibit 2. In addition, note disclosure should describe the nature of the asset impaired and the cause of the impairment, as shown in Note A of Exhibit 2.

The loss reduces the book value of the fixed asset and thus reduces the depreciation expense for future periods. If the asset could be salvaged for sale, the gain or loss on the sale would be based on the lower book value. Therefore, asset impairment accounting recognizes the loss when it is first identified, rather than at a later sale date.

[8]Fixed assets that are discontinued components, such as an operating segment, subsidiary, or asset group, should be treated as discontinued items as discussed in a later section.
[9]*Statement of Financial Accounting Standards, No. 144,* "Accounting for the Impairment or Disposal of Long-Lived Assets," Financial Accounting Standards Board (Norwalk, Connecticut: 2001).

•Exhibit 2   Unusual Items in Income Statement

Jones Corporation
Income Statement
For the Year Ended December 31, 2006

Net sales		$12,350,000
Cost of merchandise sold		5,800,000
Gross profit		$ 6,550,000
Operating expenses	$3,490,000	
Restructuring charge (Note A)	1,000,000	
Loss from asset impairment (Note A)	750,000	5,240,000
Income from continuing operations before income tax		$ 1,310,000
Income tax expense		620,000
Income from continuing operations		$ 690,000
Loss on discontinued operations (Note B)		100,000
Income before extraordinary items and cumulative effect of a change in		
accounting principle		$ 590,000
Extraordinary item:		
Gain on condemnation of land, net of applicable income tax of $65,000		150,000
Cumulative effect on prior years of changing to a different depreciation method (Note C) . . .		92,000
Net income		$ 832,000

Note A

As a result of a downturn in the economy, the company consolidated operations by closing its Dekalb, Illinois, factory on March 1 of the current year. The factory closing impaired the factory building and equipment. The building and equipment were written down by $400,000 and $350,000 to reflect their respective salvage values. In addition, 200 employees at the Dekalb facility were offered $1,000,000 in termination benefits. As of the end of the fiscal year, no obligation remains with regard to the termination benefit arrangement.

Note B

On July 1 of the current year, the electrical products division of the corporation was sold at a loss of $100,000, net of applicable income tax of $50,000. The net sales of the division for the current year were $2,900,000. The assets sold were composed of inventories, equipment, and plant totaling $2,100,000. The purchaser assumed liabilities of $600,000.

Note C

Depreciation of all property, plant, and equipment has been computed by the straight-line method in 2006. Prior to 2006, depreciation of equipment for one of the divisions had been computed on the declining-balance method. In 2006, the straight-line method was adopted for this division in order to achieve uniformity and to better match depreciation charges with the estimated economic utility of such assets. Consistent with APB Opinion No. 20, this change in depreciation has been applied to prior years. The effect of the change was to increase income by $30,000 before extraordinary items for 2006. The adjustment of $92,000 (after reduction for income tax of $88,000) to apply the new method to prior years is also included in net income for 2006.

INTEGRITY IN BUSINESS

WHEN IS AN ASSET IMPAIRED?

The asset impairment rule is designed to reduce the subjectivity of timing asset write-downs. That is, write-downs should occur when the impairment is deemed permanent. In practice, however, there still remains judgment in determining when such impairment has occurred. Ethical managers will recognize asset write-downs when they occur, not when it is most convenient. For example, the SEC investigated **Avon Corporation** for delaying the write-off of a computer software project. In settling the formal investigation, Avon had to restate its earnings to reflect the earlier write-off date.

Restructuring Charges

Restructuring charges are costs associated with involuntarily terminating employees, terminating contracts, consolidating facilities, or relocating employees. Often, these events incur initial one-time costs in order to capture long-term savings. For example, involuntarily terminated employees often receive a one-time termination or severance benefit at the time of their dismissal. Employee termination benefits are normally the most significant restructuring charges; thus, they will be the focus of this section.

Employee termination benefits arise when a plan specifying the number of terminated employees, the benefit, and the benefit timing has been authorized by senior management and communicated to the employees.[10] To illustrate, assume that the management of Jones Company communicates a plan to terminate 200 employees from the closed manufacturing plant on March 1. The plan calls for a termination benefit of $5,000 per employee. Once the plan is communicated to employees, they have the legal right to work for 60 days but may elect to leave the firm earlier. In other words, employees may be paid severance at the end of 60 days or at any time in between. The expense and liability to provide employee benefits should be recognized at its fair value on the plan communication date.[11] The fair value of this plan would be $1,000,000 (200 × $5,000), which is the aggregate expected cost of terminating the employees. Thus, the $1,000,000 restructuring charge would be recorded as follows:

Mar.	1	Restructuring Charge	1,000 0 0 0 00	
		Employee Termination Obligation		1,000 0 0 0 00

The restructuring charge is reported as a separate expense deducted from gross profit in determining income from continuing operations, as shown in Exhibit 2. The employee termination obligation would be shown as a current liability. If the plan called for expected severance payments beyond one year, then a long-term liability would be recognized. In addition, a note should disclose the nature and cause of the restructuring event and the costs associated with the type of restructuring event.

The actual benefits paid to terminated employees should be debited to the liability as employees leave the firm. For example, assume that 25 employees find other employment and leave the company on March 25. The journal entry to record the severance payment to these employees would be as follows:

Mar.	25	Employee Termination Obligation	125 0 0 0 00	
		Cash		125 0 0 0 00

Unusual Items Not Affecting Income from Continuing Operations

Some unusual items are deducted from income from continuing operations in arriving at net income. Unusual items not affecting income from continuing operations consist of discontinued operations, extraordinary items, and changes in accounting principles.

---

[10]*Statement of Financial Accounting Standards, No. 146,* "Accounting for Costs Associated with Exit or Disposal Activities," Financial Accounting Standards Board (Norwalk, Connecticut: 2002).

[11]For longer-term severance agreements, present value concepts may be required to determine fair value. We will assume short-term agreements where the time value of money is assumed to be immaterial. Present value concepts are discussed in the bonds payable chapter.

FINANCIAL REPORTING AND DISCLOSURE

ROBERT MONDAVI CORPORATION

Restructuring charges and asset impairments can be disclosed using a variety of titles on the financial statements. Often, the charges are combined under a single title on the income statement. For example, **Robert Mondavi Corporation**, a leading producer of California table wines, disclosed $12,240,000 in "special charges" on its income statement above the operating income line. These charges were explained in the notes to the financial statements as follows:

The Company changed from an operator to a sponsor role at Disney's California Adventure. With this change, the Company eliminated any further operational risk associated with the project while it continues a business relationship with Disney and maintains a presence at the theme park. As a result of this change, the Company has recorded special charges through June 30, 2002, totaling $12,240,000 or $0.47 per diluted share, primarily reflecting fixed asset write-offs, employee separation expenses and lease cancellation fees.

As can be seen in this disclosure, Mondavi chose to combine restructuring charges and fixed asset impairments under a single expense line item called special charges.

Discontinued Operations

A gain or loss from disposing of a business segment or component of an entity is reported on the income statement as a gain or loss from ***discontinued operations***. The term **business segment** refers to a major line of business for a company, such as a division or a department or a certain class of customer. A **component** of an entity is the lowest level at which the operations and cash flows can be clearly distinguished, operationally and for financial reporting purposes, from the rest of the entity.[12] Examples would be a store for a retailer, a territory for a sales organization, or a product category for a consumer products company. To illustrate the disclosure, assume that Jones Corporation has separate divisions that produce electrical products, hardware supplies, and lawn equipment. Jones sells its electrical products division at a loss. As shown in Exhibit 2, this loss is deducted from Jones' income from continuing operations (income from its hardware and lawn equipment divisions). In addition, Note B discloses the identity of the segment sold, the disposal date, a description of the segment's assets and liabilities, and the manner of disposal.

Extraordinary Items

An ***extraordinary item*** results from events and transactions that (1) are significantly different (unusual) from the typical or the normal operating activities of the business **and** (2) occur infrequently. The gains and losses resulting from natural disasters that occur infrequently, such as floods, earthquakes, and fires, are extraordinary items. Gains or losses from condemning land or buildings for public use are also extraordinary. Such gains and losses, other than those from disposing of a business segment, should be reported in the income statement as extraordinary items, as shown in Exhibit 2.

Sometimes extraordinary items result in unusual financial results. For example, **Delta Air Lines** once reported an extraordinary gain of over $5.5 million as the result of the crash of one of its 727s. The plane that crashed was insured for $6.5 million, but its book value in Delta's accounting records was $962,000.

Gains and losses on the disposal of fixed assets are *not* extraordinary items. This is because (1) they are not unusual and (2) they recur from time to time in the normal operations of a business. Likewise, gains and losses from the sale of investments are usual and recurring for most businesses.

---

[12]*Statement of Financial Accounting Standards, No. 144*, op. cit., par. 41.

Changes in Accounting Principles

Businesses are often required to change their accounting principles when the Financial Accounting Standards Board (FASB) issues a new accounting standard. In addition, a business may voluntarily change from one generally accepted accounting principle to another. For example, a corporation may change from the FIFO to the LIFO method of costing inventory to better match revenues and expenses. Changes in generally accepted accounting principles should be disclosed in the financial statements (or in notes to the statements) of the period in which they occur. This disclosure should include the following information:

1. The nature of the change.
2. The justification for the change.
3. The effect on the current year's net income.
4. The cumulative effect of the change on the net income of prior periods.

To illustrate, assume that one of Jones Corporation's divisions changes from the declining-balance method to the straight-line method of depreciation. As shown in Exhibit 2, the cumulative effect of this change is reported after the extraordinary items. The effect on the prior period is explained in Note C. If financial statements for prior periods are also presented, they should be restated as if the change had been made in the prior periods, and the effect of the restatement should be reported either on the face of the statements or in a note.

Reporting unusual items separately on the income statement allows investors to isolate the effects of these items on income and cash flows. By reporting such items, investors and other users of the financial statements can consider such factors in assessing a business's future income and cash flows.

Reporting Unusual Below-the-Line Items

The three unusual items discussed in this section are reported separately in the income statement, below the income from continuing operations, as shown in Exhibit 2 on page 485. Many different terms and formats may be used. Unlike above-the-line unusual items, the related tax effects of below-the-line items are reported either with the item with which they are associated or in the notes to the statement. Approximately 29% of U.S. companies reported one of these unusual items on their income statement for a recent fiscal year.[13]

Earnings per Common Share

objective 3

Prepare an income statement reporting earnings per share data.

The amount of net income is often used by investors and creditors in evaluating a company's profitability. However, net income by itself is difficult to use in comparing companies of different sizes. Also, trends in net income may be difficult to evaluate, using only net income, if there have been significant changes in a company's stockholders' equity. Thus, the profitability of companies is often expressed as earnings per share. **Earnings per common share (EPS)**, sometimes called **basic earnings per share**, is the net income per share of common stock outstanding during a period.

Because of its importance, earnings per share is reported in the financial press and by various investor services, such as **Moody's** and **Standard & Poor's**. Changes in earnings per share can lead to significant changes in the price of a corporation's stock in the marketplace. For example, the stock of **Texas Instruments Inc.** surged by over 12% to $16 per share after the company announced earnings per share of 6¢ as compared to Wall Street analysts' estimate of 3¢ per share.

---

[13]Determined from U.S. firms in excess of $5 billion sales on Disclosure® database.

Corporations whose stock is traded in a public market must report earnings per common share on their income statements.[14] If no preferred stock is outstanding, the earnings per common share is calculated as follows:

$$\text{Earnings per Common Share} = \frac{\text{Net Income}}{\text{Number of Common Shares Outstanding}}$$

When the number of common shares outstanding has changed during the period, a weighted average number of shares outstanding is used. If a company has preferred stock outstanding, the net income must be reduced by the amount of any preferred dividends, as shown below.

$$\text{Earnings per Common Share} = \frac{\text{Net Income} - \text{Preferred Stock Dividends}}{\text{Number of Common Shares Outstanding}}$$

Comparing the earnings per share of two or more years, based on only the net incomes of those years, could be misleading. For example, assume that Jones Corporation, whose partial income statement was presented in Exhibit 2, reported $700,000 net income for 2005. Also assume that no extraordinary or other unusual items were reported in 2005. Jones has no preferred stock outstanding and has 200,000 common shares outstanding in 2005 and 2006. The earnings per common share is $3.50 ($700,000/200,000 shares) for 2005 and $4.16 ($832,000/200,000 shares) for 2006. Comparing the two earnings per share amounts suggests that operations have improved. However, the 2006 earnings per share comparable to the $3.50 is $3.45, which is the income from continuing operations of $690,000 divided by 200,000 shares. The latter amount indicates a slight downturn in normal earnings.

When unusual below-the-line items exist, earnings per common share should be reported for those items. To illustrate, a partial income statement for Jones Corporation, showing earnings per common share, is shown in Exhibit 3. In this income statement, Jones reports all the earnings per common share amounts on the face of the income statement. However, only earnings per share amounts for income from continuing operations and net income are required to be presented on the face of

•Exhibit 3   **Income Statement with Earnings per Share**

Jones Corporation
Income Statement
For the Year Ended December 31, 2006

Earnings per common share:	
Income from continuing operations	$ 3.45
Loss on discontinued operations (Note B)	0.50
Income before extraordinary items and cumulative effect of a change	
in accounting principle	$ 2.95
Extraordinary item:	
Gain on condemnation of land, net of applicable income	
tax of $65,000	0.75
Cumulative effect on prior years of changing to a different	
depreciation method (Note C)	0.46
Net income	$ 4.16

---

[14]*Statement of Financial Accounting Standards, No. 128,* "Earnings per Share," Financial Accounting Standards Board (Norwalk, Connecticut: 1997).

the statement. The other per share amounts may be presented in the notes to the financial statements.[15]

In the preceding paragraphs, we have assumed a simple capital structure with only common stock or common stock and preferred stock outstanding. Often, however, corporations have complex capital structures with various types of securities outstanding, such as convertible preferred stock, options, warrants, and contingently issuable shares. In such cases, the possible effects of converting such securities to common stock must be calculated and reported as *earnings per common share assuming dilution or diluted earnings per share*.[16] This topic is discussed further in advanced accounting texts.

Comprehensive Income

objective 4

Describe the concept and the reporting of comprehensive income.

REAL WORLD

In the 2002 edition of *Accounting Trends & Techniques*, over 90% of the surveyed companies reported other comprehensive income, and the majority of these companies disclosed it in the statement of stockholders' equity.

Comprehensive income is defined as all changes in stockholders' equity during a period, except those resulting from dividends and stockholders' investments. Companies must report traditional net income plus or minus other comprehensive income items to arrive at comprehensive income.

Other comprehensive income items include foreign currency items, pension liability adjustments, and unrealized gains and losses on investments. These "other" comprehensive income transactions are reported in a middle ground that requires disclosure of these items but does not include them as part of reported earnings on the income statement. The FASB wanted these items disclosed separately from earnings in order to avoid potential confusion in interpreting the income statement. To the extent that other comprehensive income items give rise to tax effects, the taxes should be allocated to these items, which was illustrated for unusual below-the-line items. The cumulative effects of other comprehensive income items must be reported separately from retained earnings and paid-in capital, on the balance sheet, as *accumulated other comprehensive income*. When other comprehensive income items are not present, the income statement and balance sheet formats are similar to those we have illustrated in this and preceding chapters.

Companies may report comprehensive income on the income statement, in a separate statement of comprehensive income, or in the statement of stockholders' equity. In addition, companies may use terms other than comprehensive income, such as "total nonowner changes in equity."

To illustrate reporting for comprehensive income, assume that Triple-A Enterprises, Inc., reported comprehensive income on a separate statement, called the *statement of comprehensive income*, as follows:

Triple-A Enterprises, Inc. Statement of Comprehensive Income For the Year Ended December 31, 2006	
Net income	$8 5 0 0 00
Other comprehensive income, net of tax	9 0 00
Total comprehensive income	$8 5 9 0 00

The stockholders' equity section of the balance sheet for Triple-A Enterprises is as follows:

[15]Ibid., pars. 36 and 37.
[16]Ibid., pars. 11–39.

Triple-A Enterprises, Inc. Stockholders' Equity December 31, 2005 and 2006	2006	2005
Stockholders' equity:		
Common stock	$ 200 000 00	$ 200 000 00
Paid-in capital in excess of par	360 000 00	360 000 00
Retained earnings	165 500 00	157 000 00
Accumulated other comprehensive income	1 290 00	1 200 00
Total stockholders' equity	$222 790 00	$214 200 00

Accumulated other comprehensive income is the cumulative effect of other comprehensive income items. Thus, the additional other comprehensive income of $90 for 2006 is added to the accumulated other comprehensive income beginning balance of $1,200 to yield the December 31, 2006 balance of $1,290.

You should note that comprehensive income does not affect net income or retained earnings, as we have discussed and illustrated. In the next section, we will illustrate the determination of other comprehensive income, using unrealized gains and losses on investments.

Accounting for Investments in Stocks

objective **5**

Describe the accounting for investments in stocks.

Corporations not only issue stock, but they also purchase stocks of other companies for investment purposes. Like individuals, businesses have a variety of reasons for investing in stocks, called *equity securities*. A business may purchase stocks as a means of earning a return (income) on excess cash that it does not need for its normal operations. Such investments are usually for a short period of time. In other cases, a business may purchase the stock of another company as a means of developing or maintaining business relationships with the other company. A business may also purchase common stock as a means of gaining control of another company's operations. In these two latter cases, the business usually intends to hold the investment for a long period of time.

The equity securities in which a business invests may be classified as trading securities or available-for-sale securities. *Trading securities* are securities that management intends to actively trade for profit. Businesses holding trading securities are those whose normal operations involve buying and selling securities. Examples of such businesses include banks and insurance companies. *Available-for-sale securities* are securities that management expects to sell in the future but which are not actively traded for profit. For example, Warren Buffett, one of the wealthiest men in the world, invests through a public company called **Berkshire Hathaway Inc.** In a recent annual report, Berkshire Hathaway reported over $28 billion of equity investment holdings listed on its balance sheet as available-for-sale securities. Some of these investments include **Coca-Cola Company**, **Gillette Company**, and **American Express**. In this section, we describe and illustrate the accounting for available-for-sale equity securities. The accounting for trading securities is described and illustrated in advanced accounting texts.

Short-Term Investments in Stocks

Rather than allow excess cash to be idle until it is needed, a business may invest in available-for-sale securities. These investments are classified as *temporary investments* or **marketable securities**. Although such investments may be retained for several years, they continue to be classified as temporary, provided they meet two conditions. First, the securities are readily marketable and can be sold for cash at any time. Second, management intends to sell the securities when the business needs cash for operations.

Temporary investments in available-for-sale securities are recorded in a current asset account, *Marketable Securities*, at their cost. This cost includes all amounts spent to acquire the securities, such as broker's commissions. Any dividends received on the investment are recorded as a debit to *Cash* and a credit to *Dividend Revenue*.[17]

To illustrate, assume that on June 1 Crabtree Co. purchased 2,000 shares of Inis Corporation common stock at $89.75 per share plus a brokerage fee of $500. On October 1, Inis declared a $0.90 per share cash dividend payable on November 30. Crabtree's entries to record the stock purchase and the receipt of the dividend are as follows:

June	1	Marketable Securities	180 0 0 0 00	
		Cash		180 0 0 0 00
		Purchased 2,000 shares of Inis Corporation		
		common stock [($89.75 × 2,000 shares) + $500].		
Nov.	30	Cash	1 8 0 0 00	
		Dividend Revenue		1 8 0 0 00
		Received dividend on Inis Corporation		
		common stock (2,000 shares × $0.90).		

On the balance sheet, temporary investments are reported at their fair market value. Market values are normally available from stock quotations in financial newspapers, such as *The Wall Street Journal*. Any difference between the fair market values of the securities and their cost is an **unrealized holding gain or loss**. This gain or loss is termed "unrealized" because a transaction (the sale of the securities) is necessary before a gain or loss becomes real (realized).

To illustrate, assume that Crabtree Co.'s portfolio of temporary investments was purchased during 2006 and has the following fair market values and unrealized gains and losses on December 31, 2006:

Common Stock	Cost	Market	Unrealized Gain (Loss)
Edwards Inc.	$150,000	$190,000	$40,000
SWS Corp.	200,000	200,000	—
Inis Corporation	180,000	210,000	30,000
Bass Co.	160,000	150,000	(10,000)
Total	$690,000	$750,000	$60,000

If income taxes of $18,000 are allocated to the unrealized gain, Crabtree's temporary investments should be reported at their total cost of $690,000, plus the unrealized gain (net of applicable income tax) of $42,000 ($60,000 − $18,000), as shown in Exhibit 4.

The unrealized gain (net of applicable taxes) of $42,000 should also be reported as an *other comprehensive income item*, as we mentioned in the preceding section. For example, assume that Crabtree Co. has net income of $720,000 for the year ended December 31, 2006. Crabtree elects to report comprehensive income in the *statement of comprehensive income*, as shown in Exhibit 5. In addition, the accumu-

---

[17]Stock dividends received on an investment are not journalized, since they have no effect on the investor's assets and revenues.

•Exhibit 4   **Temporary Investments on the Balance Sheet**

Crabtree Co.
Balance Sheet (selected items)
December 31, 2006

Assets		
Current assets:		
Cash...		$119,500
Temporary investments in marketable		
securities at cost............................	$690,000	
Unrealized gain (net of applicable		
income tax of $18,000).......................	42,000	732,000
Stockholders' Equity		
Accumulated other comprehensive income..............		$ 42,000

•Exhibit 5   **Statement of Comprehensive Income**

Crabtree Co.
Statement of Comprehensive Income
For the Year Ended December 31, 2006

Net income..	$720,000
Other comprehensive income:	
Unrealized gain on temporary investments in marketable	
securities (net of applicable income tax of $18,000)...............	42,000
Comprehensive income..................................	$762,000

lated other comprehensive income on the balance sheet would also be $42,000, representing the beginning balance of zero plus other comprehensive income of $42,000, as shown in Exhibit 4.

Unrealized losses are reported in a similar manner. Unrealized gains and losses are reported as other comprehensive income items until the related securities are sold. When temporary securities are sold, the unrealized gains or losses become realized and are included in determining net income.

Long-Term Investments in Stocks

Long-term investments in stocks are not intended as a source of cash in the normal operations of the business. Rather, such investments are often held for their income, long-term gain potential, or influence over another business entity. They are reported in the balance sheet under the caption ***Investments***, which usually follows the Current Assets section.

Long-term investments in stock are treated as available-for-sale securities, as we illustrated previously for short-term available-for-sale securities. However, if the investor (the buyer of the stock) has significant influence over the operating and financing activities of the investee (company whose stock is owned), the ***equity method*** is used.

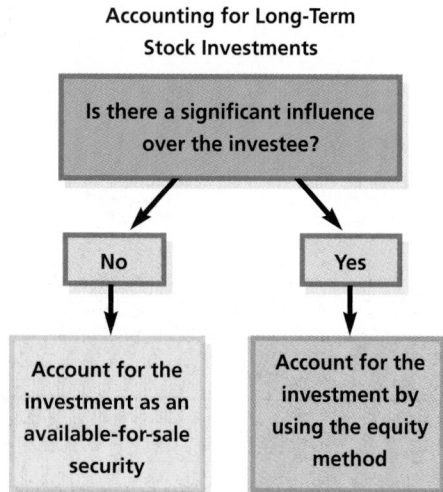

Accounting for Long-Term Stock Investments

When the investor does not have a significant influence over the investee, the investment is recorded at cost and reported at fair market value net of any applicable income tax effects. In addition, any unrealized gains and losses are reported as part of the comprehensive income.[18] For example, **Delta Air Lines** disclosed investments in **Priceline.com** preferred stock as a noncurrent investment at the appraised fair market value.

When the investor has a significant influence and the equity method is used, a stock purchase is recorded at cost, as shown previously. Evidence of significant influence includes the percentage of ownership, the existence of intercompany transactions, and the interchange of managerial personnel. Generally, if the investor owns 20% or more of the voting stock of the investee, it is assumed that the investor has significant influence over the investee.

Under the equity method, the investment is *not* subsequently adjusted to fair value. Rather, the book value of the investment is adjusted as follows:

1. The investor's share of the periodic net income of the investee is recorded as an *increase in the investment account* and as *income for the period*. Likewise, the investor's share of an investee's net loss is recorded as a *decrease in the investment account* and as a *loss for the period*.
2. The investor's share of cash dividends from the investee is recorded as an *increase in the cash account* and a *decrease in the investment account*.

To illustrate, assume that on January 2, Hally Inc. pays cash of $350,000 for 40% of the common stock and net assets of Brock Corporation. Assume also that, for the year ending December 31, Brock Corporation reports net income of $105,000 and declares and pays $45,000 in dividends. Using the equity method, Hally Inc. (the investor) records these transactions as follows:

Jan.	2	Investment in Brock Corp. Stock	350 0 0 0 00	
		Cash		350 0 0 0 00
		Purchased 40% of Brock Corp. stock.		
Dec.	31	Investment in Brock Corp. Stock	42 0 0 0 00	
		Income of Brock Corp.		42 0 0 0 00
		Recorded 40% share of Brock Corp. net		
		income of $105,000.		
Dec.	31	Cash	18 0 0 0 00	
		Investment in Brock Corp. Stock		18 0 0 0 00
		Recorded 40% share of Brock Corp. dividends.		

The combined effect of recording 40% of Brock Corporation's net income and dividends is to increase Hally's interest in the net assets of Brock by $24,000 ($42,000 − $18,000), as shown at the top of the following page.

The equity method causes the investment account to mirror the proportional changes in the book value of the investee. Thus, Brock Corporation's book value increased by $60,000 ($105,000 − $45,000), while the investment in Brock account increased by Hally's proportional share of that increase, or $24,000 ($60,000 × 40%). Both the book value of Brock Corporation and Hally's investment in Brock increased at the same rate from the original cost.

REAL WORLD

The 2002 edition of *Accounting Trends & Techniques* indicated that over 55% of the companies surveyed used the equity method to account for investments.

Assume that Hally Inc. increased its ownership in Brock Corporation to 45% at the beginning of the next year. If Brock Corporation reported net income of $80,000 and declared dividends of $50,000, by how much would Hally Inc. adjust the Investment in Brock Corp. Stock?

$13,500 [($80,000 × 45%) − ($50,000 × 45%)]

---

[18]An exception to reporting unrealized gains and losses as part of comprehensive income is made if the decrease in the market value for a stock is considered permanent. In this case, the cost of the individual stock is written down (decreased), and the amount of the write-down is included in net income.

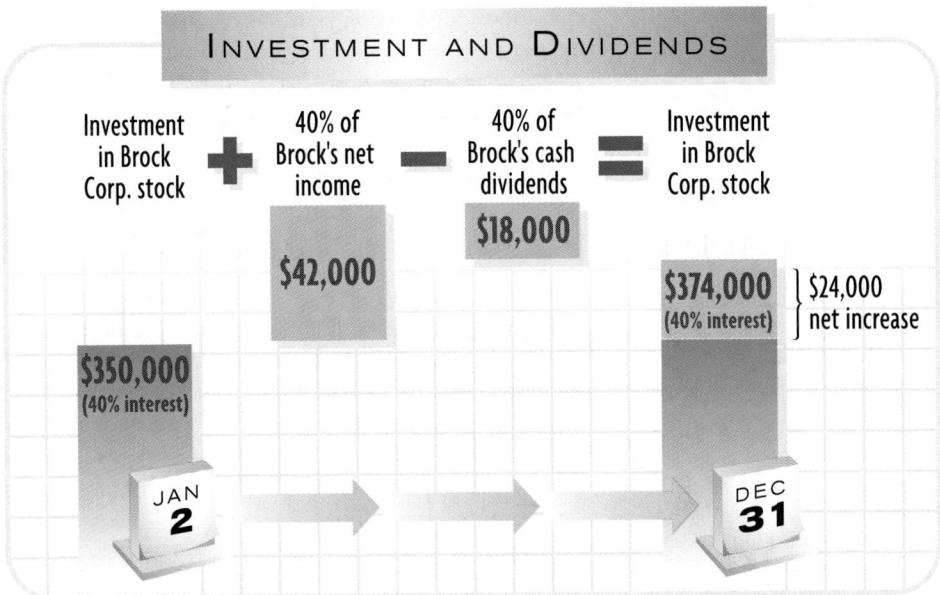

INVESTMENT AND DIVIDENDS

Sale of Investments in Stocks

Accounting for the sale of stock is the same for both short-term and long-term investments. When shares of stock are sold, the investment account is credited for the carrying amount (book value) of the shares sold. The cash or receivables account is debited for the proceeds (sales price less commission and other selling costs). Any difference between the proceeds and the carrying amount is recorded as a gain or loss on the sale and is included in determining net income.

To illustrate, assume that an investment in Drey Inc. stock has a carrying amount of $15,700 when it is sold on March 1. If the proceeds from the sale of the stock are $17,500, the entry to record the transaction is as follows:

Mar.	1	Cash	17 5 0 0 00	
		Investment in Drey Inc. Stock		15 7 0 0 00
		Gain on Sale of Investments		1 8 0 0 00

Business Combinations

objective 6

Describe alternative methods of combining businesses and how consolidated financial statements are prepared.

Each year, many businesses combine in order to produce more efficiently or to diversify product lines. Business combinations often involve complex accounting principles and terminology. The objective of this section is to introduce some of the unique terminology and concepts related to business combinations. The use and preparation of consolidated financial statements are also briefly described.

Mergers and Consolidations

One corporation may acquire all the assets and liabilities of a second corporation, which is then dissolved. This joining of two corporations is called a **merger**. The acquiring company may use cash, debt, or its own stock as the payment. Whatever the form of payment, the amount received by the dissolving corporation is distributed to its stockholders in final liquidation. For example, **Mattel Inc.** acquired **Mindscape Inc.** for $152 million in cash and stock. As a result of the merger, Mindscape no longer exists as a separate company.

A new corporation may be created, and the assets and liabilities of two or more existing corporations transferred to it. This type of combination is called a **consolidation**. The new corporation usually issues its own stock in exchange for the net assets acquired. The original corporations are then dissolved. For example, **Exxon-Mobil Corporation** became the new consolidated company that resulted from combining two individual corporations—Exxon and Mobil.

Parent and Subsidiary Corporations

I'm the top supplier of first-run syndicated programming in America. Under my roof you'll find "Wheel of Fortune" and "Jeopardy!" (the two highest-rated series in syndication), and "The Oprah Winfrey Show" (the No. 1 daytime talk show), as well as "Hollywood Squares," "Inside Edition," "Martha Stewart Living," "Bob Vila's Home Again," and "CBS Marketwatch Weekend." I also distribute "Everybody Loves Raymond," "CSI: Crime Scene Investigation," among other shows you might have heard of. My biggest recent home run is the "Dr. Phil" show. CBS bought me for $2.5 billion in 1999. Who am I? (Go to page 504 for answer.)

Business combinations may also occur when one corporation buys a controlling share of the outstanding voting stock of one or more other corporations. In this case, none of the corporations dissolve. The corporations continue as separate legal entities in a parent-subsidiary relationship. The corporation owning all or a majority of the voting stock of the other corporation is called the **parent company**. The corporation that is controlled is called the **subsidiary company**. Two or more corporations closely related through stock ownership are sometimes called **affiliated** companies. An example of an affiliated company is **ESPN, Inc.**, a subsidiary of **The Walt Disney Company**.

A corporation (the acquiring company) may acquire the controlling share of the voting common stock of another corporation (the target company) by paying cash, exchanging other assets, issuing debt, or using some combination of these methods. In addition, a parent-subsidiary relationship may be created by exchanging the voting common stock of the acquiring corporation (the parent) for the common stock of the acquired corporation (the subsidiary). Regardless if there is an outright purchase of assets or common stock or an exchange of common stock, the transaction is recorded like a normal purchase of assets, and the combination is accounted for by the **purchase method**.

Under the purchase method, the subsidiary's net assets are reported in the consolidated balance sheet at their fair market value at the time of the purchase. In some cases, a parent may pay more than the fair market value of a subsidiary's net assets because the subsidiary has prospects for high future earnings. The difference between the amount paid by the parent and the fair market value of the subsidiary's net assets is reported on the consolidated balance sheet as an intangible asset. This asset is identified as **Goodwill** or **Excess of cost of business acquired over related net assets**.

Consolidated Financial Statements

Although parent and subsidiary corporations may operate as a single economic unit, they continue to maintain separate accounting records and prepare their own periodic financial statements. At the end of the year, the financial statements of the parent and subsidiary are combined and reported as a single company. These combined financial statements are called **consolidated financial statements**. Such statements are usually identified by adding "and subsidiary(ies)" to the name of the parent corporation or by adding "consolidated" to the statement title.

To the stockholders of the parent company, consolidated financial statements are more meaningful than separate statements for each corporation. This is because the parent company, in substance, controls the subsidiaries, even though the parent and its subsidiaries are separate entities.

When a consolidated balance sheet is prepared, the ownership interest of the parent in the subsidiary's stock, which is the balance in the parent's investment in subsidiary account, must be eliminated. This is done by eliminating the parent's investment in subsidiary account against the balances of the subsidiary's stockholders' equity accounts.

If the parent owns less than 100% of the subsidiary stock, the subsidiary stock owned by outsiders is *not* eliminated but is normally reported immediately following the consolidated total liabilities. This amount is described as the **minority interest**.

When the data on the financial statements of the parent and its subsidiaries are combined to form the consolidated statements, intercompany transactions are given special attention. An example of such a transaction is the parent purchasing goods

INTEGRITY IN BUSINESS

CONFLICTS OF INTEREST

Enron Corporation, once the seventh largest company in the United States, collaped into bankruptcy in a matter of months. Most of Enron's travails were related to undisclosed losses from complex financial transactions with certain partnerships that were run by its own officers, including the CFO (chief financial officer). Enron management came under severe criticism for (1) providing minimum disclosure about these partnership investments to the investing public and (2) allowing senior officers to hold significant individual investments in these partnerships. Regarding the potential conflict of interest, Wayne Shaw, a professor of accounting, stated, "If it was the CFO, why was he put in a position where no one knew what he was doing? If the blame's being placed on one party, you have to wonder about the internal controls of the company. There's got to be checks and balances, and they weren't there." The lessons from the Enron debacle are that unconsolidated investments may require significant additional disclosures in the notes, and senior officers should avoid a conflict of interest caused by holding individual interests in the investee while being an officer of the investor.

from the subsidiary or the subsidiary loaning money to the parent. These transactions affect the individual accounts of the parent and subsidiary and thus the financial statements of both companies.[19] To illustrate, assume that P Inc. (the parent) sold merchandise to S Inc. (the subsidiary) for $90,000. The merchandise cost P Inc. $50,000. In turn, S Inc. sold the merchandise to a customer for $120,000.

The individual income statements for P Inc. and S Inc. are shown in Exhibit 6. The consolidated (combined) income statement is shown in Exhibit 7. The consolidated income statement presents the income statements for P Inc. and S Inc. as if they were one operating entity. Thus, the $90,000 sale (P Inc.) and the $90,000 cost of merchandise sold (S Inc.) are eliminated. This is because the consolidated entity cannot sell to itself or buy from itself.

•Exhibit 6   Income Statements for P Inc. and S Inc.

	P Inc.		S Inc.	
Sales		$950,000		$400,000
Cost of merchandise sold		625,000		240,000
Gross profit		$325,000		$160,000
Operating expenses:				
Selling expenses	$155,000		$55,000	
Administrative expenses	85,000	240,000	35,000	90,000
Net income		$ 85,000		$ 70,000

Many U.S. corporations own subsidiaries in foreign countries. Such corporations are often called *multinational corporations*. The financial statements of the foreign subsidiary are usually prepared in the foreign currency. Before the financial statements of foreign subsidiaries are consolidated with their domestic parent's financial statements, the amounts shown on the statements for the foreign companies must be converted to U.S. dollars.[20] For example, **General Motors Corporation** is a multinational company that consolidates its foreign subsidiaries, such as the European **Opel** division, into U.S. dollars.

---

[19]Examples of accounts often affected by intercompany transactions include *Accounts Receivable* and *Accounts Payable*, *Interest Receivable* and *Interest Income*, and *Interest Expense* and *Interest Payable*.
[20]Appendix E at the end of the text discusses and illustrates the accounting for foreign currency transactions.

communicate the plan. The expense is deducted from gross profit on the income statement.

A gain or loss resulting from the disposal of a business segment, net of related tax, should be added to or deducted from income from continuing operations on the income statement.

Gains and losses may result from events and transactions that are unusual and occur infrequently. Such extraordinary items, net of related income tax, should be added to or deducted from income from continuing operations on the income statement.

A change in an accounting principle results from the adoption of a generally accepted accounting principle different from the one used previously for reporting purposes. The effect of the change in principle on net income in the current period, as well as the cumulative effect on income of prior periods, should be disclosed in the financial statements, net of tax, below income from continuing operations.

3 Prepare an income statement reporting earnings per share data.

Earnings per share is reported on the income statements of public corporations. If there are unusual items below income from continuing operations on the income statement, the per share amount should be presented for each of these items as well as net income.

4 Describe the concept and the reporting of comprehensive income.

Comprehensive income is all changes in stockholders' equity during a period except those resulting from dividends and stockholders' investments. Companies must report traditional net income plus or minus other comprehensive income items to arrive at comprehensive income. Other comprehensive income items include transactions and events that are excluded from net income, such as unrealized gains and losses on certain investments in debt and equity securities. Accumulated other comprehensive income is separately reported in the stockholders' equity section of the balance sheet.

5 Describe the accounting for investments in stocks.

A business may purchase stocks as a means of earning a return (income) on excess cash that it does not need for its normal operations. Such investments are recorded in a marketable securities account. Their cost includes all amounts spent to acquire the securities. Any dividends received on an investment are recorded as a debit to Cash and a credit to Dividend Revenue. On the balance sheet, temporary investments are reported as available-for-sale securities at their fair market values. Any difference between the fair market values of the securities and their cost is an unrealized holding gain or loss (net of applicable taxes) that is reported as an other comprehensive income item.

Long-term investments in stocks are not intended as a source of cash in the normal operations of the business. They are reported in the balance sheet either as available-for-sale securities, and disclosed at fair value, or reported under the equity method.

The accounting for the sale of stock is the same for both short-term and long-term investments. The investment account is credited for the carrying amount (book value) of the shares sold, the cash or receivables account is debited for the proceeds, and any difference between the proceeds and the carrying amount is recorded as a gain or loss on the sale.

6 Describe alternative methods of combining businesses and how consolidated financial statements are prepared.

Businesses may combine in a merger or a consolidation. Business combinations may also occur when one corporation acquires a controlling share of the outstanding voting stock of another corporation. In this case, a parent-subsidiary relationship exists, and the companies are called affiliated companies.

Although the corporations that make up a parent-subsidiary affiliation may operate as a single economic unit, they usually continue to maintain separate accounting records and prepare their own periodic financial statements. The financial statements prepared by combining the parent and subsidiary statements are called consolidated financial statements.

When a parent corporation purchases less than 100% of the subsidiary's stock, the remaining stockholders' equity is identified as minority interest. The minority interest is reported on the consolidated balance sheet, usually following the total liabilities.

In preparing consolidated income statements for a parent and its subsidiary, all amounts from intercompany transactions, such as intercompany sales of merchandise and cost of merchandise sold, are eliminated.

7 Compute and interpret the price-earnings ratio.

The assessment of a firm's growth potential and future earnings prospects is indicated by the price-earnings ratio, or P/E ratio. It is computed by dividing the stock's market price per share at a specific date by the company's annual earnings per share.

Key Terms

accumulated other comprehensive income (490)
available-for-sale securities (491)
comprehensive income (490)
consolidated financial statements (496)
consolidation (496)
discontinued operations (487)
earnings per common share (EPS) (488)
equity method (493)

equity securities (491)
extraordinary items (487)
fixed asset impairment (484)
investments (493)
merger (495)
minority interest (496)
other comprehensive income items (490)
parent company (496)
permanent differences (483)
price-earnings ratio (498)

purchase method (496)
restructuring charge (486)
subsidiary company (496)
taxable income (481)
temporary differences (481)
temporary investments (491)
trading securities (491)
unrealized holding gain or loss (492)

Illustrative Problem

The following data were selected from the records of Botanica Greenhouses Inc. for the current fiscal year ended August 31:

Administrative expenses	$ 82,200
Cost of merchandise sold	750,000
Fixed asset impairment	115,000
Gain on condemnation of land	25,000
Income tax:	
Applicable to continuing operations	27,200
Applicable to gain on condemnation of land	10,000
Applicable to loss on discontinued operations (reduction)	24,000
Interest expense	15,200
Loss on discontinued operations	60,200
Restructuring charge	40,000
Sales	1,252,500
Selling expenses	182,100

Instructions

Prepare a multiple-step income statement, concluding with a section for earnings per share in the form illustrated in this chapter. There were 10,000 shares of common stock (no preferred) outstanding throughout the year. Assume that the gain on condemnation of land is an extraordinary item.

Solution

Botanica Greenhouses Inc.
Income Statement
For the Year Ended August 31, 2006

Sales..		$1,252,500
Cost of merchandise sold.....................		750,000
Gross profit.................................		$ 502,500
Operating expenses:		
Selling expenses........................	$182,100	
Administrative expenses.................	82,200	
Fixed asset impairment..................	115,000	
Restructuring charge	40,000	
Total operating expenses		419,300
Income from operations......................		$ 83,200
Other expense:		
Interest expense		15,200
Income from continuing operations before		
income tax.............................		$ 68,000
Income tax expense..........................		27,200
Income from continuing operations		$ 40,800
Loss on discontinued operations	$ 60,200	
Less applicable income tax	24,000	36,200
Income before extraordinary item............		$ 4,600
Extraordinary item:		
Gain on condemnation of land............	$ 25,000	
Less applicable income tax	10,000	15,000
Net income		$ 19,600
Earnings per share:		
Income from continuing operations		$4.08
Loss on discontinued operations		3.62
Income before extraordinary item		$0.46
Extraordinary item		1.50
Net income		$1.96

Self-Examination Questions (Answers at End of Chapter)

1. During its first year of operations, a corporation elected to use the straight-line method of depreciation for financial reporting purposes and MACRS in determining taxable income. If the income tax rate is 40% and the amount of depreciation expense is $60,000 under the straight-line method and $100,000 under MACRS, what is the amount of income tax deferred to future years?

   A. $16,000 C. $40,000
   B. $24,000 D. $60,000

2. A material gain resulting from condemning land for public use would be reported on the income statement as a(n):

   A. extraordinary item.
   B. other income item.
   C. restructuring charge.
   D. fixed asset impairment.

3. Gwinnett Corporation's temporary investments cost $100,000 and have a market value of $120,000 at

the end of the accounting period. Assuming a tax rate of 40%, the difference between the cost and market value would be reported as a:

A. $12,000 realized gain.

B. $12,000 unrealized gain.

C. $20,000 realized gain.

D. $20,000 unrealized gain.

4. Cisneros Corporation owns 75% of Harrell Inc. During the current year, Harrell Inc. reported net income of $150,000 and declared dividends of $40,000. How much would Cisneros Corporation increase Investment in Harrell Inc. Stock for the current year?

A. $0   C. $82,500

B. $30,000   D. $112,500

5. Harkin Company has a market price of $60 per share on December 31. The total stockholders' equity is $2,400,000, and the net income is $800,000. There are 200,000 shares outstanding. Preferred dividends are $50,000. The price-earnings ratio would be:

A. 3.

B. 15.

C. 16.

D. 20.

Class Discussion Questions

1. How would the amount of deferred income tax payable be reported in the balance sheet if (a) it is payable within one year and (b) it is payable beyond one year?

2. Maxwell Company owns an equipped plant that has a book value of $150 million. Due to a permanent decline in consumer demand for the products produced by this plant, the market value of the plant and equipment is appraised at $20 million. Describe the accounting treatment for this impairment.

3. How should the severance costs of terminated employees be accounted for?

4. During the current year, 40 acres of land that cost $200,000 were condemned for construction of an interstate highway. Assuming that an award of $350,000 in cash was received and that the applicable income tax on this transaction is 40%, how would this information be presented in the income statement?

5. Corporation X realized a material gain when its facilities at a designated floodway were acquired by the urban renewal agency. How should the gain be reported in the income statement?

6. An annual report of **Ford Motor Company** disclosed the sale of its ownership interest in **Visteon Corporation**, a major automotive components manufacturer. The estimated after-tax loss on disposal of these operations was $2.3 billion. Indicate how the loss from discontinued operations should be reported by Ford on its income statement.

7. If significant changes are made in the accounting principles applied from one period to the next, why should the effect of these changes be disclosed in the financial statements?

8. A corporation reports earnings per share of $1.38 for the most recent year and $1.10 for the preceding year. The $1.38 includes a $0.45-per-share gain from insurance proceeds related to a fully depreciated asset that was destroyed by fire.

   a. Should the composition of the $1.38 be disclosed in the financial reports?

   b. On the basis of the limited information presented, would you conclude that operations had improved or declined?

9. a. List some examples of other comprehensive income items.

   b. Does the reporting of other comprehensive income affect the determination of net income and retained earnings?

10. Why might a business invest in another company's stock?

11. How are temporary investments in marketable securities reported on the balance sheet?

12. How are unrealized gains and losses on temporary investments in marketable securities reported on the statement of comprehensive income?

13. a. What method of accounting is used for long-term investments in stock in which there is significant influence over the investee?

  b. Under what caption are long-term investments in stock reported on the balance sheet?

14. Plaster Inc. received a $0.15-per-share cash dividend on 50,000 shares of Gestalt Corporation common stock, which Plaster Inc. carries as a long-term investment. Assuming that Plaster Inc. uses the equity method of accounting for its investment in Gestalt Corporation, what account would be credited for the receipt of the $7,500 dividend?

15. Parent Corporation owns 90% of the outstanding common stock of Subsidiary Corporation, which has no preferred stock. (a) What is the term applied to the remaining 10% interest? (b) On the consolidated balance sheet, where is the amount of Subsidiary's book equity allocable to outsiders reported?

16. An annual report of **The Campbell Soup Company** reported on its income statement $2.4 million as "equity in earnings of affiliates." Journalize the entry that Campbell would have made to record this equity in earnings of affiliates.

resources for your success online at **http://warren.swlearning.com**

Remember! If you need additional help, visit South-Western's Web site. See page 28 for a description of the online and printed materials that are available. http://warren.swlearning.com

Warren Reeve Fess

Answer: King World Productions

Exercises

EXERCISE 12-1
Income tax entries
Objective 1

Journalize the entries to record the following selected transactions of Grove Monuments, Inc.:

Apr. 15. Paid the first installment of the estimated income tax for the current fiscal year ending December 31, $70,000. No entry had been made to record the liability.

June 15. Paid the second installment of $70,000.

Sept. 15. Paid the third installment of $70,000.

Dec. 31. Recorded the estimated income tax liability for the year just ended and the deferred income tax liability, based on the transactions above and the following data:

Income tax rate	40%
Income before income tax	$900,000
Taxable income according to tax return	$800,000

Jan. 15. Paid the fourth installment of $110,000.

EXERCISE 12-2
Deferred income taxes
Objective 1

Integrated Systems, Inc. recognized service revenue of $300,000 on its financial statements in 2005. Assume, however, that the Tax Code requires this amount to be recognized for tax purposes in 2006. The taxable income for 2005 and 2006 is $2,000,000 and $2,500,000, respectively. Assume a tax rate of 40%.

Prepare the journal entries to record the tax expense, deferred taxes, and taxes payable for 2005 and 2006, respectively.

EXERCISE 12-3
Fixed asset impairment
Objective 2

✓ a. $84,000,000

LightWave Communications, Inc. spent $100 million expanding its fiber optic communication network between Chicago and Los Angeles during 2004. The fiber optic network was assumed to have a 10-year life, with a $20 million salvage value, when it was put into service on January 1, 2005. The network is depreciated using the straight-line method. At the end of 2006, the expected traffic volume on the fiber optic network was only 60% of what was originally expected. The reduced traffic volume caused the fair market value of the asset to be estimated at $45 million on December 31, 2006. The loss is not expected to be recoverable.

a. Determine the book value of the network on December 31, 2006, prior to the impairment adjustment.
b. Provide the journal entry to record the fixed asset impairment on December 31, 2006.
c. Provide the balance sheet disclosure for fixed assets on December 31, 2006.

EXERCISE 12-4
Fixed asset impairment
Objective 2

Sunset Resorts, Inc. owns and manages resort properties. On January 15, 2006, one of its properties was found to be adjacent to a toxic chemical disposal site. As a result of the negative publicity, this property's bookings dropped 40% during 2006. On December 31, 2006, the accounts of the company showed the following details regarding the impaired property:

Land	$ 25,000,000
Buildings and improvements (net)	80,000,000
Equipment (net)	15,000,000
Total	$120,000,000

Management decides that closing the resort is the only option. As a result, it is estimated that the buildings and improvements will be written off completely. The land can be sold for other uses for $17 million, while the equipment can be disposed of for $4 million, net of disposal costs.

a. Provide the journal entry to record the asset impairment on December 31, 2006.
b. Provide the note disclosure for the impairment.

EXERCISE 12-5
Restructuring charge
Objective 2

✓ a. Restructuring charge, $3,600,000

Jen-King Company's board of directors approved and communicated an employee severance plan in response to a decline in demand for the company's products. The plan called for the elimination of 150 headquarters positions by providing a severance equal to 5% of the annual salary multiplied by the number of years of service. The average annual salary of the eliminated positions is $60,000. The average tenure of terminated employees is 8 years. The plan was communicated to employees on November 1, 2006. Actual termination notices will be distributed over the period between December 1, 2006, and April 1, 2007. On December 15, 2006, 40 employees received a lay-off notice and were terminated with severance.

a. Provide the appropriate journal entry for the restructuring charge.
b. Provide the journal entry to record the severance payment on December 15, 2006, assuming that the actual tenure and salary of terminated employees were consistent with the overall average.
c. Provide the balance sheet and note disclosures on December 31, 2006.

EXERCISE 12-6
Restructuring charge
Objective 2

✓ a. Restructuring charge, $3,039,200

Mango Juice Company has been suffering a downturn in its juice business due to adverse publicity regarding the caffeine content of its drink products. As a result, the company has been required to restructure operations. The board of directors approved and communicated a plan on July 1, 2006, calling for the following actions:

1. Close a juice plant on October 15, 2006. Closing, equipment relocation, and employee relocation costs are expected to be $500,000 during October.

2. Eliminate 280 plant positions. A severance will be paid to the terminated employees equal to 400% of their estimated monthly earnings payable in four quarterly installments on October 15, 2006; January 15, 2007; April 15, 2007; and July 15, 2007.

3. Terminate a juice supply contract, activating a $120,000 cancellation penalty, payable upon notice of termination. The notice will be formally delivered to the supplier on August 15, 2006.

The 280 employees earn an average of $12 per hour. The average employee works 180 hours per month.

a. Determine the total restructuring charge.
b. Provide the journal entry for the restructuring charge on July 1, 2006. (*Note:* Use Restructuring Obligation as the liability account, since the charges involve more than just employee terminations.)
c. Provide the journal entry for the October 15, 2006 employee severance payment.
d. Provide the balance sheet disclosure for December 31, 2006.
e. Provide a note disclosure for December 31, 2006.

EXERCISE 12-7
Restructuring charges and asset impairments
Objective 2

✓ *a. Severance restructuring charge, $650,000*

Conway Transportation Company has suffered losses due to increased competition in its service market from low-cost independent truckers. As a result, on December 31, 2006, the board of directors of the company approved and communicated a restructuring plan that calls for selling 50 tractor-trailers out of a fleet of 400. In addition, the plan calls for the elimination of 50 driver positions and 15 staff support positions. The market price for used tractor-trailers is depressed due to general overcapacity in the transportation industry. As a result, the market value of tractor-trailers is estimated to be only 40% of the book value of these assets. It is not believed that the impairment in fixed assets is recoverable. The cost and accumulated depreciation of the total tractor-trailer fleet on December 31 are $34 million and $9 million, respectively. The restructuring plan will provide a severance to the drivers and staff totaling $10,000 per employee, payable on March 14, 2007, which is the expected employee termination date.

a. Provide the journal entries on December 31, 2006, for the fixed asset impairment and the employee severance costs.
b. Provide the balance sheet and note disclosure on December 31, 2006.
c. Provide the journal entry for March 14, 2007.

EXERCISE 12-8
Restructuring charges and fixed asset impairment disclosure
Objective 2

REAL WORLD

The notes to the financial statements for **Maytag Corporation** provided a table of special charges, as follows:

Schedule of Special Charges
Maytag Corporation
For the Year Ended December 31, 2002 (in thousands)

Description of Reserve	Balance, Dec. 31, 2001	Charged to Earnings	Cash Utilization	Noncash Utilization	Balance, Dec. 31, 2002
Severance and related expense	$6,903	$ 4,128	$(4,629)	$ (2,292)	$4,110
Asset write-downs	0	28,627	0	(28,627)	0
Total	$6,903	$32,755	$(4,629)	$(30,919)	$4,110

The special charges include both severance-related expenses and asset impairments. The columns of the table indicate the balances and change in balances of the balance sheet accounts affected by the special charges. The notes to the financial statements also indicated the following:

The asset impairment charge was determined using estimated future cash flows through the closure date and directly reduced Property, plant and equipment on the Consolidated Balance Sheets. . . . The severance and related costs are reflected in Accrued liabilities on the Consolidated Balance Sheets.

a. Provide the journal entry to record "Special Charges" for 2002.
b. Provide the journal entry to record the cash utilization of the special charges.
c. Provide the balance sheet disclosure on December 31, 2002.

EXERCISE 12-9
Extraordinary item
Objective 2

A company received life insurance proceeds on the death of its president before the end of its fiscal year. It intends to report the amount in its income statement as an extraordinary item.

▪▪▪▪▪➤ Would this reporting be in conformity with generally accepted accounting principles? Discuss.

EXERCISE 12-10
Extraordinary item
Objective 2

REAL WORLD

For the year ended December 31, 2002, **Delta Air Lines, Inc.** provided the following note to its financial statements:

On September 22, 2001, the Air Transportation Safety and System Stabilization Act (Stabilization Act) became effective. The Stabilization Act is intended to preserve the viability of the U.S. air transportation system following the terrorist attacks on September 11, 2001 by, among other things, (1) providing for payments from the U.S. Government totaling $5 billion to compensate U.S. air carriers for losses incurred from September 11, 2001, through December 31, 2001, as a result of the September 11 terrorist attacks and (2) permitting the Secretary of Transportation to sell insurance to U.S. air carriers.

Our allocated portion of compensation under the Stabilization Act was $668 million. Due to uncertainties regarding the U.S. government's calculation of compensation, we recognized $634 million of this amount in our 2001 Consolidated Statement of Operations. We recognized the remaining $34 million of compensation in our 2002 Consolidated Statement of Operations. We received $112 million and $556 million in cash for the years ended December 31, 2002 and 2001, respectively, under the Stabilization Act.

▪▪▪▪▪➤ Do you believe that the income related to the Stabilization Act should be reported as an extraordinary item on the income statement of Delta Air Lines?

EXERCISE 12-11
Identifying extraordinary items
Objective 2

Assume that the amount of each of the following items is material to the financial statements. Classify each item as either normally recurring (NR) or extraordinary (E).

a. Interest revenue on notes receivable.
b. Uninsured flood loss. (Flood insurance is unavailable because of periodic flooding in the area.)
c. Loss on sale of fixed assets.
d. Restructuring charge related to employee termination benefits.
e. Gain on sale of land condemned for public use.
f. Uncollectible accounts expense.
g. Uninsured loss on building due to hurricane damage. The firm was organized in 1920 and had not previously incurred hurricane damage.
h. Loss on disposal of equipment considered to be obsolete because of development of new technology.

EXERCISE 12-12
Income statement
Objectives 2, 3

Wave Runner, Inc. produces and distributes equipment for sailboats. On the basis of the following data for the current fiscal year ended June 30, 2006, prepare a multiple-step income statement for Wave Runner, including an analysis of earnings per share in the form illustrated in this chapter. There were 10,000 shares of $150 par common stock outstanding throughout the year.

✓ Net income, $24,000

Administrative expenses	$ 92,400
Cost of merchandise sold	431,900
Cumulative effect on prior years of changing to a different depreciation method (decrease in income)	60,000
Gain on condemnation of land (extraordinary item)	43,000
Income tax reduction applicable to change in depreciation method	24,000
Income tax applicable to gain on condemnation of land	17,200
Income tax reduction applicable to loss from discontinued operations	36,000
Income tax applicable to ordinary income	58,800
Loss on discontinued operations	90,000
Loss from fixed asset impairment	100,000
Restructuring charge	80,000
Sales	976,400
Selling expenses	125,100

EXERCISE 12-13
Income statement

Objectives 2, 3

WHAT'S WRONG WITH THIS?

✓ *Correct EPS for net income, $8.25*

Audio Affection, Inc. sells automotive and home stereo equipment. It has 50,000 shares of $100 par common stock outstanding and 10,000 shares of $2, $100 par cumulative preferred stock outstanding as of December 31, 2006. List the errors you find in the following income statement for the year ended December 31, 2006.

Audio Affection, Inc.
Income Statement
For the Year Ended December 31, 2006

Net sales		$9,450,000
Cost of merchandise sold		7,100,000
Gross profit		$2,350,000
Operating expenses:		
Selling expenses	$820,000	
Administrative expenses	320,000	1,140,000
Income from continuing operations before income tax		$1,210,000
Income tax expense		420,000
Income from continuing operations		$ 790,000
Cumulative effect on prior years' income (decrease) of changing to a different depreciation method (net of applicable income tax of $86,000)		(204,000)
Fixed asset impairment		(30,000)
Income before condemnation of land, restructuring charge, and discontinued operations		$ 556,000
Extraordinary items:		
Gain on condemnation of land, net of applicable income tax of $80,000		120,000
Restructuring charge, net of applicable income tax of $25,500		(59,500)
Loss on discontinued operations (net of applicable income tax of $76,000)		(184,000)
Net income		$ 432,500
Earnings per common share:		
Income from continuing operations		$ 15.80
Cumulative effect on prior years' income (decrease) of changing to a different depreciation method		(4.08)
Fixed asset impairment		(0.60)
Income before extraordinary item and discontinued operations		$ 11.12
Extraordinary items:		
Gain on condemnation of land		2.40
Restructuring charge		(1.19)
Loss on discontinued operations		(3.68)
Net income		$ 8.65

EXERCISE 12-14
Earnings per share with preferred stock

Objective 3

Glow-Rite Lighting Company had earnings for 2006 of $740,000. The company had 125,000 shares of common stock outstanding during the year. In addition, the company issued 50,000 shares of $100 par value preferred stock on January 5, 2006. The preferred stock has a dividend of $6 per share. There were no transactions in either common or preferred stock during 2006.

Determine the basic earnings per share for Glow-Rite.

EXERCISE 12-15
Comprehensive income

Objective 4

REAL WORLD   SPREADSHEET

✓a. Comprehensive loss,
$240

A recent statement of comprehensive income for the **Procter & Gamble Company** was disclosed as follows (all amounts in millions):

Procter & Gamble Company
Statement of Comprehensive Income
For the Fiscal Year Ending June 30, 2002

Net earnings	$4,352
Other comprehensive income:	
Foreign currency translation	263
Net investment hedges,	
net of $238 tax benefit	(397)
Other, net of tax benefit	(106)
Total comprehensive income	$4,112

The balance sheet dated June 30, 2001, showed a retained earnings balance of $10,451 and an accumulated other comprehensive loss of $2,120. The company paid $2,823 in dividends during the fiscal year.

a. What is the total other comprehensive income or loss for Procter & Gamble for the fiscal year ended June 30, 2002?
b. What percentage decline did other comprehensive items have on net income in determining total comprehensive income?
c. What was the June 30, 2002 balance of (1) retained earnings and (2) accumulated other comprehensive income?

EXERCISE 12-16
Comprehensive income and temporary investments

Objectives 4, 5

✓c. $37,000

The statement of comprehensive income for the years ended December 31, 2006 and 2007, plus selected items from comparative balance sheets of McClain Wholesalers, Inc. are as follows:

McClain Wholesalers, Inc.
Statement of Comprehensive Income
For the Years Ended December 31, 2006 and 2007

	2006	2007
Net income	a.	$36,000
Other comprehensive income (loss), net of tax	b.	2,000
Total comprehensive income	c.	e.

McClain Wholesalers, Inc.
Selected Balance Sheet Items
December 31, 2005, 2006, and 2007

	Dec. 31, 2005	Dec. 31, 2006	Dec. 31, 2007
Temporary investments in marketable securities at fair market value, net of taxes on unrealized gains or losses	$ 26,000	d.	f.
Retained earnings	140,000	$180,000	g.
Accumulated other comprehensive income or (loss)	(5,000)	(8,000)	h.

There were no dividends or purchases or sales of temporary investments. Other comprehensive items included only after-tax unrealized gains and losses on investments.

Determine the missing lettered items.

EXERCISE 12-17
Comprehensive income and temporary investments

Objectives 4, 5

During 2006, Cosby Corporation held a portfolio of available-for-sale securities having a cost of $260,000. There were no purchases or sales of investments during the year. The market values after adjusting for the impact of taxes, at the beginning and end of the year, were $200,000 and $240,000, respectively. The net income for 2006 was $145,000, and no dividends were paid during the year. The stockholders' equity section of the balance sheet was as follows on December 31, 2005:

✓ a. Total comprehensive income, $185,000

Cosby Corporation
Stockholders' Equity
December 31, 2005

Common stock	$ 35,000
Paid-in capital in excess of par value	350,000
Retained earnings	435,000
Accumulated other comprehensive loss	(60,000)
Total	$760,000

a. Prepare a statement of comprehensive income for 2006.
b. Prepare the stockholders' equity section of the balance sheet for December 31, 2006.

EXERCISE 12-18
Temporary investments and other comprehensive income
Objectives 4, 5

✓ a. 2007 unrealized gain, $60,000

The temporary investments of Secure Connections, Inc. include only 10,000 shares of Lambert Acres Inc. common stock purchased on January 10, 2006, for $20 per share. As of the December 31, 2006 balance sheet date, assume that the share price declined to $17 per share. As of the December 31, 2007 balance sheet date, assume that the share price rose to $27 per share. The investment was held through December 31, 2007. Assume a tax rate of 40%.

a. Determine the net after-tax unrealized gain or loss from holding the Lambert Acres common stock for 2006 and 2007.
b. What is the balance of Other Accumulated Comprehensive Income or Loss for December 31, 2006, and December 31, 2007?
c. Where is Other Accumulated Comprehensive Income or Deficit disclosed on the financial statements?

EXERCISE 12-19
Temporary investments in marketable securities
Objective 5

During 2006, its first year of operations, Lyon Research Corporation purchased the following securities as a temporary investment:

Security	Shares Purchased	Cost	Cash Dividends Received
M-Labs Inc.	1,000	$29,000	$ 900
Spectrum Corp.	2,500	45,000	1,600

a. Record the purchase of the temporary investments for cash.
b. Record the receipt of the dividends.

EXERCISE 12-20
Financial statement reporting of temporary investments
Objectives 4, 5

✓ b. Comprehensive income, $73,400

Using the data for Lyon Research Corporation in Exercise 12-19, assume that as of December 31, 2006, the M-Labs Inc. stock had a market value of $28 per share and the Spectrum Corp. stock had a market value of $14 per share. For the year ending December 31, 2006, Lyon Research Corporation had net income of $80,000. Its tax rate is 40%.

a. Prepare the balance sheet presentation for the temporary investments.
b. Prepare a statement of comprehensive income presentation for the temporary investments.

EXERCISE 12-21
Entries for investment in stock, receipt of dividends, and sale of shares
Objective 5

On February 27, Ball Corporation acquired 3,000 shares of the 50,000 outstanding shares of Beach Co. common stock at 40.75 plus commission charges of $150. On July 8, a cash dividend of $1.50 per share and a 2% stock dividend were received. On December 7, 1,000 shares were sold at 49, less commission charges of $60. Record the entries to record (a) the purchase of the stock, (b) the receipt of dividends, and (c) the sale of the 1,000 shares.

EXERCISE 12-22
Entries using equity method for stock investment
Objective 5

At a total cost of $1,820,000, Joshua Corporation acquired 70,000 shares of Caleb Corp. common stock as a long-term investment. Joshua Corporation uses the equity method of accounting for this investment. Caleb Corp. has 280,000 shares of common stock outstanding, including the shares acquired by Joshua Corporation. Journalize the entries by Joshua Corporation to record the following information:

a. Caleb Corp. reports net income of $2,500,000 for the current period.
b. A cash dividend of $3.40 per common share is paid by Caleb Corp. during the current period.

EXERCISE 12-23
Equity method for stock investment—Toys "R" Us
Objective 5

REAL WORLD

Toys "R" Us Inc. is a major retailer of toys in the United States. A recent balance sheet disclosed a long-term investment in **Toys-Japan**, a public company trading on the Tokyo over-the-counter market. The balance sheet disclosure for two recent comparative years was as follows:

	Feb. 2, 2002	Feb. 3, 2001
Investment in Toys-Japan (in millions)	$123	$108

In addition, the Toys "R" Us income statement disclosed equity earnings in the Toys-Japan investment as follows (in millions):

	Feb. 2, 2002	Feb. 3, 2001
Equity in net earnings of Toys-Japan	$29	$31

The notes to the financial statements provided the following additional information about this investment:

The company accounts for its investment in the common stock of Toys-Japan under the "equity method" of accounting since the initial public offering on April 24, 2000. The quoted market value of the company's investment in Toys-Japan was $283 at February 2, 2002.

a. ▭➤ Explain the change in the investment in Toys-Japan account for fiscal year ended February 2, 2002.
b. ▭➤ Why is the Investment in Toys-Japan not recognized at market value?

EXERCISE 12-24
Consolidated financial statements
Objectives 6
✓ b. $219,000

For the current year ended September 30, the results of operations of Tennessee Corporation, and its wholly owned subsidiary, Volunteer Enterprises, are as follows:

	Tennessee Corporation		Volunteer Enterprises	
Sales		$845,000		$166,000
Cost of merchandise sold	$390,000		$68,000	
Selling expenses	125,000		34,000	
Administrative expenses	87,000		16,000	
Interest expenses (revenue)	(10,000)	592,000	10,000	128,000
Net income		$253,000		$ 38,000

During the year, Tennessee sold merchandise to Volunteer for $45,000. The merchandise was sold by Volunteer to nonaffiliated companies for $60,000. Tennessee's interest revenue was realized from a long-term loan to Volunteer.

a. Determine the amounts to be eliminated from the following items in preparing a consolidated income statement for the current year: (1) sales and (2) cost of merchandise sold.
b. Determine the consolidated net income.

EXERCISE 12-25
Price-earnings ratio calculation
Objectives 3, 7

The following comparative net income and earnings per share data are provided for **Krispy Kreme Doughnuts, Inc.,** for three recent fiscal years:

REAL WORLD

✓ a. 2001: 55.83

Year Ended	Jan. 28, 2001	Feb. 3, 2002	Feb. 2, 2003
Net income	$14,725	$26,378	$33,478
Basic earnings per share	0.30	0.49	0.61
Diluted earnings per share	0.27	0.45	0.56

The stock market prices at the end of each of the three fiscal years were as follows:

Feb. 2, 2003	$30.41
Feb. 3, 2002	37.40
Jan. 28, 2001	16.75

a. Determine the price-earnings ratio for Krispy Kreme Doughnuts, Inc. for each of the three fiscal years, using basic earnings per share and the ending stock market price.
b. ⬛▶ What conclusions can you reach by considering the price-earnings ratio?
c. ⬛▶ Why is the diluted earnings per share less than the basic earnings per share?

EXERCISE 12-26
Price-earnings ratio calculations
Objective 7

REAL WORLD

✓ a. 2001: 16.47

ExxonMobil Corp. is one of the largest companies in the world. The company explores, develops, refines, and markets petroleum products. The basic earnings per share for three comparative years were as follows:

	Years Ended Dec. 31,		
	2002	**2001**	**2000**
Basic earnings per share	$1.69	$2.23	$2.55

The market prices at the end of each year were $42, $39, and $35 for December 31, 2000, 2001, and 2002, respectively.

a. Determine the price-earnings ratio for 2000, 2001, and 2002, using end-of-year prices.
b. ⬛▶ Interpret your results over the three years.

Problems Series A

PROBLEM 12-1A
Income tax allocation
Objective 1

SPREADSHEET

✓ 1. Year-end balance, 3rd year, $16,000

Differences between the accounting methods applied to accounts and financial reports and those used in determining taxable income yielded the following amounts for the first four years of a corporation's operations:

	First Year	Second Year	Third Year	Fourth Year
Income before income taxes	$200,000	$240,000	$300,000	$400,000
Taxable income	150,000	230,000	320,000	425,000

The income tax rate for each of the four years was 40% of taxable income, and each year's taxes were promptly paid.

Instructions

1. Determine for each year the amounts described by the following captions, presenting the information in the form indicated:

	Income Tax Deducted on Income Statement	Income Tax Payments for the Year	Deferred Income Tax Payable	
Year			Year's Addition (Deduction)	Year-End Balance

2. Total the first three amount columns.

PROBLEM 12-2A

Income tax; income statement

Objectives 2, 3, 4

SPREADSHEET

✓ *Net income, $180,100*

MotoSport Inc. produces and sells off-road motorcycles and jeeps. The following data were selected from the records of MotoSport Inc. for the current fiscal year ended October 31, 2006:

Advertising expense	$ 64,000
Cost of merchandise sold	612,400
Depreciation expense—office equipment	7,000
Depreciation expense—store equipment	23,000
Gain on condemnation of land	36,400
Income tax:	
Applicable to continuing operations	92,500
Applicable to loss from discontinued operations (reduction)	12,000
Applicable to gain on condemnation of land	13,400
Interest revenue	12,000
Loss from discontinued operations	31,000
Loss from fixed asset impairment	110,000
Miscellaneous administrative expense	12,000
Miscellaneous selling expense	5,500
Office salaries expense	75,000
Rent expense	24,000
Restructuring charge	14,000
Sales	1,350,000
Sales salaries expense	140,000
Store supplies expense	6,500
Unrealized loss on temporary investments	7,000

Instructions

Prepare a multiple-step income statement, concluding with a section for earnings per share (rounded to the nearest cent) in the form illustrated in this chapter. There were 25,000 shares of common stock (no preferred) outstanding throughout the year. Assume that the gain on the condemnation of land is an extraordinary item.

PROBLEM 12-3A

Income statement; retained earnings statement; balance sheet

Objectives 1, 2, 3, 4

SPREADSHEET

✓ *Net income, $340,000*

The following data were taken from the records of Surf's Up Corporation for the year ended July 31, 2006.

Retained earnings and balance sheet data:

Accounts payable	$ 99,500
Accounts receivable	276,050
Accumulated depreciation	3,050,000
Accumulated other comprehensive income	15,000
Allowance for doubtful accounts	11,500
Cash	115,500
Common stock, $10 par (500,000 shares authorized; 251,000 shares issued)	2,510,000
Deferred income taxes payable (current portion, $4,700)	65,700
Dividends:	
Cash dividends for common stock	80,000
Cash dividends for preferred stock	100,000
Stock dividends for common stock	40,000
Dividends payable	25,000
Employee termination benefit obligation (current)	90,000
Equipment	11,819,050
Income tax payable	55,900
Interest receivable	2,500
Merchandise inventory (July 31, 2006), at lower of cost (FIFO) or market	551,500
Paid-in capital from sale of treasury stock	5,000
Paid-in capital in excess of par—common stock	996,300
Paid-in capital in excess of par—preferred stock	240,000
Patents	85,000
Preferred 6 2/3% stock, $100 par (30,000 shares authorized; 15,000 shares issued)	1,500,000
Prepaid expenses	15,900
Retained earnings, August 1, 2005	4,231,600
Temporary investments in marketable equity securities (at cost)	95,000
Treasury stock (1,000 shares of common stock at cost of $40 per share)	40,000
Unrealized gain on marketable equity securities	15,000

(continued)

Income statement data:

Administrative expenses	$ 140,000
Cost of merchandise sold	984,000
Gain on condemnation of land	30,000
Income tax:	
Applicable to continuing operations	170,000
Applicable to loss from discontinued operations	24,000
Applicable to gain on condemnation of land	10,000
Interest expense	7,500
Interest revenue	1,500
Loss from disposal of discontinued operations	104,000
Loss from fixed asset impairment	60,000
Restructuring charge	300,000
Sales	2,600,000
Selling expenses	540,000

Instructions

1. Prepare a multiple-step income statement for the year ended July 31, 2006, concluding with earnings per share. In computing earnings per share, assume that the average number of common shares outstanding was 250,000 and preferred dividends were $100,000. Assume that the gain on the condemnation of land is an extraordinary item.
2. Prepare a retained earnings statement for the year ended July 31, 2006.
3. Prepare a balance sheet in report form as of July 31, 2006.

PROBLEM 12-4A
Entries for investments in stock

Objective 5

P.A.S.S.

Theater Arts Company produces and sells theater costumes. The following transactions relate to certain securities acquired by Theater Arts Company, which has a fiscal year ending on December 31:

2004
Feb. 10. Purchased 4,000 shares of the 150,000 outstanding common shares of Haslam Corporation at 48 plus commission and other costs of $168.
June 15. Received the regular cash dividend of $0.70 a share on Haslam Corporation stock.
Dec. 15. Received the regular cash dividend of $0.70 a share plus an extra dividend of $0.05 a share on Haslam Corporation stock.

    (Assume that all intervening transactions have been recorded properly and that the number of shares of stock owned have not changed from December 31, 2004, to December 31, 2006.)

2007
Jan. 3. Purchased controlling interest in Jacob Inc. for $1,250,000 by purchasing 40,000 shares directly from the estate of the founder of Jacob. There are 100,000 shares of Jacob Inc. stock outstanding.
Apr. 1. Received the regular cash dividend of $0.70 a share and a 2% stock dividend on the Haslam Corporation stock.
July 20. Sold 1,000 shares of Haslam Corporation stock at 41. The broker deducted commission and other costs of $50, remitting the balance.
Dec. 15. Received a cash dividend at the new rate of $0.80 a share on the Haslam Corporation stock.
     31. Received $40,000 of cash dividends on Jacob Inc. stock. Jacob Inc. reported net income of $295,000 in 2007. Theater Arts uses the equity method of accounting for its investment in Jacob Inc.

Instructions
Journalize the entries for the preceding transactions.

Problems Series B

PROBLEM 12-1B
Income tax allocation

Objective 1

SPREADSHEET

✓ *1. Year-end balance, 3rd year, $52,000*

Differences between the accounting methods applied to accounts and financial reports and those used in determining taxable income yielded the following amounts for the first four years of a corporation's operations:

	First Year	Second Year	Third Year	Fourth Year
Income before income taxes	$400,000	$480,000	$600,000	$520,000
Taxable income	300,000	420,000	630,000	600,000

The income tax rate for each of the four years was 40% of taxable income, and each year's taxes were promptly paid.

Instructions

1. Determine for each year the amounts described by the following captions, presenting the information in the form indicated:

Year	Income Tax Deducted on Income Statement	Income Tax Payments for the Year	Deferred Income Tax Payable	
			Year's Addition (Deduction)	Year-End Balance

2. Total the first three amount columns.

PROBLEM 12-2B
Income tax; income statement

Objectives 2, 3, 4

SPREADSHEET

✓ *Net income, $82,000*

The following data were selected from the records of Healthy Pantry Inc. for the current fiscal year ended June 30, 2006:

Advertising expense	$ 46,000
Cost of merchandise sold	279,000
Depreciation expense—office equipment	6,000
Depreciation expense—store equipment	31,000
Gain on discontinued operations	42,500
Income tax:	
Applicable to continuing operations	32,000
Applicable to gain on discontinued operations	16,000
Applicable to loss on condemnation of land (reduction)	8,000
Insurance expense	9,000
Interest expense	18,000
Loss from condemnation of land	24,500
Loss from fixed asset impairment	90,000
Miscellaneous administrative expense	7,500
Miscellaneous selling expense	5,500
Office salaries expense	60,000
Rent expense	29,000
Restructuring charge	150,000
Sales	980,000
Sales commissions expense	145,000
Unrealized gain on temporary investments	25,000

Instructions

Prepare a multiple-step income statement, concluding with a section for earnings per share in the form illustrated in this chapter. There were 75,000 shares of common stock (no preferred) outstanding throughout the year. Assume that the loss on the condemnation of land is an extraordinary item.

PROBLEM 12-3B
Income statement; retained earnings statement; balance sheet

Objectives 1, 2, 3, 4, 5

SPREADSHEET

✓ *Net income, $277,000*

The following data were taken from the records of Skate N' Ski Corporation for the year ended October 31, 2006.

Income statement data:

Administrative expenses	$ 100,000
Cost of merchandise sold	732,000
Gain on condemnation of land	60,000
Income tax:	
Applicable to continuing operations	206,000
Applicable to loss from discontinued operations	28,800
Applicable to gain on condemnation of land	24,000
Interest expense	8,000
Interest revenue	5,000
Loss from discontinued operations	76,800
Loss from fixed asset impairment	200,000
Restructuring charge	90,000
Sales	2,020,000
Selling expenses	400,000

Retained earnings and balance sheet data:

Accounts payable	$ 89,500
Accounts receivable	309,050
Accumulated depreciation	3,050,000
Accumulated other comprehensive loss	24,000
Allowance for doubtful accounts	21,500
Cash	145,500
Common stock, $15 par (400,000 shares authorized; 152,000 shares issued)	2,280,000
Deferred income taxes payable (current portion, $4,700)	25,700
Dividends:	
Cash dividends for common stock	40,000
Cash dividends for preferred stock	100,000
Stock dividends for common stock	60,000
Dividends payable	30,000
Employee termination benefit obligation (current)	60,000
Equipment	9,541,050
Income tax payable	55,900
Interest receivable	2,500
Merchandise inventory (October 31, 2006), at lower of cost (FIFO) or market	425,000
Notes receivable	77,500
Paid-in capital from sale of treasury stock	16,000
Paid-in capital in excess of par—common stock	894,750
Paid-in capital in excess of par—preferred stock	240,000
Patents	55,000
Preferred 6 2/3% stock, $100 par (30,000 shares authorized; 15,000 shares issued)	1,500,000
Prepaid expenses	15,900
Retained earnings, November 1, 2005	2,446,150
Temporary investment in marketable equity securities	145,000
Treasury stock (2,000 shares of common stock at cost of $35 per share)	70,000
Unrealized loss on temporary equity securities	24,000

Instructions

1. Prepare a multiple-step income statement for the year ended October 31, 2006, concluding with earnings per share. In computing earnings per share, assume that the average number of common shares outstanding was 150,000 and preferred dividends were $100,000. Assume that the gain on condemnation of land is an extraordinary item.
2. Prepare a retained earnings statement for the year ended October 31, 2006.
3. Prepare a balance sheet in report form as of October 31, 2006.

PROBLEM 12-4B
Entries for investments in stock

Objective 5

P.A.S.S.

Samson Company is a wholesaler of men's hair products. The following transactions relate to certain securities acquired by Samson Company, which has a fiscal year ending on December 31:

2004
Jan.   3. Purchased 3,000 shares of the 40,000 outstanding common shares of Davidson Corporation at 67 plus commission and other costs of $468.
July   2. Received the regular cash dividend of $1.30 a share on Davidson Corporation stock.
Dec.   5. Received the regular cash dividend of $1.30 a share plus an extra dividend of $0.10 a share on Davidson Corporation stock.

(Assume that all intervening transactions have been recorded properly and that the number of shares of stock owned have not changed from December 31, 2004, to December 31, 2006.)

2007
Jan.   2. Purchased controlling interest in Comstock Inc. for $760,000 by purchasing 24,000 shares directly from the estate of the founder of Comstock. There are 80,000 shares of Comstock Inc. stock outstanding.
July   6. Received the regular cash dividend of $1.30 a share and a 3% stock dividend on the Davidson Corporation stock.
Oct. 23. Sold 750 shares of Davidson Corporation stock at 78. The broker deducted commission and other costs of $140, remitting the balance.
Dec. 10. Received a cash dividend at the new rate of $1.50 a share on the Davidson Corporation stock.
      31. Received $32,000 of cash dividends on Comstock Inc. stock. Comstock Inc. reported net income of $350,000 in 2007. Samson uses the equity method of accounting for its investment in Comstock Inc.

Instructions
Record the entries for the preceding transactions.

Special Activities

ACTIVITY 12-1
Equity method disclosure

REAL WORLD

The following note to the consolidated financial statements for **The Goodyear Tire and Rubber Co.** relates to the principles of consolidation used in preparing the financial statements:

The Company's investments in 20% to 50% owned companies in which it has the ability to exercise significant influence over operating and financial policies are accounted for by the equity method. Accordingly, the Company's share of the earnings of these companies is included in consolidated net income.

➤ Is it a requirement that Goodyear use the equity method in this situation? Explain.

ACTIVITY 12-2
Special charges analysis

The two-year comparative income statements and a note disclosure for Fleet Shoes, Inc. were as follows:

Income Statement
Fleet Shoes, Inc.
For the Years Ended December 31, 2005 and 2006

	2005	2006
Sales	$ 430,000	$ 510,000
Cost of merchandise sold	193,500	224,400
Gross profit	$ 236,500	$ 285,600
Selling and administrative expenses	(107,500)	(122,400)
Loss on fixed asset impairment		(102,000)
Income from operations	$ 129,000	$ 61,200
Income tax expense	51,600	24,480
Net income	$ 77,400	$ 36,720

Note: A fixed asset impairment of $102,000 was recognized in 2006 as the result of abandoning an order management software system. The system project was started in early 2005 and ran into significant delays and performance problems throughout 2006. It was determined that there was no incremental benefit from completing the system. Thus, the accumulated costs associated with the system were written off.

1. Construct a vertical analysis for 2005 and 2006 by determining for each line item its ratio as a percent of sales.
2. ▭▬► Interpret the performance of the company in 2006.

ACTIVITY 12-3
Extraordinary items

REAL WORLD

The following news item was published on October 7, 2001, less than one month after the September 11 terrorist incident at the World Trade Center:

Many companies already are blaming the Sept. 11 terrorist attacks for a slow-down in profits. But accounting rule-makers aren't letting them off the hook so easily. A task force of the Financial Accounting Standards Board recently decided against allowing companies to treat costs related to the disaster as an "extraordinary item" in their financial statements. That means the costs must be considered part of normal business operations and deducted from the company's operating profit.

The FASB was worried that companies would blame the attack for a variety of unrelated costs—essentially hiding bad business decisions or other problems and making profits seems better than they were.

There also was concern that it was too difficult to tell what costs were related to terrorism and what weren't. The impact of Sept. 11 has been so pervasive, affecting virtually every company, that "it almost made it ordinary," says task-force member Dick Stock.

"The task force understood this was an extraordinary event in the English-language sense of the word," says FASB Chairman Tim Lucas. "But in the final analysis, we decided it wasn't going to improve the financial-reporting system to show it as an extraordinary item." (Steve Liesman, "In Translation: What's Extraordinary—and What's Not," *The Wall Street Journal*, Sunday, October 7, 2001)

▭▬► Why would the FASB say that the September 11 terrorist incident was not "extraordinary"?

ACTIVITY 12-4
Comprehensive income

REAL WORLD

The stockholders' equity section of **YUM! Brands, Inc.**, the operator of Pizza Hut, KFC, and Taco Bell restaurants, for two recent comparative dates was as follows:

YUM! Brands, Inc.
Stockholders' Equity
December 28, 2002 and December 29, 2001
(In millions)

	2002	2001
Common stock, no par value	$1,046	$1,097
Accumulated deficit	(203)	(786)
Accumulated other comprehensive income (loss)	(249)	(207)
Total stockholders' equity	$ 594	$ 104

1. What is the "other" comprehensive income or loss for the year ended December 28, 2002?
2. ⬤▬▬➤ Explain the concept of other comprehensive income.

ACTIVITY 12-5
Ethics and professional conduct in business

ETHICS

At a recent dinner party, you met Steph Melick, the controller for Mojave Inc. Steph has worked for Mojave for the past seven years. During your conversation, you complained about having to pay your third-quarter estimated taxes on Monday, September 15. In response, Steph indicated that she always *underpays* her estimated taxes. That way, she can use her money as long as possible.
⬤▬▬➤ Is it appropriate to deliberately underpay your estimated taxes?

ACTIVITY 12-6
Ethics and professional conduct in business

ETHICS

Reed Osborn is the president and chief operating officer of MoneyScope Corporation, a developer of personal financial planning software. During the past year, MoneyScope Corporation was forced to sell 10 acres of land to the city of Houston for expansion of a freeway exit. The corporation fought the sale; but after condemnation hearings, a judge ordered it to sell the land. Because of the land's location and the fact that MoneyScope Corporation had purchased the land over 15 years ago, the corporation recorded a $0.20-per-share gain on the sale. Always looking to turn a negative into a positive, Reed has decided to announce the corporation's earnings per share of $1.05, without identifying the $0.20 impact of selling the land. Although he will retain majority ownership, Reed plans on selling 20,000 of his shares in the corporation sometime within the next month.
⬤▬▬➤ Are Reed's plans to announce earnings per share of $1.05 without mentioning the $0.20 impact of selling the land ethical and professional?

ACTIVITY 12-7
Reporting extraordinary item

Orlando Fruit Co. is in the process of preparing its annual financial statements. Orlando Fruit is a large citrus grower located in central Florida. The following is a discussion between Kevin Kirk, the controller, and Shirley Gwinn, the chief executive officer and president of Orlando Fruit Co.

Shirley: Kevin, I've got a question about your rough draft of this year's income statement.
Kevin: Sure, Shirley. What's your question?
Shirley: Well, your draft shows a net loss of $750,000.
Kevin: That's right. We'd have had a profit, except for this year's frost damage. I figured that the frost destroyed over 30% of our crop. We had a good year otherwise.
Shirley: That's my concern. I estimated that if we eliminate the frost damage, we'd show a profit of . . . let's see . . . about $250,000.
Kevin: That sounds about right.
Shirley: This income statement seems misleading. Why can't we show the loss on the frost damage separately? That way the bank and our outside investors will be able to see that this year's loss is just temporary. I'd hate to get them upset over nothing.
Kevin: Maybe we can do something. I recall from my accounting courses something about showing unusual items separately. Let's see . . . yes, I remember. They're called extraordinary items.

Assume that you have just inherited $50,000 from a distant relative, and you are considering some options for investing the money. Some of your friends have suggested that you invest it in long-term bonds. As a result, you have searched the Internet for corporate bond listings. You've identified the following listings as possible bond investments, both of which mature in the year 2028:

- **Minnesota Mining & Manufacturing Co. (3M)** 6.4% Bonds
- **Merrill Lynch & Co.** zero

The 3M bonds are selling for 114.187, while the Merrill Lynch bonds are selling for only 19.82. The 3M bonds are selling for over five and one-half times the price of the Merrill Lynch bonds. Does this mean that the Merrill Lynch bonds are a better buy? Does the 6.4% mean that if you buy the 3M bonds you can actually earn 6.4% interest? What does the "zero" mean? Does it have anything to do with the fact that the Merrill Lynch bonds are only selling for 19.82?

In this chapter, we will answer each of these questions. We first discuss the advantages and disadvantages of financing a corporation's operations by issuing debt rather than equity. We then discuss the accounting principles related to issuing long-term debt. Finally, we discuss the accounting for investments in bonds.

Financing Corporations

objective 1

Compute the potential impact of long-term borrowing on the earnings per share of a corporation.

POINT OF INTEREST

Bonds of major corporations are actively traded on bond exchanges. You can purchase bonds through a financial services firm, such as **Merrill Lynch** or **A. G. Edwards & Sons**.

Most of you have financed (purchased on credit) an automobile, a home, or a computer. Similarly, corporations often finance their operations by purchasing on credit and issuing notes or bonds. We have discussed accounts payable and notes payable in earlier chapters. A **bond** is simply a form of an interest-bearing note. Like a note, a bond requires periodic interest payments, and the face amount must be repaid at the maturity date. Bondholders are creditors of the issuing corporation, and their claims on the assets of the corporation rank ahead of stockholders.

One of the many factors that influence the decision to issue debt or equity is the effect of each alternative on earnings per share. To illustrate the possible effects, assume that a corporation's board of directors is considering the following alternative plans for financing a $4,000,000 company:

Plan 1: 100% financing from issuing common stock, $10 par
Plan 2: 50% financing from issuing preferred 9% stock, $50 par
        50% financing from issuing common stock, $10 par
Plan 3: 50% financing from issuing 12% bonds
        25% financing from issuing preferred 9% stock, $50 par
        25% financing from issuing common stock, $10 par

In each case, we assume that the stocks or bonds are issued at their par or face amount. The corporation is expecting to earn $800,000 annually, before deducting interest on the bonds and income taxes estimated at 40% of income. Exhibit 1 shows the effect of the three plans on the income of the corporation and the earnings per share on common stock.

Exhibit 1 indicates that Plan 3 yields the highest earnings per share on common stock and is thus the most attractive for common stockholders. If the estimated earnings are more than $800,000, the difference between the earnings per share to common stockholders under Plan 1 and Plan 3 is even greater.[1] However, if smaller earnings occur, Plans 2 and 3 become less attractive to common stockholders. To illustrate, the effect of earnings of $440,000 rather than $800,000 is shown in Exhibit 2.

---

[1]The higher earnings per share under Plan 3 is due to a finance concept known as **leverage**. This concept is discussed further in a later chapter.

•Exhibit 1

Effect of Alternative Financing Plans— $800,000 Earnings

	Plan 1	Plan 2	Plan 3
12% bonds	—	—	$2,000,000
Preferred 9% stock, $50 par	—	$2,000,000	1,000,000
Common stock, $10 par	$4,000,000	2,000,000	1,000,000
Total	$4,000,000	$4,000,000	$4,000,000
Earnings before interest and income tax . . .	$ 800,000	$ 800,000	$ 800,000
Deduct interest on bonds	—	—	240,000
Income before income tax	$ 800,000	$ 800,000	$ 560,000
Deduct income tax	320,000	320,000	224,000
Net income	$ 480,000	$ 480,000	$ 336,000
Dividends on preferred stock	—	180,000	90,000
Available for dividends on common stock . .	$ 480,000	$ 300,000	$ 246,000
Shares of common stock outstanding	÷ 400,000	÷ 200,000	÷ 100,000
Earnings per share on common stock	$ 1.20	$ 1.50	$ 2.46

•Exhibit 2

Effect of Alternative Financing Plans— $440,000 Earnings

	Plan 1	Plan 2	Plan 3
12% bonds	—	—	$2,000,000
Preferred 9% stock, $50 par	—	$2,000,000	1,000,000
Common stock, $10 par	$4,000,000	2,000,000	1,000,000
Total	$4,000,000	$4,000,000	$4,000,000
Earnings before interest and income tax . . .	$ 440,000	$ 440,000	$ 440,000
Deduct interest on bonds	—	—	240,000
Income before income tax	$ 440,000	$ 440,000	$ 200,000
Deduct income tax	176,000	176,000	80,000
Net income	$ 264,000	$ 264,000	$ 120,000
Dividends on preferred stock	—	180,000	90,000
Available for dividends on common stock . .	$ 264,000	$ 84,000	$ 30,000
Shares of common stock outstanding	÷ 400,000	÷ 200,000	÷ 100,000
Earnings per share on common stock	$ 0.66	$ 0.42	$ 0.30

REAL WORLD

When interest rates are low, corporations usually finance their operations with debt. For example, as interest rates fell in the early 1990s, corporations rushed to issue new debt. In one day alone, more than $4.5 billion of debt was issued.

In addition to the effect on earnings per share, the board of directors should consider other factors in deciding whether to issue debt or equity. For example, once bonds are issued, periodic interest payments and repayment of the face value of the bonds are beyond the control of the corporation. That is, if these payments are not made, the bondholders could seek court action and could force the company into bankruptcy. In contrast, a corporation is not legally obligated to pay dividends.

Characteristics of Bonds Payable

objective 2

Describe the characteristics of bonds.

A corporation that issues bonds enters into a contract, called a **bond indenture** or **trust indenture**, with the bondholders. A bond issue is normally divided into a number of individual bonds. Usually the face value of each bond, called the **principal**, is $1,000 or a multiple of $1,000. The interest on bonds may be payable annually, semiannually, or quarterly. Most bonds pay interest semiannually.

Time Warner 7.625% bonds maturing in 2031 were listed as selling for 112.698 on July 22, 2003.

The prices of bonds are quoted as a percentage of the bonds' face value. Thus, investors could purchase or sell **Wal-Mart** bonds quoted at 116.992 for $1,169.92. Likewise, bonds quoted at 109 could be purchased or sold for $1,090.

When all bonds of an issue mature at the same time, they are called **term bonds**. If the maturities are spread over several dates, they are called **serial bonds**. For example, one-tenth of an issue of $1,000,000 bonds, or $100,000, may mature 16 years from the issue date, another $100,000 in the 17th year, and so on until the final $100,000 matures in the 25th year.

Bonds that may be exchanged for other securities, such as common stock, are called **convertible bonds**. Bonds that a corporation reserves the right to redeem before their maturity are called **callable bonds**. Bonds issued on the basis of the general credit of the corporation are called **debenture bonds**.

The Present-Value Concept and Bonds Payable

objective 3

Compute the present value of bonds payable.

When a corporation issues bonds, the price that buyers are willing to pay for the bonds depends upon the following three factors:

1. The face amount of the bonds, which is the amount due at the maturity date.
2. The periodic interest to be paid on the bonds.
3. The market rate of interest.

The face amount and the periodic interest to be paid on the bonds are identified in the bond indenture. The periodic interest is expressed as a percentage of the face amount of the bond. This percentage or rate of interest is called the *contract rate* or **coupon rate**.

The **market** or *effective rate of interest* is determined by transactions between buyers and sellers of similar bonds. The market rate of interest is affected by a variety of factors, including investors' assessment of current economic conditions as well as future expectations.

If the contract rate of interest equals the market rate of interest, the bonds will sell at their face amount. If the market rate is higher than the contract rate, the bonds will sell at a *discount*, or less than their face amount. Why is this the case? Buyers are not willing to pay the face amount for bonds whose contract rate is lower than the market rate. The discount, in effect, represents the amount necessary to make up for the difference in the market and the contract interest rates. In contrast, if the market rate is lower than the contract rate, the bonds will sell at a *premium*, or more than their face amount. In this case, buyers are willing to pay more than the face amount for bonds whose contract rate is higher than the market rate.

The face amount of the bonds and the periodic interest on the bonds represent cash to be received by the buyer in the future. The buyer determines how much to pay for the bonds by computing the present value of these future cash receipts, using the market rate of interest. The concept of present value is based on the time value of money.

The time value of money concept recognizes that an amount of cash to be received today is worth more than the same amount of cash to be received in the future. For example, what would you rather have: $100 today or $100 one year from now? You would rather have the $100 today because it could be invested to earn income. For example, if the $100 could be invested to earn 10% per year, the $100 will

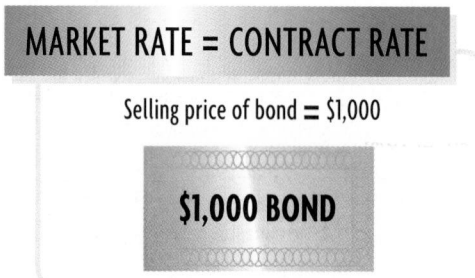

MARKET RATE = CONTRACT RATE

Selling price of bond = $1,000

$1,000 BOND

MARKET RATE > CONTRACT RATE

Selling price of bond < $1,000

$1,000 BOND — **Discount**

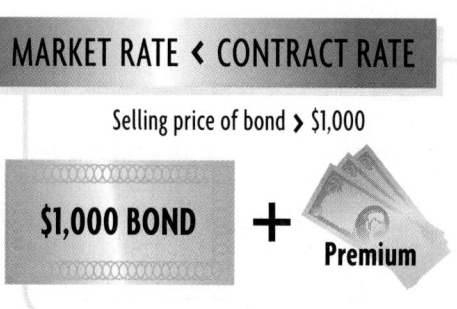

MARKET RATE < CONTRACT RATE

Selling price of bond > $1,000

$1,000 BOND + **Premium**

accumulate to $110 ($100 plus $10 earnings) in one year. In this sense, you can think of the $100 in hand today as the ***present value*** of $110 to be received a year from today. This present value is illustrated in the following time line:

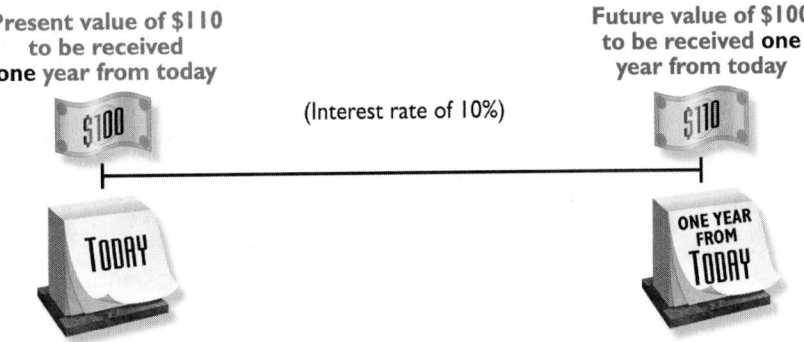

A related concept to present value is ***future value***. In the preceding illustration, the $110 to be received a year from today is the future value of $100 today, assuming an interest rate of 10%.

Present Value of the Face Amount of Bonds

The present value of the face amount of bonds is the value today of the amount to be received at a future maturity date. For example, assume that you are to receive the face value of a $1,000 bond in one year. If the market rate of interest is 10%, the present value of the face value of the $1,000 bond is $909.09 ($1,000/1.10). This present value is illustrated in the following time line:

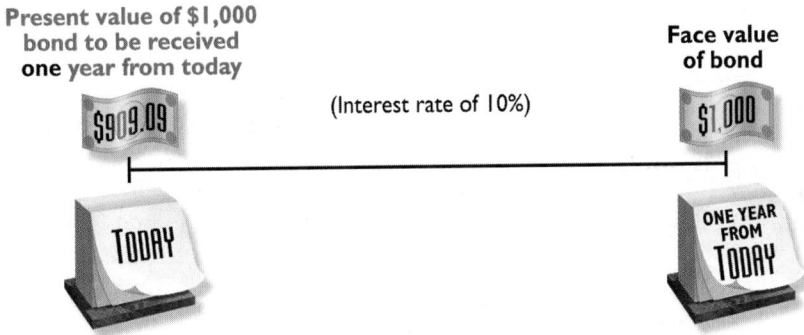

If you are to receive the face value of a $1,000 bond in two years, with interest of 10% compounded at the end of the first year, the present value is $826.45 ($909.09/1.10).[2] We illustrate this present value in the following time line:

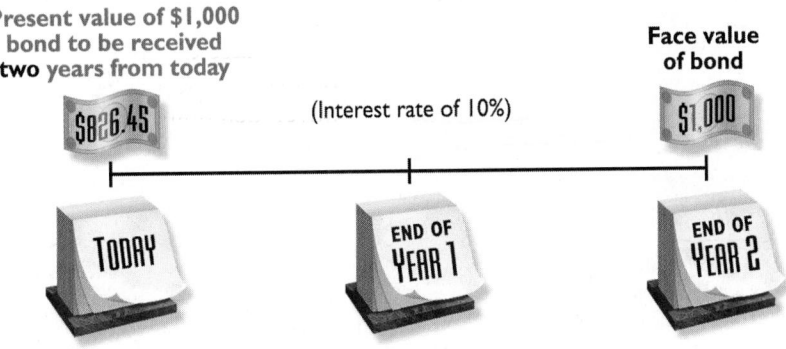

----

[2]Note that the future value of $826.45 in two years, at an interest rate of 10% compounded annually, is $1,000.

You can determine the present value of the face amount of bonds to be received in the future by a time line and a series of divisions. In practice, however, it is easier to use a table of present values. The *present value of $1 table* can be used to find the present-value factor for $1 to be received after a number of periods in the future. The face amount of the bonds is then multiplied by this factor to determine its present value. Exhibit 3 is a partial table of the present value of $1.[3]

•Exhibit 3 Present Value of $1 at Compound Interest

Periods	5%	5½%	6%	6½%	7%	10%	11%	12%	13%	14%
1	0.95238	0.94787	0.94340	0.93897	0.93458	0.90909	0.90090	0.89286	0.88496	0.87719
2	0.90703	0.89845	0.89000	0.88166	0.87344	0.82645	0.81162	0.79719	0.78315	0.76947
3	0.86384	0.85161	0.83962	0.82785	0.81630	0.75132	0.73119	0.71178	0.69305	0.67497
4	0.82270	0.80722	0.79209	0.77732	0.76290	0.68301	0.65873	0.63552	0.61332	0.59208
5	0.78353	0.76513	0.74726	0.72988	0.71299	0.62092	0.59345	0.56743	0.54276	0.51937
6	0.74622	0.72525	0.70496	0.68533	0.66634	0.56447	0.53464	0.50663	0.48032	0.45559
7	0.71068	0.68744	0.66506	0.64351	0.62275	0.51316	0.48166	0.45235	0.42506	0.39964
8	0.67684	0.65160	0.62741	0.60423	0.58201	0.46651	0.43393	0.40388	0.37616	0.35056
9	0.64461	0.61763	0.59190	0.56735	0.54393	0.42410	0.39092	0.36061	0.33288	0.30751
10	0.61391	0.58543	0.55840	0.53273	0.50835	0.38554	0.35218	0.32197	0.29459	0.26974

What is the present value of $3,000 to be received in 5 years at a market rate of interest of 14% compounded annually?

$1,558.11 ($3,000 × 0.51937)

Exhibit 3 indicates that the present value of $1 to be received in two years with a market rate of interest of 10% a year is 0.82645. Multiplying the $1,000 face amount of the bond in the preceding example by 0.82645 yields $826.45.

In Exhibit 3, the Periods column represents the number of compounding periods, and the percentage columns represent the compound interest rate per period. For example, 10% for two years compounded *annually*, as in the preceding example, is 10% for two periods. Likewise, 10% for two years compounded *semiannually* would be 5% (10% per year/2 semiannual periods) for four periods (2 years × 2 semiannual periods). Similarly, 10% for three years compounded semiannually would be 5% (10%/2) for six periods (3 years × 2 semiannual periods).

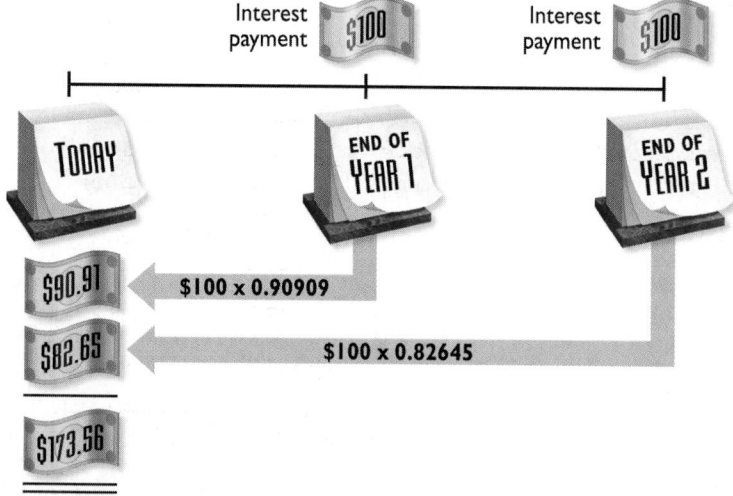

Present value of $100 interest payments to be received each year for 2 years (rounded to the nearest cent)

Present Value of the Periodic Bond Interest Payments

The present value of the periodic bond interest payments is the value today of the amount of interest to be received at the end of each interest period. Such a series of equal cash payments at fixed intervals is called an *annuity*.

The *present value of an annuity* is the sum of the present values of each cash flow. To illustrate, assume that the $1,000 bond in the preceding example pays interest of 10% annually

---

[3]To simplify the illustrations and homework assignments, the tables presented in this chapter are limited to 10 periods for a small number of interest rates, and the amounts are carried to only five decimal places. Computer programs are available for determining present value factors for any number of interest rates, decimal places, or periods. More complete interest tables, including future value tables, are presented in Appendix A.

and that the market rate of interest is also 10%. In addition, assume that the bond matures at the end of two years. The present value of the two interest payments of $100 ($1,000 × 10%) is $173.56, as shown in the time line at the bottom of page 606. It can be determined by using the present value table shown in Exhibit 3.

FINANCIAL REPORTING AND DISCLOSURE

SAFEWAY INC.

Safeway is one of the largest food and drug retailers in North America, with over 1,600 stores located in California, Oregon, Washington, Alaska, Colorado, Arizona, Texas, the Chicago metropolitan area, the Mid-Atlantic region, and Canada. During 2002, Safeway reported over $32.4 billion in revenue, income from continuing operations of $569 million, and total assets of $16 billion.

Safeway's operations are financed by notes and debentures of $7.8 billion. Of these notes and debentures, $780 million mature within the current year, and the remainder of $7 billion are long-term debt. Safeway describes its debt financing in the following notes taken from its annual report:

Notes and debentures were composed of the following at year-end (December 31)

	(in millions)	
	2002	**2001**
Commercial paper	$1,744.1	$1,723.8
Bank credit agreement, unsecured	25.3	—
9.30% Senior Secured Debentures due 2007	24.3	24.3
6.85% Senior Notes due 2004, unsecured	200.0	200.0
7.00% Senior Notes due 2007, unsecured	250.0	250.0
7.45% Senior Debentures due 2027, unsecured	150.0	150.0
3.80% Senior Notes due 2005, unsecured	225.0	—
4.80% Senior Notes due 2007, unsecured	480.0	—
5.80% Senior Notes due 2012, unsecured	800.0	—
6.05% Senior Notes due 2003, unsecured	350.0	350.0
6.50% Senior Notes due 2008, unsecured	250.0	250.0
7.00% Senior Notes due 2002, unsecured	—	600.0
7.25% Senior Notes due 2004, unsecured	400.0	400.0
7.50% Senior Notes due 2009, unsecured	500.0	500.0
6.15% Senior Notes due 2006, unsecured	700.0	700.0
6.50% Senior Notes due 2011, unsecured	500.0	500.0
7.25% Senior Debentures due 2031, unsecured	600.0	600.0
3.625% Senior Notes due 2003, unsecured	400.0	400.0
9.65% Senior Subordinated Debentures due 2004, unsecured	81.2	81.2
9.875% Senior Subordinated Debentures due 2007, unsecured	24.2	24.2
10% Senior Notes due 2002, unsecured	—	6.1
Mortgage notes payable, secured	39.7	60.5
Other notes payable, unsecured	21.6	31.7
Medium-term notes, unsecured	16.5	16.5
Short-term bank borrowings, unsecured	7.6	7.6
	$7,789.5	$6,875.9
Less current maturities	(780.3)	(639.1)
Long term portion	$7,009.2	$6,236.8

The 9.30% Senior Secured Debentures due in 2007 traded on July 23, 2003, at 120.58 and yielded a rate of return of 3.068%.

Instead of using present value of amount tables, such as Exhibit 3, separate present value tables are normally used for annuities. Exhibit 4 is a partial table of the *present value of an annuity of $1* at compound interest. It shows the present value of $1 to be received at the end of each period for various compound rates of interest. For example, the present value of $100 to be received at the end of each of the next two years at 10% compound interest per period is $173.55 ($100 × 1.73554). This amount is the same amount that we computed previously, except for rounding.

•Exhibit 4 Present Value of Annuity of $1 at Compound Interest

Periods	5%	5½%	6%	6½%	7%	10%	11%	12%	13%	14%
1	0.95238	0.94787	0.94340	0.93897	0.93458	0.90909	0.90090	0.89286	0.88496	0.87719
2	1.85941	1.84632	1.83339	1.82063	1.80802	1.73554	1.71252	1.69005	1.66810	1.64666
3	2.72325	2.69793	2.67301	2.64848	2.62432	2.48685	2.44371	2.40183	2.36115	2.32163
4	3.54595	3.50515	3.46511	3.42580	3.38721	3.16987	3.10245	3.03735	2.97447	2.91371
5	4.32948	4.27028	4.21236	4.15568	4.10020	3.79079	3.69590	3.60478	3.51723	3.43308
6	5.07569	4.99553	4.91732	4.84101	4.76654	4.35526	4.23054	4.11141	3.99755	3.88867
7	5.78637	5.68297	5.58238	5.48452	5.38929	4.86842	4.71220	4.56376	4.42261	4.28830
8	6.46321	6.33457	6.20979	6.08875	5.97130	5.33493	5.14612	4.96764	4.79677	4.63886
9	7.10782	6.95220	6.80169	6.65610	6.51523	5.75902	5.53705	5.32825	5.13166	4.94637
10	7.72174	7.53763	7.36009	7.18883	7.02358	6.14457	5.88923	5.65022	5.42624	5.21612

As we stated earlier, the amount buyers are willing to pay for a bond is the sum of the present value of the face value and the periodic interest payments, calculated by using the market rate of interest. In our example, this calculation is as follows:

What is the present value of a $10,000, 7%, 5-year bond that pays interest annually, assuming a market rate of interest of 7%?

$10,000 [($10,000 × 0.71299) + ($700 × 4.10020)]

Present value of face value of $1,000 due in 2 years at 10% compounded annually: $1,000 × 0.82645 (present value factor of $1 for 2 periods at 10%)	$ 826.45
Present value of 2 annual interest payments of $100 at 10% compounded annually: $100 × 1.73554 (present value of annuity of $1 for 2 periods at 10%)	173.55
Total present value of bonds	$1,000.00

In this example, the market rate and the contract rate of interest are the same. Thus, the present value is the same as the face value.

Accounting for Bonds Payable

objective 4

Journalize entries for bonds payable.

In the preceding section, we described and illustrated how present value concepts are used in determining how much buyers are willing to pay for bonds. In this section, we describe and illustrate how corporations record the issuance of bonds and the payment of bond interest.

Bonds Issued at Face Amount

To illustrate the journal entries for issuing bonds, assume that on January 1, 2005, a corporation issues for cash $100,000 of 12%, five-year bonds, with interest of $6,000 payable *semiannually*. The market rate of interest at the time the bonds are issued is 12%. Since the contract rate and the market rate of interest are the same, the bonds will sell at their face amount. This amount is the sum of (1) the present value of the face amount of $100,000 to be repaid in five years and (2) the present value of ten *semiannual* interest payments of $6,000 each. This computation and a time line are shown below.

Present value of face amount of $100,000 due in 5 years,
at 12% compounded semiannually: $100,000 × 0.55840
(present value of $1 for 10 periods at 6%) . . . . $ 55,840
Present value of 10 semiannual interest payments of $6,000,
at 12% compounded semiannually: $6,000 × 7.36009
(present value of annuity of $1 for 10 periods at 6%) 44,160*
Total present value of bonds $100,000

*Because the present-value tables are rounded to five decimal places, minor rounding differences may appear in the illustrations.

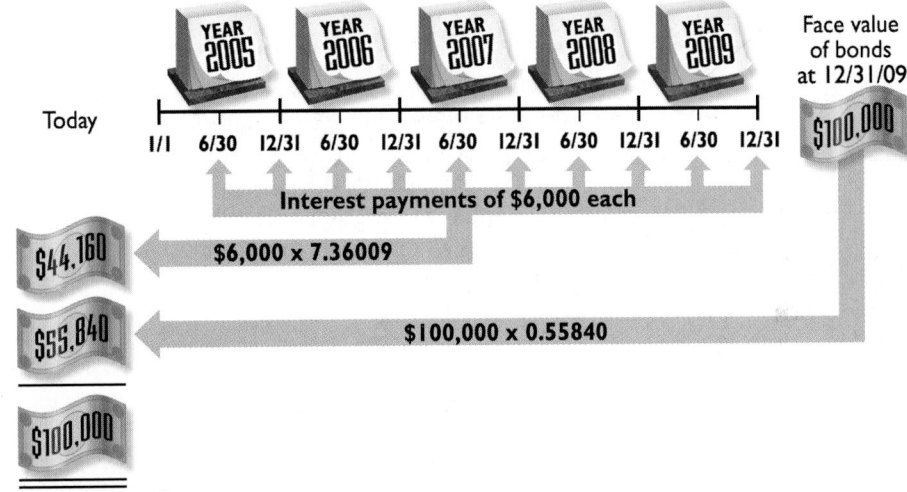

Present value of
12% bonds at
12% market rate

The following entry records the issuing of the $100,000 bonds at their face amount:

2005 Jan.	1	Cash	100 0 0 0 00	
		Bonds Payable		100 0 0 0 00
		Issued $100,000 bonds payable at		
		face amount.		

Every six months after the bonds have been issued, interest payments of $6,000 are made. The first interest payment is recorded as shown below.

June	30	Interest Expense	6 0 0 0 00	
		Cash		6 0 0 0 00
		Paid six months' interest on bonds.		

At the maturity date, the payment of the principal of $100,000 is recorded as follows:

2009 Dec.	31	Bonds Payable	100 0 0 0 00	
		Cash		100 0 0 0 00
		Paid bond principal at maturity date.		

Bonds Issued at a Discount

What if the market rate of interest is higher than the contract rate of interest? If the market rate of interest is 13% and the contract rate is 12% on the five-year, $100,000 bonds, the bonds will sell at a discount. The present value of these bonds is calculated as follows:

> **Bonds will sell at a discount when the market rate of interest is higher than the contract rate.**

Present value of face amount of $100,000 due in 5 years, at 13% compounded semiannually: $100,000 × 0.53273 (present value of $1 for 10 periods at 6½%)	$53,273
Present value of 10 semiannual interest payments of $6,000, at 13% compounded semiannually: $6,000 × 7.18883 (present value of an annuity of $1 for 10 periods at 6½%)	43,133
Total present value of bonds	$96,406

What is the present value of a $100,000, 6%, 5-year bond paying semiannual interest if the market rate of interest is 10%?

$84,556 [($100,000 × 0.61391) + ($3,000 × 7.72174)]

The two present values that make up the total are both less than the related amounts in the preceding example. This is because the market rate of interest was 12% in the first example, while the market rate of interest is 13% in this example. The present value of a future amount becomes less and less as the interest rate used to compute the present value increases.

The entry to record the issuing of the $100,000 bonds at a discount is shown below.

2005 Jan.	1	Cash		96 4 0 6 00	
		Discount on Bonds Payable		3 5 9 4 00	
		Bonds Payable			100 0 0 0 00
		Issued $100,000 bonds at discount.			

The $3,594 discount may be viewed as the amount that is needed to entice investors to accept a contract rate of interest that is below the market rate. You may think of the discount as the market's way of adjusting a bond's contract rate of interest to the higher market rate of interest. Using this logic, generally accepted accounting principles require that bond discounts be amortized as interest expense over the life of the bond.

Amortizing a Bond Discount

If the amount of a bond discount on a newly issued 6%, 5-year, $100,000 bond is $28,092, what are (a) the semiannual straight-line amortization of the discount and (b) the annual interest expense?

(a) $2,809.20, (b) $11,618.40 ($2,809.20 + $2,809.20 + $6,000)

There are two methods of amortizing a bond discount: (1) the **straight-line method** and (2) the *effective interest rate method*, often called the **interest method**. Both methods amortize the same total amount of discount over the life of the bonds. The interest method is required by generally accepted accounting principles. However, the straight-line method is acceptable if the results obtained do not materially differ from the results that would be obtained by using the interest method. Because the straight-line method illustrates the basic concept of amortizing discounts and is simpler, we will use it in this chapter. We illustrate the interest method in an appendix to this chapter.

The straight-line method of amortizing a bond discount provides for amortization in equal periodic amounts. Applying this method to the preceding example yields amortization of 1/10 of $3,594, or $359.40, each half year. The amount of the interest expense on the bonds is the same, $6,359.40 ($6,000 + $359.40) for each half year. The entry to record the first interest payment and the amortization of the related discount follows.

	2005							
	June	30	Interest Expense		6 3 5 9 40			
			Discount on Bonds Payable				3 5 9 40	
			Cash				6 0 0 0 00	
			Paid semiannual interest and					
			amortized ¹/₁₀ of bond discount.					

> Bonds will sell at a premium when the market rate of interest is less than the contract rate.

Bonds Issued at a Premium

If the market rate of interest is 11% and the contract rate is 12% on the five-year, $100,000 bonds, the bonds will sell at a premium. The present value of these bonds is computed as follows:

Present value of face amount of $100,000 due in 5 years,
   at 11% compounded semiannually: $100,000 × 0.58543
   (present value of $1 for 10 periods at 5½%) . . . . $ 58,543
Present value of 10 semiannual interest payments of $6,000,
   at 11% compounded semiannually: $6,000 × 7.53763
   (present value of an annuity of $1 for 10 periods at 5½%) 45,226
Total present value of bonds $103,769

The entry to record the issuing of the bonds is as follows:

	2005							
	Jan.	1	Cash		103 7 6 9 00			
			Bonds Payable				100 0 0 0 00	
			Premium on Bonds Payable				3 7 6 9 00	
			Issued $100,000 bonds at a premium.					

Amortizing a Bond Premium

The amortization of bond premiums is basically the same as that for bond discounts, except that interest expense is decreased. In the above example, the straight-line method yields amortization of ¹/₁₀ of $3,769, or $376.90, each half year. The entry to record the first interest payment and the amortization of the related premium is as follows:

If the amount of a bond premium on a newly issued 13%, 5-year, $100,000 bond is $11,581, what are (a) the semiannual straight-line amortization of the premium and (b) the annual interest expense?

(a) $1,158.10, (b) $10,683.80 ($13,000 − $1,158.10 − $1,158.10)

	2005							
	June	30	Interest Expense		5 6 2 3 10			
			Premium on Bonds Payable		3 7 6 90			
			Cash				6 0 0 0 00	
			Paid semiannual interest and					
			amortized ¹/₁₀ of bond premium.					

Zero-Coupon Bonds

Some corporations issue bonds that provide for only the payment of the face amount at the maturity date. Such bonds are called **zero-coupon bonds**. Because they do not provide for interest payments, these bonds sell at a large discount. For example, **Merrill Lynch**'s zero-coupon bonds maturing in 2028 were selling for 19.82.

REAL WORLD

Some bonds with high contract rates, as well as some zero-coupon bonds, are issued by weak companies. Because such bonds are high-risk bonds, they are called **junk bonds**.

The issuing price of zero-coupon bonds is the present value of their face amount. To illustrate, if the market rate of interest is 13%, the present value of $100,000 zero-coupon, five-year bonds is calculated as follows:

> Present value of $100,000 due in 5 years, at 13%
> compounded semiannually: $100,000 × 0.53273
> (present value of $1 for 10 periods at 6½%) $53,273

The accounting for zero-coupon bonds is similar to that for interest-bearing bonds that have been sold at a discount. The discount is amortized as interest expense over the life of the bonds. The entry to record the issuing of the bonds is as follows:

2005 Jan.	1	Cash	53 2 7 3 00		
		Discount on Bonds Payable	46 7 2 7 00		
		Bonds Payable		100 0 0 0 00	
		Issued $100,000 zero-coupon			
		bonds			

LET'S DANCE—A BOND WITH A TUNE

How would you like to tune into some of the royalties from David Bowie's hit song, *Let's Dance*? The British rock star has offered bonds backed by future royalties from his hit songs and albums recorded prior to 1990. In addition to *Let's Dance*, other songs include *Jean Genie*, *A Space Oddity*, *Changes*, *Diamond Dogs*, and *Rebel*.

Bowie's bonds, which have an average maturity of 10 years, pay 7.9% annual interest. Such asset-backed bonds have grown in popularity. However, this is the first time that a popular artist has made use of future royalties as asset backing. The Bowie Bonds, which are officially called Class-A royalty-backed securities, were rated AAA—the highest rating—by **Moody's Investors Service**.

Bowie is one of the most financially savvy rock stars in the world, with a well-chosen art collection and an appreciation for market trends. Bowie's principal residence is a $3.4 million, 640-acre estate in County Wicklow, Ireland, a noted tax haven. He lives there with his second wife, the supermodel and actress Iman. Still, Bowie's business man-

ager said that when he approached him with the bond idea, "he [Bowie] kind of looked at me cross-eyed and said, 'What?'"

Potential investors were reassured by the fact that Bowie never sells fewer than a million albums a year. At the time of the offering, Bowie's album, "Earthling," was near the top of the European charts. In addition, the month before the offering, he performed for a sold-out concert at New York's Madison Square Garden.

Prudential Insurance Co. isn't kidding when it says you can own a piece of the *rock*. In a private placement, Prudential purchased all of David Bowie's $55 million bonds for its general investment fund, where the money of life insurance policyholders is invested.

In addition to Bowie, other musicians who have issued royalty-backed bonds include James Brown and the heavy-metal band Iron Maiden. The Iron Maiden bonds were successfully sold for $30 million.

Bond Sinking Funds

objective **5**

Describe bond sinking funds.

A bond indenture may restrict dividend payments to stockholders as a means of increasing the likelihood that the bonds will be paid at maturity. In addition to or instead of this restriction, the bond indenture may require that funds for the payment of the face value of the bonds at maturity be set aside over the life of the bond issue. The amounts set aside are kept separate from other assets in a special fund called a **sinking fund**.

When cash is transferred to the sinking fund, it is recorded in an account called *Sinking Fund Cash*. When investments are purchased with the sinking fund cash, they are recorded in an account called *Sinking Fund Investments*. As income (interest or dividends) is received, it is recorded in an account called *Sinking Fund Revenue*.

Sinking fund revenue represents earnings of the corporation and is reported in the income statement as Other Income. The cash and the securities making up the sinking fund are reported in the balance sheet as Investments, immediately below the Current Assets section.

Bond Redemption

objective **6**

Journalize entries for bond redemptions.

REAL WORLD

Pacific Bell issued 7.5% bonds, maturing in 2033 but callable in 2023.

A corporation may call or redeem bonds before they mature. This is often done if the market rate of interest declines significantly after the bonds have been issued. In this situation, the corporation may sell new bonds at a lower interest rate and use the funds to redeem the original bond issue. The corporation can thus save on future interest expenses.

A corporation often issues callable bonds to protect itself against significant declines in future interest rates. However, callable bonds are more risky for investors, who may not be able to replace the called bonds with investments paying an equal amount of interest.

Callable bonds can be redeemed by the issuing corporation within the period of time and at the price stated in the bond indenture. Normally, the call price is above the face value. A corporation may also redeem its bonds by purchasing them on the open market.

A corporation usually redeems its bonds at a price different from that of the carrying amount (or book value) of the bonds. The ***carrying amount*** of bonds payable is the balance of the bonds payable account (face amount of the bonds) less any unamortized discount or plus any unamortized premium. If the price paid for redemption is below the bond carrying amount, the difference in these two amounts is recorded as a gain. If the price paid for the redemption is above the carrying amount, a loss is recorded. Gains and losses on the redemption of bonds are reported in the Other Income and Expense section of the income statement.

To illustrate, assume that on June 30 a corporation has a bond issue of $100,000 outstanding, on which there is an unamortized premium of $4,000. Assuming that the corporation purchases one-fourth ($25,000) of the bonds for $24,000 on June 30, the entry to record the redemption is as follows:

2005					
June	30	Bonds Payable	25 0 0 0 00		
		Premium on Bonds Payable	1 0 0 0 00		
		Cash			24 0 0 0 00
		Gain on Redemption of Bonds			2 0 0 0 00
		Redeemed $25,000 bonds for $24,000.			

In the preceding entry, only a portion of the premium relating to the redeemed bonds is written off. The difference between the carrying amount of the bonds purchased, $26,000 ($25,000 + $1,000), and the price paid for the redemption, $24,000, is recorded as a gain.

If the corporation calls the entire bond issue for $105,000 on June 30, the entry to record the redemption is as follows:

A $250,000 bond issue on which there is an unamortized discount of $20,000 is redeemed for $235,000. What is the gain or loss on the redemption of the bonds?

- -

$5,000 loss ($250,000 − $20,000 − $235,000)

2005					
June	30	Bonds Payable	100 0 0 0 00		
		Premium on Bonds Payable	4 0 0 0 00		
		Loss on Redemption of Bonds	1 0 0 0 00		
		Cash			105 0 0 0 00
		Redeemed $100,000 bonds for $105,000.			

Investments in Bonds

objective 7

Journalize entries for the purchase, interest, discount and premium amortization, and sale of bond investments.

REAL WORLD

Walt Disney's 6.375% bonds maturing in 2012 were listed as selling for 107.365 on August 1, 2003.

Throughout this chapter, we have discussed bonds and the related transactions of the issuing corporation (the debtor). However, these transactions also affect investors. In this section, we discuss the accounting for bonds from the point of view of investors.

Accounting for Bond Investments— Purchase, Interest, and Amortization

Bonds may be purchased either directly from the issuing corporation or through an organized bond exchange. Bond exchanges publish daily bond quotations. These quotations normally include the bond interest rate, maturity date, volume of sales, and the high, low, and closing prices for each corporation's bonds traded during the day. Prices for bonds are quoted as a percentage of the face amount. Thus, the price of a $1,000 bond quoted at 99.5 would be $995, while the price of a bond quoted at 104.25 would be $1,042.50.

As with other assets, the cost of a bond investment includes all costs related to the purchase. For example, for bonds purchased through an exchange, the amount paid as a broker's commission should be included as part of the cost of the investment.

When bonds are purchased between interest dates, the buyer normally pays the seller the interest accrued from the last interest payment date to the date of purchase. The amount of the interest paid is normally debited to *Interest Revenue*, since it is an offset against the amount that will be received at the next interest date.

To illustrate, assume that an investor purchases a $1,000 bond at 102 plus a brokerage fee of $5.30 and accrued interest of $10.20. The investor records the transaction as follows:

2005								
Apr.	2	Investment in Lewis Co. Bonds		1 0 2 5 30		
		Interest Revenue		1 0 20		
		Cash			1 0 3 5 50

> **A premium or discount on a bond investment is recorded in the investment account and is amortized over the remaining life of the bonds.**

The cost of the bond is recorded in a single investment account. The face amount of the bond and the premium (or discount) are normally not recorded in separate accounts. This is different from the accounting for bonds payable. Separate premium and discount accounts are usually not used by investors, because they usually do not hold bond investments until the bonds mature.

When bonds held as long-term investments are purchased at a price other than the face amount, the premium or discount should be amortized over the remaining life of the bonds. The amortization of premiums and discounts affects the investment and interest accounts as shown below.

Premium Amortization:			Discount Amortization:		
Interest Revenue	XXX		Investment in Bonds	XXX	
Investment in Bonds		XXX	Interest Revenue		XXX

The amount of the amortization can be determined by using either the straight-line or interest methods. Unlike bonds payable, the amortization of premiums and discounts on bond investments is usually recorded at the end of the period, rather than when interest is received.

To illustrate the accounting for bond investments, assume that on July 1, 2005, Crenshaw Inc. purchases $50,000 of 8% bonds of Deitz Corporation, due in $8\frac{3}{4}$ years. Crenshaw Inc. purchases the bonds directly from Deitz Corporation to yield an effective interest rate of 11%. The purchase price is $41,706 plus interest of $1,000 ($50,000 × 8% × $\frac{3}{12}$) accrued from April 1, 2005, the date of the last semiannual interest payment. Entries in the accounts of Crenshaw Inc. at the time of purchase and for the remainder of the fiscal period ending December 31, 2005, are as follows:

Calculations:

Cost of $50,000 of Deitz
    Corp. bonds $41,706
Interest accrued
    ($50,000 × 8% × $\frac{3}{12}$)   1,000
Total $42,706

$50,000 × 8% × $\frac{6}{12}$ = $2,000

$50,000 × 8% × $\frac{3}{12}$ = $1,000

Face value of bonds $50,000
Cost of bond invest.   41,706
Discount on bond
    investment $ 8,294

Number of months
    to maturity
    ($8\frac{3}{4}$ years × 12) 105 months
Monthly amortization
    ($8,294/105 months,
    rounded to nearest
    dollar) $79 per mo.
Amortization for
6 months ($79 × 6) $474

2005					
July	1	Investment in Deitz Corp. Bonds	41 7 0 6 00		
		Interest Revenue	1 0 0 0 00		
		Cash		42 7 0 6 00	
		Purchased investment in bonds, plus			
		accrued interest.			
Oct.	1	Cash	2 0 0 0 00		
		Interest Revenue		2 0 0 0 00	
		Received semiannual interest for			
		April 1 to October 1.			
Dec.	31	Interest Receivable	1 0 0 0 00		
		Interest Revenue		1 0 0 0 00	
		Adjusting entry for interest accrued			
		from October 1 to December 31.			
	31	Investment in Deitz Corp. Bonds	4 7 4 00		
		Interest Revenue		4 7 4 00	
		Adjusting entry for amortization of			
		discount for July 1 to December 31.			

The effect of these entries on the interest revenue account is shown below.

Interest Revenue

July 1	1,000	Oct. 1	2,000	
		Dec. 31	1,000	
		31	474	
	Bal. 2,474		3,474	

Accounting for Bond Investments—Sale

Many long-term investments in bonds are sold before their maturity date. When this occurs, the seller receives the sales price (less commissions and other selling costs) plus any accrued interest since the last interest payment date. Before recording the

If the Deitz Corporation bonds had been sold on September 30 instead of June 30, what would have been the amount of the loss?

$1,229 {$47,350 − [$48,342 + ($79 × 3 months)]}

Calculations:

$79 × 6 months

Carrying amount of bonds on Jan. 1, 2009	$47,868
Discount amortized, Jan. 1 to June 30, 2009	474
Carrying amount of bonds on June 30, 2009	$48,342
Proceeds of sale	47,350
Loss on sale	$ 992

cash proceeds, the seller should amortize any discount or premium for the current period up to the date of sale. Any gain or loss on the sale is then recorded when the cash proceeds are recorded. Such gains and losses are normally reported in the Other Income section of the income statement.

To illustrate, assume that the Deitz Corporation bonds in the preceding example are sold for $47,350 plus accrued interest on June 30, 2012. The *carrying amount* of the bonds (cost plus amortized discount) as of January 1, 2012 (78 months after their purchase) is $47,868 [$41,706 + ($79 per month × 78 months)]. The entries to amortize the discount for the current year and to record the sale of the bonds are as follows:

	2012							
	June	30	Investment in Deitz Corp. Bonds			474 00		
			Interest Revenue				474 00	
			Amortized discount for current year.					
		30	Cash			48 350 00		
			Loss on Sale of Investments			992 00		
			Interest Revenue				1 000 00	
			Investment in Deitz Corp. Bonds				48 342 00	
			Received interest and proceeds					
			from sale of bonds.					
			Interest for April 1 to June 30 =					
			$50,000 × 8% × ³/₁₂ = $1,000					

Corporation Balance Sheet

objective **8**

Prepare a corporation balance sheet.

In previous chapters, we illustrated the income statement and retained earnings statement for a corporation. The consolidated balance sheet in Exhibit 5 illustrates the presentation of many of the items discussed in this and preceding chapters. These items include bond sinking funds, investments in bonds, goodwill, deferred income taxes, bonds payable and unamortized discount, and minority interest in subsidiaries.

Balance Sheet Presentation of Bonds Payable

In Exhibit 5, Escoe Corporation's bonds payable are reported as long-term liabilities. If there were two or more bond issues, the details of each would be reported on the balance sheet or in a supporting schedule or note. Separate accounts are normally maintained for each bond issue.

When the balance sheet date is within one year of the maturity date of the bonds, the bonds may be classified as a current liability. This would be the case if the bonds are to be paid out of current assets. If the bonds are to be paid from a sinking fund or if they are to be refinanced with another bond issue, they should remain in the noncurrent category. In this case, the details of the retirement of the bonds are normally disclosed in a note to the financial statements.

•Exhibit 5   Balance Sheet of a Corporation

Escoe Corporation and Subsidiaries
Consolidated Balance Sheet
December 31, 2006

Assets

Current assets:

Cash and cash equivalents		$ 407,500	
Accounts and notes receivable	$ 722,000		
Less allowance for doubtful receivables	37,000	685,000	
Inventories, at lower of cost (first-in, first-out) or market		917,500	
Prepaid expenses		70,000	
Total current assets			$2,080,000

Investments:

Bond sinking fund (market value, $473,000)		$ 422,500	
Investment in bonds of Dalton Company			
(market value, $231,000)		240,000	
Total investments			662,500

	Cost	Accumulated Depreciation	Book Value	
Property, plant, and equipment				
(depreciated by the straight-line method):				
Land	$ 250,000	—	$ 250,000	
Buildings	920,000	$ 379,955	540,045	
Machinery and equipment	2,764,400	766,200	1,998,200	
Total property, plant, and equipment	$3,934,400	$1,146,155		2,788,245

Intangible assets:

Goodwill		350,000
Total assets		$5,880,745

Liabilities

Current liabilities:

Accounts payable		$ 508,810	
Income tax payable		120,500	
Dividends payable		94,000	
Accrued liabilities		81,400	
Deferred income tax payable		10,000	
Total current liabilities			$ 814,710

Long-term liabilities:

Debenture 8% bonds payable, due December 31, 2024			
(market value, $950,000)	$1,000,000		
Less unamortized discount	60,000	$ 940,000	
Minority interest in subsidiaries		115,000	
Total long-term liabilities			1,055,000

Deferred credits:

Deferred income tax payable		85,500
Total liabilities		$1,955,210

Stockholders' Equity

Paid-in capital:

Common stock, $20 par (250,000 shares authorized,			
100,000 shares issued)	$2,000,000		
Excess of issue price over par	320,000		
Total paid-in capital		$2,320,000	
Retained earnings		1,605,535	
Total stockholders' equity			3,925,535
Total liabilities and stockholders' equity			$5,880,745

The balance in Escoe's discount on bonds payable account is reported as a *deduction* from the bonds payable. Conversely, the balance in a bond premium account would be reported as an *addition* to the related bonds payable. Either on the face of the financial statements or in accompanying notes, a description of the bonds (terms, due date, and effective interest rate) and other relevant information such as sinking fund requirements should be disclosed.[4] Finally, the market (fair) value of the bonds payable should also be disclosed.

Balance Sheet Presentation of Bond Investments

Investments in bonds or other debt securities that management intends to hold to their maturity are called **held-to-maturity securities**. Such securities are classified as long-term investments under the caption Investments. These investments are reported at their cost less any amortized premium or plus any amortized discount. In addition, the market (fair) value of the bond investments should be disclosed, either on the face of the balance sheet or in an accompanying note.

Financial Analysis and Interpretation

objective 9

Compute and interpret the number of times interest charges are earned.

Some corporations, such as railroads and public utilities, have a high ratio of debt to stockholders' equity. For such corporations, analysts often assess the relative risk of the debtholders in terms of the **number of times the interest charges are earned** during the year. The higher the ratio, the greater the chance that interest payments will continue to be made if earnings decrease.[5]

The amount available to make interest payments is not affected by taxes on income. This is because interest is deductible in determining taxable income. To illustrate, the following data were taken from the 2002 annual report of **Briggs & Stratton Corporation**:

Interest expense	$44,433,000
Income before income tax	$80,510,000

The number of times interest charges are earned, 2.81, is calculated below.

$$\text{Number of times interest charges earned} = \frac{\text{Income before income tax} + \text{Interest expense}}{\text{Interest expense}}$$

$$\text{Number of times interest charges earned} = \frac{\$80,510,000 + \$44,433,000}{\$44,433,000} = 2.81$$

The number of times interest charges are earned indicates that the debtholders of Briggs & Stratton have adequate protection against a potential drop in earnings jeopardizing their receipt of interest payments. However, a final assessment should include a review of trends of past years and a comparison with industry averages.

---

[4]*Statement of Financial Accounting Standards No. 129*, "Disclosure Information About Capital Structure," Financial Accounting Standards Board (Norwalk, Connecticut: 1997).

[5]A similar analysis can also be applied to dividends on preferred stock. In such cases, net income would be divided by the amount of preferred dividends to yield the number of times preferred dividends were earned. This measure gives an indication of the relative assurance of continued dividend payments to preferred stockholders.

ppendix ## Effective Interest Rate Method of Amortization

The effective interest rate method of amortizing discounts and premiums provides for a constant rate of interest on the carrying amount of the bonds at the beginning of each period. This is in contrast to the straight-line method, which provides for a constant amount of interest expense.

The interest rate used in the interest method of amortization is the market rate on the date the bonds are issued. The carrying amount of the bonds to which the interest rate is applied is the face amount of the bonds minus any unamortized discount or plus any unamortized premium. Under the interest method, the interest expense to be reported on the income statement is computed by multiplying the effective interest rate by the carrying amount of the bonds. The difference between the interest expense computed in this way and the periodic interest payment is the amount of discount or premium to be amortized for the period.

Amortization of Discount by the Interest Method

To illustrate the interest method for amortizing bond discounts, we assume the following data from the chapter illustration of issuing $100,000 bonds at a discount:

Face value of 12%, 5-year bonds, interest compounded semiannually	$100,000
Present value of bonds at effective (market) rate of interest of 13%	96,406
Discount on bonds payable	$ 3,594

Applying the interest method to these data yields the amortization table in Exhibit 6. You should note the following items in this table:

1. The interest paid (Column A) remains constant at 6% of $100,000, the face amount of the bonds.
2. The interest expense (Column B) is computed at 6½% of the bond carrying amount at the beginning of each period. This results in an increasing interest expense each period.
3. The excess of the interest expense over the interest payment of $6,000 is the amount of discount to be amortized (Column C).

•Exhibit 6 Amortization of Discount on Bonds Payable

Interest Payment	A Interest Paid (6% of Face Amount)	B Interest Expense (6½% of Bond Carrying Amount)	C Discount Amortization (B − A)	D Unamortized Discount (D − C)	E Bond Carrying Amount ($100,000 − D)
				$3,594	$ 96,406
1	$6,000	$6,266 (6½% of $96,406)	$266	3,328	96,672
2	6,000	6,284 (6½% of $96,672)	284	3,044	96,956
3	6,000	6,302 (6½% of $96,956)	302	2,742	97,258
4	6,000	6,322 (6½% of $97,258)	322	2,420	97,580
5	6,000	6,343 (6½% of $97,580)	343	2,077	97,923
6	6,000	6,365 (6½% of $97,923)	365	1,712	98,288
7	6,000	6,389 (6½% of $98,288)	389	1,323	98,677
8	6,000	6,414 (6½% of $98,677)	414	909	99,091
9	6,000	6,441 (6½% of $99,091)	441	468	99,532
10	6,000	6,470 (6½% of $99,532)	468*	—	100,000

*Cannot exceed unamortized discount.

4. The unamortized discount (Column D) decreases from the initial balance, $3,594, to a zero balance at the maturity date of the bonds.
5. The carrying amount (Column E) increases from $96,406, the amount received for the bonds, to $100,000 at maturity.

The entry to record the first interest payment on June 30, 2005, and the related discount amortization is as follows:

2005 June	30	Interest Expense		6 2 6 6 00		
		Discount on Bonds Payable			2 6 6 00	
		Cash			6 0 0 0 00	
		Paid semiannual interest and amortized				
		bond discount for ½ year.				

If the amortization is recorded only at the end of the year, the amount of the discount amortized on December 31 would be $550. This is the sum of the first two semiannual amortization amounts ($266 and $284) from Exhibit 6.

Amortization of Premium by the Interest Method

To illustrate the interest method for amortizing bond premiums, we assume the following data from the chapter illustration of issuing $100,000 bonds at a premium:

Present value of bonds at effective (market) rate of interest of 11%	$103,769
Face value of 12%, 5-year bonds, interest compounded semiannually	100,000
Premium on bonds payable	$ 3,769

Using the interest method to amortize the above premium yields the amortization table in Exhibit 7. You should note the following items in this table:

1. The interest paid (Column A) remains constant at 6% of $100,000, the face amount of the bonds.

•Exhibit 7 Amortization of Premium on Bonds Payable

Interest Payment	A Interest Paid (6% of Face Amount)	B Interest Expense (5½% of Bond Carrying Amount)	C Premium Amortization (A – B)	D Unamortized Premium (D – C)	E Bond Carrying Amount ($100,000 + D)
				$3,769	$103,769
1	$6,000	$5,707 (5½% of $103,769)	$293	3,476	103,476
2	6,000	5,691 (5½% of $103,476)	309	3,167	103,167
3	6,000	5,674 (5½% of $103,167)	326	2,841	102,841
4	6,000	5,656 (5½% of $102,841)	344	2,497	102,497
5	6,000	5,637 (5½% of $102,497)	363	2,134	102,134
6	6,000	5,617 (5½% of $102,134)	383	1,751	101,751
7	6,000	5,596 (5½% of $101,751)	404	1,347	101,347
8	6,000	5,574 (5½% of $101,347)	426	921	100,921
9	6,000	5,551 (5½% of $100,921)	449	472	100,472
10	6,000	5,526 (5½% of $100,472)	472*	—	100,000

*Cannot exceed unamortized premium.

2. The interest expense (Column B) is computed at 5½% of the bond carrying amount at the beginning of each period. This results in a decreasing interest expense each period.
3. The excess of the periodic interest payment of $6,000 over the interest expense is the amount of premium to be amortized (Column C).
4. The unamortized premium (Column D) decreases from the initial balance, $3,769, to a zero balance at the maturity date of the bonds.
5. The carrying amount (Column E) decreases from $103,769, the amount received for the bonds, to $100,000 at maturity.

The entry to record the first interest payment on June 30, 2005, and the related premium amortization is as follows:

2005 June	30	Interest Expense		5 7 0 7 00	
		Premium on Bonds Payable		2 9 3 00	
		Cash			6 0 0 0 00
		Paid semiannual interest and amortized			
		bond premium for ½ year.			

If the amortization is recorded only at the end of the year, the amount of the premium amortized on December 31, 2005, would be $602. This is the sum of the first two semiannual amortization amounts ($293 and $309) from Exhibit 7.

Key Points

1 **Compute the potential impact of long-term borrowing on the earnings per share of a corporation.**

Three alternative plans for financing a corporation by issuing common stock, preferred stock, or bonds are illustrated in Exhibits 1 and 2. The effects of alternative financing on the earnings per share vary significantly, depending upon the level of earnings.

2 **Describe the characteristics of bonds.**

The characteristics of bonds depend upon the type of bonds issued by a corporation. Bonds that may be issued include term bonds, serial bonds, convertible bonds, callable bonds, and debenture bonds.

3 **Compute the present value of bonds payable.**

The concept of present value is based on the time value of money. That is, an amount of cash to be received at some date in the future is worth less than the same amount of cash held today. For example, if $100 cash today can be invested to earn 10% per year, the $100 today is referred to as the present value amount that is equal to $110 to be received a year from today.

A price that a buyer is willing to pay for a bond is the sum of (1) the present value of the face amount of the bonds at the maturity date and (2) the present value of the periodic interest payments.

4 **Journalize entries for bonds payable.**

The journal entry for issuing bonds payable debits Cash for the proceeds received and credits Bonds Payable for the face amount of the bonds. Any difference between the face amount of the bonds and the proceeds is debited to Discount on Bonds Payable or credited to Premium on Bonds Payable.

A discount or premium on bonds payable is amortized to interest expense over the life of the bonds. The entry to amortize a discount debits Interest Expense and credits Discount on Bonds Payable. The entry to amortize a premium debits Premium on Bonds Payable and credits Interest Expense.

5 **Describe bond sinking funds.**

A bond indenture may require that funds for the payment of the bonds at maturity be set aside over the life of the bonds. The amounts set aside are kept separate from other assets in a special fund called a sinking fund. A sinking fund is reported as an Investment on the balance sheet. Income from a sinking fund is reported as Other Income on the income statement.

6 **Journalize entries for bond redemptions.**

When a corporation redeems bonds, Bonds Payable is debited for the face amount of the bonds, the premium (discount) on bonds account is debited (credited) for its balance, Cash is credited, and any gain or loss on the redemption is recorded.

7 **Journalize entries for the purchase, interest, discount and premium amortization, and sale of bond investments.**

A long-term investment in bonds is recorded by debiting Investment in Bonds. When bonds are purchased between interest dates, the amount of the interest paid should be debited to Interest Revenue. Any discount or premium on bond investments should be amortized, using the straight-line or effective in-terest rate methods. The amortization of a discount is recorded by debiting Investment in Bonds and crediting Interest Revenue. The amortization of a premium is recorded by debiting Interest Revenue and crediting Investment in Bonds.

When bonds held as long-term investments are sold, any discount or premium for the current period should first be amortized. Cash is then debited for the proceeds of the sale, Investment in Bonds is credited for its balance, and any gain or loss is recorded.

8 **Prepare a corporation balance sheet.**

The corporation balance sheet may include bond sinking funds, investments in bonds, goodwill, deferred income taxes, bonds payable and unamortized premium or discount, and minority interest in subsidiaries.

Bonds payable are usually reported as long-term liabilities. A discount on bonds should be reported as a deduction from the related bonds payable. A premium on bonds should be reported as an addition to the related bonds payable. Investments in bonds that are held-to-maturity securities are reported as Investments at cost less any amortized premium or plus any amortized discount.

9 **Compute and interpret the number of times interest charges are earned.**

The number of times interest charges are earned during the year is a measure of the risk that interest payments to debtholders will continue to be made if earnings decrease. It is computed by dividing income before income tax plus interest expense by interest expense.

Key Terms

annuity (526)
bond (522)
bond indenture (523)
carrying amount (533)
contract rate (524)
discount (524)

effective interest rate method (530)
effective rate of interest (524)
future value (525)
held-to-maturity securities (538)
number of times interest charges
   are earned (538)

premium (524)
present value (525)
present value of an annuity (526)
sinking fund (532)

Illustrative Problem

The fiscal year of Russell Inc., a manufacturer of acoustical supplies, ends December 31. Selected transactions for the period 2005 through 2012, involving bonds payable issued by Russell Inc., are as follows:

2005
June 30. Issued $2,000,000 of 25-year, 7% callable bonds dated June 30, 2005, for cash of $1,920,000. Interest is payable semiannually on June 30 and December 31.
Dec. 31. Paid the semiannual interest on the bonds.
    31. Recorded straight-line amortization of $1,600 of discount on the bonds.
    31. Closed the interest expense account.

2006
June 30. Paid the semiannual interest on the bonds.
Dec. 31. Paid the semiannual interest on the bonds.
    31. Recorded straight-line amortization of $3,200 of discount on the bonds.
    31. Closed the interest expense account.

2012
June 30. Recorded the redemption of the bonds, which were called at 101.5. The balance in the bond discount account is $57,600 after the payment of interest and amortization of discount have been recorded. (Record the redemption only.)

Instructions

1. Journalize entries to record the preceding transactions.
2. Determine the amount of interest expense for 2005 and 2006.
3. Estimate the effective annual interest rate by dividing the interest expense for 2005 by the bond carrying amount at the time of issuance and multiplying by 2.
4. Determine the carrying amount of the bonds as of December 31, 2006.

Solution

1.

2005				
June	30	Cash	1,920 0 0 0 00	
		Discount on Bonds Payable	80 0 0 0 00	
		Bonds Payable		2,000 0 0 0 00
Dec.	31	Interest Expense	70 0 0 0 00	
		Cash		70 0 0 0 00

(continued)

2005 Dec.	31	Interest Expense	1 6 0 0 00		
		Discount on Bonds Payable		1 6 0 0 00	
	31	Income Summary	71 6 0 0 00		
		Interest Expense		71 6 0 0 00	
2006 June	30	Interest Expense	70 0 0 0 00		
		Cash		70 0 0 0 00	
Dec.	31	Interest Expense	70 0 0 0 00		
		Cash		70 0 0 0 00	
	31	Interest Expense	3 2 0 0 00		
		Discount on Bonds Payable		3 2 0 0 00	
	31	Income Summary	143 2 0 0 00		
		Interest Expense		143 2 0 0 00	
2012 June	30	Bonds Payable	2,000 0 0 0 00		
		Loss on Redemption of Bonds Payable	87 6 0 0 00		
		Discount on Bonds Payable		57 6 0 0 00	
		Cash		2,030 0 0 0 00	

2. a. 2005—$71,600
   b. 2006—$143,200

3. $71,600 ÷ $1,920,000 = 3.73% rate for six months of a year
   3.73% × 2 = 7.46% annual rate

4. Initial carrying amount of bonds $1,920,000
   Discount amortized on December 31, 2005   1,600
   Discount amortized on December 31, 2006   3,200
   Carrying amount of bonds, December 31, 2006 $1,924,800

Self-Examination Questions (Answers at End of Chapter)

1. If a corporation plans to issue $1,000,000 of 12% bonds at a time when the market rate for similar bonds is 10%, the bonds can be expected to sell at:
   A. their face amount
   B. a premium
   C. a discount
   D. a price below their face amount

2. If the bonds payable account has a balance of $500,000 and the discount on bonds payable account has a balance of $40,000, what is the carrying amount of the bonds?
   A. $460,000   C. $540,000
   B. $500,000   D. $580,000

3. The cash and securities that make up the sinking fund established for the payment of bonds at maturity are classified on the balance sheet as:

   A. current assets   C. long-term liabilities
   B. investments   D. current liabilities

4. If a firm purchases $100,000 of bonds of X Company at 101 plus accrued interest of $2,000 and pays broker's commissions of $50, the amount debited to Investment in X Company Bonds would be:
   A. $100,000   C. $103,000
   B. $101,050   D. $103,050

5. The balance in the discount on bonds payable account would usually be reported in the balance sheet in the:
   A. Current Assets section
   B. Current Liabilities section
   C. Long-Term Liabilities section
   D. Investments section

Class Discussion Questions

1. Describe the two distinct obligations incurred by a corporation when issuing bonds.
2. Explain the meaning of each of the following terms as they relate to a bond issue: (a) convertible, (b) callable, and (c) debenture.
3. What is meant by the "time value of money"?
4. What has the higher present value: (a) $10,000 to be received at the end of two years, or (b) $5,000 to be received at the end of each of the next two years?
5. If you asked your broker to purchase for you a 7% bond when the market interest rate for such bonds was 8%, would you expect to pay more or less than the face amount for the bond? Explain.
6. A corporation issues $7,500,000 of 8% bonds to yield interest at the rate of 7%. (a) Was the amount of cash received from the sale of the bonds greater or less than $7,500,000? (b) Identify the following terms related to the bond issue: (1) face amount, (2) market or effective rate of interest, (3) contract rate of interest, and (4) maturity amount.
7. If bonds issued by a corporation are sold at a premium, is the market rate of interest greater or less than the contract rate?
8. The following data relate to a $1,800,000, 6% bond issue for a selected semi-annual interest period:

Bond carrying amount at beginning of period	$1,850,000
Interest paid during period	108,000
Interest expense allocable to the period	104,400

   (a) Were the bonds issued at a discount or at a premium? (b) What is the unamortized amount of the discount or premium account at the beginning of the period? (c) What account was debited to amortize the discount or premium?
9. Assume that Mixon Co. amortizes premiums and discounts on bonds payable at the end of the year rather than when interest is paid. What accounts would be debited and credited to record (a) the amortization of a discount on bonds payable and (b) the amortization of a premium on bonds payable?
10. Would a zero-coupon bond ever sell for its face amount?
11. What is the purpose of a bond sinking fund?
12. Assume that two 25-year, 6% bond issues are identical, except that one bond issue is callable at its face amount at the end of 5 years. Which of the two bond issues do you think will sell for a lower value?
13. Bonds Payable has a balance of $800,000, and Discount on Bonds Payable has a balance of $32,500. If the issuing corporation redeems the bonds at 97, is there a gain or loss on the bond redemption?
14. Where are investments in bonds that are classified as held-to-maturity securities reported on the balance sheet?
15. At what amount are held-to-maturity investments in bonds reported on the balance sheet?

Exercises

EXERCISE 13-1
Effect of financing on earnings per share

Objective 1

✓ a. $0.48

Bridger Co., which produces and sells skiing equipment, is financed as follows:

Bonds payable, 8% (issued at face amount)	$8,000,000
Preferred $3 stock (nonparticipating), $50 par	8,000,000
Common stock, $40 par	8,000,000

Income tax is estimated at 40% of income.

Determine the earnings per share of common stock, assuming that the income before bond interest and income tax is (a) $1,600,000, (b) $2,400,000, and (c) $4,000,000.

EXERCISE 13-2
Evaluate alternative financing plans

Objective 1

⟶ Based upon the data in Exercise 13-1, discuss factors other than earnings per share that should be considered in evaluating such financing plans.

EXERCISE 13-3
Corporate financing

Objective 1

REAL WORLD

The financial statements for **Home Depot** are presented in Appendix F at the end of the text. What is the major source of financing for Home Depot?

EXERCISE 13-4
Present value of amounts due

Objective 3

Determine the present value of $100,000 to be received in three years, using an interest rate of 5%, compounded annually, as follows:

a. By successive divisions. (Round to the nearest dollar.)
b. By using the present value table in Exhibit 3.

EXERCISE 13-5
Present value of annuity

Objective 3

Determine the present value of $50,000 to be received at the end of each of four years, using an interest rate of 6%, compounded annually, as follows:

a. By successive computations, using the present value table in Exhibit 3.
b. By using the present value table in Exhibit 4.

EXERCISE 13-6
Present value of an annuity
Objective 3

On January 1, 2006, you win $25,000,000 in the state lottery. The $25,000,000 prize will be paid in equal installments of $1,000,000 over 25 years. The payments will be made on December 31 of each year, beginning on December 31, 2006. If the current interest rate is 6%, determine the present value of your winnings. Use the present value tables in Appendix A.

EXERCISE 13-7
Present value of an annuity
Objective 3

Assume the same data as in Exercise 13-6, except that the current interest rate is 12%.
⬤▭▭▭▶ Will the present value of your winnings using an interest rate of 12% be one-half the present value of your winnings using an interest rate of 6%? Why or why not?

EXERCISE 13-8
Present value of bonds payable; discount
Objectives 3, 4

Fowler Co. produces and sells bottle capping equipment for soft drink and spring water bottlers. To finance its operations, Fowler Co. issued $12,000,000 of five-year, 8% bonds with interest payable semiannually at an effective interest rate of 12%. Determine the present value of the bonds payable, using the present value tables in Exhibits 3 and 4. Round to the nearest dollar.

EXERCISE 13-9
Present value of bonds payable; premium
Objectives 3, 4

Hallelujah Alarms Co. issued $40,000,000 of five-year, 11% bonds with interest payable semiannually, at an effective interest rate of 10%. Determine the present value of the bonds payable, using the present value tables in Exhibits 3 and 4. Round to the nearest dollar.

EXERCISE 13-10
Bond price
Objectives 3, 4

REAL WORLD

Walt Disney 2.125% bonds due in 2023 were reported in *The Wall Street Journal* as selling for 103.536.
⬤▭▭▭▶ Were the bonds selling at a premium or at a discount? Explain.

EXERCISE 13-11
Entries for issuing bonds
Objective 4

Darigold Co. produces and distributes fiber optic cable for use by telecommunications companies. Darigold Co. issued $18,000,000 of 15-year, 7% bonds on April 1 of the current year, with interest payable on May 1 and November 1. The fiscal year of the company is the calendar year. Journalize the entries to record the following selected transactions for the current year:

May   1. Issued the bonds for cash at their face amount.
Nov. 1. Paid the interest on the bonds.
Dec. 31. Recorded accrued interest for two months.

EXERCISE 13-12
Entries for issuing bonds and amortizing discount by straight-line method
Objective 4
✓ b. $820,904

On the first day of its fiscal year, Monarch Company issued $8,000,000 of five-year, 8% bonds to finance its operations of producing and selling home electronics equipment. Interest is payable semiannually. The bonds were issued at an effective interest rate of 11%, resulting in Monarch Company receiving cash of $7,095,482.

a. Journalize the entries to record the following:
   1. Sale of the bonds.
   2. First semiannual interest payment. ~~(Amortization of discount is to be recorded~~ *semi* ~~annually.)~~
   3. Second semiannual interest payment.
   4. ~~Amortization of discount at~~ the end of the first year, using the straight-line method. (Round to the nearest dollar.)
b. Determine the amount of the bond interest expense for the first year.

EXERCISE 13-13
*Computing bond proceeds,
entries for bond issuing,
and amortizing premium by
straight-line method*
Objectives 3, 4

Snodgrass Corporation wholesales oil and grease products to equipment manufacturers. On March 1, 2006, Snodgrass Corporation issued $7,500,000 of five-year, 11% bonds at an effective interest rate of 10%. Interest is payable semiannually on March 1 and September 1. Journalize the entries to record the following:

a. Sale of bonds on March 1, 2006. (Use the tables of present values in Exhibits 3 and 4 to determine the bond proceeds. Round to the nearest dollar.)
b. First interest payment on September 1, 2006, and amortization of bond premium for six months, using the straight-line method. (Round to the nearest dollar.)

EXERCISE 13-14
*Entries for issuing and
calling bonds; loss*
Objectives 4, 6

Buffalo Corp., a wholesaler of office furniture, issued $12,000,000 of 30-year, 8% callable bonds on April 1, 2006, with interest payable on April 1 and October 1. The fiscal year of the company is the calendar year. Journalize the entries to record the following selected transactions:

2006
Apr. 1. Issued the bonds for cash at their face amount.
Oct. 1. Paid the interest on the bonds.
2010
Oct. 1. Called the bond issue at 102, the rate provided in the bond indenture. (Omit entry for payment of interest.)

EXERCISE 13-15
*Entries for issuing and
calling bonds; gain*
Objectives 4, 6

Safeguard Corp. produces and sells automotive and aircraft safety belts. To finance its operations, Safeguard Corp. issued $18,000,000 of 25-year, 9% callable bonds on January 1, 2006, with interest payable on January 1 and July 1. The fiscal year of the company is the calendar year. Journalize the entries to record the following selected transactions:

2006
Jan. 1. Issued the bonds for cash at their face amount.
July 1. Paid the interest on the bonds.
2012
July 1. Called the bond issue at 101, the price provided in the bond indenture. (Omit entry for payment of interest.)

EXERCISE 13-16
Reporting bonds
Objectives 5, 6, 8

WHAT'S WRONG
WITH THIS?

At the beginning of the current year, two bond issues (X and Y) were outstanding. During the year, bond issue X was redeemed and a significant loss on the redemption of bonds was reported as an extraordinary item on the income statement. At the end of the year, bond issue Y was reported as a current liability because its maturity date was early in the following year. A sinking fund of cash and securities sufficient to pay the series Y bonds was reported in the balance sheet as *Investments*. Identify the flaws in the reporting practices related to the two bond issues.

EXERCISE 13-17
*Amortizing discount on
bond investment*
Objective 7

A company purchased a $1,000, 20-year zero-coupon bond for $189 to yield 8.5% to maturity. How is the interest revenue computed?

EXERCISE 13-18
*Entries for purchase and
sale of investment in bonds;
loss*
Objective 7

Laser Vision Co. sells optical supplies to opticians and ophthalmologists. Journalize the entries to record the following selected transactions of Laser Vision Co.:

a. Purchased for cash $450,000 of Pierce Co. 8% bonds at 101½ plus accrued interest of $9,000.
b. Received first semiannual interest.
c. At the end of the first year, amortized $540 of the bond premium.
d. Sold the bonds at 99 plus accrued interest of $3,000. The bonds were carried at $453,750 at the time of the sale.

EXERCISE 13-19
Entries for purchase and sale of investment in bonds; gain

Objective 7

Inez Company develops and sells graphics software for use by architects. Journalize the entries to record the following selected transactions of Inez Company:

a. Purchased for cash $270,000 of Theisen Co. 5% bonds at 98 plus accrued interest of $2,250.
b. Received first semiannual interest.
c. Amortized $450 on the bond investment at the end of the first year.
d. Sold the bonds at 100 plus accrued interest of $4,500. The bonds were carried at $267,250 at the time of the sale.

EXERCISE 13-20
Number of times interest charges earned

Objective 9

REAL WORLD

The following data were taken from recent annual reports of **Southwest Airlines**, which operates a low-fare airline service to over 50 cities in the U.S.

	Current Year	Preceding Year
Interest expense	$106,023,000	$ 69,827,000
Income before income tax	392,682,000	827,659,000

a. Determine the number of times interest charges were earned for the current and preceding years. Round to one decimal place.
b. What conclusions can you draw?

APPENDIX
EXERCISE 13-21
Amortize discount by interest method

✓ b. $784,367

On the first day of its fiscal year, Monarch Company issued $8,000,000 of five-year, 8% bonds to finance its operations of producing and selling home electronics equipment. Interest is payable semiannually. The bonds were issued at an effective interest rate of 11%, resulting in Monarch Company receiving cash of $7,095,482.

a. Journalize the entries to record the following:
   1. Sale of the bonds.
   2. First semiannual interest payment. (Amortization of discount is to be recorded annually.)
   3. Second semiannual interest payment.
   4. Amortization of discount at the end of the first year, using the interest method. (Round to the nearest dollar.)
b. Compute the amount of the bond interest expense for the first year.

APPENDIX
EXERCISE 13-22
Amortize premium by interest method

✓ b. $777,803

Snodgrass Corporation wholesales oil and grease products to equipment manufacturers. On March 1, 2006, Snodgrass Corporation issued $7,500,000 of five-year, 11% bonds at an effective interest rate of 10%, receiving cash of $7,789,543. Interest is payable semiannually on March 1 and September 1. Snodgrass Corporation's fiscal year begins on March 1.

a. Journalize the entries to record the following:
   1. First interest payment on September 1, 2006. (Amortization of premium is to be recorded annually.)
   2. Second interest payment on March 1, 2007.
   3. Amortization of premium at the end of the first year, using the interest method. (Round to the nearest dollar.)
b. Determine the bond interest expense for the first year.

APPENDIX
EXERCISE 13-23
Compute bond proceeds, amortizing premium by interest method, and interest expense

✓ a. $33,724,853
✓ b. $95,133

Federated Paint Co. produces and sells spray painting equipment for construction contractors. On the first day of its fiscal year, Federated Paint Co. issued $32,500,000 of five-year, 12% bonds at an effective interest rate of 11%, with interest payable semiannually. Compute the following, presenting figures used in your computations.

a. The amount of cash proceeds from the sale of the bonds. (Use the tables of present values in Exhibits 3 and 4. Round to the nearest dollar.)
b. The amount of premium to be amortized for the first semiannual interest payment period, using the interest method. (Round to the nearest dollar.)

(continued)

c. The amount of premium to be amortized for the second semiannual interest payment period, using the interest method. (Round to the nearest dollar.)

d. The amount of the bond interest expense for the first year.

APPENDIX EXERCISE 13-24

Compute bond proceeds, amortizing discount by interest method, and interest expense

 a. $16,212,079

✓ b. $97,725

La Porte Co. produces and sells concrete mixing equipment. On the first day of its fiscal year, La Porte Co. issued $17,500,000 of five-year, 10% bonds at an effective interest rate of 12%, with interest payable semiannually. Compute the following, presenting figures used in your computations.

a. The amount of cash proceeds from the sale of the bonds. (Use the tables of present values in Exhibits 3 and 4.)

b. The amount of discount to be amortized for the first semiannual interest payment period, using the interest method. (Round to the nearest dollar.)

c. The amount of discount to be amortized for the second semiannual interest payment period, using the interest method. (Round to the nearest dollar.)

d. The amount of the bond interest expense for the first year.

Problems Series A

PROBLEM 13-1A
Effect of financing on earnings per share

Objective 1

SPREADSHEET

✓ 1. Plan 3: $8.10

Three different plans for financing a $20,000,000 corporation are under consideration by its organizers. Under each of the following plans, the securities will be issued at their par or face amount, and the income tax rate is estimated at 40% of income.

	Plan 1	Plan 2	Plan 3
10% bonds			$10,000,000
Preferred 6% stock, $100 par		$10,000,000	5,000,000
Common stock, $5 par	$20,000,000	10,000,000	5,000,000
Total	$20,000,000	$20,000,000	$20,000,000

Instructions

1. Determine for each plan the earnings per share of common stock, assuming that the income before bond interest and income tax is $15,000,000.

2. Determine for each plan the earnings per share of common stock, assuming that the income before bond interest and income tax is $1,600,000.

3. ▬▬➤ Discuss the advantages and disadvantages of each plan.

PROBLEM 13-2A
Present value; bond premium; entries for bonds payable transactions

Objectives 3, 4

P.A.S.S.

✓ 3. $483,920

Rest-In-Peace Corporation produces and sells burial vaults. On July 1, 2006, Rest-In-Peace Corporation issued $9,000,000 of ten-year, 12% bonds at an effective interest rate of 10%. Interest on the bonds is payable semiannually on December 31 and June 30. The fiscal year of the company is the calendar year.

Instructions

1. Journalize the entry to record the amount of the cash proceeds from the sale of the bonds. Use the tables of present values in Appendix A to compute the cash proceeds, rounding to the nearest dollar.

2. Journalize the entries to record the following:

   a. The first semiannual interest payment on December 31, 2006, and the amortization of the bond premium, using the straight-line method. (Round to the nearest dollar.)

   b. The interest payment on June 30, 2007, and the amortization of the bond premium, using the straight-line method.

3. Determine the total interest expense for 2006.

4. ▬▬➤ Will the bond proceeds always be greater than the face amount of the bonds when the contract rate is greater than the market rate of interest? Explain.

PROBLEM 13-3A
Present value; bond discount; entries for bonds payable transactions

Objectives 3, 4

P.A.S.S.

✓ *3. $668,822*

On July 1, 2005, Westwind Corporation, a wholesaler of used robotic equipment, issued $12,000,000 of ten-year, 10% bonds at an effective interest rate of 12%. Interest on the bonds is payable semiannually on December 31 and June 30. The fiscal year of the company is the calendar year.

Instructions

1. Journalize the entry to record the amount of the cash proceeds from the sale of the bonds. Use the tables of present values in Appendix A to compute the cash proceeds, rounding to the nearest dollar.
2. Journalize the entries to record the following:
   a. The first semiannual interest payment on December 31, 2005, and the amortization of the bond discount, using the straight-line method. (Round to the nearest dollar.)
   b. The interest payment on June 30, 2006, and the amortization of the bond discount, using the straight-line method.
3. Determine the total interest expense for 2005.
4. Will the bond proceeds always be less than the face amount of the bonds when the contract rate is less than the market rate of interest? Explain.

PROBLEM 13-4A
Entries for bonds payable transactions

Objectives 4, 6

SPREADSHEET
P.A.S.S.

✓ *2. a. $381,776*

The following transactions were completed by Prairie Renaissance Inc., whose fiscal year is the calendar year:

2005
July 1. Issued $8,000,000 of 5-year, 8% callable bonds dated July 1, 2005, at an effective rate of 10%, receiving cash of $7,382,236. Interest is payable semiannually on December 31 and June 30.
Dec. 31. Paid the semiannual interest on the bonds.
     31. Recorded bond discount amortization of $61,776, which was determined by using the straight-line method.
     31. Closed the interest expense account.

2006
June 30. Paid the semiannual interest on the bonds.
Dec. 31. Paid the semiannual interest on the bonds.
     31. Recorded bond discount amortization of $123,552, which was determined by using the straight-line method.
     31. Closed the interest expense account.

2007
June 30. Recorded the redemption of the bonds, which were called at 99. The balance in the bond discount account is $370,660 after payment of interest and amortization of discount have been recorded. (Record the redemption only.)

Instructions

1. Journalize the entries to record the foregoing transactions.
2. Indicate the amount of the interest expense in (a) 2005 and (b) 2006.
3. Determine the carrying amount of the bonds as of December 31, 2006.

PROBLEM 13-5A
Entries for bond investments

Objective 7

SPREADSHEET
P.A.S.S.

Danka Inc. develops and leases databases of publicly available information. The following selected transactions relate to certain securities acquired as a long-term investment by Danka Inc., whose fiscal year ends on December 31:

2005
Sept. 1. Purchased $480,000 of Sheehan Company 10-year, 8% bonds dated July 1, 2005, directly from the issuing company, for $494,750 plus accrued interest of $6,400.
Dec. 31. Received the semiannual interest on the Sheehan Company bonds.
     31. Recorded bond premium amortization of $500 on the Sheehan Company bonds. The amortization amount was determined by using the straight-line method.

(Assume that all intervening transactions and adjustments have been properly recorded and that the number of bonds owned has not changed from December 31, 2005, to December 31, 2010.)

2011

June 30. Received the semiannual interest on the Sheehan Company bonds.

Aug. 31. Sold one-half of the Sheehan Company bonds at 102 plus accrued interest. The broker deducted $400 for commission, etc., remitting the balance. Prior to the sale, $500 of premium on one-half of the bonds is to be amortized, reducing the carrying amount of those bonds to $242,875.

Dec. 31. Received the semiannual interest on the Sheehan Company bonds.

31. Recorded bond premium amortization of $750 on the Sheehan Company bonds.

Instructions

Journalize the entries to record the foregoing transactions.

APPENDIX
PROBLEM 13-6A
Entries for bonds payable transactions; interest method of amortizing bond premium

✓ 2. $506,080

Rest-In-Peace Corporation produces and sells burial vaults. On July 1, 2006, Rest-In-Peace Corporation issued $9,000,000 of ten-year, 12% bonds at an effective interest rate of 10%, receiving proceeds of $10,121,603. Interest on the bonds is payable semiannually on December 31 and June 30. The fiscal year of the company is the calendar year.

Instructions

1. Journalize the entries to record the following:
   a. The first semiannual interest payment on December 31, 2006, and the amortization of the bond premium, using the interest method. (Round to nearest dollar.)
   b. The interest payment on June 30, 2007, and the amortization of the bond premium, using the interest method. (Round to nearest dollar.)
2. Determine the total interest expense for 2006.

APPENDIX
PROBLEM 13-7A
Entries for bonds payable transactions; interest method of amortizing bond discount

✓ 2. $637,413

On July 1, 2005, Westwind Corporation, a wholesaler of used robotic equipment, issued $12,000,000 of ten-year, 10% bonds at an effective interest rate of 12%, receiving proceeds of $10,623,552. Interest on the bonds is payable semiannually on December 31 and June 30. The fiscal year of the company is the calendar year.

Instructions

1. Journalize the entries to record the following:
   a. The first semiannual interest payment on December 31, 2005, and the amortization of the bond discount, using the interest method. (Round to nearest dollar.)
   b. The interest payment on June 30, 2006, and the amortization of the bond discount, using the interest method. (Round to nearest dollar.)
2. Determine the total interest expense for 2005.

Problems Series

PROBLEM 13-1B
Effect of financing on earnings per share
Objective 1

SPREADSHEET

✓ 1. Plan 3: $2.60

Three different plans for financing a $27,000,000 corporation are under consideration by its organizers. Under each of the following plans, the securities will be issued at their par or face amount, and the income tax rate is estimated at 40% of income.

	Plan 1	Plan 2	Plan 3
12% bonds			$11,250,000
Preferred $4 stock, $50 par		$13,500,000	9,000,000
Common stock, $15 par	$27,000,000	13,500,000	6,750,000
Total	$27,000,000	$27,000,000	$27,000,000

Instructions

1. Determine for each plan the earnings per share of common stock, assuming that the income before bond interest and income tax is $4,500,000.
2. Determine for each plan the earnings per share of common stock, assuming that the income before bond interest and income tax is $2,700,000.
3. ▭▶ Discuss the advantages and disadvantages of each plan.

PROBLEM 13-2B

Present value; bond premium; entries for bonds payable transactions

Objectives 3, 4

P.A.S.S.

✓ 3. $1,037,688

Frontier Inc. produces and sells voltage regulators. On July 1, 2005, Frontier Inc. is-sued $20,000,000 of ten-year, 11% bonds at an effective interest rate of 10%. Inter-est on the bonds is payable semiannually on December 31 and June 30. The fiscal year of the company is the calendar year.

Instructions

1. Journalize the entry to record the amount of the cash proceeds from the sale of the bonds. Use the tables of present values in Appendix A to compute the cash proceeds, rounding to the nearest dollar.
2. Journalize the entries to record the following:
   a. The first semiannual interest payment on December 31, 2005, including the amortization of the bond premium, using the straight-line method.
   b. The interest payment on June 30, 2006, and the amortization of the bond pre-mium, using the straight-line method.
3. Determine the total interest expense for 2005.
4. ▭▶ Will the bond proceeds always be greater than the face amount of the bonds when the contract rate is greater than the market rate of interest? Explain.

PROBLEM 13-3B

Present value; bond discount; entries for bonds payable transactions

Objectives 3, 4

P.A.S.S.

✓ 3. $866,080

On July 1, 2005, Lamar Communications Equipment Inc. issued $18,000,000 of ten-year, 9% bonds at an effective interest rate of 10%. Interest on the bonds is payable semiannually on December 31 and June 30. The fiscal year of the company is the calendar year.

Instructions

1. Journalize the entry to record the amount of the cash proceeds from the sale of the bonds. Use the tables of present values in Appendix A to compute the cash proceeds, rounding to the nearest dollar.
2. Journalize the entries to record the following:
   a. The first semiannual interest payment on December 31, 2005, and the amorti-zation of the bond discount, using the straight-line method. (Round to the near-est dollar.)
   b. The interest payment on June 30, 2006, and the amortization of the bond dis-count, using the straight-line method.
3. Determine the total interest expense for 2005.
4. ▭▶ Will the bond proceeds always be less than the face amount of the bonds when the contract rate is less than the market rate of interest? Explain.

PROBLEM 13-4B

Entries for bonds payable transactions

Objectives 4, 6

SPREADSHEET
P.A.S.S.

✓ 2. a. $939,591

Absaroka Co. produces and sells synthetic string for tennis rackets. The following transactions were completed by Absaroka Co., whose fiscal year is the calendar year:

2005
July 1. Issued $15,000,000 of 5-year, 14% callable bonds dated July 1, 2005, at an effective rate of 12%, receiving cash of $16,104,095. Interest is payable semiannually on December 31 and June 30.
Dec. 31. Paid the semiannual interest on the bonds.
31. Recorded bond premium amortization of $110,409, which was deter-mined by using the straight-line method.
31. Closed the interest expense account.
2006
June 30. Paid the semiannual interest on the bonds.
Dec. 31. Paid the semiannual interest on the bonds.

Dec. 31. Recorded bond premium amortization of $220,818, which was determined by using the straight-line method.

31. Closed the interest expense account.

2007

July 1. Recorded the redemption of the bonds, which were called at 101. The balance in the bond premium account is $662,459 after the payment of interest and amortization of premium have been recorded. (Record the redemption only.)

Instructions

1. Journalize the entries to record the foregoing transactions.
2. Indicate the amount of the interest expense in (a) 2005 and (b) 2006.
3. Determine the carrying amount of the bonds as of December 31, 2006.

PROBLEM 13-5B
Entries for bond investments

Objective 7

SPREADSHEET
P.A.S.S.

The following selected transactions relate to certain securities acquired by Wildflower Blueprints Inc., whose fiscal year ends on December 31:

2005

Sept. 1. Purchased $400,000 of Churchill Company 20-year, 9% bonds dated July 1, 2005, directly from the issuing company, for $385,720 plus accrued interest of $6,000.

Dec. 31. Received the semiannual interest on the Churchill Company bonds.

31. Recorded bond discount amortization of $240 on the Churchill Company bonds. The amortization amount was determined by using the straight-line method.

(Assume that all intervening transactions and adjustments have been properly recorded and that the number of bonds owned has not changed from December 31, 2005, to December 31, 2009.)

2010

June 30. Received the semiannual interest on the Churchill Company bonds.

Oct. 31. Sold one-half of the Churchill Company bonds at 96½ plus accrued interest. The broker deducted $400 for commission, etc., remitting the balance. Prior to the sale, $300 of discount on one-half of the bonds was amortized, reducing the carrying amount of those bonds to $194,720.

Dec. 31. Received the semiannual interest on the Churchill Company bonds.

31. Recorded bond discount amortization of $360 on the Churchill Company bonds.

Instructions

Journalize the entries to record the foregoing transactions.

APPENDIX PROBLEM 13-6B
Entries for bonds payable transactions; interest method of amortizing bond premium

✓ 2. $1,062,312

Frontier Inc. produces and sells voltage regulators. On July 1, 2005, Frontier Inc. issued $20,000,000 of ten-year, 11% bonds at an effective interest rate of 10%, receiving proceeds of $21,246,231. Interest on the bonds is payable semiannually on December 31 and June 30. The fiscal year of the company is the calendar year.

Instructions

1. Journalize the entries to record the following:
   a. The first semiannual interest payment on December 31, 2005, and the amortization of the bond premium, using the interest method. (Round to nearest dollar.)
   b. The interest payment on June 30, 2006, and the amortization of the bond premium, using the interest method. (Round to nearest dollar.)
2. Determine the total interest expense for 2005.

APPENDIX PROBLEM 13-7B
Entries for bonds payable transactions; interest method of amortizing bond discount

On July 1, 2005, Lamar Communications Equipment Inc. issued $18,000,000 of ten-year, 9% bonds at an effective interest rate of 10%, receiving proceeds of $16,878,410. Interest on the bonds is payable semiannually on December 31 and June 30. The fiscal year of the company is the calendar year.

✓2. $843,921

Instructions

1. Journalize the entries to record the following:
   a. The first semiannual interest payment on December 31, 2005, and the amortization of the bond discount, using the interest method.
   b. The interest payment on June 30, 2006, and the amortization of the bond discount, using the interest method.
2. Determine the total interest expense for 2005.

Comprehensive Problem 4

✓2.a. Net income, $177,800

Selected transactions completed by Hubcap Products Inc. during the fiscal year ending July 31, 2006, were as follows:

a. Issued 10,000 shares of $25 par common stock at $52, receiving cash.
b. Issued 8,000 shares of $100 par preferred 8% stock at $125, receiving cash.
c. Issued $12,000,000 of 10-year, 11% bonds at an effective interest rate of 10%, with interest payable semiannually. Use the present value tables in Appendix A to determine the bond proceeds. Round to the nearest dollar.
d. Declared a dividend of $0.25 per share on common stock and $2 per share on preferred stock. On the date of record, 100,000 shares of common stock were outstanding, no treasury shares were held, and 15,000 shares of preferred stock were outstanding.
e. Paid the cash dividends declared in (d).
f. Redeemed $400,000 of 8-year, 12% bonds at 101. The balance in the bond premium account is $4,920 after the payment of interest and amortization of premium have been recorded. (Record only the redemption of the bonds payable.)
g. Purchased 5,000 shares of treasury common stock at $50 per share.
h. Declared a 2% stock dividend on common stock and a $2 cash dividend per share on preferred stock. On the date of declaration, the market value of the common stock was $51 per share. On the date of record, 100,000 shares of common stock had been issued, 5,000 shares of treasury common stock were held, and 15,000 shares of preferred stock had been issued.
i. Issued the stock certificates for the stock dividends declared in (h) and paid the cash dividends to the preferred stockholders.
j. Purchased $120,000 of Athens Sports Inc. 10-year, 15% bonds, directly from the issuing company, for $116,400 plus accrued interest of $4,500.
k. Sold, at $58 per share, 3,000 shares of treasury common stock purchased in (g).
l. Recorded the payment of semiannual interest on the bonds issued in (c) and the amortization of the premium for six months. The amortization was determined using the straight-line method. (Round the amortization to the nearest dollar.)
m. Accrued interest for four months on the Athens Sports Inc. bonds purchased in (j). Also recorded amortization of $120.

Instructions

1. Journalize the selected transactions.
2. After all of the transactions for the year ended July 31, 2006, had been posted (including the transactions recorded in (1) and all adjusting entries), the data on the following page were taken from the records of Hubcap Products Inc.
   a. Prepare a multiple-step income statement for the year ended July 31, 2006, concluding with earnings per share. In computing earnings per share, assume that the average number of common shares outstanding was 100,000 and preferred dividends were $105,000. Round earnings per share to the nearest cent.
   b. Prepare a retained earnings statement for the year ended July 31, 2006.
   c. Prepare a balance sheet in report form as of July 31, 2006.

Income statement data:

Advertising expense	$ 120,000
Cost of merchandise sold	2,799,000
Delivery expense	27,000
Depreciation expense—office buildings and equipment	20,000
Depreciation expense—store buildings and equipment	72,000
Gain on redemption of bonds	920
Income tax:	
Applicable to continuing operations	198,007
Applicable to loss from discontinued operations	80,000
Applicable to gain from redemption of bonds	120
Interest expense	622,613
Interest revenue	1,620
Loss from discontinued operations	200,000
Loss from fixed asset impairment	150,000
Miscellaneous administrative expenses	6,000
Miscellaneous selling expenses	11,000
Office rent expense	40,000
Office salaries expense	136,000
Office supplies expense	8,000
Restructuring charges	75,000
Sales	5,040,000
Sales commissions	156,000
Sales salaries expense	288,000
Store supplies expense	16,000

Retained earnings and balance sheet data:

Accounts payable	$ 175,000
Accounts receivable	450,000
Accumulated depreciation—office buildings and equipment	1,336,520
Accumulated depreciation—store buildings and equipment	3,543,000
Allowance for doubtful accounts	35,000
Bonds payable, 11%, due 2016	12,000,000
Cash	200,000
Common stock, $25 par (400,000 shares authorized;	
101,900 shares outstanding)	2,547,500
Deferred income tax payable (current portion, $7,500)	41,100
Dividends:	
Cash dividends for common stock	55,000
Cash dividends for preferred stock	105,000
Stock dividends for common stock	96,900
Dividends payable	30,000
Employee termination obligation (current)	65,000
Goodwill	432,000
Income tax payable	32,000
Interest receivable	6,000
Investment in Athens Sports Inc. bonds (long-term)	116,520
Merchandise inventory (July 31, 2006), at lower of	
cost (fifo) or market	680,000
Notes receivable	125,000
Office buildings and equipment	5,930,000
Paid-in capital from sale of treasury stock	24,000
Paid-in capital in excess of par—common stock	560,000
Paid-in capital in excess of par—preferred stock	240,000
Preferred 8% stock, $100 par (30,000 shares authorized;	
15,000 shares issued)	1,500,000
Premium on bonds payable	710,352
Prepaid expenses	25,000
Retained earnings, August 1, 2005	1,754,148
Store buildings and equipment	16,450,000
Treasury stock (2,000 shares of common stock at cost	
of $50 per share)	100,000

Special Activities

ACTIVITY 13-1
Business strategy

GROUP ACTIVITY   INTERNET

One reason that **PepsiCo**® purchased **Quaker Oats** in 2001 was to acquire rights to its sports drink, Gatorade. However, Gatorade is under increasing pressure from its competitors, including **Coca-Cola**'s Powerade®. As a result, PepsiCo is initiating an aggressive advertising campaign to promote and grow sales of Gatorade.

In groups of three or four, answer the following questions:

1. Go to the Gatorade Web site, which is linked to the text's Web site at **http://warren.swlearning.com**. (a) How and why was Gatorade developed? (b) What is Gatorade's share of the sports-drink market?
2. Drinks can be labeled as sports, lifestyle, or active thirst drinks. (a) How would you describe each of these drink labels? (b) Give an example of what you would label a sports, lifestyle, and active thirst drink.
3. Do you think PepsiCo's advertising campaign will focus on Gatorade as a sports, lifestyle, or active thirst drink? Explain.

ACTIVITY 13-2
General Electric bond issuance

ETHICS

General Electric Capital, a division of **General Electric**, uses long-term debt extensively. In early 2002, GE Capital issued $11 billion in long-term debt to investors, then within days filed legal documents to prepare for another $50 billion long-term debt issue. As a result of the $50 billion filing, the price of the initial $11 billion offering declined (due to higher risk of more debt).

> *Bill Gross, a manager of a bond investment fund, "denounced a 'lack in candor' related to GE's recent debt deal. 'It was the most recent and most egregious example of how bondholders are mistreated.' Gross argued that GE was not forthright when GE Capital recently issued $11 billion in bonds, one of the largest issues ever from a U.S. corporation. What bothered Gross is that three days after the issue the company announced its intention to sell as much as $50 billion in additional debt, warrants, preferred stock, guarantees, letters of credit and promissory notes at some future date."*

▶ In your opinion, did GE Capital act unethically by selling $11 billion of long-term debt without telling those investors that a few days later it would be filing documents to prepare for another $50 billion debt offering?

Source: Jennifer Ablan, "Gross Shakes the Bond Market; GE Calms It, a Bit," *Barron's*, March 25, 2002.

ACTIVITY 13-3
Ethics and professional conduct in business

ETHICS

Whoosh Inc. produces and sells water slides for theme parks. Whoosh Inc. has outstanding a $40,000,000, 25-year, 10% debenture bond issue dated July 1, 2001. The bond issue is due June 30, 2026. The bond indenture requires a sinking fund, which has a balance of $5,000,000 as of July 1, 2006. Whoosh Inc. is currently experiencing a shortage of funds due to a recent plant expansion. Terry Holter, treasurer of Whoosh Inc., has suggested using the sinking fund cash to temporarily relieve the shortage of funds. Terry's brother-in-law, who is trustee of the sinking fund, is willing to loan Whoosh Inc. the necessary funds from the sinking fund.

▶ Discuss whether Terry Holter is behaving in a professional manner.

ACTIVITY 13-4
Present values

Nevin's Distributors Inc. is a wholesaler of oriental rugs. The following is a luncheon conversation between Pat Cameron, the assistant controller, and Cindy Bakke, an assistant financial analyst for Nevin's.

Cindy: Pat, do you mind if I spoil your lunch and ask you an accounting question?
Pat: No, go ahead. This chicken salad sandwich is pretty bad. It smells like it's three days old, and I've already picked three bones out of it.

Cindy: Well, as you know, in finance we use present values for capital budgeting analysis, assessing financing alternatives, etc. It's probably the most important concept that I learned in school that I actually use.

Pat: So . . . ?

Cindy: I was just wondering why accountants don't use present values more.

Pat: What do you mean?

Cindy: Well, it seems to me that you ought to value all the balance sheet liabilities at their present values.

▸ How would you respond if you were Pat?

ACTIVITY 13-5
Preferred stock vs. bonds

Beacon Inc. has decided to expand its operations to owning and operating theme parks. The following is an excerpt from a conversation between the chief executive officer, Tracy Gaddis, and the vice-president of finance, Jeff Poulsen.

Tracy: Jeff, have you given any thought to how we're going to finance the acquisition of Extreme Fun Corporation?

Jeff: Well, the two basic options, as I see it, are to issue either preferred stock or bonds. The equity market is a little depressed right now. The rumor is that the Federal Reserve Bank's going to increase the interest rates either this month or next.

Tracy: Yes, I've heard the rumor. The problem is that we can't wait around to see what's going to happen. We'll have to move on this next week if we want any chance to complete the acquisition of Extreme Fun.

Jeff: Well, the bond market is strong right now. Maybe we should issue debt this time around.

Tracy: That's what I would have guessed as well. Extreme Fun's financial statements look pretty good, except for the volatility of its income and cash flows. But that's characteristic of the industry.

▸ Discuss the advantages and disadvantages of issuing preferred stock versus bonds.

ACTIVITY 13-6
Investing in bonds

GROUP ACTIVITY

Select a bond from listings that appear daily in *The Wall Street Journal*, and summarize the information related to the bond you select. Include the following information in your summary:

1. Contract rate of interest
2. Year when the bond matures
3. Current yield (effective rate of interest)
4. Closing price of bond (indicate date)
5. Other information noted about the bond, such as whether it is a zero-coupon bond (see the Explanatory Notes to the listings)

In groups of three or four, share the information you developed about the bond you selected. As a group, select one bond to invest $100,000 in and prepare a justification for your choice for presentation to the class. For example, your justification should include a consideration of risk and return.

ACTIVITY 13-7
Financing business expansion

You hold a 25% common stock interest in the family-owned business, a soft drink bottling distributorship. Your sister, who is the manager, has proposed an expansion of plant facilities at an expected cost of $10,000,000. Two alternative plans have been suggested as methods of financing the expansion. Each plan is briefly described as follows:

Plan 1. Issue $10,000,000 of 20-year, 8% notes at face amount.
Plan 2. Issue an additional 140,000 shares of $10 par common stock at $25 per share, and $6,500,000 of 20-year, 8% notes at face amount.

The balance sheet as of the end of the previous fiscal year is as follows:

North Star Bottling Co.
Balance Sheet
December 31, 2006

Assets

Current assets	$ 4,700,000
Property, plant, and equipment	10,300,000
Total assets	$15,000,000

Liabilities and Stockholders' Equity

Liabilities	$ 4,000,000
Common stock, $10	1,600,000
Paid-in capital in excess of par	160,000
Retained earnings	9,240,000
Total liabilities and stockholders' equity	$15,000,000

Net income has remained relatively constant over the past several years. The expansion program is expected to increase yearly income before bond interest and income tax from $1,000,000 in the previous year to $1,400,000 for this year. Your sister has asked you, as the company treasurer, to prepare an analysis of each financing plan.

1. Prepare a table indicating the expected earnings per share on the common stock under each plan. Assume an income tax rate of 40%.
2. a. ▭▶ Discuss the factors that should be considered in evaluating the two plans.
   b. ▭▶ Which plan offers the greater benefit to the present stockholders? Give reasons for your opinion.

ACTIVITY 13-8
Bond ratings

REAL WORLD   INTERNET

Moody's Investors Service maintains a Web site at **http://www.Moodys.com**. One of the services offered at this site is a listing of announcements of recent bond rating changes. Visit this site and read over some of these announcements. Write down several of the reasons provided for rating downgrades and upgrades. If you were a bond investor or bond issuer, would you care if Moody's changed the rating on your bonds? Why or why not?

Answers to Self-Examination Questions

1. **B** Since the contract rate on the bonds is higher than the prevailing market rate, a rational investor would be willing to pay more than the face amount, or a premium (answer B), for the bonds. If the contract rate and the market rate were equal, the bonds could be expected to sell at their face amount (answer A). Likewise, if the market rate is higher than the contract rate, the bonds would sell at a price below their face amount (answer D) or at a discount (answer C).

2. **A** The bond carrying amount is the face amount plus unamortized premium or less unamortized discount. For this question, the carrying amount is $500,000 less $40,000, or $460,000 (answer A).

3. **B** Although the sinking fund may consist of cash as well as securities, the fund is listed on the balance sheet as an investment (answer B) because it is to be used to pay the long-term liability at maturity.

4. **B** The amount debited to the investment account is the cost of the bonds, which includes the amount paid to the seller for the bonds (101% × $100,000) plus broker's commissions ($50), or $101,050 (answer B). The $2,000 of accrued interest that is paid to the seller should be debited to Interest Revenue, since it is an offset against the amount that will be received as interest at the next interest date.

5. **C** The balance of Discount on Bonds Payable is usually reported as a deduction from Bonds Payable in the Long-Term Liabilities section (answer C) of the balance sheet. Likewise, a balance in a premium on bonds payable account would usually be reported as an addition to Bonds Payable in the Long-Term Liabilities section of the balance sheet.

Noncash Investing and Financing Activities

A business may enter into investing and financing activities that do not directly involve cash. For example, it may issue common stock to retire long-term debt. Such a transaction does not have a direct effect on cash. However, the transaction does eliminate the need for future cash payments to pay interest and retire the bonds. Thus, because of their future effect on cash flows, such transactions should be reported to readers of the financial statements.

When noncash investing and financing transactions occur during a period, their effect is reported in a separate schedule. This schedule usually appears at the bottom of the statement of cash flows. For example, in such a schedule, **Amazon.com** recently disclosed the issuance of $112 million in common stock for business acquisitions. Other examples of noncash investing and financing transactions include acquiring fixed assets by issuing bonds or capital stock and issuing common stock in exchange for convertible preferred stock.

SEASONAL CASH MANAGEMENT

A business must manage its cash position so that there is enough cash on hand to pay bills and other liabilities. Cash management is particularly important for seasonal businesses, which use cash in one part of the year and generate it in another. For example, consider this assumed cash position from operations for Smart Toys, Inc., a toy retailer:

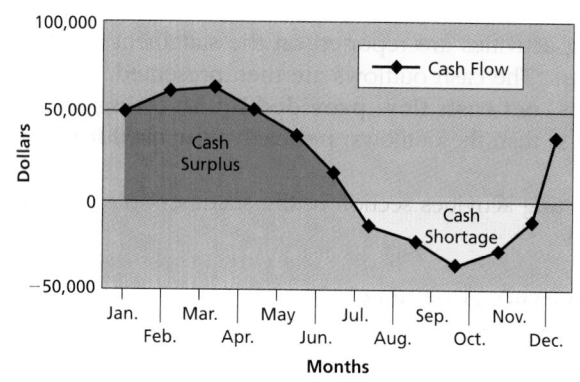

Smart Toys uses cash to purchase inventory prior to the winter holiday season. It is able to generate surplus cash by selling its inventory throughout the holiday season and into the early part of the calendar year.

If the cash required to purchase inventory exceeds Smart Toys' ability to generate operating cash flow, it may experience a cash shortage. In such a case, it must obtain short-term credit, which may be structured as a line of credit from a bank. A line of credit is an agreement that allows the business to borrow an unsecured amount of money up to some stated limit. For example, Smart Toys has a line of credit of $60,000, of which $40,000 was used during the year. Amounts drawn on a line of credit must usually be paid back within a year.

Seasonal businesses must be careful to avoid overextending their cash position during the "down cycle." For example, if Smart Toys purchases items that do not sell, a cash surplus will not be generated during the selling season.

No Cash Flow per Share

The term *cash flow per share* is sometimes reported in the financial press. Often, the term is used to mean "cash flow from operations per share." Such reporting may be misleading to users of the financial statements. For example, users might interpret cash flow per share as the amount available for dividends. This would not be the case if most of the cash generated by operations is required for repaying loans or for reinvesting in the business. Users might also think that cash flow per share is equivalent or perhaps superior to earnings per share. For these reasons, the financial statements, including the statement of cash flows, should not report cash flow per share.

Statement of Cash Flows—The Indirect Method

objective **2**

Prepare a statement of cash flows, using the indirect method.

The indirect method of reporting cash flows from operating activities is normally less costly and more efficient than the direct method. In addition, when the direct method is used, the indirect method must also be used in preparing a supplemental reconciliation of net income with cash flows from operations. The 2002 edition of *Accounting Trends & Techniques* reported that 99% of the companies surveyed used the indirect method. For these reasons, we will discuss first the indirect method of preparing the statement of cash flows.

To collect the data for the statement of cash flows, all the cash receipts and cash payments for a period could be analyzed. However, this procedure is expensive and time-consuming. A more efficient approach is to analyze the changes in the noncash balance sheet accounts. The logic of this approach is that a change in any balance sheet account (including cash) can be analyzed in terms of changes in the other balance sheet accounts. To illustrate, the accounting equation is rewritten below to focus on the cash account:

$$\text{Assets} = \text{Liabilities} + \text{Stockholders' Equity}$$
$$\text{Cash} + \text{Noncash Assets} = \text{Liabilities} + \text{Stockholders' Equity}$$
$$\text{Cash} = \text{Liabilities} + \text{Stockholders' Equity} - \text{Noncash Assets}$$

Any change in the cash account results in a change in one or more noncash balance sheet accounts. That is, if the cash account changes, then a liability, stockholders' equity, or noncash asset account must also change.

Additional data are also obtained by analyzing the income statement accounts and supporting records. For example, since the net income or net loss for the period is closed to *Retained Earnings*, a change in the retained earnings account can be partially explained by the net income or net loss reported on the income statement.

There is no order in which the noncash balance sheet accounts must be analyzed. However, it is usually more efficient to analyze the accounts in the reverse order in which they appear on the balance sheet. Thus, the analysis of retained earnings provides the starting point for determining the cash flows from operating activities, which is the first section of the statement of cash flows.

The comparative balance sheet for Rundell Inc. on December 31, 2006 and 2005, is used to illustrate the indirect method. This balance sheet is shown in Exhibit 3. Selected ledger accounts and other data are presented as needed.[2]

Retained Earnings

The comparative balance sheet for Rundell Inc. shows that retained earnings increased $80,000 during the year. Analyzing the entries posted to the retained earnings account indicates how this change occurred. The retained earnings account for Rundell Inc. is shown below.

ACCOUNT *Retained Earnings*					**ACCOUNT NO.**	
					Balance	
Date		**Item**	**Debit**	**Credit**	**Debit**	**Credit**
2006 Jan.	1	Balance				202 3 0 0 00
Dec.	31	Net income		108 0 0 0 00		310 3 0 0 00
	31	Cash dividends	28 0 0 0 00			282 3 0 0 00

[2]An appendix that discusses using a work sheet as an aid in assembling data for the statement of cash flows is presented at the end of this chapter. This appendix illustrates a work sheet that can be used with the indirect method and a work sheet that can be used with the direct method of reporting cash flows from operating activities.

•Exhibit 3 Comparative Balance Sheet

Rundell Inc.
Comparative Balance Sheet
December 31, 2006 and 2005

Assets	2006	2005	Increase Decrease*
Cash...................................	$ 97,500	$ 26,000	$ 71,500
Accounts receivable (net)...............	74,000	65,000	9,000
Inventories............................	172,000	180,000	8,000*
Land..................................	80,000	125,000	45,000*
Building..............................	260,000	200,000	60,000
Accumulated depreciation—building......	(65,300)	(58,300)	(7,000)
Total assets..........................	$618,200	$537,700	$ 80,500
Liabilities			
Accounts payable (merchandise creditors)...........................	$ 43,500	$ 46,700	$ 3,200*
Accrued expenses payable (operating expenses).................	26,500	24,300	2,200
Income taxes payable..................	7,900	8,400	500*
Dividends payable.....................	14,000	10,000	4,000
Bonds payable........................	100,000	150,000	50,000*
Total liabilities......................	$191,900	$239,400	$ 47,500*
Stockholders' Equity			
Common stock ($2 par).................	$ 24,000	$ 16,000	$ 8,000
Paid-in capital in excess of par...........	120,000	80,000	40,000
Retained earnings.....................	282,300	202,300	80,000
Total stockholders' equity..............	$426,300	$298,300	$128,000
Total liabilities and stockholders' equity....	$618,200	$537,700	$ 80,500

The retained earnings account must be carefully analyzed because some of the entries to retained earnings may not affect cash. For example, a decrease in retained earnings resulting from issuing a stock dividend does not affect cash. Such transactions are not reported on the statement of cash flows.

For Rundell Inc., the retained earnings account indicates that the $80,000 change resulted from net income of $108,000 and cash dividends declared of $28,000. The effect of each of these items on cash flows is discussed in the following sections.

Cash Flows from Operating Activities

The net income of $108,000 reported by Rundell Inc. normally is not equal to the amount of cash generated from operations during the period. This is because net income is determined using the accrual method of accounting.

Under the accrual method of accounting, revenues and expenses are recorded at different times from when cash is received or paid. For example, merchandise may be sold on account and the cash received at a later date.

Likewise, insurance expense represents the amount of insurance expired during the period. The premiums for the insurance may have been paid in a prior period. Thus, the net income reported on the income statement must be adjusted in determining cash flows from operating activities. The typical adjustments to net income are summarized in Exhibit 4.[3]

•Exhibit 4   Adjustments to Net Income—Indirect Method

Net income, per income statement		$XX
Add: Depreciation of fixed assets and amortization of intangible assets . .	$XX	
Decreases in current assets (receivables, inventories,		
prepaid expenses)	XX	
Increases in current liabilities (accounts and notes payable,		
accrued liabilities)	XX	
Losses on disposal of assets	XX	XX
Deduct: Increases in current assets (receivables, inventories,		
prepaid expenses)	$XX	
Decreases in current liabilities (accounts and notes payable,		
accrued liabilities)	XX	
Gains on disposal of assets	XX	XX
Net cash flow from operating activities		$XX

I was started in an Iowa farmhouse in 1985 by a ponytail-wearing guy who'd borrowed $10,000 from his grandmother. Today I'm a billion dollar company, employing more than 10,000 people and raking in some $6 billion annually. In 1995, I was the first manufacturer to offer on-line ordering for my kind of product. I'm a "personal technology company," offering consumers, businesses, and government agencies digital music, photography, and video services, as well as high-speed Internet connections and networking for the home and office, among other things. I'm known for my bovine design, too. Who am I? (Go to page 592 for answer.)

Some of the adjustment items in Exhibit 4 are for expenses that affect noncurrent accounts but not cash. For example, depreciation of fixed assets and amortization of intangible assets are deducted from revenue but do not affect cash.

Some of the adjustment items in Exhibit 4 are for revenues and expenses that affect current assets and current liabilities but not cash flows. For example, a sale of $10,000 on account increases accounts receivable by $10,000. However, cash is not affected. Thus, the increase in accounts receivable of $10,000 between two balance sheet dates is deducted from net income in arriving at cash flows from operating activities.

Cash flows from operating activities should not include investing or financing transactions. For example, assume that land costing $50,000 was sold for $90,000 (a gain of $40,000). The sale should be reported as an investing activity: "Cash receipts from the sale of land, $90,000." However, the $40,000 gain on the sale of the land is included in net income on the income statement. Thus, the $40,000 gain is deducted from net income in determining cash flows from operations in order to avoid "double counting" the cash flow from the gain. Likewise, losses from the sale of fixed assets are added to net income in determining cash flows from operations.

The effect of dividends payable on cash flows from operating activities is omitted from Exhibit 4. Dividends payable is omitted because dividends do not affect net income. Later in the chapter, we will discuss how dividends are reported in the statement of cash flows. In the following paragraphs, we will discuss each of the adjustments that change Rundell Inc.'s net income to "Cash flows from operating activities."

Depreciation

The comparative balance sheet in Exhibit 3 indicates that Accumulated Depreciation—Building increased by $7,000. As shown at the top of the following page, this account indicates that depreciation for the year was $7,000 for the building.

---

[3]Other items that also require adjustments to net income to obtain cash flow from operating activities include amortization of bonds payable discounts (add), losses on debt retirement (add), amortization of bonds payable premium (deduct), and gains on retirement of debt (deduct).

ACCOUNT *Accumulated Depreciation—Building*					ACCOUNT NO.		
						Balance	
Date	Item	Debit	Credit		Debit	Credit	
2006 Jan. 1	Balance					58 3 0 0 00	
Dec. 31	Depreciation for year		7 0 0 0 00			65 3 0 0 00	

Net income was $45,000 for the year. The accumulated depreciation balance increased by $15,000 over the year. There were no sales of fixed assets or changes in noncash current assets or liabilities. What is the cash flow from operations?

$60,000 ($45,000 + $15,000)

The $7,000 of depreciation expense reduced net income but did not require an outflow of cash. Thus, the $7,000 is added to net income in determining cash flows from operating activities, as follows:

Cash flows from operating activities:		
Net income	$108,000	
Add depreciation	7,000	$115,000

Current Assets and Current Liabilities

As shown in Exhibit 4, decreases in noncash current assets and increases in current liabilities are added to net income. In contrast, increases in noncash current assets and decreases in current liabilities are deducted from net income. The current asset and current liability accounts of Rundell Inc. are as follows:

	December 31		Increase
Accounts	**2006**	**2005**	**Decrease***
Accounts receivable (net)	$ 74,000	$ 65,000	$9,000
Inventories	172,000	180,000	8,000*
Accounts payable (merchandise creditors)	43,500	46,700	3,200*
Accrued expenses payable (operating expenses) . .	26,500	24,300	2,200
Income taxes payable	7,900	8,400	500*

REAL WORLD

Ford Motor Company's automotive business had a net loss of $6.6 billion but a positive cash flow from operating activities of $7.8 billion. This difference was mostly due to $5 billion of depreciation and amortization expenses and a $5 billion increase in accounts payable.

The $9,000 increase in **accounts receivable** indicates that the sales on account during the year are $9,000 more than collections from customers on account. The amount reported as sales on the income statement therefore includes $9,000 that did not result in a cash inflow during the year. Thus, $9,000 is deducted from net income.

The $8,000 decrease in **inventories** indicates that the merchandise sold exceeds the cost of the merchandise purchased by $8,000. The amount deducted as cost of merchandise sold on the income statement therefore includes $8,000 that did not require a cash outflow during the year. Thus, $8,000 is added to net income.

The $3,200 decrease in **accounts payable** indicates that the amount of cash payments for merchandise exceeds the merchandise purchased on account by $3,200. The amount reported on the income statement for cost of merchandise sold therefore excludes $3,200 that required a cash outflow during the year. Thus, $3,200 is deducted from net income.

The $2,200 increase in **accrued expenses payable** indicates that the amount incurred during the year for operating expenses exceeds the cash payments by $2,200. The amount reported on the income statement for operating expenses therefore includes $2,200 that did not require a cash outflow during the year. Thus, $2,200 is added to net income.

The $500 decrease in **income taxes payable** indicates that the amount paid for taxes exceeds the amount incurred during the year by $500. The amount reported on the income statement for income tax therefore is less than the amount paid by $500. Thus, $500 is deducted from net income.

Net income was $36,000 for the year. Accounts receivable increased $3,000, and accounts payable increased $5,000. What is the cash flow from operations?

$38,000 ($36,000 − $3,000 + $5,000)

Gain on Sale of Land

The ledger or income statement of Rundell Inc. indicates that the sale of land resulted in a gain of $12,000. As we discussed previously, the sale proceeds, which include the gain and the carrying value of the land, are included in cash flows from investing activities.[4] The gain is also included in net income. Thus, to avoid double reporting, the gain of $12,000 is deducted from net income in determining cash flows from operating activities, as shown below.

Cash flows from operating activities:
Net income $108,000
Deduct gain on sale of land   12,000

INTEGRITY IN BUSINESS

CREDIT POLICY AND CASH FLOW

Management will sometimes feel pressured to boost earnings by relaxing credit policies. Thus, they are able to create more sales on account but at a higher collection risk. The result is a temporary positive impact on the income statement. However, cash flow may be negatively impacted if high credit risk customers delay payment or are unable to pay. For example, **Lucent Technologies, Inc.**, extended billions of dollars in credit to upstart telecom companies to support Lucent's equipment sales. Loans to companies like **Winstar** and **One.Tel Ltd.** were eventually written off to the tune of $1 billion. This has prompted shareholder lawsuits accusing Lucent's directors of "mismanaging the top U.S. maker of phone equipment by lending the company's money to financially shaky customers to promote sales."

Source: *Omaha World-Herald*, "Lucent to Cut Almost Half Its Work Force; Troubled Phone Equipment Maker to Eliminate 20,000 Jobs, Take a Charge of as Much as $9 Billion," July 24, 2001.

Reporting Cash Flows from Operating Activities

We have now presented all the necessary adjustments to convert the net income to cash flows from operating activities for Rundell Inc. These adjustments are summarized in Exhibit 5 in a format suitable for the statement of cash flows.

•Exhibit 5   Cash Flows from Operating Activities—Indirect Method

Cash flows from operating activities:
Net income $108,000
Add: Depreciation . . . . $ 7,000
   Decrease in inventories   8,000
   Increase in accrued expenses   2,200   17,200
                                                                            $125,200

Deduct: Increase in accounts receivable . . . . $ 9,000
       Decrease in accounts payable   3,200
       Decrease in income taxes payable   500
       Gain on sale of land   12,000   24,700
Net cash flow from operating activities $100,500

---

[4]The reporting of the proceeds (cash flows) from the sale of land as part of investing activities is discussed later in this chapter.

FINANCIAL REPORTING AND DISCLOSURE

SIX FLAGS, INC.

The cash flows from operating activities under the indirect method often have more adjustments than illustrated in this chapter. To illustrate, the cash flows from operating activities for **Six Flags, Inc.**, an amusement park operator, is as follows:

Six Flags, Inc.
Cash Flows from Operating Activities
(Selected from the Statement of Cash Flows)
For Year Ended December 31, 2002

	2002
Cash flows from operating activities:	
Net loss	$(105,698,000)
Adjustments to reconcile net loss to net cash provided by operating activities:	
Depreciation and amortization	$ 151,849,000
Equity in operations of theme parks	(15,664,000)
Cash received from theme parks	26,679,000
Noncash compensation	9,256,000
Interest accretion on notes payable	37,818,000
Extraordinary loss on early extinguishment of debt	29,895,000
Cumulative change in accounting principle	61,054,000
Amortization of debt issuance costs	8,952,000
Loss on disposal of fixed assets	4,375,000
(Increase) decrease in accounts receivable	(3,567,000)
Increase (decrease) in inventories and prepaid expenses	2,050,000
Decrease in deposits and other assets	3,824,000
Increase (decrease) in accounts payable, deferred revenue, accrued expenses, and other liabilities	4,080,000
Increase in accrued interest payable	7,671,000
Deferred income tax benefit	(18,091,000)
Total adjustments	$ 310,181,000
Net cash provided by operating activities	$ 204,483,000

As can be seen, Six Flags had a loss of over $105 million but had positive cash flows from operating activities of over $204 million. The difference between the accrual earnings number and the cash flow from operating activities is explained by a long list of adjusting items, of which the largest is depreciation expense. Other noncash adjustments include the noncash compensation (deferred bonuses), interest revenue on non-interest-bearing notes, equity earnings (net of cash received) from partnerships, and debt issuance cost amortization (similar to discount amortizations). The cash flow impact of the extraordinary and ordinary losses are reflected in the financing and investing sections, respectively, and thus are added back in the operating activities section to avoid double-counting. The cumulative effect of the change in accounting principle was a noncash deduction in determining net income. The remaining items are the adjustments due to changes in the noncash current assets and liabilities, as described in the chapter.

Cash Flows Used for Payment of Dividends

According to the retained earnings account of Rundell Inc., shown earlier in the chapter, cash dividends of $28,000 were declared during the year. However, the dividends payable account, shown at the top of the next page, indicates that dividends of only $24,000 were paid during the year.

ACCOUNT Dividends Payable						ACCOUNT NO.
					Balance	
Date	Item	Debit	Credit	Debit	Credit	
2006 Jan. 1	Balance				10 0 0 0 00	
10	Cash paid	10 0 0 0 00		—	—	
June 20	Dividends declared		14 0 0 0 00		14 0 0 0 00	
July 10	Cash paid	14 0 0 0 00		—	—	
Dec. 20	Dividends declared		14 0 0 0 00		14 0 0 0 00	

The $24,000 of dividend payments represents a cash outflow that is reported in the financing activities section as follows:

Cash flows from financing activities:
　Cash paid for dividends $24,000

Common Stock

The common stock account increased by $8,000, and the paid-in capital in excess of par—common stock account increased by $40,000, as shown below. These increases result from issuing 4,000 shares of common stock for $12 per share.

ACCOUNT Common Stock						ACCOUNT NO.
					Balance	
Date	Item	Debit	Credit	Debit	Credit	
2006 Jan. 1	Balance				16 0 0 0 00	
Nov. 1	4,000 shares issued for cash		8 0 0 0 00		24 0 0 0 00	

ACCOUNT Paid-In Capital in Excess of Par—Common Stock						ACCOUNT NO.
					Balance	
Date	Item	Debit	Credit	Debit	Credit	
2006 Jan. 1	Balance				80 0 0 0 00	
Nov. 1	4,000 shares issued for cash		40 0 0 0 00		120 0 0 0 00	

This cash inflow is reported in the financing activities section as follows:

Cash flows from financing activities:
　Cash received from sale of common stock $48,000

Bonds Payable

The bonds payable account decreased by $50,000, as shown below. This decrease results from retiring the bonds by a cash payment for their face amount.

ACCOUNT Bonds Payable						ACCOUNT NO.
					Balance	
Date	Item	Debit	Credit	Debit	Credit	
2006 Jan. 1	Balance				150 0 0 0 00	
June 30	Retired by payment of cash					
	at face amount	50 0 0 0 00			100 0 0 0 00	

This cash outflow is reported in the financing activities section as follows:

Cash flows from financing activities:
    Cash paid to retire bonds payable $50,000

Building

The building account increased by $60,000, and the accumulated depreciation—building account increased by $7,000, as shown below.

ACCOUNT *Building* **ACCOUNT NO.**

Date		Item	Debit	Credit	Balance Debit	Balance Credit
2006 Jan.	1	Balance			200 000 00	
Dec.	27	Purchased for cash	60 000 00		260 000 00	

ACCOUNT *Accumulated Depreciation—Building* **ACCOUNT NO.**

Date		Item	Debit	Credit	Balance Debit	Balance Credit
2006 Jan.	1	Balance				58 300 00
Dec.	31	Depreciation for the year		7 000 00		65 300 00

The purchase of a building for cash of $60,000 is reported as an outflow of cash in the investing activities section, as follows:

Cash flows from investing activities:
    Cash paid for purchase of building $60,000

The credit in the accumulated depreciation—building account, shown earlier, represents depreciation expense for the year. This depreciation expense of $7,000 on the building has already been considered as an addition to net income in determining cash flows from operating activities, as reported in Exhibit 5.

Land

The $45,000 decline in the land account resulted from two separate transactions, as shown below.

ACCOUNT *Land* **ACCOUNT NO.**

Date		Item	Debit	Credit	Balance Debit	Balance Credit
2006 Jan.	1	Balance			125 000 00	
June	8	Sold for $72,000 cash		60 000 00	65 000 00	
Oct.	12	Purchased for $15,000 cash	15 000 00		80 000 00	

The first transaction is the sale of land with a cost of $60,000 for $72,000 in cash. The $72,000 proceeds from the sale are reported in the investing activities section, as follows:

A building with a cost of $145,000 and accumulated depreciation of $35,000 was sold for a $10,000 gain. How much cash was generated from this investing activity?

$120,000 ($145,000 − $35,000 + $10,000)

Cash flows from investing activities:
Cash received from sale of land (includes $12,000 gain
reported in net income) $72,000

The proceeds of $72,000 include the $12,000 gain on the sale of land and the $60,000 cost (book value) of the land. As shown in Exhibit 5, the $12,000 gain is also deducted from net income in the cash flows from operating activities section. This is necessary so that the $12,000 cash inflow related to the gain is not included twice as a cash inflow.

The second transaction is the purchase of land for cash of $15,000. This transaction is reported as an outflow of cash in the investing activities section, as follows:

Cash flows from investing activities:
Cash paid for purchase of land $15,000

Preparing the Statement of Cash Flows

The statement of cash flows for Rundell Inc. is prepared from the data assembled and analyzed above, using the indirect method. Exhibit 6 shows the statement of cash flows prepared by Rundell Inc. The statement indicates that the cash position increased by $71,500 during the year. The most significant increase in net cash flows, $100,500, was from operating activities. The most significant use of cash, $26,000, was for financing activities.

•Exhibit 6   Statement of Cash Flows—Indirect Method

Rundell Inc.
Statement of Cash Flows
For the Year Ended December 31, 2006

Cash flows from operating activities:			
Net income		$108,000	
Add: Depreciation	$ 7,000		
Decrease in inventories	8,000		
Increase in accrued expenses	2,200	17,200	
		$125,200	
Deduct: Increase in accounts receivable	$ 9,000		
Decrease in accounts payable	3,200		
Decrease in income taxes payable . . .	500		
Gain on sale of land	12,000	24,700	
Net cash flow from operating activities			$100,500
Cash flows from investing activities:			
Cash from sale of land		$ 72,000	
Less: Cash paid to purchase land	$15,000		
Cash paid for purchase of building	60,000	75,000	
Net cash flow used for investing activities			(3,000)
Cash flows from financing activities:			
Cash received from sale of common stock		$ 48,000	
Less: Cash paid to retire bonds payable	$50,000		
Cash paid for dividends	24,000	74,000	
Net cash flow used for financing activities			(26,000)
Increase in cash			$ 71,500
Cash at the beginning of the year			26,000
Cash at the end of the year			$ 97,500

INTEGRITY IN BUSINESS

MISLEADING CASH FLOWS

The Securities and Exchange Commission disagreed with a cash flow disclosure from a complex natural gas trading arrangement of **Dynegy Inc.**, a major energy provider and trader. As a result, the company was required to remove $300 million from cash flow from operations (a drop of 37%) and put it into the financing section. Although this change did not impact net cash flow from all sources, it did change the interpretation of cash flows. As quoted by one source, "the restatement is a big blow to the many investors who held onto the cash-flow statement as a beacon of truth even as their faith in earnings figure was shattered in recent months . . ." Dynegy's share price dropped 67% within two months of this announcement.

Source: Henny Sender, " 'Reliable' Cash Flow Has Shortcomings—Sums Aren't Always What They Seem," *The Wall Street Journal*, May 9, 2002.

Statement of Cash Flows—The Direct Method

objective 3

Prepare a statement of cash flows, using the direct method.

As we discussed previously, the manner of reporting cash flows from investing and financing activities is the same under the direct and indirect methods. In addition, the direct method and the indirect method will report the same amount of cash flows from operating activities. However, the methods differ in how the cash flows from operating activities data are obtained, analyzed, and reported.

To illustrate the direct method, we will use the comparative balance sheet and the income statement for Rundell Inc. In this way, we can compare the statement of cash flows under the direct method and the indirect method.

Exhibit 7 shows the changes in the current asset and liability account balances for Rundell Inc. The income statement in Exhibit 7 shows additional data for Rundell Inc.

The direct method reports cash flows from operating activities by major classes of operating cash receipts and operating cash payments. The difference between the major classes of total operating cash receipts and total operating cash payments is the net cash flow from operating activities.

Cash Received from Customers

The $1,180,000 of sales for Rundell Inc. is reported by using the accrual method. To determine the cash received from sales to customers, the $1,180,000 must be adjusted. The adjustment necessary to convert the sales reported on the income statement to the cash received from customers is summarized below.

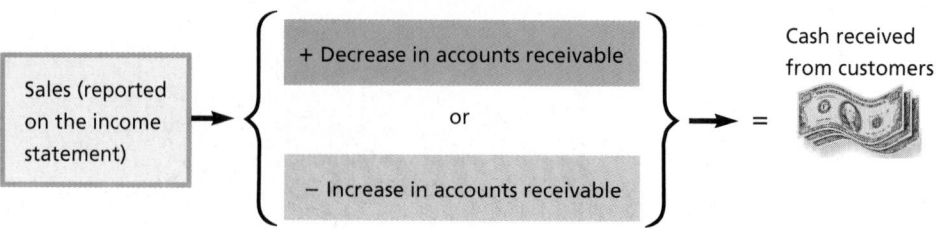

For Rundell Inc., the cash received from customers is $1,171,000, as shown below.

Sales	$1,180,000
Less increase in accounts receivable	9,000
Cash received from customers	$1,171,000

•Exhibit 7   **Balance Sheet and Income Statement Data for Direct Method**

Rundell Inc.
Schedule of Changes in Current Accounts

Accounts	December 31 2006	December 31 2005	Increase Decrease*
Cash	$ 97,500	$ 26,000	$71,500
Accounts receivable (net)	74,000	65,000	9,000
Inventories	172,000	180,000	8,000*
Accounts payable (merchandise creditors)	43,500	46,700	3,200*
Accrued expenses payable (operating expenses)	26,500	24,300	2,200
Income taxes payable	7,900	8,400	500*
Dividends payable	14,000	10,000	4,000

Rundell Inc.
Income Statement
For the Year Ended December 31, 2006

Sales		$1,180,000
Cost of merchandise sold		790,000
Gross profit		$ 390,000
Operating expenses:		
Depreciation expense	$ 7,000	
Other operating expenses	196,000	
Total operating expenses		203,000
Income from operations		$ 187,000
Other income:		
Gain on sale of land	$ 12,000	
Other expense:		
Interest expense	8,000	4,000
Income before income tax		$ 191,000
Income tax expense		83,000
Net income		$ 108,000

Sales reported on the income statement were $350,000. The accounts receivable balance declined $8,000 over the year. What was the amount of cash received from customers?

$358,000 ($350,000 + $8,000)

The additions to **accounts receivable** for sales on account during the year were $9,000 more than the amounts collected from customers on account. Sales reported on the income statement therefore included $9,000 that did not result in a cash inflow during the year. In other words, the increase of $9,000 in accounts receivable during 2006 indicates that sales on account exceeded cash received from customers by $9,000. Thus, $9,000 is deducted from sales to determine the cash received from customers. The $1,171,000 of cash received from customers is reported in the cash flows from operating activities section of the cash flow statement.

Cash Payments for Merchandise

The $790,000 of cost of merchandise sold is reported on the income statement for Rundell Inc., using the accrual method. The adjustments necessary to convert the cost of merchandise sold to cash payments for merchandise during 2006 are summarized at the top of the following page.

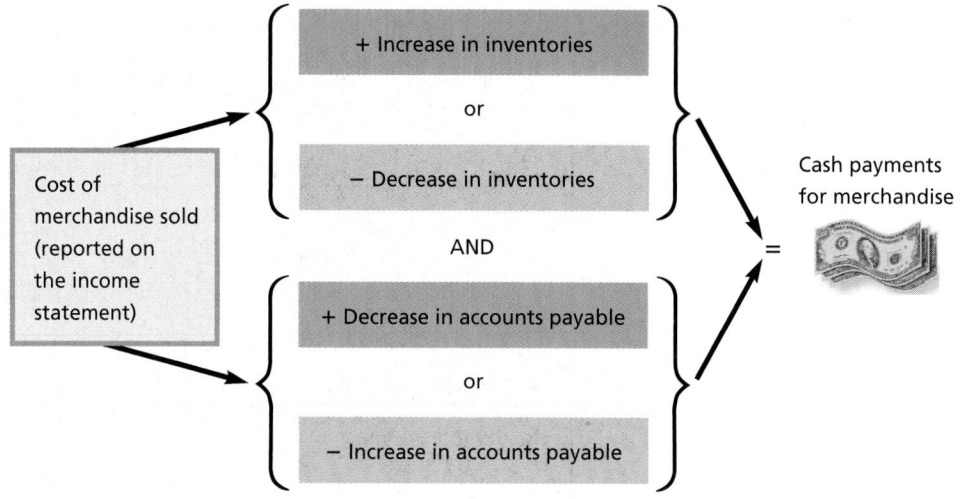

For Rundell Inc., the amount of cash payments for merchandise is $785,200, as determined below.

Cost of merchandise sold	$790,000
Deduct decrease in inventories	(8,000)
Add decrease in accounts payable	3,200
Cash payments for merchandise	$785,200

The $8,000 decrease in **inventories** indicates that the merchandise sold exceeded the cost of the merchandise purchased by $8,000. The amount reported on the income statement for cost of merchandise sold therefore includes $8,000 that did not require a cash outflow during the year. Thus, $8,000 is deducted from the cost of merchandise sold in determining the cash payments for merchandise.

The $3,200 decrease in **accounts payable** (merchandise creditors) indicates a cash outflow that is excluded from cost of merchandise sold. In other words, the decrease in accounts payable indicates that cash payments for merchandise were $3,200 more than the purchases on account during 2006. Thus, $3,200 is added to the cost of merchandise sold in determining the cash payments for merchandise.

Cash Payments for Operating Expenses

The $7,000 of depreciation expense reported on the income statement did not require a cash outflow. Thus, under the direct method, it is not reported on the statement of cash flows. The $196,000 reported for other operating expenses is adjusted to reflect the cash payments for operating expenses, as summarized below.

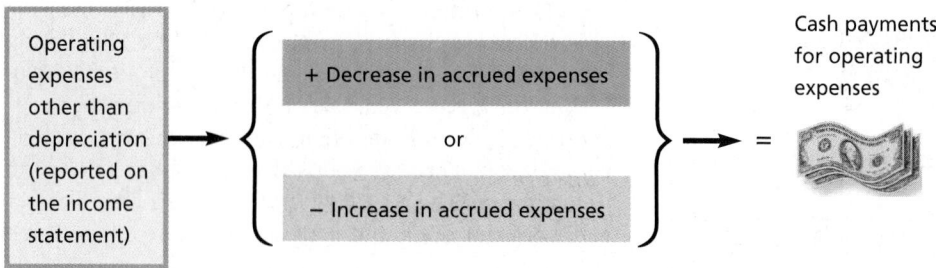

For Rundell Inc., the amount of cash payments for operating expenses is $193,800, determined as follows:

Operating expenses other than depreciation	$196,000
Deduct increase in accrued expenses	2,200
Cash payments for operating expenses	$193,800

The increase in **accrued expenses** (operating expenses) indicates that operating expenses include $2,200 for which there was no cash outflow (payment) during the year. In other words, the increase in accrued expenses indicates that the cash payments for operating expenses were $2,200 less than the amount reported as an expense during the year. Thus, $2,200 is deducted from the operating expenses on the income statement in determining the cash payments for operating expenses.

Gain on Sale of Land

The income statement for Rundell Inc. in Exhibit 7 reports a gain of $12,000 on the sale of land. As we discussed previously, the gain is included in the proceeds from the sale of land, which is reported as part of the cash flows from investing activities.

Interest Expense

The income statement for Rundell Inc. in Exhibit 7 reports interest expense of $8,000. The interest expense is related to the bonds payable that were outstanding during the year. We assume that interest on the bonds is paid on June 30 and December 31. Thus, $8,000 cash outflow for interest expense is reported on the statement of cash flows as an operating activity.

If interest payable had existed at the end of the year, the interest expense would be adjusted for any increase or decrease in interest payable from the beginning to the end of the year. That is, a decrease in interest payable would be added to interest expense and an increase in interest payable would be subtracted from interest expense. This is similar to the adjustment for changes in income taxes payable, which we will illustrate in the following paragraphs.

Cash Payments for Income Taxes

The adjustment to convert the income tax reported on the income statement to the cash basis is summarized below.

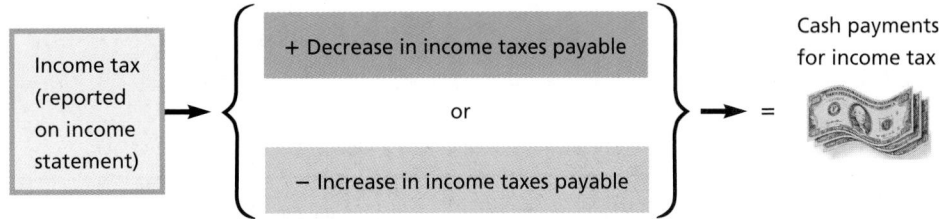

For Rundell Inc., cash payments for income tax are $83,500, determined as follows:

Income tax	$83,000
Add decrease in income taxes payable	500
Cash payments for income tax	$83,500

The cash outflow for income taxes exceeded the income tax deducted as an expense during the period by $500. Thus, $500 is added to the amount of income tax reported on the income statement in determining the cash payments for income tax.

Reporting Cash Flows from Operating Activities—Direct Method

Exhibit 8 is a complete statement of cash flows for Rundell Inc., using the direct method for reporting cash flows from operating activities. The portions of this statement that differ from the indirect method are highlighted in color. Exhibit 8 also includes the separate schedule reconciling net income and net cash flow from operating

REAL WORLD

Dell Computer Corporation is one of the few companies that has a *negative cash conversion cycle*. This means that Dell receives payment for a computer before it pays for the parts that went into that computer. This can only be done by collecting the sale with a credit card, maintaining very little inventory, and holding accounts payable open for 30 days.

•Exhibit 8   Statement of Cash Flows—Direct Method

Rundell Inc.
Statement of Cash Flows
For the Year Ended December 31, 2006

Cash flows from operating activities:			
Cash received from customers		$1,171,000	
Deduct: Cash payments for merchandise.	$785,200		
Cash payments for operating expenses. . . .	193,800		
Cash payments for interest	8,000		
Cash payments for income taxes	83,500	1,070,500	
Net cash flow from operating activities			$100,500
Cash flows from investing activities:			
Cash from sale of land		$ 72,000	
Less: Cash paid to purchase land	$ 15,000		
Cash paid for purchase of building	60,000	75,000	
Net cash flow used for investing activities			(3,000)
Cash flows from financing activities:			
Cash received from sale of common stock		$ 48,000	
Less: Cash paid to retire bonds payable	$ 50,000		
Cash paid for dividends	24,000	74,000	
Net cash flow used for financing activities			(26,000)
Increase in cash			$ 71,500
Cash at the beginning of the year			26,000
Cash at the end of the year			$ 97,500
Schedule Reconciling Net Income with Cash			
Flows from Operating Activities:			
Net income, per income statement.		$ 108,000	
Add: Depreciation.	$ 7,000		
Decrease in inventories	8,000		
Increase in accrued expenses.	2,200	17,200	
		$ 125,200	
Deduct: Increase in accounts receivable	$ 9,000		
Decrease in accounts payable	3,200		
Decrease in income taxes payable	500		
Gain on sale of land	12,000	24,700	
Net cash flow from operating activities		$ 100,500	

activities. This schedule must accompany the statement of cash flows when the direct method is used. This schedule is similar to the cash flows from operating activities section of the statement of cash flows prepared using the indirect method.

Financial Analysis and Interpretation

objective   **4**

Calculate and interpret the free cash flow.

A valuable tool for evaluating the cash flows of a business is free cash flow. *Free cash flow* is a measure of operating cash flow available for corporate purposes after providing sufficient fixed asset additions to maintain current productive capacity and dividends. Thus, free cash flow can be calculated as follows:

Cash flow from operating activities
Less: Cash used to purchase fixed assets to maintain productive
        capacity used up in producing income during the period
Less: Cash used for dividends
      Free cash flow

REAL WORLD The top five nonfinancial companies out of the Standard & Poor's 100 Index with the largest free cash flows for a recent year were as follows:

	Free Cash Flow (in millions)
Ford Motor Co.	$14,705
ExxonMobil	12,900
General Electric	10,317
Microsoft	9,967
IBM	8,595

Each of these companies are large and successful organizations. In contrast, the three organizations with the largest *negative* free cash flows were:

Lucent	$(4,839)
Delta Air Lines	(2,571)
Nextel Communications	(2,359)

Both the telecommunications equipment and airline industries were suffering significantly during this timeframe.

Source: Ronald Fink, "Adjusting the Flow," *CFO Magazine*, December 1, 2002.

Analysts often use free cash flow, rather than cash flows from operating activities, to measure the financial strength of a business. Many high-technology firms must aggressively reinvest in new technology to remain competitive. This can reduce free cash flow. For example, **Motorola**'s free cash flow is less than 10% of the cash flow from operating activities. In contrast, **Coca-Cola**'s free cash flow is approximately 75% of the cash flow from operating activities.

To illustrate, the cash flow from operating activities for **Hewlett-Packard Co.** was $5,444 million in a recent fiscal year. The statement of cash flows indicated that the cash invested in property, plant, and equipment was $1,710 million and $801 million was paid for dividends. Assuming that the amount invested in property, plant, and equipment maintained existing operations, free cash flow would be calculated as follows (in millions):

Cash flow from operating activities		$5,444
Less: Cash invested in fixed assets to		
maintain productive capacity	$1,710	
Cash for dividends	801	2,511
Free cash flow		$2,933

During this period, Hewlett-Packard generated free cash flow in excess of $2.9 billion, which was 54% of cash flows from operations and over 5% of sales. The free cash flows for the other companies in the computer industry are shown for comparison purposes below (in thousands).

	Dell Computer	Gateway Inc.	Apple Computer
Sales	$35,404,000	$4,171,325	$5,742,000
Cash flow from operating activities	$3,538,000	$ (24,667)	$ 89,000
Cash used to purchase property, plant, and equipment (assumed to maintain productive capacity)	(305,000)	(78,497)	(174,000)
Cash used to pay dividends	—	—	—
Free cash flow	$3,233,000	$(103,164)	$ (85,000)
Free cash flow as a percent of cash flow from operations	91%	NA	−96.0%
Free cash flow as a percent of sales	9%	−2.5%	−1.5%

Positive free cash flow is considered favorable. A company that has free cash flow is able to fund internal growth, retire debt, and enjoy financial flexibility. A company with no free cash flow is unable to maintain current productive capacity or dividend payouts to stockholders. Lack of free cash flow can be an early indicator of liquidity problems. Indeed, as stated by one analyst, "Free cash flow gives the company firepower to reduce debt and ultimately generate consistent, actual income."[5]

---

[5]Jill Krutick, *Fortune*, March 30, 1998, p. 106.

SPOTLIGHT ON STRATEGY

CORPORATE LIFE-CYCLE STAGES AND CASH FLOW MANAGEMENT

Many companies can expect to move through four corporate life-cycle stages, as illustrated below.

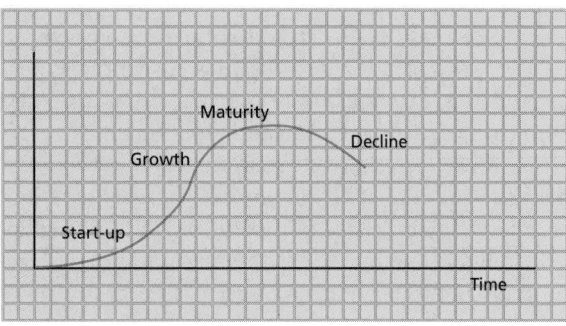

The **start-up phase** is the most risky. It has been reported that nine out of ten businesses fail during the start-up phase. During start-up, the business often generates negative cash flows from operations and thus must obtain cash from financing activities to survive. Banks usually will not lend money to start-up businesses unless there are assets to secure the loan. Thus, the start-up business must often obtain "F&F" (friends and family) financing, or equity investments by wealthy individuals, termed "angel investors."

As the start-up business begins to achieve success, it may move to the growth phase. During the **growth phase**, the business may expand operations, product offerings, channels of distribution, and facilities. A growth business may be able to generate sufficient cash flows from operations to fund the growth, such as was the case with **Microsoft**. Sometimes, however, the cash flows from operations, while positive, are not sufficient to fund future growth. In these circumstances, the growth company will seek additional sources of financing from venture capitalists, public offerings of common stock, and debt. Examples of growth companies are **Krispy Kreme Doughnuts** and **Panera Bread Company**.

Eventually, a business becomes mature. **Mature** businesses have fewer opportunities to grow and are usually under competitive pressure from other large businesses. Mature businesses generate large cash flows from operations but do not need excess cash to grow the business. As such, mature businesses will use excess cash to pay dividends or purchase treasury stock as ways to provide returns to shareholders. Examples of mature businesses are **Procter & Gamble** and **International Paper**.

Not all businesses move into the fourth stage of decline. During **decline**, business opportunities are failing, operating budgets are reduced, advertising is scaled back, facilities are sold, and dividends are cut. Businesses in decline attempt to conserve cash in order to satisfy debtors, while reducing size in an orderly manner. **Kmart** is an example of a business that has suffered a decline.

ppendix Work Sheet for Statement of Cash Flows

A work sheet may be useful in assembling data for the statement of cash flows. Whether or not a work sheet is used, the concepts of cash flow and the statements of cash flows presented in this chapter are not affected. In this appendix, we will describe and illustrate the use of work sheets for the indirect method and the direct method.

Work Sheet—Indirect Method

We will use the data for Rundell Inc., presented in Exhibit 3, as a basis for illustrating the work sheet for the indirect method. The procedures used in preparing this work sheet, shown in Exhibit 9, are outlined below.

1. List the title of each balance sheet account in the Accounts column. For each account, enter its balance as of December 31, 2005, in the first column and its balance as of December 31, 2006, in the last column. Place the credit balances in parentheses. The column totals should equal zero, since the total of the debits in a column should equal the total of the credits in a column.

2. Analyze the change during the year in each account to determine the net increase (decrease) in cash and the cash flows from operating activities, investing activities, financing activities, and the noncash investing and financing activities. Show the effect of the change on cash flows by making entries in the Transactions columns.

•Exhibit 9   Work Sheet for Statement of Cash Flows—Indirect Method

Rundell Inc.
Work Sheet for Statement of Cash Flows
For the Year Ended December 31, 2006

	Accounts	Balance Dec. 31, 2005	Transactions Debit	Transactions Credit	Balance Dec. 31, 2006	
1	Cash	26 000 00	(o) 71 500 00		97 500 00	1
2	Accounts receivable (net)	65 000 00	(n) 9 000 00		74 000 00	2
3	Inventories	180 000 00		(m) 8 000 00	172 000 00	3
4	Land	125 000 00	(k) 15 000 00	(l) 60 000 00	80 000 00	4
5	Building	200 000 00	(j) 60 000 00		260 000 00	5
6	Accumulated depreciation—building	(58 300 00)		(i) 7 000 00	(65 300 00)	6
7	Accounts payable (merchandise creditors)	(46 700 00)	(h) 3 200 00		(43 500 00)	7
8	Accrued expenses payable (operating expenses)	(24 300 00)		(g) 2 200 00	(26 500 00)	8
9	Income taxes payable	(8 400 00)	(f) 500 00		(7 900 00)	9
10	Dividends payable	(10 000 00)		(e) 4 000 00	(14 000 00)	10
11	Bonds payable	(150 000 00)	(d) 50 000 00		(100 000 00)	11
12	Common stock	(16 000 00)		(c) 8 000 00	(24 000 00)	12
13	Paid-in capital in excess of par	(80 000 00)		(c) 40 000 00	(120 000 00)	13
14	Retained earnings	(202 300 00)	(b) 28 000 00	(a) 108 000 00	(282 300 00)	14
15	Totals	0 00	237 200 00	237 200 00	0 00	15
16	Operating activities:					16
17	Net income		(a) 108 000 00			17
18	Depreciation of building		(i) 7 000 00			18
19	Decrease in inventories		(m) 8 000 00			19
20	Increase in accrued expenses		(g) 2 200 00			20
21	Increase in accounts receivable			(n) 9 000 00		21
22	Decrease in accounts payable			(h) 3 200 00		22
23	Decrease in income taxes payable			(f) 500 00		23
24	Gain on sale of land			(l) 12 000 00		24
25	Investing activities:					25
26	Sale of land		(l) 72 000 00			26
27	Purchase of land			(k) 15 000 00		27
28	Purchase of building			(j) 60 000 00		28
29	Financing activities:					29
30	Issued common stock		(c) 48 000 00			30
31	Retired bonds payable			(d) 50 000 00		31
32	Declared cash dividends			(b) 28 000 00		32
33	Increase in dividends payable		(e) 4 000 00			33
34	Net increase in cash			(o) 71 500 00		34
35	Totals		249 200 00	249 200 00		35

Analyzing Accounts

An efficient method of analyzing cash flows is to determine the type of cash flow activity that led to changes in balance sheet accounts during the period. As we analyze each noncash account, we will make entries on the work sheet for specific types of cash flow activities related to the noncash accounts. After we have analyzed all the noncash accounts, we will make an entry for the increase (decrease) in cash during the period. These entries, however, are not posted to the ledger. They only aid in assembling the data on the work sheet.

The order in which the accounts are analyzed is unimportant. However, it is more efficient to begin with the retained earnings account and proceed upward in the account listing.

Retained Earnings   The work sheet shows a Retained Earnings balance of $202,300 at December 31, 2005, and $282,300 at December 31, 2006. Thus, Retained Earnings increased $80,000 during the year. This increase resulted from two factors: (1) net income of $108,000 and (2) declaring cash dividends of $28,000. To identify the cash flows by activity, we will make two entries on the work sheet. These entries also serve to account for or explain, in terms of cash flows, the increase of $80,000.

In closing the accounts at the end of the year, the retained earnings account was credited for the net income of $108,000. The $108,000 is reported on the statement of cash flows as "cash flows from operating activities." The following entry is made in the Transactions columns on the work sheet. This entry (1) accounts for the credit portion of the closing entry (to Retained Earnings) and (2) identifies the cash flow in the bottom portion of the work sheet.

| (a) | Operating Activities—Net Income | 108,000 | |
| | Retained Earnings | | 108,000 |

In closing the accounts at the end of the year, the retained earnings account was debited for dividends declared of $28,000. The $28,000 is reported as a financing activity on the statement of cash flows. The following entry on the work sheet (1) accounts for the debit portion of the closing entry (to Retained Earnings) and (2) identifies the cash flow in the bottom portion of the work sheet.

| (b) | Retained Earnings | 28,000 | |
| | Financing Activities—Declared Cash Dividends | | 28,000 |

The $28,000 of declared dividends will be adjusted later for the actual amount of cash dividends paid during the year.

Other Accounts   The entries for the other accounts are made in the work sheet in a manner similar to entries (a) and (b). A summary of these entries is as follows:

(c)	Financing Activities—Issued Common Stock	48,000	
	Common Stock		8,000
	Paid-In Capital in Excess of Par—Common Stock		40,000
(d)	Bonds Payable	50,000	
	Financing Activities—Retired Bonds Payable		50,000
(e)	Financing Activities—Increase in Dividends Payable	4,000	
	Dividends Payable		4,000
(f)	Income Taxes Payable	500	
	Operating Activities—Decrease in Income Taxes Payable		500
(g)	Operating Activities—Increase in Accrued Expenses	2,200	
	Accrued Expenses Payable		2,200
(h)	Accounts Payable	3,200	
	Operating Activities—Decrease in Accounts Payable		3,200
(i)	Operating Activities—Depreciation of Building	7,000	
	Accumulated Depreciation—Building		7,000
(j)	Building	60,000	
	Investing Activities—Purchase of Building		60,000

(k)	Land	15,000	
	Investing Activities—Purchase of Land		15,000
(l)	Investing Activities—Sale of Land	72,000	
	Operating Activities—Gain on Sale of Land		12,000
	Land		60,000
(m)	Operating Activities—Decrease in Inventories	8,000	
	Inventories		8,000
(n)	Accounts Receivable	9,000	
	Operating Activities—Increase in Accounts Receivable		9,000
(o)	Cash	71,500	
	Net Increase in Cash		71,500

Completing the Work Sheet

After we have analyzed all the balance sheet accounts and made the entries on the work sheet, all the operating, investing, and financing activities are identified in the bottom portion of the work sheet. The accuracy of the work sheet entries is verified by the equality of each pair of the totals of the debit and credit Transactions columns.

Preparing the Statement of Cash Flows

The statement of cash flows prepared from the work sheet is identical to the statement in Exhibit 6. The data for the three sections of the statement are obtained from the bottom portion of the work sheet.

In the cash flows from operating activities section, the effect of depreciation is normally presented first. The effects of increases and decreases in current assets and current liabilities are then presented. The effects of any gains and losses on operating activities are normally reported last. The cash paid for dividends is reported as $24,000 instead of the amount of dividends declared ($28,000) less the increase in dividends payable ($4,000). Any noncash investing and financing activities are usually reported in a separate schedule at the bottom of the statement.

Work Sheet—Direct Method

As a basis for illustrating the direct method work sheet, we will use the balance sheet data for Rundell Inc. in Exhibit 3 and the income statement data in Exhibit 7. The procedures used in preparing the work sheet in Exhibit 10 are outlined below.

1. List the title of each balance sheet account in the Accounts column. For each account, enter its balance as of December 31, 2005, in the first column and its balance as of December 31, 2006, in the last column. Place the credit balances in parentheses. The column totals should equal zero, since the total of the debits in a column should equal the total of the credits in a column.
2. List the title of each income statement account and "Net income" on the work sheet.
3. Analyze the effect of each income statement item on cash flows from operating activities. Beginning with sales, enter the balance of each item in the proper Transactions column. Complete the entry in the Transactions columns to show the effect on cash flows.
4. Analyze the change during the year in each balance sheet account to determine the net increase (decrease) in cash and the cash flows from operating activities, investing activities, financing activities, and the noncash investing and financing activities. Show the effect of the change on cash flows by making entries in the Transactions columns.

•Exhibit 10   Work Sheet for Statement of Cash Flows—Direct Method

Rundell Inc.
Work Sheet for Statement of Cash Flows
For the Year Ended December 31, 2006

	Accounts	Balance Dec. 31, 2005	Transactions Debit	Transactions Credit	Balance Dec. 31, 2006	
1	**Balance Sheet**					1
2	Cash	26 000 00	(t) 71 500 00		97 500 00	2
3	Accounts receivable (net)	65 000 00	(s) 9 000 00		74 000 00	3
4	Inventories	180 000 00		(r) 8 000 00	172 000 00	4
5	Land	125 000 00	(q) 15 000 00	(e) 60 000 00	80 000 00	5
6	Building	200 000 00	(p) 60 000 00		260 000 00	6
7	Accumulated depreciation—building	(58 300 00)		(c) 7 000 00	(65 300 00)	7
8	Accounts payable (merchandise creditors)	(46 700 00)	(o) 3 200 00		(43 500 00)	8
9	Accrued expenses payable (operating expenses)	(24 300 00)		(n) 2 200 00	(26 500 00)	9
10	Income taxes payable	(8 400 00)	(m) 500 00		(7 900 00)	10
11	Dividends payable	(10 000 00)		(l) 4 000 00	(14 000 00)	11
12	Bonds payable	(150 000 00)	(k) 50 000 00		(100 000 00)	12
13	Common stock	(16 000 00)		(j) 8 000 00	(24 000 00)	13
14	Paid-in capital in excess of par	(80 000 00)		(j) 40 000 00	(120 000 00)	14
15	Retained earnings	(202 300 00)	(i) 28 000 00	(h) 108 000 00	(282 300 00)	15
16	Totals	0 00	237 200 00	237 200 00	0 00	16
17	**Income Statement**					17
18	Sales			(a)1,180 000 00		18
19	Cost of merchandise sold		(b) 790 000 00			19
20	Depreciation expense		(c) 7 000 00			20
21	Other operating expenses		(d) 196 000 00			21
22	Gain on sale of land			(e) 12 000 00		22
23	Interest expense		(f) 8 000 00			23
24	Income taxes		(g) 83 000 00			24
25	Net income		(h) 108 000 00			25
26	**Cash Flows**					26
27	Operating activities:					27
28	Cash received from customers		(a)1,180 000 00	(s) 9 000 00		28
29	Cash payments:					29
30	Merchandise		(r) 8 000 00	(b) 790 000 00		30
31				(o) 3 200 00		31
32	Operating expenses		(n) 2 200 00	(d) 196 000 00		32
33	Interest			(f) 8 000 00		33
34	Income taxes			(g) 83 000 00		34
35				(m) 500 00		35
36	Investing activities:					36
37	Sale of land		(e) 72 000 00			37
38	Purchase of land			(q) 15 000 00		38
39	Purchase of building			(p) 60 000 00		39
40	Financing activities:					40
41	Issued common stock		(j) 48 000 00			41
42	Retired bonds payable			(k) 50 000 00		42
43	Declared cash dividends			(i) 28 000 00		43
44	Increase in dividends payable		(l) 4 000 00			44
45	Net increase in cash			(t) 71 500 00		45
46	Totals		2,506 200 00	2,506 200 00		46

Analyzing Accounts

Under the direct method of reporting cash flows from operating activities, analyzing accounts begins with the income statement. As we analyze each income statement account, we will make entries on the work sheet that show the effect on cash flows from operating activities. After we have analyzed the income statement accounts, we will analyze changes in the balance sheet accounts.

The order in which the balance sheet accounts are analyzed is unimportant. However, it is more efficient to begin with the retained earnings account and proceed upward in the account listing. As each noncash balance sheet account is analyzed, we will make entries on the work sheet for the related cash flow activities. After we have analyzed all the noncash accounts, we will make an entry for the increase (decrease) in cash during the period.

Sales   The income statement for Rundell Inc. shows sales of $1,180,000 for the year. Sales for cash provide cash when the sale is made. Sales on account provide cash when customers pay their bills. The entry on the work sheet is as follows:

(a)	Operating Activities—Receipts from Customers	1,180,000	
	Sales		1,180,000

Cost of Merchandise Sold   The income statement for Rundell Inc. shows cost of merchandise sold of $790,000 for the year. The cost of merchandise sold requires cash payments for cash purchases of merchandise. For purchases on account, cash payments are made when the invoices are due. The entry on the work sheet is as follows:

(b)	Cost of Merchandise Sold	790,000	
	Operating Activities—Payments for Merchandise		790,000

Depreciation Expense   The income statement for Rundell Inc. shows depreciation expense of $7,000. Depreciation expense does not require a cash outflow and thus is not reported on the statement of cash flows. The entry on the work sheet to fully account for the depreciation expense is as follows:

(c)	Depreciation Expense	7,000	
	Accumulated Depreciation—Building		7,000

Other Accounts   The entries for the other accounts are made on the work sheet in a manner similar to entries (a), (b), and (c). A summary of these entries is as follows:

(d)	Other Operating Expenses	196,000	
	Operating Activities—Paid Operating Expenses		196,000
(e)	Investing Activities—Sale of Land	72,000	
	Land		60,000
	Gain on Sale of Land		12,000
(f)	Interest Expense	8,000	
	Operating Activities—Paid Interest		8,000
(g)	Income Taxes	83,000	
	Operating Activities—Paid Income Taxes		83,000
(h)	Net Income	108,000	
	Retained Earnings		108,000
(i)	Retained Earnings	28,000	
	Financing Activities—Declared Cash Dividends		28,000

(j)	Financing Activities—Issued Common Stock	48,000	
	Common Stock		8,000
	Paid-In Capital in Excess of Par—Common Stock		40,000
(k)	Bonds Payable	50,000	
	Financing Activities—Retired Bonds Payable		50,000
(l)	Financing Activities—Increase in Dividends Payable	4,000	
	Dividends Payable		4,000
(m)	Income Taxes Payable	500	
	Operating Activities—Cash Paid for Income Taxes		500
(n)	Operating Activities—Cash Paid for Operating Expenses	2,200	
	Accrued Expenses Payable		2,200
(o)	Accounts Payable	3,200	
	Operating Activities—Cash Paid for Merchandise		3,200
(p)	Building	60,000	
	Investing Activities—Purchase of Building		60,000
(q)	Land	15,000	
	Investing Activities—Purchase of Land		15,000
(r)	Operating Activities—Cash Paid for Merchandise	8,000	
	Inventories		8,000
(s)	Accounts Receivable	9,000	
	Operating Activities—Cash Received from Customers		9,000
(t)	Cash	71,500	
	Net Increase in Cash		71,500

Completing the Work Sheet

After we have analyzed all the income statement and balance sheet accounts and have made the entries on the work sheet, all the operating, investing, and financing activities are identified in the bottom portion of the work sheet. The mathematical accuracy of the work sheet entries is verified by the equality of each pair of the totals of the debit and credit Transactions columns.

Preparing the Statement of Cash Flows

The statement of cash flows prepared from the work sheet is identical to the statement in Exhibit 8. The data for the three sections of the statement are obtained from the bottom portion of the work sheet. Some of these data may not be reported exactly as they appear on the work sheet. The cash paid for dividends is reported as $24,000 instead of the amount of dividends declared ($28,000) less the increase in the dividends payable ($4,000).

ey Points

1 Summarize the types of cash flow activities reported in the statement of cash flows.

The statement of cash flows reports useful information about a firm's ability to generate cash from operations, maintain and expand its operating capacity, meet its financial obligations, and pay dividends.

The statement of cash flows reports cash receipts and cash payments by three types of activities: operating activities, investing activities, and financing activities.

Cash flows from operating activities are cash flows from transactions that affect net income. There are two methods of reporting cash flows from operating activities: (1) the direct method and (2) the indirect method.

Cash inflows from investing activities are cash flows from the sale of investments, fixed assets, and intangible assets. Cash outflows generally include payments to acquire investments, fixed assets, and intangible assets.

Cash inflows from financing activities include proceeds from issuing equity securities, such as preferred and common stock. Cash inflows also arise from issuing bonds, mortgage notes payable, and other long-term debt. Cash outflows from financing activities arise from paying cash dividends, purchasing treasury stock, and repaying amounts borrowed.

Investing and financing for a business may be affected by transactions that do not involve cash. The effect of such transactions should be reported in a separate schedule accompanying the statement of cash flows.

Because it may be misleading, cash flow per share is not reported in the statement of cash flows.

2 Prepare a statement of cash flows, using the indirect method.

To prepare the statement of cash flows, changes in the noncash balance sheet accounts are analyzed. This logic relies on the fact that a change in any balance sheet account can be analyzed in terms of changes in the other balance sheet accounts. Thus, by analyzing the noncash balance sheet accounts, those activities that resulted in cash flows can be identified. Although the noncash balance sheet accounts may be analyzed in any order, it is usually more efficient to begin with retained earnings. Additional data are obtained by analyzing the income statement accounts and supporting records.

3 Prepare a statement of cash flows, using the direct method.

The direct method and the indirect method will report the same amount of cash flows from operating activities. Also, the manner of reporting cash flows from investing and financing activities is the same under both methods. The methods differ in how the cash flows from operating activities data are obtained, an-alyzed, and reported. The direct method reports cash flows from operating activities by major classes of operating cash receipts and cash payments. The difference between the major classes of total operating cash receipts and total operating cash payments is the net cash flow from operating activities.

The data for reporting cash flows from operating activities by the direct method can be obtained by analyzing the cash flows related to the revenues and expenses reported on the income statement. The revenues and expenses are adjusted from the accrual basis of accounting to the cash basis for purposes of preparing the statement of cash flows.

When the direct method is used, a reconciliation of net income and net cash flow from operating activities is reported in a separate schedule. This schedule is similar to the cash flows from operating activities section of the statement of cash flows prepared using the indirect method.

4 Calculate and interpret the free cash flow.

Free cash flow is the amount of operating cash flow remaining after replacing current productive capacity and maintaining current dividends. Free cash flow is the amount of cash available to reduce debt, expand the business, or return to shareholders through increased dividends or treasury stock purchases.

ey Terms

cash flows from financing activities (561)
cash flows from investing activities (561)

cash flows from operating activities (561)
direct method (562)
free cash flow (578)

indirect method (562)
statement of cash flows (561)

Illustrative Problem

The comparative balance sheet of Dowling Company for December 31, 2007 and 2006, is as follows:

Dowling Company
Comparative Balance Sheet
December 31, 2007 and 2006

	2007	2006
Assets		
Cash	$ 140,350	$ 95,900
Accounts receivable (net)	95,300	102,300
Inventories	165,200	157,900
Prepaid expenses	6,240	5,860
Investments (long-term)	35,700	84,700
Land	75,000	90,000
Buildings	375,000	260,000
Accumulated depreciation—buildings	(71,300)	(58,300)
Machinery and equipment	428,300	428,300
Accumulated depreciation—machinery and equipment	(148,500)	(138,000)
Patents	58,000	65,000
Total assets	$1,159,290	$1,093,660
Liabilities and Stockholders' Equity		
Accounts payable (merchandise creditors)	$ 43,500	$ 46,700
Accrued expenses (operating expenses)	14,000	12,500
Income taxes payable	7,900	8,400
Dividends payable	14,000	10,000
Mortgage note payable, due 2017	40,000	0
Bonds payable	150,000	250,000
Common stock, $30 par	450,000	375,000
Excess of issue price over par—common stock	66,250	41,250
Retained earnings	373,640	349,810
Total liabilities and stockholders' equity	$1,159,290	$1,093,660

The income statement for Dowling Company is shown below.

Dowling Company
Income Statement
For the Year Ended December 31, 2007

Sales		$1,100,000
Cost of merchandise sold		710,000
Gross profit		$ 390,000
Operating expenses:		
Depreciation expense	$ 23,500	
Patent amortization	7,000	
Other operating expenses	196,000	
Total operating expenses		226,500
Income from operations		$ 163,500
Other income:		
Gain on sale of investments	$ 11,000	
Other expense:		
Interest expense	26,000	(15,000)
Income before income tax		$ 148,500
Income tax expense		50,000
Net income		$ 98,500

An examination of the accounting records revealed the following additional information applicable to 2007:

a. Land costing $15,000 was sold for $15,000.
b. A mortgage note was issued for $40,000.
c. A building costing $115,000 was constructed.
d. 2,500 shares of common stock were issued at 40 in exchange for the bonds payable.
e. Cash dividends declared were $74,670.

Instructions

1. Prepare a statement of cash flows, using the indirect method of reporting cash flows from operating activities.
2. Prepare a statement of cash flows, using the direct method of reporting cash flows from operating activities.

Solution

1.

Dowling Company
Statement of Cash Flows—Indirect Method
For the Year Ended December 31, 2007

Cash flows from operating activities:			
Net income, per income statement		$ 98,500	
Add: Depreciation	$23,500		
Amortization of patents	7,000		
Decrease in accounts receivable	7,000		
Increase in accrued expenses	1,500	39,000	
		$137,500	
Deduct: Increase in inventories	$ 7,300		
Increase in prepaid expenses	380		
Decrease in accounts payable	3,200		
Decrease in income taxes payable	500		
Gain on sale of investments	11,000	22,380	
Net cash flow from operating activities			$115,120
Cash flows from investing activities:			
Cash received from sale of:			
Investments	$60,000		
Land	15,000	$ 75,000	
Less: Cash paid for construction of building		115,000	
Net cash flow used for investing activities			(40,000)
Cash flows from financing activities:			
Cash received from issuing mortgage note payable		$ 40,000	
Less: Cash paid for dividends		70,670	
Net cash flow used for financing activities			(30,670)
Increase in cash			$ 44,450
Cash at the beginning of the year			95,900
Cash at the end of the year			$140,350
Schedule of Noncash Investing and			
Financing Activities:			
Issued common stock to retire bonds payable			$100,000

2.

Dowling Company
Statement of Cash Flows—Direct Method
For the Year Ended December 31, 2007

Cash flows from operating activities:			
Cash received from customers[1]			$1,107,000
Deduct: Cash paid for merchandise[2]	$720,500		
Cash paid for operating expenses[3]	194,880		
Cash paid for interest expense	26,000		
Cash paid for income tax[4]	50,500	991,880	
Net cash flow from operating activities			$115,120
Cash flows from investing activities:			
Cash received from sale of:			
Investments	$ 60,000		
Land	15,000	$ 75,000	
Less: Cash paid for construction of building		115,000	
Net cash flow used for investing activities			(40,000)
Cash flows from financing activities:			
Cash received from issuing mortgage note payable		$ 40,000	
Less: Cash paid for dividends[5]		70,670	
Net cash flow used for financing activities			(30,670)
Increase in cash			$ 44,450
Cash at the beginning of the year			95,900
Cash at the end of the year			$140,350

Schedule of Noncash Investing and
Financing Activities:

Issued common stock to retire bonds payable	$100,000

Computations:
[1]$1,100,000 + $7,000 = $1,107,000
[2]$710,000 + $3,200 + $7,300 = $720,500
[3]$196,000 + $380 − $1,500 = $194,880
[4]$50,000 + $500 = $50,500
[5]$74,670 + $10,000 − $14,000 = $70,670

Self-Examination Questions (Answers at End of Chapter)

1. An example of a cash flow from an operating activity is:
   A. receipt of cash from the sale of stock
   B. receipt of cash from the sale of bonds
   C. payment of cash for dividends
   D. receipt of cash from customers on account

2. An example of a cash flow from an investing activity is:
   A. receipt of cash from the sale of equipment
   B. receipt of cash from the sale of stock
   C. payment of cash for dividends
   D. payment of cash to acquire treasury stock

3. An example of a cash flow from a financing activity is:
   A. receipt of cash from customers on account
   B. receipt of cash from the sale of equipment
   C. payment of cash for dividends
   D. payment of cash to acquire land

4. Which of the following methods of reporting cash flows from operating activities adjusts net income for revenues and expenses not involving the receipt or payment of cash?
   A. Direct method   C. Reciprocal method
   B. Purchase method   D. Indirect method

5. The net income reported on the income statement for the year was $55,000, and depreciation of fixed assets for the year was $22,000. The balances of the current asset and current liability accounts at the beginning and end of the year are as follows:

	End	Beginning
Cash	$ 65,000	$ 70,000
Accounts receivable	100,000	90,000
Inventories	145,000	150,000
Prepaid expenses	7,500	8,000
Accounts payable (merchandise creditors)	51,000	58,000

The total amount reported for cash flows from operating activities in the statement of cash flows, using the indirect method, is:

A. $33,000   C. $65,500

B. $55,000   D. $77,000

Class Discussion Questions

1. What is the principal disadvantage of the direct method of reporting cash flows from operating activities?
2. What are the major advantages of the indirect method of reporting cash flows from operating activities?
3. A corporation issued $200,000 of common stock in exchange for $200,000 of fixed assets. Where would this transaction be reported on the statement of cash flows?
4. a. What is the effect on cash flows of declaring and issuing a stock dividend?
   b. Is the stock dividend reported on the statement of cash flows?
5. A retail business, using the accrual method of accounting, owed merchandise creditors (accounts payable) $290,000 at the beginning of the year and $315,000 at the end of the year. How would the $25,000 increase be used to adjust net income in determining the amount of cash flows from operating activities by the indirect method? Explain.
6. If salaries payable was $75,000 at the beginning of the year and $65,000 at the end of the year, should $10,000 be added to or deducted from income to determine the amount of cash flows from operating activities by the indirect method? Explain.
7. A long-term investment in bonds with a cost of $75,000 was sold for $80,000 cash. (a) What was the gain or loss on the sale? (b) What was the effect of the transaction on cash flows? (c) How should the transaction be reported in the statement of cash flows if cash flows from operating activities are reported by the indirect method?
8. A corporation issued $5,000,000 of 20-year bonds for cash at 105. How would the transaction be reported on the statement of cash flows?
9. Fully depreciated equipment costing $55,000 was discarded. What was the effect of the transaction on cash flows if (a) $5,000 cash is received, (b) no cash is received?
10. For the current year, Accord Company decided to switch from the indirect method to the direct method for reporting cash flows from operating activities on the statement of cash flows. Will the change cause the amount of net cash flow from operating activities to be (a) larger, (b) smaller, or (c) the same as if the indirect method had been used? Explain.
11. Name five common major classes of operating cash receipts or operating cash payments presented on the statement of cash flows when the cash flows from operating activities are reported by the direct method.
12. In a recent annual report, **eBay Inc.** reported that during the year it issued stock of $128 million for acquisitions. How would this be reported on the statement of cash flows?

REAL WORLD

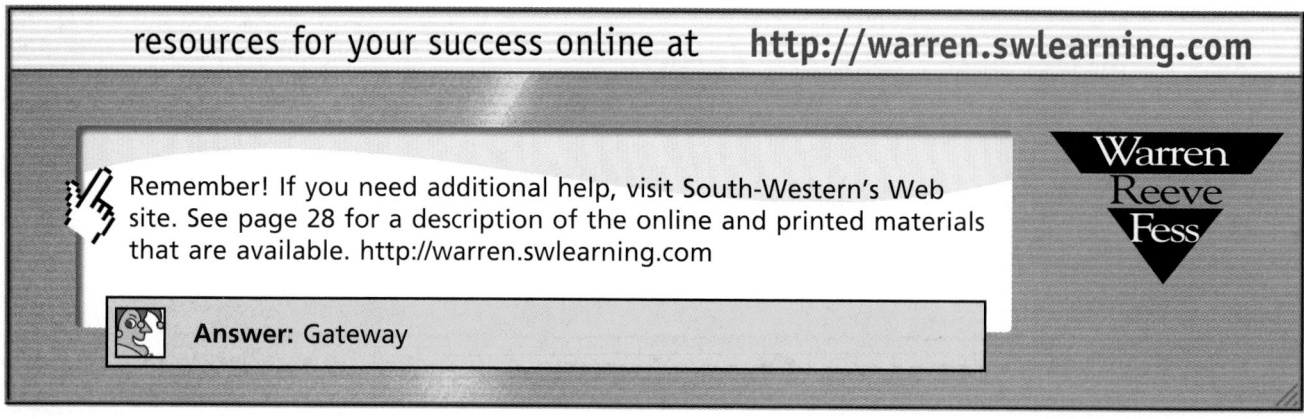

resources for your success online at **http://warren.swlearning.com**

Remember! If you need additional help, visit South-Western's Web site. See page 28 for a description of the online and printed materials that are available. http://warren.swlearning.com

Answer: Gateway

Exercises

EXERCISE 14-1
Cash flows from operating activities—net loss
Objective 1

REAL WORLD

On its income statement for a recent year, **TimeWarner Inc.**, reported a net *loss* of $4.9 billion from operations. On its statement of cash flows, it reported $5.3 billion of cash flows from operating activities.

Explain this apparent contradiction between the loss and the positive cash flows.

EXERCISE 14-2
Effect of transactions on cash flows
Objective 1

✓ *b. Cash receipt, $41,000*

State the effect (cash receipt or payment and amount) of each of the following transactions, considered individually, on cash flows:

a. Sold 5,000 shares of $30 par common stock for $45 per share.
b. Sold equipment with a book value of $42,500 for $41,000.
c. Purchased land for $120,000 cash.
d. Purchased 5,000 shares of $30 par common stock as treasury stock at $50 per share.
e. Sold a new issue of $100,000 of bonds at 101.
f. Paid dividends of $1.50 per share. There were 30,000 shares issued and 5,000 shares of treasury stock.
g. Retired $500,000 of bonds, on which there was $2,500 of unamortized discount, for $501,000.
h. Purchased a building by paying $30,000 cash and issuing a $90,000 mortgage note payable.

EXERCISE 14-3
Classifying cash flows
Objective 1

Identify the type of cash flow activity for each of the following events (operating, investing, or financing):

a. Purchased patents.
b. Purchased buildings.
c. Purchased treasury stock.
d. Sold equipment.
e. Net income.
f. Issued preferred stock.
g. Redeemed bonds.
h. Paid cash dividends.
i. Sold long-term investments.
j. Issued common stock.
k. Issued bonds.

EXERCISE 14-4
Cash flows from operating activities—indirect method
Objective 2

Indicate whether each of the following would be added to or deducted from net income in determining net cash flow from operating activities by the indirect method:

a. Increase in notes payable due in 90 days to vendors
b. Loss on disposal of fixed assets
c. Decrease in accounts payable
d. Increase in notes receivable due in 90 days from customers
e. Decrease in salaries payable
f. Decrease in prepaid expenses
g. Depreciation of fixed assets
h. Decrease in accounts receivable
i. Amortization of patent *Deprec. Exp*
j. Increase in merchandise inventory *Current asset*
k. Gain on retirement of long-term debt

EXERCISE 14-5
Cash flows from operating activities—indirect method
Objectives 1, 2

SPREADSHEET

✓ a. Cash flows from operating activities, $292,100

The net income reported on the income statement for the current year was $255,800. Depreciation recorded on equipment and a building amounted to $53,500 for the year. Balances of the current asset and current liability accounts at the beginning and end of the year are as follows:

	End of Year	Beginning of Year
Cash	$ 42,000	$ 44,200
Accounts receivable (net) *Current Asset*	65,400	67,000 *(1,600) ↓*
Inventories *Current Asset*	125,900	112,600 *13,300 ↑*
Prepaid expenses *Current Asset*	5,800	6,000 *(200) ↓*
Accounts payable (merchandise creditors) *Cur. Liab.*	61,400	67,500 *(6,100) ↓*
Salaries payable *Cur. Liability*	8,300	7,900 *400 ↑*

a. Prepare the cash flows from operating activities section of the statement of cash flows, using the indirect method.
b. ▬▬▶ If the direct method had been used, would the net cash flow from operating activities have been the same? Explain.

EXERCISE 14-6
Cash flows from operating activities—indirect method
Objective 2

SPREADSHEET

✓ Cash flows from operating activities, $96,400

The net income reported on the income statement for the current year was $75,000. Depreciation recorded on store equipment for the year amounted to $22,500. Balances of the current asset and current liability accounts at the beginning and end of the year are as follows:

	End of Year	Beginning of Year
Cash	$46,700	$43,000
Accounts receivable (net)	28,800	32,500
Merchandise inventory	54,800	49,300
Prepaid expenses	4,000	3,600
Accounts payable (merchandise creditors)	40,500	42,400
Wages payable	25,500	22,500

Prepare the cash flows from operating activities section of the statement of cash flows, using the indirect method.

EXERCISE 14-7
Determining cash payments to stockholders
Objective 2

The board of directors declared cash dividends totaling $80,000 during the current year. The comparative balance sheet indicates dividends payable of $25,000 at the beginning of the year and $20,000 at the end of the year. What was the amount of cash payments to stockholders during the year?

EXERCISE 14-8
Reporting changes in equipment on statement of cash flows
Objective 2

An analysis of the general ledger accounts indicates that office equipment, which cost $30,000 and on which accumulated depreciation totaled $10,000 on the date of sale, was sold for $25,000 during the year. Using this information, indicate the items to be reported on the statement of cash flows.

EXERCISE 14-9
Reporting changes in equipment on statement of cash flows
Objective 2

An analysis of the general ledger accounts indicates that delivery equipment, which cost $120,000 and on which accumulated depreciation totaled $40,000 on the date of sale, was sold for $75,000 during the year. Using this information, indicate the items to be reported on the statement of cash flows.

EXERCISE 14-10
Reporting land transactions on statement of cash flows
Objective 2

On the basis of the details of the following fixed asset account, indicate the items to be reported on the statement of cash flows:

ACCOUNT *Land*   **ACCOUNT NO.**

Date		Item	Debit	Credit	Balance Debit	Balance Credit
2006						
Jan.	1	Balance			900,000	
Feb.	5	Purchased for cash	300,000		1,200,000	
Oct.	30	Sold for $310,000		250,000	950,000	

EXERCISE 14-11
Reporting stockholders' equity items on statement of cash flows
Objective 2

On the basis of the following stockholders' equity accounts, indicate the items, exclusive of net income, to be reported on the statement of cash flows. There were no unpaid dividends at either the beginning or the end of the year.

ACCOUNT *Common Stock, $10 Par*   **ACCOUNT NO.**

Date		Item	Debit	Credit	Balance Debit	Balance Credit
2006						
Jan.	1	Balance, 70,000 shares				700,000
Feb.	11	12,000 shares issued for cash		120,000		820,000
June	30	4,100-share stock dividend		41,000		861,000

ACCOUNT *Paid-In Capital in Excess of Par—Common Stock*   **ACCOUNT NO.**

Date		Item	Debit	Credit	Balance Debit	Balance Credit
2006						
Jan.	1	Balance				140,000
Feb.	11	12,000 shares issued for cash		360,000		500,000
June	30	Stock dividend		102,500		602,500

ACCOUNT *Retained Earnings*   **ACCOUNT NO.**

Date		Item	Debit	Credit	Balance Debit	Balance Credit
2006						
Jan.	1	Balance				1,000,000
June	30	Stock dividend	143,500			856,500
Dec.	30	Cash dividend	240,000			616,500
	31	Net income		800,000		1,416,500

EXERCISE 14-12
Reporting land acquisition for cash and mortgage note on statement of cash flows
Objective 2

On the basis of the details of the following fixed asset account, indicate the items to be reported on the statement of cash flows:

ACCOUNT *Land*   **ACCOUNT NO.**

Date		Item	Debit	Credit	Balance Debit	Balance Credit
2006						
Jan.	1	Balance			160,000	
Feb.	10	Purchased for cash	290,000		450,000	
Nov.	20	Purchased with long-term mortgage note	200,000		650,000	

EXERCISE 14-13
Reporting issuance and retirement of long-term debt

Objective 2

On the basis of the details of the following bonds payable and related discount accounts, indicate the items to be reported in the financing section of the statement of cash flows, assuming no gain or loss on retiring the bonds:

ACCOUNT *Bonds Payable*   ACCOUNT NO.

Date		Item	Debit	Credit	Balance Debit	Balance Credit
2006						
Jan.	1	Balance				150,000
Jan.	3	Retire bonds	48,000			102,000
July	30	Issue bonds		200,000		302,000

ACCOUNT *Discount on Bonds Payable*   ACCOUNT NO.

Date		Item	Debit	Credit	Balance Debit	Balance Credit
2006						
Jan.	1	Balance			12,000	
Jan.	3	Retire bonds		4,000	8,000	
July	30	Issue bonds	15,000		23,000	
Dec.	31	Amortize discount		1,200	21,800	

EXERCISE 14-14
Determining net income from net cash flow from operating activities

Objective 2

Tiger Golf Inc. reported a net cash flow from operating activities of $105,700 on its statement of cash flows for the year ended December 31, 2006. The following information was reported in the cash flows from operating activities section of the statement of cash flows, using the indirect method:

Decrease in income taxes payable	$ 2,100
Decrease in inventories	6,400
Depreciation	11,000
Gain on sale of investments	3,600
Increase in accounts payable	4,700
Increase in prepaid expenses	2,000
Increase in accounts receivable	6,500

Determine the net income reported by Tiger Golf Inc. for the year ended December 31, 2006.

EXERCISE 14-15
Cash flows from operating activities

Objective 2

REAL WORLD   SPREADSHEET

✓ *Cash flows from operating activities, $205,006*

Selected data derived from the income statement and balance sheet of **Williams Sonoma, Inc.**, a specialty retailer of kitchen products, for a recent year are as follows:

Income Statement Data (dollars in thousands)

Net earnings	$75,096
Depreciation	81,594
Loss on sale of fixed assets	3,950
Other noncash income	7,242

Balance Sheet Data (dollars in thousands)

Decrease in accounts receivable	$ 6,025
Decrease in merchandise inventories	33,793
Increase in prepaid assets	4,511
Increase in accounts payable and other accrued expenses	4,156
Increase in income tax payable	12,145

Prepare the cash flows from operating activities section of the statement of cash flows (using the indirect method) for Williams Sonoma for the year.

EXERCISE 14-16
Cash flows from operating activities—direct method
Objective 3

✓ a. $537,000

The cash flows from operating activities are reported by the direct method on the statement of cash flows. Determine the following:

a. If sales for the current year were $510,000 and accounts receivable decreased by $27,000 during the year, what was the amount of cash received from customers?

b. If income tax expense for the current year was $29,000 and income tax payable decreased by $3,900 during the year, what was the amount of cash payments for income tax?

EXERCISE 14-17
Cash paid for merchandise purchases
Objective 3

REAL WORLD

The cost of merchandise sold for **Toys "R" Us, Inc.**, for a recent year was $7,604 million. The balance sheet showed the following current account balances (in millions):

	Balance, End of Year	Balance, Beginning of Year
Merchandise inventories	$2,041	$2,307
Accounts payable	878	1,152

Determine the amount of cash payments for merchandise.

EXERCISE 14-18
Determining selected amounts for cash flows from operating activities— direct method
Objective 3

✓ b. $79,600

Selected data taken from the accounting records of Floral Escape, Inc. for the current year ended December 31 are as follows:

	Balance, December 31	Balance, January 1
Accrued expenses (operating expenses)	$ 4,300	$ 4,900
Accounts payable (merchandise creditors)	32,100	36,800
Inventories	59,500	71,200
Prepaid expenses	2,500	3,500

During the current year, the cost of merchandise sold was $450,000 and the operating expenses other than depreciation were $80,000. The direct method is used for presenting the cash flows from operating activities on the statement of cash flows.

Determine the amount reported on the statement of cash flows for (a) cash payments for merchandise and (b) cash payments for operating expenses.

EXERCISE 14-19
Cash flows from operating activities—direct method
Objective 3

SPREADSHEET

✓ Cash flows from operating activities, $97,000

The income statement of Heart Grain Bakeries, Inc. for the current year ended June 30 is as follows:

Sales		$645,000
Cost of merchandise sold		367,800
Gross profit		$277,200
Operating expenses:		
Depreciation expense	$ 45,000	
Other operating expenses	155,400	
Total operating expenses		200,400
Income before income tax		$ 76,800
Income tax expense		25,400
Net income		$ 51,400

Changes in the balances of selected accounts from the beginning to the end of the current year are as follows:

	Increase Decrease*
Accounts receivable (net)	$12,000*
Inventories	4,200
Prepaid expenses	2,500*
Accounts payable (merchandise creditors)	8,400*
Accrued expenses (operating expenses)	2,300
Income tax payable	3,600*

Prepare the cash flows from operating activities section of the statement of cash flows, using the direct method.

EXERCISE 14-20
Cash flows from operating activities—direct method
Objective 3

SPREADSHEET

✓ Cash flows from operating activities, $27,100

The income statement for Wholly Bagel Company for the current year ended June 30 and balances of selected accounts at the beginning and the end of the year are as follows:

Sales		$265,000
Cost of merchandise sold		95,800
Gross profit		$169,200
Operating expenses:		
Depreciation expense	$ 12,500	
Other operating expenses	125,700	
Total operating expenses		138,200
Income before income tax		$ 31,000
Income tax expense		12,300
Net income		$ 18,700

	End of Year	Beginning of Year
Accounts receivable (net)	$14,800	$12,500
Inventories	38,100	32,800
Prepaid expenses	6,000	6,400
Accounts payable (merchandise creditors)	27,900	24,300
Accrued expenses (operating expenses)	7,900	8,400
Income tax payable	1,500	1,500

Prepare the cash flows from operating activities section of the statement of cash flows, using the direct method.

EXERCISE 14-21
Statement of cash flows
Objective 2

SPREADSHEET

✓ Net cash flow from operating activities, $29

The comparative balance sheet of Contemporary Millworks, Inc. for December 31, 2006 and 2005, is as follows:

	Dec. 31, 2006	Dec. 31, 2005	
Assets			
Cash	$ 50	$ 16	
Accounts receivable (net)	30	32	(2) ↓
Inventories	24	19	5 ↑
Land	35	50	(15) ↓
Equipment	32	15	17 ↑
Accumulated depreciation—equipment	(9)	(6)	(3) ↓
Total	$162	$126	
Liabilities and Stockholders' Equity			
Accounts payable (merchandise creditors)	$ 17	$ 20	(3) ↓
Dividends payable	1	—	1 ↑
Common stock, $1 par	4	2	2 ↑
Paid-in capital in excess of par—common stock	20	10	10 ↑
Retained earnings	120	94	26 ↑
Total	$162	$126	

(handwritten notes: Depr Exp – 3 ; Loss on Sale of land – 2)

The following additional information is taken from the records:

a. Land was sold for $13.
b. Equipment was acquired for cash.
c. There were no disposals of equipment during the year.
d. The common stock was issued for cash.
e. There was a $30 credit to Retained Earnings for net income.
f. There was a $4 debit to Retained Earnings for cash dividends declared.

Prepare a statement of cash flows, using the indirect method of presenting cash flows from operating activities.

EXERCISE 14-22
Statement of cash flows

Objective 2

WHAT'S WRONG WITH THIS?

List the errors you find in the following statement of cash flows. The cash balance at the beginning of the year was $70,700. All other figures are correct, except the cash balance at the end of the year.

Healthy Choice Nutrition Products, Inc.
Statement of Cash Flows
For the Year Ended December 31, 2006

Cash flows from operating activities:			
Net income, per income statement		$100,500	
Add: Depreciation	$ 49,000		
Increase in accounts receivable	10,500		
Gain on sale of investments	5,000	64,500	
		$165,000	
Deduct: Increase in accounts payable	$ 4,400		
Increase in inventories	18,300		
Decrease in accrued expenses	1,600	24,300	
Net cash flow from operating activities			$140,700
Cash flows from investing activities:			
Cash received from sale of investments		$ 85,000	
Less: Cash paid for purchase of land	$ 90,000		
Cash paid for purchase of equipment	150,100	240,100	
Net cash flow used for investing activities			(155,100)
Cash flows from financing activities:			
Cash received from sale of common stock		$107,000	
Cash paid for dividends		45,000	
Net cash flow provided by financing activities			152,000
Increase in cash			$137,600
Cash at the end of the year			105,300
Cash at the beginning of the year			$242,900

EXERCISE 14-23
Free cash flow

Objectives 2, 4

Hacienda Tile Company has 100,000 shares of common stock issued and outstanding and 1,000 shares of 8%, $100 par value preferred stock issued and outstanding. Hacienda had cash flows from operating activities of $120,000. Cash flows used for investments in property, plant, and equipment totaled $45,000, of which 60% of this investment was used to replace existing capacity. A cash dividend of $0.20 per share was declared and paid on common stock.

Determine the free cash flow for Hacienda Tile Company.

EXERCISE 14-24
Free cash flow

Objectives 2, 4

REAL WORLD

The financial statements for **Home Depot** are provided in Appendix F at the end of the text.

a. Determine the free cash flow for the years ended February 2, 2003 and February 3, 2002. Assume that 80% of capital expenditures were for new store openings, and the remaining was for remodeling and updating existing stores.
b. Determine the percent of free cash flow to operating activities and net sales.
c. Interpret your results in (a) and (b).

Problems Series A

PROBLEM 14-1A
Statement of cash flows—indirect method

Objective 2

The comparative balance sheet of Winner's Edge Sporting Goods, Inc. for December 31, 2006 and 2005, is as follows:

✓ *Net cash flow from operating activities, $163,300*

	Dec. 31, 2006	Dec. 31, 2005
Assets		
Cash	$ 464,100	$ 395,800
Accounts receivable (net)	163,200	145,700
Inventories	395,000	367,900
Investments	0	120,000
Land	160,000	0
Equipment	695,500	575,500
Accumulated depreciation—equipment	(194,000)	(168,000)
	$1,683,800	$1,436,900
Liabilities and Stockholders' Equity		
Accounts payable (merchandise creditors)	$ 228,700	$ 210,500
Accrued expenses (operating expenses)	16,500	21,400
Dividends payable	14,000	10,000
Common stock, $10 par	75,000	60,000
Paid-in capital in excess of par—common stock	265,000	175,000
Retained earnings	1,084,600	960,000
	$1,683,800	$1,436,900

The following additional information was taken from the records:

a. The investments were sold for $132,000 cash.
b. Equipment and land were acquired for cash.
c. There were no disposals of equipment during the year.
d. The common stock was issued for cash.
e. There was a $180,600 credit to Retained Earnings for net income.
f. There was a $56,000 debit to Retained Earnings for cash dividends declared.

Instructions

Prepare a statement of cash flows, using the indirect method of presenting cash flows from operating activities.

PROBLEM 14-2A
Statement of cash flows—indirect method

Objective 2

✓ *Net cash flow from operating activities, $78,400*

The comparative balance sheet of Medalist Athletic Apparel Co. at December 31, 2006 and 2005, is as follows:

	Dec. 31, 2006	Dec. 31, 2005
Assets		
Cash	$ 37,200	$ 45,300
Accounts receivable (net) *(4,200)*	61,200	65,400
Merchandise inventory *5,400*	91,000	85,600
Prepaid expenses *1,500*	5,500	4,000
Equipment	190,500	155,500
Accumulated depreciation—equipment	(41,200)	(35,800)
	$344,200	$320,000
Liabilities and Stockholders' Equity		
Accounts payable (merchandise creditors) *1700*	$ 67,100	$ 65,400
Mortgage note payable	0	95,000
Common stock, $1 par	14,000	10,000
Paid-in capital in excess of par—common stock	200,000	100,000
Retained earnings	63,100	49,600
	$344,200	$320,000

Additional data obtained from the income statement and from an examination of the accounts in the ledger for 2006 are as follows:

a. Net income, $61,500.
b. Depreciation reported on the income statement, $17,900.
c. Equipment was purchased at a cost of $47,500, and fully depreciated equipment costing $12,500 was discarded, with no salvage realized.

d. The mortgage note payable was not due until 2009, but the terms permitted earlier payment without penalty.

e. 4,000 shares of common stock were issued at $26 for cash.

f. Cash dividends declared and paid, $48,000.

Instructions

Prepare a statement of cash flows, using the indirect method of presenting cash flows from operating activities.

PROBLEM 14-3A
Statement of cash flows—indirect method

Objective 2

SPREADSHEET

✓ *Net cash flow from operating activities,* ($53,000)

The comparative balance sheet of Sunrise Juice Co. at December 31, 2006 and 2005, is as follows:

	Dec. 31, 2006	Dec. 31, 2005
Assets		
Cash	$ 405,200	$ 432,100
Accounts receivable (net)	324,100	305,700
Inventories	602,300	576,900
Prepaid expenses	10,000	12,000
Land	100,000	190,000
Buildings	650,000	400,000
Accumulated depreciation—buildings	(172,500)	(155,000)
Equipment	225,600	210,700
Accumulated depreciation—equipment	(48,100)	(56,500)
	$2,096,600	$1,915,900
Liabilities and Stockholders' Equity		
Accounts payable (merchandise creditors)	$ 399,100	$ 402,600
Bonds payable	80,000	0
Common stock, $1 par	60,000	50,000
Paid-in capital in excess of par—common stock	350,000	200,000
Retained earnings	1,207,500	1,263,300
	$2,096,600	$1,915,900

The noncurrent asset, the noncurrent liability, and the stockholders' equity accounts for 2006 are as follows:

ACCOUNT *Land* **ACCOUNT NO.**

Date		Item	Debit	Credit	Balance Debit	Balance Credit
2006						
Jan.	1	Balance			190,000	
April	20	Realized $81,000 cash from sale		90,000	100,000	

ACCOUNT *Buildings* **ACCOUNT NO.**

Date		Item	Debit	Credit	Balance Debit	Balance Credit
2006						
Jan.	1	Balance			400,000	
April	20	Acquired for cash	250,000		650,000	

ACCOUNT *Accumulated Depreciation—Buildings* **ACCOUNT NO.**

Date		Item	Debit	Credit	Balance Debit	Balance Credit
2006						
Jan.	1	Balance				155,000
Dec.	31	Depreciation for year		17,500		172,500

ACCOUNT *Equipment* **ACCOUNT NO.**

Date		Item	Debit	Credit	Balance Debit	Balance Credit
2006						
Jan.	1	Balance			210,700	
	26	Discarded, no salvage		18,000	192,700	
Aug.	11	Purchased for cash	32,900		225,600	

ACCOUNT *Accumulated Depreciation—Equipment*   **ACCOUNT NO.**

Date		Item	Debit	Credit	Balance Debit	Balance Credit
2006						
Jan.	1	Balance				56,500
	26	Equipment discarded	18,000			38,500
Dec.	31	Depreciation for year		9,600		48,100

ACCOUNT *Bonds Payable*   **ACCOUNT NO.**

Date		Item	Debit	Credit	Balance Debit	Balance Credit
2006						
May	1	Issued 20-year bonds		80,000		80,000

ACCOUNT *Common Stock, $1 Par*   **ACCOUNT NO.**

Date		Item	Debit	Credit	Balance Debit	Balance Credit
2006						
Jan.	1	Balance				50,000
Dec.	7	Issued 10,000 shares of common stock for $16 per share		10,000		60,000

ACCOUNT *Paid-In Capital in Excess of Par—Common Stock*   **ACCOUNT NO.**

Date		Item	Debit	Credit	Balance Debit	Balance Credit
2006						
Jan.	1	Balance				200,000
Dec.	7	Issued 10,000 shares of common stock for $16 per share		150,000		350,000

ACCOUNT *Retained Earnings*   **ACCOUNT NO.**

Date		Item	Debit	Credit	Balance Debit	Balance Credit
2006						
Jan.	1	Balance				1,263,300
Dec.	31	Net loss	43,800			1,219,500
	31	Cash dividends	12,000			1,207,500

Instructions

Prepare a statement of cash flows, using the indirect method of presenting cash flows from operating activities.

PROBLEM 14-4A
Statement of cash flows—direct method

Objective 3

SPREADSHEET
P.A.S.S.

✓ *Net cash flow from operating activities, $345,200*

The comparative balance sheet of Village Markets, Inc., for December 31, 2007 and 2006, is as follows:

	Dec. 31, 2007	Dec. 31, 2006
Assets		
Cash	$ 421,900	$ 456,700
Accounts receivable (net)	397,200	365,700
Inventories	658,900	623,100
Investments	—	175,000
Land	230,000	—
Equipment	590,000	450,000
Accumulated depreciation	(282,100)	(234,500)
	$2,015,900	$1,836,000
Liabilities and Stockholders' Equity		
Accounts payable (merchandise creditors)	$ 471,200	$ 456,300
Accrued expenses (operating expenses)	40,000	45,300
Dividends payable	61,000	58,000
Common stock, $1 par	23,000	20,000
Paid-in capital in excess of par—common stock	195,000	120,000
Retained earnings	1,225,700	1,136,400
	$2,015,900	$1,836,000

The income statement for the year ended December 31, 2007, is as follows:

Sales		$4,367,800
Cost of merchandise sold		2,532,000
Gross profit		$1,835,800
Operating expenses:		
Depreciation expense	$ 47,600	
Other operating expenses	1,257,900	
Total operating expenses		1,305,500
Operating income		$ 530,300
Other expense:		
Loss on sale of investments		25,000
Income before income tax		$ 505,300
Income tax expense		175,000
Net income		$ 330,300

The following additional information was taken from the records:

a. Equipment and land were acquired for cash.
b. There were no disposals of equipment during the year.
c. The investments were sold for $150,000 cash.
d. The common stock was issued for cash.
e. There was a $241,000 debit to Retained Earnings for cash dividends declared.

Instructions

Prepare a statement of cash flows, using the direct method of presenting cash flows from operating activities.

PROBLEM 14-5A
Statement of cash flows—direct method applied to Problem 14–1A

Objective 3

SPREADSHEET

✓ *Net cash flow from operating activities, $163,300*

The comparative balance sheet of Winner's Edge Sporting Goods, Inc. for December 31, 2006 and 2005, is as follows:

	Dec. 31, 2006	Dec. 31, 2005
Assets		
Cash	$ 464,100	$ 395,800
Accounts receivable (net)	163,200	145,700
Inventories	395,000	367,900
Investments	0	120,000
Land	160,000	0
Equipment	695,500	575,500
Accumulated depreciation—equipment	(194,000)	(168,000)
	$1,683,800	$1,436,900
Liabilities and Stockholders' Equity		
Accounts payable (merchandise creditors)	$ 228,700	$ 210,500
Accrued expenses (operating expenses)	16,500	21,400
Dividends payable	14,000	10,000
Common stock, $10 par	75,000	60,000
Paid-in capital in excess of par—common stock	265,000	175,000
Retained earnings	1,084,600	960,000
	$1,683,800	$1,436,900

The income statement for the year ended December 31, 2006, is as follows:

Sales		$1,580,500
Cost of merchandise sold		957,300
Gross profit		$ 623,200
Operating expenses:		
Depreciation expense	$ 26,000	
Other operating expenses	329,400	
Total operating expenses		355,400
Operating income		$ 267,800
Other income:		
Gain on sale of investments		12,000
Income before income tax		$ 279,800
Income tax expense		99,200
Net income		$ 180,600

The following additional information was taken from the records:

a. The investments were sold for $132,000 cash.
b. Equipment and land were acquired for cash.
c. There were no disposals of equipment during the year.
d. The common stock was issued for cash.
e. There was a $56,000 debit to Retained Earnings for cash dividends declared.

Instructions

Prepare a statement of cash flows, using the direct method of presenting cash flows from operating activities.

Problems Series B

PROBLEM 14-1B
Statement of cash flows—indirect method

Objective 2

SPREADSHEET

✓ *Net cash flow from operating activities, $45,900*

The comparative balance sheet of True-Tread Flooring Co. for June 30, 2006 and 2005, is as follows:

	June 30, 2006	June 30, 2005
Assets		
Cash	$ 68,900	$ 53,700
Accounts receivable (net)	89,200	85,400
Inventories	145,800	132,700
Investments	0	45,000
Land	105,500	0
Equipment	210,800	185,600
Accumulated depreciation	(52,800)	(45,100)
	$567,400	$457,300
Liabilities and Stockholders' Equity		
Accounts payable (merchandise creditors)	$104,300	$100,200
Accrued expenses (operating expenses)	15,200	14,300
Dividends payable	12,000	10,000
Common stock, $11 par	55,000	50,000
Paid-in capital in excess of par—common stock	200,000	100,000
Retained earnings	180,900	182,800
	$567,400	$457,300

The following additional information was taken from the records of True-Tread Flooring Co.:

a. Equipment and land were acquired for cash.
b. There were no disposals of equipment during the year.
c. The investments were sold for $41,000 cash.
d. The common stock was issued for cash.
e. There was a $46,100 credit to Retained Earnings for net income.
f. There was a $48,000 debit to Retained Earnings for cash dividends declared.

Instructions

Prepare a statement of cash flows, using the indirect method of presenting cash flows from operating activities.

PROBLEM 14-2B
Statement of cash flows—indirect method

Objective 2

The comparative balance sheet of Sky-Mate Luggage Company at December 31, 2006 and 2005, is as follows:

	Dec. 31, 2006	Dec. 31, 2005
Assets		
Cash	$ 184,200	$ 165,400
Accounts receivable (net)	252,100	224,300
Inventories	300,200	348,700
Prepaid expenses	9,500	8,000
Land	120,000	120,000
Buildings	600,000	425,000
Accumulated depreciation—buildings	(215,000)	(194,000)
Machinery and equipment	310,000	310,000
Accumulated depreciation—machinery & equipment	(83,500)	(75,000)
Patents	50,000	54,000
	$1,527,500	$1,386,400
Liabilities and Stockholders' Equity		
Accounts payable (merchandise creditors)	$ 284,300	$ 295,700
Dividends payable	15,000	10,000
Salaries payable	19,500	22,500
Mortgage note payable, due 2007	70,000	—
Bonds payable	—	102,000
Common stock, $1 par	22,000	20,000
Paid-in capital in excess of par—common stock	150,000	50,000
Retained earnings	966,700	886,200
	$1,527,500	$1,386,400

✓ Net cash flow from operating activities, $178,800

An examination of the income statement and the accounting records revealed the following additional information applicable to 2006:

a. Net income, $140,500.
b. Depreciation expense reported on the income statement: buildings, $21,000; machinery and equipment, $8,500.
c. Patent amortization reported on the income statement, $4,000.
d. A building was constructed for $175,000. cash
e. A mortgage note for $70,000 was issued for cash.
f. 2,000 shares of common stock were issued at $51 in exchange for the bonds payable.
g. Cash dividends declared, $60,000.

Instructions

Prepare a statement of cash flows, using the indirect method of presenting cash flows from operating activities.

PROBLEM 14-3B
*Statement of cash flows—
indirect method*

Objective 2

✓ Net cash flow from operating activities, $71,400

The comparative balance sheet of Builder's Supply Co. at December 31, 2006 and 2005, is as follows:

	Dec. 31, 2006	Dec. 31, 2005
Assets		
Cash	$ 40,400	$ 45,200
Accounts receivable (net)	95,100	87,900
Inventories	140,700	122,800
Prepaid expenses	3,900	5,000
Land	75,000	100,000
Buildings	315,000	140,000
Accumulated depreciation—buildings	(70,200)	(58,300)
Equipment	225,600	210,400
Accumulated depreciation—equipment	(81,400)	(85,900)
	$744,100	$567,100

	Dec. 31, 2006	Dec. 31, 2005
Liabilities and Stockholders' Equity		
Accounts payable (merchandise creditors)	$ 97,000	$100,500
Income tax payable	7,100	6,400
Bonds payable	40,000	—
Common stock, $1 par	32,000	30,000
Paid-in capital in excess of par—common stock	200,000	120,000
Retained earnings	368,000	310,200
	$744,100	$567,100

The noncurrent asset, the noncurrent liability, and the stockholders' equity accounts for 2006 are as follows:

ACCOUNT *Land*   **ACCOUNT NO.**

Date		Item	Debit	Credit	Balance Debit	Balance Credit
2006						
Jan.	1	Balance			100,000	
April	20	Realized $31,000 cash from sale		25,000	75,000	

ACCOUNT *Buildings*   **ACCOUNT NO.**

Date		Item	Debit	Credit	Balance Debit	Balance Credit
2006						
Jan.	1	Balance			140,000	
April	20	Acquired for cash	175,000		315,000	

ACCOUNT *Accumulated Depreciation—Buildings*   **ACCOUNT NO.**

Date		Item	Debit	Credit	Balance Debit	Balance Credit
2006						
Jan.	1	Balance				58,300
Dec.	31	Depreciation for year		11,900		70,200

ACCOUNT *Equipment*   **ACCOUNT NO.**

Date		Item	Debit	Credit	Balance Debit	Balance Credit
2006						
Jan.	1	Balance			210,400	
	26	Discarded, no salvage		24,000	186,400	
Aug.	11	Purchased for cash	39,200		225,600	

ACCOUNT *Accumulated Depreciation—Equipment*   **ACCOUNT NO.**

Date		Item	Debit	Credit	Balance Debit	Balance Credit
2006						
Jan.	1	Balance				85,900
	26	Equipment discarded	24,000			61,900
Dec.	31	Depreciation for year		19,500		81,400

ACCOUNT *Bonds Payable*   **ACCOUNT NO.**

Date		Item	Debit	Credit	Balance Debit	Balance Credit
2006						
May	1	Issued 20-year bonds		40,000		40,000

ACCOUNT *Common Stock, $1 Par*   **ACCOUNT NO.**

Date		Item	Debit	Credit	Balance Debit	Balance Credit
2006						
Jan.	1	Balance				30,000
Dec.	7	Issued 2,000 shares of common stock for $41 per share		2,000		32,000

ACCOUNT *Paid-In Capital in Excess of Par—Common Stock*   **ACCOUNT NO.**

Date		Item	Debit	Credit	Balance Debit	Balance Credit
2006						
Jan.	1	Balance				120,000
Dec.	7	Issued 2,000 shares of common stock for $41 per share		80,000		200,000

ACCOUNT *Retained Earnings*   **ACCOUNT NO.**

Date		Item	Debit	Credit	Balance Debit	Balance Credit
2006						
Jan.	1	Balance				310,200
Dec.	31	Net income		72,800		383,000
	31	Cash dividends	15,000			368,000

Instructions

Prepare a statement of cash flows, using the indirect method of presenting cash flows from operating activities.

PROBLEM 14-4B
Statement of cash flows—direct method

Objective 3

SPREADSHEET

P.A.S.S.

✓ *Net cash flow from operating activities, $110,900*

The comparative balance sheet of Heaven's Bounty Nursery Inc. for December 31, 2006 and 2007, is as follows:

	Dec. 31, 2007	Dec. 31, 2006
Assets		
Cash	$ 134,200	$154,300
Accounts receivable (net)	203,200	189,700
Inventories	267,900	243,700
Investments	—	110,000
Land	140,000	—
Equipment	290,000	210,000
Accumulated depreciation	(112,300)	(93,400)
	$ 923,000	$814,300
Liabilities and Stockholders' Equity		
Accounts payable (merchandise creditors)	$ 192,100	$175,400
Accrued expenses (operating expenses)	12,400	14,600
Dividends payable	32,100	30,400
Common stock, $1 par	10,000	8,000
Paid-in capital in excess of par—common stock	180,000	100,000
Retained earnings	496,400	485,900
	$ 923,000	$814,300

The income statement for the year ended December 31, 2007, is as follows:

Sales		$965,000
Cost of merchandise sold		503,200
Gross profit		$461,800
Operating expenses:		
Depreciation expense	$ 18,900	
Other operating expenses	258,300	
Total operating expenses		277,200
Operating income		$184,600
Other income:		
Gain on sale of investments		22,000
Income before income tax		$206,600
Income tax expense		69,400
Net income		$137,200

The following additional information was taken from the records:

a. Equipment and land were acquired for cash.
b. There were no disposals of equipment during the year.
c. The investments were sold for $132,000 cash.
d. The common stock was issued for cash.
e. There was a $126,700 debit to Retained Earnings for cash dividends declared.

Instructions

Prepare a statement of cash flows, using the direct method of presenting cash flows from operating activities.

PROBLEM 14-5B
Statement of cash flows—direct method applied to Problem 14–1B

Objective 3

SPREADSHEET

✓ *Net cash flow from operating activities, $45,900*

The comparative balance sheet of True-Tread Flooring Co. for June 30, 2006 and 2005, is as follows:

	June 30, 2006	June 30, 2005
Assets		
Cash	$ 68,900	$ 53,700
Accounts receivable (net)	89,200	85,400
Inventories	145,800	132,700
Investments	0	45,000
Land	105,500	0
Equipment	210,800	185,600
Accumulated depreciation	(52,800)	(45,100)
	$567,400	$457,300
Liabilities and Stockholders' Equity		
Accounts payable (merchandise creditors)	$104,300	$100,200
Accrued expenses (operating expenses)	15,200	14,300
Dividends payable	12,000	10,000
Common stock, $11 par	55,000	50,000
Paid-in capital in excess of par—common stock	200,000	100,000
Retained earnings	180,900	182,800
	$567,400	$457,300

The income statement for the year ended June 30, 2006, is as follows:

Sales		$945,200
Cost of merchandise sold		665,900
Gross profit		$279,300
Operating expenses:		
Depreciation expense	$ 7,700	
Other operating expenses	193,400	
Total operating expenses		201,100
Operating income		$ 78,200
Other expenses:		
Loss on sale of investments		4,000
Income before income tax		$ 74,200
Income tax expense		28,100
Net income		$ 46,100

The following additional information was taken from the records:

a. Equipment and land were acquired for cash.
b. There were no disposals of equipment during the year.
c. The investments were sold for $41,000 cash.
d. The common stock was issued for cash.
e. There was a $48,000 debit to Retained Earnings for cash dividends declared.

Instructions
Prepare a statement of cash flows, using the direct method of presenting cash flows from operating activities.

Special Activities

ACTIVITY 14-1
Ethics and professional conduct in business

Karen Holmes, president of Parisian Fashions Inc., believes that reporting operating cash flow per share on the income statement would be a useful addition to the company's just completed financial statements. The following discussion took place between Karen Holmes and Parisian Fashions' controller, Jeff May, in January, after the close of the fiscal year.

ETHICS

Karen: I have been reviewing our financial statements for the last year. I am disappointed that our net income per share has dropped by 10% from last year. This is not going to look good to our shareholders. Isn't there anything we can do about this?

Jeff: What do you mean? The past is the past, and the numbers are in. There isn't much that can be done about it. Our financial statements were prepared according to generally accepted accounting principles, and I don't see much leeway for significant change at this point.

Karen: No, no. I'm not suggesting that we "cook the books." But look at the cash flow from operating activities on the statement of cash flows. The cash flow from operating activities has increased by 20%. This is very good news—and, I might add, useful information. The higher cash flow from operating activities will give our creditors comfort.

Jeff: Well, the cash flow from operating activities is on the statement of cash flows, so I guess users will be able to see the improved cash flow figures there.

Karen: This is true, but somehow I feel that this information should be given a much higher profile. I don't like this information being "buried" in the statement of cash flows. You know as well as I do that many users will focus on the income statement. Therefore, I think we ought to include an operating cash flow per share number on the face of the income statement—someplace under the earnings per share number. In this way users will get the complete picture of our operating performance. Yes, our earnings per share dropped this year, but our cash flow from operating activities improved! And all the information is in one place where users can see and compare the figures. What do you think?

Jeff: I've never really thought about it like that before. I guess we could put the operating cash flow per share on the income statement, under the earnings per share. Users would really benefit from this disclosure. Thanks for the idea—I'll start working on it.

Karen: Glad to be of service.

➤ How would you interpret this situation? Is Jeff behaving in an ethical and professional manner?

ACTIVITY 14-2
Using the statement of cash flows

WHAT DO YOU THINK?

You are considering an investment in a new start-up company, OmniTech Inc., an Internet service provider. A review of the company's financial statements reveals a negative retained earnings. In addition, it appears as though the company has been running a negative cash flow from operating activities since the company's inception. ➤ How is the company staying in business under these circumstances? Could this be a good investment?

ACTIVITY 14-3
Analysis of cash flow from operations

The Retailing Division of Buyer's Mart, Inc. provided the following information on its cash flow from operations:

Net income	$ 450,000
Increase in accounts receivable	(540,000)
Increase in inventory	(600,000)
Decrease in accounts payable	(90,000)
Depreciation	100,000
Cash flow from operating activities	$(680,000)

The manager of the Retailing Division provided the accompanying memo with this report:

From: Senior Vice President, Retailing Division

I am pleased to report that we had earnings of $450,000 over the last period. This resulted in a return on invested capital of 10%, which is near our targets for this *division. I have been aggressive in building the revenue volume in the division. As a result, I am happy to report that we have increased the number of new credit card customers as a result of an aggressive marketing campaign. In addition, we have found some excellent merchandise opportunities. Some of our suppliers have made some of their apparel merchandise available at a deep discount. We have purchased as much of these goods as possible in order to improve profitability. I'm also happy to report that our vendor payment problems have improved. We are nearly caught up on our overdue payables balances.*

▭ ➤ Comment on the senior vice president's memo in light of the cash flow information.

ACTIVITY 14-4
Analysis of statement of cash flows

Jabari Franklin is the president and majority shareholder of Kitchens By Design, Inc., a small retail store chain. Recently, Franklin submitted a loan application for Kitchens By Design, Inc., to Montvale National Bank. It called for a $200,000, 9%, ten-year loan to help finance the construction of a building and the purchase of store equipment, costing a total of $250,000, to enable Kitchens By Design, Inc., to open a store in Montvale. Land for this purpose was acquired last year. The bank's loan officer requested a statement of cash flows in addition to the most recent income statement, balance sheet, and retained earnings statement that Franklin had submitted with the loan application.

As a close family friend, Franklin asked you to prepare a statement of cash flows. From the records provided, you prepared the following statement.

Kitchens By Design, Inc.
Statement of Cash Flows
For the Year Ended December 31, 2006

Cash flows from operating activities:			
Net income, per income statement		$ 86,400	
Add: Depreciation	$31,000		
Decrease in accounts receivable	11,500	42,500	
		$128,900	
Deduct: Increase in inventory	$12,000		
Increase in prepaid expenses	1,500		
Decrease in accounts payable	3,000		
Gain on sale of investments	7,500	24,000	
Net cash flow from operating activities			$104,900
Cash flows from investing activities:			
Cash received from investments sold		$ 42,500	
Less: Cash paid for purchase of store equipment		31,000	
Net cash flow from investing activities			11,500
Cash flows from financing activities:			
Cash paid for dividends		$ 40,000	
Net cash flow used for financing activities			(40,000)
Increase in cash			$ 76,400
Cash at the beginning of the year			27,500
Cash at the end of the year			$103,900
Schedule of Noncash Financing and			
Investing Activities:			
Issued common stock at par for land			$ 60,000

After reviewing the statement, Franklin telephoned you and commented, "Are you sure this statement is right?" Franklin then raised the following questions:

1. "How can depreciation be a cash flow?"
2. "Issuing common stock for the land is listed in a separate schedule. This transaction has nothing to do with cash! Shouldn't this transaction be eliminated from the statement?"
3. "How can the gain on sale of investments be a deduction from net income in determining the cash flow from operating activities?"

4. "Why does the bank need this statement anyway? They can compute the increase in cash from the balance sheets for the last two years."

After jotting down Franklin's questions, you assured him that this statement was "right." However, to alleviate Franklin's concern, you arranged a meeting for the following day.

a. ▭▭▷ How would you respond to each of Franklin's questions?

b. ▭▭▷ Do you think that the statement of cash flows enhances the chances of Kitchens By Design, Inc., receiving the loan? Discuss.

ACTIVITY 14-5
Statement of cash flows

REAL WORLD   **GROUP ACTIVITY**

INTERNET

This activity will require two teams to retrieve cash flow statement information from the Internet. One team is to obtain the most recent year's statement of cash flows for **Johnson & Johnson**, and the other team the most recent year's statement of cash flows for **AMR Corp.**

The statement of cash flows is included as part of the annual report information that is a required disclosure to the Securities and Exchange Commission (SEC). The SEC, in turn, provides this information online through its EDGAR service. EDGAR (Electronic Data Gathering, Analysis, and Retrieval) is the electronic archive of financial statements filed with the Securities and Exchange Commission (SEC). SEC documents can be retrieved using the EdgarScan service from **PricewaterhouseCoopers** at **http://edgarscan.pwcglobal.com**.

To obtain annual report information, type in a company name in the appropriate space. EdgarScan will list the reports available to you for the company you've selected. Select the most recent annual report filing, identified as a 10-K or 10-K405. EdgarScan provides an outline of the report, including the separate financial statements. You can double-click the income statement and balance sheet for the selected company into an Excel™ spreadsheet for further analysis.

As a group, compare the two statements of cash flows. How are Johnson & Johnson and United Airlines similar or different regarding cash flows?

Answers to Self-Examination Questions

1. **D**   Cash flows from operating activities affect transactions that enter into the determination of net income, such as the receipt of cash from customers on account (answer D). Receipts of cash from the sale of stock (answer A) and the sale of bonds (answer B) and payments of cash for dividends (answer C) are cash flows from financing activities.

2. **A**   Cash flows from investing activities include receipts from the sale of noncurrent assets, such as equipment (answer A), and payments to acquire noncurrent assets. Receipts of cash from the sale of stock (answer B) and payments of cash for dividends (answer C) and to acquire treasury stock (answer D) are cash flows from financing activities.

3. **C**   Payment of cash dividends (answer C) is an example of a financing activity. The receipt of cash from customers on account (answer A) is an operating activity. The receipt of cash from the sale of equipment (answer B) is an investing activity. The

payment of cash to acquire land (answer D) is an example of an investing activity.

4. **D**   The indirect method (answer D) reports cash flows from operating activities by beginning with net income and adjusting it for revenues and expenses not involving the receipt or payment of cash.

5. **C**   The cash flows from operating activities section of the statement of cash flows would report net cash flow from operating activities of $65,500, determined as follows:

Net income		$55,000
Add: Depreciation	$22,000	
Decrease in inventories	5,000	
Decrease in prepaid expenses	500	27,500
		$82,500
Deduct: Increase in accounts receivable	$10,000	
Decrease in accounts payable	7,000	17,000
Net cash flow from operating activities		$65,500

FINANCIAL STATEMENT ANALYSIS

objectives

After studying this chapter, you should be able to:

1 List basic financial statement analytical procedures.

2 Apply financial statement analysis to assess the solvency of a business.

3 Apply financial statement analysis to assess the profitability of a business.

4 Summarize the uses and limitations of analytical measures.

5 Describe the contents of corporate annual reports.

The Wall Street Journal reported that the common stock of **Microsoft Corporation** was selling for $26.15 per share. If you had funds to invest, would you invest in Microsoft common stock?

Microsoft is a well-known, international company. However, **United Airlines**, **WorldCom**, **Kmart**, **Polaroid**, and **Planet Hollywood** were also well-known companies. These latter companies share the common characteristic of having declared bankruptcy!

Obviously, being well-known is not necessarily a good basis for investing. Knowledge that a company has a good product, by itself, may also be an inadequate basis for investing in the company. Even with a good product, a company may go bankrupt for a variety of reasons, such as inadequate financing. For example, Planet Hollywood sought bankruptcy protection, even though it was owned and promoted by such prominent Hollywood stars as Bruce Willis, Whoopi Goldberg, and Arnold Schwarzenegger.

How, then, does one decide on the companies in which to invest? This chapter describes and illustrates common financial data that can be analyzed to assist you in making investment decisions. In addition, the contents of corporate annual reports are also discussed.

Basic Analytical Procedures

<table>
<tr><td>objective   1</td></tr>
<tr><td>List basic financial statement analytical procedures.</td></tr>
</table>

The basic financial statements provide much of the information users need to make economic decisions about businesses. In this chapter, we illustrate how to perform a complete analysis of these statements by integrating individual analytical measures.

Analytical procedures may be used to compare items on a current statement with related items on earlier statements. For example, cash of $150,000 on the current balance sheet may be compared with cash of $100,000 on the balance sheet of a year earlier. The current year's cash may be expressed as 1.5 or 150% of the earlier amount, or as an increase of 50% or $50,000.

Analytical procedures are also widely used to examine relationships within a financial statement. To illustrate, assume that cash of $50,000 and inventories of $250,000 are included in the total assets of $1,000,000 on a balance sheet. In relative terms, the cash balance is 5% of the total assets, and the inventories are 25% of the total assets.

In this chapter, we will illustrate a number of common analytical measures. The measures are not ends in themselves. They are only guides in evaluating financial and operating data. Many other factors, such as trends in the industry and general economic conditions, should also be considered.

Horizontal Analysis

The percentage analysis of increases and decreases in related items in comparative financial statements is called *horizontal analysis*. The amount of each item on the most recent statement is compared with the related item on one or more earlier statements. The amount of increase or decrease in the item is listed, along with the percent of increase or decrease.

Horizontal analysis may compare two statements. In this case, the earlier statement is used as the base. Horizontal analysis may also compare three or more statements. In this case, the earliest date or period may be used as the base for comparing all later dates or periods. Alternatively, each statement may be compared to the immediately preceding statement. Exhibit 1 is a condensed comparative balance sheet for two years for Lincoln Company, with horizontal analysis.

We cannot fully evaluate the significance of the various increases and decreases in the items shown in Exhibit 1 without additional information. Although total as-

•Exhibit 1   **Comparative Balance Sheet—Horizontal Analysis**

Lincoln Company
Comparative Balance Sheet
December 31, 2006 and 2005

	2006	2005	Increase (Decrease) Amount	Percent
Assets				
Current assets	$ 550,000	$ 533,000	$ 17,000	3.2%
Long-term investments	95,000	177,500	(82,500)	(46.5%)
Property, plant, and equipment (net)	444,500	470,000	(25,500)	(5.4%)
Intangible assets	50,000	50,000		
Total assets	$1,139,500	$1,230,500	$ (91,000)	(7.4%)
Liabilities				
Current liabilities	$ 210,000	$ 243,000	$ (33,000)	(13.6%)
Long-term liabilities	100,000	200,000	(100,000)	(50.0%)
Total liabilities	$ 310,000	$ 443,000	$(133,000)	(30.0%)
Stockholders' Equity				
Preferred 6% stock, $100 par . . .	$ 150,000	$ 150,000	—	—
Common stock, $10 par	500,000	500,000	—	—
Retained earnings	179,500	137,500	$ 42,000	30.5%
Total stockholders' equity	$ 829,500	$ 787,500	$ 42,000	5.3%
Total liabilities and stockholders' equity	$1,139,500	$1,230,500	$ (91,000)	(7.4%)

sets at the end of 2006 were $91,000 (7.4%) less than at the beginning of the year, liabilities were reduced by $133,000 (30%), and stockholders' equity increased $42,000 (5.3%). It appears that the reduction of $100,000 in long-term liabilities was achieved mostly through the sale of long-term investments.

The balance sheet in Exhibit 1 may be expanded to include the details of the various categories of assets and liabilities. An alternative is to present the details in separate schedules. Exhibit 2 is a supporting schedule with horizontal analysis.

•Exhibit 2   **Comparative Schedule of Current Assets—Horizontal Analysis**

Lincoln Company
Comparative Schedule of Current Assets
December 31, 2006 and 2005

	2006	2005	Increase (Decrease) Amount	Percent
Cash	$ 90,500	$ 64,700	$ 25,800	39.9%
Marketable securities	75,000	60,000	15,000	25.0%
Accounts receivable (net)	115,000	120,000	(5,000)	(4.2%)
Inventories	264,000	283,000	(19,000)	(6.7%)
Prepaid expenses	5,500	5,300	200	3.8%
Total current assets	$550,000	$533,000	$ 17,000	3.2%

Accounts Payable was $600,000 in the current year and $500,000 in the preceding year. What is the amount and the percentage of increase or decrease that would be shown in a balance sheet with horizontal analysis?

$100,000 or 20% ($100,000/ $500,000) increase

The decrease in accounts receivable may be due to changes in credit terms or improved collection policies. Likewise, a decrease in inventories during a period of increased sales may indicate an improvement in the management of inventories.

The changes in the current assets in Exhibit 2 appear favorable. This assessment is supported by the 24.8% increase in net sales shown in Exhibit 3.

An increase in net sales may not have a favorable effect on operating performance. The percentage increase in Lincoln Company's net sales is accompanied by a greater percentage increase in the cost of goods (merchandise) sold.[1] This has the effect of reducing gross profit. Selling expenses increased significantly, and administrative expenses increased slightly. Overall, operating expenses increased by 20.7%, whereas gross profit increased by only 19.7%.

The increase in income from operations and in net income is favorable. However, a study of the expenses and additional analyses and comparisons should be made before reaching a conclusion as to the cause.

•Exhibit 3   **Comparative Income Statement—Horizontal Analysis**

Lincoln Company Comparative Income Statement For the Years Ended December 31, 2006 and 2005				
			Increase (Decrease)	
	2006	2005	Amount	Percent
Sales	$1,530,500	$1,234,000	$296,500	24.0%
Sales returns and allowances . . .	32,500	34,000	(1,500)	(4.4%)
Net sales	$1,498,000	$1,200,000	$298,000	24.8%
Cost of goods sold	1,043,000	820,000	223,000	27.2%
Gross profit	$ 455,000	$ 380,000	$ 75,000	19.7%
Selling expenses	$ 191,000	$ 147,000	$ 44,000	29.9%
Administrative expenses	104,000	97,400	6,600	6.8%
Total operating expenses	$ 295,000	$ 244,400	$ 50,600	20.7%
Income from operations	$ 160,000	$ 135,600	$ 24,400	18.0%
Other income	8,500	11,000	(2,500)	(22.7%)
	$ 168,500	$ 146,600	$ 21,900	14.9%
Other expense	6,000	12,000	(6,000)	(50.0%)
Income before income tax	$ 162,500	$ 134,600	$ 27,900	20.7%
Income tax expense	71,500	58,100	13,400	23.1%
Net income	$ 91,000	$ 76,500	$ 14,500	19.0%

Exhibit 4 illustrates a comparative retained earnings statement with horizontal analysis. It reveals that retained earnings increased 30.5% for the year. The increase is due to net income of $91,000 for the year, less dividends of $49,000.

Vertical Analysis

A percentage analysis may also be used to show the relationship of each component to the total within a single statement. This type of analysis is called **vertical analysis**. Like horizontal analysis, the statements may be prepared in either detailed or condensed form. In the latter case, additional details of the changes in individual items may be presented in supporting schedules. In such schedules, the per-

---

[1]The term *cost of goods sold* is often used in practice in place of *cost of merchandise sold*. Such usage is followed in this chapter.

•Exhibit 4

Comparative Retained Earnings Statement— Horizontal Analysis

Lincoln Company
Comparative Retained Earnings Statement
December 31, 2006 and 2005

	2006	2005	Increase (Decrease) Amount	Increase (Decrease) Percent
Retained earnings, January 1	$137,500	$100,000	$37,500	37.5%
Net income for the year	91,000	76,500	14,500	19.0%
Total	$228,500	$176,500	$52,000	29.5%
Dividends:				
On preferred stock	$ 9,000	$ 9,000	—	—
On common stock	40,000	30,000	$10,000	33.3%
Total	$ 49,000	$ 39,000	$10,000	25.6%
Retained earnings, December 31 . . .	$179,500	$137,500	$42,000	30.5%

At the end of the current year, Accounts Payable was $600,000 and total liabilities and stockholders' equity was $1,200,000. What percent would be shown for Accounts Payable in a balance sheet with vertical analysis?

50% ($600,000/$1,200,000)

centage analysis may be based on either the total of the schedule or the statement total. Although vertical analysis is limited to an individual statement, its significance may be improved by preparing comparative statements.

In vertical analysis of the balance sheet, each asset item is stated as a percent of the total assets. Each liability and stockholders' equity item is stated as a percent of the total liabilities and stockholders' equity. Exhibit 5 is a condensed comparative balance sheet with vertical analysis for Lincoln Company.

•Exhibit 5

Comparative Balance Sheet—Vertical Analysis

Lincoln Company
Comparative Balance Sheet
December 31, 2006 and 2005

	2006 Amount	2006 Percent	2005 Amount	2005 Percent
Assets				
Current assets	$ 550,000	48.3%	$ 533,000	43.3%
Long-term investments	95,000	8.3	177,500	14.4
Property, plant, and				
equipment (net)	444,500	39.0	470,000	38.2
Intangible assets	50,000	4.4	50,000	4.1
Total assets	$1,139,500	100.0%	$1,230,500	100.0%
Liabilities				
Current liabilities	$ 210,000	18.4%	$ 243,000	19.7%
Long-term liabilities	100,000	8.8	200,000	16.3
Total liabilities	$ 310,000	27.2%	$ 443,000	36.0%
Stockholders' Equity				
Preferred 6% stock, $100 par	$ 150,000	13.2%	$ 150,000	12.2%
Common stock, $10 par	500,000	43.9	500,000	40.6
Retained earnings	179,500	15.7	137,500	11.2
Total stockholders' equity	$ 829,500	72.8%	$ 787,500	64.0%
Total liabilities and				
stockholders' equity	$1,139,500	100.0%	$1,230,500	100.0%

The major percentage changes in Lincoln Company's assets are in the current asset and long-term investment categories. In the Liabilities and Stockholders' Equity sections of the balance sheet, the greatest percentage changes are in long-term liabilities and retained earnings. Stockholders' equity increased from 64% to 72.8% of total liabilities and stockholders' equity in 2006. There is a comparable decrease in liabilities.

In a vertical analysis of the income statement, each item is stated as a percent of net sales. Exhibit 6 is a condensed comparative income statement with vertical analysis for Lincoln Company.

•Exhibit 6 Comparative Income Statement—Vertical Analysis

Lincoln Company
Comparative Income Statement
For the Years Ended December 31, 2006 and 2005

	2006		2005	
	Amount	Percent	Amount	Percent
Sales..........................	$1,530,500	102.2%	$1,234,000	102.8%
Sales returns and allowances.......	32,500	2.2	34,000	2.8
Net sales......................	$1,498,000	100.0%	$1,200,000	100.0%
Cost of goods sold	1,043,000	69.6	820,000	68.3
Gross profit....................	$ 455,000	30.4%	$ 380,000	31.7%
Selling expenses	$ 191,000	12.8%	$ 147,000	12.3%
Administrative expenses...........	104,000	6.9	97,400	8.1
Total operating expenses..........	$ 295,000	19.7%	$ 244,400	20.4%
Income from operations...........	$ 160,000	10.7%	$ 135,600	11.3%
Other income...................	8,500	0.6	11,000	0.9
	$ 168,500	11.3%	$ 146,600	12.2%
Other expense..................	6,000	0.4	12,000	1.0
Income before income tax.........	$ 162,500	10.9%	$ 134,600	11.2%
Income tax expense..............	71,500	4.8	58,100	4.8
Net income....................	$ 91,000	6.1%	$ 76,500	6.4%

The percentages of gross profit and net income to sales for a recent fiscal year for **Target Corp.** and **Wal-Mart Stores Inc.** are shown below.

REAL WORLD

	Target Corp.	Wal-Mart Stores Inc.
Gross profit to sales	31.7%	22.1%
Net income to sales	3.4%	1.8%

Wal-Mart has a significantly lower gross profit margin percentage than does Target, which is likely due to Wal-Mart's aggressive pricing strategy. However, Target's gross profit margin advantage shrinks when comparing the net income to sales ratio. Target must have larger selling and administrative expenses to sales than does Wal-Mart. Even so, Target's net income to sales is still 1.6 percentage points better than Wal-Mart.

We must be careful when judging the significance of differences between percentages for the two years. For example, the decline of the gross profit rate from 31.7% in 2005 to 30.4% in 2006 is only 1.3 percentage points. In terms of dollars of potential gross profit, however, it represents a decline of approximately $19,500 (1.3% × $1,498,000).

Common-Size Statements

Horizontal and vertical analyses with both dollar and percentage amounts are useful in assessing relationships and trends in financial conditions and operations of a business. Vertical analysis with both dollar and percentage amounts is also useful in comparing one company with another or with industry averages. Such comparisons are easier to make with the use of common-size statements. In a **_common-size statement_**, all items are expressed in percentages.

Common-size statements are useful in comparing the current period with prior periods, individual businesses, or one business with industry percentages. Industry data are often available from trade associations and financial information services. Exhibit 7 is a comparative common-size income statement for two businesses.

•Exhibit 7   Common-Size Income Statement

Lincoln Company and Madison Corporation Condensed Common-Size Income Statement For the Year Ended December 31, 2006	Lincoln Company	Madison Corporation
Sales	102.2%	102.3%
Sales returns and allowances	2.2	2.3
Net sales	100.0%	100.0%
Cost of goods sold	69.6	70.0
Gross profit	30.4%	30.0%
Selling expenses	12.8%	11.5%
Administrative expenses	6.9	4.1
Total operating expenses	19.7%	15.6%
Income from operations	10.7%	14.4%
Other income	0.6	0.6
	11.3%	15.0%
Other expense	0.4	0.5
Income before income tax	10.9%	14.5%
Income tax expense	4.8	5.5
Net income	6.1%	9.0%

Exhibit 7 indicates that Lincoln Company has a slightly higher rate of gross profit than Madison Corporation. However, this advantage is more than offset by Lincoln Company's higher percentage of selling and administrative expenses. As a result, the income from operations of Lincoln Company is 10.7% of net sales, compared with 14.4% for Madison Corporation—an unfavorable difference of 3.7 percentage points.

Other Analytical Measures

In addition to the preceding analyses, other relationships may be expressed in ratios and percentages. Often, these items are taken from the financial statements and thus are a type of vertical analysis. Comparing these items with items from earlier periods is a type of horizontal analysis.

Solvency Analysis

objective 2

Apply financial statement analysis to assess the solvency of a business.

Some aspects of a business's financial condition and operations are of greater importance to some users than others. However, all users are interested in the ability of a business to pay its debts as they are due and to earn income. The ability of a business to meet its financial obligations (debts) is called **solvency**. The ability of a business to earn income is called **profitability**.

The factors of solvency and profitability are interrelated. A business that cannot pay its debts on a timely basis may experience difficulty in obtaining credit. A lack of available credit may, in turn, lead to a decline in the business's profitability. Eventually, the business may be forced into bankruptcy. Likewise, a business that is less profitable than its competitors is likely to be at a disadvantage in obtaining credit or new capital from stockholders.

In the following paragraphs, we discuss various types of financial analyses that are useful in evaluating the solvency of a business. In the next section, we discuss various types of profitability analyses. The examples in both sections are based on

Two popular printed sources for industry ratios are available in *Annual Statement Studies* from **Robert Morris Associates** and *Industry Norms & Key Business Ratios* from **Dun's Analytical Services**. Online analysis is available from **Zacks Investment Research** site or **Market Guide's** site, both of which are linked to the text's Web site at **http://warren.swlearning.com**.

Lincoln Company's financial statements presented earlier. In some cases, data from Lincoln Company's financial statements of the preceding year and from other sources are also used. These historical data are useful in assessing the past performance of a business and in forecasting its future performance. The results of financial analyses may be even more useful when they are compared with those of competing businesses and with industry averages.

Solvency analysis focuses on the ability of a business to pay or otherwise satisfy its current and noncurrent liabilities. It is normally assessed by examining balance sheet relationships, using the following major analyses:

1. Current position analysis
2. Accounts receivable analysis
3. Inventory analysis
4. The ratio of fixed assets to long-term liabilities
5. The ratio of liabilities to stockholders' equity
6. The number of times interest charges are earned

> Solvency analysis focuses on the ability of a business to pay or otherwise satisfy its current and noncurrent liabilities.

Current Position Analysis

To be useful in assessing solvency, a ratio or other financial measure must relate to a business's ability to pay or otherwise satisfy its liabilities. Using measures to assess a business's ability to pay its current liabilities is called **current position analysis**. Such analysis is of special interest to short-term creditors.

An analysis of a firm's current position normally includes determining the working capital, the current ratio, and the quick ratio. The current and quick ratios are most useful when analyzed together and compared to previous periods and other firms in the industry.

Working Capital

The excess of the current assets of a business over its current liabilities is called working capital. The working capital is often used in evaluating a company's ability to meet currently maturing debts. It is especially useful in making monthly or other period-to-period comparisons for a company. However, amounts of working capital are difficult to assess when comparing companies of different sizes or in comparing such amounts with industry figures. For example, working capital of $250,000 may be adequate for a small local hardware store, but it would be inadequate for all of **Home Depot**.

Current Ratio

Another means of expressing the relationship between current assets and current liabilities is the ***current ratio***. This ratio is sometimes called the **working capital ratio** or **bankers' ratio**. The ratio is computed by dividing the total current assets by the total current liabilities. For Lincoln Company, working capital and the current ratio for 2006 and 2005 are as follows:

	2006	2005
Current assets	$550,000	$533,000
Current liabilities	210,000	243,000
Working capital	$340,000	$290,000
Current ratio	2.6	2.2

Microsoft Corp. maintains a high current ratio—4.2 for a recent year. Microsoft's stable and profitable software business has allowed it to develop a strong cash position coupled with no short-term notes payable.

The current ratio is a more reliable indicator of solvency than is working capital. To illustrate, assume that as of December 31, 2006, the working capital of a competitor is much greater than $340,000, but its current ratio is only 1.3. Considering these facts alone, Lincoln Company, with its current ratio of 2.6, is in a more favorable position to obtain short-term credit than the competitor, which has the greater amount of working capital.

Quick Ratio

The working capital and the current ratio do not consider the makeup of the current assets. To illustrate the importance of this consideration, the current position data for Lincoln Company and Jefferson Corporation as of December 31, 2006, are as follows:

	Lincoln Company	Jefferson Corporation
Current assets:		
Cash	$ 90,500	$ 45,500
Marketable securities	75,000	25,000
Accounts receivable (net)	115,000	90,000
Inventories	264,000	380,000
Prepaid expenses	5,500	9,500
Total current assets	$550,000	$550,000
Current liabilities	210,000	210,000
Working capital	$340,000	$340,000
Current ratio	2.6	2.6

Both companies have a working capital of $340,000 and a current ratio of 2.6. But the ability of each company to pay its current debts is significantly different. Jefferson Corporation has more of its current assets in inventories. Some of these inventories must be sold and the receivables collected before the current liabilities can be paid in full. Thus, a large amount of time may be necessary to convert these inventories into cash. Declines in market prices and a reduction in demand could also impair its ability to pay current liabilities. In contrast, Lincoln Company has cash and current assets (marketable securities and accounts receivable) that can generally be converted to cash rather quickly to meet its current liabilities.

A ratio that measures the "instant" debt-paying ability of a company is called the **quick ratio** or **acid-test ratio**. It is the ratio of the total quick assets to the total current liabilities. **Quick assets** are cash and other current assets that can be quickly converted to cash. Quick assets normally include cash, marketable securities, and receivables. The quick ratio data for Lincoln Company are as follows:

A balance sheet shows $300,000 of cash, marketable securities, and receivables, and $250,000 of inventories. Current liabilities are $200,000. What are (a) the current ratio and (b) the quick ratio?

(a) 2.75 ($550,000/$200,000);
(b) 1.5 ($300,000/$200,000)

	2006	2005
Quick assets:		
Cash	$ 90,500	$ 64,700
Marketable equity securities	75,000	60,000
Accounts receivable (net)	115,000	120,000
Total quick assets	$280,500	$244,700
Current liabilities	$210,000	$243,000
Quick ratio	1.3	1.0

Accounts Receivable Analysis

The size and makeup of accounts receivable change constantly during business operations. Sales on account increase accounts receivable, whereas collections from customers decrease accounts receivable. Firms that grant long credit terms usually have larger accounts receivable balances than those granting short credit terms. Increases or decreases in the volume of sales also affect the balance of accounts receivable.

It is desirable to collect receivables as promptly as possible. The cash collected from receivables improves solvency. In addition, the cash generated by prompt collections from customers may be used in operations for such purposes as purchasing merchandise in large quantities at lower prices. The cash may also be used for payment of dividends to stockholders or for other investing or financing purposes. Prompt collection also lessens the risk of loss from uncollectible accounts.

Accounts Receivable Turnover

The relationship between sales and accounts receivable may be stated as the **accounts receivable turnover**. This ratio is computed by dividing net sales by the average net accounts receivable.[2] It is desirable to base the average on monthly balances, which allows for seasonal changes in sales. When such data are not available, it may be necessary to use the average of the accounts receivable balance at the beginning and the end of the year. If there are trade notes receivable as well as accounts, the two may be combined. The accounts receivable turnover data for Lincoln Company are as follows.

	2006	2005
Net sales	$1,498,000	$1,200,000
Accounts receivable (net):		
Beginning of year	$ 120,000	$ 140,000
End of year	115,000	120,000
Total	$ 235,000	$ 260,000
Average (Total ÷ 2)	$ 117,500	$ 130,000
Accounts receivable turnover	12.7	9.2

The increase in the accounts receivable turnover for 2006 indicates that there has been an improvement in the collection of receivables. This may be due to a change in the granting of credit or in collection practices or both.

Number of Days' Sales in Receivables

Another measure of the relationship between sales and accounts receivable is the **number of days' sales in receivables**. This ratio is computed by dividing the net accounts receivable at the end of the year by the average daily sales. Average daily sales is determined by dividing net sales by 365 days. The number of days' sales in receivables is computed for Lincoln Company as follows:

	2006	2005
Accounts receivable (net), end of year	$115,000	$120,000
Net sales	$1,498,000	$1,200,000
Average daily sales (sales ÷ 365)	$4,104	$3,288
Number of days' sales in receivables	28.0*	36.5*

*Accounts receivable ÷ Average daily sales

The number of days' sales in receivables is an estimate of the length of time (in days) the accounts receivable have been outstanding. Comparing this measure with the credit terms provides information on the efficiency in collecting receivables. For example, assume that the number of days' sales in receivables for Grant Inc. is 40. If Grant Inc.'s credit terms are n/45, then its collection process appears to be efficient. On the other hand, if Grant Inc.'s credit terms are n/30, its collection process does not appear to be efficient. A comparison with other firms in the same industry and with prior years also provides useful information. Such comparisons may indicate efficiency of collection procedures and trends in credit management.

Inventory Analysis

A business should keep enough inventory on hand to meet the needs of its customers and its operations. At the same time, however, an excessive amount of inventory reduces solvency by tying up funds. Excess inventories also increase insurance expense, property taxes, storage costs, and other related expenses. These expenses further reduce funds that could be used elsewhere to improve operations. Finally, excess inventory also increases the risk of losses because of price declines or obsolescence of

Net sales were $960,000. The accounts receivable balance at the beginning of the year was $56,000, and at the end of the year it was $40,000. What are (a) the accounts receivable turnover and (b) the number of days' sales in receivables?

(a) 20 [$960,000/($56,000 + $40,000)/2]; (b) 15.2 days [$40,000/($960,000/365)]

---

[2]If known, **credit** sales should be used in the numerator. Because credit sales are not normally known by external users, we use net sales in the numerator.

the inventory. Two measures that are useful for evaluating the management of inventory are the inventory turnover and the number of days' sales in inventory.

Inventory Turnover

The relationship between the volume of goods (merchandise) sold and inventory may be stated as the ***inventory turnover***. It is computed by dividing the cost of goods sold by the average inventory. If monthly data are not available, the average of the inventories at the beginning and the end of the year may be used. The inventory turnover for Lincoln Company is computed as follows:

	2006	2005
Cost of goods sold	$1,043,000	$820,000
Inventories:		
Beginning of year	$ 283,000	$311,000
End of year	264,000	283,000
Total	$ 547,000	$594,000
Average (Total ÷ 2)	$ 273,500	$297,000
Inventory turnover	3.8	2.8

REAL WORLD

The inventory turnover of **McDonald's Corporation** for a recent year was 36, while for **Toys "R" Us Inc.**, it was 3.7. McDonald's inventory turnover is higher because it sells perishable food products, while toys can sit on the shelf longer without "spoiling."

The inventory turnover improved for Lincoln Company because of an increase in the cost of goods sold and a decrease in the average inventories. Differences across inventories, companies, and industries are too great to allow a general statement on what is a good inventory turnover. For example, a firm selling food should have a higher turnover than a firm selling furniture or jewelry. Likewise, the perishable foods department of a supermarket should have a higher turnover than the soaps and cleansers department. However, for each business or each department within a business, there is a reasonable turnover rate. A turnover lower than this rate could mean that inventory is not being managed properly.

Number of Days' Sales in Inventory

Another measure of the relationship between the cost of goods sold and inventory is the ***number of days' sales in inventory***. This measure is computed by dividing the inventory at the end of the year by the average daily cost of goods sold (cost of goods sold divided by 365). The number of days' sales in inventory for Lincoln Company is computed as follows:

	2006	2005
Inventories, end of year	$264,000	$283,000
Cost of goods sold	$1,043,000	$820,000
Average daily cost of goods sold (COGS ÷ 365 days)	$2,858	$2,247
Number of days' sales in inventory	92.4	125.9

The number of days' sales in inventory is a rough measure of the length of time it takes to acquire, sell, and replace the inventory. For Lincoln Company, there is a major improvement in the number of days' sales in inventory during 2006. However, a comparison with earlier years and similar firms would be useful in assessing Lincoln Company's overall inventory management.

Ratio of Fixed Assets to Long-Term Liabilities

Long-term notes and bonds are often secured by mortgages on fixed assets. The ***ratio of fixed assets to long-term liabilities*** is a solvency measure that indicates the margin of safety of the noteholders or bondholders. It also indicates the ability of the business to borrow additional funds on a long-term basis. The ratio of fixed assets to long-term liabilities for Lincoln Company is as follows:

	2006	2005
Fixed assets (net)	$444,500	$470,000
Long-term liabilities	$100,000	$200,000
Ratio of fixed assets to long-term liabilities	4.4	2.4

The major increase in this ratio at the end of 2006 is mainly due to liquidating one-half of Lincoln Company's long-term liabilities. If the company needs to borrow additional funds on a long-term basis in the future, it is in a strong position to do so.

Ratio of Liabilities to Stockholders' Equity

Claims against the total assets of a business are divided into two groups: (1) claims of creditors and (2) claims of owners. The relationship between the total claims of the creditors and owners—the **ratio of liabilities to stockholders' equity**—is a solvency measure that indicates the margin of safety for creditors. It also indicates the ability of the business to withstand adverse business conditions. When the claims of creditors are large in relation to the equity of the stockholders, there are usually significant interest payments. If earnings decline to the point where the company is unable to meet its interest payments, the business may be taken over by the creditors.

The relationship between creditor and stockholder equity is shown in the vertical analysis of the balance sheet. For example, the balance sheet of Lincoln Company in Exhibit 5 indicates that on December 31, 2006, liabilities represented 27.2% and stockholders' equity represented 72.8% of the total liabilities and stockholders' equity (100.0%). Instead of expressing each item as a percent of the total, this relationship may be expressed as a ratio of one to the other, as follows:

	2006	2005
Total liabilities	$310,000	$443,000
Total stockholders' equity	$829,500	$787,500
Ratio of liabilities to stockholders' equity	0.37	0.56

The balance sheet of Lincoln Company shows that the major factor affecting the change in the ratio was the $100,000 decrease in long-term liabilities during 2006. The ratio at the end of both years shows a large margin of safety for the creditors.

Number of Times Interest Charges Earned

Corporations in some industries, such as airlines, normally have high ratios of debt to stockholders' equity. For such corporations, the relative risk of the debtholders is normally measured as the **number of times interest charges are earned**, sometimes called the **fixed charge coverage ratio**, during the year. The higher the ratio, the lower the risk that interest payments will not be made if earnings decrease. In other words, the higher the ratio, the greater the assurance that interest payments will be made on a continuing basis. This measure also indicates the general financial strength of the business, which is of interest to stockholders and employees as well as creditors.

The amount available to meet interest charges is not affected by taxes on income. This is because interest is deductible in determining taxable income. Thus, the number of times interest charges are earned is computed as shown below.

	2006	2005
Income before income tax	$ 900,000	$ 800,000
Add interest expense	300,000	250,000
Amount available to meet interest charges	$1,200,000	$1,050,000
Number of times interest charges earned	4	4.2

REAL WORLD

The ratio of liabilities to stockholders' equity varies across industries. For example, recent annual reports of some selected companies showed the following ratio of liabilities to stockholders' equity:

Continental Airlines	7.43
Procter & Gamble	1.98
Circuit City Stores	0.66

The airline industry generally uses more debt financing than the consumer product or retail industries. Thus, the airline industry is generally considered more risky.

 What would be the number of times interest charges are earned for a company with $1,500,000, 10% debt; net income of $120,000; and a corporate tax rate of 40%?

$$\frac{[\$120,000/(1.0 - 0.4)] + \$150,000}{\$150,000} = 2.33$$

Analysis such as this can also be applied to dividends on preferred stock. In such a case, net income is divided by the amount of preferred dividends to yield the **number of times preferred dividends are earned**. This measure indicates the risk that dividends to preferred stockholders may not be paid.

FINANCIAL REPORTING AND DISCLOSURE

SARBANES-OXLEY ACT

The Sarbanes-Oxley Act became law on June 30, 2002, in response to widespread concerns about conflicts of interest between auditors and their clients, perceived weaknesses in corporate governance, and inadequate financial disclosure. Thus, Sarbanes-Oxley provided reforms in three main areas: the accounting profession, corporate governance, and financial disclosure.

Accounting Profession: A new provision in Sarbanes-Oxley prevents the independent auditor from providing other non-aligned services to a client, such as bookkeeping or internal auditing services. Providing tax services to an audit client is still acceptable. In addition, the act established a new Public Accounting Oversight Board (PAOB), consisting of five members responsible for establishing and overseeing auditing, quality control, ethics, and independence standards related to preparing audit reports.

Corporate Governance: Corporate governance refers to methods for aligning the behavior of corporate managers with the interests of shareholders. Sarbanes-Oxley added important requirements to the audit committee of the Board of Directors. The audit committee must be members of the Board of Directors and independent of management. In addition, the audit committee is required to be responsible for appointment, compensation, and oversight of the independent auditors. In addition, Sarbanes-Oxley also requires the CEO and CFO to certify the fairness of financial statements and the effectiveness of the internal controls. For example, an excerpt from the certification of a recent quarterly report of **Bank of America** by its CEO, Kenneth D. Lewis, is shown as follows:

I, Kenneth D. Lewis, certify that:

I have reviewed this quarterly report of Bank of America Corporation;

Based on my knowledge, the financial statements, and other financial information included in this quarterly report, fairly present in all material respects the financial condition, results of operations and cash flows of the (company) as of, and for, the periods presented in this quarterly report;

The . . . officers and I have disclosed, based on our most recent evaluation, to the (the company's) auditors and the audit committee . . .:

- *all significant deficiencies in the design or operation of internal controls which could adversely affect (the company's) ability to record, process, summarize and report financial data and have identified for the (company's) auditors any material weaknesses in internal controls; and*
- *any fraud, whether or not material, that involves management or other employees who have a significant role in the (company's) internal controls;*

. . .

/s/ Kenneth D. Lewis

Financial Disclosure: Sarbanes-Oxley also requires new or enhanced financial disclosures of transactions between related parties. These disclosures are prompted by a concern that such transactions are subject to a higher risk of self-dealing. In addition, the act requires material off-balance-sheet arrangements to be disclosed, such as the complex partnership transactions that led to the **Enron** failure.

Profitability Analysis

objective 3

Apply financial statement analysis to assess the profitability of a business.

The ability of a business to earn profits depends on the effectiveness and efficiency of its operations as well as the resources available to it. Profitability analysis, therefore, focuses primarily on the relationship between operating results as reported in the income statement and resources available to the business as reported in the balance sheet. Major analyses used in assessing profitability include the following:

1. Ratio of net sales to assets
2. Rate earned on total assets
3. Rate earned on stockholders' equity
4. Rate earned on common stockholders' equity
5. Earnings per share on common stock
6. Price-earnings ratio
7. Dividends per share
8. Dividend yield

> **Profitability analysis focuses on the relationship between operating results and the resources available to a business.**

Ratio of Net Sales to Assets

The ratio of net sales to assets is a profitability measure that shows how effectively a firm utilizes its assets. For example, two competing businesses have equal amounts of assets. If the sales of one are twice the sales of the other, the business with the higher sales is making better use of its assets.

In computing the ratio of net sales to assets, any long-term investments are excluded from total assets, because such investments are unrelated to normal operations involving the sale of goods or services. Assets may be measured as the total at the end of the year, the average at the beginning and end of the year, or the average of monthly totals. The basic data and the computation of this ratio for Lincoln Company are as follows:

	2006	2005
Net sales	$1,498,000	$1,200,000
Total assets (excluding long-term investments):		
Beginning of year	$1,053,000	$1,010,000
End of year	1,044,500	1,053,000
Total	$2,097,500	$2,063,000
Average (Total ÷ 2)	$1,048,750	$1,031,500
Ratio of net sales to assets	1.4	1.2

This ratio improved during 2006, primarily due to an increase in sales volume. A comparison with similar companies or industry averages would be helpful in assessing the effectiveness of Lincoln Company's use of its assets.

Rate Earned on Total Assets

The **rate earned on total assets** measures the profitability of total assets, without considering how the assets are financed. This rate is therefore not affected by whether the assets are financed primarily by creditors or stockholders.

The rate earned on total assets is computed by adding interest expense to net income and dividing this sum by the average total assets. Adding interest expense to net income eliminates the effect of whether the assets are financed by debt or equity. The rate earned by Lincoln Company on total assets is computed as follows:

	2006	2005
Net income	$ 91,000	$ 76,500
Plus interest expense	6,000	12,000
Total	$ 97,000	$ 88,500
Total assets:		
Beginning of year	$1,230,500	$1,187,500
End of year	1,139,500	1,230,500
Total	$2,370,000	$2,418,000
Average (Total ÷ 2)	$1,185,000	$1,209,000
Rate earned on total assets	8.2%	7.3%

The rate earned on total assets of Lincoln Company during 2006 improved over that of 2005. A comparison with similar companies and industry averages would be useful in evaluating Lincoln Company's profitability on total assets.

Sometimes it may be desirable to compute the **rate of income from operations to total assets**. This is especially true if significant amounts of nonoperating income and expense are reported on the income statement. In this case, any assets related to the nonoperating income and expense items should be excluded from total assets in computing the rate. In addition, using income from operations (which is before tax) has the advantage of eliminating the effects of any changes in the tax structure on the rate of earnings. When evaluating published data on rates earned on assets, you should be careful to determine the exact nature of the measure that is reported.

Rate Earned on Stockholders' Equity

Another measure of profitability is the ***rate earned on stockholders' equity***. It is computed by dividing net income by average total stockholders' equity. In contrast to the rate earned on total assets, this measure emphasizes the rate of income earned on the amount invested by the stockholders.

The total stockholders' equity may vary throughout a period. For example, a business may issue or retire stock, pay dividends, and earn net income. If monthly amounts are not available, the average of the stockholders' equity at the beginning and the end of the year is normally used to compute this rate. For Lincoln Company, the rate earned on stockholders' equity is computed as follows:

	2006	2005
Net income	$ 91,000	$ 76,500
Stockholders' equity:		
Beginning of year	$ 787,500	$ 750,000
End of year	829,500	787,500
Total	$1,617,000	$1,537,500
Average (Total ÷ 2)	$ 808,500	$ 768,750
Rate earned on stockholders' equity	11.3%	10.0%

The rate earned by a business on the equity of its stockholders is usually higher than the rate earned on total assets. This occurs when the amount earned on assets acquired with creditors' funds is more than the interest paid to creditors. This difference in the rate on stockholders' equity and the rate on total assets is called ***leverage***.

Lincoln Company's rate earned on stockholders' equity for 2006, 11.3%, is greater than the rate of 8.2% earned on total assets. The leverage of 3.1% (11.3% − 8.2%) for 2006 compares favorably with the 2.7% (10.0% − 7.3%) leverage for 2005. Exhibit 8 shows the 2006 and 2005 leverages for Lincoln Company.

 Nobody doesn't like me. Based in Chicago, I employ more than 140,000 people and my wares are sold in almost every country on earth. My food and drinks, underwear, and household products sport more than 100 brands, such as Champion, Hanes, L'eggs, Bali, Just My Size, Playtex, Wonderbra, Jimmy Dean, Ball Park, Hillshire Farms, and the Kiwi shoe care brand. My 32 "megabrands" each generate more than $100 million in annual sales. I aim to hold the No. 1 or No. 2 brand position in every category in which I compete. One of my biggest brands is my own name. Who am I? (Go to page 717 for answer.)

•Exhibit 8

Leverage

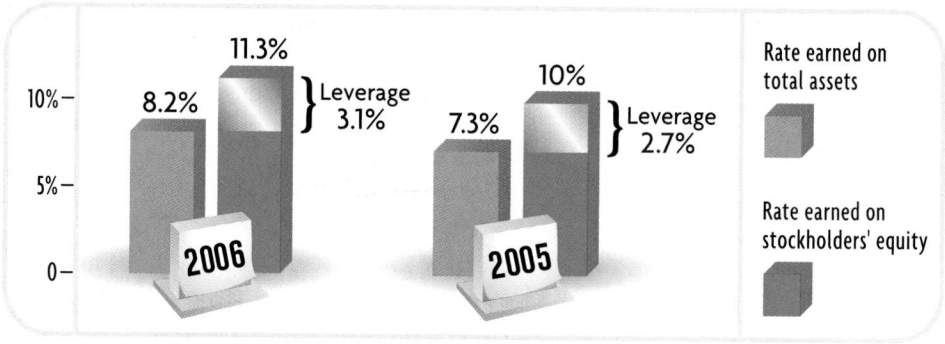

Rate Earned on Common Stockholders' Equity

A corporation may have both preferred and common stock outstanding. In this case, the common stockholders have the residual claim on earnings. The **rate earned on common stockholders' equity** focuses only on the rate of profits earned on the amount invested by the common stockholders. It is computed by subtracting preferred dividend requirements from the net income and dividing by the average common stockholders' equity.

Lincoln Company has $150,000 of 6% nonparticipating preferred stock outstanding on December 31, 2006 and 2005. Thus, the annual preferred dividend requirement is $9,000 ($150,000 × 6%). The common stockholders' equity equals the total stockholders' equity, including retained earnings, less the par of the preferred stock ($150,000). The basic data and the rate earned on common stockholders' equity for Lincoln Company are as follows:

The approximate rates earned on assets and stockholders' equity for **Adolph Coors Company** and **Anheuser-Busch Companies** for a recent fiscal year are shown below.

REAL WORLD

	Adolph Coors	Anheuser-Busch
Rate earned on assets	7%	15%
Rate earned on stockholders' equity	13%	42%

Anheuser-Busch has been more profitable and has benefited from a greater use of leverage than has Adolph Coors.

	2006	2005
Net income	$ 91,000	$ 76,500
Preferred dividends	9,000	9,000
Remainder—identified with common stock	$ 82,000	$ 67,500
Common stockholders' equity:		
Beginning of year	$ 637,500	$ 600,000
End of year	679,500	637,500
Total	$1,317,000	$1,237,500
Average (Total ÷ 2)	$ 658,500	$ 618,750
Rate earned on common stockholders' equity	12.5%	10.9%

The rate earned on common stockholders' equity differs from the rates earned by Lincoln Company on total assets and total stockholders' equity. This occurs if there are borrowed funds and also preferred stock outstanding, which rank ahead of the common shares in their claim on earnings. Thus, the concept of leverage, as we discussed in the preceding section, can also be applied to the use of funds from the sale of preferred stock as well as borrowing. Funds from both sources can be used in an attempt to increase the return on common stockholders' equity.

Earnings per Share on Common Stock

One of the profitability measures often quoted by the financial press is **earnings per share (EPS) on common stock**. It is also normally reported in the income statement in corporate annual reports. If a company has issued only one class of stock, the earnings per share is computed by dividing net income by the number of shares of stock outstanding. If preferred and common stock are outstanding, the net income is first reduced by the amount of preferred dividend requirements.[3]

---

[3] Additional details related to earnings per share were discussed in a previous chapter.

The data on the earnings per share of common stock for Lincoln Company are as follows:

	2006	2005
Net income	$91,000	$76,500
Preferred dividends	9,000	9,000
Remainder—identified with common stock	$82,000	$67,500
Shares of common stock outstanding	50,000	50,000
Earnings per share on common stock	$1.64	$1.35

Price-Earnings Ratio

Another profitability measure quoted by the financial press is the ***price-earnings (P/E) ratio*** on common stock. The price-earnings ratio is an indicator of a firm's future earnings prospects. It is computed by dividing the market price per share of common stock at a specific date by the annual earnings per share. To illustrate, assume that the market prices per common share are 41 at the end of 2006 and 27 at the end of 2005. The price-earnings ratio on common stock of Lincoln Company is computed as follows:

	2006	2005
Market price per share of common stock	$41.00	$27.00
Earnings per share on common stock	÷ 1.64	÷ 1.35
Price-earnings ratio on common stock	25	20

The price-earnings ratio indicates that a share of common stock of Lincoln Company was selling for 20 times the amount of earnings per share at the end of 2005. At the end of 2006, the common stock was selling for 25 times the amount of earnings per share.

Dividends per Share and Dividend Yield

Since the primary basis for dividends is earnings, dividends per share and earnings per share on common stock are commonly used by investors in assessing alternative stock investments. The dividends per share for Lincoln Company were $0.80 ($40,000 ÷ 50,000 shares) for 2006 and $0.60 ($30,000 ÷ 50,000 shares) for 2005.

Dividends per share can be reported with earnings per share to indicate the relationship between dividends and earnings. Comparing these two per share amounts indicates the extent to which the corporation is retaining its earnings for use in operations. Exhibit 9 shows these relationships for Lincoln Company.

•Exhibit 9   Dividends and Earnings per Share of Common Stock

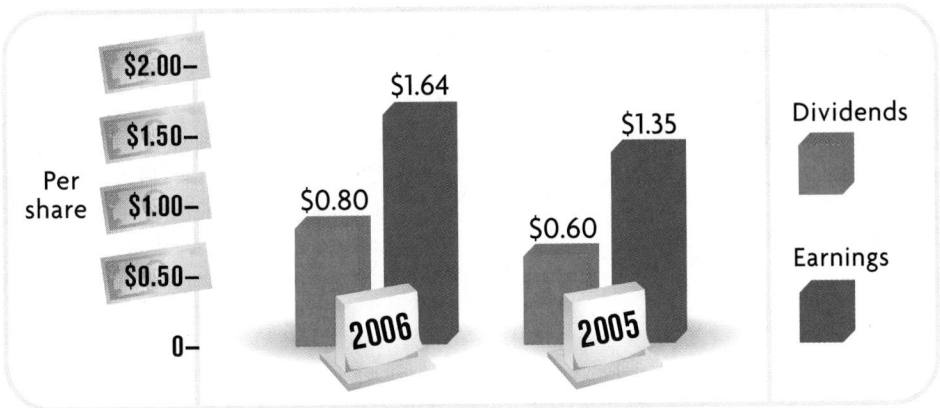

The *dividend yield* on common stock is a profitability measure that shows the rate of return to common stockholders in terms of cash dividends. It is of special interest to investors whose main investment objective is to receive current returns (dividends) on an investment rather than an increase in the market price of the investment. The dividend yield is computed by dividing the annual dividends paid per share of common stock by the market price per share on a specific date. To illustrate, assume that the market price was 41 at the end of 2006 and 27 at the end of 2005. The dividend yield on common stock of Lincoln Company is as follows:

	2006	2005
Dividends per share of common stock	$ 0.80	$ 0.60
Market price per share of common stock	÷ 41.00	÷ 27.00
Dividend yield on common stock	1.95%	2.22%

Summary of Analytical Measures

objective 4

Summarize the uses and limitations of analytical measures.

Exhibit 10 presents a summary of the analytical measures that we have discussed. These measures can be computed for most medium-size businesses. Depending on the specific business being analyzed, some measures might be omitted or additional measures could be developed. The type of industry, the capital structure, and the diversity of the business's operations usually affect the measures used. For example, analysis for an airline might include revenue per passenger mile and cost per available seat as measures. Likewise, analysis for a hotel might focus on occupancy rates.

Percentage analyses, ratios, turnovers, and other measures of financial position and operating results are useful analytical measures. They are helpful in assessing a business's past performance and predicting its future. They are not, however, a substitute for sound judgment. In selecting and interpreting analytical measures, conditions peculiar to a business or its industry should be considered. In addition, the influence of the general economic and business environment should be considered.

In determining trends, the interrelationship of the measures used in assessing a business should be carefully studied. Comparable indexes of earlier periods should also be studied. Data from competing businesses may be useful in assessing the efficiency of operations for the firm under analysis. In making such comparisons, however, the effects of differences in the accounting methods used by the businesses should be considered.

Corporate Annual Reports

objective 5

Describe the contents of corporate annual reports.

Corporations normally issue annual reports to their stockholders and other interested parties. Such reports summarize the corporation's operating activities for the past year and plans for the future. There are many variations in the order and form for presenting the major sections of annual reports. However, one section of the annual report is devoted to the financial statements, including the accompanying notes. In addition, annual reports usually include a management discussion and analysis (MDA) and an independent auditors' report. The notes, MDA, and independent auditors' report are illustrated in the 2002 annual report for **Home Depot, Inc.**, in Appendix F.

•Exhibit 10   Summary of Analytical Measures

	Method of Computation	Use
Solvency measures:		
Working capital	Current assets − Current liabilities	To indicate the ability to meet currently maturing obligations
Current ratio	$\dfrac{\text{Current assets}}{\text{Current liabilities}}$	
Quick ratio	$\dfrac{\text{Quick assets}}{\text{Current liabilities}}$	To indicate instant debt-paying ability
Accounts receivable turnover	$\dfrac{\text{Net sales}}{\text{Average accounts receivable}}$	To assess the efficiency in collecting receivables and in the management of credit
Numbers of days' sales in receivables	$\dfrac{\text{Accounts receivable, end of year}}{\text{Average daily sales}}$	
Inventory turnover	$\dfrac{\text{Cost of goods sold}}{\text{Average inventory}}$	To assess the efficiency in the management of inventory
Number of days' sales in inventory	$\dfrac{\text{Inventory, end of year}}{\text{Average daily cost of goods sold}}$	
Ratio of fixed assets to long-term liabilities	$\dfrac{\text{Fixed assets (net)}}{\text{Long-term liabilities}}$	To indicate the margin of safety to long-term creditors
Ratio of liabilities to stockholders' equity	$\dfrac{\text{Total liabilities}}{\text{Total stockholders' equity}}$	To indicate the margin of safety to creditors
Number of times interest charges earned	$\dfrac{\text{Income before income tax} + \text{Interest expense}}{\text{Interest expense}}$	To assess the risk to debtholders in terms of number of times interest charges were earned
Profitability measures:		
Ratio of net sales to assets	$\dfrac{\text{Net sales}}{\text{Average total assets (excluding long-term investments)}}$	To assess the effectiveness in the use of assets
Rate earned on total assets	$\dfrac{\text{Net income} + \text{Interest expense}}{\text{Average total assets}}$	To assess the profitability of the assets
Rate earned on stockholders' equity	$\dfrac{\text{Net income}}{\text{Average total stockholders' equity}}$	To assess the profitability of the investment by stockholders
Rate earned on common stockholders' equity	$\dfrac{\text{Net income} - \text{Preferred dividends}}{\text{Average common stockholders' equity}}$	To assess the profitability of the investment by common stockholders
Earnings per share on common stock	$\dfrac{\text{Net income} - \text{Preferred dividends}}{\text{Shares of common stock outstanding}}$	
Price-earnings ratio	$\dfrac{\text{Market price per share of common stock}}{\text{Earnings per share of common stock}}$	To indicate future earnings prospects, based on the relationship between market value of common stock and earnings
Dividends per share of common stock	$\dfrac{\text{Dividends}}{\text{Shares of common stock outstanding}}$	To indicate the extent to which earnings are being distributed to common stockholders
Dividend yield	$\dfrac{\text{Dividends per share of common stock}}{\text{Market price per share of common stock}}$	To indicate the rate of return to common stockholders in terms of dividends

Management Discussion and Analysis

A required disclosure in the annual report filed with the Securities and Exchange Commission is the ***Management Discussion and Analysis (MDA)***. The MDA provides critical information in interpreting the financial statements and assessing the future of the company.

The MDA includes an analysis of the results of operations and discusses management's opinion about future performance. It compares the prior year's income statement with the current year's to explain changes in sales, significant expenses, gross profit, and income from operations. For example, an increase in sales may be explained by referring to higher shipment volume or stronger prices.

The MDA also includes an analysis of the company's financial condition. It compares significant balance sheet items between successive years to explain changes in liquidity and capital resources. In addition, the MDA discusses significant risk exposure. For example, **Home Depot** has identified fluctuations in interest rates as its primary risk factor, since home building and improvement activities are sensitive to interest rates.

Independent Auditors' Report

Before issuing annual statements, all publicly held corporations are required to have an independent audit (examination) of their financial statements. For the financial statements of most companies, the CPAs who conduct the audit render an opinion on the fairness of the statements.

In addition, beginning in 2004, the Sarbanes-Oxley Act will require the independent auditor to provide an additional report attesting to management's assessment of internal control. This report will express the auditor's opinion on the accuracy of management's internal control assertion.[4]

---

[4]Final reporting guidelines are being formulated by appropriate professional and regulatory bodies, including the SEC, AICPA, and PAOB.

SPOTLIGHT ON STRATEGY

INVESTING STRATEGIES

How does one decide in which companies to invest? Like any other significant purchase, you would need to do some research to guide your investment decision, and that research should stem from your overall investment philosophy. If you were buying a car for performance, you would research performance characteristics, but if you were purchasing for economy, then you would research economy characteristics. You should research investment alternatives in the same way. There are four different investment philosophies that match different investment preferences: value, growth, income, and technical investing.

Value Investing
The value investor attempts to determine the intrinsic value of a business and then compare this value to the stock price. The investor is normally searching for undervalued stocks. That is, the investor attempts to discover stocks with an intrinsic value that is greater than the stock price. Value investors often look for quiet, out-of-favor, "boring" companies that have excellent financial performance. Investing in such stocks assumes that the stock price will eventually rise to match the intrinsic value. This method of investing was popularized by Benjamin Graham and is used by one of the most successful investors in the world, Warren Buffett. As stated by one author, "Graham's conviction rested on certain assumptions. First, he believed that the market frequently mispriced stocks. This mispricing was most often caused by human emotions of fear and greed. At the height of optimism, greed moved stocks beyond their intrinsic value, creating an overpriced market. At other times, fear moved prices below intrinsic value, creating an undervalued market."* Naturally, the key to successful value investing is to accurately determine a stock's intrinsic value. This will often include analyzing company financial ratios, as discussed in this chapter, relative to target ratios and industry norms.

Growth Investing
The growth investor tries to identify companies that are growing sales and earnings through new products, mar-

kets, or opportunities. Growth companies are often young companies that are still unproven but that possess unique technologies or capabilities. Investors hope to "ride the wave" of growth by purchasing these companies before their potential becomes obvious. Unlike value investors, growth investors will often purchase companies that are the "Ferraris" of the stock market. Growth investing carries the risk that the growth may not occur. Any moderation in growth can lead to severe price declines. Growth investors use many of the ratios discussed in this chapter to identify high-potential growth companies.

Income Investing
Income investors purchase common stocks for their dividend stream. High-dividend-paying companies are often in low-growth and stable industries. The stock price of such companies is usually not very volatile. Thus, the majority of the investment return comes from dividends. Many of the ratios discussed in this chapter can help identify companies with financial strength and high dividends.

Technical Investing
Investors that use technical analysis do not concern themselves with the fundamental financial strength and performance of the business but, instead, attempt to find clues of future performance from past performance. Technical investors often use charts of the historical prices in order to discover recurring price patterns that will help them determine if the stock price is near a top (signal to sell) or near a bottom (signal to buy). Technical analysts believe that the recurring patterns provide clues into market psychology and can be used to develop buy-and-sell rules. These rules are as varied as the number of investors developing them. Naturally, if everyone agreed upon a technical rule that actually predicted the future, then everyone would use the rule and it would eventually cease to work.

*Robert G. Hagstrom, *The Warren Buffett Way.*

Key Points

1 List basic financial statement analytical procedures.
The analysis of percentage increases and decreases in related items in comparative financial statements is

called horizontal analysis. The analysis of percentages of component parts to the total in a single statement is called vertical analysis.

Financial statements in which all amounts are expressed in percentages for purposes of analysis are called common-size statements.

2 Apply financial statement analysis to assess the solvency of a business.

The primary focus of financial statement analysis is the assessment of solvency and profitability. All users are interested in the ability of a business to pay its debts as they come due (solvency) and to earn income (profitability). Solvency analysis is normally assessed by examining the following balance sheet relationships: (1) current position analysis, (2) accounts receivable analysis, (3) inventory analysis, (4) the ratio of fixed assets to long-term liabilities, (5) the ratio of liabilities to stockholders' equity, and (6) the number of times interest charges are earned.

3 Apply financial statement analysis to assess the profitability of a business.

Profitability analysis focuses mainly on the relationship between operating results (income statement) and resources available (balance sheet). Major analyses used in assessing profitability include (1) the ratio of net sales to assets, (2) the rate earned on total assets, (3) the rate earned on stockholders' equity, (4) the rate earned on common stockholders' equity, (5) earnings per share on common stock, (6) the price-earnings ratio, (7) dividends per share, and (8) dividend yield.

4 Summarize the uses and limitations of analytical measures.

In selecting and interpreting analytical measures, conditions peculiar to a business or its industry should be considered. For example, the type of industry, capital structure, and diversity of the business's operations affect the measures used. In addition, the influence of the general economic and business environment should be considered.

5 Describe the contents of corporate annual reports.

Corporate annual reports normally include financial statements and the accompanying notes, the Management Discussion and Analysis, and the Independent Auditors' Report.

Key Terms

accounts receivable turnover (620)
common-size statement (616)
current ratio (618)
dividend yield (628)
earnings per share (EPS) on common stock (626)
horizontal analysis (612)
inventory turnover (621)
leverage (625)
Management Discussion and Analysis (MDA) (630)
number of days' sales in inventory (621)

number of days' sales in receivables (620)
number of times interest charges are earned (622)
price-earnings (P/E) ratio (627)
profitability (617)
quick assets (619)
quick ratio (619)
rate earned on common stockholders' equity (626)
rate earned on stockholders' equity (625)
rate earned on total assets (624)

ratio of fixed assets to long-term liabilities (621)
ratio of liabilities to stockholders' equity (622)
solvency (617)
vertical analysis (614)

Illustrative Problem

Rainbow Paint Co.'s comparative financial statements for the years ending December 31, 2006 and 2005, are as follows. The market price of Rainbow Paint Co.'s common stock was $30 on December 31, 2005, and $25 on December 31, 2006.

Rainbow Paint Co.
Comparative Income Statement
For the Years Ended December 31, 2006 and 2005

	2006	2005
Sales	$5,125,000	$3,257,600
Sales returns and allowances	125,000	57,600
Net sales	$5,000,000	$3,200,000
Cost of goods sold	3,400,000	2,080,000
Gross profit	$1,600,000	$1,120,000
Selling expenses	$ 650,000	$ 464,000
Administrative expenses	325,000	224,000
Total operating expenses	$ 975,000	$ 688,000
Income from operations	$ 625,000	$ 432,000
Other income	25,000	19,200
	$ 650,000	$ 451,200
Other expense (interest)	105,000	64,000
Income before income tax	$ 545,000	$ 387,200
Income tax expense	300,000	176,000
Net income	$ 245,000	$ 211,200

Rainbow Paint Co.
Comparative Retained Earnings Statement
For the Years Ended December 31, 2006 and 2005

	2006	2005
Retained earnings, January 1	$723,000	$581,800
Add net income for year	245,000	211,200
Total	$968,000	$793,000
Deduct dividends:		
On preferred stock	$ 40,000	$ 40,000
On common stock	45,000	30,000
Total	$ 85,000	$ 70,000
Retained earnings, December 31	$883,000	$723,000

Rainbow Paint Co.
Comparative Balance Sheet
December 31, 2006 and 2005

	2006	2005
Assets		
Current assets:		
Cash	$ 175,000	$ 125,000
Marketable securities	150,000	50,000
Accounts receivable (net)	425,000	325,000
Inventories	720,000	480,000
Prepaid expenses	30,000	20,000
Total current assets	$1,500,000	$1,000,000
Long-term investments	250,000	225,000
Property, plant, and equipment (net)	2,093,000	1,948,000
Total assets	$3,843,000	$3,173,000
Liabilities		
Current liabilities	$ 750,000	$ 650,000
Long-term liabilities:		
Mortgage note payable, 10%, due 2009	$ 410,000	—
Bonds payable, 8%, due 2012	800,000	$ 800,000
Total long-term liabilities	$1,210,000	$ 800,000
Total liabilities	$1,960,000	$1,450,000
Stockholders' Equity		
Preferred 8% stock, $100 par	$ 500,000	$ 500,000
Common stock, $10 par	500,000	500,000
Retained earnings	883,000	723,000
Total stockholders' equity	$1,883,000	$1,723,000
Total liabilities and stockholders' equity	$3,843,000	$3,173,000

Instructions

Determine the following measures for 2006:

1. Working capital
2. Current ratio
3. Quick ratio
4. Accounts receivable turnover
5. Number of days' sales in receivables
6. Inventory turnover
7. Number of days' sales in inventory
8. Ratio of fixed assets to long-term liabilities
9. Ratio of liabilities to stockholders' equity
10. Number of times interest charges earned
11. Number of times preferred dividends earned
12. Ratio of net sales to assets
13. Rate earned on total assets
14. Rate earned on stockholders' equity
15. Rate earned on common stockholders' equity
16. Earnings per share on common stock
17. Price-earnings ratio
18. Dividends per share of common stock
19. Dividend yield

Solution

(Ratios are rounded to the nearest single digit after the decimal point.)

1. Working capital: $750,000
   $1,500,000 − $750,000

2. Current ratio: 2.0
   $1,500,000 ÷ $750,000

3. Quick ratio: 1.0
   $750,000 ÷ $750,000

4. Accounts receivable turnover: 13.3
   $5,000,000 ÷ [($425,000 + $325,000) ÷ 2]

5. Number of days' sales in receivables: 31 days
   $5,000,000 ÷ 365 = $13,699
   $425,000 ÷ $13,699

6. Inventory turnover: 5.7
   $3,400,000 ÷ [($720,000 + $480,000) ÷ 2]

7. Number of days' sales in inventory: 77.3 days
   $3,400,000 ÷ 365 = $9,315
   $720,000 ÷ $9,315

8. Ratio of fixed assets to long-term liabilities: 1.7
   $2,093,000 ÷ $1,210,000

9. Ratio of liabilities to stockholders' equity: 1.0
   $1,960,000 ÷ $1,883,000

10. Number of times interest charges earned: 6.2
    ($545,000 + $105,000) ÷ $105,000

11. Number of times preferred dividends earned: 6.1
    $245,000 ÷ $40,000

12. Ratio of net sales to assets: 1.5
    $5,000,000 ÷ [($3,593,000 + $2,948,000) ÷ 2]

13. Rate earned on total assets: 10.0%
    ($245,000 + $105,000) ÷ [($3,843,000 + $3,173,000) ÷ 2]

14. Rate earned on stockholders' equity: 13.6%
$245,000 ÷ [($1,883,000 + $1,723,000) ÷ 2]

15. Rate earned on common stockholders' equity: 15.7%
($245,000 − $40,000) ÷ [($1,383,000 + $1,223,000) ÷ 2]

16. Earnings per share on common stock: $4.10
($245,000 − $40,000) ÷ 50,000

17. Price-earnings ratio: 6.1
$25 ÷ $4.10

18. Dividends per share of common stock: $0.90
$45,000 ÷ 50,000 shares

19. Dividend yield: 3.6%
$0.90 ÷ $25

Self-Examination Questions (Answers at End of Chapter)

1. What type of analysis is indicated by the following?

	Amount	Percent
Current assets	$100,000	20%
Property, plant, and equipment	400,000	80
Total assets	$500,000	100%

A. Vertical analysis   C. Profitability analysis
B. Horizontal analysis   D. Contribution margin analysis

2. Which of the following measures indicates the ability of a firm to pay its current liabilities?
A. Working capital   C. Quick ratio
B. Current ratio   D. All of the above

3. The ratio determined by dividing total current assets by total current liabilities is:

A. current ratio   C. bankers' ratio
B. working capital ratio   D. all of the above

4. The ratio of the quick assets to current liabilities, which indicates the "instant" debt-paying ability of a firm, is:
A. current ratio   C. quick ratio
B. working capital ratio   D. bankers' ratio

5. A measure useful in evaluating the efficiency in the management of inventories is:
A. working capital ratio
B. quick ratio
C. number of days' sales in inventory
D. ratio of fixed assets to long-term liabilities

Class Discussion Questions

1. What is the difference between horizontal and vertical analysis of financial statements?
2. What is the advantage of using comparative statements for financial analysis rather than statements for a single date or period?
3. The current year's amount of net income (after income tax) is 15% larger than that of the preceding year. Does this indicate an improved operating performance? Discuss.
4. How would you respond to a horizontal analysis that showed an expense increasing by over 100%?
5. How would the current and quick ratios of a service business compare?

6. For Lindsay Corporation, the working capital at the end of the current year is $5,000 greater than the working capital at the end of the preceding year, reported as follows:

	Current Year	Preceding Year
Current assets:		
Cash, marketable securities, and receivables	$34,000	$30,000
Inventories	51,000	32,500
Total current assets	$85,000	$62,500
Current liabilities	42,500	25,000
Working capital	$42,500	$37,500

Has the current position improved? Explain.

7. Why would the accounts receivable turnover ratio be different between **Wal-Mart Stores, Inc.** and **Procter & Gamble Company**?

8. A company that grants terms of n/30 on all sales has a yearly accounts receivable turnover, based on monthly averages, of 6. Is this a satisfactory turnover? Discuss.

9. a. Why is it advantageous to have a high inventory turnover?
   b. Is it possible for the inventory turnover to be too high? Discuss.
   c. Is it possible to have a high inventory turnover and a high number of days' sales in inventory? Discuss.

10. What do the following data taken from a comparative balance sheet indicate about the company's ability to borrow additional funds on a long-term basis in the current year as compared to the preceding year?

	Current Year	Preceding Year
Fixed assets (net)	$175,000	$170,000
Total long-term liabilities	70,000	85,000

11. a. Why is the rate earned on stockholders' equity by a thriving business ordinarily higher than the rate earned on total assets?
    b. Should the rate earned on common stockholders' equity normally be higher or lower than the rate earned on total stockholders' equity? Explain.

12. The net income (after income tax) of A. L. Gibson Inc. was $25 per common share in the latest year and $40 per common share for the preceding year. At the beginning of the latest year, the number of shares outstanding was doubled by a stock split. There were no other changes in the amount of stock outstanding. What were the earnings per share in the preceding year, adjusted for comparison with the latest year?

13. The price-earnings ratio for the common stock of Essian Company was 10 at December 31, the end of the current fiscal year. What does the ratio indicate about the selling price of the common stock in relation to current earnings?

14. Why would the dividend yield differ significantly from the rate earned on common stockholders' equity?

15. Favorable business conditions may bring about certain seemingly unfavorable ratios, and unfavorable business operations may result in apparently favorable ratios. For example, Sanchez Company increased its sales and net income substantially for the current year, yet the current ratio at the end of the year is lower than at the beginning of the year. Discuss some possible causes of the apparent weakening of the current position, while sales and net income have increased substantially.

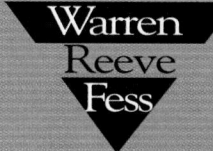
Exercises

EXERCISE 15-1
Vertical analysis of income statement
Objective 1

SPREADSHEET

✓ *2006 net income: $50,000; 10% of sales*

Revenue and expense data for Home-Mate Appliance Co. are as follows:

	2006	2005
Sales	$500,000	$450,000
Cost of goods sold	275,000	234,000
Selling expenses	90,000	94,500
Administrative expenses	60,000	63,000
Income tax expense	25,000	22,500

a. Prepare an income statement in comparative form, stating each item for both 2006 and 2005 as a percent of sales.
b. Comment on the significant changes disclosed by the comparative income statement.

EXERCISE 15-2
Vertical analysis of income statement
Objective 1

REAL WORLD

SPREADSHEET

✓ *a. Fiscal year 2002 income from continuing operations, 26.8% of revenues*

The following comparative income statement (in thousands of dollars) for the fiscal years 2001 and 2002 was adapted from the annual report of **Speedway Motorsports, Inc.**, owner and operator of several major motor speedways, such as the Atlanta, Texas, and Las Vegas Motor Speedways.

	Fiscal Year 2002	Fiscal Year 2001
Revenues:		
Admissions	$141,315	$136,362
Event-related revenue	122,172	133,289
NASCAR broadcasting revenue	77,936	67,488
Other operating revenue	34,537	38,111
Total revenue	$375,960	$375,250
Expenses and other:		
Direct expense of events	$ 69,297	$ 76,579
NASCAR purse and sanction fees	61,217	54,479
Other direct expenses	87,427	88,582
General and administrative	57,235	59,331
Total expenses and other	$275,176	$278,971
Income from continuing operations	$100,784	$ 96,279

a. Prepare a comparative income statement for fiscal years 2001 and 2002 in vertical form, stating each item as a percent of revenues. Round to one digit after the decimal place.
b. Comment on the significant changes.

EXERCISE 15-3
Common-size income statement

Objective 1

SPREADSHEET

✓ a. *Horizon net income: $105,000; 7.5% of sales*

Revenue and expense data for the current calendar year for Horizon Publishing Company and for the publishing industry are as follows. The Horizon Publishing Company data are expressed in dollars. The publishing industry averages are expressed in percentages.

	Horizon Publishing Company	Publishing Industry Average
Sales	$1,414,000	101.0%
Sales returns and allowances	14,000	1.0
Cost of goods sold	504,000	40.0
Selling expenses	574,000	39.0
Administrative expenses	154,000	10.5
Other income	16,800	1.2
Other expense	23,800	1.7
Income tax expense	56,000	4.0

a. Prepare a common-size income statement comparing the results of operations for Horizon Publishing Company with the industry average. Round to one digit after the decimal place.

b. As far as the data permit, comment on significant relationships revealed by the comparisons.

EXERCISE 15-4
Vertical analysis of balance sheet

Objective 1

SPREADSHEET

✓ *Retained earnings, Dec. 31, 2006, 46.25%*

Balance sheet data for Santa Fe Tile Company on December 31, the end of the fiscal year, are as follows:

	2006	2005
Current assets	$260,000	$200,000
Property, plant, and equipment	500,000	450,000
Intangible assets	40,000	50,000
Current liabilities	170,000	150,000
Long-term liabilities	210,000	200,000
Common stock	50,000	50,000
Retained earnings	370,000	300,000

Prepare a comparative balance sheet for 2006 and 2005, stating each asset as a percent of total assets and each liability and stockholders' equity item as a percent of the total liabilities and stockholders' equity. Round to two digits after the decimal place.

EXERCISE 15-5
Horizontal analysis of the income statement

Objective 1

SPREADSHEET

✓ a. *Net income decrease, 77.5%*

Income statement data for Scribe Paper Company for the year ended December 31, 2006 and 2005, are as follows:

	2006	2005	↑ or (↓)	%
Sales	$66,300	$85,000	(18,700)	(22%)
Cost of goods sold	32,000	40,000	(8,000)	(20%)
Gross profit	$34,300	$45,000	(10,700)	(23.8%)
Selling expenses	$24,000	$25,000	(1,000)	(4%)
Administrative expenses	7,500	6,000	1,500	25%
Total operating expenses	$31,500	$31,000	500	1.6%
Income before income tax	$ 2,800	$14,000	(11,200)	(80%)
Income tax expense	1,000	6,000	(5,000)	(83.3%)
Net income	$ 1,800	$ 8,000	(6,200)	(77.5%)

a. Prepare a comparative income statement with horizontal analysis, indicating the increase (decrease) for 2006 when compared with 2005. Round to two digits after the decimal place.

b. What conclusions can be drawn from the horizontal analysis?

EXERCISE 15-6
Current position analysis
Objective 2

✓ *2006 working capital,*
$625,000

The following data were taken from the balance sheet of Marine Equipment Company:

	Dec. 31, 2006	Dec. 31, 2005
Cash	$118,000	$ 95,000
Marketable securities	152,000	131,000
Accounts and notes receivable (net)	210,000	198,000
Inventories	345,000	326,000
Prepaid expenses	50,000	45,000
Accounts and notes payable (short-term)	190,000	208,000
Accrued liabilities	60,000	57,000

a. Determine for each year (1) the working capital, (2) the current ratio, and (3) the quick ratio.
b. What conclusions can be drawn from these data as to the company's ability to meet its currently maturing debts?

EXERCISE 15-7
Current position analysis
Objective 2

REAL WORLD

✓ *a. (1) Dec. 28, 2002*
current ratio, 1.06

PepsiCo, Inc., the parent company of Frito-Lay snack foods and Pepsi beverages, had the following current assets and current liabilities at the end of two recent years:

	Dec. 28, 2002 (in millions)	Dec. 28, 2001 (in millions)
Cash and cash equivalents	$1,638	$ 683
Short-term investments, at cost	207	966
Accounts and notes receivable, net	2,531	2,142
Inventories	1,342	1,310
Prepaid expenses and other current assets	695	752
Short-term obligations	562	354
Accounts payable and other current liabilities	4,998	4,461
Income taxes payable	492	183

a. Determine the (1) current ratio and (2) quick ratio for both years. Round to two digits after the decimal place.
b. What conclusions can you draw from these data?

EXERCISE 15-8
Current position analysis
Objective 2

**WHAT'S WRONG
WITH THIS?**

The bond indenture for the 10-year, 9½% debenture bonds dated January 2, 2005, required working capital of $350,000, a current ratio of 1.5, and a quick ratio of 1 at the end of each calendar year until the bonds mature. At December 31, 2006, the three measures were computed as follows:

1. Current assets:

Cash	$275,000	
Marketable securities	123,000	
Accounts and notes receivable (net)	172,000	
Inventories	295,000	
Prepaid expenses	35,000	
Goodwill	150,000	
Total current assets		$1,050,000
Current liabilities:		
Accounts and short-term notes payable	$375,000	
Accrued liabilities	250,000	
Total current liabilities		625,000
Working capital		$ 425,000

2. Current ratio = 1.68 ($1,050,000 ÷ $625,000)
3. Quick ratio = 1.52 ($570,000 ÷ $375,000)

a. List the errors in the determination of the three measures of current position analysis.
b. Is the company satisfying the terms of the bond indenture?

EXERCISE 15-9
Accounts receivable analysis
Objective 2

✓ *a. Accounts receivable turnover, current year, 7.1*

The following data are taken from the financial statements of Ovation Industries Inc. Terms of all sales are 1/10, n/60.

	Current Year	Preceding Year
Accounts receivable, end of year	$ 48,219	$ 52,603
Monthly average accounts receivable (net)	45,070	46,154
Net sales	320,000	300,000

a. Determine for each year (1) the accounts receivable turnover and (2) the number of days' sales in receivables. Round to nearest dollar and one digit after the decimal place.
b. What conclusions can be drawn from these data concerning accounts receivable and credit policies?

EXERCISE 15-10
Accounts receivable analysis
Objective 2

REAL WORLD

✓ *a. (1) Sears' accounts receivable turnover, 1.2*

Sears, Roebuck & Company and **Federated Department Stores, Inc.** (Macy's, Rich's, Bloomingdale's) are two of the largest department store chains in the United States. Both companies offer credit to their customers through their own credit card operations. In addition, Sears offers credit to non-Sears customers through a Sears MasterCard®. Information from the financial statements for both companies for two recent years is as follows (all numbers are in millions):

	Sears	Federated
Merchandise sales (fiscal 2002)	$35,698	$15,434
Credit card receivables—beginning	28,155	2,379
Credit card receivables—ending	30,759	2,945

a. Determine the (1) accounts receivable turnover and (2) the number of days' sales in receivables for both companies. Round to one digit after the decimal place.
b. Compare the two companies with regard to their credit card policies.

EXERCISE 15-11
Inventory analysis
Objective 2

✓ *a. Inventory turnover, 2006, 8.0*

The following data were extracted from the income statement of Mountain Sports Inc.:

	2006	2005
Sales	$656,000	$774,000
Beginning inventories	42,000	44,000
Cost of goods sold	328,000	430,000
Ending inventories	40,000	42,000

a. Determine for each year (1) the inventory turnover and (2) the number of days' sales in inventory. Round to nearest dollar and two digits after the decimal place.
b. What conclusions can be drawn from these data concerning the inventories?

EXERCISE 15-12
Inventory analysis
Objective 2

REAL WORLD

✓ *a. (1) Dell inventory turnover, 99.5*

Dell Computer Corporation and **Hewlett-Packard Corporation (HP)** compete with each other in the personal computer market. Dell's strategy is to assemble computers to customer orders, rather than for inventory. Thus, for example, Dell will build and deliver a computer within four days of a customer entering an order on a Web page. Hewlett-Packard, on the other hand, builds some computers prior to receiving an order, then sells from this inventory once an order is received. Below is selected financial information for both companies from a recent year's financial statements (in millions):

	Dell Computer Corporation	Hewlett-Packard Corporation
Sales	$35,404	$45,955
Cost of goods sold	29,055	34,573
Inventory, beginning of period	278	5,204
Inventory, end of period	306	5,797

a. Determine for both companies (1) the inventory turnover and (2) the number of days' sales in inventory. Round to one digit after the decimal place.
b. Interpret the inventory ratios by considering Dell's and Hewlett-Packard's operating strategies.

EXERCISE 15-13
Ratio of liabilities to stockholders' equity and number of times interest charges earned

Objective 2

✓ *a. Ratio of liabilities to stockholders' equity, Dec. 31, 2006, 0.54*

The following data were taken from the financial statements of Durable Structures, Inc. for December 31, 2006 and 2005:

	December 31, 2006	December 31, 2005
Accounts payable	$ 150,000	$ 140,000
Current maturities of serial bonds payable	200,000	200,000
Serial bonds payable, 8%, issued 2001, due 2011	1,000,000	1,200,000
Common stock, $1 par value	100,000	100,000
Paid-in capital in excess of par	500,000	500,000
Retained earnings	1,900,000	1,600,000

The income before income tax was $528,000 and $336,000 for the years 2006 and 2005, respectively.

a. Determine the ratio of liabilities to stockholders' equity at the end of each year. Round to two digits after the decimal place.
b. Determine the number of times the bond interest charges are earned during the year for both years.
c. What conclusions can be drawn from these data as to the company's ability to meet its currently maturing debts?

EXERCISE 15-14
Ratio of liabilities to stockholders' equity and number of times interest charges earned

Objective 2

REAL WORLD

✓ *a. Hasbro, 1.49*

Hasbro Inc. and Mattel Inc. are the two largest toy companies in North America. Condensed liabilities and stockholders' equity from a recent balance sheet are shown for each company as follows:

	Hasbro Inc.	Mattel Inc.
Current liabilities	$ 758,591,000	$1,596,981,000
Long-term debt	1,165,649,000	1,020,919,000
Deferred liabilities	91,875,000	184,203,000
Total liabilities	$2,016,115,000	$2,802,103,000
Shareholders' equity:		
Common stock, $0.50 par value	$ 104,847,000	$ 436,307,000
Additional paid-in capital	457,544,000	1,638,993,000
Retained earnings	1,622,402,000	132,900,000
Accumulated other comprehensive loss and other equity items	(71,394,000)	(307,798,000)
Treasury stock, at cost	(760,535,000)	(161,944,000)
Total stockholders' equity	$1,352,864,000	$1,738,458,000
Total liabilities and stockholders' equity	$3,368,979,000	$4,540,561,000

The income from operations and interest expense from the income statement for both companies were as follows:

	Hasbro Inc.	Mattel Inc.
Income from operations	$ 96,199,000	$430,010,000
Interest expense	103,688,000	155,132,000

a. Determine the ratio of liabilities to stockholders' equity for both companies. Round to two digits after the decimal place.
b. Determine the number of times interest charges are earned for both companies. Round to two digits after the decimal place.
c. ▭▭▭▶ Interpret the ratio differences between the two companies.

EXERCISE 15-15
Ratio of liabilities to stockholders' equity and ratio of fixed assets to long-term liabilities

Objective 2

REAL WORLD

Recent balance sheet information for two companies in the food industry, H.J. Heinz Co. and Hershey Foods Corp., are as follows (in thousands of dollars):

	H.J. Heinz	Hershey Foods
Net property, plant, and equipment	$2,250,074	$1,534,901
Current liabilities	2,509,169	606,444
Long-term debt	4,642,968	876,972
Other liabilities (pensions, deferred taxes)	1,407,607	1,223,254
Stockholders' equity	1,718,616	1,147,204

a. Determine the ratio of liabilities to stockholders' equity for both companies. Round to two digits after the decimal place.

b. Determine the ratio of fixed assets to long-term liabilities for both companies. Round to two digits after the decimal place.

c. ▬▬▶ Interpret the ratio differences between the two companies.

EXERCISE 15-16
Ratio of net sales to total assets

Objective 3

REAL WORLD

✓ a. Yellow, 2.55

Three major segments of the transportation industry are motor carriers, such as **Yellow Corp.**; railroads, such as **Union Pacific Corp.**; and transportation arrangement services, such as **C.H. Robinson Worldwide**. Recent financial statement information for these three companies is shown as follows (in thousands of dollars):

	Yellow	Union Pacific	C.H. Robinson Worldwide
Net sales	$3,276,651	$11,973,000	$3,090,072
Average total assets	1,285,777	31,551,000	683,490

a. Determine the ratio of net sales to assets for all three companies. Round to two digits after the decimal place.

b. ▬▬▶ Assume that the ratio of net sales to assets for each company represents their respective industry segment. Interpret the differences in the ratio of net sales to assets in terms of the operating characteristics of each of the respective segments.

EXERCISE 15-17
Profitability ratios

Objective 3

✓ a. Rate earned on total assets, 2007, 12.0%

The following selected data were taken from the financial statements of Yellowstone Group, Inc. for December 31, 2007, 2006, and 2005:

	December 31, 2007	December 31, 2006	December 31, 2005
Total assets	$1,450,000	$1,300,000	$1,100,000
Notes payable (8% interest)	187,500	187,500	187,500
Common stock	450,000	450,000	450,000
Preferred $10 stock, $100 par, cumulative, nonparticipating (no change during year) ..	200,000	200,000	200,000
Retained earnings	495,000	365,000	205,000

The 2007 net income was $150,000, and the 2006 net income was $180,000. No dividends on common stock were declared between 2005 and 2007.

a. Determine the rate earned on total assets, the rate earned on stockholders' equity, and the rate earned on common stockholders' equity for the years 2006 and 2007. Round to two digits after the decimal place.

b. What conclusions can be drawn from these data as to the company's profitability?

EXERCISE 15-18
Profitability ratios

Objective 3

REAL WORLD

✓ a. 2002 rate earned on total assets, 9.2%

AnnTaylor Inc. sells professional women's apparel through company-owned retail stores. Recent financial information for Ann Taylor is provided below (all numbers in thousands):

	Fiscal Year Ended	
	Feb. 1, 2003	Feb. 2, 2002
Net income	$80,158	$29,105
Interest expense	6,886	6,869

	Feb. 1, 2003	Feb. 2, 2002	Feb. 3, 2001
Total assets	$1,010,826	$883,166	$848,115
Total stockholders' equity	714,418	612,129	574,029

An analysis of 70 apparel retail companies indicates an industry average rate earned on total assets of 6% and an average rate earned on stockholders' equity of 7.8% for fiscal 2002.

a. Determine the rate earned on total assets for Ann Taylor for the fiscal years ended February 1, 2003 and February 2, 2002. Round to two digits after the decimal place.

b. Determine the rate earned on stockholders' equity for Ann Taylor for the fiscal years ended February 1, 2003 and February 2, 2002. Round to two digits after the decimal place.

c. Evaluate the two-year trend for the profitability ratios determined in (a) and (b).

d. Evaluate Ann Taylor's profit performance relative to the industry.

EXERCISE 15-19
Six measures of solvency or profitability

Objectives 2, 3

✓ *c. Ratio of net sales to assets, 1.58*

The following data were taken from the financial statements of Orion Systems Inc. for the current fiscal year:

Property, plant, and equipment (net)			$ 950,000
Liabilities:			
Current liabilities		$ 45,000	
Mortgage note payable, 7.5%, issued 1996, due 2011		680,000	
Total liabilities			$ 725,000
Stockholders' equity:			
Preferred $8 stock, $100 par, cumulative, nonparticipating (no change during year)			$ 200,000
Common stock, $10 par (no change during year)			650,000
Retained earnings:			
Balance, beginning of year	$500,000		
Net income	180,000	$680,000	
Preferred dividends	$ 16,000		
Common dividends	48,000	64,000	
Balance, end of year			616,000
Total stockholders' equity			$1,466,000
Net sales			$3,000,000
Interest expense			$ 51,000

Assuming that long-term investments totaled $200,000 throughout the year and that total assets were $2,009,000 at the beginning of the year, determine the following: (a) ratio of fixed assets to long-term liabilities, (b) ratio of liabilities to stockholders' equity, (c) ratio of net sales to assets, (d) rate earned on total assets, (e) rate earned on stockholders' equity, and (f) rate earned on common stockholders' equity. Round to two digits after the decimal place.

EXERCISE 15-20
Six measures of solvency or profitability

Objectives 2, 3

✓ *d. Price-earnings ratio, 20.83*

The balance sheet for Collier Medical, Inc. at the end of the current fiscal year indicated the following:

Bonds payable, 12% (issued in 1996, due in 2016)	$1,500,000
Preferred $10 stock, $100 par	250,000
Common stock, $20 par	2,500,000

Income before income tax was $450,000, and income taxes were $125,000 for the current year. Cash dividends paid on common stock during the current year totaled $100,000. The common stock was selling for $50 per share at the end of the year. Determine each of the following: (a) number of times bond interest charges were earned, (b) number of times preferred dividends were earned, (c) earnings per share on common stock, (d) price-earnings ratio, (e) dividends per share of common stock, and (f) dividend yield. Round to two digits after the decimal place.

EXERCISE 15-21
Earnings per share, price-earnings ratio, dividend yield

Objective 3

✓ *b. Price-earnings ratio, 20*

The following information was taken from the financial statements of Fashion Cosmetics, Inc. for December 31 of the current fiscal year:

Common stock, $12 par value (no change during the year)	$2,400,000
Preferred $9 stock, $100 par, cumulative, nonparticipating (no change during year)	600,000

The net income was $444,000 and the declared dividends on the common stock were $156,000 for the current year. The market price of the common stock is $39 per share.

For the common stock, determine the (a) earnings per share, (b) price-earnings ratio, (c) dividends per share, and (d) dividend yield. Round to two digits after the decimal place.

EXERCISE 15-22
Earnings per share

Objective 3

✓ *b. Earnings per share on common stock, $1.14*

The net income reported on the income statement of Cincinnati Soap Co. was $890,000. There were 500,000 shares of $20 par common stock and 40,000 shares of $8 cumulative preferred stock outstanding throughout the current year. The income statement included two extraordinary items: a $256,000 gain from condemnation of land and a $166,000 loss arising from flood damage, both after applicable income tax. Determine the per share figures for common stock for (a) income before extraordinary items and (b) net income.

EXERCISE 15-23
Price-earnings ratio; dividend yield

Objective 3

REAL WORLD

The table below shows the stock price, earnings per share, and dividends per share for three companies as of February 10, 2003:

	Price	Earnings per Share	Dividends per Share
Bank of America Corp.	$68.20	$5.91	$2.56
eBay, Inc.	73.56	0.85	0.00
Coca-Cola Company	40.06	1.68	0.80

a. Determine the price-earnings ratio and dividend yield for the three companies. Round to two digits after the decimal place.
b.  Explain the differences in these ratios across the three companies.

Problems Series A

PROBLEM 15-1A
Horizontal analysis for income statement

Objective 1

SPREADSHEET
P.A.S.S.

✓ *1. Net sales, 12% increase*

For 2006, Turnberry Company reported its most significant decline in net income in years. At the end of the year, Hai Chow, the president, is presented with the following condensed comparative income statement:

Turnberry Company
Comparative Income Statement
For the Years Ended December 31, 2006 and 2005

	2006	2005
Sales	$482,000	$429,000
Sales returns and allowances	6,000	4,000
Net sales	$476,000	$425,000
Cost of goods sold	216,000	180,000
Gross profit	$260,000	$245,000
Selling expenses	$109,250	$ 95,000
Administrative expenses	52,500	30,000
Total operating expenses	$161,750	$125,000
Income from operations	$ 98,250	$120,000
Other income	2,000	2,000
Income before income tax	$100,250	$122,000
Income tax expense	30,000	40,000
Net income	$ 70,250	$ 82,000

Instructions

1. Prepare a comparative income statement with horizontal analysis for the two-year period, using 2005 as the base year. Round to two digits after the decimal place.
2. To the extent the data permit, comment on the significant relationships revealed by the horizontal analysis prepared in (1).

PROBLEM 15-2A
Vertical analysis for income statement

Objective 1

SPREADSHEET
P.A.S.S.

✓ *1. Net income, 2006, 21.2%*

For 2006, Audio Tone Company initiated a sales promotion campaign that included the expenditure of an additional $13,800 for advertising. At the end of the year, Gordon Kincaid, the president, is presented with the following condensed comparative income statement:

Audio Tone Company
Comparative Income Statement
For the Years Ended December 31, 2006 and 2005

	2006	2005
Sales	$664,000	$526,000
Sales returns and allowances	4,000	6,000
Net sales	$660,000	$520,000
Cost of goods sold	257,400	213,200
Gross profit	$402,600	$306,800
Selling expenses	$138,600	$124,800
Administrative expenses	72,600	67,600
Total operating expenses	$211,200	$192,400
Income from operations	$191,400	$114,400
Other income	2,500	2,000
Income before income tax	$193,900	$116,400
Income tax expense	54,000	30,000
Net income	$139,900	$ 86,400

Instructions
1. Prepare a comparative income statement for the two-year period, presenting an analysis of each item in relationship to net sales for each of the years. Round to two digits after the decimal place.
2. To the extent the data permit, comment on the significant relationships revealed by the vertical analysis prepared in (1).

PROBLEM 15-3A
Effect of transactions on current position analysis

Objective 2

SPREADSHEET

✓ *1. Current ratio, 2.13*

Data pertaining to the current position of Anderson Lumber Company are as follows:

Cash	$240,000
Marketable securities	110,000
Accounts and notes receivable (net)	380,000
Inventories	495,000
Prepaid expenses	30,000
Accounts payable	390,000
Notes payable (short-term)	150,000
Accrued expenses	50,000

Instructions
1. Compute (a) the working capital, (b) the current ratio, and (c) the quick ratio. Round to two digits after the decimal place.
2. List the following captions on a sheet of paper:

Transaction	Working Capital	Current Ratio	Quick Ratio

Compute the working capital, the current ratio, and the quick ratio after each of the following transactions, and record the results in the appropriate columns. Consider each transaction separately and assume that only that transaction affects the data given above. Round to two digits after the decimal point.
a. Sold marketable securities at no gain or loss, $56,000.
b. Paid accounts payable, $60,000.
c. Purchased goods on account, $80,000.
d. Paid notes payable, $40,000.
e. Declared a cash dividend, $25,000.
f. Declared a common stock dividend on common stock, $28,500.

(continued)

g. Borrowed cash from bank on a long-term note, $120,000.
h. Received cash on account, $164,000.
i. Issued additional shares of stock for cash, $250,000.
j. Paid cash for prepaid expenses, $10,000.

PROBLEM 15-4A
Nineteen measures of solvency and profitability

Objectives 2, 3

SPREADSHEET

✓ *5. Number of days' sales in receivables, 69.2*

The comparative financial statements of Vision International, Inc. are as follows. The market price of Vision International, Inc. common stock was $20 on December 31, 2006.

Vision International, Inc.
Comparative Retained Earnings Statement
For the Years Ended December 31, 2006 and 2005

	Dec. 31, 2006	Dec. 31, 2005
Retained earnings, January 1	$375,000	$327,000
Add net income for year	68,000	67,000
Total	$443,000	$394,000
Deduct dividends:		
On preferred stock	$ 15,000	$ 12,000
On common stock	7,000	7,000
Total	$ 22,000	$ 19,000
Retained earnings, December 31	$421,000	$375,000

Vision International, Inc.
Comparative Income Statement
For the Years Ended December 31, 2006 and 2005

	2006	2005
Sales	$1,055,000	$966,000
Sales returns and allowances	5,000	6,000
Net sales	$1,050,000	$960,000
Cost of goods sold	400,000	390,000
Gross profit	$ 650,000	$570,000
Selling expenses	$ 270,000	$275,000
Administrative expenses	195,000	165,000
Total operating expenses	$ 465,000	$440,000
Income from operations	$ 185,000	$130,000
Other income	20,000	15,000
	$ 205,000	$145,000
Other expense (interest)	96,000	48,000
Income before income tax	$ 109,000	$ 97,000
Income tax expense	41,000	30,000
Net income	$ 68,000	$ 67,000

Vision International, Inc.
Comparative Balance Sheet
December 31, 2006 and 2005

	Dec. 31, 2006	Dec. 31, 2005
Assets		
Current assets:		
Cash	$ 165,000	$ 126,000
Marketable securities	398,000	254,000
Accounts receivable (net)	199,000	165,000
Inventories	84,000	52,000
Prepaid expenses	25,000	18,000
Total current assets	$ 871,000	$ 615,000
Long-term investments	300,000	200,000
Property, plant, and equipment (net)	1,040,000	760,000
Total assets	$2,211,000	$1,575,000

(continued)

	Dec. 31, 2006	Dec. 31, 2005
Liabilities		
Current liabilities	$ 290,000	$ 250,000
Long-term liabilities:		
Mortgage note payable, 8%, due 2011	$ 300,000	—
Bonds payable, 12%, due 2015	600,000	$ 400,000
Total long-term liabilities	$ 900,000	$ 400,000
Total liabilities	$1,190,000	$ 650,000
Stockholders' Equity		
Preferred $6 stock, $100 par	$ 250,000	$ 200,000
Common stock, $10 par	350,000	350,000
Retained earnings	421,000	375,000
Total stockholders' equity	$1,021,000	$ 925,000
Total liabilities and stockholders' equity	$2,211,000	$1,575,000

Instructions

Determine the following measures for 2006, rounding to the nearest single digit after the decimal point:

1. Working capital
2. Current ratio
3. Quick ratio
4. Accounts receivable turnover
5. Number of days' sales in receivables
6. Inventory turnover
7. Number of days' sales in inventory
8. Ratio of fixed assets to long-term liabilities
9. Ratio of liabilities to stockholders' equity
10. Number of times interest charges earned
11. Number of times preferred dividends earned
12. Ratio of net sales to assets
13. Rate earned on total assets
14. Rate earned on stockholders' equity
15. Rate earned on common stockholders' equity
16. Earnings per share on common stock
17. Price-earnings ratio
18. Dividends per share of common stock
19. Dividend yield

PROBLEM 15-5A
Solvency and profitability trend analysis

Objectives 2, 3

Sage Software Company has provided the following comparative information:

	2006	2005	2004	2003	2002
Net income	$1,200,000	$ 800,000	$ 600,000	$ 400,000	$ 300,000
Interest expense	200,000	170,000	150,000	120,000	100,000
Income tax expense	360,000	240,000	180,000	120,000	90,000
Total assets (ending balance)	6,000,000	4,500,000	3,500,000	2,600,000	2,000,000
Total stockholders' equity (ending balance)	4,000,000	2,800,000	2,000,000	1,400,000	1,000,000
Average total assets	5,250,000	4,000,000	3,050,000	2,300,000	1,800,000
Average stockholders' equity	3,400,000	2,400,000	1,700,000	1,200,000	900,000

You have been asked to evaluate the historical performance of the company over the last five years.

Selected industry ratios have remained relatively steady at the following levels for the last five years:

	2002–2006
Rate earned on total assets	15%
Rate earned on stockholders' equity	25%
Number of times interest charges earned	3.0
Ratio of liabilities to stockholders' equity	1.5

Instructions

1. Prepare four line graphs with the ratio on the vertical axis and the years on the horizontal axis for the following four ratios (rounded to two digits after the decimal place):
   a. Rate earned on total assets
   b. Rate earned on stockholders' equity
   c. Number of times interest charges earned
   d. Ratio of liabilities to stockholders' equity
   Display both the company ratio and the industry benchmark on each graph. That is, each graph should have two lines.
2. Prepare an analysis of the graphs in (1).

Problems Series B

PROBLEM 15-1B
Horizontal analysis for income statement
Objective 1

SPREADSHEET
P.A.S.S.

✓ *1. Net sales, 25% increase*

For 2006, Pet Care, Inc. reported its most significant increase in net income in years. At the end of the year, Jeff Newton, the president, is presented with the following condensed comparative income statement:

Pet Care, Inc.
Comparative Income Statement
For the Years Ended December 31, 2006 and 2005

	2006	2005
Sales	$76,200	$61,000
Sales returns and allowances	1,200	1,000
Net sales	$75,000	$60,000
Cost of goods sold	42,000	35,000
Gross profit	$33,000	$25,000
Selling expenses	$13,800	$12,000
Administrative expenses	9,000	8,000
Total operating expenses	$22,800	$20,000
Income from operations	$10,200	$ 5,000
Other income	500	500
Income before income tax	$10,700	$ 5,500
Income tax expense	2,400	1,200
Net income	$ 8,300	$ 4,300

Instructions

1. Prepare a comparative income statement with horizontal analysis for the two-year period, using 2005 as the base year. Round to two digits after the decimal place.
2. To the extent the data permit, comment on the significant relationships revealed by the horizontal analysis prepared in (1).

PROBLEM 15-2B
Vertical analysis for income statement
Objective 1

SPREADSHEET
P.A.S.S.

✓ *1. Net loss, 2006, 4.28%*

For 2006, Industrial Sanitation Systems, Inc. initiated a sales promotion campaign that included the expenditure of an additional $26,000 for advertising. At the end of the year, Alex Gonzalez, the president, is presented with the condensed comparative income statement on the following page.

Instructions

1. Prepare a comparative income statement for the two-year period, presenting an analysis of each item in relationship to net sales for each of the years. Round to two digits after the decimal place.
2. To the extent the data permit, comment on the significant relationships revealed by the vertical analysis prepared in (1).

Industrial Sanitation Systems, Inc.
Comparative Income Statement
For the Years Ended December 31, 2006 and 2005

	2006	2005
Sales	$144,000	$128,000
Sales returns and allowances	4,000	3,000
Net sales	$140,000	$125,000
Cost of goods sold	80,000	72,000
Gross profit	$ 60,000	$ 53,000
Selling expenses	$ 56,000	$ 30,000
Administrative expenses	14,000	12,000
Total operating expenses	$ 70,000	$ 42,000
Income from operations	$ (10,000)	$ 11,000
Other income	2,000	1,800
Income before income tax	$ (8,000)	$ 12,800
Income tax expense (benefit)	(2,000)	3,000
Net income (loss)	$ (6,000)	$ 9,800

PROBLEM 15-3B
Effect of transactions on current position analysis
Objective 2

SPREADSHEET

✓*1. Quick ratio, 1.34*

Data pertaining to the current position of Around Town Clothing Co. are as follows:

Cash	$120,000
Marketable securities	56,000
Accounts and notes receivable (net)	185,000
Inventories	224,000
Prepaid expenses	9,000
Accounts payable	188,000
Notes payable (short-term)	55,000
Accrued expenses	26,000

Instructions
1. Compute (a) the working capital, (b) the current ratio, and (c) the quick ratio. Round to two digits after the decimal place.
2. List the following captions on a sheet of paper:

Transaction	Working Capital	Current Ratio	Quick Ratio

Compute the working capital, the current ratio, and the quick ratio after each of the following transactions, and record the results in the appropriate columns. Consider each transaction separately and assume that only that transaction affects the data given above. Round to two digits after the decimal point.
a. Sold marketable securities at no gain or loss, $34,000.
b. Paid accounts payable, $60,000.
c. Purchased goods on account, $40,000.
d. Paid notes payable, $20,000.
e. Declared a cash dividend, $25,000.
f. Declared a common stock dividend on common stock, $16,500.
g. Borrowed cash from bank on a long-term note, $120,000.
h. Received cash on account, $86,000.
i. Issued additional shares of stock for cash, $100,000.
j. Paid cash for prepaid expenses, $9,000.

PROBLEM 15-4B
Nineteen measures of solvency and profitability
Objectives 2, 3

The comparative financial statements of Quest Polymers, Inc. are as follows. The market price of Quest Polymers, Inc. common stock was $64 on December 31, 2006.

✓9. *Ratio of liabilities to stockholders' equity, 0.6*

Quest Polymers, Inc.
Comparative Retained Earnings Statement
For the Years Ended December 31, 2006 and 2005

	Dec. 31, 2006	Dec. 31, 2005
Retained earnings, January 1	$ 645,000	$512,000
Add net income for year	361,000	221,000
Total	$1,006,000	$733,000
Deduct dividends:		
On preferred stock	$ 32,000	$ 24,000
On common stock	64,000	64,000
Total	$ 96,000	$ 88,000
Retained earnings, December 31	$ 910,000	$645,000

Quest Polymers, Inc.
Comparative Income Statement
For the Years Ended December 31, 2006 and 2005

	2006	2005
Sales	$2,830,000	$2,450,000
Sales returns and allowances	30,000	25,000
Net sales	$2,800,000	$2,425,000
Cost of goods sold	1,250,000	1,150,000
Gross profit	$1,550,000	$1,275,000
Selling expenses	$ 605,000	$ 575,000
Administrative expenses	405,000	380,000
Total operating expenses	$1,010,000	$ 955,000
Income from operations	$ 540,000	$ 320,000
Other income	40,000	30,000
	$ 580,000	$ 350,000
Other expense (interest)	79,000	34,000
Income before income tax	$ 501,000	$ 316,000
Income tax expense	140,000	95,000
Net income	$ 361,000	$ 221,000

Quest Polymers, Inc.
Comparative Balance Sheet
December 31, 2006 and 2005

	Dec. 31, 2006	Dec. 31, 2005
Assets		
Current assets:		
Cash	$ 108,000	$ 96,000
Marketable securities	320,000	126,000
Accounts receivable (net)	172,000	158,000
Inventories	325,000	265,000
Prepaid expenses	20,000	25,000
Total current assets	$ 945,000	$ 670,000
Long-term investments	250,000	200,000
Property, plant, and equipment (net)	2,100,000	1,500,000
Total assets	$3,295,000	$2,370,000
Liabilities		
Current liabilities	$ 285,000	$ 225,000
Long-term liabilities:		
Mortgage note payable, 9%, due 2011	$ 500,000	—
Bonds payable, 8.5%, due 2015	400,000	$ 400,000
Total long-term liabilities	$ 900,000	$ 400,000
Total liabilities	$1,185,000	$ 625,000
Stockholders' Equity		
Preferred $8 stock, $100 par	$ 400,000	$ 300,000
Common stock, $10 par	800,000	800,000
Retained earnings	910,000	645,000
Total stockholders' equity	$2,110,000	$1,745,000
Total liabilities and stockholders' equity	$3,295,000	$2,370,000

Instructions

Determine the following measures for 2006, rounding to nearest single digit after the decimal point:

1. Working capital
2. Current ratio
3. Quick ratio
4. Accounts receivable turnover
5. Number of days' sales in receivables
6. Inventory turnover
7. Number of days' sales in inventory
8. Ratio of fixed assets to long-term liabilities
9. Ratio of liabilities to stockholders' equity
10. Number of times interest charges earned
11. Number of times preferred dividends earned
12. Ratio of net sales to assets
13. Rate earned on total assets
14. Rate earned on stockholders' equity
15. Rate earned on common stockholders' equity
16. Earnings per share on common stock
17. Price-earnings ratio
18. Dividends per share of common stock
19. Dividend yield

PROBLEM 15-5B
Solvency and profitability trend analysis

Objectives 2, 3

Crane Plastics Company has provided the following comparative information:

	2006	2005	2004	2003	2002
Net income	$ 30,000	$ 50,000	$ 100,000	$ 150,000	$ 150,000
Interest expense	102,000	95,000	85,000	80,000	75,000
Income tax expense	9,000	15,000	30,000	45,000	45,000
Total assets (ending balance)	1,600,000	1,500,000	1,350,000	1,200,000	1,000,000
Total stockholders' equity (ending balance)	580,000	550,000	500,000	400,000	250,000
Average total assets	1,550,000	1,425,000	1,275,000	1,100,000	900,000
Average stockholders' equity	565,000	525,000	450,000	325,000	225,000

You have been asked to evaluate the historical performance of the company over the last five years.

Selected industry ratios have remained relatively steady at the following levels for the last five years:

	2002–2006
Rate earned on total assets	14%
Rate earned on stockholders' equity	20%
Number of times interest charges earned	3.0
Ratio of liabilities to stockholders' equity	2.0

Instructions

1. Prepare four line graphs with the ratio on the vertical axis and the years on the horizontal axis for the following four ratios (rounded to two digits after the decimal place):
   a. Rate earned on total assets
   b. Rate earned on stockholders' equity
   c. Number of times interest charges earned
   d. Ratio of liabilities to stockholders' equity
   Display both the company ratio and the industry benchmark on each graph. That is, each graph should have two lines.
2. Prepare an analysis of the graphs in (1).

Home Depot, Inc. Problem

FINANCIAL STATEMENT ANALYSIS

The financial statements for **Home Depot, Inc.**, are presented in Appendix F at the end of the text. The following additional information (in millions) is available:

Accounts receivable at January 28, 2001	$ 835
Inventories at January 28, 2001	6,556
Total assets at January 28, 2001	21,385
Stockholders' equity at January 28, 2001	15,005

Instructions

1. Determine the following measures for years ending February 2, 2003 and February 3, 2002, rounding to two digits after the decimal place.
   a. Working capital
   b. Current ratio
   c. Quick ratio
   d. Accounts receivable turnover
   e. Number of days' sales in receivables
   f. Inventory turnover
   g. Number of days' sales in inventory
   h. Ratio of liabilities to stockholders' equity
   i. Ratio of net sales to average total assets
   j. Rate earned on average total assets
   k. Rate earned on average common stockholders' equity
   l. Price-earnings ratio, assuming that the market price was $21.31 per share on February 2, 2003 and $49.70 on February 3, 2002.
   m. Percentage relationship of net income to net sales
2. ▭▭▭▶ What conclusions can be drawn from these analyses?

Special Activities

ACTIVITY 15-1
Analysis of financing corporate growth

WHAT DO YOU THINK?

Assume that the president of Ice Mountain Brewery made the following statement in the Annual Report to Shareholders:

"The founding family and majority shareholders of the company do not believe in using debt to finance future growth. The founding family learned from hard experience during Prohibition and the Great Depression that debt can cause loss of flexibility and eventual loss of corporate control. The company will not place itself at such risk. As such, all future growth will be financed either by stock sales to the public or by internally generated resources."

▭▭▭▶ As a public shareholder of this company, how would you respond to this policy?

ACTIVITY 15-2
Receivables and inventory turnover

Peach Computer Company has completed its fiscal year on December 31, 2006. The auditor, Sandra Blake, has approached the CFO, Travis Williams, regarding the year-end receivables and inventory levels of Peach Computer. The following conversation takes place:

Sandra: We are beginning our audit of Peach Computer and have prepared ratio analyses to determine if there have been significant changes in operations or financial position. This helps us guide the audit process. This analysis indicates that the inventory turnover has decreased from 5 to 2.8, while the accounts receivable turnover has decreased from 12 to 8. I was wondering if you could explain this change in operations.

Travis: There is little need for concern. The inventory represents computers that we were unable to sell during the holiday buying season. We are confident, however, that we will be able to sell these computers as we move into the next fiscal year.

Sandra: What gives you this confidence?

Travis: We will increase our advertising and provide some very attractive price concessions to move these machines. We have no choice. Newer technology is already out there, and we have to unload this inventory.

Sandra: . . . and the receivables?

Travis: As you may be aware, the company is under tremendous pressure to expand sales and profits. As a result, we lowered our credit standards to our commercial customers so that we would be able to sell products to a broader customer base. As a result of this policy change, we have been able to expand sales by 35%.

Sandra: Your responses have not been reassuring to me.

Travis: I'm a little confused. Assets are good, right? Why don't you look at our current ratio? It has improved, hasn't it? I would think that you would view that very favorably.

➡ Why is Sandra concerned about the inventory and accounts receivable turnover ratios and Travis's responses to them? What action may Sandra need to take? How would you respond to Travis's last comment?

ACTIVITY 15-3
Vertical analysis

The condensed income statements through income from operations for **Dell Computer Corporation** and **Apple Computer Co.** are reproduced below for recent fiscal years (numbers in millions of dollars).

	Dell Computer Corporation	Apple Computer Co.
Sales (net)	$31,168	$5,363
Cost of sales	25,661	4,128
Gross profit	$ 5,507	$1,235
Selling, general, and administrative expenses	$ 2,784	$1,138
Research and development	452	430
Special charges	482	11
Operating expenses	$ 3,718	$1,579
Income from operations	$ 1,789	$ (344)

➡ Prepare comparative common-size statements, rounding to two digits after the whole percent. Interpret the analyses.

ACTIVITY 15-4
Profitability ratios

Ford Motor Company is the second largest automobile and truck manufacturer in the United States. In addition to manufacturing motor vehicles, Ford also provides vehicle-related financing, insurance, and leasing services. Historically, people have purchased automobiles when the economy was strong and delayed automobile purchases when the economy was faltering. For this reason, Ford is considered a cyclical company. This means that when the economy does well, Ford usually prospers, while when the economy is down, Ford usually suffers.

The following information is available for three recent years (in millions of dollars except per-share amounts):

	2002	2001	2000
Net income (loss)	$ (980)	$ (5,453)	$ 3,467
Preferred dividends	15	15	15
Cash dividend per share	0.40	1.05	1.8
Average total assets	285,882	279,967	277,305
Average stockholders' equity	6,668	13,198	23,107
Average stock price	13.57	21.32	24.10
Shares outstanding for computing earnings per share	1,819	1,820	1,483

1. Calculate the following ratios for each year:
   a. Rate earned on total assets
   b. Rate earned on stockholders' equity
   c. Earnings per share
   d. Dividend yield
   e. Price-earnings ratio
2. What is the ratio of average liabilities to average stockholders' equity for 2001?
3. ▇▇▇▶ Why does Ford have so much leverage?
4. ▇▇▇▶ Explain the direction of the dividend yield and price-earnings ratio in light of Ford's profitability trend.

ACTIVITY 15-5
Projecting financial statements

INTERNET

Go to **Microsoft**'s Web site at **http://www.microsoft.com** and click on the "Investor Relations" area of Microsoft's Web environment. Select the menu item "stock info and analysis." Select the "what if" tool. With this tool, use horizontal and vertical information to create a full-year projection of the Microsoft income statement. Make the following assumptions:

Revenue growth	16%
Cost of goods sold as a percent of revenue	18%
Research and development growth	12%
Sales and marketing as a percent of sales	20%
General and administrative as a percent of sales	4%
Tax rate	35%
Diluted shares outstanding	11,000

ACTIVITY 15-6
Comprehensive profitability and solvency analysis

Marriott International Inc. and **Hilton Hotels Corp.** are two major owners and managers of lodging and resort properties in the United States. Abstracted income statement information for the two companies is as follows for a recent year:

	Marriott (in millions)	Hilton (in millions)
Operating profit before other expenses and interest	$ 590	$ 495
Other income (expenses)	(111)	48
Interest expense	(109)	(237)
Income before income taxes	$ 370	$ 306
Income tax expense	134	130
Net income	$ 236	$ 176

Balance sheet information is as follows:

	Marriott (in millions)	Hilton (in millions)
Total liabilities	$5,629	$7,498
Total stockholders' equity	3,478	1,642
Total liabilties and stockholders' equity	$9,107	$9,140

The average liabilities, stockholders' equity, and total assets were as follows:

	Marriott	Hilton
Average total liabilities	$5,300	$7,250
Average total stockholders' equity	3,373	1,713
Average total assets	8,673	8,963

1. Determine the following ratios for both companies (round to the nearest two digits after the whole percent):
   a. Rate earned on total assets
   b. Rate earned on total stockholders' equity
   c. Number of times interest charges are earned
   d. Ratio of liabilities to stockholders' equity
2. ▇▇▇▶ Analyze and compare the two companies, using the information in (1).

•Exhibit 3 Textbook Printing Operations of Goodwell Printers

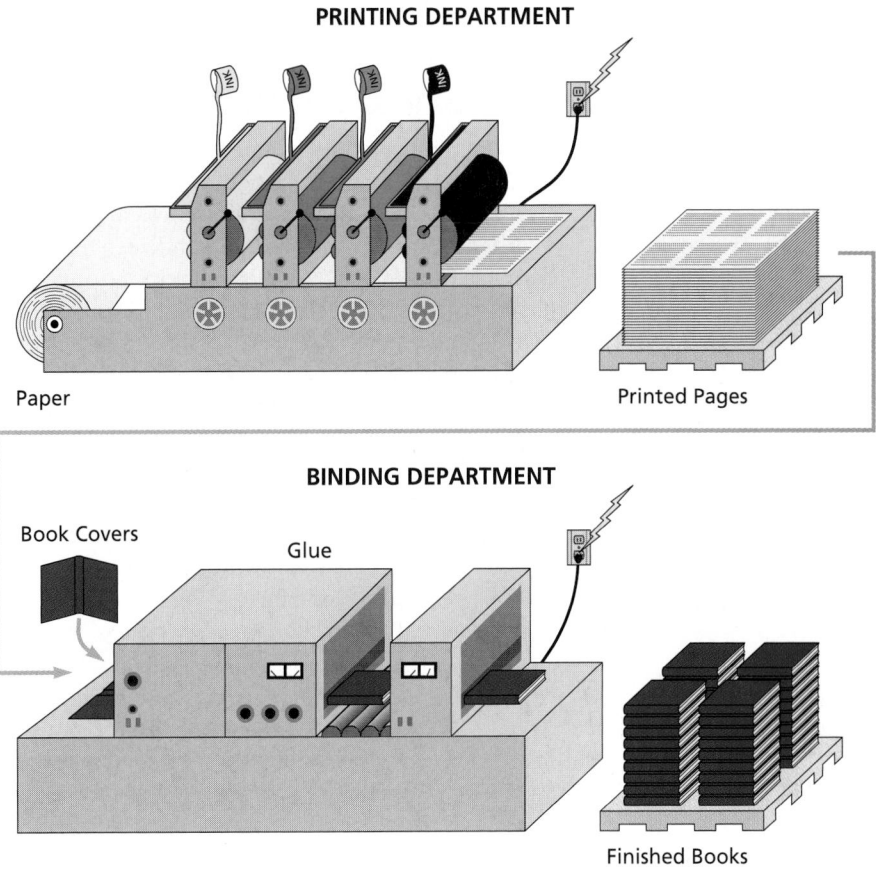

EXAMPLES OF DIRECT MATERIALS

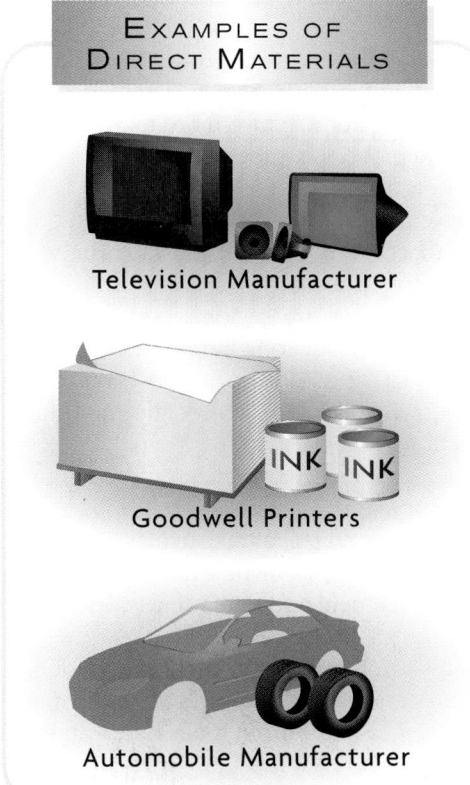

Television Manufacturer

Goodwell Printers

Automobile Manufacturer

cost. For example, the direct materials cost for Goodwell Printers would include paper and book covers.

As a practical matter, a direct materials cost must not only be an integral part of the finished product, but it must also be a significant portion of the total cost of the product. Other examples of direct materials are the electronic components for a TV manufacturer and tires for an automobile manufacturer.

The costs of materials that are not a significant portion of the total product cost are termed **indirect materials**. Indirect materials are considered a part of factory overhead, which we discuss later. For Goodwell Printers, the costs of ink and binding glue are classified as indirect materials.

Factory Labor

The cost of wages of employees who are directly involved in converting materials into the manufactured product is classified as *direct labor cost*. The direct labor cost of Goodwell Printers includes the wages of the employees who operate the printing presses. Other examples of direct labor costs are carpenters' wages for a construction contractor, mechanics' wages in an automotive repair shop, machine operators' wages in a tool manufacturing plant, and assemblers' wages in a microcomputer assembly plant.

As a practical matter, a direct labor cost must not only be an integral part of the finished product, but it must also be a significant portion of the total cost of the product. For Goodwell Printers, the printing press operators' wages are a significant portion of the total cost of each book. Labor costs that do not enter directly into the manufacture of a product are termed **indirect labor** and are recorded as factory overhead. Indirect labor for Goodwell Printers might include the salaries of maintenance, plant management, and quality control personnel.

Factory Overhead Cost

Identify whether the following costs are direct materials, direct labor, or factory overhead for an automobile assembler: tires, quality engineering salaries, assembly wages, coil steel, painter wages, plant manager salary, cleaning fluids.

Tires and coil steel—direct materials; assembly wages and painter wages—direct labor; quality engineering salaries, plant manager's salary, and cleaning fluids—factory overhead.

Costs other than direct materials cost and direct labor cost incurred in the manufacturing process are classified as *factory overhead cost*. Factory overhead is sometimes called **manufacturing overhead** or **factory burden**. Examples of factory overhead costs, in addition to indirect materials and indirect labor, are machine depreciation, factory utilities, factory supplies, and factory insurance. In addition, payments to employees for overtime and nonproductive time (such as idle time) are considered factory overhead. For many industries, factory overhead costs are becoming a larger portion of the costs of a product as manufacturing processes become more automated.

The direct materials, direct labor, and factory overhead costs are considered *product costs*, because they are associated with making a product. The costs of converting the materials into finished products consist of direct labor and factory overhead costs, which are commonly called *conversion costs*.

> **Direct materials, direct labor, and factory overhead costs are product costs.**

Cost Accounting System Overview

objective 4

Describe accounting systems used by manufacturing businesses.

Warner Bros. and other movie studios use job order cost systems to accumulate movie production and distribution costs. Costs such as actor salaries, production costs, movie print costs, and marketing costs are accumulated in a job account for a particular movie. Cost information from the job cost report can be used to control the costs of the movie while it is being produced and to determine the profitability of the movie after it has been exhibited.

An objective of a *cost accounting system* is to accumulate product costs. Product cost information is used by managers to establish product prices, control operations, and develop financial statements. In addition, the cost accounting system improves control by supplying data on the costs incurred by each manufacturing department or process.

There are two main types of cost accounting systems for manufacturing operations: job order cost systems and process cost systems. Each of the two systems is widely used, and any one manufacturer may use more than one type. In this chapter, we will illustrate the job order cost system. In the next chapter, we will illustrate the process cost system.

A *job order cost system* provides a separate record for the cost of each quantity of product that passes through the factory. A particular quantity of product is termed a *job*. A job order cost system is best suited to industries that manufacture custom goods to fill special orders from customers or that produce a high variety of products for stock. Manufacturers that use a job order cost system are sometimes called **job shops**. An example of a job shop would be an apparel manufacturer, such as **Levi Strauss**.

Many service firms also use job order cost systems to accumulate the costs associated with providing client services. For example, an accounting firm will accumulate all of the costs associated with a particular client engagement, such as accountant time, copying charges, and travel costs. Recording costs in this manner helps the accounting firm control costs during a client engagement and determines client billing and profitability.

Under a *process cost system*, costs are accumulated for each of the departments or processes within the factory. A process system is best suited for manufacturers of units of product that are not distinguishable from each other during a continuous production process. Examples would be oil refineries, paper producers, chemical processors, aluminum smelters, and food processors.

Name two types of cost systems and a typical user of each system.

Job order cost system: cabinet manufacturer, law practice, movie studio. Process cost system: food processing, paper processing, metal processing, petroleum refining.

Job Order Cost Systems for Manufacturing Businesses

objective 5

Describe and prepare summary journal entries for a job order cost accounting system.

In this section, we will illustrate the job order cost system for a manufacturing firm, Goodwell Printers. The job order system accumulates manufacturing costs by job, as shown in Exhibit 4. The **materials inventory**, sometimes called **raw materials inventory**, consists of the costs of the direct and indirect materials that have not yet entered the manufacturing process. For Goodwell Printers, the materials inventory would consist of paper, ink, glue, and book covers. The **work in process inventory** consists of direct materials costs, direct labor costs, and factory overhead costs that have entered the manufacturing process but are associated with products that have not been completed. Examples are the costs of Jobs 71 and 72 that are still in the printing process in Exhibit 4. Completed jobs that have not been sold are termed **finished goods inventory**. Examples are completed printed books from Jobs 69 and 70 shown in Exhibit 4. Upon sale, a manufacturer will record the cost of the sale as **cost of goods sold**. An example is the case of *Physics* books sold to the bookstore in Exhibit 4. The *cost of goods sold* for a manufacturer is comparable to the *cost of merchandise sold* for a merchandising business.

> **The work in process inventory consists of direct materials, direct labor, and factory overhead costs of products not yet completed.**

•**Exhibit 4**   **Flow of Manufacturing Costs**

• **Direct Labor**
• **Factory Overhead**

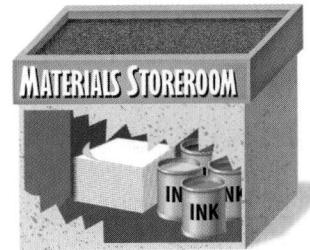

| Materials Inventory | Work In Process Inventory | Finished Goods Inventory | Cost of Goods Sold |

In a job order cost accounting system, perpetual inventory controlling accounts and subsidiary ledgers are maintained for materials, work in process, and finished goods inventories. Each inventory account is debited for all additions and is credited for all deductions. The balance of each account thus represents the balance on hand.

Materials

The procedures used to purchase, store, and issue materials to production often differ among manufacturers. Exhibit 5 shows the basic information and cost flows for the paper received and issued to production by Goodwell Printers.

Purchased materials are first received and inspected by the Receiving Department. The Receiving Department personnel prepare a **receiving report**, showing the quantity received and its condition. Some organizations now use bar code scanning devices in place of receiving reports to record and electronically transmit incoming

•Exhibit 5 Materials Information and Cost Flows

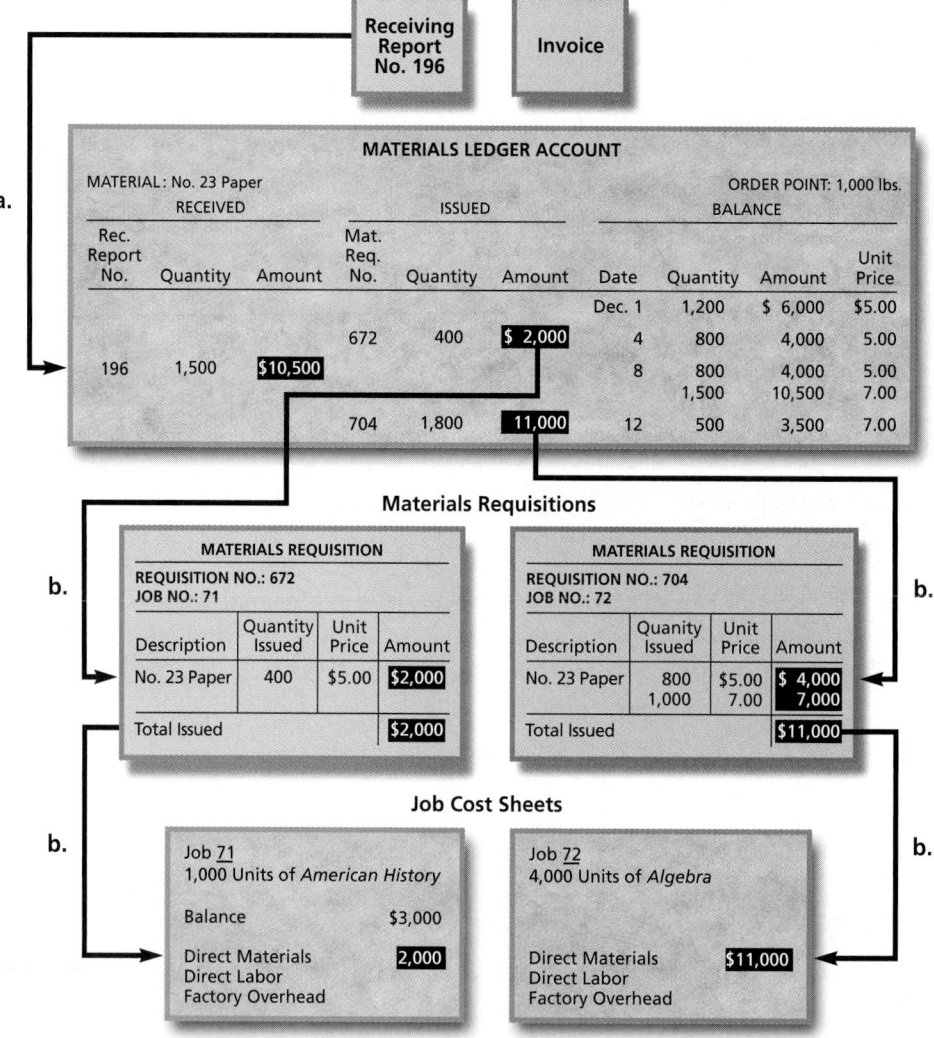

materials data. The receiving information and invoice are used to record the receipt and control the payment for purchased items. The journal entry to record Receiving Report No. 196 in Exhibit 5 is:

		a.	Materials				10	5	0	0	00					
			Accounts Payable									10	5	0	0	00
			Materials purchased during													
			December.													

The materials account in the general ledger is a controlling account. A separate account for each type of material is maintained in a subsidiary *materials ledger*. Details as to the quantity and cost of materials received are recorded in the materials ledger on the basis of the receiving reports. A typical form of a materials ledger account is illustrated in Exhibit 5.

Materials are released from the storeroom to the factory in response to *materials requisitions* from the Production Department. An illustration of a materials requisition is in Exhibit 5. The completed requisition for each job serves as the basis for posting quantities and dollar data to the job cost sheets in the case of direct materials or to factory overhead in the case of indirect materials. ***Job cost sheets***, which are illustrated in Exhibit 5, are the work in process subsidiary ledger. For Goodwell Printers, Job 71 is for 1,000 textbooks titled *American History*, while Job 72 is for 4,000 textbooks titled *Algebra*.

In Exhibit 5, the first-in, first-out costing method is used. A summary of the materials requisitions completed during the month is the basis for transferring the cost of the direct materials from the materials account in the general ledger to the controlling account for work in process. The flow of materials from the materials storeroom into production ($2,000 + $11,000) is recorded by the following entry:

b.	Work in Process	13 0 0 0 00		
	Materials			13 0 0 0 00
	Materials requisitioned to jobs.			

Many organizations are using computerized information processes that account for the flow of materials. In a computerized setting, the storeroom manager would record the release of materials into a computer, which would automatically update the subsidiary materials records.

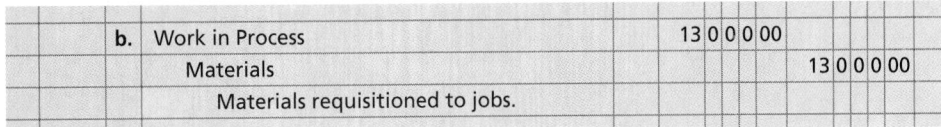

INTEGRITY IN BUSINESS

PHONY INVOICE SCAMS

A popular method for defrauding a company is to issue a phony invoice. The scam begins by initially contacting the target firm to discover details of key business contacts, business operations, and products. The swindler then uses this information to create a fictitious invoice. The invoice will include names, figures, and other details to give it the appearance of legitimacy. This type of scam can be avoided if invoices are matched with receiving documents prior to issuing a check.

Factory Labor

There are two primary objectives in accounting for factory labor. One objective is to determine the correct amount to be paid each employee for each payroll period. A second objective is to properly allocate factory labor costs to factory overhead and individual job orders.

The amount of time spent by an employee in the factory is usually recorded on **clock cards** or **in-and-out cards**. The amount of time spent by each employee and the labor cost incurred for each individual job are recorded on ***time tickets***. Exhibit 6 shows typical time ticket forms and cost flows for direct labor for Goodwell Printers.

A summary of the time tickets at the end of each month is the basis for recording the direct and indirect labor costs incurred in production. Direct labor is posted to each job cost sheet, while indirect labor is debited to Factory Overhead.[1] Goodwell Printers incurred 850 direct labor hours on Jobs 71 and 72 during December. The total direct labor costs were $11,000, divided into $3,500 for Job 71 and $7,500 for Job 72. The labor costs that flow into production are recorded by the following summary entry to the work in process controlling account:

---

[1]There are a variety of methods for recording direct labor costs. In the approach illustrated in this chapter, we assume that labor costs are automatically recorded to jobs or factory overhead when incurred. Alternatively, wages could first be debited to Factory Labor when incurred and then later distributed to jobs and factory overhead.

		c.	Work in Process		11 0 0 0 00		
			Wages Payable			11 0 0 0 00	
			Factory labor used in production				
			of jobs.				

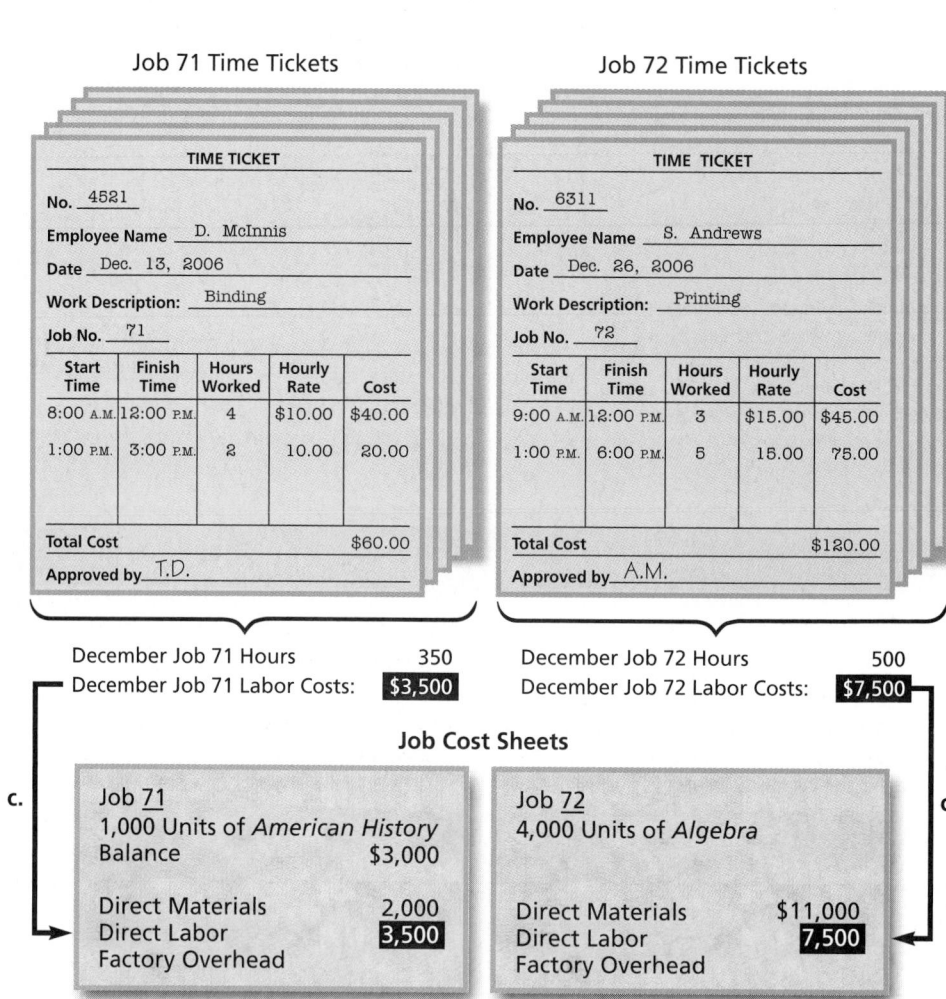

•Exhibit 6

Labor Information and Cost Flows

Job 71 Time Tickets

Job 72 Time Tickets

TIME TICKET

No. 4521
Employee Name D. McInnis
Date Dec. 13, 2006
Work Description: Binding
Job No. 71

Start Time	Finish Time	Hours Worked	Hourly Rate	Cost
8:00 A.M.	12:00 P.M.	4	$10.00	$40.00
1:00 P.M.	3:00 P.M.	2	10.00	20.00

Total Cost — $60.00
Approved by T.D.

TIME TICKET

No. 6311
Employee Name S. Andrews
Date Dec. 26, 2006
Work Description: Printing
Job No. 72

Start Time	Finish Time	Hours Worked	Hourly Rate	Cost
9:00 A.M.	12:00 P.M.	3	$15.00	$45.00
1:00 P.M.	6:00 P.M.	5	15.00	75.00

Total Cost — $120.00
Approved by A.M.

December Job 71 Hours — 350
December Job 71 Labor Costs: $3,500

December Job 72 Hours — 500
December Job 72 Labor Costs: $7,500

Job Cost Sheets

c.

Job 71
1,000 Units of *American History*
Balance — $3,000

Direct Materials — 2,000
Direct Labor — 3,500
Factory Overhead

Job 72
4,000 Units of *Algebra*

Direct Materials — $11,000
Direct Labor — 7,500
Factory Overhead

c.

As with recording direct materials, many organizations are automating the labor recording process. Employees may log their time directly into computer terminals at their workstations. Alternatively, employees may be issued magnetic cards, much like credit cards, to log in and out of work assignments that are spread across a wide geographical area. For example, **Shell Oil Company** uses a magnetic card system to track the work of maintenance crews in its refinery operations.

INTEGRITY IN BUSINESS

GHOST EMPLOYEES

Companies must guard against the fraudulent creation and cashing of payroll checks. Numerous payroll frauds involve supervisors adding fictitious employees to or failing to remove departing employees from the payroll and then cashing the check. Requiring proper authorization and approval of employee additions, removals, or changes in pay rates can minimize this type of fraud.

Factory Overhead Cost

Factory overhead includes all manufacturing costs except direct materials and direct labor. Debits to Factory Overhead come from various sources, such as indirect materials, indirect labor, factory power, and factory depreciation. For example, the factory overhead of $4,600 incurred in December for Goodwell Printers would be recorded as follows:

	d.	Factory Overhead	4 6 0 0 00			
		Materials		5 0 0 00
		Wages Payable		2 0 0 0 00
		Utilities Payable		9 0 0 00
		Accumulated Depreciation		1 2 0 0 00
		Factory overhead incurred in		
		production.		

Fred DeLuca and Peter Buck founded me in Connecticut in 1965, and Fred published a book titled "Start Small, Finish Big," in 2000. Jared has helped me grow, even as he shrank. I was first franchised in 1974 and I can feed you in Russia, Tanzania, China, Saudi Arabia, Austria, Brazil, Israel, Iceland, Jamaica, France, and more than 60 other nations. With more than 16,000 units, I recently surpassed McDonald's as the restaurant chain with the most restaurants. I began running national television commercials in 1999. I'm owned by the private company Doctor's Associates, so you can't buy stock in me. Who am I? (Go to page 681 for answer.)

Allocating Factory Overhead

Factory overhead is much different from direct labor and direct materials because it is indirectly related to the jobs. How, then, do the jobs get assigned a portion of overhead costs? The answer is through ***cost allocation***, which is the process of assigning factory overhead costs to a cost object, such as a job. The factory overhead costs are assigned to the jobs on the basis of some known measure about each job. The measure used to allocate factory overhead is frequently called an ***activity base***, **allocation base**, or **activity driver**. The estimated activity base should be a measure that reflects the consumption or use of factory overhead cost. For example, the direct labor is recorded for each job using time tickets. Thus, direct labor (hours or cost) could be used to allocate production-related factory overhead costs to each job. Likewise, direct materials costs are known about each job through the materials requisitions. Thus, materials-related factory overhead, such as Purchasing Department salaries, could logically be allocated to the job on the basis of direct materials cost.

Predetermined Factory Overhead Rate

To provide current job costs, factory overhead may be allocated or applied to production using a ***predetermined factory overhead rate***. The predetermined factory overhead rate is calculated by dividing the estimated amount of factory overhead for the forthcoming year by the estimated activity base, such as machine hours, direct materials costs, direct labor costs, or direct labor hours.

To illustrate calculating a predetermined overhead rate, assume that Goodwell Printers estimates the total factory overhead cost to be $50,000 for the year and the activity base to be 10,000 direct labor hours. The predetermined factory overhead rate would be calculated as $5 per direct labor hour, as follows:

$$\text{Predetermined factory overhead rate} = \frac{\text{Estimated total factory overhead costs}}{\text{Estimated activity base}}$$

$$\text{Predetermined factory overhead rate} = \frac{\$50,000}{10,000 \text{ direct labor hours}} = \$5 \text{ per direct labor hour}$$

Why is the predetermined overhead rate calculated from estimated numbers at the beginning of the period? The answer is to ensure timely information. If a company waited until the end of an accounting period when all overhead costs are known, the allocated factory overhead would be accurate but not timely. If the cost system is to have maximum usefulness, cost data should be available as each job is completed, even though there may be a small sacrifice in accuracy. Only through timely reporting can management make needed adjustments in pricing or in manufacturing methods and achieve the best possible combination of revenue and cost on future jobs.

A number of companies are using a new product-costing approach called activity-based costing. *Activity-based costing* is a method of accumulating and allocating factory overhead costs to products, using many overhead rates. Each rate is related to separate factory activities, such as inspecting, moving, and machining. Activity-based costing is discussed and illustrated in Chapter 25.

Applying Factory Overhead to Work in Process

As factory overhead costs are incurred, they are debited to the factory overhead account, as shown previously in transaction (d). For Goodwell Printers, factory overhead costs are applied to production at the rate of $5 per direct labor hour. The amount of factory overhead applied to each job would be recorded in the job cost sheets as shown in Exhibit 7. For example, the 850 direct labor hours used in Goodwell's December operations would all be traced to individual jobs. Job 71 used 350 labor hours, so $1,750 (350 × $5) of factory overhead would be applied to Job 71. Similarly, $2,500 (500 × $5) of factory overhead would be applied to Job 72.

•Exhibit 7

Assigning Factory Overhead to Jobs

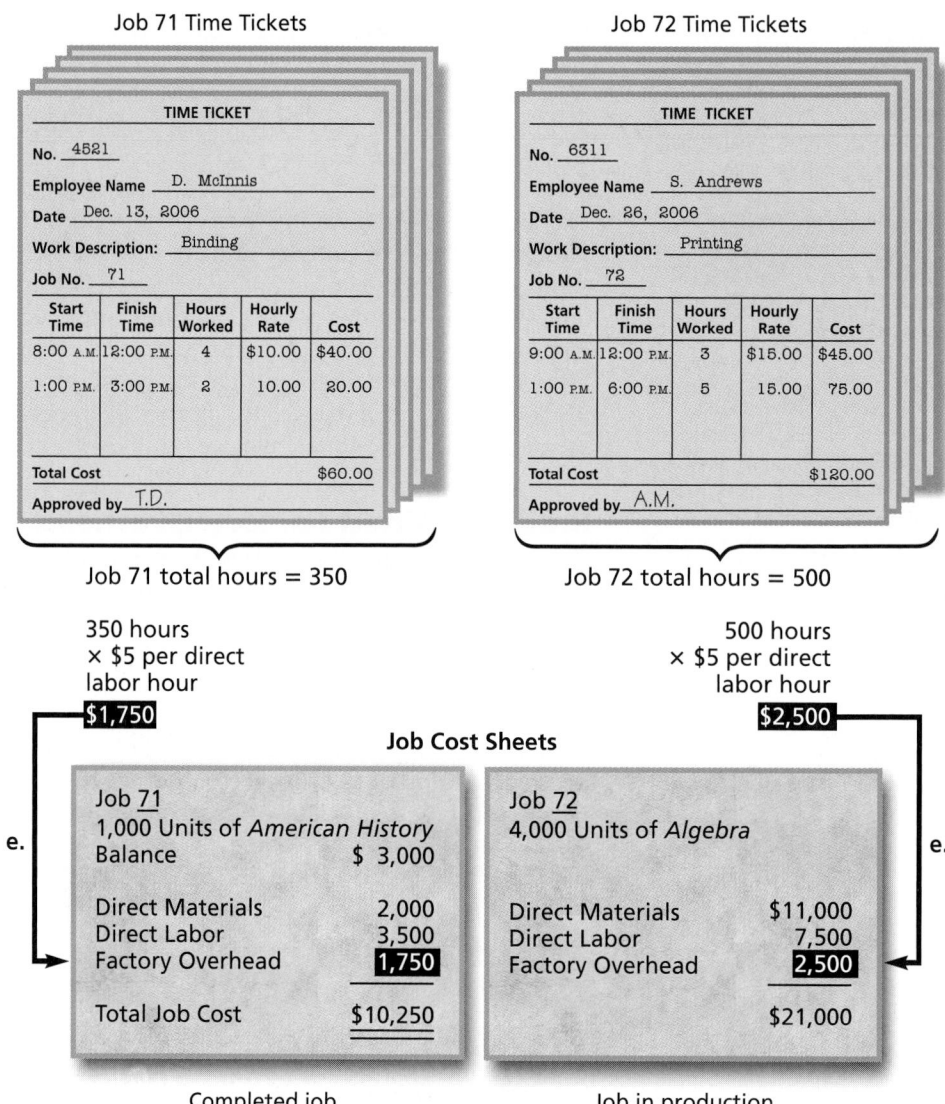

The factory overhead costs applied to production are periodically debited to the work in process account and credited to the factory overhead account. The summary entry to apply the $4,250 ($1,750 + $2,500) of factory overhead is as follows:

e.	Work in Process		4 2 5 0 00	
	Factory Overhead			4 2 5 0 00
	Factory overhead applied to jobs			
	according to the predetermined			
	overhead rate.			

Factory overhead costs are estimated to be $120,000. Direct labor hours are estimated to be 20,000 hours. Determine (a) the predetermined factory overhead rate and (b) the amount of factory overhead applied to a job with 30 direct labor hours.

(a) $6 per hour ($120,000/20,000);
(b) $180 ($6 × 30 hours)

The factory overhead costs applied and the actual factory overhead costs incurred during a period will usually differ. If the amount applied exceeds the actual costs incurred, the factory overhead account will have a credit balance. This credit is described as ***overapplied*** or **overabsorbed** *factory overhead*. If the amount applied is less than the actual costs incurred, the account will have a debit balance. This debit is described as ***underapplied*** or **underabsorbed** *factory overhead*. Both cases are illustrated in the following account for Goodwell Printers:

ACCOUNT *Factory Overhead*					**ACCOUNT NO.**	
		Post			Balance	
Date	Item	Ref.	Debit	Credit	Debit	Credit
Dec. 1	Balance					2 0 0 00
31	Factory overhead cost incurred		4 6 0 0 00		4 4 0 0 00	
31	Factory overhead cost applied			4 2 5 0 00	1 5 0 00	

Underapplied balance ⟶
Overapplied balance ⟶

If the underapplied or overapplied balance increases in only one direction and it becomes large, the balance and the overhead rate should be investigated. For example, if a large balance is caused by changes in manufacturing methods or in production goals, the factory overhead rate should be revised. On the other hand, a large underapplied balance may indicate a serious control problem caused by inefficiencies in production methods, excessive costs, or a combination of factors.

Disposal of Factory Overhead Balance

The balance in the factory overhead account is carried forward from month to month. It is reported on interim balance sheets as a deferred debit or credit. This balance should not be carried over to the next year, however, since it applies to the operations of the year just ended.

One approach for disposing of the balance of factory overhead at the end of the year is to transfer the entire balance to the cost of goods sold account.[2] To illustrate, the journal entry to eliminate Goodwell Printers' underapplied overhead balance of $150 at the end of the calendar year would be:

f.	Cost of Goods Sold		1 5 0 00	
	Factory Overhead			1 5 0 00
	Closed underapplied factory			
	overhead to cost of goods sold.			

---

[2]Alternatively, the balance may be allocated among the work in process, finished goods, and cost of goods sold balances. This approach brings the accounts into agreement with the costs actually incurred. Since this approach is a more complex calculation that adds little additional accuracy, it will not be used in this text.

Work in Process

Costs incurred for the various jobs are debited to Work in Process. Goodwell Printers' job costs described in the preceding sections may be summarized as follows:

- **Direct materials, $13,000**—Work in Process debited and Materials credited (transaction b); data obtained from summary of materials requisitions.
- **Direct labor, $11,000**—Work in Process debited and Wages Payable credited (transaction c); data obtained from summary of time tickets.
- **Factory overhead, $4,250**—Work in Process debited and Factory Overhead credited (transaction e); data obtained from summary of time tickets.

The details concerning the costs incurred on each job order are accumulated in the job cost sheets. Exhibit 8 illustrates the relationship between the job cost sheets and the work in process controlling account.

•Exhibit 8 **Job Cost Sheets and the Work in Process Controlling Account**

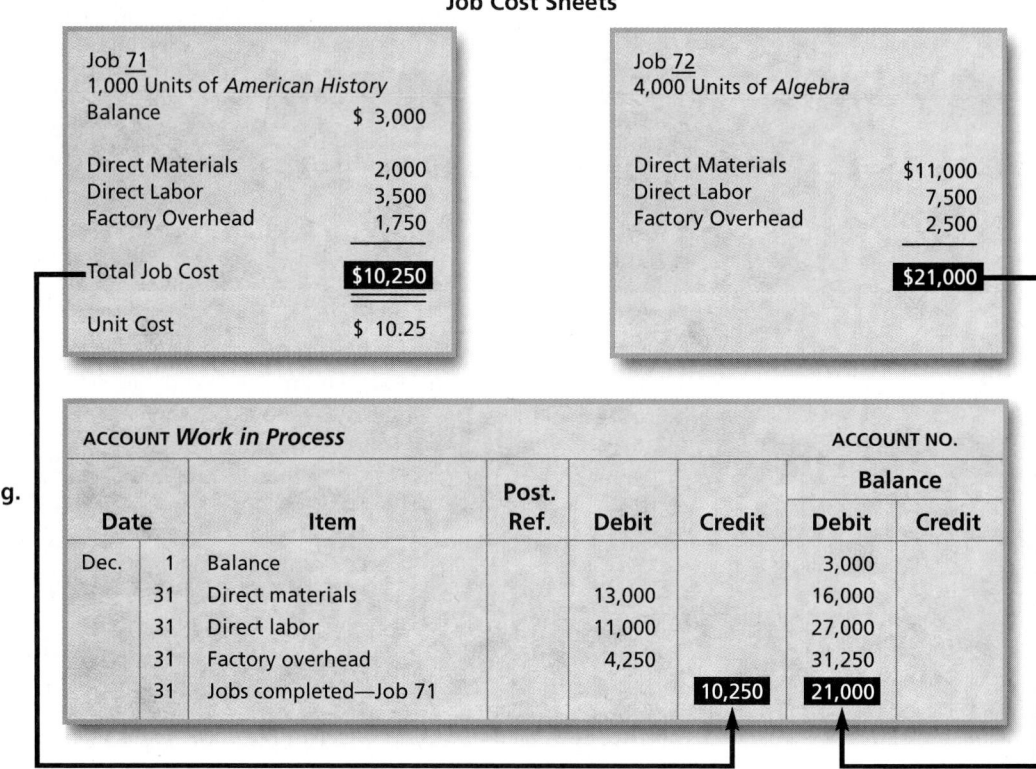

In this example, Job 71 was started in November and completed in December. The beginning December balance for Job 71 represents the costs carried over from the end of November. Job 72 was started in December but was not yet completed at the end of the month. Thus, the balance of the incomplete Job 72, or $21,000, will be shown on the balance sheet on December 31 as work in process inventory.

When Job 71 was completed, the direct materials costs, the direct labor costs, and the factory overhead costs were totaled and divided by the number of units produced to determine the cost per unit. If we assume that 1,000 units of a textbook titled *American History* were produced for Job 71, then the unit cost would be $10.25 ($10,250 ÷ 1,000).

Upon completing Job 71, the job cost sheet was removed from the cost ledger and filed for future reference. At the end of the accounting period (December), the total costs for all completed jobs during the period are determined, and the following entry is made:

g.	Finished Goods			10 2 5 0 00				
	Work in Process					10 2 5 0 00		
	Job 71 completed in December.							

Finished Goods and Cost of Goods Sold

The finished goods account is a controlling account. Its related subsidiary ledger, which has an account for each product, is called the ***finished goods ledger*** or **stock ledger**. Each account in the finished goods ledger contains cost data for the units manufactured, units sold, and units on hand. Exhibit 9 illustrates an account in the finished goods ledger.

•Exhibit 9 **Finished Goods Ledger Account**

ITEM: *American History*								
Manufactured			**Shipped**			**Balance**		
Job Order No.	Quantity	Amount	Ship Order No.	Quantity	Amount	Date	Quantity	Amount	Unit Cost
						Dec. 1	2,000	$20,000	$10.00
			643	2,000	$20,000	9	—	—	—
71	1,000	$10,250				31	1,000	10,250	10.25

Just as there are various methods of costing materials entering into production, there are various methods of determining the cost of the finished goods sold. In Exhibit 9, the first-in, first-out method is used. A summary of the cost data for the units shipped ($20,000) becomes the basis for the following entry:

h.	Cost of Goods Sold			20 0 0 0 00				
	Finished Goods					20 0 0 0 00		
	Cost of 2,000 *American History*							
	textbooks sold.							

Sales

The selling price of the goods sold is recorded by debiting Accounts Receivable (or Cash) and crediting Sales. To illustrate, assume that Goodwell Printers sold the 2,000 *American History* textbooks during December for $14 per unit.[3] The entry to the accounts receivable controlling account would be:

i.	Accounts Receivable			28 0 0 0 00				
	Sales					28 0 0 0 00		
	Revenue received from textbooks							
	sold.							

Q&A

Boxer Company completed 80,000 units at a cost of $680,000. The beginning finished goods inventory was 10,000 units at $80,000. What is the cost of goods sold for 60,000 units, assuming a FIFO cost flow?

$505,000 [$80,000 + (50,000 × $8.50)]

----

[3]The price of the textbook is the amount paid by the textbook publisher for printing the book. Printing is one small part of the total cost of the textbook. The publisher must also pay royalties, development and production costs, and selling expenses. Thus, the price of the textbook to the final user will be higher than $14.

Period Costs

In addition to product costs (direct materials, direct labor, and factory overhead), businesses also have period costs. *Period costs* are expenses that are used in generating revenue during the current period and are not involved in the manufacturing process. Period costs are generally classified into two categories: selling and administrative. **Selling expenses** are incurred in marketing the product and delivering the sold product to customers. **Administrative expenses** are incurred in the administration of the business and are not related to the manufacturing or selling functions.

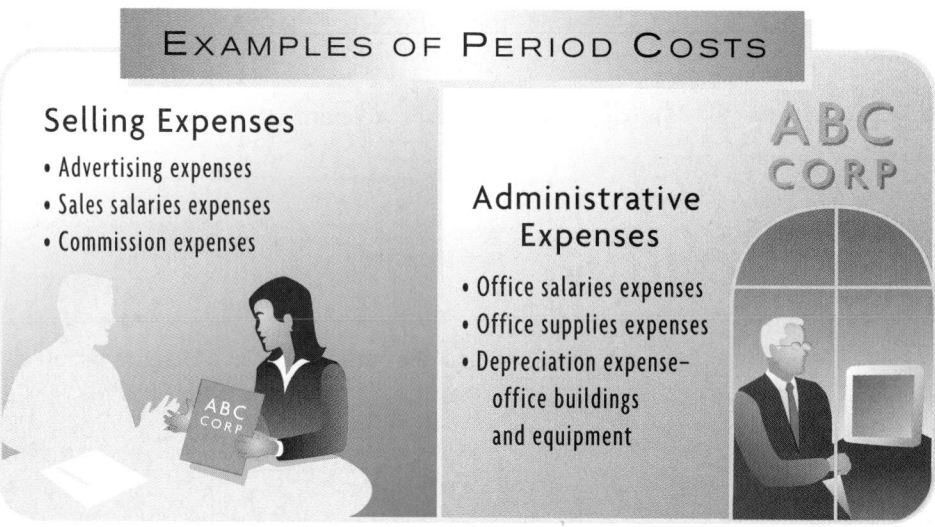

For Goodwell Printers, the following period expenses were recorded for December:

j.	Sales Salaries Expense	2 0 0 0 00		
	Office Salaries Expense	1 5 0 0 00		
	Salaries Payable		3 5 0 0 00
	Recorded December period costs.		

REAL WORLD

Service companies, such as telecommunications, insurance, banking, broadcasting, and hospitality, typically have a large portion of their total costs as period costs. This is because most service companies do not have products that can be inventoried, and hence, they do not have product costs.

Summary of Cost Flows for Goodwell Printers

Exhibit 10 shows the cost flow through the manufacturing accounts, together with summary details of the subsidiary ledgers for Goodwell Printers. Entries in the accounts are identified by letters that refer to the summary journal entries introduced in the preceding section.

The balances of the general ledger controlling accounts are supported by their respective subsidiary ledgers. The balances of the three inventory accounts—Finished Goods, Work in Process, and Materials—represent the respective ending inventories of December 31 on the balance sheet. These balances are as follows:

Materials	$ 3,500
Work in process	21,000
Finished goods	10,250

The income statement for Goodwell Printers would be as shown in Exhibit 11.

•Exhibit 10 Flow of Manufacturing Costs for Goodwell Printers

Materials

Dec. 1	6,500	(b)	13,000
(a)	10,500	(d)	500

Factory Overhead

Dec. 1	500	Dec. 1	200
(d)	900	(e)	4,250
(d)	1,200	(f)	150
(d)	2,000		

Work in Process

Dec. 1	3,000	(g)	10,250
(b)	13,000		
(e)	4,250		
(c)	11,000		

Finished Goods

Dec. 1	20,000	(h)	20,000
(g)	10,250		

Cost of Goods Sold

(h)	20,000
(f)	150

Wages Payable

	(d)	2,000
	(c)	11,000

Materials Ledger

No. 23 Paper

Dec. 1	6,000	(b)	13,000
(a)	10,500		

Glue

Dec. 1	200	(d)	200

Ink

Dec. 1	300	(d)	300

Job Cost Sheets

1,000 Units of American History, Job 71

Dec. 1	3,000
(b) Direct materials	2,000
(c) Direct labor	3,500
(e) Factory overhead	1,750
	10,250

4,000 Units of Algebra, Job 72

(b) Direct materials	11,000
(c) Direct labor	7,500
(e) Factory overhead	2,500
	21,000

Finished Goods Ledger

American History

Dec. 1	20,000	(h)	20,000
(g)	10,250		

---

a. Materials purchased during December
b. Materials requisitioned to jobs
c. Factory labor used in production of jobs
d. Factory overhead incurred in production
e. Factory overhead applied to jobs according to the predetermined overhead rate
f. Closing underapplied factory overhead to cost of goods sold
g. Job 71 completed in December
h. Cost of 2,000 *American History* textbooks sold

•Exhibit 11   Income Statement of Goodwell Printers

Goodwell Printers
Income Statement
For the Month Ended December 31, 2006

Sales		$28,000
Cost of goods sold		20,150
Gross profit		$ 7,850
Selling and administrative expenses:		
Sales salaries expense	$2,000	
Office salaries expense	1,500	
Total selling and administrative expenses		3,500
Income from operations		$ 4,350

Job Order Costing for Decision Making

objective 6

Use job order cost information for decision making.

The job order cost system that we developed in the previous sections can be used to evaluate an organization's cost performance. The unit costs for similar jobs can be compared over time to determine if costs are staying within expected ranges. If costs increase for some unexpected reason, the details in the job cost sheets can help discover the reasons.

To illustrate, Exhibit 12 shows the direct materials on the job cost sheets for Jobs 144 and 163 for a furniture company. Since both job cost sheets refer to the same type and number of chairs, the direct materials cost per unit should be about the same. However, the materials cost per chair for Job 144 is $28, while for Job 163 it is $35. The materials costs have increased since the folding chairs were produced for Job 144.

Job cost sheets can be used to investigate possible reasons for the increased cost. First, you should note that the rate for direct materials did not change. Thus, the cost increase is not related to increasing prices. What about the wood consumption? This tells us a different story. The quantity of wood used to produce 200 chairs in Job 144 is 1,600 board feet. However, Job 163 required 2,000 board feet for the same number of chairs. How can this be explained? Any one of the following explanations is possible and could be investigated further:

REAL WORLD

Major electric utilities such as **Tennessee Valley Authority**, **Consolidated Edison**, and **Pacific Gas and Electric** use job order accounting to control the costs associated with major repairs and overhauls that occur during maintenance shutdowns.

1. There was a new employee that was not adequately trained for cutting the wood for chairs. As a result, the employee improperly cut and scrapped many pieces.
2. The lumber was of poor quality. As a result, the cutting operator ended up using and scrapping additional pieces of lumber.
3. The cutting tools were in need of repair. As a result, the cutting operators miscut and scrapped many pieces of wood.
4. The operator was careless. As a result of poor work, many pieces of cut wood had to be scrapped.
5. The instructions attached to the job were incorrect. The operator cut wood according to the instructions but discovered that the pieces would not fit. As a result, many pieces had to be scrapped.

You should note that many of these explanations are not necessarily related to operator error. Poor cost performance may be the result of root causes that are outside the control of the operator.

•Exhibit 12   Comparing Data from Job Cost Sheets

Job 144
Item: 200 Standard folding chairs

	Materials Quantity (board feet)	Materials Price	Materials Amount
Direct materials:			
Wood	1,600	$3.50	$5,600
Direct materials per chair			$28

Job 163
Item: 200 Standard folding chairs

	Materials Quantity (board feet)	Materials Price	Materials Amount
Direct materials:			
Wood	2,000	$3.50	$7,000
Direct materials per chair			$35

MANAGERIAL DISCLOSURE AND ANALYSIS

DEFENSE CONTRACT ACQUISITIONS

The aerospace and defense industry uses job orders to account for program costs and revenues. Such defense programs (or contracts) are awarded by the U. S. government for various defense needs. The financial disclosures for **Northrop Grumman Systems Corp.**, a major defense contractor, include a section on contract acquisitions. Contract acquisitions are the dollar amount of contracts awarded for defense products or services for a given year. These are not the same as revenues, because some of the awarded contracts may still be unperformed, or *backlogged*. However, contract acquisitions do provide a means of evaluating a defense contractor's revenue potential. A partial listing of Northrop's recent contract acquisitions showed the following:

Aerospace electronic systems	$1,339,000,000
Air combat systems	1,594,000,000
Airborne early warning/electronic warfare	601,000,000
Airborne ground surveillance/battle management	446,000,000
Ship surface combatants	3,042,000,000

Additional disclosures indicate the aerospace electronic systems includes funding of $255 million for the Wedgetail program and $148 million for the BAT program. Air combat systems includes a $30 million increase in the F-18 program. Airborne early warning includes $231 million funding for the multiyear electronic warfare system purchase for 25 E-2C aircraft. Airborne ground surveillance includes orders for one Joint STARS aircraft, while surface combatants includes a $370 million contract award for an Aegis-class large destroyer.

Each of these programs, such as the Aegis destroyer program, is treated as a separate master program. The master program will be divided into smaller segments or jobs in what is termed a *work breakdown structure*. Costs will be accumulated by job and closed out to cost of goods sold and matched to revenue earned as contracts are completed.

Job Order Cost Systems for Professional Service Businesses

A job order cost accounting system may be useful to the management of a professional service business in planning and controlling operations. For example, an advertising agency, an attorney, and a physician all share the common characteristic of providing services to individual customers, clients, or patients. In such cases, the customer, client, or patient can be viewed as an individual job for which costs are accumulated.

Since the "product" of a service business is service, management's focus is on direct labor and overhead costs. The cost of any materials or supplies used in rendering services for a client is usually small and is normally included as part of the overhead.

The direct labor and overhead costs of rendering services to clients are accumulated in a work in process account. This account is supported by a cost ledger. A job cost sheet is used to accumulate the costs for each client's job. When a job is completed and the client is billed, the costs are transferred to a cost of services account. This account is similar to the cost of merchandise sold account for a merchandising business or the cost of goods sold account for a manufacturing business. A finished goods account and related finished goods ledger are not necessary, since the revenues associated with the services are recorded after the services have been provided. The flow of costs through a service business using a job order cost accounting system is shown in Exhibit 13.

•Exhibit 13   Flow of Costs Through a Service Business

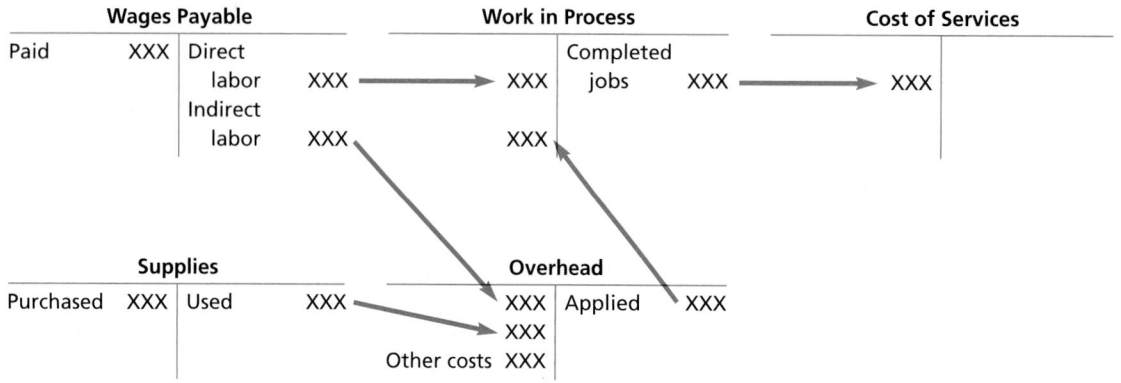

In practice, additional accounting considerations unique to service businesses may need to be considered. For example, a service business may bill clients on a weekly or monthly basis rather than waiting until a job is completed. In these situations, a portion of the costs related to each billing should be transferred from the work in process account to the cost of services account. A service business may also have advance billings that would be accounted for as deferred revenue until the services have been completed.

SPOTLIGHT ON STRATEGY

MAKING A MOVIE WITHOUT A SET (OR EVEN ACTORS)

Movie making is a high-risk venture. The movie must be completely shot and marketed before one dollar is received from the box office. If the movie is a hit, then all is well; but if it's a bomb, money will be lost. This is termed a "blockbuster" business strategy and is common to businesses that have large up-front costs in the face of uncertain follow-on revenues, such as pharmaceuticals, video games, and publishing.

The blockbuster strategy assumes that not all movies will be hits. Indeed, very few movie studios make money on all of their releases. Rather, the studio hopes to have enough hits to overcome the losses from the bombs and to make money in the end. Studios must continually create a few hits to overcome their "misses."

As the cost of movie making has increased, the risk of losing money has heightened as well. That is, the movie must become an even bigger blockbuster just to break even, much less contribute to the losses of other movies. One important approach to reining in costs is *CGI*, or *computer-generated imagery*. CGI got an important start from George Lucas, creator of the *Star Wars* movies, when he realized that he wouldn't be able to afford the miniatures and models for his original Star Wars trilogy. Lucas decided that he would have to turn to computers to create his futuristic world. Thus was born **Industrial Light +**

Magic, his digital imaging company, which is the undisputed leader in the industry. CGI has come a long way. In the early '80s, it took a Cray computer 15 to 20 minutes to render one frame on the *Last Starfighter*. In the 2000s, CGI was used in over 95% of Lucas's *Attack of the Clones*. Today, an average four-second digital effect costs between $25,000 and $125,000.

Not only has CGI played a huge role in conventional movie making, but it is also transforming animated films. The traditional method of hand drawing individual frames, or cells, for an animated feature is giving way to digital animation from companies such as Steve Job's **Pixar Animation** (*Toy Story*, *Monsters, Inc.* and *Finding Nemo*). The superiority of computer-aided animation drove **Fox Film Entertainment** to shut down its cell-animation unit and focus exclusively on CGI.

Looking to the future of movie making, it's becoming more and more difficult to distinguish between the "real" and the "digital." As Lucas was walking the set of a two-mile recreation of downtown Manhattan for another movie, he wondered why this wasn't being recreated digitally at lower cost inside the technical studios of Industrial Light + Magic. This type of question will be asked more and more by Hollywood producers.

Key Points

1 Describe the differences between managerial and financial accounting.

Managerial accounting and financial accounting serve different needs and, as such, have different characteristics. Managerial accounting serves the reporting needs of managers in meeting strategic and operational goals. Managerial accounting is not bound by a set of generally accepted accounting principles, as is financial accounting. As a result, the practice of managerial accounting is as diverse as are organizations. This additional complexity in understanding the structure of managerial accounting is offset by the degree of creativity that can be applied to managerial information needs.

2 Evaluate the organizational role of management accountants.

The financial function is generally a staff function of the organization. The chief accountant is often called the controller. The controller's function includes providing a variety of reports to support management decision making.

3 Define and illustrate materials, factory labor, and factory overhead costs.

A manufacturer converts materials into a finished product by using machinery and labor. The cost of materials that are an integral part of the manufactured product is direct materials cost. The cost of wages of employees who are involved in

converting materials into the manufactured product is direct labor cost. Costs other than direct materials and direct labor costs are factory overhead costs, including indirect materials and labor. Direct labor and factory overhead are termed conversion costs. Direct materials, direct labor, and factory overhead costs are associated with products and are called product costs.

4 Describe accounting systems used by manufacturing businesses.

A cost accounting system accumulates product costs. The cost accounting system is used by management to determine the proper product cost for inventory valuation on the financial statements, to support product pricing decisions, and to identify opportunities for cost reduction and improved production efficiency. The two primary cost accounting systems are job order and process cost systems.

5 Describe and prepare summary journal entries for a job order cost accounting system.

A job order cost system provides for a separate record of the cost of each particular quantity of product that passes through the factory. Direct materials, direct labor, and factory overhead costs are accumulated in

a subsidiary cost ledger, in which each account is represented by a job cost sheet. Work in Process is the controlling account for the cost ledger. As a job is finished, its costs are transferred to the finished goods ledger, for which Finished Goods is the controlling account.

6 Use job order cost information for decision making.

Job order cost information can support pricing and cost analysis. Managers can use job cost information to identify unusual trends and areas for cost improvement.

7 Diagram the flow of costs for a service business that uses a job order cost accounting system.

A cost flow diagram for a service business using a job order cost accounting system is shown in Exhibit 13. For a service business, the cost of materials or supplies used is normally included as part of the overhead. The direct labor and overhead costs of rendering services are accumulated in a work in process account. When a job is completed and the client is billed, the costs are transferred to a cost of services account.

ey Terms

activity base (667)
activity-based costing (668)
controller (659)
conversion costs (662)
cost (660)
cost accounting system (662)
cost allocation (667)
cost of goods sold (663)
direct labor cost (661)
direct materials cost (660)
factory overhead cost (662)

financial accounting (658)
finished goods inventory (663)
finished goods ledger (671)
job cost sheet (665)
job order cost system (662)
managerial accounting (658)
materials inventory (663)
materials ledger (664)
materials requisitions (664)
overapplied factory overhead (669)
period costs (672)

predetermined factory overhead rate (667)
process cost system (662)
product costs (662)
receiving report (663)
time tickets (665)
underapplied factory overhead (669)
work in process inventory (663)

llustrative Problem

Derby Music Company specializes in producing and packaging compact discs (CDs) for the music recording industry. Derby uses a job order cost system. The following data summarize the operations related to production for March, the first month of operations:

a. Materials purchased on account, $15,500.
b. Materials requisitioned and labor used:

	Materials	Factory Labor
Job No. 100	$2,650	$1,770
Job No. 101	1,240	650
Job No. 102	980	420
Job No. 103	3,420	1,900
Job No. 104	1,000	500
Job No. 105	2,100	1,760
For general factory use	450	650

c. Factory overhead costs incurred on account, $2,700.
d. Depreciation of machinery, $1,750.
e. Factory overhead is applied at a rate of 70% of direct labor cost.
f. Jobs completed: Nos. 100, 101, 102, 104.
g. Jobs 100, 101, and 102 were shipped, and customers were billed for $8,100, $3,800, and $3,500, respectively.

Instructions

1. Journalize the entries to record the transactions identified above.
2. Determine the account balances for Work in Process and Finished Goods.
3. Prepare a schedule of unfinished jobs to support the balance in the work in process account.
4. Prepare a schedule of completed jobs on hand to support the balance in the finished goods account.

Solution

1. a. Materials 15,500
  Accounts Payable 15,500

b. Work in Process 11,390
  Materials 11,390
  Work in Process 7,000
  Wages Payable 7,000
  Factory Overhead 1,100
  Materials 450
  Wages Payable 650

c. Factory Overhead 2,700
  Accounts Payable 2,700

d. Factory Overhead 1,750
  Accumulated Depreciation—Machinery 1,750

e. Work in Process 4,900
  Factory Overhead (70% of $7,000) 4,900

f. Finished Goods 11,548
  Work in Process 11,548

Computation of the cost of jobs finished:

Job	Direct Materials	Direct Labor	Factory Overhead	Total
Job No. 100	$2,650	$1,770	$1,239	$ 5,659
Job No. 101	1,240	650	455	2,345
Job No. 102	980	420	294	1,694
Job No. 104	1,000	500	350	1,850
				$11,548

g. Accounts Receivable 15,400
  Sales 15,400
  Cost of Goods Sold 9,698
  Finished Goods 9,698

Cost of jobs sold computation:

Job No. 100	$5,659
Job No. 101	2,345
Job No. 102	1,694
	$9,698

2. Work in Process: $11,742 ($11,390 + $7,000 + $4,900 − $11,548)
  Finished Goods: $1,850 ($11,548 − $9,698)

(continued)

3.

Schedule of Unfinished Jobs

Job	Direct Materials	Direct Labor	Factory Overhead	Total
Job No. 103	$3,420	$1,900	$1,330	$ 6,650
Job No. 105	2,100	1,760	1,232	5,092
Balance of Work in Process, March 31				$11,742

4.

Schedule of Completed Jobs

Job No. 104:

Direct materials	$1,000
Direct labor	500
Factory overhead	350
Balance of Finished Goods, March 31	$1,850

Self-Examination Questions (Answers at End of Chapter)

1. Which of the following best describes the difference between financial and managerial accounting?
   A. Managerial accounting provides information to support decisions, while financial accounting does not.
   B. Managerial accounting is not restricted to generally accepted accounting principles (GAAP), while financial accounting is restricted to GAAP.
   C. Managerial accounting does not result in financial reports, while financial accounting does result in financial reports.
   D. Managerial accounting is concerned solely with the future and does not record events from the past, while financial accounting records only events from past transactions.

2. Which of the following is *not* considered a cost of manufacturing a product?
   A. Direct materials cost   C. Sales salaries
   B. Factory overhead cost   D. Direct labor cost

3. Which of the following costs would be included as part of the factory overhead costs of a computer manufacturer?
   A. The cost of memory chips
   B. Depreciation of testing equipment
   C. Wages of computer assemblers
   D. The cost of disk drives

4. A company estimated $420,000 of factory overhead cost and 16,000 direct labor hours for the period. During the period, a job was completed with $4,500 of direct materials and $3,000 of direct labor. The direct labor rate was $15 per hour. What is the factory overhead applied to this job?
   A. $2,100   C. $78,750
   B. $5,250   D. $420,000

5. If the factory overhead account has a credit balance, factory overhead is said to be:
   A. underapplied   C. underabsorbed
   B. overapplied   D. in error

Class Discussion Questions

1. What are the major differences between managerial accounting and financial accounting?
2. a. Differentiate between a department with line responsibility and a department with staff responsibility.
   b. In an organization that has a Sales Department and a Personnel Department, among others, which of the two departments has (1) line responsibility and (2) staff responsibility?
3. a. What is the role of the controller in a business organization?
   b. Does the controller have a line or staff responsibility?

4. For a company that produces desktop computers, would memory chips be considered a direct or an indirect materials cost of each computer produced?

5. How is product cost information used by managers?

6. a. Name two principal types of cost accounting systems.
   b. Which system provides for a separate record of each particular quantity of product that passes through the factory?
   c. Which system accumulates the costs for each department or process within the factory?

7. What kind of firm would use a job order cost system?

8. **Hewlett-Packard Company** assembles ink jet printers in which a high volume of standardized units are assembled and tested. Is the job order cost system appropriate in this situation?

9. How does the use of the materials requisition help control the issuance of materials from the storeroom?

10. a. Differentiate between the clock card and the time ticket.
    b. Why should the total time reported on an employee's time tickets for a payroll period be compared with the time reported on the employee's clock cards for the same period?

11. Describe the source of the data for debiting Work in Process for (a) direct materials, (b) direct labor, and (c) factory overhead.

12. Discuss how the predetermined factory overhead rate can be used in job order cost accounting to assist management in pricing jobs.

13. a. How is a predetermined factory overhead rate calculated?
    b. Name three common bases used in calculating the rate.

14. a. What is (1) overapplied factory overhead and (2) underapplied factory overhead?
    b. If the factory overhead account has a debit balance, was factory overhead underapplied or overapplied?
    c. If the factory overhead account has a credit balance at the end of the first month of the fiscal year, where will the amount of this balance be reported on the interim balance sheet?

15. At the end of the fiscal year, there was a relatively minor balance in the factory overhead account. What procedure can be used for disposing of the balance in the account?

16. What is the difference between a product cost and a period cost?

17. How can job cost information be used to identify cost improvement opportunities?

18. Describe how a job order cost system can be used for professional service businesses.

Exercises

EXERCISE 16-1
Classify costs as materials, labor, or factory overhead
Objective 3

Indicate whether each of the following costs of a furniture manufacturer would be classified as direct materials cost, direct labor cost, or factory overhead cost:

a. Inspector salaries
b. Depreciation on woodworking machinery
c. Assembly wages
d. Wood
e. Wages of wood cutters
f. Furniture hardware
g. Saw blades
h. Supervisor salaries

EXERCISE 16-2
Classify costs as materials, labor, or factory overhead
Objective 3

REAL WORLD

Indicate whether each of the following costs of the **Procter & Gamble Company** would be classified as direct materials cost, direct labor cost, or factory overhead cost:

a. Depreciation on the St. Bernard (Cincinnati) soap plant
b. Wages paid to Packing Department employees
c. Maintenance supplies
d. Packaging materials
e. Plant manager salary of the Lima, Ohio, liquid soap plant
f. Pulp for towel and tissue products
g. Wages of Making Department employees
h. Scents and fragrances
i. Depreciation on disposable diaper converting machines
j. Salary of process engineers

EXERCISE 16-3
Classify factory overhead costs
Objective 3

REAL WORLD

Which of the following items are properly classified as part of factory overhead for **John Deere & Co.**?

a. Plant manager's salary at Greeneville, Tennessee, turf care products plant
b. Depreciation on Moline, Illinois, headquarters building
c. Property taxes on Klemme, Iowa, components plant
d. Chief financial officer's salary
e. Steel plate
f. Sales incentive fees to dealers
g. Amortization of patents on a new welding process
h. Interest expense on debt
i. Consultant fees for surveying production employee morale
j. Factory supplies used in the Kenersville, North Carolina, hydraulic excavator factory

EXERCISE 16-4
Classify costs as product or period costs
Objectives 3, 5

REAL WORLD

Classify the following costs for **Ford Motor Company** as either a product cost or a period cost.

a. Advertising
b. Tires
c. Assembly employee wages
d. Salary of marketing executive
e. Depreciation of Dearborn, Michigan, executive building
f. CEO's salary
g. Plant manager's salary
h. Depreciation on Atlanta, Georgia, assembly plant
i. Maintenance supplies
j. Glass

k. Property taxes on Kansas City, Missouri, assembly plant
l. Shipping costs
m. Travel costs used by sales personnel
n. Utility costs used in executive building
o. Stamping Department employee wages
p. Steel

EXERCISE 16-5
Concepts and terminology
Objectives 3, 5

From the choices presented in the parentheses, choose the appropriate term for completing each of the following sentences:

a. The wages of an assembly worker are normally considered a (period, product) cost.
b. Direct labor costs combined with factory overhead costs are called (product, conversion) costs.
c. Implementing automatic factory robotics equipment normally (increases, decreases) the factory overhead component of product costs.
d. Payments of cash or its equivalent or the commitment to pay cash in the future for the purpose of generating revenues are (costs, expenses).
e. Advertising expenses are usually viewed as (period, product) costs.
f. The balance sheet of a manufacturer would include an account for (cost of goods sold, work in process inventory).
g. Materials that are an integral part of the manufactured product are classified as (direct materials, materials inventory).
h. An example of factory overhead is (plant depreciation, sales office depreciation).

EXERCISE 16-6
Transactions in a job order cost system
Objective 5

Five selected transactions for the current month are indicated by letters in the following T accounts in a job order cost accounting system:

Materials	
	(a)

Work in Process	
(a)	(d)
(b)	
(c)	

Wages Payable	
	(b)

Finished Goods	
(d)	(e)

Factory Overhead	
(a)	(c)
(b)	

Cost of Goods Sold	
(e)	

Describe each of the five transactions.

EXERCISE 16-7
Cost flow relationships
Objective 5
✓ c. $276,500

The following information is available for the first month of operations of Native Arts Inc., a manufacturer of art and craft items:

Sales	$850,000
Gross profit	235,000
Indirect labor	65,000
Indirect materials	27,000
Other factory overhead	13,500
Materials purchased	305,000
Total manufacturing costs for the period	640,000
Materials inventory, end of period	20,000

Using the above information, determine the following missing amounts:

a. Cost of goods sold
b. Direct materials cost
c. Direct labor cost

EXERCISE 16-8
Cost of materials issuances by FIFO method

Objective 5

SPREADSHEET

✓ b. $880

An incomplete subsidiary ledger of wire cable for May is as follows:

RECEIVED			ISSUED			BALANCE			
Receiving Report Number	Quantity	Unit Price	Materials Requisition Number	Quantity	Amount	Date	Quantity	Amount	Unit Price
						May 1	120	$2,160	$18.00
23	190	$20.00				May 3			
			104	250		May 5			
29	140	22.00				May 19			
			117	160		May 25			

a. Complete the materials issuances and balances for the wire cable subsidiary ledger under FIFO.
b. Determine the balance of wire cable at the end of May.
c. Journalize the summary entry to transfer materials to work in process.
d. ▭▶ Explain how the materials ledger might be used as an aid in maintaining inventory quantities on hand.

EXERCISE 16-9
Entry for issuing materials

Objective 5

Materials issued for the current month are as follows:

Requisition No.	Material	Job No.	Amount
711	Steel	511	$11,200
712	Copper	514	16,450
713	Plastic	526	900
714	Abrasives	Indirect	250
715	Titanium alloy	533	36,400

Journalize the entry to record the issuance of materials.

EXERCISE 16-10
Entries for materials

Objective 5

✓ c. fabric, $40,000

Hearth and Home Furniture Company (HHC) manufactures furniture. HHC uses a job order cost system. Balances on June 1 from the materials ledger are as follows:

Fabric	$ 32,400
Polyester filling	7,300
Lumber	106,900
Glue	1,500

The materials purchased during June are summarized from the receiving reports as follows:

Fabric	$547,300
Polyester filling	103,600
Lumber	968,100
Glue	13,200

Materials were requisitioned to individual jobs as follows:

	Fabric	Polyester Filling	Lumber	Glue	Total
Job 11	$352,100	$62,300	$609,200		$1,023,600
Job 12	123,400	14,200	200,300		337,900
Job 13	64,200	10,200	181,700		256,100
Factory overhead—indirect materials				$13,500	13,500
Total	$539,700	$86,700	$991,200	$13,500	$1,631,100

The glue is not a significant cost, so it is treated as indirect materials (factory overhead).

a. Journalize the entry to record the purchase of materials in June.
b. Journalize the entry to record the requisition of materials in June.
c. Determine the June 30 balances that would be shown in the materials ledger accounts.

EXERCISE 16-11
Entry for factory labor costs
Objective 5

A summary of the time tickets for the current month follows:

Job No.	Amount	Job No.	Amount
101	$1,540	141	$ 1,630
122	1,610	Indirect labor	12,600
133	870	143	3,240
139	4,240	147	1,040

Journalize the entry to record the factory labor costs.

EXERCISE 16-12
Entry for factory labor costs
Objective 5

The weekly time tickets indicate the following distribution of labor hours for three direct labor employees:

	Hours			
	Job 111	Job 112	Job 113	Process Improvement
Harvey Daniels	18	15	2	5
Cedrick Price	6	7	25	2
Dan Zhu	9	13	15	3

The direct labor rate earned by the three employees is as follows:

Daniels	$11.50
Price	13.25
Zhu	11.40

The process improvement category includes training, quality improvement, housekeeping, and other indirect tasks.

a. Journalize the entry to record the factory labor costs for the week.
b. Assume that Jobs 111 and 112 were completed but not sold during the week and that Job 113 remained incomplete at the end of the week. How would the direct labor costs for all three jobs be reflected on the financial statements at the end of the week?

EXERCISE 16-13
Entries for direct labor and factory overhead
Objective 5

Lincoln Homes Inc. manufactures log homes. Lincoln uses a job order cost system. The time tickets from September jobs are summarized below.

Job 502	$1,470
Job 503	896
Job 504	602
Job 505	868
Factory supervision	1,730

Factory overhead is applied to jobs on the basis of a predetermined overhead rate of $18 per direct labor hour. The direct labor rate is $6 per hour.

a. Journalize the entry to record the factory labor costs.
b. Journalize the entry to apply factory overhead to production for September.

EXERCISE 16-14
Factory overhead rates, entries, and account balance
Objective 5

Detroit Motor Co. operates two factories. The company applies factory overhead to jobs on the basis of machine hours in Factory 1 and on the basis of direct labor hours in Factory 2. Estimated factory overhead costs, direct labor hours, and machine hours are as follows:

✔ b. $12.50 per direct labor hour

	Factory 1	Factory 2
Estimated factory overhead cost for fiscal year beginning April 1	$237,500	$112,500
Estimated direct labor hours for year		9,000
Estimated machine hours for year	12,500	
Actual factory overhead costs for April	$20,100	$9,450
Actual direct labor hours for April		770
Actual machine hours for April	1,035	

a. Determine the factory overhead rate for Factory 1.

b. Determine the factory overhead rate for Factory 2.

c. Journalize the entries to apply factory overhead to production in each factory for April.

d. Determine the balances of the factory accounts for each factory as of April 30, and indicate whether the amounts represent overapplied or underapplied factory overhead.

EXERCISE 16-15
Predetermined factory overhead rate
Objective 5

The AutoDoctor Body Shop uses a job order cost system to determine the cost of performing automotive body and repair work. Estimated costs and expenses for the coming period are as follows:

Auto parts	$ 675,500
Shop direct labor	490,000
Shop and repair equipment depreciation	16,900
Shop supervisor salaries	95,200
Shop property tax	19,200
Shop supplies	12,200
Advertising expense	17,300
Administrative office salaries	63,400
Administrative office depreciation expense	10,300
Total costs and expenses	$1,400,000

The average shop direct labor rate is $14 per hour.

Determine the predetermined shop overhead rate per direct labor hour.

EXERCISE 16-16
Predetermined factory overhead rate
Objective 5

✔ a. $190 per hour

Good Samaritan Medical Center has a single operating room that is used by local physicians to perform surgical procedures. The cost of using the operating room is accumulated by each patient procedure and includes the direct materials costs (drugs and medical devices), physician surgical time, and operating room overhead. On January 1 of the current year, the annual operating room overhead is estimated to be:

Disposable supplies	$124,500
Depreciation expense	24,000
Utilities	15,300
Nurse salaries	188,000
Technician wages	47,200
Total operating room overhead	$399,000

The overhead costs will be assigned to procedures based on the number of surgical room hours. The Medical Center expects to use the operating room an average of seven hours per day, six days per week. In addition, the operating room will be shut down two weeks per year for general repairs.

a. Determine the predetermined operating room overhead rate for the year.

b. LeVar Wilson had a 2.5-hour procedure on January 10. How much operating room overhead would be charged to his procedure, using the rate determined in (a)?

c. During January, the operating room was used 170 hours. The actual overhead costs incurred for January were $31,800. Determine the overhead under- or overapplied for the period.

EXERCISE 16-17
Entry for jobs completed;
cost of unfinished jobs

Objective 5

✔ b. $7,500

The following account appears in the ledger after only part of the postings have been completed for March:

Work in Process	
Balance, March 1	$15,700
Direct materials	84,700
Direct labor	63,200
Factory overhead	92,100

Jobs finished during March are summarized as follows:

Job 320	$56,800	Job 327	$23,100
Job 326	74,600	Job 350	93,700

a. Journalize the entry to record the jobs completed.
b. Determine the cost of the unfinished jobs at March 31.

EXERCISE 16-18
Entries for factory costs and
jobs completed

Objective 5

✔ d. $15,100

Creative Graphics, Inc., began printing operations on May 1. Jobs 1 and 2 were completed during the month, and all costs applicable to them were recorded on the related cost sheets. Jobs 3 and 4 are still in process at the end of the month, and all applicable costs except factory overhead have been recorded on the related cost sheets. In addition to the materials and labor charged directly to the jobs, $620 of indirect materials and $6,740 of indirect labor were used during the month. The cost sheets for the four jobs entering production during the month are as follows, in summary form:

Job 1		Job 2	
Direct materials	6,300	Direct materials	3,200
Direct labor	1,400	Direct labor	600
Factory overhead	2,520	Factory overhead	1,080
Total	10,220	Total	4,880

Job 3		Job 4	
Direct materials	8,300	Direct materials	1,100
Direct labor	1,750	Direct labor	380
Factory overhead		Factory overhead	

Journalize the summary entry to record each of the following operations for May (one entry for each operation):

a. Direct and indirect materials used.
b. Direct and indirect labor used.
c. Factory overhead applied (a single overhead rate is used based on direct labor *cost*).
d. Completion of Jobs 1 and 2.

EXERCISE 16-19
Financial statements of a
manufacturing firm

Objective 5

SPREADSHEET

✔ a. Income from
operations, $45,500

The following events took place for Mercury Shoe Company during May 2006, the first month of operations as a producer of athletic shoes:

• Purchased $155,300 of materials.
• Used $145,800 of direct materials in production.
• Incurred $94,500 of direct labor wages.
• Applied factory overhead at a rate of 75% of direct labor cost.
• Transferred $304,300 of work in process to finished goods.
• Sold goods with a cost of $300,100.
• Sold goods for $510,000.
• Incurred $116,000 of selling expenses.
• Incurred $48,400 of administrative expenses.

a. Prepare the May income statement for Mercury Shoe Company. Assume that Mercury Shoe uses the perpetual inventory method.
b. Determine the inventory balances at the end of the first month of operations.

EXERCISE 16-20
Decision making with job order costs
Objective 6

Performance Valve, Inc. is a job shop. The management of Performance uses the cost information from the job sheets to assess their cost performance. Information on the total cost, product type, and quantity of items produced is as follows:

Date	Job No.	Quantity	Product	Amount
Jan. 1	1	400	XXY	$ 7,600
Jan. 29	26	1,200	AAB	18,000
Feb. 15	43	600	AAB	9,600
Mar. 10	64	450	XXY	7,650
Mar. 31	75	900	MM	7,200
May 10	91	1,000	MM	12,000
June 20	104	400	XXY	4,800
Aug. 2	112	1,500	MM	24,000
Sept. 20	114	400	AAB	6,000
Nov. 1	126	600	XXY	6,000
Dec. 3	133	850	MM	17,850

a. Develop a graph for *each* product (three graphs), with Job No. (in date order) on the horizontal axis and unit cost on the vertical axis. Use this information to determine Performance's cost performance over time for the three products.
b. ▭▭▭▷ What additional information would you require to investigate Performance's cost performance more precisely?

EXERCISE 16-21
Decision making with job order costs
Objective 6

Engraved Awards, Inc. uses a job order cost system for determining the cost to manufacture award products (plaques and trophies). Among the company's products is an engraved plaque that is awarded to participants who complete an executive education program at a local university. The company sells the plaque to the university for $20 each.

Each plaque has a brass plate engraved with the name of the participant. Engraving requires approximately 10 minutes per name. Improperly engraved names must be redone. The plate is screwed to a walnut backboard. This assembly takes approximately 5 minutes per unit. Improper assembly must be redone using a new walnut backboard.

During the first half of the year, the university had two separate executive education classes. The job cost sheets for the two separate jobs indicated the following information:

Job 223   **March 28**

	Cost per Unit	Units	Job Cost
Direct materials:			
Wood	$ 2.00/unit	42 units	$ 84.00
Brass	2.40/unit	42 units	100.80
Engraving labor	15.00/hr.	7.0 hrs.	105.00
Assembly labor	12.00/hr.	3.5 hrs.	42.00
Factory overhead	24.00/hr.	10.5 hrs.	252.00
			$583.80
Plaques shipped			÷ 42
Cost per plaque			$ 13.90

Job 275   **May 16**

	Cost per Unit	Units	Job Cost
Direct materials:			
Wood	$ 2.00/unit	60 units	$120.00
Brass	2.40/unit	60 units	144.00
Engraving labor	15.00/hr.	10 hrs.	150.00
Assembly labor	12.00/hr.	5 hrs.	60.00
Factory overhead	24.00/hr.	15 hrs.	360.00
			$834.00
Plaques shipped			÷ 50
Cost per plaque			$ 16.68

a. Why did the cost per plaque increase from $13.90 to $16.68?
b. What improvements would you recommend for Engraved Awards, Inc.?

EXERCISE 16-22
Job order cost accounting entries for a service business
Objective 7

The law firm of Jarvis and Hunt accumulates costs associated with individual cases, using a job order cost system. The following transactions occurred during March:

Mar. 7 Charged 420 hours of professional (lawyer) time to the Masco Co. breech of contract suit to prepare for the trial, at a rate of $150 per hour.
11 Reimbursed travel costs to employees for depositions related to the Masco case, $24,000.
22 Charged 250 hours of professional time for the Masco trial at a rate of $200 per hour.
25 Received invoice from consultants Jarvis and Hunt for $45,000 for expert testimony related to the Masco trial.
30 Applied office overhead at a rate of $50 per professional hour charged to the Masco case.
31 Paid secretarial and administrative salaries of $28,000 for the month.
31 Used office supplies for the month, $4,000.
31 Paid professional salaries of $63,000 for the month.
31 Billed Masco $250,000 for successful defense of the case.

a. Provide the journal entries for each of the above transactions.
b. How much office overhead is over- or underapplied?
c. Determine the gross profit on the Masco case, assuming that over- or underapplied office overhead is closed annually to cost of services.

EXERCISE 16-23
Job order cost accounting entries for a service business
Objective 7

✓ *d. Dr. Cost of Services, $721,000*

Image Media, Inc. provides advertising services for clients across the nation. Image Media is presently working on four projects, each for a different client. Image Media accumulates costs for each account (client) on the basis of both direct costs and allocated indirect costs. The direct costs include the charged time of professional personnel and media purchases (air time and ad space). Overhead is allocated to each project as a percentage of media purchases. The predetermined overhead rate is 30% of media purchases.

On June 1, the four advertising projects had the following accumulated costs:

	March 1 Balances
Fizz4U Beverage	$105,000
First Security Bank	175,000
All-Right Rentals	54,000
SleepEzz Hotel	14,000

During June, Image Media, Inc. incurred the following direct labor and media purchase costs related to preparing advertising for each of the four accounts:

	Direct Labor	Media Purchases
Fizz4U Beverage	$ 36,000	$160,000
First Security Bank	15,000	140,000
All-Right Rentals	78,000	130,000
SleepEzz Hotel	101,000	80,000
Total	$230,000	$510,000

At the end of June, both the Fizz4U Beverage and First Security Bank campaigns were completed. The cost of completed campaigns are debited to the cost of services account.

Journalize the summary entry to record each of the following for the month:

a. Direct labor costs
b. Media purchases
c. Overhead applied
d. Completion of Fizz4U Beverage and First Security Bank campaigns

Problems Series A

PROBLEM 16-1A
Classify costs

Objectives 3, 5

The following is a list of costs that were incurred in the production and sale of lawn mowers.

a. Tires for lawn mowers.
b. Salary of factory supervisor.
c. Gasoline engines used for lawn mowers.
d. Premiums on insurance policy for factory buildings.
e. Cost of boxes used in storing and shipping lawn mowers.
f. Filter for spray gun used to paint the lawn mowers.
g. Payroll taxes on hourly assembly-line employees.
h. Rivets, bolts, and other fasteners used in lawn mowers.
i. Cash paid to outside firm for janitorial services for factory.
j. Engine oil used in mower engines prior to shipment.
k. Attorney fees for drafting a new lease for headquarters offices.
l. Maintenance costs for new factory robotics equipment, based upon hours of usage.
m. Straight-line depreciation on the robotics machinery used to manufacture the lawn mowers.
n. License fees for use of patent for lawn mower blade, based upon the number of lawn mowers produced.
o. Hourly wages of operators of robotics machinery used in production.
p. Salary of vice-president of marketing.
q. Property taxes on the factory building and equipment.
r. Factory cafeteria cashier's wages.
s. Electricity used to run the robotics machinery.
t. Commissions paid to sales representatives, based upon the number of lawn mowers sold.
u. Steel used in producing the lawn mowers.
v. Lawn mower throttle controls.
w. Telephone charges for controller's office.
x. Salary of quality control supervisor who inspects each lawn mower before it is shipped.
y. Plastic for outside housing of lawn mowers.
z. Cost of advertising in a national magazine.

Instructions
Classify each cost as either a product cost or a period cost. Indicate whether each product cost is a direct materials cost, a direct labor cost, or a factory overhead cost. Indicate whether each period cost is a selling expense or an administrative expense. Use the following tabular headings for your answer, placing an "X" in the appropriate column.

Product Costs			Period Costs	
Direct Materials Cost	Direct Labor Cost	Factory Overhead Cost	Selling Expense	Admin. Expense

PROBLEM 16-2A
Entries for costs in a job order cost system

Objective 5

P.A.S.S.

Hi-Volt Transformer Co. uses a job order cost system. The following data summarize the operations related to production for June:

a. Materials purchased on account, $635,500.
b. Materials requisitioned, $597,200, of which $36,200 was for general factory use.
c. Factory labor used, $468,100, of which $97,500 was indirect.
d. Other costs incurred on account were for factory overhead, $361,100; selling expenses, $245,000; and administrative expenses, $164,500.

e. Prepaid expenses expired for factory overhead were $21,000; for selling expenses, $14,200; and for administrative expenses, $8,600.

f. Depreciation of factory equipment was $36,000; of office equipment, $21,500; and of warehouse equipment, $9,700.

g. Factory overhead costs applied to jobs, $540,500.

h. Jobs completed, $1,436,200.

i. Cost of goods sold, $1,445,500.

Instructions

Journalize the entries to record the summarized operations.

PROBLEM 16-3A
Entries and schedules for unfinished jobs and completed jobs

Objective 5

P.A.S.S.

✓3. Work in Process balance, $6,630

Professional Printers, Inc. uses a job order cost system. The following data summarize the operations related to production for April 2006, the first month of operations:

a. Materials purchased on account, $8,100.

b. Materials requisitioned and factory labor used:

Job	Materials	Factory Labor
No. 101	$ 850	$ 680
No. 102	1,230	1,050
No. 103	630	420
No. 104	2,140	1,820
No. 105	1,250	1,100
No. 106	930	810
For general factory use	290	960

c. Factory overhead costs incurred on account, $380.

d. Depreciation of machinery and equipment, $400.

e. The factory overhead rate is $30 per machine hour. Machine hours used:

Job	Machine Hours
No. 101	7.0
No. 102	9.5
No. 103	6.0
No. 104	21.0
No. 105	13.5
No. 106	10.0
Total	67.0

f. Jobs completed: 101, 102, 103, and 105.

g. Jobs were shipped and customers were billed as follows: Job 101, $4,200; Job 102, $5,100; Job 103, $2,000.

Instructions

1. Journalize the entries to record the summarized operations.

2. Post the appropriate entries to T accounts for Work in Process and Finished Goods, using the identifying letters as dates. Insert memorandum account balances as of the end of the month.

3. Prepare a schedule of unfinished jobs to support the balance in the work in process account.

4. Prepare a schedule of completed jobs on hand to support the balance in the finished goods account.

If the working papers correlating with the textbook are not used, omit Problem 16-4A.

PROBLEM 16-4A
Job order cost sheet

Objectives 5, 6

Hampton Court Furniture Company refinishes and reupholsters furniture. Hampton uses a job order cost system. When a prospective customer asks for a price quote on a job, the estimated cost data are inserted on an unnumbered job cost sheet. If the offer is accepted, a number is assigned to the job, and the costs incurred are recorded in the usual manner on the job cost sheet. After the job is completed, reasons for the variances between the estimated and actual costs are noted on the sheet. The data are then available to management in evaluating the efficiency of operations and in preparing quotes on future jobs. On June 10, 2006, an estimate of $561.60 for reupholstering a chair and couch was given to Danzel Bishop. The estimate was based on the following data:

Estimated direct materials:	
9 meters at $18 per meter	$162.00
Estimated direct labor:	
14 hours at $10 per hour	140.00
Estimated factory overhead (35% of direct labor cost)	49.00
Total estimated costs	$351.00
Markup (60% of production costs)	210.60
Total estimate	$561.60

On June 16, the chair and couch were picked up from the residence of Danzel Bishop, 1900 Peachtree, Atlanta, with a commitment to return it on July 16. The job was completed on July 11.

The related materials requisitions and time tickets are summarized as follows:

Materials Requisition No.	Description	Amount
U642	4 meters at $18	$ 72
U651	8 meters at $18	144

Time Ticket No.	Description	Amount
1519	8 hours at $10	$ 80
1520	7 hours at $10	70

Instructions

1. Complete that portion of the job order cost sheet that would be prepared when the estimate is given to the customer.
2. ▬▬▶ Assign number 00-8-38 to the job, record the costs incurred, and complete the job order cost sheet. Comment on the reasons for the variances between actual costs and estimated costs. For this purpose, assume that three meters of materials were spoiled, the factory overhead rate has been proved to be satisfactory, and an inexperienced employee performed the work.

PROBLEM 16-5A
Analyzing manufacturing cost accounts
Objective 5

SPREADSHEET

✓ G. $184,646

Alpine Bliss Ski Company manufactures snow skis in a wide variety of lengths and styles. The following incomplete ledger accounts refer to transactions that are summarized for January:

Materials

Jan. 1	Balance	10,000	Jan. 31	Requisitions	(A)
31	Purchases	110,000			

Work in Process

Jan. 1	Balance	(B)	Jan. 31	Completed jobs	(F)
31	Materials	(C)			
31	Direct labor	(D)			
31	Factory overhead applied	(E)			

Finished Goods

Jan. 1	Balance	0	Jan. 31	Cost of goods sold	(G)
31	Completed jobs	(F)			

Wages Payable

			Jan. 31	Wages incurred	74,200

17

PROCESS COST SYSTEMS

objectives

After studying this chapter, you should be able to:

1 Distinguish between job order costing and process costing systems.

2 Explain and illustrate the physical flows and cost flows for a process manufacturer.

3 Calculate and interpret the accounting for completed and partially completed units under the fifo method.

4 Prepare a cost of production report.

5 Prepare journal entries for transactions of a process manufacturer.

6 Use cost of production reports for decision making.

7 Contrast just-in-time processing with conventional manufacturing practices.

PHOTO: © DIGITAL VISION/GETTY IMAGES

If you bake cookies, the ingredients would include flour, sugar, and shortening. These ingredients would all be added at the beginning of the baking process by mixing them in a bowl. After mixing, do you have cookies? No. Why? Because they aren't baked (converted). But are they 100% complete with respect to materials? Yes, all the materials have been added to the baking process. When will they be cookies? When they are 100% complete with respect to materials *and* baking.

Now, assume that you ask the question, "How much cost have I incurred in baking cookies after 15 minutes (out of 30 minutes) of baking time?" The answer would require that you separate the ingredients and the electricity costs. These two costs are incurred in the baking process at different rates, and so it is convenient to identify them separately. The ingredient costs have all been incurred, since they were all introduced at the beginning of the process. The electricity costs, however, are a different story. Since the baking is only 50% complete, only 50% of the electricity costs (for the oven) have been incurred in the baking process. Therefore, the answer to the question is that all the materials costs and half the electricity costs have been incurred in the baking process after 15 minutes of baking.

In this chapter, we apply these concepts to manufacturers that use a process cost system. After introducing process costing, we discuss decision making with process cost system reports. We conclude the chapter with a brief discussion of just-in-time cost systems.

Comparing Job Order Costing and Process Costing

objective 1

Distinguish between job order costing and process costing systems.

REAL WORLD

Industries and examples of companies that may use process cost systems are:

Industry	Example Company
Automobile	General Motors
Beverages	Coca-Cola
Chemicals	Dow Chemical
Food	Campbell Soup
Forest and paper products	Georgia Pacific
Metals	Alcoa
Petroleum refining	ExxonMobil
Pharmaceuticals	Merck
Soap and cosmetics	Procter & Gamble

As we discussed in the previous chapter, the job order cost system is best suited to industries that make special orders for customers or manufacture different products in groups. Industries that may use job order cost systems include special-order printing, custom-made tailoring, furniture manufacturing, shipbuilding, aircraft building, and construction. Process manufacturing is different from job-order manufacturing. **Process manufacturers** typically use large machines to process a flow of raw materials into a finished state. For example, a petro-chemical business processes crude oil through numerous refining steps to produce higher grades of oil until gasoline is produced. The cost accounting system used by process manufacturers is called the **process cost system**.

In some ways, the process cost and job order cost systems are similar. Both systems accumulate product costs—direct materials, direct labor, and factory overhead—and allocate these costs to the units produced. Both systems maintain perpetual inventory accounts with subsidiary ledgers for materials, work in process, and finished goods. Both systems also provide product cost data to management for planning, directing, improving, controlling, and decision making. The main difference between the two systems is the form in which the product costs are accumulated and reported.

Exhibit 1 illustrates the main differences between the job order and process cost systems. In a job order cost system, product costs are accumulated by job and are summarized on job cost sheets. The job cost sheets provide unit cost information and can be used by management for product pricing, cost control, and inventory valuation. The process manufacturer does not manufacture according to "jobs." Rather, costs are accumulated by department. Each unit of product that passes through the department is similar. Thus, the production costs reported by each department provide unit cost information that can be used by management for cost control. In

•Exhibit 1 Job Order and Process Cost Systems Compared

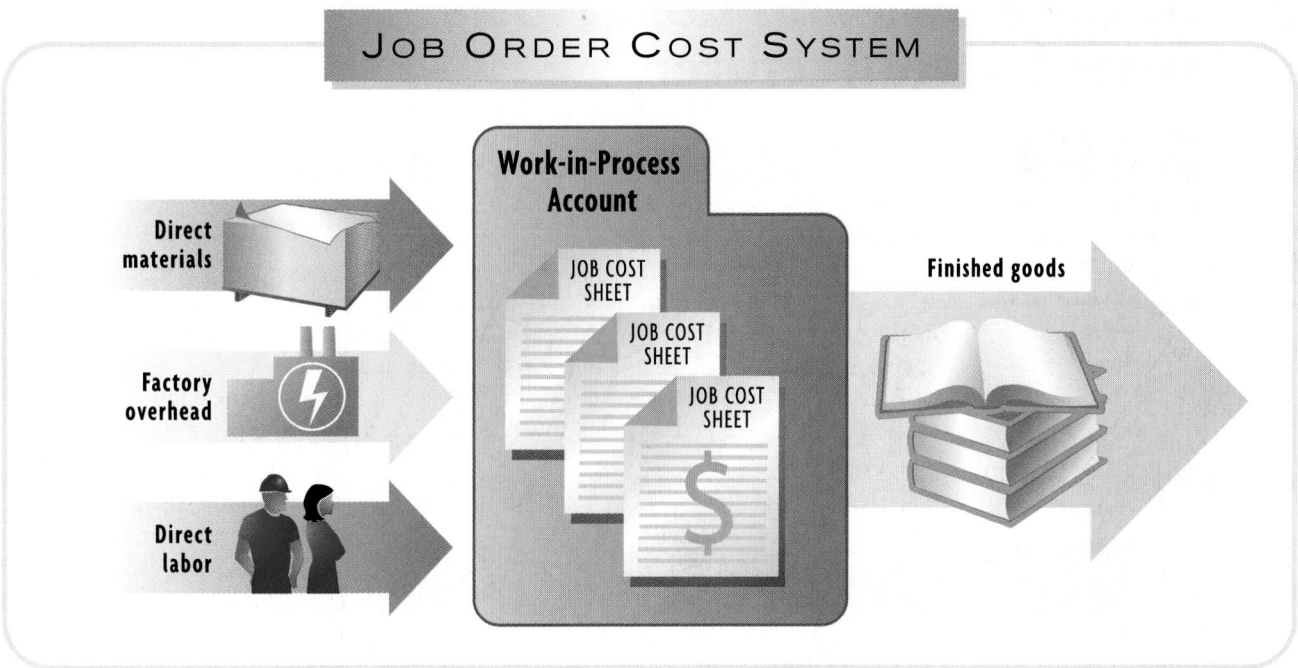

JOB ORDER COST SYSTEM

Direct materials

Factory overhead

Direct labor

Work-in-Process Account

JOB COST SHEET

JOB COST SHEET

JOB COST SHEET

Finished goods

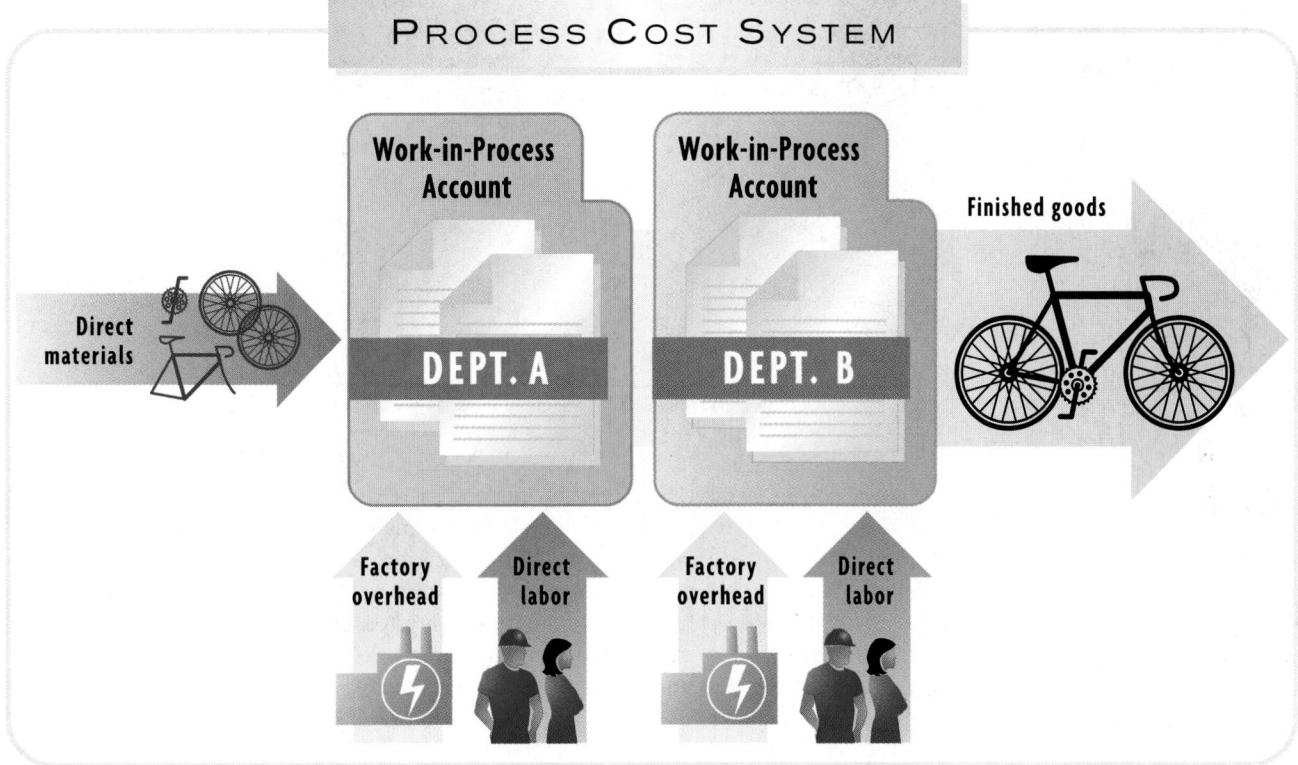

PROCESS COST SYSTEM

Direct materials

Work-in-Process Account

DEPT. A

Work-in-Process Account

DEPT. B

Finished goods

Factory overhead   **Direct labor**

Factory overhead   **Direct labor**

Process manufacturers accumulate costs by department.

a job order cost system, the work in process inventory at the end of the accounting period is the sum of the job cost sheets for partially completed jobs. In a process cost system, the amount of work in process inventory is determined by allocating costs between completed and partially completed units within a department.

Physical Flows and Cost Flows for a Process Manufacturer

<image name="objective">objective **2**</image>

Explain and illustrate the physical flows and cost flows for a process manufacturer.

Materials costs are a large portion of the costs for most process manufacturers. Often, the materials costs can be as high as 70% of the total manufacturing costs. Thus, accounting for materials costs is very important for process operations.

Exhibit 2 illustrates the physical flow of materials for a steel processor. Direct materials in the form of scrap metal are placed into a furnace in the Melting Department. The Melting Department uses conversion costs (direct labor and factory overhead) during the melting process. The molten metal is then transferred to the Casting Department, where it is poured into an ingot casting. The Casting Department also uses conversion costs during the casting process. The ingot castings are transferred to the finished goods inventory for shipment to customers.

•Exhibit 2

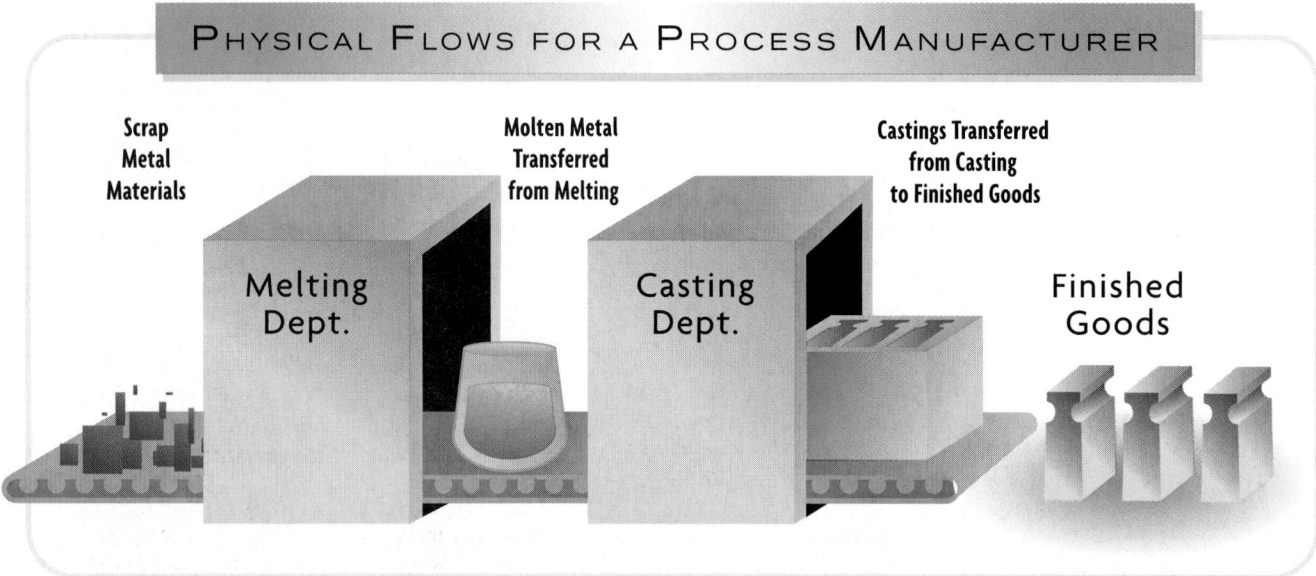

PHYSICAL FLOWS FOR A PROCESS MANUFACTURER

Scrap Metal Materials — Melting Dept. — Molten Metal Transferred from Melting — Casting Dept. — Castings Transferred from Casting to Finished Goods — Finished Goods

The cost flows in a process cost system reflect the physical materials flows and are illustrated in Exhibit 3. Purchased materials are debited to Materials (a) and credited to Accounts Payable (not shown). Direct materials (scrap metal) used by the Melting Department are debited to Work in Process—Melting and credited to Materials (b). In addition, indirect materials and other overhead incurred are debited to department factory overhead accounts and credited to Materials (d) and other accounts. Direct labor in the Melting Department is debited to the department's work in process account (c) and credited to Wages Payable (not shown). Applied factory overhead is debited to Work in Process—Melting, using a predetermined overhead rate (e). The cost of completed production from the Melting Department is transferred to the Casting Department by debiting Work in Process—Casting and crediting Work in Process—Melting (f). The transferred costs include the direct materials and conversion costs for completed production of the Melting Department. The direct labor and applied factory overhead costs in the Casting Department are debited to Work in Process—Casting (g and h). The cost of the finished ingots is transferred out of the Casting Department by debiting Finished Goods and crediting Work in Process—Casting (i). The cost of ingots sold to customers is transferred out of finished goods with a debit to Cost of Goods Sold and a credit to Finished Goods (j).

•Exhibit 3   Cost Flows for a Process Manufacturer

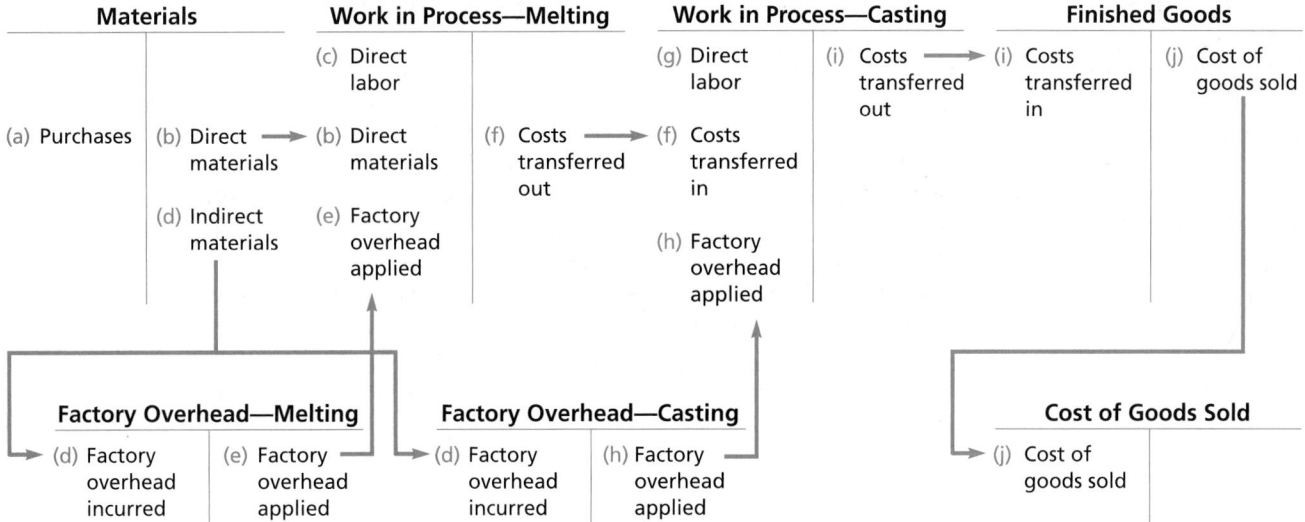

<table>
<tr><th>Materials</th><th>Work in Process—Melting</th><th>Work in Process—Casting</th><th>Finished Goods</th></tr>
</table>

Materials
(a) Purchases | (b) Direct materials → (d) Indirect materials

Work in Process—Melting
(c) Direct labor
(b) Direct materials
(e) Factory overhead applied
(f) Costs transferred out →

Work in Process—Casting
(g) Direct labor
(f) Costs transferred in
(h) Factory overhead applied
(i) Costs transferred out →

Finished Goods
(i) Costs transferred in
(j) Cost of goods sold

Factory Overhead—Melting
(d) Factory overhead incurred | (e) Factory overhead applied

Factory Overhead—Casting
(d) Factory overhead incurred | (h) Factory overhead applied

Cost of Goods Sold
(j) Cost of goods sold

MANAGERIAL DISCLOSURE AND ANALYSIS

NORTHROP GRUMMAN CORPORATION

Northrop Grumman is a defense contractor that designs, develops, and manufactures a wide variety of defense electronics and systems, aerospace management systems, precision weapons, marine systems, logistic systems, and automation and information systems. Northrop Grumman has operations in 44 states and 25 countries, serving U.S. and international military, government, and commercial customers. Along with other projects, Northrop provides systems for the F-16 and F-22 fighter aircraft, the Longbow Apache helicopter, and the B-2 Stealth Bomber.

In an attempt to improve its manufacturing operations, Northrop videotaped a mechanic in its Palmdale, Califor-

nia, plant, whose job was to apply approximately 70 feet of tape to the B-2 bomber. The mechanic walked away from the airplane 26 times and took three hours to gather the necessary chemicals, hoses, gauges, and other material needed just to start, and the total job took 8.4 hours. The diagram on the left shows the path of the mechanic in performing this job.

By designing prepackaged kits for the job, the mechanic did not have to leave the plane at all, and the total time to perform the job dropped to 1.62 hours. The diagram on the right shows the path of the mechanic using the prepackaged kits.

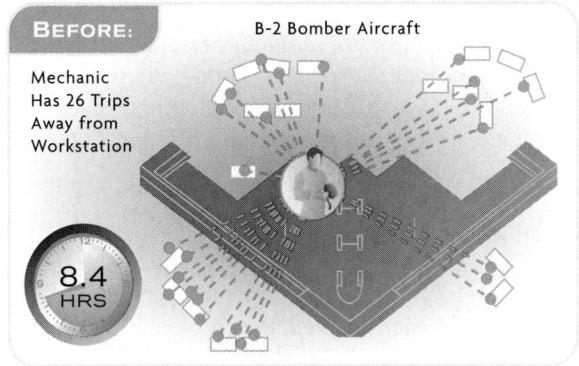

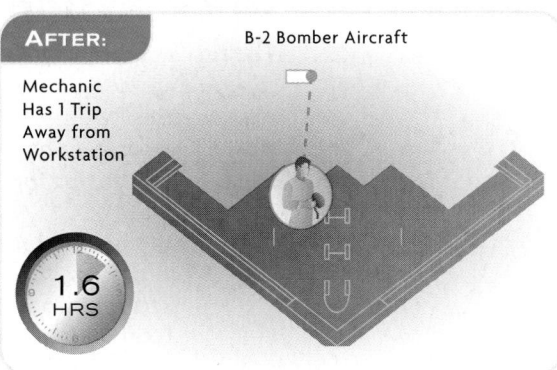

Source: Andrew Pollack, "Aerospace Gets Japan's Message," *The New York Times*, March 9, 1999.

The First-In, First-Out (Fifo) Method

objective   **3**

Calculate and interpret the accounting for completed and partially completed units under the fifo method.

I'm an international giant that manufactures, markets, and distributes branded beverages and confectionery products in nearly 200 nations. My brands include Dr Pepper, 7 UP, Canada Dry, A&W, Snapple, Hawaiian Punch, and Mott's. I employ some 40,000 people and rake in about $8 billion per year. I'm the world's third-largest soft drink company. I'm acquiring Adams from Pfizer for $4.2 billion. (Adams, known for its gum, sports such brand names as Trident, Dentyne, and Hall's medicated.) Once merged, I'll be the world's No. 2 chewing gum company, tied for No. 1 in global confections. Who am I? (Go to page 726 for answer.)

In a process cost system, the accountant determines the cost transferred out and thus the amount remaining in inventory for each department. To determine this cost, the accountant must make a cost flow assumption. Like merchandise inventory, costs can be assumed to flow through the manufacturing process using the first-in, first-out (fifo) or average cost methods. Because the ***first-in, first-out (fifo) method*** is often the same as the physical flow of units, we use the fifo method in this chapter.[1]

Most process manufacturers have more than one department. In the illustrations that follow, McDermott Steel Inc. has two departments, Melting and Casting. McDermott melts scrap metal and then pours the molten metal into an ingot casting.

To illustrate the first-in, first-out method, we will simplify by using only the Melting Department of McDermott Steel Inc. The following data for the Melting Department are for July 2006:

Inventory in process, July 1, 500 tons:		
Direct materials cost, for 500 tons	$24,550	
Conversion costs, for 500 tons, 70% completed	3,600	
Total inventory in process, July 1		$28,150
Direct materials cost for July, 1,000 tons		50,000
Conversion costs for July		9,690
Goods transferred to Casting in July (includes units in process on July 1), 1,100 tons		?
Inventory in process, July 31, 400 tons, 25% completed as to conversion costs		?

We assume that all materials used in the department are added at the beginning of the process, and conversion costs (direct labor and factory overhead) are incurred evenly throughout the melting process. The objective is to determine the cost of goods completed and the ending inventory valuation, which are represented by the question marks. We determine these amounts by using the following four steps:

1. Determine the units to be assigned costs.
2. Calculate equivalent units of production.
3. Determine the cost per equivalent unit.
4. Allocate costs to transferred and partially completed units.

Step 1: Determine the Units to Be Assigned Costs

The first step in our illustration is to determine the units to be assigned costs. A unit can be any measure of completed production, such as tons, gallons, pounds, barrels, or cases. We use tons as the definition for units in McDermott Steel.

McDermott Steel had 1,500 tons of direct materials charged to production in the Melting Department for July, as shown below.

Total tons charged to production:	
In process, July 1	500 tons
Received from materials storeroom	1,000
Total units accounted for by the Melting Department	1,500 tons

There are three categories of units to be assigned costs for an accounting period: **(A)** units in beginning in-process inventory, **(B)** units started and completed during the period, and **(C)** units in ending in-process inventory. Exhibit 4 illustrates these

---

[1]The average cost method is illustrated in an appendix to this chapter.

categories in the Melting Department for July. The 500-ton beginning inventory **(A)** was completed and transferred to the Casting Department. McDermott Steel started another 1,000 tons of material into the process during July. Of the 1,000 tons introduced in July, 400 tons were left incomplete at the end of the month **(C)**. Thus, only 600 of the 1,000 tons were actually started and completed in July **(B)**.

•Exhibit 4   July Units to Be Costed—Melting Department

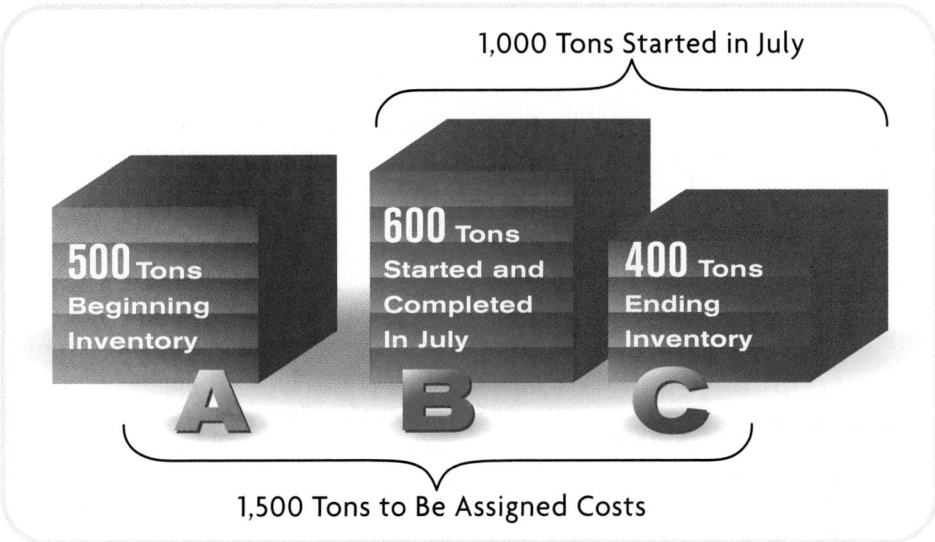

The total units (tons) to be assigned costs for McDermott Steel can be summarized as shown below.

(A)	Inventory in process, July 1, completed in July	500 tons
(B)	Started and completed in July	600
	Transferred out to the Casting Department in July	1,100
(C)	Inventory in process, July 31	400
	Total tons to be assigned costs	1,500 tons

Note that the total tons to be assigned costs equals the total tons accounted for by the department. The three unit categories (**A**, **B**, and **C**) are used in the remaining steps to determine the cost transferred to the Casting Department and the cost remaining in work in process inventory at the end of the period.

INTEGRITY IN BUSINESS

SUVS VS. CARS

All the major automobile manufacturers produce sport utility vehicles (SUVs), which have a history of safety concerns. One major concern is the compatibility of SUVs and cars. Since many SUVs are built on truck frames, an SUV can sweep over a car's frame in crashes with a car built lower to the ground. In side crashes, the danger is even worse for the car passengers, since the SUV frame will impact the car's weaker doors and windows. In addition, SUVs are heavier, thus providing better protection to the SUV passengers but at the expense of the car occupants.

What, if anything, should manufacturers of SUVs do? Recently, the auto industry voluntarily appointed groups to address the issues of frontal- and side-impact crashes involving SUVs and cars. This was done partially in response to regulatory pressure by Congress and the government.

Source: Karen Lundegaard, "Effort Under Way to Increase Safety for Car Passengers in SUV Wrecks," *The Wall Street Journal*, February 14, 2003.

Department 2 received 2,400 tons from Department 1. During the period, Department 2 completed 2,600 tons and had 600 tons of work in process at the beginning of the period. The ending work in process inventory was 400 tons. How many tons were started and completed during the period?

- -

2,000 tons (2,400 − 400, or 2,600 − 600)

Step 2: Calculate Equivalent Units of Production

Process manufacturers often have some partially processed materials remaining in production at the end of a period. In these cases, the costs of production must be allocated between the units that have been completed and transferred to the next process (or finished goods) and those that are only partially completed and remain within the department. This allocation can be determined by using the equivalent units of production.

The ***equivalent units of production*** are the number of units that *could have been* completed within a given accounting period. In contrast, **whole units** are the number of units in production during a period, whether or not completed. For example, assume that 400 whole units are in work in process at the end of a period. If the units are 25% complete, the number of equivalent units in process is 100 (400 × 25%).

> **The equivalent units of production are the number of units that could have been completed during a period.**

Equivalent units for materials and conversion costs are usually determined separately because they are often introduced at different times or at different rates in the production process. In contrast, direct labor and factory overhead are combined together as conversion costs because they are often incurred in production at the same time and rate.

Materials Equivalent Units

To allocate materials costs between the completed and partially completed units, it is necessary to determine how materials are added during the manufacturing process. In the case of McDermott Steel, the materials are added at the beginning of the melting process. In other words, the melting process cannot begin without the scrap metal. The equivalent unit computation for materials in July is as follows:

	Total Whole Units	Percent Materials Added in July	Equivalent Units for Direct Materials
Inventory in process, July 1	500	0%	0
Started and completed in July (1,100 − 500)	600	100%	600
Transferred out to Casting Dept. in July	1,100	—	600
Inventory in process, July 31	400	100%	400
Total tons to be assigned cost	1,500		1,000

Department 3 had 400 tons in beginning work in process inventory (30% complete). During the period, 5,800 tons were completed. The ending work in process inventory was 600 tons (60% complete). What are the equivalent units for direct materials if materials are added at the beginning of the process?

- -

6,000 tons (5,800 − 400 + 600)

The whole units from Step 1 are multiplied by the percentage of materials that are added in July for the in-process inventories and units started and completed. The equivalent units for direct materials are illustrated in Exhibit 5.

The direct materials for the 500 tons of July 1 in-process inventory were introduced in June. Thus, no materials units were added in July for the inventory in process on July 1. All of the 600 tons started and completed in July were 100% complete with respect to materials. Thus, 600 equivalent units of materials were added in July. All the materials for the July 31 in-process inventory were introduced at the beginning of the process. Thus, 400 equivalent units of material for the July 31 in-process inventory were added in July.

Conversion Equivalent Units

The conversion costs are usually incurred evenly throughout a process. For example, direct labor, utilities, and machine depreciation are usually used uniformly during processing. Thus, the conversion equivalent units are added in July in direct relation to the percentage of processing completed in July. The computations for July are as follows:

	Total Whole Units	Percent Conversion Completed in July	Equivalent Units for Conversion
Inventory in process, July 1	500	30%	150
Started and completed in July (1,100 − 500)	600	100%	600
Transferred out to Casting Dept. in July	1,100	—	750
Inventory in process, July 31	400	25%	100
Total tons to be assigned cost	1,500		850

•Exhibit 5   Direct Materials Equivalent Units

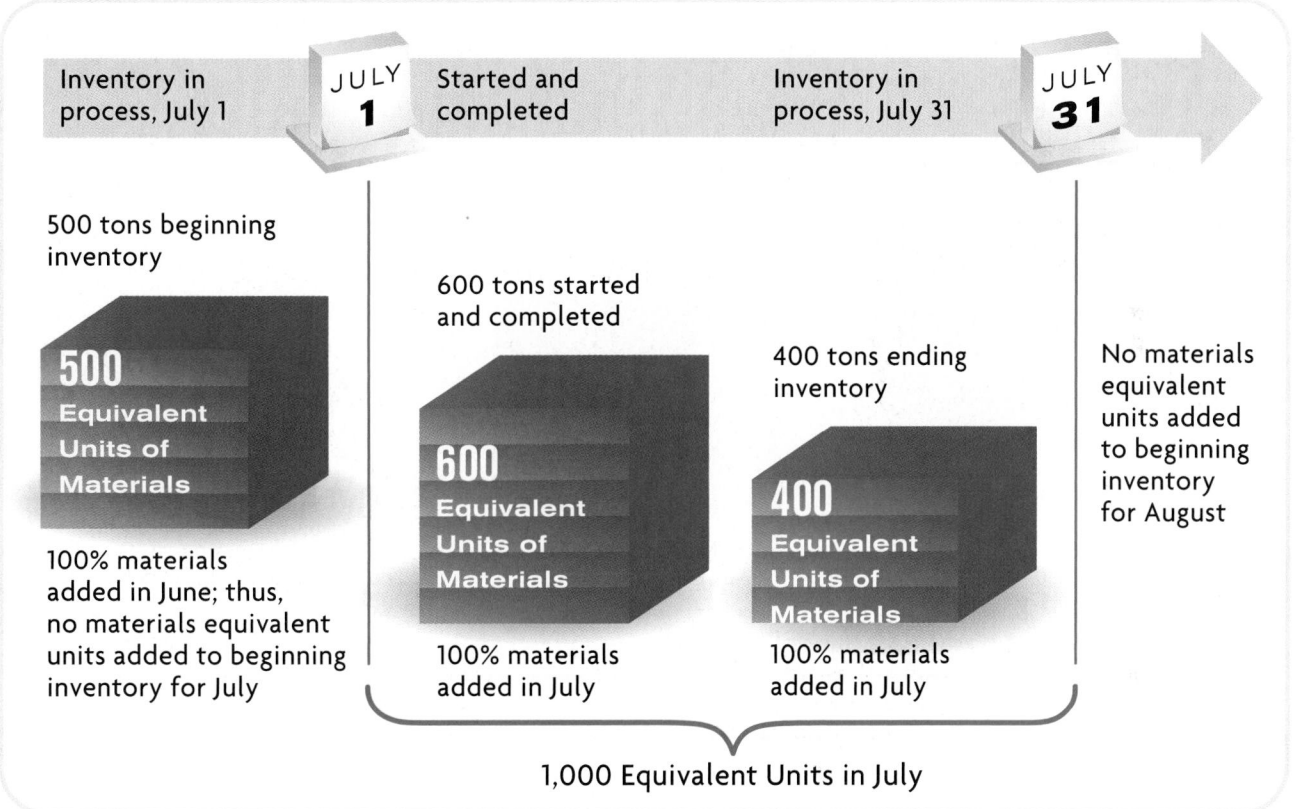

Department 3 had 400 tons in beginning work in process inventory (30% complete). During the period, 5,800 tons were completed. The ending work in process inventory was 600 tons (60% complete). What are the equivalent units for conversion costs?

6,040 tons [(70% × 400) + (5,800 − 400) + (60% × 600)]

The whole units from Step 1 are multiplied by the percentage of conversion completed in July for the in-process inventories and units started and completed. The equivalent units for conversion are illustrated in Exhibit 6.

The conversion equivalent units of the July 1 in-process inventory are 30% of the 500 tons, or 150 equivalent units. Since 70% of the conversion had been completed on July 1, only 30% of the conversion effort for these tons was incurred in July. All the units started and completed used converting effort in July. Thus, conversion equivalent units are 100% of these tons. The equivalent units for the July 31 in-process inventory are 25% of the 400 tons because only 25% of the converting has been completed with respect to these tons in July.

Step 3: Determine the Cost per Equivalent Unit

In Step 3, we calculate the cost per equivalent unit. The July equivalent unit totals for McDermott Steel's Melting Department are reproduced from Step 2 as follows:

	Equivalent Units	
	Direct Materials	**Conversion**
Inventory in process, July 1	0	150
Started and completed in July (1,100 − 500)	600	600
Transferred out to Casting Dept. in July	600	750
Inventory in process, July 31	400	100
Total tons to be assigned cost	1,000	850

•Exhibit 6   Conversion Equivalent Units

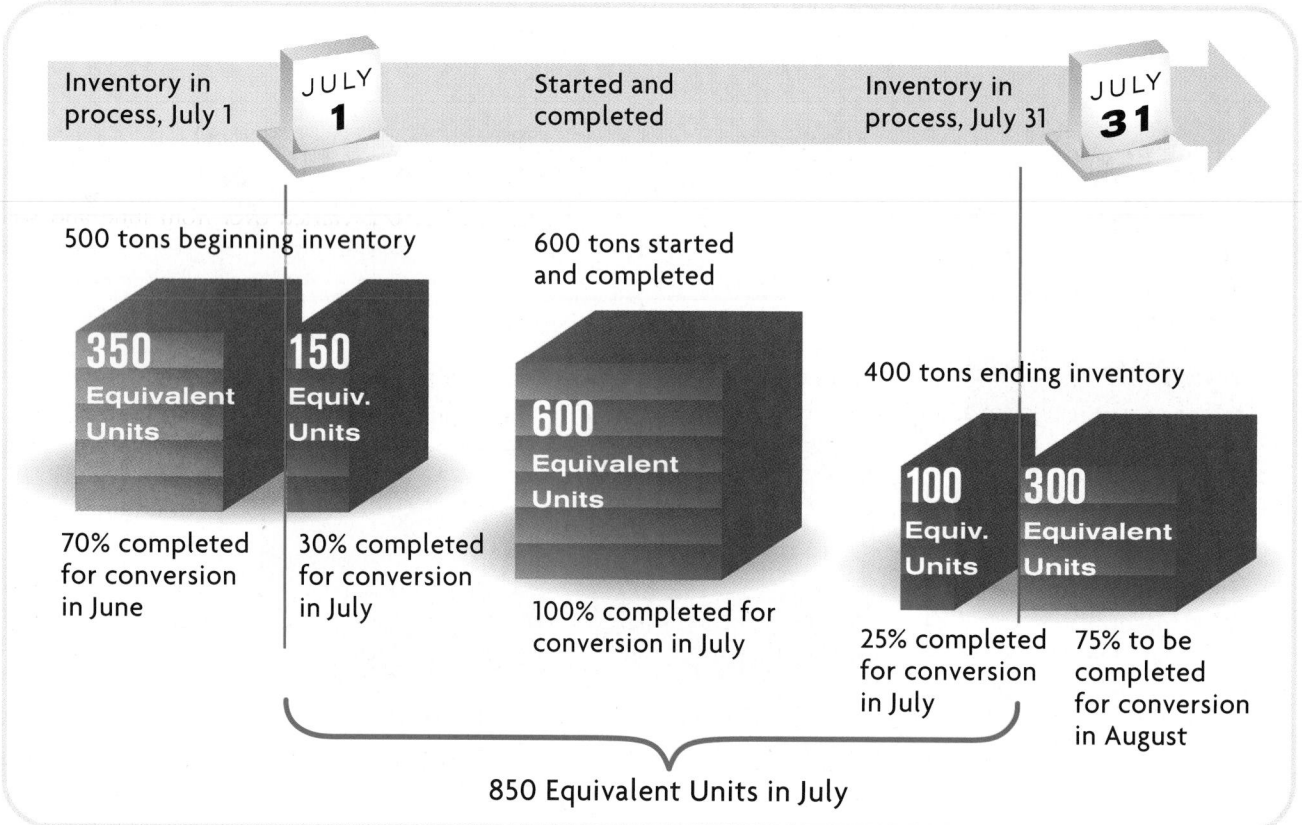

The ***cost per equivalent unit*** is determined by dividing the direct materials and conversion costs incurred in July by the respective total equivalent units for direct materials and conversion costs. The direct materials and conversion costs were given at the beginning of this illustration. These calculations are as follows:

Equivalent unit cost for direct materials:

$$\frac{\$50,000 \text{ direct materials cost}}{1,000 \text{ direct materials equivalent units}} = \begin{array}{l}\$50.00 \text{ per equivalent} \\ \text{unit of direct materials}\end{array}$$

Equivalent unit cost for conversion:

$$\frac{\$9,690 \text{ conversion cost}}{850 \text{ conversion equivalent units}} = \begin{array}{l}\$11.40 \text{ per equivalent} \\ \text{unit of conversion}\end{array}$$

We will use these rates in Step 4 to allocate the direct materials and conversion costs to the completed and partially completed units.

Step 4: Allocate Costs to Transferred and Partially Completed Units

In Step 4, we multiply the equivalent unit rates by their respective equivalent units of production in order to determine the cost of transferred and partially completed units. The cost of the July 1 in-process inventory, completed and transferred out to the Casting Department, is determined as follows:

What costs are included in the $28,150 beginning work in process inventory for McDermott Steel?

70% of the conversion cost and all of the materials costs for 500 tons.

	Direct Materials Costs	Conversion Costs	Total Costs
Inventory in process, July 1 balance			$28,150
Equivalent units for completing the July 1 in-process inventory	0	150	
Equivalent unit cost	×$50.00	×$11.40	
Cost of completed July 1 in-process inventory	0	$1,710	1,710
Cost of July 1 in-process inventory transferred to Casting Department			$29,860

The July 1 in-process inventory cost of $28,150 is carried over from June and will be transferred to Casting. The cost required to finish the July 1 in-process inventory is $1,710, which consists of conversion costs required to complete the remaining 30% of the processing. This total does not include direct materials costs, since these costs were added at the beginning of the process in June. The conversion costs required to complete the beginning inventory are added to the balance carried over from the previous month to yield a total cost of the completed July 1 in-process inventory of $29,860.

The 600 units started and completed in July receive 100% of their direct materials and conversion costs in July. The costs associated with the units started and completed are determined by multiplying the equivalent units in Step 2 by the unit costs in Step 3, as follows:

	Direct Materials Costs	Conversion Costs	Total Costs
Units started and completed in July	600	600	
Equivalent unit cost	×$50.00	×$11.40	
Cost to complete the units started and completed in July	$ 30,000	$ 6,840	$36,840

The total cost transferred to the Casting Department is the sum of the beginning inventory cost from the previous period ($28,150), the additional costs incurred in July to complete the beginning inventory ($1,710), and the costs incurred for the units started and completed in July ($36,840). Thus, the total cost transferred to Casting is $66,700.

The units of ending inventory have not been transferred, so they must be valued at July 31. The costs associated with the partially completed units in the ending inventory are determined by multiplying the equivalent units in Step 2 by the unit costs in Step 3, as follows:

	Direct Materials Costs	Conversion Costs	Total Costs
Equivalent units in ending inventory	400	100	
Equivalent unit cost	×$50.00	×$11.40	
Cost of ending inventory	$ 20,000	$ 1,140	$21,140

The units in the ending inventory have received 100% of their materials in July. Thus, the materials cost incurred in July for the ending inventory is $20,000, or 400 equivalent units of materials multiplied by $50. The conversion cost incurred in July for the ending inventory is $1,140, which is 100 equivalent units of conversion (400 units, 25% complete) for the ending inventory multiplied by $11.40. Summing the conversion and materials costs, the total ending inventory cost is $21,140.

Bringing It All Together: The Cost of Production Report

objective   4

Prepare a cost of production report.

A *cost of production report* is normally prepared for each processing department at periodic intervals. The July cost of production report for McDermott Steel's Melting Department is shown in Exhibit 7. As can be seen on the report, the two question marks from page 788 can now be determined. The cost of goods transferred

•**Exhibit 7**   Cost of Production Report for McDermott Steel's Melting Department—FIFO

McDermott Steel Inc.
Cost of Production Report—Melting Department
For the Month Ended July 31, 2006

UNITS	Whole Units (Step 1)	Equivalent Units (Step 2) Direct Materials	Conversion
Units charged to production:			
Inventory in process, July 1	500		
Received from materials storeroom	1,000		
Total units accounted for by the Melting Dept.	1,500		
Units to be assigned cost:			
Inventory in process, July 1 (70% completed)	500	0	150
Started and completed in July	600	600	600
Transferred to Casting Department in July	1,100	600	750
Inventory in process, July 31 (25% complete)	400	400	100
Total units to be assigned cost	1,500	1,000	850

COSTS	Direct Materials	Costs Conversion	Total Costs
Unit costs (Step 3):			
Total costs for July in Melting Dept.	$50,000	$9,690	
Total equivalent units (from Step 2 above)	÷ 1,000	÷ 850	
Cost per equivalent unit	$ 50.00	$11.40	
Costs charged to production:			
Inventory in process, July 1			$28,150
Costs incurred in July			59,690
Total costs accounted for by the Melting Dept.			$87,840
Costs allocated to completed and partially completed units (Step 4):			
Inventory in process, July 1—balance			$28,150
To complete inventory in process, July 1	$ 0	$1,710[a]	1,710
Started and completed in July	30,000[b]	6,840[c]	36,840
Transferred to Casting Dept. in July			$66,700
Inventory in process, July 31	$20,000[d]	$1,140[e]	21,140
Total costs assigned by the Melting Dept.			$87,840

[a]150 units × $11.40 = $1,710   [b]600 units × $50.00 = $30,000   [c]600 units × $11.40 = $6,840   [d]400 units × $50.00 = $20,000   [e]100 units × $11.40 = $1,140

to the Casting Department in July was $66,700, while the cost of the ending work in process in the Melting Department on July 31 is $21,140.

The report summarizes the four previous steps by providing the following production quantity and cost data:

1. The units for which the department is accountable and the disposition of those units.
2. The production costs incurred by the department and the allocation of those costs between completed and partially completed units.

The cost of production report is also used to control costs. Each department manager is responsible for the units entering production and the costs incurred in the department. Any failure to account for all costs and any significant differences in unit product costs from one month to another should be investigated.

Journal Entries for a Process Cost System

objective 5

Prepare journal entries for transactions of a process manufacturer.

To illustrate the journal entries to record the cost flows in a process costing system, we will use the July transactions for McDermott Steel. The entries in summary form for these transactions are shown here and on the following page. In practice, transactions would be recorded daily.

		JOURNAL			
Date		Description	Post. Ref.	Debit	Credit
	a.	Materials		62 000 00	
		Accounts Payable			62 000 00
		Materials purchased on account.			
	b.	Work in Process—Melting		50 000 00	
		Factory Overhead—Melting		4 000 00	
		Factory Overhead—Casting		3 000 00	
		Materials			57 000 00
		Materials requisitioned.			
	c.	Work in Process—Melting		5 000 00	
		Work in Process—Casting		4 500 00	
		Wages Payable			9 500 00
		Direct labor used.			
	d.	Factory Overhead—Melting		1 000 00	
		Factory Overhead—Casting		7 000 00	
		Accumulated Depreciation			8 000 00
		Depreciation expenses.			
	e.	Work in Process—Melting		4 690 00	
		Work in Process—Casting		9 640 00	
		Factory Overhead—Melting			4 690 00
		Factory Overhead—Casting			9 640 00
		Factory overhead applied.			
	f.	Work in Process—Casting		66 700 00	
		Work in Process—Melting			66 700 00
		Melting Department transferred			
		$66,700 to Casting Department			
		(from Exhibit 7).			

g.	Finished Goods		78 6 0 0 00		
	Work in Process—Casting			78 6 0 0 00
	Casting Department transferred			
	$78,600 to Finished Goods.			
h.	Cost of Goods Sold		73 7 0 0 00	
	Finished Goods			73 7 0 0 00
	Goods sold.			

Exhibit 8 shows the flow of costs for each transaction. Note that the highlighted amounts in Exhibit 8 were determined from assigning the costs charged to production in the Melting Department. These amounts were computed and are shown at the bottom of the cost of production report for the Melting Department in Exhibit 7. Likewise, the amount transferred out of the Casting Department to Finished Goods would have also been determined from a cost of production report for the Casting Department.

•Exhibit 8 McDermott Steel's Cost Flows

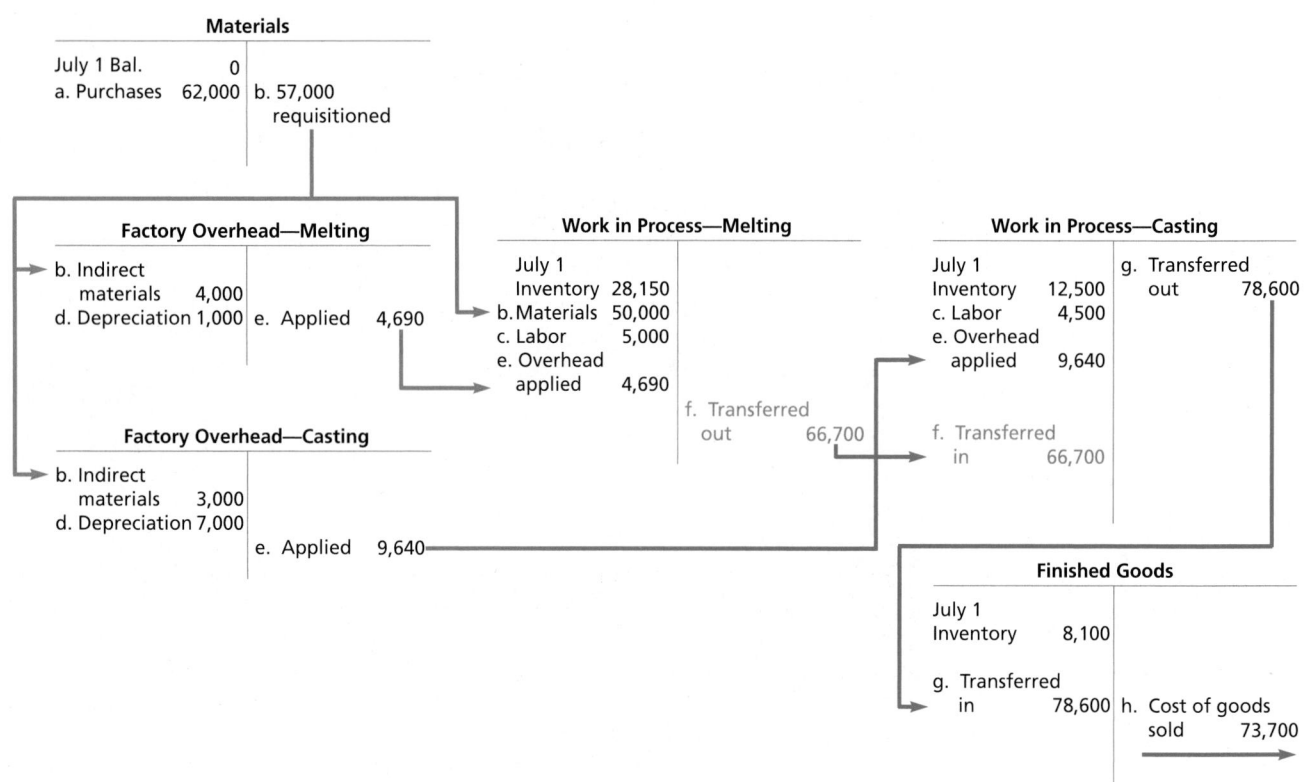

Using the Cost of Production Report for Decision Making

objective **6**

Use cost of production reports for decision making.

The cost of production report is one source of information that may be used by managers to control and improve operations. A cost of production report will normally list costs in greater detail than in Exhibit 7. This greater detail helps management isolate problems and opportunities. To illustrate, assume that the Blending

Department of Holland Beverage Company prepared cost of production reports for April and May. In addition, assume that the Blending Department had no beginning or ending work in process inventory either month. Thus, in this simple case, there is no need to determine equivalent units of production for allocating costs between completed and partially completed units. The cost of production reports for April and May in the Blending Department are as follows:

Cost of Production Reports
Holland Beverage Company—Blending Department
For the Months Ended April 30 and May 31, 2006

	April	May
Direct materials	$ 20,000	$ 40,600
Direct labor	15,000	29,400
Energy	8,000	20,000
Repairs	4,000	8,000
Tank cleaning	3,000	8,000
Total	$ 50,000	$ 106,000
Units completed	÷ 100,000	÷ 200,000
Cost per unit	$ 0.50	$ 0.53

Note that the preceding reports provide more cost detail than simply reporting direct materials and conversion costs. The May results indicate that total unit costs have increased from $0.50 to $0.53, or 6% from the previous month. What caused this increase? To determine the possible causes for this increase, the cost of production report may be restated in per-unit terms, as shown below.

Blending Department Per-Unit
Expense Comparisons

	April	May	% Change
Direct materials	$0.200	$0.203	1.50%
Direct labor	0.150	0.147	−2.00%
Energy	0.080	0.100	25.00%
Repairs	0.040	0.040	0.00%
Tank cleaning	0.030	0.040	33.33%
Total	$0.500	$0.530	6.00%

Both energy and tank cleaning per-unit costs have increased dramatically in May. Further investigation should focus on these costs. For example, an increasing trend in energy may indicate that the machines are losing fuel efficiency, thereby requiring the company to purchase an increasing amount of fuel. This unfavorable trend could motivate management to repair the machines. The tank cleaning costs could be investigated in a similar fashion.

In addition to unit production cost trends, managers of process manufacturers are also concerned about yield trends. **Yield** is the ratio of the materials output quantity to the input quantity. A yield less than one occurs when the output quantity is less than the input quantity due to materials losses during the process. For example, if 1,000 pounds of sugar entered the packing operation, and only 980 pounds of sugar were packed, the yield would be 98%. Two percent or 20 pounds of sugar were lost or spilled during the packing process.

REAL WORLD

Middle Tennessee Lumber Company produces cabinet and furniture panels from various hardwoods. The company purchased new computer and sawing technology that improved the cutting yield by approximately 10%. The cutting yield is the ratio of finished panel board feet to the number of board feet input to the sawing operation. The new equipment scans the rough-cut lumber with a laser beam. The scanned information is input to a software program that calculates the optimum cutting pattern for minimizing trim waste. The wood is then sent to a computer-controlled saw, which proceeds to cut the board according to the calculations from the laser scan.

Just-in-Time Processing

objective 7

Contrast just-in-time processing with conventional manufacturing practices.

The objective of many companies is to produce products with high quality, low cost, and instant availability. One approach to achieving this objective is to implement just-in-time processing. **Just-in-time processing (JIT)** is a philosophy that focuses on reducing time and cost and eliminating poor quality. A JIT system achieves production efficiencies and flexibility by reorganizing the traditional production process.

In a traditional production process (illustrated in Exhibit 9), a product moves from process to process as each function or step is completed. Each worker is assigned a specific job, which is performed repeatedly as unfinished products are received from the preceding department. For example, a furniture manufacturer might use seven production departments to perform the operating functions necessary to manufacture furniture, as shown in the diagram in Exhibit 9.

•Exhibit 9

TRADITIONAL PRODUCTION LINE

Furniture Manufacturer

Wood — CUTTING DEPARTMENT — DRILLING DEPARTMENT — SANDING DEPARTMENT — STAINING DEPARTMENT — VARNISHING DEPARTMENT — UPHOLSTERY DEPARTMENT — ASSEMBLY DEPARTMENT — Finished Goods

POINT OF INTEREST

The Internet complements a just-in-time processing strategy. **Ford Motor Company** states that the impact of the Internet is the equivalent of "the moving assembly line of the 21st Century." This is because the Internet will connect the whole supply chain—from customers to suppliers—to create a fast and efficient manufacturing system. As stated by William Clay Ford, Chairman of Ford Motor, "The automobile is about to undergo the most profound and revolutionary changes it's seen since the Model T first hit the streets."

For the furniture maker in the illustration, manufacturing would begin in the Cutting Department, where the wood would be cut to design specifications. Next, the Drilling Department would perform the drilling function, after which the Sanding Department would sand the wood, the Staining Department would stain the furniture, and the Varnishing Department would apply varnish and other protective coatings. Then, the Upholstery Department would add fabric and other materials. Finally, the Assembly Department would assemble the furniture to complete the process.

In the traditional production process, production supervisors attempt to enter enough materials into the process to keep all the manufacturing departments operating. Some departments, however, may process materials more rapidly than others. In addition, if one department stops production because of machine breakdowns, for example, the preceding departments usually continue production in order to avoid idle time. This may result in a build-up of work in process inventories in some departments.

In a just-in-time system, processing functions are combined into work centers, sometimes called **manufacturing cells**. For example, the seven departments illustrated above for the furniture manufacturer might be reorganized into three work centers. As shown in the diagram in Exhibit 10, Work Center One would perform the cutting, drilling, and sanding functions, Work Center Two would perform the staining and varnishing functions, and Work Center Three would perform the upholstery and assembly functions.

In the traditional production line, a worker typically performs only one function. However, in a work center in which several functions take place, the workers are often cross-trained to perform more than one function. Research has indicated that

•Exhibit 10

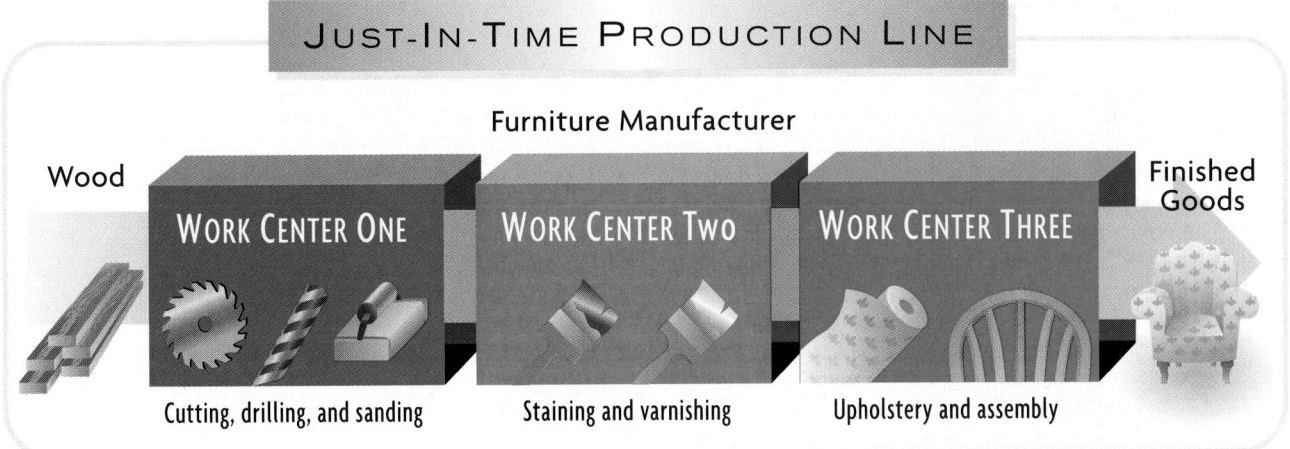

JUST-IN-TIME PRODUCTION LINE

Furniture Manufacturer

Wood — WORK CENTER ONE — WORK CENTER TWO — WORK CENTER THREE — Finished Goods

Cutting, drilling, and sanding   Staining and varnishing   Upholstery and assembly

REAL WORLD

American automakers are continuing to look for ways to be more efficient and catch up with their offshore rivals. One basis of competition is the number of direct labor hours per vehicle (HPV). The "Big 3" reported the following HPV statistics for 2003:

Ford	26.14
General Motors	24.40
Chrysler	28.04

The best plant in the United States was Nissan's Smyrna, Tennessee operations, with 15.74 HPV. While **Ford**, **GM**, and **Chrysler** are all improving their productivity, they are still lagging behind **Toyota**, **Honda**, and **Nissan**, which have many North American plants at less than 22 HPV.

Source: *Harbour Report North America 2003*, Harbour and Associates.

workers who perform several manufacturing functions identify better with the end product. This creates pride in the product and improves quality and productivity.

Implementing JIT may also result in reorganizing service activities. Specifically, the service activities may be assigned to individual work centers, rather than to centralized service departments. For example, each work center may be assigned the responsibility for the repair and maintenance of its machinery and equipment. Accepting this responsibility creates an environment in which workers gain a better understanding of the production process and the machinery. In turn, workers tend to take better care of the machinery, which decreases repairs and maintenance costs, reduces machine downtime, and improves product quality.

In a JIT system, wasted motion from moving the product and materials is reduced. The product is often placed on a movable carrier that is centrally located in the work center. After the workers in a work center have completed their activities with the product, the entire carrier and any additional materials are moved just in time to satisfy the demand or need of the next work center. In this sense, the product is said to be "pulled through." Each work center is connected to other work centers through information contained on Kanbans, which is a Japanese term for cards.

The experience of **Caterpillar Inc.** illustrates the impact of JIT. Before implementing JIT, an average transmission would travel 10 miles through the factory and require 1,000 pieces of paper for materials, labor, and movement transactions. After implementing JIT, Caterpillar improved manufacturing so that an average transmission traveled only 200 feet and required only 10 pieces of paper.

In summary, the primary benefit of JIT systems is the increased efficiency of operations, which is achieved by eliminating waste and simplifying the production process. At the same time, JIT systems emphasize continuous improvement in the manufacturing process and the improvement of product quality.

Appendix   Average Cost Method

A manufacturer uses a cost flow assumption in determining the costs flowing into, out of, and remaining in each manufacturing department. In this chapter, we illustrated the first-in, first-out cost flow assumption for the Melting Department of McDermott Steel Inc. In this appendix, we illustrate the average cost flow method for Gemini Steel Corporation.

P&G'S "PIT STOPS"

What do **Procter & Gamble** and Formula One racing have in common? The answer begins with P&G's Packing Department, which is where detergents and other products are filled on a "pack line." Containers move down the pack line and are filled with products from a multihead packing machine. When it was time to change from a 36-oz. to a 54-oz. *Tide* box, for example, the changeover involved stopping the line, adjusting guide rails, retrieving items from the tool room, placing items back in the tool room, changing and cleaning the pack heads, and performing routine maintenance. Changing the pack line could be a very difficult process and typically took up to eight hours. Management realized that it was important to reduce this time significantly in order to become more flexible and cost efficient in packing products. Where could they learn how to do changeovers faster? They turned to Formula One racing, reasoning that a pit stop was much like a changeover. As a result, P&G videotaped actual Formula One pit stops. These videos were used to form the following principles for conducting a fast changeover:

- Position the tools near their point of use on the line prior to stopping the line, to reduce time going back and forth to the tool room.
- Arrange the tools in the exact order of work, so that no time is wasted looking for a tool.
- Have each employee perform a very specific task during the changeover.
- Design the workflow so that employees don't interfere with each other.
- Have each employee in position at the moment the line is stopped.
- Train each employee, and practice, practice, practice.
- Put a stop watch on the changeover process.
- Plot improvements over time on a visible chart.

As a result of these changes, P&G was able to reduce pack-line changeover time from eight hours to 20 minutes. This allowed them to produce a much larger variety of products every day and to improve the cost performance of the Packing Department.

Determining Costs Under the Average Cost Method

Gemini's operations are similar to those of McDermott Steel in that Gemini melts scrap metal and then pours the molten metal into an ingot casting. Like McDermott Steel, Gemini has two manufacturing departments, Melting and Casting. To illustrate the average cost method, we simplify by using only the Melting Department of Gemini Steel. The manufacturing data for the Melting Department for July 2006 are as follows:

Work in process inventory, July 1, 500 tons (70% completed)	$28,050
Direct materials cost incurred in July, 1,000 tons	50,000
Direct labor cost incurred in July	4,000
Factory overhead applied in July	4,350
Total production costs to account for	$86,400
Cost of goods transferred to Casting in July (includes units in process on July 1), 1,100 tons	?
Cost of work in process inventory, July 31, 400 tons, 25% completed as to conversion costs	?

Using the average cost method, our objective is to allocate the total costs of production of $86,400 to the 1,100 tons completed and transferred to the Casting Department and the costs of the remaining 400 tons in the ending work in process inventory. These costs are represented in the preceding table by two question marks. We determine these amounts by using the following four steps:

1. Determine the units to be assigned costs.
2. Calculate equivalent units of production.
3. Determine the cost per equivalent unit.
4. Allocate costs to transferred and partially completed units.

Step 1: Determine the Units to Be Assigned Costs

The first step in our illustration is to determine the units to be assigned costs. A unit can be any measure of completed production, such as tons, gallons, pounds, barrels, or cases. We use tons as the definition for units in Gemini Steel.

Gemini Steel's Melting Department had 1,500 tons of direct materials to account for during July, as shown here:

Total tons to account for:	
Work in process, July 1	500 tons
Received from materials storeroom	1,000
Total units to account for by the Melting Department	1,500 tons

There are two categories of units to be assigned costs for the period: (1) units completed and transferred out and (2) units in the ending work in process inventory. During July, the Melting Department completed and transferred 1,100 tons to the Casting Department. Of the 1,000 tons started in July, 600 tons were completed and transferred to the Casting Department. Thus, the ending work in process inventory consists of 400 tons.

The total units (tons) to be assigned costs for Gemini Steel can be summarized as follows:

(1) Transferred out to the Casting Department in July	1,100 tons
(2) Work in process inventory, July 31	400
Total tons to be assigned costs	1,500 tons

Note that the total units (tons) to be assigned costs (1,500 tons) equals the total units to account for (1,500 tons).

Step 2: Calculate Equivalent Units of Production

Gemini Steel has 400 tons of whole units in the work in process inventory for the Melting Department on July 31. Since these units are 25% complete, the number of equivalent units in process in the Melting Department on July 31 is 100 tons (400 tons $\times$ 0.25). Since the units transferred to the Casting Department have been completed, the whole units (1,100 tons) transferred are the same as the equivalent units transferred.

The total equivalent units of production for the Melting Department is determined by adding the equivalent units in the ending work in process inventory to the units transferred and completed during the period as shown here:

Equivalent units completed and transferred to the Casting Department during July	1,100 tons
Equivalent units in ending work in process, July 31	100
Total equivalent units	1,200 tons

Step 3: Determine the Cost per Equivalent Unit

Materials and conversion costs are often combined in computing cost per equivalent unit under the average cost method. In doing so, the cost per equivalent unit is determined by dividing the total production costs by the total equivalent units of production as follows:

$$\text{Cost per equivalent unit} = \frac{\text{Total production costs}}{\text{Total equivalent units}} = \frac{\$86,400}{1,200 \text{ tons}} = \$72$$

We use the cost per equivalent unit in Step 4 to allocate the production costs to the completed and partially completed units.

Step 4: Allocate Costs to Transferred and Partially Completed Units

In Step 4, we multiply the cost per equivalent unit by the equivalent units of production to determine the cost of transferred and partially completed units. For the Melting Department, these costs are determined as shown:

(1) Transferred out to the Casting Depart. (1,100 tons × $72)	$79,200
(2) Work in process inventory, July 31 (400 tons × 0.25 complete × $72)	7,200
Total production costs assigned	$86,400

The Cost of Production Report

The July cost of production report for Gemini Steel's Melting Department is shown in Exhibit 11. The cost of production report in Exhibit 11 summarizes the following:

1. The units for which the department is accountable and the disposition of those units.
2. The production costs incurred by the department and the allocation of those costs between completed and partially completed units.

•Exhibit 11   Cost of Production Report for Gemini Steel's Melting Department

GEMINI STEEL CORPORATION
Cost of Production Report—Melting Department
For the Month Ended July 31, 2006

Units	Whole Units (Step 1)	Equivalent Units of Production (Step 2)
Units to account for during production:		
Work in process inventory, July 1	500	
Received from materials storeroom	1,000	
Total units accounted for by the Melting Dept.	1,500	
Units to be assigned cost:		
Transferred to Casting Department in July	1,100	1,100
Inventory in process, July 31 (25% complete)	400	100
Total units to be assigned cost	1,500	1,200
Costs		
Cost per equivalent unit (Step 3):		
Total production costs for July in Melting Dept.		$86,400
Total equivalent units (from Step 2 above)		÷ 1,200
Cost per equivalent unit		$ 72
Costs assigned to production:		
Inventory in process, July 1		$28,050
Direct materials and conversion costs incurred in July		58,350
Total production costs accounted for by the Melting Dept.		$86,400
Costs allocated to transferred and partially completed units (Step 4):		
Transferred to Casting Dept. in July (1,100 units × $72)		$79,200
Inventory in process, July 31 (400 units × 0.25 × $72)		7,200
Total costs assigned by the Melting Dept.		$86,400

ey Points

1 Distinguish between job order costing and process costing systems.

The process cost system is best suited for industries that mass-produce identical units of a product that often have passed through a sequence of processes on a continuous basis. In process cost accounting, costs are charged to processing departments, and the cost of the finished unit is determined by dividing the total cost incurred in each process by the number of units produced.

2 Explain and illustrate the physical flows and cost flows for a process manufacturer.

Materials are introduced, converted, and passed from one department to the next department or to finished goods. The accumulated costs transferred from preceding departments and the costs of direct materials and direct labor incurred in each processing department are debited to the related work in process account in a process cost system. Each work in process account is also debited for the factory overhead applied.

3 Calculate and interpret the accounting for completed and partially completed units under the fifo method.

Frequently, partially processed materials remain in various stages of production in a department at the end of a period. In this case, the manufacturing costs must be allocated between the units that have been completed and those that are only partially completed and remain within the department. To allocate processing costs between the output completed and the inventory of goods within the department under fifo, it is necessary to determine the number of equivalent units of production during the period for the beginning inventory, units started and completed currently, and the ending inventory.

4 Prepare a cost of production report.

A cost of production report is prepared periodically for each processing department. It summarizes (1) the units for which the department is accountable and the disposition of those units and (2) the production costs incurred by the department and the allocation of those costs. The report is used to control costs and improve the process.

5 Prepare journal entries for transactions of a process manufacturer.

Summary journal entries for common process manufacturer transactions are illustrated for McDermott Steel in the text. Basic entries include debit-ing the processing department work in process account for direct materials, direct labor, and applied factory overhead costs incurred in production. Costs for completed units are credited to the transferring department's work in process account and debited to the receiving department's work in process account.

6 Use cost of production reports for decision making.

The cost of production report provides information for controlling and improving operations. Most cost of production reports include the detailed manufacturing costs incurred for completing production during the period. Analyzing trends in each of these costs over time can provide insights about process performance.

7 Contrast just-in-time processing with conventional manufacturing practices.

The just-in-time processing philosophy focuses on reducing time, cost, and poor quality within the process. This is accomplished by combining process functions into work centers, assigning overhead services directly to the cells, involving the employees in process improvement efforts, eliminating wasteful activities, and reducing the amount of work in process inventory required to fulfill production targets.

ey Terms

cost of production report (714)
cost per equivalent unit (712)
equivalent units of production (710)

first-in, first-out (fifo) method (708)
just-in-time processing (JIT) (718)
manufacturing cells (718)

process cost system (704)
process manufacturers (704)
yield (717)

Illustrative Problem

Southern Aggregate Company manufactures concrete by a series of four processes. All materials are introduced in Crushing. From Crushing, the materials pass through Sifting, Baking, and Mixing, emerging as finished concrete. All inventories are costed by the first-in, first-out method.

The balances in the accounts Work in Process—Mixing and Finished Goods were as follows on May 1, 2006:

Work in Process—Mixing (2,000 units, 1/4 completed)	$13,700
Finished Goods (1,800 units at $8.00 a unit)	14,400

The following costs were charged to Work in Process—Mixing during May:

Direct materials transferred from Baking:	
15,200 units at $6.50 a unit	$98,800
Direct labor	17,200
Factory overhead	11,780

During May, 16,000 units of concrete were completed, and 15,800 units were sold. Inventories on May 31 were as follows:

Work in Process—Mixing: 1,200 units, 1/2 completed	
Finished Goods: 2,000 units	

Instructions

1. Prepare a cost of production report for the Mixing Department.
2. Determine the cost of goods sold (indicate number of units and unit costs).
3. Determine the finished goods inventory, May 31, 2006.

Solution

1.

Southern Aggregate Company
Cost of Production Report—Mixing Department
For the Month Ended May 31, 2006

		Equivalent Units	
UNITS	Whole Units	Direct Materials	Conversion
Units charged to production:			
Inventory in process, May 1	2,000		
Received from Baking	15,200		
Total units accounted for by the Mixing Dept.	17,200		
Units to be assigned cost:			
Inventory in process, May 1 (25% completed)	2,000	0	1,500
Started and completed in May	14,000	14,000	14,000
Transferred to finished goods in May	16,000	14,000	15,500
Inventory in process, May 31 (50% complete)	1,200	1,200	600
Total units to be assigned cost	17,200	15,200	16,100

COSTS		Costs		
		Direct Materials	Conversion	Total Costs
Unit costs:				
Total cost for May in Mixing		$ 98,800	$ 28,980	
Total equivalent units (from above)		÷15,200	÷16,100	
Cost per equivalent unit		$ 6.50	$ 1.80	
Costs charged to production:				
Inventory in process, May 1				$ 13,700
Costs incurred in May				127,780
Total costs accounted for by the Mixing Dept.				$141,480

		Direct Materials	Conversion	Total Costs
Costs allocated to completed and partially completed units:				
Inventory in process, May 1—balance				$13,700
To complete inventory in process, May 1		$ 0	$ 2,700 (a)	2,700
Started and completed in May		91,000 (b)	25,200 (c)	116,200
Transferred to finished goods in May				$132,600
Inventory in process, May 31		$ 7,800 (d)	$ 1,080 (e)	8,880
Total costs assigned by the Mixing Department				$141,480

(a) 1,500 × $1.80 = $2,700   (c) 14,000 × $1.80 = $25,200   (e) 600 × $1.80 = $1,080
(b) 14,000 × $6.50 = $91,000   (d) 1,200 × $6.50 = $7,800

2. Cost of goods sold:

1,800 units at $8.00	$ 14,400	(from finished goods beginning inventory)
2,000 units at $8.20*	16,400	(from work in process beginning inventory)
12,000 units at $8.30**	99,600	(from May production started and completed)
15,800 units	$130,400	

*($13,700 + $2,700) ÷ 2,000
**$116,200 ÷ 14,000

3. Finished goods inventory, May 31:

2,000 units at $8.30 $16,600

Self-Examination Questions (Answers at End of Chapter)

1. For which of the following businesses would the process cost system be most appropriate?
   A. Custom furniture manufacturer
   B. Commercial building contractor
   C. Crude oil refinery
   D. Automobile repair shop

2. There were 2,000 pounds in process at the beginning of the period in the Packing Department. Packing received 24,000 pounds from the Blending Department during the month, of which 3,000 pounds were in process at the end of the month. How many pounds were completed and transferred to finished goods from the Packing Department?
   A. 23,000   C. 26,000
   B. 21,000   D. 29,000

3. Information relating to production in Department A for May is as follows:

May	1	Balance, 1,000 units, ¾ completed	$22,150
	31	Direct materials, 5,000 units	75,000
	31	Direct labor	32,500
	31	Factory overhead	16,250

If 500 units were one-fourth completed at May 31, 5,500 units were completed during May, and inventories are costed by the first-in, first-out method, what was the number of equivalent units of production with respect to conversion costs for May?
   A. 4,500   C. 5,500
   B. 4,875   D. 6,000

4. Based on the data presented in Question 3, what is the conversion cost per equivalent unit?
   A. $10   C. $25
   B. $15   D. $32

5. Information from the accounting system revealed the following:

	Day 1	Day 2	Day 3	Day 4	Day 5
Materials	$ 20,000	$18,000	$ 22,000	$ 20,000	$ 20,000
Electricity	2,500	3,000	3,500	4,000	4,700
Maintenance	4,000	3,750	3,400	3,000	2,800
Total costs	$ 26,500	$24,750	$ 28,900	$ 27,000	$ 27,500
Pounds produced	÷10,000	÷9,000	÷11,000	÷10,000	÷10,000
Cost per unit	$ 2.65	$ 2.75	$ 2.63	$ 2.70	$ 2.75

Which of the following statements best interprets this information?

A. The total costs are out of control.
B. The product costs have steadily increased because of higher electricity costs.
C. Electricity costs have steadily increased because of lack of maintenance.
D. The unit costs reveal a significant operating problem.

Class Discussion Questions

1. Which type of cost system, process or job order, would be best suited for each of the following: (a) custom jewelry manufacturer, (b) paper manufacturer, (c) automobile repair shop, (d) building contractor, (e) TV assembler? Give reasons for your answers.
2. In job order cost accounting, the three elements of manufacturing cost are charged directly to job orders. Why is it not necessary to charge manufacturing costs in process cost accounting to job orders?
3. In a job order cost system, direct labor and factory overhead applied are debited to individual jobs. How are these items treated in a process cost system and why?
4. What are transferred-out materials?
5. What are the four steps for determining the cost of goods completed and the ending inventory?
6. What is meant by the term *equivalent units*?
7. Why is the cost per equivalent unit often determined separately for direct materials and conversion costs?
8. What is the purpose for determining the cost per equivalent unit?
9. Domingo Company is a process manufacturer with two production departments, Departments A and B. All direct materials are introduced in Department A from the materials store area. What is included in the cost transferred to Department B?
10. How is actual factory overhead accounted for in a process manufacturer?
11. What is the most important purpose of the cost of production report?
12. How are cost of production reports used for controlling and improving operations?
13. How is "yield" determined for a process manufacturer?
14. What is just-in-time processing?
15. How does just-in-time processing differ from the conventional manufacturing process?

Exercises

EXERCISE 17-1
Entries for materials cost flows in a process cost system
Objective 2

REAL WORLD   SPREADSHEET

Hershey Foods Corporation manufactures chocolate confectionery products. The three largest raw materials are cocoa beans, sugar, and dehydrated milk. These raw materials first go into the Blending Department. The blended product is then sent to the Molding Department, where the bars of candy are formed. The candy is then sent to the Packing Department, where the bars are wrapped and boxed. The boxed candy is then sent to the distribution center, where it is eventually sold to food brokers and retailers.

Show the accounts debited and credited for each of the following business events:

a. Materials used by the Blending Department.
b. Transfer of blended product to the Molding Department.
c. Transfer of candy to the Packing Department.
d. Transfer of boxed candy to the distribution center.
e. Sale of boxed candy.

EXERCISE 17-2
Flowchart of accounts related to service and processing departments
Objective 2

REAL WORLD

Alcoa Inc. is the world's largest producer of aluminum products. One product that Alcoa manufactures is aluminum sheet products for the aerospace industry. The entire output of the Smelting Department is transferred to the Rolling Department. Part of the fully processed goods from the Rolling Department are sold as rolled sheet, and the remainder of the goods are transferred to the Converting Department for further processing into sheared sheet.

Prepare a chart of the flow of costs from the processing department accounts into the finished goods accounts and then into the cost of goods sold account. The relevant accounts are as follows:

Cost of Goods Sold	Finished Goods—Rolled Sheet
Materials	Finished Goods—Sheared Sheet
Factory Overhead—Smelting Department	Work in Process—Smelting Department
Factory Overhead—Rolling Department	Work in Process—Rolling Department
Factory Overhead—Converting Department	Work in Process—Converting Department

EXERCISE 17-3
Entries for flow of factory costs for process cost system
Objectives 2, 5

REAL WORLD

The **Domino Sugar Corporation** manufactures a sugar product by a continuous process, involving three production departments—Refining, Sifting, and Packing. Assume that records indicate that direct materials, direct labor, and applied factory overhead for the first department, Refining, were $245,000, $112,000, and $81,600, respectively. Also, work in process in the Refining Department at the beginning of the period totaled $24,000, and work in process at the end of the period totaled $38,000.

Journalize the entries to record (a) the flow of costs into the Refining Department during the period for (1) direct materials, (2) direct labor, and (3) factory overhead, and (b) the transfer of production costs to the second department, Sifting.

EXERCISE 17-4
Factory overhead rate, entry for applying factory overhead, and factory overhead account balance
Objectives 2, 5
✓ *a. 120%*

The chief cost accountant for Doolittle Beverage Co. estimated that total factory overhead cost for the Blending Department for the coming fiscal year beginning February 1 would be $936,000, and total direct labor costs would be $780,000. During February, the actual direct labor cost totaled $64,500, and factory overhead cost incurred totaled $75,000.

a. What is the predetermined factory overhead rate based on direct labor cost?
b. Journalize the entry to apply factory overhead to production for February.
c. What is the February 28 balance of the account Factory Overhead—Blending Department?
d. Does the balance in (c) represent overapplied or underapplied factory overhead?

EXERCISE 17-5
Equivalent units of production

Objective 3

✓ *Direct materials, 12,900 units*

The Converting Department of Rhino Napkin Company had 1,800 units in work in process at the beginning of the period, which were 75% complete. During the period, 13,500 units were completed and transferred to the Packing Department. There were 1,200 units in process at the end of the period, which were 40% complete. Direct materials are placed into the process at the beginning of production. Determine the number of equivalent units of production with respect to direct materials and conversion costs.

EXERCISE 17-6
Equivalent units of production

Objective 3

✓ *a. Conversion, 88,745 units*

Units of production data for the two departments of Havana Cable and Wire Company for July of the current fiscal year are as follows:

	Drawing Department	Winding Department
Work in process, July 1	4,500 units, 35% completed	2,000 units, 55% completed
Completed and transferred to next processing department during July	86,000 units	84,800 units
Work in process, July 31	5,400 units, 80% completed	3,200 units, 18% completed

If all direct materials are placed in process at the beginning of production, determine the direct materials and conversion equivalent units of production for July for (a) the Drawing Department and (b) the Winding Department.

EXERCISE 17-7
Equivalent units of production

Objectives 2, 3

✓ *b. Conversion, 179,000*

The following information concerns production in the Finishing Department for July. All direct materials are placed in process at the beginning of production.

ACCOUNT *Work in Process—Finishing Department*   **ACCOUNT NO.**

Date		Item	Debit	Credit	Balance Debit	Balance Credit
July	1	Bal., 10,000 units, ³/₅ completed			67,000	
	31	Direct materials, 180,000 units	396,000		463,000	
	31	Direct labor	558,480		1,021,480	
	31	Factory overhead	837,720		1,859,200	
	31	Goods finished, 175,000 units		1,748,200	111,000	
	31	Bal.—units, ²/₃ completed			111,000	

a. Determine the number of units in work in process inventory at the end of the month.
b. Determine the equivalent units of production for direct materials and conversion costs in July.

EXERCISE 17-8
Costs per equivalent unit

Objective 3

✓ *2. Conversion cost per equivalent unit, $7.80*

a. Based upon the data in Exercise 17-7, determine the following:
    1. Direct materials cost per equivalent unit.
    2. Conversion cost per equivalent unit.
    3. Cost of the beginning work in process completed during July.
    4. Cost of units started and completed during July.
    5. Cost of the ending work in process.
b. Assuming that the direct materials cost is the same for June and July, did the conversion cost per equivalent unit increase, decrease, or remain the same in July?

EXERCISE 17-9
Equivalent units of production

Objectives 2, 3

REAL WORLD

The **Kellogg Company** manufactures cold cereal products, such as *Frosted Flakes* and *Special K*. Assume that the Inventory in Process on October 1 for the Packing Department included 1,800 pounds of cereal in the packing machine hopper. In addition, there were 1,200 empty 24-oz. boxes held in the package carousel of the packing machine. During October, 24,000 boxes of 24-oz. cereal were packaged. Conversion costs are incurred when a box is filled with cereal. On October 31, the packing machine hopper held 750 pounds of cereal, and the package carousel held 500 empty 24-oz. boxes. Assume that once a box is filled with cereal, it is immediately transferred to the finished goods warehouse.

Determine the equivalent units of production for cereal, boxes, and conversion costs for October. An equivalent unit is defined as "pounds" for cereal and "24-oz. boxes" for boxes and conversion costs.

EXERCISE 17-10
Costs per equivalent unit
Objective 3

✓ *c. $3.72*

Enviro Wood Products Inc. completed and transferred 120,000 particle board units of production from the Pressing Department. There was no beginning inventory in process in the department. The ending in-process inventory was 7,500 units, which were ³⁄₅ complete as to conversion cost. All materials are added at the beginning of the process. Direct materials cost incurred was $474,300, direct labor cost incurred was $69,720, and factory overhead applied was $29,880.

Determine the following for the Pressing Department:

a. Total conversion cost
b. Conversion cost per equivalent unit
c. Direct materials cost per equivalent unit

EXERCISE 17-11
Equivalent units of production and related costs
Objective 3

SPREADSHEET

✓ *a. 4,000 units*

The charges to Work in Process—Assembly Department for a period, together with information concerning production, are as follows. All direct materials are placed in process at the beginning of production.

Work in Process—Assembly Department			
Bal., 2,500 units, 40% completed	8,225	To Finished Goods, 54,500 units	?
Direct materials, 56,000 units @ $1.85	103,600		
Direct labor	75,210		
Factory overhead	112,815		
Bal. _?_ units, 25% completed	?		

Determine the following:

a. The number of units in work in process inventory at the end of the period.
b. Equivalent units of production for direct materials and conversion.
c. Costs per equivalent unit for direct materials and conversion.
d. Cost of the units started and completed during the period.

EXERCISE 17-12
Cost of units completed and in process
Objective 3

✓ *1. $13,400*

a. Based upon the data in Exercise 17-11, determine the following:
   1. Cost of beginning work in process inventory completed this period.
   2. Cost of units transferred to finished goods during the period.
   3. Cost of ending work in process inventory.
   4. Cost per unit of beginning work in process completed during the period.
b. Did the production costs change from the preceding period? Explain.
c. Assuming that the direct materials cost per unit did not change from the preceding period, did the conversion costs per equivalent unit increase, decrease, or remain the same for the current period?

EXERCISE 17-13
Errors in equivalent unit computation
Objective 3

WHAT'S WRONG WITH THIS?

Fondue Oil Refining Company processes gasoline. At April 1 of the current year, 4,500 units were ²⁄₃ completed in the Blending Department. During April, 18,000 units entered the Blending Department from the Refining Department. During April, the units in process at the beginning of the month were completed. Of the 18,000 units entering the department, all were completed except 6,200 units that were ¹⁄₅ completed. The equivalent units for conversion costs for April for the Blending Department were computed as follows:

Equivalent units of production in April:	
To process units in inventory on April 1:	
4,500 × ²⁄₃	3,000
To process units started and completed in April:	
18,000 − 4,500	13,500
To process units in inventory on April 30:	
6,200 × ¹⁄₅	1,240
Equivalent units of production	17,740

List the errors in the computation of equivalent units for conversion costs for the Blending Department for April.

EXERCISE 17-14
Cost per equivalent unit
Objectives 2, 3

✓a. 47,500 units

The following information concerns production in the Forging Department for November. All direct materials are placed into the process at the beginning of production, and conversion costs are incurred evenly throughout the process. The beginning inventory consists of $60,000 of direct materials.

ACCOUNT *Work in Process—Forging Department*   **ACCOUNT NO.**

Date		Item	Debit	Credit	Balance Debit	Balance Credit
Nov.	1	Bal., 7,500 units, 60% completed			75,750	
	30	Direct materials, 48,000 units	396,000		471,750	
	30	Direct labor	64,800		536,550	
	30	Factory overhead	97,200		633,750	
	30	Goods transferred, _?_ units		?	?	
	30	Bal., 8,000 units, 25% completed			?	

a. Determine the number of units transferred to the next department.
b. Determine the cost per equivalent unit of direct materials and conversion.
c. Determine the cost of units started and completed in November.

EXERCISE 17-15
Costs per equivalent unit and production costs
Objective 3

✓a. $86,550

Based upon the data in Exercise 17-14, determine the following:

a. Cost of beginning work in process inventory completed in November.
b. Cost of units transferred to the next department during November.
c. Cost of ending work in process inventory on November 30.
d. Cost per equivalent unit of direct materials and conversion included in the November 1 beginning work in process.
e. The November increase or decrease in cost per equivalent unit for direct materials and conversion.

EXERCISE 17-16
Cost of production report
Objective 4

SPREADSHEET

✓d. $7,020

The debits to Work in Process—Cooking Department for Euphrates Company for January 2006, together with information concerning production, are as follows:

Work in process, January 1, 1,500 pounds, 30% complete		$ 6,753*
*Direct materials (1,500 × $2.75)	$4,125	
Conversion (1,500 × 30% × $5.84)	2,628	
	$6,753	
Beans added during January, 63,500 pounds		177,800
Conversion costs during January		278,080
Work in process, January 31, 1,800 pounds, 25% completed		?
Goods finished during January, 63,200 pounds		?

All direct materials are placed in process at the beginning of production. Prepare a cost of production report, presenting the following computations:

a. Direct materials and conversion equivalent units of production for January.
b. Direct materials and conversion cost per equivalent unit for January.
c. Cost of goods finished during January.
d. Cost of work in process at January 31, 2006.

EXERCISE 17-17
Cost of production report
Objective 4

Prepare a cost of production report for the Cutting Department of Bogart Carpet Company for March 2006, using the following data and assuming that all materials are added at the beginning of the process:

SPREADSHEET

✓ *Conversion rate, $4.75*

Work in process, March 1, 8,000 units, 75% complete		$ 70,400*
*Direct materials (8,000 × $5.20)	$41,600	
Conversion (8,000 × 75% × $4.80)	28,800	
	$70,400	

Materials added during March from Weaving Dept., 215,000 units	1,128,750
Direct labor for March	402,040
Factory overhead for March	603,060
Goods finished during March (includes goods in process, March 1), 214,000 units	—
Work in process, March 31, 9,000 units, 40% completed	—

EXERCISE 17-18
Cost of production and journal entries
Objectives 2, 3, 5
✓ *b. $14,800*

Parsley Metal Works Company casts blades for turbine engines. Within the Casting Department, alloy is first melted in a crucible, then poured into molds to produce the castings. On October 1, there were 750 pounds of alloy in process, which were 40% complete as to conversion. The Work in Process balance for these 750 pounds was $32,700, determined as follows:

Direct materials (750 × $26)	$19,500
Conversion (750 × 40% × $44)	13,200
	$32,700

During October, the Casting Department was charged $249,200 for 8,900 pounds of alloy and $162,540 for direct labor. Factory overhead is applied to the department at a rate of 150% of direct labor. The department transferred out 9,250 pounds of finished castings to the Machining Department. The October 31 inventory in process was 20% complete as to conversion.

a. Prepare the following October journal entries for the Casting Department:
   1. The materials charged to production.
   2. The conversion costs charged to production.
   3. The completed production transferred to the Machining Department.
b. Determine the Work in Process—Casting Department October 31 balance.

EXERCISE 17-19
Decision making
Objective 6

Hoffman Bottling Company bottles popular beverages. The beverages are produced by blending concentrate with water and sugar. The concentrate is purchased from a concentrate producer. The concentrate producer sets higher prices for the more popular concentrate flavors. Below is a simplified cost of production report separating the cost of bottling the four flavors.

	Orange	Cola	Lemon-Lime	Root Beer
Concentrate	$ 3,600	$33,000	$21,000	$1,800
Water	1,200	9,000	6,000	600
Sugar	2,000	15,000	10,000	1,000
Bottles	4,400	33,000	22,000	2,200
Flavor changeover	3,000	1,800	1,200	3,000
Conversion cost	1,600	7,500	5,000	800
Total cost	$15,800	$99,300	$65,200	$9,400
Number of cases	4,000	30,000	20,000	2,000

Beginning and ending work in process inventories are negligible, so are omitted from the cost of production report. The flavor changeover cost represents the cost of cleaning the bottling machines between production runs of different flavors.
➤ Prepare a memo to the production manager analyzing this comparative cost information. In your memo, provide recommendations for further action, along with supporting schedules showing the total cost per case and cost per case by cost element.

EXERCISE 17-20
Decision making
Objective 6

Sharp Images Inc. produces film products for cameras. One of the processes for this operation is a coating (solvent spreading) operation, where chemicals are coated on to film stock. There has been some concern about the cost performance of this operation. As a result, you have begun an investigation. You first discover that all input prices have not changed for the last six months. If there is a problem, it is related to the quantity of input. You have discovered three possible problems from some of the operating personnel whose quotes follow:

Operator 1: "I've been keeping an eye on my operating room instruments. I feel as though our energy consumption is becoming less efficient."

Operator 2: "Every time the coating machine goes down, we produce waste on shutdown and subsequent startup. It seems like during the last half year we have had more unscheduled machine shutdowns than in the past. Thus, I feel as though our yields must be dropping."

Operator 3: "My sense is that our coating costs are going up. It seems to me like we are spreading a thicker coating than we should. Perhaps the coating machine needs to be recalibrated."

The Coating Department had no beginning or ending inventories for any month during the study period. The following data from the cost of production report are made available:

	January	February	March	April	May	June
Materials	$ 53,760	$ 67,200	$ 60,480	$ 50,400	$ 53,760	$ 67,200
Coating cost	15,360	21,120	21,600	20,160	22,272	30,720
Conversion cost (incl. energy)	38,400	48,000	43,200	36,000	38,400	48,000
Pounds input to the process	320,000	400,000	360,000	300,000	320,000	400,000
Pounds transferred out	153,600	192,000	172,800	144,000	153,600	192,000

Use the preceding information to discover the problem in the operation.

EXERCISE 17-21
Just-in-time manufacturing
Objective 7

The following are some quotes provided by a number of managers at Casagrande Machining Company regarding the company's planned move toward a just-in-time manufacturing system:

Director of Purchasing: *I'm very concerned about moving to a just-in-time system for materials. What would happen if one of our suppliers were unable to make a shipment? A supplier could fall behind in production or have a quality problem. Without some safety stock in our materials, our whole plant would shut down.*

Director of Manufacturing: *If we go to just-in-time, I think our factory output will drop. We need in-process inventory in order to "smooth out" the inevitable problems that occur during manufacturing. For example, if a machine that is used to process a product breaks down, I would starve the next machine if I don't have in-process inventory between the two machines. If I have in-process inventory, then I can keep the next operation busy while I fix the broken machine. Thus, the in-process inventories give me a safety valve that I can use to keep things running when things go wrong.*

Director of Sales: *I'm afraid we'll miss some sales if we don't keep a large stock of items on hand just in case demand increases. It only makes sense to me to keep large inventories in order to assure product availability for our customers.*

How would you respond to these managers?

APPENDIX
EXERCISE 17-22
Equivalent units of production: average cost method
✓ a. 11,100

The Converting Department of Zhao Napkin Company uses the average cost method and had 1,200 units in work in process that were 60% complete at the beginning of the period. During the period, 10,500 units were completed and transferred to the Packing Department. There were 600 units in process that were 30% complete at the end of the period.

a. Determine the number of whole units to be accounted for and to be assigned costs for the period.

b. Determine the number of equivalent units of production for the period.

APPENDIX EXERCISE 17-23
Equivalent units of production: average cost method

✓ a. 77,600 units to be accounted for

Units of production data for the two departments of Southern Cable and Wire Company for October of the current fiscal year are as follows:

	Drawing Department	Winding Department
Work in process, October 1	2,000 units, 65% completed	1,400 units, 30% completed
Completed and transferred to next processing department during October	74,000 units	73,000 units
Work in process, October 31	3,600 units, 75% completed	2,400 units, 20% completed

Each department uses the average cost method.

a. Determine the number of whole units to be accounted for and to be assigned costs and the equivalent units of production for the Drawing Department.
b. Determine the number of whole units to be accounted for and to be assigned costs and the equivalent units of production for Winding Department.

APPENDIX EXERCISE 17-24
Equivalent units of production: average cost method

✓ a. 27,500

The following information concerns production in the Finishing Department for March. The Finishing Department uses the average cost method.

ACCOUNT *Work in Process—Finishing Department*   **ACCOUNT NO.**

Date		Item	Debit	Credit	Balance Debit	Balance Credit
Mar.	1	Bal., 14,000 units, 40% completed			38,000	
	31	Direct materials, 103,000 units	240,000		278,000	
	31	Direct labor	68,000		346,000	
	31	Factory overhead	40,800		386,800	
	31	Goods transferred, 89,500 units		304,842	81,958	
	31	Bal., _?_ units, 60% completed			81,958	

a. Determine the number of units in work in process inventory at the end of the month.
b. Determine the number of whole units to be accounted for and to be assigned costs and the equivalent units of production for March.

APPENDIX EXERCISE 17-25
Equivalent units of production and related costs

SPREADSHEET

✓ b. 71,080 units

The charges to Work in Process—Baking Department for a period as well as information concerning production are as follows. The Baking Department uses the average cost method, and all direct materials are placed in process during production.

Work in Process—Baking Department			
Bal., 8,000 units, 70% completed	75,000	To Finished Goods, 70,000 units	?
Direct materials, 67,400 units	148,280		
Direct labor	35,000		
Factory overhead	18,932		
Bal., 5,400 units, 20% completed	?		

Determine the following:

a. Determine the number of whole units to be accounted for and to be assigned costs.
b. Determine the number of equivalent units of production.
c. Determine the cost per equivalent unit.
d. Determine the cost of the units transferred to Finished Goods.
e. Determine the cost of ending Work in Process.

APPENDIX EXERCISE 17-26
Cost per equivalent unit: average cost method

The following information concerns production in the Forging Department for September. The Forging Department uses the average cost method.

✓ a. $12.85

ACCOUNT *Work in Process—Forging Department*   **ACCOUNT NO.**

Date		Item	Debit	Credit	Balance Debit	Balance Credit
Sept.	1	Bal., 5,500 units, 40% completed			53,000	
	30	Direct materials, 36,000 units	284,400		337,400	
	30	Direct labor	83,385		420,785	
	30	Factory overhead	83,706		504,491	
	30	Goods transferred, 38,300 units		?	?	
	30	Bal., 3,200 units, 30% completed			?	

a. Determine the cost per equivalent unit.
b. Determine the cost of the units transferred to Finished Goods.
c. Determine the cost of ending Work in Process.

APPENDIX EXERCISE 17-27
Cost of production report: average cost method

SPREADSHEET

✓ *Cost per equivalent unit, $1.72*

The increases to Work in Process—Cooking Department for Better Beans Company for January 2006 as well as information concerning production are as follows:

Work in process, January 1, 800 pounds, 30% complete	$ 1,050
Beans added during January, 48,600 pounds	58,320
Conversion costs during January	25,254
Work in process, January 31, 500 pounds, 60% completed	—
Goods finished during January, 48,900 pounds	—

Prepare a cost of production report, using the average cost method.

APPENDIX EXERCISE 17-28
Cost of production report: average cost method

SPREADSHEET

✓ *Cost per equivalent unit, $5.58*

Prepare a cost of production report for the Cutting Department of Arizona Carpet Company for July 2006. Use the average cost method with the following data:

Work in process, July 1, 10,000 units, 70% complete	$ 50,000
Materials added during July from Weaving Dept., 182,000 units	837,200
Direct labor for July	71,160
Factory overhead for July	50,504
Goods finished during July (includes goods in process, July 1), 178,000 units	—
Work in process, July 31, 14,000 units, 20% completed	—

Problems Series A

PROBLEM 17-1A
Entries for process cost system

Objectives 2, 5

P.A.S.S.

✓ *2. Materials January 31 balance, $13,554*

Gaffney Soap Company manufactures powdered detergent. Phosphate is placed in process in the Making Department, where it is turned into granulars. The output of Making is transferred to the Packing Department, where packaging is added at the beginning of the process. On January 1, Gaffney Soap Company had the following inventories:

Finished Goods	$28,440
Work in Process—Making	6,444
Work in Process—Packing	11,610
Materials	4,320

Departmental accounts are maintained for factory overhead, which both have zero balances on January 1.

Manufacturing operations for January are summarized as follows:

a. Materials purchased on account $286,020
b. Materials requisitioned for use:
    Phosphate—Making Department $202,320
    Packaging—Packing Department 66,060
    Indirect materials—Making Department 5,760
    Indirect materials—Packing Department 2,646
c. Labor used:
    Direct labor—Making Department $122,220
    Direct labor—Packing Department 76,860
    Indirect labor—Making Department 25,740
    Indirect labor—Packing Department 42,660
d. Depreciation charged on fixed assets:
    Making Department $22,500
    Packing Department 16,920
e. Expired prepaid factory insurance:
    Making Department $4,680
    Packing Department 1,800
f. Applied factory overhead:
    Making Department $57,600
    Packing Department 64,800
g. Production costs transferred from Making Dept. to Packing Dept. $378,846
h. Production costs transferred from Packing Dept. to finished goods $584,460
i. Cost of goods sold during the period $594,900

Instructions

1. Journalize the entries to record the operations, identifying each entry by letter.
2. Compute the January 31 balances of the inventory accounts.
3. Compute the January 31 balances of the factory overhead accounts.

PROBLEM 17-2A
Entries for process cost system

Objectives 2, 5

P.A.S.S.

Petra Refining Company processes gasoline. Petroleum is placed in production in the Refining Department and, after processing, is transferred to the Blending Department, where detergents are added. The finished blended gasoline emerges from the Blending Department.

There were no inventories of work in process at the beginning or at the end of December 2006. Finished goods inventory at December 1 was 7,500 barrels of gasoline at a total cost of $285,000.

Transactions related to manufacturing operations for December are summarized as follows:

a. Materials purchased on account, $727,800.
b. Materials requisitioned for use: Refining, $626,250 ($618,450 entered directly into the product); Blending, $86,400 ($81,300 entered directly into the product).
c. Labor costs incurred: Refining, $159,450 ($124,800 entered directly into the product); Blending, $66,900 ($47,100 entered directly into the product).
d. Miscellaneous costs and expenses incurred on account: Refining, $19,800; Blending, $6,450.
e. Expiration of various prepaid expenses: Refining, $6,000; Blending, $2,250.
f. Depreciation charged on plant assets: Refining, $53,100; Blending, $18,450.
g. Factory overhead applied to production, based on processing hours: $123,000 for Refining and $50,100 for Blending.
h. Output of Refining: 26,250 barrels.
i. Output of Blending: 26,250 barrels of gasoline.
j. Sales on account: 30,000 barrels of gasoline at $50 per barrel. Credits to the finished goods account are to be made according to the first-in, first-out method.

Instructions

Journalize the entries to record the transactions, identifying each by letter. Include as an explanation for entry (j) the number of barrels and the cost per barrel of gasoline sold.

PROBLEM 17-3A
Cost of production report
Objectives 3, 4

SPREADSHEET

✓ *Conversion rate per equivalent unit, $1.75*

Lady Ann's Chocolate Company processes chocolate into candy bars. The process begins by placing direct materials (raw chocolate, milk, and sugar) into the Blending Department. All materials are placed into production at the beginning of the blending process. After blending, the milk chocolate is then transferred to the Molding Department, where the milk chocolate is formed into candy bars. The following is a partial work in process account of the Blending Department at March 31, 2006:

ACCOUNT *Work in Process—Blending Department*				ACCOUNT NO.	
				Balance	
Date	**Item**	**Debit**	**Credit**	**Debit**	**Credit**
Mar. 1	Bal., 6,000 units, 45% completed			42,540	
31	Direct materials, 180,000 units	1,125,000		1,167,540	
31	Direct labor	126,210		1,293,750	
31	Factory overhead	189,315		1,483,065	
31	Goods finished, 178,500 units		?		
31	Bal. _?_ units, 60% completed			?	

Instructions

1. Prepare a cost of production report, and identify the missing amounts for the Work in Process—Blending Department account.
2. Assuming that the March 1 Work in Process inventory includes direct materials of $37,680, determine the increase or decrease in March in the cost per equivalent unit for direct materials and conversion as compared to February.

PROBLEM 17-4A
Equivalent units and related costs; cost of production report; entries
Objectives 3, 4, 5

SPREADSHEET

✓ *Transferred to finished goods, $846,467*

Northway Chemical Company manufactures specialty chemicals by a series of three processes, all materials being introduced in the Distilling Department. From the Distilling Department, the materials pass through the Reaction and Filling Departments, emerging as finished chemicals.

The balance in the account Work in Process—Filling was as follows on December 1, 2006:

Work in Process—Filling Department
(1,200 units, 30% completed):
Direct materials (1,200 × $15.20) $18,240
Conversion (1,200 × 30% × $8.15)   2,934
                                           $21,174

The following costs were charged to Work in Process—Filling during December:

Direct materials transferred from Reaction
Department: 36,400 units at $15.25 a unit $555,100
Direct labor   119,443
Factory overhead   179,160

During December, 36,100 units of specialty chemicals were completed. Work in Process—Filling Department on December 31 was 1,500 units, 45% completed.

Instructions

1. Prepare a cost of production report for the Filling Department for December.
2. Journalize the entries for costs transferred from Reaction to Filling and the cost of goods transferred to finished goods.
3. Determine the increase or decrease in the cost per equivalent unit from November to December for direct materials and conversion costs.
4. ▬▬▶ Discuss the uses of the cost of production report and the results of (3).

PROBLEM 17-5A
Work in process account data for two months; cost of production reports
Objectives 2, 3, 4, 5

Isotonic Aluminum Company uses a process cost system to record the costs of manufacturing rolled aluminum, which requires a series of four processes. The inventory of Work in Process—Rolling on September 1, 2006, and debits to the account during September were as follows:

✓ 1. c. Transferred to finished goods in September, $8,061,960

Bal., 4,500 units, 1/3 completed:
Direct materials (4,500 × $38.60)	$173,700	
Conversion (4,500 × 1/3 × $11.74)	17,610	
	$191,310	
From Smelting Dept., 160,000 units	6,200,000	
Direct labor	765,600	
Factory overhead	1,146,000	

During September, 4,500 units in process on September 1 were completed, and of the 160,000 units entering the department, all were completed except 5,000 units that were ⁴⁄₅ completed.

Charges to Work in Process—Rolling for October were as follows:

From Smelting Department, 175,000 units	$6,797,000
Direct labor	826,080
Factory overhead	1,239,120

During October, the units in process at the beginning of the month were completed, and of the 175,000 units entering the department, all were completed except 6,500 units that were ²⁄₅ completed.

Instructions

1. Enter the balance as of September 1, 2006, in a four-column account for Work in Process—Rolling. Record the debits and the credits in the account for September. Construct a cost of production report and present computations for determining (a) equivalent units of production for materials and conversion, (b) equivalent costs per unit, (c) cost of goods finished, differentiating between units started in the prior period and units started and finished in September, and (d) work in process inventory.
2. Provide the same information for October by recording the October transactions in the four-column work in process account. Construct a cost of production report, and present the October computations (a through d) listed in (1).
3. ▬▶ Comment on the change in cost per equivalent unit for August through October for direct materials and conversion cost.

APPENDIX PROBLEM 17-6A
Cost of production report: average cost method

✓ Cost per equivalent unit, $11.40

Reynolds Coffee Company roasts and packs coffee beans. The process begins in the Roasting Department. From the Roasting Department, the coffee beans are transferred to the Packing Department. The following is a partial work in process account of the Roasting Department at July 31, 2006:

ACCOUNT **Work in Process—Roasting Department**   ACCOUNT NO.

Date		Item	Debit	Credit	Balance Debit	Balance Credit
July	1	Bal., 20,000 units, 60% completed			132,000	
	31	Direct materials, 320,000 units	2,000,000		2,132,000	
	31	Direct labor	636,100		2,768,100	
	31	Factory overhead	954,000		3,722,100	
	31	Goods finished, 317,500 units		?	?	
	31	Bal. _?_ units, 40% completed			?	

Instructions

Prepare a cost of production report, using the average cost method, and identify the missing amounts for the Work in Process—Roasting Department account.

APPENDIX PROBLEM 17-7A
Equivalent units and related costs; cost of production report: average cost method

Montana's Choice Flour Company manufactures flour by a series of three processes, beginning in the Milling Department. From the Milling Department, the materials pass through the Sifting and Packaging Departments, emerging as packaged refined flour.

SPREADSHEET

✓ *Transferred to Packaging Dept., $878,400*

The balance in the account Work in Process—Sifting Department was as follows on October 1, 2006:

Work in Process—Sifting Department (18,000 units, 80% completed) $25,200

The following costs were charged to Work in Process—Sifting Department during October:

Direct materials transferred from Milling Department: 490,000 units $686,000
Direct labor   71,200
Factory overhead   106,800

During October, 488,000 units of flour were completed. Work in Process—Sifting Department on October 31 was 20,000 units, 30% completed.

Instructions

Prepare a cost of production report for the Sifting Department for October, using the average cost method.

Problems Series B

PROBLEM 17-1B
Entries for process cost system

Objectives 2, 5

P.A.S.S.

✓ *Materials July 31 balance, $32,375*

Rimrock Carpet Company manufactures carpets. Fiber is placed in process in the Spinning Department, where it is spun into yarn. The output of the Spinning Department is transferred to the Tufting Department, where carpet backing is added at the beginning of the process and the process is completed. On July 1, Rimrock Carpet Company had the following inventories:

Finished Goods $40,750
Work in Process—Spinning Department   7,250
Work in Process—Tufting Department   30,375
Materials   23,250

Departmental accounts are maintained for factory overhead, and both have zero balances on July 1.

Manufacturing operations for July are summarized as follows:

a. Materials purchased on account $915,500
b. Materials requisitioned for use:
   Fiber—Spinning Department $611,625
   Carpet backing—Tufting Department 240,375
   Indirect materials—Spinning Department 42,500
   Indirect materials—Tufting Department 11,875
c. Labor used:
   Direct labor—Spinning Department $292,750
   Direct labor—Tufting Department 207,125
   Indirect labor—Spinning Department 115,375
   Indirect labor—Tufting Department 67,750
d. Depreciation charged on fixed assets:
   Spinning Department $79,000
   Tufting Department 39,000
e. Expired prepaid factory insurance:
   Spinning Department $17,500
   Tufting Department 15,000
f. Applied factory overhead:
   Spinning Department $256,250
   Tufting Department 131,250
g. Production costs transferred from Spinning Dept. to Tufting Dept. $1,142,875
h. Production costs transferred from Tufting Dept. to finished goods $1,725,125
i. Cost of goods sold during the period $1,741,250

Instructions

1. Journalize the entries to record the operations, identifying each entry by letter.
2. Compute the July 31 balances of the inventory accounts.
3. Compute the July 31 balances of the factory overhead accounts.

PROBLEM 17-2B
Entries for process cost system
Objectives 2, 5

P.A.S.S.

Hawkeye Bakery Company manufactures cookies. Materials are placed in production in the Baking Department and after processing are transferred to the Packing Department, where packing materials are added. The finished products emerge from the Packing Department.

There were no inventories of work in process at the beginning or at the end of August 2006. Finished goods inventory at August 1 was 900 cases of cookies at a total cost of $40,500.

Transactions related to manufacturing operations for August are summarized as follows:

a. Materials purchased on account, $504,000.
b. Materials requisitioned for use: Baking Department, $399,600 ($387,000 entered directly into the product); Packing Department, $90,000 ($81,000 entered directly into the product).
c. Labor costs incurred: Baking Department, $175,500 ($163,800 entered directly into the product); Packing Department, $131,760 ($126,000 entered directly into the product).
d. Miscellaneous costs and expenses incurred on account: Baking Department, $18,540; Packing Department, $7,740.
e. Depreciation charged on fixed assets: Baking Department, $27,900; Packing Department, $13,140.
f. Expiration of various prepaid expenses: Baking Department, $4,320; Packing Department, $1,980.
g. Factory overhead applied to production, based on machine hours: $75,600 for Baking and $37,800 for Packing.
h. Output of Baking Department: 19,800 cases.
i. Output of Packing Department: 19,800 cases of cookies.
j. Sales on account: 20,160 cases of cookies at $90. Credits to the finished goods account are to be made according to the first-in, first-out method.

Instructions

Journalize the entries to record the transactions, identifying each by letter. Include as an explanation for entry (j) the number of cases and the cost per case of cookies sold.

PROBLEM 17-3B
Cost of production report
Objectives 3, 4

SPREADSHEET

✓ *Conversion cost per equivalent unit, $5.35*

Grizzly Coffee Company roasts and packs coffee beans. The process begins by placing coffee beans into the Roasting Department. From the Roasting Department, coffee beans are then transferred to the Packing Department. The following is a partial work in process account of the Roasting Department at October 31, 2006:

ACCOUNT *Work in Process—Roasting Department*   **ACCOUNT NO.**

Date		Item	Debit	Credit	Balance Debit	Balance Credit
Oct.	1	Bal., 14,500 units, ¹/₅ completed			54,578	
	31	Direct materials, 315,000 units	819,000		873,578	
	31	Direct labor	678,380		1,551,958	
	31	Factory overhead	1,017,570		2,569,528	
	31	Goods finished, 316,700 units		?		
	31	Bal. _?_ units, ¹/₄ completed			?	

Instructions

1. Prepare a cost of production report, and identify the missing amounts for the Work in Process—Roasting Department account. *(continued)*

2. Assuming that the October 1 Work in Process inventory includes $39,150 of direct materials, determine the cost per equivalent unit for direct materials and conversion in the beginning work in process inventory.

PROBLEM 17-4B
Equivalent units and related costs; cost of production report; entries

Objectives 3, 4, 5

SPREADSHEET

✓ *Transferred to Packaging Dept., $944,820*

Montana Wheat Flour Company manufactures flour by a series of three processes, beginning with wheat grain being introduced in the Milling Department. From the Milling Department, the materials pass through the Sifting and Packaging Departments, emerging as packaged refined flour.

The balance in the account Work in Process—Sifting Department was as follows on May 1, 2006:

Work in Process—Sifting Department (24,000 units, ³/₄ completed):
Direct materials (24,000 × $1.25) $30,000
Conversion (24,000 × ³/₄ × $0.44)   7,920
                                     $37,920

The following costs were charged to Work in Process—Sifting Department during May:

Direct materials transferred from Milling Department:
575,000 units at $1.20 a unit $690,000
Direct labor   102,960
Factory overhead   154,440

During May, 572,000 units of flour were completed. Work in Process—Sifting Department on May 31 was 27,000 units, ²/₃ completed.

Instructions
1. Prepare a cost of production report for the Sifting Department for May.
2. Journalize the entries for costs transferred from Milling to Sifting and the costs transferred from Sifting to Packaging.
3. Determine the increase or decrease in the cost per equivalent unit from April to May for direct materials and conversion costs.
4. ▬▬▶ Discuss the uses of the cost of production report and the results of (3).

PROBLEM 17-5B
Work in process account data for two months; cost of production reports

Objectives 2, 3, 4, 5

SPREADSHEET

✓ *1. c. Transferred to finished goods in July, $822,960*

Spence Soup Co. uses a process cost system to record the costs of processing soup, which requires a series of three processes. The inventory of Work in Process—Filling on July 1 and debits to the account during July 2006 were as follows:

Bal., 1,800 units, ¹/₃ completed:
Direct materials (1,800 × $4.72) $8,496
Conversion (1,800 × ¹/₃ × $2.10)   1,260
                                        $9,756

From Cooking Dept., 120,000 units $570,000
Direct labor   101,564
Factory overhead   152,200

During July, 1,800 units in process on July 1 were completed, and of the 120,000 units entering the department, all were completed except 2,000 units that were ¹/₄ completed.

Charges to Work in Process—Filling for August were as follows:

From Cooking Dept., 140,000 units $669,200
Direct labor   121,480
Factory overhead   182,000

During August, the units in process at the beginning of the month were completed, and of the 140,000 units entering the department, all were completed except 2,500 units that were ³/₅ completed.

Instructions

1. Enter the balance as of July 1, 2006, in a four-column account for Work in Process—Filling. Record the debits and the credits in the account for July. Construct a cost of production report, and present computations for determining (a) equivalent units of production for materials and conversion, (b) equivalent costs per unit, (c) cost of goods finished, differentiating between units started in the prior period and units started and finished in July, and (d) work in process inventory.
2. Provide the same information for August by recording the August transactions in the four-column work in process account. Construct a cost of production report, and present the August computations (a through d) listed in (1).
3. ➤ Comment on the change in cost per equivalent unit for June through August for direct materials and conversion costs.

APPENDIX PROBLEM 17-6B

Cost of production report: average cost method

SPREADSHEET

✓ *Cost per equivalent unit, $9.35*

Valdez Coffee Company roasts and packs coffee beans. The process begins in the Roasting Department. From the Roasting Department, the coffee beans are transferred to the Packing Department. The following is a partial work in process account of the Roasting Department at March 31, 2006:

ACCOUNT *Work in Process—Roasting Department*   **ACCOUNT NO.**

Date		Item	Debit	Credit	Balance Debit	Balance Credit
Mar.	1	Bal., 13,800 units, 80% completed			114,600	
	31	Direct materials, 258,000 units	1,444,800		1,559,400	
	31	Direct labor	335,000		1,894,400	
	31	Factory overhead	562,406		2,456,806	
	31	Goods finished, 260,500 units		?	?	
	31	Bal. _?_ units, 20% completed			?	

Instructions

Prepare a cost of production report, using the average cost method, and identify the missing amounts for the Work in Process—Roasting Department account.

APPENDIX PROBLEM 17-7B

Equivalent units and related costs; cost of production report: average cost method

SPREADSHEET

✓ *Transferred to Packaging Dept., $1,014,000*

Baker's Choice Flour Company manufactures flour by a series of three processes, beginning in the Milling Department. From the Milling Department, the materials pass through the Sifting and Packaging Departments, emerging as packaged refined flour.

The balance in the account Work in Process—Sifting Department was as follows on July 1, 2006:

Work in Process—Sifting Department (25,800 units, 75% completed) $38,700

The following costs were charged to Work in Process—Sifting Department during July:

Direct materials transferred from Milling Department: 640,000 units	$736,000
Direct labor	148,742
Factory overhead	96,720

During July, 650,000 units of flour were completed. Work in Process—Sifting Department on July 31 was 15,800 units, 25% completed.

Instructions

Prepare a cost of production report for the Sifting Department for July, using the average cost method.

Special Activities

ACTIVITY 17-1
Ethics and professional conduct in business

ETHICS

You are the division controller for Margie's Cookie Company. Margie's has introduced a new chocolate chip cookie called Full of Chips, and it is a success. As a result, the product manager responsible for the launch of this new cookie was promoted to division vice-president and became your boss. A new product manager, Wilkin, has been brought in to replace the promoted manager. Wilkin notices that the Full of Chips cookie uses a lot of chips, which increases the cost of the cookie. As a result, Wilkin has ordered that the amount of chips used in the cookies be reduced by 10%. The manager believes that a 10% reduction in chips will not adversely affect sales, but will reduce costs, and hence improve margins. The increased margins would help Wilkin meet profit targets for the period.

You are looking over some cost of production reports segmented by cookie line. You notice that there is a drop in the materials costs for Full of Chips. On further investigation, you discover why the chip costs have declined (fewer chips). Both you and Wilkin report to the division vice-president, who was the original product manager for Full of Chips. You are trying to decide what to do, if anything.

➤ Discuss the options you might consider.

ACTIVITY 17-2
Accounting for materials costs

REAL WORLD   WHAT DO YOU THINK?

In papermaking operations for companies such as **International Paper, Inc.**, wet pulp is fed into paper machines, which press and dry pulp into a continuous sheet of paper. The paper is formed at very high speeds (60 mph). Once the paper is formed, the paper is rolled onto a reel at the back end of the paper machine. One of the characteristics of paper making is the creation of "broke" paper. Broke is paper that fails to satisfy quality standards and is therefore rejected for final shipment to customers. Broke is recycled back to the beginning of the process by combining the recycled paper with virgin (new) pulp material. The combination of virgin pulp and recycled broke is sent to the paper machine for papermaking. Broke is fed into this recycle process continuously from all over the facility.

In this industry it is typical to charge the papermaking operation with the cost of direct materials, which is a mixture of virgin materials and broke. Broke has a much lower cost than does virgin pulp. Therefore, the more broke in the mixture, the lower the average cost of direct materials to the department. Papermaking managers will frequently comment on the importance of broke for keeping their direct materials costs down.

a. ➤ How do you react to this accounting procedure?
b. ➤ What "hidden costs" are not considered when accounting for broke as described above?

ACTIVITY 17-3
Analyzing unit costs

Pierce Can Company manufactures cans for the canned food industry. The operations manager of a can manufacturing operation wants to conduct a cost study investigating the relationship of tin content in the material (can stock) to the energy cost for enameling the cans. The enameling was necessary to prepare the cans for labeling. A higher percentage of tin content in the can stock increases the cost of material. The operations manager believed there was a relationship between the tin content and energy costs for enameling. During the analysis period the amount of tin content in the steel can stock was increased for every month, from April to September. The following operating reports were available from the controller:

	April	May	June	July	August	September
Energy	$ 13,000	$ 28,800	$ 24,200	$ 14,000	$ 16,200	$ 15,000
Materials	12,000	30,000	28,600	18,900	25,200	29,000
Total cost	$ 25,000	$ 58,800	$ 52,800	$ 32,900	$ 41,400	$ 44,000
Units produced	÷100,000	÷240,000	÷220,000	÷140,000	÷180,000	÷200,000
Cost per unit	$ 0.250	$ 0.245	$ 0.240	$ 0.235	$ 0.230	$ 0.220

Differences in materials unit costs were entirely related to the amount of tin content. Interpret this information and report to the operations manager your recommendations with respect to tin content.

ACTIVITY 17-4
Decision making

Jim Shepherd, plant manager of Covershot Paper Company's papermaking mill, was looking over the cost of production reports for July and August for the Papermaking Department. The reports revealed the following:

	July	August
Pulp and chemicals	$300,000	$307,000
Conversion cost	150,000	153,000
Total cost	$450,000	$460,000
Number of tons	÷ 1,250	÷ 1,150
Cost per ton	$ 360	$ 400

Jim was concerned about the growth in the cost per ton from the output of the department. As a result, he asked the plant controller to perform a study to help explain these results. The controller, Kim Meehan, began the analysis by performing some interviews of key plant personnel in order to understand what the problem might be. Excerpts from an interview with Earl Townes, a paper machine operator, follow:

Earl: We have two papermaking machines in the department. I have no data, but I think paper machine 1 is applying too much pulp, and thus is wasting both conversion and materials resources. We haven't had repairs on paper machine 1 in a while. Maybe this is the problem.

Kim: How does too much pulp result in wasted resources?

Earl: Well, you see, if too much pulp is applied, then we will waste pulp material. The customer will not pay for the extra weight. Thus, we just lose that amount of material. Also, when there is too much pulp, the machine must be slowed down in order to complete the drying process. This results in a waste of conversion costs.

Kim: Do you have any other suspicions?

Earl: Well, as you know, we have two products—green paper and yellow paper. They are identical except for the color. The color is added to the paper-making process in the paper machine. I think that during August these two color papers have been behaving very differently. I don't have any data, but it just seems as though the amount of waste associated with the green paper has increased.

Kim: Why is this?

Earl: I understand that there has been a change in specifications for the green paper, starting near the beginning of August. This change could be causing the machines to run poorly when making green paper. If this is the case, the cost per ton would increase for green paper.

Kim also asked for a computer printout providing greater detail on August's operating results.

Computer run: 09085   September 9   Requested by: Kim Meehan

Papermaking Department—August detail

Paper Machine	Color	Materials Costs	Conversion Costs	Tons
1	Green	35,800	17,400	120
1	Yellow	41,700	21,200	140
1	Green	44,600	22,500	150
1	Yellow	36,100	18,100	120
2	Green	38,300	18,800	160
2	Yellow	41,300	19,900	170
2	Green	35,600	18,100	150
2	Yellow	33,600	17,000	140
Total		307,000	153,000	1,150

Assuming that you're Kim Meehan, write a memo to Jim Shephard with a recommendation to management. You should analyze the August data to determine whether the paper machine or the paper color explains the increase in the unit cost from July. Include any supporting schedules that are appropriate.

ACTIVITY 17-5
Process costing companies

GROUP ACTIVITY

The following categories represent typical process manufacturing industries:

Beverages	Metals
Chemicals	Petroleum refining
Food	Pharmaceuticals
Forest and paper products	Soap and cosmetics

In each category, identify one company (following your instructor's specific instructions) and determine the following:

1. Typical products manufactured by the selected company, including brand names.
2. Typical raw materials used by the selected company.
3. Types of processes used by the selected company.

Use annual reports, the Internet, or library resources in doing this activity.

nswers to Self-Examination Questions

1. **C**   The process cost system is most appropriate for a business where manufacturing is conducted by continuous operations and involves a series of uniform production processes, such as the processing of crude oil (answer C). The job order cost system is most appropriate for a business where the product is made to customers' specifications, such as custom furniture manufacturing (answer A), commercial building construction (answer B), or automobile repair shop (answer D).

2. **A**   The total pounds transferred to finished goods (23,000) are the 2,000 in-process pounds at the beginning of the period plus the number of pounds started and completed during the month, 21,000 (24,000 − 3,000). Answer B incorrectly assumes that the beginning inventory is not transferred during the month. Answer C assumes that all 24,000 pounds started during the month are transferred to finished goods, instead of only the portion started and completed. Answer D incorrectly adds all the numbers together.

3. **B**   The number of units that could have been produced from start to finish during a period is termed equivalent units. The 4,875 equivalent units (answer B) is determined as follows:

To process units in inventory on May 1 (1,000 × ¼)	250
To process units started and completed in May (5,500 units − 1,000 units)	4,500
To process units in inventory on May 31 (500 units × ¼)	125
Equivalent units of production in May	4,875

4. **A**   The conversion costs (direct labor and factory overhead) totaling $48,750 are divided by the number of equivalent units (4,875) to determine the unit conversion cost of $10 (answer A).

5. **C**   The electricity costs have increased, and maintenance costs have decreased. Answer C would be a reasonable explanation for these results. The total costs, materials costs, and costs per unit do not reveal any type of pattern over the time period. In fact, the materials costs have stayed at exactly $2.00 per pound over the time period. This demonstrates that aggregated numbers can sometimes hide underlying information that can be used to improve the process.

18

COST BEHAVIOR AND COST-VOLUME-PROFIT ANALYSIS

objectives

After studying this chapter, you should be able to:

1 Classify costs by their behavior as variable costs, fixed costs, or mixed costs.

2 Compute the contribution margin, the contribution margin ratio, and the unit contribution margin, and explain how they may be useful to managers.

3 Using the unit contribution margin, determine the break-even point and the volume necessary to achieve a target profit.

4 Using a cost-volume-profit chart and a profit-volume chart, determine the break-even point and the volume necessary to achieve a target profit.

5 Calculate the break-even point for a business selling more than one product.

6 Compute the operating leverage and the margin of safety, and explain how managers use these concepts.

7 List the assumptions underlying cost-volume-profit analysis.

What are the costs of operating your car? You will normally pay a license plate (tag) fee once a year. This cost does not change, regardless of the number of miles you drive. On the other hand, the total amount you spend on gasoline during the year changes on a day-to-day basis as you drive. The more you drive, the more you spend on gasoline.

How does such operating cost information affect you? Information on how your car's operating costs behave could be relevant in planning a summer vacation. For example, you might be trying to decide between taking an airline flight or driving your car to your vacation destination. In this case, your license plate fee and annual car insurance costs will not change, regardless of whether you drive your car or fly. Thus, these costs would not affect your decision. However, the estimated cost of gasoline and routine maintenance would affect your decision.

As in operating your car, all of the costs of operating a business do not behave in the same way. In this chapter, we discuss commonly used methods for classifying costs according to how they change. We also discuss how management uses cost-volume-profit analysis as a tool in making decisions.

Cost Behavior

objective 1

Classify costs by their behavior as variable costs, fixed costs, or mixed costs.

Knowing how costs behave is useful to management for a variety of purposes. For example, knowing how costs behave allows managers to predict profits as sales and production volumes change. Knowing how costs behave is also useful for estimating costs. Estimated costs, in turn, affect a variety of management decisions, such as whether to use excess machine capacity to produce and sell a product at a reduced price.

Cost behavior refers to the manner in which a cost changes as a related activity changes. To understand cost behavior, two factors must be considered. First, we must identify the activities that are thought to relate to the cost incurred. Such activities are called *activity bases* (or *activity drivers*). Second, we must specify the range of activity over which the changes in the cost are of interest. This range of activity is called the *relevant range*.

To illustrate, hospital administrators must plan and control hospital food costs. To fully understand why food costs change, the activity that causes cost to be incurred must be identified. In the case of food costs, the feeding of patients is a major cause of these costs. The number of patients *treated* by the hospital would not be a good activity base, since some patients are outpatients who do not stay in the hospital. The number of patients who *stay* in the hospital, however, is a good activity base for studying food costs. Once the proper activity base is identified, food costs can then be analyzed over the range of the number of patients who normally stay in the hospital (the relevant range).

Three of the most common classifications of cost behavior are variable costs, fixed costs, and mixed costs.

Variable Costs

When the level of activity is measured in units produced, direct materials and direct labor costs are generally classified as variable costs. *Variable costs* are costs that vary in proportion to changes in the level of activity. For example, assume that Jason Inc. produces stereo sound systems under the brand name of J-Sound. The parts for the stereo systems are purchased from outside suppliers for $10 per unit and are assembled in Jason Inc.'s Waterloo plant. The direct materials costs for Model JS-12 for the relevant range of 5,000 to 30,000 units of production are shown at the top of the next page.

Number of Units of Model JS-12 Produced	Direct Materials Cost per Unit	Total Direct Materials Cost
5,000 units	$10	$ 50,000
10,000	10	100,000
15,000	10	150,000
20,000	10	200,000
25,000	10	250,000
30,000	10	300,000

Variable costs are the same per unit, while the total variable cost changes in proportion to changes in the activity base. For Model JS-12, for example, the direct materials cost for 10,000 units ($100,000) is twice the direct materials cost for 5,000 units ($50,000). The total direct materials cost varies in proportion to the number of units produced because the direct materials cost per unit ($10) is the same for all levels of production. Thus, producing 20,000 additional units of JS-12 will increase the direct materials cost by $200,000 (20,000 × $10), producing 25,000 additional units will increase the materials cost by $250,000, and so on.

Exhibit 1 illustrates how the variable costs for direct materials for Model JS-12 behave in total and on a per-unit basis as production changes.

•Exhibit 1   Variable Cost Graphs

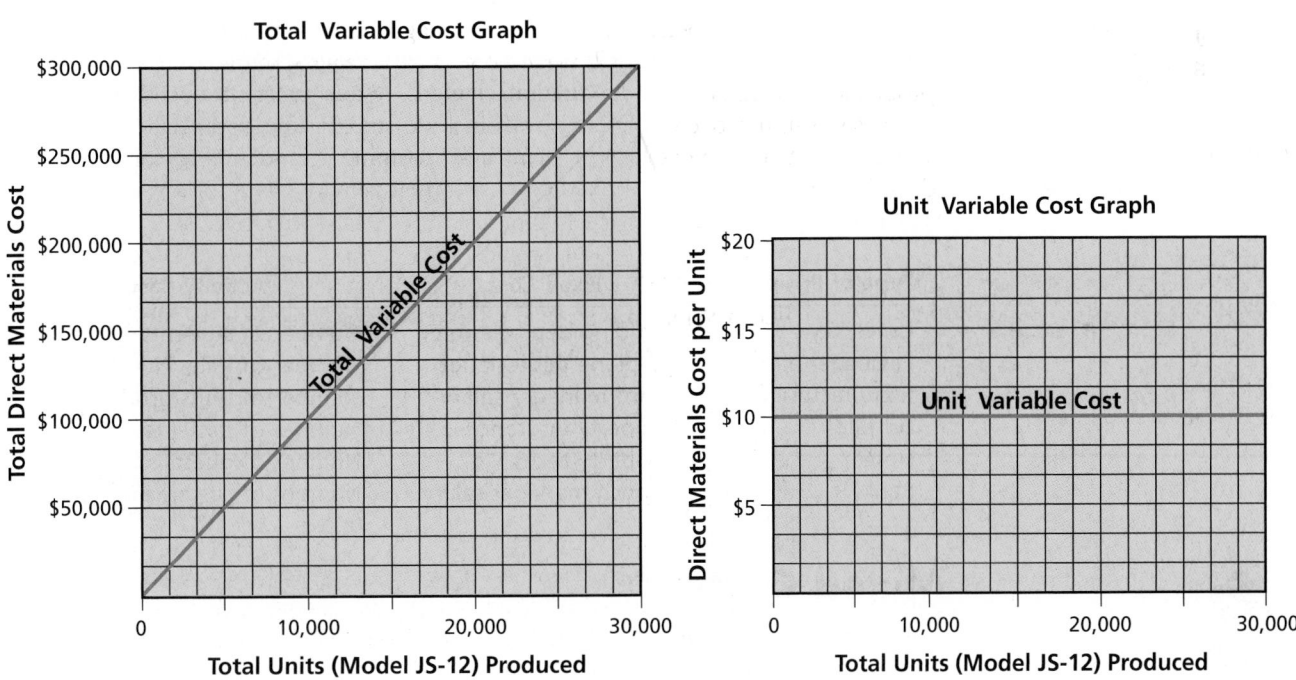

There are a variety of activity bases used by managers for evaluating cost behavior. The following list provides some examples of variable costs, along with their related activity bases for various types of businesses.

Type of Business	Cost	Activity Base
University	Instructor salaries	Number of classes
Passenger airline	Fuel	Number of miles flown
Manufacturing	Direct materials	Number of units produced
Hospital	Nurse wages	Number of patients
Hotel	Maid wages	Number of guests
Bank	Teller wages	Number of banking transactions

Fixed Costs

Fixed costs are costs that remain the same in total dollar amount as the level of activity changes. To illustrate, assume that Minton Inc. manufactures, bottles, and distributes La Fleur Perfume at its Los Angeles plant. The production supervisor at the Los Angeles plant is Jane Sovissi, who is paid a salary of $75,000 per year. The relevant range of activity for a year is 50,000 to 300,000 bottles of perfume. Sovissi's salary is a fixed cost that does not vary with the number of units produced. Regardless of the number of bottles produced within the range of 50,000 to 300,000 bottles, Sovissi receives a salary of $75,000.

Although the total fixed cost remains the same as the number of bottles produced changes, the fixed cost per bottle changes. As more bottles are produced, the total fixed costs are spread over a larger number of bottles, and thus the fixed cost per bottle decreases. This relationship is shown below for Jane Sovissi's $75,000 salary.

Number of Bottles of Perfume Produced	Total Salary for Jane Sovissi	Salary per Bottle of Perfume Produced
50,000 bottles	$75,000	$1.500
100,000	75,000	0.750
150,000	75,000	0.500
200,000	75,000	0.375
250,000	75,000	0.300
300,000	75,000	0.250

Exhibit 2 illustrates how the fixed cost of Jane Sovissi's salary behaves in total and on a per-unit basis as production changes. When units produced is the measure of activity, examples of fixed costs include straight-line depreciation of factory equipment, insurance on factory plant and equipment, and salaries of factory supervisors. Other examples of fixed costs and their activity bases for a variety of businesses are as follows:

Type of Business	Fixed Cost	Activity Base
University	Building depreciation	Number of students
Passenger airline	Airplane depreciation	Number of miles flown
Manufacturing	Plant manager salary	Number of units produced
Hospital	Property insurance	Number of patients
Hotel	Property taxes	Number of guests
Bank	Branch manager salary	Number of customer accounts

Mixed Costs

REAL WORLD

A salesperson's compensation can be a mixed cost comprised of a salary (fixed portion) plus a commission as a percent of sales (variable portion).

A **mixed cost** has characteristics of both a variable and a fixed cost. For example, over one range of activity, the total mixed cost may remain the same. It thus behaves as a fixed cost. Over another range of activity, the mixed cost may change in proportion to changes in the level of activity. It thus behaves as a variable cost. Mixed costs are sometimes called *semivariable* or *semifixed* costs.

To illustrate, assume that Simpson Inc. manufactures sails, using rented machinery. The rental charges are $15,000 per year, plus $1 for each machine hour used over 10,000 hours. If the machinery is used 8,000 hours, the total rental charge is $15,000. If the machinery is used 20,000 hours, the total rental charge is $25,000 [$15,000 + (10,000 hours × $1)], and so on. Thus, if the level of activity is measured in machine hours and the relevant range is 0 to 40,000 hours, the rental charges are a fixed cost up to 10,000 hours and a variable cost thereafter. This mixed cost behavior is shown graphically in Exhibit 3.

In analyses, mixed costs are usually separated into their fixed and variable components. The **high-low method** is a cost estimation technique that may be used for

•Exhibit 2   Fixed Cost Graphs

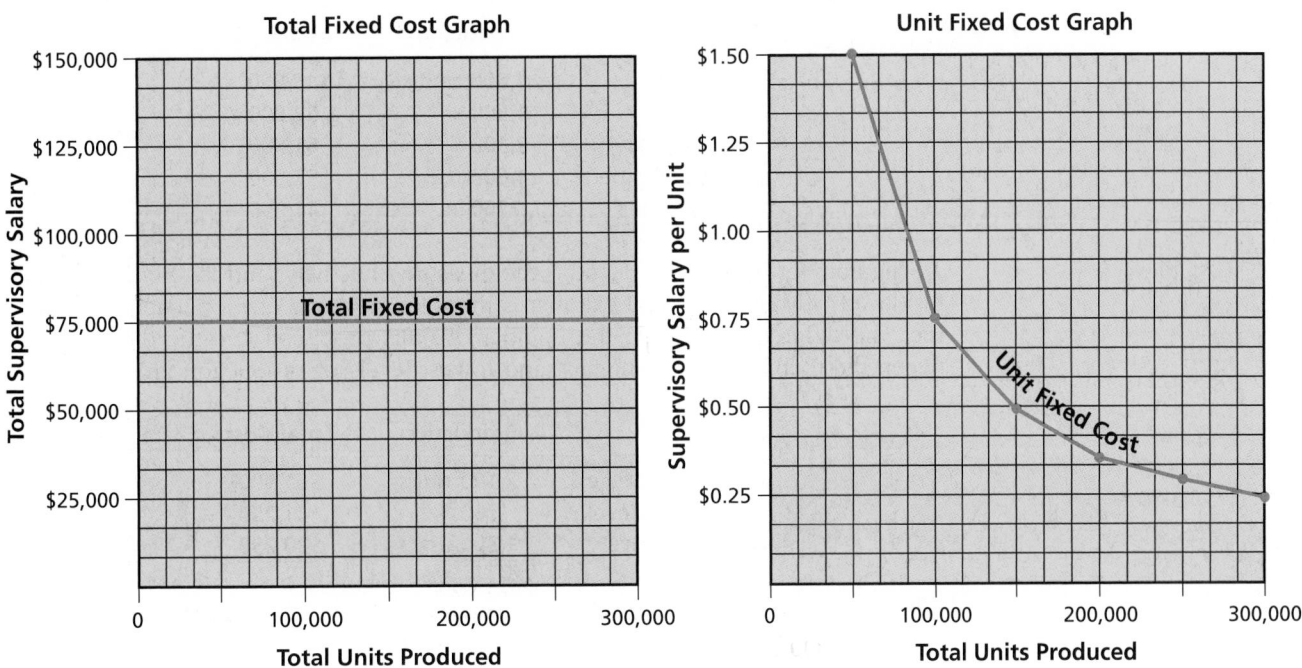

•Exhibit 3   Mixed Costs

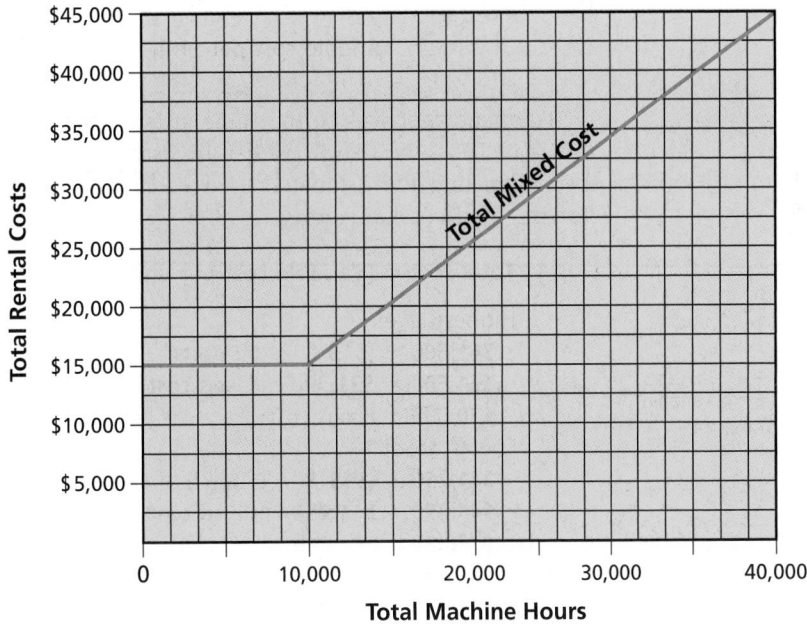

this purpose.[1] The high-low method uses the highest and lowest activity levels and their related costs to estimate the variable cost per unit and the fixed cost component of mixed costs.

---

[1]Other methods of estimating costs, such as the scattergraph method and the least squares method, are discussed in cost accounting textbooks.

To illustrate, assume that the Equipment Maintenance Department of Kason Inc. incurred the following costs during the past five months:

	Production	Total Cost
June	1,000 units	$45,550
July	1,500	52,000
August	2,100	61,500
September	1,800	57,500
October	750	41,250

The number of units produced is the measure of activity, and the number of units produced between June and October is the relevant range of production. For Kason Inc., the difference between the number of units produced and the difference between the total cost at the highest and lowest levels of production are as follows:

	Production	Total Cost
Highest level	2,100 units	$61,500
Lowest level	750	41,250
Difference	1,350 units	$20,250

Since the total fixed cost does not change with changes in volume of production, the $20,250 difference in the total cost is the change in the total variable cost. Hence, dividing the difference in the total cost by the difference in production provides an estimate of the variable cost per unit. For Kason Inc., this estimate is $15, as shown below.

$$\text{Variable cost per unit} = \frac{\text{Difference in total cost}}{\text{Difference in production}}$$

$$\text{Variable cost per unit} = \frac{\$20,250}{1,350 \text{ units}} = \$15$$

The fixed cost will be the same at both the highest and the lowest levels of production. Thus, the fixed cost can be estimated at either of these levels. This is done by subtracting the estimated total variable cost from the total cost, using the following total cost equation:

Total cost = (Variable cost per unit × Units of production) + Fixed cost

Highest level:
  $61,500 = ($15 × 2,100 units) + Fixed cost
  $61,500 = $31,500 + Fixed cost
  $30,000 = Fixed cost
Lowest level:
  $41,250 = ($15 × 750 units) + Fixed cost
  $41,250 = $11,250 + Fixed cost
  $30,000 = Fixed cost

The manufacturing cost at the highest production level of 2,500 units is $125,000. The manufacturing cost at the lowest production level of 1,000 units is $80,000. Using the high-low method, what are (a) the variable cost per unit and (b) the total fixed cost?

(a) $30 per unit [($125,000 − $80,000) ÷ (2,500 − 1,000)]; (b) $50,000 [$125,000 − ($30 × 2,500)]

The total equipment maintenance cost for Kason Inc. can thus be analyzed as a $30,000 fixed cost and a $15-per-unit variable cost. Using these amounts in the total cost equation, the total equipment maintenance cost at other levels of production can be estimated.

Summary of Cost Behavior Concepts

The following table summarizes the cost behavior attributes of variable costs and fixed costs:

	Effect of Changing Activity Level	
Cost	**Total Amount**	**Per-Unit Amount**
Variable	Increases and decreases proportionately with activity level.	Remains the same regardless of activity level.
Fixed	Remains the same regardless of activity level.	Increases and decreases inversely with activity level.

Examples of common variable, fixed, and mixed costs when the number of units produced is the activity base are:

Variable Cost	**Fixed Cost**	**Mixed Cost**
Direct materials	Depreciation expense	Quality Control Department salaries
Direct labor	Property taxes	Purchasing Department salaries
Electricity expense	Officer salaries	Maintenance expenses
Sales commissions	Insurance expense	Warehouse expenses

Mixed costs contain a fixed cost component that is incurred even if nothing is produced. For analyses, the fixed and variable cost components of mixed costs should be separated. Separating costs into their variable and fixed components for reporting purposes can be useful for decision making. One method of reporting variable and fixed costs is called **variable costing** or **direct costing**. Under variable costing, only the variable manufacturing costs (direct materials, direct labor, and variable factory overhead) are included in the product cost. The fixed factory overhead is an expense of the period in which it is incurred.[2]

Cost-Volume-Profit Relationships

objective 2

Compute the contribution margin, the contribution margin ratio, and the unit contribution margin, and explain how they may be useful to managers.

After costs have been classified as fixed and variable, their effect on revenues, volume, and profits can be studied by using cost-volume-profit analysis. **Cost-volume-profit analysis** is the systematic examination of the relationships among selling prices, sales and production volume, costs, expenses, and profits.

Cost-volume-profit analysis provides management with useful information for decision making. For example, cost-volume-profit analysis may be used in setting selling prices, selecting the mix of products to sell, choosing among marketing strategies, and analyzing the effects of changes in costs on profits. In today's business environment, management must make such decisions quickly and accurately. As a result, the importance of cost-volume-profit analysis has increased in recent years.

Contribution Margin Concept

One relationship among cost, volume, and profit is the contribution margin. The **contribution margin** is the excess of sales revenues over variable costs. The contribution margin concept is especially useful in business planning because it gives insight into the profit potential of a firm. To illustrate, the income statement of Lambert Inc. in Exhibit 4 has been prepared in a contribution margin format.

---

[2]The variable costing concept is discussed more fully in the next chapter.

•Exhibit 4

**Contribution Margin
Income Statement**

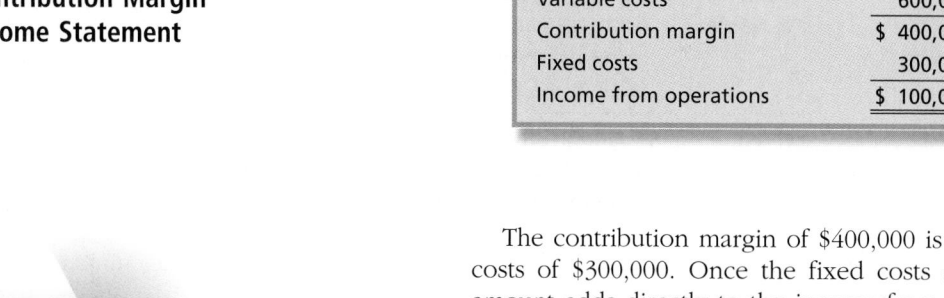

Sales	$1,000,000
Variable costs	600,000
Contribution margin	$ 400,000
Fixed costs	300,000
Income from operations	$ 100,000

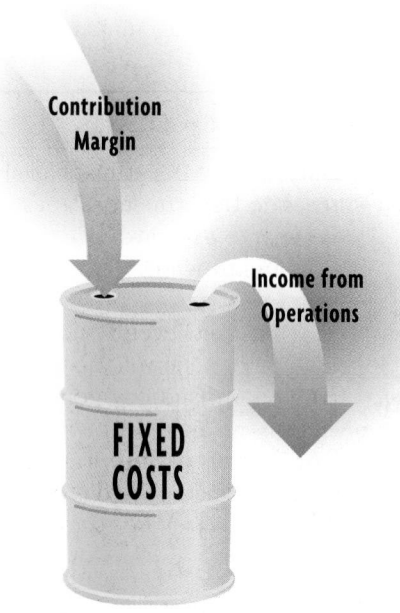

Contribution
Margin

Income from
Operations

FIXED
COSTS

The contribution margin of $400,000 is available to cover the fixed costs of $300,000. Once the fixed costs are covered, any remaining amount adds directly to the income from operations of the company. Consider the graphic to the left. The fixed costs are a bucket and the contribution margin is water filling the bucket. Once the bucket is filled, the overflow represents income from operations. Up until the point of overflow, however, the contribution margin contributes to fixed costs (filling the bucket).

Contribution Margin Ratio

The contribution margin can also be expressed as a percentage. The **contribution margin ratio**, sometimes called the **profit-volume ratio**, indicates the percentage of each sales dollar available to cover the fixed costs and to provide income from operations. For Lambert Inc., the contribution margin ratio is 40%, as computed below.

$$\text{Contribution margin ratio} = \frac{\text{Sales} - \text{Variable costs}}{\text{Sales}}$$

$$\text{Contribution margin ratio} = \frac{\$1,000,000 - \$600,000}{\$1,000,000} = 40\%$$

The contribution margin ratio measures the effect of an increase or a decrease in sales volume on income from operations. For example, assume that the management of Lambert Inc. is studying the effect of adding $80,000 in sales orders. Multiplying the contribution margin ratio (40%) by the change in sales volume ($80,000) indicates that income from operations will increase $32,000 if the additional orders are obtained. The validity of this analysis is illustrated by the following contribution margin income statement of Lambert Inc.:

Sales	$1,080,000
Variable costs ($1,080,000 × 60%)	648,000
Contribution margin ($1,080,000 × 40%)	$ 432,000
Fixed costs	300,000
Income from operations	$ 132,000

Variable costs as a percentage of sales are equal to 100% minus the contribution margin ratio. Thus, in the above income statement, the variable costs are 60% (100% − 40%) of sales, or $648,000 ($1,080,000 × 60%). The total contribution margin, $432,000, can also be computed directly by multiplying the sales by the contribution margin ratio ($1,080,000 × 40%).

In using the contribution margin ratio in analysis, factors other than sales volume, such as variable cost per unit and sales price, are assumed to remain constant. If such factors change, their effect must be considered.

The contribution margin ratio is also useful in setting business policy. For example, if the contribution margin ratio of a firm is large and production is at a level below 100% capacity, a large increase in income from operations can be expected from an increase in sales volume. A firm in such a position might decide to devote more effort to sales promotion because of the large change in income from operations that will result from changes in sales volume. In contrast, a firm with a small contribution margin ratio will probably want to give more attention to reducing costs before attempting to promote sales.

Unit Contribution Margin

Sales are 20,000 units at $12 per unit, variable costs are $9 per unit, and fixed costs are $25,000. What are (a) the contribution margin ratio, (b) the unit contribution margin, and (c) the income from operations?

(a) 25% [($240,000 − $180,000) ÷ $240,000]; (b) $3 per unit ($12 − $9); (c) $35,000 ($240,000 − $180,000 − $25,000)

The unit contribution margin is also useful for analyzing the profit potential of proposed projects. The **unit contribution margin** is the sales price less the variable cost per unit. For example, if Lambert Inc.'s unit selling price is $20 and its unit variable cost is $12, the unit contribution margin is $8 ($20 − $12).

The *contribution margin ratio* is most useful when the increase or decrease in sales volume is measured in sales *dollars*. The *unit contribution margin* is most useful when the increase or decrease in sales volume is measured in sales *units* (quantities). To illustrate, assume that Lambert Inc. sold 50,000 units. Its income from operations is $100,000, as shown in the following contribution margin income statement:

Sales (50,000 units × $20)	$1,000,000
Variable costs (50,000 units × $12)	600,000
Contribution margin (50,000 units × $8)	$ 400,000
Fixed costs	300,000
Income from operations	$ 100,000

If Lambert Inc.'s sales could be increased by 15,000 units, from 50,000 units to 65,000 units, its income from operations would increase by $120,000 (15,000 units × $8), as shown below.

Sales (65,000 units × $20)	$1,300,000
Variable costs (65,000 units × $12)	780,000
Contribution margin (65,000 units × $8)	$ 520,000
Fixed costs	300,000
Income from operations	$ 220,000

REAL WORLD

A $200-per-night room at the **Four Seasons** hotel may have a variable cost, including maids' salaries, laundry, soap, and utilities, of only $25 per night and thus a high unit contribution margin per room. The high contribution margin per unit is necessary to cover the high fixed costs for the hotel.

Unit contribution margin analyses can provide useful information for managers. The preceding illustration indicates, for example, that Lambert could spend up to $120,000 for special advertising or other product promotions to increase sales by 15,000 units.

Mathematical Approach to Cost-Volume-Profit Analysis

objective **3**

Using the unit contribution margin, determine the break-even point and the volume necessary to achieve a target profit.

Accountants use various approaches for expressing the relationship of costs, sales (volume), and income from operations (operating profit). The mathematical approach is one approach that is used often in practice.

The mathematical approach to cost-volume-profit analysis uses equations (1) to determine the units of sales necessary to achieve the break-even point in operations or (2) to determine the units of sales necessary to achieve a target or desired profit.

We will next describe and illustrate these equations and their use by management in profit planning.

Break-Even Point

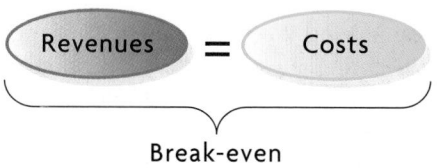

The ***break-even point*** is the level of operations at which a business's revenues and expired costs are exactly equal. At break-even, a business will have neither an income nor a loss from operations. The break-even point is useful in business planning, especially when expanding or decreasing operations.

To illustrate the computation of the break-even point, assume that the fixed costs for Barker Corporation are estimated to be $90,000. The unit selling price, unit variable cost, and unit contribution margin for Barker Corporation are as follows:

Unit selling price	$25
Unit variable cost	15
Unit contribution margin	$10

The break-even point is 9,000 units, which can be computed by using the following equation:

$$\text{Break-even sales (units)} = \frac{\text{Fixed costs}}{\text{Unit contribution margin}}$$

$$\text{Break-even sales (units)} = \frac{\$90,000}{\$10} = 9{,}000 \text{ units}$$

The following income statement verifies the preceding computation:

Sales (9,000 units × $25)	$225,000
Variable costs (9,000 units × $15)	135,000
Contribution margin	$ 90,000
Fixed costs	90,000
Income from operations	$ 0

The break-even point is affected by changes in the fixed costs, unit variable costs, and the unit selling price. Next, we will briefly describe the effect of each of these factors on the break-even point.

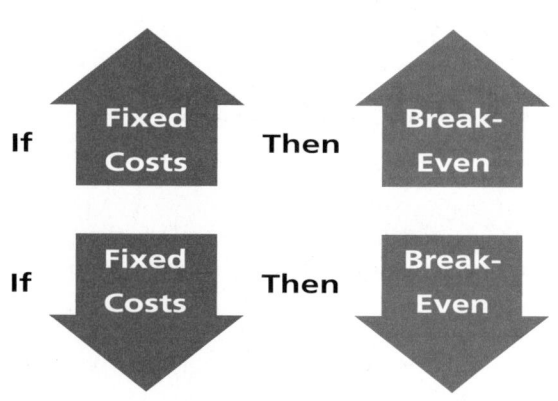

Effect of Changes in Fixed Costs

Although fixed costs do not change in total with changes in the level of activity, they may change because of other factors. For example, changes in property tax rates or factory supervisors' salaries change fixed costs. Increases in fixed costs will raise the break-even point. Likewise, decreases in fixed costs will lower the break-even point.

To illustrate, assume that Bishop Co. is evaluating a proposal to budget an additional $100,000 for advertising. Fixed costs before the additional advertising are estimated at $600,000, and the unit contribution margin is $20. The break-even point before the additional expense is 30,000 units, computed as follows:

$$\text{Break-even sales (units)} = \frac{\text{Fixed costs}}{\text{Unit contribution margin}}$$

$$\text{Break-even sales (units)} = \frac{\$600,000}{\$20} = 30,000 \text{ units}$$

If the additional amount is spent, the fixed costs will increase by $100,000 and the break-even point will increase to 35,000 units, computed as follows:

$$\text{Break-even sales (units)} = \frac{\text{Fixed costs}}{\text{Unit contribution margin}}$$

$$\text{Break-even sales (units)} = \frac{\$700,000}{\$20} = 35,000 \text{ units}$$

The $100,000 increase in the fixed costs requires an additional 5,000 units ($100,000 ÷ $20) of sales to break even. In other words, an increase in sales of 5,000 units is required in order to generate an additional $100,000 of total contribution margin (5,000 units × $20) to cover the increased fixed costs.

Effect of Changes in Unit Variable Costs

Although unit variable costs are not affected by changes in volume of activity, they may be affected by other factors. For example, changes in the price of direct materials and the wages for factory workers providing direct labor will change unit variable costs. Increases in unit variable costs will raise the break-even point. Likewise, decreases in unit variable costs will lower the break-even point. For example, when fuel prices rise or decline, there is a direct impact on the break-even freight load for the **Union Pacific** railroad.

To illustrate, assume that Park Co. is evaluating a proposal to pay an additional 2% commission on sales to its salespeople as an incentive to increase sales. Fixed costs are estimated at $840,000, and the unit selling price, unit variable cost, and unit contribution margin before the additional 2% commission are as follows:

Unit selling price	$250
Unit variable cost	145
Unit contribution margin	$105

The break-even point is 8,000 units, computed as follows:

$$\text{Break-even sales (units)} = \frac{\text{Fixed costs}}{\text{Unit contribution margin}}$$

$$\text{Break-even sales (units)} = \frac{\$840,000}{\$105} = 8,000 \text{ units}$$

If the sales commission proposal is adopted, variable costs will increase by $5 per unit ($250 × 2%). This increase in the variable costs will decrease the unit contribution margin by $5 (from $105 to $100). Thus, the break-even point is raised to 8,400 units, computed as follows:

$$\text{Break-even sales (units)} = \frac{\text{Fixed costs}}{\text{Unit contribution margin}}$$

$$\text{Break-even sales (units)} = \frac{\$840,000}{\$100} = 8,400 \text{ units}$$

At the original break-even point of 8,000 units, the new unit contribution margin of $100 would provide only $800,000 to cover fixed costs of $840,000. Thus,

an additional 400 units of sales will be required in order to provide the additional $40,000 (400 units × $100) contribution margin necessary to break even.

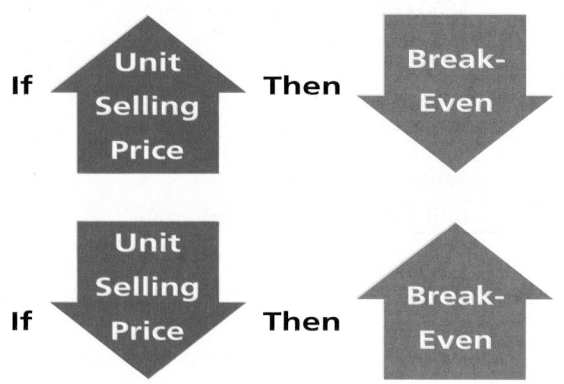

Effect of Changes in the Unit Selling Price

Increases in the unit selling price will lower the break-even point, while decreases in the unit selling price will raise the break-even point. To illustrate, assume that Graham Co. is evaluating a proposal to increase the unit selling price of its product from $50 to $60. The following data have been gathered:

	Current	Proposed
Unit selling price	$50	$60
Unit variable cost	30	30
Unit contribution margin	$20	$30
Total fixed costs	$600,000	$600,000

The break-even point based on the current selling price is 30,000 units, computed as follows:

$$\text{Break-even sales (units)} = \frac{\text{Fixed costs}}{\text{Unit contribution margin}}$$

$$\text{Break-even sales (units)} = \frac{\$600,000}{\$20} = 30,000 \text{ units}$$

If the selling price is increased by $10 per unit, the break-even point is decreased to 20,000 units, computed as follows:

$$\text{Break-even sales (units)} = \frac{\text{Fixed costs}}{\text{Unit contribution margin}}$$

$$\text{Break-even sales (units)} = \frac{\$600,000}{\$30} = 20,000 \text{ units}$$

The increase of $10 per unit in the selling price increases the unit contribution margin by $10. Thus, the break-even point decreases by 10,000 units (from 30,000 units to 20,000 units).

Summary of Effects of Changes on Break-Even Point

The break-even point in sales (units) moves in the same direction as changes in the variable cost per unit and fixed costs. In contrast, the break-even point in sales (units) moves in the opposite direction to changes in the sales price per unit. A summary of the impact of these changes on the break-even point in sales (units) is shown below.

The selling price for a product is $60 per unit. The variable cost is $35 per unit, while fixed costs are $80,000. What are the following amounts: (a) the break-even point in sales units and (b) the break-even point if the selling price were increased to $67 per unit?

- -

(a) 3,200 units [$80,000 ÷ ($60 − $35)]; (b) 2,500 units [$80,000 ÷ ($67 − $35)]

Type of Change	Direction of Change	Effect of Change on Break-Even Sales (Units)
Fixed cost	Increase	Increase
	Decrease	Decrease
Variable cost per unit	Increase	Increase
	Decrease	Decrease
Unit sales price	Increase	Decrease
	Decrease	Increase

Target Profit

At the break-even point, sales and costs are exactly equal. However, the break-even point is not the goal of most businesses. Rather, managers seek to maximize profits. By modifying the break-even equation, the sales volume required to earn a target or desired amount of profit may be estimated. For this purpose, target profit is added to the break-even equation as shown below.

$$\text{Sales (units)} = \frac{\text{Fixed costs} + \text{Target profit}}{\text{Unit contribution margin}}$$

To illustrate, assume that fixed costs are estimated at $200,000, and the desired profit is $100,000. The unit selling price, unit variable cost, and unit contribution margin are as follows:

Unit selling price	$75
Unit variable cost	45
Unit contribution margin	$30

The sales volume necessary to earn the target profit of $100,000 is 10,000 units, computed as follows:

$$\text{Sales (units)} = \frac{\text{Fixed costs} + \text{Target profit}}{\text{Unit contribution margin}}$$

$$\text{Sales (units)} = \frac{\$200,000 + \$100,000}{\$30} = 10,000 \text{ units}$$

The following income statement verifies this computation:

The sales price is $140 per unit, variable costs are $60 per unit, and fixed costs are $240,000. What would be (a) the break-even point in sales units and (b) the break-even point in sales units if a target profit of $50,000 is desired?

(a) 3,000 units [$240,000 ÷ ($140 − $60)]; (b) 3,625 units [($240,000 + $50,000) ÷ ($140 − $60)]

Sales (10,000 units × $75)	$750,000
Variable costs (10,000 units × $45)	450,000
Contribution margin (10,000 units × $30)	$300,000
Fixed costs	200,000
Income from operations	$100,000

← Target profit

INTEGRITY IN BUSINESS

PREDICTING BREAK-EVEN

The SEC requires management to provide forward-looking statements about known trends, events, or uncertainties impacting their business. These disclosures are required as part of the management discussion and analysis portion of the SEC annual report (10-K). Often, as part of these disclosures, companies operating with losses will predict when they anticipate to break even. For example, **Ford** **Motor Co.** stated in its 2001 annual report that "based on these [*vehicle demand assumptions*] and other assumptions (e.g., assumptions regarding marketing costs, which are expected to be higher in 2002), we expect 2002 earnings (excluding unusual items) to be about break even." (Emphasis added.)

Graphic Approach to Cost-Volume-Profit Analysis

objective 4

Using a cost-volume-profit chart and a profit-volume chart, determine the break-even point and the volume necessary to achieve a target profit.

Cost-volume-profit analysis can be presented graphically as well as in equation form. Many managers prefer the graphic format because the income or loss from operations (operating profit or loss) for different levels of sales can readily be determined. Next, we describe two graphic approaches that managers find useful.

Cost-Volume-Profit (Break-Even) Chart

A *cost-volume-profit chart*, sometimes called a **break-even chart**, may assist management in understanding relationships among costs, sales, and operating profit or loss. To illustrate, the cost-volume-profit chart in Exhibit 5 is based on the following data:

Unit selling price	$50
Unit variable cost	30
Unit contribution margin	$20
Total fixed costs	$100,000

•**Exhibit 5** Cost-Volume-Profit Chart

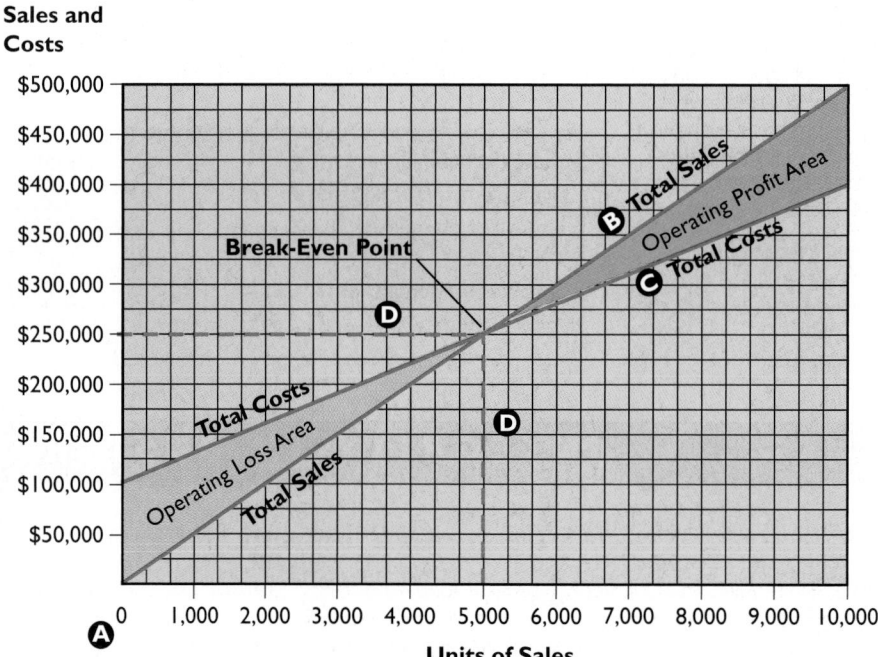

We constructed the cost-volume-profit chart in Exhibit 5 as follows:

A. Volume expressed in units of sales is indicated along the horizontal axis. The range of volume shown on the horizontal axis should reflect the *relevant range* in which the business expects to operate. Dollar amounts representing total sales and costs are indicated along the vertical axis.

B. A sales line is plotted by beginning at zero on the left corner of the graph. A second point is determined by multiplying any units of sales on the horizontal axis by the unit sales price of $50. For example, for 10,000 units of sales, the total sales would be $500,000 (10,000 units × $50). The sales line is drawn upward to the right from zero through the $500,000 point.

C. A cost line is plotted by beginning with total fixed costs, $100,000, on the vertical axis. A second point is determined by multiplying any units of sales on the horizontal axis by the unit variable costs and adding the fixed costs. For example, for 10,000 units of sales, the total estimated costs would be $400,000 [(10,000 units × $30) + $100,000]. The cost line is drawn upward to the right from $100,000 on the vertical axis through the $400,000 point.

D. Horizontal and vertical lines are drawn at the intersection point of the sales and cost lines, which is the break-even point, and the areas representing operating profit and operating loss are identified.

In Exhibit 5, the dotted lines drawn from the intersection point of the total sales line and the total cost line identify the break-even point in total sales dollars and units. The break-even point is $250,000 of sales, which represents a sales volume of 5,000 units. Operating profits will be earned when sales levels are to the right of the break-even point (operating profit area). Operating losses will be incurred when sales levels are to the left of the break-even point (operating loss area).

Changes in the unit selling price, total fixed costs, and unit variable costs can be analyzed by using a cost-volume-profit chart. Using the data in Exhibit 5, assume that a proposal to reduce fixed costs by $20,000 is to be evaluated. In this case, the total fixed costs would be $80,000 ($100,000 − $20,000). As shown in Exhibit 6, the total cost line should be redrawn, starting at the $80,000 point (total fixed costs) on the vertical axis. A second point is determined by multiplying any units of sales on the horizontal axis by the unit variable costs and adding the fixed costs. For example, for 10,000 units of sales, the total estimated costs would be $380,000 [(10,000 units × $30) + $80,000]. The cost line is drawn upward to the right from $80,000 on the vertical axis through the $380,000 point. The revised cost-volume-profit chart in Exhibit 6 indicates that the break-even point decreases to $200,000 or 4,000 units of sales.

•Exhibit 6   Revised Cost-Volume-Profit Chart

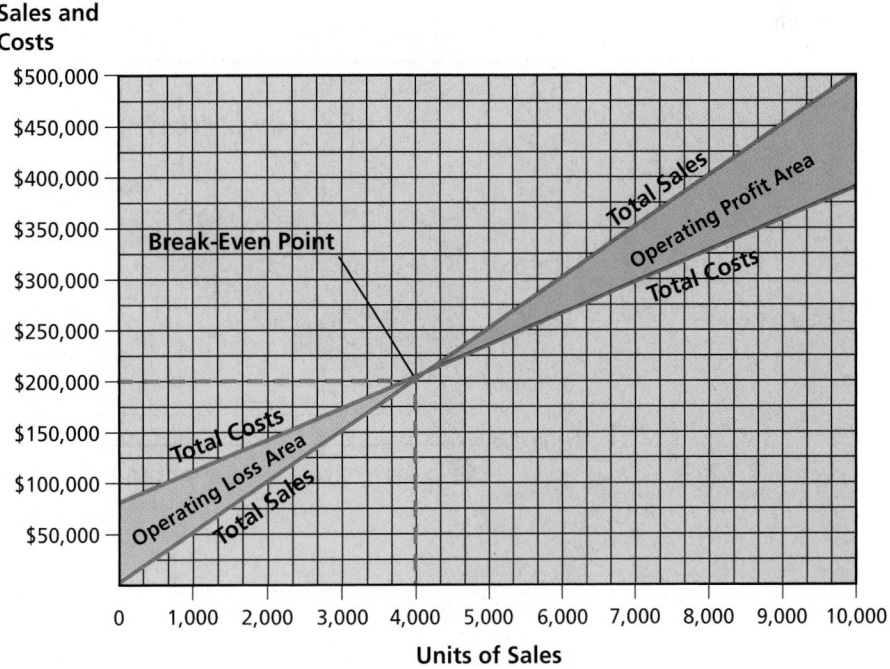

Profit-Volume Chart

Another graphic approach to cost-volume-profit analysis, the **_profit-volume chart_**, focuses on profits. This is in contrast to the cost-volume-profit chart, which focuses on sales and costs. The profit-volume chart plots only the difference between total sales and total costs (or profits). In this way, the profit-volume chart allows managers to determine the operating profit (or loss) for various levels of operations.

To illustrate, assume that the profit-volume chart in Exhibit 7 is based on the same data as used in Exhibit 5. These data are as follows:

Unit selling price	$50
Unit variable cost	30
Unit contribution margin	$20
Total fixed costs	$100,000

The maximum operating loss is equal to the fixed costs of $100,000. Assuming that the maximum unit sales within the relevant range is 10,000 units, the maximum operating profit is $100,000, computed as follows:

Sales (10,000 units × $50)	$500,000
Variable costs (10,000 units × $30)	300,000
Contribution margin (10,000 units × $20)	$200,000
Fixed costs	100,000
Operating profit	$100,000	← Maximum profit

•Exhibit 7 Profit-Volume Chart

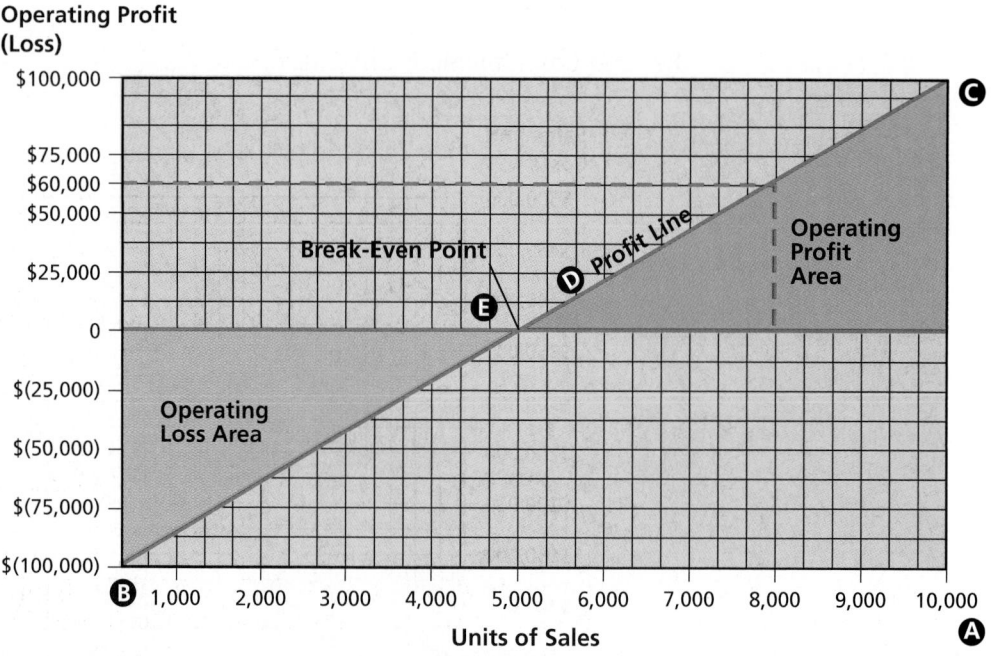

We constructed the profit-volume chart in Exhibit 7 as follows:

A. Volume expressed in units of sales is indicated along the horizontal axis. The range of volume shown on the horizontal axis should reflect the *relevant range* in

Many NBA franchises, such as the **Los Angeles Lakers**, state that their financial goal is to break even during the regular season and to make their profit during the playoffs, or basketball's so called "second season." The deeper the team goes into the playoffs, the greater the operating profit earned above break-even from additional ticket sales and TV revenues.

which the business expects to operate. In this illustration, the maximum number of sales units within the relevant range is assumed to be 10,000 units. Dollar amounts indicating operating profits and losses are shown along the vertical axis.

B. A point representing the maximum operating loss is plotted on the vertical axis at the left. This loss is equal to the total fixed costs at the zero level of sales.

C. A point representing the maximum operating profit within the relevant range is plotted on the right.

D. A diagonal profit line is drawn connecting the maximum operating loss point with the maximum operating profit point.

E. The profit line intersects the horizontal zero operating profit line at the break-even point expressed in units of sales, and the areas indicating operating profit and loss are identified.

In Exhibit 7, the break-even point is 5,000 units of sales, which is equal to total sales of $250,000 (5,000 units × $50). Operating profit will be earned when sales levels are to the right of the break-even point (operating profit area). Operating losses will be incurred when sales levels are to the left of the break-even point (operating loss area). For example, at sales of 8,000 units, an operating profit of $60,000 will be earned, as shown in Exhibit 7.

The effect of changes in the unit selling price, total fixed costs, and unit variable costs on profit can be analyzed using a profit-volume chart. To illustrate, using the data in Exhibit 7, we will evaluate the effect on profit of an increase of $20,000 in fixed costs. In this case, the total fixed costs would be $120,000 ($100,000 + $20,000), and the maximum operating loss would also be $120,000. If the maximum sales within the relevant range is 10,000 units, the maximum operating profit would be $80,000, computed as follows:

Sales (10,000 units × $50)	$500,000
Variable costs (10,000 units × $30)	300,000
Contribution margin (10,000 units × $20)	$200,000
Fixed costs	120,000
Operating profit	$ 80,000

← Revised maximum profit

I'm the nation's largest turkey processor. I trace my history back to 1891, when a son of German immigrants founded me in Minnesota. I debuted the world's first canned ham in 1926 and a year later had salesmen selling from "sausage trucks." In 1937, I introduced a now-famous luncheon meat made of spiced ham. My brands include Dinty Moore, Herb-Ox, Chi-Chi's, House of Tsang, Pataks, and Little Sizzlers. In 1986, I bought Jennie-O, the premier turkey-product maker. I rake in more than $4 billion annually and have increased my dividends for 31 consecutive years. Who am I? (Go to page 772 for answer.)

A revised profit-volume chart is constructed by plotting the maximum operating loss and maximum operating profit points and drawing the revised profit line. The original and the revised profit-volume charts are shown in Exhibit 8.

The revised profit-volume chart indicates that the break-even point is 6,000 units of sales. This is equal to total sales of $300,000 (6,000 units × $50). The operating loss area of the chart has increased, while the operating profit area has decreased under the proposed change in fixed costs.

Use of Computers in Cost-Volume-Profit Analysis

With computers, the graphic approach and the mathematical approach to cost-volume-profit analysis are easy to use. Managers can vary assumptions regarding selling prices, costs, and volume and can immediately see the effects of each change on the break-even point and profit. Such an analysis is called a **"what if" analysis** or **sensitivity analysis**.

•Exhibit 8   Original Profit-Volume Chart and Revised Profit-Volume Chart

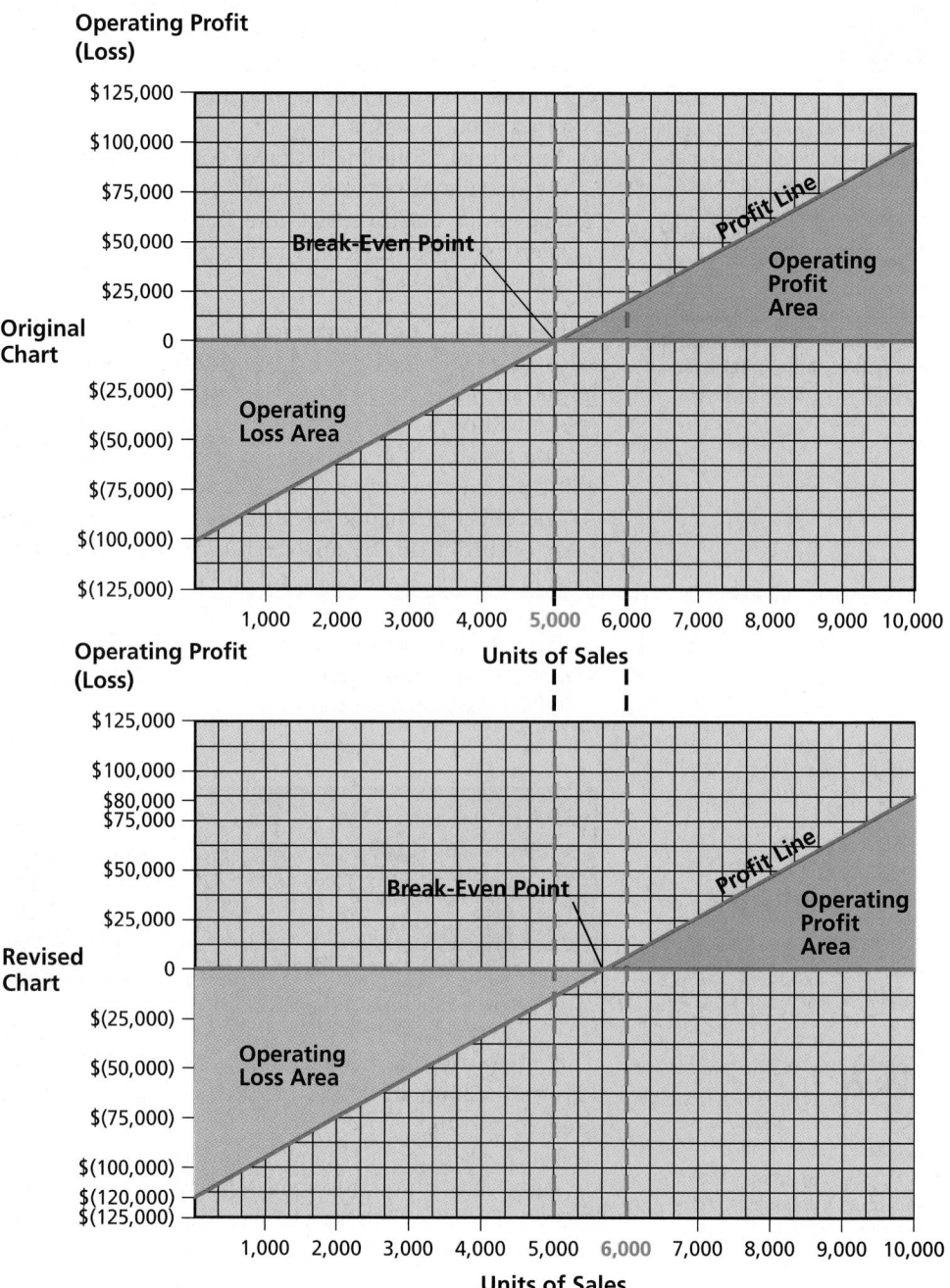

Sales Mix Considerations

objective **5**

Calculate the break-even point for a business selling more than one product.

In most businesses, more than one product is sold at varying selling prices. In addition, the products often have different unit variable costs, and each product makes a different contribution to profits. Thus, the sales volume necessary to break even or to earn a target profit for a business selling two or more products depends upon the sales mix. The ***sales mix*** is the relative distribution of sales among the various products sold by a business.

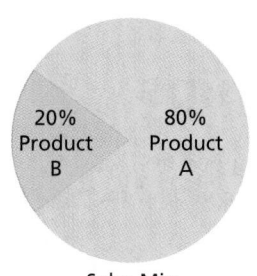

Sales Mix

To illustrate the calculation of the break-even point for a company that sells more than one product, assume that Cascade Company sold 8,000 units of Product A and 2,000 units of Product B during the past year. The sales mix for products A and B can be expressed as percentages (80% and 20%) or as a ratio (80:20).

Cascade Company's fixed costs are $200,000. The unit selling prices, unit variable costs, and unit contribution margins for products A and B are as follows:

Product	Unit Selling Price	Unit Variable Cost	Unit Contribution Margin
A	$ 90	$70	$20
B	140	95	45

In computing the break-even point, it is useful to think of the individual products as components of one overall enterprise product. For Cascade Company, this overall enterprise product is called E. We can think of the unit selling price of E as equal to the total of the unit selling prices of products A and B, multiplied by their sales mix percentages. Likewise, we can think of the unit variable cost and unit contribution margin of E as equal to the total of the unit variable costs and unit contribution margins of products A and B, multiplied by the sales mix percentages. These computations are as follows:

Unit selling price of E: ($90 × 0.8) + ($140 × 0.2) = $100
Unit variable cost of E: ($70 × 0.8) + ($ 95 × 0.2) = $ 75
Unit contribution margin of E: ($20 × 0.8) + ($ 45 × 0.2) = $ 25

The break-even point of 8,000 units of E can be determined in the normal manner as follows:

$$\text{Break-even sales (units)} = \frac{\text{Fixed costs}}{\text{Unit contribution margin}}$$

$$\text{Break-even sales (units)} = \frac{\$200,000}{\$25} = 8,000 \text{ units}$$

Since the sales mix for products A and B is 80% and 20%, the break-even quantity of A is 6,400 units (8,000 units × 80%) and B is 1,600 units (8,000 units × 20%). This analysis can be verified in the following income statement:

	Product A	Product B	Total
Sales:			
6,400 units × $90	$576,000		$576,000
1,600 units × $140		$224,000	224,000
Total sales	$576,000	$224,000	$800,000
Variable costs:			
6,400 units × $70	$448,000		$448,000
1,600 units × $95		$152,000	152,000
Total variable costs	$448,000	$152,000	$600,000
Contribution margin	$128,000	$ 72,000	$200,000
Fixed costs			200,000
Income from operations			$ 0	← Break-even point

The effects of changes in the sales mix on the break-even point can be determined by repeating this analysis, assuming a different sales mix.

Special Cost-Volume-Profit Relationships

objective **6**

Compute the operating leverage and the margin of safety, and explain how managers use these concepts.

Some additional relationships useful to managers can be developed from cost-volume-profit data. Two of these relationships are the operating leverage and the margin of safety.

Operating Leverage

The relative mix of a business's variable costs and fixed costs is measured by the *operating leverage*. It is computed as follows:

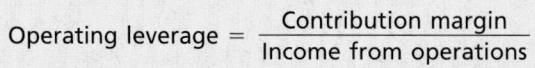

$$\text{Operating leverage} = \frac{\text{Contribution margin}}{\text{Income from operations}}$$

REAL WORLD

One type of business that has high operating leverage is what is called a "network" business—one in which service is provided over a network that moves either goods or information. Examples of network businesses include **American Airlines, Verizon Communications, Yahoo!**, and **Union Pacific**.

Since the difference between contribution margin and income from operations is fixed costs, companies with large amounts of fixed costs will generally have a high operating leverage. Thus, companies in capital-intensive industries, such as the airline and automotive industries, will generally have a high operating leverage. A low operating leverage is normal for companies in industries that are labor-intensive, such as professional services.

Managers can use operating leverage to measure the impact of changes in sales on income from operations. A high operating leverage indicates that a small increase in sales will yield a large percentage increase in income from operations. In contrast, a low operating leverage indicates that a large increase in sales is necessary to significantly increase income from operations. To illustrate, assume the following operating data for Jones Inc. and Wilson Inc.:

	Jones Inc.	Wilson Inc.
Sales	$400,000	$400,000
Variable costs	300,000	300,000
Contribution margin	$100,000	$100,000
Fixed costs	80,000	50,000
Income from operations	$ 20,000	$ 50,000

What is the operating leverage for a company with sales of $410,000, variable costs of $250,000, and fixed costs of $80,000?
....
2.0 [($410,000 − $250,000) ÷ ($410,000 − $250,000 − $80,000)]

Both companies have the same sales, the same variable costs, and the same contribution margin. Jones Inc. has larger fixed costs than Wilson Inc. and, as a result, a lower income from operations and a higher operating leverage. The operating leverage for each company is computed as follows:

Jones Inc.

$$\text{Operating leverage} = \frac{\$100,000}{\$20,000} = 5$$

Wilson Inc.

$$\text{Operating leverage} = \frac{\$100,000}{\$50,000} = 2$$

Jones Inc.'s operating leverage indicates that, for each percentage point change in sales, income from operations will change five times that percentage. In contrast, for each percentage point change in sales, the income from operations of Wilson Inc. will change only two times that percentage. For example, if sales increased by 10% ($40,000) for each company, income from operations will increase by 50% (10% × 5), or $10,000 (50% × $20,000), for Jones Inc. The sales increase of $40,000 will increase income from operations by only 20% (10% × 2), or $10,000 (20% × $50,000), for Wilson Inc. The validity of this analysis is shown as follows:

	Jones Inc.	Wilson Inc.
Sales	$440,000	$440,000
Variable costs	330,000	330,000
Contribution margin	$110,000	$110,000
Fixed costs	80,000	50,000
Income from operations	$ 30,000	$ 60,000

For Jones Inc., even a small increase in sales will generate a large percentage increase in income from operations. Thus, Jones's managers may be motivated to think of ways to increase sales. In contrast, Wilson's managers might attempt to increase operating leverage by reducing variable costs and thereby change the cost structure.

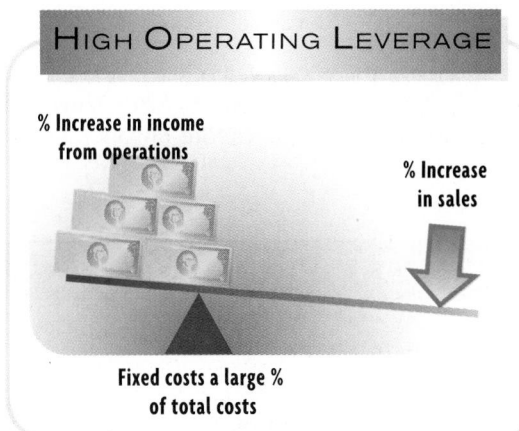

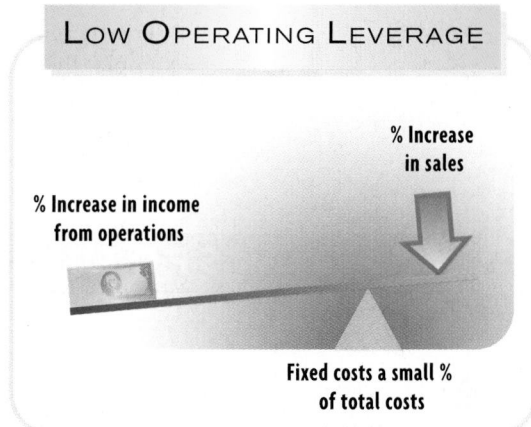

MANAGERIAL DISCLOSURE AND ANALYSIS

OPERATING LEVERAGE IN THE AIRLINE INDUSTRY

The commercial airline industry has high operating leverage. The annual fixed costs of the airplanes, ground facilities, and service network are high relative to the variable costs, such as fuel. Thus, when this industry operates above break-even, it is very profitable; however, at below break-even, the industry generates large losses. To help assess the break-even point, **Delta Air Lines, Inc.**, provided the following disclosure in its annual report to the Securities and Exchange Commission (10-K):

	2001	2000	Change
Revenue passengers enplaned (thousands)	104,943	119,930	(12)%
Revenue passenger miles (millions)	101,717	112,998	(10)%
Available seat miles (millions)	147,837	154,974	(5)%
Passenger load factor	68.8%	72.9%	(4.1) pts
Breakeven passenger load factor	74.7%	64.8%	9.9 pts

As can be seen, the number of passengers that flew with Delta dropped by 12% between 2000 and 2001. This decrease was largely the result of the 9/11 terrorist incident. The total number of miles flown by these passengers (revenue passenger miles) dropped by 10% over the same time period. Delta adjusted its operating capacity to the drop in demand by reducing the available seat miles by five percent. The available seat miles is the number of available (sold or unsold) seats multiplied by the number of miles flown. As a result, the passenger load (passenger miles divided by the available passenger miles) dropped by 4.1%. Unfortunately, the higher costs attributed to the 9/11 incident have increased the break-even load factor by almost 10 full percentage points. This caused Delta to swing from nearly eight points above break-even in 2000 (72.9 − 64.8) to nearly six points below break-even in 2001 (68.8 − 74.7).

Margin of Safety

The difference between the current sales revenue and the sales at the break-even point is called the ***margin of safety***. It indicates the possible decrease in sales that may occur before an operating loss results. For example, if the margin of safety is low, even a small decline in sales revenue may result in an operating loss.

If sales are $250,000, the unit selling price is $25, and sales at the break-even point are $200,000, the margin of safety is 20%, computed as follows:

$$\text{Margin of safety} = \frac{\text{Sales} - \text{Sales at break-even point}}{\text{Sales}}$$

$$\text{Margin of safety} = \frac{\$250,000 - \$200,000}{\$250,000} = 20\%$$

The margin of safety may also be stated in terms of units. In this illustration, for example, the margin of safety of 20% is equivalent to $50,000 ($250,000 × 20%). In units, the margin of safety is 2,000 units ($50,000 ÷ $25). Thus, the current sales of $250,000 may decline $50,000 or 2,000 units before an operating loss occurs.

SPOTLIGHT ON STRATEGY

MANAGING THE POWER STACK

Electric utility companies, such as **Duke Energy Corporation**, generate electricity by using a variety of means, such as nuclear, coal, and oil/gas generating facilities. Power companies manage their various power generation resources to match the demand for power, using what is termed the "power stack." The power stack matches demand for power by arranging generating facilities in the order of cost per kilowatt-hour. The least cost per kilowatt-hour facilities satisfy initial demand at the bottom of the stack, while the highest cost per kilowatt-hour power sources are placed at the top of the stack for peak loads, as illustrated below.

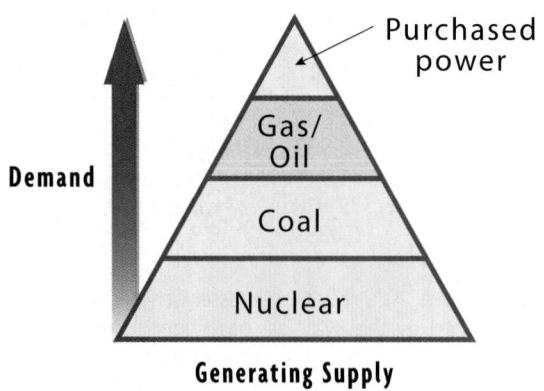

The lowest cost facilities form what is termed "base load." If the power company uses nuclear power facilities, these will often be placed in base load. Nuclear power plants have a high fixed cost but a low variable fuel cost. These facilities are very efficient at high utilization levels; thus, they form the base of the power stack. As demand increases, power generation facilities with lower fixed costs and higher variable fuel costs are switched on. Coal plants are usually next in the stack, followed by gas- or oil-fired turbines. Lastly, during the peak demands of summer, the power company may be required to purchase electricity in the power market. This power is usually the most expensive power available, but it is also the most flexible because it requires no fixed costs.

Managing power generating resources in this way gives management the ability to price electricity to customers according to the time of day they demand power. For example, a factory willing to run during the night can receive a price discount because power generated during the lower-demand night hours comes from lower in the power stack. Likewise, when a power company sells electricity in the power market, management must know the stack location for the power sales in order to remain profitable.

As the U.S. power market becomes more deregulated, a company's understanding of its power stack will become critical to business success.

ssumptions of Cost-Volume-Profit Analysis

objective **7**

List the assumptions underlying cost-volume-profit analysis.

The reliability of cost-volume-profit analysis depends upon the validity of several assumptions. The primary assumptions are as follows:

1. Total sales and total costs can be represented by straight lines.
2. Within the relevant range of operating activity, the efficiency of operations does not change.
3. Costs can be accurately divided into fixed and variable components.
4. The sales mix is constant.
5. There is no change in the inventory quantities during the period.

These assumptions simplify cost-volume-profit analysis. Since they are often valid for the relevant range of operations, cost-volume-profit analysis is useful to decision making.[3]

Key Points

1 Classify costs by their behavior as variable costs, fixed costs, or mixed costs.

Cost behavior refers to the manner in which a cost changes as a related activity changes. Variable costs are costs that vary in total in proportion to changes in the level of activity. Fixed costs are costs that remain the same in total dollar amount as the level of activity changes. A mixed cost has attributes of both a variable and a fixed cost.

2 Compute the contribution margin, the contribution margin ratio, and the unit contribution margin, and explain how they may be useful to managers.

The contribution margin concept is useful in business planning because it gives insight into the profit potential of a firm. The contribution margin is the excess of sales revenues over variable costs. The contribution margin ratio is computed as follows:

$$\text{Contribution margin ratio} = \frac{\text{Sales} - \text{Variable costs}}{\text{Sales}}$$

The unit contribution margin is the excess of the unit selling price over the unit variable cost.

3 Using the unit contribution margin, determine the break-even point and the volume necessary to achieve a target profit.

The mathematical approach to cost-volume-profit analysis uses the unit contribution margin concept and the following equations to determine the break-even point and the volume necessary to achieve a target profit for a business:

$$\text{Break-even sales (units)} = \frac{\text{Fixed costs}}{\text{Unit contribution margin}}$$

$$\text{Sales (units)} = \frac{\text{Fixed costs + Target profit}}{\text{Unit contribution margin}}$$

4 Using a cost-volume-profit chart and a profit-volume chart, determine the break-even point and the volume necessary to achieve a target profit.

A cost-volume-profit chart focuses on the relationships among costs, sales, and operating profit or loss. Preparing and using a cost-volume-profit chart to determine the break-even point and the volume necessary to achieve a target profit are illustrated in this chapter.

The profit-volume chart focuses on profits rather than on revenues and costs. Preparing and using a profit-volume chart to determine the break-even point and the volume necessary to achieve a target profit are illustrated in this chapter.

5 Calculate the break-even point for a business selling more than one product.

Calculating the break-even point for a business selling two or more products is based upon a specified sales mix. Given the sales mix, the break-even point can be computed, using the methods illustrated for Cascade Company in this chapter.

6 Compute the operating leverage and the margin of safety, and explain how managers use these concepts.

Operating leverage is computed as follows:

$$\text{Operating leverage} = \frac{\text{Contribution margin}}{\text{Income from operations}}$$

Operating leverage is useful in measuring the impact of changes in sales on income from operations without preparing formal income

---

[3]The impact of violating these assumptions is discussed in advanced accounting texts.

statements. For example, a high operating leverage indicates that a small increase in sales will yield a large percentage increase in income from operations.

The margin of safety as a percentage of current sales is computed as follows:

Margin of safety =

$$\frac{\text{Sales} - \text{Sales at break-even point}}{\text{Sales}}$$

The margin of safety is useful in evaluating past operations and in planning future operations. For example, if the margin of safety is low, even a small decline in sales revenue will result in an operating loss.

7 **List the assumptions underlying cost-volume-profit analysis.**

The primary assumptions underlying cost-volume-profit analysis are as follows:

1. Total sales and total costs can be represented by straight lines.
2. Within the relevant range of operating activity, the efficiency of operations does not change.
3. Costs can be accurately divided into fixed and variable components.
4. The sales mix is constant.
5. There is no change in the inventory quantities during the period.

Key Terms

activity bases (drivers) (746)
break-even point (754)
contribution margin (751)
contribution margin ratio (752)
cost behavior (746)
cost-volume-profit analysis (751)

cost-volume-profit chart (758)
fixed costs (748)
high-low method (748)
margin of safety (766)
mixed cost (748)
operating leverage (764)

profit-volume chart (760)
relevant range (746)
sales mix (762)
unit contribution margin (753)
variable costing (751)
variable costs (746)

Illustrative Problem

Wyatt Inc. expects to maintain the same inventories at the end of the year as at the beginning of the year. The estimated fixed costs for the year are $288,000, and the estimated variable costs per unit are $14. It is expected that 60,000 units will be sold at a price of $20 per unit. Maximum sales within the relevant range are 70,000 units.

Instructions
1. What is (a) the contribution margin ratio and (b) the unit contribution margin?
2. Determine the break-even point in units.
3. Construct a cost-volume-profit chart, indicating the break-even point.
4. Construct a profit-volume chart, indicating the break-even point.
5. What is the margin of safety?

Solution

1. a. Contribution margin ratio = $\dfrac{\text{Sales} - \text{Variable costs}}{\text{Sales}}$

Contribution margin ratio = $\dfrac{(60,000 \text{ units} \times \$20) - (60,000 \text{ units} \times \$14)}{(60,000 \text{ units} \times \$20)}$

Contribution margin ratio = $\dfrac{\$1,200,000 - \$840,000}{\$1,200,000} = \dfrac{\$360,000}{\$1,200,000}$

Contribution margin ratio = 30%

b. Unit contribution margin = Unit selling price − Unit variable costs
Unit contribution margin = $20 − $14 = $6

2. Break-even sales (units) = $\dfrac{\text{Fixed costs}}{\text{Unit contribution margin}}$

Break-even sales (units) = $\dfrac{\$288,000}{\$6}$ = 48,000 units

3. **Sales and Costs**

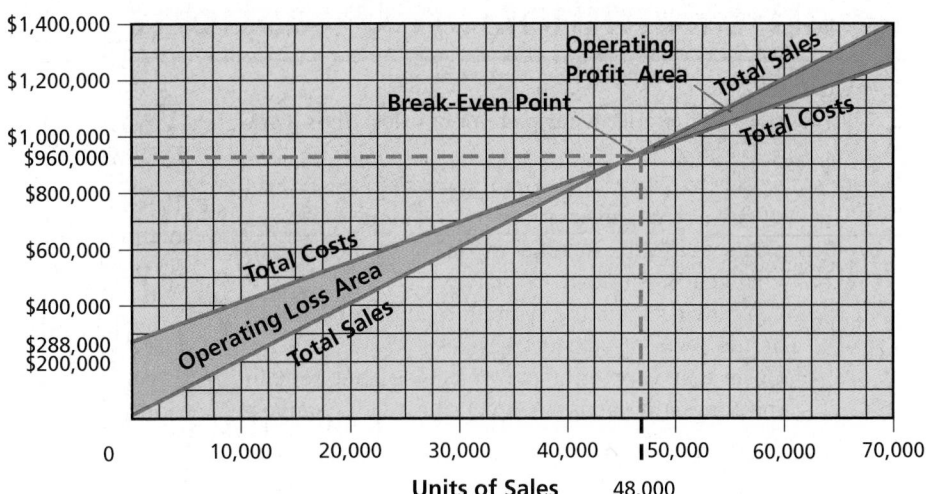

4. **Operating Profit (Loss)**

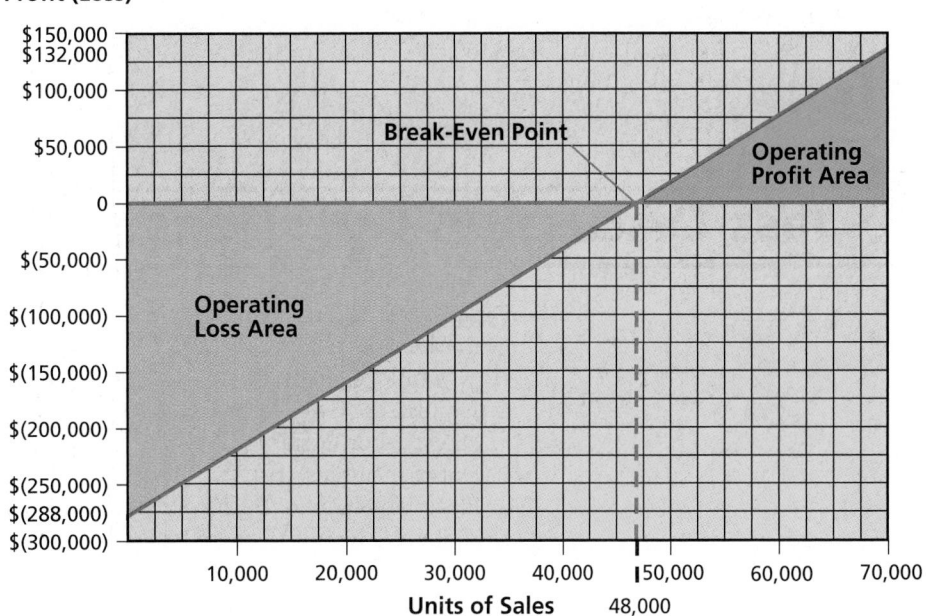

5. Margin of safety:

Expected sales (60,000 units × $20)	$1,200,000
Break-even point (48,000 units × $20)	960,000
Margin of safety	$ 240,000

or

$$\text{Margin of safety} = \frac{\text{Sales} - \text{Sales at break-even point}}{\text{Sales}}$$

$$\text{Margin of safety} = \frac{\$240,000}{\$1,200,000} = 20\%$$

Self-Examination Questions (Answers at End of Chapter)

1. Which of the following statements describes variable costs?
   A. Costs that vary on a per-unit basis as the level of activity changes.
   B. Costs that vary in total in direct proportion to changes in the level of activity.
   C. Costs that remain the same in total dollar amount as the level of activity changes.
   D. Costs that vary on a per-unit basis, but remain the same in total as the level of activity changes.

2. If sales are $500,000, variable costs are $200,000, and fixed costs are $240,000, what is the contribution margin ratio?
   A. 40%   C. 52%
   B. 48%   D. 60%

3. If the unit selling price is $16, the unit variable cost is $12, and fixed costs are $160,000, what are the break-even sales (units)?

A. 5,714 units   C. 13,333 units
B. 10,000 units   D. 40,000 units

4. Based on the data presented in Question 3, how many units of sales would be required to realize income from operations of $20,000?
   A. 11,250 units   C. 40,000 units
   B. 35,000 units   D. 45,000 units

5. Based on the following operating data, what is the operating leverage?

Sales	$600,000
Variable costs	240,000
Contribution margin	$360,000
Fixed costs	160,000
Income from operations	$200,000

A. 0.8   B. 1.2   C. 1.8   D. 4.0

Class Discussion Questions

1. Describe how total variable costs and unit variable costs behave with changes in the level of activity.
2. How would each of the following costs be classified if units produced is the activity base?
   a. Direct labor costs
   b. Direct materials cost
   c. Electricity costs of $0.20 per kilowatt-hour
3. Describe the behavior of (a) total fixed costs and (b) unit fixed costs as the level of activity increases.
4. How would each of the following costs be classified if units produced is the activity base?
   a. Straight-line depreciation of plant and equipment
   b. Salary of factory supervisor ($80,000 per year)
   c. Property insurance premiums of $5,000 per month on plant and equipment
5. In cost analyses, how are mixed costs treated?
6. Which of the following graphs illustrates how total variable costs behave with changes in total units produced?

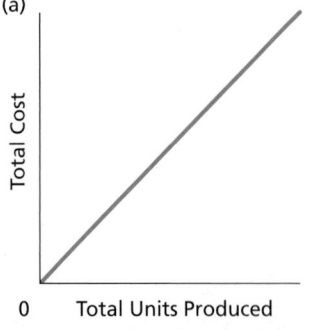

(a)

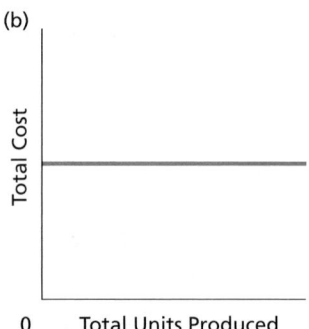

(b)

7. Which of the following graphs illustrates how unit variable costs behave with changes in total units produced?

(a)

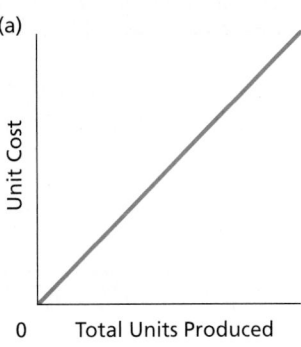

(b)

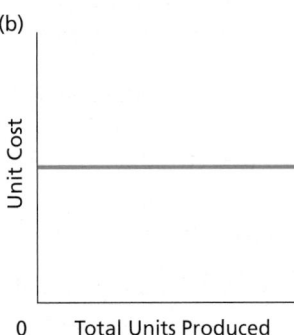

8. Which of the following graphs best illustrates fixed costs per unit as the activity base changes?

(a)

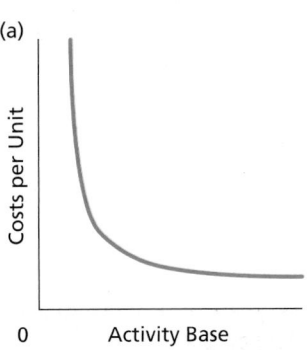

(b)

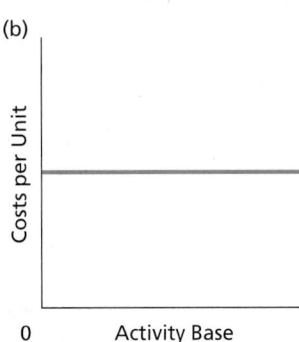

9. In applying the high-low method of cost estimation, how is the total fixed cost estimated?

10. If fixed costs increase, what would be the impact on the (a) contribution margin? (b) income from operations?

11. An examination of the accounting records of Hudson Company disclosed a high contribution margin ratio and production at a level below maximum capacity. Based on this information, suggest a likely means of improving income from operations. Explain.

12. If the unit cost of direct materials is decreased, what effect will this change have on the break-even point?

13. If insurance rates are increased, what effect will this change in fixed costs have on the break-even point?

14. Both Simmons Company and Pate Company had the same sales, total costs, and income from operations for the current fiscal year; yet Simmons Company had a lower break-even point than Pate Company. Explain the reason for this difference in break-even points.

15. How does the sales mix affect the calculation of the break-even point?

16. What does operating leverage measure, and how is it computed?

Exercises

EXERCISE 18-1
Classify costs
Objective 1

Following is a list of various costs incurred in producing frozen pizzas. With respect to the production and sale of frozen pizzas, classify each cost as either variable, fixed, or mixed.

1. Refrigerant used in refrigeration equipment
2. Straight-line depreciation on the production equipment
3. Packaging
4. Property insurance premiums, $1,500 per month plus $0.005 for each dollar of property over $3,000,000
5. Property taxes, $50,000 per year on factory building and equipment
6. Pension cost, $0.50 per employee hour on the job
7. Hourly wages of inspectors
8. Dough
9. Hourly wages of machine operators
10. Janitorial costs, $3,000 per month
11. Rent on warehouse, $5,000 per month plus $5 per square foot of storage used
12. Tomato paste
13. Electricity costs, $0.08 per kilowatt-hour
14. Salary of plant manager
15. Pepperoni

EXERCISE 18-2
Identify cost graphs
Objective 1

The following cost graphs illustrate various types of cost behavior:

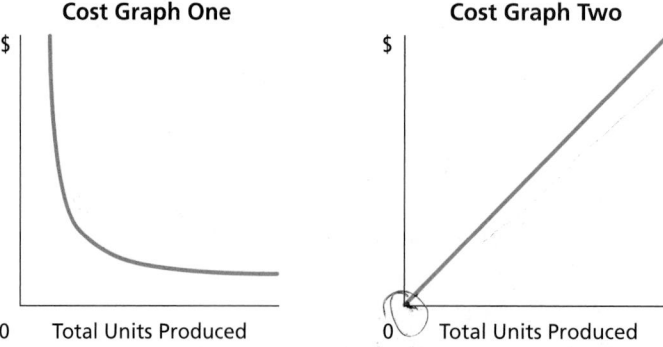

Cost Graph One

$

0   Total Units Produced

Cost Graph Two

$

0   Total Units Produced

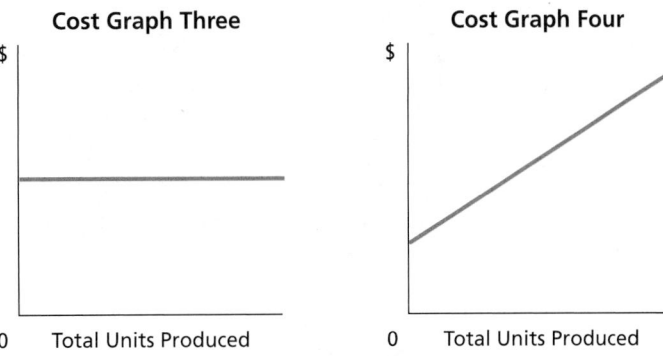

For each of the following costs, identify the cost graph that best illustrates its cost behavior as the number of units produced increases.

a. Total direct materials cost
b. Salary of quality control supervisor, $4,000 per month
c. Electricity costs of $2,000 per month plus $0.02 per kilowatt-hour
d. Per-unit direct labor cost
e. Per-unit cost of straight-line depreciation on factory equipment

EXERCISE 18-3
Identify activity bases
Objective 1

REAL WORLD

For **Ohio State University**, match each cost in the following table with the activity base most appropriate to it. An activity base may be used more than once, or not used at all.

Cost:
1. Admissions office salaries
2. Record office salaries
3. Housing personnel wages
4. Supplies
5. Instructor salaries
6. Financial aid office salaries

Activity Base:
a. Number of enrollment applications
b. Number of financial aid applications
c. Student credit hours
d. Number of enrolled students and alumni
e. Number of students living on campus
f. Number of student/athletes

EXERCISE 18-4
Identify activity bases
Objective 1

From the following list of activity bases for an automobile dealership, select the base that would be most appropriate for each of these costs: (1) preparation costs (cleaning, oil, and gasoline costs) for each car received, (2) salespersons' commission of 3% of the sales price for each car sold, and (3) administrative costs for ordering cars.

a. Dollar amount of cars sold
b. Dollar amount of cars on hand
c. Dollar amount of cars received
d. Dollar amount of cars ordered
e. Number of cars received
f. Number of cars on hand
g. Number of cars ordered
h. Number of cars sold

EXERCISE 18-5
Identify fixed and variable costs
Objective 1

REAL WORLD

Intuit Inc. develops and sells software products for the personal finance market, including popular titles such as Quicken® and TurboTax®. Classify each of the following costs and expenses for this company as either variable or fixed to the number of units produced and sold:

a. Packaging costs
b. Salaries of software developers
c. Salaries of customer support personnel
d. CDs
e. Sales commissions
f. Advertising
g. Straight-line depreciation of computer equipment
h. Shipping expenses
i. Wages of telephone order assistants
j. Property taxes on general offices
k. User's guides
l. President's salary

EXERCISE 18-6
*Relevant range and fixed
and variable costs*

Objective 1

SPREADSHEET

✓ a. $4.00

Digital Image Video Inc. manufactures compact disks within a relevant range of 200,000 to 400,000 disks per year. Within this range, the following partially completed manufacturing cost schedule has been prepared:

CDs produced	200,000	300,000	400,000
Total costs:			
Total variable costs	$800,000	(d)	(j)
Total fixed costs	180,000	(e)	(k)
Total costs	$980,000	(f)	(l)
Cost per unit:			
Variable cost per unit	(a)	(g)	(m)
Fixed cost per unit	(b)	(h)	(n)
Total cost per unit	(c)	(i)	(o)

Complete the cost schedule, identifying each cost by the appropriate letter (a) through (o).

EXERCISE 18-7
High-low method

Objective 1

SPREADSHEET

✓ a. $19.50 per unit

Keepsake Gifts, Inc. has decided to use the high-low method to estimate the total cost and the fixed and variable cost components of the total cost. The data for the highest and lowest levels of production are as follows:

	Units Produced	Total Costs
Highest level	15,000	$432,500
Lowest level	5,000	$237,500

a. Determine the variable cost per unit and the fixed cost.
b. Based on (a), estimate the total cost for 12,000 units of production.

EXERCISE 18-8
*High-low method for
service company*

Objective 1

SPREADSHEET

✓ Fixed cost, $740,000

Thoroughbred Railroad decided to use the high-low method and operating data from the past six months to estimate the fixed and variable components of transportation costs. The activity base used by Thoroughbred Railroad is a measure of railroad operating activity, termed "gross-ton miles," which is the total number of tons multiplied by the miles moved.

	Transportation Costs	Gross-Ton Miles
January	$1,463,000	595,000
February	1,372,000	540,000
March	1,322,000	485,000
April	1,641,000	740,000
May	1,522,000	670,000
June	1,748,000	840,000

Determine the variable cost per gross-ton mile and the fixed cost.

EXERCISE 18-9
Contribution margin ratio

Objective 2

✓ a. 35%

a. Collier Company budgets sales of $560,000, fixed costs of $125,000, and variable costs of $364,000. What is the contribution margin ratio for Collier Company?
b. If the contribution margin ratio for Morris Company is 42%, sales were $264,000, and fixed costs were $100,000, what was the income from operations?

EXERCISE 18-10
*Contribution margin and
contribution margin ratio*

Objective 2

REAL WORLD

For a recent year, **McDonald's Corporation** had the following sales and expenses (in millions):

Sales	$14,870
Food and packaging	$ 3,802
Payroll	2,901
Occupancy (rent, depreciation, etc.)	3,551
General, selling, and administrative expenses	1,919
	$12,173
Income from operations	$ 2,697

✓ b. 49.76%

Assume that the variable costs consist of food and packaging, payroll, and 40% of the general, selling, and administrative expenses.

a. What is McDonald's contribution margin? Round to the nearest million.
b. What is McDonald's contribution margin ratio? Round to two decimal places.
c. How much would income from operations increase if same-store sales increased by $300 million for the coming year, with no change in the contribution margin ratio or fixed costs?

EXERCISE 18-11
Break-even sales and sales to realize income from operations
Objective 3

✓ b. 21,750 units

For the current year ending March 31, Chow Company expects fixed costs of $345,600, a unit variable cost of $32, and a unit selling price of $50.

a. Compute the anticipated break-even sales (units).
b. Compute the sales (units) required to realize income from operations of $45,900.

EXERCISE 18-12
Break-even sales
Objective 3

REAL WORLD

✓ a. 61,288,032 barrels

The **Anheuser Busch Corporation** reported the following operating information for a recent year (in millions):

Net sales	$12,911
Cost of goods sold	$ 7,950
Marketing and distribution	2,256
	$10,206 ← T.C.
Income from operations	$ 2,705*

*Before special items

In addition, Anheuser Busch sold 107 million barrels of beer during the year. Assume that variable costs were 70% of the cost of goods sold and 45% of marketing and distribution expenses. Assume that the remaining costs are fixed. For the following year, assume that Anheuser Busch expects pricing, variable costs per barrel, and fixed costs to remain constant, except that new distribution and general office facilities are expected to increase fixed costs by $110 million.
Rounding to the nearest cent:

a. Compute the break-even sales (barrels) for the current year.
b. Compute the anticipated break-even (barrels) for the following year.

EXERCISE 18-13
Break-even sales
Objective 3

✓ a. 7,200 units

Currently, the unit selling price of a product is $250, the unit variable cost is $175, and the total fixed costs are $540,000. A proposal is being evaluated to increase the unit selling price to $300.

a. Compute the current break-even sales (units).
b. Compute the anticipated break-even sales (units), assuming that the unit selling price is increased and all costs remain constant.

EXERCISE 18-14
Break-even analysis
Objective 3

The **Junior League of Tampa, Florida**, collected recipes from members and published a cookbook entitled *Life of the Party*. The book will sell for $18 per copy. The chairwoman of the cookbook development committee estimated that the league needed to sell 14,000 books to break even on its $120,000 investment. What is the variable cost per unit assumed in the Junior League's analysis? Round to the nearest cent.

EXERCISE 18-15
Break-even analysis
Objective 3

REAL WORLD

The America Online division of **Time Warner Inc.** has fueled its growth by using aggressive promotion strategies. One of these strategies is to send compact disk software to potential customers, offering free AOL service for a period of time. Assume that during a given promotional campaign, AOL mailed 800,000 disks to potential customers, offering three months' free service. In addition, assume the following information:

Cost per disk (including mailing)	$3.00
Number of months an average new customer stays with the service (including the three free months)	30 months
Revenue per month per customer account	$20.00
Variable cost per month per customer account	$2.00

Determine the number of new customer accounts needed to break even on the cost of the promotional campaign. In forming your answer, (1) treat the cost of mailing the disk as a fixed cost, and (2) treat the revenue less variable cost per account for the service period as the unit contribution margin.

EXERCISE 18-16
Break-even analysis
Objective 3

REAL WORLD

Nextel Communications Inc. is one of the largest digital wireless service providers in the United States. In a recent year, it had 8,666,500 million handsets (accounts) that generated revenue of $7,689,000,000. Costs and expenses for the year were as follows:

Cost of revenue $2,869,000,000
Selling, general, and administrative expenses 3,020,000,000
Depreciation 1,746,000,000

Assume that 70% of the cost of revenue and 40% of the selling, general, and administrative expenses are variable to the number of handsets (accounts).

a. What is Nextel's break-even number of accounts, using the data and assumptions above? Round per-unit calculations to the nearest dollar.
b. How much revenue per account would be sufficient for Nextel to break even if the number of accounts remained constant?

EXERCISE 18-17
Cost-volume-profit chart
Objective 4

✔ *b. $1,800,000*

For the coming year, Peters Inc. anticipates fixed costs of $450,000, a unit variable cost of $45, and a unit selling price of $60. The maximum sales within the relevant range are $2,400,000.

a. Construct a cost-volume-profit chart.
b. Estimate the break-even sales (dollars) by using the cost-volume-profit chart constructed in (a).
c.  What is the main advantage of presenting the cost-volume-profit analysis in graphic form rather than equation form?

EXERCISE 18-18
Profit-volume chart
Objective 4

✔ *b. $150,000*

Using the data for Peters Inc. in Exercise 18–17, (a) determine the maximum possible operating loss, (b) compute the maximum possible income from operations, (c) construct a profit-volume chart, and (d) estimate the break-even sales (units) by using the profit-volume chart constructed in (c).

EXERCISE 18-19
Break-even chart
Objective 4

Name the following chart, and identify the items represented by the letters (a) through (f).

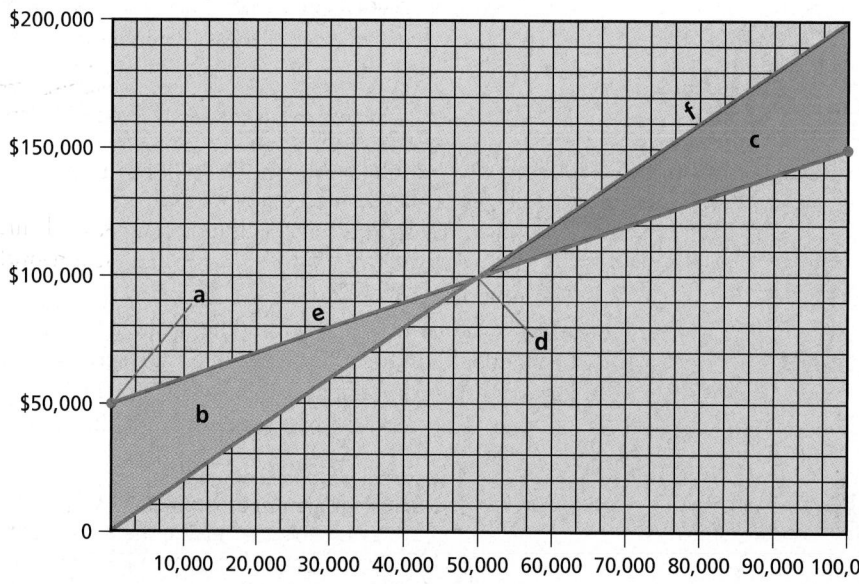

EXERCISE 18-20
Break-even chart
Objective 4

Name the following chart, and identify the items represented by the letters (a) through (f).

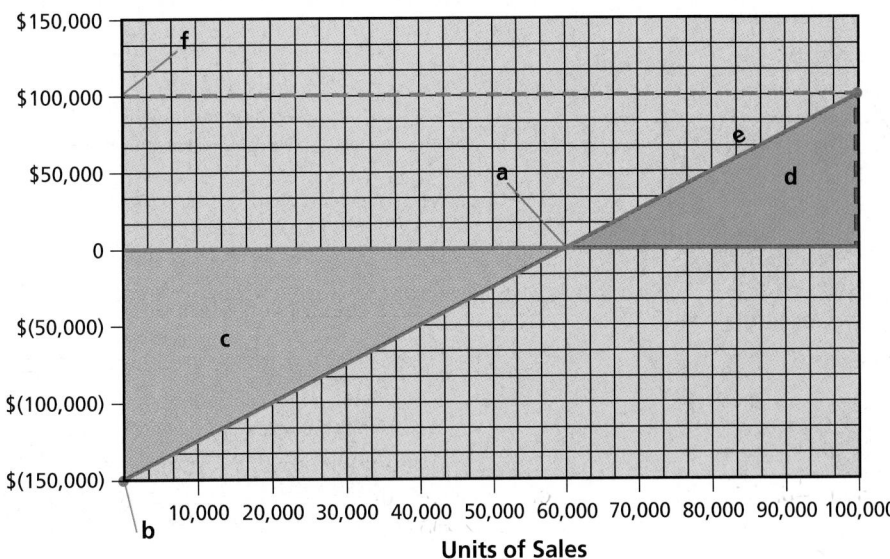

EXERCISE 18-21
Sales mix and break-even sales
Objective 5

SPREADSHEET

✓a. 200,000 units

Salted Munchies, Inc. manufactures and sells two products, potato chips and pretzels. The fixed costs are $300,000, and the sales mix is 60% potato chips and 40% pretzels. The unit selling price and the unit variable cost for each product are as follows:

Products	Unit Selling Price	Unit Variable Cost
Potato Chips	$2.80	$1.10
Pretzels	2.00	0.80

a. Compute the break-even sales (units) for the overall product, E.
b. How many units of each product, potato chips and pretzels, would be sold at the break-even point?

EXERCISE 18-22
Break-even sales and sales mix for a service company
Objective 5

SPREADSHEET

✓a. 60 seats

Sun Airways provides air transportation services between New York and Miami. A single New York to Miami round-trip flight has the following operating statistics:

Fuel	$3,690
Flight crew salaries	7,510
Airplane depreciation	3,200
Variable cost per passenger—business class	58
Variable cost per passenger—tourist class	34
Round-trip ticket price—business class	400
Round-trip ticket price—tourist class	240

It is assumed that the fuel, crew salaries, and airplane depreciation are fixed, regardless of the number of seats sold for the round-trip flight.

a. Compute the break-even number of seats sold on a single round-trip flight for the overall product. Assume that the overall product is 25% business class and 75% tourist class tickets.
b. How many business class and tourist class seats would be sold at the break-even point?

EXERCISE 18-23
Margin of safety
Objective 6

✓a. (2) 25%

a. If Lambert Company, with a break-even point at $300,000 of sales, has actual sales of $400,000, what is the margin of safety expressed (1) in dollars and (2) as a percentage of sales?

(continued)

b. If the margin of safety for Ingram Company was 25%, fixed costs were $450,000, and variable costs were 60% of sales, what was the amount of actual sales (dollars)? (*Hint:* Determine the break-even in sales dollars first.)

EXERCISE 18-24
Break-even and margin of safety relationships
Objective 6

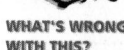

WHAT'S WRONG
WITH THIS?

At a recent staff meeting, the question of discontinuing Product Q from the product line was being discussed. The chief financial analyst reported the following current monthly data for Product Q:

Units of sales	20,000
Break-even units	23,000
Margin of safety in units	3,000

For what reason would you question the validity of these data?

EXERCISE 18-25
Operating leverage
Objective 6

SPREADSHEET

✓ a. Abdel, 1.20

Abdel Inc. and Hui Inc. have the following operating data:

	Abdel	Hui
Sales	$150,000	$200,000
Variable costs	90,000	125,000
Contribution margin	$ 60,000	$ 75,000
Fixed costs	10,000	60,000
Income from operations	$ 50,000	$ 15,000

a. Compute the operating leverage for Abdel Inc. and Hui Inc.
b. How much would income from operations increase for each company if the sales of each increased by 20%?
c. Why is there a difference in the increase in income from operations for the two companies? Explain.

Problems Series A

PROBLEM 18-1A
Classify costs
Objective 1

Forty-Niner Company manufactures blue jeans for distribution to several major retail chains. The following costs are incurred in the production and sale of blue jeans:

a. Salary of designers
b. Salesperson's salary, $12,000 plus 3% of the total sales
c. Rental costs of warehouse, $2,000 per month plus $1 per square foot of storage used
d. Brass buttons
e. Consulting fee of $50,000 paid to industry specialist for marketing advice
f. Legal fees paid to attorneys in defense of the company in a patent infringement suit, $20,000 plus $100 per hour
g. Electricity costs of $0.07 per kilowatt-hour
h. Blue denim fabric
i. Hourly wages of sewing machine operators
j. Janitorial supplies, $2,000 per month
k. Salary of production vice-president
l. Straight-line depreciation on sewing machines
m. Leather for patches identifying each jean style
n. Rent on experimental equipment, $25,000 per year
o. Shipping boxes used to ship orders
p. Sewing supplies
q. Property taxes on property, plant, and equipment
r. Thread

s. Blue dye

t. Insurance premiums on property, plant, and equipment, $10,000 per year plus $3 per $10,000 of insured value over $5,000,000

Instructions

Classify the preceding costs as either fixed, variable, or mixed. Use the following tabular headings and place an "X" in the appropriate column. Identify each cost by letter in the cost column.

Cost	Fixed Cost	Variable Cost	Mixed Cost

PROBLEM 18-2A

Break-even sales under present and proposed conditions

Objectives 2, 3

SPREADSHEET

✓ 2. (a) $32.50

Concord Instruments Company, operating at full capacity, sold 60,000 units at a price of $62.50 per unit during 2006. Its income statement for 2006 is as follows:

Sales		$3,750,000
Cost of goods sold		1,500,000
Gross profit		$2,250,000
Operating expenses:		
Selling expenses	$1,200,000	
Administrative expenses	300,000	
Total operating expenses		1,500,000
Income from operations		$ 750,000

The division of costs between fixed and variable is as follows:

	Fixed	Variable
Cost of sales	40%	60%
Selling expenses	25%	75%
Administrative expenses	50%	50%

Management is considering a plant expansion program that will permit an increase of $600,000 in yearly sales. The expansion will increase fixed costs by $180,000, but will not affect the relationship between sales and variable costs.

Instructions

1. Determine for 2006 the total fixed costs and the total variable costs.
2. Determine for 2006 (a) the unit variable cost and (b) the unit contribution margin.
3. Compute the break-even sales (units) for 2006.
4. Compute the break-even sales (units) under the proposed program.
5. Determine the amount of sales (units) that would be necessary under the proposed program to realize the $750,000 of income from operations that was earned in 2006.
6. Determine the maximum income from operations possible with the expanded plant.
7. If the proposal is accepted and sales remain at the 2006 level, what will the income or loss from operations be for 2007?
8. ➤ Based on the data given, would you recommend accepting the proposal? Explain.

PROBLEM 18-3A

Break-even sales and cost-volume-profit chart

Objectives 3, 4

✓ 1. 9,000 units

For the coming year, India Ink Company anticipates a unit selling price of $400, a unit variable cost of $300, and fixed costs of $900,000.

Instructions

1. Compute the anticipated break-even sales (units).
2. Compute the sales (units) required to realize income from operations of $150,000.
3. Construct a cost-volume-profit chart, assuming maximum sales of 16,000 units within the relevant range.
4. Determine the probable income (loss) from operations if sales total 7,000 units.

PROBLEM 18-4A

Break-even sales and cost-volume-profit chart

Objectives 3, 4

Last year, Fifth Dimension Beauty Products Inc. had sales of $400,000, based on a unit selling price of $80. The variable cost per unit was $55, and fixed costs were $125,000. The maximum sales within Fifth Dimension's relevant range are 10,000

✓ *1. 5,000 units*

units. Fifth Dimension is considering a proposal to spend an additional $40,000 on billboard advertising during the current year in an attempt to increase sales and utilize unused capacity.

Instructions

1. Construct a cost-volume-profit chart indicating the break-even sales for last year. Verify your answer, using the break-even equation.
2. Using the cost-volume-profit chart prepared in (1), determine (a) the income from operations for last year and (b) the maximum income from operations that could have been realized during the year. Verify your answers arithmetically.
3. Construct a cost-volume-profit chart indicating the break-even sales for the current year, assuming that a noncancelable contract is signed for the additional billboard advertising. No changes are expected in the unit selling price or other costs. Verify your answer, using the break-even equation.
4. Using the cost-volume-profit chart prepared in (3), determine (a) the income from operations if sales total 8,000 units and (b) the maximum income from operations that could be realized during the year. Verify your answers arithmetically.

PROBLEM 18-5A
Sales mix and break-even sales

Objective 5

SPREADSHEET

✓ *1. 19,700 units*

Data related to the expected sales of golf balls and tennis balls for Medalist Inc. for the current year, which is typical of recent years, are as follows:

Products	Unit Selling Price	Unit Variable Cost	Sales Mix
Golf balls	$36.00	$10.00	30%
Tennis balls	8.00	3.00	70%

The estimated fixed costs for the current year are $222,610.

Instructions

1. Determine the estimated units of sales of the overall product necessary to reach the break-even point for the current year.
2. Based on the break-even sales (units) in (1), determine the unit sales of both golf balls and tennis balls for the current year.
3. ▭▶ Assume that the sales mix was 70% golf balls and 30% tennis balls. Compare the break-even point with that in (1). Why is it so different?

PROBLEM 18-6A
Contribution margin, break-even sales, cost-volume-profit chart, margin of safety, and operating leverage

Objectives 2, 3, 4, 6

SPREADSHEET

✓ *2. 40%*

Cascade Outdoor Products Inc. expects to maintain the same inventories at the end of 2006 as at the beginning of the year. The total of all production costs for the year is therefore assumed to be equal to the cost of goods sold. With this in mind, the various department heads were asked to submit estimates of the costs for their departments during 2006. A summary report of these estimates is as follows:

	Estimated Fixed Cost	Estimated Variable Cost (per unit sold)
Production costs:		
Direct materials	—	$132.30
Direct labor	—	115.30
Factory overhead	$264,000	24.50
Selling expenses:		
Sales salaries and commissions	245,000	12.70
Advertising	75,000	—
Travel	39,500	—
Miscellaneous selling expense	24,500	6.70
Administrative expenses:		
Office and officers' salaries	220,000	—
Supplies	15,000	6.30
Miscellaneous administrative expense	17,000	2.20
Total	$900,000	$300.00

It is expected that 6,000 units will be sold at a price of $500 a unit. Maximum sales within the relevant range are 10,000 units.

Instructions
1. Prepare an estimated income statement for 2006.
2. What is the expected contribution margin ratio?
3. Determine the break-even sales in units.
4. Construct a cost-volume-profit chart indicating the break-even sales.
5. What is the expected margin of safety?
6. Determine the operating leverage.

Problems Series B

PROBLEM 18-1B
Classify costs
Objective 1

Hearth & Home Furniture Company manufactures sofas for distribution to several major retail chains. The following costs are incurred in the production and sale of sofas:

a. Legal fees paid to attorneys in defense of the company in a patent infringement suit, $10,000 plus $75 per hour
b. Rental costs of warehouse, $10,000 per month
c. Wood for framing the sofas
d. Salary of designers
e. Foam rubber for cushion fillings
f. Sewing supplies
g. Hourly wages of sewing machine operators
h. Property taxes on property, plant, and equipment
i. Electricity costs of $0.02 per kilowatt-hour
j. Straight-line depreciation on factory equipment
k. Cartons used to ship sofas
l. Fabric for sofa coverings
m. Salary of production vice-president
n. Insurance premiums on property, plant, and equipment, $5,000 per year plus $20 per $10,000 of insured value over $8,000,000
o. Employer's FICA taxes on controller's salary of $125,000
p. Springs
q. Rent on experimental equipment, $25 for every sofa produced
r. Consulting fee of $15,000 paid to efficiency specialists
s. Janitorial supplies, $10 for each sofa produced
t. Salesperson's salary, $12,000 plus 5% of the selling price of each sofa sold

Instructions
Classify the preceding costs as either fixed, variable, or mixed. Use the following tabular headings and place an "X" in the appropriate column. Identify each cost by letter in the Cost column.

Cost	Fixed Cost	Variable Cost	Mixed Cost

PROBLEM 18-2B
Break-even sales under present and proposed conditions
Objectives 2, 3

SPREADSHEET

✓ *3. 21,000 units*

Cajun Foods, Inc., operating at full capacity, sold 29,200 units at a price of $90 per unit during 2006. Its income statement for 2006 is as follows:

Sales		$2,628,000
Cost of goods sold		1,600,000
Gross profit		$1,028,000
Operating expenses:		
Selling expenses	$300,000	
Administrative expenses	400,000	
Total operating expenses		700,000
Income from operations		$ 328,000

The division of costs between fixed and variable is as follows:

	Fixed	Variable
Cost of sales	25%	75%
Selling expenses	40%	60%
Administrative expenses	80%	20%

Management is considering a plant expansion program that will permit an increase of $432,000 in yearly sales. The expansion will increase fixed costs by $140,000, but will not affect the relationship between sales and variable costs.

Instructions

1. Determine for 2006 the total fixed costs and the total variable costs.
2. Determine for 2006 (a) the unit variable cost and (b) the unit contribution margin.
3. Compute the break-even sales (units) for 2006.
4. Compute the break-even sales (units) under the proposed program.
5. Determine the amount of sales (units) that would be necessary under the proposed program to realize the $328,000 of income from operations that was earned in 2006.
6. Determine the maximum income from operations possible with the expanded plant.
7. If the proposal is accepted and sales remain at the 2006 level, what will the income or loss from operations be for 2007?
8. ➧ Based on the data given, would you recommend accepting the proposal? Explain.

PROBLEM 18-3B
Break-even sales and cost-volume-profit chart

Objectives 3, 4

✓ *1. 14,000 units*

For the coming year, Texas Leathergoods Company anticipates a unit selling price of $75, a unit variable cost of $30, and fixed costs of $630,000.

Instructions

1. Compute the anticipated break-even sales (units).
2. Compute the sales (units) required to realize income from operations of $94,500.
3. Construct a cost-volume-profit chart, assuming maximum sales of 40,000 units within the relevant range.
4. Determine the probable income (loss) from operations if sales total 32,000 units.

PROBLEM 18-4B
Break-even sales and cost-volume-profit chart

Objectives 3, 4

✓ *1. 1,400 units*

Last year, Cell-Tec Mobile Phone Co. had sales of $459,900, based on a unit selling price of $210. The variable cost per unit was $120, and fixed costs were $126,000. The maximum sales within Cell-Tec's relevant range are 3,000 units. Cell-Tec is considering a proposal to spend an additional $47,700 on billboard advertising during the current year in an attempt to increase sales and utilize unused capacity.

Instructions

1. Construct a cost-volume-profit chart indicating the break-even sales for last year. Verify your answer, using the break-even equation.
2. Using the cost-volume-profit chart prepared in (1), determine (a) the income from operations for last year and (b) the maximum income from operations that could have been realized during the year. Verify your answers arithmetically.
3. Construct a cost-volume-profit chart indicating the break-even sales for the current year, assuming that a noncancelable contract is signed for the additional billboard advertising. No changes are expected in the selling price or other costs. Verify your answer, using the break-even equation.
4. Using the cost-volume-profit chart prepared in (3), determine (a) the income from operations if sales total 2,300 units and (b) the maximum income from operations that could be realized during the year. Verify your answers arithmetically.

PROBLEM 18-5B
Sales mix and break-even sales

Objective 5

Data related to the expected sales of 12″ and 16″ pizzas for Pietro's Pizza, Inc. for the current year, which is typical of recent years, are as follows:

✓ 1. 53,000 units

Products	Unit Selling Price	Unit Variable Cost	Sales Mix
12" Pizza	$ 8.00	$3.00	20%
16" Pizza	11.00	4.50	80%

The estimated fixed costs for the current year are $328,600.

Instructions

1. Determine the estimated units of sales of the overall product necessary to reach the break-even point for the current year.
2. Based on the break-even sales (units) in (1), determine the unit sales of both 12" and 16" pizzas for the current year.
3. ▭▭▶ Assume that the sales mix was 80% 12" and 20% 16" pizzas. Compare the break-even point with that in (1). Why is it so different?

PROBLEM 18-6B
Contribution margin, break-even sales, cost-volume-profit chart, margin of safety, and operating leverage

Objectives 2, 3, 4, 6

✓ 2. 37.5%

Cabot Co. expects to maintain the same inventories at the end of 2006 as at the beginning of the year. The total of all production costs for the year is therefore assumed to be equal to the cost of goods sold. With this in mind, the various department heads were asked to submit estimates of the costs for their departments during 2006. A summary report of these estimates is as follows:

	Estimated Fixed Cost	Estimated Variable Cost (per unit sold)
Production costs:		
Direct materials	—	$ 8.80
Direct labor	—	4.20
Factory overhead	$ 83,500	1.90
Selling expenses:		
Sales salaries and commissions	37,300	1.30
Advertising	12,500	—
Travel	3,200	—
Miscellaneous selling expense	4,200	1.00
Administrative expenses:		
Office and officers' salaries	75,400	—
Supplies	5,000	0.20
Miscellaneous administrative expense	3,900	2.60
Total	$225,000	$20.00

It is expected that 20,000 units will be sold at a price of $32 a unit. Maximum sales within the relevant range are 30,000 units.

Instructions

1. Prepare an estimated income statement for 2006.
2. What is the expected contribution margin ratio?
3. Determine the break-even sales in units.
4. Construct a cost-volume-profit chart indicating the break-even sales.
5. What is the expected margin of safety?
6. Determine the operating leverage.

Special Activities

ACTIVITY 18-1
Ethics and professional conduct in business

Brian Jeffries is a financial consultant to Diamond Properties Inc., a real estate syndicate. Diamond Properties Inc. finances and develops commercial real estate (office buildings). The completed projects are then sold as limited partnership interests to individual investors. The syndicate makes a profit on the sale of these partnership interests. Brian provides financial information for the offering prospectus, which is a

ETHICS

document that provides the financial and legal details of the limited partnership offerings. In one of the projects, the bank has financed the construction of a commercial office building at a rate of 6% for the first four years, after which time the rate jumps to 10% for the remaining 26 years of the mortgage. The interest costs are one of the major ongoing costs of a real estate project. Brian has reported prominently in the prospectus that the break-even occupancy for the first four years is 60%. This is the amount of office space that must be leased to cover the interest and general upkeep costs over the first four years. The 60% break-even is very low and thus communicates a low risk to potential investors. Brian uses the 60% break-even rate as a major marketing tool in selling the limited partnership interests. Buried in the fine print of the prospectus is additional information that would allow an astute investor to determine that the break-even occupancy will jump to 85% after the fourth year because of the contracted increase in the mortgage interest rate. Brian believes prospective investors are adequately informed as to the risk of the investment.

Comment on the ethical considerations of this situation.

ACTIVITY 18-2
Break-even sales, contribution margin

REAL WORLD   WHAT DO YOU THINK?

"For a student, a grade of 65 percent is nothing to write home about. But for the airline . . . [industry], filling 65 percent of the seats . . . is the difference between profit and loss.

The [economy] might be just strong enough to sustain all the carriers on a cash basis, but not strong enough to bring any significant profitability to the industry. . . . For the airlines . . . , the emphasis will be on trying to consolidate routes and raise ticket prices. . . ."

The airline industry is notorious for boom and bust cycles. Why is airline profitability very sensitive to these cycles? Do you think that during a down cycle the strategy to consolidate routes and raise ticket prices is reasonable? What would make this strategy succeed or fail? Why?

Source: Edwin McDowell, "Empty Seats, Empty Beds, Empty Pockets," *New York Times*, January 6, 1992, p. C3.

ACTIVITY 18-3
Break-even analysis

Northern Lights Studios has finished a new DVD movie offering, *Keeping in Balance*. Management is now considering its marketing strategies. The following information is available:

Anticipated sales price per unit	$25
Variable cost per unit*	$5
Anticipated volume	750,000
Movie production costs	$10,000,000
Anticipated advertising	$5,000,000

*The cost of the DVD disk, packaging, and copying costs.

Two managers, Julie Wilson and Steve Harris, had the following discussion of ways to increase the profitability of this new offering.

Julie: I think we need to think of some way to increase our profitability. Do you have any ideas?

Steve: Well, I think the best strategy would be to become aggressive on price.

Julie: How aggressive?

Steve: If we drop the price to $20 per unit and maintain our advertising budget at $5,000,000, I think we will generate sales of 1,600,000 units.

Julie: I think that's the wrong way to go. You're giving too much up on price. Instead, I think we need to follow an aggressive advertising strategy.

Steve: How aggressive?

Julie: If we increase our advertising to a total of $8,000,000, we should be able to increase sales volume to 1,500,000 units without any change in price.

Steve: I don't think that's reasonable. We'll never cover the increased advertising costs.

Which strategy is best: Do nothing? Follow the advice of Steve Harris? Or follow Julie Wilson's strategy?

ACTIVITY 18-4
Variable costs and activity bases in decision making

WHAT DO YOU THINK?

The owner of Personal Shirts, Inc., a T-shirt printing company, is planning direct labor needs for the upcoming year. The owner has provided you with the following information for next year's plans:

	One Color	Two Color	Three Color	Four Color	Total
Number of T-shirts	300	800	900	1,000	3,000

Each color on the T-shirt must be printed one at a time. Thus, for example, a four-color T-shirt will need to be run through the silk screen operation four separate times. The total production volume last year was 2,000 T-shirts, as shown below.

	One Color	Two Color	Three Color	Total
Number of T-shirts	300	800	900	2,000

As you can see, the four-color T-shirt is a new product offering for the upcoming year. The owner believes that the expected 1,000-unit increase in volume from last year means that direct labor expenses should increase by 50% (1,000/2,000). What do you think?

ACTIVITY 18-5
Variable costs and activity bases in decision making

Sales volume has been dropping at Koinonia Publishing Company. During this time, however, the Shipping Department manager has been under severe financial constraints. The manager knows that most of the Shipping Department's effort is related to pulling inventory from the warehouse for each order and performing the paperwork. The paperwork involves preparing shipping documents for each order. Thus, the pulling and paperwork effort associated with each sales order is essentially the same, regardless of the size of the order. The Shipping Department manager has discussed the financial situation with senior management. Senior management has responded by pointing out that sales volume has been dropping, so that the amount of work in the Shipping Department should be dropping. Thus, senior management told the Shipping Department manager that costs should be decreasing in the department.

The Shipping Department manager prepared the following information:

Month	Sales Volume	Number of Customer Orders	Sales Volume per Order
January	$95,000	500	$190
February	93,600	520	180
March	90,100	530	170
April	90,000	600	150
May	89,900	620	145
June	85,000	625	136
July	81,900	630	130
August	80,000	640	125

Given this information, how would you respond to senior management?

ACTIVITY 18-6
Break-even analysis

GROUP ACTIVITY

Break-even analysis is one of the most fundamental tools for managing any kind of business unit. Consider the management of your school. In a group, brainstorm some applications of break-even analysis at your school. Identify three areas where break-even analysis might be used. For each area, identify the revenues, variable costs, and fixed costs that would be used in the calculation.

**nswers to Self-Examination Questions**

1. **B** Variable costs vary in total in direct proportion to changes in the level of activity (answer B). Costs that vary on a per-unit basis as the level of activity changes (answer A) or remain constant in total dollar amount as the level of activity changes (answer C), or both (answer D), are fixed costs.

2. **D** The contribution margin ratio indicates the percentage of each sales dollar available to cover the fixed costs and provide income from operations and is determined as follows:

$$\text{Contribution margin ratio} = \frac{\text{Sales} - \text{Variable costs}}{\text{Sales}}$$

$$\text{Contribution margin ratio} = \frac{\$500,000 - \$200,000}{\$500,000}$$

$$= 60\%$$

3. **D** The break-even sales of 40,000 units (answer D) is computed as follows:

$$\text{Break-even sales (units)} = \frac{\text{Fixed costs}}{\text{Unit contribution margin}}$$

$$\text{Break-even sales (units)} = \frac{\$160,000}{\$4} = 40,000 \text{ units}$$

4. **D** Sales of 45,000 units are required to realize income from operations of $20,000, computed as follows:

$$\text{Sales (units)} = \frac{\text{Fixed costs} + \text{Target profit}}{\text{Unit contribution margin}}$$

$$\text{Sales (units)} = \frac{\$160,000 + \$20,000}{\$4} = 45,000 \text{ units}$$

5. **C** The operating leverage is 1.8, computed as follows:

$$\text{Operating leverage} = \frac{\text{Contribution margin}}{\text{Income from operations}}$$

$$\text{Operating leverage} = \frac{\$360,000}{\$200,000} = 1.8$$

19

PROFIT REPORTING FOR MANAGEMENT ANALYSIS

objectives

After studying this chapter, you should be able to:

1 Describe and illustrate income reporting under variable costing and absorption costing.

2 Describe and illustrate income analysis under variable costing and absorption costing.

3 Describe and illustrate management's use of variable costing and absorption costing for controlling costs, pricing products, planning production, analyzing market segments, and analyzing contribution margins.

4 Illustrate contribution margin reporting for products, territories, and salespersons.

5 Explain changes in contribution margin as a result of quantity and price factors.

6 Describe and illustrate contribution margin reporting and analysis for service firms.

You are interested in obtaining a temporary job during the summer, and you have three different job options. How would you evaluate these options? Naturally, there are many things to consider, including how much income each job would provide.

Determining the income from each job may not be as simple as comparing the rates of pay per hour. For example, a job as an office clerk at a local company pays $7 per hour. A job delivering pizza pays $10 per hour (including estimated tips), although you must use your own transportation. A job working in a store located in a beach resort over 500 miles away from your home pays $8 per hour. All three jobs offer work for 40 hours per week for the whole summer. If these options were ranked according to their pay per hour, the pizza delivery job would appear to be the most attractive. However, the costs associated with each job must also be evaluated. For example, the office job may require that you pay for downtown parking and purchase office clothes. The pizza delivery job will require you to pay for gas and maintenance for your car. The resort job will require you to move to the resort city and incur additional living costs. Only by considering the direct costs for each job will you be able to determine which job will provide you the most income.

Just as you should evaluate the relative financial impact of various choices, so must a business evaluate the financial impact of its choices. In this chapter we will discuss how businesses measure profitability, using absorption costing and variable costing. After illustrating and comparing these concepts, we discuss how businesses use them for controlling costs, pricing products, planning production, analyzing market segments, and analyzing contribution margins.

The Income Statement Under Variable Costing and Absorption Costing

One of the most important items affecting a business's net income is the cost of goods sold. In many cases, the cost of goods sold is larger than all of the other expenses combined. The cost of goods sold can be determined under either the absorption costing or variable costing concept.

Under **absorption costing**, all manufacturing costs are included in finished goods and remain there as an asset until the goods are sold. Absorption costing is necessary in determining historical costs for financial reporting to external users and for tax reporting.

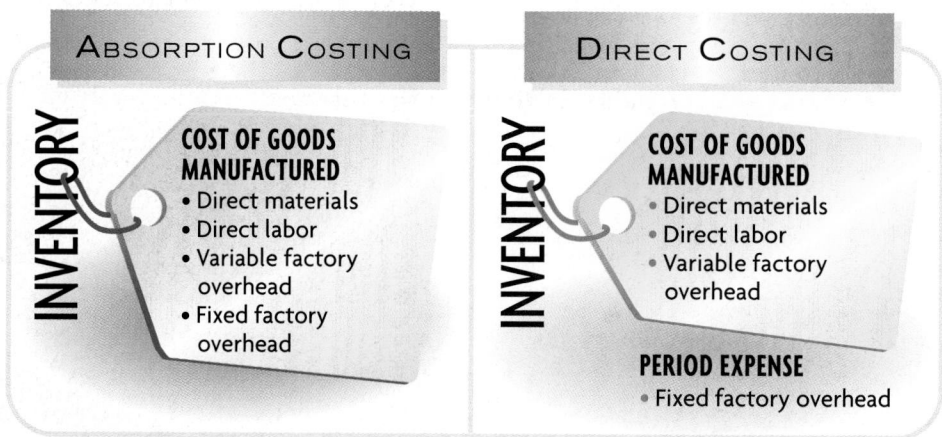

Variable costing may be more useful to management in making decisions. In **variable costing**, which is also called **direct costing**, the cost of goods manufactured is composed only of *variable* manufacturing costs—costs that increase or decrease as the volume of production rises or falls. These costs are the direct materials, direct labor, and only those factory overhead costs that vary with the rate of production. The remaining factory overhead costs, which are fixed or nonvariable costs, are generally related to the productive capacity of the manufacturing plant and are not affected by changes in the quantity of product manufactured. Thus, the fixed factory overhead does not become a part of the cost of goods manufactured but is treated as an expense of the period in which it is incurred.

To illustrate the difference between the variable costing income statement and the absorption costing income statement, assume that Belling Co. manufactured 15,000 units at the following costs:

	Total Cost	Number of Units	Unit Cost
Manufacturing costs:			
Variable	$375,000	15,000	$25
Fixed	150,000	15,000	10
Total	$525,000		$35
Selling and administrative expenses:			
Variable ($5 per unit sold)	$ 75,000		
Fixed	50,000		
Total	$125,000		

> **The variable costing income statement includes only variable manufacturing costs in the cost of goods sold.**

The units sell at a price of $50, as shown in the variable costing income statement for Belling Co. in Exhibit 1. In this income statement, variable costs are separated from fixed costs. The variable cost of goods sold, which includes the variable manufacturing costs, is deducted from sales to yield the ***manufacturing margin*** of $375,000. The variable selling and administrative expenses of $75,000 are deducted from the manufacturing margin to yield the contribution margin of $300,000. Thus, the ***contribution margin*** is sales less variable costs, as we defined in the previous chapter. The income from operations of $100,000 is then determined by deducting fixed costs of $200,000 from the contribution margin.

Exhibit 2 shows the absorption costing income statement prepared for Belling Co. The absorption costing income statement does not distinguish between variable and

•Exhibit 1   Variable Costing Income Statement

A company has sales of $450,000, cost of goods sold of $300,000, variable cost of goods sold of $220,000, and variable selling expenses of $50,000. What are (a) its manufacturing margin and (b) its contribution margin?

(a) $230,000 ($450,000 − $220,000); (b) $180,000 ($230,000 − $50,000)

Sales (15,000 × $50)		$750,000
Variable cost of goods sold (15,000 × $25)		375,000
Manufacturing margin		$375,000
Variable selling and administrative expenses		75,000
Contribution margin		$300,000
Fixed costs:		
Fixed manufacturing costs	$150,000	
Fixed selling and administrative expenses	50,000	200,000
Income from operations		$100,000

fixed costs. All manufacturing costs are included in the cost of goods sold. Deducting cost of goods sold from sales yields the $225,000 gross profit. Deducting selling and administrative expenses then yields income from operations of $100,000.

•Exhibit 2   **Absorption Costing Income Statement**

Sales (15,000 × $50).	$750,000
Cost of goods sold (15,000 × $35)	525,000
Gross profit	$225,000
Selling and administrative expenses ($75,000 + $50,000)	125,000
Income from operations	$100,000

REAL WORLD

Different parts of the world emphasize different approaches to reporting income. For example, Scandinavian companies have a strong variable costing tradition, while German cost accountants have developed some of the most advanced absorption costing practices in the world.

Income from Operations When Units Manufactured Equal Units Sold

In Exhibits 1 and 2, 15,000 units were manufactured and sold. Both the variable and the absorption costing income statements reported the same income from operations of $100,000. Thus, when the number of units manufactured equals the number of units sold, income from operations will be the same under both methods.

Income from Operations When Units Manufactured Exceed Units Sold

When the number of units manufactured exceeds the number of units sold, the variable costing income from operations will be *less* than the absorption costing income from operations. To illustrate, assume that in the preceding example only 12,000 units of the 15,000 units manufactured were sold. Exhibit 3 shows the two income statements that result.

The $30,000 difference ($70,000 − $40,000) in the amount of income from operations is due to the different treatment of the fixed manufacturing costs. The entire amount of the $150,000 of fixed manufacturing costs is included as an expense of the period in the variable costing statement. The ending inventory in the absorption

•Exhibit 3   **Units Manufactured Exceed Units Sold**

Variable Costing Income Statement		
Sales (12,000 × $50)		$600,000
Variable cost of goods sold:		
Variable cost of goods manufactured (15,000 × $25).	$375,000	
Less ending inventory (3,000 × $25).	75,000	
Variable cost of goods sold.		300,000
Manufacturing margin		$300,000
Variable selling and administrative expenses (12,000 × $5).		60,000
Contribution margin		$240,000
Fixed costs:		
Fixed manufacturing costs	$150,000	
Fixed selling and administrative expenses.	50,000	200,000
Income from operations.		$ 40,000

•Exhibit 3
(concluded)

Absorption Costing Income Statement		
Sales (12,000 × $50).....................................		$600,000
Cost of goods sold:		
Cost of goods manufactured (15,000 × $35)	$525,000	
Less ending inventory (3,000 × $35).......................	105,000	
Cost of goods sold		420,000
Gross profit		$180,000
Selling and administrative expenses ($60,000 + $50,000)		110,000
Income from operations		$ 70,000

Fixed costs are $40 per unit and variable costs are $120 per unit. Production exceeded sales by 5,000 units. What is the difference in the variable costing and absorption costing income from operations?

Variable costing income from operations will be $200,000 ($40 per unit × 5,000) less than absorption costing income from operations.

costing statement includes $30,000 (3,000 units × $10) of fixed manufacturing costs. This $30,000 is excluded from the current cost of goods sold in the absorption costing statement and is thus deferred to a future period.

Income from Operations When Units Manufactured Are Less than Units Sold

When the number of units manufactured is less than the number of units sold, the variable costing income from operations will be *greater* than the absorption costing income from operations. To illustrate, assume that 5,000 units of inventory were on hand at the beginning of a period, 10,000 units were manufactured during the period, and 15,000 units were sold (10,000 units manufactured during the period plus the 5,000 units on hand at the beginning of the period) at $50 per unit. The manufacturing costs and selling and administrative expenses are as follows. Exhibit 4 shows the two income statements prepared from this information.

	Total Cost	Number of Units	Unit Cost
Beginning inventory:			
Manufacturing costs:			
Variable	$125,000	5,000	$25
Fixed	50,000	5,000	10
Total	$175,000		$35
Current period:			
Manufacturing costs:			
Variable	$250,000	10,000	$25
Fixed	150,000	10,000	15
Total	$400,000		$40
Selling and administrative expenses:			
Variable ($5 per unit sold)	$ 75,000		
Fixed	50,000		
Total	$125,000		

The $50,000 difference ($100,000 − $50,000) in the income from operations is caused by the different treatment of the fixed manufacturing costs. The beginning inventory in the absorption costing income statement includes $50,000 (5,000 units × $10) of fixed manufacturing costs incurred in the preceding period. By being included in the beginning inventory, this $50,000 is included in the cost of goods sold

•Exhibit 4 Units Manufactured Are Less than Units Sold

Variable Costing Income Statement		
Sales (15,000 × $50)...		$750,000
Variable cost of goods sold:		
Beginning inventory (5,000 × $25)........................	$125,000	
Variable cost of goods manufactured (10,000 × $25)..........	250,000	
Variable cost of goods sold............................		375,000
Manufacturing margin..		$375,000
Variable selling and administrative expenses (15,000 × $5).......		75,000
Contribution margin...		$300,000
Fixed costs:		
Fixed manufacturing costs................................	$150,000	
Fixed selling and administrative expenses	50,000	200,000
Income from operations		$100,000

The beginning inventory is 8,000 units, all of which are sold during the period. The beginning inventory fixed costs are $60 per unit, and variable costs are $300 per unit. What is the difference in the variable costing and absorption costing income from operations, assuming no ending inventory?

Variable costing income from operations will be $480,000 ($60 per unit × 8,000) greater than absorption costing income from operations.

Absorption Costing Income Statement		
Sales (15,000 × $50)...		$750,000
Cost of goods sold:		
Beginning inventory (5,000 × $35)........................	$175,000	
Cost of goods manufactured (10,000 × $40)	400,000	
Cost of goods sold		575,000
Gross profit		$175,000
Selling and administrative expenses ($75,000 + $50,000)		125,000
Income from operations.......................................		$ 50,000

for the current period. Under variable costing, however, this $50,000 was included as an expense in an income statement of a prior period. Therefore, none of it is included as an expense in the current income statement.

Comparing Income from Operations Under the Two Concepts

The two preceding examples illustrate the effects of the variable costing and absorption costing concepts on income from operations when the number of units sold do *not* equal the number of units produced. These effects are summarized below.

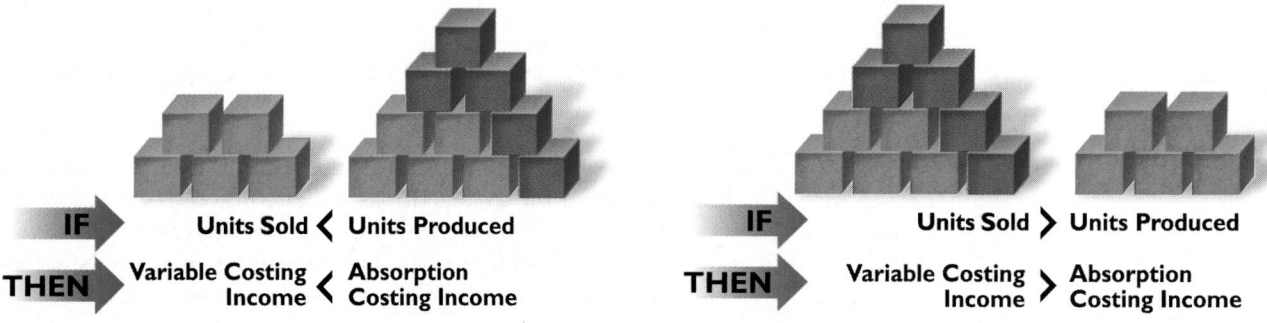

Income Analysis Under Variable Costing and Absorption Costing

Describe and illustrate income analysis under variable costing and absorption costing.

As we have illustrated, the income from operations under variable costing can differ from the income from operations under absorption costing. This difference results from changes in the quantity of the finished goods inventory, which are caused by differences in the levels of sales and production. In analyzing and evaluating operations, management should be aware of the possible effects of changing inventory levels under the two concepts. To illustrate, assume that Frand Manufacturing Company has no beginning inventory and sales are estimated to be 20,000 units at $75 per unit, regardless of production levels. Assume further that the following two proposed production levels are being evaluated by the management of Frand Manufacturing Company:

Proposal 1: 20,000 Units to Be Manufactured and Sold

	Total Cost	Number of Units	Unit Cost
Manufacturing costs:			
Variable	$ 700,000	20,000	$35
Fixed	400,000	20,000	20
Total costs	$1,100,000		$55
Selling and administrative expenses:			
Variable ($5 per unit sold)	$ 100,000		
Fixed	100,000		
Total expenses	$ 200,000		

Proposal 2: 25,000 Units to Be Manufactured; 20,000 Units to Be Sold

	Total Cost	Number of Units	Unit Cost
Manufacturing costs:			
Variable	$ 875,000	25,000	$35
Fixed	400,000	25,000	16
Total costs	$1,275,000		$51
Selling and administrative expenses:			
Variable ($5 per unit sold)	$ 100,000		
Fixed	100,000		
Total expenses	$ 200,000		

If Frand Manufacturing Company manufactures 20,000 units, which is an amount equal to the estimated sales, income from operations under absorption costing would be $200,000. However, the income from operations could be increased by $80,000 by manufacturing 25,000 units and adding 5,000 units to the finished goods inventory. The absorption costing income statements illustrating this effect are shown in Exhibit 5.

•Exhibit 5

**Absorption Costing
Income Statements for
Two Production Levels**

	Frand Manufacturing Company Absorption Costing Income Statements	
	20,000 Units Manufactured	**25,000 Units Manufactured**
Sales (20,000 units × $75)	$1,500,000	$1,500,000
Cost of goods sold:		
Cost of goods manufactured:		
(20,000 units × $55)	$1,100,000	
(25,000 units × $51)		$1,275,000
Less ending inventory:		
(5,000 units × $51)		255,000
Cost of goods sold	$1,100,000	$1,020,000
Gross profit	$ 400,000	$ 480,000
Selling and administrative expenses		
($100,000 + $100,000)	200,000	200,000
Income from operations	$ 200,000	$ 280,000

Variable costs are $100 per unit, and fixed costs are $50,000. Sales are estimated to be 4,000 units. (a) How much would absorption costing income from operations differ between a plan to produce 4,000 units and 5,000 units? (b) How much would variable costing income from operations differ between the two production plans?

(a) $10,000 greater for 5,000 units of production [1,000 units × ($50,000 ÷ 5,000), or 4,000 units × ($12.50 − $10.00)];
(b) There would be no difference in income from operations.

The $80,000 increase in income from operations would be caused by allocating the fixed manufacturing costs of $400,000 over a greater number of units of production. Specifically, an increase in production from 20,000 units to 25,000 units meant that the fixed manufacturing costs per unit decreased from $20 ($400,000 ÷ 20,000 units) to $16 ($400,000 ÷ 25,000 units). Thus, the cost of goods sold when 25,000 units are manufactured would be $4 per unit less, or $80,000 less in total (20,000 units sold × $4). Since the cost of goods sold is less, income from operations is $80,000 more when 25,000 units rather than 20,000 units are manufactured.

Under variable costing, income from operations would have been $200,000, regardless of the amount by which units manufactured exceeded sales, because no fixed manufacturing costs are allocated to the units manufactured. To illustrate, Exhibit 6 presents the variable costing income statements for Frand Manufacturing Company for the production of 20,000 units, 25,000 units, and 30,000 units. In each case, the income from operations is $200,000.

As illustrated, if absorption costing is used, management should be careful in analyzing income from operations when large changes in inventory levels occur.

INTEGRITY IN BUSINESS

PRODUCTION VS. DEMAND

Aligning production to demand is a critical decision in business. Managers must not allow the temporary benefits of excess production through higher absorption of fixed costs guide their decisions. Likewise, if demand falls, production should be dropped and inventory liquidated to match the new demand level, even though earnings will be penalized. The following interchange provides an example of an appropriate response to lowered demand for **H.J. Heinz Company**:

Analyst's question: *Could you talk for a moment about manufacturing costs during the quarter? You had highlighted that they were up and that gross margins at Heinz USA were down. Why was that the case?*

Heinz executive's response: *Yeah. The manufacturing costs were somewhat up . . . as we improve our inventory position, obviously you've got less inventory to spread your fixed costs over, so you'll take what accountants would call an absorption hit as we reduce costs. And that will be something that as we pull down inventory over the years, that will be an additional P&L cost hurdle that we need to overcome.*

Management operating with integrity will lower production and inventory to lower demand levels, even though there will be an adverse impact on published financial statements.

•Exhibit 6

Variable Costing Income Statements for Three Production Levels

Frand Manufacturing Company
Variable Costing Income Statements

	20,000 Units Manufactured	25,000 Units Manufactured	30,000 Units Manufactured
Sales (20,000 units × $75).......	$1,500,000	$1,500,000	$1,500,000
Variable cost of goods sold:			
Variable cost of goods			
manufactured:			
(20,000 units × $35).......	$ 700,000		
(25,000 units × $35).......		$ 875,000	
(30,000 units × $35).......			$1,050,000
Less ending inventory:			
(0 units × $35)	0		
(5,000 units × $35)........		175,000	
(10,000 units × $35).......			350,000
Variable cost of goods sold....	$ 700,000	$ 700,000	$ 700,000
Manufacturing margin..........	$ 800,000	$ 800,000	$ 800,000
Variable selling and administrative			
expenses...................	100,000	100,000	100,000
Contribution margin............	$ 700,000	$ 700,000	$ 700,000
Fixed costs:			
Fixed manufacturing costs	$ 400,000	$ 400,000	$ 400,000
Fixed selling and administrative			
expenses	100,000	100,000	100,000
Total fixed costs	$ 500,000	$ 500,000	$ 500,000
Income from operations........	$ 200,000	$ 200,000	$ 200,000

Managers could misinterpret increases or decreases in income from operations, due to mere changes in inventory levels, to be the result of business events, such as changes in sales volume, prices, or costs.

Many accountants believe that variable costing should be used for evaluating operating performance because absorption costing encourages management to produce inventory. This is because producing inventory absorbs fixed costs and causes the income from operations to appear higher, as we have illustrated previously. In the long run, building inventory without the promise of future sales may lead to higher handling, storage, financing, and obsolescence costs.

Management's Use of Variable Costing and Absorption Costing

objective **3**

Describe and illustrate management's use of variable costing and absorption costing for controlling costs, pricing products, planning production, analyzing market segments, and analyzing contribution margins.

Managerial accountants should carefully analyze each situation in evaluating whether variable costing or absorption costing reports would be more useful to management. In many situations, preparing reports under both concepts provides useful insights. In the following paragraphs, we discuss such reports and their advantages and disadvantages to management in making decisions related to the items identified in Exhibit 7.

Controlling Costs

All costs are controllable in the long run by someone within a business, but they are not all controllable at the same level of management. For example, plant supervisors,

•Exhibit 7 Accounting Reports and Management Decisions

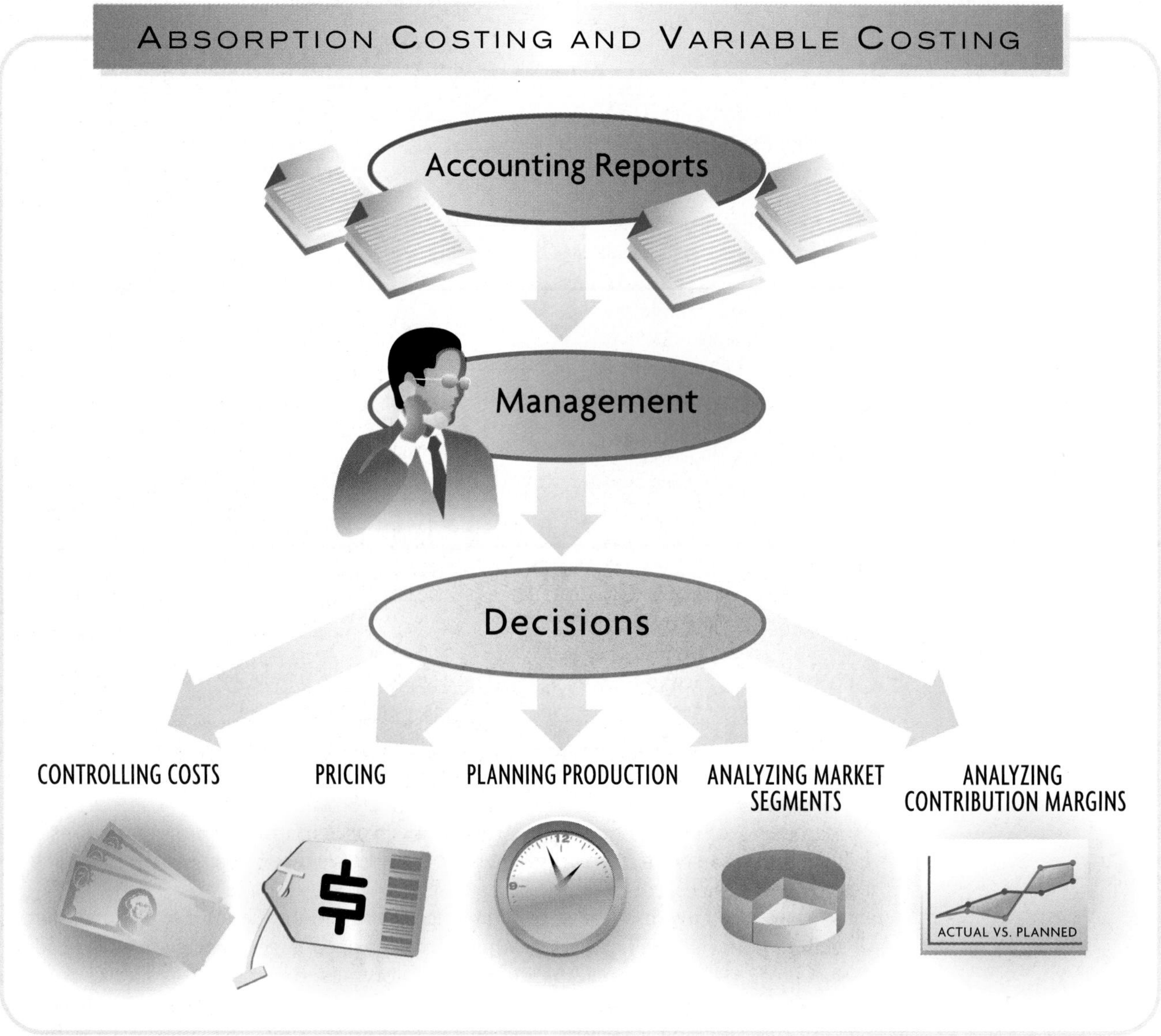

ABSORPTION COSTING AND VARIABLE COSTING

Accounting Reports

Management

Decisions

CONTROLLING COSTS   PRICING   PLANNING PRODUCTION   ANALYZING MARKET SEGMENTS   ANALYZING CONTRIBUTION MARGINS

ACTUAL VS. PLANNED

REAL WORLD

Most chemical companies, such as **Union Carbide** or **Dow Chemical**, use variable costing to evaluate the profitability of their operations. These approaches prevent fixed costs outside of managers' control to be used for evaluation purposes.

as members of operating management, are responsible for controlling the use of direct materials in their departments. They have no control, however, of insurance costs related to the buildings housing their departments. For a specific level of management, **controllable costs** are costs that can be influenced by management at that level, and **noncontrollable costs** are costs that another level of management controls. This distinction is useful in fixing the responsibility for incurring costs and for reporting costs to those responsible for their control.

Variable manufacturing costs are controlled at the operating level. If the product's cost includes only variable manufacturing costs, the cost can be controlled by operating management. The fixed factory overhead costs are normally the responsibility of a higher level of management. When the fixed factory overhead costs are reported as a separate item in the variable costing income statement, they are easier to identify and control than when they are spread among units of product, as they are under absorption costing.

As in the case with the fixed and variable manufacturing costs, the control of the variable and fixed operating expenses is usually the responsibility of different levels of management. Under variable costing, the variable selling and administrative expenses are reported separately from the fixed selling and administrative expenses. Because they are reported in this manner, both types of operating expenses are easier to identify and control than is the case under absorption costing.

Pricing Products

Many factors enter into determining the selling price of a product. The cost of making the product is clearly significant. Microeconomic theory states that income is maximized by expanding output to the volume where the revenue realized by the sale of an additional unit (marginal revenue) equals the cost of that unit (marginal cost). Although the degree of accuracy assumed in economic theory is rarely achieved, the concepts of marginal revenue and marginal cost are useful in setting selling prices.

In the short run, a business is committed to its existing manufacturing facilities. The pricing decision should be based upon making the best use of such capacity. The fixed costs cannot be avoided, but the variable costs can be eliminated if the company does not manufacture the product. The selling price of a product, therefore, should at least be equal to the variable costs of making and selling it. Any price above this minimum selling price contributes an amount toward covering fixed costs and providing income. Variable costing procedures yield data that emphasize these relationships.

In the long run, plant capacity can be increased or decreased. If a business is to continue operating, the selling prices of its products must cover all costs and provide a reasonable income. Hence, in establishing pricing policies for the long run, information provided by absorption costing procedures is needed.

The results of a research study indicated that the companies studied used absorption costing in making routine pricing decisions. However, these companies regularly used variable costing as a basis for setting prices in many short-run situations.

There are no simple solutions to most pricing problems. Consideration must be given to many factors of varying importance. Accounting can contribute by preparing analyses of various pricing plans for both the short run and the long run. Additional analyses useful for product pricing are further described and illustrated in a later chapter.

Planning Production

Planning production also has both short-run and long-run implications. In the short run, production is limited to existing capacity. Operating decisions must be made quickly before opportunities are lost. For example, a company manufacturing products with a seasonal demand may have an opportunity to obtain an off-season order that will not interfere with its production schedule nor reduce the sales of its other products. The relevant factors for such a short-run decision are the additional revenues and the additional variable costs associated with the off-season order. If the revenues from the special order will provide a contribution margin, the order should be accepted because it will increase the company's income from operations. For long-run planning, management must also consider the fixed costs.

Analyzing Market Segments

Market analysis is performed by the sales and marketing function in order to determine the profit contributed by market segments. A **_market segment_** is a portion of business that can be assigned to a manager for profit responsibility. Examples of market segments include sales territories, products, salespersons, and customers. Variable costing can provide significant insight to decision making regarding such segments. We will illustrate contribution margin reporting for market segments in the next section.

Contribution Margin Reporting for Market Segments

objective 4

Illustrate contribution margin reporting for products, territories, and salespersons.

Businesses develop contribution margin reports by meaningful market segments. Most companies will develop product segment reports, since products provide different levels of profitability. Beyond product segments, companies may emphasize geographic, customer, distribution channel, or salesperson segments. For example, **McDonald's Corporation** analyzes geographic segments. Geographic segments are more meaningful for McDonald's than are customer segments. It is difficult, and probably meaningless, to try to distinguish McDonald's customers. However, McDonald's geographic segments are unique. For example, the operating results of restaurants in the United States are different from those in Asia or Europe.

To illustrate contribution margin reporting for market segments, assume the following data for March 2006 for Camelot Fragrance Company. Camelot Fragrance Company manufactures and sells the Gwenevere perfume line for women and the Lancelot cologne line for men. For simplicity, we assume that the inventories are negligible and are thus disregarded in the reports that follow.

	Northern Territory	Southern Territory	Total
Sales:			
Gwenevere	$60,000	$30,000	$ 90,000
Lancelot	20,000	50,000	70,000
Total territory sales	$80,000	$80,000	$160,000
Variable production costs:			
Gwenevere (12% of sales)	$ 7,200	$ 3,600	$ 10,800
Lancelot (12% of sales)	2,400	6,000	8,400
Total variable production cost by territory	$ 9,600	$ 9,600	$ 19,200
Promotion costs:			
Gwenevere (variable at 30% of sales)	$18,000	$ 9,000	$ 27,000
Lancelot (variable at 20% of sales)	4,000	10,000	14,000
Total promotion cost by territory	$22,000	$19,000	$ 41,000
Sales commissions:			
Gwenevere (variable at 20% of sales)	$12,000	$ 6,000	$ 18,000
Lancelot (variable at 10% of sales)	2,000	5,000	7,000
Total sales commissions by territory	$14,000	$11,000	$ 25,000

This information can be used by Camelot Fragrance Company to prepare a sales territory, product, and salesperson profitability analysis. Each of these is discussed on the following pages.

Sales Territory Profitability Analysis

An income statement presenting the contribution margin by sales territories is often useful to management in evaluating past performance and in directing future sales efforts. Sales territory profitability analysis may lead management to reduce costs in lower-profit sales territories or to increase sales effort in higher-profit territories. For example, **The Coca-Cola Company** earns over 75% of its total corporate profits outside of the United States. This information motivates the Coca-Cola management to continue expanding operations and sales efforts around the world.

There are many possible explanations for profit differences between territories, including differences in pricing, sales unit volumes, media rates, selling costs, and the types of products sold. To illustrate the analysis of profit differences by sales territory, Exhibit 8 shows the contribution margin by sales territory for Camelot Fragrance Company.

•Exhibit 8

Contribution Margin by Sales Territory Report

Camelot Fragrance Company Contribution Margin by Sales Territory For the Month Ended March 31, 2006				
	Northern Territory		**Southern Territory**	
Sales		$80,000		$80,000
Variable cost of goods sold . . .		9,600		9,600
Manufacturing margin		$70,400		$70,400
Variable selling expenses:				
Promotion costs	$22,000		$19,000	
Sales commissions	14,000	36,000	11,000	30,000
Contribution margin		$34,400		$40,400
Contribution margin ratio		43%		50.5%

REAL WORLD

Rite-Aid Corporation recently reported that its gross margins increased as a result of a shift in sales mix from prescription toward generic drug sales.

The contribution margin for each territory consists of the sales less the variable costs associated with producing and selling products in each territory. In addition to the contribution margin, the contribution margin ratio (contribution margin divided by sales) for each territory is useful in evaluating sales territories and directing operations toward more profitable activities. For the Northern Territory, the contribution margin ratio is 43% ($34,400 ÷ $80,000), and for the Southern Territory the ratio is 50.5% ($40,400 ÷ $80,000). Although each territory had the same sales, the contribution margin ratios are different. Why is this?

In this case, the difference in territory profit performance can be explained by the difference in sales mix between the two territories. **Sales mix**, sometimes referred to as *product mix*, is defined as the relative distribution of sales among the various products sold. From the assumed information, the Southern Territory had a higher relative proportion of Lancelot sales than did the Northern Territory. If the Lancelot line is more profitable than the Gwenevere line, then we would expect the Southern Territory's overall profitability to be higher than the Northern Territory's, as shown in Exhibit 8. To verify the difference between the profitabilities of the two products, product profitability analysis may be performed.

Product Profitability Analysis

REAL WORLD

Customer, territory, product, and salesperson profit analysis is done by using a "data warehouse." A data warehouse is a relational database of revenue and cost information that can be divided into many different profit views. For example, **Johnson and Johnson**'s data warehouse, called Darwin, enables managers from fifty countries around the world to see various profit views at the click of a mouse.

Management should focus its sales efforts on those products that will provide the maximum total contribution margin. An income statement presenting the contribution margin by products is often used by management to guide product-related sales and promotional efforts. For example, **Ford**'s *Expedition* sport utility vehicle is one of its most profitable models. Ford uses this information to motivate higher production levels and promotion effort for this brand.

Some products are more profitable than others due to differences with respect to pricing, manufacturing costs, advertising support, or salesperson support. To illustrate the analysis of these differences, Exhibit 9 shows the contribution margin by product for Camelot Fragrance Company.

As you can see, Lancelot's contribution margin ratio is greater than Gwenevere's, even though both product lines have the same manufacturing margin as a percent of sales (88%). The higher contribution margin ratio is the result of Lancelot's lower promotion costs and sales commissions as a percent of sales. The sales territory profitability

•**Exhibit 9**

Contribution Margin by
Product Line Report

Camelot Fragrance Company
Contribution Margin by Product Line
For the Month Ended March 31, 2006

	Gwenevere		Lancelot	
Sales		$90,000		$70,000
Variable cost of goods sold . . .		10,800		8,400
Manufacturing margin		$79,200		$61,600
Variable selling expenses:				
Promotion costs	$27,000		$14,000	
Sales commissions	18,000	45,000	7,000	21,000
Contribution margin		$34,200		$40,600
Contribution margin ratio		38%		58%

analysis and the product profitability analysis both indicate the superior profit performance of the Lancelot line. Thus, management should emphasize the Lancelot product line in its marketing plans, try to reduce the promotion and sales commission expenses associated with Gwenevere sales, or increase the price of Gwenevere.

Salesperson Profitability Analysis

In addition to the sales territory and product profitability analyses, sales managers may wish to evaluate the performance of salespersons. This may be done with a salesperson profitability analysis.

A report to management for use in evaluating the sales performance of each salesperson could include total sales, variable cost of goods sold, variable selling expenses, contribution margin, and contribution margin ratio. Exhibit 10 illustrates such a report for three salespersons in the Northern Territory of Camelot Fragrance Company.

•**Exhibit 10**

Contribution Margin by
Salesperson Report

Camelot Fragrance Company
Contribution Margin by Salesperson—Northern Territory
For the Month Ended March 31, 2006

	Inez Rodriguez	Tom Ginger	Beth Williams	Northern Territory— Total
Sales	$20,000	$20,000	$40,000	$80,000
Variable cost of goods sold . .	2,400	2,400	4,800	9,600
Manufacturing margin	$17,600	$17,600	$35,200	$70,400
Variable selling expenses:				
Promotion costs	$ 5,000	$ 5,000	$12,000	$22,000
Sales commissions	3,000	3,000	8,000	14,000
	$ 8,000	$ 8,000	$20,000	$36,000
Contribution margin	$ 9,600	$ 9,600	$15,200	$34,400
Contribution margin ratio . . .	48%	48%	38%	43%
Sales mix (% Lancelot sales) . .	50%	50%	0	25%

The additional information provided on the total sales and costs of all three salespersons agrees with the total sales and costs for the Northern Territory in Exhibit 8. Thus, this report provides the Northern Territory manager with a more detailed analysis of the territory's performance. The report indicates that Beth Williams produced the greatest contribution margin for the company but had the lowest contribution margin ratio. Beth Williams sold $40,000 of product, which is twice as much product as the other two salespersons. However, Beth Williams sold only the Gwenevere product line, which has the lowest contribution margin ratio (from Exhibit 9). The other two salespersons sold equal amounts of Gwenevere and Lancelot. These two salespersons had higher contribution margin ratios because of the sales of the higher-margin Lancelot line. The territory manager could use this report to encourage Rodriguez and Ginger to sell more total product, while encouraging Williams to place more selling effort on the Lancelot line.

Other factors should also be considered in evaluating salespersons' performance. For example, sales growth rates, years of experience, customer service, territory size, and actual performance compared to budgeted performance may also be important.

MANAGERIAL DISCLOSURE AND ANALYSIS

MCDONALD'S CORPORATION

McDonald's Corporation is the largest restaurant company in the world, representing 2.6% of the restaurants and 6.3% of the sales of all restaurants in the United States. McDonald's annual report identifies revenues and costs for its company-owned restaurants separately from its franchised restaurants. Assume that the food, paper, payroll, and benefit costs are variable and that occupancy and other operating expenses are fixed. A contribution margin and income from operations can be constructed for the company-owned restaurants as follows:

McDonald's Corporation
Company-Owned Restaurant Contribution Margin and Income from Operations
For the Year Ended December 31, 2002 (in thousands)

Sales		$11,499,600
Variable restaurant expenses:		
Food and paper	$3,917,400	
Payroll and employee benefits	3,078,200	
Total variable restaurant operating costs		6,995,600
Contribution margin		$ 4,504,000
Occupancy and other operating expenses		2,911,000
Income from operations		$ 1,593,000

The annual report also indicates that McDonald's has 9,000 company-owned restaurants. Dividing the numbers above by 9,000 yields the contribution margin and income from operations *per restaurant* as follows:

Sales	$1,277,733
Variable restaurant expenses	777,289
Contribution margin	$ 500,444
Occupancy and other operating expenses	323,444
Income from operations	$ 177,000

In addition, McDonald's segments this information by its major operating regions, such as the United States, Europe, Latin America, Canada, and Asia. McDonald's can use this information for pricing products; evaluating the sensitivity of store profitability to changes in sales volume, prices, and costs; analyzing profitability by geographic segments; and evaluating the contribution of the company-owned stores to overall corporate profitability.

Contribution Margin Analysis

objective **5**

Explain changes in contribution margin as a result of quantity and price factors.

The contribution margin concept can be used to assist managers in planning and controlling operations by focusing on the differences between planned and actual contribution margins. These differences, as well as the causes of the differences, can be systematically explained using **contribution margin analysis**.

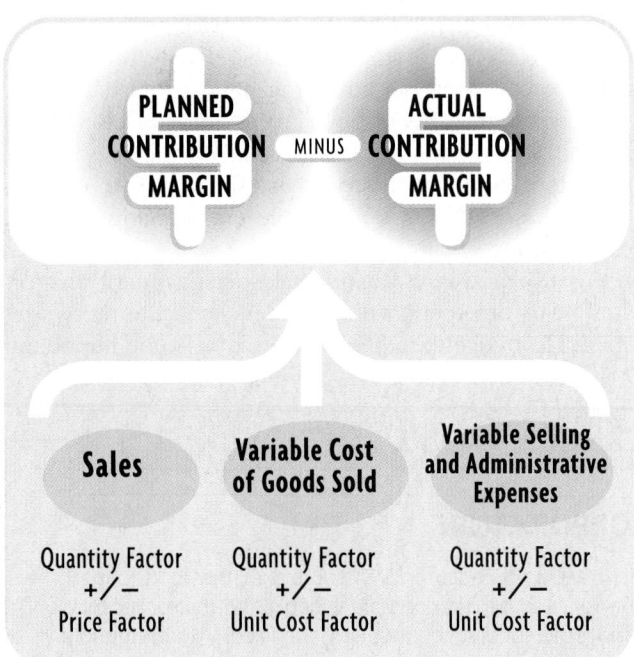

Since contribution margin is the excess of sales over variable costs, a difference between the planned and actual contribution margin can be caused by (1) an increase or decrease in the amount of sales or (2) an increase or decrease in the amount of variable costs. An increase or decrease in either element may in turn be due to (1) an increase or decrease in the number of units sold or (2) an increase or decrease in the unit sales price or unit cost. The effect of these two factors on either sales or variable costs may be stated as follows:

1. ***Quantity factor***—the effect of a difference in the number of units sold, assuming no change in unit sales price or unit cost. The quantity factor is the difference between the actual quantity sold and the planned quantity sold, multiplied by the planned unit sales price or unit cost.

2. Unit ***price factor*** or **unit cost factor**—the effect of a difference in unit sales price or unit cost on the number of units sold. The unit price or unit cost factor is the difference between the actual unit price or unit cost and the planned unit price or unit cost, multiplied by the actual quantity sold.

We will use the following data for Noble Inc. for the year ended December 31, 2006, as a basis for illustrating contribution margin analysis. For the sake of simplicity, we will assume a single commodity. The analysis would be more complex if several different commodities were sold, but the basic principles would not be affected.

	Actual	Planned	Increase or (Decrease)
Sales	$937,500	$800,000	$137,500
Less: Variable cost of goods sold	$425,000	$350,000	$ 75,000
Variable selling and administrative expenses	162,500	125,000	37,500
Total	$587,500	$475,000	$112,500
Contribution margin	$350,000	$325,000	$ 25,000
Number of units sold	125,000	100,000	
Per unit:			
Sales price	$7.50	$8.00	
Variable cost of goods sold	$3.40	$3.50	
Variable selling and administrative expenses	$1.30	$1.25	

The analysis of these data in Exhibit 11 shows that the favorable increase of $25,000 in the contribution margin was due in large part to an increase in the number of units sold. This increase was partially offset by a decrease in the unit sales price and an increase in the unit cost for variable selling and administrative expenses. The decrease in the unit cost for the variable cost of goods sold was an additional favorable result of 2006 operations.

The information presented in the contribution margin analysis report is useful to management in evaluating past performance and in planning future operations. For example, the impact of the $0.50 reduction in the unit sales price on the number of units sold and on the total sales for the year is useful information that management can use in determining whether further price reductions might be desirable.

•Exhibit 11   Contribution Margin Analysis Report

Noble Inc.
Contribution Margin Analysis
For the Year Ended December 31, 2006

Increase in amount of sales attributed to:			
Quantity factor:			
Increase in number of units sold in 2006		25,000	
Planned sales price in 2006		× $8.00	$200,000
Price factor:			
Decrease in unit sales price in 2006		$(0.50)	
Number of units sold in 2006		×125,000	(62,500)
Net increase in amount of sales			$137,500
Increase in amount of variable cost of goods sold attributed to:			
Quantity factor:			
Increase in number of units sold in 2006	25,000		
Planned unit cost in 2006	× $3.50	$ 87,500	
Unit cost factor:			
Decrease in unit cost in 2006	$(0.10)		
Number of units sold in 2006	×125,000	(12,500)	
Net increase in amount of variable cost of goods sold		$ 75,000	
Increase in amount of variable selling and administrative expenses attributed to:			
Quantity factor:			
Increase in number of units sold in 2006	25,000		
Planned unit cost in 2006	× $1.25	$ 31,250	
Unit cost factor:			
Increase in unit cost in 2006	$0.05		
Number of units sold in 2006	×125,000	6,250	
Net increase in the amount of variable selling and administrative expenses		$ 37,500	
Net increase in amount of variable costs			112,500
Increase in contribution margin			$ 25,000

The contribution margin analysis report also highlights the impact of changes in unit variable costs and expenses. For example, the $0.05 increase in the unit variable selling and administrative expenses might be a result of increased advertising expenditures. If so, the increase in the number of units sold in 2006 could be attributed to both the $0.50 price reduction and the increased advertising.

Contribution Margin Reporting and Analysis for Service Firms

objective 6

Describe and illustrate contribution margin reporting and analysis for service firms.

The previous sections illustrated contribution margin reporting and analysis for manufacturing firms. Service firms also prepare contribution margin reports and use these reports for analyzing market segments and performing contribution margin analyses.

Contribution Margin Report

Unlike a manufacturing firm, a service firm does not make a product for sale. As a result, service firms do not have inventory and thus do not allocate fixed costs to inventory using absorption costing concepts. Service firms can, however, report and analyze contribution margin as the difference between revenues and variable costs.

To illustrate, Blue Skies Airlines Inc. operates a small commercial airline. The fixed and variable costs associated with operating Blue Skies are shown in Exhibit 12.

•Exhibit 12

Costs of Blue Skies Airlines

Cost	Amount	Cost Behavior	Activity Base
Depreciation expense	$3,600,000	Fixed	
Food and beverage service expense	444,000	Variable	Number of passengers
Fuel expense	4,080,000	Variable	Number of miles flown
Rental expense	800,000	Fixed	
Selling expense	3,256,000	Variable	Number of passengers
Wages expense	6,120,000	Variable	Number of miles flown

As discussed in the prior chapter, a cost is fixed or variable by defining its behavior relative to changes in an activity base. The activity base in a manufacturing firm is often the number of units produced and sold. A service firm, however, may have multiple activity bases. For example, some airline costs, such as food and beverage costs, vary with the number of passengers. An airline also has costs that vary with the number of miles flown, such as fuel and wage costs. As a result, we must be careful in analyzing changes in costs to be sure that we properly identify the underlying activity changes. For example, if an airline increases the average number of passengers flown per flight, called the *load factor*, but not the number of flights, then only the selling and food and beverage costs will increase. The fuel and wage costs will not change because the number of miles flown is unchanged.[1]

The contribution margin and income from operations report for Blue Skies, assuming revenue of $19,238,000, is shown in Exhibit 13. In comparing this report to the variable costing income statement for a manufacturing firm, you will notice that there are no cost of goods sold, inventory, or manufacturing margin. However, as shown in Exhibit 13, contribution margin is reported separately from income from operations.

•Exhibit 13

Contribution Margin and Income from Operations Report

Blue Skies Airlines Inc.
Contribution Margin and Income from Operations Report
For the Month Ended April 30, 2006

Revenue		$19,238,000
Variable costs:		
Fuel expense	$4,080,000	
Wages expense	6,120,000	
Food and beverage service expense	444,000	
Selling expenses...........................	3,256,000	
Total variable costs		13,900,000
Contribution margin.............................		$ 5,338,000
Fixed costs:		
Depreciation expense.......................	$3,600,000	
Rental expense	800,000	
Total fixed costs		4,400,000
Income from operations		$ 938,000

---

[1]Fuel costs may increase somewhat due to added passenger weight, traffic volume, or weather. Our examples are simplified to focus only on the major cost behavior patterns.

Market Segment Analysis

As is the case with a manufacturing firm, the contribution margin report for service firms can be prepared to evaluate the contribution margin of market segments. The following table illustrates typical segments used in various service industries:

Service Industry	Market Segments
Electric power	Regions, customer types (industrial, consumer)
Banking	Customer types (commercial, retail), products (loans, savings accounts)
Airlines	Products (passengers, cargo), routes
Railroads	Products (commodity type), routes
Hotels	Hotel properties
Telecommunications	Customer type (commercial, retail), service type (voice, data)
Health care	Procedure, payment type (Medicare, insured)

The contribution margin report for Blue Skies Airlines can be segmented by the various routes (city pairs) flown by the airline. Management would use such a report to evaluate the relative contribution to profitability of the various city pairs served by the airline. To illustrate, assume that Blue Skies serves three city pairs: Chicago/Atlanta, Atlanta/Los Angeles, and Los Angeles/Chicago. The contribution margin report is constructed by identifying the revenues and variable costs for each of the segments. The following information was determined from corporate records for the month of April for each route:

	Chicago/Atlanta	Atlanta/LA	LA/Chicago
Average ticket price per passenger	$400	$1,075	$805
Total passengers served	16,000	7,000	6,600
Total miles flown	56,000	88,000	60,000

The variable costs are as follows:

Fuel	$ 20 per mile
Wages	30 per mile
Food and beverage service	15 per passenger
Selling	110 per passenger

A contribution margin report by segment is illustrated in Exhibit 14. You should note that the sum of the segment contribution margins in Exhibit 14 is equal to the total contribution margin shown in Exhibit 13.

As can be seen from the report, the Chicago/Atlanta route has the lowest contribution margin ratio, while the Atlanta/Los Angeles route has the highest contribution margin ratio. We discuss the implications of Exhibit 14 for management decision making next.

Contribution Margin Analysis

The management of Blue Skies is concerned about the low contribution margin ratio on the Chicago/Atlanta route. To improve the contribution margin of this route, management decreased the ticket price from $400 to $380 in May. The price reduction increased the number of tickets sold (passengers) on the existing flights from 16,000 to 20,000. That is, the load factor increased. In addition, the price for fuel increased,

 Founded in Michigan in 1927 as the Kna-Shoe Manufacturing Co., I churned out doll furniture and cabinets. Despite a name that suggests sloth, I ring up more than $2 billion in sales annually. My brand names include Alexvale, American Drew, Bauhaus, Centurion, Clayton Marcus, Hammary, HickoryMark, Kincaid, Pennsylvania House and Sam Moore. I'm a major player in residential furniture and contract furniture for the hospitality and assisted-living markets. I invented the recliner, first as a folding wood-slat porch chair. Suggested names for it included Sit-N-Snooze, Slack-Back or Comfort Carrier. Later designs were the Hi-Lo Matic, the Lectra-Lounger and the Oasis. Who am I? (Go to page 812 for answer.)

•Exhibit 14 Contribution Margin Report by Segment

Blue Skies Airlines Inc.
Contribution Margin by Route Report
For the Month Ended April 30, 2006

	Chicago/ Atlanta	Atlanta/ Los Angeles	Los Angeles/ Chicago	Total
Revenue				
(ticket price × No. of passengers)	$ 6,400,000	$ 7,525,000	$ 5,313,000	$19,238,000
Aircraft fuel				
($20 × No. of miles flown)	(1,120,000)	(1,760,000)	(1,200,000)	(4,080,000)
Wages and benefits				
($30 × No. of miles flown)	(1,680,000)	(2,640,000)	(1,800,000)	(6,120,000)
Food and beverage service				
($15 × No. of passengers)	(240,000)	(105,000)	(99,000)	(444,000)
Selling expenses				
($110 × No. of passengers)	(1,760,000)	(770,000)	(726,000)	(3,256,000)
Contribution margin	$ 1,600,000	$ 2,250,000	$ 1,488,000	$ 5,338,000
Contribution margin ratio*	25%	30%	28%	28%

*Contribution margin ÷ revenue

causing the cost per mile to increase from $20 to $22. The following data were used for the contribution margin analysis for the month of May, assuming planned results in May were as in April:

	Chicago/Atlanta Route		
	Actual, May	Planned, May	Increase (Decrease)
Revenue	$7,600,000	$6,400,000	$1,200,000
Less variable expenses:			
Aircraft fuel	$1,232,000	$1,120,000	$ 112,000
Wages and benefits	1,680,000	1,680,000	—
Food and beverage service	300,000	240,000	60,000
Selling expenses and commissions	2,200,000	1,760,000	440,000
Total	$5,412,000	$4,800,000	$ 612,000
Contribution margin	$2,188,000	$1,600,000	$ 588,000
Contribution margin ratio	29%	25%	
Number of miles flown	56,000	56,000	
Number of passengers flown	20,000	16,000	
Per unit:			
Ticket price	$ 380	$ 400	
Fuel expense	22	20	
Wages expense	30	30	
Food and beverage service expense	15	15	
Selling expenses	110	110	

The highlighted numbers indicate the actual changes from the planned May results. The data can be used to develop a contribution margin analysis report similar to our previous example in Exhibit 11. The analysis in Exhibit 15 provides the various quantity and price factors that are impacted by the changes.

•Exhibit 15   Contribution Margin Analysis Report—Service Company

Blue Skies Airlines Inc.
Contribution Margin Analysis
For the Month Ended May 31, 2006

Increase in revenue attributed to:			
Quantity factor:			
Increase in the number of tickets sold in May	4,000		
Planned price	× $400	$1,600,000	
Price factor:			
Decrease in the ticket price in May	$(20)		
Number of tickets sold in May	× 20,000	(400,000)	
Net increase in revenue			$1,200,000
Increase in fuel costs attributed to:			
Unit cost factor:			
Increase in unit cost in May	$2.00		
Number of miles flown	× 56,000		
Net increase in fuel costs			(112,000)
Increase in food and beverage service attributed to:			
Quantity factor:			
Increase in the number of tickets sold in May	4,000		
Planned unit cost in May	× $15.00		
Net increase in food and beverage service costs			(60,000)
Increase in selling costs and commissions attributed to:			
Quantity factor:			
Increase in the number of tickets sold in May	4,000		
Planned unit cost in May	× $110		
Net increase in selling costs			(440,000)
Increase in contribution margin			$ 588,000

The contribution margin analysis indicates that the decrease in price generated an additional $1,200,000 in revenue. This amount consists of $1,520,000 from increased tickets sold and a $320,000 revenue reduction from the reduced ticket price. The increased fuel costs (by $2 per mile) reduced the contribution margin by $112,000. The increased tickets sold also increased the food and beverage service costs by $60,000 and the selling costs by $440,000. The net increase in contribution margin from management's actions is $588,000, indicating that their actions were successful.

SPOTLIGHT ON STRATEGY

DELIVERING A VALUE PROPOSITION

How does a company command premium prices from a product or service? One way is by providing the customer an attractive value proposition. A *value proposition* is the bundle of *experiences* provided to a customer by a product or service. A successful value proposition will provide a set of experiences superior to the competition at a price that is both accepted by the customer and profitable for the company. For example, consider book retailers **Barnes and Noble** and **Amazon.com**. Barnes and Noble retail stores provide the following value proposition:

1. Friendly and fun book-buying atmosphere
2. Book-related activities, such as entertainment, coffee, readings, children's area, book discussions, and book signings
3. Browsing
4. Wide assortment of titles
5. Ability to physically touch and read sample pages of the book
6. Impulse purchasing and immediate gratification (if title is in stock)
7. Assisted search

Amazon.com offers a different value proposition that is more related to the convenience of purchasing a book:

1. Automated self-search features that allow a customer to easily find books by title, author, or topic
2. Very large assortment of titles
3. Convenient shopping from one's home or business
4. Delivery to the customer location within days of ordering
5. Convenient online transaction processing with One Click® ordering
6. Online reviews and information about unfamiliar titles
7. Ability to read sample pages of the book electronically
8. Automated suggestions for books that match a buyer's tastes and preferences

What is clear is that both retailers are not simply "selling books" but are providing a set of experiences that are related to book buying. These experiences set Barnes and Noble and Amazon.com apart in the bookselling marketplace. That is, the experiences delivered by Barnes and Noble are difficult for Amazon.com to deliver, and likewise, the experiences of Amazon.com are difficult for the Barnes and Noble retail stores to deliver. As a result, the consumer market appears to be supporting both value propositions. The profitability of each company will depend on its ability to maintain its unique value propositions and command pricing that is accepted by customers and covers the costs of delivering this value.

Key Points

1 Describe and illustrate income reporting under variable costing and absorption costing.

Under absorption costing, direct materials, direct labor, and factory overhead become part of the cost of goods manufactured. Under variable costing, the cost of goods manufactured is composed of only variable costs—the direct materials, direct labor, and only those factory overhead costs that vary with the rate of production. The fixed factory overhead costs do not become a part of the cost of goods manufactured but are considered an expense of the period.

Deducting the variable cost of goods sold from sales in the variable costing income statement yields the manufacturing margin. Deducting the variable selling and administrative expenses from the manufacturing margin yields the contribution margin. Deducting the fixed costs from the contribution margin yields the income from operations.

The difference in the income reported under variable costing and absorption costing is summarized in the following table:

Units Manufactured	
Equal units sold	Variable costing income equals absorption costing income.
Exceed units sold	Variable costing income is less than absorption costing income.
Less than units sold	Variable costing income is greater than absorption costing income.

2 Describe and illustrate income analysis under variable costing and absorption costing.

Management should be aware of the effects of changes in inventory levels on income from operations reported under variable costing and absorption costing. If absorption costing is used, managers could misinterpret increases or decreases in income from operations due to changes in inventory levels to be the result of operating efficiencies or inefficiencies.

3 Describe and illustrate management's use of variable costing and absorption costing for controlling costs, pricing products, planning production, analyzing market segments, and analyzing contribution margins.

Variable costing is especially useful at the operating level of management because the amount of variable manufacturing costs are controllable at this level. The fixed factory overhead costs are ordinarily controllable by a higher level of management.

In the short run, variable costing may be useful in establishing the selling price of a product. This price should be at least equal to the variable costs of making and selling the product. In the long run, however, absorption costing is useful in establishing selling prices because all costs must be covered and a reasonable amount of operating income must be earned.

4 Illustrate contribution margin reporting for products, territories, and salespersons.

Variable costing can make a significant contribution to management decision making in analyzing and evaluating market segments, such as territories, products, salespersons, and customers. The revenues and variable costs can be allocated to the market segments. Segment contribution margin can be used by managers to support price decisions, evaluate cost changes, and plan volume changes.

5 Explain changes in contribution margin as a result of quantity and price factors.

Contribution margin analysis is the systematic examination of differences between planned and actual contribution margins. These differences can be caused by (1) an increase or decrease in the amount of sales or (2) an increase or decrease in the amount of variable costs. An increase or decrease in either element may in turn be due to (1) an increase or decrease in the number of units sold or (2) an increase or decrease in the unit sales price or unit cost. The effect of these two factors on either sales or variable costs may be stated as follows:

1. **Quantity factor**—The effect of a difference in the number of units sold, assuming no change in unit sales price or unit cost. The quantity factor is the difference between the actual quantity sold and the planned quantity sold, multiplied by the planned unit sales price or unit cost.

2. **Unit price or unit cost factor**—The effect of a difference in unit sales price or unit cost on the number of units sold. The unit price or unit cost factor is the difference between the actual unit price or unit cost and the planned unit price or unit cost, multiplied by the actual quantity sold.

6 Describe and illustrate contribution margin reporting and analysis for service firms.

Service firms will not have inventories, manufacturing margin, cost of goods sold, or differences in income from operations between variable and absorption costing. Service firms can report contribution margin as the difference between revenues and variable costs. Service firms can report contribution margin for market segments. In addition, service firms can use contribution margin analysis to plan and control operations.

Key Terms

absorption costing (788)
contribution margin (789)
contribution margin analysis (801)
controllable cost (796)

manufacturing margin (789)
market segment (797)
noncontrollable cost (796)
price factor (802)

quantity factor (802)
sales mix (799)
variable costing (788)

Illustrative Problem

During the current period, McLaughlin Company sold 60,000 units of product at $30 per unit. At the beginning of the period, there were 10,000 units in inventory and McLaughlin Company manufactured 50,000 units during the period. The manufacturing costs and selling and administrative expenses were as follows:

	Total Cost	Number of Units	Unit Cost
Beginning inventory:			
Direct materials	$ 67,000	10,000	$ 6.70
Direct labor	155,000	10,000	15.50
Variable factory overhead	18,000	10,000	1.80
Fixed factory overhead	20,000	10,000	2.00
Total	$ 260,000		$26.00
Current period costs:			
Direct materials	$ 350,000	50,000	$ 7.00
Direct labor	810,000	50,000	16.20
Variable factory overhead	90,000	50,000	1.80
Fixed factory overhead	100,000	50,000	2.00
Total	$1,350,000		$27.00
Selling and administrative expenses:			
Variable	$ 65,000		
Fixed	45,000		
Total	$ 110,000		

Instructions

1. Prepare an income statement based on the variable costing concept.
2. Prepare an income statement based on the absorption costing concept.
3. Give the reason for the difference in the amount of income from operations in 1 and 2.

Solution

1.

Variable Costing Income Statement

Sales (60,000 × $30)		$1,800,000
Variable cost of goods sold:		
Beginning inventory (10,000 × $24)	$ 240,000	
Variable cost of goods manufactured (50,000 × $25)	1,250,000	
Variable cost of goods sold		1,490,000
Manufacturing margin		$ 310,000
Variable selling and administrative expenses		65,000
Contribution margin		$ 245,000
Fixed costs:		
Fixed manufacturing costs	$ 100,000	
Fixed selling and administrative expenses	45,000	145,000
Income from operations		$ 100,000

2.

Absorption Costing Income Statement

Sales (60,000 × $30)		$1,800,000
Cost of goods sold:		
Beginning inventory (10,000 × $26)	$ 260,000	
Cost of goods manufactured (50,000 × $27)	1,350,000	
Cost of goods sold		1,610,000
Gross profit		$ 190,000
Selling and administrative expenses ($65,000 + $45,000)		110,000
Income from operations		$ 80,000

3. The difference of $20,000 ($100,000 − $80,000) in the amount of income from operations is attributable to the different treatment of the fixed manufacturing costs. The beginning inventory in the absorption costing income statement includes $20,000 (10,000 units × $2) of fixed manufacturing costs incurred in the preceding period. This $20,000 was included as an expense in a variable costing income statement of a prior period. Therefore, none of it is included as an expense in the current period variable costing income statement.

Self-Examination Questions (Answers at End of Chapter)

1. Sales were $750,000, the variable cost of goods sold was $400,000, the variable selling and administrative expenses were $90,000, and fixed costs were $200,000. The contribution margin was:
   A. $60,000
   B. $260,000
   C. $350,000
   D. none of the above

2. During a year in which the number of units manufactured exceeded the number of units sold, the income from operations reported under the absorption costing concept would be:
   A. larger than the income from operations reported under the variable costing concept.
   B. smaller than the income from operations reported under the variable costing concept.
   C. the same as the income from operations reported under the variable costing concept.
   D. none of the above.

3. The beginning inventory consists of 6,000 units, all of which are sold during the period. The beginning inventory fixed costs are $20 per unit, and variable costs are $90 per unit. What is the difference in income from operations between variable and absorption costing?
   A. Variable costing income from operations is $540,000 less than under absorption costing.
   B. Variable costing income from operations is $660,000 greater than under absorption costing.
   C. Variable costing income from operations is $120,000 less than under absorption costing.
   D. Variable costing income from operations is $120,000 greater than under absorption costing.

4. Variable costs are $70 per unit and fixed costs are $150,000. Sales are estimated to be 10,000 units. How much would absorption costing income from operations differ between a plan to produce 10,000 units and 12,000 units?
   A. $150,000 greater for 12,000 units
   B. $150,000 less for 12,000 units
   C. $25,000 greater for 12,000 units
   D. $25,000 less for 12,000 units

5. If actual sales totaled $800,000 for the current year (80,000 units at $10 each) and planned sales were $765,000 (85,000 units at $9 each), the difference between actual and planned sales due to the quantity factor is:
   A. a $50,000 increase
   B. a $35,000 increase
   C. a $45,000 decrease
   D. none of the above

Class Discussion Questions

1. What types of costs are customarily included in the cost of manufactured products under (a) the absorption costing concept and (b) the variable costing concept?
2. Which type of manufacturing cost (direct materials, direct labor, variable factory overhead, fixed factory overhead) is included in the cost of goods manufactured under the absorption costing concept but is excluded from the cost of goods manufactured under the variable costing concept?
3. Which of the following costs would be included in the cost of a manufactured product according to the variable costing concept: (a) direct labor, (b) depreciation on factory building, (c) salary of factory supervisor, (d) electricity purchased

to operate factory equipment, (e) property taxes on factory building, (f) rent on factory building, (g) direct materials?

4. In the following equations, based on the variable costing income statement, identify the items designated by X:

a. Net sales − X = manufacturing margin

b. Manufacturing margin − X = contribution margin

c. Contribution margin − X = income from operations

5. In the variable costing income statement, how are the fixed manufacturing costs reported and how are the fixed selling and administrative expenses reported?

6. If the quantity of the ending inventory is larger than that of the beginning inventory, will the amount of income from operations determined by absorption costing be more than or less than the amount determined by variable costing? Explain.

7. Since all costs of operating a business are controllable, what is the significance of the term *noncontrollable cost?*

8. Discuss how financial data prepared on the basis of variable costing can assist management in the development of short-run pricing policies.

9. How might management analyze sales territory profitability?

10. Why might management analyze product profitability?

11. Explain why rewarding sales personnel on the basis of total sales might not be in the best interests of a business whose goal is to maximize profits.

12. Discuss the two factors affecting both sales and variable costs to which a change in contribution margin can be attributed.

13. How is the quantity factor for an increase or decrease in the amount of sales computed in using contribution margin analysis?

14. How is the unit cost factor for an increase or decrease in the amount of variable cost of goods sold computed in using contribution margin analysis?

15. Provide examples of market segments for an entertainment company, such as **The Walt Disney Co.**

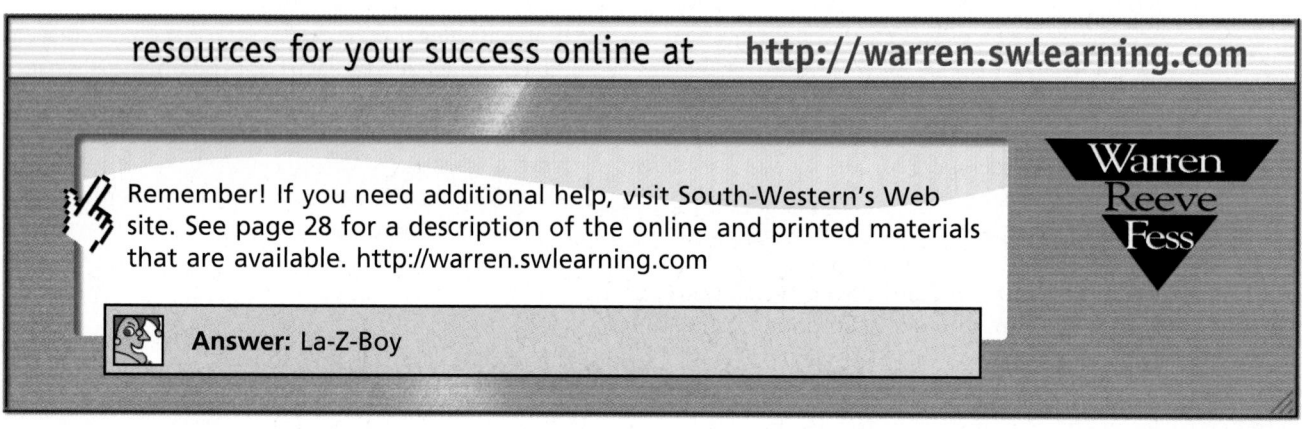

resources for your success online at   http://warren.swlearning.com

Remember! If you need additional help, visit South-Western's Web site. See page 28 for a description of the online and printed materials that are available. http://warren.swlearning.com

Answer: La-Z-Boy

Exercises

EXERCISE 19-1
Inventory valuation under absorption costing and variable costing

Objective 1

✔ *b. Inventory, $98,875*

At the end of the first year of operations, 2,500 units remained in the finished goods inventory. The unit manufacturing costs during the year were as follows:

Direct materials	$25.00
Direct labor	11.10
Fixed factory overhead cost	4.20
Variable factory overhead cost	3.45

What would be the cost of the finished goods inventory reported on the balance sheet under (a) the absorption costing concept and (b) the variable costing concept?

EXERCISE 19-2
Income statements under absorption costing and variable costing

Objective 1

SPREADSHEET

✔ *a. Income from operations, $264,000*

Laser Audio Inc. assembles and sells CD players. The company began operations on May 1, 2006, and operated at 100% of capacity during the first month. The following data summarize the results for May:

Sales (10,000 units)		$1,900,000
Production costs (12,000 units):		
Direct materials	$780,000	
Direct labor	420,000	
Variable factory overhead	208,800	
Fixed factory overhead	122,400	1,531,200
Selling and administrative expenses:		
Variable selling and administrative expenses	$260,000	
Fixed selling and administrative expenses	100,000	360,000

a. Prepare an income statement according to the absorption costing concept.
b. Prepare an income statement according to the variable costing concept.
c. ✎ What is the reason for the difference in the amount of income from operations reported in (a) and (b)?

EXERCISE 19-3
Income statements under absorption costing and variable costing

Objective 1

SPREADSHEET

✔ *b. Income from operations, $657,000*

Milan Fashions Inc. manufactures and sells women's clothes. The company began operations on August 1, 2006, and operated at 100% of capacity (30,000 units) during the first month, creating an ending inventory of 2,000 units. During September, the company produced 28,000 garments during the month but sold 30,000 units at $110 per unit. The September manufacturing costs and selling and administrative expenses were as follows:

	Total Cost	Number of Units Produced	Unit Cost
Manufacturing costs in Sept. beginning inventory:			
Variable	$ 96,000	2,000	$48.00
Fixed	22,400	2,000	11.20
Total	$ 118,400		$59.20
September manufacturing costs:			
Variable	$1,344,000	28,000	$48.00
Fixed	336,000	28,000	12.00
Total	$1,680,000		$60.00
Selling and administrative expenses:			
Variable ($21.40 per unit sold)	$ 642,000		
Fixed	225,000		
Total	$ 867,000		

(continued)

a. Prepare an income statement according to the absorption costing concept for September.

b. Prepare an income statement according to the variable costing concept for September.

c.  What is the reason for the difference in the amount of income from operations reported in (a) and (b)?

EXERCISE 19-4
Cost of goods manufactured, using variable costing and absorption costing

Objective 1

✓ b. Unit cost of goods manufactured, $39,000

On August 31, the end of the first year of operations, Tower Equipment Company manufactured 900 units and sold 800 units. The following income statement was prepared, based on the variable costing concept:

Tower Equipment Company
Variable Costing Income Statement
For the Year Ended August 31, 2006

Sales		$41,600,000
Variable cost of goods sold:		
Variable cost of goods manufactured	$24,300,000	
Less inventory, August 31	2,700,000	
Variable cost of goods sold		21,600,000
Manufacturing margin		$20,000,000
Variable selling and administrative expenses		4,300,000
Contribution margin		$15,700,000
Fixed costs:		
Fixed manufacturing costs	$10,800,000	
Fixed selling and administrative expenses	2,800,000	13,600,000
Income from operations		$ 2,100,000

Determine the *unit* cost of goods manufactured, based on (a) the variable costing concept and (b) the absorption costing concept.

EXERCISE 19-5
Variable costing income statement

Objective 1

SPREADSHEET

✓ Income from operations, $5,745

On April 30, the end of the first month of operations, East Texas Petroleum Company prepared the following income statement, based on the absorption costing concept:

East Texas Petroleum Company
Absorption Costing Income Statement
For the Month Ended April 30, 2006

Sales (3,700 units)		$88,800
Cost of goods sold:		
Cost of goods manufactured (4,000 units)	$64,000	
Less inventory, April 30 (300 units)	4,800	
Cost of goods sold		59,200
Gross profit		$29,600
Selling and administrative expenses		22,550
Income from operations		$ 7,050

If the fixed manufacturing costs were $17,400 and the variable selling and administrative expenses were $7,000, prepare an income statement according to the variable costing concept.

EXERCISE 19-6
Absorption costing income statement

Objective 1

On September 30, the end of the first month of operations, Olde English Furniture Company prepared the following income statement, based on the variable costing concept:

✓ Income from operations, $167,870

Olde English Furniture Company
Variable Costing Income Statement
For the Month Ended September 30, 2007

Sales (8,000 units)		$960,000
Variable cost of goods sold:		
Variable cost of goods manufactured	$470,000	
Less inventory, September 30 (1,400 units)	70,000	
Variable cost of goods sold		400,000
Manufacturing margin		$560,000
Variable selling and administrative expenses		245,000
Contribution margin		$315,000
Fixed costs:		
Fixed manufacturing costs	$122,200	
Fixed selling and administrative expenses	43,130	165,330
Income from operations		$149,670

Prepare an income statement under absorption costing.

EXERCISE 19-7
Variable costing income statement

Objective 1

✓ a. Income from operations, $6,678

The following data were adapted from a recent income statement of **Procter & Gamble Company**:

	(in millions)
Net sales	$40,238
Operating costs:	
Cost of products sold	$20,989
Marketing, administrative, and other expenses	12,571
Total operating costs	$33,560
Income from operations	$ 6,678

Assume that the variable amount of each category of operating costs is as follows:

	(in millions)
Cost of products sold	$15,000
Marketing, administrative, and other expenses	6,900

a. Based on the above data, prepare a variable costing income statement for Procter & Gamble Company, assuming that the company maintained constant inventory levels during the period.
b.  If Procter & Gamble reduced its inventories during the period, what impact would that have on the income from operations determined under absorption costing?

EXERCISE 19-8
Estimated income statements, using absorption and variable costing

Objectives 1, 2

✓ a. 1. Income from operations, $31,500 (8,000 units)

Prior to the first month of operations ending March 31, 2006, Advanced Filters Inc. estimated the following operating results:

Sales (8,000 × $85)	$680,000
Manufacturing costs (8,000 units):	
Direct materials	408,000
Direct labor	100,000
Variable factory overhead	50,000
Fixed factory overhead	54,000
Fixed selling and administrative expenses	12,200
Variable selling and administrative expenses	24,300

The company is evaluating a proposal to manufacture 9,000 units instead of 8,000 units, thus creating an ending inventory of 1,000 units. Manufacturing the additional units will not change sales, unit variable factory overhead costs, total fixed factory overhead cost, or total selling and administrative expenses.

(continued)

a. Prepare an estimated income statement, comparing operating results if 8,000 and 9,000 units are manufactured, in the (1) absorption costing format and (2) variable costing format.

b. 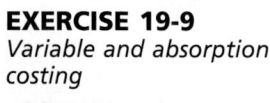 What is the reason for the difference in income from operations reported for the two levels of production by the absorption costing income statement?

EXERCISE 19-9
Variable and absorption costing

Objectives 2, 3

WHAT'S WRONG
WITH THIS?

Aspen Boot Company manufactures and sells three types of boots. The income statements prepared under the absorption costing method for the three boots are as follows:

Aspen Boot Company
Product Income Statements—Absorption Costing
For the Year Ended December 31, 2006

	Hiking Boots	Fishing Boots	Ski Boots
Revenues	$590,000	$500,000	$430,000
Cost of goods sold	310,000	230,000	260,000
Gross profit	$280,000	$270,000	$170,000
Selling and administrative expenses	200,000	150,000	225,000
Income from operations	$ 80,000	$120,000	$ (55,000)

In addition, you have determined the following information with respect to allocated fixed costs:

	Hiking Boots	Fishing Boots	Ski Boots
Fixed costs:			
Cost of goods sold	$70,000	$55,000	$60,000
Selling and administrative expenses	60,000	50,000	70,000

These fixed costs are used to support all three product lines. In addition, you have determined that the inventory is negligible.

The management of the company has deemed the profit performance of the ski boot line as unacceptible. As a result, it has decided to eliminate the ski boot line. Management does not expect to be able to increase sales in the other two lines. However, as a result of eliminating the ski boot line, management expects the profits of the company to increase by $55,000.

a. 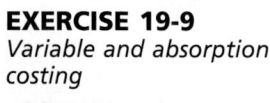 Do you agree with management's decision and conclusions?

b. Prepare a profit report under the variable costing approach for the three products.

c. Use the report in (b) to determine the profit impact of eliminating the ski boot line, assuming no other changes.

EXERCISE 19-10
Variable and absorption costing

Objective 1

REAL WORLD   SPREADSHEET

✓ a. *Contribution margin,*
$3,903.30

Whirlpool Corporation had the following abbreviated income statement for a recent year:

	(in millions)
Net sales	$11,016
Cost of goods sold	$ 8,464
Selling, administrative, and other expenses	1,860
Total expenses	$10,324
Income from operations	$ 692

The company reported depreciation of $405 million for the recent year. Assume that 60% of the depreciation was related to manufacturing property, plant, and equipment. In addition, assume that there were an additional $2,200 million fixed manufacturing costs and $600 million fixed selling, administrative, and other costs for the year.

The finished goods inventories at the beginning and end of the year from the balance sheet were as follows:

January 1	$949 million
December 31	$928 million

Assume that 30% of the beginning and ending inventory consists of fixed costs.

a. Prepare an income statement according to the variable costing concept for Whirlpool Corporation for the recent year.
b. ▰▰▰▰▶ What is the reason for the difference in the amount of income from operations reported under the absorption costing and variable costing concepts?

EXERCISE 19-11
Change in sales mix and contribution margin
Objective 4

Hancock Pen Company manufactures ballpoint and fountain pens and is operating at less than full capacity. Market research indicates that 5,000 additional ballpoint pens and 7,500 additional fountain pens could be sold. The income from operations by unit of product is as follows:

	Ballpoint Pen	Fountain Pen
Sales price	$5.50	$15.00
Variable cost of goods sold	2.80	8.30
Manufacturing margin	$2.70	$ 6.70
Variable selling and administrative expenses	1.00	2.50
Contribution margin	$1.70	$ 4.20
Fixed manufacturing costs	0.50	1.00
Income from operations	$1.20	$ 3.20

Prepare an analysis indicating the increase or decrease in total profitability if 5,000 additional ballpoint pens and 7,500 additional fountain pens are produced and sold, assuming that there is sufficient capacity for the additional production.

EXERCISE 19-12
Product profitability analysis
Objective 4

SPREADSHEET

✓ *Console contribution margin, $240,000*

X-C TV Inc. manufactures and sells two styles of televisions, table top and console, from a single manufacturing facility. The manufacturing facility operates at 100% of capacity. The following per unit information is available for the two products:

	Table Top	Console
Sales price	$240	$500
Variable cost of goods sold	135	210
Manufacturing margin	$105	$290
Variable selling expenses	45	90
Contribution margin	$ 60	$200
Fixed expenses	25	165
Income from operations	$ 35	$ 35

In addition, the following unit volume information for the period is as follows:

	Table Top	Console
Sales unit volume	2,000	1,200

a. Prepare a contribution margin report by product.
b. ▰▰▰▰▶ What advice would you give to the management of X-C TV Inc.?

EXERCISE 19-13
Territory and product profitability analysis
Objective 4

SPREADSHEET

Cycle Sport Inc. manufactures and sells two styles of bicycles, touring and mountain. These bicycles are sold in two countries, the Netherlands and France. Information about the two bicycles is as follows:

	Touring Bike	Mountain Bike
Sales price	$605	$400
Variable cost of goods sold per unit	240	225
Manufacturing margin per unit	$365	$175
Variable selling expense per unit	250	75
Contribution margin per unit	$115	$100

✓ *a. France contribution margin, $860,000*

The sales unit volume for the territories and products for the period is as follows:

	Netherlands	France
Touring Bike	8,000	4,000
Mountain Bike	0	4,000

a. Prepare a contribution margin report by sales territory.

b. ▶ What advice would you give to the management of Cycle Sport Inc.?

EXERCISE 19-14
Sales territory and salesperson profitability analysis
Objective 4

SPREADSHEET

✓ *a. Luis A. contribution margin, $144,000*

HCA Hardware Company manufactures and sells a wide variety of hardware products to retailers in the Northern and Southern regions. There are two salespersons assigned to each territory. Higher commission rates go to the most experienced salespersons. The following sales statistics are available for each salesperson:

	Northern		Southern	
	Connie M.	Luis A.	Barry L.	Tamara T.
Average per unit:				
Sales price	$70.00	$60.00	$80.00	$55.00
Variable cost of goods sold	$42.00	$24.00	$48.00	$22.00
Commission rate	8%	12%	12%	8%
Units sold	5,800	5,000	4,000	7,000
Manufacturing margin ratio	40%	60%	40%	60%

a. 1. Prepare a contribution margin by salesperson report.
   2. Interpret the report.
b. 1. Prepare a contribution margin by territory report. Round to two decimal places.
   2. Interpret the report.

EXERCISE 19-15
Segment profitability analysis
Objective 4

REAL WORLD   SPREADSHEET

✓ *a. North America contribution margin, $1,330*

Provided below are the equipment and machinery segment sales for **Caterpillar, Inc.** for a recent year.

Caterpillar, Inc.
Equipment and Machinery Segment Sales
(in millions)

	Asia/Pacific	Europe/Africa/ Middle East (EAME)	Latin America	Power Products	North America
Sales	$1,660	$2,828	$1,313	$5,736	$5,575

The Power Products segment designs, manufactures, and markets engines. The geographic segments sell Caterpillar equipment to their respective regions.
    Assume that the following information is also available:

	Asia/Pacific	Europe/Africa/ Middle East (EAME)	Latin America	Power Products	North America
Variable cost of goods sold as a percent of sales	50%	60%	45%	60%	52%
Dealer commissions as a percent of sales	8%	12%	8%	5%	8%
Variable promotion expenses (in millions)	$400	$450	$300	$750	$900

a. Use the sales information and the additional assumed information to prepare a segment contribution margin statement. Round to two decimal places.
b. Prepare a table showing the manufacturing margin, dealer commissions, and variable promotion expenses as a percent of sales for each territory. Round to two decimal places.
c. ▶ Use the information in (a) and (b) to interpret the segment performance.

EXERCISE 19-16
Segment contribution margin analysis

Objective 4, 6

REAL WORLD

✓ a. Video, $1,948.10, 35%

The operating revenues of the four largest business segments for **Viacom, Inc.** for a recent year are shown below. Each segment includes a number of businesses, of which the largest is indicated in parentheses.

Viacom, Inc. Segment Revenues (in millions)	
Cable Networks (MTV)	$4,727
Television (CBS)	7,490
Infinity (radio stations)	3,755
Entertainment (Paramount Pictures)	3,647
Video (Blockbuster Video)	5,566

Assume that the variable costs as a percent of sales for each segment are as follows:

Cable Networks	15%
Television	15%
Infinity	10%
Entertainment	25%
Video	65%

a. Determine the contribution margin and contribution margin ratio for each segment from the above information. Round to two digits after the decimal place.
b. ▭▭▭▶ Why is the contribution margin ratio for the video segment smaller than for the other segments?
c. ▭▭▭▶ Does your answer to (a) mean that the other segments are more profitable businesses than the video segment?

EXERCISE 19-17
Contribution margin analysis—sales

Objective 4

SPREADSHEET

New Sound Music Company sells recorded CD music. Management decided early in the year to reduce the price of the CD in order to increase sales volume. As a result, for the year ended December 31, 2006, the sales increased by $10,500 from the planned level of $144,500. The following information is available from the accounting records for the year ended December 31, 2006:

	Actual	Planned	Difference— Increase (Decrease)
Sales	$155,000	$144,500	$10,500
Number of units sold	10,000	8,500	1,500
Sales price	$15.50	$17.00	$(1.50)
Variable cost per unit	$6.00	$6.00	0

a. Prepare an analysis of the sales quantity and price factors.
b. ▭▭▭▶ Did the price decrease generate sufficient volume to result in a net increase in contribution margin if the actual variable cost per unit was $6, as planned?

EXERCISE 19-18
Contribution margin analysis—sales

Objective 4

SPREADSHEET

✓ Sales quantity factor, $(77,500)

The following data for Highland Products Inc. are available:

For the Year Ended December 31, 2006	Actual	Planned	Difference— Increase or (Decrease)
Sales	$2,211,000	$2,154,500	$ 56,500
Less:			
Variable cost of goods sold	$1,206,000	$1,195,400	$ 10,600
Variable selling and administrative expenses	214,400	243,250	(28,850)
Total variable costs	$1,420,400	$1,438,650	$(18,250)
Contribution margin	$ 790,600	$ 715,850	$ 74,750
Number of units sold	13,400	13,900	
Per unit:			
Sales price	$165.00	$155.00	
Variable cost of goods sold	90.00	86.00	
Variable selling and administrative expenses	16.00	17.50	

Prepare an analysis of the sales quantity and price factors.

EXERCISE 19-19
Contribution margin analysis—variable costs

Objective 4

SPREADSHEET

✓ *Variable cost of goods sold price factor, $53,600*

Based upon the data in Exercise 19-18, prepare a contribution analysis of the variable costs for Highland Products Inc. for the year ended December 31, 2006.

EXERCISE 19-20
Contribution margin reporting and analysis— service company

Objectives 5, 6

SPREADSHEET

The actual and planned data for Erudite University for the Fall term were as follows:

	Actual	Planned
Enrollment	4,400	4,000
Tuition per credit hour	$110	$120
Credit hours	66,000	48,000
Registration, records, and marketing cost per enrolled student	$280	$280
Instructional costs per credit hour	$69	$65
Depreciation on classrooms and equipment	$890,000	$890,000

Registration, records, and marketing costs vary by the number of enrolled students, while instructional costs vary by the number of credit hours. Depreciation is a fixed cost.

a. Prepare a report showing the contribution margin and income from operations for the Fall term.
b. Prepare a contribution margin analysis report comparing planned with actual performance for the Fall term.

EXERCISE 19-21
Contribution margin reporting—service company

Objectives 4, 6

SPREADSHEET

Coastal Railroad Company transports commodities between three routes (city-pairs): Atlanta/Baltimore, Baltimore/Pittsburgh, and Pittsburgh/Atlanta. Significant costs, their cost behavior, and activity rates for July 2006 are as follows:

Cost	Amount	Cost Behavior	Activity Rate
Labor costs for loading and unloading railcars	$264,000	Variable	$55 per railcar
Fuel costs	477,000	Variable	12 per train-mile
Train crew labor costs	278,250	Variable	7 per train-mile
Switchyard labor costs	168,000	Variable	35 per railcar
Track and equipment depreciation	200,000	Fixed	
Maintenance	125,000	Fixed	

Operating statistics from the management information system reveal the following for July:

	Atlanta/ Baltimore	Baltimore/ Pittsburgh	Pittsburgh/ Atlanta	Total
Number of train-miles	14,000	8,750	17,000	39,750
Number of rail cars	500	2,800	1,500	4,800
Revenue per rail car	$620	$290	$500	

a. Prepare a contribution margin report by route for Coastal Railroad Company for the month of July.
b. Evaluate the route performance of the railroad.

EXERCISE 19-22
Contribution margin reporting and analysis—service company
Objectives 5, 6

SPREADSHEET

The management of Coastal Railroad Company introduced in Exercise 19-21 improved the profitability of the Atlanta/Baltimore route in August by reducing the price of a railcar from $620 to $550. This price reduction increased the demand for rail services. Thus, the number of railcars increased by 400 railcars to a total of 900 railcars. This was accomplished by increasing the size of each train but not the number of trains. Thus, the number of train-miles was unchanged. All the activity rates remained unchanged.

a. Prepare a contribution margin report for the Atlanta/Baltimore route for August.
b. Prepare a contribution margin analysis report to evaluate management's actions in August. Assume that the August base plan was the same as July.

Problems Series A

PROBLEM 19-1A
Absorption and variable costing income statements
Objectives 1, 2

SPREADSHEET

✓ 2. Income from operations, $193,000

During the first month of operations ended August 31, 2007, Miracle Kitchen Appliance Company manufactured 1,420 refrigerators, of which 1,360 were sold. Operating data for the month are summarized as follows:

Sales		$924,800
Manufacturing costs:		
Direct materials	$340,800	
Direct labor	134,900	
Variable manufacturing cost	63,900	
Fixed manufacturing cost	99,400	639,000
Selling and administrative expenses:		
Variable	$ 81,600	
Fixed	34,000	115,600

Instructions
1. Prepare an income statement based on the absorption costing concept.
2. Prepare an income statement based on the variable costing concept.
3. ▭▬▶ Explain the reason for the difference in the amount of income from operations reported in (1) and (2).

PROBLEM 19-2A
Income statements under absorption costing and variable costing
Objectives 1, 2

SPREADSHEET

✓ 2. Contribution margin, $59,520

The demand for solvent, one of numerous products manufactured by Albany Products Inc., has dropped sharply because of recent competition from a similar product. The company's chemists are currently completing tests of various new formulas, and it is anticipated that the manufacture of a superior product can be started on November 1, one month hence. No changes will be needed in the present production facilities to manufacture the new product because only the mixture of the various materials will be changed.

The controller has been asked by the president of the company for advice on whether to continue production during October or to suspend the manufacture of solvent until November 1. The controller has assembled the following pertinent data:

Albany Products Inc.
Income Statement—Solvent
For the Month Ended September 30, 2007

Sales (3,200 units)	$304,000
Cost of goods sold	255,440
Gross profit	$ 48,560
Selling and administrative expenses	43,700
Income from operations	$ 4,860

The production costs and selling and administrative expenses, based on production of 3,200 units in September, are as follows:

Direct materials	$ 38.00 per unit
Direct labor	14.50 per unit
Variable manufacturing cost	11.70 per unit
Variable selling and administrative expenses	6.00 per unit
Fixed manufacturing costs	50,000 for September
Fixed selling and administrative expenses	24,500 for September

Sales for October are expected to drop about 25% below those of the preceding month. No significant changes are anticipated in the fixed costs or variable costs per unit. No extra costs will be incurred in discontinuing operations in the portion of the plant associated with solvent. The inventory of solvent at the beginning and end of October is expected to be inconsequential.

Instructions

1. Prepare an estimated income statement in absorption costing form for October for solvent, assuming that production continues during the month.
2. Prepare an estimated income statement in variable costing form for October for solvent, assuming that production continues during the month.
3. What would be the estimated loss in income from operations if the solvent production were temporarily suspended for October?
4. ▆▆▆▆► What advice should the controller give to management?

PROBLEM 19-3A
Absorption and variable costing income statements for two months and analysis

Objectives 1, 2

SPREADSHEET

✓ *1. b. Income from operations, $69,240*

During the first month of operations ended July 31, 2006, Sound Off Shirt Company produced 39,000 T-shirts, of which 36,000 were sold. Operating data for the month are summarized as follows:

Sales		$450,000
Manufacturing costs:		
Direct materials	$241,800	
Direct labor	62,400	
Variable manufacturing cost	35,100	
Fixed manufacturing cost	34,320	373,620
Selling and administrative expenses:		
Variable	$ 18,000	
Fixed	12,600	30,600

During August, Sound Off Shirt Company produced 33,000 T-shirts and sold 36,000 shirts. Operating data for August are summarized as follows:

Sales		$450,000
Manufacturing costs:		
Direct materials	$204,600	
Direct labor	52,800	
Variable manufacturing cost	29,700	
Fixed manufacturing cost	34,320	321,420
Selling and administrative expenses:		
Variable	$ 18,000	
Fixed	12,600	30,600

Instructions

1. Using the absorption costing concept, prepare income statements for (a) July and (b) August.
2. Using the variable costing concept, prepare income statements for (a) July and (b) August.
3. a. ▆▆▆▆► Explain the reason for the differences in the amount of income from operations in (1) and (2) for July.
   b. ▆▆▆▆► Explain the reason for the differences in the amount of income from operations in (1) and (2) for August.
4. ▆▆▆▆► Based upon your answers to (1) and (2), did Sound Off Shirt Company operate more profitably in July or in August? Explain.

PROBLEM 19-4A
Salespersons' report and analysis

Objective 4

SPREADSHEET

✓ *1. Severinsen contribution margin ratio, 18.2%*

River City Band Instrument Company employs seven salespersons to sell and distribute its product throughout the state. Data taken from reports received from the salespersons during the year ended December 31, 2007, are as follows:

Salesperson	Total Sales	Variable Cost of Goods Sold	Variable Selling Expenses
Alpert	$500,000	$300,000	$100,000
Armstrong	540,000	340,000	105,000
Goodman	600,000	325,000	105,000
Hirt	490,000	305,000	80,000
Kenny G.	480,000	280,000	90,000
Marsalis	525,000	300,000	100,000
Severinsen	550,000	330,000	120,000

Instructions

1. Prepare a table indicating contribution margin, variable cost of goods sold as a percent of sales, variable selling expenses as a percent of sales, and contribution margin ratio by salesperson. Round to the nearest tenth of a percent.
2. Which salesperson generated the highest contribution margin ratio for the year and why?
3. ⬛▬▶ Briefly list factors other than contribution margin that should be considered in evaluating the performance of salespersons.

PROBLEM 19-5A
Variable costing income statement and effect on income of change in operations

Objective 4

SPREADSHEET

✓ *1. Income from operations, $105,000*

Alaskan Coat Company manufactures three sizes of winter coats, small (S), medium (M), and large (L). The income statement has consistently indicated a net loss for the M size, and management is considering three proposals: (1) continue Size M, (2) discontinue Size M and reduce total output accordingly, or (3) discontinue Size M and conduct an advertising campaign to expand the sales of Size S so that the entire plant capacity can continue to be used.

If Proposal 2 is selected and Size M is discontinued and production curtailed, the annual fixed production costs and fixed operating expenses could be reduced by $50,000 and $32,000, respectively. If Proposal 3 is selected, it is anticipated that an additional annual expenditure of $40,000 for the rental of additional warehouse space would yield an increase of 130% in Size S sales volume. It is also assumed that the increased production of Size S would utilize the plant facilities released by the discontinuance of Size M.

The sales and costs have been relatively stable over the past few years, and they are expected to remain so for the foreseeable future. The income statement for the past year ended June 30, 2006, is as follows:

	Size			
	S	**M**	**L**	**Total**
Sales	$560,000	$620,000	$850,000	$2,030,000
Cost of goods sold:				
Variable costs	$250,000	$300,000	$350,000	$ 900,000
Fixed costs	70,000	110,000	140,000	320,000
Total cost of goods sold	$320,000	$410,000	$490,000	$1,220,000
Gross profit	$240,000	$210,000	$360,000	$ 810,000
Less operating expenses:				
Variable expenses	$110,000	$145,000	$160,000	$ 415,000
Fixed expenses	70,000	100,000	120,000	290,000
Total operating expenses	$180,000	$245,000	$280,000	$ 705,000
Income from operations	$ 60,000	$ (35,000)	$ 80,000	$ 105,000

Instructions

1. Prepare an income statement for the past year in the variable costing format. Use the following headings:

(continued)

	Size		
S	M	L	Total

Data for each style should be reported through contribution margin. The fixed costs should be deducted from the total contribution margin, as reported in the "Total" column, to determine income from operations.

2. Based on the income statement prepared in (1) and the other data presented, determine the amount by which total annual income from operations would be reduced below its present level if Proposal 2 is accepted.

3. Prepare an income statement in the variable costing format, indicating the projected annual income from operations if Proposal 3 is accepted. Use the following headings:

	Size	
S	L	Total

Data for each style should be reported through contribution margin. The fixed costs should be deducted from the total contribution margin as reported in the "Total" column. For purposes of this problem, the expenditure of $40,000 for the rental of additional warehouse space can be added to the fixed operating expenses.

4. By how much would total annual income increase above its present level if Proposal 3 is accepted? Explain.

PROBLEM 19-6A
Contribution margin analysis
Objective 5

SPREADSHEET

✔ 1. Sales quantity factor, ($40,000)

Alpha Industries Inc. manufactures only one product. For the year ended December 31, 2006, the contribution margin decreased by $5,000 from the planned level of $140,000. The president of Alpha Industries Inc. has expressed some concern about this decrease and has requested a follow-up report.

The following data have been gathered from the accounting records for the year ended December 31, 2006:

	Actual	Planned	Difference— Increase (Decrease)
Sales	$405,000	$400,000	$ 5,000
Less: Variable cost of goods sold	162,000	170,000	(8,000)
Variable selling and administrative expense	108,000	90,000	18,000
Total	$270,000	$260,000	$10,000
Contribution margin	$135,000	$140,000	$ (5,000)
Number of units sold	9,000	10,000	
Per unit:			
Sales price	$45.00	$40.00	
Variable cost of goods sold	18.00	17.00	
Variable selling and administrative expenses	12.00	9.00	

Instructions

1. Prepare a contribution margin analysis report for the year ended December 31, 2006.

2. At a meeting of the board of directors on January 30, 2007, the president, after reviewing the contribution margin analysis report, made the following comment:

It looks as if the price increase of $5.00 had the effect of decreasing sales volume. However, this was a favorable tradeoff. The variable cost of goods sold was less than planned. Apparently, we are efficiently managing our variable cost of goods sold. However, the variable selling and administrative expenses appear out of control. Let's look into these expenses and get them under control! Also, let's consider increasing the sales price to $50 and continue this favorable tradeoff between higher price and lower volume.

Do you agree with the president's comment? Explain.

Problems Series B

PROBLEM 19-1B
Absorption and variable costing income statements
Objectives 1, 2

SPREADSHEET

✓ *2. Contribution margin, $215,775*

During the first month of operations ended June 30, 2006, Connectex Modem Company manufactured 7,200 modems, of which 6,850 were sold. Operating data for the month are summarized as follows:

Sales		$787,750
Manufacturing costs:		
Direct materials	$345,600	
Direct labor	100,800	
Variable manufacturing cost	86,400	
Fixed manufacturing cost	39,600	572,400
Selling and administrative expenses:		
Variable	$ 65,075	
Fixed	20,550	85,625

Instructions
1. Prepare an income statement based on the absorption costing concept.
2. Prepare an income statement based on the variable costing concept.
3. Explain the reason for the difference in the amount of income from operations reported in (1) and (2).

PROBLEM 19-2B
Income statements under absorption costing and variable costing
Objectives 1, 2

SPREADSHEET

✓ *2. Contribution margin, $165,600*

The demand for shampoo, one of numerous products manufactured by Aphrodite Inc., has dropped sharply because of recent competition from a similar product. The company's chemists are currently completing tests of various new formulas, and it is anticipated that the manufacture of a superior product can be started on March 1, one month hence. No changes will be needed in the present production facilities to manufacture the new product because only the mixture of the various materials will be changed.

The controller has been asked by the president of the company for advice on whether to continue production during February or to suspend the manufacture of shampoo until March 1. The controller has assembled the following pertinent data:

Aphrodite Inc.
Income Statement—Shampoo
For the Month Ended January 31, 2006

Sales (80,000 units)	$896,000
Cost of goods sold	724,000
Gross profit	$172,000
Selling and administrative expenses	178,000
Loss from operations	$ (6,000)

The production costs and selling and administrative expenses, based on production of 80,000 units in January, are as follows:

Direct materials	$ 2.10 per unit
Direct labor	2.75 per unit
Variable manufacturing cost	1.20 per unit
Variable selling and administrative expenses	1.70 per unit
Fixed manufacturing costs	240,000 for January
Fixed selling and administrative expenses	42,000 for January

Sales for February are expected to drop about 40% below those of the preceding month. No significant changes are anticipated in the fixed costs or variable costs per unit. No extra costs will be incurred in discontinuing operations in the portion of the plant associated with shampoo. The inventory of shampoo at the beginning and end of February is expected to be inconsequential.

Instructions

1. Prepare an estimated income statement in absorption costing form for February for shampoo, assuming that production continues during the month.
2. Prepare an estimated income statement in variable costing form for February for shampoo, assuming that production continues during the month.
3. What would be the estimated loss in income from operations if the shampoo production were temporarily suspended for February?
4. ▭▷ What advice should the controller give to management?

PROBLEM 19-3B
Absorption and variable costing income statements for two months and analysis

Objectives 1, 2

SPREADSHEET

✓ *2. a. Manufacturing margin, $18,480*

During the first month of operations ended May 31, 2006, Holiday Bakery Inc. baked 3,000 cakes, of which 2,800 were sold. Operating data for the month are summarized as follows:

Sales		$35,000
Baking costs:		
Direct materials	$10,800	
Direct labor	4,500	
Variable manufacturing cost	2,400	
Fixed manufacturing cost	3,900	21,600
Selling and administrative expenses:		
Variable	$ 3,360	
Fixed	980	4,340

During June, Holiday Bakery Inc. baked 2,600 cakes and sold 2,800 cakes. Operating data for June are summarized as follows:

Sales		$35,000
Baking costs:		
Direct materials	$9,360	
Direct labor	3,900	
Variable manufacturing cost	2,080	
Fixed manufacturing cost	3,900	19,240
Selling and administrative expenses:		
Variable	$3,360	
Fixed	980	4,340

Instructions

1. Using the absorption costing concept, prepare income statements for (a) May and (b) June.
2. Using the variable costing concept, prepare income statements for (a) May and (b) June.
3. a. ▭▷ Explain the reason for the differences in the amount of income from operations in (1) and (2) for May.
   b. ▭▷ Explain the reason for the differences in the amount of income from operations in (1) and (2) for June.
4. ▭▷ Based upon your answers to (1) and (2), did Holiday Bakery operate more profitably in May or in June? Explain.

PROBLEM 19-4B
Salespersons' report and analysis

Objective 4

SPREADSHEET

✓ *1. Marvin contribution margin ratio, 30.2%*

Western Wear Depot Inc. employs seven salespersons to sell and distribute its product throughout the state. Data taken from reports received from the salespersons during the year ended June 30, 2007, are as follows:

Salesperson	Total Sales	Variable Cost of Goods Sold	Variable Selling Expenses
Cooper	$350,000	$170,000	$ 70,000
Eastwood	420,000	200,000	85,000
Ladd	500,000	250,000	110,000
Marvin	480,000	230,000	105,000
Newman	420,000	200,000	110,000
Redford	540,000	240,000	100,000
Wayne	490,000	225,000	105,000

Instructions

1. Prepare a table indicating contribution margin, variable cost of goods sold as a percent of sales, variable selling expenses as a percent of sales, and contribution margin ratio by salesperson (round to nearest tenth of a percent).
2. Which salesperson generated the highest contribution margin ratio for the year and why?
3. ➤ Briefly list factors other than contribution margin that should be considered in evaluating the performance of salespersons.

PROBLEM 19-5B
Variable costing income statement and effect on income of change in operations

Objective 4

SPREADSHEET

✓ 3. Income from operations, $203,000

Auditorium Seating Company manufactures three sizes of folding chairs, small (S), medium (M), and large (L). The income statement has consistently indicated a net loss for the M size, and management is considering three proposals: (1) continue Size M, (2) discontinue Size M and reduce total output accordingly, or (3) discontinue Size M and conduct an advertising campaign to expand the sales of Size S so that the entire plant capacity can continue to be used.

If Proposal 2 is selected and Size M is discontinued and production curtailed, the annual fixed production costs and fixed operating expenses could be reduced by $140,000 and $20,000 respectively. If Proposal 3 is selected, it is anticipated that an additional annual expenditure of $80,000 for the salary of an assistant brand manager (classified as a fixed operating expense) would yield an increase of 150% in Size S sales volume. It is also assumed that the increased production of Size S would utilize the plant facilities released by the discontinuance of Size M.

The sales and costs have been relatively stable over the past few years, and they are expected to remain so for the foreseeable future. The income statement for the past year ended January 31, 2006, is as follows:

	S	M	L	Total
Size				
Sales	$1,040,000	$1,250,000	$1,100,000	$3,390,000
Cost of goods sold:				
Variable costs	$ 560,000	$ 780,000	$ 625,000	$1,965,000
Fixed costs	235,000	340,000	290,000	865,000
Total cost of goods sold	$ 795,000	$1,120,000	$ 915,000	$2,830,000
Gross profit	$ 245,000	$ 130,000	$ 185,000	$ 560,000
Less operating expenses:				
Variable expenses	$ 120,000	$ 145,000	$ 120,000	$ 385,000
Fixed expenses	32,000	50,000	25,000	107,000
Total operating expenses	$ 152,000	$ 195,000	$ 145,000	$ 492,000
Income from operations	$ 93,000	$ (65,000)	$ 40,000	$ 68,000

Instructions

1. Prepare an income statement for the past year in the variable costing format. Use the following headings:

S	M	L	Total
Size			

Data for each style should be reported through contribution margin. The fixed costs should be deducted from the total contribution margin, as reported in the "Total" column, to determine income from operations.
2. Based on the income statement prepared in (1) and the other data presented above, determine the amount by which total annual income from operations would be reduced below its present level if Proposal 2 is accepted.
3. Prepare an income statement in the variable costing format, indicating the projected annual income from operations if Proposal 3 is accepted. Use the following headings:

(continued)

Size		
S	L	Total

Data for each style should be reported through contribution margin. The fixed costs should be deducted from the total contribution margin as reported in the "Total" column. For purposes of this problem, the additional expenditure of $80,000 for the assistant brand manager's salary can be added to the fixed operating expenses.

4. By how much would total annual income increase above its present level if Proposal 3 is accepted? Explain.

PROBLEM 19-6B
Contribution margin analysis
Objective 5

SPREADSHEET

✓ *1. Sales price factor, ($44,000)*

Signal Electronics Company manufactures only one product. For the year ended December 31, 2006, the contribution margin decreased by $18,500 from the planned level of $200,000. The president of Signal Electronics Company has expressed serious concern about this decrease and has requested a follow-up report.

The following data have been gathered from the accounting records for the year ended December 31, 2006:

	Actual	Planned	Difference— Increase or (Decrease)
Sales	$616,000	$600,000	$ 16,000
Less:			
Variable cost of goods sold	341,000	325,000	16,000
Variable selling and administrative expenses	93,500	75,000	18,500
Total	$434,500	$400,000	$ 34,500
Contribution margin	$181,500	$200,000	$(18,500)
Number of units sold	5,500	5,000	
Per unit:			
Sales price	$112.00	$120.00	
Variable cost of goods sold	62.00	65.00	
Variable selling and administrative expenses	17.00	15.00	

Instructions

1. Prepare a contribution margin analysis report for the year ended December 31, 2006.
2. At a meeting of the board of directors on January 30, 2007, the president, after reviewing the contribution margin analysis report, made the following comment:

"It looks as if the price decrease of $8.00 had the effect of increasing sales. However, we lost control over the variable cost of goods sold and variable selling and administrative expenses. Let's look into these expenses and get them under control! Also, let's consider decreasing the sales price to $100 to increase sales further."

Do you agree with the president's comment? Explain.

Special Activities

ACTIVITY 19-1
Ethics and professional conduct in business

ETHICS

The Sporting Goods Division of Glenn Diversified Industries Inc. uses absorption costing for profit reporting. The general manager of the Sporting Goods Division is concerned about meeting the income objectives of the division. At the beginning of the reporting period, the division had an adequate supply of inventory. The general manager has decided to increase production of goods in the plant in order to allocate fixed manufacturing cost over a greater number of units. Unfortunately, the increased production cannot be sold and will increase the inventory. However, the impact on earnings will be positive, because the lower cost per unit will be matched against sales. The general manager has come to Eric Peters, the controller, to determine exactly how much additional production is required in order to increase net income enough to meet the division's profit objectives. Peters analyzes the data and determines that the inventory will need to be increased by 30% in order to absorb enough fixed costs and meet the income objective. Peters reports this information to the division manager.

➤ Discuss whether Peters is acting in an ethical manner.

ACTIVITY 19-2
Inventories under absorption costing

WHAT DO YOU THINK?

Powertronics Enterprises manufactures power converters for the electronics industry and has just completed its first year of operations. The following discussion took place between the controller, Ted Andrews, and the company president, Lisa Jenkins:

Lisa: I've been looking over our first year's performance by quarters. Our earnings have been increasing each quarter, even though our sales have been flat and our prices and costs have not changed. Why is this?

Ted: Our actual sales have stayed even throughout the year, but we've been increasing the utilization of our factory every quarter. By keeping our factory utilization high, we will keep our costs down by allocating the fixed plant costs over a greater number of units. Naturally, this causes our cost per unit to be lower than it would be otherwise.

Lisa: Yes, but what good is it if we have been unable to sell everything that we make? Our inventory is also increasing.

Ted: This is true. However, our unit costs are lower because of the additional production. When these lower costs are matched against sales, it has a positive impact on our earnings.

Lisa: Are you saying that we are able to create additional earnings merely by building inventory? Can this be true?

Ted: Well, I've never thought about it quite that way . . . but I guess so.

Lisa: And another thing. What will happen if we begin to reduce our production in order to liquidate the inventory? Don't tell me our earnings will go down even though our production effort drops!

Ted: Well . . .

Lisa: There must be a better way. I'd like our quarterly income statements to reflect what's really going on. I don't want our income reports to reward building inventory and penalize reducing inventory.

Ted: I'm not sure what I can do—we have to follow generally accepted accounting principles.

1. ➤ Why does reporting income under generally accepted accounting principles "reward" building inventory and "penalize" reducing inventory?
2. ➤ What advice would you give to Ted in responding to Lisa's concern about the present method of profit reporting?

ACTIVITY 19-3
Margin analysis

CardioMed Inc. manufactures and sells devices used in cardiovascular surgery. The company has two salespersons, Lancaster and Johnson.

A contribution margin by salesperson report was prepared as follows:

CardioMed Inc.
Contribution Margin by Salesperson

	Lancaster	Johnson
Sales	$240,000	$300,000
Variable cost of goods sold	96,000	210,000
Manufacturing margin	$144,000	$ 90,000
Variable promotion expenses	$ 80,000	$ 10,000
Variable sales commission expenses	40,000	50,000
	$120,000	$ 60,000
Contribution margin	$ 24,000	$ 30,000
Manufacturing margin as a percent of sales (manufacturing margin ratio)	60.00%	30.00%
Contribution margin ratio	10.00%	10.00%

▭▬► Interpret the report, and provide recommendations to the two salespersons for improving profitability.

ACTIVITY 19-4
Margin analysis

Elite Chef Inc. manufactures and sells kitchen cooking products throughout the state. The company employs four salespersons. The following contribution margin by salesperson analysis was prepared:

Elite Chef Inc.
Contribution Margin Analysis by Salesperson

	Childs	Tipton	Huang	Chavez
Sales	$120,000	$150,000	$140,000	$100,000
Variable cost of goods sold	48,000	75,000	70,000	50,000
Manufacturing margin	$ 72,000	$ 75,000	$ 70,000	$ 50,000
Variable selling expenses:				
Commissions	$ 6,000	$ 7,500	$ 7,000	$ 5,000
Promotion expenses	24,000	45,000	42,000	30,000
Total variable selling expenses	$ 30,000	$ 52,500	$ 49,000	$ 35,000
Contribution margin	$ 42,000	$ 22,500	$ 21,000	$ 15,000

1. Calculate the manufacturing margin as a percent of sales and the contribution margin ratio for each salesperson.
2. ▭▬► Explain the results of the analysis.

ACTIVITY 19-5
Contribution margin analysis

DiVinci Art Supply Company sells artistic supplies to retailers in three different states, Texas, Oklahoma, and Kansas. The following profit analysis by state was prepared by the company:

	Texas	Oklahoma	Kansas
Revenue	$320,000	$380,000	$300,000
Cost of goods sold	160,000	200,000	150,000
Gross profit	$160,000	$180,000	$150,000
Selling expenses	100,000	80,000	50,000
Income from operations	$ 60,000	$100,000	$100,000

The following fixed costs have also been provided:

	Texas	Oklahoma	Kansas
Fixed manufacturing costs	$70,000	$40,000	$40,000
Fixed selling expenses	60,000	30,000	20,000

In addition, assume that inventories have been negligible.

Management believes it could increase state sales by 25%, without increasing any of the fixed costs, by spending an additional $10,000 per state on advertising.

1. Prepare a contribution margin by state report for DiVinci Art Supply Company.
2. Determine how much state operating profit will be generated for an additional $10,000 per state on advertising.
3. ▭▬► Which state will provide the greatest profit return for a $10,000 increase in advertising? Why?

ACTIVITY 19-6
Absorption costing

GROUP ACTIVITY

Robbins Company is a family-owned business in which you own 20% of the common stock and your brothers and sisters own the remaining shares. The employment contract of Robbins's new president, Glen Edwards, stipulates a base salary of $90,000 per year plus 7% of income from operations in excess of $1,000,000. Robbins uses the absorption costing method of reporting income from operations, which has averaged approximately $1,000,000 for the past several years.

Sales for 2006, Edwards' first year as president of Robbins Company, are estimated at 100,000 units at a selling price of $60 per unit. To maximize the use of Robbins's productive capacity, Edwards has decided to manufacture 150,000 units, rather than the 100,000 units of estimated sales. The beginning inventory at January 1, 2006, is insignificant in amount, and the manufacturing costs and selling and administrative expenses for the production of 100,000 and 150,000 units are as follows:

100,000 Units to Be Manufactured

	Total Cost	Number of Units	Unit Cost
Manufacturing costs:			
Variable	$3,200,000	100,000	$32
Fixed	600,000	100,000	6
Total	$3,800,000		$38
Selling and administrative expenses:			
Variable	$ 900,000		
Fixed	300,000		
Total	$1,200,000		

150,000 Units to Be Manufactured

	Total Cost	Number of Units	Unit Cost
Manufacturing costs:			
Variable	$4,800,000	150,000	$32
Fixed	600,000	150,000	4
Total	$5,400,000		$36
Selling and administrative expenses:			
Variable	$ 900,000		
Fixed	300,000		
Total	$1,200,000		

1. In one group, prepare an absorption costing income statement for the year ending December 31, 2006, based upon sales of 100,000 units and the manufacture of 100,000 units. In the other group, conduct the same analysis, assuming production of 150,000 units.
2. ━━━▶ Explain the difference in the income from operations reported in (1).
3. Compute Edwards' total salary for the year 2006, based on sales of 100,000 units and the manufacture of 100,000 units (Group 1) and 150,000 units (Group 2). Compare your answers.
4. ━━━▶ In addition to maximizing the use of Robbins Company's productive capacity, why might Edwards wish to manufacture 150,000 units rather than 100,000 units?
5. ━━━▶ Can you suggest an alternative way in which Edwards' salary could be determined, using a base salary of $90,000 and 7% of income from operations in excess of $1,000,000, so that the salary could not be increased by simply manufacturing more units?

nswers to Self-Examination Questions

1. **B** The contribution margin of $260,000 (answer B) is determined by deducting all of the variable costs ($400,000 + $90,000) from sales ($750,000).
2. **A** In a period in which the number of units manufactured exceeds the number of units sold, the income from operations reported under the absorption costing concept is larger than the income from operations reported under the variable costing concept (answer A). This is because a portion of the fixed manufacturing costs are deferred when the absorption costing concept is used. This deferment has the effect of excluding a portion of the fixed manufacturing costs from the current cost of goods sold.

3. **D** (6,000 units × $20 per unit). Answer A incorrectly calculates the difference in income from operations using the variable cost per unit, while Answer B incorrectly calculates the difference in income from operations using the total cost per unit. Answer C is incorrect because variable costing income from operations will be greater than absorption costing income from operations when units manufactured is less than units sold.

4. **C** [2,000 units × ($150,000 ÷ 12,000)]. Answers A and B incorrectly calculate the difference in income from operations using variable cost per unit. When production exceeds sales, absorption costing will include fixed costs in the ending inventory, which causes cost of goods sold to decline and income from operations to increase. Thus, income from operations would not decline (answer D) for a production level of 12,000 units.

5. **C** A difference between planned and actual sales can be attributed to a unit price factor. The $45,000 decrease (answer C) attributed to the quantity factor is determined as follows:

Decrease in number of units sold	5,000
Planned unit sales price	× $9
Quantity factor—decrease	$45,000

The unit price factor can be determined as follows:

Increase in unit sales price	$1
Actual number of units sold	× 80,000
Price factor—increase	$80,000

The increase of $80,000 attributed to the price factor less the decrease of $45,000 attributed to the quantity factor accounts for the $35,000 increase in total sales.

20

BUDGETING

objectives

After studying this chapter, you should be able to:

1 Describe budgeting, its objectives, and its impact on human behavior.

2 Describe the basic elements of the budget process, the two major types of budgeting, and the use of computers in budgeting.

3 Describe the master budget for a manufacturing business.

4 Prepare the basic income statement budgets for a manufacturing business.

5 Prepare balance sheet budgets for a manufacturing business.

You may have financial goals for your life. To achieve these goals, it is necessary to plan for future expenses. For example, you may consider taking a part-time job to save money for school expenses for the coming school year. How much money would you need to earn and save in order to pay these expenses? One way to answer this question would be to prepare a budget. For example, a budget would show an estimate of your expenses associated with school, such as tuition, fees, and books. In addition, you would have expenses for day-to-day living, such as rent, food, and clothing. You might also have expenses for travel and entertainment. Once the school year begins, you can use the budget as a tool for guiding your spending priorities during the year.

The budget is used in businesses in much the same way as it can be used in personal life. For example, **DaimlerChrysler** uses budgeting to determine the number of cars to be produced, number of shifts to operate, number of people to be employed, and amount of material to be purchased. The budget provides the company a "game plan" for the year. In this chapter, you will see how budgets can be used for financial planning and control.

Nature and Objectives of Budgeting

objective **1**

Describe budgeting, its objectives, and its impact on human behavior.

If you were driving across the country, you might plan your trip with the aid of a road map. The road map would lay out your route across the country, identify stopovers, and reduce your chances of getting lost. In the same way, a ***budget*** charts a course for a business by outlining the plans of the business in financial terms. Like the road map, the budget can help a company navigate through the year and reduce negative outcomes.

Although budgets are normally associated with profit-making businesses, they also play an important role in operating most units of government. For example, budgets are important in managing rural school districts and small villages as well as agencies of the federal government. Budgets are also important for managing the operations of churches, hospitals, and other nonprofit institutions. Individuals and families also use budgeting techniques in managing their financial affairs. In this chapter, we emphasize the principles of budgeting in the context of a business organized for profit.

POINT OF INTEREST The chart below shows the estimated portion of your total monthly income that should be budgeted for various living expenses.

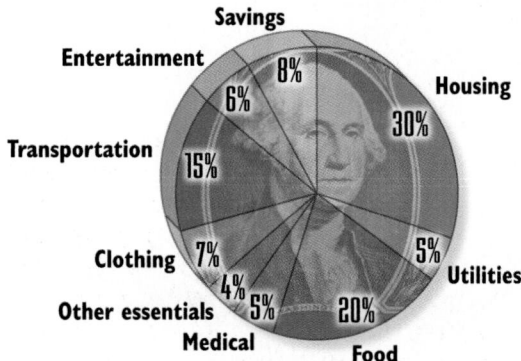

Source: Consumer Credit Counseling Service

Objectives of Budgeting

Budgeting involves (1) establishing specific goals, (2) executing plans to achieve the goals, and (3) periodically comparing actual results with the goals. These goals include both the overall business goals as well as the specific goals for the individual units within the business. Establishing specific goals for future operations is part of the *planning* function of management, while executing actions to meet the goals is the *directing* function of management. Periodically comparing actual results with these goals and taking appropriate action is the *controlling* function of management. The relationships of these functions are illustrated in Exhibit 1.

Planning

A set of goals is often necessary to guide and focus individual and group actions. For example, students set academic goals, athletes set athletic goals, employees set career goals, and businesses set financial goals. In the same way, budgeting supports the planning process by requiring all organizational units to establish their

•Exhibit 1   Planning, Directing, and Controlling

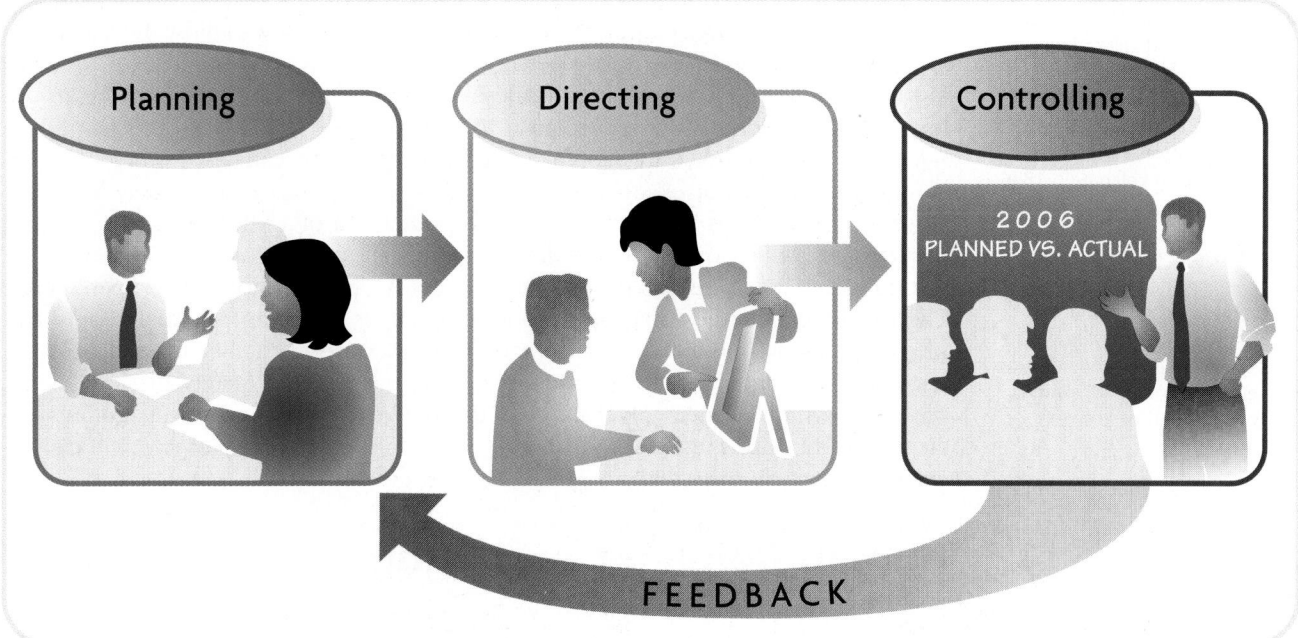

goals for the upcoming period. These goals, in turn, motivate individuals and groups to perform at high levels. For example, **Charles Schwab Corp.**, a major financial services company, recently used its budget process to reduce planned expenditures for professional services, advertising, development, and administrative support by $200 million. Using the budget to communicate these expectations throughout the organization helped Schwab reduce expenses during a severe business downturn.

Planning not only motivates employees to attain goals but also improves overall decision making. During the planning phase of the budget process, all viewpoints are considered, options identified, and cost reduction opportunities assessed. This effort leads to better decision making for the organization. As a result, the budget process may reveal opportunities or threats that were not known prior to the budget planning process. For example, the financial planning process helped **Microsoft Corporation** plan its expansion into the hardware segments of the home electronics market with Xbox® and Tablet PC®.

Directing

Once the budget plans are in place, they can be used to direct and coordinate operations in order to achieve the stated goals. For example, your goal to receive an "A" in a course would result in certain activities, such as reading the book, completing assignments, participating in class, and studying for exams. Such actions are fairly easy to direct and coordinate. A business, however, is much more complex and requires more formal direction and coordination. The budget is one way to direct and coordinate business activities and units to achieve stated goals. The budgetary units of an organization are called ***responsibility centers***. Each responsibility center is led by a manager who has the authority over and responsibility for the unit's performance.

If there is a change in the external environment, the budget process can also be used by unit managers to readjust the operations. For example, **SKI Ltd.** uses weather information to plan expenditures at its Killington and Mt. Snow ski resorts in Vermont. When the weather is forecasted to turn cold and dry, the company increases expenditures in snow-making activities and adds to the staff in order to serve a greater number of skiers.

Controlling

As time passes, the actual performance of an operation can be compared against the planned goals. This provides prompt feedback to employees about their performance. If necessary, employees can use such **feedback** to adjust their activities in the future. For example, a salesperson may be given a quota to achieve $100,000 in sales for the period. If the actual sales are only $75,000, the salesperson can use this feedback about underperformance to change sales tactics and improve future sales. Feedback is not only helpful to individuals, but it can also redirect a complete organization. For example, **McDonalds' Corporation** recently decided to reverse its growth plans by closing stores and pulling out of a few countries as a result of reporting its first quarterly loss since becoming a public company in 1965.

Comparing actual results to the plan also helps prevent unplanned expenditures. The budget encourages employees to establish their spending priorities. For example, departments in universities have budgets to support faculty travel to conferences and meetings. The travel budget communicates to the faculty the upper limit on travel. Often, desired travel exceeds the budget. Thus, the budget requires the faculty to prioritize travel-related opportunities. In the next chapter, we will discuss comparing actual costs with budgeted costs in greater detail.

Human Behavior and Budgeting

In the budgeting process, business, team, and individual goals are established. Human behavior problems can arise if (1) the budget goal is unachievable (too tight), (2) the budget goal is very easy to achieve (too loose), or (3) the budget goals of the business conflict with the objectives of employees (goal conflict).

Setting Budget Goals Too Tightly

People can become discouraged if performance expectations are set too high. For example, would you be inspired or discouraged by a guitar instructor expecting you to play like Eric Clapton after only a few lessons? You'd probably be discouraged. This same kind of problem can occur in businesses if employees view budget goals as unrealistic or unachievable. In such a case, the budget discourages employees from achieving the goals. On the other hand, aggressive but attainable goals are likely to inspire employees to achieve the goals. Therefore, it is important that employees (managers and nonmanagers) be involved in establishing reasonable budget estimates.

Involving all employees encourages cooperation both within and among departments. It also increases awareness of each department's importance to the overall objectives of the company. Employees view budgeting more positively when they have an opportunity to participate in the budget-setting process. This is because employees with a greater sense of control over the budget process will have a greater commitment to achieving its goals. In such cases, budgets are valuable planning tools that increase the possibility of achieving business goals.

Setting Budget Goals Too Loosely

Although it is desirable to establish attainable goals, it is undesirable to plan lower goals than may be possible. Such budget "padding" is termed **budgetary slack**. An example of budgetary slack is including spare employees in the plan. Managers may plan slack in the budget in order to provide a "cushion" for unexpected events or improve the appearance of operations. Budgetary slack can be avoided if lower- and mid-level managers are required to support their spending requirements with operational plans.

Slack budgets can cause employees to develop a "spend it or lose it" mentality. This often occurs at the end of the budget period when actual spending is less than the budget. Employees may attempt to spend the remaining budget (purchase equipment, hire consultants, purchase supplies) in order to avoid having the budget cut next period.

REAL WORLD

There is strong evidence that loose budgets may be appropriate in settings involving high uncertainty, such as research and development. The loose budget acts as a "shock absorber," giving managers maneuvering room to minimize work disruptions.

REAL WORLD The state of Illinois' budget process requires unspent budget monies to be returned to the state when the fiscal year ends. According to the state Comptroller, this encourages "an orgy of spending" at the end of a fiscal year. Directors fearing future budget cuts if they leave anything unspent order airline tickets, training, and computer equipment, all during the last days of the fiscal year.

POINT OF INTEREST A student's question, "Will this be on the test?" is evidence of goal conflict. The student's narrow incentive goal is to pass the test, while the instructor's broader objective is to convey a body of knowledge.

Setting Conflicting Budget Goals

Goal conflict occurs when individual self-interest differs from business objectives. This can happen when management establishes individual goals that conflict with overall business objectives. Often, such conflicts are subtle. For example, the Sales Department manager may be given a sales goal, while the Manufacturing Department manager may be given a cost reduction goal. It is possible for both goals to conflict. The Sales Department may increase sales by promising customers small product deviations that are difficult and unprofitable to make. This would increase sales at the expense of Manufacturing's expense reduction goal and impact the overall profitability objectives of the firm. Likewise, Manufacturing may schedule the plant for maximum manufacturing efficiency with little regard for actual customer product demand. This would reduce manufacturing costs at the expense of the sales goal and reduce the overall profitability of the firm. Goal conflict can be avoided if budget goals are carefully designed for consistency across all areas of the organization.

INTEGRITY IN BUSINESS

BUDGET GAMES

The budgeting system is designed to plan and control a business. However, it is common for the budget to be "gamed" by its participants. For example, cost center managers may pad their budgets with excess resources. In this way, the managers have additional resources for unexpected events during the period. If the budget is being used to establish the incentive plan, then sales managers have incentives to understate the sales potential of a territory in order to ensure hitting their quotas. Other times, managers engage in "land grabbing," which occurs when they overstate the sales potential of a territory in order to guarantee access to resources. If cost center managers believe that unspent resources will not roll over to future periods, then they may be encouraged to "spend it or lose it," causing wasteful expenditures. These types of problems can be partially overcome by separating the budget into planning and incentive components. This is why many organizations have parallel budget processes, one for resource planning and another, more challenging budget for motivating managers.

Budgeting Systems

objective 2

Describe the basic elements of the budget process, the two major types of budgeting, and the use of computers in budgeting.

REAL WORLD **Western Digital Corporation**, a computer hard drive manufacturer, introduced a new Web-based B&P (budget and planning) system to perform a continuous rolling budget. According to the financial executives at the company, "We're never [again] comparing results to old operating plans that were set months ago." Rather, the more frequent budget cycle enables senior managers to react to changing business conditions with revised and updated budgets.

Budgeting systems vary among businesses because of such factors as organizational structure, complexity of operations, and management philosophy. Differences in budget systems are even more significant among different types of businesses, such as manufacturers and service businesses. The details of a budgeting system used by an automobile manufacturer such as **Ford** would obviously differ from a service company such as **American Airlines**. However, the basic budgeting concepts illustrated in the following paragraphs apply to all types of businesses and organizations.

The budgetary period for operating activities normally includes the fiscal year of a business. A year is short enough that future operations can be estimated fairly accurately, yet long enough that the future can be viewed in a broad context. However, to achieve effective control, the annual budgets are usually subdivided into shorter time periods, such as quarters of the year, months, or weeks.

A variation of fiscal-year budgeting, called **continuous budgeting**, maintains a twelve-month projection into the future. The twelve-month budget is continually revised by removing the data for the period just ended and adding estimated budget data for the same period next year, as shown in Exhibit 2.

•Exhibit 2

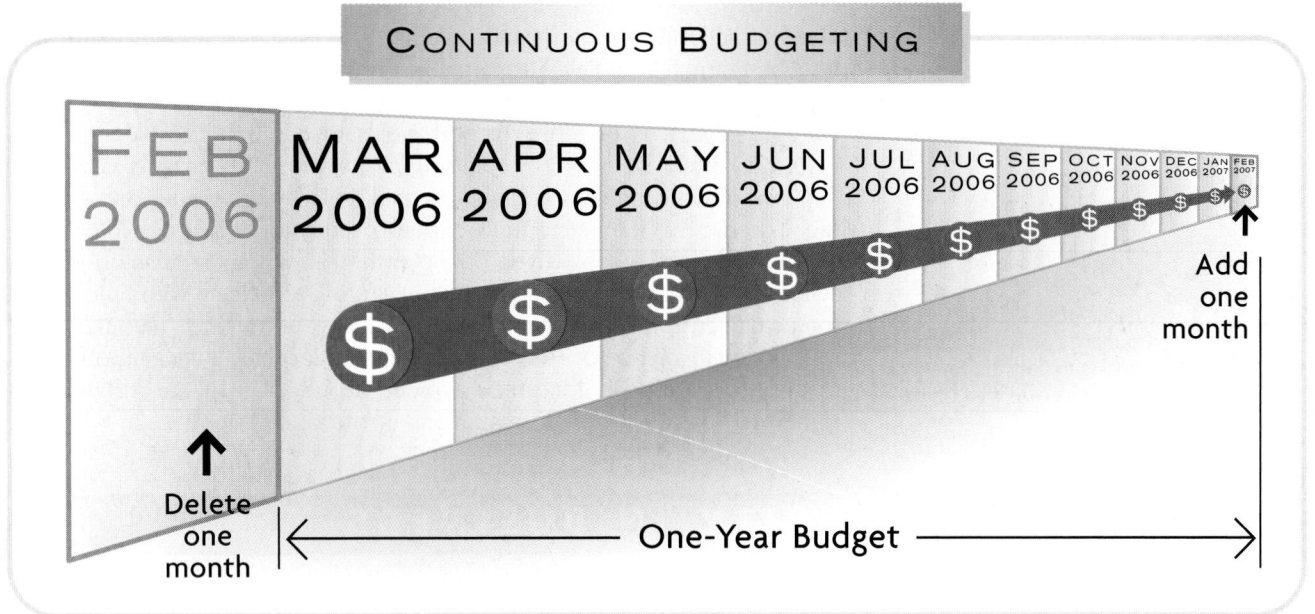

CONTINUOUS BUDGETING

FEB 2006

MAR 2006 APR 2006 MAY 2006 JUN 2006 JUL 2006 AUG 2006 SEP 2006 OCT 2006 NOV 2006 DEC 2006 JAN 2007 FEB 2007

Add one month

Delete one month

One-Year Budget

REAL WORLD

Lockheed Martin Corporation used a zero-based budgeting approach, called risk-based budgeting, to identify cost savings during the downsizing of some of its military and weapons programs. Lockheed Martin divided its operations into core and supplemental activities. Core activities were spared from deep budget cuts, but supplemental activities were evaluated for possible budget reductions.

Developing budgets for the next fiscal year usually begins several months prior to the end of the current year. This responsibility is normally assigned to a budget committee. Such a committee often consists of the budget director and such high-level executives as the controller, the treasurer, the production manager, and the sales manager. Once the budget has been approved, the budget process is monitored and summarized by the Accounting Department, which reports to the committee.

There are several methods of developing budget estimates. One method, termed **_zero-based budgeting_**, requires managers to estimate sales, production, and other operating data as though operations are being started for the first time. This approach has the benefit of taking a fresh view of operations each year. A more common approach is to start with last year's budget and revise it for actual results and expected changes for the coming year. Two major budgets using this approach are the static budget and the flexible budget.

Static Budget

A **_static budget_** shows the expected results of a responsibility center for only one activity level. Once the budget has been determined, it is not changed, even if the activity changes. Static budgeting is used by many service companies and for some administrative functions of manufacturing companies, such as purchasing, engineering, and accounting. For example, the Assembly Department manager for Colter Manufacturing Company prepared the static budget for the upcoming year, shown in Exhibit 3.

A disadvantage of static budgets is that they do not adjust for changes in activity levels. For example, assume that the actual amounts spent by the Assembly Department of Colter Manufacturing totaled $72,000, which is $12,000 or 20% ($12,000 ÷ $60,000) more than budgeted. Is this good news or bad news? At first you might think that this is a bad result. However, this conclusion may not be valid, since static budget results may be difficult to interpret. To illustrate, assume that the assembly manager constructed the budget based on plans to assemble _8,000_ units during the year. However, if _10,000_ units were actually produced, should the additional $12,000 in spending in excess of the budget be considered "bad news"? Maybe not. The Assembly Department provided 25% (2,000 units ÷ 8,000 units) more output for only 20% more cost.

•Exhibit 3 Static Budget

Colter Manufacturing Company
Assembly Department Budget
For the Year Ending July 31, 2006

Direct labor	$40,000
Electric power	5,000
Supervisor salaries	15,000
Total department costs	$60,000

MANAGERIAL DISCLOSURE AND ANALYSIS

NASHVILLE'S BUDGET

By law, government entities must provide budget information to its citizens. This information can often be found on the government entity's Web site. For example, excerpts from the budget for Nashville, Tennessee, are as follows:

City of Nashville Budget (General Fund)
Fiscal Year 2003

Revenues

Property taxes	$246,488,785
Sales taxes	79,509,853
Licenses	64,295,575
Federal and state transfers	81,373,539
Other	105,618,371
Total revenues	$577,286,123

Expenses

General government	$ 97,086,083
Fiscal administration	21,359,829
Administration of justice	42,890,268
Law enforcement	164,953,968
Fire prevention	27,927,212
Public health and welfare	53,667,025
Public works, highways, and streets	44,828,934
Recreation and community support	72,341,443
Other	52,231,361
Total expenses	$577,286,123

This budget shows the source of city revenues and where the dollars are spent. Property taxes are the greatest revenue source, and law enforcement is the largest expense of the General Fund (excluding schools). Note that as for most city and state governments, the revenue and expense budgets must balance. Each of the line items in the General Fund budget has greater detail at a lower level. For example, the Nashville city budget indicates that the "Fiscal Administration" is comprised of four line items, as follows:

Fiscal Administration

Finance	$ 9,282,120
Assessor of property	6,574,521
Trustee	2,018,973
County clerk	3,484,215
Total fiscal administration	$21,359,829

Flexible Budget

Flexible budgets show expected results for several activity levels.

Unlike static budgets, *flexible budgets* show the expected results of a responsibility center for several activity levels. You can think of a flexible budget as a series of static budgets for different levels of activity. Such budgets are especially useful in estimating and controlling factory costs and operating expenses. Exhibit 4 is a flexible budget for the annual manufacturing expense in the Assembly Department of Colter Manufacturing Company.

•Exhibit 4 Flexible Budget

Colter Manufacturing Company Assembly Department Budget For the Year Ending July 31, 2006			
Units of production	8,000	9,000	10,000
Variable cost:			
Direct labor ($5 per unit)	$40,000	$45,000	$50,000
Electric power ($0.50 per unit)	4,000	4,500	5,000
Total variable cost	$44,000	$49,500	$55,000
Fixed cost:			
Electric power	$ 1,000	$ 1,000	$ 1,000
Supervisor salaries	15,000	15,000	15,000
Total fixed cost	$16,000	$16,000	$16,000
Total department costs	$60,000	$65,500	$71,000

REAL WORLD

Many hospitals use flexible budgeting to plan the number of nurses for patient floors. These budgets use a measure termed "relative value units." A relative value unit is a measure of effort related to a nursing activity, such as feeding the patient or verifying vital signs. The total relative value units for a floor can be determined from a computer simulation, based on the number of patients on the floor and the type of illnesses. Naturally, the more patients and the more severe their illnesses, the higher the total relative value units. The total relative units can then be translated into the number of nurses required to support the patients.

At the beginning of the period, the Assembly Department budgeted direct labor of $45,000 and supervisor salaries of $30,000 for 5,000 hours of production. The department actually completed 6,000 hours of production. What is the appropriate total budget for the department, assuming that it uses flexible budgeting?

- -

$84,000 [($9 × 6,000) + $30,000]

When constructing a flexible budget, we first identify the relevant activity levels. In Exhibit 4, there are 8,000, 9,000, and 10,000 units of production. Alternative activity bases, such as machine hours or direct labor hours, may be used in measuring the volume of activity. Second, we identify the fixed and variable cost components of the costs being budgeted. For example, in Exhibit 4, the electric power cost is separated into its fixed cost ($1,000 per month) and variable cost ($0.50 per unit). Lastly, we prepare the budget for each activity level by multiplying the variable cost per unit by the activity level and then adding the monthly fixed cost.

With a flexible budget, the department manager can be evaluated by comparing actual expenses to the budgeted amount for actual activity. For example, if Colter Manufacturing Company's Assembly Department actually spent $72,000 to produce 10,000 units, the manager would be considered over budget by $1,000 ($72,000 − $71,000). Under the static budget in Exhibit 3, the department was $12,000 over budget. This comparison is illustrated in Exhibit 5. The flexible budget for the Assembly Department is much more accurate than the static budget, because budget amounts adjust for changes in activity.

Computerized Budgeting Systems

In developing budgets, many firms use computerized budgeting systems. Such systems speed up and reduce the cost of preparing the budget. This is especially true when large quantities of data need to be processed. Computers are also useful in continuous budgeting. Reports that compare actual results with amounts budgeted can also be prepared on a timely basis through the use of computerized systems. For example, **Fujitsu** used Enterprise Resource Planning (ERP) software to streamline its budgeting process from 6–8 weeks down to 10 to 15 days.

Managers often use computer spreadsheets or simulation models to represent the operating and budget relationships. By using computer simulation models, the impact of various operating alternatives on the budget can be assessed. For example, the budget can be revised to show the impact of a proposed change in indirect labor wage rates. Likewise, the budgetary effect of a proposed product line can be determined.

•Exhibit 5

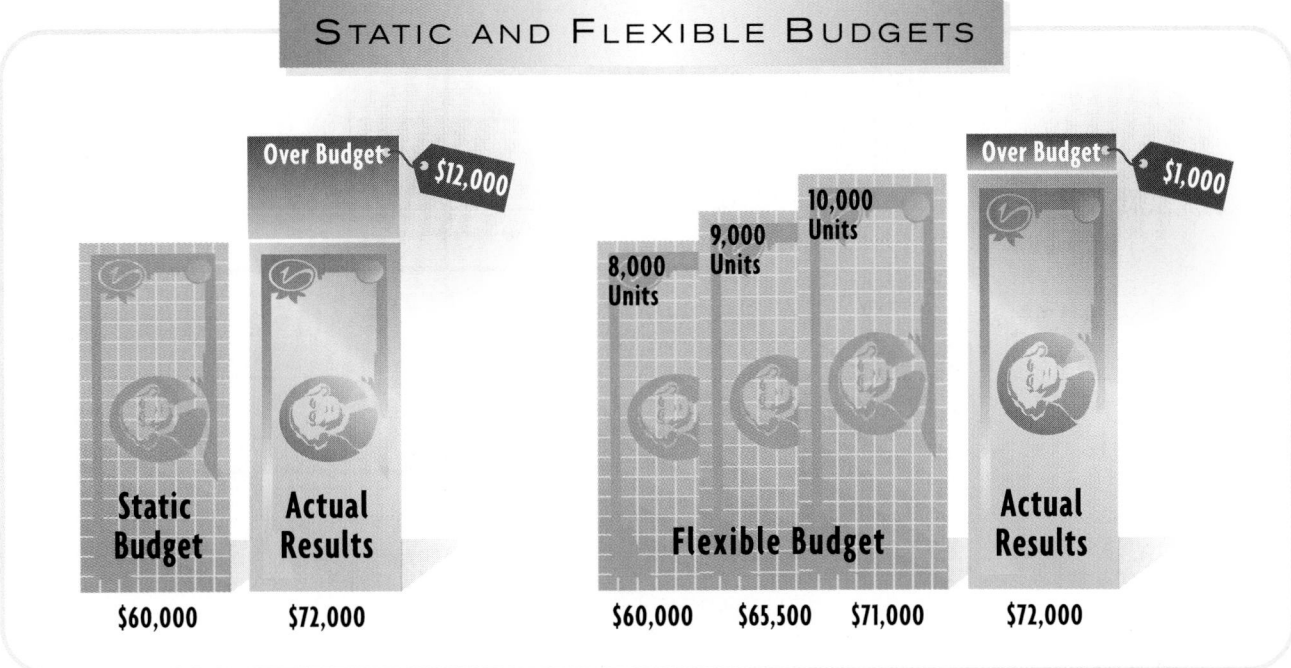

STATIC AND FLEXIBLE BUDGETS

Static Budget	Actual Results			Flexible Budget		Actual Results
$60,000	$72,000			$60,000 $65,500 $71,000		$72,000

A common objective of using computer-based budgeting is to tie all the budgets of the organization together. The newest budgeting and planning (B&P) systems are accomplishing this by using Web-based applications to tie thousands of employees together. In the next section, we will illustrate how a company ties its budgets together to develop a complete plan.

Master Budget

objective **3**

Describe the master budget for a manufacturing business.

Manufacturing operations require a series of budgets that are linked together in a ***master budget***. The major parts of the master budget are as follows:

Budgeted Income Statement	Budgeted Balance Sheet
Sales budget	Cash budget
Cost of goods sold budget:	Capital expenditures budget
Production budget	
Direct materials purchases budget	
Direct labor cost budget	
Factory overhead cost budget	
Selling and administrative expenses budget	

Exhibit 6 shows the relationship among the income statement budgets. The budget process begins by estimating sales. The sales information is then provided to the various units for estimating the production and selling and administrative expenses budgets. The production budgets are used to prepare the direct materials purchases, direct labor cost, and factory overhead cost budgets. These three budgets are used to develop the cost of goods sold budget. Once these budgets and the selling and administrative expenses budget have been completed, the budgeted income statement can be prepared, as we illustrate in the following section.

•Exhibit 6

Income Statement Budgets

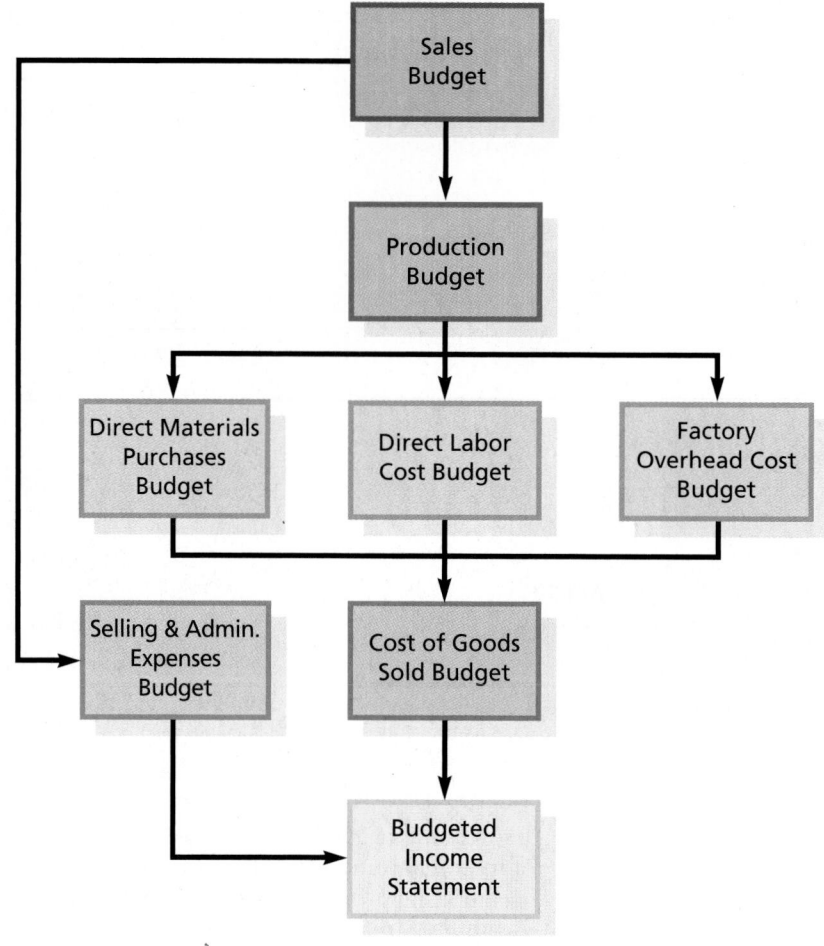

After the budgeted income statement has been developed, the budgeted balance sheet can be prepared. Two major budgets comprising the budgeted balance sheet are the cash budget and the capital expenditures budget, which we illustrate later in the chapter.

Income Statement Budgets

objective **4**

Prepare the basic income statement budgets for a manufacturing business.

In the following sections, we will illustrate the major elements of the income statement budget. We will use a small manufacturing business, Elite Accessories Inc., as the basis for our illustration.

Sales Budget

The *sales budget* normally indicates for each product (1) the quantity of estimated sales and (2) the expected unit selling price. These data are often reported by regions or by sales representatives.

In estimating the quantity of sales for each product, past sales volumes are often used as a starting point. These amounts are revised for factors that are expected to affect future sales, such as the factors listed below.

- backlog of unfilled sales orders
- planned advertising and promotion
- expected industry and general economic conditions
- productive capacity

- projected pricing policy
- findings of market research studies

Once an estimate of the sales volume is obtained, the expected sales revenue can be determined by multiplying the volume by the expected unit sales price. Exhibit 7 is the sales budget for Elite Accessories Inc.

•Exhibit 7

Sales Budget

Elite Accessories Inc. Sales Budget For the Year Ending December 31, 2006			
Product and Region	**Unit Sales Volume**	**Unit Selling Price**	**Total Sales**
Wallet:			
East	287,000	$12.00	$ 3,444,000
West	241,000	12.00	2,892,000
Total	528,000		$ 6,336,000
Handbag:			
East	156,400	$25.00	$ 3,910,000
West	123,600	25.00	3,090,000
Total	280,000		$ 7,000,000
Total revenue from sales			$13,336,000

For control purposes, management can compare actual sales and budgeted sales by product, region, or sales representative. Management would investigate any significant differences and take possible corrective actions.

Production Budget

Production should be carefully coordinated with the sales budget to ensure that production and sales are kept in balance during the period. The number of units to be manufactured to meet budgeted sales and inventory needs for each product is set forth in the ***production budget***. The budgeted volume of production is determined as follows:

Sales of 45,000 units are budgeted for the period. The estimated beginning inventory is 3,000 units, and the desired ending inventory is 5,000 units. What is the budgeted production (in units) for the period?

47,000 units (45,000 units + 5,000 units − 3,000 units)

Expected units to be sold
\+ Desired units in ending inventory
\− Estimated units in beginning inventory
Total units to be produced

Exhibit 8 is the production budget for Elite Accessories Inc.

Direct Materials Purchases Budget

The production budget is the starting point for determining the estimated quantities of direct materials to be purchased. Multiplying these quantities by the expected unit purchase price determines the total cost of direct materials to be purchased.

Materials required for production
\+ Desired ending materials inventory
\− Estimated beginning materials inventory
Direct materials to be purchased

•**Exhibit 8**

Production Budget

Elite Accessories Inc.
Production Budget
For the Year Ending December 31, 2006

	Units	
	Wallet	**Handbag**
Expected units to be sold (from Exhibit 7)	528,000	280,000
Plus desired ending inventory, December 31, 2006	80,000	60,000
Total	608,000	340,000
Less estimated beginning inventory, January 1, 2006 . . .	88,000	48,000
Total units to be produced	520,000	292,000

In Elite Accessories Inc.'s production operations, leather and lining are required for wallets and handbags. The quantity of direct materials expected to be used for each unit of product is as follows:

Wallet:
    Leather: 0.30 square yard per unit
    Lining: 0.10 square yard per unit

Handbag:
    Leather: 1.25 square yards per unit
    Lining: 0.50 square yard per unit

Based on these data and the production budget, the **direct materials purchases budget** is prepared. As shown in the budget in Exhibit 9, for Elite Accessories Inc. to produce 520,000 wallets, 156,000 square yards (520,000 units × 0.30 square yard per unit) of leather are needed. Likewise, to produce 292,000 handbags, 365,000

•**Exhibit 9**

Direct Materials Purchases Budget

Elite Accessories Inc.
Direct Materials Purchases Budget
For the Year Ending December 31, 2006

	Direct Materials		
	Leather	**Lining**	**Total**
Square yards required for production:			
Wallet (Note A)	156,000	52,000	
Handbag (Note B)	365,000	146,000	
Plus desired inventory, December 31, 2006	20,000	12,000	
Total	541,000	210,000	
Less estimated inventory, January 1, 2006	18,000	15,000	
Total square yards to be purchased	523,000	195,000	
Unit price (per square yard)	× $4.50	× $1.20	
Total direct materials to be purchased	$2,353,500	$234,000	$2,587,500

Note A: Leather: 520,000 units × 0.30 sq. yd. per unit = 156,000 sq. yds.
           Lining: 520,000 units × 0.10 sq. yd. per unit = 52,000 sq. yds.

Note B: Leather: 292,000 units × 1.25 sq. yds. per unit = 365,000 sq. yds.
           Lining: 292,000 units × 0.50 sq. yd. per unit = 146,000 sq. yds.

square yards (292,000 units × 1.25 square yards per unit) of leather are needed. We can compute the needs for lining in a similar manner. Then adding the desired ending inventory for each material and deducting the estimated beginning inventory determines the amount of each material to be purchased. Multiplying these amounts by the estimated cost per square yard yields the total materials purchase cost.

The direct materials purchases budget helps management maintain inventory levels within reasonable limits. For this purpose, the timing of the direct materials purchases should be coordinated between the purchasing and production departments.

Direct Labor Cost Budget

The production budget also provides the starting point for preparing the direct labor cost budget. For Elite Accessories Inc., the labor requirements for each unit of product are estimated as follows:

Wallet:
Cutting Department: 0.10 hour per unit
Sewing Department: 0.25 hour per unit

Handbag:
Cutting Department: 0.15 hour per unit
Sewing Department: 0.40 hour per unit

Budgeted production is 22,000 units. Each unit requires 0.70 pound of steel and 0.20 direct labor hour. Steel is purchased for $45 per pound, and direct labor is $18 per hour. Steel has an estimated beginning inventory of 700 units and a desired ending inventory of 200 units. For the period, what is the budgeted (a) direct materials purchases and (b) direct labor cost?

(a) $670,500 {[(22,000 units × 0.70 lb.) + 200 lbs. − 700 lbs.] × $45}; (b) $79,200 (22,000 units × 0.20 hr. × $18)

Based on these data and the production budget, Elite Accessories Inc. prepares the direct labor budget. As shown in the budget in Exhibit 10, for Elite Accessories Inc. to produce 520,000 wallets, 52,000 hours (520,000 units × 0.10 hour per unit) of labor in the Cutting Department are required. Likewise, to produce 292,000 handbags, 43,800 hours (292,000 units × 0.15 hour per unit) of labor in the Cutting Department are required. In a similar manner, we can determine the direct labor hours needed in the Sewing Department to meet the budgeted production. Multiplying the direct labor hours for each department by the estimated department hourly rate yields the total direct labor cost for each department.

•Exhibit 10

Direct Labor Cost Budget

Elite Accessories Inc. Direct Labor Cost Budget For the Year Ending December 31, 2006			
	Cutting	**Sewing**	**Total**
Hours required for production:			
Wallet (Note A)	52,000	130,000	
Handbag (Note B)	43,800	116,800	
Total	95,800	246,800	
Hourly rate	× $12.00	× $15.00	
Total direct labor cost	$1,149,600	$3,702,000	$4,851,600

Note A: Cutting Department: 520,000 units × 0.10 hour per unit = 52,000 hours
Sewing Department: 520,000 units × 0.25 hour per unit = 130,000 hours

Note B: Cutting Department: 292,000 units × 0.15 hour per unit = 43,800 hours
Sewing Department: 292,000 units × 0.40 hour per unit = 116,800 hours

The direct labor needs should be coordinated between the production and personnel departments. This ensures that there will be enough labor available for production.

Factory Overhead Cost Budget

The estimated factory overhead costs necessary for production make up the factory overhead cost budget. This budget usually includes the total estimated cost for each item of factory overhead, as shown in Exhibit 11.

•**Exhibit 11**

Factory Overhead Cost Budget

Elite Accessories Inc. Factory Overhead Cost Budget For the Year Ending December 31, 2006	
Indirect factory wages	$ 732,800
Supervisor salaries	360,000
Power and light	306,000
Depreciation of plant and equipment	288,000
Indirect materials	182,800
Maintenance	140,280
Insurance and property taxes	79,200
Total factory overhead cost	$2,089,080

A business may prepare supporting departmental schedules, in which the factory overhead costs are separated into their fixed and variable cost elements. Such schedules enable department managers to direct their attention to those costs for which they are responsible and to evaluate performance.

Cost of Goods Sold Budget

The direct materials purchases budget, direct labor cost budget, and factory overhead cost budget are the starting point for preparing the *cost of goods sold budget*. To illustrate, these data are combined with the desired ending inventory and the estimated beginning inventory data below to determine the budgeted cost of goods sold shown in Exhibit 12.

Estimated inventories on January 1, 2006:		Desired inventories on December 31, 2006:	
Finished goods	$1,095,600	Finished goods	$1,565,000
Work in process	214,400	Work in process	220,000

Selling and Administrative Expenses Budget

The sales budget is often used as the starting point for estimating the selling and administrative expenses. For example, a budgeted increase in sales may require more advertising. Exhibit 13, on page 848, is a selling and administrative expenses budget for Elite Accessories Inc.

Detailed supporting schedules are often prepared for major items in the selling and administrative expenses budget. For example, an advertising expense schedule for the Marketing Department should include the advertising media to be used (newspaper, direct mail, television), quantities (column inches, number of pieces, minutes), and the cost per unit. Attention to such details results in realistic budgets. Effective control results from assigning responsibility for achieving the budget to department supervisors.

•Exhibit 12   Cost of Goods Sold Budget

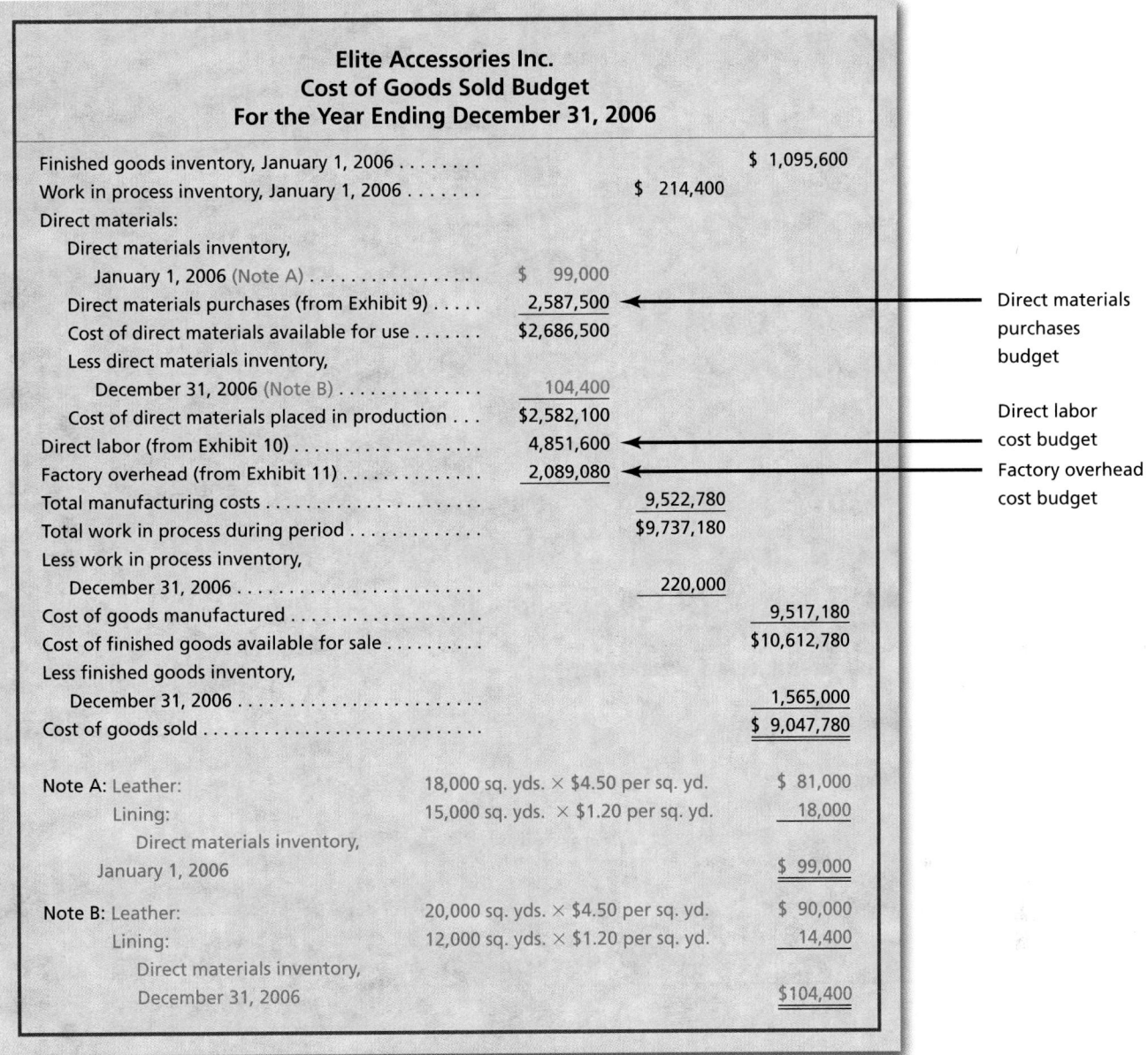

Elite Accessories Inc.
Cost of Goods Sold Budget
For the Year Ending December 31, 2006

Finished goods inventory, January 1, 2006		$ 1,095,600
Work in process inventory, January 1, 2006	$ 214,400	
Direct materials:		
Direct materials inventory, January 1, 2006 (Note A)	$ 99,000	
Direct materials purchases (from Exhibit 9)	2,587,500	
Cost of direct materials available for use	$2,686,500	
Less direct materials inventory, December 31, 2006 (Note B)	104,400	
Cost of direct materials placed in production . . .	$2,582,100	
Direct labor (from Exhibit 10)	4,851,600	
Factory overhead (from Exhibit 11)	2,089,080	
Total manufacturing costs	9,522,780	
Total work in process during period	$9,737,180	
Less work in process inventory, December 31, 2006	220,000	
Cost of goods manufactured		9,517,180
Cost of finished goods available for sale		$10,612,780
Less finished goods inventory, December 31, 2006		1,565,000
Cost of goods sold		$ 9,047,780

Direct materials purchases budget

Direct labor cost budget

Factory overhead cost budget

Note A: Leather:	18,000 sq. yds. × $4.50 per sq. yd.	$ 81,000
Lining:	15,000 sq. yds. × $1.20 per sq. yd.	18,000
Direct materials inventory, January 1, 2006		$ 99,000
Note B: Leather:	20,000 sq. yds. × $4.50 per sq. yd.	$ 90,000
Lining:	12,000 sq. yds. × $1.20 per sq. yd.	14,400
Direct materials inventory, December 31, 2006		$104,400

Budgeted Income Statement

The budgets for sales, cost of goods sold, and selling and administrative expenses, combined with the data on other income, other expense, and income tax, are used to prepare the budgeted income statement. Exhibit 14 is a budgeted income statement for Elite Accessories Inc.

The budgeted income statement summarizes the estimates of all phases of operations. This allows management to assess the effects of the individual budgets on profits for the year. If the budgeted net income is too low, management could review and revise operating plans in an attempt to improve income.

•Exhibit 13   Selling and Administrative Expenses Budget

Elite Accessories Inc.
Selling and Administrative Expenses Budget
For the Year Ending December 31, 2006

Selling expenses:		
Sales salaries expense	$715,000	
Advertising expense	360,000	
Travel expense	115,000	
Total selling expenses		$1,190,000
Administrative expenses:		
Officers' salaries expense	$360,000	
Office salaries expense	258,000	
Office rent expense	34,500	
Office supplies expense	17,500	
Miscellaneous administrative expenses	25,000	
Total administrative expenses		695,000
Total selling and administrative expenses		$1,885,000

•Exhibit 14   Budgeted Income Statement

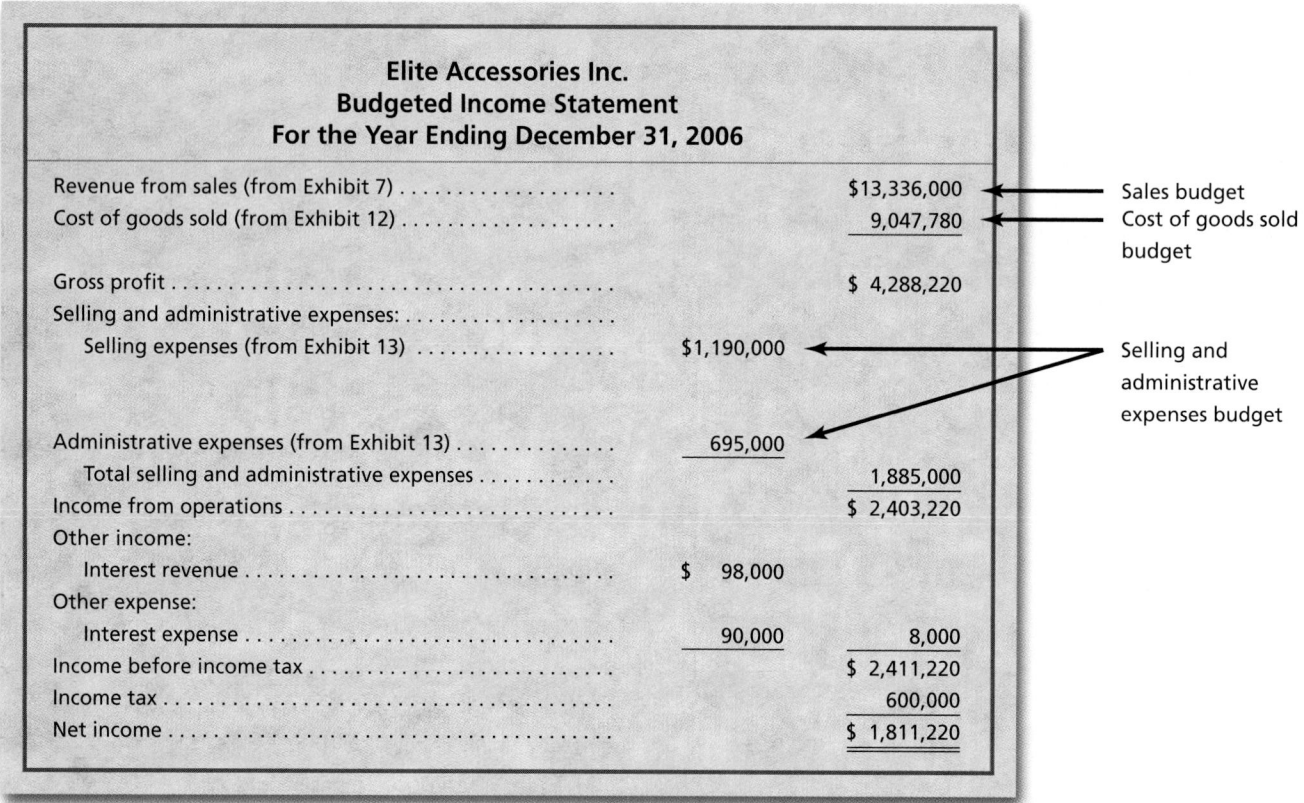

Elite Accessories Inc.
Budgeted Income Statement
For the Year Ending December 31, 2006

Revenue from sales (from Exhibit 7)		$13,336,000	← Sales budget
Cost of goods sold (from Exhibit 12)		9,047,780	← Cost of goods sold budget
Gross profit		$ 4,288,220	
Selling and administrative expenses:			
Selling expenses (from Exhibit 13)	$1,190,000		← Selling and administrative expenses budget
Administrative expenses (from Exhibit 13)	695,000		
Total selling and administrative expenses		1,885,000	
Income from operations		$ 2,403,220	
Other income:			
Interest revenue	$ 98,000		
Other expense:			
Interest expense	90,000	8,000	
Income before income tax		$ 2,411,220	
Income tax		600,000	
Net income		$ 1,811,220	

Balance Sheet Budgets

objective **5**

Prepare balance sheet budgets for a manufacturing business.

Balance sheet budgets are used by managers to plan financing, investing, and cash objectives for the firm. The balance sheet budgets illustrated for Elite Accessories Inc. in the following sections are the cash budget and the capital expenditures budget.

Cash Budget

The **cash budget** is one of the most important elements of the budgeted balance sheet. The cash budget presents the expected receipts (inflows) and payments (outflows) of cash for a period of time.

> **The cash budget presents the expected receipts and payments of cash for a period of time.**

Information from the various operating budgets, such as the sales budget, the direct materials purchases budget, and the selling and administrative expenses budget, affects the cash budget. In addition, the capital expenditures budget, dividend policies, and plans for equity or long-term debt financing also affect the cash budget.

We illustrate the monthly cash budget for January, February, and March 2006, for Elite Accessories Inc. We begin by developing the estimated cash receipts and estimated cash payments portion of the cash budget.

Estimated Cash Receipts

Estimated cash receipts are planned additions to cash from sales and other sources, such as issuing securities or collecting interest. A supporting schedule can be used in determining the collections from sales. To illustrate this schedule, assume the following information for Elite Accessories Inc.:

Accounts receivable, January 1, 2006 . . . . $370,000

	January	February	March
Budgeted sales	$1,080,000	$1,240,000	$970,000

Elite Accessories Inc. expects to sell 10% of its merchandise for cash. Of the remaining 90% of the sales on account, 60% are expected to be collected in the month of the sale and the remainder in the next month.

Using this information, we prepare the schedule of collections from sales, shown in Exhibit 15. The cash receipts from sales on account are determined by adding the amounts collected from credit sales earned in the current period (60%) and the amounts accrued from sales in the previous period as accounts receivable (40%).

Estimated Cash Payments

Estimated cash payments are planned reductions in cash from manufacturing costs, selling and administrative expenses, capital expenditures, and other sources, such as buying securities or paying interest or dividends. A supporting schedule can be used in estimating the cash payments for manufacturing costs. To illustrate, the schedule shown in Exhibit 16 is based on the following information for Elite Accessories:

Accounts payable, January 1, 2006 . . . . $190,000

	January	February	March
Manufacturing costs	$840,000	$780,000	$812,000

Depreciation expense on machines is estimated to be $24,000 per month and is included in the manufacturing costs. The accounts payable were incurred for manufacturing costs. Elite Accessories Inc. expects to pay 75% of the manufacturing costs in the month in which they are incurred and the balance in the next month.

•Exhibit 15

Schedule of Collections from Sales

A company collects 25% of its sales in the month of the sale and 75% in the month following the sale. If sales are budgeted to be $750,000 for March and $900,000 for April, what are the budgeted cash receipts for April?

$787,500 [($750,000 × 0.75) + ($900,000 × 0.25)]

Elite Accessories Inc.
Schedule of Collections from Sales
For the Three Months Ending March 31, 2006

	January	February	March
Receipts from cash sales:			
Cash sales (10% × current month's sales— Note A)	$108,000	$ 124,000	$ 97,000
Receipts from sales on account:			
Collections from prior month's sales (40% of previous month's credit sales—Note B)	$370,000	$ 388,800	$446,400
Collections from current month's sales (60% of current month's credit sales—Note C)	583,200	669,600	523,800
Total receipts from sales on account	$953,200	$1,058,400	$970,200

Note A: $108,000 = $1,080,000 × 10%
$124,000 = $1,240,000 × 10%
$ 97,000 = $ 970,000 × 10%

Note B: $370,000, given as January 1, 2006 Accounts Receivable balance
$388,800 = $1,080,000 × 90% × 40%
$446,400 = $1,240,000 × 90% × 40%

Note C: $583,200 = $1,080,000 × 90% × 60%
$669,600 = $1,240,000 × 90% × 60%
$523,800 = $ 970,000 × 90% × 60%

•Exhibit 16

Schedule of Payments for Manufacturing Costs

Elite Accessories Inc.
Schedule of Payments for Manufacturing Costs
For the Three Months Ending March 31, 2006

	January	February	March
Payments of prior month's manufacturing costs {[25% × previous month's manufacturing costs (less depreciation)]—Note A}	$190,000	$204,000	$189,000
Payments of current month's manufacturing costs {[75% × current month's manufacturing costs (less depreciation)]—Note B}	612,000	567,000	591,000
Total payments	$802,000	$771,000	$780,000

Note A: $190,000, given as January 1, 2006 Accounts Payable balance
$204,000 = ($840,000 − $24,000) × 25%
$189,000 = ($780,000 − $24,000) × 25%

Note B: $612,000 = ($840,000 − $24,000) × 75%
$567,000 = ($780,000 − $24,000) × 75%
$591,000 = ($812,000 − $24,000) × 75%

In Exhibit 16, the cash payments are determined by adding the amounts paid from costs incurred in the current period (75%) and the amounts accrued as a liability from costs in the previous period (25%). The $24,000 of depreciation must be excluded from all calculations, since depreciation is a noncash expense that should not be included in the cash budget.

Completing the Cash Budget

To complete the cash budget for Elite Accessories Inc., as shown in Exhibit 17, assume that Elite Accessories Inc. is expecting the following:

Cash balance on January 1	$280,000
Quarterly taxes paid on March 31	150,000
Quarterly interest expense paid on January 10	22,500
Quarterly interest revenue received on March 21	24,500
Sewing equipment purchased in February	274,000

In addition, monthly selling and administrative expenses, which are paid in the month incurred, are estimated as follows:

	January	February	March
Selling and administrative expenses	$160,000	$165,000	$145,000

•Exhibit 17 Cash Budget

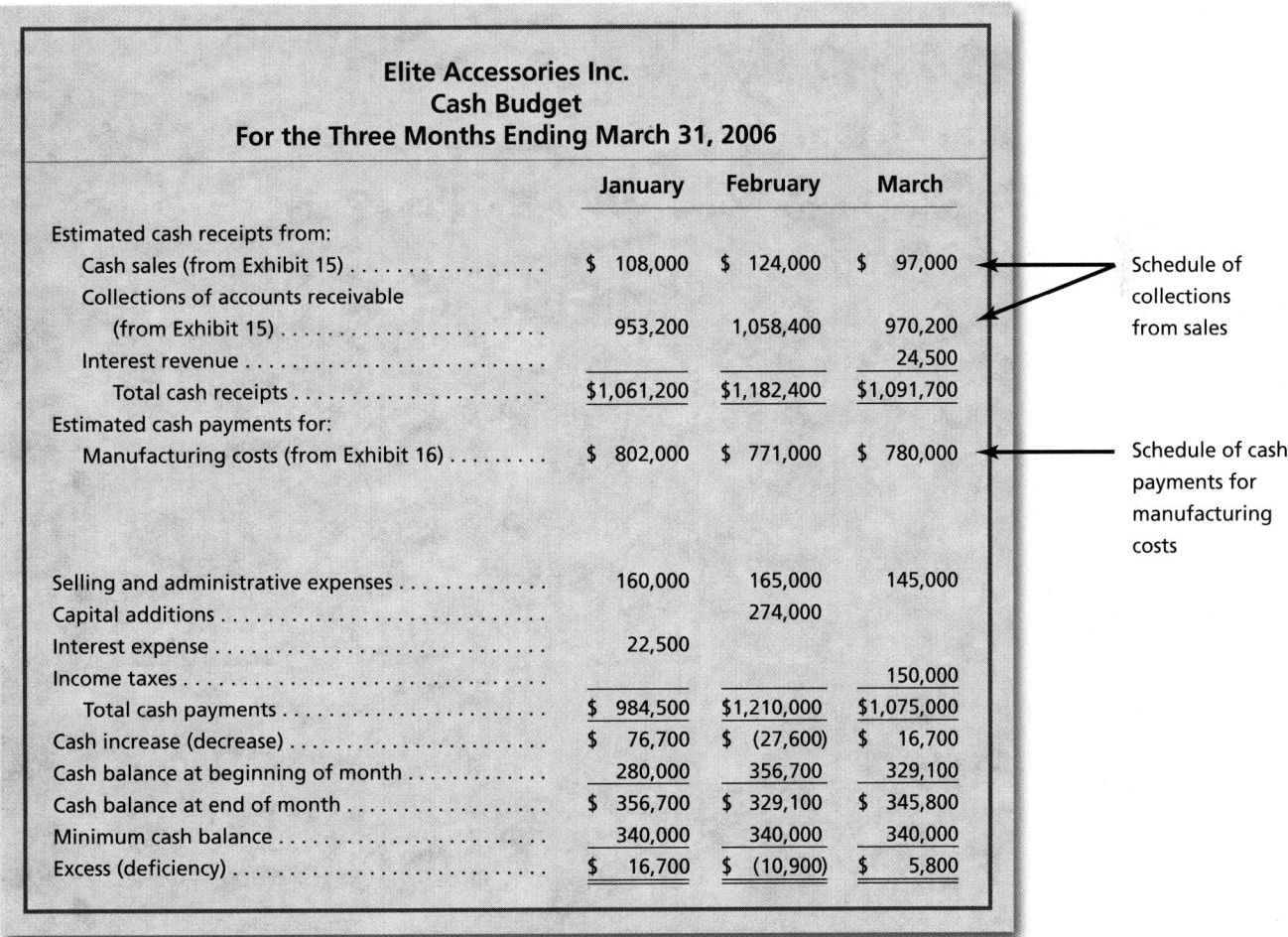

Elite Accessories Inc.
Cash Budget
For the Three Months Ending March 31, 2006

	January	February	March
Estimated cash receipts from:			
Cash sales (from Exhibit 15)	$ 108,000	$ 124,000	$ 97,000
Collections of accounts receivable			
(from Exhibit 15)	953,200	1,058,400	970,200
Interest revenue			24,500
Total cash receipts	$1,061,200	$1,182,400	$1,091,700
Estimated cash payments for:			
Manufacturing costs (from Exhibit 16)	$ 802,000	$ 771,000	$ 780,000
Selling and administrative expenses	160,000	165,000	145,000
Capital additions		274,000	
Interest expense	22,500		
Income taxes			150,000
Total cash payments	$ 984,500	$1,210,000	$1,075,000
Cash increase (decrease)	$ 76,700	$ (27,600)	$ 16,700
Cash balance at beginning of month	280,000	356,700	329,100
Cash balance at end of month	$ 356,700	$ 329,100	$ 345,800
Minimum cash balance	340,000	340,000	340,000
Excess (deficiency)	$ 16,700	$ (10,900)	$ 5,800

Schedule of collections from sales

Schedule of cash payments for manufacturing costs

We can compare the estimated cash balance at the end of the period with the minimum balance required by operations. Assuming that the minimum cash balance for Elite Accessories Inc. is $340,000, we can determine any expected excess or deficiency.

The minimum cash balance protects against variations in estimates and for unexpected cash emergencies. For effective cash management, much of the minimum cash balance should be deposited in income-producing securities that can be readily converted to cash. U.S. Treasury Bills or Notes are examples of such securities.

Capital Expenditures Budget

The *capital expenditures budget* summarizes plans for acquiring fixed assets. Such expenditures are necessary as machinery and other fixed assets wear out, become obsolete, or for other reasons need to be replaced. In addition, expanding plant facilities may be necessary to meet increasing demand for a company's product.

The useful life of many fixed assets extends over long periods of time. In addition, the amount of the expenditures for such assets may vary from year to year. It is normal to project the plans for a number of periods into the future in preparing the capital expenditures budget. Exhibit 18 is a five-year capital expenditures budget for Elite Accessories Inc.

•Exhibit 18 Capital Expenditures Budget

Item	2006	2007	2008	2009	2010
\multicolumn{6}{l}{**Elite Accessories Inc.**}
Machinery—Cutting Department	$400,000			$280,000	$360,000
Machinery—Sewing Department	274,000	$260,000	$560,000	200,000	
Office equipment		90,000			60,000
Total	$674,000	$350,000	$560,000	$480,000	$420,000

Elite Accessories Inc.
Capital Expenditures Budget
For the Five Years Ending December 31, 2010

The capital expenditures budget should be considered in preparing the other operating budgets. For example, the estimated depreciation of new equipment affects the factory overhead cost budget and the selling and administrative expenses budget. The plans for financing the capital expenditures may also affect the cash budget.

Budgeted Balance Sheet

The budgeted balance sheet estimates the financial condition at the end of a budget period. The budgeted balance sheet assumes that all operating budgets and financing plans are met. It is similar to a balance sheet based on actual data in the accounts. For this reason, we do not illustrate a budgeted balance sheet for Elite Accessories Inc. If the budgeted balance sheet indicates a weakness in financial position, revising the financing plans or other plans may be necessary. For example, a large amount of long-term debt in relation to stockholders' equity might require revising financing plans for capital expenditures. Such revisions might include issuing equity rather than debt.

SPOTLIGHT ON STRATEGY

ALIGNING THE BUDGETING SYSTEM WITH STRATEGY

A business unit of a company can adopt either a build strategy or a harvest strategy. A *build* strategy is one where the business is designing, launching, and growing new products and markets. Build strategies often require short-term profit sacrifice in order to grow market share. HDTVs are an example of a product managed under a build strategy. A *harvest* strategy is often employed for business units with mature products enjoying high market share in low-growth industries. Harvest strategies maximize short-term earnings and cash flow, sometimes at the expense of market share. Often the term "cash cow" is used to describe a product managed under a harvest strategy. Tobacco is an example of such a product. Compared to the harvest strategy, a build strategy often has greater uncertainty, unpredictability, and change. Build strategies are usually employed in evolving product/market segments; thus, the competitive battle for market share is often fierce and unpredictable. The differences between build and harvest strategies imply different budgeting approaches. That is, the budget approach is contingent upon the strategy.

The build strategy should employ a budget approach that is flexible to the inherent uncertainty of the business. Thus, budgets should adapt to changing conditions by allowing periodic revisions and flexible targets. Often the managers controlled by the budget will participate in setting budget targets, so that all uncertainties are considered. In addition, the budget will complement other, more subjective, evaluation criteria. Overall, the budget serves as a short-term planning tool to guide management in executing an uncertain and evolving product market strategy.

Under the harvest strategy, the business is often much more stable and is managed to maximize profitability and cash flow. Cost control is much more important in a harvest strategy; thus, the budget is used to restrict the actions of managers. The budget is established with ambitious cost reduction targets, allowing little room for negotiation or revision. In addition, the managers controlled by the budget often do not participate in its development. Rather, the budget is imposed. In a harvest business, the budget is the major control tool and is often not supplemented with other more subjective performance measures.

The descriptions above provide the extreme ends of a continuum. Real-world budget systems will blend tight vs. loose, objective vs. subjective, short-term vs. long-term, programmed vs. interactive, and mechanistic vs. flexible characteristics to fit the strategy. Budgeting systems are not "one size fits all" solutions but must adapt to the underlying business conditions.

Key Points

1 Describe budgeting, its objectives, and its impact on human behavior.

Budgeting involves (1) establishing specific goals, (2) executing plans to achieve the goals, and (3) periodically comparing actual results with these goals. In addition, budget goals should be established to avoid problems in human behavior. Thus, budgets should not be set too tightly, too loosely, or with goal conflict.

2 Describe the basic elements of the budget process, the two major types of budgeting, and the use of computers in budgeting.

The budget process is initiated by a budget committee. The annual estimates received by the budget committee should be carefully studied, analyzed, revised, and finally integrated together into the budget. Two major types of budgets are the static budget and the flexible budget. The static budget does not adjust with changes in activity, while the flexible budget does adjust with changes in activity. Computers can be useful in speeding up the budgetary process and in preparing timely budget performance reports. In addition, simulation models can be used to determine the impact of operating alternatives on various budgets.

3 Describe the master budget for a manufacturing business.

The master budget consists of the budgeted income statement and budgeted balance sheet. These two budgets are developed from detailed budgets that are described in the next two objectives.

4 Prepare the basic income statement budgets for a manufacturing business.

The basic income statement budgets are the sales budget, production budget, direct materials purchases budget, direct labor cost budget, factory overhead cost budget, cost of goods sold budget, and selling and administrative expenses budget.

5 Prepare balance sheet budgets for a manufacturing business.

Both the cash budget and the capital expenditures budget can be used in preparing the budgeted balance sheet. The cash budget consists of budgeted cash receipts and budgeted cash payments. The capital expenditures budget is an important tool for planning expenditures for fixed assets.

Key Terms

budget (834)

budgetary slack (836)

capital expenditures budget (852)

cash budget (849)

continuous budgeting (837)

cost of goods sold budget (846)

direct materials purchases budget (844)

flexible budget (839)

goal conflict (837)

master budget (841)

production budget (843)

responsibility center (835)

sales budget (842)

static budget (838)

zero-based budgeting (838)

Illustrative Problem

Selected information concerning sales and production for Cabot Co. for July 2006 are summarized as follows:

a. Estimated sales:

Product K: 40,000 units at $30.00 per unit

Product L: 20,000 units at $65.00 per unit

b. Estimated inventories, July 1, 2006:

Material A:	4,000 lbs.	Product K: 3,000 units at $17 per unit	$ 51,000
Material B:	3,500 lbs.	Product L: 2,700 units at $35 per unit	94,500
		Total	$145,500

There were no work in process inventories estimated for July 1, 2006.

c. Desired inventories at July 31, 2006:

Material A:	3,000 lbs.	Product K: 2,500 units at $17 per unit	$ 42,500
Material B:	2,500 lbs.	Product L: 2,000 units at $35 per unit	70,000
		Total	$112,500

There were no work in process inventories desired for July 31, 2006.

d. Direct materials used in production:

	Product K	Product L
Material A:	0.7 lb. per unit	3.5 lbs. per unit
Material B:	1.2 lbs. per unit	1.8 lbs. per unit

e. Unit costs for direct materials:

Material A: $4.00 per lb.

Material B: $2.00 per lb.

f. Direct labor requirements:

	Department 1	Department 2
Product K	0.4 hour per unit	0.15 hour per unit
Product L	0.6 hour per unit	0.25 hour per unit

g.

	Department 1	Department 2
Direct labor rate	$12.00 per hour	$16.00 per hour

h. Estimated factory overhead costs for July:

Indirect factory wages	$200,000
Depreciation of plant and equipment	40,000
Power and light	25,000
Indirect materials	34,000
Total	$299,000

Instructions

1. Prepare a sales budget for July.
2. Prepare a production budget for July.
3. Prepare a direct materials purchases budget for July.
4. Prepare a direct labor cost budget for July.
5. Prepare a cost of goods sold budget for July.

Solution

1.

Cabot Co.
Sales Budget
For the Month Ending July 31, 2006

Product	Unit Sales Volume	Unit Selling Price	Total Sales
Product K	40,000	$30.00	$1,200,000
Product L	20,000	65.00	1,300,000
Total revenue from sales . . .			$2,500,000

2.

Cabot Co.
Production Budget
For the Month Ending July 31, 2006

	Units	
	Product K	Product L
Sales	40,000	20,000
Plus desired inventories at July 31, 2006	2,500	2,000
Total	42,500	22,000
Less estimated inventories, July 1, 2006	3,000	2,700
Total production	39,500	19,300

3.

Cabot Co.
Direct Materials Purchases Budget
For the Month Ending July 31, 2006

	Direct Materials		
	Material A	**Material B**	**Total**
Units required for production:			
Product K (39,500 × lbs. per unit)	27,650 lbs.*	47,400 lbs.*	
Product L (19,300 × lbs. per unit)	67,550**	34,740**	
Plus desired units of inventory,			
July 31, 2006	3,000	2,500	
Total	98,200 lbs.	84,640 lbs.	
Less estimated units of inventory,			
July 1, 2006	4,000	3,500	
Total units to be purchased	94,200 lbs.	81,140 lbs.	
Unit price	× $4.00	× $ 2.00	
Total direct materials purchases	$376,800	$162,280	$539,080

*27,650 = 39,500 × 0.7   47,400 = 39,500 × 1.2
**67,550 = 19,300 × 3.5   34,740 = 19,300 × 1.8

4.

Cabot Co.
Direct Labor Cost Budget
For the Month Ending July 31, 2006

	Department 1	Department 2	Total
Hours required for production:			
Product K (39,500 × hours per unit) . . .	15,800*	5,925*	
Product L (19,300 × hours per unit) . . .	11,580**	4,825**	
Total	27,380	10,750	
Hourly rate	× $12.00	× $16.00	
Total direct labor cost	$328,560	$172,000	$500,560

*15,800 = 39,500 × 0.4   5,925 = 39,500 × 0.15
**11,580 = 19,300 × 0.6   4,825 = 19,300 × 0.25

5.

Cabot Co.
Cost of Goods Sold Budget
For the Month Ending July 31, 2006

Finished goods inventory, July 1, 2006		$ 145,500
Direct materials:		
Direct materials inventory, July 1, 2006—(Note A)	$ 23,000	
Direct materials purchases	539,080	
Cost of direct materials available for use	$562,080	
Less direct materials inventory, July 31, 2006—(Note B) . . .	17,000	
Cost of direct materials placed in production	$545,080	
Direct labor	500,560	
Factory overhead.	299,000	
Cost of goods manufactured		1,344,640
Cost of finished goods available for sale		$1,490,140
Less finished goods inventory, July 31, 2006		112,500
Cost of goods sold		$1,377,640

Note A:

Material A	4,000 lbs.	at $4.00 per lb.	$16,000
Material B	3,500 lbs.	at $2.00 per lb.	7,000
Direct materials inventory, July 1, 2006			$23,000

Note B:

Material A	3,000 lbs.	at $4.00 per lb.	$12,000
Material B	2,500 lbs.	at $2.00 per lb.	5,000
Direct materials inventory, July 31, 2006			$17,000

Self-Examination Questions (Answers at End of Chapter)

1. A tight budget may create:
   A. budgetary slack
   B. discouragement
   C. a flexible budget
   D. a "spend it or lose it" mentality

2. The first step of the budget process is:
   A. plan   C. control
   B. direct   D. feedback

3. Static budgets are often used by:
   A. production departments
   B. administrative departments
   C. responsibility centers
   D. capital projects

4. The total estimated sales for the coming year is 250,000 units. The estimated inventory at the be-ginning of the year is 22,500 units, and the desired inventory at the end of the year is 30,000 units. The total production indicated in the production budget is:
   A. 242,500 units   C. 280,000 units
   B. 257,500 units   D. 302,500 units

5. Dixon Company expects $650,000 of credit sales in March and $800,000 of credit sales in April. Dixon historically collects 70% of its sales in the month of sale and 30% in the following month. How much cash does Dixon expect to collect in April?
   A. $800,000   C. $755,000
   B. $560,000   D. $1,015,000

Class Discussion Questions

1. What are the three major objectives of budgeting?
2. What is the manager's role in a responsibility center?
3. Briefly describe the type of human behavior problems that might arise if budget goals are set too tightly.
4. Why should all levels of management and all departments participate in preparing and submitting budget estimates?
5. Give an example of budgetary slack.
6. What behavioral problems are associated with setting a budget too loosely?
7. What behavioral problems are associated with establishing conflicting goals within the budget?
8. When would a company use zero-based budgeting?
9. Under what circumstances would a static budget be appropriate?
10. How do computerized budgeting systems aid firms in the budgeting process?
11. What is the first step in preparing a master budget?
12. Why should the production requirements set forth in the production budget be carefully coordinated with the sales budget?
13. Why should the timing of direct materials purchases be closely coordinated with the production budget?
14. In preparing the budget for the cost of goods sold, what are the three budgets from which data on relevant estimates of quantities and costs are combined with data on estimated inventories?
15. a. Discuss the purpose of the cash budget.
    b. If the cash for the first quarter of the fiscal year indicates excess cash at the end of each of the first two months, how might the excess cash be used?
16. How does a schedule of collections from sales assist in preparing the cash budget?
17. Give an example of how the capital expenditures budget affects other operating budgets.

resources for your success online at **http://warren.swlearning.com**

Remember! If you need additional help, visit South-Western's Web site. See page 28 for a description of the online and printed materials that are available. http://warren.swlearning.com

Warren Reeve Fess

Answer: Heinz

Exercises

EXERCISE 20-1
Personal cash budget
Objectives 2, 5

At the beginning of the 2006 school year, Hakim Davis decided to prepare a cash budget for the months of September, October, November, and December. The budget must plan for enough cash on December 31 to pay the spring semester tuition. The following information relates to the budget:

SPREADSHEET

✓ *December 31 cash balance, $2,690*

Cash balance, September 1 (from a summer job)	$6,000
Purchase season football tickets in September	180
Additional entertainment for each month	250
Pay fall semester tuition on September 3	3,250
Pay rent at the beginning of each month	400
Pay for food each month	320
Pay apartment deposit on September 2 (to be returned December 15)	500
Part-time job earnings each month (net of taxes)	1,000

a. Prepare a cash budget for September, October, November, and December.
b. Are the budgets prepared as static budgets or flexible budgets?
c. ⬛▬▶ What are the budget implications for Hakim Davis?

EXERCISE 20-2
Flexible budget for selling and administrative expenses

Objectives 2, 4

SPREADSHEET

✓ *Total selling and administrative expenses at $130,000 sales, $51,200*

Central Industrial Supply Company uses flexible budgets that are based on the following data:

Sales commissions	5% of sales
Advertising expense	15% of sales
Miscellaneous selling expense	$2,000 plus 3% of sales
Office salaries expense	$10,000 per month
Office supplies expense	2% of sales
Miscellaneous administrative expense	$1,500 per month plus 4% of sales

Prepare a flexible selling and administrative expenses budget for May 2006, for sales volumes of $100,000, $115,000, and $130,000. (Use Exhibit 4 as a model.)

EXERCISE 20-3
Static budget vs. flexible budget

Objectives 2, 4

SPREADSHEET

P.A.S.S.

✓ *b. Excess of actual over budget for March, $28,000*

The production supervisor of the Molding Department for Towers Company agreed to the following monthly static budget for the upcoming year:

Towers Company
Molding Department
Monthly Production Budget

Wages	$648,000
Utilities	108,000
Depreciation	70,000
Total	$826,000

The actual amount spent and the actual units produced in the first three months of 2006 in the Molding Department were as follows:

	Amount Spent	Units Produced
January	$775,000	55,000
February	720,000	50,000
March	665,000	45,000

The Molding Department supervisor has been very pleased with this performance, since actual expenditures have been less than the monthly budget. However, the plant manager believes that the budget should not remain fixed for every month but should "flex" or adjust to the volume of work that is produced in the Molding Department. Additional budget information for the Molding Department is as follows:

Wages per hour	$18.00
Utility cost per direct labor hour	$3.00
Direct labor hours per unit	0.60
Planned unit production	60,000

a. Prepare a flexible budget for the actual units produced for January, February, and March in the Molding Department.
b. ⬛▬▶ Compare the flexible budget with the actual expenditures for the first three months. What does this comparison suggest?

EXERCISE 20-4
Flexible budget for Fabrication Department

Objective 2

REAL WORLD   SPREADSHEET

✓ *Total department cost at 15,000 units, $1,139,000*

Steelcase Corporation is one of the largest manufacturers of office furniture in the United States. In Grand Rapids, Michigan, it produces filing cabinets in two departments: Fabrication and Trim Assembly. Assume the following information for the Fabrication Department:

Steel per filing cabinet	40 pounds
Direct labor per filing cabinet	24 minutes
Supervisor salaries	$125,000 per month
Depreciation	$30,000 per month
Direct labor rate	$14 per hour
Steel cost	$1.50 per pound

Prepare a flexible budget for 15,000, 17,500, and 20,000 filing cabinets for the month of May 2006, similar to Exhibit 4, assuming that inventories are not significant.

EXERCISE 20-5
Sales and production budgets

Objective 4

SPREADSHEET

✓ *b. Model DL total production, 7,410 units*

Harmony Audio Company manufactures two models of speakers, DL and XL. Based on the following production and sales data for September 2007, prepare (a) a sales budget and (b) a production budget.

	DL	XL
Estimated inventory (units), September 1	350	120
Desired inventory (units), September 30	410	100
Expected sales volume (units):		
East Region	4,200	3,000
West Region	3,150	2,200
Unit sales price	$125.00	$180.00

EXERCISE 20-6
Professional fees budget

Objective 4

SPREADSHEET

✓ *Total professional fees, $13,050,500*

Jeffries and Valdez, CPAs, offer three types of services to clients: auditing, tax, and computer consulting. Based on experience and projected growth, the following billable hours have been estimated for the year ending December 31, 2006:

	Billable Hours
Audit Department:	
Staff	32,500
Partners	4,800
Tax Department:	
Staff	28,700
Partners	3,950
Computer Consulting Department:	
Staff	24,600
Partners	5,700

The average billing rate for staff is $110 per hour, and the average billing rate for partners is $250 per hour. Prepare a professional fees budget for Jeffries and Valdez, CPAs, for the year ending December 31, 2006, using the following column headings and showing the estimated professional fees by type of service rendered:

Billable Hours	Hourly Rate	Total Revenue

EXERCISE 20-7
Professional labor cost budget

Objective 4

SPREADSHEET

✓ *Staff total labor cost, $4,290,000*

Based on the data in Exercise 20-6 and assuming that the average compensation per hour for staff is $50 and for partners is $150, prepare a professional labor cost budget for Jeffries and Valdez, CPAs, for the year ending December 31, 2006. Use the following column headings:

Billable Hours Required	
Staff	**Partners**

EXERCISE 20-8
Direct materials purchases budget

Objective 4

SPREADSHEET

✓ *Total cheese purchases, $103,142*

Taste of Italy Frozen Pizza Inc. has determined from its production budget the following estimated production volumes for 12″ and 16″ frozen pizzas for August 2006:

	Units	
	12″ Pizza	**16″ Pizza**
Budgeted production volume	18,200	24,600

There are three direct materials used in producing the two types of pizza. The quantities of direct materials expected to be used for each pizza are as follows:

	12″ Pizza	**16″ Pizza**
Direct materials:		
Dough	1.00 lb. per unit	1.50 lbs. per unit
Tomato	0.50	0.80
Cheese	0.70	1.10

In addition, Taste of Italy has determined the following information about each material:

	Dough	**Tomato**	**Cheese**
Estimated inventory, August 1, 2006	600 lbs.	180 lbs.	480 lbs.
Desired inventory, August 31, 2006	450 lbs.	240 lbs.	350 lbs.
Price per pound	$1.40	$2.20	$2.60

Prepare August's direct materials purchases budget for Taste of Italy Frozen Pizza Inc.

EXERCISE 20-9
Direct materials purchases budget

Objective 4

REAL WORLD   SPREADSHEET

✓ *Concentrate budgeted purchases, $91,040*

Coca-Cola Enterprises is the largest bottler of Coca-Cola® in North America. The company purchases Coke® and Sprite® concentrate from **The Coca-Cola Company**, dilutes and mixes the concentrate with carbonated water, and then fills the blended beverage into cans or plastic 2-liter bottles. Assume that the estimated production for Coke and Sprite 2-liter bottles at the Chattanooga, Tennessee, bottling plant are as follows for the month of September:

Coke	178,000 two-liter bottles
Sprite	142,000 two-liter bottles

In addition, assume that the concentrate costs $80 per pound for both Coke and Sprite and is used at a rate of 0.2 pound per 100 liters of carbonated water in blending Coke and 0.15 pound per 100 liters of carbonated water in blending Sprite. Assume that two-liter bottles cost $0.09 per bottle and carbonated water costs $0.04 per liter.

Prepare a direct materials purchases budget for September 2006, assuming no changes between beginning and ending inventories for all three materials.

EXERCISE 20-10
Direct materials purchases budget

Objective 4

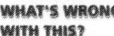

WHAT'S WRONG   SPREADSHEET
WITH THIS?

✓ *Total steel belt purchases, $952,200*

Anticipated sales for Goodman Tire Company were 36,000 passenger car tires and 16,000 truck tires. There were no anticipated beginning finished goods inventories for either product. The planned ending finished goods inventories were 2,500 units for each product. Rubber and steel belts are used in producing passenger car and truck tires according to the following table:

	Passenger Car	**Truck**
Rubber	25 lbs. per unit	60 lbs. per unit
Steel belts	3 lbs. per unit	8 lbs. per unit

The purchase prices of rubber and steel are $2.80 and $3.60 per pound, respectively. The desired ending inventories of rubber and steel belts are 40,000 and 6,000 pounds, respectively. The estimated beginning inventories for rubber and steel belts are 70,000 and 5,000 pounds, respectively.

The following materials purchases budget was prepared for Goodman Tire Company:

Goodman Tire Company
Direct Materials Purchases Budget
For the Year Ending December 31, 2006

	Rubber	Steel Belts	Total
Units required for production:			
Passenger tires	900,000 lbs.	108,000 lbs.	
Truck tires	960,000	128,000	
Total	1,860,000 lbs.	236,000 lbs.	
Unit price	× $2.80	× $3.60	
Total direct materials purchases	$5,208,000	$849,600	$6,057,600

Correct the direct materials purchases budget for Goodman Tire Company.

EXERCISE 20-11
Direct labor cost budget
Objective 4

SPREADSHEET

✔ *Total direct labor cost, Assembly, $136,680*

Ace Racket Company manufactures two types of tennis rackets, the Junior and Ace Master models. The production budget for August for the two rackets is as follows:

	Junior	Ace Master
Production budget	5,300 units	19,600 units

Both rackets are produced in two departments, Forming and Assembly. The direct labor hours required for each racket are estimated as follows:

	Forming Department	Assembly Department
Junior	0.20 hour per unit	0.30 hour per unit
Ace Master	0.30 hour per unit	0.50 hour per unit

The direct labor rate for each department is as follows:

Forming Department	$19.00 per hour
Assembly Department	$12.00 per hour

Prepare the direct labor cost budget for August 2006.

EXERCISE 20-12
Direct labor budget—service business
Objective 4

SPREADSHEET

✔ *Average weekday total, $1,848*

City Suites Hotels, Inc., operates a downtown hotel property that has 200 rooms. On average, 80% of City Suites' rooms are occupied on weekdays, and 40% are occupied during the weekend. The manager has asked you to develop a direct labor budget for the housekeeping and restaurant staff. You have determined that the housekeeping staff requires 45 minutes to clean each occupied room. The housekeeping staff is paid $9 per hour. The restaurant has four full-time staff (8-hour day) on duty, regardless of occupancy. However, for every 20 occupied rooms, an additional person is brought in for the 8-hour day. The restaurant staff is paid $8 per hour.

To aid your budget preparations, determine the estimated housekeeping and restaurant direct labor cost for an average weekday and weekend day.

EXERCISE 20-13
Production and direct labor cost budgets
Objective 4

REAL WORLD   SPREADSHEET

Levi Strauss & Co. manufactures jeans and slacks under a variety of brand names, such as Dockers® and 501 Jeans®. Slacks and jeans are assembled by a variety of different sewing operations. Assume that the sales budget for Dockers and 501 Jeans shows estimated sales of 21,600 and 43,400 pairs, respectively, for March 2006. The finished goods inventory is assumed as follows:

	Dockers	501 Jeans
March 1 estimated inventory	300	140
March 31 desired inventory	250	100

✓a. Total production of
501 Jeans, 43,360

Assume the following direct labor data per 10 pairs of Dockers and 501 Jeans for four different sewing operations:

| | Direct Labor per 10 Pairs | |
	Dockers	501 Jeans
Inseam	15 minutes	12 minutes
Outerseam	20	14
Pockets	5	8
Zipper	6	6
Total	46 minutes	40 minutes

a. Prepare a production budget for March.
b. Prepare the March direct labor cost budget for the four sewing operations, assuming an $11 wage per hour for the inseam and outerseam sewing operations and a $13 wage per hour for the pocket and zipper sewing operations.

EXERCISE 20-14
Factory overhead cost budget
Objective 4

SPREADSHEET

✓*Total variable factory overhead costs, $229,000*

Dutch Shoe Company budgeted the following costs for anticipated production for January 2006:

Advertising expenses	$260,000	Production supervisor wages	$115,000
Manufacturing supplies	12,000	Production control salaries	32,000
Power and light	45,000	Executive officer salaries	210,000
Sales commissions	280,000	Materials management salaries	25,000
Factory insurance	22,000	Factory depreciation	19,000

Prepare a factory overhead cost budget, separating variable and fixed costs. Assume that factory insurance and depreciation are the only fixed costs.

EXERCISE 20-15
Cost of goods sold budget
Objective 4

SPREADSHEET

✓*Cost of goods sold, $1,143,100*

Union Chemical Company uses oil to produce two types of plastic products, P1 and P2. Union purchased 25,000 barrels of oil in April for $30 per barrel. Direct labor used in the chemical process was $140,000 for April. Factory overhead totaled $250,000 during April. The inventories on April 1 were estimated to be:

Oil	$14,200
P1	8,300
P2	9,100
Work in process	12,300

The desired inventories on April 30 were:

Oil	$12,100
P1	8,500
P2	9,900
Work in process	10,300

Use the preceding information to prepare a cost of goods sold budget for April.

EXERCISE 20-16
Cost of goods sold budget
Objective 4

SPREADSHEET

✓*Cost of goods sold, $379,030*

The controller of Heritage Ceramics, Inc. wishes to prepare a cost of goods sold budget for June. The controller assembled the following information for constructing the cost of goods sold budget:

Direct materials:	Enamel	Paint	Porcelain	Total
Total direct materials purchases budgeted for June	$31,350	$4,970	$104,240	$140,560
Estimated inventory, June 1, 2006	1,250	2,400	4,540	8,190
Desired inventory, June 30, 2006	2,000	2,150	5,000	9,150

Direct labor cost:	Kiln Department	Decorating Department	Total
Total direct labor cost budgeted for June	$36,500	$123,600	$160,100

Finished goods inventories:	Dish	Bowl	Figurine	Total
Estimated inventory, June 1, 2006	$4,180	$3,270	$2,670	$10,120
Desired inventory, June 30, 2006	3,250	3,940	3,150	10,340

Work in process inventories:	
Estimated inventory, June 1, 2006	$2,900
Desired inventory, June 30, 2006	1,350

Budgeted factory overhead costs for June:	
Indirect factory wages	$54,700
Depreciation of plant and equipment	14,600
Power and light	5,300
Indirect materials	3,400
Total	$78,000

Use the preceding information to prepare a cost of goods sold budget for June 2006.

EXERCISE 20-17
Schedule of cash collections of accounts receivable
Objective 5

SPREADSHEET

✓ *Total cash collected in May, $437,600*

Lion Heart Company was organized on March 1, 2006. Projected sales for each of the first three months of operations are as follows:

March	$400,000
April	480,000
May	425,000

The company expects to sell 10% of its merchandise for cash. Of sales on account, 60% are expected to be collected in the month of the sale, 30% in the month following the sale, and the remainder in the second month following the sale.

Prepare a schedule indicating cash collections from sales for March, April, and May.

EXERCISE 20-18
Schedule of cash collections of accounts receivable
Objective 5

SPREADSHEET

✓ *Total cash collected in January, $254,000*

Star Office Supplies Inc. has "cash and carry" customers and account customers. Star estimates that 40% of monthly sales are to cash customers, while the remaining sales are to credit customers. Of the credit customers, 20% pay their accounts in the month of sale, while the remaining 80% pay their accounts in the month following the month of sale. Projected sales for the first three months of 2006 are:

January	$200,000
February	240,000
March	225,000

The Accounts Receivable balance on December 31, 2005, was $150,000.

Prepare a schedule of cash collections from sales for January, February, and March.

EXERCISE 20-19
Schedule of cash payments
Objective 5

SPREADSHEET

✓ *Total cash payments in August, $105,625*

Distance Learning Systems Inc. was organized on May 31, 2006. Projected selling and administrative expenses for each of the first three months of operations are as follows:

June	$104,200
July	116,500
August	122,000

Depreciation, insurance, and property taxes represent $15,000 of the estimated monthly expenses. The annual insurance premium was paid on May 31, and property taxes for the year will be paid in December. Three-fourths of the remainder of the expenses are expected to be paid in the month in which they are incurred, with the balance to be paid in the following month.

Prepare a schedule indicating cash payments for selling and administrative expenses for June, July, and August.

EXERCISE 20-20
Schedule of cash payments

Objective 5

SPREADSHEET

✔ *Total cash payments in December, $121,330*

The Zone Fitness Center is planning its cash payments for operations for the fourth quarter (October–December), 2007. The Accrued Expenses Payable balance on October 1 is $21,400. The budgeted expenses for the next three months are as follows:

	October	November	December
Salaries	$ 57,400	$ 65,300	$ 71,500
Utilities	5,000	5,400	6,100
Other operating expenses	46,900	51,300	62,300
Total	$109,300	$122,000	$139,900

Other operating expenses include $12,400 of monthly depreciation expense and $800 of monthly insurance expense that was prepaid for the year on March 1 of the current year. Of the remaining expenses, 70% are paid in the month in which they are incurred, with the remainder paid in the following month. The Accrued Expenses Payable balance on October 1 relates to the expenses incurred in September.

Prepare a schedule of cash payments for operations for October, November, and December.

EXERCISE 20-21
Capital expenditures budget

Objective 5

SPREADSHEET

✔ *Total capital expenditures in 2005, $6,000,000*

On January 1, 2005, the controller of O'Brian Manufacturing Company is planning capital expenditures for the years 2005–2008. The following interviews helped the controller collect the necessary information for the capital expenditures budget.

Director of Facilities: A construction contract was signed in late 2004 for the construction of a new factory building at a contract cost of $10,000,000. The construction is scheduled to begin in 2005 and be completed in 2006.

Vice-President of Manufacturing: Once the new factory building is finished, we plan to purchase $1.7 million in equipment in late 2006. I expect that an additional $400,000 will be needed early in the following year (2007) to test and install the equipment before we can begin production. If sales continue to grow, I expect we'll need to invest another million in equipment in 2008.

Vice-President of Marketing: We have really been growing lately. I wouldn't be surprised if we need to expand the size of our new factory building in 2008 by at least 45%. Fortunately, we expect inflation to have minimal impact on construction costs over the next four years.

Director of Information Systems: We need to upgrade our information systems to wireless network technology. It doesn't make sense to do this until after the new factory building is completed and producing product. During 2007, once the factory is up and running, we should equip the whole facility with wireless technology. I think it would cost us $1,800,000 today to install the technology. However, prices have been dropping by 20% per year, so it should be less expensive at a later date.

President: I am excited about our long-term prospects. My only short-term concern is financing the $6,000,000 of construction costs on the portion of the new factory building scheduled to be completed in 2005.

Use the interview information above to prepare a capital expenditures budget for O'Brian Manufacturing Company for the years 2005–2008.

Problems Series A

PROBLEM 20-1A
Forecast sales volume and sales budget

Objective 4

Protect-Ex Security Devices Inc. prepared the following sales budget for the current year:

SPREADSHEET

✓ *3. Total revenue from sales, $29,893,800*

Protect-Ex Security Devices Inc.
Sales Budget
For the Year Ending December 31, 2006

Product and Area	Unit Sales Volume	Unit Selling Price	Total Sales
Home Alert System:			
United States	25,800	$240	$ 6,192,000
Europe	6,900	240	1,656,000
Asia	4,500	240	1,080,000
Total	37,200		$ 8,928,000
Business Alert System:			
United States	12,300	$850	$10,455,000
Europe	5,300	850	4,505,000
Asia	3,900	850	3,315,000
Total	21,500		$18,275,000
Total revenue from sales			$27,203,000

At the end of December 2006, the following unit sales data were reported for the year:

	Unit Sales	
	Home Alert System	**Business Alert System**
United States	26,832	12,546
Europe	6,693	5,353
Asia	4,680	3,705

For the year ending December 31, 2007, unit sales are expected to follow the patterns established during the year ending December 31, 2006. The unit selling price for the Home Alert System is expected to increase to $280, and the unit selling price for the Business Alert System is expected to be increased to $870, effective January 1, 2007.

Instructions

1. Compute the increase or decrease of actual unit sales for the year ended December 31, 2006, over budget. Place your answers in a columnar table with the following format:

	Unit Sales, Year Ended 2006		Increase (Decrease) Actual Over Budget	
	Budget	**Actual Sales**	**Amount**	**Percent**
Home Alert System:				
United States				
Europe				
Asia				
Business Alert System:				
United States				
Europe				
Asia				

2. Assuming that the trend of sales indicated in (1) is to continue in 2007, compute the unit sales volume to be used for preparing the sales budget for the year ending December 31, 2007. Place your answers in a columnar table similar to that in (1) above but with the following column heads. Round budgeted units to the nearest unit.

2006 Actual Units	Percentage Increase (Decrease)	2007 Budgeted Units (rounded)

3. Prepare a sales budget for the year ending December 31, 2007.

PROBLEM 20-2A
Sales, production, direct materials, and direct labor budgets

Objective 4

SPREADSHEET

✓ 3. Total direct materials purchases, $4,972,211

The budget director of Royal Furniture Company requests estimates of sales, production, and other operating data from the various administrative units every month. Selected information concerning sales and production for July 2006 is summarized as follows:

a. Estimated sales of King and Prince chairs for July by sales territory:

Northern Domestic:
King . . . .   5,700 units at $600 per unit
Prince . . . .   6,900 units at $450 per unit
Southern Domestic:
King . . . .   3,600 units at $620 per unit
Prince . . . .   4,000 units at $460 per unit
International:
King . . . .   1,100 units at $700 per unit
Prince . . . .   1,300 units at $500 per unit

b. Estimated inventories at July 1:

Direct materials: Finished products:
Fabric . . . . 4,300 sq. yds.   King . . . . 840 units
Wood . . . . 6,300 lineal ft.   Prince . . . . 280 units
Filler . . . . 2,500 cu. ft.
Springs . . . . 7,500 units

c. Desired inventories at July 31:

Direct materials: Finished products:
Fabric . . . . 4,500 sq. yds.   King . . . . 700 units
Wood . . . . 5,700 lineal ft.   Prince . . . . 300 units
Filler . . . . 2,700 cu. ft.
Springs . . . . 7,000 units

d. Direct materials used in production:

In manufacture of King: In manufacture of Prince:
Fabric . . . 4 sq. yds. per unit of product   Fabric . . . 3.2 sq. yds. per unit of product
Wood . . . 30 lineal ft. per unit of product   Wood . . . 20 lineal ft. per unit of product
Filler . . . . 3.5 cu. ft. per unit of product   Filler . . . . 3.0 cu. ft. per unit of product
Springs . . 12 units per unit of product   Springs . . 10 units per unit of product

e. Anticipated purchase price for direct materials:

Fabric . . . . . . $9.00 per square yard   Filler . . . . $4.50 per cubic foot
Wood . . . . . . 6.00 per lineal foot   Springs . . . . . . 2.50 per unit

f. Direct labor requirements:

King:
Framing Department . . . . 2.0 hours at $13 per hour
Cutting Department . . . . 0.5 hour at $10 per hour
Upholstery Department . . . . 2.5 hours at $12 per hour
Prince:
Framing Department . . . . 1.5 hours at $13 per hour
Cutting Department . . . . 0.4 hour at $10 per hour
Upholstery Department . . . . 1.8 hours at $12 per hour

Instructions
1. Prepare a sales budget for July.
2. Prepare a production budget for July.
3. Prepare a direct materials purchases budget for July.
4. Prepare a direct labor cost budget for July.

PROBLEM 20-3A
Budgeted income statement and supporting budgets

Objective 4

SPREADSHEET

✓ *4. Total direct labor cost in Assembly Dept., $56,460*

The budget director of Sport Gear Inc., with the assistance of the controller, treasurer, production manager, and sales manager, has gathered the following data for use in developing the budgeted income statement for August 2006:

a. Estimated sales for August:

Batting helmet	3,400 units at $60 per unit
Football helmet	7,200 units at $125 per unit

b. Estimated inventories at August 1:

Direct materials:		Finished products:	
Plastic	950 lbs.	Batting helmet	255 units at $21 per unit
Foam lining	470 lbs.	Football helmet	390 units at $40 per unit

c. Desired inventories at August 31:

Direct materials:		Finished products:	
Plastic	1,140 lbs.	Batting helmet	230 units at $21 per unit
Foam lining	450 lbs.	Football helmet	350 units at $40 per unit

d. Direct materials used in production:

In manufacture of batting helmet:		In manufacture of football helmet:	
Plastic	1.40 lbs. per unit of product	Plastic	3.20 lbs. per unit of product
Foam lining ..	0.60 lb. per unit of product	Foam lining ..	1.20 lbs. per unit of product

e. Anticipated cost of purchases and beginning and ending inventory of direct materials:

Plastic	$5.00 per lb.
Foam lining	$2.00 per lb.

f. Direct labor requirements:

Batting helmet:	
Molding Department	0.16 hour at $12 per hour
Assembly Department	0.40 hour at $10 per hour
Football helmet:	
Molding Department	0.25 hour at $12 per hour
Assembly Department	0.60 hour at $10 per hour

g. Estimated factory overhead costs for August:

Indirect factory wages	$95,000	Power and light	$12,000
Depreciation of plant and equipment	25,000	Insurance and property tax	9,700

h. Estimated operating expenses for August:

Sales salaries expense	$255,600
Advertising expense	125,300
Office salaries expense	82,300
Depreciation expense—office equipment	6,200
Telephone expense—selling	4,700
Telephone expense—administrative	900
Travel expense—selling	42,100
Office supplies expense	4,000
Miscellaneous administrative expense	5,000

i. Estimated other income and expense for August:

Interest revenue	$12,500
Interest expense	15,700

j. Estimated tax rate: 35%

Instructions

1. Prepare a sales budget for August.
2. Prepare a production budget for August.
3. Prepare a direct materials purchases budget for August.
4. Prepare a direct labor cost budget for August.
5. Prepare a factory overhead cost budget for August.
6. Prepare a cost of goods sold budget for August. Work in process at the beginning of August is estimated to be $12,300, and work in process at the end of August is desired to be $13,200.
7. Prepare a selling and administrative expenses budget for August.
8. Prepare a budgeted income statement for August.

PROBLEM 20-4A
Cash budget
Objective 5

SPREADSHEET

✓ *1. June deficiency,*
$38,700

The controller of Digital Storage, Inc. instructs you to prepare a monthly cash budget for the next three months. You are presented with the following budget information:

	April	May	June
Sales	$90,000	$140,000	$150,000
Manufacturing costs	42,000 →22,000	48,000 →28,000	50,000 → 30,000
Selling and administrative expenses	35,000	36,000	40,000
Capital expenditures	—	—	60,000

The company expects to sell about 10% of its merchandise for cash. Of sales on account, 70% are expected to be collected in full in the month following the sale and the remainder the following month. Depreciation, insurance, and property tax expense represent $20,000 of the estimated monthly manufacturing costs. The annual insurance premium is paid in July, and the annual property taxes are paid in November. Of the remainder of the manufacturing costs, 80% are expected to be paid in the month in which they are incurred and the balance in the following month.

Current assets as of April 1 include cash of $40,000, marketable securities of $65,000, and accounts receivable of $109,600 ($85,000 from March sales and $24,600 from February sales). Current liabilities as of April 1 include a $50,000, 12%, 90-day note payable due June 20 and $25,000 of accounts payable incurred in March for manufacturing costs. All selling and administrative expenses are paid in cash in the period they are incurred. It is expected that $3,000 in dividends will be received in April. An estimated income tax payment of $32,000 will be made in May. Digital Storage's regular quarterly dividend of $10,000 is expected to be declared in May and paid in June. Management desires to maintain a minimum cash balance of $35,000.

Instructions

1. Prepare a monthly cash budget and supporting schedules for April, May, and June.
2. On the basis of the cash budget prepared in (1), what recommendation should be made to the controller?

PROBLEM 20-5A
Budgeted income statement and balance sheet
Objectives 4, 5

SPREADSHEET

✓ *1. Net income, $531,750*

As a preliminary to requesting budget estimates of sales, costs, and expenses for the fiscal year beginning January 1, 2007, the following tentative trial balance as of December 31, 2006, is prepared by the Accounting Department of Thomas Marcus Apparel Co.:

Cash	$ 122,500	
Accounts Receivable	246,700	
Finished Goods	157,800	
Work in Process	37,800	
Materials	57,800	
Prepaid Expenses	4,500	
Plant and Equipment	620,000	
Accumulated Depreciation—Plant and Equipment		$ 267,000
Accounts Payable		184,500
Common Stock, $15 par		450,000
Retained Earnings		345,600
	$1,247,100	$1,247,100

Factory output and sales for 2007 are expected to total 25,000 units of product, which are to be sold at $115 per unit. The quantities and costs of the inventories at December 31, 2007, are expected to remain unchanged from the balances at the beginning of the year.

Budget estimates of manufacturing costs and operating expenses for the year are summarized as follows:

	Estimated Costs and Expenses	
	Fixed (Total for Year)	Variable (Per Unit Sold)
Cost of goods manufactured and sold:		
Direct materials	—	$28.00
Direct labor	—	9.50
Factory overhead:		
Depreciation of plant and equipment	$ 45,000	—
Other factory overhead	15,000	4.80
Selling expenses:		
Sales salaries and commissions	121,000	12.00
Advertising	105,800	—
Miscellaneous selling expense	11,500	2.25
Administrative expenses:		
Office and officers salaries	84,500	7.50
Supplies	4,700	1.50
Miscellaneous administrative expense	2,000	1.20

Balances of accounts receivable, prepaid expenses, and accounts payable at the end of the year are not expected to differ significantly from the beginning balances. Federal income tax of $285,000 on 2007 taxable income will be paid during 2007. Regular quarterly cash dividends of $1.75 a share are expected to be declared and paid in March, June, September, and December. It is anticipated that fixed assets will be purchased for $180,000 cash in May.

Instructions

1. Prepare a budgeted income statement for 2007.
2. Prepare a budgeted balance sheet as of December 31, 2007, with supporting calculations.

Problems Series B

PROBLEM 20-1B
Forecast sales volume and sales budget

Objective 4

SPREADSHEET

✓ 3. *Total revenue from sales, $2,021,549*

Classic Art Frame Company prepared the following sales budget for the current year:

Classic Art Frame Company
Sales Budget
For the Year Ending December 31, 2006

Product and Area	Unit Sales Volume	Unit Selling Price	Total Sales
8″ × 10″ Frame:			
East	28,000	$12.00	$ 336,000
Central	21,000	12.00	252,000
West	34,500	12.00	414,000
Total	83,500		$1,002,000
12″ × 16″ Frame:			
East	14,000	$20.00	$ 280,000
Central	12,500	20.00	250,000
West	16,000	20.00	320,000
Total	42,500		$ 850,000
Total revenue from sales			$1,852,000

At the end of December 2006, the following unit sales data were reported for the year:

	Unit Sales	
	8″ × 10″ Frame	12″ × 16″ Frame
East	28,980	14,350
Central	21,840	12,750
West	33,051	15,136

For the year ending December 31, 2007, unit sales are expected to follow the patterns established during the year ending December 31, 2006. The unit selling price for the 8″ × 10″ frame is expected to change to $13, and the unit selling price for the 12″ × 16″ frame is expected to change to $22, effective January 1, 2007.

Instructions

1. Compute the increase or decrease of actual unit sales for the year ended December 31, 2006, over budget. Place your answers in a columnar table with the following format:

	Unit Sales, Year Ended 2006		Increase (Decrease) Actual Over Budget	
	Budget	Actual Sales	Amount	Percent
8″ × 10″ Frame:				
East				
Central				
West				
12″ × 16″ Frame:				
East				
Central				
West				

2. Assuming that the trend of sales indicated in (1) is to continue in 2007, compute the unit sales volume to be used for preparing the sales budget for the year ending December 31, 2007. Place your answers in a columnar table similar to that in (1) above but with the following column heads. Round budgeted units to the nearest unit.

2006 Actual Units	Percentage Increase (Decrease)	2007 Budgeted Units (rounded)

3. Prepare a sales budget for the year ending December 31, 2007.

PROBLEM 20-2B
Sales, production, direct materials, and direct labor budgets

Objective 4

SPREADSHEET

✓ *3. Total direct materials purchases, $6,498,540*

The budget director of New England Outdoor Grill Company requests estimates of sales, production, and other operating data from the various administrative units every month. Selected information concerning sales and production for May 2006 is summarized as follows:

a. Estimated sales for May by sales territory:

Maine:
Backyard Chef ...... 4,200 units at $900 per unit
Master Chef .... 1,800 units at $1,500 per unit
Vermont:
Backyard Chef ...... 3,600 units at $850 per unit
Master Chef .... 1,500 units at $1,400 per unit
New Hampshire:
Backyard Chef ...... 4,000 units at $950 per unit
Master Chef .... 1,900 units at $1,600 per unit

b. Estimated inventories at May 1:

Direct materials:
Grates . . . . 1,000 units
Stainless steel . . . . 2,500 lbs.
Burner subassemblies . . . . . . 600 units
Shelves . . . . 400 units

Finished products:
Backyard Chef . . . . 1,500 units
Master Chef . . . . 400 units

c. Desired inventories at May 31:

Direct materials:
Grates . . . . 800 units
Stainless steel . . . . 1,900 lbs.
Burner subassemblies . . . . . . 800 units
Shelves . . . . 480 units

Finished products:
Backyard Chef . . . . 1,200 units
Master Chef . . . . 500 units

d. Direct materials used in production:

In manufacture of Backyard Chef:
Grates . . . . 2 units per unit of product
Stainless steel . . . . 25 lbs. per unit of product
Burner subassemblies . . . . 1 unit per unit of product
Shelves . . . . 2 units per unit of product
In manufacture of Master Chef:
Grates . . . . 6 units per unit of product
Stainless steel . . . . 65 lbs. per unit of product
Burner subassemblies . . . . 2 units per unit of product
Shelves . . . . 3 units per unit of product

e. Anticipated purchase price for direct materials:

Grates . . . . $16 per unit
Stainless steel . . . . $4 per lb.

Burner subassemblies . . . . . . $125 per unit
Shelves . . . . $8 per unit

f. Direct labor requirements:

Backyard Chef:
Stamping Department . . . . . . 0.50 hour at $14 per hour
Forming Department . . . . 0.75 hour at $12 per hour
Assembly Department . . . . 1.50 hours at $10 per hour
Master Chef:
Stamping Department . . . . . . 0.60 hour at $14 per hour
Forming Department . . . . 1.50 hours at $12 per hour
Assembly Department . . . . 2.50 hours at $10 per hour

Instructions
1. Prepare a sales budget for May.
2. Prepare a production budget for May.
3. Prepare a direct materials purchases budget for May.
4. Prepare a direct labor cost budget for May.

PROBLEM 20-3B
Budgeted income statement and supporting budgets

Objective 4

SPREADSHEET

✓ *4. Total direct labor cost in Slitting Dept., $288,810*

The budget director of Precious Memories Film Company, with the assistance of the controller, treasurer, production manager, and sales manager, has gathered the following data for use in developing the budgeted income statement for October 2006:

a. Estimated sales for October:

Instant Image . . . . 32,500 units at $75 per unit
Pro Image . . . . 26,400 units at $110 per unit

b. Estimated inventories at October 1:

Direct materials:
Celluloid . . . . 2,700 lbs.
Silver . . . . 3,000 ozs.

Finished products:
Instant Image . . . . . . 4,800 units at $35 per unit
Pro Image . . . . 2,400 units at $55 per unit

c. Desired inventories at October 31:

Direct materials:		Finished products:	
Celluloid	3,400 lbs.	Instant Image	5,400 units at $35 per unit
Silver	2,900 ozs.	Pro Image	1,900 units at $55 per unit

d. Direct materials used in production:

In manufacture of Instant Image:		In manufacture of Pro Image:	
Celluloid . . .	0.40 lb. per unit of product	Celluloid . . .	0.60 lb. per unit of product
Silver	2.50 ozs. per unit of product	Silver	4.00 ozs. per unit of product

e. Anticipated cost of purchases and beginning and ending inventory of direct materials:

Celluloid . . . . $1.80 per lb.   Silver . . . . $7.00 per oz.

f. Direct labor requirements:

Instant Image:
    Coating Department . . . . . .   0.20 hour at $15 per hour
    Slitting Department . . . .   0.25 hour at $18 per hour
Pro Image:
    Coating Department . . . . . .   0.40 hour at $15 per hour
    Slitting Department . . . .   0.30 hour at $18 per hour

g. Estimated factory overhead costs for October:

Indirect factory wages	$600,000	Power and light	$46,000
Depreciation of plant and equipment	145,000	Insurance and property tax	18,400

h. Estimated operating expenses for October:

Sales salaries expense	$685,000
Advertising expense	146,500
Office salaries expense	224,800
Depreciation expense—office equipment	5,300
Telephone expense—selling	5,000
Telephone expense—administrative	1,900
Travel expense—selling	38,500
Office supplies expense	3,000
Miscellaneous administrative expense	4,200

i. Estimated other income and expense for October:

Interest revenue	$18,900
Interest expense	12,300

j. Estimated tax rate: 40%

Instructions
1. Prepare a sales budget for October.
2. Prepare a production budget for October.
3. Prepare a direct materials purchases budget for October.
4. Prepare a direct labor cost budget for October.
5. Prepare a factory overhead cost budget for October.
6. Prepare a cost of goods sold budget for October. Work in process at the beginning of October is estimated to be $28,500, and work in process at the end of October is estimated to be $34,200.
7. Prepare a selling and administrative expenses budget for October.
8. Prepare a budgeted income statement for October.

PROBLEM 20-4B
Cash budget
Objective 5

SPREADSHEET

✓ 1. October deficiency,
$48,500

The controller of Frozen Delight Ice Cream Co. instructs you to prepare a monthly cash budget for the next three months. You are presented with the following budget information:

	August	September	October
Sales	$610,000	$700,000	$825,000
Manufacturing costs	320,000	350,000	400,000
Selling and administrative expenses	180,000	210,000	225,000
Capital expenditures			140,000

The company expects to sell about 10% of its merchandise for cash. Of sales on account, 60% are expected to be collected in full in the month following the sale and the remainder the following month. Depreciation, insurance, and property tax expense represent $30,000 of the estimated monthly manufacturing costs. The annual insurance premium is paid in July, and the annual property taxes are paid in November. Of the remainder of the manufacturing costs, 80% are expected to be paid in the month in which they are incurred and the balance in the following month.

Current assets as of August 1 include cash of $55,000, marketable securities of $85,000, and accounts receivable of $680,000 ($500,000 from July sales and $180,000 from June sales). Current liabilities as of August 1 include a $100,000, 10%, 90-day note payable due October 20 and $60,000 of accounts payable incurred in July for manufacturing costs. All selling and administrative expenses are paid in cash in the period they are incurred. It is expected that $1,500 in dividends will be received in August. An estimated income tax payment of $42,000 will be made in September. Frozen Delight's regular quarterly dividend of $15,000 is expected to be declared in September and paid in October. Management desires to maintain a minimum cash balance of $45,000.

Instructions

1. Prepare a monthly cash budget and supporting schedules for August, September, and October.
2. ▬▬▶ On the basis of the cash budget prepared in (1), what recommendation should be made to the controller?

PROBLEM 20-5B
Budgeted income statement and balance sheet
Objectives 4, 5

SPREADSHEET

✓ 1. Net income, $118,600

As a preliminary to requesting budget estimates of sales, costs, and expenses for the fiscal year beginning January 1, 2007, the following tentative trial balance as of December 31, 2006, is prepared by the Accounting Department of Signature Pen Co.:

Cash	$ 85,000	
Accounts Receivable	104,700	
Finished Goods	74,800	
Work in Process	25,600	
Materials	46,700	
Prepaid Expenses	2,400	
Plant and Equipment	340,000	
Accumulated Depreciation—Plant and Equipment		$135,200
Accounts Payable		59,000
Common Stock, $10 par		200,000
Retained Earnings		285,000
	$679,200	$679,200

Factory output and sales for 2007 are expected to total 200,000 units of product, which are to be sold at $4.50 per unit. The quantities and costs of the inventories at December 31, 2007, are expected to remain unchanged from the balances at the beginning of the year.

Budget estimates of manufacturing costs and operating expenses for the year are summarized as follows:

	Estimated Costs and Expenses	
	Fixed (Total for Year)	Variable (Per Unit Sold)
Cost of goods manufactured and sold:		
Direct materials	—	$0.90
Direct labor	—	0.35
Factory overhead:		
Depreciation of plant and equipment	$42,000	—
Other factory overhead	8,000	0.25
Selling expenses:		
Sales salaries and commissions	50,000	0.40
Advertising	60,000	—
Miscellaneous selling expense	4,300	0.12
Administrative expenses:		
Office and officers salaries	65,100	0.15
Supplies	4,000	0.05
Miscellaneous administrative expense	3,000	0.08

Balances of accounts receivable, prepaid expenses, and accounts payable at the end of the year are not expected to differ significantly from the beginning balances. Federal income tax of $85,000 on 2007 taxable income will be paid during 2007. Regular quarterly cash dividends of $0.60 a share are expected to be declared and paid in March, June, September, and December. It is anticipated that fixed assets will be purchased for $50,000 cash in May.

Instructions
1. Prepare a budgeted income statement for 2007.
2. Prepare a budgeted balance sheet as of December 31, 2007, with supporting calculations.

Special Activities

ACTIVITY 20-1
Ethics and professional conduct in business

The director of marketing for Eastern Computer Co., Callie Keller, had the following discussion with the company controller, Isaiah Johnson, on July 26 of the current year:

Callie: Isaiah, it looks like I'm going to spend much less than indicated on my July budget.

Isaiah: I'm glad to hear it.

Callie: Well, I'm not so sure it's good news. I'm concerned that the president will see that I'm under budget and reduce my budget in the future. The only reason that I look good is that we've delayed an advertising campaign. Once the campaign hits in September, I'm sure my actual expenditures will go up. You see, we are also having our sales convention in September. Having the advertising campaign and the convention at the same time is going to kill my September numbers.

Isaiah: I don't think that's anything to worry about. We all expect some variation in actual spending month to month. What's really important is staying within the budgeted targets for the year. Does that look as if it's going to be a problem?

Callie: I don't think so, but just the same, I'd like to be on the safe side.

Isaiah: What do you mean?

Callie: Well, this is what I'd like to do. I want to pay the convention-related costs in advance this month. I'll pay the hotel for room and convention space and purchase the airline tickets in advance. In this way, I can charge all these expenditures to July's budget. This would cause my actual expenses to come close to budget for July. Moreover, when the big advertising campaign hits in

September, I won't have to worry about expenditures for the convention on my September budget as well. The convention costs will already be paid. Thus, my September expenses should be pretty close to budget.

Isaiah: I can't tell you when to make your convention purchases, but I'm not too sure that it should be expensed on July's budget.

Callie: What's the problem? It looks like "no harm, no foul" to me. I can't see that there's anything wrong with this—it's just smart management.

▭➤ How should Isaiah Johnson respond to Callie Keller's request to expense the advanced payments for convention-related costs against July's budget?

ACTIVITY 20-2
Evaluating budgeting systems

REAL WORLD

Children's Hospital of the King's Daughter in Norfolk, Virginia, introduced a new budgeting method that allowed the hospital's annual plan to be updated for changes in operating plans. For example, if the budget was based on 400 patient-days and the actual count rose to 450 patient-days, the variable costs of staffing, lab work, and medication costs could be adjusted to reflect this change. The budget manager stated, "I work with hospital directors to turn data into meaningful information and effect change before the month ends."

a. What budgeting methods are being used under the new approach?

b. ▭➤ Why are these methods superior to the former approaches?

ACTIVITY 20-3
Service company static decision making

A bank manager of MetroBank Financial Inc. uses the managerial accounting system to track the costs of operating the various departments within the bank. The departments include Cash Management, Trust Commercial Loans, Mortgage Loans, Operations, Credit Card, and Branch Services. The budget and actual results for the Operations Department are as follows:

Resources	Budget	Actual
Salaries	$150,000	$150,000
Benefits	30,000	30,000
Supplies	45,000	42,000
Travel	20,000	30,000
Training	25,000	30,000
Overtime	25,000	20,000
Total	$295,000	$302,000
Excess of actual over budget	$ 7,000	

a. ▭➤ What information is provided by the budget? Specifically, what questions can the bank manager ask of the Operations Department manager?

b. ▭➤ What information does the budget fail to provide? Specifically, could the budget information be presented differently to provide even more insight for the bank manager?

ACTIVITY 20-4
Objectives of the master budget

REAL WORLD

Dominos Inc. operates pizza delivery and carryout restaurants. The annual report describes its business as follows:

We offer a focused menu of high-quality, value priced pizza with three types of crust (Hand-Tossed, Thin Crust, and Deep Dish), along with buffalo wings, bread sticks, cheesy bread, CinnaStix®, and Coca-Cola® products. Our hand-tossed pizza is made from fresh dough produced in our regional distribution centers. We prepare every pizza using real cheese, pizza sauce made from fresh tomatoes, and a choice of high-quality meat and vegetable toppings in generous portions. Our focused menu and use of premium ingredients enable us to consistently and efficiently produce the highest-quality pizza.

Over the 41 years since our founding, we have developed a simple, cost-efficient model. We offer a limited menu, our stores are designed for delivery and carry-out, and we do not generally offer dine-in service. As a result, our stores require relatively small, lower-rent locations and limited capital expenditures.

> How would a master budget support planning, directing, and control for Dominos?

ACTIVITY 20-5
Integrity and evaluating budgeting systems

The city of Glendale has an annual budget cycle that begins on July 1 and ends on June 30. At the beginning of each budget year, an annual budget is established for each department. The annual budget is divided by 12 months to provide a constant monthly static budget. On June 30, all unspent budgeted monies for the budget year from the various city departments must be "returned" to the General Fund. Thus, if department heads fail to use their budget by year-end, they will lose it. A budget analyst prepared a chart of the difference between the monthly actual and budgeted amounts for the recent fiscal year. The chart was as follows:

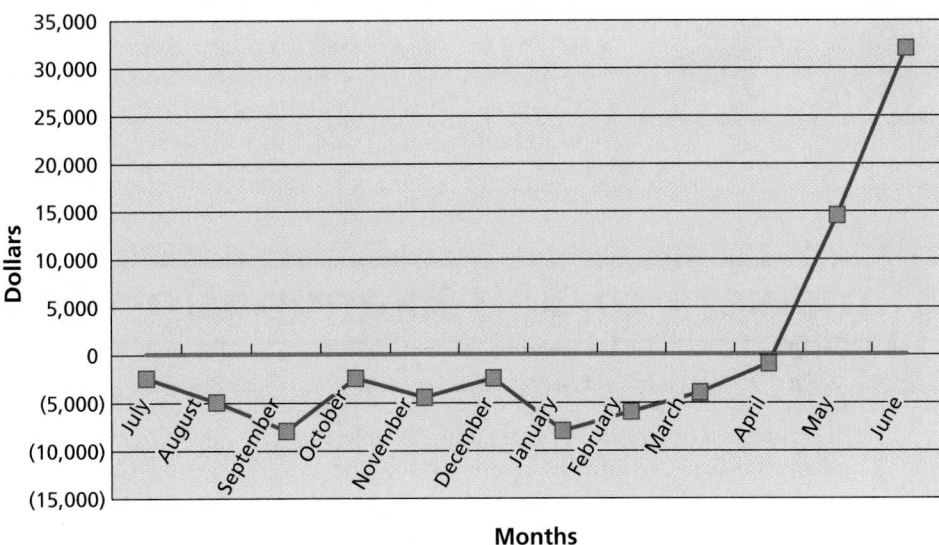

a. > Interpret the chart.
b. > Suggest an improvement in the budget system.

ACTIVITY 20-6
Objectives of budgeting

At the beginning of the year, Ted Frey decided to prepare a cash budget for the year, based upon anticipated cash receipts and payments. The estimates in the budget represent a "best guess." The budget is as follows:

Expected annual cash receipts:		
Salary from part-time job	$10,000	
Salary from summer job	4,000	
Total receipts		$14,000
Expected annual cash payments:		
Tuition	$ 4,500	
Books	400	
Rent	3,500	
Food	2,500	
Utilities	800	
Entertainment	4,000	
Total payments		15,700
Net change in cash		$ (1,700)

1. > What does this budget suggest? In what ways is this information useful to Ted?
2. a. > Some items in the budget are more certain than are others. Which items are the most certain? Which items are the most uncertain? What are the implications of these different levels of certainty to Ted's planning?

b. ━━▶ Some payment items are more controllable than others. Assuming that Ted plans to go to school, classify the items as controllable, partially controllable, or not controllable. What are the implications of controllable items to planning?

3. ━━▶ What actions could Ted take in order to avoid having the anticipated shortfall of $1,700 at the end of the year?

4. ━━▶ What does this budget fail to consider, and what are the implications of these omissions to Ted's planning?

ACTIVITY 20-7
Budget for a state government

GROUP ACTIVITY

INTERNET

In a group, find the home page of the state in which you presently live. The state's home page, if it has one, will be in the form: **http://www.state.stateabbreviation.us/**. At the home page site, search for annual budget information. If you are unable to find the budget of your state, then go to the state of Ohio's budget page at **http://www.state.oh.us/obm/** to complete this activity.

1. What are the budgeted sources of revenue and their percentage breakdown?
2. What are the major categories of budgeted expenditures (or appropriations) and their percentage breakdown?
3. Is the projected budget in balance?

Answers to Self-Examination Questions

1. **B** Individuals can be discouraged with budgets that appear too tight or unobtainable. Flexible budgeting (answer C) provides a series of budgets for varying rates of activity and thereby builds into the budgeting system the effect of fluctuations in the level of activity. Budgetary slack (answer A) comes from a loose budget, not a tight budget. A "spend it or lose it" mentality (answer D) is often associated with loose budgets.

2. **A** The first step of the budget process is to develop a plan. Once plans are established, management may direct actions (answer B). The results of actions can be controlled (answer C) by comparing them to the plan. This feedback (answer D) can be used by management to change plans or redirect actions.

3. **B** Administrative departments (answer B), such as Purchasing or Human Resources, will often use static budgeting. Production departments (answer A)

frequently use flexible budgets. Responsibility centers (answer C) can use either static or flexible budgeting. Capital expenditure budgets are used to plan capital projects (answer D).

4. **B** The total production indicated in the production budget is 257,500 units (answer B), which is computed as follows:

Sales	250,000 units
Plus desired ending inventory	30,000 units
Total	280,000 units
Less estimated beginning inventory	22,500 units
Total production	257,500 units

5. **C** Dixon expects to collect 70% of April sales ($560,000) plus 30% of the March sales ($195,000) in April, for a total of $755,000 (answer C). Answer A is 100% of April sales. Answer B is 70% of April sales. Answer D adds 70% of both March and April sales.

21

PERFORMANCE EVALUATION USING VARIANCES FROM STANDARD COSTS

objectives

After studying this chapter, you should be able to:

1 Describe the types of standards and how they are established for businesses.

2 Explain and illustrate how standards are used in budgeting.

3 Calculate and interpret direct materials price and quantity variances.

4 Calculate and interpret direct labor rate and time variances.

5 Calculate and interpret factory overhead controllable and volume variances.

6 Journalize the entries for recording standards in the accounts and prepare an income statement that includes variances from standard.

7 Explain how standards may be used for nonmanufacturing expenses.

8 Explain and provide examples of nonfinancial performance measures.

When you play a sport, you are evaluated with respect to how well you perform compared to a standard or to a competitor. In bowling, for example, your score is compared to a perfect score of 300 or to the score of your competitors. In this class, you are compared to performance standards. These standards are often described in terms of letter grades, which provide a measure of how well you achieved the class objectives. On your job, you are also evaluated according to performance standards.

Just as your class performance is evaluated, managers are evaluated according to goals and plans. Performance is often measured as the difference between actual results and planned results. In this chapter, we will discuss and illustrate the ways in which business performance is evaluated.

Standards

objective 1

Describe the types of standards and how they are established for businesses.

What are standards? **Standards** are performance goals. Service, merchandising, and manufacturing businesses may all use standards to evaluate and control operations. For example, long-haul drivers for **United Parcel Service** are expected to drive a standard distance per day. Salespersons for **The Limited** are expected to meet sales standards.

Manufacturers normally use standard costs for each of the three manufacturing costs: direct materials, direct labor, and factory overhead. Accounting systems that use standards for these costs are called *standard cost systems*. These systems enable management to determine how much a product should cost (*standard cost*), how much it does cost (actual cost), and the causes of any difference (*cost variances*). When actual costs are compared with standard costs, only the exceptions or variances are reported for cost control. This reporting by the *principle of exceptions* allows management to focus on correcting the variances. Thus, using standard costs assists management in controlling costs and in motivating employees to focus on costs.

Standard cost systems are commonly used with job order and process systems. Automated manufacturing operations may also integrate standard cost data with the computerized system that directs operations. Such systems detect and report variances automatically and make adjustments to operations in progress.

Setting Standards

Setting standards is both an art and a science. The standard-setting process normally requires the joint efforts of accountants, engineers, and other management personnel. The accountant plays an essential role by expressing in dollars and cents the results of judgments and studies. Engineers contribute to the standard-setting process by identifying the materials, labor, and machine requirements needed to produce the product. For example, engineers determine the direct materials requirements by studying the materials specifications for products and estimating normal spoilage in production. Time and motion studies may be used to determine the length of time required for each manufacturing operation. Engineering studies may also be used to determine standards for factory overhead, such as the amount of power needed to operate machinery.

Setting standards often begins with analyzing past operations. However, standards are not just an extension of past costs, and caution must be used in relying on past cost data. For example, inefficiencies may be contained within past costs. In addition, changes in technology, machinery, or production methods may make past costs irrelevant for future operations.

Types of Standards

Standards imply an acceptable level of production efficiency. One of the major objectives in setting standards is to motivate workers to achieve efficient operations.

Like the budgets we discussed earlier, tight, unrealistic standards may have a negative impact on performance. This is because workers may become frustrated with an inability to meet the standards and may give up trying to do their best. Such standards can be achieved only under perfect operating conditions, such as no idle time, no machine breakdowns, and no materials spoilage. These standards are called *ideal standards* or **theoretical standards**. Although ideal standards are not widely used, a few firms use ideal standards to motivate changes and improvement. Such an approach is termed "Kaizen costing." Kaizen is a Japanese term meaning "continuous improvement."

Standards that are too loose might not motivate employees to perform at their best. This is because the standard level of performance can be reached too easily. As a result, operating performance may be lower than what could be achieved.

Most companies use *currently attainable standards* (sometimes called **normal standards**). These standards can be attained with reasonable effort. Such standards allow for normal production difficulties and mistakes, such as materials spoilage and machine breakdowns. When reasonable standards are used, employees become more focused on cost and are more likely to put forth their best efforts.

An example from the game of golf illustrates the distinction between ideal and normal standards. In golf, "par" is an *ideal* standard for most players. Each player's USGA (United States Golf Association) handicap is the player's *normal* standard. The motivation of average players is to beat their handicaps because they may view beating par as unrealistic. Normal and ideal standards are illustrated as follows:

Mohawk Forest Products had a normal standard cost for a premium grade paper of $2,900 per ton, while the ideal cost was $1,342 per ton. The company used the ideal standard to motivate cost improvement. The resulting improvements allowed the company to reduce the normal standard cost to $1,738 per ton.

Currently
attainable
(personal best)

Ideal
(world record)

Reviewing and Revising Standards

Standard costs should be continuously reviewed and should be revised when they no longer reflect operating conditions. Inaccurate standards may distort management decision making and may weaken management's ability to plan and control operations.

Standards should not be revised, however, just because they differ from actual costs. They should be revised only when they no longer reflect the operating conditions that they were intended to measure. For example, the direct labor standard would not be revised simply because workers were unable to meet properly determined standards. On the other hand, standards should be revised when prices, product designs, labor rates, or manufacturing methods change. For example, when aluminum beverage cans were redesigned to taper slightly at the top of the can, manufacturers reduced the standard amount of aluminum per can because less aluminum was required for the top piece of the tapered can.

Support and Criticism of Standards

Standards are used to value inventory and to plan and control costs. Companies are also using standards to assess performance at lower levels of the organization, for shorter accounting periods, and for an increasing number of costs.

Using standards for performance evaluation has been criticized by some. For example, critics assert that standards limit improvement of operations by discouraging improvement beyond the standard. Regardless of this criticism, standards are widely used. Most managers strongly support standard cost systems and regard standards as critical for running large businesses efficiently.

INTEGRITY IN BUSINESS

STANDARDS IN ETHICAL CONDUCT

Harris Interactive annually ranks American corporations in terms of reputation. The ranking is based upon how respondents rate corporations on 20 attributes in six major areas. The six areas are emotional appeal, products and services, financial performance, workplace environment, social responsibility, and vision and leadership. What are the five highest and lowest ranked companies in its 2001 survey? The five highest (best) ranked companies were **Johnson & Johnson**, **Harley-Davidson**, **Coca-Cola**, **United Parcel Service (UPS)**, and **General Mills**. The five lowest (worst) companies were **Enron**, **Global Crossing**, **WorldCom**, **Andersen Worldwide**, and **Adelphia**. Not surprisingly, every one of these latter companies was involved in corporate scandal that ended in bankruptcy.

Source: Ronald Alsop, "Scandal-Filled Year Takes Toll on Companies' Good Names," *The Wall Street Journal*, February 12, 2003.

Budgetary Performance Evaluation

objective **2**

Explain and illustrate how standards are used in budgeting.

As we discussed in the previous chapter, the master budget assists a company in planning, directing, and controlling performance. In the remainder of this chapter, we will discuss using the master budget for control purposes. The control function, or budgetary performance evaluation, compares the actual performance against the budget.

We illustrate budget performance evaluation using Western Rider Inc., a manufacturer of blue jeans. Western Rider Inc. uses standard manufacturing costs in its budgets. The standards for direct materials, direct labor, and factory overhead are separated into two components: (1) a price standard and (2) a quantity standard. Multiplying these two elements together yields the standard cost per unit for a given manufacturing cost category, as shown for style XL jeans in Exhibit 1.

•Exhibit 1 Standard Cost for XL Jeans

Manufacturing Costs	Standard Price	×	Standard Quantity per Pair	=	Standard Cost per Pair of XL Jeans
Direct materials	$5.00 per square yard		1.5 square yards		$ 7.50
Direct labor	$9.00 per hour		0.80 hour per pair		7.20
Factory overhead	$6.00 per hour		0.80 hour per pair		4.80
Total standard cost per pair					$19.50

The standard price and quantity are separated because the means of controlling them are normally different. For example, the direct materials price per square yard is controlled by the Purchasing Department, and the direct materials quantity per pair is controlled by the Production Department.

As we illustrated in the previous chapter, the budgeted costs at planned volumes are included in the master budget at the beginning of the period. The standard amounts budgeted for materials purchases, direct labor, and factory overhead are determined by multiplying the standard costs per unit by the *planned* level of production. At the end of the month, the standard costs per unit are multiplied by the *actual* production and compared to the actual costs. To illustrate, assume that Western Rider produced and sold 5,000 pairs of XL jeans. It incurred direct materials costs of $40,150, direct labor costs of $38,500, and factory overhead costs of $22,400. The **budget performance report** shown in Exhibit 2 summarizes the actual costs, the standard amounts for the actual level of production achieved, and the differences between the two amounts. These differences are called **cost variances**. A *favorable* cost variance occurs when the actual cost is less than the standard cost (at actual volumes). An *unfavorable* variance occurs when the actual cost exceeds the standard cost (at actual volumes).

•Exhibit 2 Budget Performance Report

Western Rider Inc.
Budget Performance Report
For the Month Ended June 30, 2006

Manufacturing Costs	Actual Costs	Standard Cost at Actual Volume (5,000 pairs of XL Jeans)*	Cost Variance— (Favorable) Unfavorable
Direct materials	$ 40,150	$37,500	$2,650
Direct labor	38,500	36,000	2,500
Factory overhead	22,400	24,000	(1,600)
Total manufacturing costs	$101,050	$97,500	$3,550

*5,000 pairs × $7.50 per pair = $37,500
 5,000 pairs × $7.20 per pair = $36,000
 5,000 pairs × $4.80 per pair = $24,000

Actual cost < Standard cost at actual volumes: Favorable cost variance

Actual cost > Standard cost at actual volumes: Unfavorable cost variance

Based on the information in the budget performance report, management can investigate major differences and take corrective action. In Exhibit 2, for example, the direct materials cost variance is an unfavorable $2,650. There are two possible explanations for this variance: (1) the amount of blue denim used per pair of blue jeans was different than expected, and/or (2) the purchase price of blue denim was different than expected. In the next sections, we will illustrate how to separate the price and quantity variances for direct materials, the rate and time variances for direct labor, and the controllable and volume variances for factory overhead.

The relationship of these variances to the total manufacturing cost variance is shown at the top of the following page.

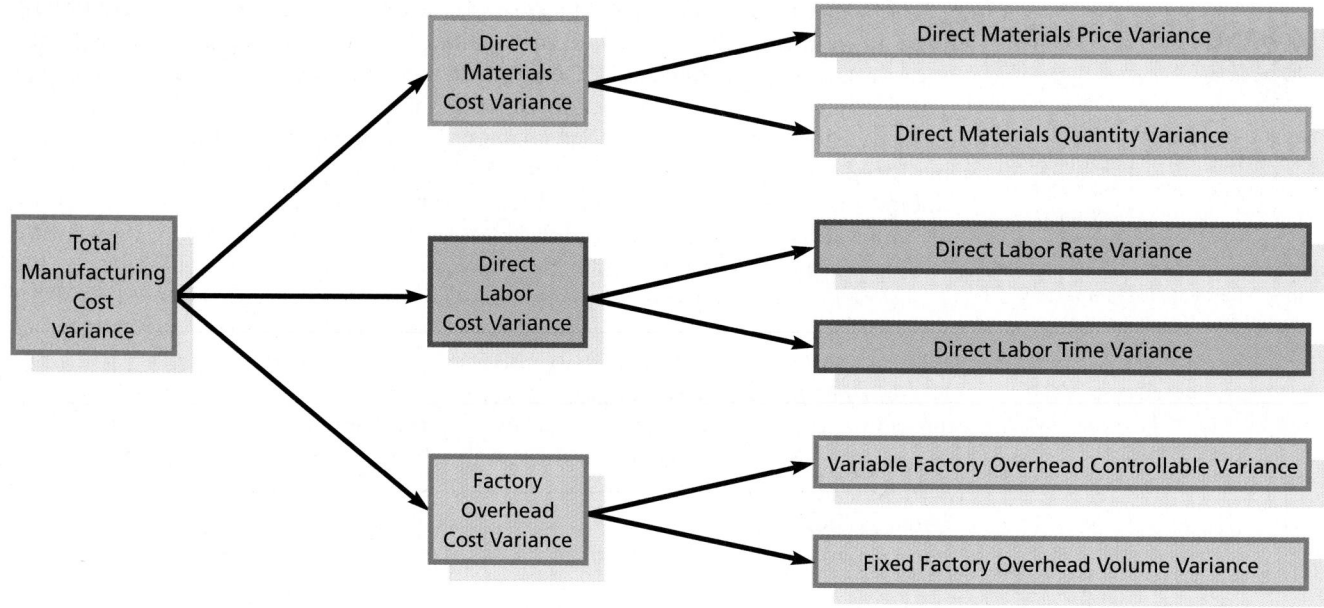

Direct Materials Variances

objective 3

Calculate and interpret direct materials price and quantity variances.

What caused Western Rider Inc.'s unfavorable materials variance of $2,650? Recall that the direct materials standards from Exhibit 1 are as follows:

> Price standard: $5.00 per square yard
> Quantity standard: 1.5 square yards per pair of XL jeans

To determine the number of standard square yards of denim budgeted, multiply the actual production for June 2006 (5,000 pairs) by the quantity standard (1.5 square yards per pair). Then multiply the standard square yards by the standard price per square yard ($5.00) to determine the *standard* budgeted cost at the actual volume. The calculation is shown as follows:

Standard square yards per pair of jeans	1.5 sq. yards
Actual units produced	× 5,000 pairs of jeans
Standard square yards of denim budgeted for actual production	7,500 sq. yards
Standard price per square yard	× $5.00
Standard direct materials cost at actual production (same as Exhibit 2)	$37,500

This calculation assumes that there is no change in the beginning and ending materials inventories. Thus, the amount of materials budgeted for production equals the amount purchased.

Assume that the *actual* total cost for denim used during June 2006 was as follows:

Actual quantity of denim used in production	7,300 sq. yards
Actual price per square yard	× $5.50
Total actual direct materials cost (same as Exhibit 2)	$40,150

Most restaurants use standards to control the amount of food served to customers. For example, **Darden Restaurants Inc.**, the operator of the **Red Lobster** chain, establishes standards for the number of shrimp, scallops, or clams on a seafood plate. In the same way, **Keystone Foods, Inc.**, a major food supplier to **McDonald's**, uses standards to carefully control the size and weight of chicken nuggets.

A product requires 6 standard pounds per unit. The standard price is $4.50 per pound. If 3,000 units required 18,500 pounds, which were purchased at $4.35 per pound, what is the direct materials (1) price variance and (2) quantity variance?

- -

(1) $2,775 favorable [($4.35 − $4.50) × 18,500 lbs.]; (2) $2,250 unfavorable [(18,500 lbs. − 18,000 lbs.) × $4.50]

The total unfavorable cost variance of $2,650 ($40,150 − $37,500) results from an excess price per square yard of $0.50 and using 200 fewer square yards of denim. These two reasons can be reported as two separate variances, as shown in the next sections.

Direct Materials Price Variance

The ***direct materials price variance*** is the difference between the actual price per unit ($5.50) and the standard price per unit ($5.00), multiplied by the actual quantity used (7,300 square yards). If the actual price per unit exceeds the standard price per unit, the variance is unfavorable, as shown for Western Rider Inc. If the actual price per unit is less than the standard price per unit, the variance is favorable. The calculation for Western Rider Inc. is as follows:

Price variance:

Actual price per unit	$5.50 per square yard
Standard price per unit	5.00 per square yard
Price variance—unfavorable	$0.50 per square yard × actual qty., 7,300 sq. yds. = $3,650 U

Direct Materials Quantity Variance

The ***direct materials quantity variance*** is the difference between the actual quantity used (7,300 square yards) and the standard quantity at actual production (7,500 square yards), multiplied by the standard price per unit ($5.00). If the actual quantity of materials used exceeds the standard quantity budgeted, the variance is unfavorable. If the actual quantity of materials used is less than the standard quantity, the variance is favorable, as shown for Western Rider Inc.:

Quantity variance:

Actual quantity	7,300 square yards
Standard quantity at actual production	7,500
Quantity variance—favorable	(200) square yards × standard price, $5.00 = ($1,000) F

Direct Materials Variance Relationships

The direct materials variances can be illustrated by making the three calculations shown in Exhibit 3.

•Exhibit 3   **Direct Materials Variance Relationships**

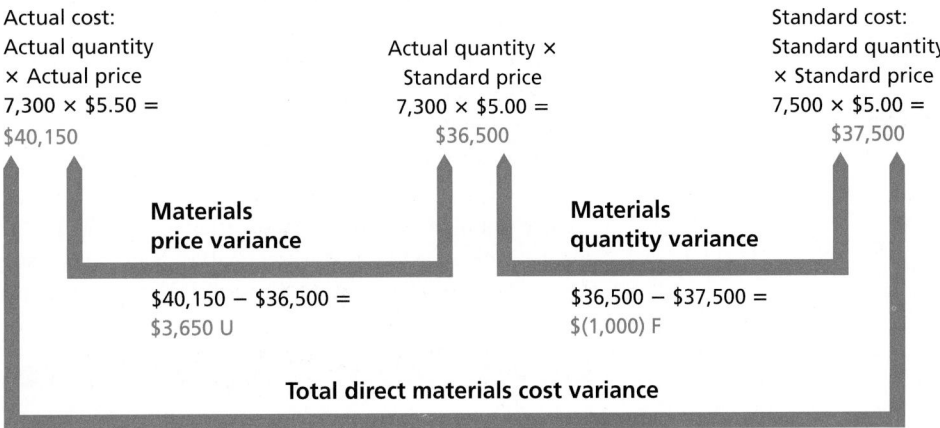

Reporting Direct Materials Variances

The direct materials quantity variance should be reported to the proper operating management level for corrective action. For example, an unfavorable quantity variance might have been caused by malfunctioning equipment that has not been properly maintained or operated. However, unfavorable materials quantity variances are not always caused by operating departments. For example, the excess materials usage may be caused by purchasing inferior raw materials. In this case, the Purchasing Department should be held responsible for the variance.

The materials price variance should normally be reported to the Purchasing Department, which may or may not be able to control this variance. If materials of the same quality could have been purchased from another supplier at the standard price, the variance was controllable. On the other hand, if the variance resulted from a marketwide price increase, the variance may not be controllable.

Direct Labor Variances

objective 4

Calculate and interpret direct labor rate and time variances.

REAL WORLD

The **Internal Revenue Service** publishes a time standard for completing a tax return. The average 1040EZ return is expected to require 3 hours and 46 minutes to prepare.

REAL WORLD

Hospitals are now developing cost standards for various categories of procedures. Variances from standard cost can be accumulated by procedure, by patient, or by doctor. Doctor variances occur when a doctor consistently prescribes treatment that varies from the standard. Doctors who have consistent unfavorable variances may be asked to review their treatment decisions.

Western Rider Inc.'s direct labor cost variance can also be separated into two parts. Recall that the direct labor standards from Exhibit 1 are as follows:

> Rate standard: $9.00 per hour
> Time standard: 0.80 hour per pair of XL jeans

The actual production (5,000 pairs) is multiplied by the time standard (0.80 hour per pair) to determine the number of standard direct labor hours budgeted. The standard direct labor hours are then multiplied by the standard rate per hour ($9.00) to determine the *standard* direct labor cost at actual volumes. These calculations are shown below.

Standard direct labor hours per pair of XL jeans	0.80 direct labor hours
Actual units produced	× 5,000 pairs of jeans
Standard direct labor hours budgeted for actual production	4,000 direct labor hours
Standard rate per direct labor hour	× $9.00
Standard direct labor cost at actual production (same as Exhibit 2)	$36,000

Assume that the *actual* total cost for direct labor during June 2006 was as follows:

Actual direct labor hours used in production	3,850 direct labor hours
Actual rate per direct labor hour	× $10.00
Total actual direct labor cost (same as Exhibit 2)	$ 38,500

The total unfavorable cost variance $2,500 ($38,500 − $36,000) results from an excess rate of $1.00 per direct labor hour and using 150 fewer direct labor hours. These two reasons can be reported as two separate variances, as we discuss next.

Direct Labor Rate Variance

The **direct labor rate variance** is the difference between the actual rate per hour ($10.00) and the standard rate per hour ($9.00), multiplied by the actual hours worked (3,850 hours). If the actual rate per hour is less than the standard rate per hour, the variance is favorable. If the actual rate per hour exceeds the standard rate per hour, the variance is unfavorable, as shown below for Western Rider Inc.

Rate variance:

Actual rate	$10.00 per hour
Standard rate	9.00
Rate variance—unfavorable	$ 1.00 per hour × actual time, 3,850 hours = $3,850 U

Direct Labor Time Variance

The *direct labor time variance* is the difference between the actual hours worked (3,850 hours) and the standard hours at actual production (4,000 hours), multiplied by the standard rate per hour ($9.00). If the actual hours worked exceed the standard hours, the variance is unfavorable. If the actual hours worked are less than the standard hours, the variance is favorable, as shown below for Western Rider Inc.

Time variance:

Actual hours	3,850 direct labor hours
Standard hours at actual production	4,000
Time variance—favorable	(150) direct labor hours × standard rate, $9.00 = ($1,350) F

Direct Labor Variance Relationships

The direct labor variances can be illustrated by making the three calculations shown in Exhibit 4.

•Exhibit 4   Direct Labor Variance Relationships

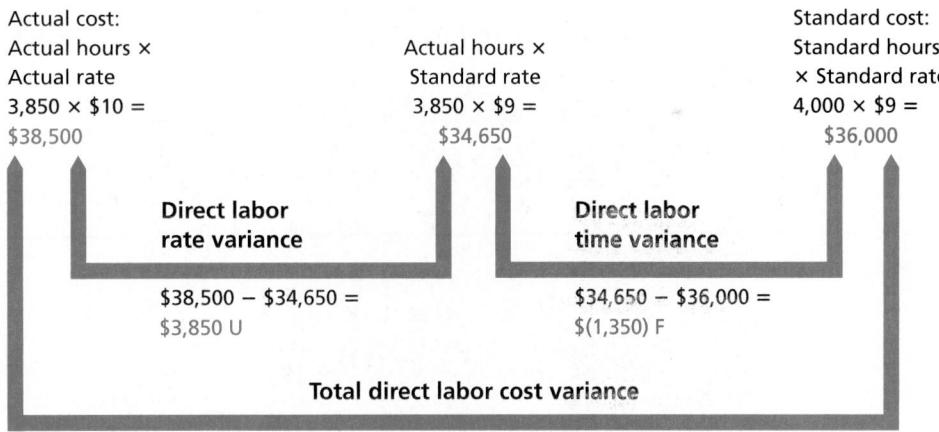

A product requires 2.5 standard hours per unit at a standard hourly rate of $12 per hour. If 800 units required 1,920 hours at an hourly rate of $12.30 per hour, what is the direct labor (1) rate variance and (2) time variance?

- -

(1) $576 unfavorable [($12.30 − $12.00) × 1,920 hours]; (2) $960 favorable [(1,920 hrs. − 2,000 hrs.) × $12.00]

REAL WORLD

In highly automated industries, such as chemical, metal, food, and paper processing, direct labor variances are rarely used. This is because factory employees run and maintain equipment, and thus the cost of their labor is part of factory overhead.

Reporting Direct Labor Variances

Controlling direct labor cost is normally the responsibility of the production supervisors. To aid them, reports analyzing the cause of any direct labor variance may be prepared. Differences between standard direct labor hours and actual direct labor hours can be investigated. For example, a time variance may be incurred because of the shortage of skilled workers. Such variances may be uncontrollable unless they are related to high turnover rates among employees, in which case the cause of the high turnover should be investigated.

Likewise, differences between the rates paid for direct labor and the standard rates can be investigated. For example, unfavorable rate variances may be caused by the improper scheduling and use of workers. In such cases, skilled, highly paid workers may be used in jobs that are normally performed by unskilled, lower-paid workers. In this case, the unfavorable rate variance should be reported for corrective action to the managers who schedule work assignments.

Factory Overhead Variances

objective | 5

Calculate and interpret factory overhead controllable and volume variances.

Factory overhead costs are more difficult to manage than are direct labor and materials costs. This is because the relationship between production volume and indirect costs is not easy to determine. For example, when production is increased, the direct materials will increase. But what about the Engineering Department overhead? The relationship between production volume and cost is less clear for the Engineering Department. Companies normally respond to this difficulty by separating factory overhead into variable and fixed costs. For example, manufacturing supplies are considered variable to production volume, whereas straight-line plant depreciation is considered fixed. In the following sections, we discuss the approaches used to budget and control factory overhead by separating overhead into fixed and variable components.

The Factory Overhead Flexible Budget

A flexible budget may be used to determine the impact of changing production on fixed and variable factory overhead costs. The standard overhead rate is determined by dividing the budgeted factory overhead costs by the standard amount of productive activity, such as direct labor hours. Exhibit 5 is a flexible factory overhead budget for Western Rider Inc.

•**Exhibit 5** **Factory Overhead Cost Budget Indicating Standard Factory Overhead Rate**

Western Rider Inc.
Factory Overhead Cost Budget
For the Month Ending June 30, 2006

Percent of normal capacity	80%	90%	100%	110%
Units produced	5,000	5,625	6,250	6,875
Direct labor hours (0.80 hour per unit)	4,000	4,500	5,000	5,500
Budgeted factory overhead:				
Variable costs:				
Indirect factory wages	$ 8,000	$ 9,000	$10,000	$11,000
Power and light	4,000	4,500	5,000	5,500
Indirect materials	2,400	2,700	3,000	3,300
Total variable cost	$14,400	$16,200	$18,000	$19,800
Fixed costs:				
Supervisory salaries	$ 5,500	$ 5,500	$ 5,500	$ 5,500
Depreciation of plant and equipment	4,500	4,500	4,500	4,500
Insurance and property taxes	2,000	2,000	2,000	2,000
Total fixed cost	$12,000	$12,000	$12,000	$12,000
Total factory overhead cost	$26,400	$28,200	$30,000	$31,800

Factory overhead rate per direct labor hour, $30,000 ÷ 5,000 hours = $6.00

In Exhibit 5, the standard factory overhead cost rate is $6.00. It is determined by dividing the total budgeted cost of 100% of normal capacity by the standard hours required at 100% of normal capacity, or $30,000 ÷ 5,000 hours = $6.00 per hour. This rate can be subdivided into $3.60 per hour for variable factory overhead ($18,000 ÷ 5,000 hours) and $2.40 per hour for fixed factory overhead ($12,000 ÷ 5,000 hours).

Variances from standard for factory overhead cost result from:

1. Actual variable factory overhead cost greater or less than budgeted variable factory overhead for actual production.
2. Actual production at a level above or below 100% of normal capacity.

The first factor results in the controllable variance for variable overhead costs. The second factor results in a volume variance for fixed overhead costs. We will discuss each of these variances next.

I was created in 1937 as a spin-off from one of the world's leading makers of weaving machinery. I unveiled my first small car in 1947 and 12 years later, in Brazil, I opened the first of many production plants in other countries. Today I'm the planet's third-largest automaker, cranking out more than 5.8 million vehicles annually—about one every six seconds. My brands are known for their high quality. Vehicles account for 90 percent of my revenues but I also dabble in forklifts, telecommunications, pre-fab housing, and leisure boats. Who am I? (Go to page 901 for answer.)

Variable Factory Overhead Controllable Variance

The variable factory overhead **controllable variance** is the difference between the actual variable overhead incurred and the budgeted variable overhead for actual production. The controllable variance measures the *efficiency* of using variable overhead resources. Thus, if the actual variable overhead is less than the budgeted variable overhead, the variance is favorable. If the actual variable overhead exceeds the budgeted variable overhead, the variance is unfavorable.

To illustrate, recall that Western Rider Inc. produced 5,000 pairs of XL jeans in June. Each pair requires 0.80 standard labor hour for production. As a result, Western Rider Inc. had 4,000 standard hours at actual production (5,000 jeans × 0.80 hour). This represents 80% of normal productive capacity (4,000 hours ÷ 5,000 hours). The standard variable overhead at 4,000 hours worked, according to the budget in Exhibit 5, was $14,400 (4,000 direct labor hours × $3.60). The following actual factory overhead costs were incurred in June:

Actual costs:	
Variable factory overhead	$10,400
Fixed factory overhead	12,000
Total actual factory overhead	$22,400

The controllable variance can be calculated as follows:

Controllable variance:	
Actual variable factory overhead	$10,400
Budgeted variable factory overhead for actual amount produced (4,000 hrs. × $3.60)	14,400
Variance—favorable	$ (4,000) F

The variable factory overhead controllable variance indicates management's ability to keep the factory overhead costs within the budget limits. Since variable factory overhead costs are normally controllable at the department level, responsibility for controlling this variance usually rests with department supervisors.

Fixed Factory Overhead Volume Variance

Using currently attainable standards, Western Rider Inc. set its budgeted normal capacity at 5,000 direct labor hours. This is the amount of expected capacity that management believes will be used under normal business conditions. You should note that this amount may be much less than the total available capacity if management believes demand will be low.

U.S. airlines use a variety of non-financial measures, such as on-time performance, lost baggage, and customer complaints. These nonfinancial measures are used to balance customer satisfaction with cost reduction. Many airlines have admitted going too far in cutting costs. For example, **Northwest Airlines** increased the frequency of steam-cleaning its planes' lavatories from every 14 days to every 9 days. **America West** upgraded food and installed in-flight phones. **Delta Air Lines** added baggage handlers and gate agents to reduce waiting time during arrivals and departures.

variances. Unfortunately, the fast work resulted in poor quality that, in turn, created difficulty in the assembly operation. The company decided to use both a labor time standard *and* a quality standard in order to encourage employees to consider both the speed and quality of their work.

In the preceding example, nonfinancial performance measures brought additional perspectives, such as quality of work, to evaluating performance. Some additional examples of nonfinancial performance measures are as follows:

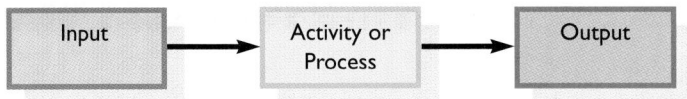

Nonfinancial Performance Measures

Inventory turnover
On-time delivery
Elapsed time between a customer order and product delivery
Customer preference rankings compared to competitors
Response time to a service call
Time to develop new products
Employee satisfaction
Number of customer complaints

Nonfinancial measures can be linked to either the inputs or outputs of an activity or process. A ***process*** is a sequence of activities linked together for performing a particular task. For example, the procurement process consists of the "create purchase order" and "select vendor" activities that are performed in procuring materials. The relationship between a process or activity and its inputs and outputs is shown as follows:

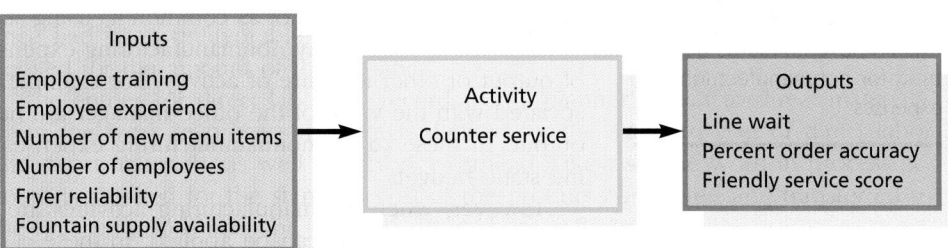

To illustrate nonfinancial measures for a single activity, consider the counter service activity of a fast food restaurant. The following input/output relationship could be identified:

Inputs	Activity	Outputs
Employee training	Counter service	Line wait
Employee experience		Percent order accuracy
Number of new menu items		Friendly service score
Number of employees		
Fryer reliability		
Fountain supply availability		

The outputs of the counter service activity include the customer line wait, order accuracy, and service experience. The inputs that impact these outputs include the number of employees, level of employee experience and training, reliability of the french fryer, menu complexity, fountain drink supply, and the like. Also, note that the inputs for one activity could be the outputs of another. For example, fryer reliability is an input to the counter service activity, but is an output of the french frying activity. Moving back, fryer maintenance would be an input to the french frying activity. Thus, a chain of inputs and outputs can be developed between a set of connected activities or processes. The fast food restaurant can develop a set of linked nonfinancial performance measures across the chain of inputs and outputs. The output measures tell management how the activity is performing, such as keeping the line wait to a minimum. The input measures are the *levers* that impact the activity's performance. Thus, if the fast food restaurant line wait is too long, then the input measures might indicate a need for more training, more employees, or better fryer reliability.

Solution

1.

Direct Materials Cost Variance

Quantity variance:		
Actual quantity	1,600 pounds	
Standard quantity	1,500	
Variance—unfavorable	100 pounds × standard price, $35	$ 3,500
Price variance:		
Actual price	$32.00 per pound	
Standard price	35.00	
Variance—favorable	$ (3.00) per pound × actual quantity, 1,600	(4,800)
Total direct materials cost variance—favorable		$(1,300)

2.

Direct Labor Cost Variance

Time variance:		
Actual time	4,500 hours	
Standard time	4,800 hours	
Variance—favorable	(300) hours × standard rate, $11	$(3,300)
Rate variance:		
Actual rate	$11.80	
Standard rate	11.00	
Variance—unfavorable	$ 0.80 per hour × actual time, 4,500 hrs.	3,600
Total direct labor cost variance—unfavorable		$ 300

3.

Factory Overhead Cost Variance

Variable factory overhead—controllable variance:		
Actual variable factory overhead cost incurred	$12,300	
Budgeted variable factory overhead for 4,800 hours	11,520*	
Variance—unfavorable		$ 780
Fixed factory overhead—volume variance:		
Budgeted hours at 100% of normal capacity	5,500 hours	
Standard hours for actual production	4,800	
Productive capacity not used	700 hours	
Standard fixed factory overhead cost rate	× $3.50 hours	
Variance—unfavorable		2,450
Total factory overhead cost variance—unfavorable		$3,230

*4,800 hrs. × $2.40 = $11,520

Self-Examination Questions (Answers at End of Chapter)

1. The actual and standard direct materials costs for producing a specified quantity of product are as follows:

Actual:	51,000 pounds at $5.05	$257,550
Standard:	50,000 pounds at $5.00	$250,000

The direct materials price variance is:
A. $50 unfavorable   C. $2,550 unfavorable
B. $2,500 unfavorable   D. $7,550 unfavorable

2. Bower Company produced 4,000 units of product. Each unit requires 0.5 standard hour. The standard labor rate is $12 per hour. Actual direct labor for the period was $22,000 (2,200 hours × $10 per hour). The direct labor time variance is:
A. 200 hours unfavorable   C. $4,000 favorable
B. $2,000 unfavorable   D. $2,400 unfavorable

3. The actual and standard factory overhead costs for producing a specified quantity of product are as follows:

Actual:	Variable factory overhead	$72,500	
	Fixed factory overhead	40,000	$112,500
Standard:	19,000 hours at $6		
	($4 variable and $2 fixed)		114,000

If 1,000 hours were unused, the fixed factory overhead volume variance would be:

A. $1,500 favorable   C. $4,000 unfavorable

B. $2,000 unfavorable   D. $6,000 unfavorable

4. Ramathan Company produced 6,000 units of product Y, which is 80% of capacity. Each unit required 0.25 standard machine hour for production. The standard variable factory overhead rate is $5.00 per machine hour. The actual variable factory overhead incurred during the period was $8,000. The variable factory overhead controllable variance is:

A. $500 favorable   C. $1,875 favorable

B. $500 unfavorable   D. $1,875 unfavorable

5. Applegate Company has a normal budgeted capacity of 200 machine hours. Applegate produced 600 units. Each unit requires a standard 0.2 machine hour to complete. The standard fixed factory overhead is $12.00 per hour, determined at normal capacity. The fixed factory overhead volume variance is:

A. $4,800 unfavorable   C. $960 favorable

B. $4,800 favorable   D. $960 unfavorable

Class Discussion Questions

1. What are the basic objectives in the use of standard costs?
2. How can standards be used by management to help control costs?
3. What is meant by reporting by the "principle of exceptions," as the term is used in reference to cost control?
4. How often should standards be revised?
5. How are standards used in budgetary performance evaluation?
6. a. What are the two variances between the actual cost and the standard cost for direct materials?
   b. Discuss some possible causes of these variances.
7. The materials cost variance report for Nickols Inc. indicates a large favorable materials price variance and a significant unfavorable materials quantity variance. What might have caused these offsetting variances?
8. a. What are the two variances between the actual cost and the standard cost for direct labor?
   b. Who generally has control over the direct labor cost?
9. A new assistant controller recently was heard to remark: "All the assembly workers in this plant are covered by union contracts, so there should be no labor variances." Was the controller's remark correct? Discuss.
10. a. Describe the two variances between the actual costs and the standard costs for factory overhead.
    b. What is a factory overhead cost variance report?
11. What are budgeted fixed costs at normal volume?
12. If variances are recorded in the accounts at the time the manufacturing costs are incurred, what does a debit balance in Direct Materials Price Variance represent?
13. If variances are recorded in the accounts at the time the manufacturing costs are incurred, what does a credit balance in Direct Materials Quantity Variance represent?
14. Would the use of standards be appropriate in a nonmanufacturing setting, such as a fast food restaurant?
15. Briefly explain why firms might use nonfinancial performance measures.

Exercises

EXERCISE 21-1
Standard direct materials cost per unit

Objective 2

SPREADSHEET

Sharon's Chocolate Company produces chocolate bars. The primary materials used in producing chocolate bars are cocoa, sugar, and milk. The standard costs for a batch of chocolate (1,000 bars) are as follows:

Ingredient	Quantity	Price
Cocoa	455 pounds	$0.20 per pound
Sugar	175 pounds	$0.40 per pound
Milk	100 gallons	$1.19 per gallon

Determine the standard direct materials cost per bar of chocolate.

EXERCISE 21-2
Standard product cost

Objective 2

SPREADSHEET

Austin Furniture Company manufactures unfinished oak furniture. Austin uses a standard cost system. The direct labor, direct materials, and factory overhead standards for an unfinished dining room table are as follows:

Direct labor:	standard rate	$15.00 per hour
	standard time per unit	3.5 hours
Direct materials (oak):	standard price	$7.50 per board foot
	standard quantity	20 board feet
Variable factory overhead:	standard rate	$2.20 per direct labor hour
Fixed factory overhead:	standard rate	$0.80 per direct labor hour

Determine the standard cost per dining room table.

EXERCISE 21-3
Budget performance report

Objective 2

SPREADSHEET

✓ *b. Direct labor cost variance, $64 F*

Sams Bottle Company (SBC) manufactures plastic 2-liter bottles for the beverage industry. The cost standards per 100 2-liter bottles are as follows:

Cost Category	Standard Cost per 100 2-Liter Bottles
Direct labor	$1.26
Direct materials	5.04
Factory overhead	0.35
Total	$6.65

At the beginning of July, SBC management planned to produce 600,000 bottles. The actual number of bottles produced for July was 640,000 bottles. The actual costs for July of the current year were as follows:

Cost Category	Actual Cost for the Month Ended July 31, 2006
Direct labor	$ 8,000
Direct materials	32,600
Factory overhead	2,500
Total	$43,100

a. Prepare the July manufacturing standard cost budget (direct labor, direct materials, and factory overhead) for SBC, assuming planned production.
b. Prepare a budget performance report for manufacturing costs, showing the total cost variances for direct materials, direct labor, and factory overhead for July.
c. ▐▬▬▶ Interpret the budget performance report.

EXERCISE 21-4
Direct materials variances
Objective 3
✓ *a. Price variance, $19,275 F*

The following data relate to the direct materials cost for the production of 4,000 automobile tires:

Actual:	128,500 pounds at $1.85	$237,725
Standard:	126,750 pounds at $2.00	$253,500

a. Determine the price variance, quantity variance, and total direct materials cost variance.
b. ▐▬▬▶ To whom should the variances be reported for analysis and control?

EXERCISE 21-5
Standard direct materials cost per unit from variance data
Objectives 2, 3

The following data relating to direct materials cost for October of the current year are taken from the records of Zig's Toys Inc., a manufacturer of plastic toys:

Quantity of direct materials used	39,000 pounds
Actual unit price of direct materials	$1.42 per pound
Units of finished product manufactured	7,500 units
Standard direct materials per unit of finished product	5 pounds
Direct materials quantity variance—unfavorable	$2,025
Direct materials price variance—unfavorable	$2,730

Determine the standard direct materials cost per unit of finished product, assuming that there was no inventory of work in process at either the beginning or the end of the month.

EXERCISE 21-6
Standard product cost, direct materials variance
Objectives 2, 3

REAL WORLD   SPREADSHEET

✓ *a. $0.78 per pound*

H.J. Heinz Company uses standards to control its materials costs. Assume that a batch of ketchup (1,600 pounds) has the following standards:

	Standard Quantity	Standard Price
Whole tomatoes	2,500 pounds	$0.30 per pound
Vinegar	120 gallons	2.40 per gallon
Corn syrup	15 gallons	6.50 per gallon
Salt	50 pounds	2.25 per pound

The actual materials in a batch may vary from the standard due to tomato characteristics. Assume that the actual quantity of materials for batch W196 were:

2,600 pounds of tomatoes
108 gallons of vinegar
17 gallons of corn syrup
49 pounds of salt

a. Determine the standard unit materials cost per pound for a standard batch.
b. Determine the direct materials quantity variance for batch W196.

EXERCISE 21-7
Direct labor variances
Objective 4
✓ *a. Rate variance, $2,776 U*

The following data relate to labor cost for production of 12,500 cellular telephones:

Actual:	17,350 hours at $18.16	$315,076
Standard:	17,500 hours at $18.00	$315,000

a. Determine the rate variance, time variance, and total direct labor cost variance.
b. ◖▬▬► Discuss what might have caused these variances.

EXERCISE 21-8
Direct labor variances
Objective 4

✓a. Time variance, $1,575 F

Big Sky Bicycle Company manufactures mountain bikes. The following data for March of the current year are available:

Quantity of direct labor used	1,300 hours
Actual rate for direct labor	$16.40 per hour
Bicycles completed in March	250
Standard direct labor per bicycle	5.60 hours
Standard rate for direct labor	$15.75 per hour
Planned bicycles for March	200

a. Determine the direct labor rate and time variance.
b. How much direct labor should be debited to Work in Process?

EXERCISE 21-9
Direct materials and direct labor variances
Objectives 2, 3, 4

✓Direct materials quantity variance, $720 F

At the beginning of April, Mountain Fresh Printers Company budgeted 12,000 books to be printed in April at standard direct materials and direct labor costs as follows:

Direct materials	$24,000
Direct labor	21,600
Total	$45,600

The standard materials price is $0.40 per pound. The standard direct labor rate is $12 per hour. At the end of April, the actual direct materials and direct labor costs were as follows:

Actual direct materials	$24,880
Actual direct labor	23,940
Total	$48,820

There were no direct materials price or direct labor rate variances for April. In addition, assume no changes in the direct materials inventory balances in April. Mountain Fresh Printers Company actually produced 12,800 units during April.

Determine the direct materials quantity and direct labor time variances.

EXERCISE 21-10
Flexible overhead budget
Objective 5

SPREADSHEET

✓Total factory overhead, 12,000 hrs: $132,000

Jarrett Wood Products Company prepared the following factory overhead cost budget for the Press Department for February 2006, during which it expected to require 9,000 hours of productive capacity in the department:

Variable overhead cost:		
Indirect factory labor	$25,200	
Power and light	4,050	
Indirect materials	19,800	
Total variable cost		$ 49,050
Fixed overhead cost:		
Supervisory salaries	$32,400	
Depreciation of plant and equipment	27,000	
Insurance and property taxes	7,200	
Total fixed cost		66,600
Total factory overhead cost		$115,650

Assuming that the estimated costs for March are the same as for February, prepare a flexible factory overhead cost budget for the Press Department for March for 6,000, 9,000, and 12,000 hours of production.

EXERCISE 21-11
Factory overhead cost variances
Objective 5

✓Volume variance, $9,250 U

The following data relate to factory overhead cost for the production of 25,000 computers:

Actual:	Variable factory overhead	$500,000
	Fixed factory overhead	74,000
Standard:	35,000 hours at $16	560,000

If productive capacity of 100% was 40,000 hours and the factory overhead cost budgeted at the level of 35,000 standard hours was $569,250, determine the variable factory overhead controllable variance, fixed factory overhead volume variance, and total factory overhead cost variance. The fixed factory overhead rate was $1.85 per hour.

EXERCISE 21-12
Factory overhead cost variances

Objective 5

✓ a. $2,050 F

Flossmoor Textiles Corporation began October with a budget for 25,000 hours of production in the Weaving Department. The department has a full capacity of 30,000 hours under normal business conditions. The budgeted overhead at the planned volumes at the beginning of October was as follows:

Variable overhead	$ 70,000
Fixed overhead	48,000
Total	$118,000

The actual factory overhead was $122,250 for October. The actual fixed factory overhead was as budgeted. During October, the Weaving Department had standard hours at actual production volume of 27,250 hours.

a. Determine the variable factory overhead controllable variance.
b. Determine the fixed factory overhead volume variance.

EXERCISE 21-13
Factory overhead cost variance report

Objective 5

SPREADSHEET

✓ Net controllable variance, $1,250 U

Tri-State Molded Products Inc. prepared the following factory overhead cost budget for the Trim Department for July 2006, during which it expected to use 18,000 hours for production:

Variable overhead cost:		
Indirect factory labor	$44,100	
Power and light	10,800	
Indirect materials	28,800	
Total variable cost		$ 83,700
Fixed overhead cost:		
Supervisory salaries	$30,000	
Depreciation of plant and equipment	27,300	
Insurance and property taxes	20,700	
Total fixed cost		78,000
Total factory overhead cost		$161,700

Tri-State Molded Products has available 24,000 hours of monthly productive capacity in the Trim Department under normal business conditions. During July, the Trim Department actually used 20,000 hours for production. The actual fixed costs were as budgeted. The actual variable overhead for July was as follows:

Actual variable factory overhead cost:	
Indirect factory labor	$48,750
Power and light	13,000
Indirect materials	32,500
Total variable cost	$94,250

Construct a factory overhead cost variance report for the Trim Department for July.

EXERCISE 21-14
Recording standards in accounts

Objective 6

Thexton Manufacturing Company incorporates standards in the accounts and identifies variances at the time the manufacturing costs are incurred. Journalize the entries to record the following transactions:

a. Purchased 1,200 units of copper tubing on account at $43.50 per unit. The standard price is $40.00 per unit.
b. Used 825 units of copper tubing in the process of manufacturing 120 air conditioners. Seven units of copper tubing are required, at standard, to produce one air conditioner.

EXERCISE 21-15
Income statement indicating standard cost variance

Objective 6

SPREADSHEET

✓ *Income before income tax, $206,500*

The following data were taken from the records of Beartooth Company for January 2006:

Administrative expenses	$ 55,000
Cost of goods sold (at standard)	812,500
Direct materials price variance—favorable	1,500
Direct materials quantity variance—unfavorable	2,750
Direct labor rate variance—favorable	1,000
Direct labor time variance—unfavorable	3,750
Variable factory overhead controllable variance—favorable	4,750
Fixed factory overhead volume variance—unfavorable	10,000
Interest expense	2,375
Sales	1,200,000
Selling expenses	114,375

Prepare an income statement for presentation to management.

EXERCISE 21-16
Variance calculations

Objective 5

WHAT'S WRONG
WITH THIS?

The data related to Ruby River Sporting Goods Company's factory overhead cost for the production of 45,000 units of product are as follows:

Actual:	Variable factory overhead	$258,950
	Fixed factory overhead	210,000
Standard:	72,000 hours at $6.30 ($3.50 for variable factory overhead)	453,600

Productive capacity at 100% of normal was 75,000 hours, and the factory overhead cost budgeted at the level of 72,000 standard hours was $462,000. Based upon these data, the chief cost accountant prepared the following variance analysis:

Variable factory overhead controllable variance:		
Actual variable factory overhead cost incurred	$258,950	
Budgeted variable factory overhead for 72,000 hours	252,000	
Variance—unfavorable		$ 6,950
Fixed factory overhead volume variance:		
Normal productive capacity at 100%	75,000 hours	
Standard for amount produced	72,000	
Productive capacity not used	3,000 hours	
Standard variable factory overhead rate	× $6.30	
Variance—unfavorable		18,900
Total factory overhead cost variance—unfavorable		$25,850

Identify the errors in the factory overhead cost variance analysis.

EXERCISE 21-17
Standards for nonmanufacturing expenses

Objective 7

✓ *a. $1,440*

Wild Rose Hospital began using standards to evaluate its Admissions Department. The standard was broken into two types of admissions as follows:

Type of Admission	Standard Time to Complete Admission Record
Unscheduled admission	40 minutes
Scheduled admission	20 minutes

The unscheduled admission took longer, since name, address, and insurance information needed to be determined at the time of admission. Information was collected on scheduled admissions prior to the admissions, which was less time consuming.

The Admissions Department employs two full-time people (40 productive hours per week, with no overtime) at $18 per hour. For the most recent week, the department handled 54 unscheduled and 160 scheduled admissions.

a. How much was actually spent on labor for the week?
b. What are the standard hours for the actual volume for the week? Round to one digit after the decimal place.
c. Calculate a time variance, and report how well the department performed for the week.

EXERCISE 21-18
Standards for nonmanufacturing operations

Objectives 2, 4, 7

REAL WORLD

✓ b. $1,080 F

One of the operations in the **U.S. Post Office** is a mechanical mail sorting operation. In this operation, letter mail is sorted at a rate of one letter per second. The letter is mechanically sorted from a three-digit code input by an operator sitting at a keyboard. The manager of the mechanical sorting operation wishes to determine the number of temporary employees to hire for December. The manager estimates that there will be an additional 31,104,000 pieces of mail in December, due to the upcoming holiday season.

Assume that the sorting operators are temporary employees. The union contract requires that temporary employees be hired for one month at a time. Each temporary employee is hired to work 160 hours in the month.

a. How many temporary employees should the manager hire for December?
b. If each employee earns a standard $18 per hour, what would be the labor time variance if there were 31,320,000 additional letters sorted in December?

EXERCISE 21-19
Nonfinancial performance measures

Objective 8

City College wishes to monitor the efficiency and quality of its course registration process.

a. Identify three input and three output measures for this process.
b. Why would City College use nonfinancial measures for monitoring this process?

EXERCISE 21-20
Nonfinancial performance measures

Objective 8

Highcountry.com is an Internet retailer of sporting good products. Customers order sporting goods from the company, using an online catalog. The company processes these orders and delivers the requested product from the company's warehouse. The company wants to provide customers with an excellent purchase experience in order to expand the business with favorable word-of-mouth and to drive repeat business. To help monitor performance, the company developed a set of performance measures for its order placement and delivery process.

> Average computer response time to customer "clicks"
> Dollar amount of returned goods
> Elapsed time between customer order and product delivery
> Maintenance dollars divided by hardware investment
> Number of customer complaints divided by the number of orders
> Number of misfilled orders
> Number of orders per warehouse employee
> Number of page faults or errors due to software programming errors
> Server (computer) downtime
> System capacity divided by customer demands
> Training dollars per programmer

Identify the input and output measures related to the order placement and delivery process.

Problems Series A

PROBLEM 21-1A
Direct materials and direct labor variance analysis

Objectives 2, 3, 4

✓ c. Direct labor time variance, $2,304 F

Integrated Fixtures Company manufactures faucets in a small manufacturing facility. The faucets are made from zinc. Manufacturing has 62 employees. Each employee presently provides 38 hours of labor per week. Information about a production week is as follows:

Standard wage per hour	$16.00
Standard labor time per faucet	15 minutes
Standard number of pounds of zinc	1.8 pounds
Standard price per pound of zinc	$9.00
Actual price per pound of zinc	$8.80

(continued)

Actual pounds of zinc used during the week	18,175 lbs.
Number of faucets produced during the week	10,000
Actual wage per hour	$16.25
Actual hours per week	2,356 hours

Instructions

Determine (a) the standard cost per unit for direct materials and direct labor, (b) the price variance, quantity variance, and total direct materials cost variance, and (c) the rate variance, time variance, and total direct labor cost variance.

PROBLEM 21-2A
Flexible budgeting and variance analysis

Objectives 2, 3, 4

SPREADSHEET

✓1. b. Time variance, $430 F

Hahn Coat Company makes women's and men's coats. Both products require filler and lining material. The following planning information has been made available:

| | Standard Quantity | | |
	Women's Coats	Men's Coats	Standard Price per Unit
Filler	2 lbs.	3.5 lbs.	$28.00
Liner	5 yds.	8 yds.	$ 4.00
Standard labor time	0.20 hr.	0.30 hr.	
Planned production	2,000 units	3,500 units	
Standard labor rate	$14.00 per hour	$15.00 per hour	

Hahn Coat does not expect there to be any beginning or ending inventories of filler and lining material.

At the end of the budget year, Hahn Coat experienced the following actual results:

	Women's Coats	Men's Coats
Actual production	2,800	4,000

	Actual Price per Unit	Actual Quantity Purchased and Used
Filler	$27.50	20,100
Liner	4.10	45,300

	Actual Labor Rate	Actual Labor Hours Used
Woman's Coat	$13.60	615
Man's Coat	15.20	1,120

The expected beginning inventory and desired ending inventory were realized.

Instructions

1. Prepare the following variance analyses, based on the actual results and production levels at the end of the budget year:
   a. Direct materials price, quantity, and total variance.
   b. Direct labor rate, time, and total variance.
2. ▬▬▶ Why are the standard amounts in (1) based on the actual production at the end of the year instead of the planned production at the beginning of the year?

PROBLEM 21-3A
Direct materials, direct labor, and factory overhead cost variance analysis

Objectives 3, 4, 5

✓a. Price variance, $21,930 U

Ikon Tire Co. manufactures automobile tires. Standard costs and actual costs for direct materials, direct labor, and factory overhead incurred for the manufacture of 36,000 tires were as follows:

	Standard Costs	Actual Costs
Direct materials	72,000 pounds at $4.50	73,100 pounds at $4.80
Direct labor	18,000 hours at $18.00	18,500 hours at $17.88
Factory overhead	Rates per direct labor hour, based on 100% of normal capacity of 20,000 direct labor hours:	
	Variable cost, $2.40	$42,870 variable cost
	Fixed cost, $3.75	$75,000 fixed cost

Each tire requires 0.50 hour of direct labor.

Instructions

Determine (a) the price variance, quantity variance, and total direct materials cost variance, (b) the rate variance, time variance, and total direct labor cost variance, and (c) variable factory overhead controllable variance, the fixed factory overhead volume variance, and total factory overhead cost variance.

PROBLEM 21-4A
Standard factory overhead variance report
Objective 5

SPREADSHEET
P.A.S.S.

✓ *Net controllable variance, $900 F*

Wethington Company, a manufacturer of disposable medical supplies, prepared the following factory overhead cost budget for the Assembly Department for October 2006. The company expected to operate the department at 100% of normal capacity of 25,000 hours.

Variable costs:		
Indirect factory wages	$220,000	
Power and light	160,000	
Indirect materials	40,000	
Total variable cost		$420,000
Fixed costs:		
Supervisory salaries	$120,000	
Depreciation of plant and equipment	95,000	
Insurance and property taxes	27,000	
Total fixed cost		242,000
Total factory overhead cost		$662,000

During October, the department operated at 23,750 hours, and the factory overhead costs incurred were indirect factory wages, $207,500; power and light, $153,200; indirect materials, $37,400; supervisory salaries, $120,000; depreciation of plant and equipment, $95,000; and insurance and property taxes, $27,000.

Instructions

Prepare a factory overhead cost variance report for October. To be useful for cost control, the budgeted amounts should be based on 23,750 hours.

PROBLEM 21-5A
Standards for nonmanufacturing expenses
Objectives 4, 7, 8

✓ *2. $90 F*

The Radiology Department provides imaging services for Mercy Medical Center. One important activity in the Radiology Department is transcribing tape-recorded analyses of images into a written report. The manager of the Radiology Department determined that the average transcriptionist could type 600 lines of a report in an hour. The plan for the first week in July called for 69,000 typed lines to be written. The Radiology Department has three transcriptionists. Each transcriptionist is hired from an employment firm that requires that temporary employees be hired for a minimum of a 40-hour week. Transcriptionists are paid $18.00 per hour. The manager offered a bonus if the department could type more than 72,000 lines for the week, without overtime. Due to high service demands, the transcriptionists typed more lines in the first week of July than planned. The actual amount of lines typed in the first week of July was 75,000 lines, without overtime. As a result, the bonus caused the average transcriptionist hourly rate to increase to $20.00 per hour during the first week in July.

Instructions

1. If the department typed 69,000 lines according to the original plan, what would have been the labor time variance?
2. What was the labor time variance as a result of typing 75,000 lines?
3. What was the labor rate variance as a result of the bonus?
4. The manager is trying to determine if a better decision would have been to hire a temporary transcriptionist to meet the higher typing demands in the first week of July, rather than paying out the bonus. If another employee was hired from the employment firm, what would have been the labor time variance in the first week?

5. ⬛▶ Which decision is better, paying the bonus or hiring another transcriptionist?

6. ⬛▶ Are there any performance-related issues that the labor time and rate variances fail to consider? Explain.

Problems Series B

PROBLEM 21-1B
Direct materials and direct labor variance analysis

Objectives 2, 3, 4

✓ c. Rate variance, $108 U

Dresses by Audrey Inc. manufactures silk dresses in a small manufacturing facility. Manufacturing has 20 employees. Each employee presently provides 36 hours of productive labor per week. Information about a production week is as follows:

Standard wage per hour	$10.65
Standard labor time per dress	20 minutes
Standard number of yards of silk per dress	3.8 yards
Standard price per yard of silk	$2.75
Actual price per yard of silk	$2.80
Actual yards of silk used during the week	7,500 yards
Number of dresses produced during the week	2,100
Actual wage per hour	$10.80
Actual hours per week	720 hours

Instructions
Determine (a) the standard cost per dress for direct materials and direct labor, (b) the price variance, quantity variance, and total direct materials cost variance, and (c) the rate variance, time variance, and total direct labor cost variance.

PROBLEM 21-2B
Flexible budgeting and variance analysis

Objectives 2, 3, 4

SPREADSHEET

✓ 1. a. Direct materials quantity variance, $1,700 U

Phillis' Chocolate Company makes dark chocolate and light chocolate. Both products require cocoa and sugar. The following planning information has been made available:

	Standard Quantity		
	Dark Chocolate	Light Chocolate	Standard Price per Pound
Cocoa	12 lbs.	8 lbs.	$8.00
Sugar	10 lbs.	16 lbs.	$1.50
Standard labor time	0.25 hr.	0.40 hr.	
Planned production	3,400 cases	4,400 cases	
Standard labor rate	$16.20 per hour	$16.15 per hour	

Phillis' Chocolate does not expect there to be any beginning or ending inventories of cocoa or sugar.

At the end of the budget year, Phillis' Chocolate had the following actual results:

	Dark Chocolate	Light Chocolate
Actual production (cases)	3,000	5,000

	Actual Price per Pound	Actual Pounds Purchased and Used
Cocoa	$7.75	75,500
Sugar	1.68	113,800

	Actual Labor Rate	Actual Labor Hours Used
Dark chocolate	$16.40	800
Light chocolate	16.40	1,800

Instructions
1. Prepare the following variance analyses, based on the actual results and production levels at the end of the budget year:
   a. Direct materials price, quantity, and total variance.
   b. Direct labor rate, time, and total variance.

2. Why are the standard amounts in (1) based on the actual production for the year instead of the planned production for the year?

PROBLEM 21-3B
Direct materials, direct labor, and factory overhead cost variance analysis

Objectives 3, 4, 5

✓ *c. Controllable variance, $190 F*

Rigsby Resins Company processes a base chemical into plastic. Standard costs and actual costs for direct materials, direct labor, and factory overhead incurred for the manufacture of 2,700 units of product were as follows:

	Standard Costs	Actual Costs
Direct materials	6,750 pounds at $6.20	6,900 pounds at $6.15
Direct labor	2,160 hours at $20.10	2,200 hours at $20.50
Factory overhead	Rates per direct labor hour, based on 100% of normal capacity of 2,100 direct labor hours:	
	Variable cost, $2.75	$5,750 variable cost
	Fixed cost, $16.50	$34,650 fixed cost

Each unit requires 0.8 hour of direct labor.

Instructions
Determine (a) the price variance, quantity variance, and total direct materials cost variance, (b) the rate variance, time variance, and total direct labor cost variance, and (c) variable factory overhead controllable variance, the fixed factory overhead volume variance, and total factory overhead cost variance.

PROBLEM 21-4B
Standard factory overhead variance report

Objective 5

SPREADSHEET
P.A.S.S.

✓ *Volume variance, $2,620 F*

Old Faithful Inc., a manufacturer of construction equipment, prepared the following factory overhead cost budget for the Welding Department for July 2006. The company expected to operate the department at 100% of normal capacity of 5,000 hours.

Variable costs:		
Indirect factory wages	$14,750	
Power and light	8,000	
Indirect materials	9,250	
Total variable cost		$32,000
Fixed costs:		
Supervisory salaries	$17,000	
Depreciation of plant and equipment	41,250	
Insurance and property taxes	7,250	
Total fixed cost		65,500
Total factory overhead cost		$97,500

During July, the department operated at 5,200 standard hours, and the factory overhead costs incurred were indirect factory wages, $15,000; power and light, $8,500; indirect materials, $9,450; supervisory salaries, $17,000; depreciation of plant and equipment, $41,250; and insurance and property taxes, $7,250.

Instructions
Prepare a factory overhead cost variance report for July. To be useful for cost control, the budgeted amounts should be based on 5,200 hours.

PROBLEM 21-5B
Standards for nonmanufacturing expenses

Objectives 4, 7, 8

✓ *3. $640 U*

Infosystems.com Software Company does software development. One important activity in software development is writing software code. The manager of the WritePro Development Team determined that the average software programmer could write 40 lines of code in an hour. The plan for the first week in May called for 6,320 lines of code to be written on the WritePro product. The WritePro Team has four programmers. Each programmer is hired from an employment firm that requires that temporary employees be hired for a minimum of a 40-hour week. Programmers are paid $30.00 per hour. The manager offered a bonus if the team could generate more than 6,600 lines for the week, without overtime. Due to a project emergency, the programmers wrote more code in the first week of May than planned. The actual amount of code written in the first week of May was 7,000 lines, without overtime. As a result, the bonus caused the average programmer's hourly rate to increase to $34.00 per hour during the first week in May.

Instructions

1. If the team generated 6,320 lines of code according to the original plan, what would have been the labor time variance?
2. What was the actual labor time variance as a result of generating 7,000 lines of code?
3. What was the labor rate variance as a result of the bonus?
4. The manager is trying to determine if a better decision would have been to hire a temporary programmer to meet the higher programming demand in the first week of May, rather than paying out the bonus. If another employee was hired from the employment firm, what would have been the labor time variance in the first week?
5. ▬▶ Which decision is better, paying the bonus or hiring another programmer?
6. ▬▶ Are there any performance-related issues that the labor time and rate variances fail to consider? Explain.

Special Activities

ACTIVITY 21-1
Ethics and professional conduct in business

ETHICS

Cecil Hogan is a cost analyst with Manhattan Insurance Company. Manhattan is applying standards to its claims payment operation. Claims payment is a repetitive operation that could be evaluated with standards. Cecil used time and motion studies to identify an ideal standard of 36 claims processed per hour. The Claims Processing Department manager, Lynn Weese, has rejected this standard and has argued that the standard should be 30 claims processed per hour. Lynn and Cecil were unable to agree, so they decided to discuss this matter openly at a joint meeting with the vice-president of operations, who would arbitrate a final decision. Prior to the meeting, Cecil wrote the following memo to the VP.

To: Taylor Meadows, Vice-President of Operations
From: Cecil Hogan
Re: Standards in the Claims Processing Department

As you know, Lynn and I are scheduled to meet with you to discuss our disagreement with respect to the appropriate standards for the Claims Processing Department. I have conducted time and motion studies and have determined that the ideal standard is 36 claims processed per hour. Lynn argues that 30 claims processed per hour would be more appropriate. I believe she is trying to "pad" the budget with some slack. I'm not sure what she is trying to get away with, but I believe a tight standard will drive efficiency up in her area. I hope you will agree when we meet with you next week.

▬▶ Discuss the ethical and professional issues in this situation.

ACTIVITY 21-2
Nonfinancial performance measures

The senior management of Moncrief Company has proposed the following three performance measures for the company:

1. Net income as a percent of stockholders' equity
2. Revenue growth
3. Employee satisfaction

Management believes these three measures combine both financial and nonfinancial measures and are thus superior to using just financial measures.

⬛➤ What advice would you give Moncrief Company for improving on its performance measurement system?

ACTIVITY 21-3
Nonfinancial performance measures

REAL WORLD

WHAT DO YOU THINK?

At the Soladyne Division of **Rogers Corporation**, the controller used a number of measures to provide managers information about the performance of a just-in-time (JIT) manufacturing operation. Three measures used by the company are:

- Scrap Index: The sales dollar value of scrap for the period.
- Orders Past Due: Sales dollar value of orders that were scheduled for shipment, but were not shipped during the period.
- Buyer Misery Index: Number of different customers that have orders that are late (scheduled for shipment, but not shipped).

1. ⬛➤ Why do you think the scrap index is measured at sales dollar value, rather than at cost?
2. ⬛➤ How is the "orders past due" measure different from the "buyer's misery index," or are the two measures just measuring the same thing?

ACTIVITY 21-4
Variance interpretation

You have been asked to investigate some cost problems in the Assembly Department of JeVo Electronics Inc., a consumer electronics company. To begin your investigation, you have obtained the following budget performance report for the department for the last quarter:

JeVo Electronics Inc.—Assembly Department
Quarterly Budget Performance Report

	Standard Quantity at Standard Rates	Actual Quantity at Standard Rates	Quantity Variances
Direct labor	$ 78,750	$113,750	$35,000 U
Direct materials	148,750	192,500	43,750 U
Total	$227,500	$306,250	$78,750 U

The following reports were also obtained:

JeVo Electronics Inc.—Purchasing Department
Quarterly Budget Performance Report

	Actual Quantity at Standard Rates	Actual Quantity at Actual Rates	Price Variance
Direct materials	$218,750	$192,500	$26,250 F

JeVo Electronics Inc.—Fabrication Department
Quarterly Budget Performance Report

	Standard Quantity at Standard Rates	Actual Quantity at Standard Rates	Quantity Variances
Direct labor	$122,500	$101,500	$21,000 F
Direct materials	70,000	70,000	0
Total	$192,500	$171,500	$21,000 F

You also interviewed the Assembly Department supervisor. Excerpts from the interview follow.

Q: *What explains the poor performance in your department?*
A: *Listen, you've got to understand what it's been like in this department recently. Lately, it seems no matter how hard we try, we can't seem to make the standards. I'm not sure what is going on, but we've been having a lot of problems lately.*

Q: *What kind of problems?*

A: *Well, for instance, all this quarter we've been requisitioning purchased parts from the material storeroom, and the parts just didn't fit together very well. I'm not sure what is going on, but during most of this quarter we've had to scrap and sort purchased parts—just to get our assemblies put together. Naturally, all this takes time and material. And that's not all.*

Q: *Go on.*

A: *All this quarter, the work that we've been receiving from the Fabrication Department has been shoddy. I mean, maybe around 20% of the stuff that comes in from Fabrication just can't be assembled. The fabrication is all wrong. As a result, we've had to scrap and rework a lot of the stuff. Naturally, this has just shot our quantity variances.*

➤ Interpret the variance reports in light of the comments by the Assembly Department supervisor.

ACTIVITY 21-5
Variance interpretation

Thirsty Ear Inc. is a small manufacturer of electronic musical instruments. The plant manager received the following variable factory overhead report for the period:

	Actual	Budgeted Variable Factory Overhead at Actual Production
Supplies	$28,000	$26,520
Power and light	35,000	33,990
Indirect factory wages	26,112	20,400
Total	$89,112	$80,910

Actual units produced: 10,200 (85% of practical capacity)

The plant manager is not pleased with the $8,202 unfavorable variable factory overhead controllable variance and has come to discuss the matter with the controller. The following discussion occurred:

Plant Manager: I just received this factory report for the latest month of operation. I'm not very pleased with these figures. Before these numbers go to headquarters, you and I will need to reach an understanding.

Controller: Go ahead, what's the problem?

Plant Manager: What's the problem? Well, everything. Look at the variance. It's too large. If I understand the accounting approach being used here, you are assuming that my costs are variable to the units produced. Thus, as the production volume declines, so should these costs. Well, I don't believe that these costs are variable at all. I think they are fixed costs. As a result, when we operate below capacity, the costs really don't go down at all. I'm being penalized for costs I have no control over at all. I need this report to be redone to reflect this fact. If anything, the difference between actual and budget is essentially a volume variance. Listen, I know that you're a team player. You really need to reconsider your assumptions on this one.

➤ If you were in the controller's position, how would you respond to the plant manager?

ACTIVITY 21-6
Government performance review

GROUP ACTIVITY   INTERNET

Municipal governments are discovering that you can control only what you measure. As a result, many municipal governments are introducing nonfinancial performance measures to help improve municipal services. In a group, use the Google® search engine to perform a search for "municipal government performance measurement." Google will provide a list of Internet sites that outline various city efforts in using nonfinancial performance measures. As a group, report on the types of measures used by one of the cities from the search.

nswers to Self-Examination Questions

1. **C** The unfavorable direct materials price variance of $2,550 is determined as follows:

Actual price	$5.05 per pound
Standard price	5.00
Price variance—unfavorable	$0.05 per pound

$0.05 × 51,000 actual pounds = $2,550

2. **D** The unfavorable direct labor time variance of $2,400 is determined as follows:

Actual direct labor time	2,200
Standard direct labor time	2,000
Direct labor time variance—unfavorable	200 × $12 standard rate = $2,400

3. **B** The unfavorable factory overhead volume variance of $2,000 is determined as follows:

Productive capacity not used	1,000 hours
Standard fixed factory overhead cost rate	× $2
Factory overhead volume variance—unfavorable	$2,000

4. **B** The controllable variable factory overhead variance is determined as follows:

6,000 units × 0.25 hour = 1,500 hours
1,500 hours × $5.00 per hour = $7,500

Actual variable overhead:	$8,000
Less: Budgeted variable overhead at actual volume	7,500
Unfavorable controllable variance	$ 500

5. **D** The fixed factory overhead volume variance can be determined as follows:

Actual production in standard hours:
   600 units × 0.2 machine hour = 120 machine hours

Practical capacity	200 machine hours
Standard hours at actual production	120
Idle capacity	80 machine hours

80 hours × $12.00 = $960 unfavorable volume variance

22

PERFORMANCE EVALUATION FOR DECENTRALIZED OPERATIONS

objectives

After studying this chapter, you should be able to:

1 List and explain the advantages and disadvantages of decentralized operations.

2 Prepare a responsibility accounting report for a cost center.

3 Prepare responsibility accounting reports for a profit center.

4 Compute and interpret the rate of return on investment, the residual income, and the balanced scorecard for an investment center.

5 Explain how the market price, negotiated price, and cost price approaches to transfer pricing may be used by decentralized segments of a business.

Have you ever wondered if there is an economic reason why large retail stores, such as **J.C.Penney Co.** and **Sears**, are divided into departments? Typically, these stores include a Men's Department, Women's Department, Cosmetics Department, Gift Department, and Furnishings Department. Each department usually has a manager who is responsible for the financial performance of the department. The store may be the responsibility of a store manager, and a group of stores within a particular geographic area may be the responsibility of a division or district manager. If you were to be hired by a department store chain, you would probably begin your career in a department. Running a department would be a valuable experience before becoming responsible for a complete store. Likewise, responsibility for a complete store provides excellent training for other management positions.

In this chapter, we will focus on the role of accounting in assisting managers in planning and controlling organizational units, such as divisions, stores, and departments.

Centralized and Decentralized Operations

SunTrust Banks Inc., a major regional bank, centralized its administrative banking regions from 30 to 15, while simultaneously decentralizing customer functions by expanding its local presidents from 30 to 50. A senior manager of the bank stated, "We're trying to do two things. We're trying to drive revenue production by further leveraging our best talent and by giving our field units more time to focus exclusively on the customer. And we're trying to capture the opportunity of further efficiency by consolidating other things that are not directly customer-related."

Source: David Broaks, "Centralize or Decentralize—SunTrust Picks Both," *American Banker*, June 2002.

objective 1

List and explain the advantages and disadvantages of decentralized operations.

A **centralized** business is one in which all major planning and operating decisions are made by top management. For example, a one-person, owner/manager-operated business is centralized because all plans and decisions are made by one person. In a small owner/manager-operated business, centralization may be desirable. This is because the owner/manager's close supervision ensures that the business will be operated in the way the owner/manager wishes.

Separating a business into ***divisions*** or operating units and delegating responsibility to unit managers is called ***decentralization***. In a decentralized business, the unit managers are responsible for planning and controlling the operations of their units.

Divisions are often structured around common functions, products, customers, or regions. For example, **Delta Air Lines** is organized around *functions*, such as the Flight Operations Division. The **Procter & Gamble Company** is organized around common *products*, such as the Soap Division, which sells a wide array of cleaning products. The **Norfolk Southern Corporation** decentralizes its railroad operations into Eastern, Western, and Northern regional divisions.

There is no one best amount of decentralization for all businesses. In some companies, division managers have authority over all operations, including fixed asset acquisitions and retirements. In other companies, division managers have authority over profits but not fixed asset acquisitions and retirements. The proper amount of decentralization for a company depends on its advantages and disadvantages for the company's unique circumstances.

Advantages of Decentralization

As a business grows, it becomes more difficult for top management to maintain close daily contact with all operations. In such cases, delegating authority to managers closest to the operations usually results in better decisions. These managers often anticipate and react to operating data more quickly than could top management. In addition, as a company expands into a wide range of products and services, it becomes more difficult for top management to maintain operating expertise in all product lines and services. Decentralization allows managers to focus on acquiring expertise in their areas of responsibility. For example, in a company that maintains operations in insurance, banking, and health care, managers could become "experts" in their area of operation and responsibility.

Decentralized decision making also provides excellent training for managers. This may be a factor in helping a company retain quality managers. Since the art of management is best acquired through experience, delegating responsibility allows managers to acquire and develop managerial expertise early in their careers.

Businesses that work closely with customers, such as hotels, are often decentralized. This helps managers create good customer relations by responding quickly to customers' needs. In addition, because managers of decentralized operations tend to identify with customers and with operations, they are often more creative in suggesting operating and product improvements.

Disadvantages of Decentralization

A primary disadvantage of decentralized operations is that decisions made by one manager may negatively affect the profitability of the entire company. For example, the Pizza Hut chain added chicken to its menu and ended up taking business away from KFC. Then KFC retaliated with a blistering ad campaign against Pizza Hut. This happened even though both chains are part of the same company, **Yum Brands, Inc.**!

Another potential disadvantage of decentralized operations is duplicating assets and costs in operating divisions. For example, each manager of a product line might have a separate sales force and administrative office staff. Centralizing these personnel could save money. For example, **McDonald's Corporation** recently reduced the number of operating divisions in the United States from five to three in order to cut administrative expenses.

Responsibility Accounting

In a decentralized business, an important function of accounting is to assist unit managers in evaluating and controlling their areas of responsibility, called **responsibility centers**. *Responsibility accounting* is the process of measuring and reporting operating data by responsibility center. Three common types of responsibility centers are cost centers, profit centers, and investment centers. These three responsibility centers differ in their scope of responsibility, as shown below.

Cost Center	Profit Center	Investment Center
	Revenue	Revenue
Cost	− Cost	− Cost
	Profit	Profit
		Investment in assets

A department in a manufacturing facility would likely be what type of performance center?

Cost center

Responsibility Accounting for Cost Centers

objective 2

Prepare a responsibility accounting report for a cost center.

In a **cost center**, the unit manager has responsibility and authority for controlling the costs incurred. For example, the supervisor of the Power Department has responsibility for the costs incurred in providing power. A cost center manager does not make decisions concerning sales or the amount of fixed assets invested in the center.

Since managers of cost centers have responsibility and authority over costs, responsibility accounting for cost centers focuses on costs. To illustrate, the budget performance reports in Exhibit 1 are part of a responsibility accounting system. These reports aid the managers in controlling costs.

In Exhibit 1, the reports prepared for the department supervisors show the budgeted and actual manufacturing costs for their departments. The supervisors can use these reports to focus on areas of significant difference, such as the difference between the budgeted and actual materials cost. The supervisor of Department 1 in Plant A may use additional information from a scrap report to determine why materials are over budget. Such a report might show that materials were scrapped as a result of machine malfunctions, improper use of machines by employees, or low quality materials.

For higher levels of management, responsibility accounting reports are usually more summarized than for lower levels of management. In Exhibit 1, for example, the budget performance report for the plant manager summarizes budget and actual cost data for the departments under the manager's supervision. This report en-

•Exhibit 1

Responsibility Accounting Reports for Cost Centers

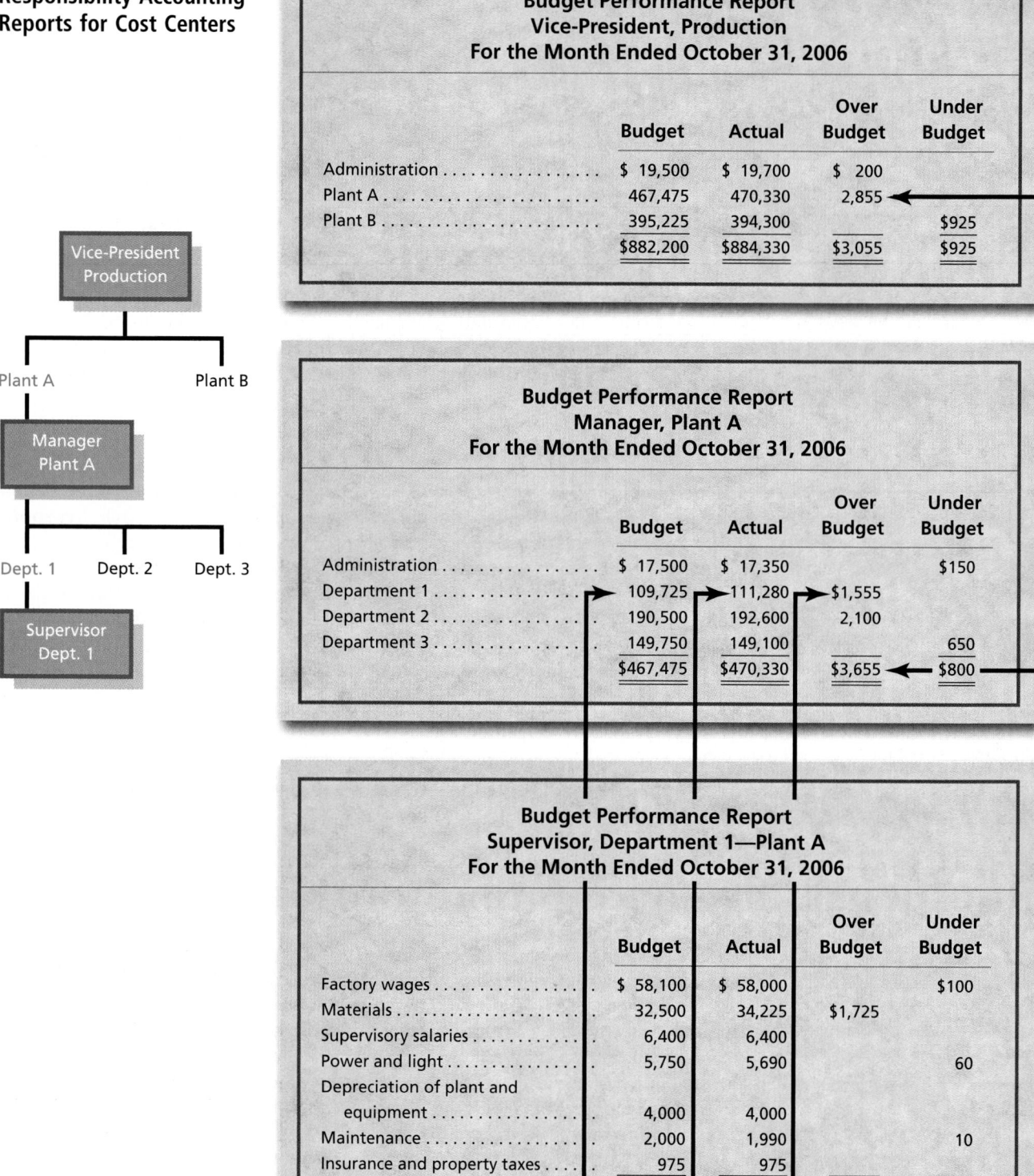

Budget Performance Report
Vice-President, Production
For the Month Ended October 31, 2006

	Budget	Actual	Over Budget	Under Budget
Administration	$ 19,500	$ 19,700	$ 200	
Plant A	467,475	470,330	2,855	
Plant B	395,225	394,300		$925
	$882,200	$884,330	$3,055	$925

Budget Performance Report
Manager, Plant A
For the Month Ended October 31, 2006

	Budget	Actual	Over Budget	Under Budget
Administration	$ 17,500	$ 17,350		$150
Department 1	109,725	111,280	$1,555	
Department 2	190,500	192,600	2,100	
Department 3	149,750	149,100		650
	$467,475	$470,330	$3,655	$800

Budget Performance Report
Supervisor, Department 1—Plant A
For the Month Ended October 31, 2006

	Budget	Actual	Over Budget	Under Budget
Factory wages	$ 58,100	$ 58,000		$100
Materials	32,500	34,225	$1,725	
Supervisory salaries	6,400	6,400		
Power and light	5,750	5,690		60
Depreciation of plant and equipment	4,000	4,000		
Maintenance	2,000	1,990		10
Insurance and property taxes	975	975		
	$109,725	$111,280	$1,725	$170

Vice-President Production

Plant A   Plant B

Manager Plant A

Dept. 1   Dept. 2   Dept. 3

Supervisor Dept. 1

ables the plant manager to identify the department supervisors responsible for major differences. Likewise, the report for the vice-president of production summarizes the cost data for each plant. The plant managers can thus be held responsible for major differences in budgeted and actual costs in their plants.

Cost centers may vary in size from a small department to an entire manufacturing plant. In addition, cost centers may exist within other cost centers. For example, we could view an entire university as a cost center, and each college and department within the university could also be a cost center, as shown in Exhibit 2.

•Exhibit 2

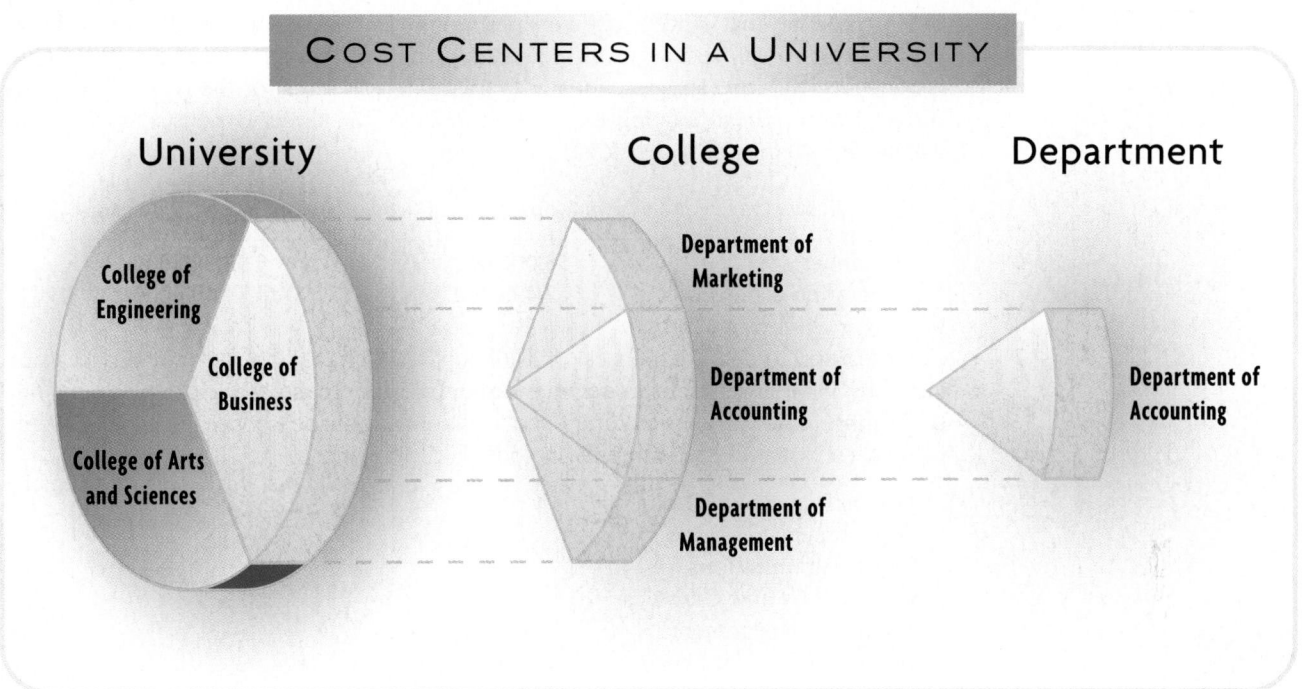

COST CENTERS IN A UNIVERSITY

University — College of Engineering, College of Business, College of Arts and Sciences

College — Department of Marketing, Department of Accounting, Department of Management

Department — Department of Accounting

Responsibility Accounting for Profit Centers

objective 3

Prepare responsibility accounting reports for a profit center.

In a ***profit center***, the unit manager has the responsibility and the authority to make decisions that affect both costs and revenues (and thus profits). Profit centers may be divisions, departments, or products. For example, a consumer products company might organize its brands (product lines) as divisional profit centers. The manager of each brand could have responsibility for product cost and decisions regarding revenues, such as setting sales prices. The manager of a profit center does not make decisions concerning the fixed assets invested in the center. For example, the brand manager of a consumer products company does not make the decision to expand the plant capacity for the brand.

Profit centers are often viewed as an excellent training assignment for new managers. For example, Lester B. Korn, Chairman and Chief Executive Officer of **Korn/Ferry International**, offered the following strategy for young executives en route to top management positions:

Get Profit-Center Responsibility—Obtain a position where you can prove yourself as both a specialist with particular expertise and a generalist who can exercise leadership, authority, and inspire enthusiasm among colleagues and subordinates.

Profit centers may be divisions, departments, or products.

Responsibility accounting reports usually show the revenues, expenses, and income from operations for the profit center. The profit center income statement should include only revenues and expenses that are controlled by the manager. **Controllable revenues** are revenues earned by the profit center. ***Controllable expenses*** are costs that can be influenced (controlled) by the decisions of profit center managers. For example, the manager of the Men's Department at **Nordstrom** most likely controls the salaries of department personnel, but does not control the property taxes of the store.

Service Department Charges

We will illustrate profit center income reporting for the Nova Entertainment Group (NEG). Assume that NEG is a diversified entertainment company with two operating divisions organized as profit centers: the Theme Park Division and the Movie Production Division. The revenues and operating expenses for the two divisions are shown below. The operating expenses consist of the direct expenses, such as the wages and salaries of a division's employees.

	Theme Park Division	Movie Production Division
Revenues	$6,000,000	$2,500,000
Operating expenses	2,495,000	405,000

In addition to direct expenses, divisions may also have expenses for services provided by internal centralized **service departments**. These service departments are often more efficient at providing service than are outside service providers. Examples of such service departments include the following:

- Research and Development
- Government Relations
- Telecommunications
- Publications and Graphics
- Facilities Management
- Purchasing
- Information Systems
- Payroll Accounting
- Transportation
- Personnel Administration

A profit center's income from operations should reflect the cost of any internal services used by the center. To illustrate, assume that NEG established a Payroll Accounting Department. The costs of the payroll services, called **service department charges**, are charged to NEG's profit centers, as shown in Exhibit 3.

Which of the following departments—Legal Department, Fabrication Department, MIS Department, Maintenance Department—are examples of service departments?

Legal Department, MIS Department, and Maintenance Department

•**Exhibit 3**

Payroll Accounting Department Charges to NEG's Theme Park and Movie Production Division

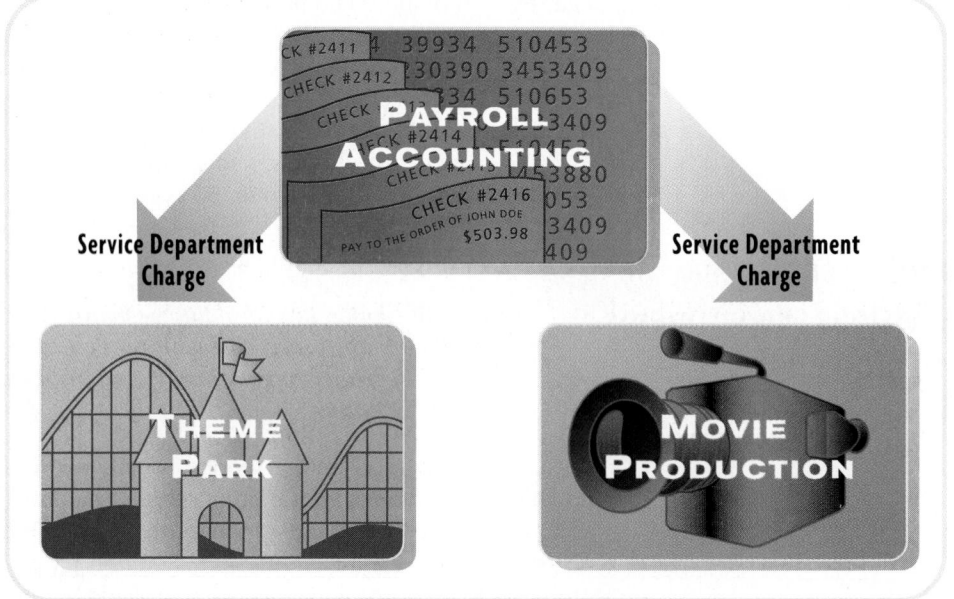

Service department charges are *indirect expenses* to a profit center. They are similar to the expenses that would be incurred if the profit center had purchased the services from a source outside the company. A profit center manager has control over such expenses if the manager is free to choose *how much* service is used from the service department.

To illustrate service department charges, assume that NEG has two other service departments—Purchasing and Legal, in addition to Payroll Accounting. The expenses for the year ended December 31, 2006, for each service department are as follows:

Purchasing	$400,000
Payroll Accounting	255,000
Legal	250,000
Total	$905,000

An **activity base** for each service department is used to charge service department expenses to the Theme Park and Movie Production Divisions. The activity base for each service department is a measure of the services performed. For NEG, the service department activity bases are as follows:

Department	Activity Base
Purchasing	Number of purchase requisitions
Payroll Accounting	Number of payroll checks
Legal	Number of billed hours

The use of services by the Theme Park and Movie Production Divisions is as follows:

	Service Usage		
	Purchasing	Payroll Accounting	Legal
Theme Park Division	25,000 purchase requisitions	12,000 payroll checks	100 billed hrs.
Movie Production Division	15,000	3,000	900
Total	40,000 purchase requisitions	15,000 payroll checks	1,000 billed hrs.

The rates at which services are charged to each division are called **service department charge rates**. These rates are determined by dividing each service department's expenses by the total service usage as follows:

$$\text{Purchasing: } \frac{\$400,000}{40,000 \text{ purchase requisitions}} = \$10 \text{ per purchase requisition}$$

$$\text{Payroll Accounting: } \frac{\$255,000}{15,000 \text{ payroll checks}} = \$17 \text{ per payroll check}$$

$$\text{Legal: } \frac{\$250,000}{1,000 \text{ hours}} = \$250 \text{ per hour}$$

The use of services by the Theme Park and Movie Production Divisions is multiplied by the service department charge rates to determine the charges to each division, as shown in Exhibit 4.

The Theme Park Division employs many temporary and part-time employees who are paid weekly. This is in contrast to the Movie Production Division, which has a more permanent payroll that is paid on a monthly basis. As a result, the Theme Park Division requires 12,000 payroll checks. This results in a large service charge from Payroll Accounting to the Theme Park Division. In contrast, the Movie Production Division uses many legal services for contract negotiations. Thus, there is a large service charge from Legal to the Movie Production Division.

•Exhibit 4

Service Department
Charges to NEG Divisions

Nova Entertainment Group
Service Department Charges to NEG Divisions
For the Year Ended December 31, 2006

Service Department	Theme Park Division	Movie Production Division
Purchasing (Note A)	$250,000	$150,000
Payroll Accounting (Note B)	204,000	51,000
Legal (Note C)	25,000	225,000
Total service department charges	$479,000	$426,000

Note A:
25,000 purchase requisitions × $10 per purchase requisition = $250,000
15,000 purchase requisitions × $10 per purchase requisition = $150,000
Note B:
12,000 payroll checks × $17 per check = $204,000
3,000 payroll checks × $17 per check = $51,000
Note C:
100 hours × $250 per hour = $25,000
900 hours × $250 per hour = $225,000

If sales are $500,000, the cost of goods sold is $285,000, selling expenses are $85,000, and service department charges are $53,000, what is the income from operations?

$77,000 ($500,000 − $285,000 − $85,000 − $53,000)

Profit Center Reporting

The divisional income statements for NEG are presented in Exhibit 5. These statements show the service department charges to the divisions.

The ***income from operations*** is a measure of a manager's performance. In evaluating the profit center manager, the income from operations should be compared over time to a budget. It should not be compared across profit centers, since the profit centers are usually different in terms of size, products, and customers.

•Exhibit 5

Divisional Income
Statements—NEG

Nova Entertainment Group
Divisional Income Statements
For the Year Ended December 31, 2006

	Theme Park Division	Movie Production Division
Revenues*	$6,000,000	$2,500,000
Operating expenses	2,495,000	405,000
Income from operations before		
service department charges	$3,505,000	$2,095,000
Less service department charges:		
Purchasing	$ 250,000	$ 150,000
Payroll Accounting	204,000	51,000
Legal	25,000	225,000
Total service department		
charges	$ 479,000	$ 426,000
Income from operations	$3,026,000	$1,669,000

*For a profit center that sells products, the income statement would show: Net sales − Cost of goods sold = Gross profit. The selling and administrative expenses would be deducted from the gross profit to get the income from operations before service department charges.

Responsibility Accounting for Investment Centers

Compute and interpret the rate of return on investment, the residual income, and the balanced scorecard for an investment center.

In an ***investment center***, the unit manager has the responsibility and the authority to make decisions that affect not only costs and revenues but also the assets invested in the center. Investment centers are widely used in highly diversified companies organized by divisions.

The manager of an investment center has more authority and responsibility than the manager of a cost center or a profit center. The manager of an investment center occupies a position similar to that of a chief operating officer or president of a company and is evaluated in much the same way.

Since investment center managers have responsibility for revenues and expenses, income from operations is an important part of investment center reporting. In addition, because the manager has responsibility for the assets invested in the center, two additional measures of performance are often used. These measures are the rate of return on investment and residual income. Top management often compares these measures across investment centers to reward performance and assess investment in the centers.

To illustrate, assume that DataLink Inc. is a cellular phone company that has three regional divisions, Northern, Central, and Southern. Condensed divisional income statements for the investment centers are shown in Exhibit 6.

•**Exhibit 6**   Divisional Income Statements—DataLink Inc.

	Northern Division	Central Division	Southern Division
DataLink Inc.			
Divisional Income Statements			
For the Year Ended December 31, 2006			
Revenues	$560,000	$672,000	$750,000
Operating expenses	336,000	470,400	562,500
Income from operations before service department charges	$224,000	$201,600	$187,500
Service department charges	154,000	117,600	112,500
Income from operation	$ 70,000	$ 84,000	$ 75,000

Using only income from operations, the Central Division is the most profitable division. However, income from operations does not reflect the amount of assets invested in each center. For example, if the amount of assets invested in the Central Division is twice that of the other divisions, then the Central Division would be the least profitable in terms of the rate of return on these assets.

Rate of Return on Investment

Since investment center managers also control the amount of assets invested in their centers, they should be held accountable for the use of these assets. One measure that considers the amount of assets invested is the ***rate of return on investment***

(ROI) or **rate of return on assets**. It is one of the most widely used measures for investment centers and is computed as follows:

$$\text{Rate of return on investment (ROI)} = \frac{\text{Income from operations}}{\text{Invested assets}}$$

The rate of return on investment is useful because the three factors subject to control by divisional managers (revenues, expenses, and invested assets) are used in its computation. By measuring profitability relative to the amount of assets invested in each division, the rate of return on investment can be used to compare divisions. The higher the rate of return on investment, the better the division utilizes its assets to generate income. To illustrate, the rate of return on investment for each division of DataLink Inc., based on the book value of invested assets, is as follows:

	Northern Division	Central Division	Southern Division
Income from operations	$ 70,000	$ 84,000	$ 75,000
Invested assets	$350,000	$700,000	$500,000
Rate of return on investment	20%	12%	15%

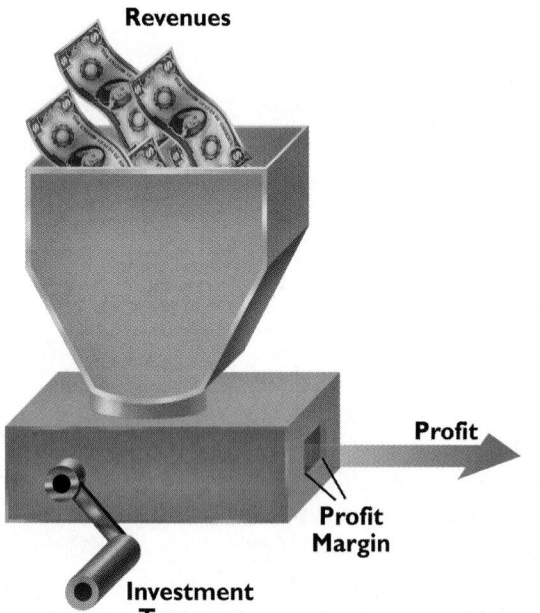

Revenues

Profit

Profit Margin

Investment Turnover

Although the Central Division generated the largest income from operations, its rate of return on investment (12%) is the lowest. Hence, relative to the assets invested, the Central Division is the least profitable division. In comparison, the rate of return on investment of the Northern Division is 20% and the Southern Division is 15%. One way to analyze these differences is by using an expanded formula, called the DuPont formula, for the rate of return on investment. The **DuPont formula**, created by a financial executive of **E.I. DuPont De Nemours & Co.** in 1919, states that the rate earned on total assets is the product of two factors.

The first factor is the ratio of income from operations to sales, often called the **profit margin**. The second factor is the ratio of sales to invested assets, often called the **investment turnover**. In the illustration at the left, profits can be earned by either increasing the investment turnover (turning the crank faster), by increasing the profit margin (increasing the size of the opening), or both.

Using the DuPont formula yields the same rate of return on investment for the Northern Division, 20%, as computed previously.

$$\text{Rate of return on investment (ROI)} = \text{Profit margin} \times \text{Investment turnover}$$

$$\text{Rate of return on investment (ROI)} = \frac{\text{Income from operations}}{\text{Sales}} \times \frac{\text{Sales}}{\text{Invested assets}}$$

$$\text{ROI} = \frac{\$\ 70,000}{\$560,000} \times \frac{\$560,000}{\$350,000}$$

$$\text{ROI} = 12.5\% \times 1.6$$
$$\text{ROI} = 20\%$$

The DuPont formula for the rate of return on investment is useful in evaluating and controlling divisions. This is because the profit margin and the investment turnover focus on the underlying operating relationships of each division.

The profit margin component focuses on profitability by indicating the rate of profit earned on each sales dollar. If a division's profit margin increases, and all other factors remain the same, the division's rate of return on investment will increase. For example, a division might add more profitable products to its sales mix and thereby increase its overall profit margin and rate of return on investment.

The investment turnover component focuses on efficiency in using assets and indicates the rate at which sales are generated for each dollar of invested assets. The more sales per dollar invested, the greater the efficiency in using the assets. If a division's investment turnover increases, and all other factors remain the same, the division's rate of return on investment will increase. For example, a division might attempt to increase sales through special sales promotions or reduce inventory assets by using just-in-time principles, either of which would increase investment turnover.

The rate of return on investment, using the DuPont formula for each division of DataLink Inc., is summarized as follows:

> The profit margin indicates the rate of profit on each sales dollar. The investment turnover indicates the rate of sales on each dollar of invested assets.

$$\text{Rate of return on investment (ROI)} = \frac{\text{Income from operations}}{\text{Sales}} \times \frac{\text{Sales}}{\text{Invested assets}}$$

$$\text{Northern Division (ROI)} = \frac{\$70,000}{\$560,000} \times \frac{\$560,000}{\$350,000}$$

$$\text{ROI} = 12.5\% \times 1.6$$
$$\text{ROI} = 20\%$$

$$\text{Central Division (ROI)} = \frac{\$84,000}{\$672,000} \times \frac{\$672,000}{\$700,000}$$

$$\text{ROI} = 12.5\% \times 0.96$$
$$\text{ROI} = 12\%$$

$$\text{Southern Division (ROI)} = \frac{\$75,000}{\$750,000} \times \frac{\$750,000}{\$500,000}$$

$$\text{ROI} = 10\% \times 1.5$$
$$\text{ROI} = 15\%$$

Although the Northern and Central Divisions have the same profit margins, the Northern Division investment turnover (1.6) is larger than that of the Central Division (0.96). Thus, by using its invested assets more efficiently, the Northern Division's rate of return on investment is higher than the Central Division's. The Southern Division's profit margin of 10% and investment turnover of 1.5 are lower than those of the Northern Division. The product of these factors results in a return on investment of 15% for the Southern Division, compared to 20% for the Northern Division.

To determine possible ways of increasing the rate of return on investment, the profit margin and investment turnover for a division may be analyzed. For example, if the Northern Division is in a highly competitive industry in which the profit margin cannot be easily increased, the division manager might focus on increasing the investment turnover. To illustrate, assume that the revenues of the Northern Division could be increased by $56,000 through increasing operating expenses, such as advertising, to $385,000. The Northern Division's income from operations will increase from $70,000 to $77,000, as shown below.

Income from operations is $35,000, invested assets are $140,000, and sales are $437,500. What is the (a) profit margin, (b) investment turnover, and (c) rate of return on investment?

- -

(a) 8% ($35,000/$437,500); (b) 3.125 ($437,500/$140,000); (c) 25% (8% × 3.125, or $35,000/$140,000)

Revenues ($560,000 + $56,000)	$616,000
Operating expenses	385,000
Income from operations before service department charges	$231,000
Service department charges	154,000
Income from operations	$ 77,000

The rate of return on investment for the Northern Division, using the DuPont formula, is recomputed as follows:

$$\text{Rate of return on investment (ROI)} = \frac{\text{Income from operations}}{\text{Sales}} \times \frac{\text{Sales}}{\text{Invested assets}}$$

$$\text{Northern Division revised ROI} = \frac{\$ 77,000}{\$616,000} \times \frac{\$616,000}{\$350,000}$$

$$\text{ROI} = 12.5\% \times 1.76$$
$$\text{ROI} = 22\%$$

REAL WORLD

Mars, Inc., candy company uses ROI as a measure of responsibility center performance. In its equation, total assets are measured at replacement cost instead of book value. As a result, it believes that its ROI gives management an incentive to replace equipment with the latest technology, since adding new equipment does not penalize the ROI with a larger denominator.

Although the Northern Division's profit margin remains the same (12.5%), the investment turnover has increased from 1.6 to 1.76, an increase of 10% (0.16 ÷ 1.6). The 10% increase in investment turnover also increases the rate of return on investment by 10% (from 20% to 22%).

In addition to using it as a performance measure, the rate of return on investment may assist management in other ways. For example, in considering a decision to expand the operations of DataLink Inc., management might consider giving priority to the Northern Division because it earns the highest rate of return on investment. If the current rates of return on investment are maintained in the future, an investment in the Northern Division will return 20 cents (20%) on each dollar invested. In contrast, investments in the Central Division will earn only 12 cents per dollar invested, and investments in the Southern Division will return only 15 cents per dollar.

A disadvantage of the rate of return on investment as a performance measure is that it may lead divisional managers to reject new investments that could be profitable for the company as a whole. For example, the Northern Division of DataLink Inc. has an overall rate of return on investment of 20%. The minimum acceptable

MANAGERIAL DISCLOSURE AND ANALYSIS

TIME WARNER

The annual report of public companies must provide segment disclosure information identifying revenues, income from operations, and total assets. This information can be used with the DuPont formula to calculate the return on investment (ROI) for the segments of a company. For example, **Time Warner Inc.** operates three major segments:

1. *Cable:* Cable television systems, such as TWI Cable.

2. *Filmed Entertainment:* Warner Bros. and New Line Cinema studios and television production.
3. *Networks:* Cable television and broadcast network programming, such as Turner Networks, Home Box Office, and the WB.

The DuPont formulas for these three segments, as derived from a recent annual report, are as follows:

	Profit Margin	×	Investment Turnover	=	Return on Investment
Cable	−2.4%		0.11		−0.3%
Filmed Entertainment	3.2%		0.42		1.3%
Networks	9.6%		0.27		2.6%

As can be seen from these data, Time Warner's three segments all have very low investment turnovers, at less than 0.50. The Cable segment has a strikingly low investment turnover at 0.11. The profit margins for Cable are negative, while the Filmed Entertainment segment has a weak profit margin of 3.2%. The Networks boasted the best margins at nearly 10%. Multiplying the profit margin by the investment turnover yields the ROI. The ROI is weak for all three segments. This information indicates that the Cable segment's profit margins and investment turnover must be improved. Expanding the number of subscribers or services, such as high-speed Internet services, could help improve both the profit margin and investment turnover of this segment. The Filmed Entertainment segment could improve profit margins and investment turnover by producing more blockbuster hits, such as *Lord of the Rings*. The Networks segment is very sensitive to advertising revenue. Advertising revenues were depressed from an industry slowdown. However, as the advertising cycle returns to health, the Networks segment should benefit.

rate of return on investment for DataLink Inc. is 10%. The manager of the Northern Division has the opportunity of investing in a new project that is estimated will earn a 17% rate of return. If the manager of the Northern Division invests in the project, however, the Northern Division's overall rate of return will decrease from 20%. Thus, the division manager might decide to reject the project, even though the investment would exceed DataLink's minimum acceptable rate of return on investment. The CFO of **Millennium Chemicals Inc.** referred to a similar situation by stating: "We had too many divisional executives who failed to spend money on capital projects with more than satisfactory returns because those projects would have lowered the average return on assets of their particular business."

Residual Income

An additional measure of evaluating divisional performance—residual income—is useful in overcoming some of the disadvantages associated with the rate of return on investment. **Residual income**[1] is the excess of income from operations over a minimum acceptable income from operations, as illustrated below.

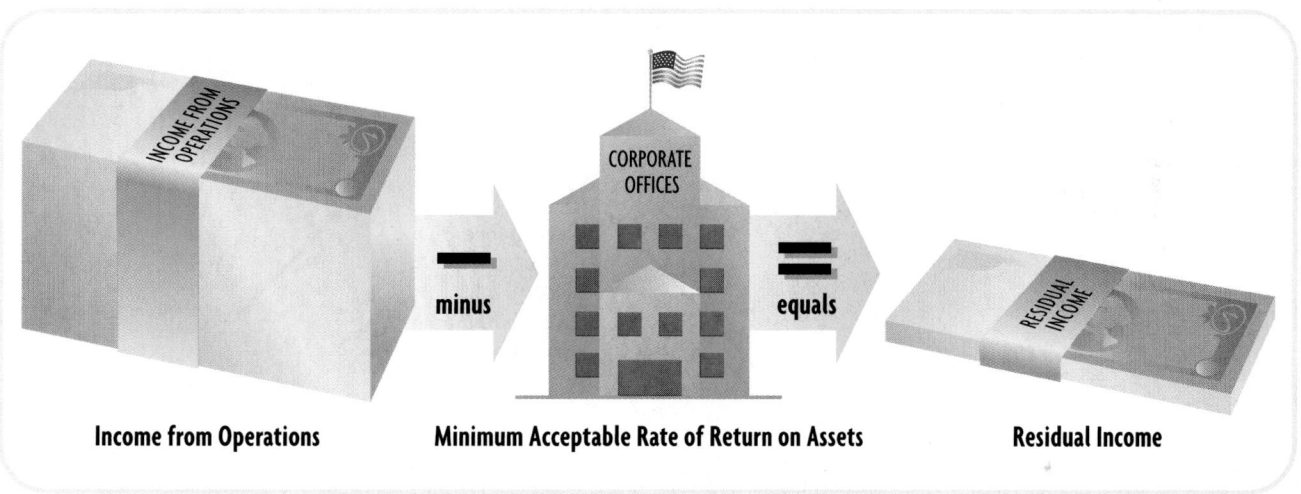

Income from Operations — Minimum Acceptable Rate of Return on Assets = Residual Income

The minimum acceptable income from operations is normally computed by multiplying a minimum rate of return by the amount of divisional assets. The minimum rate is set by top management, based on such factors as the cost of financing the business operations. To illustrate, assume that DataLink Inc. has established 10% as the minimum acceptable rate of return on divisional assets. The residual incomes for the three divisions are as follows:

The International Division has income from operations of $87,000 and assets of $240,000. The minimum acceptable rate of return on assets is 12%. What is the residual income for the division?

$58,200 [$87,000 − ($240,000 × 12%)]

	Northern Division	Central Division	Southern Division
Income from operations	$70,000	$84,000	$75,000
Minimum acceptable income from operations as a percent of assets:			
$350,000 × 10%	35,000		
$700,000 × 10%		70,000	
$500,000 × 10%			50,000
Residual income	$35,000	$14,000	$25,000

[1]Another popular term for residual income is Economic Value Added (EVA), which has been trademarked by the consulting firm **Stern Stewart & Co.**

REAL WORLD

Briggs & Stratton, a small engine manufacturer, uses residual income selectively in its business. In its engine plant, residual income was replaced with traditional productivity measures because the employees did not control investments in the plant. However, residual income was used with great success in the foundry because workers had influence on investments and other drivers of residual income, such as equipment uptime, scrap, rework, and attendance.

The Northern Division has more residual income than the other divisions, even though it has the least amount of income from operations. This is because the assets on which to earn a minimum acceptable rate of return are less for the Northern Division than for the other divisions.

The major advantage of residual income as a performance measure is that it considers both the minimum acceptable rate of return and the total amount of the income from operations earned by each division. Residual income encourages division managers to maximize income from operations in excess of the minimum. This provides an incentive to accept any project that is expected to have a rate of return in excess of the minimum. Thus, the residual income number supports both divisional and overall company objectives.

The Balanced Scorecard[2]

In addition to financial divisional performance measures, many companies are also relying on nonfinancial divisional measures. One popular evaluation approach is the **balanced scorecard**. The balanced scorecard is a set of financial and nonfinancial measures that reflect multiple performance dimensions of a business. A common balanced scorecard design measures performance in the innovation and learning, customer, internal, and financial dimensions of a business. These four areas can be diagrammed as shown in Exhibit 7.

•Exhibit 7

The Balanced Scorecard

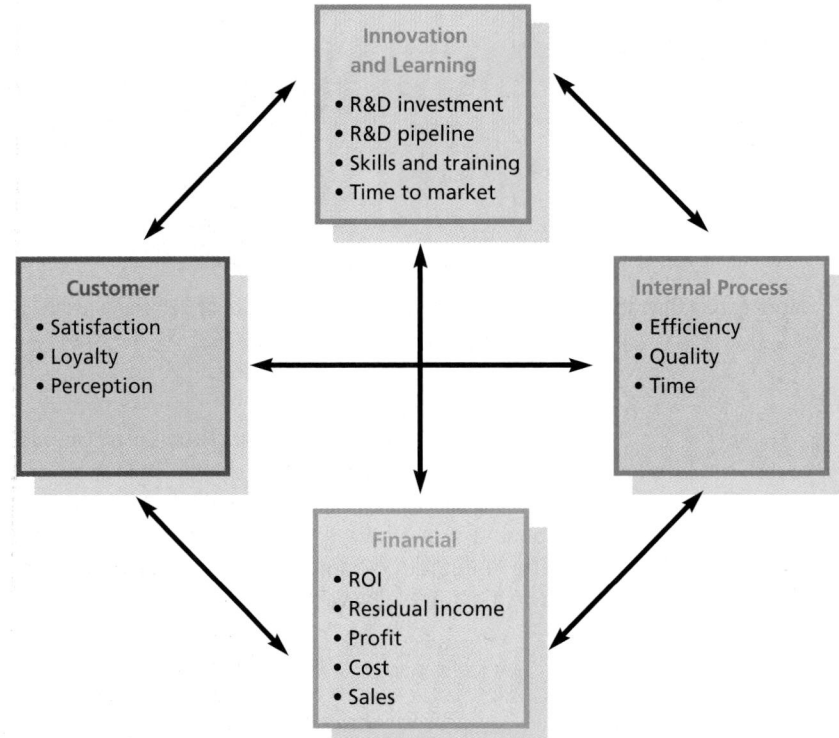

REAL WORLD

Pitney Bowes, a manufacturer of mail metering equipment, developed a balanced scorecard around financial, customer loyalty, competition, employees, and partner dimensions. The final system was placed on the firm's internal Web site, using a "traffic light" approach, where red, yellow, and green are used to indicate when a measure is below, at, or above target.

The *innovation and learning* perspective measures the amount of innovation in an organization. For example, a drug company, such as **Merck**, would measure the number of drugs in its FDA (Food and Drug Administration) approval pipeline, the amount of research and development (R&D) spending per period, and the length of time it takes to turn ideas into marketable products. Managing the performance of its R&D processes is critical to Merck's longer-term prospects and thus would be an

---

[2]The balanced scorecard was developed by R. S. Kaplan and D. P. Norton and explained in *The Balanced Scorecard: Translating Strategy into Action* (Cambridge: Harvard Business School Press, 1996).

additional performance perspective beyond the financial numbers. The *customer* perspective would measure customer satisfaction, loyalty, and perceptions. For example, **Amazon.com** measures the number of repeat visitors to its Web site as a measure of customer loyalty. Amazon.com needs repeat business because the costs to acquire a new customer are very high. The *internal process* perspective measures the effectiveness and efficiency of internal business processes. For example, **DaimlerChrysler** measures quality by the average warranty claims per automobile, measures efficiency by the average labor hours per automobile, and measures the average time to assemble each automobile. The *financial* perspective measures the economic performance of the responsibility center as we have illustrated in the previous sections of this chapter. All companies will use financial measures. The measures most commonly used are income from operations as a percent of sales and rate of return on investment.

The balanced scorecard is designed to reveal the underlying nonfinancial drivers, or causes, of financial performance. For example, if a business improves customer satisfaction, this will likely lead to improved financial performance. In addition, the balanced scorecard helps managers consider trade-offs between short- and long-term performance. For example, additional investment in research and development (R&D) would penalize the short-term financial perspective, because R&D is an expense that reduces income from operations. However, the innovation perspective would measure additional R&D expenditures favorably, because current R&D expenditures will lead to future profits from new products. The balanced scorecard will motivate the manager to invest in new R&D, even though it is recognized as a current period expense. A survey by Bain & Co., a consulting firm, indicated that 62% of large companies use the balanced scorecard.[3] Thus, the balanced scorecard is gaining acceptance because of its ability to reveal the underlying causes of financial performance, while helping managers consider the short- and long-term implications of their decisions.

I'm a global giant, reeling in some $7 billion in sales annually. Brands in my big plastic bin include Sharpie, Paper Mate, Parker, Waterman, Rubbermaid, Blue Ice, Calphalon, Little Tikes, Graco, Levolor, Kirsch, Shur-Line, and Eldon. Based in Freeport, Ill., I employ roughly 50,000 people worldwide. The two merged companies that make up my name began by selling curtain rods and toy balloons. I'm one of the most diverse injection-molding and blow-molding companies in the world. My biggest customer is Wal-Mart. Named the most powerful brand in the home products industry in 2001, I'm "how life gets organized." Who am I? (Go to page 937 for answer.)

Transfer Pricing

o b j e c t i v e **5**

Explain how the market price, negotiated price, and cost price approaches to transfer pricing may be used by decentralized segments of a business.

When divisions transfer products or render services to each other, a ***transfer price*** is used to charge for the products or services. Since transfer prices affect the goals for both divisions, setting these prices is a sensitive matter for division managers.

Transfer prices should be set so that overall company income is increased when goods are transferred between divisions. As we will illustrate, however, transfer prices may be misused in such a way that overall company income suffers.

In the following paragraphs, we discuss various approaches to setting transfer prices. Exhibit 8 shows the range of prices that results from common approaches to setting transfer prices.[4] Transfer prices can be set as low as the variable cost per unit or as high as the market price. Often, transfer prices are negotiated at some point between variable cost per unit and market price.

Transfer prices may be used when decentralized units are organized as cost, profit, or investment centers. To illustrate, we will use a packaged snack food company (Wilson Company) with no service departments and two operating divisions (Eastern and Western) organized as investment centers. Condensed divisional income statements for Wilson Company, assuming no transfers between divisions, are shown in Exhibit 9.

---

[3]Bain & Co., "Management Tools 2003."
[4]The discussion in this chapter highlights the essential concepts of transfer pricing. In-depth discussion of transfer pricing can be found in advanced texts.

•**Exhibit 8**

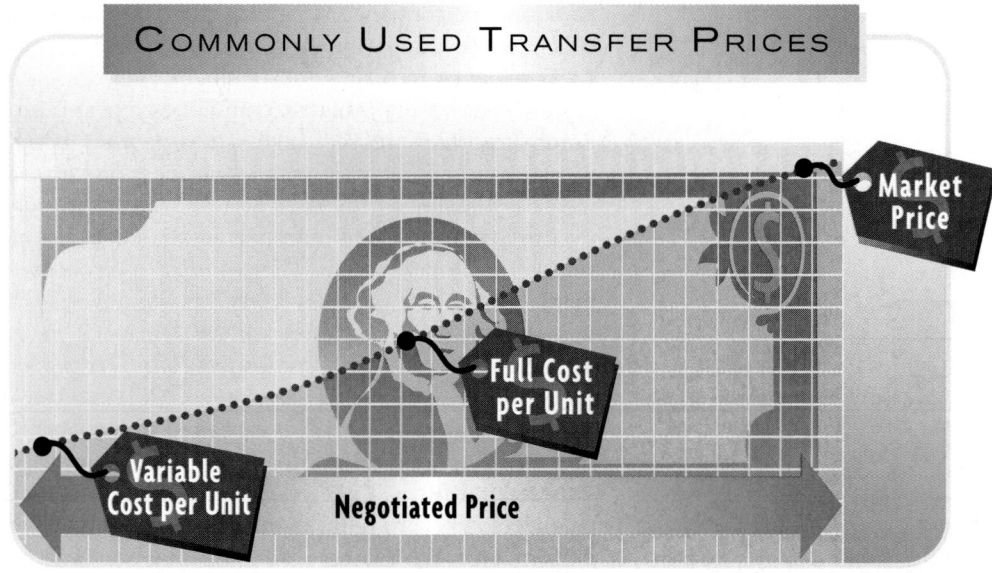

COMMONLY USED TRANSFER PRICES

Market Price

Full Cost per Unit

Variable Cost per Unit

Negotiated Price

•**Exhibit 9**

Income Statement—
No Transfers Between
Divisions

	Eastern Division	Western Division	Total
Wilson Company Divisional Income Statements For the Year Ended December 31, 2006			
Sales:			
50,000 units × $20 per unit	$1,000,000		$1,000,000
20,000 units × $40 per unit		$800,000	800,000
			$1,800,000
Expenses:			
Variable:			
50,000 units × $10 per unit . . .	$ 500,000		$ 500,000
20,000 units × $30* per unit . .		$600,000	600,000
Fixed	300,000	100,000	400,000
Total expenses	$ 800,000	$700,000	$1,500,000
Income from operations	$ 200,000	$100,000	$ 300,000

*$20 of the $30 per unit represents materials costs, and the remaining $10 per unit represents other variable conversion expenses incurred within the Western Division.

Market Price Approach

Using the ***market price approach***, the transfer price is the price at which the product or service transferred could be sold to outside buyers. If an outside market exists for the product or service transferred, the current market price may be a proper transfer price.

To illustrate, assume that materials used by Wilson Company in producing snack food in the Western Division are currently purchased from an outside supplier at $20 per unit. The same materials are produced by the Eastern Division. The Eastern Division is operating at full capacity of 50,000 units and can sell all it produces to either the Western Division or to outside buyers. A transfer price of $20 per unit (the market price) has no effect on the Eastern Division's income or total company income. The Eastern Division will earn revenues of $20 per unit on all its production and sales, regardless of who buys its product. Likewise, the Western Division will pay $20 per unit for materials (the market price). Thus, the use of the market price as the transfer price has no effect on the Eastern Division's income or total company income. In this situation, the use of the market price as the transfer price is proper. The condensed divisional income statements for Wilson Company in this case are also shown in Exhibit 9.

Negotiated Price Approach

If unused or excess capacity exists in the supplying division (the Eastern Division), and the transfer price is equal to the market price, total company profit may not be maximized. This is because the manager of the Western Division will be indifferent toward purchasing materials from the Eastern Division or from outside suppliers. Thus, the Western Division may purchase the materials from outside suppliers. If, however, the Western Division purchases the materials from the Eastern Division, the difference between the market price of $20 and the variable costs of the Eastern Division can cover fixed costs and contribute to company profits. When the negotiated price approach is used in this situation, the manager of the Western Division is encouraged to purchase the materials from the Eastern Division.

The *negotiated price approach* allows the managers of decentralized units to agree (negotiate) among themselves as to the transfer price. The only constraint on the negotiations is that the transfer price be less than the market price but greater than the supplying division's variable costs per unit.

To illustrate the use of the negotiated price approach, assume that instead of a capacity of 50,000 units, the Eastern Division's capacity is 70,000 units. In addition, assume that the Eastern Division can continue to sell only 50,000 units to outside buyers. A transfer price less than $20 would encourage the manager of the Western Division to purchase from the Eastern Division. This is because the Western Division's materials cost per unit would decrease, and its income from operations would increase. At the same time, a transfer price above the Eastern Division's variable costs per unit of $10 (from Exhibit 9) would encourage the manager of the Eastern Division to use the excess capacity to supply materials to the Western Division. In doing so, the Eastern Division's income from operations would increase.

We continue the illustration with the aid of Exhibit 10, assuming that Wilson Company's division managers agree to a transfer price of $15 for the Eastern Division's product. By purchasing from the Eastern Division, the Western Division's materials cost would be $5 per unit less. At the same time, the Eastern Division would increase its sales by $300,000 (20,000 units × $15 per unit) and increase its income by $100,000 ($300,000 sales − $200,000 variable costs). The effect of reducing the Western Division's materials cost by $100,000 (20,000 units × $5 per unit) is to increase its income by $100,000. Therefore, Wilson Company's income is increased by $200,000 ($100,000 reported by the Eastern Division and $100,000 reported by the Western Division), as shown in the condensed income statements in Exhibit 10.

In this illustration, any transfer price less than the market price of $20 but greater than the Eastern Division's unit variable costs of $10 would increase each division's income. In addition, overall company profit would increase by $200,000. By establishing a range of $20 to $10 for the transfer price, each division manager has an incentive to negotiate the transfer of the materials.

Cost Price Approach

Under the *cost price approach*, cost is used to set transfer prices. With this approach, a variety of cost concepts may be used. For example, cost may refer to either total product cost per unit or variable product cost per unit. If total product cost per unit is used, direct materials, direct labor, and factory overhead are included in the transfer price. If variable product cost per unit is used, the fixed factory overhead component of total product cost is excluded from the transfer price.

Either actual costs or standard (budgeted) costs may be used in applying the cost price approach. If actual costs are used, inefficiencies of the producing division are

•Exhibit 10

Income Statements—Negotiated Transfer Price

Wilson Company
Divisional Income Statements
For the Year Ended December 31, 2006

	Eastern Division	Western Division	Total
Sales:			
50,000 units × $20 per unit	$1,000,000		$1,000,000
20,000 units × $15 per unit	300,000		300,000
20,000 units × $40 per unit		$800,000	800,000
	$1,300,000	$800,000	$2,100,000
Expenses:			
Variable:			
70,000 units × $10 per unit . . .	$ 700,000		$ 700,000
20,000 units × $25* per unit . .		$500,000	500,000
Fixed	300,000	100,000	400,000
Total expenses	$1,000,000	$600,000	$1,600,000
Income from operations	$ 300,000	$200,000	$ 500,000

*$10 of the $25 are variable conversion expenses incurred solely within the Western Division, and $15 per unit represents the transfer price per unit from the Eastern Division.

transferred to the purchasing division. Thus, there is little incentive for the producing division to control costs carefully. For this reason, most companies use standard costs in the cost price approach. In this way, differences between actual and standard costs remain with the producing division for cost control purposes.

When division managers have responsibility for cost centers, the cost price approach to transfer pricing is proper and is often used. The cost price approach may not be proper, however, for decentralized operations organized as profit or investment centers. In profit and investment centers, division managers have responsibility for both revenues and expenses. The use of cost as a transfer price ignores the supplying division manager's responsibility for revenues. When a supplying division's sales are all intracompany transfers, for example, using the cost price approach prevents the supplying division from reporting any income from operations. A cost-based transfer price may therefore not motivate the division manager to make intracompany transfers, even though they are in the best interests of the company.

INTEGRITY IN BUSINESS

SHIFTING INCOME THROUGH TRANSFER PRICES

Transfer prices effectively shift tax burdens of multinational corporations across different countries. For example, assume that a multinational corporation has one division in the United States and another division outside the United States. If the tax rate is lower outside the United States, the corporation has incentives to shift income to the division outside the United States. Setting the U.S. division's purchase transfer prices high and selling transfer prices low can achieve this. For example, a recent Government Accounting Office (GAO) report found that some U.S. subsidiaries bought safety pins at $29 per piece and sold pianos for $50 each and tractor tires for $7.89 each. To control this behavior, the tax codes in the United States and most other countries require transfer prices at "Basic Arm's-Length Standard" (BALS), which is often interpreted as market price. However, even within this standard, there is subjectivity. Thus, financial managers must be careful to set transfer prices to meet economic objectives within the constraints of the transfer pricing laws of the countries in which they conduct business, or they could be subject to significant fines and legal action.

SPOTLIGHT ON STRATEGY

"ASSET LIGHT" STRATEGIES IN "ASSET HEAVY" INDUSTRIES

The asset strategies of various companies in a given industry can be explained by examining the DuPont formula. The relationships can be graphed with the investment turnover on the vertical axis and the profit margin on the horizontal axis. Thus, each firm can be plotted on the graph according to its unique profit margin and investment turnover combination. A graph for the freight transportation industry is shown below. Each point on the graph is a firm in the freight transportation industry. For example, **FedEx Corp.** is shown in the graph as having a 5.6% profit margin and a 1.49 investment turnover. Other firms plotted on the graph are trucking companies, such as **Yellow Corp.**, railroads, such as **Union Pacific Corp.**, and logistics service providers, such as **C.H. Robinson Worldwide**.

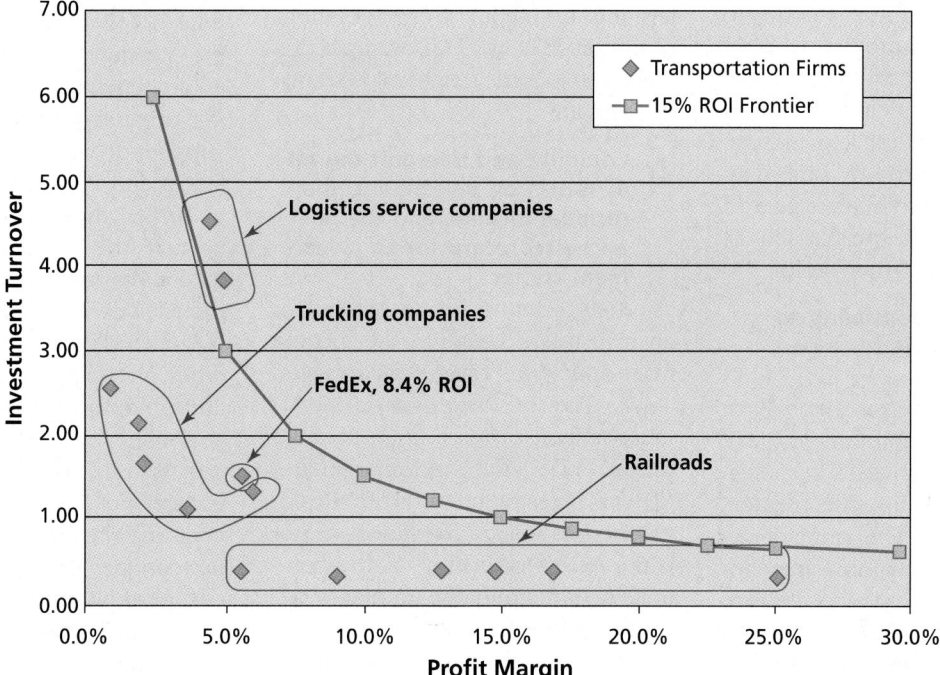

The 15% ROI frontier represents all the combinations of profit margin and return on investment that, when multiplied, equal 15%. Thus, a 15% ROI can also be achieved by many different combinations of profit margin and investment turnover. The closer a firm is to the frontier, the closer it is to a 15% ROI.

The freight transportation industry exhibits a number of different strategies. For example, the railroads are all very asset intensive; thus, their investment turnovers are the lowest of all the firms (all below 0.4). The trucking firms all have higher investment turnover than the railroads, but their profit margins are mostly lower. The trucking firms generally have ROIs of 4%–6%, which is slightly better than the railroads.

The two logistics service companies are able to exceed the 15% ROI frontier. Both companies have the highest investment turnover in the industry, while earning profit margins comparable to the truckers. These firms accomplish this by providing "door-to-door" logistics services without owning the trucks, trains, or planes that provide this service. That is, these companies arrange, manage, and purchase shipping services on behalf of their customers. This is an example of an "asset light" strategy. The logistics service companies rely on other "asset heavy" companies to supply the shipping service, while earning a margin from managing the complex logistical details.

Key Points

1 List and explain the advantages and disadvantages of decentralized operations.

The advantages of decentralization may include better decisions by the managers closest to the operations, more time for top management to focus on strategic planning, training for managers, improved ability to serve customers and respond to their needs, and improved manager morale. The disadvantages of decentralization may include failure of the company to maximize profits because decisions made by one manager may affect other managers in such a way that the profitability of the entire company may suffer.

2 Prepare a responsibility accounting report for a cost center.

Since managers of cost centers have responsibility and authority to make decisions regarding costs, responsibility accounting for cost centers focuses on costs. The primary accounting tools for planning and controlling costs for a cost center are budgets and budget performance reports. An example of a budget performance report is shown in Exhibit 1.

3 Prepare responsibility accounting reports for a profit center.

In preparing a profitability report for a profit center, operating expenses are subtracted from revenues in order to determine the income from operations before service department charges. Service department charges are then subtracted in order to determine the income from operations of the profit center. An example of a divisional income statement is shown in Exhibit 5.

4 Compute and interpret the rate of return on investment, the residual income, and the balanced scorecard for an investment center.

The rate of return on investment for an investment center is the income from operations divided by invested assets. The rate of return on investment may also be computed as the product of (1) the profit margin and (2) the investment turnover. Residual income for an investment center is the excess of income from operations over a minimum amount of desired income from operations. The balanced scorecard combines nonfinancial measures in order to help managers consider the underlying causes of financial performance and tradeoffs between short-term and long-term performance.

5 Explain how the market price, negotiated price, and cost price approaches to transfer pricing may be used by decentralized segments of a business.

Under the market price approach, the transfer price is the price at which the product or service transferred could be sold to outside buyers. Market price should be used when the supplier division is able to sell to outsiders and is operating at capacity.

Under the negotiated price approach, the managers of decentralized units agree (negotiate) among themselves as to the transfer price. Negotiated prices should be used when the supplier division is operating below capacity.

Under the cost price approach, cost is used as the basis for setting transfer prices. A variety of cost concepts may be used, such as total product cost per unit or variable product cost per unit. In addition, actual costs or standard (budgeted) costs may be used. The cost price approach should be used for supplier divisions that are organized as cost centers.

Key Terms

balanced scorecard (928)
controllable expenses (919)
cost center (917)
cost price approach (931)
decentralization (916)
division (916)
DuPont formula (924)

income from operations (922)
investment center (923)
investment turnover (924)
market price approach (930)
negotiated price approach (931)
profit center (919)
profit margin (924)

rate of return on investment (ROI) (923)
residual income (927)
responsibility accounting (917)
service department charges (920)
transfer price (929)

Illustrative Problem

Quinn Company has two divisions, Domestic and International. Invested assets and condensed income statement data for each division for the past year ended December 31 are as follows:

	Domestic Division	International Division
Revenues	$675,000	$480,000
Operating expenses	450,000	372,400
Service department charges	90,000	50,000
Invested assets	600,000	384,000

Instructions

1. Prepare condensed income statements for the past year for each division.
2. Using the DuPont formula, determine the profit margin, investment turnover, and rate of return on investment for each division.
3. If management's minimum acceptable rate of return is 10%, determine the residual income for each division.

Solution

1.

Quinn Company
Divisional Income Statements
For the Year Ended December 31, 2006

	Domestic Division	International Division
Revenues	$675,000	$480,000
Operating expenses	450,000	372,400
Income from operations before		
service department charges	$225,000	$107,600
Service department charges	90,000	50,000
Income from operations	$135,000	$ 57,600

2.

$$\text{Rate of return on investment (ROI)} = \text{Profit margin} \times \text{Investment turnover}$$

$$\text{Rate of return on investment (ROI)} = \frac{\text{Income from operations}}{\text{Sales}} \times \frac{\text{Sales}}{\text{Invested assets}}$$

Domestic Division: $\text{ROI} = \dfrac{\$135,000}{\$675,000} \times \dfrac{\$675,000}{\$600,000}$

$$\text{ROI} = 20\% \times 1.125$$
$$\text{ROI} = 22.5\%$$

International Division: $\text{ROI} = \dfrac{\$ 57,600}{\$480,000} \times \dfrac{\$480,000}{\$384,000}$

$$\text{ROI} = 12\% \qquad \times 1.25$$
$$\text{ROI} = 15\%$$

3. Domestic Division: $75,000 [$135,000 − (10% × $600,000)]
   International Division: $19,200 [$57,600 − (10% × $384,000)]

Self-Examination Questions (Answers at End of Chapter)

1. When the manager has the responsibility and authority to make decisions that affect costs and revenues but no responsibility for or authority over assets invested in the department, the department is called:
   A. a cost center
   B. a profit center
   C. an investment center
   D. a service department

2. The Accounts Payable Department has expenses of $600,000 and makes 150,000 payments to the various vendors who provide products and services to the divisions. Division A has income from operations of $900,000, before service department charges, and requires 60,000 payments to vendors. If the Accounts Payable Department is treated as a service department, what is Division A's income from operations?
   A. $300,000
   B. $900,000
   C. $660,000
   D. $540,000

3. Division A of Kern Co. has sales of $350,000, cost of goods sold of $200,000, operating expenses of $30,000, and invested assets of $600,000. What is the rate of return on investment for Division A?
   A. 20%
   B. 25%
   C. 33%
   D. 40%

4. Division L of Liddy Co. has a rate of return on investment of 24% and an investment turnover of 1.6. What is the profit margin?
   A. 6%
   B. 15%
   C. 24%
   D. 38%

5. Which approach to transfer pricing uses the price at which the product or service transferred could be sold to outside buyers?
   A. Cost price approach
   B. Negotiated price approach
   C. Market price approach
   D. Standard cost approach

Class Discussion Questions

1. Differentiate between a cost center and a profit center.
2. Differentiate between a profit center and an investment center.
3. In what major respect would budget performance reports prepared for the use of plant managers of a manufacturing business with cost centers differ from those prepared for the use of the various department supervisors who report to the plant managers?
4. For what decisions is the manager of a cost center *not* responsible?
5. **Weyerhaeuser Company** developed a system that assigns service department expenses to user divisions on the basis of actual services consumed by the division. Here are a number of Weyerhaeuser's activities in its central financial services department:

   REAL WORLD

   • Payroll
   • Accounts payable
   • Accounts receivable
   • Database administration—report preparation

   For each activity, identify an output measure that could be used to charge user divisions for service.
6. What is the major shortcoming of using income from operations as a performance measure for investment centers?
7. Why should the factors under the control of the investment center manager (revenues, expenses, and invested assets) be considered in computing the rate of return on investment?
8. In a decentralized company in which the divisions are organized as investment centers, how could a division be considered the least profitable even though it earned the largest amount of income from operations?

9. How does using the rate of return on investment facilitate comparability between divisions of decentralized companies?
10. The rates of return on investment for Harmon Co.'s three divisions, A, B, and C, are 20%, 17%, and 15%, respectively. In expanding operations, which of Harmon Co.'s divisions should be given priority? Explain.
11. Why would a firm use a balanced scorecard in evaluating divisional performance?
12. What is the objective of transfer pricing?
13. When is the negotiated price approach preferred over the market price approach in setting transfer prices?
14. Why would standard cost be a more appropriate transfer cost between cost centers than actual cost?
15. When using the negotiated price approach to transfer pricing, within what range should the transfer price be established?

---

resources for your success online at **http://warren.swlearning.com**

Remember! If you need additional help, visit South-Western's Web site. See page 28 for a description of the online and printed materials that are available. http://warren.swlearning.com

Warren Reeve Fess

Answer: Newell Rubbermaid

Exercises

EXERCISE 22-1
Budget performance reports for cost centers

Objective 2

✓ c. $1,650

Partially completed budget performance reports for Air-Cool Company, a manufacturer of air conditioners, are provided below.

Air-Cool Company
Budget Performance Report—Vice-President, Production
For the Month Ended April 30, 2006

Plant	Budget	Actual	Over Budget	Under Budget
St. Louis Plant	$258,900	$257,800		$1,100
Tempe Plant	185,700	184,700		1,000
Syracuse Plant	(g)	(h)	$ (i)	
	$ (j)	$ (k)	$ (l)	$2,100

Air-Cool Company
Budget Performance Report—Manager, Syracuse Plant
For the Month Ended April 30, 2006

Department	Budget	Actual	Over Budget	Under Budget
Compressor Assembly	$ (a)	$ (b)	$ (c)	
Electronic Assembly	53,200	53,900	700	
Final Assembly	85,700	85,400		$300
	$ (d)	$ (e)	$ (f)	$300

Video Division	180 computers	4,200 checks
Audio Division	120	7,800
Total	300 computers	12,000 checks

The service department charges of the Computer Support Department and the Accounts Payable Department are considered controllable by the divisions. Corporate administrative expenses are not considered controllable by the divisions. The revenues, cost of goods sold, and operating expenses for the two divisions are as follows:

	Video	Audio
Revenues	$4,000,000	$3,400,000
Cost of goods sold	2,100,000	1,600,000
Operating expenses	750,000	700,000

Prepare the divisional income statements for the two divisions.

EXERCISE 22-8
Corrections to service department charges
Objective 3

WHAT'S WRONG WITH THIS? SPREADSHEET

✓ *b. Income from operations, Cargo Division, $1,275,000*

Pegasus Airlines Inc. has two divisions organized as profit centers, the Passenger Division and the Cargo Division. The following divisional income statements were prepared:

Pegasus Airlines Inc.
Divisional Income Statements
For the Year Ended October 31, 2006

		Passenger Division		Cargo Division
Revenues		$3,000,000		$3,000,000
Operating expenses		1,500,000		1,250,000
Income from operations before				
service department charges		$1,500,000		$1,750,000
Less service department charges:				
Training	$250,000		$250,000	
Flight scheduling	300,000		300,000	
Reservations	400,000	950,000	400,000	950,000
Income from operations		$ 550,000		$ 800,000

The service department charge rate for the service department costs was based on revenues. Since the revenues of the two divisions were the same, the service department charges to each division were also the same.

The following additional information is available:

	Passenger Division	Cargo Division	Total
Number of flight personnel trained	200	50	250
Number of flights	150	250	400
Number of reservations requested	20,000	—	20,000

a. Does the income from operations for the two divisions accurately measure performance?
b. Correct the divisional income statements, using the activity bases provided above in revising the service department charges.

EXERCISE 22-9
Profit center responsibility reporting
Objectives 3, 5

Sierra Sporting Goods Co. operates two divisions—the Camping Equipment Division and the Ski Equipment Division. The following income and expense accounts were provided from the trial balance as of June 30, 2006, the end of the current fiscal year, after all adjustments, including those for inventories, were recorded and posted:

Sales—Camping Equipment Division	$380,000
Sales—Ski Equipment Division	575,000
Cost of Goods Sold—Camping Equipment Division	205,000
Cost of Goods Sold—Ski Equipment Division	275,000
Sales Expense—Camping Equipment Division	60,000
Sales Expense—Ski Equipment Division	82,000
Administrative Expense—Camping Equipment Division	38,800
Administrative Expense—Ski Equipment Division	51,200
Advertising Expense	25,800
Transportation Expense	20,140
Accounts Receivable Collection Expense	11,620
Warehouse Expense	60,000

SPREADSHEET

✓ *Income from operations, Camping Equipment Division, $10,840*

The bases to be used in allocating expenses, together with other essential information, are as follows:

a. Advertising expense—incurred at headquarters, charged back to divisions on the basis of usage: Camping Equipment Division, $11,200; Ski Equipment Division, $14,600.

b. Transportation expense—charged back to divisions at a transfer price of $3.80 per bill of lading: Camping Equipment Division, 2,400 bills of lading; Ski Equipment Division, 2,900 bills of lading.

c. Accounts receivable collection expense—incurred at headquarters, charged back to divisions at a transfer price of $2.80 per invoice: Camping Equipment Division, 1,800 sales invoices; Ski Equipment Division, 2,350 sales invoices.

d. Warehouse expense—charged back to divisions on the basis of floor space used in storing division products: Camping Equipment Division, 10,000 square feet; Ski Equipment Division, 5,000 square feet.

Prepare a divisional income statement with two column headings: Camping Equipment Division and Ski Equipment Division. Provide supporting schedules for determining service department charges.

EXERCISE 22-10
Rate of return on investment
Objective 4

✓ *a. Milk Division, 25%*

The income from operations and the amount of invested assets in each division of Wisconsin Dairy Company are as follows:

	Income from Operations	Invested Assets
Cheese Division	$104,000	$ 800,000
Milk Division	160,000	640,000
Butter Division	297,600	1,240,000

a. Compute the rate of return on investment for each division.
b. Which division is the most profitable per dollar invested?

EXERCISE 22-11
Residual income
Objective 4

✓ *a. Cheese Division, $(16,000)*

Based on the data in Exercise 22-10, assume that management has established a 15% minimum acceptable rate of return for invested assets.

a. Determine the residual income for each division.
b. Which division has the most residual income?

EXERCISE 22-12
Determining missing items in rate of return computation
Objective 4

✓ *d. 1.5*

One item is omitted from each of the following computations of the rate of return on investment:

Rate of return on investment	=	Profit margin	×	Investment turnover
21%	=	15%	×	(a)
(b)	=	8%	×	1.75
18%	=	(c)	×	0.75
27%	=	18%	×	(d)
(e)	=	12%	×	2.0

Determine the missing items, identifying each by the appropriate letter.

EXERCISE 22-13
Profit margin, investment turnover, and rate of return on investment

Objective 4

✓ a. ROI, 12.6%

The condensed income statement for the New England Division of Eastern Gas Co. is as follows (assuming no service department charges):

Sales	$700,000
Cost of goods sold	320,000
Gross profit	$380,000
Administrative expenses	222,500
Income from operations	$157,500

The manager of the New England Division is considering ways to increase the rate of return on investment.

a. Using the DuPont formula for rate of return on investment, determine the profit margin, investment turnover, and rate of return on investment of the New England Division, assuming that $1,250,000 of assets have been invested in the New England Division.
b. If expenses could be reduced by $39,375 without decreasing sales, what would be the impact on the profit margin, investment turnover, and rate of return on investment for the New England Division?

EXERCISE 22-14
Rate of return on investment

Objective 4

REAL WORLD

✓ Media Networks ROI, 3.79%

The Walt Disney Corporation has four major sectors, described as follows:

- **Media Networks:** The ABC television and radio network, Disney channel, ESPN, A&E, E!, and Disney.com.
- **Parks and Resorts:** Disney World, Disney Land, Disney Cruise Line, and other resort properties.
- **Studio Entertainment:** Walt Disney Pictures, Touchstone Pictures, Hollywood Pictures, Miramax, and Disney theatrical productions.
- **Consumer Products:** Character merchandising, Disney stores, books, and magazines

Disney recently reported sector income from operations, revenue, and invested assets (in millions) as follows:

	Income from Operations	Revenue	Invested Assets
Media Networks	$ 986	$9,733	$26,038
Parks and Resorts	1,169	6,465	11,305
Studio Entertainment	273	6,662	7,879
Consumer Products	394	2,509	1,125

a. Use the DuPont formula to determine the rate of return on investment for the four Disney sectors. Round to four digits after the decimal place.
b. ▬▬▶ How do the four sectors differ in their profit margin, investment turnover, and return on investment?

EXERCISE 22-15
Determining missing items in rate of return and residual income computations

Objective 4

✓ c. $15,450

Data for Midas Mining Company is presented in the following table of rates of return on investment and residual incomes:

Invested Assets	Income from Operations	Rate of Return on Investment	Minimum Rate of Return	Minimum Acceptable Income from Operations	Residual Income
$515,000	$77,250	(a)	12%	(b)	(c)
$335,000	(d)	(e)	(f)	$50,250	$16,750
$220,000	(g)	14%	(h)	$35,200	(i)
$450,000	$54,000	(j)	10%	(k)	(l)

Determine the missing items, identifying each item by the appropriate letter.

EXERCISE 22-16
Determining missing items from computations

Objective 4

✓ a. (e) $750,000

Data for the North, East, South, and West Divisions of Columbia Wireless Communication Company are as follows:

	Sales	Income from Operations	Invested Assets	Rate of Return on Investment	Profit Margin	Investment Turnover
North	$365,000	(a)	(b)	20%	16%	(c)
East	(d)	$60,000	(e)	(f)	12.5%	0.64
South	$326,000	(g)	$407,500	12%	(h)	(i)
West	$850,000	$119,000	$680,000	(j)	(k)	(l)

a. Determine the missing items, identifying each by the letters (a) through (l).
b. Determine the residual income for each division, assuming that the minimum acceptable rate of return established by management is 10%.
c. Which division is the most profitable in terms of (1) return on investment and (2) residual income?

EXERCISE 22-17
Rate of return on investment, residual income

Objective 4

REAL WORLD

Hilton Hotels Corp. provides lodging services around the world. The company is separated into three major divisions:

- **Hotel ownership:** Hotels owned and operated by Hilton.
- **Managing and franchising:** Hotels franchised to others or managed for others.
- **Timeshare:** Resort properties managed for timeshare vacation owners.

Financial information for each division, from a recent annual report, is as follows (in millions):

	Hotel Ownership	Managing and Franchising	Timeshare
Revenues	$2,388	$342	$320
Income from operations	470	290	86
Total assets	4,542	668	333

a. Use the DuPont formula to determine the return on investment for each of the Hilton business divisions. Round to four digits after the decimal place.
b. Determine the residual income for each division, assuming a minimum acceptable income of 15% of total assets.
c. ▭▭▷ Interpret your results.

EXERCISE 22-18
Balanced scorecard

Objective 4

REAL WORLD

The **American Express Company** is a major financial services company, noted for its American Express® card. Below are some of the performance measures used by the company in its balanced scorecard.

Average cardmember spending	Number of merchant signings
Cards in force	Number of card choices
Earnings growth	Number of new card launches
Hours of credit consultant training	Return on equity
Investment in information technology	Revenue growth
Number of Internet features	

For each measure, identify whether the measure best fits the innovation, customer, internal process, or financial dimension of the balanced scorecard.

EXERCISE 22-19
Balanced scorecard

Objective 4

REAL WORLD

Several years ago, **United Parcel Service (UPS)** believed that the Internet was going to change the parcel delivery market and would require UPS to become a more nimble and customer-focused organization. As a result, UPS replaced its old measurement system, which was 90% oriented toward financial performance, with a balanced scorecard. The scorecard emphasized four "point of arrival" measures, which were:

1. Customer satisfaction index—a measure of customer satisfaction.
2. Employee relations index—a measure of employee sentiment and morale.
3. Competitive position—delivery performance relative to competition.
4. Time in transit—the time from order entry to delivery.

a. Why did UPS introduce a balanced scorecard and nonfinancial measures in its new performance measurement system?
b. Why do you think UPS included a factor measuring employee sentiment?

EXERCISE 22-20
Decision on transfer pricing
Objective 5
✓ a. $3,500,000

Materials used by the Truck Division of Monumental Motors are currently purchased from outside suppliers at a cost of $260 per unit. However, the same materials are available from the Component Division. The Component Division has unused capacity and can produce the materials needed by the Truck Division at a variable cost of $190 per unit.

a. If a transfer price of $210 per unit is established and 50,000 units of materials are transferred, with no reduction in the Component Division's current sales, how much would Monumental Motors' total income from operations increase?
b. How much would the Truck Division's income from operations increase?
c. How much would the Component Division's income from operations increase?

EXERCISE 22-21
Decision on transfer pricing
Objective 5
✓ b. $1,000,000

Based on the Monumental Motors data in Exercise 22-20, assume that a transfer price of $240 has been established and that 50,000 units of materials are transferred, with no reduction in the Component Division's current sales.

a. How much would Monumental Motors' total income from operations increase?
b. How much would the Truck Division's income from operations increase?
c. How much would the Component Division's income from operations increase?
d. If the negotiated price approach is used, what would be the range of acceptable transfer prices and why?

Problems Series A

PROBLEM 22-1A
Budget performance report for a cost center
Objective 2

SPREADSHEET
P.A.S.S.

Quill Net.Com, Inc. sells books over the Internet. The International Division is organized as a cost center. The budget for the International Division for the month ended April 30, 2006, is as follows (in millions):

Software engineer salaries	$155
Customer service salaries	85
Logistics salaries	170
Marketing salaries	240
Warehouse wages	105
Equipment depreciation	32
Insurance and property taxes	23
Total	$810

During April, the costs incurred in the International Division were as follows:

Software engineer salaries	$152
Customer service salaries	109
Logistics salaries	168
Marketing salaries	269
Warehouse wages	101
Equipment depreciation	32
Insurance and property taxes	22
Total	$853

Instructions
1. Prepare a budget performance report for the director of the International Division for the month of April.
2. For which costs might the director be expected to request supplemental reports?

PROBLEM 22-2A
Profit center responsibility reporting

Objective 3

SPREADSHEET

✔ 1. Income from operations, Coastal Division, $263,100

A.G. Bell Communications Company has three regional divisions organized as profit centers. The Chief Executive Officer (CEO) evaluates divisional performance, using income from operations as a percent of revenues. The following quarterly income and expense accounts were provided from the trial balance as of December 31, 2006:

Revenues—Central Division	$ 620,000
Revenues—Coastal Division	856,000
Revenues—Metro Division	1,180,000
Operating Expenses—Central Division	370,000
Operating Expenses—Coastal Division	495,700
Operating Expenses—Metro Division	675,200
Corporate Expenses—Shareholder Relations	65,000
Corporate Expenses—Customer Support	192,000
Corporate Expenses—Central Accounting	102,000
General Corporate Officers' Salaries	190,000

The company operates three service departments: Shareholder Relations, Customer Support, and Central Accounting. The Shareholder Relations Department conducts a variety of services for shareholders of the company. The Customer Support Department is the company's telephone point of contact for new service, complaints, and requests for repair. The department believes that the number of customer calls is an activity base for this work. The Central Accounting Department provides reports for division management. The department believes that the number of reports is an activity base for this work. The following additional information has been gathered:

	Central	Coastal	Metro
Number of customer calls	4,000	4,600	7,400
Number of accounting reports	800	1,400	1,200

Instructions

1. Prepare quarterly income statements showing income from operations for the three divisions. Use three column headings: Central, Coastal, and Metro.
2. Identify the most successful division according to the profit margin. Round whole percentages to two decimal places.
3. ▬▬▶ Provide a recommendation to the CEO for a better method for evaluating the performance of the divisions. In your recommendation, identify the major weakness of the present method.

PROBLEM 22-3A
Divisional income statements and rate of return on investment analysis

Objective 4

SPREADSHEET

✔ 2. Cereal Division, ROI, 10.08%

Hearty Morning Food Company is a diversified food products company with three operating divisions organized as investment centers. Condensed data taken from the records of the three divisions for the year ended June 30, 2006, are as follows:

	Cereal Division	Fruit Juice Division	Bread Division
Sales	$1,050,000	$1,400,000	$800,000
Cost of goods sold	760,000	900,000	520,000
Operating expenses	164,000	290,000	120,000
Invested assets	1,250,000	2,000,000	640,000

The management of Hearty Morning Food Company is evaluating each division as a basis for planning a future expansion of operations.

Instructions

1. Prepare condensed divisional income statements for the three divisions, assuming that there were no service department charges.
2. Using the DuPont formula for rate of return on investment, compute the profit margin, investment turnover, and rate of return on investment for each division.
3. ▬▬▶ If available funds permit the expansion of operations of only one division, which of the divisions would you recommend for expansion, based on (1) and (2)? Explain.

PROBLEM 22-4A
Effect of proposals on divisional performance

Objective 4

SPREADSHEET

✓1. ROI, 17.60%

A condensed income statement for the Music Division of Memphis Sounds Inc. for the year ended December 31, 2006, is as follows:

Sales	$410,000
Cost of goods sold	177,500
Gross profit	$232,500
Operating expenses	187,400
Income from operations	$ 45,100

Assume that the Music Division received no charges from service departments. The president of Memphis Sounds has indicated that the division's rate of return on a $256,250 investment must be increased to at least 20% by the end of the next year if operations are to continue. The division manager is considering the following three proposals:

Proposal 1: Transfer recording equipment with a book value of $51,250 to other divisions at no gain or loss and lease similar equipment. The annual lease payments would exceed the amount of depreciation expense on the old equipment by $12,300. This increase in expense would be included as part of the cost of goods sold. Sales would remain unchanged.

Proposal 2: Purchase new and more efficient disk reproduction equipment and thereby reduce the cost of goods sold by $53,300. Sales would remain unchanged, and the old equipment, which has no remaining book value, would be scrapped at no gain or loss. The new equipment would increase invested assets by an additional $256,250 for the year.

Proposal 3: Reduce invested assets by discontinuing a label. This action would eliminate sales of $70,000, cost of goods sold of $38,900, and operating expenses of $37,000. Assets of $43,750 would be transferred to other divisions at no gain or loss.

Instructions
1. Using the DuPont formula for rate of return on investment, determine the profit margin, investment turnover, and rate of return on investment for the Music Division for the past year.
2. Prepare condensed estimated income statements and calculate the invested assets for each proposal.
3. Using the DuPont formula for rate of return on investment, determine the profit margin, investment turnover, and rate of return on investment for each proposal.
4. Which of the three proposals would meet the required 20% rate of return on investment?
5. If the Music Division were in an industry where the profit margin could not be increased, how much would the investment turnover have to increase to meet the president's required 20% rate of return on investment?

PROBLEM 22-5A
Divisional performance analysis and evaluation

Objective 4

SPREADSHEET

✓2. Men's Division ROI, 22.5%

The vice-president of operations of Swift Shoe Company is evaluating the performance of two divisions organized as investment centers. Invested assets and condensed income statement data for the past year for each division are as follows:

	Men's Division	Women's Division
Sales	$480,000	$620,000
Cost of goods sold	275,000	376,000
Operating expenses	115,000	120,000
Invested assets	400,000	775,000

Instructions
1. Prepare condensed divisional income statements for the year ended December 31, 2006, assuming that there were no service department charges.
2. Using the DuPont formula for rate of return on investment, determine the profit margin, investment turnover, and rate of return on investment for each division.

3. If management desires a minimum acceptable rate of return of 20%, determine the residual income for each division.
4. ▭▭▶ Discuss the evaluation of the two divisions, using the performance measures determined in (1), (2), and (3).

PROBLEM 22-6A
Transfer pricing
Objective 5

SPREADSHEET

✓ *3. Total income from operations, $706,000*

Parker Packaging Company manufactures cardboard and packaging products, with two operating divisions, the Cardboard and Packaging Divisions. Condensed divisional income statements, which involve no intracompany transfers and which include a breakdown of expenses into variable and fixed components, are as follows:

Parker Packaging Company
Divisional Income Statements
For the Year Ended December 31, 2006

	Cardboard Division	Packaging Division	Total
Sales:			
10,000 units × $105 per unit	$1,050,000		$1,050,000
15,000 units × $190 per unit		$2,850,000	2,850,000
			$3,900,000
Expenses:			
Variable:			
10,000 units × $72 per unit	$ 720,000		$ 720,000
15,000 units × $135* per unit		$2,025,000	2,025,000
Fixed	155,000	360,000	515,000
Total expenses	$ 875,000	$2,385,000	$3,260,000
Income from operations	$ 175,000	$ 465,000	$ 640,000

*$105 of the $135 per case represents materials costs, and the remaining $30 per case represents other variable conversion expenses incurred within the Packaging Division.

The Cardboard Division is presently producing 10,000 cases out of a total capacity of 12,000 cases. Materials used in producing the Packaging Division's product are currently purchased from outside suppliers at a price of $105 per case. The Cardboard Division is able to produce the materials used by the Packaging Division. Except for the possible transfer of materials between divisions, no changes are expected in sales and expenses.

Instructions
1. ▭▭▶ Would the market price of $105 per case be an appropriate transfer price for Parker Packaging Company? Explain.
2. ▭▭▶ If the Packaging Division purchases 2,000 cases from the Cardboard Division, rather than externally, at a negotiated transfer price of $80 per case, how much would the income from operations of each division and the total company income from operations increase?
3. Prepare condensed divisional income statements for Parker Packaging Company, based on the data in (2).
4. ▭▭▶ If a transfer price of $100 per case is negotiated, how much would the income from operations of each division and the total company income from operations increase?
5. a. ▭▭▶ What is the range of possible negotiated transfer prices that would be acceptable for Parker Packaging Company?
   b. Assuming that the managers of the two divisions cannot agree on a transfer price, what price would you suggest as the transfer price?

Problems Series B

PROBLEM 22-1B
Budget performance report for a cost center

Objective 2

SPREADSHEET
P.A.S.S.

The Eastern District of CableVision Inc. is organized as a cost center. The budget for the Eastern District of CableVision Inc. for the month ended September 30, 2006, is as follows:

Sales salaries	$ 542,300
System administration salaries	296,400
Customer service salaries	101,300
Billing salaries	65,300
Maintenance	179,500
Depreciation of plant and equipment	61,000
Insurance and property taxes	27,300
Total	$1,273,100

During September, the costs incurred in the Eastern District were as follows:

Sales salaries	$ 541,600
System administration salaries	296,100
Customer service salaries	118,700
Billing salaries	64,900
Maintenance	180,500
Depreciation of plant and equipment	61,000
Insurance and property taxes	27,400
Total	$1,290,200

Instructions

1. Prepare a budget performance report for the manager of the Eastern District of CableVision Inc. for the month of September.
2. ✏ For which costs might the supervisor be expected to request supplemental reports?

PROBLEM 22-2B
Profit center responsibility reporting

Objective 3

SPREADSHEET

✓ 1. Income from operations, Northern Division, $182,500

Bi-Coastal Railroad Company organizes its three divisions, the Northwest, Western, and Northern Regions, as profit centers. The Chief Executive Officer (CEO) evaluates divisional performance, using income from operations as a percent of revenues. The following quarterly income and expense accounts were provided from the trial balance as of December 31, 2007:

Revenues—NW Region	$1,450,000
Revenues—W Region	2,350,000
Revenues—N Region	1,950,000
Operating Expenses—NW Region	950,000
Operating Expenses—W Region	1,750,000
Operating Expenses—N Region	1,430,000
Corporate Expenses—Dispatching	500,000
Corporate Expenses—Equipment	525,000
Corporate Expenses—Treasurer	350,000
General Corporate Officers' Salaries	650,000

The company operates three service departments: the Dispatching Department, the Equipment Department, and the Treasurer's Department. The Dispatching Department manages the scheduling and releasing of complete trains. The Equipment Department manages the railroad car inventories. It makes sure the right freight cars are at the right place at the right time. The Treasurer's Department conducts a variety of services for the company as a whole. The following additional information has been gathered:

	Northwest	Western	Northern
Number of scheduled trains	500	850	650
Number of railroad cars in inventory	6,000	8,000	7,000

Instructions

1. Prepare quarterly income statements showing income from operations for the three divisions. Use three column headings: Northwest, Western, and Northern.
2. Identify the most successful division according to the profit margin. Round whole percentages to two decimal places.
3. ▬▬▶ Provide a recommendation to the CEO for a better method for evaluating the performance of the divisions. In your recommendation, identify the major weakness of the present method.

PROBLEM 22-3B
Divisional income statements and rate of return on investment analysis

Objective 4

SPREADSHEET

✓ *2. Retail Broker Division ROI, 12.0%*

Eagle Financial Inc. is a diversified investment company with three operating divisions organized as investment centers. Condensed data taken from the records of the three divisions for the year ended December 31, 2006, are as follows:

	Retail Broker Division	E-trade Division	Mutual Fund Division
Fee revenue	$ 750,000	$280,000	$ 900,000
Operating expenses	390,000	257,600	729,000
Invested assets	3,000,000	80,000	1,125,000

The management of Eagle Financial Inc. is evaluating each division as a basis for planning a future expansion of operations.

Instructions

1. Prepare condensed divisional income statements for the three divisions, assuming that there were no service department charges.
2. Using the DuPont formula for rate of return on investment, compute the profit margin, investment turnover, and rate of return on investment for each division.
3. ▬▬▶ If available funds permit the expansion of operations of only one division, which of the divisions would you recommend for expansion, based on (1) and (2)? Explain.

PROBLEM 22-4B
Effect of proposals on divisional performance

Objective 4

SPREADSHEET

✓ *3. Proposal 3 ROI, 17.28%*

A condensed income statement for the Golf Equipment Division of Scottish Pride Inc. for the year ended January 31, 2006, is as follows:

Sales	$2,400,000
Cost of goods sold	1,325,000
Gross profit	$1,075,000
Operating expenses	727,000
Income from operations	$ 348,000

Assume that the Golf Equipment Division received no charges from service departments.

The president of Scottish Pride Inc. has indicated that the division's rate of return on a $2,000,000 investment must be increased to at least 20% by the end of the next year if operations are to continue. The division manager is considering the following three proposals:

Proposal 1: Transfer equipment with a book value of $500,000 to other divisions at no gain or loss and lease similar equipment. The annual lease payments would exceed the amount of depreciation expense on the old equipment by $36,000. This increase in expense would be included as part of the cost of goods sold. Sales would remain unchanged.

Proposal 2: Reduce invested assets by discontinuing a product line. This action would eliminate sales of $250,000, cost of goods sold of $161,500, and operating expenses of $20,000. Assets of $280,000 would be transferred to other divisions at no gain or loss.

Proposal 3: Purchase new and more efficient machinery and thereby reduce the cost of goods sold by $84,000. Sales would remain unchanged, and the old machinery, which has no remaining book value, would be scrapped at no gain or loss. The new machinery would increase invested assets by $500,000 for the year.

Instructions

1. Using the DuPont formula for rate of return on investment, determine the profit margin, investment turnover, and rate of return on investment for the Golf Equipment Division for the past year.
2. Prepare condensed estimated income statements and calculate the invested assets for each proposal.
3. Using the DuPont formula for rate of return on investment, determine the profit margin, investment turnover, and rate of return on investment for each proposal.
4. Which of the three proposals would meet the required 20% rate of return on investment?
5. If the Golf Equipment Division were in an industry where the profit margin could not be increased, how much would the investment turnover have to increase to meet the president's required 20% rate of return on investment? Round to two digits after the decimal place.

PROBLEM 22-5B
Divisional performance analysis and evaluation
Objective 4

SPREADSHEET

✓ *2. Office Division ROI, 30%*

The vice-president of operations of Holland Commercial Furniture Company is evaluating the performance of two divisions organized as investment centers. Invested assets and condensed income statement data for the past year for each division are as follows:

	Office Division	Hotel Division
Sales	$1,200,000	$1,800,000
Cost of goods sold	650,000	1,100,000
Operating expenses	250,000	250,000
Invested assets	1,000,000	3,600,000

Instructions

1. Prepare condensed divisional income statements for the year ended July 31, 2006, assuming that there were no service department charges.
2. Using the DuPont formula for rate of return on investment, determine the profit margin, investment turnover, and rate of return on investment for each division.
3. If management's minimum acceptable rate of return is 15%, determine the residual income for each division.
4. ▶ Discuss the evaluation of the two divisions, using the performance measures determined in (1), (2), and (3).

PROBLEM 22-6B
Transfer pricing
Objective 5

SPREADSHEET

✓ *4. Instruments Division, $110,000*

Allied Instrument Company is a diversified aerospace company, with two operating divisions, Electronics and Instruments Divisions. Condensed divisional income statements, which involve no intracompany transfers and which include a breakdown of expenses into variable and fixed components, are as follows:

Allied Instrument Company
Divisional Income Statements
For the Year Ended December 31, 2006

	Electronics Division	Instruments Division	Total
Sales:			
800 units × $1,650 per unit	$1,320,000		$1,320,000
1,250 units × $2,480 per unit		$3,100,000	3,100,000
			$4,420,000
Expenses:			
Variable:			
800 units × $970 per unit	$ 776,000		$ 776,000
1,250 units × $1,950* per unit		$2,437,500	2,437,500
Fixed	244,000	318,000	562,000
Total expenses	$1,020,000	$2,755,500	$3,775,500
Income from operations	$ 300,000	$ 344,500	$ 644,500

*$1,650 of the $1,950 per unit represents materials costs, and the remaining $300 per unit represents other variable conversion expenses incurred within the Instruments Division.

The Electronics Division is presently producing 800 units out of a total capacity of 1,000 units. Materials used in producing the Instruments Division's product are currently purchased from outside suppliers at a price of $1,650 per unit. The Electronics Division is able to produce the components used by the Instruments Division. Except for the possible transfer of materials between divisions, no changes are expected in sales and expenses.

Instructions

1.  Would the market price of $1,650 per unit be an appropriate transfer price for Allied Instrument Company? Explain.
2.  If the Instruments Division purchases 200 units from the Electronics Division, rather than externally, at a negotiated transfer price of $1,450 per unit, how much would the income from operations of each division and total company income from operations increase?
3. Prepare condensed divisional income statements for Allied Instrument Company, based on the data in (2).
4.  If a transfer price of $1,100 per unit is negotiated, how much would the income from operations of each division and total company income from operations increase?
5. a.  What is the range of possible negotiated transfer prices that would be acceptable for Allied Instrument Company?
   b. Assuming that the managers of the two divisions cannot agree on a transfer price, what price would you suggest as the transfer price?

Special Activities

ACTIVITY 22-1
Ethics and professional conduct in business

ETHICS

Jolly Giant Company has two divisions, the Can Division and the Food Division. The Food Division may purchase cans from the Can Division or from outside suppliers. The Can Division sells can products both internally and externally. The market price for cans is $100 per 1,000 cans. Dan Jacobs is the controller of the Food Division, and Bonnie Clark is the controller of the Can Division. The following conversation took place between Dan and Bonnie:

Dan: I hear you are having problems selling cans out of your division. Maybe I can help.

Bonnie: You've got that right. We're producing and selling at only 70% of our capacity to outsiders. Last year we were selling all we could make. It would help a great deal if your division would divert some of your purchases to our division so we could use up our capacity. After all, we are part of the same company.

Dan: What kind of price could you give me?

Bonnie: Well, you know as well as I that we are under strict profit responsibility in our divisions, so I would expect to get market price, $100 for 1,000 cans.

Dan: I'm not so sure we can swing that. I was expecting a price break from a "sister" division.

Bonnie: Hey, I can only take this "sister" stuff so far. If I give you a price break, our profits will fall from last year's levels. I don't think I could explain that. I'm sorry, but I must remain firm—market price. After all, it's only fair—that's what you would have to pay from an external supplier.

Dan: Fair or not, I think we'll pass. Sorry we couldn't have helped.

 Was Dan behaving ethically by trying to force the Can Division into a price break? Comment on Bonnie's reactions.

ACTIVITY 22-2
Service department charges

The Accounting Department of Faber University asked the Publications Department to prepare a brochure for the Masters of Accountancy program. The Publications Department delivered the brochures and charged the Accounting Department a rate that was 20% higher than could be obtained from an outside printing company. The policy of the university required the Accounting Department to use the internal publications group for brochures. The Publications Department claimed that it had a drop in demand for its services during the fiscal year, so it had to charge higher prices in order to recover its payroll and fixed costs.

➤ Should the cost of the brochure be transferred to the Accounting Department in order to hold the department head accountable for the cost of the brochure? What changes in policy would you recommend?

ACTIVITY 22-3
Evaluating divisional performance

The three divisions of Hollywood Media Enterprises are Broadcasting, Music, and Publications. The divisions are structured as investment centers. The following responsibility reports were prepared for the three divisions for the prior year:

	Broadcasting	Music	Publications
Revenues	$ 600,000	$1,400,000	$500,000
Operating expenses	240,000	800,000	100,000
Income from operations before service department charges	$ 360,000	$ 600,000	$400,000
Service department charges:			
Promotion	$ 100,000	$ 200,000	$176,000
Legal	50,000	40,000	80,000
	$ 150,000	$ 240,000	$256,000
Income from operations	$ 210,000	$ 360,000	$144,000
Invested assets	$1,500,000	$3,000,000	$900,000

1. Which division is making the best use of invested assets and thus should be given priority for future capital investments?
2. ➤ Assuming that the minimum acceptable rate of return on new projects is 10%, would all investments that produce a return in excess of 10% be accepted by the divisions?
3. ➤ Can you identify opportunities for improving the company's financial performance?

ACTIVITY 22-4
Evaluating division performance over time

The Snack Foods Division of Diversified Foods Inc. has been experiencing revenue and profit growth during the years 2005–2007. The divisional income statements are provided below.

Diversified Foods Inc.
Divisional Income Statements, Snack Foods Division
For the Years Ended December 31, 2005–2007

	2005	2006	2007
Sales	$420,000	$540,000	$650,000
Cost of goods sold	264,000	310,000	342,500
Gross profit	$156,000	$230,000	$307,500
Operating expenses	93,000	116,600	145,000
Income from operations	$ 63,000	$113,400	$162,500

Assume that there are no charges from service departments. The vice-president of the division, Kevin Duncan, is proud of his division's performance over the last three years. The president of Diversified Foods Inc., LaToya Crawford, is discussing the division's performance with Kevin, as follows:

Kevin: As you can see, we've had a successful three years in the Snack Foods Division.
LaToya: I'm not too sure.

Kevin: What do you mean? Look at our results. Our income from operations has nearly tripled, while our profit margins are improving.

LaToya: I am looking at your results. However, your income statements fail to include one very important piece of information; namely, the invested assets. You have been investing a great deal of assets into the division. You had $210,000 in invested assets in 2005, $540,000 in 2006, and $1,300,000 in 2007.

Kevin: You are right. I've needed the assets in order to upgrade our technologies and expand our operations. The additional assets are one reason we have been able to grow and improve our profit margins. I don't see that this is a problem.

LaToya: The problem is that we must maintain a 20% rate of return on invested assets.

1. Determine the profit margins for the Snack Foods Division for 2005–2007.
2. Calculate the investment turnover for the Snack Foods Division for 2005–2007.
3. Calculate the rate of return on investment for the Snack Foods Division for 2005–2007.
4. ▭▶ Evaluate the division's performance over the 2005–2007 time period. Why was LaToya concerned about the performance?

ACTIVITY 22-5
Evaluating division performance

Leisure World Inc. is a privately held diversified company with five separate divisions organized as investment centers. A condensed income statement for the Sporting Goods Division for the past year, assuming no service department charges, is as follows:

Leisure World Inc.—Sporting Goods Division
Income Statement
For the Year Ended December 31, 2006

Sales	$16,000,000
Cost of goods sold	10,100,000
Gross profit	$ 5,900,000
Operating expenses	1,900,000
Income from operations	$ 4,000,000

The manager of the Sporting Goods Division was recently presented with the opportunity to add an additional product line, which would require invested assets of $12,000,000. A projected income statement for the new product line is as follows:

New Product Line
Projected Income Statement
For the Year Ended December 31, 2007

Sales	$7,500,000
Cost of goods sold	4,200,000
Gross profit	$3,300,000
Operating expenses	2,100,000
Income from operations	$1,200,000

The Sporting Goods Division currently has $20,000,000 in invested assets, and Leisure World Inc.'s overall rate of return on investment, including all divisions, is 8%. Each division manager is evaluated on the basis of divisional rate of return on investment, and a bonus equal to $10,000 for each percentage point by which the division's rate of return on investment exceeds the company average is awarded each year.

The President is concerned that the manager of the Sporting Goods Division rejected the addition of the new product line, when all estimates indicated that the product line would be profitable and would increase overall company income. You have been asked to analyze the possible reasons why the Sporting Goods Division manager rejected the new product line.

1. Determine the rate of return on investment for the Sporting Goods Division for the past year.

Many of the decisions that you make depend on comparing the estimated costs of alternatives. The payoff from such comparisons is described in the following report from a University of Michigan study.

Richard Nisbett and two colleagues quizzed Michigan faculty members and university seniors on such questions as how often they walk out on a bad movie, refuse to finish a bad meal, start over on a weak term paper, or abandon a research project that no longer looks promising. They believe that people who cut their losses this way are following sound economic rules: calculating the net benefits of alternative courses of action, writing off past costs that can't be recovered, and weighing the opportunity to use future time and effort more profitably elsewhere.

They find that among faculty members, those who use cost-benefit reasoning in this fashion—being more likely to give up on research that isn't getting anywhere or using labor-saving devices as often as possible—have higher salaries relative to their age and departments. Not surprisingly, economists are more likely to apply the approach than professors of humanities or biology.

Among students, those who have learned to use cost-benefit analysis frequently are apt to have far better grades than their Scholastic Aptitude Test scores would have predicted. Again, the more economics courses the students have, the more likely they are to apply cost-benefit analysis outside the classroom.

Dr. Nisbett concedes that for many Americans, cost-benefit rules often appear to conflict with such traditional principles as "never give up" and "waste not, want not."

Managers must also consider the effects of alternative decisions on their businesses. In this chapter, we discuss differential analysis, which reports the effects of alternative decisions on total revenues and costs. We also describe and illustrate practical approaches to setting product prices. Finally, we discuss how production bottlenecks influence product mix and pricing decisions.

Source: Alan L. Otten, "Economic Perspective Produces Steady Yields," from People Patterns, *The Wall Street Journal*, March 31, 1992, p. B1.

Differential Analysis

objective 1

Prepare a differential analysis report for decisions involving leasing or selling equipment, discontinuing an unprofitable segment, manufacturing or purchasing a needed part, replacing usable fixed assets, processing further or selling an intermediate product, or accepting additional business at a special price.

Planning for future operations involves decision making. For some decisions, revenue and cost data from the accounting records may be useful. However, the revenue and cost data for use in evaluating courses of future operations or choosing among competing alternatives are often not available in the accounting records and must be estimated.

Consider:

- The decision by **General Motors** to purchase on-board communications products from **Delphi Automotive Systems** instead of making them internally.
- The decision by **Marriott** hotels to accept a special price from a bid placed on **priceline.com**.
- The decision by **United Airlines** to discontinue service to New Zealand.

In each of these decisions, the estimated revenues and costs were **relevant**. The relevant revenues and costs focus on the differences between each alternative. Costs that have been incurred in the past are not relevant to the decision. These costs are called **sunk costs**.

Differential revenue is the amount of increase or decrease in revenue expected from a course of action as compared with an alternative. To illustrate, assume that certain equipment is being used to manufacture calculators, which are expected to generate revenue of $150,000. If the equipment could be used to make digital clocks,

The irrelevancy of sunk cost is sometimes difficult to apply in practice. Psychologists believe this is because acknowledging a sunk cost is the same as admitting to a past mistake. For example, one study compared the playing time of players selected in the first round of the **NBA** draft with other players. The study found that poor-performing first-round draftees received more court time than players with better performance but smaller contracts. Apparently, the owners felt that they had to prove that the big contract wasn't wasted, even though it meant having the wrong players on the court.

Decision	Differential Analysis
Alternative A	
	Differential revenue
or	− Differential costs
	Differential income or loss
Alternative B	

which would generate revenue of $175,000, the differential revenue from making and selling digital clocks is $25,000.

Differential cost is the amount of increase or decrease in cost that is expected from a course of action as compared with an alternative. For example, if an increase in advertising expenditures from $100,000 to $150,000 is being considered, the differential cost of the action is $50,000.

Differential income or loss is the difference between the differential revenue and the differential costs. Differential income indicates that a particular decision is expected to be profitable, while a differential loss indicates the opposite.

Differential analysis focuses on the effect of alternative courses of action on the relevant revenues and costs. For example, if a manager must decide between two alternatives, differential analysis would involve comparing the differential revenues of the two alternatives with the differential costs.

In this chapter, we will discuss the use of differential analysis in analyzing the following alternatives:

1. Leasing or selling equipment.
2. Discontinuing an unprofitable segment.
3. Manufacturing or purchasing a needed part.
4. Replacing usable fixed assets.
5. Processing further or selling an intermediate product.
6. Accepting additional business at a special price.

Lease or Sell

Management may have a choice between leasing or selling a piece of equipment that is no longer needed in the business. In deciding which option is best, management may use differential analysis. To illustrate, assume that Marcus Company is considering disposing of equipment that cost $200,000 and has $120,000 of accumulated depreciation to date. Marcus Company can sell the equipment through a broker for $100,000 less a 6% commission. Alternatively, Potamkin Company (the lessee) has offered to lease the equipment for five years for a total of $160,000. At the end of the fifth year of the lease, the equipment is expected to have no residual value. During the period of the lease, Marcus Company (the lessor) will incur repair, insurance, and property tax expenses estimated at $35,000. Exhibit 1 shows Marcus Company's analysis of whether to lease or sell the equipment.

Note that in Exhibit 1, the $80,000 book value ($200,000 − $120,000) of the equipment is a sunk cost and is not considered in the analysis. The $80,000 is a cost that resulted from a previous decision. It is not affected by the alternatives now being considered in leasing or selling the equipment. The relevant factors to be considered are the differential revenues and differential costs associated with the lease or sell decision. This analysis is verified by the traditional analysis in Exhibit 2.

The alternatives presented in Exhibits 1 and 2 were relatively simple. However, regardless of the complexity, the approach to differential analysis is basically the same. Two additional factors that often need to be considered are (1) differential revenue from investing the funds generated by the alternatives and (2) any income tax differential. In Exhibit 1, there could be differential interest revenue related to investing the cash flows from the two alternatives. Any income tax differential would be related to the differences in the timing of the income from the alternatives and the differences in the amount of

Marcus Company

Sell Equipment to — Broker

OR

Lease Equipment to — Potamkin Company

•Exhibit 1

Differential Analysis Report—Lease or Sell

Proposal to Lease or Sell Equipment June 22, 2006			
Differential revenue from alternatives:			
Revenue from lease		$160,000	
Revenue from sale		100,000	
Differential revenue from lease			$60,000
Differential cost of alternatives:			
Repair, insurance, and property tax expenses		$ 35,000	
Commission expense on sale		6,000	
Differential cost of lease			29,000
Net differential income from the lease alternative			**$31,000**

•Exhibit 2

Traditional Analysis

Lease or Sell			
Lease alternative:			
Revenue from lease		$160,000	
Depreciation expense for remaining five years	$80,000		
Repair, insurance, and property tax expenses	35,000	115,000	
Net gain			$45,000
Sell alternative:			
Sales price		$100,000	
Book value of equipment	$80,000		
Commission expense	6,000	86,000	
Net gain			14,000
Net differential income from the lease alternative			**$31,000**

Many companies that manufacture expensive equipment give customers the choice of leasing the equipment. For example, construction equipment from **Caterpillar Inc.** can either be purchased outright or leased through Caterpillar's financial services subsidiary. **IBM** makes its large mainframe computers available by lease, as does **Xerox** with its copy machines.

Product A has a loss from operations of $18,000 and fixed costs of $25,000. Product B has a loss from operations of $12,000 and fixed costs of $8,000. All remaining products have income from operations of $75,000 and fixed costs of $30,000. (1) Which product(s) should be discontinued, and (2) what would be the estimated income from operations if the action in (1) is taken?

----

(1) Product B; (2) $79,000
($75,000 + $4,000)

investment income. In the next chapter, we will consider these factors on management decisions.

Discontinue a Segment or Product

When a product or a department, branch, territory, or other segment of a business is generating losses, management may consider eliminating the product or segment. It is often assumed, sometimes in error, that the total income from operations of a business would be increased if the operating loss could be eliminated. Discontinuing the product or segment usually eliminates all of the product or segment's variable costs (direct materials, direct labor, sales commissions, and so on). However, if the product or segment is a relatively small part of the business, the fixed costs (depreciation, insurance, property taxes, and so on) may not be decreased by discontinuing it. It is possible in this case for the total operating income of a company to decrease rather than increase by eliminating the product or segment. To illustrate, the income statement for Battle Creek Cereal Co. presented in Exhibit 3 is for a normal year ending August 31, 2006.

Because Bran Flakes incurs annual losses, management is considering discontinuing it. Total annual operating income of $80,000 ($40,000 Toasted Oats + $40,000 Corn Flakes) might seem to be indicated by the income statement in Exhibit 3 if Bran Flakes is discontinued.

Discontinuing Bran Flakes, however, would actually decrease operating income by $15,000, to $54,000 ($69,000 − $15,000). This is shown by the differential analysis report in Exhibit 4, in which we assume that discontinuing Bran Flakes would have no effect on fixed costs and expenses. The traditional analysis in Exhibit 5 verifies the differential analysis in Exhibit 4.

•Exhibit 3

Income (Loss) by Product

Battle Creek Cereal Co.
Condensed Income Statement
For the Year Ended August 31, 2006

	Corn Flakes	Toasted Oats	Bran Flakes	Total
Sales	$500,000	$400,000	$100,000	$1,000,000
Cost of goods sold:				
Variable costs	$220,000	$200,000	$ 60,000	$ 480,000
Fixed costs	120,000	80,000	20,000	220,000
Total cost of goods sold	$340,000	$280,000	$ 80,000	$ 700,000
Gross profit	$160,000	$120,000	$ 20,000	$ 300,000
Operating expenses:				
Variable expenses	$ 95,000	$ 60,000	$ 25,000	$ 180,000
Fixed expenses	25,000	20,000	6,000	51,000
Total operating expenses ...	$120,000	$ 80,000	$ 31,000	$ 231,000
Income (loss) from operations	$ 40,000	$ 40,000	$ (11,000)	$ 69,000

•Exhibit 4

Differential Analysis Report—Discontinue an Unprofitable Segment

Proposal to Discontinue Bran Flakes
September 29, 2006

Differential revenue from annual sales of Bran Flakes:		
Revenue from sales		$100,000
Differential cost of annual sales of Bran Flakes:		
Variable cost of goods sold	$60,000	
Variable operating expenses	25,000	85,000
Annual differential income from sales of Bran Flakes ..		**$ 15,000**

•Exhibit 5 Traditional Analysis

Proposal to Discontinue Bran Flakes
September 29, 2006

	Bran Flakes, Toasted Oats, and Corn Flakes	Discontinue Bran Flakes*	Toasted Oats and Corn Flakes
Sales	$1,000,000	$100,000	$900,000
Cost of goods sold:			
Variable costs	$ 480,000	$ 60,000	$420,000
Fixed costs	220,000	—	220,000
Total cost of goods sold	$ 700,000	$ 60,000	$640,000
Gross profit	$ 300,000	$ 40,000	$260,000
Operating expenses:			
Variable expenses	$ 180,000	$ 25,000	$155,000
Fixed expenses	51,000	—	51,000
Total operating expenses	$ 231,000	$ 25,000	$206,000
Income (loss) from operations	**$ 69,000**	**$ 15,000**	**$ 54,000**

*Fixed costs are assumed to remain unchanged with the discontinuance of Bran Flakes.

In Exhibit 5, only the short-term (one year) effects of discontinuing Bran Flakes are considered. When eliminating a product or segment, management may also consider the long-term effects. For example, the plant capacity made available by discontinuing Bran Flakes might be eliminated. This could reduce fixed costs. Some employees may have to be laid off, and others may have to be relocated and retrained. Further, there may be a related decrease in sales of more profitable products to those customers who were attracted by the discontinued product.

MANAGERIAL DISCLOSURE AND ANALYSIS

MATTEL'S SEGMENT PROFITABILITY

Mattel Inc., the largest U.S. toy manufacturer, reported the following domestic operating segment information for a recent year:

	Girls	Boys—Entertainment	Infant & Preschool
Revenues	$1,380,208	$766,073	$1,282,221
Operating income	389,788	110,004	187,009
Depreciation	42,338	33,505	28,054

Mattel segments its business by type of customer. The Girls segment includes sales of Barbie®, the Boys segment includes sales of Hot Wheels® and Matchbox®, and the Infant segment includes sales of Fisher-Price® toys. All the segments are profitable. The estimated contribution margin (revenues − operating income + depreciation) in each segment is high. The Girls segment is the most profitable per sales dollar (28.2%), and the Boys and Infant segments are about equal in their profitability per sales dollar (14.3% and 14.6%, respectively). The discontinuance of any of these segments would cause Mattel's overall corporate income to decline.

REAL WORLD

Nike, Inc., does not make shoes but buys 100% of its shoe manufacturing from outside suppliers. Nike, Inc., believes that its strengths are in designing, marketing, distributing, and selling athletic shoes. Thus, Nike focuses on the parts of the business where it believes that it adds the greatest value to the customer and thus the greatest profitability to the company.

Part K can be purchased for $30 per unit. Part K can be manufactured internally using $7.50 of direct materials and 0.75 hour of direct labor at $12 per direct labor hour (dlh). Factory overhead is applied at a rate of $20 per direct labor hour. ($7 per dlh is fixed.) What is the cost savings or penalty from manufacturing the part internally?

$3.75 cost savings {$30 − [$7.50 + (0.75 × $12) + (0.75 × $13)]}

Make or Buy

The assembly of many parts is often a major element in manufacturing some products, such as automobiles. These parts may be made by the product's manufacturer, or they may be purchased. For example, some of the parts for an automobile, such as the motor, may be produced by the automobile manufacturer. Other parts, such as tires, may be purchased from other manufacturers. In addition, in manufacturing motors, such items as spark plugs and nuts and bolts may be acquired from suppliers.

Management uses differential costs to decide whether to make or buy a part. For example, if a part is purchased, management has concluded that it is less costly to buy the part than to manufacture it. Make or buy options often arise when a manufacturer has excess productive capacity in the form of unused equipment, space, and labor.

The differential analysis is similar, whether management is considering making a part that is currently being purchased or purchasing a part that is currently being made. To illustrate, assume that an automobile manufacturer has been purchasing instrument panels for $240 a unit. The factory is currently operating at 80% of capacity, and no major increase in production is expected in the near future. The cost per unit of manufacturing an instrument panel internally, including fixed costs, is estimated as follows:

Direct materials	$ 80
Direct labor	80
Variable factory overhead	52
Fixed factory overhead	68
Total cost per unit	$280

If the *make* price of $280 is simply compared with the *buy* price of $240, the decision is to buy the instrument panel. However, if unused capacity could be used in manufacturing the part, there would be no increase in the total amount of fixed factory overhead costs. Thus, only the variable factory overhead costs need to be considered. The relevant costs are summarized in the differential report in Exhibit 6.

Other possible effects of a decision to manufacture the instrument panel should also be considered. For example, capacity committed to the instrument panel may not be available for more production opportunities in the future. This decision may affect employees. It may also affect future business relations with the instrument panel supplier, who may provide other essential parts. The company's decision to manufacture instrument panels might jeopardize the timely delivery of these other parts.

•Exhibit 6

Differential Analysis Report—Make or Buy

Proposal to Manufacture Instrument Panels **February 15, 2006**		
Purchase price of an instrument panel		$240.00
Differential cost to manufacture:		
Direct materials	$80.00	
Direct labor	80.00	
Variable factory overhead	52.00	212.00
Cost savings from manufacturing an instrument panel . .		**$ 28.00**

INTEGRITY IN BUSINESS

RELATED-PARTY TRANSACTIONS

The make-or-buy decision can be complicated if the purchase (buy) is being made by a related party. A related party is one in which there is direct or indirect control of one party over another or the presence of a family member in a transaction. Such dependence or familiarity may interfere with the appropriateness of the business transaction. One investor has said, "Related parties are akin to steroids used by athletes. If you're an athlete and you can cut the mustard, you don't need steroids to make yourself stronger or faster. By the same token, if you're a good company, you don't need related parties or deals that don't make sense." While related-party transactions are legal, GAAP (FASB Statement No. 56) and the Sarbanes/Oxley Act require that they must be disclosed under the presumption that such transactions are less than arm's length.

Source: Herb Greenburg, "Poor Relations: The Problem with Related-Party Transactions," *Fortune Advisor* (February 5, 2001), p. 198.

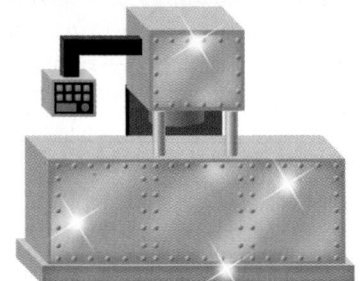

Replace Equipment

The usefulness of fixed assets may be reduced long before they are considered to be worn out. For example, equipment may no longer be efficient for the purpose for which it is used. On the other hand, the equipment may not have reached the point of complete inadequacy. Decisions to replace usable fixed assets should be based on relevant costs. The relevant costs are the future costs of continuing to use the equipment versus replacement. The book values of the fixed assets being replaced are sunk costs and are irrelevant.

To illustrate, assume that a business is considering the disposal of several identical machines having a total book value of $100,000 and an estimated remaining life of five years. The old machines can be sold for $25,000. They can be replaced by a single high-speed machine at a cost of $250,000. The new machine has an estimated useful life of five years and no residual value. Analyses indicate an estimated annual reduction in variable manufacturing costs from $225,000 with the old machine to $150,000 with the new machine. No other changes in the manufacturing costs or the operating expenses are expected. The relevant costs are summarized in the differential report in Exhibit 7.

•Exhibit 7

Differential Analysis Report—Replace Equipment

Proposal to Replace Equipment
November 28, 2006

Annual variable costs—present equipment	$225,000	
Annual variable costs—new equipment	150,000	
Annual differential decrease in cost	$ 75,000	
Number of years applicable	× 5	
Total differential decrease in cost	$375,000	
Proceeds from sale of present equipment	25,000	400,000
Cost of new equipment		250,000
Net differential decrease in cost, 5-year total		$150,000
Annual net differential decrease in cost—new equipment		**$ 30,000**

Other factors are often important in equipment replacement decisions. For example, differences between the remaining useful life of the old equipment and the estimated life of the new equipment could exist. In addition, the new equipment might improve the overall quality of the product, resulting in an increase in sales volume. Additional factors could include the time value of money and other uses for the cash needed to purchase the new equipment.[1]

The amount of income that is forgone from an alternative use of an asset, such as cash, is called an **opportunity cost**. For example, your opportunity cost of attending school is the income forgone from lost work hours. Although the opportunity cost does not appear as a part of historical accounting data, it is useful in analyzing alternative courses of action. To illustrate, assume that the cash outlay of $250,000 for the new equipment, less the $25,000 proceeds from the sale of the present equipment, could be invested to yield a 10% return. Thus, the annual opportunity cost related to the purchase of the new equipment is $22,500 (10% × $225,000).

---

[1]The importance of the time value of money in equipment replacement decisions is discussed in the next chapter.

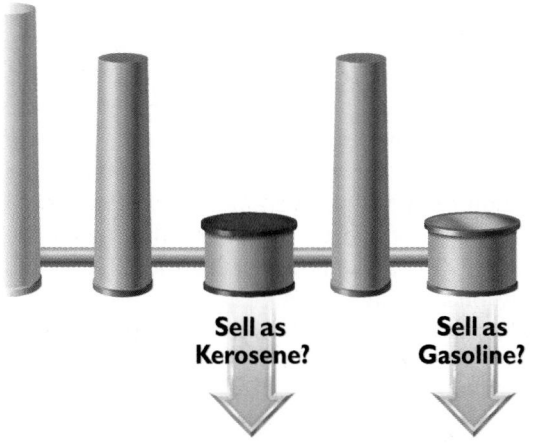

Sell as Kerosene?

Sell as Gasoline?

Process or Sell

When a product is manufactured, it progresses through various stages of production. Often a product can be sold at an intermediate stage of production, or it can be processed further and then sold. In deciding whether to sell a product at an intermediate stage or to process it further, differential analysis is useful. The differential revenues from further processing are compared to the differential costs of further processing. The costs of producing the intermediate product do not change, regardless of whether the intermediate product is sold or processed further. Thus, these costs are not differential costs and are irrelevant to the decision to process further.

To illustrate, assume that a business produces kerosene in batches of 4,000 gallons. Standard quantities of 4,000 gallons of direct materials are processed, which cost $0.60 per gallon. Kerosene can be sold without further processing for $0.80 per gallon. It can be processed further to yield gasoline, which can be sold for $1.25 per gallon. Gasoline requires additional processing costs of $650 per batch, and 20% of the gallons of kerosene will evaporate during production. Exhibit 8 summarizes the differential revenues and costs in deciding whether to process kerosene to produce gasoline.

Product T is produced for $2.50 per gallon ($1.00 fixed cost) and can be sold without additional processing for $3.50 per gallon. Product T can be processed further into Product V at a cost of $1.60 per gallon ($0.90 fixed). Product V can be sold for $4.00 per gallon. What is the differential income or loss per gallon from processing Product T into Product V?

$0.20 loss [$4.00 − $3.50 − $1.60 + $0.90]

•**Exhibit 8**   Differential Analysis Report—Process or Sell

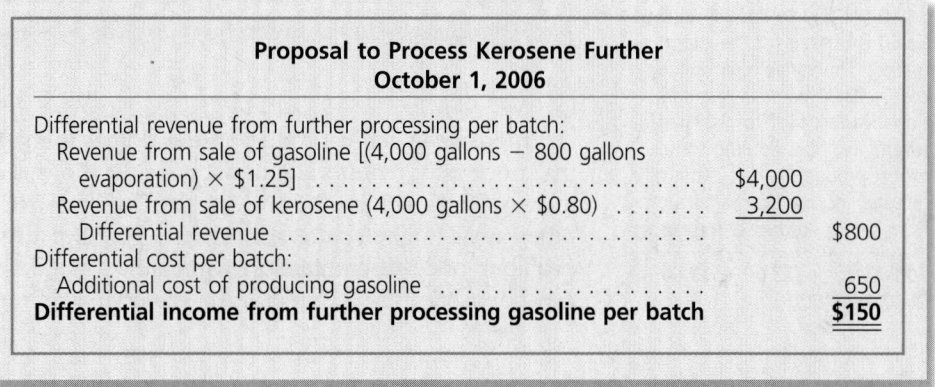

Proposal to Process Kerosene Further
October 1, 2006

Differential revenue from further processing per batch:		
Revenue from sale of gasoline [(4,000 gallons − 800 gallons evaporation) × $1.25]	$4,000	
Revenue from sale of kerosene (4,000 gallons × $0.80)	3,200	
Differential revenue		$800
Differential cost per batch:		
Additional cost of producing gasoline		650
Differential income from further processing gasoline per batch		**$150**

The differential income from further processing kerosene into gasoline is $150 per batch. The initial cost of producing the intermediate kerosene, $2,400 (4,000 gallons × $0.60), is not considered in deciding whether to process kerosene further. This initial cost will be incurred, regardless of whether gasoline is produced.

Accept Business at a Special Price

Differential analysis is also useful in deciding whether to accept additional business at a special price. The differential revenue that would be provided from the additional business is compared to the differential costs of producing and delivering the product to the customer. If the company is operating at full capacity, any additional production will increase both fixed and variable production costs. If, however, the normal production of the company is below full capacity, additional business may be undertaken without increasing fixed production costs. In this case, the differential costs of the additional production are the variable manufacturing costs. If operating expenses increase because of the additional business, these expenses should also be considered.

REAL WORLD

The Internet is forcing many companies toward "dynamic" pricing. For example, in **priceline.com's** "name your price" format, customers tell the company what they are willing to pay and then the company must decide if it is willing to sell at that price.

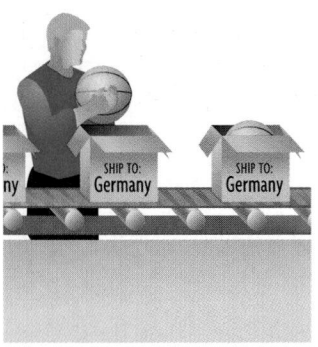

To illustrate, assume that the monthly capacity of a sporting goods business is 12,500 basketballs. Current sales and production are averaging 10,000 basketballs per month. The current manufacturing cost of $20 per unit consists of variable costs of $12.50 and fixed costs of $7.50. The normal selling price of the product in the domestic market is $30. The manufacturer receives from an exporter an offer for 5,000 basketballs at $18 each. Production can be spread over a three-month period without interfering with normal production or incurring overtime costs. Pricing policies in the domestic market will not be affected. Simply comparing the sales price of $18 with the present unit manufacturing cost of $20 indicates that the offer should be rejected. However, by focusing only on the differential cost, which in this case is the variable cost, the decision is different. Exhibit 9 shows the differential analysis report for this decision.

•Exhibit 9   Differential Analysis Report—Sell at Special Price

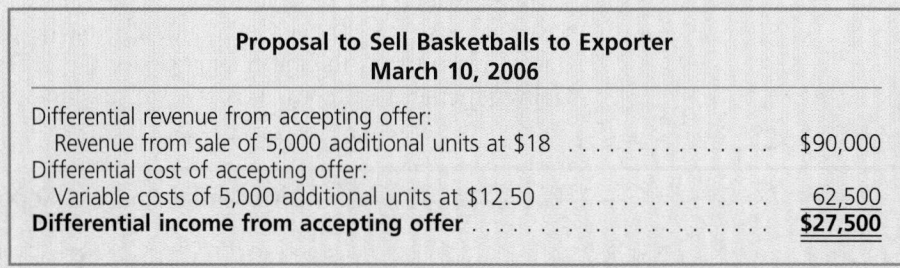

Proposal to Sell Basketballs to Exporter
March 10, 2006

Differential revenue from accepting offer:	
Revenue from sale of 5,000 additional units at $18	$90,000
Differential cost of accepting offer:	
Variable costs of 5,000 additional units at $12.50	62,500
Differential income from accepting offer	**$27,500**

Product D is normally sold for $4.40 per unit. A special price of $3.60 is offered for the export market. The variable production cost is $3.00 per unit. An additional export tariff of 10% of revenue will be required for all export products. What is the differential income or loss per unit from selling Product D for export?

$0.24 income [$3.60 − $3.00 − (0.10 × $3.60)]

Proposals to sell a product in the domestic market at prices lower than the normal price may require additional considerations. For example, it may be unwise to increase sales volume in one territory by price reductions if sales volume is lost in other areas. Manufacturers must also conform to the Robinson-Patman Act, which prohibits price discrimination within the United States unless differences in prices can be justified by different costs of serving different customers.

Setting Normal Product Selling Prices

objective   2

Determine the selling price of a product, using the total cost, product cost, and variable cost concepts.

Differential analysis may be useful in deciding to lower selling prices for special short-run decisions, such as whether to accept business at a price lower than the normal price. In such cases, the minimum short-run price is set high enough to cover all variable costs. Any price above this minimum price will improve profits in the short run. In the long run, however, the normal selling price must be set high enough to cover all costs and expenses (both fixed and variable) and provide a reasonable profit. Otherwise, the business may not survive.

The normal selling price can be viewed as the target selling price to be achieved in the long run. The basic approaches to setting this price are as follows:

Market Methods	**Cost-Plus Methods**
1. Demand-based methods	1. Total cost concept
2. Competition-based methods	2. Product cost concept
	3. Variable cost concept

McDonald's Corporation evaluated the *Extra Value Meals* concept and determined that combination meals priced at a discount would create additional revenue from customer "trade-ups" from *a la carte* purchases. The concept was so successful that it has become an industry standard.

Managers using the market methods refer to the external market to determine the price. Demand-based methods set the price according to the demand for the product. If there is high demand for the product, then the price may be set high, while lower demand may require the price to be set low. An example of setting different prices according to the demand for the product is found in the telecommunications industry, with low weekend rates and high business day rates for long-distance telephone calls.

Competition-based methods set the price according to the price offered by competitors. For example, if a competitor reduces the price, then management may be required to adjust the price to meet the competition. The market-based pricing approaches are discussed in greater detail in marketing courses, so we will not expand upon them here.

Managers using the cost-plus methods price the product in order to achieve a target profit. Managers add to the cost an amount called a **markup**, so that all costs plus a profit are included in the selling price. In the following paragraphs, we describe and illustrate the three cost concepts often used in applying the cost-plus approach: (1) total cost, (2) product cost, and (3) variable cost. A cost reduction method that uses market-method pricing, called target costing, is discussed later in this section.

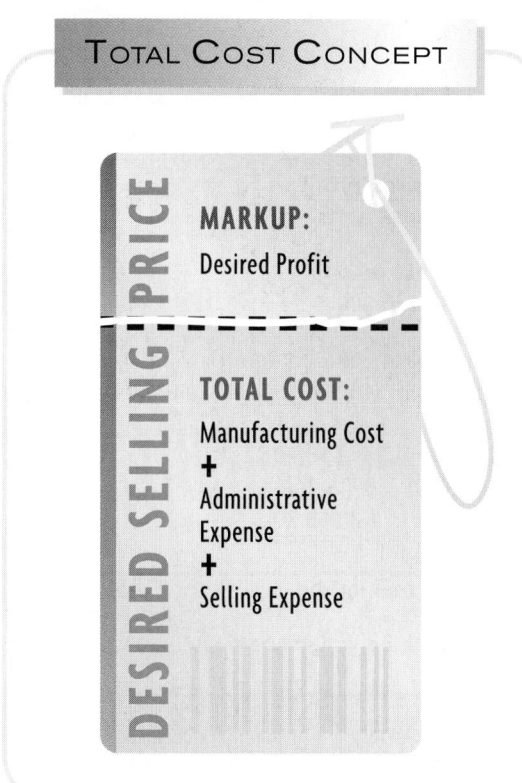

Total Cost Concept

Using the **total cost concept**, all costs of manufacturing a product plus the selling and administrative expenses are included in the cost amount to which the markup is added. Since all costs and expenses are included in the cost amount, the dollar amount of the markup equals the desired profit.

The first step in applying the total cost concept is to determine the total cost of manufacturing the product. This cost includes the costs of direct materials, direct labor, and factory overhead and should be available from the accounting records. The next step is to add the estimated selling and administrative expenses to the total cost of manufacturing the product. The cost amount per unit is then computed by dividing the total costs by the total units expected to be produced and sold.

After the cost amount per unit has been determined, the dollar amount of the markup is determined. For this purpose, the markup is expressed as a percentage of cost. This percentage is then multiplied by the cost amount per unit. The dollar amount of the markup is then added to the cost amount per unit to arrive at the selling price.

The markup percentage for the total cost concept is determined by applying the following formula:

$$\text{Markup percentage} = \frac{\text{Desired profit}}{\text{Total costs}}$$

The numerator of the formula is only the desired profit. This is because all costs and expenses are included in the cost amount to which the markup is added. The denominator of the formula is the total costs.

To illustrate, assume that the costs for calculators of Digital Solutions Inc. are as follows:

Variable costs:	
Direct materials	$ 3.00 per unit
Direct labor	10.00
Factory overhead	1.50
Selling and administrative expenses	1.50
Total	$ 16.00 per unit
Fixed costs:	
Factory overhead	$50,000
Selling and administrative expenses	20,000

 I trace my roots back to Blue Ribbon Sports, a 1962 partnership between an athlete and an Oregon track coach. In 1971, the coach was inspired by his breakfast waffles to improve running shoes. Today I employ more than 20,000 people on six continents. I'm named after the winged Greek goddess of victory and rake in nearly $10 billion annually. My brands include Cole Haan and Bauer. I'm No. 2 in soccer and a new big player in golf. Nearly half my sales are generated internationally and apparel accounts for about 30 percent of sales. I recycle sneakers, too. Who am I? (Go to page 977 for answer.)

Digital Solutions Inc. desires a profit equal to a 20% rate of return on assets, $800,000 of assets are devoted to producing calculators, and 100,000 units are expected to be produced and sold. The calculators' total cost is $1,670,000, or $16.70 per unit, computed as follows:

Variable costs ($16.00 × 100,000 units)		$1,600,000
Fixed costs:		
Factory overhead	$50,000	
Selling and administrative expenses	20,000	70,000
Total costs		$1,670,000
Total cost per calculator ($1,670,000 ÷ 100,000 units)		$16.70

The desired profit is $160,000 (20% × $800,000), and the markup percentage for a calculator is 9.6%, computed as follows:

$$\text{Markup percentage} = \frac{\text{Desired profit}}{\text{Total costs}}$$

$$\text{Markup percentage} = \frac{\$160,000}{\$1,670,000} = 9.6\%$$

Based on the total cost per unit and the markup percentage for a calculator, Digital Solutions Inc. would price each calculator at $18.30 per unit, as shown below.

Total cost per calculator	$16.70
Markup ($16.70 × 9.6%)	1.60
Selling price	$18.30

The ability of the selling price of $18.30 to generate the desired profit of $160,000 is shown by the following income statement:

Digital Solutions Inc.
Income Statement
For the Year Ended December 31, 2006

Sales (100,000 units × $18.30)		$1,830,000
Expenses:		
Variable (100,000 units × $16.00)	$1,600,000	
Fixed ($50,000 + $20,000)	70,000	1,670,000
Income from operations		$ 160,000

The total cost concept of applying the cost-plus approach to product pricing is often used by contractors who sell products to government agencies. In many cases, government contractors are required by law to be reimbursed for their products on a total-cost-plus-profit basis.

INTEGRITY IN BUSINESS

PRICE FIXING

Federal law prevents companies competing in similar markets from sharing cost and price information, or what is commonly termed "price fixing." For example, the Federal Trade Commission brought a suit against the major record labels and music retailers for conspiring to set CD prices at a minimum level, or MAP (minimum advertised price). In settling the suit, the major labels ceased their MAP policies and provided $143 million in cash and CDs for consumers.

Product Cost Concept

Product Cost Concept

Using the **_product cost concept_**, only the costs of manufacturing the product, termed the product cost, are included in the cost amount to which the markup is added. Estimated selling expenses, administrative expenses, and profit are included in the markup. The markup percentage is determined by applying the following formula:

$$\text{Markup percentage} = \frac{\text{Desired profit} + \text{Total selling and administrative expenses}}{\text{Total manufacturing costs}}$$

The numerator of the markup percentage formula is the desired profit plus the total selling and administrative expenses. These expenses must be included in the markup, since they are not included in the cost amount to which the markup is added. The denominator of the formula includes the costs of direct materials, direct labor, and factory overhead.

To illustrate, assume the same data used in the preceding illustration. The manufacturing cost for Digital Solutions Inc.'s calculator is $1,500,000, or $15 per unit, computed as follows:

Direct materials ($3 × 100,000 units)		$ 300,000
Direct labor ($10 × 100,000 units)		1,000,000
Factory overhead:		
Variable ($1.50 × 100,000 units)	$150,000	
Fixed	50,000	200,000
Total manufacturing costs		$1,500,000
Manufacturing cost per calculator ($1,500,000 ÷ 100,000 units) . .		$15

The desired profit is $160,000 (20% × $800,000), and the total selling and administrative expenses are $170,000 [(100,000 units × $1.50 per unit) + $20,000]. The markup percentage for a calculator is 22%, computed as follows:

$$\text{Markup percentage} = \frac{\text{Desired profit} + \text{Total selling and administrative expenses}}{\text{Total manufacturing costs}}$$

$$\text{Markup percentage} = \frac{\$160,000 + \$170,000}{\$1,500,000}$$

$$\text{Markup percentage} = \frac{\$330,000}{\$1,500,000} = 22\%$$

REAL WORLD

Federal Express Corporation decided to abandon its flat price strategy in favor of setting the price based on the distance a parcel travels. As a result, prices decreased on many short-distance parcels, while prices increased on long-distance shipments. This decision was made because FedEx could no longer ignore the differential costs associated with shipping short and long distances.

Based on the manufacturing cost per calculator and the markup percentage, Digital Solutions Inc. would price each calculator at $18.30 per unit, as shown below.

Manufacturing cost per calculator	$15.00
Markup ($15 × 22%)	3.30
Selling price	$18.30

VARIABLE COST CONCEPT

MARKUP:
Total Fixed Costs
+
Desired Profit

VARIABLE COST:
Variable Manufacturing Cost
+
Variable Administrative and Selling Expenses

DESIRED SELLING PRICE

Variable Cost Concept

The **variable cost concept** emphasizes the distinction between variable and fixed costs in product pricing. Using the variable cost concept, only variable costs are included in the cost amount to which the markup is added. All variable manufacturing costs, as well as variable selling and administrative expenses, are included in the cost amount. Fixed manufacturing costs, fixed selling and administrative expenses, and profit are included in the markup.

The markup percentage is determined by applying the following formula:

$$\text{Markup percentage} = \frac{\text{Desired profit} + \text{Total fixed costs}}{\text{Total variable costs}}$$

The numerator of the markup percentage formula is the desired profit plus the total fixed manufacturing costs and the total fixed selling and administrative expenses. These costs and expenses must be included in the markup, since they are not included in the cost amount to which the markup is added. The denominator of the formula includes the total variable costs.

To illustrate, assume the same data used in the two preceding illustrations. The calculator variable cost is $1,600,000, or $16.00 per unit, computed as follows:

Variable costs:	
Direct materials ($3 × 100,000 units)	$ 300,000
Direct labor ($10 × 100,000 units)	1,000,000
Factory overhead ($1.50 × 100,000 units)	150,000
Selling and administrative expenses ($1.50 × 100,000 units)	150,000
Total variable costs	$1,600,000
Variable cost per calculator ($1,600,000 ÷ 100,000 units)	$16.00

The desired profit is $160,000 (20% × $800,000), the total fixed manufacturing costs are $50,000, and the total fixed selling and administrative expenses are $20,000. The markup percentage for a calculator is 14.4%, computed as follows:

$$\text{Markup percentage} = \frac{\text{Desired profit} + \text{Total fixed costs}}{\text{Total variable costs}}$$

$$\text{Markup percentage} = \frac{\$160,000 + \$50,000 + \$20,000}{\$1,600,000}$$

$$\text{Markup percentage} = \frac{\$230,000}{\$1,600,000} = 14.4\%$$

Based on the variable cost per calculator and the markup percentage, Digital Solutions Inc. would price each calculator at $18.30 per unit, as shown below.

Variable cost per calculator	$16.00
Markup ($16.00 × 14.4%)	2.30
Selling price	$18.30

Choosing a Cost-Plus Approach Cost Concept

Product Z has a total cost of $30 per unit. Of this amount, $10 per unit is selling and administrative costs. The total variable cost is $18 per unit. The desired profit is $3 per unit. Determine the markup percentage on (1) total cost, (2) product cost, and (3) variable cost.

----

(1) 10% ($3 ÷ $30); (2) 65% [($10 + $3) ÷ $20]; (3) 83.3% [($12 + $3) ÷ $18]

All three cost concepts produced the same selling price ($18.30) for Digital Solutions Inc. In practice, however, the three cost concepts are usually not viewed as alternatives. Each cost concept requires different estimates of costs and expenses. This difficulty and the complexity of the manufacturing operations should be considered in choosing a cost concept.

To reduce the costs of gathering data, estimated (standard) costs rather than actual costs may be used with any of the three cost concepts. However, management should exercise caution when using estimated costs in applying the cost-plus approach. The estimates should be based on normal (attainable) operating levels and not theoretical (ideal) levels of performance. In product pricing, the use of estimates based on ideal- or maximum-capacity operating levels might lead to setting product prices too low. In this case, the costs of such factors as normal spoilage or normal periods of idle time might not be considered.

The decision-making needs of management are also an important factor in selecting a cost concept for product pricing. For example, managers who often make special pricing decisions are more likely to use the variable cost concept. In contrast, a government defense contractor would be more likely to use the total cost concept.

Activity-Based Costing

As illustrated in the preceding paragraphs, costs are an important consideration in setting product prices. To more accurately measure the costs of producing and selling products, some companies use activity-based costing. **Activity-based costing (ABC)** identifies and traces activities to specific products.

Activity-based costing may be useful in making product pricing decisions where manufacturing operations involve large amounts of factory overhead. In such cases, traditional overhead allocation using activity bases such as units produced or machine hours may yield inaccurate cost allocations. This, in turn, may result in distorted product costs and product prices. By providing more accurate product cost allocations, activity-based costing aids in setting product prices that will cover costs and expenses.[2]

Target Costing

A method that combines market-based pricing with a cost reduction emphasis is **target costing**. Under target costing, a future selling price is anticipated, using the demand-based methods or the competition-based methods discussed previously. The targeted cost is determined by *subtracting* a desired profit from the expected selling price. In contrast, the three cost-plus concepts discussed previously begin with a given cost and *add* a markup to determine the selling price.

Target costing is used to motivate cost reduction as shown in Exhibit 10. The bar at the left in Exhibit 10 shows the actual cost and profit that can be earned during the present time period for a particular product. The bar at the right shows that the market price is expected to decline in the future. Thus, to earn a profit, a target cost is estimated as the difference between the expected market price and the desired profit. This target cost establishes a product cost objective that will maintain competitiveness and profitability.

Since the target cost is less than the current cost, managers must plan and remove cost from the design and manufacture of the product. The planned cost reduction is sometimes referred to as the cost "drift." Cost can be removed from a product in a variety of ways, such as by simplifying the design, reducing the cost

[2]Activity-based costing is further discussed and illustrated in a later chapter.

•Exhibit 10 Target Cost Concept

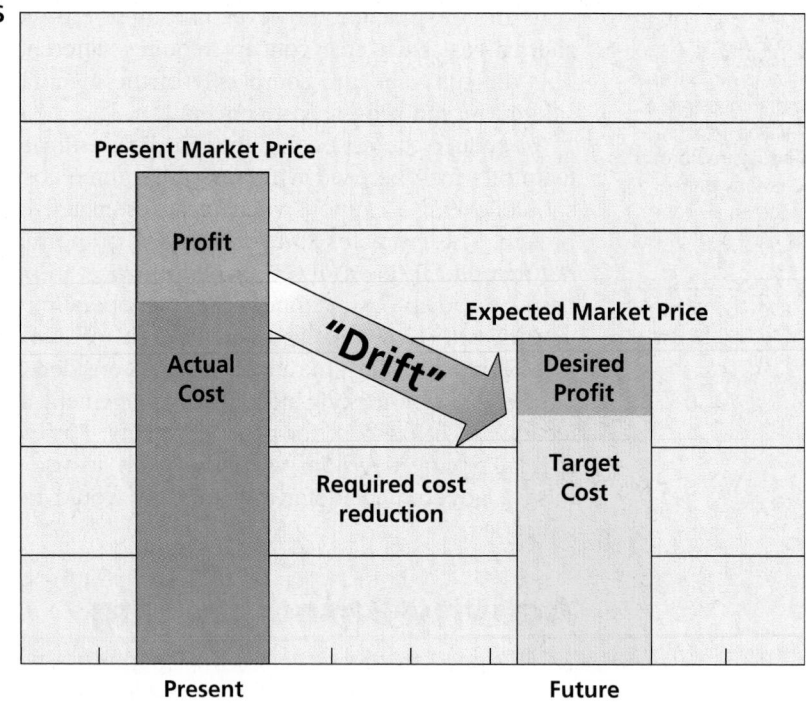

of direct materials, reducing the direct labor content, or eliminating waste from manufacturing operations. Using the target cost concept in this way provides managers with a road map for making improvements and gauging the success of their efforts over time. Target costing is especially useful in highly competitive markets that require continual product cost reductions to remain competitive.

WHAT IS A PRODUCT?

A product is often thought of in terms beyond just its physical attributes. For example, why a customer buys a product usually impacts how a business markets the product. Other considerations, such as warranty needs, servicing needs, and perceived quality, also affect business strategies.

Consider the four different types of products listed below. For these products, the frequency of purchase, the profit per unit, and the number of retailers differ. As a result, the sales and marketing approach for each product differs.

Product	Type of Product	Frequency of Purchase	Profit per Unit	Number of Retailers	Sales/Marketing Approach
Snickers®	Convenience	Often	Low	Many	Mass advertising
Sony® TV	Shopping	Occasional	Moderate	Many	Mass advertising; personal selling
Diamond ring	Specialty	Seldom	High	Few	Personal selling
Prearranged funeral	Unsought	Rare	High	Few	Aggressive selling

Product Profitability and Pricing Under Production Bottlenecks

objective   **3**

Calculate the relative profitability of products in bottleneck production environments.

An important consideration influencing production volumes and prices is production bottlenecks. A production **bottleneck** (or **constraint**) occurs at the point in the process where the demand for the company's product exceeds the ability to produce the product. The **theory of constraints (TOC)** is a manufacturing strategy that focuses on reducing the influence of bottlenecks on a process.

Product Profitability Under Production Bottlenecks

When a company has a bottleneck in its production process, it should attempt to maximize its profitability, subject to the influence of the bottleneck. To illustrate, assume that Snapp-Off Tool Company makes three types of wrenches: small, medium, and large. All three products are processed through a heat treatment operation, which hardens the steel tools. Snapp-Off Tool's heat treatment process is operating at full capacity and is a production bottleneck. The product contribution margin per unit and the number of hours of heat treatment used by each type of wrench are as follows:

The sand in the hourglass can pass only as fast as the narrowest point in the glass will allow.

Bottleneck

	Small Wrench	Medium Wrench	Large Wrench
Sales price per unit	$130	$140	$160
Variable cost per unit	40	40	40
Contribution margin per unit	$ 90	$100	$120
Heat treatment hours per unit	1	4	8

The large wrench appears to be the most profitable product because its contribution margin per unit is the greatest. However, the contribution margin per unit can be a misleading indicator of profitability in a bottleneck operation. The correct measure of performance is the value of each bottleneck hour, or the contribution margin per bottleneck hour. Using this measure, each product has a much different profitability when compared to the contribution margin per unit information, as shown in Exhibit 11.

The small wrench produces the most contribution margin per bottleneck (heat treatment) hour used, while the large wrench produces the smallest profit per bottleneck hour. Thus, the small wrench is the most profitable product. This information is the opposite of that implied by the unit contribution margin profit.

Product A has a contribution margin of $15 per unit. Product B has a contribution margin of $20 per unit. Product A requires 3 furnace hours, while Product B requires 5 furnace hours. Determine the most profitable product, assuming that the furnace is a bottleneck.

- -

Product A ($15 ÷ 3 hours = $5 per hour, which is greater than $20 ÷ 5 hours, or $4 per hour)

•Exhibit 11   Contribution Margin per Bottleneck Hour

	Small Wrench	Medium Wrench	Large Wrench
Sales price	$130	$140	$160
Variable cost per unit	40	40	40
Contribution margin per unit	$ 90	$100	$120
Bottleneck (heat treatment) hours per unit . . .	÷ 1	÷ 4	÷ 8
Contribution margin per bottleneck hour	$ 90	$ 25	$ 15

REAL WORLD

Latrobe Steel Division of **Timken Company** originally used total cost plus a markup to price its steel products. However, Latrobe discovered that one of its machines was a bottleneck in its operation. It recalculated the profitability of its products, based on the contribution margin per hour of constraint. The results showed that some products that had appeared only marginally profitable had, in fact, a high contribution margin per bottleneck hour. This analysis caused Latrobe management to change the product mix in favor of products with high contribution margins per constraint hour. Management estimated that these changes improved income from operations by 20%.

Product Pricing Under Production Bottlenecks

Each hour of a bottleneck delivers profit to the company. When a company has a production bottleneck, the contribution margin per hour of bottleneck provides a measure of the product's relative profitability. This information can also be used to adjust the product price to better reflect the value of the product's use of a bottleneck. Products that use a large number of bottleneck hours per unit require more contribution margin than products that use few bottleneck hours per unit. For example, Snapp-Off Tool Company should increase the price of the large wrench in order to deliver more contribution margin per bottleneck hour.

To determine the price of the large wrench that would equate its profitability to the small wrench, we need to solve the following equation:

$$\text{Contribution margin per bottleneck hour per small wrench} = \frac{\text{Revised price of large wrench} - \text{Variable cost per large wrench}}{\text{Bottleneck hours per large wrench}}$$

$$\$90 = \frac{\text{Revised price of large wrench} - \$40}{8}$$

$$\$720 = \text{Revised price of large wrench} - \$40$$
$$\$760 = \text{Revised price of large wrench}$$

The large wrench's price would need to be increased to $760 in order to deliver the same contribution margin per bottleneck hour as does the small wrench, as verified below.

Revised price of large wrench	$760
Less: Variable cost per unit of large wrench	40
Contribution margin per unit of large wrench	$720
Bottleneck hours per unit of large wrench	÷ 8
Revised contribution margin per bottleneck hour	$ 90

At a price of $760, the company would be indifferent between producing and selling the small wrench or the large wrench, all else being equal. This analysis assumes that there is unlimited demand for the products. If the market were unwilling to purchase the large wrench at this price, then the company should produce the small wrench.

SPOTLIGHT ON STRATEGY

ALTERNATIVE PRICING APPROACHES

At various times, a business may use alternative pricing approaches, often as a supplement to the traditional cost-plus pricing of products. Some of these alternative approaches are described below.

- **Price skimming** is normally short-term in nature and is used when a business has a new product that is unique in the marketplace. Because of the lack of competing products, the business sets the price at an artificially high level. It anticipates that it will have to lower the price once competitors enter the market. In the meantime, however, it will be able to earn high profits that can be used to cover the costs of developing the product. For example, **Samsung** is initially setting the price for its new video cell phones at around $600. Eventually, as technology matures and competitors enter the market, the price for these phones will likely fall.

- **Psychological pricing** is based on two behavioral tendencies of customers. First, customers often assume that the higher the price of a product, the higher the quality. Thus, for a special occasion, a novice wine buyer might be more inclined to purchase a higher-priced bottle of wine than a lower-priced bottle. Second, consumers are more likely to purchase a product priced just below the next whole number. For example, retailers often price products at $899 or $895, rather than $900. This type of pricing, called *odd-even*

pricing, is used to imply bargains, even though the price difference between the odd and even number is insignificant.

- **Bundle pricing** involves grouping two related products together and pricing them as a single product. For example, appliance retailers often bundle a clothes washer and dryer together at a price that is less than the sum of the price of the washer and dryer separately. Other examples of bundle pricing include "value meals" in fast food restaurants and software bundled with PCs. Bundling products at a slightly reduced total price is intended to generate additional sales that otherwise might not have been made.

- **Dynamic pricing** is used when the price of a product changes depending upon supply, demand, time of day, season, weather conditions, and other factors. An example is the pricing of airline tickets. The price often depends on when the reservation is made, the degree of competition in the local market, number of seats already sold, and the time of day. Thus, the price of a ticket to fly between two cities can vary greatly. A business executive requiring an immediate one-day ahead round-trip ticket that departs in the morning and arrives back home in the evening will be charged a premium price. Another traveler with the same city-to-city destination can save money by reserving a ticket weeks ahead and flying during the off-peak midday hours.

Key Points

1 **Prepare a differential analysis report for decisions involving leasing or selling equipment, discontinuing an unprofitable segment, manufacturing or purchasing a needed part, replacing usable fixed assets, processing further or selling an intermediate product, or accepting additional business at a special price.**

Differential analysis reports for leasing or selling, discontinuing a segment or product, making or buying, replacing equipment, processing or selling, and accepting business at a special price are illustrated in the text. Each analysis focuses on the differential revenues and/or costs of the alternative courses of action.

2 **Determine the selling price of a product, using the total cost, product cost, and variable cost concepts.**

The three cost concepts commonly used in applying the cost-plus approach to product pricing are summarized as follows.

Cost Concept	Covered in Cost Amount	Covered in Markup
Total cost	Total costs	Desired profit
Product cost	Total manufacturing costs	Desired profit + Total selling and administrative expenses
Variable cost	Total variable costs	Desired profit + Total fixed costs

The markup percentages used in applying each cost concept are as follows:

Total cost concept:

$$\text{Markup percentage} = \frac{\text{Desired profit}}{\text{Total costs}}$$

Product cost concept:

$$\text{Markup percentage} = \frac{\text{Desired profit} + \text{Total selling and admin. expenses}}{\text{Total manufacturing costs}}$$

Variable cost concept:

$$\text{Markup percentage} = \frac{\text{Desired profit} + \text{Total fixed costs}}{\text{Total variable costs}}$$

Activity-based costing can be used to provide more accurate cost information in applying cost-plus concepts when indirect costs are insignificant. Target costing combines market-based methods with a cost-reduction emphasis.

3 Calculate the relative profitability of products in bottleneck production environments.

The profitability of a product in a bottleneck production environment may not be accurately shown in the contribution margin product report. Instead, the best measure of profitability is determined by dividing the contribution margin per unit by the bottleneck hours per unit. The resulting measure indicates the product's profitability per hour of bottleneck use. This information can be used to support product pricing decisions.

Key Terms

activity-based costing (ABC) (969)
bottleneck (971)
differential analysis (957)
differential cost (957)
differential revenue (956)

markup (965)
opportunity cost (962)
product cost concept (967)
sunk cost (956)
target costing (969)

theory of constraints (TOC) (971)
total cost concept (965)
variable cost concept (968)

Illustrative Problem

Inez Company recently began production of a new product, M, which required the investment of $1,600,000 in assets. The costs of producing and selling 80,000 units of Product M are estimated as follows:

Variable costs:		
Direct materials	$ 10.00	per unit
Direct labor	6.00	
Factory overhead	4.00	
Selling and administrative expenses	5.00	
Total	$ 25.00	per unit
Fixed costs:		
Factory overhead	$800,000	
Selling and administrative expenses	400,000	

Inez Company is currently considering establishing a selling price for Product M. The president of Inez Company has decided to use the cost-plus approach to product pricing and has indicated that Product M must earn a 10% rate of return on invested assets.

Instructions

1. Determine the amount of desired profit from the production and sale of Product M.
2. Assuming that the total cost concept is used, determine (a) the cost amount per unit, (b) the markup percentage, and (c) the selling price of Product M.
3. Assuming that the product cost concept is used, determine (a) the cost amount per unit, (b) the markup percentage, and (c) the selling price of Product M.
4. Assuming that the variable cost concept is used, determine (a) the cost amount per unit, (b) the markup percentage, and (c) the selling price of Product M.
5. Assume that for the current year, the selling price of Product M was $42 per unit. To date, 60,000 units have been produced and sold, and analysis of the domestic

market indicates that 15,000 additional units are expected to be sold during the remainder of the year. Recently, Inez Company received an offer from Wong Inc. for 4,000 units of Product M at $28 each. Wong Inc. will market the units in Korea under its own brand name, and no additional selling and administrative expenses associated with the sale will be incurred by Inez Company. The additional business is not expected to affect the domestic sales of Product M, and the additional units could be produced during the current year, using existing capacity. (a) Prepare a differential analysis report of the proposed sale to Wong Inc. (b) Based upon the differential analysis report in (a), should the proposal be accepted?

Solution

1. $160,000 ($1,600,000 × 10%)

2. a. Total costs:

Variable ($25 × 80,000 units)	$2,000,000
Fixed ($800,000 + $400,000)	1,200,000
Total	$3,200,000

Cost amount per unit: $3,200,000 ÷ 80,000 units = $40.00

b. Markup percentage = $\dfrac{\text{Desired profit}}{\text{Total costs}}$

Markup percentage = $\dfrac{\$160,000}{\$3,200,000}$ = 5%

c.

Cost amount per unit	$40.00
Markup ($40 × 5%)	2.00
Selling price	$42.00

3. a. Total manufacturing costs:

Variable ($20 × 80,000 units)	$1,600,000
Fixed factory overhead	800,000
Total	$2,400,000

Cost amount per unit: $2,400,000 ÷ 80,000 units = $30.00

b. Markup percentage = $\dfrac{\text{Desired profit} + \text{Total selling and administrative expenses}}{\text{Total manufacturing costs}}$

Markup percentage = $\dfrac{\$160,000 + \$400,000 + (\$5 \times 80,000\ \text{units})}{\$2,400,000}$

Markup percentage = $\dfrac{\$160,000 + \$400,000 + \$400,000}{\$2,400,000}$

Markup percentage = $\dfrac{\$960,000}{\$2,400,000}$ = 40%

c.

Cost amount per unit	$30.00
Markup ($30 × 40%)	12.00
Selling price	$42.00

4. a. Variable cost amount per unit: $25
Total variable costs: $25 × 80,000 units = $2,000,000

b. Markup percentage = $\dfrac{\text{Desired profit} + \text{Total fixed costs}}{\text{Total variable costs}}$

Markup percentage = $\dfrac{\$160,000 + \$800,000 + \$400,000}{\$2,000,000}$

Markup percentage = $\dfrac{\$1,360,000}{\$2,000,000}$ = 68%

c. Cost amount per unit	$25.00
Markup ($25 × 68%)	17.00
Selling price	$42.00

5. a.

Proposal to Sell to Wong Inc.

Differential revenue from accepting offer:	
Revenue from sale of 4,000 additional units at $28	$112,000
Differential cost from accepting offer:	
Variable production costs of 4,000 additional units at $20	80,000
Differential income from accepting offer	$ 32,000

b. The proposal should be accepted.

Self-Examination Questions (Answers at End of Chapter)

1. Marlo Company is considering discontinuing a product. The costs of the product consist of $20,000 fixed costs and $15,000 variable costs. The variable operating expenses related to the product total $4,000. What is the differential cost?
   A. $19,000   C. $35,000
   B. $15,000   D. $39,000

2. Victor Company is considering disposing of equipment that was originally purchased for $200,000 and has $150,000 of accumulated depreciation to date. The same equipment would cost $310,000 to replace. What is the sunk cost?
   A. $50,000   C. $200,000
   B. $150,000   D. $310,000

3. Henry Company is considering spending $100,000 for a new grinding machine. This amount could be invested to yield a 12% return. What is the opportunity cost?
   A. $112,000   C. $12,000
   B. $88,000   D. $100,000

4. For which cost concept used in applying the cost-plus approach to product pricing are fixed manufacturing costs, fixed selling and administrative expenses, and desired profit allowed for in determining the markup?
   A. Total cost   C. Variable cost
   B. Product cost   D. Standard cost

5. Mendosa Company produces three products. All the products use a furnace operation, which is a production bottleneck. The following information is available:

	Product 1	Product 2	Product 3
Unit volume—March	1,000	1,500	1,000
Per unit information:			
Sales price	$35	$33	$29
Variable cost	15	15	15
Contribution margin	$20	$18	$14
Furnace hours	4	3	2

From a profitability perspective, which product should be emphasized in April's advertising campaign?
   A. Product 1   C. Product 3
   B. Product 2   D. All three

Class Discussion Questions

1. Explain the meaning of (a) differential revenue, (b) differential cost, and (c) differential income.

2. It was reported that **Exabyte**, a fast growing (100-fold in four years) Colorado marketer of tape drives, has decided to purchase key components of its product from others. For example, **Sony** provides Exabyte with mechanical decks, and **Solectron** provides circuit boards. Exabyte's chief executive officer, Peter Behrendt, states, "If we'd tried to build our own plants, we could never have

REAL WORLD

grown that fast or maybe survived." The decision to purchase key product components is an example of what type of decision illustrated in this chapter?

3. In the long run, the normal selling price must be set high enough to cover what factors?

4. A company could sell a building for $500,000 or lease it for $5,000 per month. What would need to be considered in determining if the lease option would be preferred?

5. A chemical company has a commodity-grade and premium-grade product. Why might the company elect to process the commodity-grade product further to the premium-grade product?

6. A company accepts incremental business at a special price that exceeds the variable cost. What other issues must the company consider in deciding whether to accept the business?

7. A company fabricates a component at a cost of $4.00. A supplier offers to supply the same component for $3.60. Under what circumstances is it reasonable to purchase from the supplier?

8. Many fast-food restaurant chains, such as **McDonald's**, will occasionally discontinue restaurants in their system. What are some financial considerations in deciding to eliminate a store?

9. Why might the use of ideal standards in applying the cost-plus approach to product pricing lead to setting product prices that are too low?

10. Although the cost-plus approach to product pricing may be used by management as a general guideline, what are some examples of other factors that managers should also consider in setting product prices?

11. What method of determining product cost may be appropriate in settings where the manufacturing process is complex?

12. How does the target cost concept differ from cost-plus approaches?

13. Under what circumstances is it appropriate to use the target cost concept?

14. What is a production bottleneck?

15. What is the appropriate measure of a product's value when a firm is operating under production bottlenecks?

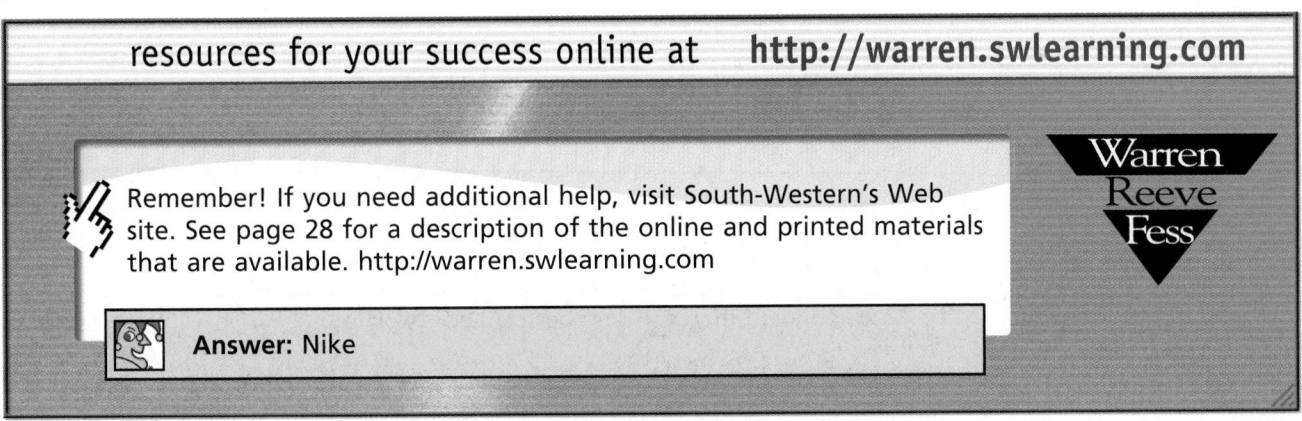

resources for your success online at **http://warren.swlearning.com**

Remember! If you need additional help, visit South-Western's Web site. See page 28 for a description of the online and printed materials that are available. http://warren.swlearning.com

Warren
Reeve
Fess

Answer: Nike

Exercises

EXERCISE 23-1
Lease or sell decision

Objective 1

Tenney Construction Company is considering selling excess machinery with a book value of $210,000 (original cost of $320,000 less accumulated depreciation of $110,000) for $180,000 less a 5% brokerage commission. Alternatively, the machinery can be leased for a total of $200,000 for five years, after which it is expected

✓ *a. Differential revenue from lease, $20,000*

to have no residual value. During the period of the lease, Tenney Construction Company's costs of repairs, insurance, and property tax expenses are expected to be $24,000.

a. Prepare a differential analysis report, dated January 3, 2006, for the lease or sell decision.

b. ▆▆▆▶ On the basis of the data presented, would it be advisable to lease or sell the machinery? Explain.

EXERCISE 23-2
Differential analysis report for a discontinued product
Objective 1

✓ *a. Differential cost of annual sales, $401,400*

A condensed income statement by product line for Nordic Beverage Inc. indicated the following for Diet Kola for the past year:

Sales	$486,000
Cost of goods sold	258,000
Gross profit	$228,000
Operating expenses	260,000
Loss from operations	$ (32,000)

It is estimated that 20% of the cost of goods sold represents fixed factory overhead costs and that 25% of the operating expenses are fixed. Since Diet Kola is only one of many products, the fixed costs will not be materially affected if the product is discontinued.

a. Prepare a differential analysis report, dated January 3, 2006, for the proposed discontinuance of Diet Kola.

b. ▆▆▆▶ Should Diet Kola be retained? Explain.

EXERCISE 23-3
Differential analysis report for a discontinued product
Objective 1

✓ *a. Differential income: bowls, $34,580*

The condensed product-line income statement for Century Ceramics Company for the current year is as follows:

Century Ceramics Company
Product-Line Income Statement
For the Year Ended December 31, 2006

	Bowls	Plates	Cups
Sales	$96,000	$122,000	$79,000
Cost of goods sold	51,000	68,000	51,000
Gross profit	$45,000	$ 54,000	$28,000
Selling and administrative expenses	28,000	31,000	34,000
Income from operations	$17,000	$ 23,000	$ (6,000)

Fixed costs are 18% of the cost of goods sold and 30% of the selling and administrative expenses. Century Ceramics assumes that fixed costs would not be materially affected if the Cups line were discontinued.

a. Prepare a differential analysis report for all three products for 2006.
b. ▆▆▆▶ Should the Cups line be retained? Explain.

EXERCISE 23-4
Segment analysis
Objective 1

The **Charles Schwab Corporation** is one of the more innovative brokerage and financial service companies in the United States. The company recently provided information about its major business segments as follows (in millions):

	Individual Investor	Institutional Investor	Capital Markets
Revenues	$2,531	$827	$315
Income from operations	245	272	18
Depreciation	294	51	26

a. ▆▆▆▶ How do you believe Schwab defines the difference between the "Individual Investor" and "Institutional Investor" segments?
b. Provide a specific example of a variable and fixed cost in the "Individual Investor" segment.

c. Estimate the contribution margin for each segment.

d. If Schwab decided to sell its "Institutional Investor" accounts to another company, estimate how much operating income would decline?

EXERCISE 23-5
Decision to discontinue a product
Objective 1

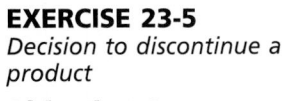

WHAT'S WRONG
WITH THIS?

On the basis of the following data, the general manager of Sole Mates Inc. decided to discontinue Children's Shoes because it reduced income from operations by $22,000. What is the flaw in this decision?

Sole Mates Inc.
Product-Line Income Statement
For the Year Ended August 31, 2006

	Children's Shoes	Men's Shoes	Women's Shoes	Total
Sales	$130,000	$300,000	$500,000	$930,000
Costs of goods sold:				
Variable costs	$ 90,000	$150,000	$220,000	$460,000
Fixed costs	30,000	60,000	120,000	210,000
Total cost of goods sold	$120,000	$210,000	$340,000	$670,000
Gross profit	$ 10,000	$ 90,000	$160,000	$260,000
Operating expenses:				
Variable expenses	$ 20,000	$ 45,000	$ 95,000	$160,000
Fixed expenses	12,000	20,000	25,000	57,000
Total operating expenses	$ 32,000	$ 65,000	$120,000	$217,000
Income (loss) from operations	$ (22,000)	$ 25,000	$ 40,000	$ 43,000

EXERCISE 23-6
Make-or-buy decision
Objective 1

SPREADSHEET

✓a. Cost savings from making, $1.00 per case

Advent Computer Company has been purchasing carrying cases for its portable computers at a delivered cost of $51 per unit. The company, which is currently operating below full capacity, charges factory overhead to production at the rate of 40% of direct labor cost. The fully absorbed unit costs to produce comparable carrying cases are expected to be:

Direct materials	$20.00
Direct labor	24.00
Factory overhead (40% of direct labor)	9.60
Total cost per unit	$53.60

If Advent Computer Company manufactures the carrying cases, fixed factory overhead costs will not increase and variable factory overhead costs associated with the cases are expected to be 25% of the direct labor costs.

a. Prepare a differential analysis report, dated June 5, 2006, for the make-or-buy decision.

b. On the basis of the data presented, would it be advisable to make the carrying cases or to continue buying them? Explain.

EXERCISE 23-7
Make-or-buy decision
Objective 1

SPREADSHEET

The International Pet Association (IPA) employs five people in its Publication Department. These people lay out pages for pamphlets, brochures, and other publications for the IPA membership. The pages are delivered to an outside company for printing. The company is considering an outside publication service for the layout work. The outside service is quoting a price of $16 per layout page. The budget for the Publication Department for 2006 is as follows:

Salaries	$200,000
Benefits	40,000
Supplies	35,000
Office expenses	20,000
Office depreciation	22,000
Computer depreciation	30,000
Total	$347,000

The department expects to lay out 18,000 pages for 2006. The computers have an estimated salvage value of $6,000. The Publication Department office space would be used for future administrative needs, if the department's function were purchased from the outside.

a. Prepare a differential analysis report, dated December 15, 2005, for the make-or-buy decision, considering the 2006 differential revenues and costs.
b. On the basis of your analysis in (a), should the page layout work be purchased from an outside company?
c. What additional considerations might factor into the decision making?

EXERCISE 23-8
Machine replacement decision
Objective 1

SPREADSHEET

✓ *a. Annual differential income, $10,000*

A company is considering replacing an old piece of machinery, which cost $520,000 and has $300,000 of accumulated depreciation to date, with a new machine that costs $445,000. The old equipment could be sold for $85,000. The variable production costs associated with the old machine are estimated to be $160,000 for six years. The variable production costs for the new machine are estimated to be $90,000 for six years.

a. Determine the differential annual income or loss from replacing the old machine.
b. What is the sunk cost in this situation?

EXERCISE 23-9
Differential analysis report for machine replacement
Objective 1

SPREADSHEET

✓ *a. Annual differential increase in costs, $2,000*

IC Electronics Company assembles circuit boards by using a manually operated machine to insert electronic components. The original cost of the machine is $140,000, the accumulated depreciation is $110,000, its remaining useful life is 10 years, and its salvage value is negligible. On January 20, 2006, a proposal was made to replace the present manufacturing procedure with a fully automatic machine that will cost $225,000. The automatic machine has an estimated useful life of 10 years and no significant salvage value. For use in evaluating the proposal, the accountant accumulated the following annual data on present and proposed operations:

	Present Operations	Proposed Operations
Sales	$280,000	$280,000
Direct materials	87,500	87,500
Direct labor	43,500	—
Power and maintenance	8,000	28,000
Taxes, insurance, etc.	4,000	7,000
Selling and administrative expenses	70,000	70,000

a. Prepare a differential analysis report for the proposal to replace the machine. Include in the analysis both the net differential change in costs anticipated over the 10 years and the net annual differential change in costs anticipated.
b. Based only on the data presented, should the proposal be accepted?
c. ▬▬➤ What are some of the other factors that should be considered before a final decision is made?

EXERCISE 23-10
Sell or process further
Objective 1
✓ *a. $205*

Daniels Lumber Company incurs a cost of $445 per hundred board feet in processing certain "rough-cut" lumber, which it sells for $615 per hundred board feet. An alternative is to produce a "finished-cut" at a total processing cost of $560 per hundred board feet, which can be sold for $820 per hundred board feet. For these alternatives, what is the amount of (a) the differential revenue, (b) differential cost, and (c) differential income?

EXERCISE 23-11
Sell or process further
Objective 1

AM Coffee Company produces Columbian coffee in batches of 8,000 pounds. The standard quantity of materials required in the process are 8,000 pounds, which cost $5.00 per pound. Columbian coffee can be sold without further processing for $8.80 per pound. Columbian coffee can also be processed further to yield Decaf Columbian, which can be sold for $11.20 per pound. The processing into Decaf Columbian re-

✓ c. $11.70

quires additional processing costs of $18,520 per batch. The additional processing will also cause a 5% loss of product due to evaporation.

a. Prepare a differential analysis report for the decision to sell or process further.
b. Should AM sell Columbian coffee or process further and sell Decaf Columbian?
c. Determine the price of Decaf Columbian that would cause neither an advantage or disadvantage for processing further and selling Decaf Columbian.

EXERCISE 23-12
Decision on accepting additional business
Objective 1

✓ a. Differential income, $91,000

Outdoor Denim Co. has an annual plant capacity of 60,000 units, and current production is 45,000 units. Monthly fixed costs are $40,000, and variable costs are $21 per unit. The present selling price is $36 per unit. On January 18, 2006, the company received an offer from Barker Company for 13,000 units of the product at $28 each. Barker Company will market the units in a foreign country under its own brand name. The additional business is not expected to affect the domestic selling price or quantity of sales of Outdoor Denim Co.

a. Prepare a differential analysis report for the proposed sale to Barker Company.
b. ▬▬▬► Briefly explain the reason why accepting this additional business will increase operating income.
c. What is the minimum price per unit that would produce a contribution margin?

EXERCISE 23-13
Accepting business at a special price
Objective 1

Genesis Company expects to operate at 90% of productive capacity during May. The total manufacturing costs for May for the production of 20,000 batteries are budgeted as follows:

Direct materials	$242,000
Direct labor	85,000
Variable factory overhead	29,000
Fixed factory overhead	60,000
Total manufacturing costs	$416,000

The company has an opportunity to submit a bid for 1,000 batteries to be delivered by May 31 to a government agency. If the contract is obtained, it is anticipated that the additional activity will not interfere with normal production during May or increase the selling or administrative expenses. What is the unit cost below which Genesis Company should not go in bidding on the government contract?

EXERCISE 23-14
Decision on accepting additional business
Objective 1

✓ a. Differential revenue, $1,400,000

Dunkirk Tire and Rubber Company has capacity to produce 160,000 tires. Dunkirk presently produces and sells 130,000 tires for the North American market at a price of $90 per tire. Dunkirk is evaluating a special order from a European automobile company, Continental Motors. Continental is offering to buy 20,000 tires for $70 per tire. Dunkirk's accounting system indicates that the total cost per tire is as follows:

Direct materials	$30
Direct labor	12
Factory overhead (40% variable)	18
Selling and administrative expenses (50% variable)	15
Total	$75

Dunkirk pays a selling commission equal to 5% of the selling price on North American orders, which is included in the variable portion of the selling and administrative expenses. However, this special order would not have a sales commission. If the order was accepted, the tires would be shipped overseas for an additional shipping cost of $4.00 per tire. In addition, Continental has made the order conditional on receiving European safety certification. Dunkirk estimates that this certification would cost $140,000.

a. Prepare a differential analysis report dated August 4, 2006, for the proposed sale to Continental Motors.
b. What is the minimum price per unit that would be financially acceptable to Dunkirk?

EXERCISE 23-22
Product pricing under bottlenecked operations

Objective 3

✓ *Medium, $220*

Based on the data presented in Exercise 23-21, assume that Safe-Tee Glass wanted to price all products so that they produced the same profit potential as the highest profit product. What would be the prices of all three products that would produce the largest profit?

Problems Series A

PROBLEM 23-1A
Differential analysis report involving opportunity costs

Objective 1

SPREADSHEET

✓ 3. $820,000

On December 1, Thoroughbred Distribution Company is considering leasing a building and buying the necessary equipment to operate a public warehouse. Alternatively, the company could use the funds to invest in $600,000 of 8% U.S. Treasury bonds that mature in 14 years. The bonds could be purchased at face value. The following data have been assembled:

Cost of equipment	$600,000
Life of equipment	14 years
Estimated residual value of equipment	$ 90,000
Yearly costs to operate the warehouse, excluding depreciation of equipment	$110,000
Yearly expected revenues—years 1–7	$230,000
Yearly expected revenues—years 8–14	$180,000

Instructions

1. Prepare a report as of December 1, 2006, presenting a differential analysis of the proposed operation of the warehouse for the 14 years as compared with present conditions.
2. Based on the results disclosed by the differential analysis, should the proposal be accepted?
3. If the proposal is accepted, what is the total estimated income from operations of the warehouse for the 14 years?

PROBLEM 23-2A
Differential analysis report for machine replacement proposal

Objective 1

SPREADSHEET

Ohio Tooling Company is considering replacing a machine that has been used in its factory for two years. Relevant data associated with the operations of the old machine and the new machine, neither of which has any estimated residual value, are as follows:

Old Machine

Cost of machine, 8-year life	$ 96,000
Annual depreciation (straight-line)	12,000
Annual manufacturing costs, excluding depreciation	23,000
Annual nonmanufacturing operating expenses	9,500
Annual revenue	45,000
Current estimated selling price of the machine	54,000

New Machine

Cost of machine, 6-year life	$114,000
Annual depreciation (straight-line)	19,000
Estimated annual manufacturing costs, exclusive of depreciation	10,000

Annual nonmanufacturing operating expenses and revenue are not expected to be affected by purchase of the new machine.

Instructions

1. Prepare a differential analysis report as of March 22, 2006, comparing operations utilizing the new machine with operations using the present equipment. The analy-

sis should indicate the differential income that would result over the 6-year period if the new machine is acquired.

2. ▭▬➤ List other factors that should be considered before a final decision is reached.

PROBLEM 23-3A
Differential analysis report for sales promotion proposal

Objective 1

SPREADSHEET

✓ *1. Differential income, tennis shoe, $183,000*

Strider Athletic Shoe Company is planning a one-month campaign for April to promote sales of one of its two shoe products. A total of $105,000 has been budgeted for advertising, contests, redeemable coupons, and other promotional activities. The following data have been assembled for their possible usefulness in deciding which of the products to select for the campaign.

	Tennis Shoe	Walking Shoe
Unit selling price	$102	$96
Unit production costs:		
Direct materials	$ 24	$18
Direct labor	10	8
Variable factory overhead	6	5
Fixed factory overhead	10	15
Total unit production costs	$ 50	$46
Unit variable selling expenses	14	18
Unit fixed selling expenses	12	16
Total unit costs	$ 76	$80
Operating income per unit	$ 26	$16

No increase in facilities would be necessary to produce and sell the increased output. It is anticipated that 6,000 additional units of tennis shoes or 8,000 additional units of walking shoes could be sold without changing the unit selling price of either product.

Instructions

1. Prepare a differential analysis report as of March 3, 2006, presenting the additional revenue and additional costs anticipated from the promotion of tennis shoes and walking shoes.

2. ▭▬➤ The sales manager had tentatively decided to promote tennis shoes, estimating that operating income would be increased by $51,000 ($26 operating income per unit for 6,000 units, less promotion expenses of $105,000). The manager also believed that the selection of walking shoes would increase operating income by $23,000 ($16 operating income per unit for 8,000 units, less promotion expenses of $105,000). State briefly your reasons for supporting or opposing the tentative decision.

PROBLEM 23-4A
Differential analysis report for further processing

Objective 1

SPREADSHEET

✓ *Differential revenue, $18,000*

The management of White Metals Inc. is considering whether to process aluminum ingot further into rolled aluminum. Rolled aluminum can be sold for $1,440 per ton, and ingot can be sold without further processing for $920 per ton. Ingot is produced in batches of 50 tons by smelting 60 tons of bauxite, which costs $450 per ton. Rolled aluminum will require additional processing costs of $385 per ton of ingot, and 1.125 tons of ingot will produce 1 ton of rolled aluminum.

Instructions

1. Prepare a report as of February 20, 2006, presenting a differential analysis associated with the further processing of aluminum ingot to produce rolled aluminum.

2. ▭▬➤ Briefly report your recommendations.

PROBLEM 23-5A
Product pricing using the cost-plus approach concepts; differential analysis report for accepting additional business

Safety-Bright Company recently began production of a new product, the halogen light, which required the investment of $1,000,000 in assets. The costs of producing and selling 20,000 halogen lights are estimated as follows:

Variable costs per unit:		Fixed costs:	
Direct materials	$28.00	Factory overhead	$200,000
Direct labor	12.00	Selling and administrative expenses	80,000
Factory overhead	5.00		
Selling and administrative expenses	5.00		
Total	$50.00		

Safety-Bright Company is currently considering establishing a selling price for the halogen light. The president of Safety-Bright Company has decided to use the cost-plus approach to product pricing and has indicated that the halogen light must earn a 15% rate of return on invested assets.

Instructions

1. Determine the amount of desired profit from the production and sale of the halogen light.
2. Assuming that the total cost concept is used, determine (a) the cost amount per unit, (b) the markup percentage (rounded to two decimal places), and (c) the selling price of the halogen light.
3. Assuming that the product cost concept is used, determine (a) the cost amount per unit, (b) the markup percentage, and (c) the selling price of the halogen light. Round to the nearest cent.
4. Assuming that the variable cost concept is used, determine (a) the cost amount per unit, (b) the markup percentage, and (c) the selling price of the halogen light.
5. ⬛▸ Comment on any additional considerations that could influence establishing the selling price for the halogen light.
6. Assume that as of June 1, 2006, 7,000 units of halogen light have been produced and sold during the current year. Analysis of the domestic market indicates that 10,000 additional units of the halogen light are expected to be sold during the remainder of the year at the normal product price determined under the total cost concept. On June 5, Safety-Bright Company received an offer from Lights Inc. for 2,000 units of the halogen light at $49 each. Lights Inc. will market the units in Japan under its own brand name, and no additional selling and administrative expenses associated with the sale will be incurred by Safety-Bright Company. The additional business is not expected to affect the domestic sales of the halogen light, and the additional units could be produced using existing capacity.
   a. Prepare a differential analysis report of the proposed sale to Lights Inc.
   b. Based upon the differential analysis report in (a), should the proposal be accepted?

PROBLEM 23-6A
Product pricing and profit analysis with bottleneck operations

Objectives 1, 3

SPREADSHEET

✓ *3. Ester price, $115.40*

Quality Chemical Company produces three products: ethylene, butane, and ester. Each of these products has high demand in the market, and Quality Chemical is able to sell as much as it can produce of all three. The reaction operation is a bottleneck in the process and is running at 100% of capacity. Quality Chemical is attempting to determine how to improve profitability for the chemical operations. The variable conversion cost is $6 per process hour. The fixed cost is $990,000. In addition, the cost analyst was able to determine the following information about the three products:

	Ethylene	Butane	Ester
Budgeted units produced	6,000	6,000	6,000
Total process hours per unit	2	2	1.5
Reactor hours per unit	0.8	0.5	0.4
Price per unit	$152	$125	$114
Direct materials cost per unit	$100	$ 80	$ 80

The reaction operation is part of the total process for each of these three products. So, for example, 0.8 of the 2 hours required to process Ethylene are associated with the reactor.

Instructions

1. Determine the contribution margin per unit for each product.
2. Provide an analysis to determine the relative product profitabilities, assuming that the reactor is a bottleneck.
3. Assume that management wishes to improve profitability by increasing prices on selected products. At what price would Ethylene and Ester need to be offered in order to produce the same relative profitability as Butane?

Problems Series B

PROBLEM 23-1B
Differential analysis report involving opportunity costs

Objective 1

SPREADSHEET

✓ 3. $212,000

On July 1, Starlight Stores Inc. is considering leasing a building and purchasing the necessary equipment to operate a retail store. Alternatively, the company could use the funds to invest in $250,000 of 6% U.S. Treasury bonds that mature in 18 years. The bonds could be purchased at face value. The following data have been assembled:

Cost of store equipment	$250,000
Life of store equipment	18 years
Estimated residual value of store equipment	$ 30,000
Yearly costs to operate the store, excluding depreciation of store equipment	$ 64,000
Yearly expected revenues—years 1–9	$ 84,000
Yearly expected revenues—years 10–18	$ 92,000

Instructions

1. Prepare a report as of July 1, 2006, presenting a differential analysis of the proposed operation of the store for the 18 years as compared with present conditions.
2. Based on the results disclosed by the differential analysis, should the proposal be accepted?
3. If the proposal is accepted, what would be the total estimated income from operations of the store for the 18 years?

PROBLEM 23-2B
Differential analysis report for machine replacement decision

Objective 1

SPREADSHEET

Keystone Printing Company is considering replacing a machine that has been used in its factory for two years. Relevant data associated with the operations of the old machine and the new machine, neither of which has any estimated residual value, are as follows:

Old Machine	
Cost of machine, 10-year life	$360,000
Annual depreciation (straight-line)	36,000
Annual manufacturing costs, excluding depreciation	345,000
Annual nonmanufacturing operating expenses	215,000
Annual revenue	740,000
Current estimated selling price of machine	190,000

New Machine	
Cost of machine, 8-year life	$580,000
Annual depreciation (straight-line)	72,500
Estimated annual manufacturing costs, exclusive of depreciation	276,000

Annual nonmanufacturing operating expenses and revenue are not expected to be affected by purchase of the new machine.

(continued)

Instructions

1. Prepare a differential analysis report as of August 11, 2006, comparing operations utilizing the new machine with operations using the present equipment. The analysis should indicate the total differential income that would result over the 8-year period if the new machine is acquired.

2. ▭▭▶ List other factors that should be considered before a final decision is reached.

PROBLEM 23-3B
Differential analysis report for sales promotion proposal

Objective 1

SPREADSHEET

✓ *1. Cologne differential income, $120,000*

Lilac Cosmetics Company is planning a one-month campaign for May to promote sales of one of its two cosmetics products. A total of $90,000 has been budgeted for advertising, contests, redeemable coupons, and other promotional activities. The following data have been assembled for their possible usefulness in deciding which of the products to select for the campaign:

	Cologne	Perfume
Unit selling price	$52	$65
Unit production costs:		
Direct materials	$ 8	$12
Direct labor	4	6
Variable factory overhead	3	4
Fixed factory overhead	8	8
Total unit production costs	$23	$30
Unit variable selling expenses	16	20
Unit fixed selling expenses	4	2
Total unit costs	$43	$52
Operating income per unit	$ 9	$13

No increase in facilities would be necessary to produce and sell the increased output. It is anticipated that 10,000 additional units of cologne or 9,000 additional units of perfume could be sold without changing the unit selling price of either product.

Instructions

1. Prepare a differential analysis report as of April 5, 2006, presenting the additional revenue and additional costs anticipated from the promotion of cologne and perfume.

2. ▭▭▶ The sales manager had tentatively decided to promote perfume, estimating that operating income would be increased by $27,000 ($13 operating income per unit for 9,000 units, less promotion expenses of $90,000). The manager also believed that the selection of cologne would have no impact on operating income ($9 operating income per unit for 10,000 units, less promotion expenses of $90,000). State briefly your reasons for supporting or opposing the tentative decision.

PROBLEM 23-4B
Differential analysis report for further processing

Objective 1

SPREADSHEET

✓ *Differential revenue, $7,600*

The management of Caribbean Sugar Company is considering whether to process further raw sugar into refined sugar. Refined sugar can be sold for $1.85 per pound, and raw sugar can be sold without further processing for $1.10 per pound. Raw sugar is produced in batches of 20,000 pounds by processing 90,000 pounds of sugar cane, which costs $0.25 per pound. Refined sugar will require additional processing costs of $0.33 per pound of raw sugar, and 1.25 pounds of raw sugar will produce 1 pound of refined sugar.

Instructions

1. Prepare a report as of May 30, 2006, presenting a differential analysis of the further processing of raw sugar to produce refined sugar.

2. ▭▭▶ Briefly report your recommendations.

PROBLEM 23-5B
Product pricing using the cost-plus approach concepts; differential analysis report for accepting additional business

Objectives 1, 2

✓*2. b. Markup percentage, 5%*

Display Labs Inc. recently began production of a new product, flat panel displays, which required the investment of $2,500,000 in assets. The costs of producing and selling 25,000 units of flat panel displays are estimated as follows:

Variable costs per unit:		Fixed costs:	
Direct materials	$170	Factory overhead	$1,500,000
Direct labor	40	Selling and administrative expenses	500,000
Factory overhead	50		
Selling and administrative expenses	20		
Total	$280		

Display Labs Inc. is currently considering establishing a selling price for flat panel displays. The president of Display Labs has decided to use the cost-plus approach to product pricing and has indicated that the displays must earn an 18% rate of return on invested assets.

Instructions

1. Determine the amount of desired profit from the production and sale of flat panel displays.
2. Assuming that the total cost concept is used, determine (a) the cost amount per unit, (b) the markup percentage, and (c) the selling price of flat panel displays.
3. Assuming that the product cost concept is used, determine (a) the cost amount per unit, (b) the markup percentage, and (c) the selling price of flat panel displays.
4. Assuming that the variable cost concept is used, determine (a) the cost amount per unit, (b) the markup percentage, and (c) the selling price of flat panel displays.
5. ▭▬▶ Comment on any additional considerations that could influence establishing the selling price for flat panel displays.
6. Assume that as of September 1, 2006, 17,000 units of flat panel displays have been produced and sold during the current year. Analysis of the domestic market indicates that 5,000 additional units are expected to be sold during the remainder of the year at the normal product price determined under the total cost concept. On September 3, Display Labs Inc. received an offer from Kane Company for 3,000 units of flat panel displays at $275 each. Kane Company will market the units in Canada under its own brand name, and no additional selling and administrative expenses associated with the sale will be incurred by Display Labs Inc. The additional business is not expected to affect the domestic sales of flat panel displays, and the additional units could be produced using existing capacity.
   a. Prepare a differential analysis report of the proposed sale to Kane Company.
   b. Based upon the differential analysis report in (a), should the proposal be accepted?

PROBLEM 23-6B
Product pricing and profit analysis with bottleneck operations

Objectives 1, 3

SPREADSHEET

✓*3. High Grade price, $536*

Mohawk Valley Steel Company produces three grades of steel: high, good, and regular grade. Each of these products (grades) has high demand in the market, and Mohawk Valley is able to sell as much as it can produce of all three. The furnace operation is a bottleneck in the process and is running at 100% of capacity. Mohawk Valley is attempting to determine how to improve profitability for the steel operations. The variable conversion cost is $8 per process hour. The fixed cost is $1,530,000. In addition, the cost analyst was able to determine the following information about the three products:

	High Grade	Good Grade	Regular Grade
Budgeted units produced	5,000	5,000	5,000
Total process hours per unit	12	12	10
Furnace hours per unit	6	4	2
Price per unit	$350	$325	$300
Direct materials cost per unit	$140	$125	$120

(continued)

The furnace operation is part of the total process for each of these three products. So, for example, 6 of the 12 hours required to process High Grade steel are associated with the furnace.

Instructions

1. Determine the contribution margin per unit for each product.
2. Provide an analysis to determine the relative product profitabilities, assuming that the furnace is a bottleneck.
3. Assume that management wishes to improve profitability by increasing prices on selected products. At what price would High and Good Grades need to be offered in order to produce the same relative profitability as Regular Grade steel?

Special Activities

ACTIVITY 23-1
Product pricing

ETHICS

Marcia Sanchez is a cost accountant for Bearings Inc. Ted Crowe, vice-president of marketing, has asked Marcia to meet with representatives of Bearings' major competitor to discuss product cost data. Crowe indicates that the sharing of these data will enable Bearings to determine a fair and equitable price for its products.

→ Would it be ethical for Sanchez to attend the meeting and share the relevant cost data?

ACTIVITY 23-2
Decision on accepting additional business

A manager of Dutch's Sporting Goods Company is considering accepting an order from an overseas customer. This customer has requested an order for 20,000 dozen golf balls at a price of $15.00 per dozen. The variable cost to manufacture a dozen golf balls is $13.00 per dozen. The full cost is $17.00 per dozen. Dutch's has a normal selling price of $23.00 per dozen. Dutch's plant has just enough excess capacity on the second shift to make the overseas order.

→ What are some considerations in accepting or rejecting this order?

ACTIVITY 23-3
Accept business at a special price

REAL WORLD

INTERNET

If you are not familiar with **priceline.com**, go to its Web site. Assume that an individual bids $50 on priceline.com for a room in Dallas, Texas, on August 24. Assume that August 24 is a Saturday, with low expected room demand in Dallas at a **Marriott** hotel, so there is excess room capacity. The fully allocated cost per room per day is assumed from hotel records as follows:

Housekeeping labor cost*	$25
Hotel depreciation expense	37
Cost of room supplies (soap, paper, etc.)	5
Laundry labor and material cost*	10
Cost of desk staff	5
Utility cost (mostly air conditioning)	3
Total cost per room per day	$85

*Both housekeeping and laundry staff include many part-time workers, so that workload can be matched to demand.

Should Marriott accept the customer bid for a night in Dallas on August 24 at a price of $50?

ACTIVITY 23-4
Product profitability with production constraints

Peer Glass Company produces glass products for the automobile industry. The company produces three types of products: small, medium, and large windows. One of the process steps in glass making involves a furnace operation. Presently, the furnace runs 24 hours per day, seven days per week. The following per-unit information is available about the three major product lines:

	Small Window	Medium Window	Large Window
Sales price	$14.00	$24.00	$32.00
Variable cost	8.00	16.00	20.00
Contribution margin	$ 6.00	$ 8.00	$12.00
Furnace hours	2	4	5

The product manager of Peer Glass Company believes that the company should increase incremental sales effort on the large window, since the contribution margin per unit is the highest.

▶ Respond to this suggestion. What recommendations would you suggest to improve profitability?

ACTIVITY 23-5
Make or buy decision

The president of Shield Materials Inc., Jason Sheppard, asked the controller, Jill Mayfield, to provide an analysis of a make vs. buy decision for material TS-101. The material is presently processed in Shield's Roanoke facility. TS-101 is used in processing of final products in the facility. Mayfield determined the following unit production costs for the material as of March 15, 2006:

Direct materials	$ 7.20
Direct labor	2.50
Variable factory overhead	1.20
Fixed factory overhead	2.00
Total production costs per unit	$12.90

In addition, material TS-101 requires special hazardous material handling. This special handling adds an additional cost of $1.50 for each unit produced.

Material TS-101 can be purchased from an overseas supplier. The supplier does not presently do business with Shield Materials. This supplier promises monthly delivery of the material at a price of $9.60 per unit, plus transportation cost of $0.40 per unit. In addition, Shield would need to incur additional administrative costs to satisfy import regulations for hazardous material. These additional administrative costs are estimated to be $0.80 per purchased unit. Each purchased unit would also require special hazardous material handling of $1.50 per unit.

a. Prepare a differential analysis report to support Mayfield's recommendation on whether to continue making material TS-101 or whether to purchase the material from the overseas supplier.
b. ▶ What additional considerations should Mayfield address in the recommendation?

ACTIVITY 23-6
Cost-plus and target costing concepts

The following conversation took place between Cedrick James, vice-president of marketing, and Lee Wright, controller of Gem Computer Company:

Cedrick: I am really excited about our new computer coming out. I think it will be a real market success.

Lee: I'm really glad you think so. I know that our price is one variable that will determine if it's a success. If our price is too high, our competitors will be the ones with the market success.

Cedrick: Don't worry about it. We'll just mark our product cost up by 25% and it will all work out. I know we'll make money at those markups. By the way, what does the estimated product cost look like?

Lee: Well, there's the rub. The product cost looks as if it's going to come in at around $2,400. With a 25% markup, that will give us a selling price of $3,000.

Cedrick: I see your concern. That's a little high. Our research indicates that computer prices are dropping by about 20% per year and that this type of computer should be selling for around $2,500 when we release it to the market.

Lee: I'm not sure what to do.

Cedrick: Let me see if I can help. How much of the $2,400 is fixed cost?

Lee: About $400.

Cedrick: There you go. The fixed cost is sunk. We don't need to consider it in our pricing decision. If we reduce the product cost by $400, the new price with a 25% markup would be right at $2,500. Boy, I was really worried for a minute there. I knew something wasn't right.

a.  If you were Lee, how would you respond to Cedrick's solution to the pricing problem?

b.  How might target costing be used to help solve this pricing dilemma?

ACTIVITY 23-7
Internet marketing

GROUP ACTIVITY   INTERNET

Many businesses are offering their products and services over the Internet. Some of these companies and their Internet addresses are listed below.

Company Name	Internet Address (URL)	Product
Delta Air Lines	http://www.delta.com	air travel
Amazon.com, Inc.	http://www.amazon.com	books
Dell Computer Company	http://www.dell.com	personal computers

a. In groups of three, assign each person in your group to one of the Internet sites listed above. For each site, determine the following:
  1. A product (or service) description.
  2. A product price.
  3. A list of costs that are required to produce and sell the product selected in (1) as listed in the annual report on SEC form 10-K.
  4. Whether the costs identified in (3) are fixed costs or variable costs.

b. Which of the three products do you believe has the largest markup on variable cost?

Answers to Self-Examination Questions

1. **A** Differential cost is the amount of increase or decrease in cost that is expected from a particular course of action compared with an alternative. For Marlo Company, the differential cost is $19,000 (answer A). This is the total of the variable product costs ($15,000) and the variable operating expenses ($4,000), which would not be incurred if the product is discontinued.

2. **A** A sunk cost is not affected by later decisions. For Victor Company, the sunk cost is the $50,000 (answer A) book value of the equipment, which is equal to the original cost of $200,000 (answer C) less the accumulated depreciation of $150,000 (answer B).

3. **C** The amount of income that could have been earned from the best available alternative to a proposed use of cash is the opportunity cost. For Henry Company, the opportunity cost is 12% of $100,000, or $12,000 (answer C).

4. **C** Under the variable cost concept of product pricing (answer C), fixed manufacturing costs, fixed administrative and selling expenses, and desired profit

are allowed for in determining the markup. Only desired profit is allowed for in the markup under the total cost concept (answer A). Under the product cost concept (answer B), total selling and administrative expenses and desired profit are allowed for in determining the markup. Standard cost (answer D) can be used under any of the cost-plus approaches to product pricing.

5. **C** Product 3 has the highest unit contribution margin per bottleneck hour ($14/2 = $7). Product 1 (answer A) has the largest contribution margin per unit, but the lowest unit contribution per bottleneck hour ($20/4 = $5), so it is the least profitable product in the constrained environment. Product 2 (answer B) has the highest total profitability in March (1,500 units × $18), but this does not suggest that it has the highest profit potential. Product 2's unit contribution per bottleneck hour ($18/3 = $6) is between Products 1 and 3. Answer D is not true, since the products all have different profit potential in terms of unit contribution margin per bottleneck hour.

CAPITAL INVESTMENT ANALYSIS

objectives

After studying this chapter, you should be able to:

1 Explain the nature and importance of capital investment analysis.

2 Evaluate capital investment proposals, using the following methods: average rate of return, cash payback, net present value, and internal rate of return.

3 List and describe factors that complicate capital investment analysis.

4 Diagram the capital rationing process.

Why are you paying tuition, studying this text, and spending time and money on a higher education? Most people believe that the money and time spent now will return them more income in the future. In other words, a higher education is an investment in future earning ability. How would you know if this investment is worth it? One method would be to compare the cost of a higher education against the estimated future increased earning power. The more your future increased earnings exceed the investment, the more attractive the investment. As you will see in this chapter, the same is true for business investments in fixed assets. Business organizations analyze potential capital investments by using various methods that compare investment costs to future earnings and cash flows.

In this chapter, we will describe analyses useful for making investment decisions, which may involve thousands, millions, or even billions of dollars. We will emphasize the similarities and differences among the most commonly used methods of evaluating investment proposals, as well as the uses of each method. We will also discuss qualitative considerations affecting investment analyses. Finally, we will discuss considerations complicating investment analyses and the process of allocating available investment funds among competing proposals.

Nature of Capital Investment Analysis

Explain the nature and importance of capital investment analysis.

How do companies decide to make significant investments such as the following?

- **Yum Brands Inc.** adds 375 new international Taco Bell, Pizza Hut, and KFC units.
- **The Walt Disney Company** commits to investing $315 million to build a new theme park in Hong Kong.
- **Carnival Corporation** commits $6 billion to build 13 luxury cruise ships throughout the mid 2000s.

Companies use capital investment analysis to help evaluate long-term investments. *Capital investment analysis* (or **capital budgeting**) is the process by which management plans, evaluates, and controls investments in fixed assets. Capital investments involve the long-term commitment of funds and affect operations for many years. Thus, these investments must earn a reasonable rate of return, so that the business can meet its obligations to creditors and provide dividends to stockholders. Because capital investment decisions are some of the most important decisions that management makes, capital investment analysis must be carefully developed and implemented.

A capital investment program should encourage employees to submit proposals for capital investments. It should communicate to employees the long-range goals of the business, so that useful proposals are submitted. All reasonable proposals should be considered and evaluated with respect to economic costs and benefits. The program may reward employees whose proposals are accepted.

Methods of Evaluating Capital Investment Proposals

objective   **2**

Evaluate capital investment proposals, using the following methods: average rate of return, cash payback, net present value, and internal rate of return.

Capital investment evaluation methods can be grouped into the following two categories:

1. Methods that do not use present values
2. Methods that use present values

Two methods that do not use present values are (1) the average rate of return method and (2) the cash payback method. Two methods that use present values are (1) the net present value method and (2) the internal rate of return method. These methods consider the time value of money. The ***time value of money concept*** recognizes that an amount of cash invested today will earn income and therefore has value over time.

Management often uses a combination of methods in evaluating capital investment proposals. Each method has advantages and disadvantages. In addition, some of the computations are complex. Computers, however, can perform the computations quickly and easily. Computers can also be used to analyze the impact of changes in key estimates in evaluating capital investment proposals.

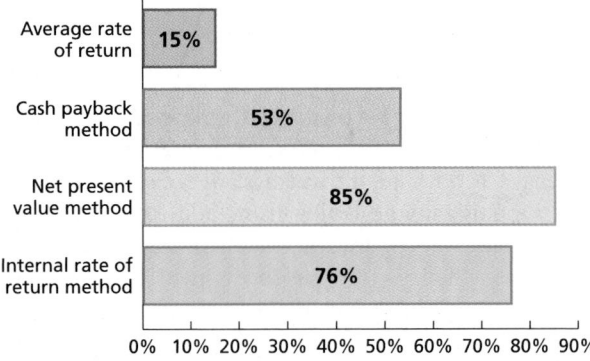

REAL WORLD A CFO survey of capital investment analysis methods used by large U.S. companies reported the following:

Percentage of Respondents Reporting the Use of the Method as "Always" or "Often"

Source: Patricia A. Ryan and Glenn P. Ryan, "Capital Budgeting Practices of the Fortune 1000: How Have Things Changed?" *Journal of Business and Management* (Winter 2002).

Methods that Ignore Present Value

The average rate of return and the cash payback methods are easy to use. These methods are often initially used to screen proposals. Management normally sets minimum standards for accepting proposals, and those not meeting these standards are dropped from further consideration. If a proposal meets the minimum standards, it is often subject to further analysis.

The methods that ignore present value are often useful in evaluating capital investment proposals that have relatively short useful lives. In such cases, the timing of the cash flows is less important.

Average Rate of Return Method

The ***average rate of return***, sometimes called the **accounting rate of return**, is a measure of the average income as a percent of the average investment in fixed assets. The average rate of return is determined by using the following equation:

$$\text{Average rate of return} = \frac{\text{Estimated average annual income}}{\text{Average investment}}$$

The numerator is the average of the annual income expected to be earned from the investment over the investment life, after deducting depreciation. The denominator is the average book value over the investment life. Thus, if straight-line depreciation and no residual value are assumed, the average investment over the useful life is equal to one-half of the original cost.[1]

---

[1]The average investment is the midpoint of the depreciable cost of the asset. Since a fixed asset is never depreciated below its residual value, this midpoint is determined by adding the original cost of the asset to the estimated residual value and dividing by 2.

To illustrate, assume that management is considering the purchase of a machine at a cost of $500,000. The machine is expected to have a useful life of 4 years, with no residual value, and to yield total income of $200,000. The estimated average annual income is therefore $50,000 ($200,000 ÷ 4), and the average investment is $250,000 [($500,000 + $0 residual value) ÷ 2]. Thus, the average rate of return on the average investment is 20%, computed as follows:

$$\text{Average rate of return} = \frac{\text{Estimated average annual income}}{\text{Average investment}}$$

$$\text{Average rate of return} = \frac{\$200,000 \div 4}{(\$500,000 + \$0) \div 2} = 20\%$$

The average rate of return of 20% should be compared with the minimum rate for such investments. If the average rate of return equals or exceeds the minimum rate, the machine should be purchased.

When several capital investment proposals are considered, the proposals can be ranked by their average rates of return. The higher the average rate of return, the more desirable the proposal. For example, assume that management is considering two capital investment proposals and has computed the following average rates of return:

What is the average rate of return for a project that is estimated to yield total income of $273,600 over three years, cost $690,000, and has a $70,000 residual value?

24% [($273,600 ÷ 3)/($690,000 + $70,000) ÷ 2]

	Proposal A	Proposal B
Estimated average annual income	$ 30,000	$ 36,000
Average investment	$120,000	$180,000
Average rate of return:		
$30,000 ÷ $120,000	25%	
$36,000 ÷ $180,000		20%

If only the average rate of return is considered, Proposal A, with an average rate of return of 25%, would be preferred over Proposal B.

In addition to being easy to compute, the average rate of return method has several advantages. One advantage is that it includes the amount of income earned over the entire life of the proposal. In addition, it emphasizes accounting income, which is often used by investors and creditors in evaluating management performance. Its main disadvantage is that it does not directly consider the expected cash flows from the proposal and the timing of these cash flows.

> **The average rate of return method considers the amount of income earned over the life of a proposal.**

Cash Payback Method

Cash flows are important because cash can be reinvested. Very simply, the capital investment uses cash and must therefore return cash in the future in order to be successful.

The expected period of time that will pass between the date of an investment and the complete recovery in cash (or equivalent) of the amount invested is the **cash payback period**. To simplify the analysis, the revenues and expenses other than depreciation related to operating fixed assets are assumed to be all in the form of cash. The excess of the cash flowing in from revenue over the cash flowing out for expenses is termed **net cash flow**. The time required for the net cash flow to equal the initial outlay for the fixed asset is the payback period.

To illustrate, assume that the proposed investment in a fixed asset with an 8-year life is $200,000. The annual cash revenues from the investment are $50,000, and the annual cash expenses are $10,000. Thus, the annual net cash flow is expected to be $40,000 ($50,000 − $10,000). The estimated cash payback period for the investment is 5 years, computed as follows:

$$\frac{\$200,000}{\$40,000} = \text{5-year cash payback period}$$

A project has estimated annual net cash flows of $30,000. It is estimated to cost $105,000. What is the cash payback period?

3½ years ($105,000 ÷ $30,000)

In this illustration, the annual net cash flows are equal ($40,000 per year). If these annual net cash flows are *not* equal, the cash payback period is determined by adding the annual net cash flows until the cumulative sum equals the amount of the proposed investment. To illustrate, assume that for a proposed investment of $400,000, the annual net cash flows and the cumulative net cash flows over the proposal's 6-year life are as follows:

Year	Net Cash Flow	Cumulative Net Cash Flow
1	$ 60,000	$ 60,000
2	80,000	140,000
3	105,000	245,000
4	155,000	400,000
5	100,000	500,000
6	90,000	590,000

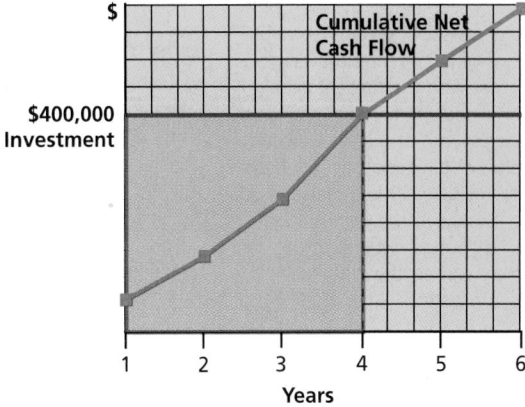

The cumulative net cash flow at the end of the fourth year equals the amount of the investment, $400,000. Thus, the payback period is 4 years. If the amount of the proposed investment had been $450,000, the cash payback period would occur during the fifth year. If the net cash flows are uniform during the period, the cash payback period would be 4½ years.

The cash payback method is widely used in evaluating proposals for investments in new projects. A short payback period is desirable, because the sooner the cash is recovered, the sooner it becomes available for reinvestment in other projects. In addition, there is less possibility of losses from economic conditions, out-of-date assets, and other unavoidable risks when the payback period is short. The cash payback period is also important to bankers and other creditors who may be depending upon net cash flow for repaying debt related to the capital investment. The sooner the cash is recovered, the sooner the debt or other liabilities can be paid. Thus, the cash payback method is especially useful to managers whose primary concern is liquidity.

One of the disadvantages of the cash payback method is that it ignores cash flows occurring after the payback period. In addition, the cash payback method does not use present value concepts in valuing cash flows occurring in different periods. In the next section, we will review present value concepts and introduce capital investment methods that use present value.

Present Value Methods

An investment in fixed assets may be viewed as acquiring a series of net cash flows over a period of time. The period of time over which these net cash flows will be received may be an important factor in determining the value of an investment. Present value methods use both the amount and the timing of net cash flows in evaluating an investment. Before illustrating how these methods are used in capital investment analysis, we will review basic present value concepts.[2]

Present Value Concepts

Present value concepts can be divided into the *present value of an amount* and the *present value of an annuity*. We describe and illustrate these two concepts next.

I began in 1910 as the Shwayder Trunk Manufacturing Company of Colorado. In 1941, I introduced a new "Streamlite" line that was tapered and looked like leather and also featured the name of a shaggy Biblical figure. In 1969 I launched the revolutionary hard-sided Saturn, the first polypropylene case supported by injection-molded shells. My Oyster became the fastest selling item of its kind of all time. I acquired the Lark brand in 1984 and American Tourister in 1993. In the '90s, I ventured into footwear and clothing. My fiscal 2001 sales topped $750 million. I provide world-proof solutions for travelers' needs. Who am I? (Go to page 1012 for answer.)

----

[2]Present value calculations were introduced in accounting for bond liabilities. Present value concepts are developed again here in order to reinforce that introduction.

Present Value of an Amount   If you were given the choice, would you prefer to receive $1 now or $1 three years from now? You should prefer to receive $1 now, because you could invest the $1 and earn interest for three years. As a result, the amount you would have after three years would be greater than $1.

To illustrate, assume that on January 1, 2006, you invest $1 in an account that earns 12% interest compounded annually. After one year, the $1 will grow to $1.12 ($1 × 1.12), because interest of 12¢ is added to the investment. The $1.12 earns 12% interest for the second year. Interest earning interest is called **compounding**. By the end of the second year, the investment has grown to $1.254 ($1.12 × 1.12). By the end of the third year, the investment has grown to $1.404 ($1.254 × 1.12). Thus, if money is worth 12%, you would be equally satisfied with $1 on January 1, 2006, or $1.404 three years later.

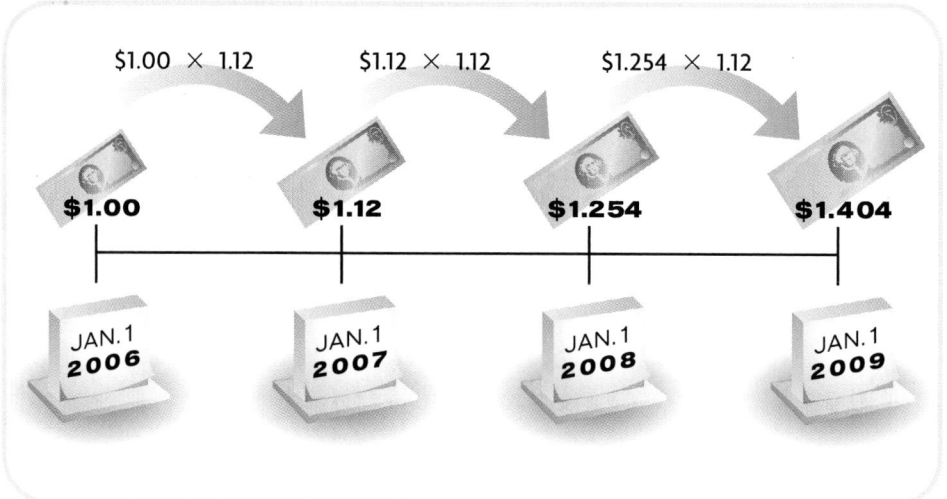

On January 1, 2006, what is the present value of $1.404 to be received on January 1, 2009? This is a present value question. The answer can be determined with the aid of a present value of $1 table. For example, the partial table in Exhibit 1 indicates that the present value of $1 to be received three years hence, with earnings compounded at the rate of 12% a year, is 0.712. Multiplying 0.712 by $1.404 yields $1, which is the present value that started the compounding process.[3]

•Exhibit 1   Partial Present Value of $1 Table

	Present Value of $1 at Compound Interest				
Year	6%	10%	12%	15%	20%
1	0.943	0.909	0.893	0.870	0.833
2	0.890	0.826	0.797	0.756	0.694
3	0.840	0.751	0.712	0.658	0.579
4	0.792	0.683	0.636	0.572	0.482
5	0.747	0.621	0.567	0.497	0.402
6	0.705	0.564	0.507	0.432	0.335
7	0.665	0.513	0.452	0.376	0.279
8	0.627	0.467	0.404	0.327	0.233
9	0.592	0.424	0.361	0.284	0.194
10	0.558	0.386	0.322	0.247	0.162

[3]The present value factors in the table are rounded to three decimal places. More complete tables of both present values and future values are in Appendix A.

Present Value of an Annuity   An *annuity* is a series of equal net cash flows at fixed time intervals. Annuities are very common in business. For example, monthly rental, salary, and bond interest cash flows are all examples of annuities. The *present value of an annuity* is the sum of the present values of each cash flow. In other words, the present value of an annuity is the amount of cash that is needed today to yield a series of equal net cash flows at fixed time intervals in the future.

To illustrate, the present value of a $100 annuity for five periods at 12% could be determined by using the present value factors in Exhibit 1. Each $100 net cash flow could be multiplied by the present value of $1 at 12% factor for the appropriate period and summed to determine a present value of $360.50, as shown in the following timeline:

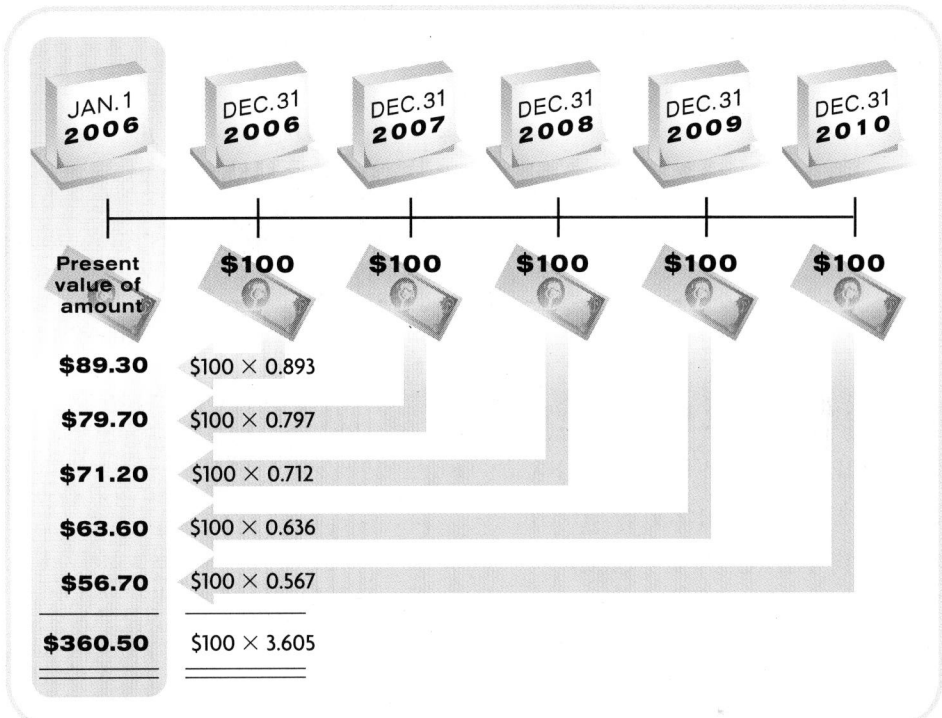

Using a present value of an annuity table is a simpler approach. Exhibit 2 is a partial table of present value of annuity factors.[4] These factors are merely the sum of the present value of $1 factors in Exhibit 1 for the number of annuity periods. Thus, 3.605 in the annuity table (Exhibit 2) is the sum of the five individual present value of $1 factors at 12%. Multiplying $100 by 3.605 yields the same amount ($360.50) that was determined in the preceding illustration by five successive multiplications.

Net Present Value Method

The *net present value method* analyzes capital investment proposals by comparing the initial cash investment with the present value of the net cash flows. It is sometimes called the **discounted cash flow method**. The interest rate (return) used in net present value analysis is set by management. This rate, sometimes termed the **hurdle rate**, is often based upon such factors as the nature of the business, the purpose of the investment, the cost of securing funds for the investment, and the minimum desired rate of return. If the net present value of the cash flows expected from a proposed investment equals or exceeds the amount of the initial investment, the proposal is desirable.

To illustrate, assume a proposal to acquire $200,000 of equipment with an expected useful life of five years (no residual value) and a minimum desired rate of return of

REAL WORLD

A 55-year-old bank janitor won a $5 million lottery jackpot, payable in 21 annual installments of $240,245. Unfortunately, the bank janitor died after collecting only one payment. What happens to the remaining unclaimed payments? In this case, the lottery winnings were auctioned off for the benefit of the janitor's estate. The winning bid approximated the present value of the remaining cash flows, or about $2.1 million.

---

[4]Expanded tables for the present value of an annuity are in Appendix A.

•Exhibit 2 Partial Present Value of an Annuity Table

Present Value of an Annuity of $1 at Compound Interest					
Year	6%	10%	12%	15%	20%
1	0.943	0.909	0.893	0.870	0.833
2	1.833	1.736	1.690	1.626	1.528
3	2.673	2.487	2.402	2.283	2.106
4	3.465	3.170	3.037	2.855	2.589
5	4.212	3.791	3.605	3.353	2.991
6	4.917	4.355	4.111	3.785	3.326
7	5.582	4.868	4.564	4.160	3.605
8	6.210	5.335	4.968	4.487	3.837
9	6.802	5.759	5.328	4.772	4.031
10	7.360	6.145	5.650	5.019	4.192

> **The net present value method compares an investment's initial cash outflow with the present value of its cash inflows.**

10%. The present value of the net cash flow for each year is computed by multiplying the net cash flow for the year by the present value factor of $1 for that year. For example, the $70,000 net cash flow to be received on December 31, 2006, is multiplied by the present value of $1 for one year at 10% (0.909). Thus, the present value of the $70,000 is $63,630. Likewise, the $60,000 net cash flow on December 31, 2007, is multiplied by the present value of $1 for two years at 10% (0.826) to yield $49,560, and so on. The amount to be invested, $200,000, is then subtracted from the total present value of the net cash flows, $202,900, to determine the net present value, $2,900, as shown below. The net present value indicates that the proposal is expected to recover the investment and provide more than the minimum rate of return of 10%.

When capital investment funds are limited and the alternative proposals involve different amounts of investment, it is useful to prepare

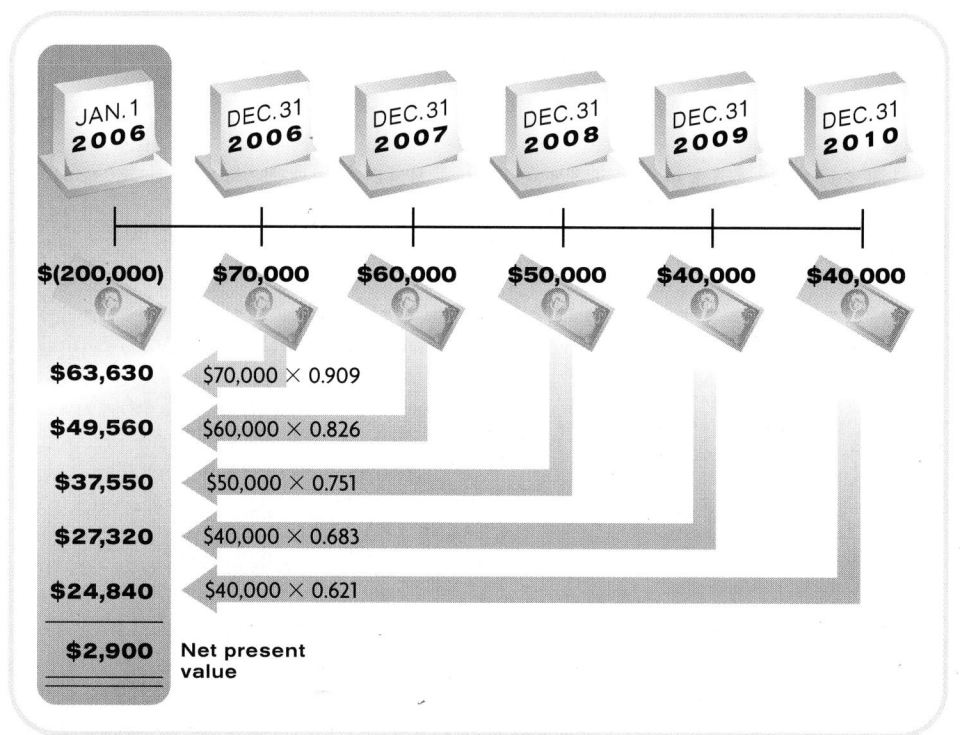

a ranking of the proposals by using a present value index. The ***present value index*** is calculated by dividing the total present value of the net cash flow by the amount to be invested. The present value index for the investment in the previous illustration is calculated as follows:

$$\text{Present value index} = \frac{\text{Total present value of net cash flow}}{\text{Amount to be invested}}$$

$$= \frac{\$202,900}{\$200,000} = 1.0145$$

If a business is considering three alternative proposals and has determined their net present values, the present value index for each proposal is as follows:

	Proposal A	Proposal B	Proposal C
Total present value of net cash flow..	$107,000	$86,400	$93,600
Amount to be invested	100,000	80,000	90,000
Net present value	$ 7,000	$ 6,400	$ 3,600
Present value index	1.07 ($107,000 ÷ $100,000)	1.08 ($86,400 ÷ $80,000)	1.04 ($93,600 ÷ $90,000)

A project has estimated annual net cash flows of $50,000 for seven years and is estimated to cost $240,000. Assume a minimum rate of return of 12%. For this project, what is the (1) net present value and (2) present value index? (3) Should the project be accepted, based on this analysis?

----

(1) ($11,800) [($50,000 × 4.564) − $240,000]; (2) 0.95 (rounded) ($228,200 ÷ $240,000); (3) No.

Although Proposal A has the largest net present value, the present value indices indicate that it is not as desirable as Proposal B. That is, Proposal B returns $1.08 present value per dollar invested, whereas Proposal A returns only $1.07. Proposal B requires an investment of $80,000, compared to an investment of $100,000 for Proposal A. Management should consider the possible use of the $20,000 difference between Proposal A and Proposal B investments before making a final decision.

An advantage of the net present value method is that it considers the time value of money. A disadvantage is that the computations are more complex than those for the methods that ignore present value.

Internal Rate of Return Method

The ***internal rate of return method*** uses present value concepts to compute the rate of return from the net cash flows expected from capital investment proposals. This method is sometimes called the **time-adjusted rate of return method**. It is similar to the net present value method, in that it focuses on the present value of the net cash flows. However, the internal rate of return method starts with the net cash flows and, in a sense, works backwards to determine the rate of return expected from the proposal.

To illustrate, assume that management is evaluating a proposal to acquire equipment costing $33,530. The equipment is expected to provide annual net cash flows of $10,000 per year for five years. If we assume a rate of return of 12%, we can calculate the present value of the net cash flows, using the present value of an annuity table in Exhibit 2. These calculations are shown in Exhibit 3.

•Exhibit 3   Net Present Value Analysis at 12%

Annual net cash flow (at the end of each of five years)	$10,000
Present value of an annuity of $1 at 12% for 5 years (Exhibit 2)	× 3.605
Present value of annual net cash flows	$36,050
Less amount to be invested	33,530
Net present value	$ 2,520

In Exhibit 3, the $36,050 present value of the cash inflows, based on a 12% rate of return, is greater than the $33,530 to be invested. Therefore, the internal rate of return must be greater than 12%. Through trial-and-error procedures, the rate of return that equates the $33,530 cost of the investment with the present value of the net cash flows is determined to be 15%, as shown below.

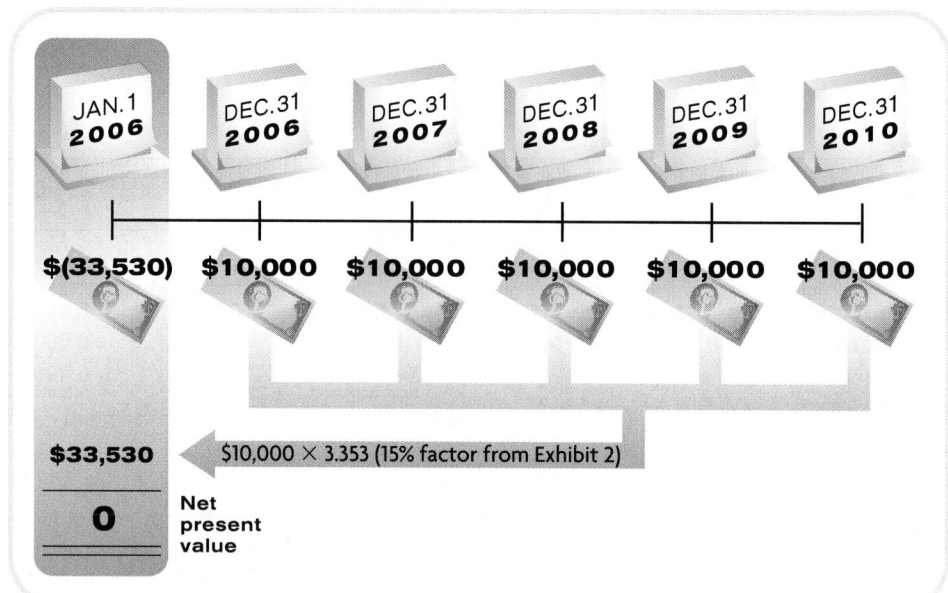

Such trial-and-error procedures are time-consuming. However, when equal annual net cash flows are expected from a proposal, as in the illustration, the calculations are simplified by using the following procedures:[5]

1. Determine a present value factor for an annuity of $1 by dividing the amount to be invested by the equal annual net cash flows, as follows:

$$\text{Present value factor for an annuity of \$1} = \frac{\text{Amount to be invested}}{\text{Equal annual net cash flows}}$$

2. In the present value of an annuity of $1 table, locate the present value factor determined in (1). First locate the number of years of expected useful life of the investment in the Year column, and then proceed horizontally across the table until you find the present value factor computed in (1).
3. Identify the internal rate of return by the heading of the column in which the present value factor in (2) is located.

To illustrate, assume that management is considering a proposal to acquire equipment costing $97,360. The equipment is expected to provide equal annual net cash flows of $20,000 for seven years. The present value factor for an annuity of $1 is **4.868**, calculated as follows:

Present value factor for an annuity of $1

$$= \frac{\text{Amount to be invested}}{\text{Equal annual net cash flows}}$$

$$= \frac{\$97,360}{\$20,000} = 4.868$$

What is the internal rate of return for a project estimated to cost $208,175 and provide annual net cash flows of $55,000 for six years?

- -

15% ($208,175 ÷ $55,000 = 3.785, the present value of an annuity factor for six periods at 15%)

---

[5]Equal annual net cash flows are assumed in order to simplify the illustration. If the annual net cash flows are not equal, the calculations are more complex, but the basic concepts are the same.

For a period of seven years, the partial present value of an annuity of $1 table indicates that the factor **4.868** is related to a percentage of **10%**, as shown below. Thus, 10% is the internal rate of return for this proposal.

Present Value of an Annuity of $1 at Compound Interest			
Year	6%	10%	12%
1	0.943	0.909	0.893
2	1.833	1.736	1.690
3	2.673	2.487	2.402
4	3.465	3.170	3.037
5	4.212	3.791	3.605
6	4.917	4.355	4.111
7	5.582	4.868	4.564
8	6.210	5.335	4.968
9	6.802	5.759	5.328
10	7.360	6.145	5.650

REAL WORLD

The minimum acceptable rate of return for **Owens-Corning Fiberglass** is 18%; for **General Electric**, it is 20%. David Devonshire, CFO of Owens-Corning, states, "I'm here to challenge anyone— even the CEO—who gets emotionally attached to a project that doesn't reach our benchmark."

If the minimum acceptable rate of return for similar proposals is 10% or less, then the proposed investment should be considered acceptable. When several proposals are considered, management often ranks the proposals by their internal rates of return. The proposal with the highest rate is considered the most desirable.

The primary advantage of the internal rate of return method is that the present values of the net cash flows over the entire useful life of the proposal are considered. In addition, by determining a rate of return for each proposal, all proposals are compared on a common basis. The primary disadvantage of the internal rate of return method is that the computations are more complex than for some of the other methods. However, spreadsheet software programs have internal rate of return functions that simplify the calculation.

MANAGERIAL DISCLOSURE AND ANALYSIS

PANERA BREAD COMPANY

The **Panera Bread Company** owns, operates, and franchises bakery-cafes throughout the United States. A recent annual report to the Securities and Exchange Commission (SEC Form 10-K) disclosed the following information about an average company-owned store:

Operating profit	$280,000
Depreciation	60,000
Investment	760,000

Assume that the operating profit and depreciation will remain unchanged for the next ten years. In addition, assume that the investment salvage value will equal the original investment due to rising real estate values. The average rate of return and internal rate of return can then be estimated. The average rate of return on a company-owned store is:

$$\frac{\$280,000}{\$760,000} = 36.8\%$$

The internal rate of return is calculated by first determining the present value of an annuity of $1:

$$\text{Present value of an annuity of \$1: } \frac{\$760,000}{(\$280,000 + \$60,000)} = 2.24$$

For a period of three years, this factor implies an internal rate of return of nearly 15% (from Exhibit 2). However, if we more realistically assumed these cash flows for ten years, Panera's company-owned stores generate an estimated internal rate of return of approximately 44% (from a spreadsheet calculation). Clearly, both investment evaluation methods indicate a highly successful business.

Factors that Complicate Capital Investment Analysis

objective **3**

List and describe factors that complicate capital investment analysis.

In the preceding discussion, we described four widely used methods of evaluating capital investment proposals. In practice, additional factors may have an impact on the outcome of a capital investment decision. In the following paragraphs, we discuss some of the most important of these factors: the federal income tax, unequal lives of alternative proposals, leasing, uncertainty, changes in price levels, and qualitative factors.

Income Tax

In many cases, the impact of the federal income tax on capital investment decisions can be material. For example, in determining depreciation for federal income tax purposes, useful lives that are much shorter than the actual useful lives are often used. Also, depreciation can be calculated by methods that approximate the 200-percent declining-balance method. Thus, depreciation for tax purposes often exceeds the depreciation for financial statement purposes in the early years of an asset's use. The tax reduction in these early years is offset by higher taxes in the later years, so that accelerated depreciation does not result in a long-run saving in taxes. However, the timing of the cash outflows for income taxes can have a significant impact on capital investment analysis.[6]

8-Year Life

TRUCK

5-Year Life

COMPUTER NETWORK

Unequal Proposal Lives

In the preceding discussion, the illustrations of the methods of analyzing capital investment proposals were based on the assumption that alternative proposals had the same useful lives. In practice, however, alternative proposals may have unequal lives. To illustrate, assume that alternative investments, a truck and computers, are being compared. The truck has a useful life of 8 years, and the computer network has a useful life of 5 years. Each proposal requires an initial investment of $100,000, and the company desires a rate of return of 10%. The expected cash flows and net present value of each alternative are shown in Exhibit 4. Because of the unequal useful lives of the two proposals, however, the net present values in Exhibit 4 are not comparable.

To make the proposals comparable for the analysis, they can be adjusted to end at the same time. This can be done by assuming that the truck is to be sold at the end of 5 years. The residual value of the truck must be estimated at the end of 5 years, and this value must then be included as a cash flow at that date. Both proposals will then cover 5 years, and net present value analysis can be used to compare the two proposals over the same 5-year period. If the truck's estimated residual value is $40,000 at the end of year 5, the net present value for the truck exceeds the net present value for the computers by $1,835 ($18,640 − $16,805), as shown in Exhibit 5. Therefore, the truck may be viewed as the more attractive of the two proposals.

---

[6]The impact of income taxes on capital investment analysis is described and illustrated in advanced textbooks.

•Exhibit 4   Net Present Value Analysis—Unequal Lives of Proposals

	Truck		
Year	**Present Value of $1 at 10%**	**Net Cash Flow**	**Present Value of Net Cash Flow**
1	0.909	$ 30,000	$ 27,270
2	0.826	30,000	24,780
3	0.751	25,000	18,775
4	0.683	20,000	13,660
5	0.621	15,000	9,315
6	0.564	15,000	8,460
7	0.513	10,000	5,130
8	0.467	10,000	4,670
Total		$155,000	$112,060
Amount to be invested			100,000
Net present value			$ 12,060

	Computers		
Year	**Present Value of $1 at 10%**	**Net Cash Flow**	**Present Value of Net Cash Flow**
1	0.909	$ 30,000	$ 27,270
2	0.826	30,000	24,780
3	0.751	30,000	22,530
4	0.683	30,000	20,490
5	0.621	35,000	21,735
Total		$155,000	$116,805
Amount to be invested			100,000
Net present value			$ 16,805

•Exhibit 5

Net Present Value Analysis—Equalized Lives of Proposals

	Truck—Revised to 5-Year Life		
Year	**Present Value of $1 at 10%**	**Net Cash Flow**	**Present Value of Net Cash Flow**
1	0.909	$ 30,000	$ 27,270
2	0.826	30,000	24,780
3	0.751	25,000	18,775
4	0.683	20,000	13,660
5	0.621	15,000	9,315
5 (Residual value)	0.621	40,000	24,840
Total		$160,000	$118,640
Amount to be invested			100,000
Net present value			$ 18,640

Truck NPV > Computers NPV

Lease versus Capital Investment

Leasing fixed assets has become common in many industries. For example, hospitals often lease diagnostic and other medical equipment. Leasing allows a business to use fixed assets without spending large amounts of cash to purchase them. In addition, management may believe that a fixed asset has a high risk of becoming obsolete. This risk may be reduced by leasing rather than purchasing the asset. Also, the *Internal Revenue Code* allows the lessor (the owner of the asset) to pass tax deductions on to the lessee (the party leasing the asset). These provisions of the tax law have made leasing assets more attractive. For example, a company that pays $50,000 per year for leasing a $200,000 fixed asset with a life of 8 years is permitted to deduct from taxable income the annual lease payments.

In many cases, before a final decision is made, management should consider leasing assets instead of purchasing them. Normally, leasing assets is more costly than purchasing because the lessor must include in the rental price not only the costs associated with owning the assets but also a profit. Nevertheless, using the methods

of evaluating capital investment proposals, management should consider whether it is more profitable to lease rather than purchase an asset.

Uncertainty

All capital investment analyses rely on factors that are uncertain. For example, the estimates related to revenues, expenses, and cash flows are uncertain. The long-term nature of capital investments suggests that some estimates are likely to involve uncertainty. Errors in one or more of the estimates could lead to incorrect decisions.

Changes in Price Levels

In performing investment analysis, management must be concerned about changes in price levels. Price levels may change due to **inflation**, which occurs when general price levels are rising. Thus, while general prices are rising, the returns on an investment must exceed the rising price level, or else the cash returned on the investment becomes less valuable over time.

Price levels may also change for foreign investments as the result of currency exchange rates. **Currency exchange rates** are the rates at which currency in another country can be exchanged for U.S. dollars. If the amount of local dollars that can be exchanged for one U.S. dollar increases, then the local currency is said to be weakening to the dollar. Thus, if a company made an investment in another country where the local currency was weakening, it would adversely impact the return on that investment as expressed in U.S. dollars. This is because the expected amount of local currency returned on the investment would purchase fewer U.S. dollars.[7]

Management should attempt to anticipate future price levels and consider their effects on the estimates used in capital investment analyses. Changes in anticipated price levels could significantly affect the analyses.

Qualitative Considerations

Some benefits of capital investments are qualitative in nature and cannot be easily estimated in dollar terms. If management does not consider these qualitative considerations, the quantitative analyses may suggest rejecting a worthy investment.

Qualitative considerations in capital investment analysis are most appropriate for strategic investments. Strategic investments are those that are designed to affect a company's long-term ability to generate profits. Strategic investments often have many uncertainties and intangible benefits. Unlike capital investments that are designed to cut costs, strategic investments have very few "hard" savings. Instead, they may affect future revenues, which are difficult to estimate. An example of a strategic investment is **Nucor's** decision to be the first to invest in a new continuous casting technology that had the potential to make thin gauge sheet steel and thus open new product markets. Nucor's new investment was justified more on the strategic

---

INTEGRITY IN BUSINESS

ASSUMPTION FUDGING

The results of any capital budgeting analysis depend on many subjective estimates, such as the cash flows, discount rate, time period, and total investment amount. The results of the analysis should be used to either support or reject a project. Capital budgeting should not be used in reverse. That is, the analyst should not work backwards, filling in assumed numbers that will produce the desired net present value. Such a reverse approach reduces the credibility of the entire process.

---

[7]Accounting for foreign currency transactions is discussed in Appendix E.

importance of the investment than on the economic analysis. As it turned out, the investment was very successful.

Qualitative considerations that may influence capital investment analysis include product quality, manufacturing flexibility, employee morale, manufacturing productivity, and market opportunity. Many of these qualitative factors may be as important, if not more important, than the results of quantitative analysis.

Capital Rationing

objective 4

Diagram the capital rationing process.

Funding for capital projects may be obtained from issuing bonds or stock or from operating cash. *Capital rationing* is the process by which management allocates these funds among competing capital investment proposals. In this process, management often uses a combination of the methods described in this chapter. Exhibit 6 portrays the capital rationing decision process.

In capital rationing, alternative proposals are initially screened by establishing minimum standards for the cash payback and the average rate of return. The proposals that survive this screening are further analyzed, using the net present value and internal rate of return methods. Throughout the capital rationing process, qualitative factors related to each proposal should also be considered. For example, the acquisition of new, more efficient equipment that eliminates several jobs could lower employee morale to a level that could decrease overall plant productivity. Alternatively, new equipment might improve the quality of the product and thus increase consumer satisfaction and sales.

The final steps in the capital rationing process are ranking the proposals according to management's criteria, comparing the proposals with the funds available, and selecting the proposals to be funded. Funded proposals are included in the **capital expenditures budget** to aid the planning and financing of operations. Unfunded proposals may be reconsidered if funds later become available.

SPOTLIGHT ON STRATEGY

INTEL'S "CAPACITY IS STRATEGY"

Andy Grove, Chairman of **Intel Corporation**, has stated, "You know that saying, 'The Internet changes everything'? People now are backing away from it; but I say, just wait five years. Hundreds of billions of dollars we now spend on voice telecommunications will become a freebie—just like [Cisco CEO] John Chambers has said. . . . The entire entertainment industry will be digitally distributed over broadband networks. [Media companies are] going to tip over, because one of them, with its back to the wall, will make the transition, and the others will have to follow. . . . Houses will be wireless, broadband will be delivered wirelessly, and home and portable computers and consumer electronics are going to be built to facilitate all of the above. Okay, it hasn't happened in the first five years; it's going to take ten. And there will be a lot of pain for some. But it will happen, and we'll all benefit."

Intel Corporation is betting $10 billion on four state-of-the-art computer chip factories (fabs) that Andy Grove's vision of the future is true. Intel's management believes that "capacity is strategy." As Grove says, "Henry Ford used it to revolutionize the automobile industry; the Japanese did it to push us out of the memory-chip business 25 years ago; we used it a decade ago to ignite the PC industry. Now we're using it again so we can broaden our business beyond the PC." By having the most capacity of the latest technology, Intel believes that it will be able to have the lowest cost and highest quality chip products. These new plants will produce chips that embed wireless technology, dubbed the "Radio Free Intel" strategy. Electronic devices having these new chips will be able to search and connect to wireless networks effortlessly and continuously, thus providing consumers ready access to broadband services. Intel is making a bold move. But this is not new. Over the years, Intel has made huge investments in its chip factories. As Grove has said, "Our fabs are fields of dreams. We build them and hope people will come." So far, Intel has been right.

Source: Intel's $10 Billion Gamble, *Fortune*, November 11, 2002.

•Exhibit 6   Capital Rationing Decision Process

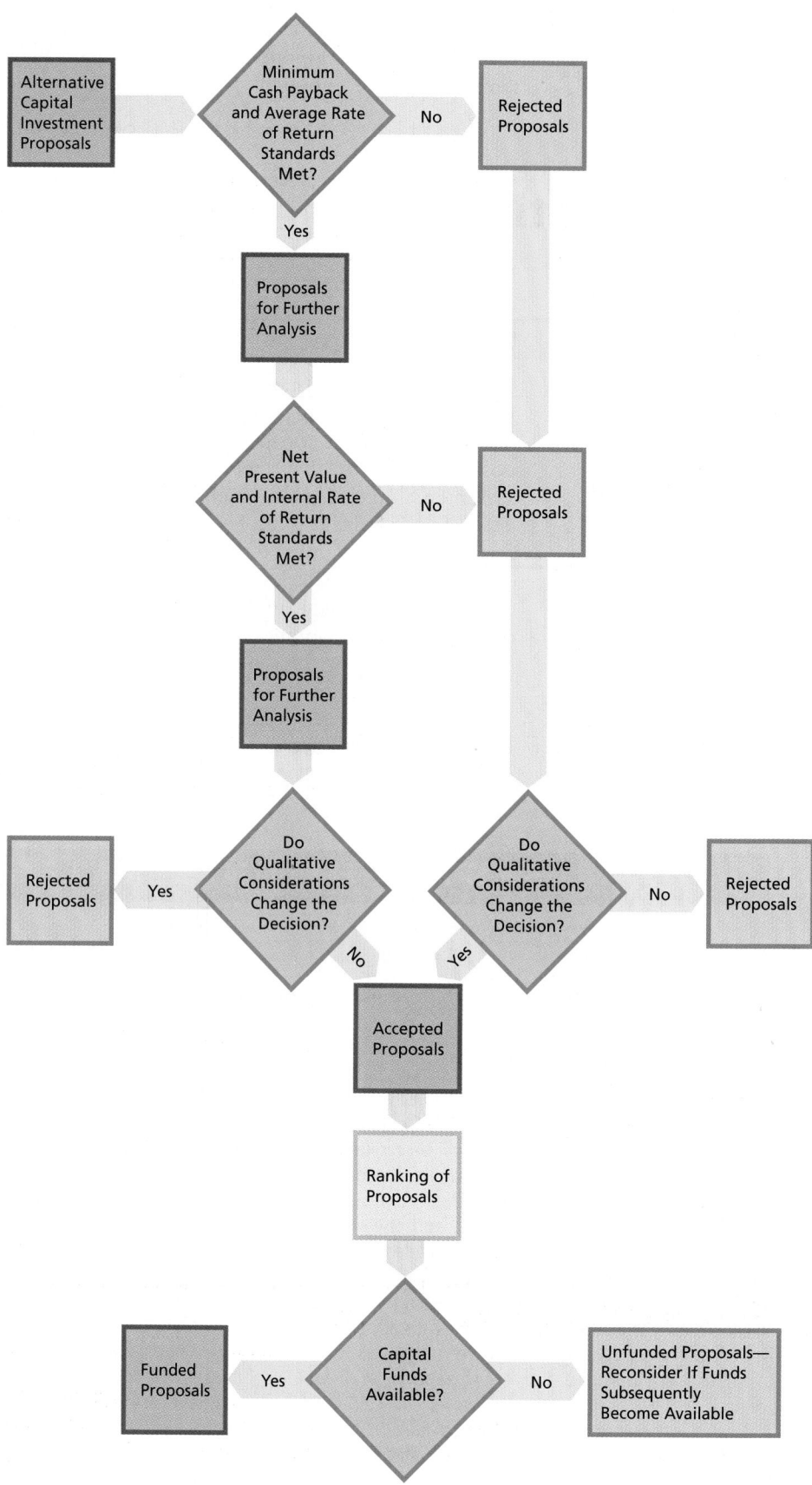

Key Points

1 Explain the nature and importance of capital investment analysis.

Capital investment analysis is the process by which management plans, evaluates, and controls investments involving fixed assets. Capital investment analysis is important to a business because such investments affect profitability for a long period of time.

2 Evaluate capital investment proposals, using the following methods: average rate of return, cash payback, net present value, and internal rate of return.

The average rate of return method measures the expected profitability of an investment in fixed assets. It is calculated using the following formula:

$$\text{Average rate of return} = \frac{\text{Estimated average annual income}}{\text{Average investment}}$$

The expected period of time that will pass between the date of an investment and the complete recovery in cash (or equivalent) of the amount invested is the cash payback period. Investment proposals with the shortest cash payback are considered the most desirable.

The net present value method uses present values to compute the net present value of the cash flows expected from a proposal. The net present value of the cash flows are then compared across proposals. The present value of a cash flow is computed by looking up the present value of $1 from a table of present values and multiplying it by the amount of the future cash flow, as shown in the text.

The internal rate of return method uses present values to compute the rate of return from the net cash flows expected from capital investment proposals. When equal annual net cash flows are expected from a proposal, the computations are simplified by using a table of the present value of an annuity, as shown in the text.

3 List and describe factors that complicate capital investment analysis.

Factors that may complicate capital investment analysis include the impact of the federal income tax, unequal lives of alternative proposals, leasing, uncertainty, changes in price levels, and qualitative considerations. A brief description of the effect of each of these factors appears in the text.

4 Diagram the capital rationing process.

Capital rationing refers to the process by which management allocates available investment funds among competing capital investment proposals. A diagram of the capital rationing process appears in Exhibit 6.

Key Terms

annuity (999)
average rate of return (995)
capital investment analysis (994)
capital rationing (1007)
cash payback period (996)

currency exchange rate (1006)
inflation (1006)
internal rate of return method (1001)
net present value method (999)

present value concept (997)
present value index (1001)
present value of an annuity (999)
time value of money concept (995)

Illustrative Problem

The capital investment committee of Hopewell Company is currently considering two projects. The estimated income from operations and net cash flows expected from each project are as follows:

	Project A		Project B	
Year	Income from Operations	Net Cash Flow	Income from Operations	Net Cash Flow
1	$ 6,000	$ 22,000	$13,000	$ 29,000
2	9,000	25,000	10,000	26,000
3	10,000	26,000	8,000	24,000
4	8,000	24,000	8,000	24,000
5	11,000	27,000	3,000	19,000
	$44,000	$124,000	$42,000	$122,000

Each project requires an investment of $80,000. Straight-line depreciation will be used, and no residual value is expected. The committee has selected a rate of 15% for purposes of the net present value analysis.

Instructions

1. Compute the following:
   a. The average rate of return for each project.
   b. The net present value for each project. Use the present value of $1 table appearing in this chapter.
2. Why is the net present value of Project B greater than Project A, even though its average rate of return is less?
3. Prepare a summary for the capital investment committee, advising it on the relative merits of the two projects.

Solution

1. a. Average rate of return for Project A:

$$\frac{\$44,000 \div 5}{(\$80,000 + \$0) \div 2} = 22\%$$

Average rate of return for Project B:

$$\frac{\$42,000 \div 5}{(\$80,000 + \$0) \div 2} = 21\%$$

b. Net present value analysis:

Year	Present Value of $1 at 15%	Net Cash Flow Project A	Net Cash Flow Project B	Present Value of Net Cash Flow Project A	Present Value of Net Cash Flow Project B
1	0.870	$ 22,000	$ 29,000	$19,140	$25,230
2	0.756	25,000	26,000	18,900	19,656
3	0.658	26,000	24,000	17,108	15,792
4	0.572	24,000	24,000	13,728	13,728
5	0.497	27,000	19,000	13,419	9,443
Total		$124,000	$122,000	$82,295	$83,849
Amount to be invested				80,000	80,000
Net present value				$ 2,295	$ 3,849

2. Project B has a lower average rate of return than Project A because Project B's total income from operations for the five years is $42,000, which is $2,000 less than Project A's. Even so, the net present value of Project B is greater than that of Project A, because Project B has higher cash flows in the early years.

3. Both projects exceed the selected rate established for the net present value analysis. Project A has a higher average rate of return, but Project B offers a larger net present value. Thus, if only one of the two projects can be accepted, Project B would be the more attractive.

Self-Examination Questions (Answers at End of Chapter)

1. Methods of evaluating capital investment proposals that ignore present value include:
   A. average rate of return
   B. cash payback
   C. both A and B
   D. neither A nor B

2. Management is considering a $100,000 investment in a project with a 5-year life and no residual value. If the total income from the project is expected to be $60,000 and recognition is given to the effect of straight-line depreciation on the investment, the average rate of return is:
   A. 12% C. 60%
   B. 24% D. 75%

3. The expected period of time that will elapse between the date of a capital investment and the complete recovery of the amount of cash invested is called:

   A. the average rate of return period
   B. the cash payback period
   C. the net present value period
   D. the internal rate of return period

4. A project that will cost $120,000 is estimated to generate cash flows of $25,000 per year for eight years. What is the net present value of the project, assuming an 11% required rate of return? (Use the present value tables in Appendix A.)
   A. ($38,214) C. $55,180
   B. $8,653 D. $75,000

5. A project is estimated to generate cash flows of $40,000 per year for 10 years. The cost of the project is $226,009. What is the internal rate of return for this project?
   A. 8% C. 12%
   B. 10% D. 14%

Class Discussion Questions

1. What are the principal objections to the use of the average rate of return method in evaluating capital investment proposals?
2. Discuss the principal limitations of the cash payback method for evaluating capital investment proposals.
3. Why would the average rate of return differ from the internal rate of return on the same project?
4. What information does the cash payback period ignore that is included by the net present value method?
5. Your boss has suggested that a one-year payback period is the same as a 100% average rate of return. Do you agree?
6. Why would the cash payback method understate the attractiveness of a project with a large salvage value?
7. Why would the use of the cash payback period for analyzing the financial performance of theatrical releases from a motion picture production studio be supported over the net present value method?
8. A net present value analysis used to evaluate a proposed equipment acquisition indicated a $9,750 net present value. What is the meaning of the $9,750 as it relates to the desirability of the proposal?
9. Two projects have an identical net present value of $5,000. Are both projects equal in desirability?
10. What are the major disadvantages of the use of the net present value method of analyzing capital investment proposals?
11. What are the major disadvantages of the use of the internal rate of return method of analyzing capital investment proposals?
12. What provision of the Internal Revenue Code is especially important to consider in analyzing capital investment proposals?

13. What method can be used to place two capital investment proposals with unequal useful lives on a comparable basis?
14. What are the major advantages of leasing a fixed asset rather than purchasing it?
15. Give an example of a qualitative factor that should be considered in a capital investment analysis related to acquiring automated factory equipment.
16. **Monsanto**, a large chemical and fibers company, invested $37 million in state-of-the-art systems to improve process control, laboratory automation, and local area network (LAN) communications. The investment was not justified merely on cost savings but was also justified on the basis of qualitative considerations. Monsanto management viewed the investment as a critical element toward achieving its vision of the future. What qualitative and quantitative considerations do you believe Monsanto would have considered in its strategic evaluation of these investments?

REAL WORLD

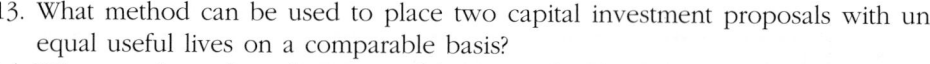

resources for your success online at **http://warren.swlearning.com**

Remember! If you need additional help, visit South-Western's Web site. See page 28 for a description of the online and printed materials that are available. http://warren.swlearning.com

Warren
Reeve
Fess

Answer: Samsonite

Exercises

EXERCISE 24-1
Average rate of return
Objective 2

SPREADSHEET

✓ *Testing Equipment, 12.5%*

The following data are accumulated by Environmental Services Inc. in evaluating two competing capital investment proposals:

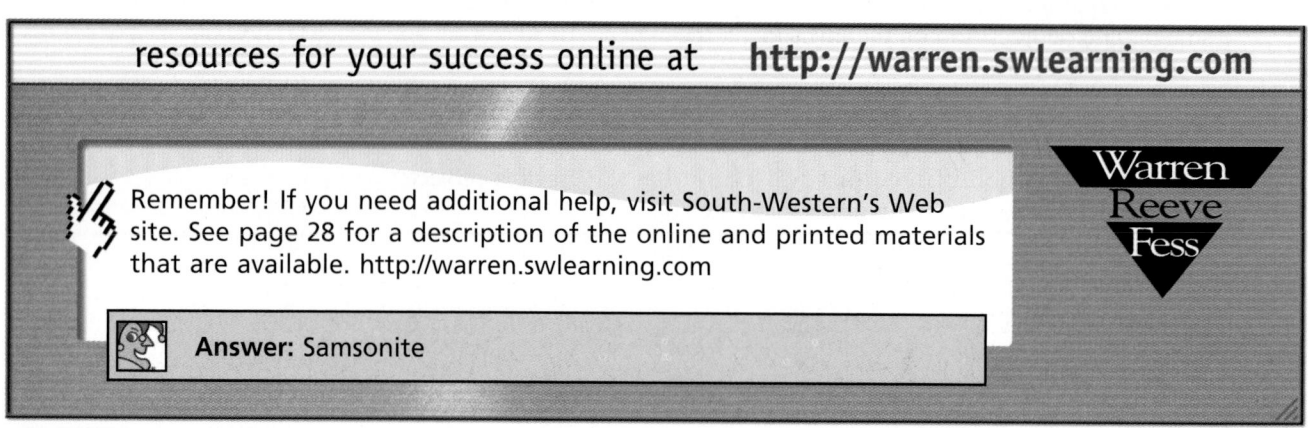

	Testing Equipment	Centrifuge
Amount of investment	$42,000	$56,000
Useful life	4 years	5 years
Estimated residual value	-0-	-0-
Estimated total income over the useful life	$10,500	$12,250

Determine the expected average rate of return for each proposal.

EXERCISE 24-2
Average rate of return—cost savings
Objective 2

General Bearings Company is considering an investment in equipment that will replace direct labor. The equipment has a cost of $94,000, with a $6,000 residual value and an 8-year life. The equipment will replace one employee who has an average wage of $26,000 per year. In addition, the equipment will have operating and energy costs of $8,250 per year.

Determine the average rate of return on the equipment, giving effect to straight-line depreciation on the investment.

EXERCISE 24-3
Average rate of return—new product
Objective 2

Pocket Communications Inc. is considering an investment in new equipment that will be used to manufacture a PDA (personal data assistant). The PDA is expected to generate additional annual sales of 4,500 units at $325 per unit. The equipment has a cost of $870,000, residual value of $30,000, and a 10-year life. The equipment

✓ *Average annual income, $135,000*

can only be used to manufacture the PDA. The cost to manufacture the PDA is shown below.

Cost per unit:	
Direct labor	$ 42.00
Direct materials	195.00
Factory overhead (including depreciation)	58.00
Total cost per unit	$295.00

Determine the average rate of return on the equipment.

EXERCISE 24-4
Calculate cash flows
Objective 2

SPREADSHEET

✓ *Year 1: ($120,800)*

Green Thumb Inc. is planning to invest $238,000 in a new garden tool that is expected to generate additional sales of 8,000 units at $36 each. The $238,000 investment includes $54,000 for initial launch-related expenses and $184,000 for equipment that has a 15-year life and a $10,000 residual value. Selling expenses related to the new product are expected to be 5% of sales revenue. The cost to manufacture the product includes the following per unit costs:

Direct labor	$ 6.00
Direct materials	11.75
Fixed factory overhead—depreciation	1.45
Variable factory overhead	1.80
Total	$21.00

Determine the net cash flows for the first year of the project, years 2–14, and for the last year of the project.

EXERCISE 24-5
Cash payback period
Objective 2

✓ *Proposal 1: 5 years*

First Charter Bank Corporation is evaluating two capital investment proposals for a drive-up ATM, each requiring an investment of $250,000 and each with an 8-year life and expected total net cash flows of $400,000. Location 1 is expected to provide equal annual net cash flows of $50,000, and Location 2 is expected to have the following unequal annual net cash flows:

Year 1	$80,000	Year 5	$37,500
Year 2	70,000	Year 6	37,500
Year 3	50,000	Year 7	37,500
Year 4	50,000	Year 8	37,500

Determine the cash payback period for both proposals.

EXERCISE 24-6
Cash payback method
Objective 2

SPREADSHEET

✓ *a. Cosmetics: 5 years*

Personal Care Products Company is considering an investment in one of two new product lines. The investment required for either product line is $550,000. The net cash flows associated with each product are as follows:

	Liquid Soap	Cosmetics
Year 1	$150,000	$110,000
2	140,000	110,000
3	130,000	110,000
4	130,000	110,000
5	100,000	110,000
6	90,000	110,000
7	70,000	110,000
8	70,000	110,000
Total	$880,000	$880,000

a. Recommend a product offering to Personal Care Products Company, based on the cash payback period for each product line.
b. ▭▭▶ Why is one product line preferred over the other, even though they both have the same total net cash flows through eight periods?

EXERCISE 24-7
Net present value method
Objective 2

SPREADSHEET

✓ a. NPV ($9,310)

The following data are accumulated by Pilot Atlas Company in evaluating the purchase of $340,000 of equipment, having a 4-year useful life:

	Net Income	Net Cash Flow
Year 1	$ 65,000	$150,000
Year 2	35,000	120,000
Year 3	(10,000)	75,000
Year 4	(10,000)	75,000

a. Assuming that the desired rate of return is 12%, determine the net present value for the proposal. Use the table of the present value of $1 appearing in this chapter.
b. ▭▭▭➤ Would management be likely to look with favor on the proposal? Explain.

EXERCISE 24-8
Net present value method
Objective 2

SPREADSHEET

✓ a. $24

Metro-Goldwyn-Mayer, Inc. (MGM), is a major producer and distributor of theatrical and television filmed entertainment. Regarding theatrical films, MGM states, "Our feature films are exploited through a series of sequential domestic and international distribution channels, typically beginning with theatrical exhibition. Thereafter, feature films are first made available for home video generally six months after theatrical release; for pay television, one year after theatrical release; and for syndication, approximately three to five years after theatrical release."

Assume that MGM releases a film that cost $100 million (excluding depreciation) and grosses $125 million at the box office in 2006. The film requires $40 million of advertising during the release. One year later, by the end of 2007, the film is expected to earn MGM $90 million in home video sales at a net cash margin of 30% of sales. By the end of 2008, the film is expected to earn MGM $20 million from pay TV; and by the end of 2009, the film is expected to earn $5 million from syndication.

a. Determine the net present value of the film if the desired rate of return is 20%. Use the table of present value of $1 appearing in Exhibit 1 of this chapter. Round to the nearest whole million dollars.
b. ▭▭▭➤ Under the assumptions provided here, is the film expected to be financially successful?

EXERCISE 24-9
Net present value method—annuity
Objective 2

✓ a. $60,000

Crowe Excavation Company is planning an investment of $235,000 for a bulldozer. The bulldozer is expected to operate for 1,500 hours per year for five years. Customers will be charged $98 per hour for bulldozer work. The bulldozer operator is paid an hourly wage of $22 per hour. The bulldozer is expected to require annual maintenance costing $12,000. The bulldozer uses fuel that is expected to cost $28 per hour of bulldozer operation.

a. Determine the equal annual net cash flows from operating the bulldozer.
b. Determine the net present value of the investment, assuming that the desired rate of return is 10%. Use the table of present values of an annuity of $1 in the chapter. Round to the nearest dollar.
c. ▭▭▭➤ Should Crowe invest in the bulldozer, based on this analysis?

EXERCISE 24-10
Net present value—unequal lives
Objectives 2, 3

SPREADSHEET

✓ *Net present value, Apartment Complex, $42,400*

Bellco Development Company has two competing projects: an apartment complex and an office building. Both projects have an initial investment of $775,000. The net cash flows estimated for the two projects are as follows:

	Net Cash Flow	
Year	Apartment Complex	Office Building
1	$220,000	$300,000
2	200,000	300,000
3	200,000	275,000
4	180,000	275,000
5	150,000	
6	120,000	
7	90,000	
8	60,000	

The estimated residual value of the Apartment Complex at the end of year 4 is $420,000.

Determine which project should be favored, comparing the net present values of the two projects and assuming a minimum rate of return of 15%. Use the table of present values in the chapter.

EXERCISE 24-11
Net present value method
Objective 2

REAL WORLD

✓*Net investment,*
$1,693,000

IHOP Corporation franchises breakfast-oriented restaurants throughout North America. The average development costs for a new restaurant were reported by IHOP as follows:

Land	$ 667,000
Building	800,000
Equipment	341,000
Site improvements	185,000
Total	$1,993,000

IHOP develops the restaurant properties. IHOP indicates that the franchisee pays an initial franchise fee of $300,000 for a newly developed restaurant. IHOP also receives revenues from the franchisee as follows: (1) a royalty equal to 4.5% of the restaurant's sales; (2) income from the leasing of the restaurant and related equipment; and (3) revenue from the sale of certain proprietary products, primarily pancake mixes.

IHOP reported that franchise operators earned annual revenues averaging $1,500,000 per restaurant. Assume that the net cash flows received by IHOP for lease payments and sale of proprietary products (items 2 and 3 above) average $175,000 per year per restaurant, for ten years. Assume further that the franchise operator can purchase the property for $600,000 at the end of the lease term.

Determine IHOP's net present value for a new restaurant, assuming a 10-year life, no change in annual revenues, and a 10% desired rate of return. Use the present value tables appearing in Exhibits 1 and 2 in this chapter.

EXERCISE 24-12
Net present value method
Objective 2

REAL WORLD

✓*a. $91,200,000*

Carnival Corp. has recently placed into service some of the largest cruise ships in the world. One of these ships, the **Carnival Glory**, can hold up to 3,000 passengers and cost $510 million to build. Assume the following additional information:

- The average occupancy rate for the new ship is estimated to be 80% of capacity.
- There will be 300 cruise days per year.
- The variable expenses per passenger are estimated to be $75 per cruise day.
- The revenue per passenger is expected to be $310 per cruise day.
- The fixed expenses for running the ship, other than depreciation, are estimated to be $78,000,000 per year.
- The ship has a service life of 10 years, with a salvage value of $85,000,000 at the end of 10 years.

a. Determine the annual net cash flow from operating the cruise ship.
b. Determine the net present value of this investment, assuming a 12% minimum rate of return. Use the present value tables provided in the chapter in determining your answer.
c. Assume that Carnival Corp. decided to increase its price so that the revenue increased to $320 per passenger per cruise day. Would this allow Carnival Corp. to earn a 15% rate of return on the cruise ship investment, assuming no change in any of the other assumptions? Use the present value tables provided in the chapter in determining your answer.

EXERCISE 24-13
Present value index
Objective 2

Animated Media Inc. has computed the net present value for capital expenditure proposals A and B, using the net present value method. Relevant data related to the computation are as follows:

✓ *Proposal A, 0.96*

	Proposal A	Proposal B
Total present value of net cash flow	$308,256	$158,895
Amount to be invested	321,100	148,500
Net present value	$ (12,844)	$ 10,395

Determine the present value index for each proposal.

EXERCISE 24-14
Net present value method and present value index
Objective 2

✓ *b. Packing Machine, 1.13*

Victory Sporting Goods Company is considering an investment in one of two machines. The sewing machine will increase productivity from sewing 120 baseballs per hour to sewing 170 per hour. The contribution margin is $0.75 per baseball. Assume that any increased production of baseballs can be sold. The second machine is an automatic packaging machine for the golf ball line. The packaging machine will reduce packing labor cost. The labor cost saved is equivalent to $20 per hour. The sewing machine will cost $311,600, have an 8-year life, and will operate for 2,000 hours per year. The packing machine will cost $126,690, have an 8-year life, and will operate for 1,600 hours per year. Victory seeks a minimum rate of return of 15% on its investments.

a. Determine the net present value for the two machines. Use the table of present values of an annuity of $1 in the chapter. Round to the nearest dollar.
b. Determine the present value index for the two machines. Round to 2 decimal places.
c. If Victory has sufficient funds for only one of the machines and qualitative factors are equal between the two machines, in which machine should it invest?

EXERCISE 24-15
Average rate of return, cash payback period, net present value method
Objective 2

✓ *b. 5 years*

Western Rail Inc. is considering acquiring equipment at a cost of $468,800. The equipment has an estimated life of 10 years and no residual value. It is expected to provide yearly net cash flows of $93,760. The company's minimum desired rate of return for net present value analysis is 12%.
Compute the following:

a. The average rate of return, giving effect to straight-line depreciation on the investment.
b. The cash payback period.
c. The net present value. Use the table of the present value of an annuity of $1 appearing in this chapter. Round to the nearest dollar.

EXERCISE 24-16
Internal rate of return method
Objective 2

✓ *a. 4.968*

The internal rate of return method is used by Rustic Renovations Inc. in analyzing a capital expenditure proposal that involves an investment of $74,520 and annual net cash flows of $15,000 for each of the 8 years of its useful life.

a. Determine a present value factor for an annuity of $1 which can be used in determining the internal rate of return.
b. Using the factor determined in (a) and the present value of an annuity of $1 table appearing in this chapter, determine the internal rate of return for the proposal.

EXERCISE 24-17
Internal rate of return method
Objective 2

REAL WORLD

IBM Corporation recently saved $250 million over three years by implementing supply chain software that reduced the cost of components used in its manufacture of computers. If we assume that the savings occurred equally over the three years and the cost of implementing the new software was $190,250,000, what would be the internal rate of return for this investment? Use the present value of an annuity of $1 table found in Exhibit 2 in determining your answer.

EXERCISE 24-18
Internal rate of return method—two projects
Objective 2

✓ a. Delivery truck, 12%

Mr. Pop Popcorn Company is considering two possible investments: a delivery truck or a bagging machine. The delivery truck would cost $36,506 and could be used to deliver an additional 40,000 bags of popcorn per year. Each bag of popcorn can be sold for a contribution margin of $0.35. The delivery truck operating expenses, excluding depreciation, are $0.32 per mile for 16,000 miles per year. The bagging machine would replace an old bagging machine, and its net investment cost would be $27,555. The new machine would require 2 fewer hours of direct labor per day. Direct labor is $14 per hour. There are 260 operating days in the year. Both the truck and the bagging machine are estimated to have 6-year lives. The minimum rate of return is 11%. However, Mr. Pop has funds to invest in only *one* of the projects.

a. Compute the approximate internal rate of return for each investment. Use the table of present values of an annuity of $1 in the chapter.

b. Provide a memo to management with a recommendation.

EXERCISE 24-19
Net present value method and internal rate of return method
Objective 2

✓ a. ($7,474)

Empire Healthcare Corp. is proposing to spend $84,434 on a 7-year project whose estimated net cash flows are $18,500 for each of the seven years.

a. Compute the net present value, using a rate of return of 15%. Use the table of present values of an annuity of $1 in the chapter.

b. Based on the analysis prepared in (a), is the rate of return (1) more than 15%, (2) 15%, or (3) less than 15%? Explain.

c. Determine the internal rate of return by computing a present value factor for an annuity of $1 and using the table of the present value of an annuity of $1 presented in the text.

EXERCISE 24-20
Identify error in capital investment analysis calculations
Objective 2

WHAT'S WRONG WITH THIS?

Portable Technologies Inc. is considering the purchase of automated machinery that is expected to have a useful life of 4 years and no residual value. The average rate of return on the average investment has been computed to be 25%, and the cash payback period was computed to be 4.5 years.

Do you see any reason to question the validity of the data presented? Explain.

EXERCISE 24-21
Changing prices
Objective 3

International Foods Inc. invested $1,000,000 to build a plant in a foreign country. The labor and materials used in production are purchased locally. The plant expansion was estimated to produce an internal rate of return of 20% in U.S. dollar terms. Due to a currency crisis, the currency exchange rate between the local currency and the U.S. dollar doubled from 4 local units per U.S. dollar to 8 local units per U.S. dollar.

a. Assume that the plant produced and sold product in the local economy. Explain what impact this change in the currency exchange rate would have on the project's internal rate of return.

b. Assume that the plant produced product in the local economy but exported the product back to the U.S. for sale. Explain what impact the change in the currency exchange rate would have on the project's internal rate of return under this assumption.

Problems Series A

PROBLEM 24-1A
Average rate of return method, net present value method, and analysis

Objective 2

SPREADSHEET

✓1. a. 16%

The capital investment committee of Eastern Trucking Inc. is considering two investment projects. The estimated income from operations and net cash flows from each investment are as follows:

	Warehouse		Parcel Tracking Technology	
Year	Income from Operations	Net Cash Flow	Income from Operations	Net Cash Flow
1	$ 44,000	$154,000	$ 25,000	$135,000
2	44,000	154,000	35,000	145,000
3	44,000	154,000	45,000	155,000
4	44,000	154,000	55,000	165,000
5	44,000	154,000	60,000	170,000
Total	$220,000	$770,000	$220,000	$770,000

Each project requires an investment of $550,000. Straight-line depreciation will be used, and no residual value is expected. The committee has selected a rate of 12% for purposes of the net present value analysis. *ROR. on total (5yrs.*

Instructions
1. Compute the following:
   a. The average rate of return for each investment.
   b. The net present value for each investment. Use the present value of $1 table appearing in this chapter.
2. ▬▬▶ Prepare a brief report for the capital investment committee, advising it on the relative merits of the two projects.

PROBLEM 24-2A
Cash payback period, net present value method, and analysis

Objective 2

SPREADSHEET

✓1. b. Teen, $71,710

Lifestyle Publications Inc. is considering two new magazine products. The estimated net cash flows from each product are as follows:

Year	Home and Garden	Today's Teen
1	$220,000	$150,000
2	200,000	270,000
3	180,000	190,000
4	40,000	30,000
5	30,000	30,000
Total	$670,000	$670,000

Each product requires an investment of $420,000. A rate of 15% has been selected for the net present value analysis.

Instructions
1. Compute the following for each project:
   a. Cash payback period.
   b. The net present value. Use the present value of $1 table appearing in this chapter.
2. ▬▬▶ Prepare a brief report advising management on the relative merits of each of the two products.

PROBLEM 24-3A
Net present value method, present value index, and analysis

Objective 2

Mid-West Bancorp Inc. wishes to evaluate three capital investment projects by using the net present value method. Relevant data related to the projects are summarized as follows:

✓2. Branch office, 0.98

	Branch Office Expansion	Computer System Upgrade	Install Internet Bill-Pay
Amount to be invested	$520,000	$380,000	$625,000
Annual net cash flows:			
Year 1	260,000	200,000	325,000
Year 2	240,000	195,000	310,000
Year 3	220,000	185,000	305,000

Instructions

1. Assuming that the desired rate of return is 20%, prepare a net present value analysis for each project. Use the present value of $1 table appearing in this chapter.
2. Determine a present value index for each project. Round to 2 decimal places.
3. ▄▄▄▄► Which project offers the largest amount of present value per dollar of investment? Explain.

PROBLEM 24-4A
Net present value method, internal rate of return method, and analysis

Objective 2

✓1. a. Radio station, $80,640

The management of West Coast Media Inc. is considering two capital investment projects. The estimated net cash flows from each project are as follows:

Year	Radio Station	TV Station
1	$180,000	$480,000
2	180,000	480,000
3	180,000	480,000
4	180,000	480,000

The radio station requires an investment of $466,020, while the TV station requires an investment of $1,370,400. No residual value is expected from either project.

Instructions

1. Compute the following for each project:
   a. The net present value. Use a rate of 12% and the present value of an annuity of $1 table appearing in this chapter.
   b. A present value index. Round to 2 decimal places.
2. Determine the internal rate of return for each project by (a) computing a present value factor for an annuity of $1 and (b) using the present value of an annuity of $1 table appearing in this chapter.
3. ▄▄▄▄► What advantage does the internal rate of return method have over the net present value method in comparing projects?

PROBLEM 24-5A
Evaluate alternative capital investment decisions

Objectives 2, 3

✓1. Site B, $134,550

The investment committee of Mr. Bob Restaurants Inc. is evaluating two restaurant sites. The sites have different useful lives, but each requires an investment of $465,000. The estimated net cash flows from each site are as follows:

	Net Cash Flows	
Year	Site A	Site B
1	$140,000	$210,000
2	140,000	210,000
3	140,000	210,000
4	140,000	210,000
5	140,000	
6	140,000	

The committee has selected a rate of 15% for purposes of net present value analysis. It also estimates that the residual value at the end of each restaurant's useful life is $0, but at the end of the fourth year, Site A's residual value would be $300,000.

Instructions

1. For each site, compute the net present value. Use the present value of an annuity of $1 table appearing in this chapter. (Ignore the unequal lives of the projects.)

2. For each site, compute the net present value, assuming that Site A is adjusted to a 4-year life for purposes of analysis. Use the present value of $1 table appearing in this chapter.

3. ▬▬▶ Prepare a report to the investment committee, providing your advice on the relative merits of the two sites.

PROBLEM 24-6A
Capital rationing decision involving four proposals

Objectives 2, 4

SPREADSHEET

✓ *5. Proposal B, 1.36*

Data Stream Communications Inc. is considering allocating a limited amount of capital investment funds among four proposals. The amount of proposed investment, estimated income from operations, and net cash flow for each proposal are as follows:

	Investment	Year	Income from Operations	Net Cash Flow
Proposal A:	$720,000	1	$ 76,000	$220,000
		2	76,000	220,000
		3	76,000	220,000
		4	36,000	180,000
		5	36,000	180,000
Proposal B:	$124,000	1	$ 15,200	$ 40,000
		2	59,200	84,000
		3	15,200	40,000
		4	5,200	30,000
		5	(4,800)	20,000
Proposal C:	$300,000	1	$ 20,000	$ 80,000
		2	20,000	80,000
		3	20,000	80,000
		4	20,000	80,000
		5	(10,000)	50,000
Proposal D:	$225,000	1	$ 35,000	$ 80,000
		2	35,000	80,000
		3	20,000	65,000
		4	20,000	65,000
		5	20,000	65,000

The company's capital rationing policy requires a maximum cash payback period of three years. In addition, a minimum average rate of return of 10% is required on all projects. If the preceding standards are met, the net present value method and present value indexes are used to rank the remaining proposals.

Instructions

1. Compute the cash payback period for each of the four proposals.
2. Giving effect to straight-line depreciation on the investments and assuming no estimated residual value, compute the average rate of return for each of the four proposals. Round to 1 decimal place.
3. Using the following format, summarize the results of your computations in (1) and (2). By placing a check mark in the appropriate column at the right, indicate which proposals should be accepted for further analysis and which should be rejected.

Proposal	Cash Payback Period	Average Rate of Return	Accept for Further Analysis	Reject
A				
B				
C				
D				

4. For the proposals accepted for further analysis in (3), compute the net present value. Use a rate of 10% and the present value of $1 table appearing in this chapter. Round to the nearest dollar.
5. Compute the present value index for each of the proposals in (4). Round to 2 decimal places.

6. Rank the proposals from most attractive to least attractive, based on the present values of net cash flows computed in (4).

7. Rank the proposals from most attractive to least attractive, based on the present value indexes computed in (5). Round to 2 decimal places.

8. ⬛⬛⬛⮞ Based upon the analyses, comment on the relative attractiveness of the proposals ranked in (6) and (7).

Problems Series B

PROBLEM 24-1B
Average rate of return method, net present value method, and analysis
Objective 2

SPREADSHEET

✓ *1. a. 22.5%*

The capital investment committee of Nature's Beauty Landscaping Company is considering two capital investments. The estimated income from operations and net cash flows from each investment are as follows:

| | Greenhouse | | Skid Loader | |
Year	Income from Operations	Net Cash Flow	Income from Operations	Net Cash Flow
1	$ 9,000	$ 25,000	$19,000	$ 35,000
2	9,000	25,000	14,000	30,000
3	9,000	25,000	9,000	25,000
4	9,000	25,000	4,000	20,000
5	9,000	25,000	(1,000)	15,000
	$45,000	$125,000	$45,000	$125,000

Each project requires an investment of $80,000. Straight-line depreciation will be used, and no residual value is expected. The committee has selected a rate of 10% for purposes of the net present value analysis.

Instructions

1. Compute the following:
   a. The average rate of return for each investment.
   b. The net present value for each investment. Use the present value of $1 table appearing in this chapter.
2. ⬛⬛⬛⮞ Prepare a brief report for the capital investment committee, advising it on the relative merits of the two investments.

PROBLEM 24-2B
Cash payback period, net present value method, and analysis
Objective 2

SPREADSHEET

✓ *1. b. Plant Expansion, $10,810*

Audio Zone Inc. is considering two investment projects. The estimated net cash flows from each project are as follows:

Year	Plant Expansion	Retail Store Expansion
1	$ 270,000	$ 250,000
2	250,000	250,000
3	220,000	240,000
4	250,000	240,000
5	260,000	270,000
Total	$1,250,000	$1,250,000

Each project requires an investment of $740,000. A rate of 20% has been selected for the net present value analysis.

Instructions

1. Compute the following for each project:
   a. Cash payback period.
   b. The net present value. Use the present value of $1 table appearing in this chapter. *(continued)*

2. ▭▭▷ Prepare a brief report advising management on the relative merits of each of the two projects.

PROBLEM 24-3B
Net present value method, present value index, and analysis

Objective 2

SPREADSHEET

✓2. Railcars, 0.95

Columbia Railroad Company wishes to evaluate three capital investment proposals by using the net present value method. Relevant data related to the proposals are summarized as follows:

	Route Expansion	Acquire Railcars	New Maintenance Yard
Amount to be invested	$840,000	$490,000	$420,000
Annual net cash flows:			
Year 1	420,000	225,000	210,000
Year 2	380,000	200,000	200,000
Year 3	350,000	180,000	180,000

Instructions
1. Assuming that the desired rate of return is 15%, prepare a net present value analysis for each proposal. Use the present value of $1 table appearing in this chapter.
2. Determine a present value index for each proposal. Round to two decimal places.
3. ▭▭▷ Which proposal offers the largest amount of present value per dollar of investment? Explain.

PROBLEM 24-4B
Net present value method, rate of return method, and analysis

Objective 2

✓1. a. Generating unit, $79,800

The management of Northern Utilities Inc. is considering two capital investment projects. The estimated net cash flows from each project are as follows:

Year	Generating Unit	Distribution Network Expansion
1	$600,000	$160,000
2	600,000	160,000
3	600,000	160,000
4	600,000	160,000

The generating unit requires an investment of $1,822,200, while the distribution network expansion requires an investment of $456,800. No residual value is expected from either project.

Instructions
1. Compute the following for each project:
   a. The net present value. Use a rate of 10% and the present value of an annuity of $1 table appearing in this chapter.
   b. A present value index. Round to 2 decimal places.
2. Determine the internal rate of return for each project by (a) computing a present value factor for an annuity of $1 and (b) using the present value of an annuity of $1 table appearing in this chapter.
3. ▭▭▷ What advantage does the internal rate of return method have over the net present value method in comparing projects?

PROBLEM 24-5B
Evaluate alternative capital investment decisions

Objectives 2, 3

SPREADSHEET

✓2. Project II, $78,460

The investment committee of Heartland Insurance Co. is evaluating two projects. The projects have different useful lives, but each requires an investment of $200,000. The estimated net cash flows from each project are as follows:

	Net Cash Flows	
Year	Project I	Project II
1	$65,000	$97,500
2	65,000	97,500
3	65,000	97,500
4	65,000	97,500
5	65,000	
6	65,000	

The committee has selected a rate of 15% for purposes of net present value analysis. It also estimates that the residual value at the end of each project's useful life is $0, but at the end of the fourth year, Project I's residual value would be $140,000.

Instructions

1. For each project, compute the net present value. Use the present value of an annuity of $1 table appearing in this chapter. (Ignore the unequal lives of the projects.)
2. For each project, compute the net present value, assuming that Project I is adjusted to a 4-year life for purposes of analysis. Use the present value of $1 table appearing in this chapter.
3.  Prepare a report to the investment committee, providing your advice on the relative merits of the two projects.

PROBLEM 24-6B
Capital rationing decision involving four proposals

Objectives 2, 4

SPREADSHEET

✓*5. Proposal B, 1.25*

Jefferson Capital Group is considering allocating a limited amount of capital investment funds among four proposals. The amount of proposed investment, estimated income from operations, and net cash flow for each proposal are as follows:

	Investment	Year	Income from Operations	Net Cash Flow
Proposal A:	$500,000	1	$ 40,000	$140,000
		2	40,000	140,000
		3	40,000	140,000
		4	(20,000)	80,000
		5	(20,000)	80,000
Proposal B:	$225,000	1	$ 55,000	$100,000
		2	35,000	80,000
		3	15,000	60,000
		4	15,000	60,000
		5	15,000	60,000
Proposal C:	$600,000	1	$100,000	$220,000
		2	80,000	200,000
		3	60,000	180,000
		4	60,000	180,000
		5	30,000	150,000
Proposal D:	$300,000	1	$ 65,000	$125,000
		2	35,000	95,000
		3	0	60,000
		4	0	60,000
		5	0	60,000

The company's capital rationing policy requires a maximum cash payback period of three years. In addition, a minimum average rate of return of 10% is required on all projects. If the preceding standards are met, the net present value method and present value indexes are used to rank the remaining proposals.

Instructions

1. Compute the cash payback period for each of the four proposals.
2. Giving effect to straight-line depreciation on the investments and assuming no estimated residual value, compute the average rate of return for each of the four proposals. Round to 1 decimal place.
3. Using the following format, summarize the results of your computations in (1) and (2). By placing a check mark in the appropriate column at the right, indicate which proposals should be accepted for further analysis and which should be rejected.

Proposal	Cash Payback Period	Average Rate of Return	Accept for Further Analysis	Reject
A				
B				
C				
D				

4. For the proposals accepted for further analysis in (3), compute the net present value. Use a rate of 10% and the present value of $1 table appearing in this chapter. Round to the nearest dollar.

5. Compute the present value index for each of the proposals in (4). Round to 2 decimal places.

6. Rank the proposals from most attractive to least attractive, based on the present values of net cash flows computed in (4).

7. Rank the proposals from most attractive to least attractive, based on the present value indexes computed in (5).

8. ▭▭▭➤ Based upon the analyses, comment on the relative attractiveness of the proposals ranked in (6) and (7).

Special Activities

ACTIVITY 24-1
Ethics and professional conduct in business

ETHICS

Kelly McClung was recently hired as a cost analyst by Continental Medical Supplies Inc. One of Kelly's first assignments was to perform a net present value analysis for a new warehouse. Kelly performed the analysis and calculated a present value index of 0.75. The plant manager, I. M. Madd, is very intent on purchasing the warehouse because he believes that more storage space is needed. I. M. Madd asks Kelly into his office and the following conversation takes place.

I. M.: McClung, you're new here, aren't you?

Kelly: Yes, sir.

I. M.: Well, McClung, let me tell you something. I'm not at all pleased with the capital investment analysis that you performed on this new warehouse. I need that warehouse for my production. If I don't get it, where am I going to place our output?

Kelly: Hopefully with the customer, sir.

I. M.: Now don't get smart with me.

Kelly: No, really, I was being serious. My analysis does not support constructing a new warehouse. There is no way that I can get the numbers to make this a favorable investment. In fact, it seems to me that purchasing a warehouse does not add much value to the business. We need to be producing product to satisfy customer orders, not to fill a warehouse.

I. M.: Listen, you need to understand something. The headquarters people will not allow me to build the warehouse if the numbers don't add up. I know as well as you that many assumptions go into your net present value analysis. Why don't you relax some of your assumptions so that the financial savings will offset the cost?

Kelly: I'm willing to discuss my assumptions with you. Maybe I overlooked something.

I. M.: Good. Here's what I want you to do. I see in your analysis that you don't project greater sales as a result of the warehouse. It seems to me, if we can store more goods, then we will have more to sell. Thus, logically, a larger warehouse translates into more sales. If you incorporate this into your analysis, I think you'll see that the numbers will work out. Why don't you work it through and come back with a new analysis. I'm really counting on you on this one. Let's get off to a good start together and see if we can get this project accepted.

▭▭▭➤ What is your advice to Kelly?

ACTIVITY 24-2
Personal investment analysis

A Masters of Accountancy degree at Mid-State University would cost $12,000 for an additional fifth year of education beyond the bachelor's degree. Assume that all tuition is paid at the beginning of the year. A student considering this investment must evaluate the present value of cash flows from possessing a graduate degree versus holding only the undergraduate degree. Assume that the average student with an undergraduate degree is expected to earn an annual salary of $40,000 per year (assumed to be paid at the end of the year) for ten years. Assume that the average student with a graduate Masters of Accountancy degree is expected to earn an annual salary of $50,000 per year (assumed to be paid at the end of the year) for nine years after graduation. Assume a minimum rate of return of 10%.

1. Determine the net present value of cash flows from an undergraduate degree. Use the present value tables provided in this chapter.
2. Determine the net present value of cash flows from a Masters of Accountancy degree, assuming no salary is earned during the graduate year of schooling.
3. ▭▶ What is the net advantage or disadvantage of pursuing a graduate degree under these assumptions?

ACTIVITY 24-3
Investment analysis and qualitative considerations

The plant manager of Griffin Equipment Company is considering the purchase of a new robotic assembly plant. The new robotic line will cost $1,250,000. The manager believes that the new investment will result in direct labor savings of $250,000 per year for ten years.

1. What is the payback period on this project?
2. What is the net present value, assuming a 10% rate of return?
3. ▭▶ What else should the manager consider in the analysis?

ACTIVITY 24-4
Qualitative issues in investment analysis

REAL WORLD

The following are some selected quotes from senior executives:

CEO, **Worthington Industries** (a high technology steel company): *"We try to find the best technology, stay ahead of the competition, and serve the customer. . . . We'll make any investment that will pay back quickly . . . but if it is something that we really see as a must down the road, payback is not going to be that important."*

Chairman of **Amgen** (a biotech company): *"You cannot really run the numbers, do net present value calculations, because the uncertainties are really gigantic . . . You decide on a project you want to run, and then you run the numbers [as a reality check on your assumptions]. Success in a business like this is much more dependent on tracking rather than on predicting, much more dependent on seeing results over time, tracking and adjusting and readjusting, much more dynamic, much more flexible."*

Chief Financial Officer of **Merck & Co.** (a pharmaceutical company): *". . . at the individual product level—the development of a successful new product requires on the order of $230 million in R&D, spread over more than a decade—discounted cash flow style analysis does not become a factor until development is near the point of manufacturing scale-up effort. Prior to that point, given the uncertainties associated with new product development, it would be lunacy in our business to decide that we know exactly what's going to happen to a product once it gets out."*

▭▶ Explain the role of capital investment analysis for these companies.

ACTIVITY 24-5
Analyze cash flows

You are considering an investment of $360,000 in either Project A or Project B for Lion Studios Inc. In discussing the two projects with an advisor, you decided that, for the risk involved, a return of 12% on the cash investment would be required. For this purpose, you estimated the following economic factors for the projects:

	Project A	Project B
Useful life	4 years	4 years
Residual value	-0-	-0-
Net income:		
Year 1	$ 65,000	$ 25,000
2	50,000	40,000
3	40,000	58,000
4	25,000	64,200

Have you ever had to request service repairs on an appliance at your home? The repair person may arrive and take five minutes to replace a part, yet the bill may indicate a charge for a minimum amount that is more than five minutes of work. Why might the service person have a minimum charge just for showing up? The answer is that the service person must charge for the time and expense of coming to your house. In a sense, the bill reflects two elements of service: the cost of coming to your house and the cost of providing the service. The first portion of the cost reflects the time required to "set up" the job, while the second part of the cost reflects the cost of performing the service. Notice that the setup charge will be the same, whether the repairs take five minutes or five hours. In contrast, the second portion of the bill that reflects the actual service performed varies with the time on the job. Like the repair person, companies must be careful to cost their products and services to reflect the different activities involved in producing the product. Otherwise, the cost of products and services may be distorted and lead to improper management decisions.

In this chapter we will explain and illustrate three different methods of allocating factory overhead to products. In addition, we will explain how product cost distortions can result from improper factory overhead allocation. We will end the chapter by explaining and illustrating how overhead costs can be allocated to services.

Product Costing Allocation Methods

objective 1

Identify three methods used for allocating factory overhead costs to products.

How does **Toyota Motor Company** determine if its *Avalon* automobile is a profitable product? First, it needs to determine the revenues earned from selling the cars. Most companies have accounting systems that trace revenues to individual product lines. In addition, however, Toyota needs to subtract the cost of manufacturing *Avalon* cars in order to determine the profit from *Avalon* sales. Toyota's cost accounting system provides this cost information. Determining the cost of the *Avalon*, or any other product, is termed ***product costing***.

We introduced product costing in the job order costing chapter. We stated that product costs consist of direct materials, direct labor, and factory overhead. The direct materials and direct labor are direct to the product. However, factory overhead is often indirect to products and must be allocated. In this chapter we will illustrate three different factory overhead allocation approaches: (1) the single plantwide factory overhead rate method, (2) the multiple production department factory overhead rate method, and (3) the activity-based costing method.

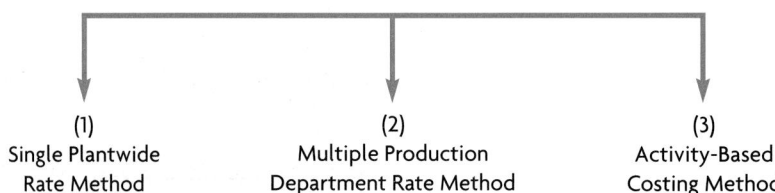

Three Factory Overhead Allocation Methods

(1)	(2)	(3)
Single Plantwide Rate Method	Multiple Production Department Rate Method	Activity-Based Costing Method

How does an accountant know which method to use? In this chapter we will illustrate each of the three methods and identify the conditions favoring each method. Managers should be concerned about which method is selected because the method of allocation determines the accuracy of the resulting product cost. Accurate product costs support management decisions, such as determining product mix, establishing product price, or determining whether or not to emphasize a product line. For example, after implementing a more accurate factory overhead cost allocation system, a senior manager at **Kraft Foods** remarked, "I expect to see that there are some products we definitely should not be manufacturing and some other products that we should be committing many more resources to . . . . [The cost system] should affect our long-term decisions on which businesses Kraft should be in."[1] Thus, factory overhead allocation is not just necessary for financial reporting purposes, but it also contributes to management decision making.

Single Plantwide Factory Overhead Rate Method

objective 2

Use a single plantwide factory overhead rate for product costing.

REAL WORLD

Many professional service companies use a single overhead rate in determining their prices and job profitability. For example, medical, legal, and accounting services develop hourly rates that will provide a profit after covering labor and overhead.

As we discussed in a previous chapter, companies may use a predetermined factory overhead rate to allocate factory overhead costs to products. Under the **single plantwide factory overhead rate method**, all of the factory overhead is allocated to all the products, using only one rate.

To illustrate, assume that Ruiz Company manufactures two products, snowmobiles and lawnmowers. Both products are manufactured in a single factory. In addition, there is $1,600,000 of factory overhead budgeted for the period. The factory overhead consists of factory and equipment depreciation, factory power, factory supplies, and indirect labor.

Under the single plantwide factory overhead rate method, the $1,600,000 budgeted factory overhead is applied to all products by using one rate. This rate is computed by dividing the total budgeted factory overhead cost by the total budgeted (estimated) plantwide allocation base as follows:

$$\text{Single plantwide factory overhead rate} = \frac{\text{Total budgeted factory overhead cost}}{\text{Total budgeted plantwide allocation base}}$$

The budgeted allocation base is a measure of operating activity in the factory. Common allocation bases would include direct labor hours, direct labor dollars, and machine hours.

Assume that Ruiz Company allocates factory overhead to the two products on the basis of budgeted direct labor hours. The total budgeted direct labor hours can be determined by multiplying the manufacturing volume by the direct labor hours per unit. Ruiz Company plans to manufacture 1,000 units of each product. Snowmobiles and lawnmowers both require 10 direct labor hours per unit to manufacture. The total budgeted plantwide direct labor hours is 20,000, as shown below.

Snowmobile: 1,000 units × 10 direct labor hours = 10,000 direct labor hours
Lawnmower: 1,000 units × 10 direct labor hours = 10,000
                                                  20,000 direct labor hours

The single plantwide factory overhead rate is $80 per direct labor hour, determined as follows:

$$\text{Single plantwide factory overhead rate} = \frac{\$1,600,000}{20,000 \text{ direct labor hours}}$$

$$= \$80 \text{ per direct labor hour}$$

This plantwide rate of $80 per direct labor hour can be used to allocate factory overhead to each product, as shown on the following page.

---

[1]R. Cooper, R. S. Kaplan, L. S. Maisel, E. Morrissey, and R. M. Oehm, *Implementing Activity-Based Cost Management: Moving from Analysis to Action* (Institute of Management Accountants, 1992), p. 269.

	Single Plantwide Factory Overhead Rate	×	Direct Labor Hours per Unit	=	Factory Overhead Cost per Unit
Snowmobile	$80 per direct labor hour	×	10 direct labor hours	=	$800
Lawnmower	$80 per direct labor hour	×	10 direct labor hours	=	$800

The factory overhead allocated to each unit of product is the same. This is because each product used the same number of direct labor hours.

The effects of using the single plantwide factory overhead rate method are summarized for Ruiz Company in Exhibit 1.

REAL WORLD

Many military contractors use a single plantwide rate for allocating factory overhead costs to products, such as jet fighters. This approach is satisfactory when all products in the plant are manufactured under cost plus profit margin contracts to a single customer, such as the Department of Defense. The factory overhead is rationally and systematically allocated to products and is thus "paid for" under the contract terms. However, cost distortions can still occur. This is one reason why government contractors sometimes make "$200 flashlights" that could be purchased at the local hardware store for $5.

•Exhibit 1

Single Plantwide Factory Overhead Rate Method—Ruiz Company

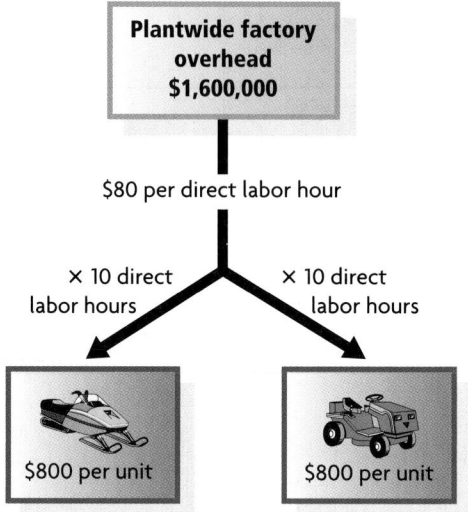

Lin Company has budgeted $500,000 of factory overhead and 25,000 direct labor hours. How much factory overhead is allocated to a product that uses 22 direct labor hours?

$440 [22 hours × ($500,000 ÷ 25,000 hours)]

The greatest advantage of the single plantwide overhead rate method is that it is simple and inexpensive to apply in practice. Using a plantwide rate, we assume that the factory overhead costs are consumed in the same way by all products. For example, for Ruiz Company, we assume that all factory overhead can be accurately allocated to the two products based on the total number of direct labor hours consumed by each product. For companies that manufacture one or very few products, this assumption may be true. However, if the company manufactures many different types of products that consume factory overhead costs in different ways, then the assumption may not be true. In such a situation, a single plantwide rate may not accurately allocate factory overhead to the products. A solution may be to use multiple production department factory overhead rates, which we illustrate in the next section.

INTEGRITY IN BUSINESS

FALSE CLAIMS ACT

The **U.S. Government** purchases military equipment from defense contractors, such as **Lockheed Martin Corp.** and **Northrop Grumman Corp.** Defense contracts often allow companies to recover their costs plus some profit. The overhead allocation method is important in determining the correct amounts to be recovered. Due to the complexity of determining cost recoveries, the Department of Defense audits the amount charged for work performed under contract. In the event of disagreement between the contractor and the government, the U.S. Government may sue the company under the False Claims Act. This Act is a set of laws used for recovering false claims in government contracting. For example, the **Newport News** shipyard was recently sued under the False Claims Act for allegedly including $72 million of research and development costs for a commercial tanker program in an overhead rate applied to Navy work.

Multiple Production Department Factory Overhead Rate Method

When production departments *differ significantly* in their manufacturing processes, factory overhead costs are likely to be incurred differently in each department. For example, a fabrication department that uses equipment may require more depreciation, power, and maintenance than would an assembly department that uses people. In addition, different products may consume the factory overhead from each production department in different proportions. For example, some products may use more of the fabrication department, while others use more of the assembly department. Under these conditions, the factory overhead costs may be more accurately allocated using multiple production department factory overhead rates.

The ***multiple production department factory overhead rate method*** uses different rates for each production department to allocate factory overhead to products. This is in contrast to the single plantwide rate method, which uses only one rate to allocate plantwide factory overhead to the products. Exhibit 2 illustrates how these two methods differ.

•Exhibit 2

Comparison of Single Plantwide Rate and Multiple Production Department Rate Methods

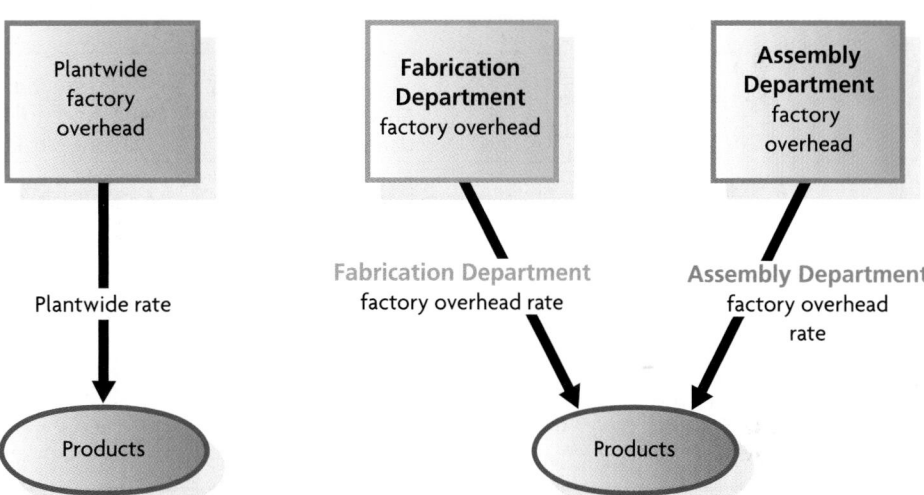

To illustrate the multiple production department factory overhead rate method, assume that Ruiz Company has two production departments, Fabrication and Assembly. Also assume that the factory overhead associated with the Fabrication Department is $1,030,000, and the factory overhead associated with the Assembly Department is $570,000.[2] The Fabrication Department has nearly twice the factory overhead of the Assembly Department because of the additional machinery-related factory overhead, such as power, equipment depreciation, and factory supplies. Note that the $1,600,000 of budgeted factory overhead in the two production departments equals the budgeted plantwide factory overhead.

Production Department Factory Overhead Rates and Allocation

The **production department factory overhead rates** are determined by dividing the budgeted production department factory overhead by the budgeted allocation

---

[2]The factory overhead is allocated to production departments by using methods that are discussed in advanced texts.

POINT OF INTEREST

A company may use different allocation bases for different departments. For example, a machine-intensive department may use machine hours as an allocation base, and a labor-intensive department may use labor hours as an allocation base. However, in situations where one employee operates one machine, machine hours and labor hours will be equal and will yield the same allocation results.

base for each department. For Ruiz Company, direct labor hours are used as the allocation base for each production department. Each production department uses 10,000 direct labor hours. Thus, the factory overhead rates for the two departments are determined as follows:

$$\text{Fabrication department factory overhead rate} = \frac{\$1,030,000}{10,000 \text{ dlh}}$$

$$= \$103 \text{ per direct labor hour}$$

$$\text{Assembly department factory overhead rate} = \frac{\$570,000}{10,000 \text{ dlh}}$$

$$= \$57 \text{ per direct labor hour}$$

Recall that each product requires ten direct labor hours. We will now assume some additional information about these hours. The snowmobile requires eight direct labor hours in the Fabrication Department and two direct labor hours in the Assembly Department. The lawnmower requires two direct labor hours in the Fabrication Department and eight in the Assembly Department.

Factory overhead is allocated to each product by multiplying the direct labor hours used by each product in each department by the production department factory overhead rate. Exhibit 3 shows this process for Ruiz Company.

•Exhibit 3 Allocating Factory Overhead to Products—Ruiz Company

	Allocation-Base Usage per Unit	×	Production Department Factory Overhead Rate	=	Allocated Factory Overhead per Unit of Product
Snowmobile					
Fabrication Department	8 direct labor hours	×	$103 per dlh	=	$824
Assembly Department	2 direct labor hours	×	$ 57 per dlh	=	114
Total factory overhead cost per snowmobile					$938
Lawnmower					
Fabrication Department	2 direct labor hours	×	$103 per dlh	=	$206
Assembly Department	8 direct labor hours	×	$ 57 per dlh	=	456
Total factory overhead cost per lawnmower					$662

The multiple production department rate allocation method for Ruiz Company is summarized in Exhibit 4. You should note that the production department factory

•Exhibit 4

Multiple Production Department Rate Method—Ruiz Company

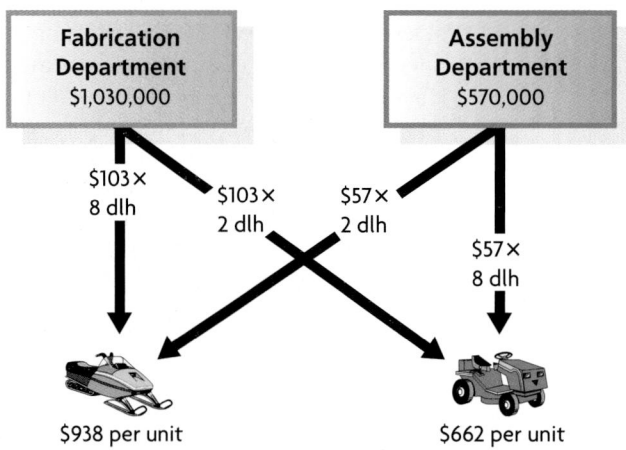

POINT OF INTEREST

A company may develop factory overhead rates for each class of machine, rather than for a department. This allows for more precise allocation of machine costs to products in machine-intensive operations.

overhead rates are not the same for each department. The Fabrication Department is more expensive in terms of factory overhead per direct labor hour than is the Assembly Department. In addition, the snowmobile uses more Fabrication Department direct labor hours than does the lawnmower. As a result, the total overhead allocated to each snowmobile is greater than that allocated to each lawnmower.

Distortion in Product Costs—Single Plantwide versus Multiple Production Department Factory Overhead Rates

For Ruiz Company, the following table shows the difference in the factory overhead per unit for each product, using the single plantwide and the multiple production department factory overhead rate methods:

	Factory Overhead Cost per Unit	
	Single Plantwide Rate	Multiple Production Department Rates
Snowmobile	$800	$938
Lawnmower	800	662

Product A requires 12 labor hours in Department 1 and 4 labor hours in Department 2. The factory overhead budgeted is $800,000 for Department 1 and $200,000 for Department 2. Both departments have 8,000 direct labor hours budgeted for the period. What is the factory overhead allocated to Product A under the multiple production department rate method?

$1,300 [($800,000 ÷ 8,000) × 12 hours + ($200,000 ÷ 8,000) × 4 hours]

> **The single plantwide factory overhead rate distorts product cost by averaging high and low factory overhead costs.**

Which method is correct? In this case, the single plantwide factory overhead rate distorts the product cost by averaging the differences between the high factory overhead costs in the Fabrication Department and the low factory overhead costs in the Assembly Department. Using the single plantwide rate, we assume that all factory overhead is directly related to a single allocation base representing the entire plant. In many plants, this assumption is not realistic. Thus, using a single plantwide rate may result in product cost distortion.

In general, the following conditions may indicate that a single plantwide factory overhead rate will lead to distorted product costs:

Condition 1: Differences in production department factory overhead rates. There are significant differences in the factory overhead rates across different production departments. That is, some departments have high rates, while others have low rates.

and

Condition 2: Differences in the ratios of allocation-base usage. The products require different ratios of allocation base-usage across the departments.

Exhibit 5 illustrates both conditions for Ruiz Company. Condition 1 exists because the factory overhead rate for the Fabrication Department is $103 per direct labor hour, while the rate for the Assembly Department is only $57 per direct labor hour. This condition, by itself, will not cause product cost distortion. However, Condition 2 also exists. The snowmobile consumes 8 direct labor hours in the Fabrication Department, while the lawnmower consumes only 2 direct labor hours (8:2 ratio). The opposite is the case in the Assembly Department (2:8 ratio). Since both conditions exist, the product costs calculated using the single plantwide factory overhead rate are distorted. If Ruiz Company used the $800 product cost to determine its pricing strategy for both products, it would likely *underprice* the snowmobile and *overprice* the lawnmower. Eventually, Ruiz might be shut out of the lawnmower business due to this pricing error. If Ruiz used the multiple production department factory overhead rate approach, however, its product costs would be more accurate, and thus it would have a better starting point for making pricing decisions.

•Exhibit 5

Conditions for Product Cost Distortion—Ruiz Company

Fabrication Department	Assembly Department

Condition 1: Differences in production department factory overhead rates

$103 per direct labor hour

$57 per direct labor hour

Condition 2: Differences in the ratios of allocation-base usage

8 direct labor hours	2 direct labor hours
2 direct labor hours	8 direct labor hours

Activity-Based Costing Method

objective **4**

Use activity-based costing for product costing.

In today's more complex manufacturing systems, product costs may still be distorted when multiple production department factory overhead rates are used. One way to avoid this distortion is by using the ***activity-based costing (ABC) method***. This approach allocates factory overhead more accurately than does the multiple production department rate method.

The activity-based costing method uses cost of activities to determine product costs. Under this method, factory overhead costs are initially accounted for in ***activity cost pools***. These cost pools are related to a given activity, such as machine usage, inspections, moving, production setups, and engineering activities. In contrast, when multiple production department factory overhead rates are used, factory overhead costs are first accounted for in production departments. Exhibit 6 illustrates how these two approaches compare.

•Exhibit 6 Multiple Production Department Factory Overhead Rate Method vs. Activity-Based Costing

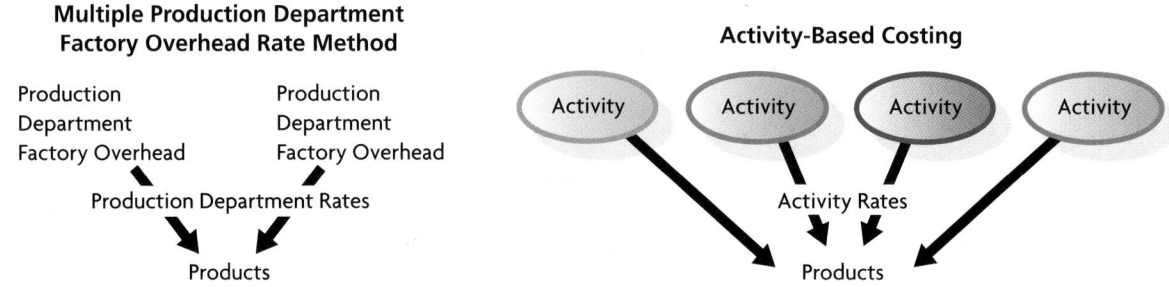

To illustrate the activity-based costing method, assume that Ruiz Company has five activities. Two activities are the fabrication and assembly production activities. We now call these *activities*, rather than *departments*, because the factory overhead costs in these pools are more closely related to their activity bases than under the multiple department factory overhead rate method.

Ruiz has three additional activities, which are described below.

Another term for "setup" is "changeover." This term is often used in continuous process industries. For example, reactors, paper machines, and rolling mills are "changed over" to produce a different product. Often, machine characteristics are changed while the process continues running ("on the fly"). Such changeovers are still costly, however, because the machines will make low-quality product for a period of time during the changeover.

- *Setup*—the activity of changing the characteristics of a machine to prepare for manufacturing a different product. Often, a production run requires a **setup**. For example, changing a stamping machine from stamping the body for a snowmobile to stamping the body for a lawnmower would require stopping the machine and changing the die. The work associated with changing the die is a setup activity.
- *Quality control inspection*—the activity of inspecting the product for defects. For example, a snowmobile inspection may require the snowmobile to be run for several hours and then be disassembled to test for component strength, fit, and function.
- *Engineering changes*—the activity of processing changes in product design characteristics. An **engineering change order (ECO)** initiates an administrative process to change the design of a product. For example, to change the type of blade assembled in a lawnmower would require an engineering change order.

We will assume the following budgeted factory overhead associated with each activity:

Activity Cost Pool	Amount
Fabrication	$ 530,000
Assembly	70,000
Setup	480,000
Quality control inspection	312,000
Engineering changes	208,000
Total budgeted factory overhead	$1,600,000

The **U.S. Postal Service** has initiated a new activity-based costing system, called PostalOne!, which will track the real costs associated with processing and delivering each class of mail.

The total budgeted factory overhead to be allocated is still $1,600,000. However, the budgeted factory overhead has now been divided into cost pools. The costs in the fabrication and assembly pools are less than the costs in the production departments from the previous section because the production departments included costs that were not closely related to fabrication and assembly activities. These costs, which total $1,000,000 ($480,000 + $312,000 + $208,000), are now related to their own activity pools, namely setup, quality control inspection, and engineering changes.

Activity Rates and Allocation

Activity rates are determined by dividing the budgeted activity cost pool by the total estimated activity base.

The activity cost pools are assigned to products, using factory overhead rates for each activity. These rates are often called **activity rates** because they are related to activities. Activity rates are determined by dividing the cost budgeted for each activity pool by the estimated activity base for that pool. We use the term **activity base**, rather than allocation base, since the base is related to an activity cost pool. For example, the activity rate for the setup activity would be determined by dividing the setup budgeted cost pool by the number of estimated setups. Setup cost would be related to a product by multiplying the setup activity rate by the number of setups used by that particular product.

To determine each activity-base quantity, assume the following additional information about the snowmobiles and lawnmowers for Ruiz Company:

- *Snowmobiles:* Ruiz Company estimates that the total production for snowmobiles will be 1,000 units. Snowmobiles are a new product, and the engineers are still

tinkering with design changes. Thus, there are 12 engineering change orders estimated for the period. In addition, the snowmobile production run is expected to be set up 100 times during the period, or 10 units per production run (1,000 units total production ÷ 100 setups). For quality control purposes, 100 snowmobiles (10% of total production) will be inspected.

• *Lawnmowers:* Ruiz Company estimates that the total production for lawnmowers will also be 1,000 units. Lawnmowers are a mature and stable product that has been produced by Ruiz Company for many years. Thus, Ruiz Company expects the lawnmower to have only four engineering changes for the period. Due to its long history of successful production of lawnmowers, Ruiz expects fewer quality problems; thus, only four lawnmowers (0.4% of production) will be quality-control inspected. In addition, the lawnmower production run is expected to be set up 20 times during the period, or 50 units per production run (1,000 units total production ÷ 20 setups).

The estimated **activity-base usage quantities** are the total activity-base quantities related to each product. These quantities reflect differences with respect to using setup, quality control inspection, and engineering change activities, as we noted in the preceding paragraphs. In addition, each product uses different amounts of direct labor hours in the fabrication and assembly activities, as we noted in an earlier section. The estimated activity-base usage quantities for all 1,000 units of production for each product are shown in Exhibit 7.

•Exhibit 7   Estimated Activity-Base Usage Quantities—Ruiz Company

| | Activities | | | | |
Products	Fabrication	Assembly	Setup	Quality Control Inspections	Engineering Changes
Snowmobile	8,000 dlh	2,000 dlh	100 setups	100 inspections	12 ECOs
Lawnmower	2,000	8,000	20	4	4
Total activity base	10,000 dlh	10,000 dlh	120 setups	104 inspections	16 ECOs

The activity rates for each activity can now be determined by dividing the budgeted activity cost pool by the total estimated activity base from Exhibit 7. These activity rates are shown in Exhibit 8.

•Exhibit 8   Activity Rates—Ruiz Company

Activity	Budgeted Activity Cost Pool	÷	Estimated Activity Base	=	Activity Rate
Fabrication	$530,000	÷	10,000 direct labor hours	=	$53 per direct labor hour
Assembly	$ 70,000	÷	10,000 direct labor hours	=	$7 per direct labor hour
Setup	$480,000	÷	120 setups	=	$4,000 per setup
Quality control inspections	$312,000	÷	104 inspections	=	$3,000 per inspection
Engineering changes	$208,000	÷	16 engineering changes	=	$13,000 per engineering change order

The product costs for the snowmobile and lawnmower are computed by multiplying the activity rate by the related activity-base quantity for each product. The total of these costs for each product is the total factory overhead cost for that product. This amount is divided by the total number of units of that product budgeted for manufacture in the period. This result, as shown in Exhibit 9, is the factory overhead cost per unit.

•Exhibit 9 Activity-Based Product Cost Calculations

	Snowmobile				Lawnmower			
Activity	**Activity-Base Usage**	**×**	**Activity Rate**	**= Activity Cost**	**Activity-Base Usage**	**×**	**Activity Rate**	**= Activity Cost**
Fabrication	8,000 dlh	×	$ 53	= $ 424,000	2,000 dlh	×	$ 53	= $106,000
Assembly	2,000 dlh	×	7	= 14,000	8,000 dlh	×	7	= 56,000
Setup	100 setups	×	4,000	= 400,000	20 setups	×	4,000	= 80,000
Quality control inspections	100 inspections	×	3,000	= 300,000	4 inspections	×	3,000	= 12,000
Engineering changes	12 ECOs	×	13,000	= 156,000	4 ECOs	×	13,000	= 52,000
Total factory overhead cost				$1,294,000				$306,000
Budgeted units of production				÷ 1,000				÷ 1,000
Factory overhead cost per unit				$ 1,294				$ 306

The setup activity is estimated to cost $260,000 to support 520 setups. Product A is produced in average run lengths of 160 units and has an estimated production of 20,000 units. How much setup activity should be allocated to Product A?

$62,500 [$500 per setup ($260,000 ÷ 520 setups) × 125 setups (20,000 units ÷ 160 units)]

The activity-based costing method for Ruiz Company is summarized in Exhibit 10. Compare Exhibit 10 with Exhibit 4. In both exhibits, multiple rates are used. In Exhibit 4, production department factory overhead costs were allocated to products on the basis of the production department factory overhead rates. In contrast, under activity-based costing, the activity cost pools are allocated to the products on the basis of each activity's own unique activity rate.

Distortion in Product Costs—Multiple Production Department Factory Overhead Rate Method versus Activity-Based Costing

The factory overhead costs per unit for Ruiz Company across all three allocation methods are shown below.

	Factory Overhead Cost per Unit— Three Cost Allocation Methods		
	Single Plantwide Rate	**Multiple Production Department Rates**	**Activity-Based Costing**
Snowmobile	$800	$938	$1,294
Lawnmower	800	662	306

•Exhibit 10   Activity-Based Costing Method—Ruiz Company

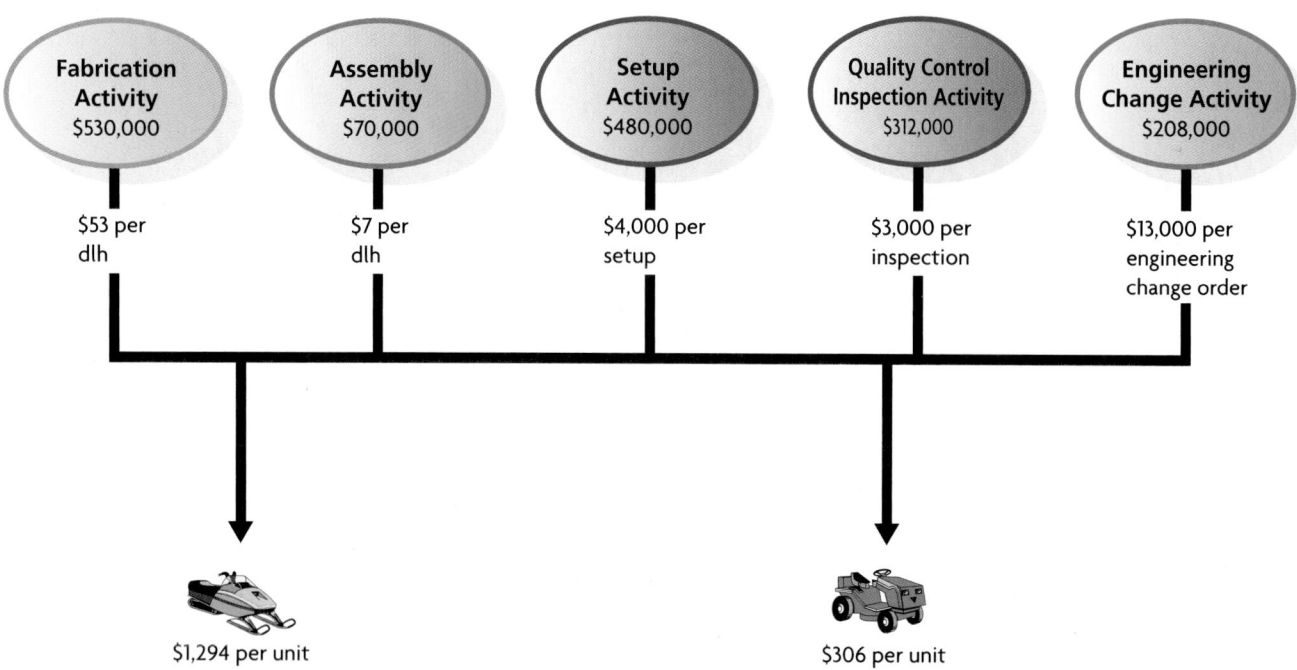

$1,294 per unit $306 per unit

REAL WORLD

Procter & Gamble used activity-based costing information to simplify its business by standardizing product formulas and packaging, to reduce promotions, to eliminate marginal brands, and to standardize advertising campaigns.

REAL WORLD

A recent survey showed that 20% of the surveyed companies had adopted activity-based costing.

Source: "2001 Survey on Cost Management Practices," IMA.

As you can see, the activity-based costing method produced different product costs than did the multiple department factory overhead rate method. What caused these differences, and which method is more accurate? The answer lies in how the $1,000,000 of setup, quality control, and engineering change activities were treated. Under the multiple production department factory overhead rate method, this factory overhead was included in the production department factory overhead and allocated to products on the basis of direct labor hours. However, each product did *not* consume *activities* in proportion to its direct labor hours. Namely, the snowmobile consumed a larger portion of the setup, quality control inspection, and engineering change activities, even though each product consumed 10,000 labor hours. As a result, activity-based costing allocates more of this factory overhead cost to the snowmobile and less to the lawnmower than did the multiple production department factory overhead rate method. In summary, the activity-based costing method provided the most accurate product costs because activities were consumed in different proportions than the direct labor used in the two products.

The Dangers of Product Cost Distortion

Product cost distortion can lead to bad management decisions, and bad decisions can lead to business disasters. To illustrate, **ArvinMeritor, Inc.** conducted an activity-based costing study after one of its best-selling axles had begun losing market share. The study found that incorrect factory overhead cost allocations had "overcosted" its highest-volume axle by roughly 20%, while underestimating the cost of low-volume axles by as much as 40%. Since the sales prices were based on these estimated costs, ArvinMeritor had underpriced its low-volume axles and overpriced its high-volume axles. As a result, competitors had begun to attract customers away from ArvinMeritor's best-selling, high-volume axles. Without the activity-based costing analysis, ArvinMeritor could well have discovered that it was gradually being forced out of the high-volume axle business—not by choice, but because of inaccurate product costing and bad pricing decisions.

MANAGERIAL DISCLOSURE AND ANALYSIS

FIDELITY INVESTMENTS

Fidelity Investments, an integrated financial services company, recently shifted its strategic focus from the "mutual fund owner" to that of the "household." Fidelity believed that a household owned assets beyond those placed by a single fund owner and thus was a more comprehensive view of its business opportunity. As a result, the company implemented an activity-based costing system to evaluate its costs. The result was a profit management system that changed the focus of the organization.

The activity-based costing system showed management the revenues and costs of acquiring and managing assets by household wealth segment. For example, Fidelity used its activity-based costing system to tailor its sales and marketing strategies to different wealth segments. Thus, a higher wealth segment could afford more personal sales attention, while less wealthy segments would rely on less costly sales activities, such as mass mail.

Activity-Based Costing for Selling and Administrative Expenses

REAL WORLD

ExxonMobil Corporation has analyzed the cost of its selling and administrative activities to better determine the cost of its lubrication products. In addition, the activity information helped ExxonMobil discover the relative costs of serving customers directly versus through distributors. Examples of selling and administrative activities used in its activity-based costing analysis included sales, maintenance, engineering calls, distributor calls, order taking, market research, and advertising.

objective 5

Use activity-based costing to allocate selling and administrative expenses to products.

Generally accepted accounting principles require that selling and administrative expenses be treated as period expenses on the income statement prepared for external users. However, accountants may allocate selling and administrative expenses to products in preparing product profitability reports for management. A traditional method is to allocate selling and administrative expenses to the products, based on product sales volumes. However, products may consume activities in ways that are unrelated to their sales volumes. When this occurs, activity-based costing may provide a more accurate allocation approach.

To illustrate, assume that Abacus Company has two products, Ipso and Facto. Both products have the same total sales volume. However, both products are not the same in terms of how they consume selling and administrative activities. Exhibit 11 identifies some of these differences.

If the selling and administrative expenses of Abacus Company were allocated on the basis of sales volumes, both products would be allocated the same amount, since they both have the same sales volume. Does this seem correct? Should both products have the same selling and administrative expenses? No, they should not. Ipso is much less complex and hence less expensive than Facto. The activity-based costing approach would allocate the selling and administrative activities to each product based on its individual differences in consuming these activities. For example, assume that the field service activity of Abacus Company had a budgeted cost of $150,000. Additionally, assume that 100 warranty claims were estimated for the period. Using warranty claims as the activity base, the cost per warranty claim would be $1,500 [$150,000/100 claims]. Thus, if Ipso had 10 warranty claims and Facto had 90 warranty claims, Ipso would be allocated $15,000 (10 × $1,500) of field service activity, while Facto would be allocated $135,000 (90 × $1,500) of this activity. Allocating selling and administrative expenses using activity-based costing would result in more accurate product profitability reports for Abacus Company management.

For some companies, selling and administrative expenses may be more related to customer behaviors than to differences in products. That is, some customers may demand more service and selling activities than other customers. In such cases, activity-based cost reports can be developed to show the impact of these differences on customer profitability. For example, a recent survey of manufacturers (suppliers) indicated that **Wal-Mart** has earned the distinction of being the easiest, and often

•**Exhibit 11**

Selling and
Administrative Activity
Product Differences

Selling and Administrative Activities	Ipso	Facto
Post-sale technical support	Product is easy to use by the customer.	Product requires specialized training in order to be used by the customer.
Order writing	Product requires no technical information from the customer.	Product requires detailed technical information from the customer.
Promotional support	Product requires no promotional effort.	Product requires extensive promotional effort.
Order entry	Product is purchased in large volumes per order.	Product is purchased in small volumes per order.
Customer return processing	Product has few customer returns.	Product has many customer returns.
Shipping document preparation	Product is shipped domestically.	Product is shipped internationally, requiring customs and export documents.
Shipping and handling	Product is not hazardous.	Product is hazardous, requiring specialized shipping and handling.
Field service	Product has few warranty claims.	Product has many warranty claims.

most profitable, retailer with which to do business.[3] In the next section, we will see how service companies can also use activity-based costing to evaluate their costs to serve customers.

INTEGRITY IN BUSINESS

PERIOD AND PRODUCT COSTS

The selling and administrative expenses must be expensed on the income statement as a period cost, according to GAAP. These costs may be allocated to products for internal reporting but must not be included as a product cost for external reporting.

Activity-Based Costing in Service Businesses

objective **6**

Use activity-based costing in a service business.

Service companies have a need to determine the cost of services in order to make pricing, promoting, and other decisions with regard to service offerings. Many service companies find that single and multiple department overhead rate methods may lead to distortions similar to those of manufacturing firms. Thus, many service companies are now using activity-based costing for determining the cost of providing services to *customers*.

[3]As reported in Jerry Useem, "One Nation Under Wal-Mart" *Fortune*, February 18, 2003.

To illustrate activity-based costing for a service company, assume that Hopewell Hospital uses an activity-based costing system to determine how hospital overhead is allocated to patients. Hopewell Hospital first determines the activity cost pools and then allocates the activity cost pools to patients, using activity rates. We will assume that the activities of Hopewell Hospital include admitting, radiological testing, operating room, pathological testing, and dietary and laundry. Each activity cost pool has an estimated activity base measuring the output of the activity. The cost of activities is allocated to patients by multiplying the activity rate by the number of activity-base usage quantities consumed by each patient. Exhibit 12 illustrates the activity-based costing method for Hopewell Hospital.

Each activity rate shown in Exhibit 12 is determined by dividing the budgeted activity cost pool by the estimated activity-base quantity. To illustrate, assume that the radiological testing activity cost pool budget is $960,000, and the total estimated activity-base quantity is 3,000 images. The activity rate of $320 per image is calculated as follows:

$$\text{Radiological testing activity rate} = \frac{\$960,000}{3,000 \text{ images}} = \$320 \text{ per image}$$

•Exhibit 12 Activity-Based Costing Method—Hopewell Hospital

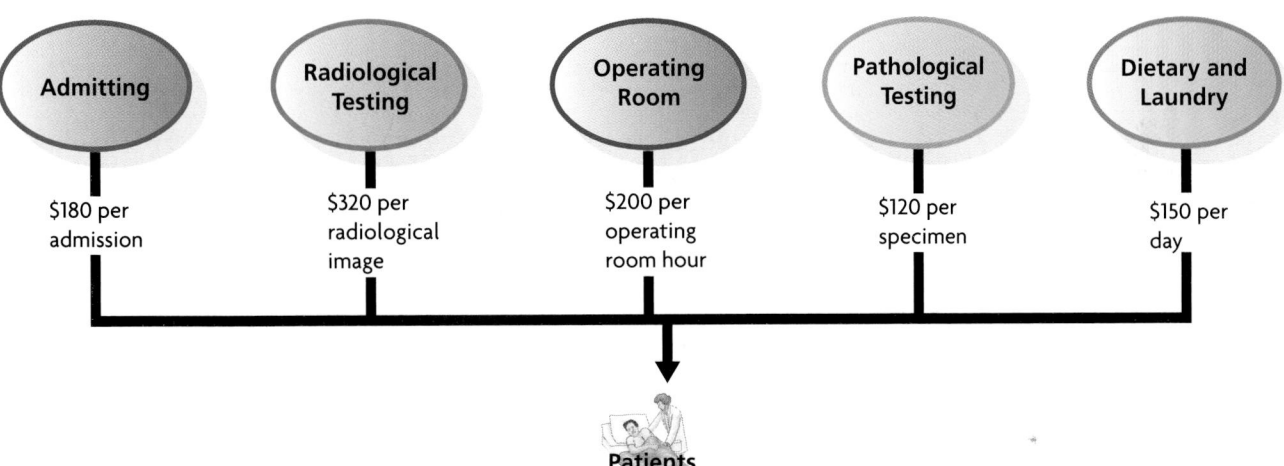

The activity rates for the other activities are determined in a similar manner. These activity rates are used to allocate costs to patients. To illustrate, assume that Mary Wilson was a patient of the hospital. The hospital overhead cost associated with services (activities) performed for Mary Wilson is determined by multiplying the activity-base quantity for Mary Wilson's stay in the hospital by the activity rate. The sum of the costs across the activities is the total hospital overhead cost of services performed for Mary Wilson. These calculations are shown below.

Patient Name: Mary Wilson

Activity	Activity-Base Usage	×	Activity Rate	=	Activity Cost
Admitting	1 admission	×	$180 per admission	=	$ 180
Radiological testing	2 images	×	320 per image	=	640
Operating room	4 hours	×	200 per hour	=	800
Pathological testing	1 specimen	×	120 per specimen	=	120
Dietary and laundry	7 days	×	150 per day	=	1,050
Total					$2,790

The patient activity costs can be combined with the direct costs, such as drugs and supplies, and reported with the revenues earned for each patient in a customer profitability report. A partial customer profitability report for Hopewell Hospital is shown in Exhibit 13.

The report in Exhibit 13 can be used by the administrators to guide decisions on pricing or service delivery. For example, there was a large loss on services provided to Brian Birini. Further investigation might reveal that services provided to Birini were out of line with what would be allowed for reimbursement by the insurance company. As a result, future losses could be avoided by lobbying for a higher insurance reimbursement or aligning the services closer to the revenues allowed by the insurance company.

•Exhibit 13

Customer Profitability
Report

Hopewell Hospital Customer (Patient) Profitability Report For the Period Ending December 31, 2003				
	Adcock, Kim	Birini, Brian	Conway, Don	Wilson, Mary
Revenues	$9,500	$21,400	$5,050	$3,300
Less: Patient costs:				
Drugs and supplies	$ 400	$ 1,000	$ 300	$ 200
Admitting	180	180	180	180
Radiological testing	1,280	2,560	1,280	640
Operating room	2,400	6,400	1,600	800
Pathological testing	240	600	120	120
Dietary and laundry	4,200	14,700	1,050	1,050
Total patient costs	$8,700	$25,440	$4,530	$2,990
Income from operations	$ 800	$ (4,040)	$ 520	$ 310

SPOTLIGHT ON STRATEGY

FINDING THE RIGHT NICHE

Businesses often attempt to divide a market into its unique characteristics, called market segmentation. Once a market segment is identified, product, price, promotion, and location strategies are tailored to fit that market. This is a better approach for many products and services than following a "one size fits all" strategy. For example, the McDonald's "Happy Meal" is targeted to the children's market segment, while the "Quarter Pounder" is targeted to more adult segments. The following table lists popular forms of segmentation and their common characteristics:

Form of Segmentation	Characteristics
Demographic	Age, education, gender, income, race
Geographic	Region, city, country
Psychographic	Lifestyle, values, attitudes
Benefit	Benefits provided
Volume	Light vs. heavy use

Examples for each of these forms of segmentation are as follows:

Demographic: Cadillac automobiles are targeted to an older, more affluent segment.
Geographic: Pro sports teams offer merchandise in their home cities.

Psychographic: The Body Shop markets all-natural beauty products to consumers who value cosmetic products that have not been animal-tested.
Benefit: TCBY frozen yogurt shops market a low-fat product that tastes good.
Volume: Delta Air Lines provides additional benefits, such as class upgrades, free air travel, and boarding priority, to its frequent fliers.

Key Points

1 Identify three methods used for allocating factory overhead costs to products.

There are three basic cost allocation methods used for determining the cost of products: the single plantwide factory overhead rate method, the multiple production department factory overhead rate method, and the activity-based costing method.

2 Use a single plantwide factory overhead rate for product costing.

A single plantwide factory overhead rate can be used to allocate all plant overhead to all products, based on the formula below. The single plantwide factory overhead rate is simple to apply, but it can lead to significant product cost distortions.

$$\text{Single plantwide factory overhead rate} = \frac{\text{Total budgeted factory overhead costs}}{\text{Total budgeted plantwide allocation base}}$$

3 Use multiple production department factory overhead rates for product costing.

Product costing using multiple production department factory overhead rates requires identifying the factory overhead associated with the production departments. Using these rates will result in greater accuracy than using single plantwide factory overhead rates when:

1. There are significant differences in the factory overhead rates across different production departments.

and

2. The products require different ratios of allocation-base usage in each production department.

4 Use activity-based costing for product costing.

Activity-based costing requires factory overhead to be budgeted to activity cost pools. The activity cost pools are allocated to products by multiplying activity rates by the activity-base quantity consumed for each product. Using activity rates rather than multiple production department factory overhead rates may result in more accurate product costs when products consume activities in ratios that are unrelated to their departmental allocation bases.

5 Use activity-based costing to allocate selling and administrative expenses to products.

Selling and administrative expenses can be allocated to products for management profit reporting, using activity-based costing. The traditional approach to allocating selling and administrative expenses is by the relative sales volumes of the products. Activity-based costing would be preferred when the products use selling and administrative activities in ratios that are unrelated to their sales volumes.

6 Use activity-based costing in a service business.

Activity-based costing may be applied in service settings to determine the cost of individual service offerings. Service costs are determined by multiplying activity rates by the amount of activity-base quantities consumed by the customer using the service offering. Such information can support service pricing and profitability analysis.

Key Terms

activity base (1035)
activity cost pools (1034)
activity rate (1035)
activity-base usage quantity (1036)
activity-based costing (ABC) method (1034)

engineering change order (ECO) (1035)
multiple production department factory overhead rate method (1031)
product costing (1028)

setup (1035)
single plantwide factory overhead rate method (1029)

Illustrative Problem

Hammer Company plans to use activity-based costing to determine its product costs. It presently uses a single plantwide factory overhead rate for allocating factory overhead to products, based on direct labor hours. The total factory overhead cost is as follows:

Department	Factory Overhead
Production Support	$1,225,000
Production (factory overhead only)	175,000
Total cost	$1,400,000

The company determined that it performed four major activities in the Production Support Department. These activities, along with their budgeted costs, are as follows:

Production Support Activities	Budgeted Cost
Setup	$ 428,750
Production control	245,000
Quality control	183,750
Materials management	367,500
Total	$1,225,000

Hammer Company estimated the following activity-base usage quantities and units produced for each of its three products:

Products	Number of Units	Direct Labor Hrs.	Setups	Production Orders	Inspections	Material Requisitions
Product K	10,000	25,000	80	80	35	320
Product L	2,000	10,000	40	40	40	400
Product M	50,000	140,000	5	5	0	30
Total cost	62,000	175,000	125	125	75	750

Instructions

1. Determine the factory overhead cost per unit for Products K, L, and M under the single plantwide factory overhead rate method. Use direct labor hours as the activity base.
2. Determine the factory overhead cost per unit for Products K, L, and M under activity-based costing.
3. Which method provides more accurate product costing? Why?

Solution

1. Single plantwide factory overhead rate $= \dfrac{\$1,400,000}{175,000 \text{ direct labor hours}}$

$= \$8$ per direct labor hour

Factory overhead cost per unit:

	Product K	Product L	Product M
Number of direct labor hours	25,000	10,000	140,000
Single plantwide factory overhead rate	× $8/dlh	× $8/dlh	× $8/dlh
Total factory overhead	$200,000	$ 80,000	$1,120,000
Number of units	÷ 10,000	÷ 2,000	÷ 50,000
Cost per unit	$ 20.00	$ 40.00	$ 22.40

2. Under activity-based costing, an activity rate must be determined for each activity pool:

Activity	Activity Cost Pool Budget	÷	Estimated Activity Base	=	Activity Rate
Setup	$428,750	÷	125 setups	=	$3,430 per setup
Production control	$245,000	÷	125 production orders	=	$1,960 per production order

Activity	Activity Cost Pool Budget	÷	Estimated Activity Base	=	Activity Rate
Quality control	$183,750	÷	75 inspections	=	$2,450 per inspection
Materials management	$367,500	÷	750 requisitions	=	$490 per requisition
Production	$175,000	÷	175,000 direct labor hours	=	$1 per direct labor hour

These activity rates can be used to determine the activity-based factory overhead cost per unit as follows:

Product K

Activity	Activity-Base Usage	×	Activity Rate	=	Activity Cost
Setup	80 setups	×	$3,430	=	$274,400
Production control	80 production orders	×	1,960	=	156,800
Quality control	35 inspections	×	2,450	=	85,750
Materials management	320 requisitions	×	490	=	156,800
Production	25,000 direct labor hrs.	×	1	=	25,000
Total factory overhead					$698,750
Unit volume					÷ 10,000
Factory overhead cost per unit					$ 69.88

Product L

Activity	Activity-Base Usage	×	Activity Rate	=	Activity Cost
Setup	40 setups	×	$3,430	=	$137,200
Production control	40 production orders	×	1,960	=	78,400
Quality control	40 inspections	×	2,450	=	98,000
Materials management	400 requisitions	×	490	=	196,000
Production	10,000 direct labor hrs.	×	1	=	10,000
Total factory overhead					$519,600
Unit volume					÷ 2,000
Factory overhead cost per unit					$ 259.80

Product M

Activity	Activity-Base Usage	×	Activity Rate	=	Activity Cost
Setup	5 setups	×	$3,430	=	$ 17,150
Production control	5 production orders	×	1,960	=	9,800
Quality control	0 inspections	×	2,450	=	0
Materials management	30 requisitions	×	490	=	14,700
Production	140,000 direct labor hrs.	×	1	=	140,000
Total factory overhead					$181,650
Unit volume					÷ 50,000
Factory overhead cost per unit					$ 3.63

3. Activity-based costing is more accurate, compared to the single plantwide factory overhead rate method. Activity-based costing properly shows that Product M is actually less expensive to make, while the other two products are more expensive to make. The reason is that the single plantwide factory overhead rate method fails to account for activity costs correctly. The setup, production control, quality control, and materials management activities are all performed on products in rates that are different from their volumes. For example, Product L requires many of these activities relative to its actual unit volume. Product L requires 40 setups over a volume of 2,000 units (average production run size = 50 units), while Product M has only 5 setups over 50,000 units (average production run size = 10,000 units). Thus, Product L requires greater support costs relative to Product M.

Product M requires minimum activity support because it is scheduled in large batches and requires no inspections (has high quality) and few requisitions. The other two products exhibit the opposite characteristics.

Self-Examination Questions (Answers at End of Chapter)

1. Which of the following statements is most accurate?
   A. The single plantwide factory overhead rate method will usually provide management with accurate product costs.
   B. Activity-based costing can be used by management to determine accurate profitability for each product.
   C. The multiple production department factory overhead rate method will usually result in more product cost distortion than the single plantwide factory overhead rate method.
   D. Generally accepted accounting principles require activity-based costing methods for inventory valuation.

2. San Madeo Company had the following factory overhead costs:

Power	$120,000
Indirect labor	60,000
Equipment depreciation	500,000

   The factory is budgeted to work 20,000 direct labor hours in the upcoming period. San Madeo uses a single plantwide factory overhead rate based on direct labor hours. What is the overhead cost per unit associated with Product M, if Product M uses 6 direct labor hours per unit in the factory?
   A. $34   C. $204
   B. $54   D. $150

3. Which of the following activity bases would best be used to allocate setup activity to products?
   A. Number of inspections
   B. Direct labor hours
   C. Direct machine hours
   D. Number of production runs

4. Production Department 1 (PD1) and Production Department 2 (PD2) had factory overhead budgets of $26,000 and $48,000, respectively. Each department was budgeted for 5,000 direct labor hours of production activity. Product T required 5 direct labor hours in PD1 and 2 direct labor hours in PD2. What is the factory overhead cost associated with a unit of Product T, assuming that factory overhead is allocated using the multiple production department rate method?
   A. $26.00   C. $45.20
   B. $40.40   D. $58.40

5. The following activity rates are associated with moving rail cars by train:
   $4 per gross ton mile
   $50 per rail car switch
   $200 per rail car

   A train with 20 rail cars traveled 100 miles. Each rail car carried 10 tons of product. Each rail car was switched 2 times. What is the total cost of moving this train?
   A. $5,400   C. $44,100
   B. $10,000   D. $86,000

Class Discussion Questions

1. How does a company use product costing?
2. Why would it be appropriate for a company that builds aircraft carriers for the Navy to use a single overhead rate?
3. Why would management be concerned about the accuracy of product costs?
4. Why is the sum of product costs under alternative factory overhead cost allocation methods equal?
5. Why would a manufacturing company with multiple production departments still prefer to use a single plantwide overhead rate?
6. How do the multiple production department and the single plantwide factory overhead rate methods differ?
7. How are multiple production department factory overhead rates determined?
8. How is the allocation base for a production department selected?
9. Under what two conditions would the multiple production department factory overhead rate method provide more accurate product costs than the single plantwide factory overhead rate method?

10. How does activity-based costing differ from the multiple production department factory overhead rate method?

11. Shipping, selling, marketing, sales order processing, return processing, and advertising activities can be related to products by using activity-based costing. Would allocating these activities to products for financial statement reporting be acceptable according to GAAP?

12. What would happen to net income if the activities noted in Question 11 were allocated to products for financial statement reporting and the inventory increased?

13. Under what circumstances might the activity-based costing method provide more accurate product costs than the multiple production department factory overhead rate method?

14. When might activity-based costing be preferred over using a relative amount of product sales in allocating selling and administrative expenses to products?

15. How can activity-based costing be used in service companies?

16. How would a telecommunications company use activity-based costing in conducting profit analysis?

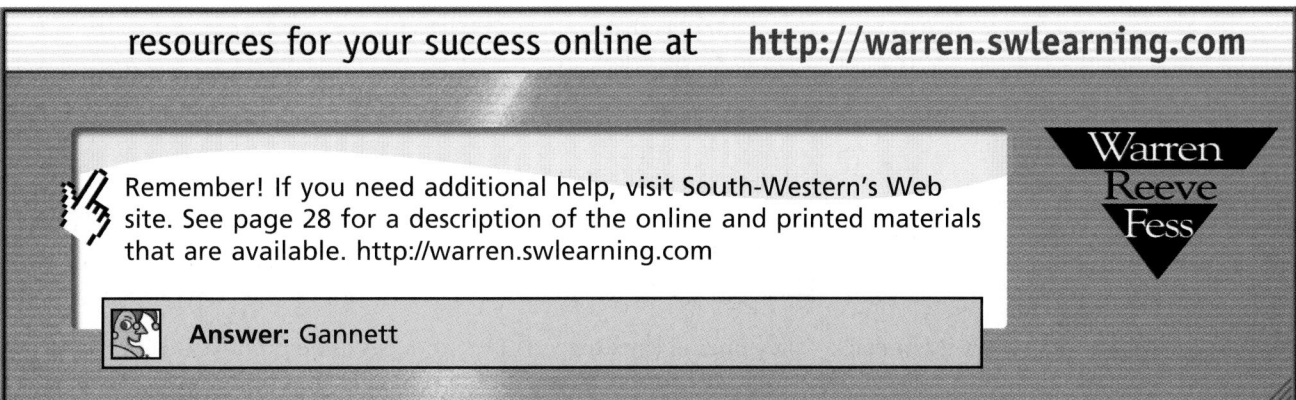

Remember! If you need additional help, visit South-Western's Web site. See page 28 for a description of the online and printed materials that are available. http://warren.swlearning.com

Answer: Gannett

Exercises

EXERCISE 25-1
Single plantwide factory overhead rate
Objective 2

Spacely Company's Fabrication Department incurred $125,000 of factory overhead cost in producing gears and sprockets. The two products consumed a total of 4,000 direct machine hours. Of that amount, sprockets consumed 1,800 direct machine hours.

Determine the total amount of factory overhead that should be allocated to sprockets.

EXERCISE 25-2
Single plantwide factory overhead rate
Objective 2

SPREADSHEET

✓ a. $28 per direct labor hour

Brass Tones Inc. makes three musical instruments: trumpets, tubas, and trombones. The budgeted factory overhead cost is $140,840. Factory overhead is allocated to the three products on the basis of direct labor hours. The products have the following budgeted production volume and direct labor hours per unit:

	Budgeted Production Volume	Direct Labor Hours per Unit
Trumpets	2,400 units	0.8
Tubas	900	1.5
Trombones	1,600	1.1

a. Determine the single plantwide factory overhead rate.

b. Use the factory overhead rate in (a) to determine the amount of total and per unit factory overhead allocated to each of the three products.

EXERCISE 25-3
Single plantwide factory overhead rate

Objective 2

SPREADSHEET

✓ a. $67 per processing hour

Salty-Snack Food Company manufactures three types of snack foods: tortilla chips, potato chips and pretzels. The company has budgeted the following costs for the upcoming period:

Factory depreciation	$102,500
Indirect labor	333,300
Factory electricity	32,400
Indirect materials	61,100
Selling expenses	170,000
Administrative expenses	90,700
Total costs	$790,000

Factory overhead is allocated to the three products on the basis of processing hours. The products had the following production budget and processing hours per case:

	Budgeted Production Volume (Cases)	Processing Hours per Case
Tortilla chips	15,000	0.12
Potato chips	32,000	0.15
Pretzels	13,000	0.10
Total	60,000	

a. Determine the single plantwide factory overhead rate.
b. Use the factory overhead rate in (a) to determine the amount of total and per case factory overhead allocated to each of the three products under generally accepted accounting principles.

EXERCISE 25-4
Product costs and product profitability reports, using a single plantwide factory overhead rate

Objective 2

SPREADSHEET

✓ c. Pistons gross profit, $50,400

Merrimack Valley Engine Parts Inc. (MVEP) produces three products—pistons, valves, and cams—for the heavy equipment industry. MVEP has a very simple production process and product line and uses a single plantwide factory overhead rate to allocate overhead to the three products. The factory overhead rate is based on direct labor hours. Information about the three products is as follows:

	Budgeted Volume (Units)	Direct Labor Hours per Unit	Price per Unit	Direct Materials per Unit
Pistons	4,000	0.20	$48.00	$24.50
Valves	16,000	0.14	15.80	5.80
Cams	1,000	0.12	38.75	16.40

The estimated direct labor rate is $24 per direct labor hour. There are no beginning or ending inventories. The budgeted factory overhead for MVEP is $96,380.

a. Determine the plantwide factory overhead rate.
b. Determine the factory overhead and direct labor cost per unit for each product.
c. Use the information above to construct a budgeted gross profit report by product line. Include the gross profit as a percent of sales in the last line of your report.
d. ▬▬▶ What does the report in (c) indicate to you?

EXERCISE 25-5
Multiple production department factory overhead rate method

Objective 3

SPREADSHEET

Duluth Glove Company produces three types of gloves: small, medium, and large. A glove pattern is first stenciled onto leather in the Pattern Department. The stenciled patterns are then sent to the Cut and Sew Department, where the final glove is cut and sewed together. Duluth uses the multiple production department factory overhead rate method of allocating factory overhead costs. Its factory overhead costs were budgeted as follows:

Pattern Department overhead	$ 80,000
Cut and Sew Department overhead	320,000
Total	$400,000

The direct labor estimated for each production department was as follows:

Pattern Department	2,500 direct labor hours
Cut and Sew Department	4,000
Total	6,500 direct labor hours

Direct labor is used to allocate the production department overhead to the products. The direct labor hours per unit for each product for each production department were obtained from the engineering records as follows:

Production Departments	Small Glove	Medium Glove	Large Glove
Pattern Department	0.02	0.04	0.08
Cut and Sew Department	0.05	0.06	0.08
Direct labor hours per unit	0.07	0.10	0.16

a. Determine the two production department factory overhead rates.
b. Use the two production department factory overhead rates to determine the factory overhead per unit for each product.

EXERCISE 25-6
Single plantwide and multiple production department factory overhead rate methods and product cost distortion

Objectives 2, 3

✓ b. Portable computer, $420 per unit

Peach Computer Company manufactures a desktop and portable computer through two production departments, Assembly and Testing. Presently, the company uses a single plantwide factory overhead rate for allocating factory overhead to the two products. However, management is considering using the multiple production department factory overhead rate method. The following factory overhead was budgeted for Peach:

Assembly Department	$ 360,000
Testing Department	690,000
Total	$1,050,000

Direct machine hours were estimated as follows:

Assembly Department	3,000 hours
Testing Department	2,000
Total	5,000 hours

In addition, the direct machine hours (dmh) used to produce a unit of each product in each department were determined from engineering records, as follows:

	Desktop	Portable
Assembly Department	0.75 dmh	1.20 dmh
Testing Department	0.50	0.80
Total machine hours per unit	1.25 dmh	2.00 dmh

a. Determine the per unit factory overhead allocated to the desktop and portable computers under the single plantwide factory overhead rate method, using direct machine hours as the allocation base.
b. Determine the per unit factory overhead allocated to the desktop and portable computers under the multiple production department factory overhead rate method, using direct machine hours as the allocation base for each department.
c. ▆▆▆▶ Recommend to management a product costing approach, based on your analyses in (a) and (b). Support your recommendation.

EXERCISE 25-7
Single plantwide and multiple production department factory overhead rate methods and product cost distortion

Objectives 2, 3

The management of Saginaw Engines Inc. manufactures gasoline and diesel engines through two production departments, Fabrication and Assembly. Management needs accurate product cost information in order to guide product strategy. Presently, the company uses a single plantwide factory overhead rate for allocating factory overhead to the two products. However, management is considering using the multiple production department factory overhead rate method. The following factory overhead was budgeted for Saginaw:

✔ *b. Diesel engine, $653 per unit*

Fabrication Department factory overhead	$570,000
Assembly Department factory overhead	249,000
Total	$819,000

Direct labor hours were estimated as follows:

Fabrication Department	3,000 hours
Assembly Department	3,000
Total	6,000 hours

In addition, the direct labor hours (dlh) used to produce a unit of each product in each department were determined from engineering records, as follows:

Production Departments	Gasoline Engine	Diesel Engine
Fabrication Department	1 dlh	3 dlh
Assembly Department	3	1
Direct labor hours per unit	4 dlh	4 dlh

a. Determine the per unit factory overhead allocated to the gasoline and diesel engines under the single plantwide factory overhead rate method, using direct labor hours as the activity base.
b. Determine the per unit factory overhead allocated to the gasoline and diesel engines under the multiple production department factory overhead rate method, using direct labor hours as the activity base for each department.
c. ▬▬▶ Recommend to management a product costing approach, based on your analyses in (a) and (b). Support your recommendation.

EXERCISE 25-8
Identifying activity bases in an activity-based cost system

Objective 4

Quantum Systems Inc. uses activity-based costing to determine product costs. For each activity listed in the left column, match an appropriate activity base from the right column. You may use items in the activity base list more than once or not at all.

Activity	Activity Base
Customer return processing	Engineering change orders
Electric power	Kilowatt-hours used
Human resources	Number of customer orders
Invoice and collecting	Number of customer returns
Machine depreciation	Number of customers
Materials handling	Number of direct labor hours
Order shipping	Number of inspections
Payroll	Number of machine hours
Production control	Number of material moves
Production setup	Number of payroll checks processed
Purchasing	Number of production orders
Quality control	Number of purchase orders
	Number of setups

EXERCISE 25-9
Product costs using activity rates

Objective 4

✔ *b. $45,500*

Net Gift Registry Inc. sells china and flatware over the Internet. For the next period, the budgeted cost of the sales order processing activity is $99,400, and 14,200 sales orders are estimated to be processed.

a. Determine the activity rate of the sales order processing activity.
b. Determine the amount of sales order processing cost that china would receive if it had 6,500 sales orders.

EXERCISE 25-10
Product costs using activity rates

Objective 4

Cardio Max Equipment Company manufactures stationary bicycles and rowing machines. The products are produced in its Fabrication and Assembly production departments. In addition to production activities, several other activities are required to produce the two products. These activities and their associated activity rates are as follows:

✓ *Rowing machine activity cost per unit, $47.36*

Activity	Activity Rate
Fabrication	$25 per machine hour
Assembly	$8 per direct labor hour
Setup	$50 per setup
Inspecting	$24 per inspection
Production scheduling	$15 per production order
Purchasing	$10 per purchase order

The activity-base usage quantities and units produced for each product were as follows:

Activity Base	Stationary Bicycle	Rowing Machine
Machine hours	1,796	988
Direct labor hours	448	176
Setups	45	16
Inspections	700	400
Production orders	70	12
Purchase orders	180	120
Units produced	800	800

Use the activity rate and usage information to calculate the total activity cost and activity cost per unit for each product.

EXERCISE 25-11
Activity rates and product costs using activity-based costing
Objective 4

✓ *b. Dining room lighting fixtures, $67.50 per unit*

Modern Lighting Inc. manufactures entry and dining room lighting fixtures. Five activities are used in manufacturing the fixtures. These activities and their associated activity cost pools and activity bases are as follows:

Activity	Activity Cost Pool (Budgeted)	Activity Base
Casting	$261,000	Machine hours
Assembly	112,200	Direct labor hours
Inspecting	35,000	Number of inspections
Setup	75,000	Number of setups
Materials handling	34,000	Number of loads

Corporate records were obtained to estimate the amount of activity to be used by the two products. The estimated activity-base usage quantities and units produced are provided in the table below.

Activity Base	Entry	Dining	Total
Machine hours	5,000	4,000	9,000
Direct labor hours	4,100	6,100	10,200
Number of inspections	1,800	700	2,500
Number of setups	220	80	300
Number of loads	750	250	1,000
Units Produced			
Number of units	5,916	3,280	9,196

a. Determine the activity rate for each activity.
b. Use the activity rates in (a) to determine the total and per unit activity costs associated with each product.

EXERCISE 25-12
Activity cost pools, activity rates, and product costs using activity-based costing
Objective 4

Elite Gourmet Inc. is estimating the activity cost associated with producing ovens and refrigerators. The indirect labor can be traced into four separate activity pools, based on time records provided by the employees. The budgeted activity cost and activity base information are provided as follows:

✓ b. Oven, $89.42 per unit

Activity	Activity Pool Cost	Activity Base
Procurement	$150,000	Number of purchase orders
Scheduling	8,400	Number of production orders
Materials handling	37,500	Number of moves
Product development	24,650	Number of engineering changes
Total cost	$220,550	

The estimated activity-base usage and unit information for Elite Gourmet's two product lines was determined from corporate records as follows:

	Number of Purchase Orders	Number of Production Orders	Number of Moves	Number of Engineering Changes	Units
Ovens	700	220	450	130	1,500
Refrigerators	500	130	300	40	2,000
Totals	1,200	350	750	170	3,500

a. Determine the activity rate for each activity cost pool.
b. Determine the activity-based cost per unit of each product.

EXERCISE 25-13
Activity-based costing and product cost distortion

Objectives 2, 4

SPREADSHEET

✓ c. CD, $3.96

Digital Media is considering a change to activity-based product costing. The company produces two products, compact disks (CDs) and data cartridges, in a single production department. The production department is estimated to require 4,000 direct labor hours. The total indirect labor is budgeted to be $480,000.

Time records from indirect labor employees revealed that they spent 35% of their time setting up production runs and 65% of their time supporting actual production.

The following information about CDs and data cartridges was determined from the corporate records:

	Number of Setups	Direct Labor Hours	Units
CDs	400	2,000	50,000
Data cartridges	1,200	2,000	50,000
Total	1,600	4,000	100,000

a. Determine the indirect labor cost per unit allocated to CDs and data cartridges under a single plantwide factory overhead rate system.
b. Determine the activity pools and activity rates for the indirect labor under activity-based costing. Assume two activity pools—one for setup and the other for production support.
c. Determine the activity cost per unit for indirect labor allocated to each product under activity-based costing.
d. ▬▬▶ Why are the per unit allocated costs in (a) different from the per unit activity cost assigned to the products in (c)?

EXERCISE 25-14
Multiple production department factory overhead rate method

Objective 3

SPREADSHEET

✓ b. Blender, $16.02 per unit

Handy Kitchen Appliance Company manufactures small kitchen appliances. The product line consists of blenders and toaster ovens. Handy Kitchen presently uses the multiple production department factory overhead rate method. The factory overhead is as follows:

Assembly Department	$205,000
Test and Pack Department	135,000
Total	$340,000

The direct labor information for the production of 10,000 units of each product is as follows:

	Assembly Department	Test and Pack Department
Blender	450 dlh	800 dlh
Toaster oven	800	450
Total	1,250 dlh	1,250 dlh

Handy Kitchen used direct labor hours to allocate production department factory overhead to products.

a. Determine the two production department factory overhead rates.
b. Determine the total factory overhead and the factory overhead per unit allocated to each product.

EXERCISE 25-15
Activity-based costing and product cost distortion

Objective 4

SPREADSHEET

✓ *b. Blender, $18.27 per unit*

The management of Handy Kitchen Appliance Company in Exercise 25-14 has asked you to use activity-based costing to allocate factory overhead costs to the two products. You have determined that $60,000 of factory overhead from each of the production departments can be associated with setup activity ($120,000 in total). Company records indicate that blenders required 275 setups, while the toaster ovens required only 125 setups. Each product has a production volume of 10,000 units.

a. Determine the three activity rates (assembly, test and pack, and setup).
b. Determine the total factory overhead and factory overhead per unit allocated to each product.

EXERCISE 25-16
Single plantwide rate and activity-based costing

Objectives 2, 4

REAL WORLD   SPREADSHEET

✓ *a. Low, Col. C., 103.15%*

Whirlpool Corporation conducted an activity-based costing study of its Evansville, Indiana plant in order to identify its most profitable products. Assume that we select three representative refrigerators (out of 333): one low-, one medium-, and one high-volume refrigerator. Additionally, we assume the following activity-base information for each of the three refrigerators:

Three Representative Refrigerators	Number of Machine Hours	Number of Setups	Number of Sales Orders	Number of Units
Refrigerator—Low Volume	25	18	42	120
Refrigerator—Medium Volume	297	20	150	1,400
Refrigerator—High Volume	860	10	120	4,300

Prior to conducting the study, the factory overhead allocation was based on a single machine hour rate. The machine hour rate was $280 per hour. After conducting the activity-based costing study, assume that three activities were used to allocate the factory overhead. The new activity rate information is assumed to be as follows:

	Machining Activity	Setup Activity	Sales Order Processing Activity
Activity rate	$180	$400	$60

a. Complete the following table, using the single machine hour rate to determine the per unit factory overhead for each refrigerator (Column A) and the three activity-based rates to determine the activity-based factory overhead per unit (Column B). Finally, compute the percent change in per unit allocation from the single to activity-based rate methods (Column C). Round to two decimal places.

	Column A	Column B	Column C
Product Volume Class	Single Rate Overhead Allocation per Unit	ABC Overhead Allocation per Unit	Percent Change in Allocation (Col. B − Col. A)/Col. A
Low			
Medium			
High			

b. ▅▅▅► Why is the traditional overhead rate per machine hour greater under the single rate method than under the activity-based method?

c. ▅▅▅► Interpret Column C in your table from part (a).

EXERCISE 25-17
Evaluating selling and administrative cost allocations

Objective 5

WHAT'S WRONG WITH THIS?

Zeeland Furniture Company has two major product lines with the following characteristics:

Commercial office furniture: Few large orders, little advertising support, shipments in full truckloads, and low handling complexity

Home office furniture: Many small orders, large advertising support, shipments in partial truckloads, and high handling complexity

The company produced the following profitability report for management:

Zeeland Furniture Company
Product Profitability Report
For the Year Ended December 31, 2006

	Commercial Office Furniture	Home Office Furniture	Total
Revenue	$2,400,000	$1,200,000	$3,600,000
Cost of goods sold	1,500,000	700,000	2,200,000
Gross profit	$ 900,000	$ 500,000	$1,400,000
Selling and administrative expenses	600,000	300,000	900,000
Income from operations	$ 300,000	$ 200,000	$ 500,000

The selling and administrative expenses are allocated to the products on the basis of relative sales dollars.

▅▅▅► Evaluate the accuracy of this report and recommend an alternative approach.

EXERCISE 25-18
Construct and interpret a product profitability report, allocating selling and administrative expenses

Objective 5

SPREADSHEET

✓ *b. Generators operating profit-to-sales, 22%*

Power Serve Equipment Company manufactures power equipment. Power Serve has two primary products—generators and air compressors. The following report was prepared by the controller for Power Serve's senior marketing management:

	Generators	Air Compressors	Total
Revenue	$1,800,000	$950,000	$2,750,000
Cost of goods sold	1,350,000	712,500	2,062,500
Gross profit	$ 450,000	$237,500	$ 687,500
Selling and administrative expenses			253,500
Income from operations			$ 434,000

The marketing management team was concerned that the selling and administrative expenses were not traced to the products. Marketing management believed that some products consumed larger amounts of selling and administrative expense than did other products. To verify this, the controller was asked to prepare a complete product profitability report, using activity-based costing.

The controller determined that selling and administrative expenses consisted of two activities: sales order processing and post-sale customer service. The controller was able to determine the activity base and activity rate for each activity, as shown below.

Activity	Activity Base	Activity Rate
Sales order processing	Sales orders	$ 90 per sales order
Post-sale customer service	Service requests	$300 per customer service request

The controller determined the following additional information about each product:

	Generators	Air Compressors
Number of sales orders	300	800
Number of service requests	90	425

a. Determine the activity cost of each product for sales order processing and post-sale customer service activities.
b. Use the information in (a) to prepare a complete product profitability report. Calculate the gross profit to sales and the income from operations to sales percentages for each product.
c.  Interpret the product profitability report. How should management respond to the report?

EXERCISE 25-19
Activity-based costing and customer profitability

Objective 6

REAL WORLD   SPREADSHEET

✓ *a. Customer 1, $2,615*

Square D Corporation manufactures power distribution equipment for commercial customers, such as hospitals and manufacturers. Activity-based costing was used to determine customer profitability. Customer service activities were assigned to individual customers, using the following assumed customer service activities, activity base, and activity rate:

Customer Service Activity	Activity Base	Activity Rate
Bid preparation	Number of bid requests	$145/request
Shipment	Number of shipments	$28/shipment
Support standard items	Number of standard items ordered	$45/std. item
Support nonstandard items	Number of nonstandard items ordered	110/nonstd. item

Assume that the company had the following gross profit information for three representative customers:

	Customer 1	Customer 2	Customer 3
Revenue	$18,500	$27,750	$40,000
Cost of goods sold	10,175	14,430	24,000
Gross profit	$ 8,325	$13,320	$16,000
Gross profit as a percent of sales	45%	48%	40%

The administrative records indicated that the activity-base usage quantities for each customer were as follows:

Activity Base	Customer 1	Customer 2	Customer 3
Number of bid requests	8	18	5
Number of shipments	20	36	18
Number of standard items ordered	30	45	50
Number of nonstandard items ordered	24	55	12

a. Prepare a customer profitability report showing (1) the income from operations after customer service activities and (2) the income from operations after customer service activities as a percent of sales. Prepare the report with a column for each customer. Round percentages to the nearest whole percent.
b.  Interpret the table in part (a).

EXERCISE 25-20
Activity-based costing for a hospital

Objective 6

SPREADSHEET

✓ *a. Patient M, $6,210*

Memorial Hospital plans to use activity-based costing to assign hospital indirect costs to the care of patients. The hospital has identified the following activities and activity rates for the hospital indirect costs:

Activity	Activity Rate
Room and meals	$175 per day
Radiology	$280 per image
Pharmacy	$35 per physician order
Chemistry lab	$90 per test
Operating room	$700 per operating room hour

The records of two representative patients were analyzed, using the activity rates. The activity information associated with the two patients is as follows:

	Patient M	Patient T
Number of days	7 days	3 days
Number of images	4 images	2 images
Number of physician orders	5 orders	1 order
Number of tests	6 tests	2 tests
Number of operating room hours	4.5 hours	1 hour

a. Determine the activity cost associated with each patient.
b. ▣▬▶ Why is the total activity cost different for the two patients?

EXERCISE 25-21
Activity-based costing in an insurance company

Objectives 5, 6

SPREADSHEET

✓a. Auto, $893,250

Safe Hands Insurance Company carries three major lines of insurance: auto, workers' compensation, and homeowners. The company has prepared the following report for 2007:

Safe Hands Insurance Company
Product Profitability Report
For the Year Ended December 31, 2007

	Auto	Workers' Comp.	Homeowners
Premium revenue	$5,000,000	$4,000,000	$6,000,000
Less estimated claims	3,250,000	2,600,000	3,900,000
Underwriting income	$1,750,000	$1,400,000	$2,100,000
Underwriting income as a percent of premium revenue	35%	35%	35%

Management is concerned that the administrative expenses may make some of the insurance lines unprofitable. However, the administrative expenses have not been allocated to the insurance lines. The controller has suggested that the administrative expenses could be assigned to the insurance lines, using activity-based costing. The administrative expenses are comprised of five activities. The activities and their rates are as follows:

	Activity Rates
New policy processing	$180 per new policy
Cancellation processing	$290 per cancellation
Claim audits	$580 per claim audit
Claim disbursements processing	$125 per disbursement
Premium collection processing	$40 per premium collected

Activity-base usage data for each line of insurance was retrieved from the corporate records and is shown below.

	Auto	Workers' Comp.	Homeowners
Number of new policies	1,100	1,200	2,600
Number of canceled policies	450	150	1,350
Number of audited claims	325	110	720
Number of claim disbursements	350	140	750
Number of premiums collected	7,400	1,200	12,000

a. Complete the product profitability report through the administrative activities. Determine the income from operations as a percent of premium revenue, rounded to one decimal place.
b. ▣▬▶ Interpret the report.

Problems Series A

PROBLEM 25-1A

Single plantwide factory overhead rate

Objective 2

✓*1. b. $240 per machine hour*

Comfort Farms Dairy Company manufactures three products—whole milk, skim milk, and cream—in two production departments, Blending and Packing. The factory overhead for Comfort Farms is $672,000.

The three products consume both machine hours and direct labor hours in the two production departments as follows:

	Direct Labor Hours	Machine Hours
Blending Department		
Whole milk	200	800
Skim milk	240	750
Cream	60	250
	500	1,800
Packing Department		
Whole milk	460	400
Skim milk	520	450
Cream	120	150
	1,100	1,000
Total	1,600	2,800

Instructions

1. Determine the single plantwide factory overhead rate, using each of the following allocation bases: (a) direct labor hours and (b) machine hours.
2. Determine the product factory overhead costs, using (a) the direct labor hour plantwide factory overhead rate and (b) the machine hour plantwide factory overhead rate.

PROBLEM 25-2A

Multiple production department factory overhead rates

Objective 3

✓*2. Cream, $89,400*

The management of Comfort Farms Dairy, described in Problem 25-1A, now plans to use the multiple production department factory overhead rate method. The total factory overhead associated with each department is as follows:

Blending Department	$540,000
Packing Department	132,000
Total	$672,000

Instructions

1. Determine the multiple production department factory overhead rates, using machine hours for the Blending Department and direct labor hours for the Packing Department.
2. Determine the product factory overhead costs, using the multiple production department rates in (1).

PROBLEM 25-3A

Activity-based and department rate product costing and product cost distortions

Objectives 3, 4

SPREADSHEET

✓*4. CD players, $490,720 and $61.34*

Real Audio Inc. manufactures two products, receivers and CD players. The factory overhead incurred is as follows:

Indirect labor	$ 560,000
Subassembly Department	440,000
Final Assembly Department	340,000
Total	$1,340,000

The activity base associated with the two production departments is direct labor hours. The indirect labor can be assigned to two different activities as follows:

During a portion of the year, Mercy collected patient information for three selected procedures, as shown below.

	Activity-Base Usage
Procedure A	
Number of patients	200
Average length of stay	× 6 days
Patient days	1,200
Weighted care units	16,000
Procedure B	
Number of patients	400
Average length of stay	× 2 days
Patient days	800
Weighted care units	4,200
Procedure C	
Number of patients	800
Average length of stay	× 3 days
Patient days	2,400
Weighted care units	25,000

Private insurance reimburses the hospital for these activities at a fixed daily rate of $300 per patient day for all three procedures.

Instructions
1. Determine the activity rates.
2. Determine the activity cost for each procedure.
3. Determine the excess or deficiency of reimbursements over activity cost.
4.  Interpret your results.

Special Activities

ACTIVITY 25-1
Ethics and professional conduct in business

ETHICS

The controller of Summit Systems Inc. devised a new costing system based on tracing the cost of activities to products. The controller was able to measure post-manufacturing activities, such as selling, promotional, and distribution activities, and allocate these activities to products in order to have a more complete view of the company's product costs. This effort produced better strategic information about the relative profitability of product lines. In addition, the controller used the same product cost information for inventory valuation on the financial statements. Surprisingly, the controller discovered that the company's reported net income was larger under this scheme than under the traditional costing approach.

 Why was the net income larger, and how would you react to the controller's action?

ACTIVITY 25-2
Identifying product cost distortion

WHAT DO YOU THINK?

Mr. Fizz Beverage Company manufactures soft drinks. Information about two products is as follows:

	Volume	Sales Price per Case	Gross Profit per Case
Jamaican Punch	10,000 cases	$30	$12
King Kola	800,000 cases	30	12

It is known that both products have the same direct materials and direct labor costs per case. Mr. Fizz allocates factory overhead to products by using a single plantwide factory overhead rate, based on direct labor cost. Additional information about the two products is as follows:

Jamaican Punch: Requires extensive process preparation and sterilization prior to processing. The ingredients are from Jamaica, requiring complex import controls. The formulation is complex, and it is thus difficult to maintain quality. Lastly, the product is sold in small (less than full truckload) orders.

King Kola: Requires minor process preparation and sterilization prior to processing. The ingredients are acquired locally. The formulation is simple, and it is easy to maintain quality. Lastly, the product is sold in large bulk (full truckload) orders.

➤ Explain the product profitability report in light of the additional data.

ACTIVITY 25-3
Activity-based costing

REAL WORLD

Acordia, Inc. is an insurance brokerage company that classified insurance products as either "easy" or "difficult." Easy and difficult products were defined as follows:

Easy: Electronic claims, few inquiries, mature product
Difficult: Paper claims, complex claims to process, many inquiries, a new product with complex options

The company originally allocated processing and service expenses on the basis of revenue. Under this traditional allocation approach, the product profitability report revealed the following:

	Easy Product	Difficult Product	Total
Revenue	$600	$400	$1,000
Processing and service expenses	420	280	700
Income from operations	$180	$120	$ 300
Operating income margin	30%	30%	30%

Acordia decided to use activity-based costing to allocate the processing and service expenses. The following activity-based costing analysis of the same data illustrates a much different profit picture for the two types of products.

	Easy Product	Difficult Product	Total
Revenue	$600	$ 400	$1,000
Processing and service expenses	183	517	700
Income from operations	$417	$(117)	$ 300
Operating income margin	70%	(29%)	30%

➤ Explain why the activity-based profitability report reveals different information from the traditional sales allocation report.

Source: Dan Patras and Kevin Clancy, "ABC in the Service Industry: Product Line Profitability at Acordia, Inc." *As Easy as ABC Newsletter,* Issue 12, Spring 1993.

ACTIVITY 25-4
Using a product profitability report to guide strategic decisions

The controller of Audio Escape Inc. prepared the following product profitability report for management, using activity-based costing methods for allocating both the factory overhead and the marketing expenses. As such, the controller has confidence in the accuracy of this report. In addition, the controller interviewed the vice-president of marketing, who indicated that the floor loudspeakers were an older product that was highly recognized in the marketplace. The ribbon loudspeakers were a new product that was recently launched. The ribbon loudspeakers are a new technology that have no competition in the marketplace, and it is hoped that they will become an important future addition to the company's product portfolio. Initial indications are that the product is well received by customers. The controller believes that the manufacturing costs for all three products are in line with expectations.

	Floor Loudspeakers	Bookshelf Loudspeakers	Ribbon Loudspeakers	Totals
Sales	$8,000,000	$50,000,000	$25,000,000	$83,000,000
Less cost of goods sold	5,400,000	30,000,000	24,000,000	59,400,000
Gross profit	$2,600,000	$20,000,000	$ 1,000,000	$23,600,000
Less marketing expenses	2,800,000	4,000,000	600,000	7,400,000
Income from operations	$ (200,000)	$16,000,000	$ 400,000	$16,200,000

1. Calculate the gross profit and income from operations to sales ratios for each product.
2. ▭▭▭▶ Write a memo using the product profitability report and the calculations in (1) to make recommendations to management with respect to strategies for the three products.

ACTIVITY 25-5
Product cost distortion

Luis Lopez, president of Digital Assistant Inc., was reviewing the product profitability reports with the controller, Yolanda Greene. The following conversation took place:

Luis: I've been reviewing the product profitability reports. Our high-volume calculator, the T-100, appears to be unprofitable, while some of our lower-volume specialty calculators in the T-900 series appear to be very profitable. These results do not make sense to me. How are the product profits determined?

Yolanda: First, we identify the revenues associated with each product line. This information comes directly from our sales order system and is very accurate. Next, we identify the direct materials and direct labor associated with making each of the calculators. Again, this information is very accurate. The final cost that must be considered is the factory overhead. Factory overhead is allocated to the products, based on the direct labor hours used to assemble the calculator.

Luis: What about distribution, promotion, and other post-manufacturing costs that can be associated with the product?

Yolanda: According to generally accepted accounting principles, we expense them in the period that they are incurred and do not treat them as product costs.

Luis: Another thing, you say that you allocate factory overhead according to direct labor hours. Yet I know that the T-900 series specialty products have very low volumes but require extensive engineering, testing, and materials management effort. They are our newer, more complex products. It seems that these sources of factory overhead will end up being allocated to the T-100 line because it is the high-volume and therefore high direct labor hour product. Yet the T-100 line is easy to make and requires very little support from our engineering, testing, and materials management personnel.

Yolanda: I'm not too sure. I do know that our product costing approach is similar to that used by many different types of companies. I don't think we could all be wrong.

▭▭▭▶ Is Lopez's concern valid and how might Greene redesign the cost allocation system to address Lopez's concern?

ACTIVITY 25-6
Allocating bank administrative costs

Banks have a variety of products, such as savings accounts, checking accounts, certificates of deposit (CDs), and loans. Assume that you were assigned the task of determining the administrative costs of "savings accounts" as a complete product line. What are some of the activities associated with savings accounts? In answering this question, consider the activities that you might perform with your savings account. For each activity, what would be an activity base that could be used to allocate the activity cost to the savings account product line?

Answers to Self-Examination Questions

1. **B** Activity-based costing provides accurate product costs, which can be used for strategic product profitability analysis. The single plantwide factory overhead rate method (answer A) can distort the individual product costs under a variety of reasonable conditions. The multiple production department factory overhead rate method will lead to less (not more) distortion than the single plantwide factory overhead rate method (answer C). Generally accepted accounting principles do not require activity-based costing for inventory valuation (answer D).

2. **C** The single plantwide factory overhead rate is $34 per hour (answer A), determined as $680,000 ÷ 20,000 hours. This rate is multiplied by 6 direct labor hours per unit of Product M to determine the correct overhead per unit of $204. The total overhead should be used in the numerator in determining the overhead rate, not just power and indirect labor (answer B) or equipment depreciation (answer D).

3. **D** The number of production runs best relates the activity cost of setup to the products. Number of inspections, direct labor hours, and direct machine hours (answers A , B, and C) will likely have very little logical association with the costs incurred in setting up production runs.

4. **C** PD1 rate: $26,000/5,000 dlh = $5.20 per dlh
   PD2 rate: $48,000/5,000 dlh = $9.60 per dlh
   Product T: (5 dlh × $5.20) + (2 dlh × $9.60) = $45.20

5. **D** (100 miles × 20 cars × 10 tons × $4) + ($200 × 20 cars) + (20 cars × 2 switches × $50) = $80,000 + $4,000 + $2,000 = $86,000

COST MANAGEMENT FOR JUST-IN-TIME ENVIRONMENTS

objectives

After studying this chapter, you should be able to:

1 Compare and contrast just-in-time (JIT) manufacturing practices with traditional manufacturing practices.

2 Apply just-in-time manufacturing practices to a traditional manufacturing illustration.

3 Describe the implications of a just-in-time manufacturing philosophy on cost accounting and performance measurement systems.

4 Apply just-in-time practices to a non-manufacturing setting.

5 Describe and illustrate activity analysis for improving operations.

When you order the salad bar at the local restaurant, you are able to serve yourself at your own pace. There is no waiting for the waitress to take the order or for the cook to prepare the meal. You are able to move directly to the salad bar and select from various offerings. You might wish to have salad with lettuce, cole slaw, bacon bits, croutons, and salad dressing. The offerings are arranged in a row so that you can build your salad as you move down the salad bar.

Many manufacturers are attempting to produce each product directly to customer requirements, in much the same way that the salad bar is designed to satisfy each customer's specific requirements. Like customers at the salad bar, products move through a production process as they are built for each customer's unique needs.

In this chapter, we will discuss the just-in-time philosophy and illustrate the managerial accounting principles and tools used in just-in-time environments. We will then discuss the cost management issues appropriate for the just-in-time environment. We will complete the chapter by discussing and illustrating the accounting for quality costs.

Just-in-Time Principles

<table>
<tr><td>objective</td><td>1</td></tr>
</table>

Compare and contrast just-in-time (JIT) manufacturing practices with traditional manufacturing practices.

The operating methods used by many companies are undergoing significant change. Companies are recognizing the need to produce products and services with high quality, low cost, and instant availability. Achieving these objectives requires a change in the methods of manufacturing products and delivering services. One approach reflecting these changes is the just-in-time philosophy. ***Just-in-time (JIT)***, sometimes called **short-cycle** or **lean manufacturing**, focuses on reducing time, cost, and poor quality within manufacturing and nonmanufacturing processes.

We will first discuss just-in-time principles within a manufacturing setting. Exhibit 1 lists some of the just-in-time manufacturing principles and the traditional manufacturing principles. In the following paragraphs, we briefly discuss each of the just-in-time principles. We will then address the accounting implications of these principles.

•Exhibit 1   Operating Principles of Just-in-Time versus Traditional Manufacturing

Issue	Just-in-Time Manufacturing	Traditional Manufacturing
Inventory	Reduces inventory.	Increases inventory to "buffer" or protect against process problems.
Lead time	Reduces lead time.	Increases lead time as a buffer against uncertainty.
Setup time	Reduces setup time.	Disregards setup time as an improvement priority.
Production layout	Emphasizes product-oriented layout.	Emphasizes process-oriented layout.
Role of the employee	Emphasizes team-oriented employee involvement.	Emphasizes work of individuals, following manager instructions.
Production scheduling policy	Emphasizes pull manufacturing.	Emphasizes push manufacturing.
Quality	Emphasizes zero defects.	Tolerates defects.
Suppliers	Emphasizes supplier partnering.	Treats suppliers as "arm's-length," independent entities.

Reducing Inventory

Supporters of just-in-time manufacturing view inventory as wasteful and unnecessary. They argue that inventory may hide underlying production problems. For example, they point out that inventory is often used to maintain sales and production levels during various production interruptions, such as machine breakdowns, manufacturing schedule changes, transportation delays, and unexpected scrap and rework. An important focus in just-in-time manufacturing is to remove these production problems so that the materials, work in process, and finished goods inventory levels can be reduced or eliminated.

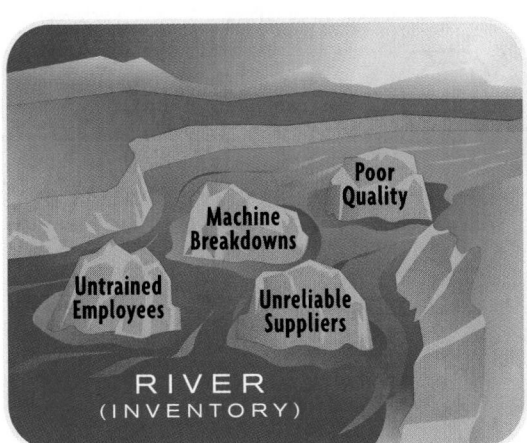

The role of inventory can be explained by referring to a river. Inventory is the water in a river, while the rocks at the bottom of the river are the production problems. When the water level is high, all the rocks at the bottom of the river are hidden. That is, inventory hides the production problems. However, as the water level drops, the rocks become exposed, one by one. Reducing inventory reveals production problems. Once these problems are fixed, the "water level" can be reduced even further to expose more "rocks" for elimination until an efficient, effective production process is achieved.

INTEGRITY IN BUSINESS

THE INVENTORY SHIFT

Some managers take a short-cut to reducing inventory by shifting inventory to their suppliers. With this tactic, the hard work of improving processes is avoided. Enlightened managers realize that such tactics often have short-lived savings. Suppliers will eventually increase their prices to compensate for the additional inventory holding costs, thus resulting in no savings.

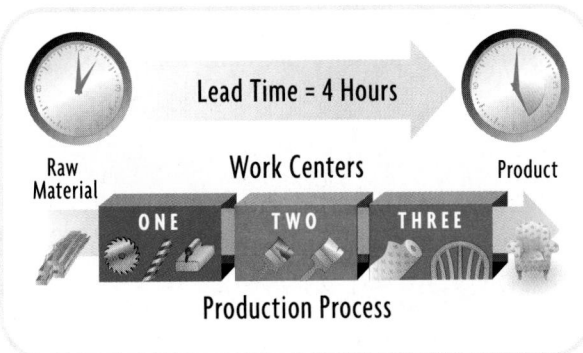

Reducing Lead Times

Lead time, sometimes called **throughput time**, is a measure of the time that elapses between starting a unit of product into the beginning of a process and completing the unit of product. As shown in the illustration, if a product begins the process at 1:00 P.M. and is completed at 5:00 P.M., the lead time is four hours.

Reducing lead times can be an objective for products manufactured in the plant or any other item that is produced through a process. For example, lead times could be reduced for processing sales orders, invoices, insurance applications, or hospital patients.

The total lead time can be divided into value-added and nonvalue-added time portions, as shown in Exhibit 2. *Value-added lead time* is the time required to actually manufacture a unit of a product. It is the conversion time for a unit. For example, value-added lead time would include the time to drill and pack parts for shipment. The *value-added ratio* is the ratio of the value-added lead time to the total lead time. *Nonvalue-added lead time* is the time that a unit of product sits in inventories or moves unnecessarily. Nonvalue-added lead time occurs in poor production processes. In a well-functioning process, the product should spend very little time waiting in inventory, because inventory is at a minimum. The product should also spend little time moving, because operations are sequenced closely.

•**Exhibit 2**

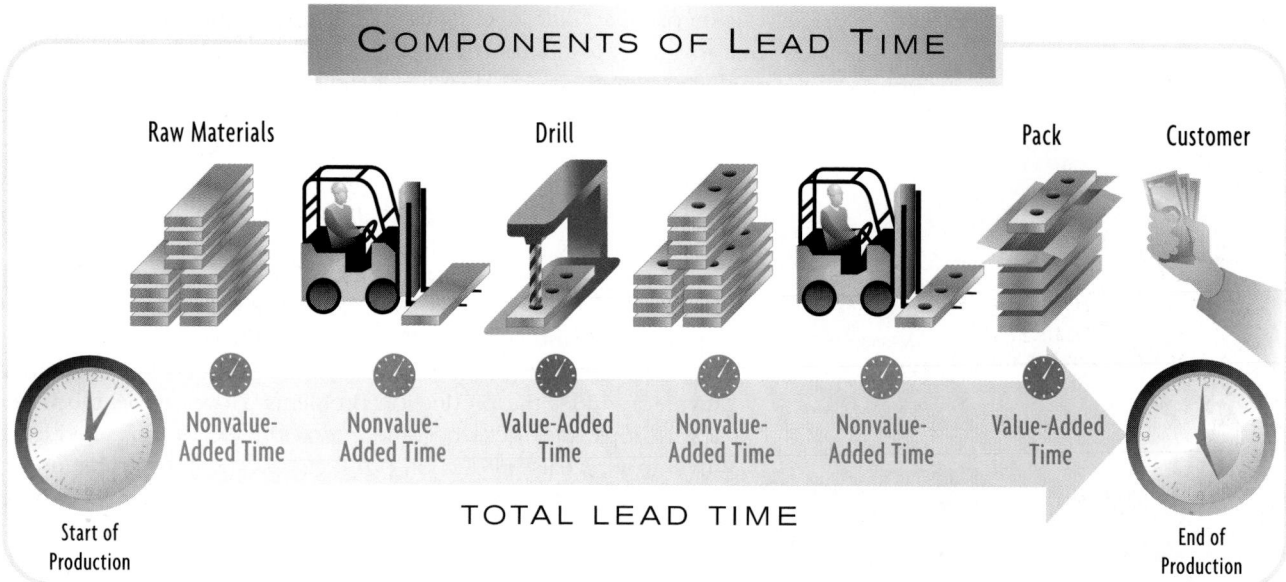

COMPONENTS OF LEAD TIME

Just-in-time concepts have allowed **Boeing Company** to slash the time it takes to deliver a commercial plane from 1½ years to 10 months.

Just-in-time manufacturing attempts to make the nonvalue-added lead time very short, thereby reducing the cost and improving the speed of production. Reducing nonvalue-added lead time is often directly related to reducing inventory. Organizations that use many work in process inventory locations may discover that the value-added ratio can be as little as 5% of the total lead time.

Reducing Setup Time

As we introduced in the previous chapter, a *setup* is the effort required to prepare an operation for a new production run. For example, a beverage company's bottling line would need to be cleaned between flavor changes. If setups are long and expensive, the production run (*batch*) must be large in order to recover the setup cost. Large batches increase inventory, and larger inventories add to lead time. Exhibit 3 is a diagram of the relationship between setup times and lead time.

•**Exhibit 3**

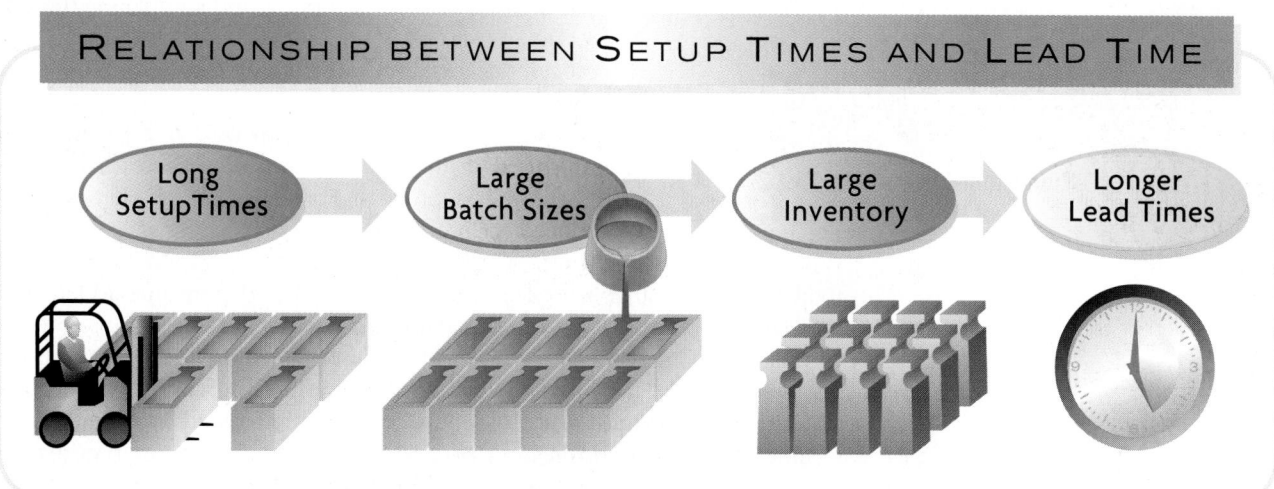

RELATIONSHIP BETWEEN SETUP TIMES AND LEAD TIME

Exhibit 4 illustrates the impact of batch sizes on lead times, using a product that is manufactured in two identical processes (X and Y) that require three operations

•Exhibit 4   **Impact of Batch Sizes on Lead Times**

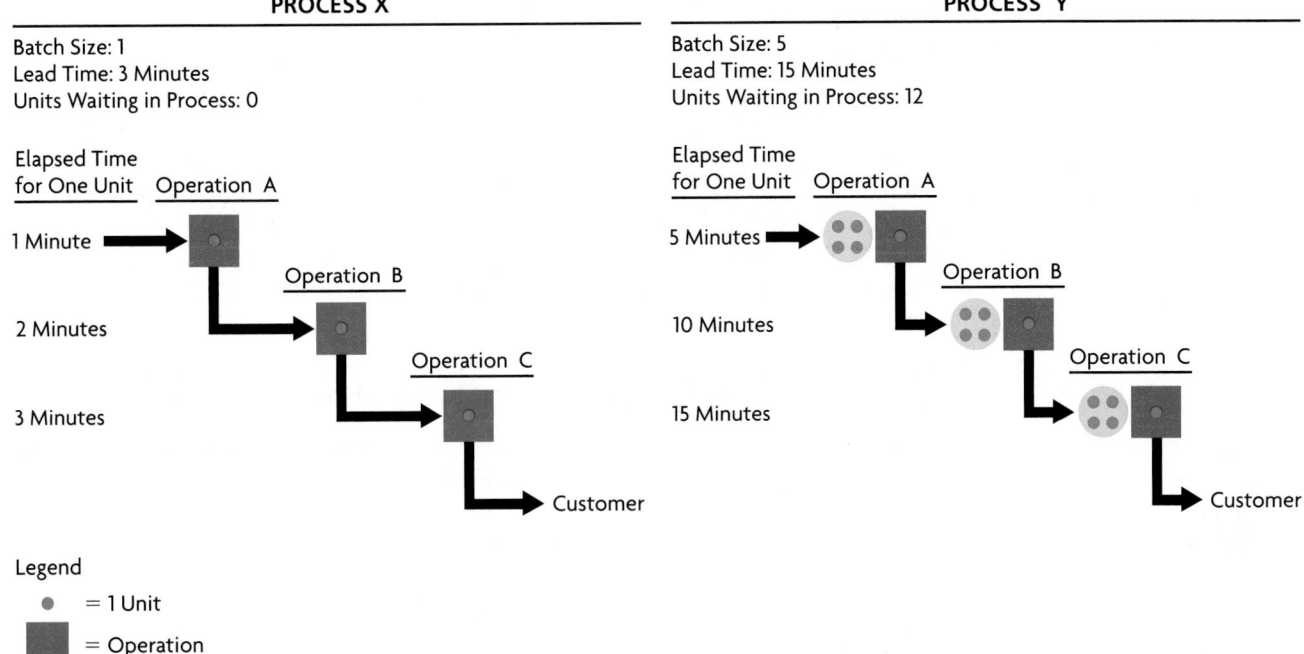

Legend

- ● = 1 Unit
- ■ = Operation
- ● = Waiting in Process

REAL WORLD

Tech Industries required five hours and 84 separate steps to set up a large injection molding machine. A videotape of the setup showed that the operator climbed a ladder to the top of the machine 35 times, walked around the machine 37 times, and left the area for tools 12 times, for over 3,000 yards of walking. The improvement team reorganized the setup so that the operator climbed the machine only seven times, walked around the machine 12 times, and never left the area for tools. These improvements reduced the number of process steps from 84 to 19 and the setup time from five hours to one hour.

in each process in the order of A, B, and C. The product requires one minute of processing inside each operation. In Process X, the batch size is one unit, while in Process Y, the batch size is five units. Process X has only three units in process—one unit being produced in each of three operations. The lead time for any particular unit in Process X is three minutes, while for Process Y, it is 15 minutes. In Process Y, three units are being produced in the operating departments, while the other 12 are stored as work in process inventory. Each unit waits its "turn" while other units in the batch are being processed. At each operation, one unit takes five minutes to complete the operation—four minutes waiting its "turn" and one minute in production. The four minutes that each part "waits its turn" at each operation is called *within-batch wait time.* Of the 15 minutes total lead time, 12 minutes represents the within-batch wait time for all three operations (3 operations × 4 minutes). Thus, 80% (12 minutes ÷ 15 minutes) of the lead time in Process Y is nonvalue-added.

Organizations that use just-in-time practices try to reduce setup times to reduce the batch size. Once batch sizes are reduced, the work in process inventory and wait time are reduced, thus reducing overall lead time.

To illustrate, assume that Automotive Components Inc. manufactures a batch of 40 engine starters through three processes: machining, assembly, and testing. Each unit in the batch requires the following processing times:

Processing Time per Unit	
Machining	6 minutes
Assembly	10
Testing	8
Total	24 minutes

After machining, it takes 10 minutes to move the machined batch to assembly. It then takes 15 minutes to move the assembled batch to testing. The lead time can be analyzed as follows:

	Lead Times	Percent of Total
Value-added lead time	24 minutes	2.5%
Nonvalue-added lead time:		
Within-batch wait time [24 min. × (40 − 1)]	936	95.0
Move time	25	2.5
Total	985 minutes	100.0%

A product manufactured in batches of 25 units is produced through three stages of production: forging, machining, and assembly. Each unit requires 10 minutes forging, 16 minutes machining, and 8 minutes assembly. What is the within-batch wait time?

----

816 minutes [34 minutes × (25 units − 1 unit)]

Approximately 97.5% of the lead time is consumed by nonvalue-added waiting and moving. How could Automotive Components improve its lead time performance? First, it could reduce setups so that the batch size could be reduced to one piece, termed *one-piece flow*. Second, it could move the processes closer to each other so that the move time is eliminated. With these two steps, the total lead time would approach the value-added lead time.

Emphasizing Product-Oriented Layout

Organizing work around products is called a ***product-oriented layout*** (or **product cells**), while organizing work around processes is called a ***process-oriented layout***. Just-in-time methods favor organizing work around products rather than processes. Organizing work around products reduces the amount of materials movement, coordination between operations, and work in process inventory. As a result, lead time and production costs are reduced.

To illustrate, **Hallmark Cards** at one time processed greeting card design work through separate Art, Layout, and Preproduction Departments. These departments were organized around the processes for designing a new greeting card. Hallmark decided that this traditional method of organizing work was slowing down the designing of new cards, while increasing their cost. As a result, Hallmark reorganized the greeting card design activity around each holiday. Layout, art, and preproduction activities were arranged together into single cells according to each type of holiday. Hallmark now has a Valentine's Day cell, a Mother's Day cell, and cells for other major holidays.

REAL WORLD

Sony has organized a small team of four employees to completely assemble a camcorder, doing everything from soldering to testing. The new line reduces assembly time from 70 minutes to 15 minutes per camera. "There is no future in conventional conveyor lines. They are a tool that conforms to the person with the least ability," states a Sony representative.

Emphasizing Employee Involvement

Employee involvement is a management approach that grants employees the responsibility and authority to make decisions about operations, rather than relying solely on management instructions. This decision-making authority requires accounting and other information to be made available to all employees.

Employee involvement uses teams organized in product cells, rather than just the efforts of isolated, individual employees. Such employee teams can be **cross-trained** to perform any operation within the product cell. For example, employees learn how to operate several different machines within their product cell. Moreover, team members are trained to perform functions traditionally handled by centralized service departments. For example, direct labor employees may perform their own maintenance, quality control, housekeeping, and production improvement work. When direct labor employees perform such indirect functions, the distinction between direct and indirect labor cost becomes less important.

REAL WORLD

Kenney Manufacturing Company, a manufacturer of window shades, estimated that 50% of its window shade process was nonvalue-added. By using pull manufacturing and changing the line layout, it was able to reduce inventory by 82% and lead time by 84%.

Emphasizing Pull Manufacturing

Another important just-in-time principle is to produce items only as they are needed by the customer. This principle is called ***pull manufacturing*** (or **make to order**). In pull manufacturing, the status of the next operation determines when products are moved or produced. If the next operation is busy, then production stops so that material does not pile up in front of the busy operation. If the next operation is ready, then product can be produced or moved to that operation.

The system that accomplishes pull manufacturing is often called *kanban*, which is Japanese for "cards." Electronic cards or containers signal production quantities to be filled by the feeder operation. The cards link the customer back through each stage of production. When a consumer purchases a product, a card triggers assembly of a replacement product, which in turn triggers cards to manufacture the components required for the assembly. This creates a flow of parts and products that move to the drumbeat of customer demand.

In contrast, the traditional approach is to schedule production based on forecasted customer requirements. This principle is called **push manufacturing** (or **make to stock**). In push manufacturing, product is released for manufacturing without reference to line status but according to a production schedule. The schedule "pushes" product to inventory ahead of known customer demand. As a result, manufacturers using push manufacturing will generally have more inventory than those of manufacturers using pull manufacturing. As stated by one consultant, "If your manufacturing operations are still set up around guessing demand, you will forever be in a loop of producing and holding the wrong items and not having enough of what the customer actually wants."[1]

Emphasizing Zero Defects

Just-in-time manufacturing practices strive to eliminate poor quality. Poor quality results in an increased need for inspection, more production interruptions, an increased need for rework, additional recordkeeping for scrap, a higher cost from scrap, and additional warranty costs. Thus, one of the primary objectives of just-in-time manufacturing is to improve the process so that products are made right the first time.

Emphasizing Supplier Partnering

Another just-in-time manufacturing practice is entering into long-term agreements with suppliers. Developing long-term customer/supplier relationships is called **supplier partnering**. Partnering encourages suppliers to develop a commitment to the manufacturer so that materials purchased will be high-quality, low-cost, and on-time.

REAL WORLD

Maytag Corporation's CEO recently stated: "Our vision for the future includes flexibility in manufacturing so that we can take an order electronically or over the phone, manufacture it with the features specified, and be ready to ship it within a week."

MANAGERIAL DISCLOSURE AND ANALYSIS

CONTINGENT RISKS OF JUST-IN-TIME

The objective of just-in-time is to reduce the amount of inventory and improve the lead time. However, reducing direct materials inventory exposes the purchaser to disrupted supply from volatile demand, labor strikes, transportation delays, and equipment interruptions. As a result, manufacturers will often reduce the risk of disrupted supplies by providing suppliers guaranteed purchase commitments. Such commitments give the supplier confidence to reserve manufacturing capacity, hold safety-stock inventory, and make commitments to *their* suppliers. Using purchase commitments in this way is an example of supplier partnering. However, these commitments can expose the purchasing company to a contingent financial obligation. As such, purchase commitments are a risk that must be disclosed in the annual report filed with the Security and Exchange Commission and in the notes to the financial statements. **Cisco Systems, Inc.** disclosed its purchase commitment risk with suppliers as follows:

Manufacturing capacity and component supply constraints could be significant issues for us. We use several contract manufacturers and suppliers to provide manufacturing services for our products. During the normal course of business, in order to reduce manufacturing lead times and ensure adequate component supply, we enter into agreements with certain contract manufacturers and suppliers that allow them to procure inventory based upon criteria as defined by us. If we fail to anticipate customer demand properly, an oversupply of parts could result in excess or obsolete components which could adversely affect our gross margins. . . . Furthermore, as a result of binding price or purchase commitments with suppliers, we may be obligated to purchase components at prices that are higher than those available in the current market. In the event that we become committed to purchase components at prices in excess of the current market price when the components are actually utilized, our gross margins could decrease.

---

[1]Quoted by David Rucker of TBM Institute in "E-biz Requires Leaner Operations, More Integration," Jennifer Shah, *Electronic Buyer News*, July 31, 2000.

Supplier partnering often involves working to improve supplier operations by employing just-in-time principles. Thus, the just-in-time approach does not stop within the four walls of the factory but extends to the supplier's manufacturing operations as well. The result is an effective and efficient production chain that operates from raw materials to the final consumer. In addition, electronic data interchange and the Internet are used to improve the information flows between suppliers and customers. ***Electronic data interchange (EDI)*** is a method of using computers to electronically communicate orders, relay information, and make or receive payments from one organization to another. In addition, a supplier partner can electronically transmit engineering and design support for supplied parts.

Applying a Just-in-Time Approach to Anderson Metal Fabricators

<table>
<tr><td>objective 2</td></tr>
</table>

Apply just-in-time manufacturing practices to a traditional manufacturing illustration.

To illustrate just-in-time manufacturing principles, we will assume that Anderson Metal Fabricators (AMF) makes two types of metal covers, large and small, for electronic test equipment. Metal covers are made by stamping a pattern of the cover from sheet steel, much like a cookie cutter stamps cookies out of dough. The stamped patterns are then sent through a punching operation, which punches holes on the pattern for fasteners. The last operation is the forming operation, where the pattern is bent into a cover and fasteners are attached.

Traditional Operations—AMF

Exhibit 5 illustrates the plant layout of AMF as a traditional manufacturer. The facility is divided into three major production departments: Stamping, Punching, and Forming. This is an example of the process-oriented layout found in many traditional manufacturing operations. AMF has many machines in each department. Within each department, partially completed products are stored in work in process inventory, waiting to be worked on by the next department. The Maintenance and Tooling Department is in a centralized location within the plant. Customers order product from the finished goods inventory. Departments receive their production schedules and work instructions based on forecasted demand, which is an example of push manufacturing.

Following the traditional approach, AMF's purchasing function attempts to supply the correct amount of raw materials according to production schedules. Extra raw materials are ordered "just in case" a shipment is missed, delayed, or incorrect. Likewise, uncertainty about the final output of any department, because of machine breakdowns, scrap, rework, or production inefficiency, causes managers to increase work in process inventory. For example, the large work in process inventory in the Stamping Department keeps the Punching Department from running out of stampings when the stamping machines break down. Finally, the machines within AMF's departments must be set up to change production between the small and large covers.

Just-in-Time Operations—AMF

The management of AMF wishes to introduce a new product, the medium-size metal cover. Unfortunately, the existing production capacity and space will not support the increased production. As a result, AMF management has decided to use just-in-time principles in order to better utilize the existing productive capacity and space.

Exhibit 6 illustrates the just-in-time operations for AMF. To apply just-in-time principles, management revised the department structure. Instead of the production departments being organized around the various operational processes, they are now

•Exhibit 5

Traditional Operations—AMF

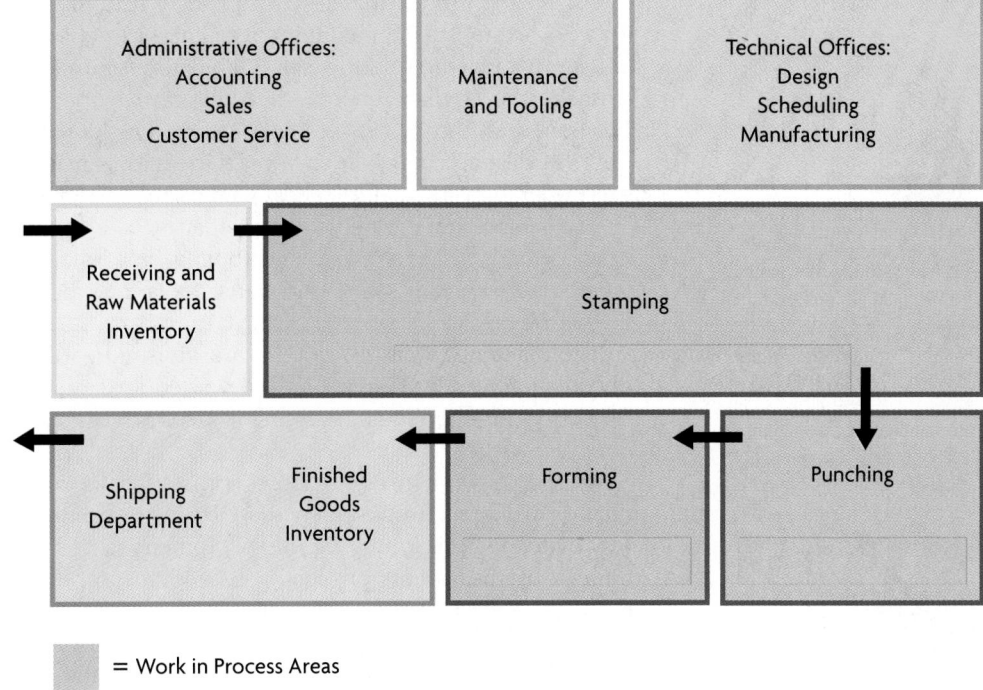

= Work in Process Areas

organized around the three product lines (small, medium, and large covers). This product-oriented layout was accomplished by taking the machines and the people in each of the old departments and separating them into three product production cells. For example, the Stamping Department machines were separated to form the first position in three separate product cells.

•Exhibit 6

Just-in-Time Operations—AMF

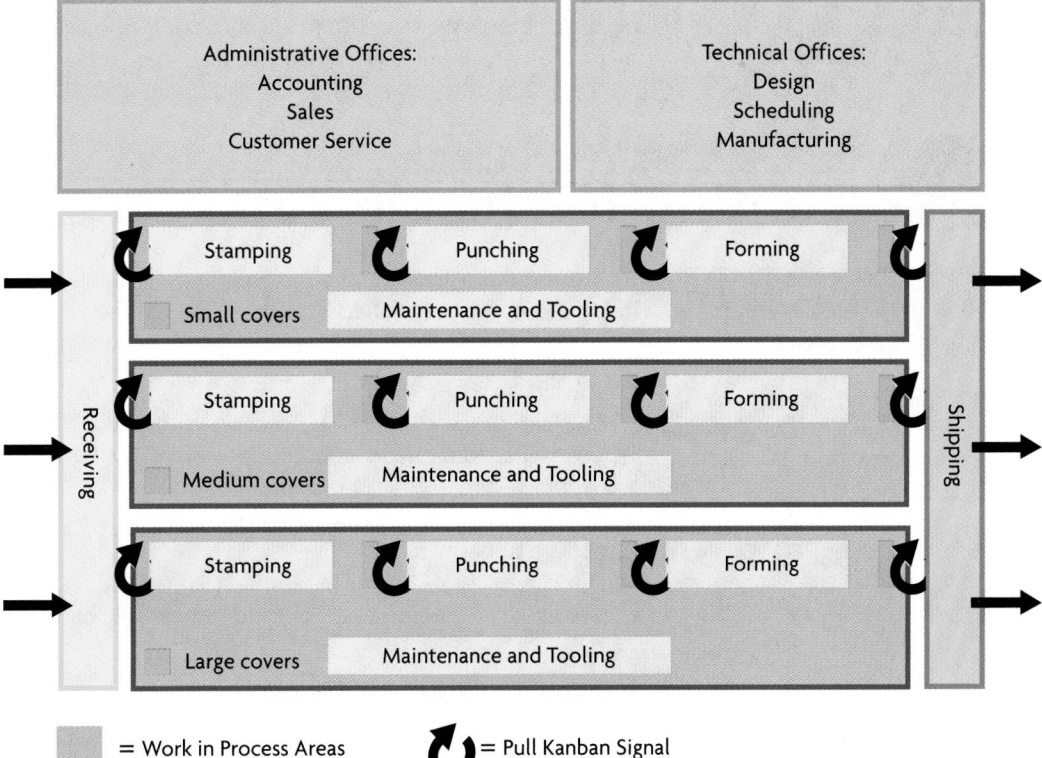

= Work in Process Areas   = Pull Kanban Signal

General Motors' first new assembly plant in over a decade is being designed with a leaner, more flexible layout. The building is about half the traditional size. Rather than centralized shipping and receiving areas, it features widely dispersed loading docks so suppliers can feed parts directly to the assembly process.

What features of AMF's new process are consistent with just-in-time manufacturing principles?

Product-oriented layout, elimination of setups, close physical distance between operations, decentralized maintenance and tooling, reduction of inventories (materials, work in process, and finished goods), increased employee involvement in improving the process, use of supplier partnering to increase quality and delivery frequency of incoming parts, and application of pull manufacturing.

Since each product has its own product cell, there is no longer any need for setups. For example, the medium cover line has no setups because only medium covers are manufactured in this cell. Eliminating setup time releases productive capacity to make the medium covers. In addition, the operations within a product cell are positioned physically close to each other in order to minimize move time. The close physical distance between each machine allows materials to be transferred between each operation in small batches, using kanban signals.

The Maintenance and Tooling Department was decentralized. Each product cell now includes a maintenance and tooling function. This allows equipment to be repaired more quickly, since the parts, tools, and personnel are physically closer to the problem.

The materials, work in process, and finished goods inventory storage space is reduced significantly. Eliminating the wasted space used for inventory provides room for producing the medium covers. Thus, AMF is able to expand production without investing in new facilities.

AMF orders raw materials only as they are needed for production. In the just-in-time environment, trucks often arrive daily or even more frequently, with just enough raw materials to last until the next shipment arrives. The raw materials are received directly by the various product cells, without inspection, because suppliers guarantee zero defects through supplier partnering.

Minimal work in process inventory exists between the product cells because of employee involvement to reduce the mistakes and errors within the process. Thus, AMF's employees have improved quality, while reducing machine failures, scrap, and rework. Normally, small work in process inventory levels would cause AMF to risk a loss in productivity through unexpected manufacturing stoppages. However, the process improvements will allow AMF's production to continue without risk of shutdown, even with reduced inventory. As a result of these improvements, the nonvalue-added lead time has been significantly reduced.

Operations do not produce product just to remain busy and improve machine utilization. In pull manufacturing, operations respond only to customer orders. As a result, all operations within a cell operate at the same pace. This practice avoids a buildup of work in process inventory from "out-running" slower operations. If customer demand slows, then the production pace will also be slowed to match the demand. Employees can then use the extra time to work on improving the process or to move to other cells where product demand is high.

Accounting for Just-in-Time Operations

objective 3

Describe the implications of a just-in-time manufacturing philosophy on cost accounting and performance measurement systems.

In just-in-time operations, the accounting system will have the characteristics listed below. Each of these characteristics is described in the following paragraphs.

* *Fewer transactions.* The accounting system is simpler because there are fewer transactions to record.
* *Combined accounts.* All in-process work is combined with raw materials to form a new account, **Raw and In Process (RIP) Inventory**, while the direct labor becomes part of the conversion cost.
* *Nonfinancial performance measures.* There is a greater emphasis on nonfinancial performance measures.
* *Direct tracing of overhead.* Indirect labor is directly assigned to product production cells, requiring less factory overhead allocation to products.

Fewer Transactions

The traditional process cost accounting system accumulates the cost incurred in a department and then transfers this cost to the next department. Thus, materials are recorded into and out of work in process inventories as production moves through the factory. Recording the flow of costs through a plant in this way leads to control of departmental costs. However, since each department has transactions flowing in and out, the traditional cost accounting system has many transactions to record, accumulate, correct, and report. This adds cost, complexity, and delay in reporting accounting information.

In the just-in-time production process, the need for accounting cost control is much less, because lower inventories make problems much more visible on the factory floor. That is, managers don't need an accounting report to indicate problems, since any problems are immediately visible to them. Thus, the accounting system can be simplified by eliminating the accumulation and transfer of costs as products move through the production process. Such simplification is termed **backflush accounting**. In backflush accounting, costs are transferred from combined material and conversion cost accounts directly to finished production without transferring costs through intermediate departmental work in process accounts. We illustrate the use of combined accounts in this way in the next section.

Combined Accounts

Since the just-in-time manufacturer attempts to eliminate inventory, including raw materials, there is no need for a separate materials account. For example, **Saturn Corporation** has receiving areas all around the perimeter of its factory. In this way, raw materials can be delivered by trucks to a receiving area that is located near the point of use on the assembly line. Thus, there is no need for a separate materials inventory location or a materials account, since materials are introduced immediately into production. Many just-in-time manufacturers debit all materials and conversion costs to *Raw and In Process Inventory* and thus combine materials and work in process costs in one account.

The direct labor cost classification is often not used by just-in-time manufacturers. This is because the employees in product cells perform many tasks, some of which could be classified as direct, such as performing operations, and some as indirect, such as performing inspections. From an accounting perspective, the product cell labor cost is combined with other cell overhead costs to form the total product cell conversion cost.

To illustrate these accounting concepts, assume that the annual budgeted conversion cost for AMF's medium-cover product cell is $2,400,000. These costs will support 1,920 planned hours of production. The cell conversion cost rate is determined by dividing the annual budgeted conversion cost by the planned production hours to yield $1,250 per hour, as shown below. This rate is similar to a predetermined factory overhead rate, except that it includes all conversion costs in the numerator.

$$\text{Budgeted cell conversion cost rate} = \frac{\$2,400,000 \text{ budgeted conversion cost}}{1,920 \text{ planned production hours}}$$

$$= \$1,250 \text{ per hour}$$

The medium-cover product cell is expected to require 0.02 hour of manufacturing time per unit. Thus, the conversion cost is estimated to be $25 per unit, as shown below.

0.02 hour per unit × $1,250 conversion cost per hour =
$25 conversion cost per unit

To illustrate the recording of transactions in AMF's just-in-time operations, assume that the following selected transactions occurred during April:

REAL WORLD

At **Caterpillar, Inc.**, traditional plant layouts required a transmission assembly to travel as much as 10 miles as it moved to different operations. Its progress was tracked by more than 1,000 pieces of paper. Caterpillar then reorganized its work flows, using just-in-time approaches. As a result, the transmission assembly travel distance was reduced to 200 feet, with an average of 10 pieces of paper used to track each transmission.

A company using just-in-time principles purchased 5,000 parts for $50 per part. These parts were used to make 5,000 units, each unit requiring 15 minutes of cell assembly time. The cell conversion cost is estimated at $250 per hour. What are the appropriate journal entries to record these two transactions?

Raw and In Process Inventory	250,000	
Accounts Payable		250,000
Raw and In Process Inventory	312,500	
Factory Overhead		312,500
[(15 min./60 min.) × $250 × 5,000]		

•Exhibit 12

Cost of Quality Report— Gifford Company

Gifford Company			
Cost of Quality Report			
Quality Cost Classification	Quality Cost	Percent of Total Quality Cost	Percent of Total Sales
Prevention	$ 180,000	12.00%	3.6%
Appraisal	210,000	14.00	4.2
Internal failure	735,000	49.00	14.7
External failure	375,000	25.00	7.5
Total	$1,500,000	100.00%	30.0%

REAL WORLD

Bank One, a large regional bank, performed a quality control activity analysis. The analysis indicated the following percentage of costs allocated to each classification:

External Failure 18%

Appraisal 45%

Internal Failure 27%

Prevention 10%

As a result of this study, Bank One was able to justify greater investments in prevention activities to improve customer service at lower operating costs.

As you can see, 12% of the total quality cost is the cost of preventing quality problems and 14% is the cost of appraisal activities, while the remaining 74% is for internal and external failures. In addition, internal and external failure-related costs are equal to 22.2% of sales. Gifford Company is not spending a sufficient amount of money in prevention and appraisal activities, while the amount of money spent on internal and external failure activities is too high. This information can be used by Gifford Company to improve quality by focusing on prevention and appraisal activities and thus reducing internal and external failure costs and total quality costs.

Value-Added/Nonvalue-Added Activity Analysis

In the preceding section, the quality control activities of Gifford Company were classified as prevention, appraisal, internal failure, and external failure costs. Alternatively, activities may be classified as value-added and nonvalue-added. A **value-added activity** is one that is necessary to meet customer requirements. A **nonvalue-added activity** is *not* required by the customer but exists because of mistakes, errors, omissions, and other process failures. To illustrate, Exhibit 13 shows the value-added and nonvalue-added classification for the quality control activities for Gifford Company.[4]

•Exhibit 13

Value-Added/Nonvalue-Added Quality Control Activities

Quality Control Activities	Activity Cost	Classification
Design engineering	$ 55,000	Value-added
Disposing of rejected materials	160,000	Nonvalue-added
Finished goods inspection	140,000	Value-added
Materials inspection	70,000	Value-added
Preventive maintenance	80,000	Value-added
Processing returned materials	150,000	Nonvalue-added
Disposing of scrap	195,000	Nonvalue-added
Assessing vendor quality	45,000	Value-added
Rework	380,000	Nonvalue-added
Warranty work	225,000	Nonvalue-added
Total activity cost	$1,500,000	

---

[4]We use the quality control activities for illustrating the value-added and nonvalue-added activities in this section. However, a value-added/nonvalue-added activity analysis can be done for any activity in a business, not just quality control activities.

As you can see, the internal and external failure costs are classified as nonvalue-added, while the prevention and appraisal costs are classified as value-added.[5] A summary of the value-added and nonvalue-added activities can be developed to show the percentage of the value-added and nonvalue-added costs to the total costs, as follows:

Classification	Amount	Percent
Value-added	$ 390,000	26%
Nonvalue-added	1,110,000	74
Total	$1,500,000	100%

For Gifford Company, 74% of the studied activities are nonvalue-added. This information should further motivate management to make improvements to reduce nonvalued-added activities.

Activity Analysis for Processes

Activity analysis can also be used to evaluate the cost of business processes. A ***process*** is a sequence of activities that converts an input into an output. That is, a process is a set of activities linked together by common inputs and outputs. Examples of common business processes include procurement, product development, manufacturing, distribution, and sales order fulfillment. Exhibit 14 shows a simplified sales order fulfillment process for Masters Company. This process converts a customer order (the input) into a product received by the customer (the output) through a series of four activities.

•Exhibit 14 Sales Order Fulfillment Process

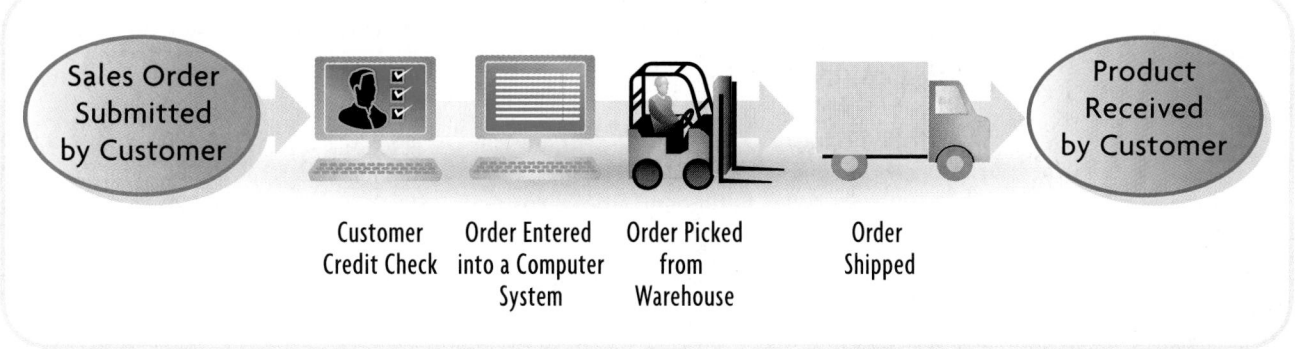

	Customer Credit Check	Order Entered into a Computer System	Order Picked from Warehouse	Order Shipped	

*Operators driving forklifts receive a list of orders, drive to stocking locations within the warehouse, pick the orders, and then transport them back to an area to prepare for shipment.

An activity analysis can be used to determine the cost of the activities of this process. To illustrate, assume that an activity analysis determined that the cost of the four activities in Masters Company sales order fulfillment process was as follows:

---

[5]Some believe that appraisal costs are nonvalue-added. They argue that if the product had been made correctly, then no inspection would be required. We will take a less strict view and assume that appraisal costs are value-added.

Sales Order Fulfillment Activities	Activity Cost	Percent of Total Process Cost
Customer credit check	$14,400	18%
Order entering	9,600	12
Order picking	36,000	45
Order shipping	20,000	25
Total sales order fulfillment process cost	$80,000	100%

The total cost of performing the sales order fulfillment process is $80,000. The order picking activity represents 45% of the total process cost. If we assume that 10,000 sales orders were submitted and eventually shipped through this process, the process could be calculated to average $8 per shipped order ($80,000 ÷ 10,000 shipped orders).

Management can use process cost information to support cost improvement activity. For example, assume that Masters Company management set a cost improvement target of $6 per shipped order. A $2 reduction per shipped order would require this process to be improved by either eliminating unnecessary or wasteful work or improving processing method efficiency. In this case, Masters Company determines that cost can be improved by eliminating unnecessary credit check work and by improving the picking activity efficiency.

Specifically, management determines that not all customer orders need to go through credit check, just the new orders from new customers. If Masters assumes that the process will ship 10,000 orders during the next period, it is estimated that this change would require the credit check activity to process only 2,500 sales orders, or 25% of the total. In addition, management introduces a more efficient warehouse product layout. This layout reduces the cost of picking orders by 35%. The cost savings from these two efforts and their impact on the cost of the sales order fulfillment process can be evaluated as follows:

Activity	Activity Cost Prior to Improvement	Activity Cost After Improvement	Activity Cost Savings
Customer credit check	$14,400	$ 3,600[1]	$10,800
Order entering	9,600	9,600	0
Order picking	36,000	23,400[2]	12,600
Order shipping	20,000	20,000	0
Total sales order fulfillment process cost	$80,000	$56,600	$23,400
Cost per shipped order (total divided by 10,000 orders shipped)	$8.00	$5.66	

[1]$14,400 × 25%
[2]$36,000 × 65%

Management's improvement activities would generate a savings of $23,400 during a period in which 10,000 sales orders are shipped.[6] This savings would reduce the cost from $8.00 to $5.66 per sales order shipped, thus exceeding management's improvement target.

More complex analyses can be performed by integrating activity-based process analysis into the budgeting system. In this way, process activity costs could be segregated into fixed and variable costs, and thus planned and controlled, using flexible budgets as discussed in a previous chapter. The use of activity-based process analysis in this way is discussed in advanced managerial accounting texts.

---

[6]This analysis assumes that the activity costs are variable to the inputs and outputs of the process. While this is likely true for processes primarily using labor, such as a sales order fulfillment process, other types of processes may have significant fixed costs that would not change with changes of inputs and outputs.

SPOTLIGHT ON STRATEGY

SPEED TO MARKET

We have all heard the expression "time is money." One area where this expression is especially true is in reducing the *time to market*, or the time it takes to move from product concept to final production. The shorter this time frame, the faster a company is able to earn profits from an idea and match the product design with customer tastes and preferences. New information technology, termed product life cycle management (PLM) software, can help companies reduce the time to market. **Lockheed Martin**, the largest defense contractor in the United States, replaced fax machines, clipboards, and spreadsheets with an integrated system for designing the new Joint Strike Fighter, the world's first "paperless plane." Currently, the system puts engineering drawings, manufacturing guidelines, and parts simulations online, so that nearly 3,000 engineers across 80 different companies are able to collaborate on the design. **Procter & Gamble**, the largest consumer-packaged-goods manufacturer in the United States, created a database of over 250,000 approved product formulas, chemicals, and packaging materials. As a result, P&G chemists were able to find the approved orange dye needed for the new Citrus Breeze® dishwashing liquid,

thus saving two months of safety testing. In the past, "only if someone in beauty care talked to someone in fabric and home care would that information have been shared." Companies can also rapidly introduce new technologies into existing products by using a *make-to-order* manufacturing strategy. Under a make-to-order strategy, a company is not concerned with first selling an existing inventory of older models before introducing a newer model. As stated by **Dell Computer Company** regarding its renowned make-to-order (build-to-order) manufacturing strategy:

The Company's build-to-order manufacturing process is designed to allow the Company to quickly produce customized computer systems and to achieve rapid inventory turnover and reduced inventory levels, which lessens the Company's exposure to the risk of declining inventory values. This flexible manufacturing process also allows the Company to quickly incorporate new technologies or components into its product offerings.

Sources: Andrew Raskin, "A Faster Ride to Market," *Business 2.0*, October 2002; Dell Computer Corporation Annual Report to the SEC.

Key Points

1 **Compare and contrast just-in-time (JIT) manufacturing practices with traditional manufacturing practices.**

The just-in-time manufacturing philosophy uses different principles than do traditional manufacturing methods. Just-in-time attempts to reduce lead time, while traditional methods attempt to lengthen lead time to provide a time buffer for uncertainty. Just-in-time emphasizes a product-oriented production layout, rather than a process-oriented layout. Just-in-time emphasizes a team-oriented work environment, while the traditional approach is more individual-oriented. Just-in-time views setup time reduction as a high-priority item. With reduced setup times, just-in-time manufacturers can emphasize pull manufacturing, rather than push

manufacturing. Just-in-time manufacturers must emphasize high quality, since there is very little inventory to protect production against quality problems. Finally, just-in-time manufacturers emphasize supplier partnering in order to improve the quality and delivery of incoming materials.

2 **Apply just-in-time manufacturing practices to a traditional manufacturing illustration.**

The just-in-time philosophy was illustrated for Anderson Metal Fabricators (AMF). In the illustration, AMF was able to add a new product line without increasing the size of its facility. This was done by using just-in-time principles to eliminate the space normally used for inventory. This space could now be used for producing the new product line.

3 **Describe the implications of a just-in-time manufacturing philosophy on cost accounting and performance measurement systems.**

The just-in-time philosophy has implications for cost accounting. The cost accounting system will have fewer transactions, will combine the materials and work in process accounts, and will account for direct labor as a part of cell conversion cost. Just-in-time will use nonfinancial reporting measures and result in more direct tracing of factory overhead to product cells.

4 **Apply just-in-time practices to a nonmanufacturing setting.**

Just-in-time principles can be used in service businesses and administrative processes. For example, hospitals are removing delays in serving patients by improving admission, testing, and recovery processes. This is accomplished by designing product-focused hospital units that use cross-trained caregivers in the delivery of hospital care.

5 **Describe and illustrate activity analysis for improving operations.**

Companies use activity analysis to identify the costs of quality, which include prevention, appraisal, internal failure, and external failure costs. The quality cost activities may be reported on a Pareto chart, which visually highlights the most expensive quality cost categories. In addition, the quality costs can be summarized in a quality cost report by each of the four major classifications. An alternative method for categorizing activities is by value-added and non-value-added classifications. An activity analysis can also be used to determine the cost of processes. Process costs can be improved by either improving processing methods or eliminating unnecessary or wasteful work.

Key Terms

activity analysis (1083)
appraisal costs (1083)
backflush accounting (1079)
cost of quality report (1085)
costs of quality (1083)
electronic data interchange (EDI) (1076)
employee involvement (1074)
external failure costs (1083)
internal failure costs (1083)

just-in-time (JIT) manufacturing (1070)
lead time (1071)
nonfinancial measure (1080)
nonvalue-added activity (1086)
nonvalue-added lead time (1071)
Pareto chart (1084)
prevention costs (1083)
process (1087)
process-oriented layout (1074)

product-oriented layout (1074)
pull manufacturing (1074)
push manufacturing (1075)
Raw and In Process (RIP) Inventory (1078)
supplier partnering (1075)
value-added activity (1086)
value-added lead time (1071)
value-added ratio (1071)

Illustrative Problem

Krisco Company operates under the just-in-time philosophy. As such, it has a production cell for its microwave ovens. The conversion cost for 2,400 hours of production is budgeted for the year at $4,800,000.

During January, 2,000 microwave ovens were started and completed. Each oven requires six minutes of cell processing time. The materials cost for each oven is $100.

Instructions

1. Determine the budgeted cell conversion cost per hour.
2. Determine the manufacturing cost per unit.
3. Journalize the entry to record the costs charged to the production cell in January.
4. Journalize the entry to record the costs transferred to finished goods.

Solution

1. Budgeted cell conversion cost rate $= \dfrac{\$4,800,000}{2,400 \text{ hours}} = \$2,000$ per cell hour

2.

Materials	$100 per unit
Conversion cost [($2,000 per hour ÷ 60 min.) × 6 min]	200
Total	$300 per unit

3.

		Debit	Credit
1	Raw and In Process Inventory	200 0 0 0 00	
2	Accounts Payable		200 0 0 0 00
3	To record materials costs.		
4	(2,000 units × $100 per unit).		
5			
6	Raw and In Process Inventory	400 0 0 0 00	
7	Conversion Costs		400 0 0 0 00
8	To record conversion costs.		
9	(2,000 units × $200 per unit).		
10			
11	**4.** Finished Goods (2,000 × $300 per unit)	600 0 0 0 00	
12	Raw and In Process Inventory		600 0 0 0 00
13	To record finished production.		

Self-Examination Questions (Answers at End of Chapter)

1. Which of the following is not a characteristic of the just-in-time philosophy?
   A. Product-oriented layout
   B. Push manufacturing (make to stock)
   C. Short lead times
   D. Reducing setup time as a critical improvement priority

2. Accounting in a just-in-time environment is best described as:
   A. more complex.
   B. focused on direct labor.
   C. providing detailed variance reports.
   D. providing less transaction control.

3. The product cell for Dynah Company has budgeted conversion costs of $420,000 for the year. The cell is planned to be available 2,100 hours for production. Each unit requires $12.50 of materials cost. The cell started and completed 700 units. The cell process time for the product is 15 minutes per unit. What is the cost debited to finished goods for the period?
   A. $8,750   C. $43,750
   B. $35,000   D. $140,000

4. In-process inspection activities are an example of what type of quality cost?
   A. Prevention
   B. Appraisal
   C. Internal failure
   D. External failure

5. A Pareto chart is used to display:
   A. a ranking of attribute totals, by category, in the form of a bar chart.
   B. important trends in the form of a line chart.
   C. percentage information in the form of a pie chart.
   D. a listing of attribute totals, by category, in a table.

Class Discussion Questions

1. What is the benefit of ...e processing?
   ... nonvalue-added lead time?
2. What are some e... ...ted layout preferred by just-in-time manufacturers over a ...ayout?
3. Why is a pr... ...time related to lead time?
   proce...just-in-time manufacturers favor pull or "make to order" manufacturing?
4. ...y would a just-in-time manufacturer strive to produce zero defects?

7. How is supplier partnering different from traditional supplier relationships?
8. Why does accounting in a just-in-time environment result in fewer transactions?
9. Why is a "raw and in process inventory" account used by just-in-time manufacturers, rather than separately reporting materials and work in process?
10. Why is the direct labor cost category eliminated in many just-in-time environments?
11. How does accounting under a just-in-time environment provide less transaction control?
12. What are some possible explanations for the actual conversion cost per unit being greater than the budgeted cost per unit in a just-in-time production cell?
13. What just-in-time principles might a hospital use?
14. What is the benefit of an activity analysis?
15. How does a Pareto chart assist management?
16. What is the benefit of identifying nonvalue-added activities?
17. What ways can the cost of a process be improved?

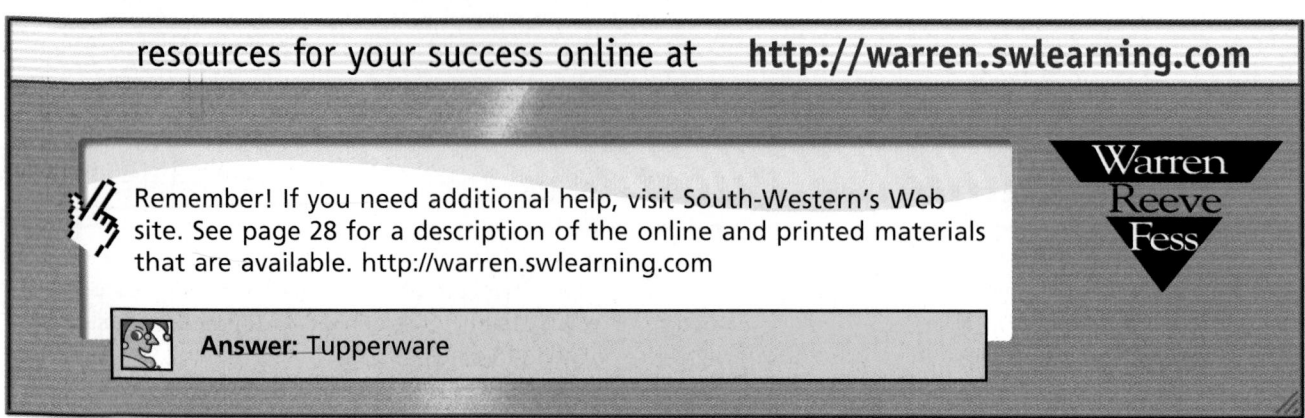

resources for your success online at   **http://warren.swlearning.com**

Remember! If you need additional help, visit South-Western's Web site. See page 28 for a description of the online and printed materials that are available. http://warren.swlearning.com

Warren Reeve Fess

Answer: Tupperware

Exercises

EXERCISE 26-1
Just-in-time principles
Objective 1

The Chief Executive Officer (CEO) of Sun-Ray Windows Inc. has just returned from a management seminar describing the benefits of the just-in-time philosophy. The CEO issued the following statement after returning from the conference:

This company will become a just-in-time manufacturing company. Presently, we have too much inventory. To become just-in-time we need to eliminate the excess inventory. Therefore, I want all employees to begin reducing inventories until we are just-in-time. Thank you for your cooperation.

How would you respond to the CEO's statement?

EXERCISE 26-2
Just-in-time as a strategy
Objective 1

The American textile industry has moved much of its operations offshore in the pursuit of lower labor ... tion in 1962 to over ... Textile imports have risen from 2% of all textile production ... mass-market apparel items ... 4. Offshore manufacturers make long runs of standard ... ships, requiring significant time ... then brought to the United States in container ... tail customers must accurately forec... riginal order and delivery. As a result, re-

Assuming that you work for a U... im... mands for imported apparel items.

recommend responding to the low-cost impo... '> company, how would you

EXERCISE 26-3
Lead time reduction—service company
Objectives 1, 4

Sentry Insurance Company takes ten days to make payments on insurance claims. Claims are processed through three departments: Data Input, Claims Audit, and Claims Adjustment. The three departments are on different floors, approximately one hour apart from each other. Claims are processed in batches of 100. Each batch of 100 claims moves through the three departments on a wheeled cart. Management is concerned about customer dissatisfaction caused by the long lead time for claim payments.

How might this process be changed so that the lead time could be reduced significantly?

EXERCISE 26-4
Just-in-time principles
Objective 1

Duke Shirt Company manufactures various styles of men's casual wear. Shirts are cut and assembled by a workforce that is paid by piece rate. This means that they are paid according to the amount of work completed during a period of time. To illustrate, if the piece rate is $0.10 per sleeve assembled, and the worker assembles 700 sleeves during the day, then the worker would be paid $70 (700 × $0.10) for the day's work.

The company is considering adopting a just-in-time manufacturing philosophy by organizing work cells around various types of products and employing pull manufacturing. However, no change is expected in the compensation policy. On this point, the manufacturing manager stated the following:

"Piecework compensation provides an incentive to work fast. Without it, the workers will just goof off and expect a full day's pay. We can't pay straight hourly wages—at least not in this industry."

How would you respond to the manufacturing manager's comments?

EXERCISE 26-5
Lead time analysis
Objective 1

WHAT DO YOU THINK?

Kiddie Kuddles Inc. manufactures toy stuffed animals. The direct labor time required to cut, sew, and stuff a toy is 12 minutes per unit. The company makes two types of stuffed toys—a lion and a bear. The lion is assembled in lot sizes of 50 units per batch, while the bear is assembled in lot sizes of 5 units per batch. Since each product has direct labor time of 12 minutes per unit, management has determined that the lead time for each product is 12 minutes.

Is management correct? What are the lead times for each product?

EXERCISE 26-6
Reduce setup time
Objective 1

Cleveland Cams Inc. has analyzed the setup time on its computer-controlled lathe. The setup requires changing the type of fixture that holds a part. The average setup time has been 160 minutes, consisting of the following steps:

Turn off machine and remove fixture from lathe	5 minutes
Go to tool room with fixture	25
Record replacement of fixture to tool room	15
Return to lathe	25
Clean lathe	15
Return to tool room	25
Record withdrawal of new fixture from tool room	20
Return to lathe	25
Install new fixture and turn on machine	5
Total setup time	160 minutes

a. Why should management be concerned about improving setup time?
b. What do you recommend to Cleveland Cams Inc. for improving setup time?
c. How much time would be required for a setup, using your suggestion in (b)?

EXERCISE 26-7
Calculate lead time
Objective 1

Concord Machining Company machines metal parts for the automotive industry. Under the traditional manufacturing approach, the parts are machined through two processes: Milling and Finishing. Parts are produced in batch sizes of 60 parts. A part requires 4 minutes in milling and 6 minutes in finishing. The move time between the two operations for a complete batch is 15 minutes.

Under the just-in-time philosophy, the part is produced in a cell that includes both the milling and finishing operations. The operating time is unchanged; however, the batch size is reduced to 4 parts and the move time is eliminated.

Determine the value-added, nonvalue-added, total lead time, and the value-added ratio under the traditional and just-in-time manufacturing methods. Round whole percentages to two decimal places.

EXERCISE 26-8
Calculate lead time

Objective 1

Flash Memories Inc. is considering a new just-in-time product cell. The present manufacturing approach produces a product in four separate steps. The production batch sizes are 60 units. The process time for each step is as follows:

Process Step 1	5 minutes
Process Step 2	3 minutes
Process Step 3	11 minutes
Process Step 4	6 minutes

The time required to move each batch between steps is 15 minutes. In addition, the time to move raw materials to Process Step 1 is also 15 minutes, and the time to move completed units from Process Step 4 to finished goods inventory is 15 minutes.

The new just-in-time layout will allow the company to reduce the batch sizes from 60 units to 5 units. The time required to move each batch between steps and the inventory locations will be reduced to 3 minutes. The processing time in each step will stay the same.

Determine the value-added, nonvalue-added, total lead times, and the value-added ratio under the present and proposed production approaches. Round whole percentages to two decimal places.

EXERCISE 26-9
Lead time calculation—doctor's office

Objectives 1, 4

✔ b. 130 minutes

Ellen Chow caught the flu and needed to see the doctor. Chow called to set up an appointment and was told to come in at 1:00 P.M. Chow arrived at the doctor's office promptly at 1:00 P.M. The waiting room had twelve other people in it. Patients were admitted from the waiting room in FIFO (first-in, first-out) order at a rate of five minutes per patient. After waiting until her turn, a nurse finally invited Chow to an examining room. Once in the examining room, Chow waited another 20 minutes before a nurse arrived to take some basic readings (temperature, blood pressure). The nurse needed five minutes to collect the clinical information. After the nurse left, Chow waited 15 additional minutes before the doctor arrived. The doctor arrived and diagnosed the flu and provided a prescription for antibiotics. This took the doctor 10 minutes. Before leaving the doctor's office, Chow waited 15 minutes at the business office to pay for the office visit.

Chow spent 5 minutes walking next door to fill the prescription at the pharmacy. There were four people in front of Chow, each person requiring 5 minutes to fill and purchase his or her prescription. Chow finally arrived home 20 minutes after paying for her prescription.

a. What time does Chow arrive home?
b. How much of the total elapsed time from 1:00 P.M. until when Chow arrived home was nonvalue-added time?
c. Why does the doctor require patients to wait so long for service?

EXERCISE 26-10
Supplier partnering

Objective 1

REAL WORLD

The following is an excerpt from a recent article discussing supplier relationships with the Big Three North American automakers.

"The Big Three select suppliers on the basis of lowest price and annual price reductions," said Neil De Koker, president of the Original Equipment Suppliers Association. "They look globally for the lowest parts prices from the lowest cost countries," De Koker said. "There is little trust and respect. Collaboration is missing." Japanese auto makers want long-term supplier relationships. They select suppliers as a person would a mate. The Big Three are quick to beat down prices with methods such as electronic auctions or rebidding work to a competitor. The Japanese are equally tough on price but are committed to maintaining supplier continuity. "They work with you to arrive

*at a competitive price, and they are willing to pay because they want long-term part-nering," said Carl Code, a vice president at Ernie Green Industries. "They [**Honda** and **Toyota**] want suppliers to make enough money to stay in business, grow and bring them innovation." The Big Three's supply chain model is not much different from the one set by Henry Ford. In 1913, he set up the system of independent sup-plier firms operating at arm's length on short-term contracts. One consequence of the Big Three's low-price-at-all-costs mentality is that suppliers are reluctant to offer them their cutting-edge technology out of fear the contract will be resourced before the research and development costs are recouped.*

a. Contrast the Japanese supplier model with that of the Big Three.
b. Why might a supplier prefer the Japanese model?
c. What benefits might accrue to the Big Three by adopting the Japanese supplier practices?

Source: Robert Sherefkin and Amy Wilson, "Suppliers Prefer Japanese Business Model," *Rubber & Plastics News*, March 17, 2003, Vol. 24, No. 11.

EXERCISE 26-11
Employee involvement
Objective 1

REAL WORLD

Quickie Designs Inc. uses teams in the manufacture of lightweight wheelchairs. Two features of its team approach are team hiring and peer reviews. Under team hiring, the team recruits, interviews, and hires new team members from within the organization. Using peer reviews, the team evaluates each member of the team with regard to quality, knowledge, teamwork, goal performance, attendance, and safety. These reviews provide feedback to the team member for improvement.

How do these two team approaches differ from using managers to hire and evaluate employees?

EXERCISE 26-12
Accounting issues in a just-in-time environment
Objective 3

WHAT'S WRONG WITH THIS?

Vision Electronics Company has recently implemented a just-in-time manufacturing approach. A production department manager has approached the controller with the following comments:

I am very upset with our accounting system now that we have implemented our new just-in-time manufacturing methods. It seems as if all I'm doing is paperwork. Our product is moving so fast through the manufacturing process that the paperwork can hardly keep up. For example, it just doesn't make sense to me to fill out daily labor reports. The employees are assigned to complete cells, performing many different tasks. I can't keep up with direct labor reports on each individual task. I thought we were trying to eliminate waste. Yet the information requirements of the accounting system are slowing us down and adding to overall lead time. Moreover, I'm still getting my monthly variance reports. I don't think that these are necessary. I have nonfinancial performance measures that are more timely than these reports. Besides, the employees don't really understand accounting variances. How about giving some information that I can really use?

What accounting system changes would you suggest in light of the pro-duction department manager's criticisms?

EXERCISE 26-13
Just-in-time journal entries
Objective 3
✓ b. $225

Digi-Tek Inc. uses a just-in-time strategy to manufacture DVD players. The company manufactures DVDs through a single product cell. The budgeted conversion cost for the year is $837,000 for 1,860 production hours. Each unit requires 30 minutes of cell process time. During March, 310 DVDs are manufactured in the cell. The estimated materials cost per unit is $175. The following summary transactions took place dur-ing March:

1. Materials are purchased for March production.
2. Conversion costs were applied to production.
3. 310 DVDs are assembled and placed in finished goods.
4. 300 DVDs are sold for $500 per unit.

(continued)

a. Determine the budgeted cell conversion cost per hour.
b. Determine the budgeted cell conversion cost per unit.
c. Journalize the summary transactions (1)–(4) for March.

EXERCISE 26-14
Just-in-time journal entries
Objective 3
✓ a. $70

Jen-Light Inc. manufactures lighting fixtures, using just-in-time manufacturing methods. Style BB-01 has a materials cost per unit of $22. The budgeted conversion cost for the year is $147,000 for 2,100 production hours. A unit of Style BB-01 requires 12 minutes of cell production time. The following transactions took place during June:

1. Materials were acquired to assemble 850 Style BB-01 units for June.
2. Conversion costs were applied to production.
3. 850 units of Style BB-01 were started and completed in June.
4. 830 units of Style BB-01 were sold in June for $55 per unit.

a. Determine the budgeted cell conversion cost per hour.
b. Determine the budgeted cell conversion cost per unit.
c. Journalize the summary transactions (1)–(4) for June.

EXERCISE 26-15
Just-in-time—fast food restaurant
Objective 4

The management of Burger Stop fast-food franchise wants to provide hamburgers quickly to customers. It has been using a process by which precooked hamburgers are prepared and placed under hot lamps. These hamburgers are then sold to customers. In this process, every customer receives the same type of hamburger and dressing (ketchup, onions, mustard). If a customer wants something different, then a "special order" must be cooked to the customer's requirements. This requires the customer to wait several minutes, which often slows down the service line. Burger Stop has been receiving more and more special orders from customers, which has been slowing service down considerably.

a. ▶ How would you describe the present Burger Stop service delivery system?
b. ▶ How might you use just-in-time principles to provide customers quick service, yet still allow them to custom order their burgers?

EXERCISE 26-16
Pareto chart
Objective 5

A-Plus Micro Circuits Inc. manufactures RAM memory chips for personal computers. An activity analysis was conducted, and the following activity costs were identified with the manufacture and sale of memory chips:

Activities	Activity Cost
Correct shipment errors	$ 96,000
Disposing of scrap	180,000
Emergency equipment maintenance	120,000
Employee training	24,000
Final inspection	114,000
Inspecting incoming materials	30,000
Preventive equipment maintenance	36,000
Processing customer returns	144,000
Scrap reporting	60,000
Supplier development	12,000
Warranty claims	384,000
Total	$1,200,000

Prepare a Pareto chart of these activities.

EXERCISE 26-17
Cost of quality report
Objective 5

SPREADSHEET

✓ a. Appraisal, 12.0% of total costs

a. Using the information in Exercise 26-16, prepare a cost of quality report. Assume that the sales for the period were $6,000,000.
b. ▶ Interpret the cost of quality report.

EXERCISE 26-18
Pareto chart for a service company

Objective 5

Infoquest Cable Company provides cable TV and Internet service to the local community. The activities and activity costs of Infoquest Cable are identified as follows:

Activities	Activity Cost
Billing error correction	$ 45,000
Cable signal testing	120,000
Reinstalling service (installed incorrectly the first time)	90,000
Repairing satellite equipment	22,500
Repairing underground cable connections to the customer	26,250
Replacing old technology cable with higher quality cable	157,500
Replacing old technology signal switches with higher quality switches	202,500
Responding to customer home repair requests	56,250
Training employees	30,000
Total	$750,000

Prepare a Pareto chart of these activities.

EXERCISE 26-19
Cost of quality and value-added/nonvalue-added reports

Objective 5

SPREADSHEET

✓ *a. External failure, 29% of total costs*

a. Using the activity data in Exercise 26-18, prepare a cost of quality report. Assume that sales are $2,500,000. Round percentages to two decimal places.
b. Using the activity data in Exercise 26-18, prepare a value-added/nonvalue-added analysis.
c. ▬▬▶ Interpret the information in (a) and (b).

EXERCISE 26-20
Process activity analysis

Objectives 4, 5

SPREADSHEET

✓ *b. $45 per claim payment*

Gann Insurance Company has a process for making payments on insurance claims as follows:

An activity analysis revealed that the cost of these activities was as follows:

Receiving claim	$ 28,800
Adjusting claim	113,400
Paying claim	37,800

This process includes only the cost of processing the claim payments, not the actual amount of the claim payments. The adjusting activity involves verifying and estimating the amount of the claim.

The process received, adjusted, and paid 4,000 claims during the period. All claims were treated identically in this process.

To improve the cost of this process, management has determined that claims should be segregated into two categories. Claims under $1,000 and claims greater than $1,000: claims under $1,000 would not be adjusted but would be accepted upon the insured's evidence of claim. Claims above $1,000 would be adjusted. It is estimated that 60% of the claims are under $1,000 and would thus be paid without adjustment. It is also estimated that the additional effort to segregate claims would add 10% to the "receiving claim" activity cost.

a. Develop a table showing the percent of activity cost to the total process cost for the claim payment activities.

(continued)

b. Determine the average total process cost per claim payment, assuming 4,000 total claims.

c. Prepare a table showing the changes in the activity costs as a result of the changes proposed by management.

d. Estimate the average cost per claim payment, assuming that the changes proposed by management are enacted for 4,000 total claims.

EXERCISE 26-21
Process activity analysis
Objective 5

SPREADSHEET

✓ b. $15 per check

The procurement process for Baker Company includes a series of activities that transforms a materials requisition into a vendor check. The process begins with a request for materials. The requesting department prepares and sends a materials request form to the Purchasing Department. The Purchasing Department then places a request for a quote to vendors. Vendors prepare bids in response to the request for a quote. A vendor is selected based on the lowest bid. A purchase order to the low-bid vendor is prepared. The vendor delivers the materials to the company, whereupon a receiving ticket is prepared. Payment to the vendor is authorized if the materials request form, receiving ticket, and vendor invoice are in agreement. These three documents fail to agree 45% of the time, initiating effort to reconcile the differences. Once the three documents agree, a check is issued. The process can be diagrammed as follows:

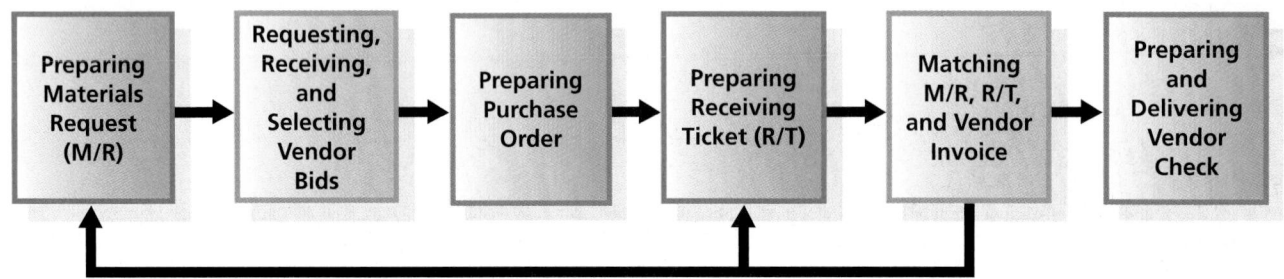

An activity analysis indicated the following activity costs with this process:

Preparing materials request	$ 31,500
Requesting, receiving, and selecting vendor bids	99,000
Preparing purchase order	22,500
Preparing receiving ticket	40,500
Matching M/R, R/T, and invoice	54,000
Correcting reconciliation differences	157,500
Preparing and delivering vendor check	45,000
Total process activity cost	$450,000

On average, the process handles 30,000 individual requests for materials that result in 30,000 individual checks to vendors.

Management proposes to improve this process in two ways. First, the Purchasing Department will develop a preapproved vendor list for which orders can be placed without a request for quote. It is expected that this will reduce the need for requesting and receiving vendor bids by 70%. Second, additional training and standardization will be provided to reduce errors introduced into the materials requisition form and receiving tickets. It is expected that this will reduce the number of reconciliations from 45% to 9%, over an average of 30,000 payments.

a. Develop a table showing the percent of activity cost to the total process cost for the procurement activities.

b. Determine the average total process cost per vendor check, assuming 30,000 checks.

c. Prepare a table showing the improvements in the activity costs as a result of the changes proposed by management.
d. Estimate the average cost per vendor check, assuming that the changes proposed by management are enacted for 30,000 total checks.

Problems Series A

PROBLEM 26-1A
Just-in-time principles
Objective 1

✓ 3. $3.00 per frame

Hawg Wild Motorcycle Company manufactures a variety of motorcycles. Hawg's purchasing policy requires that the purchasing agents place each quarter's purchasing requirements out for bid. This is because the Purchasing Department is evaluated solely by its ability to get the lowest purchase prices. The lowest cost bidder receives the order for the next quarter (90 days). To make its motorcycles, Hawg Wild requires 7,200 frames per quarter. Hawg Wild received two frame bids for the third quarter, as follows:

* *Durable Forging Company:* $242 per frame. Delivery schedule: 80 frames per working day (90 days in the quarter).
* *Temper Forging Company:* $240 per frame. Delivery schedule: 7,200 frames at the beginning of July to last for three months.

Hawg Wild accepted Temper Forging Company's bid because it was the low-cost bid.

Instructions
1. ▬▬▶ Comment on Hawg Wild's purchasing policy.
2. ▬▬▶ What are the additional (hidden) costs, beyond price, of Temper Forging Company's bid? Why weren't these costs considered?
3. Considering just inventory financing costs, what is the additional cost per frame of Temper Forging Company's bid if the cost of money is 10%? (*Hint:* Determine the average value of frame inventory held for the quarter and multiply by the quarterly interest charge.)

PROBLEM 26-2A
Lead time
Objective 1

SPREADSHEET

✓ 1. Total wait time, 6,050 minutes

Bon Appetit Appliance Company manufactures home kitchen appliances. The manufacturing process includes stamping, final assembly, testing, and shipping. In the stamping operation, a number of individuals are responsible for stamping the steel outer surface of the appliance. The stamping operation is set up prior to each run. A run of 120 stampings is completed after each setup. A setup requires 100 minutes. The parts wait for the setup to be completed before stamping begins. Each stamping requires 5 minutes of operating time. After each batch is completed, the operator moves the stamped covers to the final assembly area. This move takes 15 minutes to complete.

The final assembly for each appliance unit requires 24 minutes and is also done in batches of 120 appliance units. The batch of 120 appliance units is moved into the test building, which is across the street. The move takes 25 minutes. In the final test, the 120-unit batch is tested one at a time. Each test requires 8 minutes. The completed units are sent to shipping for packaging and final shipment to customers. A complete batch of 120 units is sent from final assembly to shipping. The Shipping Department is located next to final assembly. Thus, there is no move time between these two operations. Packaging and shipment labeling requires 13 minutes per unit.

Instructions
1. Determine the amount of value-added and nonvalue-added lead time and the value-added ratio in this process for an average kitchen appliance in a batch of 120 units. Round percentages to two decimal places. Categorize the nonvalue-added time into wait and move time.
2. ▬▬▶ How could this process be improved so as to reduce the amount of waste in the process?

PROBLEM 26-3A
Just-in-time accounting

Objective 3

SPREADSHEET

✓ *4. Raw and In Process Inventory, $30,000*

Pin Drop Technologies Inc. manufactures and assembles two major types of telephone assemblies—a desk phone and a mobile phone. The process consists of a just-in-time cell for each product. The data that follow concern only the mobile phone just-in-time cell.

For the year, Pin Drop Technologies Inc. budgeted the following costs for the mobile phone production cell:

Conversion Cost Categories	Budget
Labor	$101,000
Supplies	34,000
Utilities	12,000
Total	$147,000

Pin Drop plans 3,500 hours of production for the mobile phone cell for the year. The materials cost is $80 per unit. Each assembly requires 16 minutes of cell assembly time. There was no October 1 inventory for either Raw and In Process Inventory or Finished Goods Inventory.

The following summary events took place in the mobile phone cell during October:

a. Electronic parts were purchased to produce 13,500 mobile phone assemblies in October.
b. Conversion costs were applied for 13,125 units of production in October.
c. 13,125 units were started and completed in October.
d. 12,900 units were shipped to customers at a price of $185 per unit.

Instructions
1. Determine the budgeted cell conversion cost per hour.
2. Determine the budgeted cell conversion cost per unit.
3. Journalize the summary transactions (a) through (d).
4. Determine the ending balance in Raw and In Process Inventory and Finished Goods Inventory.
5. ▭▭▭▶ How does the accounting in a JIT environment differ from traditional accounting?

PROBLEM 26-4A
Pareto chart and cost of quality report—manufacturing company

Objective 5

✓ *3. Nonvalue-added, 35%*

The president of Elegon & Fashions Inc. has been concerned about the growth in costs over the last several years. The president asked the controller to perform an activity analysis to gain a better insight into these costs. The activity analysis revealed the following:

Activity	Activity Cost
Correcting invoice errors	$ 16,200
Disposing of incoming materials with poor quality	19,800
Disposing of scrap	34,200
Expediting late production	43,200
Final inspection	30,600
Inspecting incoming materials	9,000
Inspecting work in process	37,800
Preventive machine maintenance	23,400
Producing product	133,200
Responding to customer quality complaints	12,600
Total	$360,000

The production process is complicated by quality problems, requiring the production manager to expedite production and dispose of scrap.

Instructions
1. Prepare a Pareto chart of the company activities.
2. Use the activity cost information to determine the percentages of total costs that are prevention, appraisal, internal failure, external failure, and not costs of quality.
3. Determine the percentages of total costs that are value- and nonvalue-added.
4. ▭▭▭▶ Interpret the information.

Problems Series B

PROBLEM 26-1B
Just-in-time principles
Objective 1

✓ 3. $0.16 per pound

Ready Electric Co. manufactures light bulbs. Ready's purchasing policy requires that the purchasing agents place each quarter's purchasing requirements out for bid. This is because the Purchasing Department is evaluated solely by its ability to get the lowest purchase prices. The lowest cost bidder receives the order for the next quarter (90 working days).

To make its bulb products, Ready requires 24,300 pounds of glass per quarter. Ready received two glass bids for the second quarter, as follows:

- *Prism Glass Company:* $16.00 per pound of glass. Delivery schedule: 24,300 pounds at the beginning of April to last for 3 months.
- *Reflection Glass Company:* $16.10 per pound of glass. Delivery schedule: 270 pounds per working day (90 days in the quarter).

Ready accepted Prism Glass Company's bid because it was the low-cost bid.

Instructions

1. ▭► Comment on Ready's purchasing policy.
2. ▭► What are the additional (hidden) costs, beyond price, of Prism Glass Company's bid? Why weren't these costs considered?
3. Considering just inventory financing costs, what is the additional cost per pound of Prism Glass Company's bid if the cost of money is 8%? (*Hint:* Determine the average value of glass inventory held for the quarter and multiply by the quarterly interest charge.)

PROBLEM 26-2B
Lead time
Objective 1

SPREADSHEET

✓ 1. Total wait time, 1,356 minutes

Bass Sound Audio Company manufactures electronic stereo equipment. The manufacturing process includes printed circuit (PC) card assembly, final assembly, testing, and shipping. In the PC card assembly operation, a number of individuals are responsible for assembling electronic components into printed circuit boards. Each operator is responsible for soldering components according to a given set of instructions. Operators work on batches of 40 printed circuit boards. Each board requires 8 minutes of assembly time. After each batch is completed, the operator moves the assembled cards to the final assembly area. This move takes 20 minutes to complete.

The final assembly for each stereo unit requires 15 minutes and is also done in batches of 40 units. A batch of 40 stereos is moved into the test building, which is across the street. The move takes 30 minutes. Before conducting the test, the test equipment must be set up for the particular stereo model. The test setup requires 30 minutes. The units wait while the setup is performed. In the final test, the 40-unit batch is tested one at a time. Each test requires 5 minutes. The completed batch, after all testing, is sent to shipping for packaging and final shipment to customers. A complete batch of 40 units is sent from final assembly to shipping. The Shipping Department is located next to final assembly. Thus, there is no move time between these two operations. Packaging and labeling requires 6 minutes per unit.

Instructions

1. Determine the amount of value-added and nonvalue-added lead time and the value-added ratio in this process for an average stereo unit in a batch of 40 units. Round percentages to two decimal places. Categorize the nonvalue-added time into wait and move time.
2. ▭► How could this process be improved so as to reduce the amount of waste in the process?

PROBLEM 26-3B
Just-in-time accounting
Objective 3

Display Tek Inc. manufactures and assembles automobile instrument panels for both Burton Motors and National Motors. The process consists of a just-in-time product cell for each customer's instrument assembly. The data that follow concern only the Burton just-in-time cell.

✓ *4. Raw and In Process
Inventory, $93,750*

For the year, Display Tek Inc. budgeted the following costs for the Burton production cell:

Conversion Cost Categories	Budget
Labor	$662,000
Supplies	112,000
Utilities	36,000
Total	$810,000

Display Tek Inc. plans 4,500 hours of production for the Burton cell for the year. The materials cost is $125 per instrument assembly. Each assembly requires 24 minutes of cell assembly time. There was no June 1 inventory for either Raw and In Process Inventory or Finished Goods Inventory.

The following summary events took place in the Burton cell during June:

a. Electronic parts and wiring were purchased to produce 12,000 instrument assemblies in June.
b. Conversion costs were applied for the production of 11,250 units in June.
c. 11,250 units were started and completed in June.
d. 11,000 units were shipped to customers at a price of $400 per unit.

Instructions

1. Determine the budgeted cell conversion cost per hour.
2. Determine the budgeted cell conversion cost per unit.
3. Journalize the summary transactions (a) through (d).
4. Determine the ending balance in Raw and In Process Inventory and Finished Goods Inventory.
5. ▭▶ How does the accounting in a JIT environment differ from traditional accounting?

PROBLEM 26-4B
Pareto chart and cost of quality report—service company

Objectives 4, 5

✓ *3. Nonvalue-added, 61.50%*

The controller of Guardian Insurance Company, W.E. Payup, has been asked to perform an activity analysis of its optical scanning center. The optical scanning center reads application, claims, and adjustment information into the computer. The result of the activity analysis is summarized as follows:

Activities	Activity Cost
Correcting errors identified by customers (claim, check, application errors)	$108,000
Correcting jams	85,500
Correcting scan errors	54,000
Loading	27,000
Logging-in control codes (for later reconciliation)	20,250
Program scanner	18,000
Rerunning job due to scan reading errors	29,250
Scanning	58,500
Verifing scan accuracy via reconciling totals	27,000
Verifing scanner accuracy with test run	22,500
Total	$450,000

Instructions

1. Prepare a Pareto chart of the department activities.
2. Use the activity cost information to determine the percentages of total department costs that are prevention, appraisal, internal failure, external failure, and not costs of quality. Round percentages to two decimal places.
3. Determine the percentages of the total department costs that are value- and nonvalue-added.
4. ▭▶ Interpret the information.

Special Activities

ACTIVITY 26-1
Ethics and professional conduct in business

ETHICS

In June, Calico Company introduced a new performance measurement system in manufacturing operations. One of the new performance measures was lead time. The lead time was determined by tagging a random sample of items with a log sheet throughout the month. This log sheet recorded the time that the item started and the time that it ended production, as well as all steps in between. The controller collected the log sheets and calculated the average lead time of the tagged products. This number was reported to central management and was used to evaluate the performance of the plant manager. The plant was under extreme pressure to reduce lead time because of poor lead time results reported in June.

The following memo was intercepted by the controller.

> Date: July 1
> To: Hourly Employees
> From: Plant Manager
>
> During last month, you noticed that some of the products were tagged with a log sheet. This sheet records the time that a product enters production and the time that it leaves production. The difference between these two times is termed the "lead time." Our plant is evaluated on improving lead time. From now on, I ask all of you to keep an eye out for the tagged items. When you receive a tagged item, it is to receive special attention. Work on that item first, and then immediately move it to the next operation. Under no circumstances should tagged items wait on any other work that you have. Naturally, report accurate information. I insist that you record the correct times on the log sheet as the product goes through your operations.

How should the controller respond to this discovery?

ACTIVITY 26-2
Just-in-time principles

Heaters Inc. manufactures electric space heaters. While the CEO, Brian Baily, is visiting the production facility, the following conversation takes place with the plant manager, Karen Alvarez:

Brian: As I walk around the facility, I can't help noticing all the materials inventories. What's going on?

Karen: I have found our suppliers to be very unreliable in meeting their delivery commitments. Thus, I keep a lot of materials on hand so as to not risk running out and shutting down production.

Brian: Not only do I see a lot of materials inventory, but there also seems to be a lot of finished goods inventory on hand. Why is this?

Karen: As you know, I am evaluated on maintaining a low cost per unit. The one way that I am able to reduce my unit costs is by producing as many space heaters as possible. This allows me to spread my fixed costs over a larger base. When orders are down, the excess production builds up as inventory, as we are seeing now. But don't worry—I'm really keeping our costs down this way.

Brian: I'm not so sure. It seems that this inventory must cost us something.

Karen: Not really. I'll eventually use the materials and we'll eventually sell the finished goods. By keeping the plant busy, I'm using our plant assets wisely. This is reflected in the low unit costs that I'm able to maintain.

If you were Baily, how would you respond to Alvarez? What recommendations would you provide Alvarez?

ACTIVITY 26-3
Just-in-time principles

Renaissance Labs Inc. prepared the following performance graphs for the prior year:

Total Manufacturing Lead Time

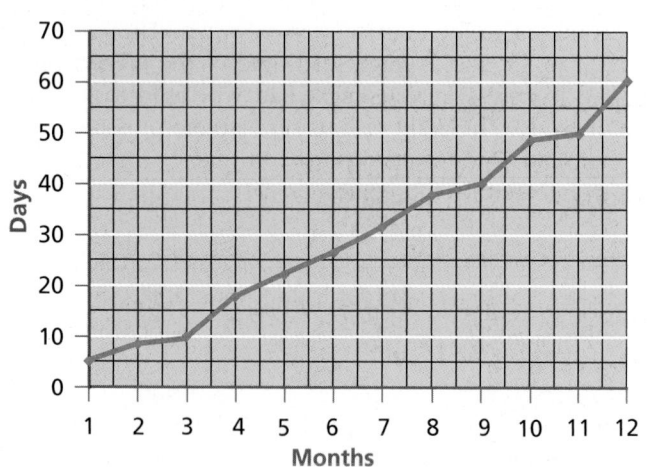

Percent of Sales Orders Filled on Time

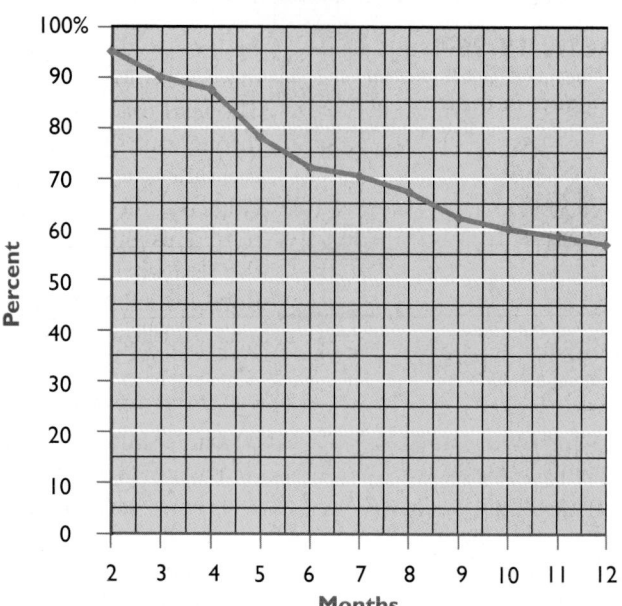

Total Inventory Dollars (in 000s)

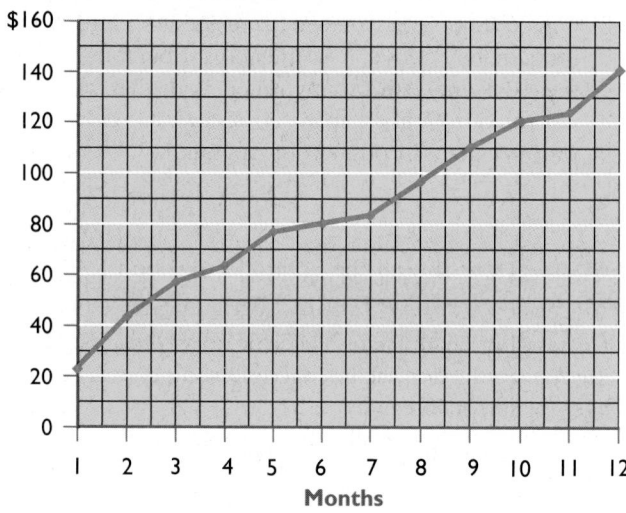

What do these charts appear to indicate?

ACTIVITY 26-4
Value-added and nonvalue-added activity costs

Laredo Company prepared the following factory overhead report from its general ledger:

Indirect labor	$500,000
Fringe benefits	60,000
Supplies	110,000
Depreciation	230,000
Total	$900,000

The management of Laredo Company was dissatisfied with this report and asked the controller to prepare an activity analysis of the same information. This activity analysis was as follows:

Processing sales orders	$216,000	24%
Disposing scrap	198,000	22
Expediting work orders	162,000	18
Producing parts	126,000	14
Resolving supplier quality problems	90,000	10
Reissuing corrected purchase orders	72,000	8
Expediting customer orders	36,000	4
Total	$900,000	100%

Interpret the activity analysis by identifying value-added and nonvalue-added activity costs. How does the activity cost report differ from the general ledger report?

ACTIVITY 26-5
Lead time

GROUP ACTIVITY

In groups of two to four people, visit a sit-down restaurant and do a lead time study. If more than one group chooses to visit the same restaurant, choose different times for your visits. Note the time when you walk in the door of the restaurant and the time when you walk out the door after you have eaten. The difference between these two times is the total lead time of your restaurant experience. While in the restaurant, determine the time spent on nonvalue-added time, such as wait time, and the time spent on value-added eating time. Note the various activities and the time required to perform each activity during your visit to the restaurant. Compare your analyses, identifying possible reasons for differences in the times recorded by groups that visited the same restaurant.

Answers to Self-Examination Questions

1. **B** The just-in-time philosophy embraces a product-oriented layout (answer A), making lead times short (answer C), and reducing setup times (answer D). Pull manufacturing, the opposite of push manufacturing (answer B), is also a just-in-time principle.

2. **D** Accounting in a just-in-time environment should not be complex (answer A), not focus on direct labor (answer B) because it is combined with other conversion costs, and not provide detailed variance reporting (answer C) because of a higher reliance on nonfinancial performance measures. However, the just-in-time accounting environment will have fewer transaction control features than the traditional system (answer D).

3. **C** $420,000\2,100 hours = $200 per hour
   $200 per hour × 0.25 hour = $50 per unit
   700 units × ($50 + $12.50) = $43,750

4. **B** Appraisal costs (answer B) are the costs of inspecting and testing activities, which include detecting, measuring, evaluating, and auditing products and processes. Prevention (answer A) activities are incurred to prevent defects from occurring during the design and delivery of products or services. Internal failure costs (answer C) are associated with defects that are discovered by the organization before the product or service is delivered to the consumer. External failure costs (answer D) are the costs incurred after defective units or service have been delivered to consumers.

5. **A** A Pareto chart is a bar chart that ranks attribute totals by category (answer A). A line chart (answer B), a pie chart (answer C), and a table listing (answer D) are other ways of displaying information, but they are not Pareto charts.

Present Value of Ordinary Annuity of $1 per Period: $p_{\bar{n}\backslash i} = \dfrac{1 - \dfrac{1}{(1 + i)^n}}{i}$

n＼i	5%	5.5%	6%	6.5%	7%	8%
1	0.95238	0.94787	0.94340	0.93897	0.93458	0.92593
2	1.85941	1.84632	1.83339	1.82063	1.80802	1.78326
3	2.72325	2.69793	2.67301	2.64848	2.62432	2.57710
4	3.54595	3.50515	3.46511	3.42580	3.38721	3.31213
5	4.32948	4.27028	4.21236	4.15568	4.10020	3.99271
6	5.07569	4.99553	4.91732	4.84101	4.76654	4.62288
7	5.78637	5.68297	5.58238	5.48452	5.38923	5.20637
8	6.46321	6.33457	6.20979	6.08875	5.97130	5.74664
9	7.10782	6.95220	6.80169	6.65610	6.51523	6.24689
10	7.72174	7.53763	7.36009	7.18883	7.02358	6.71008
11	8.30641	8.09254	7.88688	7.68904	7.49867	7.13896
12	8.86325	8.61852	8.38384	8.15873	7.94269	7.53608
13	9.39357	9.11708	8.85268	8.59974	8.35765	7.90378
14	9.89864	9.58965	9.29498	9.01384	8.74547	8.22424
15	10.37966	10.03758	9.71225	9.40267	9.10791	8.55948
16	10.83777	10.46216	10.10590	9.76776	9.44665	8.85137
17	11.27407	10.86461	10.47726	10.11058	9.76322	9.12164
18	11.68959	11.24607	10.82760	10.43247	10.05909	9.37189
19	12.08532	11.60765	11.15812	10.73471	10.33560	9.60360
20	12.46221	11.95038	11.46992	11.01851	10.59401	9.81815
21	12.82115	12.27524	11.76408	11.28498	10.83553	10.01680
22	13.16300	12.58317	12.04158	11.53520	11.06124	10.20074
23	13.48857	12.87504	12.30338	11.77014	11.27219	10.37106
24	13.79864	13.15170	12.55036	11.99074	11.46933	10.52876
25	14.09394	13.41393	12.78336	12.19788	11.65358	10.67478
26	14.37518	13.66250	13.00317	12.39237	11.82578	10.80998
27	14.64303	13.89810	13.21053	12.57500	11.98671	10.93516
28	14.89813	14.12142	13.40616	12.74648	12.13711	11.05108
29	15.14107	14.33310	13.59072	12.90749	12.27767	11.15841
30	15.37245	14.53375	13.76483	13.05868	12.40904	11.25778
31	15.59281	14.72393	13.92909	13.20063	12.53181	11.34980
32	15.80268	14.90420	14.08404	13.33393	12.64656	11.43500
33	16.00255	15.07507	14.23023	13.45909	12.75379	11.51389
34	16.19290	15.23703	14.36814	13.57661	12.85401	11.58693
35	16.37420	15.39055	14.49825	13.68696	12.94767	11.65457
40	17.15909	16.04612	15.04630	14.14553	13.33171	11.92461
45	17.77407	16.54773	15.45583	14.48023	13.60552	12.10840
50	18.25592	16.93152	15.76186	14.72452	13.80075	12.23348

Present Value of Ordinary Annuity of \$1 per Period: $p_{\overline{n}|i} = \dfrac{1 - \dfrac{1}{(1+i)^n}}{i}$

$n \backslash i$	9%	10%	11%	12%	13%	14%
1	0.91743	0.90909	0.90090	0.89286	0.88496	0.87719
2	1.75911	1.73554	1.71252	1.69005	1.66810	1.64666
3	2.53130	2.48685	2.44371	2.40183	2.36115	2.32163
4	3.23972	3.16986	3.10245	3.03735	2.97447	2.91371
5	3.88965	3.79079	3.69590	3.60478	3.51723	3.43308
6	4.48592	4.35526	4.23054	4.11141	3.99755	3.88867
7	5.03295	4.86842	4.71220	4.56376	4.42261	4.28830
8	5.53482	5.33493	5.14612	4.96764	4.79677	4.63886
9	5.99525	5.75902	5.53705	5.32825	5.13166	4.94637
10	6.41766	6.14457	5.88923	5.65022	5.42624	5.21612
11	6.80519	6.49506	6.20652	5.93770	5.68694	5.45273
12	7.16072	6.81369	6.49236	6.19437	5.91765	5.66029
13	7.48690	7.10336	6.74987	6.42355	6.12181	5.84236
14	7.78615	7.36669	6.96187	6.62817	6.30249	6.00207
15	8.06069	7.60608	7.19087	6.81086	6.46238	6.14217
16	8.31256	7.82371	7.37916	6.97399	6.60388	6.26506
17	8.54363	8.02155	7.54879	7.11963	6.72909	6.37286
18	8.75562	8.20141	7.70162	7.24967	6.83991	6.46742
19	8.95012	8.36492	7.83929	7.36578	6.93797	6.55037
20	9.12855	8.51356	7.96333	7.46944	7.02475	6.62313
21	9.29224	8.64869	8.07507	7.56200	7.10155	6.68696
22	9.44242	8.77154	8.17574	7.64465	7.16951	6.74294
23	9.58021	8.88322	8.26643	7.71843	7.22966	6.79206
24	9.70661	8.98474	8.34814	7.78432	7.28288	6.83514
25	9.82258	9.07704	8.42174	7.84314	7.32998	6.87293
26	9.92897	9.16094	8.48806	7.89566	7.37167	6.90608
27	10.02658	9.23722	8.54780	7.94255	7.40856	6.93515
28	10.11613	9.30657	8.60162	7.98442	7.44120	6.96066
29	10.19828	9.36961	8.65011	8.02181	7.47009	6.98304
30	10.27365	9.42691	8.69379	8.05518	7.49565	7.00266
31	10.34280	9.47901	8.73315	8.08499	7.51828	7.01988
32	10.40624	9.52638	8.76860	8.11159	7.53830	7.03498
33	10.46444	9.56943	8.80054	8.13535	7.55602	7.04823
34	10.51784	9.60858	8.82932	8.15656	7.57170	7.05985
35	10.56682	9.64416	8.85524	8.17550	7.58557	7.07005
40	10.75736	9.77905	8.95105	8.24378	7.63438	7.10504
45	10.88118	9.86281	9.00791	8.28252	7.66086	7.12322
50	10.96168	9.91481	9.04165	8.30450	7.67524	7.13266

Future Amount of $1 at Compound Interest Due in n Periods: $A_{\overline{n}|i} = (1 + i)^n$

$n \backslash i$	5%	5.5%	6%	6.5%	7%	8%
1	1.05000	1.05500	1.06000	1.06500	1.07000	1.08000
2	1.10250	1.11303	1.12360	1.13423	1.14490	1.16640
3	1.15762	1.17424	1.19102	1.20795	1.22504	1.25971
4	1.21551	1.23882	1.26248	1.28647	1.31080	1.36049
5	1.27628	1.30696	1.33823	1.37009	1.40255	1.46933
6	1.34100	1.37884	1.41852	1.45914	1.50073	1.58687
7	1.40710	1.45468	1.50363	1.55399	1.60578	1.71382
8	1.54347	1.53469	1.59385	1.65500	1.71819	1.85093
9	1.55133	1.61909	1.68948	1.76257	1.83846	1.99900
10	1.62890	1.70814	1.79085	1.87714	1.96715	2.15892
11	1.71034	1.80209	1.89830	1.99915	2.10485	2.33164
12	1.79586	1.90121	2.01220	2.12910	2.25219	2.51817
13	1.88565	2.00577	2.13293	2.26749	2.40984	2.71962
14	1.97993	2.11609	2.26091	2.41487	2.57853	2.93719
15	2.07893	2.23248	2.39656	2.57184	2.75903	3.17217
16	2.18288	2.35526	2.54035	2.73901	2.95216	3.42594
17	2.29202	2.48480	2.69277	2.91705	3.15882	3.70002
18	2.40662	2.62147	2.85434	3.10665	3.37993	3.99602
19	2.52695	2.76565	3.02560	3.30859	3.61653	4.31570
20	2.65330	2.91776	3.20714	3.52365	3.86968	4.66096
21	2.78596	3.07823	3.39956	3.75268	4.14056	5.03383
22	2.92526	3.24754	3.60354	3.99661	4.43040	5.43654
23	3.07152	3.42615	3.81975	4.25639	4.74053	5.87146
24	3.22510	3.61459	4.04894	4.53305	5.07237	6.34118
25	3.38636	3.81339	4.29187	4.82770	5.42743	6.84848
26	3.55567	4.02313	4.54938	5.14150	5.80735	7.39635
27	3.73346	4.24440	4.82235	5.47570	6.21387	7.98806
28	3.92013	4.47784	5.11169	5.83162	6.64884	8.62711
29	4.11614	4.72412	5.41839	6.21067	7.11426	9.31728
30	4.32194	4.98395	5.74349	6.61437	7.61226	10.06266
31	4.53804	5.25807	6.08810	7.04430	8.14511	10.86767
32	4.76494	5.54726	6.45339	7.50218	8.71527	11.73708
33	5.00319	5.85236	6.84059	7.98982	9.32534	12.67605
34	5.25335	6.17424	7.25102	8.50916	9.97811	13.69013
35	5.51602	6.51383	7.68609	9.06225	10.67658	14.78534
40	7.03999	8.51331	10.28572	12.41607	14.97446	21.72452
45	8.98501	11.12655	13.76461	17.01110	21.00245	31.92045
50	11.46740	14.54196	18.42015	23.30668	29.45702	46.90161

Future Amount of \$1 at Compound Interest Due in n Periods: $A_{\bar{n}\backslash i} = (1 + i)^n$

$n \backslash i$	9%	10%	11%	12%	13%	14%
1	1.09000	1.10000	1.11000	1.12000	1.13000	1.14000
2	1.18810	1.21000	1.23210	1.25440	1.27690	1.29960
3	1.29503	1.33100	1.36763	1.40493	1.44290	1.48154
4	1.41158	1.46410	1.51807	1.57352	1.63047	1.68896
5	1.53862	1.61051	1.68506	1.76234	1.84244	1.92541
6	1.67710	1.77156	1.87041	1.97382	2.08195	2.19497
7	1.82804	1.94872	2.07616	2.21068	2.35261	2.50227
8	1.99256	2.14359	2.30454	2.47596	2.65844	2.85259
9	2.17189	2.35795	2.55804	2.77308	3.00404	3.25195
10	2.36736	2.59374	2.83942	3.10585	3.39457	3.70722
11	2.58043	2.85312	3.15176	3.47855	3.83586	4.22623
12	2.81266	3.13843	3.49845	3.89598	4.33452	4.81790
13	3.06580	3.45227	3.88328	4.36349	4.89801	5.49241
14	3.34173	3.79750	4.31044	4.88711	5.53475	6.26135
15	3.64248	4.17725	4.78459	5.47357	6.25427	7.13794
16	3.97031	4.59497	5.31089	6.13039	7.06733	8.13725
17	4.32763	5.05447	5.89509	6.86604	7.98608	9.27646
18	4.71712	5.55992	6.54355	7.68997	9.02427	10.57517
19	5.14166	6.11591	7.26334	8.61276	10.19742	12.05569
20	5.60441	6.72750	8.06231	9.64629	11.52309	13.74349
21	6.10881	7.40025	8.94917	10.80385	13.02109	15.66758
22	6.65860	8.14028	9.93357	12.10031	14.71383	17.86104
23	7.25787	8.95430	11.02627	13.55235	16.62663	20.36158
24	7.91108	9.84973	12.23916	15.17863	18.78809	23.21221
25	8.62308	10.83471	13.58546	17.00006	21.23054	26.46192
26	9.39916	11.91818	15.07986	19.04007	23.99051	30.16658
27	10.24508	13.10999	16.73865	21.32488	27.10928	34.38991
28	11.16714	14.42099	18.57990	23.88387	30.63349	39.20449
29	12.17218	15.86309	20.62369	26.74993	34.61584	44.69312
30	13.26768	17.44940	22.89230	29.95992	39.11590	50.95016
31	14.46177	19.19434	25.41045	33.55511	44.20096	58.08318
32	15.76333	21.11378	28.20560	37.58173	49.94709	66.21483
33	17.18203	23.22515	31.30821	42.09153	56.44021	75.48490
34	18.72841	25.54767	34.75212	47.14252	63.77744	86.05279
35	20.41397	28.10244	38.57485	52.79962	72.06851	98.10018
40	31.40942	45.25926	65.00087	93.05097	132.78155	188.88351
45	48.32729	72.89048	109.53024	163.98760	244.64140	363.67907
50	74.35752	117.39085	184.56483	289.00219	450.73593	700.23299

Future Amount of Ordinary Annuity of \$1 per Period: $A_{\overline{n}|i} = \frac{(1 + i)^n - 1}{i}$

n＼i	5%	5.5%	6%	6.5%	7%	8%
1	1.00000	1.00000	1.00000	1.00000	1.00000	1.00000
2	2.05000	2.05500	2.06000	2.06500	2.07000	2.08000
3	3.15250	3.16802	3.18360	3.19922	3.21490	3.24640
4	4.31012	4.34227	4.37462	4.40717	4.43994	4.50611
5	5.52563	5.58109	5.63709	5.69364	5.75074	5.86660
6	6.80191	6.88805	6.97532	7.06373	7.15329	7.33593
7	8.14201	8.26689	8.39384	8.52287	8.65402	8.92280
8	9.54911	9.72157	9.89747	10.07688	10.25980	10.63663
9	11.02656	11.25626	11.49132	11.73185	11.97799	12.48756
10	12.57789	12.87535	13.18080	13.49442	13.81645	14.48656
11	14.20679	14.58350	14.97184	15.37156	15.78360	16.64549
12	15.91713	16.38559	16.86994	17.37071	17.88845	18.97713
13	17.71298	18.28680	18.88214	19.49981	20.14064	21.49530
14	19.59863	20.29257	21.01505	21.76730	22.55049	24.21492
15	21.57856	22.40866	23.27597	24.18217	25.12902	27.15211
16	23.65749	24.64114	25.67253	26.75401	27.88805	30.32428
17	25.84037	28.99640	28.21288	29.49302	30.84022	33.75023
18	28.13238	29.48120	30.90565	32.41007	33.99903	37.45024
19	30.53900	32.10267	33.75999	35.51672	37.37896	41.44626
20	33.06595	34.86832	36.78559	38.82531	40.99549	45.76196
21	35.71925	37.78608	39.99273	42.34895	44.86518	50.42292
22	38.50521	40.86431	43.39229	46.10164	49.00574	55.45676
23	41.43048	44.11185	46.99583	50.09824	53.43614	60.89330
24	44.50200	47.53800	50.81558	54.35463	58.17667	66.76476
25	47.72710	51.15259	54.86451	58.88768	63.24904	73.10594
26	51.11345	54.96598	59.15638	63.71538	68.67647	79.95442
27	54.66913	58.98911	63.70577	68.85688	74.48382	87.35077
28	58.40258	63.23351	68.52811	74.33257	80.69769	95.33883
29	62.32271	67.71135	73.62980	80.16419	87.34653	103.96594
30	66.43885	72.43548	79.05819	86.37486	94.46079	113.28321
31	70.76079	77.41943	84.80168	92.98923	102.07304	123.34587
32	75.29883	82.67750	90.88978	100.03353	110.21815	134.21354
33	80.06377	88.22476	97.34316	107.53571	118.93342	145.95062
34	85.06696	94.07712	104.18376	115.52553	128.25876	158.62667
35	90.32031	100.25136	111.43478	124.03469	138.23688	172.31680
40	120.79977	136.60561	154.76197	175.63192	199.63511	259.05652
45	159.70016	184.11917	212.74351	246.32459	285.74931	386.50562
50	209.34800	246.21748	290.33591	343.17967	406.52893	573.77016

Future Amount of Ordinary Annuity of $1 per Period: $A_{\overline{n}|i} = (1 + i)^n - 1/i$

$n \diagdown i$	9%	10%	11%	12%	13%	14%
1	1.00000	1.00000	1.00000	1.00000	1.00000	1.00000
2	2.09000	2.10000	2.11000	2.12000	2.13000	2.14000
3	3.27810	3.31000	3.34210	3.37440	3.40690	3.43960
4	4.57313	4.64100	4.70973	4.77933	4.84980	4.92114
5	5.98471	6.10510	6.22780	6.35285	6.48027	6.61010
6	7.52334	7.71561	7.91286	8.11519	8.32271	8.53552
7	9.20044	9.48717	9.78327	10.08901	10.40466	10.73049
8	11.02847	11.43589	11.85943	12.29969	12.75726	13.23276
9	13.02104	13.57948	14.16397	14.77566	15.41571	16.08535
10	15.19293	15.93742	16.72201	17.54874	18.41975	19.33730
11	17.56029	18.53117	19.56143	20.65458	21.81432	23.04452
12	20.14072	21.38428	22.71319	24.13313	25.65018	27.27075
13	22.95338	24.52271	26.21164	28.02911	29.98470	32.08865
14	26.01919	27.97498	30.09492	32.39260	34.88271	37.58107
15	29.36092	31.77248	34.40536	37.27972	40.41746	43.84241
16	33.00340	35.94973	39.18995	42.75328	46.67173	50.98035
17	36.97370	40.54470	44.50084	48.88367	53.73906	59.11760
18	41.30134	45.59917	50.39594	55.74972	61.72514	68.39407
19	46.01846	51.15909	56.93949	63.43968	70.74941	78.96923
20	51.16012	57.27500	64.20283	72.05244	80.94683	91.02493
21	56.76453	64.00250	72.26514	81.69874	92.46992	104.76842
22	62.87334	71.40275	81.21431	92.50258	105.49101	120.43600
23	69.53194	79.54302	91.14788	104.60289	120.20484	138.29704
24	76.78981	88.49733	102.17415	118.15524	136.83147	158.65862
25	84.70090	98.34706	114.41331	133.33387	155.61956	181.87083
26	93.32398	109.18176	127.99877	150.33393	176.85010	208.33274
27	102.72314	121.09994	143.07864	169.37401	200.84061	238.49933
28	112.96822	134.20994	159.81729	190.69889	227.94989	272.88923
29	124.13536	148.63093	178.39719	214.58275	258.58338	312.09373
30	136.30754	164.49402	199.02088	241.33268	293.19922	356.78685
31	149.57522	181.94342	221.91317	271.29261	332.31511	407.73701
32	164.03699	201.13777	247.32362	304.84772	376.51608	465.82019
33	179.80032	222.25154	275.52922	342.42945	426.46317	532.03501
34	196.98234	245.47670	306.83744	384.52098	482.90338	607.51991
35	215.71076	271.02437	341.58955	431.66350	546.68082	693.57270
40	337.88244	442.59256	581.82607	767.09142	1013.70424	1342.02510
45	525.85873	718.90484	986.63856	1358.23003	1874.16463	2590.56480
50	815.08356	1163.90853	1668.77115	2400.01825	3459.50712	4994.52135

appendix B

Alternative Methods of Recording Deferrals

As discussed in Chapter 3, deferrals are created by recording a transaction in a way that delays or defers the recognition of an expense or a revenue. Deferrals may be either deferred expenses (prepaid expenses) or deferred revenues (unearned revenues).

In Chapter 2, deferred expenses (prepaid expenses) were debited to an *asset* account at the time of payment. As an alternative, deferred expenses may be debited to an *expense* account at the time of payment. In Chapter 2, deferred revenues (unearned revenues) were credited to a *liability* account at the time of receipt. As an alternative, deferred revenues may be credited to a *revenue* account at the time of receipt. This appendix describes and illustrates these alternative methods of recording deferred expenses and deferred revenues.

Deferred Expenses (Prepaid Expenses)

As a basis for illustrating the alternative methods of recording deferred expenses, the insurance premium paid by NetSolutions in Chapter 2 is used. The amounts related to this insurance are as follows:

Prepayment of insurance for 24 months, starting December 1	$2,400
Insurance premium expired during December	100
Unexpired insurance premium at the end of December	$2,300

Based on the above data, the entries to account for the deferred expense (prepaid insurance) recorded initially as an *asset* are shown in the journal and T accounts in Exhibit 1. The adjusting entry in Exhibit 1 was shown in Chapter 3. The entries to account for the prepaid insurance recorded initially as an *expense* are shown in the journal and T accounts in Exhibit 2.

•Exhibit 1

Prepaid Expense Recorded Initially as Asset

Initial entry (to record initial payment):

Dec. 1	Prepaid Insurance	2,400	
	Cash		2,400

Adjusting entry (to transfer amount *used* to the proper *expense* account):

Dec. 31	Insurance Expense	100	
	Prepaid Insurance		100

Closing entry (to close income statement accounts with debit balances):

Income Summary		XXXX	
	Supplies Expense		XXXX
	Insurance Expense		100

Prepaid Insurance

Dec. 1	2,400	Dec. 31 Adjusting	100

Insurance Expense

Dec. 31 Adjusting	100	Dec. 31 Closing	100

•Exhibit 2

Prepaid Expense Recorded Initially as Expense

Initial entry (to record initial payment):

Dec. 1	Insurance Expense	2,400	
	Cash		2,400

Adjusting entry (to transfer amount *unused* to the proper *asset* account):

Dec. 31	Prepaid Insurance	2,300	
	Insurance Expense		2,300

Closing entry (to close income statement accounts with debit balances):

Income Summary		XXXX	
	Supplies Expense		XXXX
	Insurance Expense		100

Prepaid Insurance

Dec. 31 Adjusting	2,300		

Insurance Expense

Dec. 1	2,400	Dec. 31 Adjusting	2,300
		31 Closing	100

Either of the two methods of recording deferred expenses (prepaid expenses) may be used. As illustrated in Exhibits 1 and 2, both methods result in the same account balances after the adjusting entries have been recorded. Therefore, the amounts reported as expenses in the income statement and as assets on the balance sheet will not be affected by the method used. To avoid confusion, the method used by a business for each kind of prepaid expense should be followed consistently from year to year.

Some businesses record all deferred expenses using one method. Other businesses use one method to record the prepayment of some expenses and the other method for other expenses. Initial debits to the asset account are logical for prepayments of insurance, which are usually for periods of one to three years. On the other hand, rent on a building may be prepaid on the first of each month. The prepaid rent will expire by the end of the month. In this case, it is logical to record the payment of rent by initially debiting an expense account rather than an asset account.

Deferred Revenues (Unearned Revenues)

To illustrate the alternative methods of recording deferred revenues, we will use the rent received by NetSolutions in Chapter 2. NetSolutions rented land on December 1 to a local retailer for use as a parking lot for three months and received $360 for the entire three months. On December 31, $120 (1/3 × $360) of the rent has been earned, and $240 (2/3 × $360) of the rent is still unearned.

Based on the above data, the entries to account for the deferred revenue (unearned rent) recorded initially as a liability are shown in the journal and ledger in Exhibit 3. The adjusting entry in Exhibit 3 was shown in Chapter 3. The entries to account for the unearned rent recorded initially as revenue are shown in the journal and ledger in Exhibit 4.

As illustrated in Exhibits 3 and 4, both methods result in the same account balances after the adjusting entries have been recorded. Therefore, the amounts reported as revenues in the income statement and as liabilities on the balance sheet will not be affected by the method used. Either of the methods may be used for all

•**Exhibit 3**				•**Exhibit 4**			
Unearned Revenue Recorded Initially as Liability				**Unearned Revenue Recorded Initially as Revenue**			

Exhibit 3				Exhibit 4			
Initial entry (to record initial receipt):				Initial entry (to record initial receipt):			
Dec. 1	Cash	360		Dec. 1	Cash	360	
	Unearned Rent		360		Rent Revenue		360
Adjusting entry (to transfer amount *earned* to proper *revenue* account):				Adjusting entry (to transfer amount *unearned* to proper *liability* account):			
Dec. 31	Unearned Rent	120		Dec. 31	Rent Revenue	240	
	Rent Revenue		120		Unearned Rent		240
Closing entry (to close income statement accounts with credit balances):				Closing entry (to close income statement accounts with credit balances):			
Dec. 31	Fees Earned	XXXX		Dec. 31	Fees Earned	XXXX	
	Rent Revenue	120			Rent Revenue	120	
	Income Summary		XXXX		Income Summary		XXXX

Unearned Rent

Dec. 31	Adjusting	120	Dec. 1		360

Rent Revenue

Dec. 31	Closing	120	Dec. 31	Adjusting	120

Unearned Rent

			Dec. 31	Adjusting	240

Rent Revenue

Dec. 31	Adjusting	240	Dec. 1		360
31	Closing	120			

revenues received in advance. Alternatively, the first method may be used for advance receipts of some kinds of revenue and the second method for other kinds. To avoid confusion, the method used by a business for each kind of unearned revenue should be followed consistently from year to year.

Reversing Entries for Deferrals

As discussed in the appendix at the end of Chapter 4, the use of reversing entries is optional. However, the use of reversing entries generally simplifies the analysis of transactions and reduces the likelihood of errors in the subsequent recording of transactions. Normally, reversing entries are prepared for deferrals in the following two cases:

1. When a deferred expense (prepaid expense) is initially recorded as an expense.
2. When a deferred revenue (unearned revenue) is initially recorded as a revenue.

The entry to reverse the adjustment to record the prepaid insurance in Exhibit 2 is as follows:

Jan.	1	Insurance Expense	2,300	
		Prepaid Insurance		2,300

The entry to reverse the adjustment to record the unearned rent in Exhibit 4 is as follows:

Jan.	1	Unearned Rent	240	
		Rent Revenue		240

Exercises

EXERCISE B-1
Adjusting entries for office supplies

The office supplies purchased during the year total $4,570, and the amount of office supplies on hand at the end of the year is $460.

a. Record the following transactions directly in T accounts for Office Supplies and Office Supplies Expense, using the system of initially recording supplies as an asset: (1) purchases for the period; (2) adjusting entry at the end of the period. Identify each entry by number.
b. Record the following transactions directly in T accounts for Office Supplies and Office Supplies Expense, using the system of initially recording supplies as an expense: (1) purchases for the period; (2) adjusting entry at the end of the period. Identify each entry by number.

EXERCISE B-2
Adjusting entries for prepaid insurance

During the first year of operations, insurance premiums of $11,400 were paid. At the end of the year, unexpired premiums totaled $4,175. Journalize the adjusting entry at the end of the year, assuming that (a) prepaid expenses were initially recorded as assets and (b) prepaid expenses were initially recorded as expenses.

EXERCISE B-3
Adjusting entries for advertising revenue

The unearned advertising revenues collected in advance during the year total $482,800, and the unearned advertising revenue at the end of the year is $112,500.

a. Record the following transactions directly in T accounts for Unearned Advertising Revenue and Advertising Revenue, using the system of initially recording advertising fees as a liability: (1) revenues received during the period; (2) adjusting entry at the end of the period. Identify each entry by number.
b. Record the following transactions directly in T accounts for Unearned Advertising Revenue and Advertising Revenue, using the system of initially recording advertising fees as revenue: (1) revenues received during the period; (2) adjusting entry at the end of the period. Identify each entry by number.

EXERCISE B-4
Year-end entries for deferred revenues

In its first year of operation, Martin Publishing Co. received $3,275,000 in advance from advertising contracts and $9,195,000 in advance from magazine subscriptions, crediting the two amounts to Unearned Advertising Revenue and Circulation Revenue, respectively. At the end of the year, the unearned advertising revenue amounts to $396,000, and the circulation revenue amounts to $3,150,000. Journalize the adjusting entries that should be made at the end of the year.

appendix C

Special Journals and Subsidiary Ledgers

In the beginning chapters of this text, all transactions for NetSolutions were manually recorded in an all-purpose (two-column) journal. The journal entries were then posted individually to the accounts in the ledger. Such manual accounting systems are simple to use and easy to understand. Manually kept records may serve a business reasonably well when the amount of data collected, stored, and used is relatively small. For a large business with a large database, however, such manual processing is too costly and too time-consuming. For example, a large company such as **AT&T** has millions of long-distance telephone fees earned on account with millions of customers daily. Each telephone fee on account requires an entry debiting Accounts Receivable and crediting Fees Earned. In addition, a record of each customer's receivable must be kept. Clearly, a simple manual system would not serve the business needs of AT&T.

When a business has a large number of similar transactions, using an all-purpose journal is inefficient and impractical. In such cases, special journals are useful. In addition, the manual system can be supplemented or replaced by a computerized system. Although we will illustrate the manual use of special journals and subsidiary ledgers, the basic principles described in the following paragraphs also apply to a computerized accounting system.

Special Journals

One method of processing data more efficiently in a manual accounting system is to expand the all-purpose two-column journal to a multicolumn journal. Each column in a multicolumn journal is used only for recording transactions that affect a certain account. For example, a special column could be used only for recording debits to the cash account, and another special column could be used only for recording credits to the cash account. The addition of the two special columns would eliminate the writing of *Cash* in the journal for every receipt and every payment of cash. Also, there would be no need to post each individual debit and credit to the cash account. Instead, the *Cash Dr.* and *Cash Cr.* columns could be totaled periodically and only the totals posted. In a similar way, special columns could be added for recording credits to Fees Earned, debits and credits to Accounts Receivable and Accounts Payable, and for other entries that are often repeated.

An all-purpose multicolumn journal may be adequate for a small business that has many transactions of a similar nature. However, a journal that has many columns for recording many different types of transactions is impractical for larger businesses.

> **Special journals are a method of summarizing transactions.**

The next logical extension of the accounting system is to replace the single multicolumn journal with several ***special journals***. Each special journal is designed to be used for recording a single kind of transaction that occurs frequently. For example, since most businesses have many transactions in which cash is paid out, they will likely use a special journal for recording cash payments. Likewise, they will use another special journal for recording cash receipts. Special journals are a method of summarizing transactions, which is a basic feature of any accounting system.

The format and number of special journals that a business uses depends upon the nature of the business. A business that gives credit might use a special journal designed for recording only revenue from services provided on credit. On the other hand, a business that does not give credit would have no need for such a journal. In other cases, record-keeping costs may be reduced by using supporting documents as special journals.

The transactions that occur most often in a small- to medium-size service business and the special journals in which they are recorded are as follows:

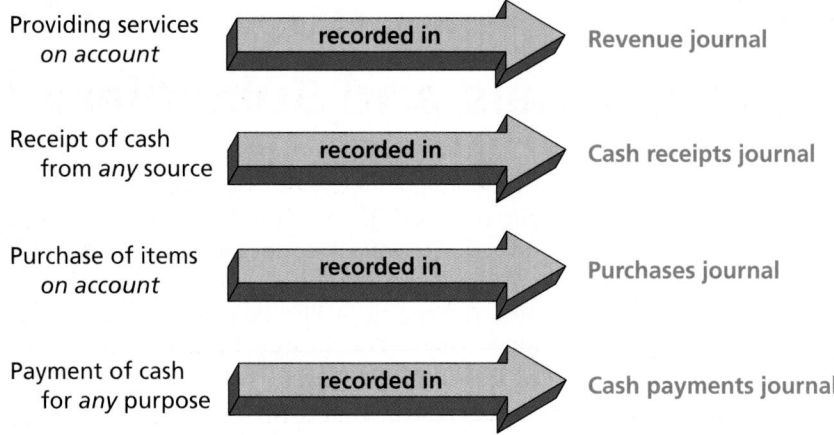

The all-purpose two-column journal, called the **general journal** or simply the **journal**, can be used for entries that do not fit into any of the special journals. For example, adjusting and closing entries are recorded in the general journal.

Subsidiary Ledgers

An accounting system should be designed to provide information on the amounts due from various customers (accounts receivable) and amounts owed to various creditors (accounts payable). A separate account for each customer and creditor could be added to the ledger. However, as the number of customers and creditors increases, the ledger becomes awkward to use when it includes many customers and creditors.

A large number of individual accounts with a common characteristic can be grouped together in a separate ledger called a **subsidiary ledger**. The primary ledger, which contains all of the balance sheet and income statement accounts, is then called the **general ledger**. Each subsidiary ledger is represented in the general ledger by a summarizing account, called a **controlling account**. The sum of the balances of the accounts in a subsidiary ledger must equal the balance of the related controlling account. Thus, you may think of a subsidiary ledger as a secondary ledger that supports a controlling account in the general ledger.

> **The sum of the balances of the subsidiary ledger accounts must equal the balance of the related controlling account.**

The individual accounts with customers are arranged in alphabetical order in a subsidiary ledger called the **accounts receivable subsidiary ledger**, or **customers ledger**. The controlling account in the general ledger that summarizes the debits and credits to the individual customer accounts is *Accounts Receivable*. The individual accounts with creditors are arranged in alphabetical order in a subsidiary ledger called the **accounts payable subsidiary ledger**, or **creditors ledger**. The related controlling account in the general ledger is *Accounts Payable*. The relationship between the general ledger and these subsidiary ledgers is illustrated in Exhibit 1.

In the following paragraphs, we illustrate special journals and subsidiary ledgers in a manual accounting system for NetSolutions. To simplify the illustration, we will use a minimum number of transactions. We will focus our discussion on two common operating cycles: (1) the revenue and collection cycle and (2) the purchase and payment cycle. We will assume that NetSolutions had the following selected general ledger balances on March 1, 2006:

Account Number	Account	Balance
11	Cash	$6,200
12	Accounts Receivable	3,400
14	Supplies	2,500
18	Office Equipment	2,500
21	Accounts Payable	1,230

•Exhibit 1 General Ledger and Subsidiary Ledgers

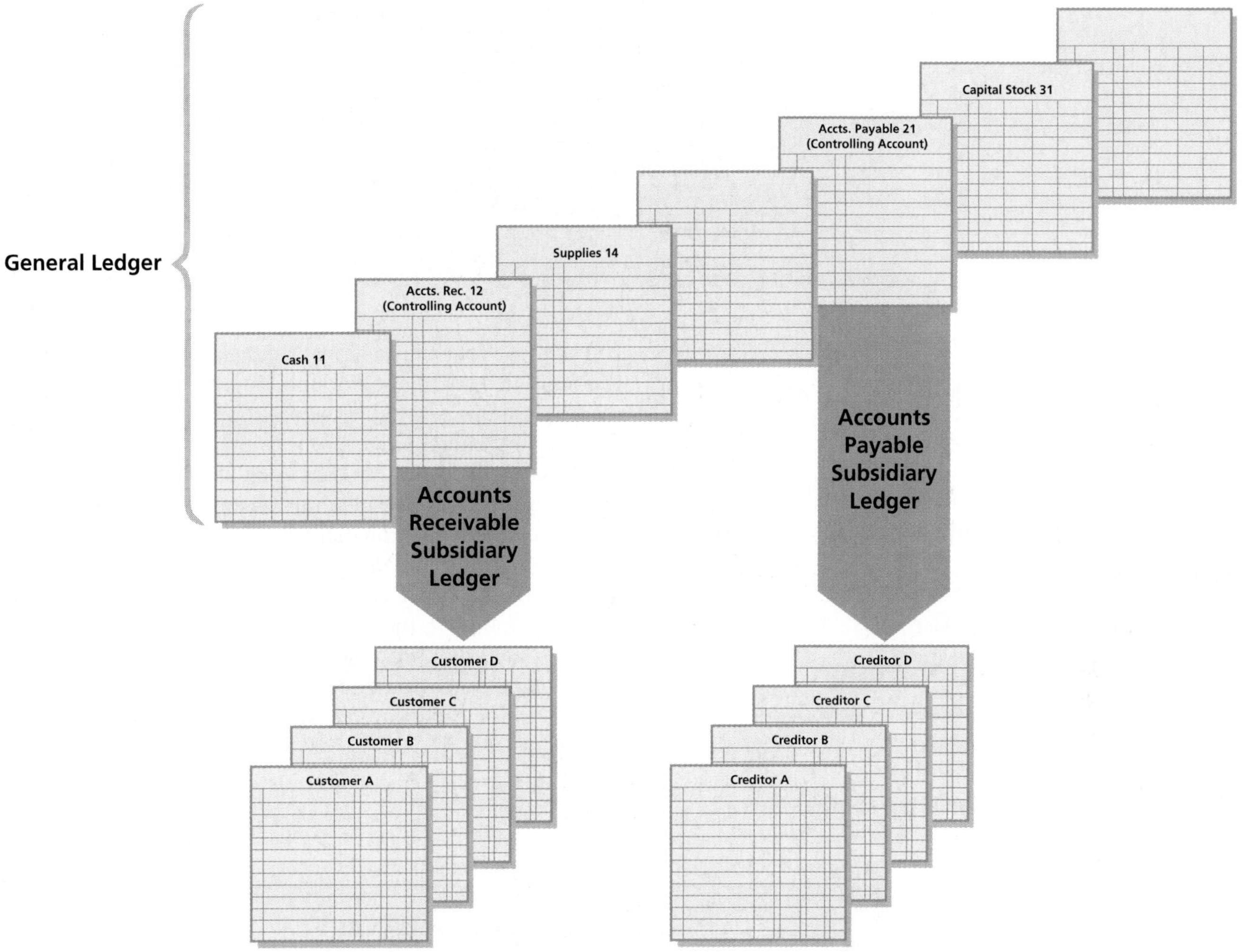

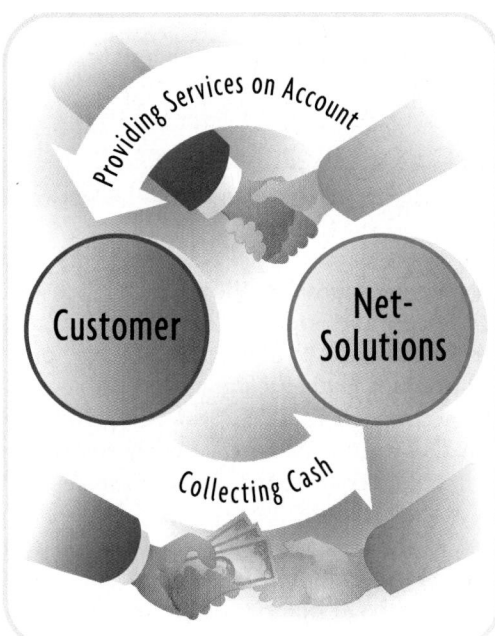

The Revenue and Collection Cycle

The **revenue and collection cycle** for NetSolutions consists of providing services on account and collecting cash from customers. Revenues earned on account create a customer receivable and will be recorded in a revenue journal. Customers' accounts receivable are collected and will be recorded in a cash receipts journal.

Internal control is enhanced by separating the function of recording revenue transactions in the revenue journal from recording cash collections in the cash receipts journal. For example, if these duties are separated, it is more difficult for one person to embezzle cash collections and manipulate the accounting records.

Revenue Journal

The **revenue journal** is used only for recording **fees earned on account**. *Cash fees earned would be recorded in the cash receipts journal.* The sale of products is recorded in a **sales journal**, which is similar to the revenue journal. We will compare the efficiency of using a revenue journal with a general journal by assuming that NetSolutions recorded the following revenue transactions in a general journal:

2006 Mar.	2	Accounts Receivable—MyMusicClub.com	12/✔	2 2 0 0 00			
		Fees Earned	41		2 2 0 0 00
	6	Accounts Receivable—RapZone.com	12/✔	1 7 5 0 00			
		Fees Earned	41		1 7 5 0 00
	18	Accounts Receivable—Web Cantina	12/✔	2 6 5 0 00			
		Fees Earned	41		2 6 5 0 00
	27	Accounts Receivable—MyMusicClub.com	12/✔	3 0 0 0 00			
		Fees Earned	41		3 0 0 0 00

> The general journal entry on March 2 is posted as a $2,200 debit to Accounts Receivable in the general ledger, a $2,200 debit to MyMusicClub.com in the accounts receivable subsidiary ledger, and a $2,200 credit to Fees Earned in the general ledger.

For these four transactions, NetSolutions recorded eight account titles and eight amounts. In addition, NetSolutions made 12 postings to the ledgers—four to Accounts Receivable in the general ledger, four to the accounts receivable subsidiary ledger (indicated by each check mark), and four to Fees Earned in the general ledger. These transactions could be recorded more efficiently in a revenue journal, as shown in Exhibit 2. In each revenue transaction, the amount of the debit to Accounts Receivable is the same as the amount of the credit to Fees Earned. Therefore, only a single amount column is necessary. The date, invoice number, customer name, and amount are entered separately for each transaction.

•**Exhibit 2**   Revenue Journal

					REVENUE JOURNAL			Page 35	
		Date	Invoice No.	Account Debited			Post. Ref.	Accts. Rec. Dr. Fees Earned Cr.	
1	2006 Mar.	2	615	MyMusicClub.com				2 2 0 0 00	1
2		6	616	RapZone.com				1 7 5 0 00	2
3		18	617	Web Cantina				2 6 5 0 00	3
4		27	618	MyMusicClub.com				3 0 0 0 00	4
5		31						9 6 0 0 00	5

The basic procedure of posting from a revenue journal is shown in Exhibit 3. A single monthly total is posted to Accounts Receivable and Fees Earned in the general ledger. Each transaction, such as the $2,200 debit to MyMusicClub.com, must also be posted individually to a customer account in the accounts receivable subsidiary ledger. These postings to customer accounts should be made frequently. In this way, management has information on the current balance of each customer's account. Since the balances in the customer accounts are usually debit balances, the three-column account form shown in the exhibit is often used.

To provide a trail of the entries posted to the subsidiary ledger, the source of these entries is indicated in the *Posting Reference* column of each account by inserting the letter *R* (for revenue journal) and the page number of the revenue journal. A check mark (✔) instead of a number is then inserted in the *Posting Reference* column of the revenue journal, as shown in Exhibit 3.

•Exhibit 3   Revenue Journal Postings to Ledgers

REVENUE JOURNAL   Page 35

	Date	Invoice No.	Account Debited	Post. Ref.	Accts. Rec. Dr. Fees Earned Cr.	
	2006					
1	Mar. 2	615	MyMusicClub.com	✔	2,200	1
2	6	616	RapZone.com	✔	1,750	2
3	18	617	Web Cantina	✔	2,650	3
4	27	618	MyMusicClub.com	✔	3,000	4
5	31				9,600	5
6					(12) (41)	6

GENERAL LEDGER

ACCOUNT   Accounts Receivable   **Account No. 12**

Date	Item	Post. Ref.	Dr.	Cr.	Balance Dr.	Balance Cr.
2006						
Mar. 1	Balance	✔			3,400	
31		R35	9,600		13,000	

ACCOUNT   Fees Earned   **Account No. 41**

Date	Item	Post. Ref.	Dr.	Cr.	Balance Dr.	Balance Cr.
2006						
Mar. 31		R35		9,600		9,600

ACCOUNTS RECEIVABLE SUBSIDIARY LEDGER

NAME: MyMusicClub.com

Date	Item	Post. Ref.	Dr.	Cr.	Balance
2006					
Mar. 2		R35	2,200		2,200
27		R35	3,000		5,200

NAME: RapZone.com

Date	Item	Post. Ref.	Dr.	Cr.	Balance
2006					
Mar. 6		R35	1,750		1,750

NAME: Web Cantina

Date	Item	Post. Ref.	Dr.	Cr.	Balance
2006					
Mar. 1	Balance	✔			3,400
18		R35	2,650		6,050

If a customer's account has a credit balance, that fact should be indicated by an asterisk or parentheses in the *Balance* column. When an account's balance is zero, a line may be drawn in the *Balance* column.

At the end of each month, the amount column of the revenue journal is totaled. This total is equal to the sum of the month's debits to the individual accounts in the subsidiary ledger. It is posted in the general ledger as a debit to Accounts Receivable and a credit to Fees Earned, as shown in Exhibit 3. The respective account numbers (12 and 41) are then inserted below the total in the revenue journal to indicate that the posting is completed, as shown in Exhibit 3. In this way, all of the transactions for fees earned during the month are posted to the general ledger only once—at the end of the month—greatly simplifying the posting process.

Cash Receipts Journal

All transactions that involve the receipt of cash are recorded in a **cash receipts journal**. Thus, the cash receipts journal has a column entitled *Cash Dr.*, as shown in Exhibit 4. All transactions recorded in the cash receipts journal will involve an entry in the *Cash Dr.* column. For example, on March 28 NetSolutions received cash of $2,200 from MyMusicClub.com and entered that amount in the *Cash Dr.* column.

•Exhibit 4   Cash Receipts Journal and Postings

CASH RECEIPTS JOURNAL   Page 14

	Date	Account Credited	Post. Ref.	Other Accounts Cr.	Accounts Receivable Cr.	Cash Dr.	
1	2006 Mar. 1	Rent Revenue	42	400		400	1
2	19	Web Cantina	✔		3,400	3,400	2
3	28	MyMusicClub.com	✔		2,200	2,200	3
4	30	RapZone.com	✔		1,750	1,750	4
5	31			400	7,350	7,750	5
6				(✔)	(12)	(11)	6

GENERAL LEDGER

ACCOUNT   Rent Revenue   Account No. 42

Date	Item	Post. Ref.	Dr.	Cr.	Balance Dr.	Balance Cr.
2006 Mar. 1		CR14		400		400

ACCOUNT   Accounts Receivable   Account No. 12

Date	Item	Post. Ref.	Dr.	Cr.	Balance Dr.	Balance Cr.
2006 Mar. 1	Balance	✔			3,400	
31		R35	9,600		13,000	
31		CR14		7,350	5,650	

ACCOUNT   Cash   Account No. 11

Date	Item	Post. Ref.	Dr.	Cr.	Balance Dr.	Balance Cr.
2006 Mar. 1	Balance	✔			6,200	
31		CR14	7,750		13,950	

ACCOUNTS RECEIVABLE SUBSIDIARY LEDGER

NAME: MyMusicClub.com

Date	Item	Post. Ref.	Dr.	Cr.	Balance
2006 Mar. 2		R35	2,200		2,200
27		R35	3,000		5,200
28		CR14		2,200	3,000

NAME: RapZone.com

Date	Item	Post. Ref.	Dr.	Cr.	Balance
2006 Mar. 6		R35	1,750		1,750
30		CR14		1,750	—

NAME: Web Cantina

Date	Item	Post. Ref.	Dr.	Cr.	Balance
2006 Mar. 1	Balance	✔			3,400
18		R35	2,650		6,050
19		CR14		3,400	2,650

The kinds of transactions in which cash is received and how often they occur determine the titles of the other columns. For NetSolutions, the most frequent source of cash is collections from customers. Thus, the cash receipts journal in Exhibit 4 has an *Accounts Receivable Cr.* column. On March 28, when MyMusicClub.com made a payment on its account, NetSolutions entered *MyMusicClub.com* in the *Account Credited* column and entered *2,200* in the *Accounts Receivable Cr.* column.

The *Other Accounts Cr.* column in Exhibit 4 is used for recording credits to any account for which there is no special credit column. For example, NetSolutions received cash on March 1 for rent. Since no special column exists for Rent Revenue, NetSolutions entered *Rent Revenue* in the *Account Credited* column and entered *400* in the *Other Accounts Cr.* column.

Postings from the cash receipts journal to the ledgers of NetSolutions are also shown in Exhibit 4. This posting process is similar to that of the revenue journal. At regular intervals, each amount in the *Other Accounts Cr.* column is posted to the proper account in the general ledger. The posting is indicated by inserting the account number in the *Posting Reference* column of the cash receipts journal. The posting reference *CR* (for cash receipts journal) and the proper page number are inserted in the *Posting Reference* columns of the accounts.

The amounts in the *Accounts Receivable Cr.* column are posted individually to the customer accounts in the accounts receivable subsidiary ledger. These postings should be made frequently. The posting reference *CR* and the proper page number are inserted in the *Posting Reference* column of each customer's account. A check mark is placed in the *Posting Reference* column of the cash receipts journal to show that each amount has been posted. None of the individual amounts in the *Cash Dr.* column is posted separately.

At the end of the month, all of the amount columns are totaled. The debits should equal the credits. Because each amount in the *Other Accounts Cr.* column has been posted individually to a general ledger account, a check mark is inserted below the column total to indicate that no further action is needed. The totals of the *Accounts Receivable Cr.* and *Cash Dr.* columns are posted to the proper accounts in the general ledger, and their account numbers are inserted below the totals to show that the postings have been completed.

Accounts Receivable Control and Subsidiary Ledger

After all posting has been completed for the month, the sum of the balances in the accounts receivable subsidiary ledger should be compared with the balance of the accounts receivable controlling account in the general ledger. If the controlling account and the subsidiary ledger do not agree, the error or errors must be located and corrected. The balances of the individual customer accounts may be summarized in a schedule of accounts receivable. The total of NetSolutions' schedule of accounts receivable, $5,650, agrees with the balance of its accounts receivable controlling account on March 31, 2006, as shown below.

Accounts Receivable— (Controlling)		NetSolutions Schedule of Accounts Receivable March 31, 2006	
Balance, March 1, 2006	$3,400	MyMusicClub.com	$3,000
Total debits (from revenue journal)	9,600	RapZone.com	0
Total credits (from cash receipts journal)	(7,350)	Web Cantina	2,650
Balance, March 31, 2006	$5,650	Total accounts receivable	$5,650

The Purchase and Payment Cycle

The **purchase and payment cycle** for NetSolutions consists of purchases on account and payments of cash to suppliers. To make purchases of supplies and other items on account requires establishing a supplier account payable. These transactions will be recorded in a purchases journal. The payments of suppliers' accounts payable will be recorded in the cash payments journal.

Internal control is enhanced by separating the function of recording purchases in the purchases journal from recording cash payments in the cash payments journal.

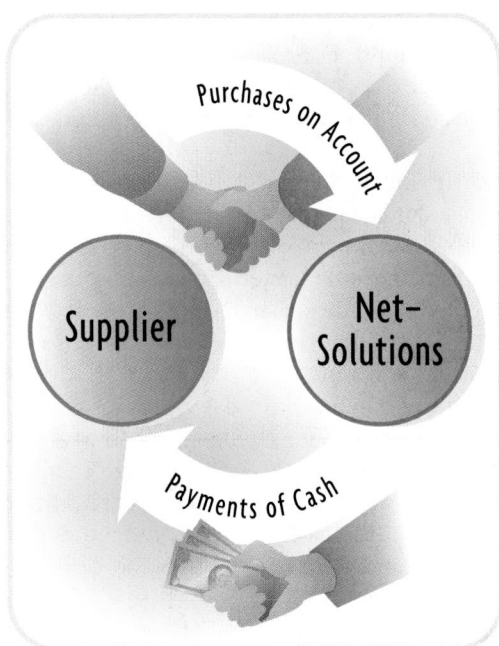

Separating duties in this way prevents an individual from establishing a fictitious supplier and then collecting payments for fictitious purchases from this supplier.

Purchases Journal

The ***purchases journal*** is designed for recording all **purchases on account**. *Cash purchases would be recorded in the cash payments journal*. The purchases journal has a column entitled *Accounts Payable Cr.* The purchases journal also has special columns for recording debits to the accounts most often affected. Since NetSolutions makes frequent debits to its supplies account, a *Supplies Dr.* column is included for these transactions. For example, as shown in Exhibit 5, NetSolutions recorded the purchase of supplies on March 3 by entering *600* in the *Supplies Dr.* column, *600* in the *Accounts Payable Cr.* column, and *Howard Supplies* in the *Account Credited* column.

The *Other Accounts Dr.* column in Exhibit 5 is used to record purchases, on account, of any item for which there is no special debit column. The title of the account to be debited is entered in the *Other Accounts* column, and the amount is entered in the *Amount* column. For example, NetSolutions recorded the purchase of office equipment on account on March 12 by entering *Office Equipment* in the *Other Accounts Dr.* column, *2,800* in the *Amount* column, *2,800* in the *Accounts Payable Cr.* column, and *Jewett Business Systems* in the *Account Credited* column.

Postings from the purchases journal to the ledgers of NetSolutions are also shown in Exhibit 5. The principles used in posting the purchases journal are similar to those used in posting the revenue and cash receipts journals. The source of the entries posted to the subsidiary and general ledgers is indicated in the *Posting Reference* column of each account by inserting the letter *P* (for purchases journal) and the page number of the purchases journal. A check mark (✔) is inserted in the *Posting Reference* column of the purchases journal after each credit is posted to a creditor's account in the accounts payable subsidiary ledger.

At regular intervals, the amounts in the *Other Accounts Dr.* column are posted to the accounts in the general ledger. As each amount is posted, the related general ledger account number is inserted in the *Posting Reference* column of the *Other Accounts* section.

At the end of each month, the amount columns in the purchases journal are totaled. The sum of the two debit column totals should equal the sum of the credit column.

The totals of the *Accounts Payable Cr.* and *Supplies Dr.* columns are posted to the appropriate general ledger accounts in the usual manner, with the related account numbers inserted below the column totals. Because each amount in the *Other Accounts Dr.* column was posted individually, a check mark is placed below the $2,800 total to show that no further action is needed.

Cash Payments Journal

The special columns for the ***cash payments journal*** are determined in the same manner as for the revenue, cash receipts, and purchases journals. The determining factors are the kinds of transactions to be recorded and how often they occur.

The cash payments journal has a *Cash Cr.* column, as shown in Exhibit 6 on page C-10. All transactions recorded in the cash payments journal will involve an entry in this column. Payments to creditors on account happen often enough to require an *Accounts Payable Dr.* column. Debits to creditor accounts for invoices paid are recorded in the *Accounts Payable Dr.* column. For example, on March 15 NetSolutions paid $1,230 on its account with Grayco Supplies. NetSolutions recorded this transaction by entering *1,230* in the *Accounts Payable Dr.* column, *1,230* in the *Cash Cr.* column, and *Grayco Supplies* in the *Account Debited* column.

•Exhibit 5   Purchases Journal and Postings

PURCHASES JOURNAL   Page 11

	Date	Account Credited	Post. Ref.	Accounts Payable Cr.	Supplies Dr.	Other Accounts Dr.	Post. Ref.	Amount	
	2006								
1	Mar. 3	Howard Supplies	✔	600	600				1
2	7	Donnelly Supplies	✔	420	420				2
3	12	Jewett Business Systems	✔	2,800		Office Equipment	18	2,800	3
4	19	Donnelly Supplies	✔	1,450	1,450				4
5	27	Howard Supplies	✔	960	960				5
6	31			6,230	3,430			2,800	6
7				(21)	(14)			(✔)	7

GENERAL LEDGER

ACCOUNT   Accounts Payable   Account No. 21

Date	Item	Post. Ref.	Dr.	Cr.	Balance
2006					
Mar. 1	Balance	✔			1,230
31		P11		6,230	7,460

ACCOUNT   Supplies   Account No. 14

Date	Item	Post. Ref.	Dr.	Cr.	Balance
2006					
Mar. 1	Balance	✔			2,500
31		P11	3,430		5,930

ACCOUNT   Office Equipment   Account No. 18

Date	Item	Post. Ref.	Dr.	Cr.	Balance
2006					
Mar. 1	Balance	✔			2,500
12		P11	2,800		5,300

ACCOUNTS PAYABLE SUBSIDIARY LEDGER

NAME: Donnelly Supplies

Date	Item	Post. Ref.	Dr.	Cr.	Balance
2006					
Mar. 7		P11		420	420
19		P11		1,450	1,870

NAME: Grayco Supplies

Date	Item	Post. Ref.	Dr.	Cr.	Balance
2006					
Mar. 1	Balance	✔			1,230

NAME: Howard Supplies

Date	Item	Post. Ref.	Dr.	Cr.	Balance
2006					
Mar. 3		P11		600	600
27		P11		960	1,560

NAME: Jewett Business Systems

Date	Item	Post. Ref.	Dr.	Cr.	Balance
2006					
Mar. 12		P11		2,800	2,800

NetSolutions makes all payments by check. As each transaction is recorded in the cash payments journal, the related check number is entered in the column at the right of the *Date* column. The check numbers are helpful in controlling cash payments, and they provide a useful cross-reference.

The *Other Accounts Dr.* column is used for recording debits to any account for which there is no special column. For example, NetSolutions paid $1,600 on March

•Exhibit 6   Cash Payments Journal and Postings

CASH PAYMENTS JOURNAL   Page 7

	Date	Ck. No.	Account Debited	Post. Ref.	Other Accounts Dr.	Accounts Payable Dr.	Cash Cr.	
	2006							
1	Mar. 2	150	Rent Expense	52	1,600		1,600	1
2	15	151	Grayco Supplies	✔		1,230	1,230	2
3	21	152	Jewett Business Systems	✔		2,800	2,800	3
4	22	153	Donnelly Supplies	✔		420	420	4
5	30	154	Utilities Expense	54	1,050		1,050	5
6	31	155	Howard Supplies	✔		600	600	6
7	31				2,650	5,050	7,700	7
8					(✔)	(21)	(11)	8

GENERAL LEDGER

ACCOUNT   Accounts Payable   Account No. 21

Date	Item	Post. Ref.	Dr.	Cr.	Balance
2006					
Mar. 1	Balance	✔			1,230
31		P11		6,230	7,460
31		CP7	5,050		2,410

ACCOUNT   Cash   Account No. 11

Date	Item	Post. Ref.	Dr.	Cr.	Balance
2006					
Mar. 1	Balance	✔			6,200
31		CR14	7,750		13,950
31		CP7		7,700	6,250

ACCOUNT   Rent Expense   Account No. 52

Date	Item	Post. Ref.	Dr.	Cr.	Balance
2006					
Mar. 2		CP7	1,600		1,600

ACCOUNT   Utilities Expense   Account No. 54

Date	Item	Post. Ref.	Dr.	Cr.	Balance
2006					
Mar. 30		CP7	1,050		1,050

ACCOUNTS PAYABLE SUBSIDIARY LEDGER

NAME: Donnelly Supplies

Date	Item	Post. Ref.	Dr.	Cr.	Balance
2006					
Mar. 7		P11		420	420
19		P11		1,450	1,870
22		CP7	420		1,450

NAME: Grayco Supplies

Date	Item	Post. Ref.	Dr.	Cr.	Balance
2006					
Mar. 1	Balance	✔			1,230
15		CP7	1,230		—

NAME: Howard Supplies

Date	Item	Post. Ref.	Dr.	Cr.	Balance
2006					
Mar. 3		P11		600	600
27		P11		960	1,560
31		CP7	600		960

NAME: Jewett Business Systems

Date	Item	Post. Ref.	Dr.	Cr.	Balance
2006					
Mar. 12		P11		2,800	2,800
21		CP7	2,800		—

2 for rent. The transaction was recorded by entering *Rent Expense* in the space provided and *1,600* in the *Other Accounts Dr.* and *Cash Cr.* columns.

Postings from the cash payments journal to the ledgers of NetSolutions are also shown in Exhibit 6. The amounts entered in the *Accounts Payable Dr.* column are posted to the individual creditor accounts in the accounts payable subsidiary ledger. These postings should be made frequently. After each posting, *CP* (for cash payments journal) and the page number of the journal are inserted in the *Posting Reference* column of the account. A check mark is placed in the *Posting Reference* column of the cash payments journal to indicate that each amount has been posted.

At regular intervals, each item in the *Other Accounts Dr.* column is also posted individually to an account in the general ledger. The posting is indicated by writing the account number in the *Posting Reference* column of the cash payments journal.

At the end of the month, each of the amount columns in the cash payments journal is totaled. The sum of the two debit totals is compared with the credit total to determine their equality. A check mark is placed below the total of the *Other Accounts Dr.* column to indicate that no further action is needed. When each of the totals of the other two columns is posted to the general ledger, an account number is inserted below each column total.

Accounts Payable Control and Subsidiary Ledger

After all posting has been completed for the month, the sum of the balances in the accounts payable subsidiary ledger should be compared with the balance of the accounts payable controlling account in the general ledger. If the controlling account and the subsidiary ledger do not agree, the error or errors must be located and corrected. The balances of the individual supplier accounts may be summarized in a schedule of accounts payable. The total of NetSolutions' schedule of accounts payable, $2,410, agrees with the balance of the accounts payable controlling account on March 31, 2006, as shown below.

Accounts Payable— (Controlling)		NetSolutions Schedule of Accounts Payable March 31, 2006	
Balance, March 1, 2006	$1,230	Donnelly Supplies	$1,450
Total credits (from purchases journal)	6,230	Grayco Supplies	0
Total debits		Howard Supplies	960
(from cash payments journal)	(5,050)	Jewett Business Systems	0
Balance, March 31, 2006	$2,410	Total	$2,410

Exercises

EXERCISE C-1
Identify journals

Assuming the use of a two-column (all-purpose) general journal, a revenue journal, and a cash receipts journal as illustrated in this chapter, indicate the journal in which each of the following transactions should be recorded:

a. Providing services for cash.
b. Receipt of cash from sale of office equipment.
c. Sale of office supplies on account, at cost, to a neighboring business.
d. Closing of dividends account at the end of the year.
e. Receipt of cash refund from overpayment of taxes.
f. Receipt of cash for rent.
g. Sale of capital stock for cash.
h. Providing services on account.
i. Receipt of cash on account from a customer.
j. Adjustment to record accrued salaries at the end of the year.

EXERCISE C-2
Identify journals

Assuming the use of a two-column (all-purpose) general journal, a purchases journal, and a cash payments journal as illustrated in this chapter, indicate the journal in which each of the following transactions should be recorded:

a. Payment of six months' rent in advance.
b. Purchase of office supplies on account.
c. Purchase of office supplies for cash.
d. Adjustment to prepaid rent at the end of the month.
e. Adjustment to prepaid insurance at the end of the month.
f. Purchase of office equipment for cash.
g. Purchase of an office computer on account.
h. Advance payment of a one-year fire insurance policy on the office.
i. Adjustment to record accrued salaries at the end of the period.
j. Adjustment to record depreciation at the end of the month.
k. Purchase of services on account.

EXERCISE C-3
Identify postings from revenue journal

Using the following revenue journal for Delta Consulting Co., identify each of the posting references, indicated by a letter, as representing (1) posting to general ledger accounts, or (2) posting to subsidiary ledger accounts.

REVENUE JOURNAL

Date	Invoice No.	Account Debited	Post. Ref.	Accounts Receivable Dr. Fees Earned Cr.
2006				
Nov. 1	772	Environmental Safety Co.	(a)	$2,625
10	773	Greenberg Co.	(b)	1,050
20	774	Smith and Smith	(c)	1,600
27	775	Envirolab	(d)	965
30				$6,240
				(e)

EXERCISE C-4
Identify transactions in accounts receivable ledger

The debits and credits from three related transactions are presented in the following customer's account taken from the accounts receivable subsidiary ledger.

NAME *Good Times Catering*
ADDRESS *1319 Elm Street*

Date	Item	Post. Ref.	Debit	Credit	Balance
2006					
Nov. 3		R50	570		570
9		J9		80	490
13		CR38		490	—

Describe each transaction, and identify the source of each posting.

EXERCISE C-5
Identify transactions in accounts payable ledger account

The debits and credits from three related transactions are presented in the following creditor's account taken from the accounts payable ledger.

NAME *Echo Co.*
ADDRESS *1717 Kirby Street*

Date	Item	Post. Ref.	Debit	Credit	Balance
2006					
Feb. 6		P34		12,200	12,200
10		J10	400		11,800
16		CP37	11,800		—

Describe each transaction, and identify the source of each posting.

EXERCISE C-6
Identify postings from purchases journal

Using the following purchases journal, identify each of the posting references, indicated by a letter, as representing (1) a posting to a general ledger account, (2) a posting to a subsidiary ledger account, or (3) that no posting is required.

PURCHASES JOURNAL   Page 49

| | | | | | | Other Accounts Dr. | | |
| | | | Accounts | Store | Office | | | |
Date	Account Credited	Post. Ref.	Payable Cr.	Supplies Dr.	Supplies Dr.	Account	Post. Ref.	Amount
2006								
April 4	Corter Supply Co.	(a)	4,200		4,200			
6	Coastal Insurance Co.	(b)	5,325			Prepaid Insurance	(c)	5,325
11	Keller Bros.	(d)	2,000			Office Equipment	(e)	2,000
13	Taylor Products	(f)	1,675	1,400	275			
20	Keller Bros.	(g)	5,500			Store Equipment	(h)	5,500
27	Miller Supply Co.	(i)	2,740	2,740				
30			21,440	4,140	4,475			12,825
			(j)	(k)	(l)			(m)

Problems

PROBLEM C-1
Revenue journal; accounts receivable and general ledgers

SPREADSHEET

✓ 1. Revenue journal, total fees earned, $10,715

SafeGuard Security Services was established on August 15, 2006, to provide security services. The services provided during the remainder of the month are listed below.

Aug. 18. Jacob Co., Invoice No. 1, $920 on account.
    20. Ro-Gain Co., Invoice No. 2, $650 on account.
    22. Great Northern Co., Invoice No. 3, $2,480 on account.
    27. Carson Co., Invoice No. 4, $1,870 on account.
    28. Bower Co., Invoice No. 5, $950 on account.
    28. Ro-Gain Co., $575 in exchange for supplies.
    30. Ro-Gain Co., Invoice No. 6, $2,860 on account.
    31. Great Northern Co., Invoice No. 7, $985 on account.

Instructions

1. Journalize the transactions for August, using a single-column revenue journal and a two-column general journal. Post to the following customer accounts in the accounts receivable ledger, and insert the balance immediately after recording each entry: Bower Co.; Carson Co.; Great Northern Co.; Jacob Co.; Ro-Gain Co.

2. Post the revenue journal to the following accounts in the general ledger, inserting the account balances only after the last postings:

        12   Accounts Receivable
        14   Supplies
        41   Fees Earned

3. a. What is the sum of the balances of the accounts in the subsidiary ledger at August 31?
    b. What is the balance of the controlling account at August 31?

4. Assume that on September 1, the state in which SafeGuard operates begins requiring that sales tax be collected on accounting services. Briefly explain how the revenue journal may be modified to accommodate sales of services on account requiring the collection of a state sales tax.

PROBLEM C-2
Revenue and cash receipts journals; accounts receivable and general ledgers

Transactions related to revenue and cash receipts completed by Broadway Engineering Services during the period November 2–30, 2006, are as follows:

✓ 3. Total cash receipts, $30,410

Nov. 2. Issued Invoice No. 717 to Yamura Co., $6,420.

    3. Received cash from AGI Co. for the balance owed on its account.

    7. Issued Invoice No. 718 to Dover Co., $4,120.

    10. Issued Invoice No. 719 to Ross and Son, $10,140.

    Post revenue and collections to the accounts receivable subsidiary ledger.

    14. Received cash from Dover Co. for the balance owed on November 1.

    16. Issued Invoice No. 720 to Dover Co., $8,320.

    Post revenue and collections to the accounts receivable subsidiary ledger.

    19. Received cash from Yamura Co. for the balance due on invoice of November 2.

    20. Received cash from Dover Co. for invoice of November 7.

    23. Issued Invoice No. 721 to AGI Co., $8,950.

    30. Recorded cash fees earned, $4,550.

    30. Received office equipment of $9,000 in partial settlement of balance due on the Ross and Son account.

    Post revenue and collections to the accounts receivable subsidiary ledger.

Instructions

1. Insert the following balances in the general ledger as of November 1:

11	Cash	$18,940
12	Accounts Receivable	15,320
18	Office Equipment	32,600
41	Fees Earned	—

2. Insert the following balances in the accounts receivable subsidiary ledger as of November 1:

AGI Co.	$12,340
Dover Co.	2,980
Ross and Son	—
Yamura Co.	—

3. Prepare a single-column revenue journal and a cash receipts journal. Use the following column headings for the cash receipts journal: Fees Earned, Accounts Receivable, and Cash. The Fees Earned column is used to record cash fees. Insert a check mark (✓) in the Post. Ref. Column.

4. Using the two special journals and the two-column general journal, journalize the transactions for November. Post to the accounts receivable subsidiary ledger, and insert the balances at the points indicated in the narrative of transactions. Determine the balance in the customer's account before recording a cash receipt.

5. Total each of the columns of the special journals, and post the individual entries and totals to the general ledger. Insert account balances after the last posting.

6. Determine that the subsidiary ledger agrees with the controlling account in the general ledger.

PROBLEM C-3

Purchases, accounts payable account, and accounts payable ledger

✓ 3. Total accounts payable credit, $23,660

Arc-Tangent Surveyors provides survey work for construction projects. The office staff use office supplies, while surveying crews use field supplies. Purchases on account completed by Arc-Tangent Surveyors during May 2006 are as follows:

May 1. Purchased field supplies on account from Wendell Co., $3,720.

    3. Purchased office supplies on account from Lassiter Co., $320.

    8. Purchased field supplies on account from Timberland Supply, $2,010.

    12. Purchased field supplies on account from Wendell Co., $2,000.

    15. Purchased office supplies on account from J-Mart Co., $485.

    19. Purchased office equipment on account from Eskew Co., $6,500.

    23. Purchased field supplies on account from Timberland Supply, $2,450.

    26. Purchased office supplies on account from J-Mart Co., $575.

    30. Purchased field supplies on account from Timberland Supply, $5,600.

Instructions

1. Insert the following balances in the general ledger as of May 1:

14	Field Supplies	$ 5,300
15	Office Supplies	1,230
18	Office Equipment	18,400
21	Accounts Payable	3,240

2. Insert the following balances in the accounts payable subsidiary ledger as of May 1:

Eskew Co.	$2,200
J-Mart Co.	620
Lassiter Co.	420
Timberland Supply	—
Wendell Co.	—

3. Journalize the transactions for May, using a purchases journal similar to the one illustrated in this chapter. Prepare the purchases journal with columns for Accounts Payable, Field Supplies, Office Supplies, and Other Accounts. Post to the creditor accounts in the accounts payable ledger immediately after each entry.
4. Post the purchases journal to the accounts in the general ledger.
5. a. What is the sum of the balances in the subsidiary ledger at May 31?
   b. What is the balance of the controlling account at May 31?

PROBLEM C-4
Purchases and cash payments journals; accounts payable and general ledgers

P.A.S.S.

✓ 1. Total cash payments, $111,400

Black Gold Exploration Co. was established on March 15, 2006, to provide oil-drilling services. Black Gold uses field equipment (rigs and pipe) and field supplies (drill bits and lubricants) in its operations. Transactions related to purchases and cash payments during the remainder of March are as follows:

Mar. 16. Issued Check No. 1 in payment of rent for the remainder of March, $2,400.
   16. Purchased field equipment on account from PMI Sales, Inc., $32,400.
   17. Purchased field supplies on account from Culver Supply Co., $12,300.
   18. Issued Check No. 2 in payment of field supplies, $1,400, and office supplies, $440.
   20. Purchased office supplies on account from Castle Office Supply Co., $3,060.
       Post the journals to the accounts payable subsidiary ledger.
   24. Issued Check No. 3 to PMI Sales, Inc., in payment of March 16 invoice.
   26. Issued Check No. 4 to Culver Supply Co. in payment of March 17 invoice.
   28. Issued Check No. 5 to purchase land from the owner, $38,000.
   28. Purchased office supplies on account from Castle Office Supply Co., $3,600.
       Post the journals to the accounts payable subsidiary ledger.
   30. Purchased the following from PMI Sales, Inc. on account: field supplies, $18,500, and office equipment, $16,400.
   30. Issued Check No. 6 to Castle Office Supply Co. in payment of March 20 invoice.
   30. Purchased field supplies on account from Culver Supply Co., $9,200.
   31. Issued Check No. 7 in payment of salaries, $21,400.
   31. Acquired land in exchange for field equipment having a cost of $13,100.
       Post the journals to the accounts payable subsidiary ledger.

Instructions

1. Journalize the transactions for March. Use a purchases journal and a cash payments journal, similar to those illustrated in this chapter, and a two-column general journal. Set debit columns for Field Supplies, Office Supplies, and Other Accounts in the purchases journal. Refer to the following partial chart of accounts:

11	Cash	19	Land
14	Field Supplies	21	Accounts Payable
15	Office Supplies	61	Salary Expense
17	Field Equipment	71	Rent Expense
18	Office Equipment		

At the points indicated in the narrative of transactions, post to the following accounts in the accounts payable ledger:

> Castle Office Supply Co.
> Culver Supply Co.
> PMI Sales, Inc.

2. Post the individual entries (Other Accounts columns of the purchases journal and the cash payments journal; both columns of the general journal) to the appropriate general ledger accounts.
3. Total each of the columns of the purchases journal and the cash payments journal, and post the appropriate totals to the general ledger. (Because the problem does not include transactions related to cash receipts, the cash account in the ledger will have a credit balance.)
4. Prepare a schedule of accounts payable.

PROBLEM C-5
All journals and general ledger; trial balance

P.A.S.S.

✓ *2. Total cash receipts, $75,095*

The transactions completed by Paul Revere Courier Company during May 2006, the first month of the fiscal year, were as follows:

May 1. Issued Check No. 205 for May rent, $900.
   2. Purchased a vehicle on account from McIntyre Sales Co., $26,800.
   3. Purchased office equipment on account from Office Mate, Inc., $4,500.
   5. Issued Invoice No. 91 to Martin Co., $7,230.
   6. Received check for $6,245 from Baker Co. in payment of invoice.
   7. Issued Invoice No. 92 to Trent Co., $4,340.
   9. Issued Check No. 206 for fuel expense, $680.
   10. Received check for $10,890 from Sing Co. in payment of invoice.
   10. Issued Check No. 207 to Office City in payment of $510 invoice.
   10. Issued Check No. 208 to Bastille Co. in payment of $2,010 invoice.
   11. Issued Invoice No. 93 to Joy Co., $5,200.
   11. Issued Check No. 209 to Porter Co. in payment of $270 invoice.
   12. Received check for $7,230 from Martin Co. in payment of invoice.
   13. Issued Check No. 210 to McIntyre Sales Co. in payment of $26,800 invoice.
   16. Cash fees earned for May 1–16, $14,450.
   16. Issued Check No. 211 for purchase of a vehicle, $31,400.
   17. Issued Check No. 212 for miscellaneous administrative expenses, $280.
   18. Purchased maintenance supplies on account from Bastille Co., $1,480.
   18. Received check for rent revenue on office space, $1,400.
   19. Purchased the following on account from Master Supply Co.: maintenance supplies, $1,950, and office supplies, $550.
   20. Issued Check No. 213 in payment of advertising expense, $6,800.
   20. Used maintenance supplies with a cost of $3,000 to repair vehicles.
   21. Purchased office supplies on account from Office City, $610.
   24. Issued Invoice No. 94 to Sing Co., $11,530.
   25. Received check for $15,680 from Baker Co. in payment of invoice.
   25. Issued Invoice No. 95 to Trent Co., $5,900.
   26. Issued Check No. 214 to Office Mate, Inc. in payment of $4,500 invoice.
   30. Issued Check No. 215 in payment of driver salaries, $27,500.
   31. Issued Check No. 216 in payment of office salaries, $16,750.
   31. Issued Check No. 217 for office supplies, $230.
   31. Cash fees earned for May 17–31, $19,200.

Instructions
1. Enter the following account balances in the general ledger as of May 1:

11	Cash	$ 57,900	41	Fees Earned	—
12	Accounts Receivable	32,815	42	Rent Revenue	—
14	Maintenance Supplies	6,150	51	Driver Salaries Expense	—
15	Office Supplies	2,580	52	Maintenance Supplies	
16	Office Equipment	14,370		Expense	—
17	Accumulated Depreciation		53	Fuel Expense	—
	—Office Equipment	3,000	61	Office Salaries Expense	—
18	Vehicles	48,000	62	Rent Expense	—
19	Accumulated Depreciation		63	Advertising Expense	—
	—Vehicles	13,590	64	Miscellaneous Adminis-	
21	Accounts Payable	2,790		trative Expense	—
31	Capital Stock	60,000			
32	Retained Earnings	82,435			

2. Journalize the transactions for May 2006, using the following journals similar to those illustrated in this chapter: single-column revenue journal, cash receipts journal, purchases journal (with columns for Accounts Payable, Maintenance Supplies, Office Supplies, and Other Accounts), cash payments journal, and two-column general journal. Assume that the daily postings to the individual accounts in the accounts payable ledger and the accounts receivable ledger have been made.
3. Post the appropriate individual entries to the general ledger.
4. Total each of the columns of the special journals, and post the appropriate totals to the general ledger; insert the account balances.
5. Prepare a trial balance.
6. Verify the agreement of each subsidiary ledger with its controlling account. The sum of the balances of the accounts in the subsidiary ledgers as of May 31 are as follows:

Accounts receivable	$26,970
Accounts payable	4,590

June 8.   Returned merchandise purchased on account from Owen Clothing on
          June 5, $500.

Accounts Payable—Owen Clothing	500	
Purchases Returns and Allowances		500

Under the perpetual inventory system, returns would be recorded as a credit to the merchandise inventory account at their cost of $500.

June 15.   Paid Owen Clothing for purchase of June 5, less return of $500 and
           discount of $590 [($30,000 − $500) × 2%].

Accounts Payable—Owen Clothing	29,500	
Cash		28,910
Purchases Discounts		590

Under a perpetual inventory system, a purchases discount account is not used. Instead the merchandise inventory account is credited for the amount of the discount, $590.

June 18.   Sold merchandise on account to Jones Co., $12,500, 1/10, n/30. The cost of
           the merchandise sold was $9,000.

Accounts Receivable—Jones Co.	12,500	
Sales		12,500

The entry to record the sale is the same under both systems. Under the perpetual inventory system, the cost of merchandise sold and the reduction in merchandise inventory would also be recorded on the date of sale.

June 21.   Received merchandise returned on account from Jones Co., $4,000.
           The cost of the merchandise returned was $2,800.

Sales Returns and Allowances	4,000	
Accounts Receivable—Jones Co.		4,000

The entry to record the sales return is the same under both systems. In addition, the cost of the merchandise returned would be debited to the merchandise inventory account and credited to the cost of merchandise sold account under the perpetual inventory system.

June 22.   Purchased merchandise from Norcross Clothiers, $15,000, terms FOB
           shipping point, 2/15, n/30, with prepaid transportation charges of
           $750 added to the invoice.

Purchases	15,000	
Transportation In	750	
Accounts Payable—Norcross Clothiers		15,750

This entry is similar to the June 5 entry for the purchase of merchandise. Since the transportation terms were FOB shipping point, the prepaid freight charges of $750 must be added to the invoice cost of $15,000. Under the perpetual inventory system, the purchase is recorded in the merchandise inventory account at the cost of $15,750 (invoice price plus transportation).

June 28.   Received $8,415 as payment on account from Jones Co., less return of
           June 21 and less discount of $85 [($12,500 − $4,000) × 1%].

Cash	8,415	
Sales Discounts	85	
Accounts Receivable—Jones Co.		8,500

This entry is the same under the perpetual inventory system.

June 29.   Received $19,600 from cash sales. The cost of the merchandise sold
           was $13,800.

Cash	19,600	
Sales		19,600

The entry to record the sale is the same under both systems. Under the perpetual inventory system, the cost of merchandise sold and the reduction in merchandise inventory would also be recorded on the date of sale.

The multiple-step income statement under the periodic inventory system is illustrated in Exhibit 1. The multiple-step income statement under a perpetual inventory system is similar, except that the cost of merchandise sold is reported as a single amount.

Chart of Accounts for a Periodic Inventory System

Exhibit 2 on page D-5 is the chart of accounts for NetSolutions when a periodic inventory system is used. The periodic inventory accounts related to merchandising transactions are shown in color.

End-of-Period Procedures in a Periodic Inventory System

The end-of-period procedures are generally the same for the periodic and perpetual inventory systems. In the remainder of this appendix, we will discuss the differences in procedures for the two systems that affect the work sheet, the adjusting entries, and the closing entries. As the basis for illustrations, we will use the data for NetSolutions, presented in Chapter 5.

Work Sheet

The differences in the work sheet for a merchandising business that uses the periodic inventory system are highlighted in the work sheet for NetSolutions in Exhibit 3 on page D-6. As we illustrated earlier, accounts for purchases, purchases returns and allowances, purchases discounts, and transportation in are used in a periodic inventory system.

Under the periodic inventory system, the merchandise inventory account, throughout the accounting period, shows the inventory at the beginning of the period. The merchandise inventory on January 1, 2007, $59,700, is a part of the merchandise available for sale. At the end of the period, the beginning inventory amount in the ledger is replaced with the ending inventory amount. To update the inventory account, two adjusting entries are used.[2] The first adjusting entry transfers the beginning inventory balance to Income Summary. This entry, shown below, has the effect of increasing the cost of merchandise sold and decreasing net income.

Dec. 31	Income Summary	59,700	
	Merchandise Inventory		59,700

---

[2]Another method of updating the merchandise inventory account at the end of the period is called the *closing method*. This method adjusts the merchandise inventory through the use of closing entries. This method may not be appropriate for use in computerized accounting systems. Since the financial statements are the same under both methods and since computerized accounting systems are used by most businesses, the closing method is not illustrated.

•Exhibit 1 Multiple-Step Income Statement—Periodic Inventory System

NetSolutions
Income Statement
For the Year Ended December 31, 2007

Revenue from sales:			
Sales			$720,185
Less: Sales returns and allowances		$ 6,140	
Sales discounts		5,790	11,930
Net sales			$708,255
Cost of merchandise sold:			
Merchandise inventory, January 1, 2007			$ 59,700
Purchases		$521,980	
Less: Purchases returns and allowances	$9,100		
Purchases discounts	2,525	11,625	
Net purchases		$510,355	
Add transportation in		17,400	
Cost of merchandise purchased		$527,755	
Merchandise available for sale		$587,455	
Less merchandise inventory,			
December 31, 2007		62,150	
Cost of merchandise sold			525,305
Gross profit			$182,950
Operating expenses:			
Selling expenses:			
Sales salaries expense	$ 56,230		
Advertising expense	10,860		
Depreciation expense—store equipment	3,100		
Miscellaneous selling expense	630		
Total selling expenses		$ 70,820	
Administrative expenses:			
Office salaries expense	$ 21,020		
Rent expense	8,100		
Depreciation expense—office equipment	2,490		
Insurance expense	1,910		
Office supplies expense	610		
Miscellaneous administrative expense	760		
Total administrative expenses		34,890	
Total operating expenses			105,710
Income from operations			$ 77,240
Other income and expense:			
Rent revenue		$ 600	
Interest expense		2,440	1,840
Net income			$ 75,400

After the first adjusting entry has been recorded and posted, the balance of the merchandise inventory account is zero. The second adjusting entry records the cost of the merchandise on hand at the end of the period by debiting Merchandise Inventory. Since the merchandise inventory at December 31, 2007, $62,150, is subtracted from the cost of merchandise available for sale in determining the cost of

•Exhibit 2 Chart of Accounts—Periodic Inventory System

Balance Sheet Accounts		Income Statement Accounts	
	100 Assets		400 Revenues
110	Cash	410	Sales
111	Notes Receivable	411	Sales Returns and Allowances
112	Accounts Receivable	412	Sales Discounts
115	Merchandise Inventory		
116	Office Supplies		500 Costs and Expenses
117	Prepaid Insurance	510	Purchases
120	Land	511	Purchases Returns and
123	Store Equipment		Allowances
124	Accumulated Depreciation—	512	Purchases Discounts
	Store Equipment	513	Transportation In
125	Office Equipment	520	Sales Salaries Expense
126	Accumulated Depreciation—	521	Advertising Expense
	Office Equipment	522	Depreciation Expense—Store
			Equipment
	200 Liabilities	523	Transportation Out
210	Accounts Payable	529	Miscellaneous Selling Expense
211	Salaries Payable	530	Office Salaries Expense
212	Unearned Rent	531	Rent Expense
215	Notes Payable	532	Depreciation Expense—Office
			Equipment
	300 Stockholders' Equity	533	Insurance Expense
310	Capital Stock	534	Office Supplies Expense
311	Retained Earnings	539	Misc. Administrative Expense
312	Dividends		
313	Income Summary		600 Other Income
		610	Rent Revenue
			700 Other Expense
		710	Interest Expense

merchandise sold, Income Summary is credited. This credit has the effect of decreasing the cost of merchandise available for sale during the period, $587,455, by the cost of the unsold merchandise. The second adjusting entry is shown below.

Dec. 31   Merchandise Inventory   62,150
                   Income Summary   62,150

After the second adjusting entry has been recorded and posted, the balance of the merchandise inventory account is the amount of the ending inventory. The accounts for Merchandise Inventory and Income Summary after both entries have been posted would appear in T account form as follows:

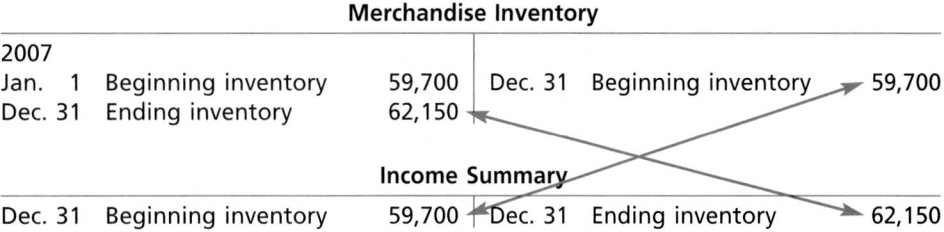

Merchandise Inventory

2007					
Jan. 1	Beginning inventory	59,700	Dec. 31	Beginning inventory	59,700
Dec. 31	Ending inventory	62,150			

Income Summary

Dec. 31	Beginning inventory	59,700	Dec. 31	Ending inventory	62,150

No separate adjusting entry can be made for merchandise inventory shrinkage in a periodic inventory system. This is because no perpetual inventory records are available to show what inventory should be on hand at the end of the period.

•Exhibit 3   Work Sheet—Periodic Inventory System

NetSolutions
Work Sheet
For the Year Ended December 31, 2007

Account Title	Trial Balance Dr.	Trial Balance Cr.	Adjustments Dr.	Adjustments Cr.	Adjusted Trial Balance Dr.	Adjusted Trial Balance Cr.	Income Statement Dr.	Income Statement Cr.	Balance Sheet Dr.	Balance Sheet Cr.
Cash	52,950				52,950				52,950	
Accounts Receivable	91,080				91,080				91,080	
Merchandise Inventory	59,700		(b)62,150	(a)59,700	62,150				62,150	
Office Supplies	1,090			(c) 610	480				480	
Prepaid Insurance	4,560			(d) 1,910	2,650				2,650	
Land	20,000				20,000				20,000	
Store Equipment	27,100				27,100				27,100	
Accum. Depr.—Store Equipment		2,600		(e) 3,100		5,700				5,700
Office Equipment	15,570				15,570				15,570	
Accum. Depr.—Office Equipment		2,230		(f) 2,490		4,720				4,720
Accounts Payable		22,420				22,420				22,420
Salaries Payable				(g) 1,140		1,140				1,140
Unearned Rent		2,400	(h) 600			1,800				1,800
Notes Payable (final payment, 2017)		25,000				25,000				25,000
Capital Stock		25,000				25,000				25,000
Retained Earnings		128,800				128,800				128,800
Dividends	18,000				18,000				18,000	
Income Summary			(a)59,700	(b)62,150	59,700	62,150	59,700	62,150		
Sales		720,185				720,185		720,185		
Sales Returns and Allowances	6,140				6,140		6,140			
Sales Discounts	5,790				5,790		5,790			
Purchases	521,980				521,980		521,980			
Purchases Returns & Allowances		9,100				9,100		9,100		
Purchases Discounts		2,525				2,525		2,525		
Transportation In	17,400				17,400		17,400			
Sales Salaries Expense	55,450		(g) 780		56,230		56,230			
Advertising Expense	10,860				10,860		10,860			
Depr. Expense—Store Equipment			(e) 3,100		3,100		3,100			
Miscellaneous Selling Expense	630				630		630			
Office Salaries Expense	20,660		(g) 360		21,020		21,020			
Rent Expense	8,100				8,100		8,100			
Depr. Expense—Office Equipment			(f) 2,490		2,490		2,490			
Insurance Expense			(d) 1,910		1,910		1,910			
Office Supplies Expense			(c) 610		610		610			
Misc. Administrative Expense	760				760		760			
Rent Revenue				(h) 600		600		600		
Interest Expense	2,440				2,440		2,440			
	940,260	940,260	131,700	131,700	1,009,140	1,009,140	719,160	794,560	289,980	214,580
Net Income							75,400			75,400
							794,560	794,560	289,980	289,980

(a) Beginning merchandise inventory, $59,700.
(b) Ending merchandise inventory, $62,150.
(c) Office supplies used, $610 ($1,090 − $480).
(d) Insurance expired, $1,910.
(e) Depreciation of store equipment, $3,100.

(f) Depreciation of office equipment, $2,490.
(g) Salaries accrued but not paid (sales salaries, $780; office salaries, $360), $1,140.
(h) Rent earned from amount received in advance, $600.

One disadvantage of the periodic inventory system is that inventory shrinkage cannot be measured.[3]

Completing the Work Sheet

After all of the necessary adjustments have been entered on the work sheet, the work sheet is completed in the normal manner. An exception to the usual practice of extending only account balances is Income Summary. Both the debit and credit amounts for Income Summary are extended to the Adjusted Trial Balance columns. Extending both amounts aids in the preparation of the income statement because the debit adjustment (the beginning inventory of $59,700) and the credit adjustment (the ending inventory of $62,150) are reported as part of the cost of merchandise sold.

The purchases, purchases discounts, purchases returns and allowances, and transportation in accounts are extended to the Income Statement Columns of the work sheet, since they are used in computing the cost of merchandise sold. You should note that the two merchandise inventory amounts in Income Summary are extended to the Income Statement columns. After all of the items have been extended to the statement columns, the four columns are totaled and the net income or net loss is determined.

Financial Statements

The financial statements for NetSolutions are essentially the same under both the perpetual and periodic inventory systems. The main difference is that the cost of goods is reported as a single amount under the perpetual system. Exhibit 1 illustrates the manner in which cost of merchandise sold is reported in a multiple-step income statement when the periodic inventory system is used.[4]

Adjusting and Closing Entries

The adjusting entries are the same under both inventory systems, except for merchandise inventory. As indicated previously, two adjusting entries for beginning and ending merchandise inventory are necessary in a periodic inventory system.

The closing entries differ in the periodic inventory system in that there is no cost of merchandise sold account to be closed to Income Summary. Instead, the purchases, purchases discounts, purchases returns and allowances, and transportation in accounts are closed to Income Summary.[5] To illustrate, the adjusting and closing entries under a periodic inventory system for NetSolutions are shown below and on the following page.

		JOURNAL			Page 16	
	Date	Description	Post. Ref.	Debit	Credit	
1		Adjusting Entries				1
2	2007 Dec. 31	Income Summary	312	59 7 0 0 00		2
3		Merchandise Inventory	115		59 7 0 0 00	3
4						4
5	31	Merchandise Inventory	115	62 1 5 0 00		5
6		Income Summary	312		62 1 5 0 00	6
7						7

(continued)

---

[3]Any inventory shrinkage that does exist is part of the cost of merchandise sold and is reported on the income statement, since a smaller ending inventory is deducted from other merchandise available for sale.

[4]The single-step income statement would be the same for both the perpetual and the periodic inventory systems.

[5]The balance of Income Summary, after the merchandise inventory adjustments and the first two closing entries have been posted, is the net income or net loss for the period.

		Description	Post. Ref.	Debit	Credit	
8	31	Office Supplies Expense	534	6 1 0 00		8
9		Office Supplies	116		6 1 0 00	9
10						10
11	31	Insurance Expense	533	1 9 1 0 00		11
12		Prepaid Insurance	117		1 9 1 0 00	12
13						13
14	31	Depreciation Expense—Store Equip.	522	3 1 0 0 00		14
15		Accumulated Depr.—Store Equip.	124		3 1 0 0 00	15
16						16
17	31	Depreciation Expense—Office Equip.	532	2 4 9 0 00		17
18		Accumulated Depr.—Office Equip.	126		2 4 9 0 00	18
19						19
20	31	Sales Salaries Expense	520	7 8 0 00		20
21		Office Salaries Expense	530	3 6 0 00		21
22		Salaries Payable	211		1 1 4 0 00	22
23						23
24	31	Unearned Rent	212	6 0 0 00		24
25		Rent Revenue	610		6 0 0 00	25

				JOURNAL		**Page 17**	
	Date		Description	Post. Ref.	Debit	Credit	
1			Closing Entries				1
2	2007 Dec.	31	Sales	410	720 1 8 5 00		2
3			Purchases Returns and Allowances	511	9 1 0 0 00		3
4			Purchases Discounts	512	2 5 2 5 00		4
5			Rent Revenue	610	6 0 0 00		5
6			Income Summary	313		732 4 1 0 00	6
7							7
8		31	Income Summary	313	659 4 6 0 00		8
9			Sales Returns and Allowances	411		6 1 4 0 00	9
10			Sales Discounts	412		5 7 9 0 00	10
11			Purchases	510		521 9 8 0 00	11
12			Transportation In	513		17 4 0 0 00	12
13			Sales Salaries Expense	520		56 2 3 0 00	13
14			Advertising Expense	521		10 8 6 0 00	14
15			Depreciation Exp.—Store Equip.	522		3 1 0 0 00	15
16			Miscellaneous Selling Expense	529		6 3 0 00	16
17			Office Salaries Expense	530		21 0 2 0 00	17
18			Rent Expense	531		8 1 0 0 00	18
19			Depreciation Exp.—Office Equip.	532		2 4 9 0 00	19
20			Insurance Expense	533		1 9 1 0 00	20
21			Office Supplies Expense	534		6 1 0 00	21
22			Miscellaneous Administrative Exp.	539		7 6 0 00	22
23			Interest Expense	710		2 4 4 0 00	23
24							24
25		31	Income Summary	313	75 4 0 0 00		25
26			Retained Earnings	311		75 4 0 0 00	26
27							27
28		31	Retained Earnings	311	18 0 0 0 00		28
29			Dividends	312		18 0 0 0 00	29

Exercises

EXERCISE D-1
Purchases-related transactions—periodic inventory system

Journalize entries for the following related transactions, assuming that Mountain Gallery, Inc. uses the periodic inventory system.

a. Purchased $12,000 of merchandise from Yellowstone Co. on account, terms 2/10, n/30.
b. Discovered that some of the merchandise was defective and returned items with an invoice price of $2,500, receiving credit.
c. Paid the amount owed on the invoice within the discount period.
d. Purchased $9,000 of merchandise from Glacier, Inc. on account, terms 1/10, n/30.
e. Paid the amount owed on the invoice within the discount period.

EXERCISE D-2
Sales-related transactions—periodic inventory system

Journalize entries for the following related transactions, assuming that Aveda Company uses the periodic inventory system.

July 6 Sold merchandise to a customer for $18,500, terms FOB shipping point, 2/10, n/30.
  6 Paid the transportation charges of $420, debiting the amount to Accounts Receivable.
  9 Issued a credit memorandum for $4,700 to the customer for merchandise returned.
  16 Received a check for the amount due from the sale.

EXERCISE D-3
Adjusting entries for merchandise inventory—periodic inventory system

Data assembled for preparing the work sheet for Meridian Co. for the fiscal year ended December 31, 2006, included the following:

Merchandise inventory as of January 1, 2006	$475,000
Merchandise inventory as of December 31, 2006	$528,300

Journalize the two adjusting entries for merchandise inventory that would appear on the work sheet, assuming that the periodic inventory system is used.

EXERCISE D-4
Identification of missing items from income statement—periodic inventory system

For (a) through (i), identify the items designated by "X" and "Y."

a. Sales $-$ (X + Y) = Net sales
b. Purchases $-$ (X + Y) = Net purchases
c. Net purchases + X = Cost of merchandise purchased
d. Merchandise inventory (beginning) + Cost of merchandise purchased = X
e. Merchandise available for sale $-$ X = Cost of merchandise sold
f. Net sales $-$ Cost of merchandise sold = X
g. Gross profit $-$ Operating expenses = X
h. X + Y = Operating expenses
i. Income from operations + X $-$ Y = Net income

EXERCISE D-5
Multiple-step income statement—periodic inventory system

✓ *Gross profit: $230,560*

Selected data for Canyon Ferry Stores Company for the year ended December 31, 2006, are as follows:

Merchandise inventory, January 1	$ 85,760	Sales	$1,288,000
Merchandise inventory, December 31	102,240	Sales discounts	10,400
Purchases	1,051,200	Sales returns and allowances	13,920
Purchases discounts	12,800	Transportation in	36,000
Purchases returns and allowances	24,800		

Prepare a multiple-step income statement through gross profit for Canyon Ferry Stores Company for the current year ended December 31.

EXERCISE D-6
Adjusting and closing entries—periodic inventory system

Selected account titles and related amounts appearing in the Income Statement and Balance Sheet columns of the work sheet of Southern Bell Company for the year ended December 31 are listed in alphabetical order as follows:

Administrative Expenses	$ 72,000	Purchases Discounts	$ 14,000
Building	312,500	Purchases Returns and Allowances	9,000
Capital Stock	80,000	Retained Earnings	353,080
Cash	58,500	Salaries Payable	4,220
Dividends	40,000	Sales	1,450,000
Interest Expense	2,500	Sales Discounts	18,000
Merchandise Inventory (1/1)	300,000	Sales Returns and Allowances	32,000
Merchandise Inventory (12/31)	275,000	Selling Expenses	240,200
Notes Payable	25,000	Store Supplies	7,700
Office Supplies	10,600	Transportation In	21,300
Purchases	820,000		

All selling expenses have been recorded in the account entitled Selling Expenses, and all administrative expenses have been recorded in the account entitled Administrative Expenses. Assuming that Southern Bell Company uses the periodic inventory system, journalize (a) the adjusting entries for merchandise inventory and (b) the closing entries.

Problems

PROBLEM D-1
Sales-related and purchase-related transactions—periodic inventory system

The following were selected from among the transactions completed by Infinet Shops, Inc., during November of the current year:

Nov. 2. Purchased merchandise on account from Loftin Co., list price $24,000, trade discount 25%, terms FOB destination, 2/10, n/30.

8. Sold merchandise for cash, $8,100.

9. Purchased merchandise on account from Chestnut Co., $12,000, terms FOB shipping point, 2/10, n/30, with prepaid transportation costs of $180 added to the invoice.

10. Returned $3,000 of merchandise purchased on November 2 from Loftin Co.

11. Sold merchandise on account to Fawcett Co., list price $2,500, trade discount 20%, terms 1/10, n/30.

12. Paid Loftin Co. on account for purchase of November 2, less return of November 10 and discount.

15. Sold merchandise on nonbank credit cards and reported accounts to the card company, American Express, $9,850.

19. Paid Chestnut Co. on account for purchase of November 9, less discount.

21. Received cash on account from sale of November 11 to Fawcett Co., less discount.

25. Sold merchandise on account to Clemons Co., $3,000, terms 1/10, n/30.

28. Received cash from American Express for nonbank credit card sales of November 15, less $380 service fee.

30. Received merchandise returned by Clemons Co. from sale on November 25, $1,700.

Instructions
Journalize the transactions for Infinet Shops, Inc., in a two-column general journal.

PROBLEM D-2
Sales-related and purchase-related transactions—periodic inventory system

The following were selected from among the transactions completed by Copra Sentry Company during July of the current year:

July 3. Purchased merchandise on account from Swanson Co., list price $60,000, trade discount 30%, terms FOB shipping point, 2/10, n/30, with prepaid transportation costs of $1,200 added to the invoice.

4. Purchased merchandise on account from Lambert Co., $8,000, terms FOB destination, 1/10, n/30.

7. Sold merchandise on account to Walsh Co., list price $12,000, trade discount 20%, terms 2/10, n/30.

9. Returned merchandise purchased on July 4 from Lambert Co., $1,300.

13. Paid Swanson Co. on account for purchase of July 3, less discount.

14. Paid Lambert Co. on account for purchase of July 4, less return of July 9 and discount.

17. Received cash on account from sale of July 7 to Walsh Co., less discount.

19. Sold merchandise on nonbank credit cards and reported accounts to the card company, American Express, $7,450.

22. Sold merchandise on account to Wu Co., $4,420, terms 2/10, n/30.

24. Sold merchandise for cash, $4,350.

25. Received merchandise returned by Wu Co. from sale on July 22, $1,610.

31. Received cash from American Express for nonbank credit card sales of July 19, less $290 service fee.

Instructions

Journalize the transactions for Copra Sentry Co. in a two-column general journal.

PROBLEM D-3
Sales-related and purchase-related transactions for seller and buyer—periodic inventory system

P.A.S.S.

The following selected transactions were completed during May between Simkins Company and Burk Co.:

May 6. Simkins Company sold merchandise on account to Burk Co., $18,500, terms FOB destination, 2/15, n/eom.

6. Simkins Company paid transportation costs of $600 for delivery of merchandise sold to Burk Co. on May 6.

10. Simkins Company sold merchandise on account to Burk Co., $15,750, terms FOB shipping point, n/eom.

11. Burk Co. returned merchandise purchased on account on May 6 from Simkins Company, $5,500.

14. Burk Co. paid transportation charges of $300 on May 10 purchase from Simkins Company.

17. Simkins Company sold merchandise on account to Burk Co., $30,000, terms FOB shipping point, 1/10, n/30. Simkins prepaid transportation costs of $1,750, which were added to the invoice.

21. Burk Co. paid Simkins Company for purchase of May 6, less discount and less return of May 11.

27. Burk Co. paid Simkins Company on account for purchase of May 17, less discount.

31. Burk Co. paid Simkins Company on account for purchase of May 10.

Instructions

Journalize the May transactions for (1) Simkins Company and for (2) Burk Co.

PROBLEM D-4
Preparation of work sheet, financial statements, and adjusting and closing entries—periodic inventory system

The accounts and their balances in the ledger of Sunshine Sports Co. on December 31, 2006, are as follows:

P.A.S.S.

✓ *1. Net income: $222,950*

Cash	$ 28,000	Sales Discounts	$ 7,100
Accounts Receivable	142,500	Purchases	500,000
Merchandise Inventory	200,000	Purchases Returns and Allowances	10,100
Prepaid Insurance	9,700	Purchases Discounts	4,900
Store Supplies	4,250	Transportation In	11,200
Office Supplies	2,100	Sales Salaries Expense	81,400
Store Equipment	132,000	Advertising Expense	45,000
Accumulated Depreciation—		Depreciation Expense—	
Store Equipment	40,300	Store Equipment	—
Office Equipment	50,000	Store Supplies Expense	—
Accumulated Depreciation—		Miscellaneous Selling Expense	1,600
Office Equipment	17,200	Office Salaries Expense	44,000
Accounts Payable	56,700	Rent Expense	26,000
Salaries Payable	—	Insurance Expense	—
Unearned Rent	1,200	Depreciation Expense—	
Note Payable (final payment, 2013)	100,000	Office Equipment	—
Capital Stock	50,000	Office Supplies Expense	—
Retained Earnings	109,600	Miscellaneous Administrative	
Dividends	40,000	Expense	1,650
Income Summary	—	Rent Revenue	—
Sales	960,000	Interest Expense	11,600
Sales Returns and Allowances	11,900		

The data needed for year-end adjustments on December 31 are as follows:

Merchandise inventory on December 31		$215,000
Insurance expired during the year		4,800
Supplies on hand on December 31:		
Store supplies		1,300
Office supplies		750
Depreciation for the year:		
Store equipment		7,500
Office equipment		3,800
Salaries payable on December 31:		
Sales salaries	$4,000	
Office salaries	2,000	6,000
Unearned rent on December 31		400

Instructions

1. Prepare a work sheet for the fiscal year ended December 31, listing all accounts in the order given.
2. Prepare a multiple-step income statement.
3. Prepare a retained earnings statement.
4. Prepare a report form of balance sheet, assuming that the current portion of the note payable is $10,000.
5. Journalize the adjusting entries.
6. Journalize the closing entries.

appendix E

Foreign Currency Transactions

In this appendix, we describe and illustrate the accounting for transactions in which a U.S. company sells products or services to foreign companies or buys foreign products or services. If transactions with foreign companies require payment or receipt in U.S. dollars, no special accounting problems arise.[1] Such transactions are recorded as we described and illustrated earlier in this text. For example, the sale of merchandise to a Japanese company that is billed in and paid for in dollars would be recorded by the U.S. company in the normal manner. However, if the transaction is billed and payment is to be received in Japanese yen, the U.S. company may incur an exchange gain or loss. Some foreign manufacturers have begun building manufacturing plants in the United States, which avoids such gains and losses for denominated sales. For example, **BMW** has constructed its first U.S. plant.

Realized Currency Exchange Gains and Losses

When a U.S. company receives foreign currency, the amount must be converted to its equivalent in U.S. dollars for recording in the accounts. When payment is to be made in a foreign currency, U.S. dollars must be exchanged for the foreign currency for payment. To illustrate, assume that a U.S. company purchases merchandise from a British company that requires payment in British pounds. In this case, U.S. dollars ($) must be exchanged for British pounds (£) to pay for the merchandise. This exchange of one currency for another involves using an exchange rate. The **_exchange rate_** is the rate at which one unit of currency (the dollar, for example) can be converted into another currency (the British pound, for example).

To continue the example, assume that the U.S. company had purchased merchandise for £1,000 from a British company on June 1, when the exchange rate was $1.40 per British pound. Thus, $1,400 must be exchanged for £1,000 to make the purchase.[2] The U.S. company records the transaction in dollars, as follows:

June	1	Merchandise Inventory		1 4 0 0 00	
		Cash			1 4 0 0 00
		Payment of Invoice No. 1725 from			
		W. A. Sterling Co., £1,000; exchange			
		rate, $1.40 per British pound.			

Instead of a cash purchase, the purchase may be made on account. In this case, the exchange rate may change between the date of purchase and the date of payment of the account payable in the foreign currency. In practice, exchange rates vary daily.

To illustrate, assume that the preceding purchase was made on account. The entry to record it is as follows:

---

[1]This discussion is from the point of view of a U.S. company. Unless otherwise indicated, the reference to the dollar refers to the U.S. dollar rather than a dollar of another country, such as Canada.

[2]Foreign exchange rates are quoted in major financial reporting services. Because the exchange rates are quite volatile, those used in this chapter are assumed rates.

June	1	Merchandise Inventory		1 4 0 0 00			
		Accounts Payable—W. A. Sterling Co.				1 4 0 0 00	
		Purchase on account; Invoice					
		No. 1725 from W. A. Sterling Co.,					
		£1,000; exchange rate, $1.40 per					
		British pound.					

Assume that on the date of payment, June 15, the exchange rate was $1.45 per pound. The £1,000 account payable must be settled by exchanging $1,450 (£1,000 × $1.45) for £1,000. In this case, the U.S. company incurs an exchange loss of $50 because $1,450 was needed to settle a $1,400 account payable. The cash payment is recorded as follows:

June	15	Accounts Payable—W. A. Sterling Co.		1 4 0 0 00			
		Exchange Loss		5 0 00			
		Cash				1 4 5 0 00	
		Cash paid on Invoice No. 1725, for					
		£1,000, or $1,400, when exchange					
		rate was $1.45 per pound.					

We can analyze all transactions with foreign companies in the manner described. For example, assume that a sale on account for $1,000 to a Swiss company on May 1 was billed in Swiss francs. The cost of the merchandise sold was $600, and the selling company uses a perpetual inventory system. If the exchange rate was $0.25 per Swiss franc (F) on May 1, the transaction is recorded as follows:

May	1	Accounts Receivable—D. W. Robinson Co.		1 0 0 0 00			
		Sales				1 0 0 0 00	
		Invoice No. 9772, F4,000; exchange					
		rate, $0.25 per Swiss franc.					
	1	Cost of Merchandise Sold		6 0 0 00			
		Merchandise Inventory				6 0 0 00	

Assume that the exchange rate increases to $0.30 per Swiss franc on May 31 when cash is received. In this case, the U.S. company realizes an exchange gain of $200. This gain is realized because the F4,000, which had a value of $1,000 on the date of sale, has increased in value to $1,200 (F4,000 × $0.30) on May 31 when the payment is received. The receipt of the cash is recorded as follows:

May	31	Cash		1 2 0 0 00			
		Accounts Receivable—D. W. Robinson Co.				1 0 0 0 00	
		Exchange Gain				2 0 0 00	
		Cash received on Invoice No. 9772,					
		for F4,000, $1,000, when exchange					
		rate was $0.30 per Swiss franc.					

Unrealized Currency Exchange Gains and Losses

In the previous examples, the transactions were completed by either the receipt or the payment of cash. On the date the cash was received or paid, any related exchange gain or loss was realized and was recorded in the accounts. However, financial statements may be prepared between the date of the sale or purchase on account and the date the cash is received or paid. In this case, any exchange gain or loss created by a change in exchange rates between the date of the original transaction and the balance sheet date must be recorded. Such an exchange gain or loss is reported in the financial statements as an unrealized exchange gain or loss.

To illustrate, assume that a sale on account for $1,000 had been made to a German company on December 20 and had been billed in euros. The cost of merchandise sold was $700. On this date, the exchange rate was $1.25 per euro. The transaction is recorded as follows:

Dec.	20	Accounts Receivable—T. A. Mueller Inc.	1 0 0 0 00	
		Sales		1 0 0 0 00
		Invoice No. 1793, 800 euros; exchange		
		rate, $1.25 per euro.		
	20	Cost of Merchandise Sold	7 0 0 00	
		Merchandise Inventory		7 0 0 00

Assume that the exchange rate decreases to $1.20 per euro on December 31, the date of the balance sheet. Thus, the $1,000 account receivable on December 31 has a value of only $960 (800 euros × $1.20). This unrealized loss of $40 ($1,000 − $960) is recorded as follows:

Dec.	31	Exchange Loss	4 0 00	
		Accounts Receivable—T. A. Mueller Inc.		4 0 00
		Invoice No. 1793, 800 euros × $0.05		
		decrease in exchange rate.		

Any additional change in the exchange rate during the following period is recorded when the cash is received. To continue the illustration, assume that the exchange rate declines from $1.20 to $1.18 per euro by January 19, when the 800 euros are received. The receipt of the cash on January 19 is recorded as follows:

Jan.	19	Cash (800 euros × $1.18)	9 4 4 00	
		Exchange Loss (800 euros × $0.02)	1 6 00	
		Accounts Receivable—T. A. Mueller Inc.		9 6 0 00
		Cash received on Invoice No. 1793,		
		for 800 euros, or $44, when exchange		
		rate was $1.18 per euro.		

In contrast, assume that in the preceding example the exchange rate increases between December 31 and January 19. In this case, an exchange gain would be recorded on January 19. For example, if the exchange rate increases from $1.20 to $1.24 per euro during this period, Exchange Gain would be credited for $32 (800 euros × $0.04).

A balance in the exchange loss account at the end of the fiscal period is reported in the Other Expense section of the income statement. A balance in the exchange gain account is reported in the Other Income section.

Exercises

EXERCISE E-1
Entries for sales made in foreign currency

The E-Cube Toy Company makes sales on account to several Swedish companies that it bills in kronas. Journalize the entries for the following selected transactions completed during the current year, assuming that E-Cube uses the perpetual inventory system:

Mar. 9. Sold merchandise on account, 30,000 kronas; exchange rate, $0.12 per krona. The cost of merchandise sold was $2,100.

Apr. 8. Received cash from sale of March 9, 30,000 kronas; exchange rate, $0.13 per krona.

July 13. Sold merchandise on account, 27,000 kronas; exchange rate, $0.14 per krona. The cost of merchandise sold was $2,400.

Aug. 17. Received cash from sale of July 13, 27,000 kronas; exchange rate, $0.13 per krona.

EXERCISE E-2
Entries for purchases made in foreign currency

Crossroads Care Inc. sells artificial arms and legs to hospitals and physicians. It purchases merchandise from a German company that requires payment in Euros. Journalize the entries for the following selected transactions completed during the current year, assuming that Crossroads Care Inc. uses the perpetual inventory system:

Oct.   3. Purchased merchandise on account, net 30, 20,000 Euros; exchange rate, $0.99 per Euro.

Nov. 2. Paid invoice of October 3; exchange rate, $1.01 per Euro.

     29. Purchased merchandise on account, net 30, 15,000 Euros; exchange rate, $1.00 per Euro.

Dec. 19. Paid invoice of Nov. 2; exchange rate, $0.98 per Euro.

Problems

PROBLEM E-1
Foreign currency transactions

P.A.S.S.

Outdoor Sports is a wholesaler of sports equipment, including golf clubs and gym sets. It sells to and purchases from companies in Canada and the Philippines. These transactions are settled in the foreign currency. The following selected transactions were completed during the current fiscal year:

Feb. 10. Sold merchandise on account to Manco Company, net 30, 600,000 pesos; exchange rate, $0.018 per Philippines peso. The cost of merchandise sold was $6,000.

Mar. 12. Received cash from Manco Company; exchange rate, $0.017 per Philippines peso.

     20. Purchased merchandise on account from Fossum Inc., net 30, $20,000 Canadian; exchange rate, $0.65 per Canadian dollar.

Apr. 11. Issued check for amount owed to Fossum Inc.; exchange rate, $0.63 per Canadian dollar.

June 27. Sold merchandise on account to Hu Company, net 30, 400,000 pesos; exchange rate, $0.016 per Philippines peso. The cost of merchandise sold was $3,800.

July 27. Received cash from Hu Company; exchange rate, $0.017 per Phillipines peso.

Oct. 8. Purchased merchandise on account from Chevalier Company, net 30, $50,000 Canadian; exchange rate, $0.64 per Canadian dollar.

Nov. 7. Issued check for amount owed to Chevalier Company; exchange rate, $0.65 per Canadian dollar.

Dec. 15. Sold merchandise on account to Cassandra Company, net 30, $120,000 Canadian; exchange rate, $0.65 per Canadian dollar. The cost of merchandise sold was $50,000.

16. Purchased merchandise on account from Juan Company, net 30, 500,000 pesos; exchange rate, $0.017 per Philippines peso.

31. Recorded unrealized currency exchange gain and/or loss on transactions of December 15 and 16. Exchange rates on December 31: $0.66 per Canadian dollar; $0.018 per Philippines peso.

Instructions

1. Journalize the entries to record the transactions and adjusting entries for the year, assuming that Outdoor Sports uses the perpetual inventory system.
2. Journalize the entries to record the payment of the December 16 purchase, on January 15, when the exchange rate was $0.016 per Philippines peso, and the receipt of cash from the December 15 sale, on January 17, when the exchange rate was $0.67 per Canadian dollar.

The Home Depot Annual Report

2002 ANNUAL REPORT

MANAGEMENT'S DISCUSSION AND ANALYSIS
OF RESULTS OF OPERATIONS AND FINANCIAL CONDITION
THE HOME DEPOT, INC. AND SUBSIDIARIES

SELECTED CONSOLIDATED STATEMENTS OF EARNINGS DATA

The data below reflect selected sales data, the percentage relationship between sales and major categories in the Consolidated Statements of Earnings and the percentage change in the dollar amounts of each of the items.

		Fiscal Year[1]		Percentage Increase (Decrease) In Dollar Amounts	
	2002	2001	2000	2002 vs. 2001	2001 vs. 2000
NET SALES	100.0%	100.0%	100.0%	8.8%	17.1%
GROSS PROFIT	31.1	30.2	29.9	12.1	18.0
Operating Expenses:					
Selling and Store Operating	19.2	19.0	18.6	10.0	19.4
Pre-Opening	0.2	0.2	0.3	(17.9)	(17.6)
General and Administrative	1.7	1.7	1.8	7.2	12.0
Total Operating Expenses	21.1	20.9	20.7	9.5	18.2
OPERATING INCOME	10.0	9.3	9.2	18.2	17.7
Interest Income (Expense):					
Interest and Investment Income	0.1	0.1	0.1	49.1	12.8
Interest Expense	(0.0)	(0.1)	(0.1)	32.1	33.3
Interest, net	0.1	–	–	68.0	(3.8)
EARNINGS BEFORE PROVISION FOR INCOME TAXES	10.1	9.3	9.2	18.5	17.5
Provision for Income Taxes	3.8	3.6	3.6	15.4	16.9
NET EARNINGS	6.3%	5.7%	5.6%	20.4%	17.9%
SELECTED SALES DATA [2]					
Number of Transactions (000s)	1,160,994	1,090,975	936,519	6.4%	16.5%
Average Sale per Transaction	$ 49.43	$ 48.64	$ 48.65	1.6	–
Weighted Average Weekly Sales per Operating Store	$772,000	$812,000	$864,000	(4.9)	(6.0)
Weighted Average Sales per Square Foot [3]	$ 370.21	$ 387.93	$ 414.68	(4.6)	(6.5)

[1] Fiscal years 2002, 2001 and 2000 refer to the fiscal years ended February 2, 2003, February 3, 2002 and January 28, 2001, respectively. Fiscal years 2002 and 2000 include 52 weeks, while fiscal year 2001 includes 53 weeks.

[2] Includes all retail locations in excess of 50,000 square feet and, therefore, excludes Apex Supply Company, Georgia Lighting, Maintenance Warehouse, Your "other" Warehouse, Designplace Direct (formerly National Blinds and Wallpaper) and HD Builder Solutions Group locations.

[3] Adjusted to reflect the first 52 weeks of the 53-week fiscal year in 2001.

FORWARD-LOOKING STATEMENTS

Certain statements made herein regarding implementation of store initiatives, store openings, capital expenditures and the effect of adopting certain accounting standards constitute "forward-looking statements" as defined in the Private Securities Litigation Reform Act of 1995. These statements are subject to various risks and uncertainties that could cause actual results to differ materially from our historical experience and our present expectations. These risks and uncertainties include, but are not limited to, fluctuations in and the overall condition of the U.S. economy, stability of costs and availability of sourcing channels, conditions affecting new store development, our ability to implement new technologies and processes, our ability to attract, train and retain highly-qualified associates, unanticipated weather conditions, the impact of competition and the effects of regulatory and litigation matters. You should not place undue reliance on such forward-looking statements as such statements speak only as of the date on which they are made. Additional information concerning these and other risks and uncertainties is contained in our periodic filings with the Securities and Exchange Commission.

RESULTS OF OPERATIONS

For an understanding of the significant factors that influenced our performance during the past three fiscal years, the following discussion should be read in conjunction with the consolidated financial statements and the notes to consolidated financial statements presented in this annual report.

MANAGEMENT'S DISCUSSION AND ANALYSIS
OF RESULTS OF OPERATIONS AND FINANCIAL CONDITION (CONTINUED)
THE HOME DEPOT, INC. AND SUBSIDIARIES

Fiscal year ended February 2, 2003 ("fiscal 2002") compared to fiscal year ended February 3, 2002 ("fiscal 2001")

Fiscal 2002 included 52 weeks as compared to 53 weeks in fiscal 2001. Net sales for fiscal 2002 increased 8.8% to $58.2 billion from $53.6 billion in fiscal 2001. This increase was attributable to the 203 new stores opened during fiscal 2002 and full year sales from the 204 new stores opened during fiscal 2001. The increase was partially offset by the net sales attributable to the additional week in fiscal 2001 of $880 million.

Comparable store-for-store sales were flat in fiscal 2002, reflecting a number of internal and external factors. In the spring and early summer, we experienced some inventory out-of-stock positions as we transitioned through our new in-store Service Performance Improvement ("SPI") initiative, in which our stores handle and receive inventory at night. In addition, comparable store-for-store sales were negatively impacted by the level of merchandise resets implemented throughout the year, which disrupted in-store service and had a negative impact on our customers' experience in our stores. Kitchen and bath, plumbing and paint categories experienced strong comparable store-for-store sales growth for the year, which offset price deflation and the resulting comparable store-for-store sales decline in commodity categories such as lumber.

In order to meet our customer service objectives, we strategically open stores near market areas served by existing strong performing stores ("cannibalize") to enhance service levels, gain incremental sales and increase market penetration. As of the end of fiscal 2002, certain new stores cannibalized 21% of our existing stores and we estimate that store cannibalization reduced total comparable store-for-store sales by approximately 4%, or about the same percentage as in the prior year. As we heavily cannibalized our most productive divisions, the weighted average weekly sales per store decreased during fiscal 2002 to $772,000 from $812,000 in the prior year. Additionally, we believe that our sales performance has been, and could continue to be, negatively impacted by the level of competition that we encounter in various markets. However, due to the highly-fragmented U.S. home improvement industry, in which we estimate our market share is approximately 10%, measuring the impact on our sales by our competitors is extremely difficult.

During fiscal 2002, we continued the implementation or expansion of a number of in-store initiatives. We believe these initiatives will increase customer loyalty and operating efficiencies as they are fully implemented in the stores. The professional business customer ("Pro") initiative adds programs to our stores to enhance service levels to the Pro customer base. As of the end of fiscal 2002, the Pro initiative was in 1,135 stores or 74% of total stores, compared to 535 stores or 40% of total stores as of the end of fiscal 2001. This initiative is still in its early stages as approximately half of our stores implemented the Pro initiative in

fiscal 2002. We expect to add the Pro initiative to an additional 204 stores by the end of fiscal 2003. As the Pro initiative matures within the stores in which it has been implemented, we expect to generate improvements in operating performance.

We continued to implement the Appliance initiative which was started in the third quarter of fiscal 2001. The Appliance initiative offers customers an assortment of in-stock name brand appliances, including General Electric® and Maytag®, and offers the ability to special order over 2,300 additional related products through computer kiosks located in the stores. In the stores which have implemented the Appliance initiative, we have enhanced the offering of appliances through 1,500 to 2,000 square feet of dedicated appliance selling space. Comparable store-for-store sales in the appliance category increased by approximately 23% in fiscal 2002. The Appliance initiative was in 743 or 48% of our stores as of the end of fiscal 2002, compared to 73 or 5% of our stores as of the end of fiscal 2001. We expect to add the Appliance initiative to an additional 671 stores by the end of fiscal 2003.

We also continued to implement our Designplace initiative. This initiative offers an enhanced shopping experience to our design and décor customers by providing personalized service from specially-trained associates and an enhanced merchandise selection in an attractive setting. Although the Designplace initiative is in its early stages, stores generally show a positive sales trend after implementation. The Designplace initiative was in 873 or 57% of our stores as of the end of fiscal 2002, compared to 205 or 15% of our stores as of the end of fiscal 2001. We expect to add the Designplace initiative to an additional 556 stores by the end of fiscal 2003.

In addition, we continued to drive our services programs, which focus primarily on providing products and services to our do-it-for-me customers. These programs are offered through Home Depot and EXPO Design Center stores. We also arrange for the provision of flooring installation services to homebuilders through HD Builder Solutions Group, Inc. Net service revenues for fiscal 2002 increased 25% to $2.0 billion from $1.6 billion for fiscal 2001.

Gross profit as a percent of sales was 31.1% for fiscal 2002 compared to 30.2% for fiscal 2001. The rate increase was attributable to a reduction in the cost of merchandise sold which resulted from centralized purchasing, as we continued rationalizing vendor and sku assortments. Enhanced inventory control, resulting in lower shrink levels, and an increase in direct import penetration to 8% in fiscal 2002 from 6% in fiscal 2001 also positively impacted the gross profit rate.

Operating expenses as a percent of sales were 21.1% for fiscal 2002 compared to 20.9% for fiscal 2001. Included in operating expenses are selling and store operating expenses which, as a percent of sales, increased to 19.2% in fiscal 2002 from 19.0% in fiscal 2001. The increase in selling and store

MANAGEMENT'S DISCUSSION AND ANALYSIS
OF RESULTS OF OPERATIONS AND FINANCIAL CONDITION (CONTINUED)
THE HOME DEPOT, INC. AND SUBSIDIARIES

operating expenses was primarily attributable to higher costs associated with merchandise resets and store renovations as we invested in new signage, fixtures and general maintenance of our stores, a continued investment in store leadership positions in our stores and rising workers' compensation expense due in part to medical cost inflation. These increases were partially offset by a decrease in store payroll expense which resulted from improvement in labor productivity and effective wage rate management.

Pre-opening expenses as a percent of sales were 0.2% for both fiscal 2002 and fiscal 2001. We opened 203 new stores in fiscal 2002 as compared to 204 new stores in fiscal 2001.

General and administrative expenses as a percent of sales were 1.7% for both fiscal 2002 and fiscal 2001.

Interest and investment income as a percent of sales was 0.1% for both fiscal 2002 and 2001. Interest expense as a percent of sales was 0.0% for fiscal 2002 and 0.1% for fiscal 2001.

Our combined federal and state effective income tax rate decreased to 37.6% for fiscal 2002 from 38.6% for fiscal 2001. The decrease in fiscal 2002 was attributable to higher tax credits and a lower effective state income tax rate compared to fiscal 2001.

Fiscal 2001 compared to fiscal year ended January 28, 2001 ("fiscal 2000")

Fiscal 2001 included 53 weeks as compared to 52 weeks in fiscal 2000. Net sales for fiscal 2001 increased 17.1% to $53.6 billion from $45.7 billion in fiscal 2000. This increase was attributable to, among other things, the 204 new stores opened during fiscal 2001 and full year sales from the 204 new stores opened during fiscal 2000. Approximately $880 million of the increase in sales was attributable to the additional week in fiscal 2001. Comparable store-for-store sales were flat in fiscal 2001 due to the weak economic environment resulting from certain factors including, but not limited to, low consumer confidence and high unemployment.

Gross profit as a percent of sales was 30.2% for fiscal 2001 compared to 29.9% for fiscal 2000. The rate increase was primarily attributable to a lower cost of merchandise resulting from product line reviews, purchasing synergies created by our newly centralized merchandising structure and an increase in the number of tool rental centers from 342 at the end of fiscal 2000 to 466 at the end of fiscal 2001.

Operating expenses as a percent of sales were 20.9% for fiscal 2001 compared to 20.7% for fiscal 2000. Included in operating expenses are selling and store operating expenses which, as a percent of sales, increased to 19.0% in fiscal 2001 from 18.6% in fiscal 2000. The increase was primarily attributable to growth in store occupancy costs resulting from higher depreciation and property taxes due to our investment in new stores, combined with increased energy costs. Also, credit card transaction fees were higher than the prior year due to increased penetration of total credit sales. These increases were partially offset by a decrease in store payroll expense due to an improvement in labor productivity which resulted from initiatives inside the store and new systems enhancements.

Store initiatives included our SPI initiative which was introduced to every Home Depot store in fiscal 2001. Under SPI our stores receive and handle inventory at night, allowing our associates to spend more time with customers during peak selling hours. In addition, our Pro program was in 535 of our Home Depot stores at the end of fiscal 2001, providing dedicated store resources to serve the specific needs of professional customers.

Pre-opening expenses as a percent of sales were 0.2% for fiscal 2001 and 0.3% for fiscal 2000. We opened 204 new stores in both fiscal 2001 and 2000. The decrease was primarily due to shorter pre-opening periods as we re-engineered our store opening process.

General and administrative expenses as a percent of sales were 1.7% for fiscal 2001 compared to 1.8% for fiscal 2000. This decrease was primarily due to cost savings associated with the reorganization of certain components of our organizational structure, such as the centralization of our merchandising organization and our focus on expense control in areas such as travel.

Interest and investment income as a percent of sales was 0.1% for both fiscal 2001 and 2000. Interest expense as a percent of sales was 0.1% for both fiscal 2001 and 2000.

Our combined federal and state effective income tax rate decreased to 38.6% for fiscal 2001 from 38.8% for fiscal 2000. The decrease in fiscal 2001 was attributable to higher tax credits and a lower effective state income tax rate compared to fiscal 2000.

LIQUIDITY AND CAPITAL RESOURCES

Cash flow generated from operations provides us with a significant source of liquidity. For fiscal 2002, cash provided by operations decreased to $4.8 billion from $6.0 billion in fiscal 2001. The decrease was primarily due to a 7.9% increase in average inventory per store resulting from our focus on improving our in-stock position in fiscal 2002.

During fiscal 2002, we experienced a significant growth in days payable outstanding to 42 days at the end of fiscal 2002 from 34 days at the end of fiscal 2001. The growth in days payable is the result of our efforts to move our payment terms to industry averages. We have realized the majority of the benefit from our renegotiated payment terms.

MANAGEMENT'S DISCUSSION AND ANALYSIS
OF RESULTS OF OPERATIONS AND FINANCIAL CONDITION (CONTINUED)
THE HOME DEPOT, INC. AND SUBSIDIARIES

Cash used in investing activities decreased to $2.9 billion in fiscal 2002 from $3.5 billion in fiscal 2001. Capital expenditures decreased to $2.7 billion in fiscal 2002 from $3.4 billion in fiscal 2001. This decrease was due primarily to a shift in the timing of spending for future store openings. We opened 203 new stores in fiscal 2002 compared to 204 new stores in fiscal 2001. We own 195 and 188 of the stores opened in fiscal 2002 and fiscal 2001, respectively, and lease the remainder.

We plan to open 206 stores in fiscal 2003, including 6 Home Depot Landscape Supply stores, and expect total capital expenditures to be approximately $4.0 billion, which includes a higher level of investment in store remodeling, technology and other initiatives as compared to fiscal 2002.

Cash used in financing activities in fiscal 2002 was $2.2 billion compared with $173 million in fiscal 2001. This change is primarily due to the repurchase of approximately 68.6 million shares of our common stock for $2 billion, pursuant to the Share Repurchase Program approved by our Board of Directors in July 2002.

We have a commercial paper program that allows borrowings for up to a maximum of $1 billion. As of February 2, 2003, there were no borrowings outstanding under the program. In connection with the program, we have a back-up credit facility with a consortium of banks for up to $800 million. The credit facility, which expires in September 2004, contains various restrictive covenants, none of which are expected to impact our liquidity or capital resources.

We use capital and operating leases, as well as three off-balance sheet leases created under structured financing arrangements, to finance about 22% of our real estate. The net present value of capital lease obligations is reflected in our Consolidated Balance Sheets in Long-Term Debt. The three off-balance sheet leases were created to purchase land and fund the construction of certain stores, office buildings and distribution centers. Two of these lease agreements involve a special purpose entity ("SPE") which meets the criteria for non-consolidation established by generally accepted accounting principles and is not owned by or affiliated with our Company, management or officers. Operating and off-balance sheet leases are not reflected in our Consolidated Balance Sheets in accordance with generally accepted accounting principles.

As of the end of fiscal 2002, our long-term debt-to-equity ratio was 6.7%. If the estimated net present value of future payments under the operating and off-balance sheet leases were capitalized, our long-term debt-to-equity ratio would increase to 28.5%.

The following table summarizes our significant contractual obligations and commercial commitments as of February 2, 2003 (amounts in millions):

| Contractual Obligations[1] | Total | Payments Due By Fiscal Year | | | |
		2003	2004-2005	2006-2007	Thereafter
Long-Term Debt	$1,051	$ 2	$502	$502	$ 45
Capital Lease Obligations	834	44	89	93	608
Operating Leases	7,308	541	988	864	4,915

| Commercial Commitments[2] | Total | Amount of Commitment Expiration Per Fiscal Year | | | |
		2003	2004-2005	2006-2007	Thereafter
Letters of Credit	$ 930	$921	$ 9	$ –	$ –
Guarantees	799	–	72	504	223

[1] Contractual obligations include long-term debt comprised primarily of $1 billion of Senior Notes further discussed in "Quantitative and Qualitative Disclosures about Market Risk" and future minimum lease payments under capital and operating leases, which include off-balance sheet leases, used in the normal course of business.

[2] Commercial commitments include letters of credit for certain business transactions and guarantees provided under the off-balance sheet leases. We issue letters of credit for insurance programs, import purchases and construction contracts. Under the three off-balance sheet leases for certain stores, office buildings and distribution centers, we have provided residual value guarantees. The estimated maximum amount of the residual value guarantees at the end of the leases is $799 million. The leases expire at various dates during fiscal 2005 through 2008 with two of the leases having an option to renew through 2025. Events or circumstances that would require us to perform under the guarantees include 1) our default on the leases with the assets being sold for less than the initial book value, or 2) we decide not to purchase the assets at the end of the leases and the sale of the assets results in proceeds less than the initial book value of the assets. Our guarantees are limited to 82% of the initial book value of the assets. The expiration dates of the residual value guarantees as disclosed in the table above are based on the expiration of the leases; however, the expiration dates will change if the leases are renewed.

MANAGEMENT'S DISCUSSION AND ANALYSIS
OF RESULTS OF OPERATIONS AND FINANCIAL CONDITION (CONTINUED)
THE HOME DEPOT, INC. AND SUBSIDIARIES

As of February 2, 2003, we had approximately $2.3 billion in cash and short-term investments. We believe that our current cash position, cash flow generated from operations, funds available from the $1 billion commercial paper program and the ability to obtain alternate sources of financing should be sufficient to enable us to complete our capital expenditure programs through the next several fiscal years.

QUANTITATIVE AND QUALITATIVE DISCLOSURES ABOUT MARKET RISK
Our exposure to market risk results primarily from fluctuations in interest rates. Although we have international operating entities, our exposure to foreign currency rate fluctuations is not significant to our financial condition and results of operations. Our objective for holding derivative instruments is primarily to decrease the volatility of earnings and cash flow associated with fluctuations in interest rates.

We have financial instruments that are sensitive to changes in interest rates. These instruments include primarily fixed rate debt. As of February 2, 2003, we had $500 million of $5^3/_8\%$ Senior Notes and $500 million of $6^1/_2\%$ Senior Notes outstanding. The market values of the publicly traded $5^3/_8\%$ and $6^1/_2\%$ Senior Notes as of February 2, 2003, were approximately $538 million and $537 million, respectively. We have an interest rate swap agreement, with the notional amount of $300 million, that swaps fixed rate interest on $300 million of our $500 million $5^3/_8\%$ Senior Notes for a variable interest rate equal to LIBOR plus 30 basis points and expires on April 1, 2006.

IMPACT OF INFLATION AND CHANGING PRICES
Although we cannot accurately determine the precise effect of inflation on operations, we do not believe inflation has had a material effect on sales or results of operations.

CRITICAL ACCOUNTING POLICIES
Our significant accounting policies are disclosed in Note 1 to our consolidated financial statements. The following discussion addresses our most critical accounting policies, which are those that are both important to the portrayal of our financial condition and results of operations and that require significant judgment or use of complex estimates.

REVENUE RECOGNITION
We recognize revenue, net of estimated returns, at the time the customer takes possession of the merchandise or receives services. We estimate the liability for sales returns based on our historical return levels. The methodology used is consistent with other retailers. We believe that our estimate for sales returns is an accurate reflection of future returns. When we receive payment from customers before the customer has taken possession of the merchandise or the service has been performed, the amount received is recorded in Deferred Revenue in the accompanying Consolidated Balance Sheets.

INVENTORY
Our inventory is stated at the lower of cost (first-in, first-out) or market, with approximately 93% valued under the retail method and the remainder under the cost method. Retailers with many different types of merchandise at low unit cost with a large number of transactions frequently use the retail method. Under the retail method, inventory is stated at cost which is determined by applying a cost-to-retail ratio to the ending retail value of inventory. As our inventory retail value is adjusted regularly to reflect market conditions, our inventory methodology approximates the lower of cost or market. Accordingly, there were no significant valuation reserves related to our inventory as of February 2, 2003 and February 3, 2002. In addition, we reduce our ending inventory value for estimated losses related to shrink. This estimate is determined based upon analysis of historical shrink losses and recent shrink trends.

SELF INSURANCE
We are self-insured for certain losses related to general liability, product liability, workers' compensation and medical claims. Our liability represents an estimate of the ultimate cost of claims incurred as of the balance sheet date. The estimated liability is not discounted and is established based upon analysis of historical data and actuarial estimates, and is reviewed by management and third party actuaries on a quarterly basis to ensure that the liability is appropriate. While we believe these estimates are reasonable based on the information currently available, if actual trends, including the severity or frequency of claims, medical cost inflation, or fluctuations in premiums, differ from our estimates, our results of operations could be impacted.

CHANGE IN ACCOUNTING FOR STOCK-BASED COMPENSATION
During fiscal 2002 and all fiscal years prior, we elected to account for our stock-based compensation plans under Accounting Principles Board Opinion No. 25 ("APB 25"), "Accounting for Stock Issued to Employees," which requires the recording of compensation expense for some, but not all, stock-based compensation, rather than the alternative accounting permitted by Statement of Financial Accounting Standards ("SFAS") No. 123, "Accounting for Stock-Based Compensation."

In December 2002, SFAS No. 148, "Accounting for Stock-Based Compensation – Transition and Disclosure," was issued, which provides three alternative methods of transition for a voluntary change to the fair value method of accounting for stock-based compensation in accordance with SFAS No. 123.

MANAGEMENT'S DISCUSSION AND ANALYSIS
OF RESULTS OF OPERATIONS AND FINANCIAL CONDITION (CONTINUED)
THE HOME DEPOT, INC. AND SUBSIDIARIES

Effective February 3, 2003, we adopted the fair value method of recording compensation expense related to all stock options granted after February 2, 2003, in accordance with SFAS Nos. 123 and 148. Accordingly, the fair value of stock options as determined on the date of grant using the Black-Scholes option-pricing model will be expensed over the vesting period of the related stock options. The estimated negative impact on diluted earnings per share is approximately $.02 for fiscal 2003. The actual impact may differ from this estimate as the estimate is based upon a number of factors including, but not limited to, the number of stock options granted and the fair value of the stock options on the date of grant.

RECENT ACCOUNTING PRONOUNCEMENTS
In January 2003, the Financial Accounting Standards Board ("FASB") issued Interpretation No. 46, "Consolidation of Variable Interest Entities." Interpretation No. 46 requires consolidation of a variable interest entity if a company's variable interest absorbs a majority of the entity's losses or receives a majority of the entity's expected residual returns, or both. We do not have a variable interest in the SPE created as part of our off-balance sheet structured financing arrangements and, therefore, we are not required to consolidate the SPE. We do not expect Interpretation No. 46 to have any impact on our consolidated financial statements.

In January 2003, the Emerging Issues Task Force issued EITF 02-16, "Accounting by a Customer (Including a Reseller) for Certain Consideration Received from a Vendor," which states that cash consideration received from a vendor is presumed to be a reduction of the prices of the vendor's products or services and should, therefore, be characterized as a reduction of Cost of Merchandise Sold when recognized in our Consolidated Statements of Earnings. That presumption is overcome when the consideration is either a reimbursement of specific, incremental, identifiable costs incurred to sell the vendor's products, or a payment for assets or services delivered to the vendor. EITF 02-16 is effective for arrangements entered into after December 31, 2002. We are currently assessing the impact of the adoption of EITF 02-16 and do not expect the adoption to materially impact net earnings in fiscal 2003. We do, however, expect that certain payments received from our vendors that are currently reflected as a reduction in advertising expense, which is classified as Selling and Store Operating Expense, will be reclassified as a reduction of Cost of Merchandise Sold.

In December 2002, the FASB issued Interpretation No. 45, "Guarantor's Accounting and Disclosure Requirements for Guarantees, Including Indirect Guarantees of Indebtedness of Others," which provides for additional disclosures to be made by a guarantor in its interim and annual financial statements about its obligations and requires, under certain circumstances, a guarantor to recognize, at the inception of a guarantee, a liability for the fair value of the obligation undertaken in issuing the guarantee. We have adopted the disclosure requirements for the fiscal year ended February 2, 2003. We do not expect the recognition and measurement provisions of Interpretation No. 45 for guarantees issued or modified after December 31, 2002, to have a material impact on our consolidated financial statements.

CONSOLIDATED STATEMENTS OF EARNINGS

THE HOME DEPOT, INC. AND SUBSIDIARIES

	Fiscal Year Ended[1]		
amounts in millions, except per share data	February 2, 2003	February 3, 2002	January 28, 2001
NET SALES	$58,247	$53,553	$45,738
Cost of Merchandise Sold	40,139	37,406	32,057
GROSS PROFIT	18,108	16,147	13,681
Operating Expenses:			
Selling and Store Operating	11,180	10,163	8,513
Pre-Opening	96	117	142
General and Administrative	1,002	935	835
Total Operating Expenses	12,278	11,215	9,490
OPERATING INCOME	5,830	4,932	4,191
Interest Income (Expense):			
Interest and Investment Income	79	53	47
Interest Expense	(37)	(28)	(21)
Interest, net	42	25	26
EARNINGS BEFORE PROVISION FOR INCOME TAXES	5,872	4,957	4,217
Provision for Income Taxes	2,208	1,913	1,636
NET EARNINGS	$ 3,664	$ 3,044	$ 2,581
Weighted Average Common Shares	2,336	2,335	2,315
BASIC EARNINGS PER SHARE	$ 1.57	$ 1.30	$ 1.11
Diluted Weighted Average Common Shares	2,344	2,353	2,352
DILUTED EARNINGS PER SHARE	$ 1.56	$ 1.29	$ 1.10

[1] Fiscal years ended February 2, 2003 and January 28, 2001 include 52 weeks. Fiscal year ended February 3, 2002 includes 53 weeks.

See accompanying notes to consolidated financial statements.

CONSOLIDATED BALANCE SHEETS

THE HOME DEPOT, INC. AND SUBSIDIARIES

amounts in millions, except per share data	February 2, 2003	February 3, 2002
ASSETS		
Current Assets:		
Cash and Cash Equivalents	$ 2,188	$ 2,477
Short-Term Investments, including current maturities of long-term investments	65	69
Receivables, net	1,072	920
Merchandise Inventories	8,338	6,725
Other Current Assets	254	170
Total Current Assets	11,917	10,361
Property and Equipment, at cost:		
Land	5,560	4,972
Buildings	9,197	7,698
Furniture, Fixtures and Equipment	4,074	3,403
Leasehold Improvements	872	750
Construction in Progress	724	1,049
Capital Leases	306	257
	20,733	18,129
Less Accumulated Depreciation and Amortization	3,565	2,754
Net Property and Equipment	17,168	15,375
Notes Receivable	107	83
Cost in Excess of the Fair Value of Net Assets Acquired, net of accumulated amortization of $50 at February 2, 2003 and $49 at February 3, 2002	575	419
Other Assets	244	156
	$30,011	$26,394
LIABILITIES AND STOCKHOLDERS' EQUITY		
Current Liabilities:		
Accounts Payable	$ 4,560	$ 3,436
Accrued Salaries and Related Expenses	809	717
Sales Taxes Payable	307	348
Deferred Revenue	998	851
Income Taxes Payable	227	211
Other Accrued Expenses	1,134	938
Total Current Liabilities	8,035	6,501
Long-Term Debt, excluding current installments	1,321	1,250
Other Long-Term Liabilities	491	372
Deferred Income Taxes	362	189
STOCKHOLDERS' EQUITY		
Common Stock, par value $0.05; authorized: 10,000 shares, issued and outstanding 2,362 shares at February 2, 2003 and 2,346 shares at February 3, 2002	118	117
Paid-In Capital	5,858	5,412
Retained Earnings	15,971	12,799
Accumulated Other Comprehensive Loss	(82)	(220)
Unearned Compensation	(63)	(26)
Treasury Stock, at cost, 69 shares at February 2, 2003	(2,000)	—
Total Stockholders' Equity	19,802	18,082
	$30,011	$26,394

See accompanying notes to consolidated financial statements.

CONSOLIDATED STATEMENTS OF STOCKHOLDERS' EQUITY AND COMPREHENSIVE INCOME

THE HOME DEPOT, INC. AND SUBSIDIARIES

amounts in millions, except per share data	Common Stock Shares	Amount	Paid-In Capital	Retained Earnings	Accumulated Other Comprehensive Income (Loss)	Treasury Stock Shares	Amount	Unearned Compensation	Total Stockholders' Equity	Comprehensive Income[1]
BALANCE, JANUARY 30, 2000	2,304	$115	$4,319	$ 7,941	$ (27)	–	$ –	$ (7)	$12,341	
Net Earnings	–	–	–	2,581	–	–	–	–	2,581	$2,581
Shares Issued Under Employee Stock Purchase and Option Plans	20	1	348	–	–	–	–	1	350	
Tax Effect of Sale of Option Shares by Employees	–	–	137	–	–	–	–	–	137	
Translation Adjustments	–	–	–	–	(40)	–	–	–	(40)	(40)
Stock Compensation Expense	–	–	6	–	–	–	–	–	6	
Cash Dividends ($0.16 per share)	–	–	–	(371)	–	–	–	–	(371)	
Comprehensive Income										$2,541
BALANCE, JANUARY 28, 2001	2,324	$116	$4,810	$10,151	$ (67)	–	$ –	$ (6)	$15,004	
Net Earnings	–	–	–	3,044	–	–	–	–	3,044	$3,044
Shares Issued Under Employee Stock Purchase and Option Plans	22	1	448	–	–	–	–	(20)	429	
Tax Effect of Sale of Option Shares by Employees	–	–	138	–	–	–	–	–	138	
Translation Adjustments	–	–	–	–	(124)	–	–	–	(124)	(124)
Unrealized Loss on Derivative	–	–	–	–	(29)	–	–	–	(29)	(18)
Stock Compensation Expense	–	–	16	–	–	–	–	–	16	
Cash Dividends ($0.17 per share)	–	–	–	(396)	–	–	–	–	(396)	
Comprehensive Income										$2,902
BALANCE, FEBRUARY 3, 2002	2,346	$117	$5,412	$12,799	$(220)	–	$ –	$(26)	$18,082	
Net Earnings	–	–	–	3,664	–	–	–	–	3,664	$3,664
Shares Issued Under Employee Stock Purchase and Option Plans	16	1	366	–	–	–	–	(37)	330	
Tax Effect of Sale of Option Shares by Employees	–	–	68	–	–	–	–	–	68	
Translation Adjustments	–	–	–	–	109	–	–	–	109	109
Realized Loss on Derivative	–	–	–	–	29	–	–	–	29	18
Stock Compensation Expense	–	–	12	–	–	–	–	–	12	
Repurchase of Common Stock	–	–	–	–	–	(69)	(2,000)	–	(2,000)	
Cash Dividends ($0.21 per share)	–	–	–	(492)	–	–	–	–	(492)	
Comprehensive Income										$3,791
BALANCE, FEBRUARY 2, 2003	2,362	$118	$5,858	$15,971	$ (82)	(69)	$(2,000)	$(63)	$19,802	

[1] Components of comprehensive income are reported net of related income taxes.

See accompanying notes to consolidated financial statements.

CONSOLIDATED STATEMENTS OF CASH FLOWS

THE HOME DEPOT, INC. AND SUBSIDIARIES

	Fiscal Year Ended[1]		
amounts in millions	February 2, 2003	February 3, 2002	January 28, 2001
CASH FLOWS FROM OPERATIONS:			
Net Earnings	$3,664	$3,044	$2,581
Reconciliation of Net Earnings to Net Cash Provided by Operations:			
Depreciation and Amortization	903	764	601
Increase in Receivables, net	(38)	(119)	(246)
Increase in Merchandise Inventories	(1,592)	(166)	(1,075)
Increase in Accounts Payable and Accrued Liabilities	1,394	1,878	268
Increase in Deferred Revenue	147	200	486
Increase in Income Taxes Payable	83	272	151
Increase (Decrease) in Deferred Income Taxes	173	(6)	108
Other	68	96	(78)
Net Cash Provided by Operations	4,802	5,963	2,796
CASH FLOWS FROM INVESTING ACTIVITIES:			
Capital Expenditures, net of $49, $5 and $16 of non-cash capital expenditures in fiscal 2002, 2001 and 2000, respectively	(2,749)	(3,393)	(3,558)
Payments for Businesses Acquired, net	(235)	(190)	(26)
Proceeds from Sales of Businesses, net	22	64	–
Proceeds from Sales of Property and Equipment	105	126	95
Purchases of Investments	(583)	(85)	(39)
Proceeds from Maturities of Investments	506	25	30
Other	–	(13)	(32)
Net Cash Used in Investing Activities	(2,934)	(3,466)	(3,530)
CASH FLOWS FROM FINANCING ACTIVITIES:			
(Repayments) Issuances of Commercial Paper Obligations, net	–	(754)	754
Proceeds from Long-Term Debt	1	532	32
Repayments of Long-Term Debt	–	–	(29)
Repurchase of Common Stock	(2,000)	–	–
Proceeds from Sale of Common Stock, net	326	445	351
Cash Dividends Paid to Stockholders	(492)	(396)	(371)
Net Cash (Used in) Provided by Financing Activities	(2,165)	(173)	737
Effect of Exchange Rate Changes on Cash and Cash Equivalents	8	(14)	(4)
(Decrease) Increase in Cash and Cash Equivalents	(289)	2,310	(1)
Cash and Cash Equivalents at Beginning of Year	2,477	167	168
Cash and Cash Equivalents at End of Year	$2,188	$2,477	$ 167
SUPPLEMENTAL DISCLOSURE OF CASH PAYMENTS MADE FOR:			
Interest, net of interest capitalized	$ 50	$ 18	$ 16
Income Taxes	$1,951	$1,685	$1,386

[1] *Fiscal years ended February 2, 2003, and January 28, 2001, include 52 weeks. Fiscal year ended February 3, 2002, includes 53 weeks.*

See accompanying notes to consolidated financial statements.

NOTES TO CONSOLIDATED FINANCIAL STATEMENTS

THE HOME DEPOT, INC. AND SUBSIDIARIES

1 SUMMARY OF SIGNIFICANT ACCOUNTING POLICIES

BUSINESS, CONSOLIDATION AND PRESENTATION

The Home Depot, Inc. and subsidiaries (the "Company") operate Home Depot stores, which are full-service, warehouse-style stores averaging approximately 108,000 square feet in size. The stores stock approximately 40,000 to 50,000 different kinds of building materials, home improvement supplies and lawn and garden products that are sold primarily to do-it-your-selfers, but also to home improvement contractors, trades-people and building maintenance professionals. In addition, the Company operates EXPO Design Center stores, which offer products and services primarily related to design and renovation projects, Home Depot Landscape Supply stores which service landscape professionals and garden enthusiasts with lawn, landscape and garden products and Home Depot Supply stores serving primarily professional customers. The Company also operates one Home Depot Floor Store, a test store that offers only flooring products and installation services. At the end of fiscal 2002, the Company was operating 1,532 stores in total, which included 1,370 Home Depot stores, 52 EXPO Design Center stores, 5 Home Depot Supply stores, 3 Home Depot Landscape Supply stores and 1 Home Depot Floor Store in the United States ("U.S."); 89 Home Depot stores in Canada and 12 Home Depot stores in Mexico. Included in the Company's Consolidated Balance Sheet at February 2, 2003, were $1.2 billion of net assets of the Canada and Mexico operations.

The consolidated results include several wholly-owned subsidiaries. The Company offers facilities maintenance and repair products as well as wallpaper and custom window treatments via direct shipment through its subsidiaries, Maintenance Warehouse America Corp. and National Blinds and Wallpaper, Inc. (doing business as Designplace Direct). Georgia Lighting, Inc. is a specialty lighting designer, distributor and retailer to both commercial and retail customers. The Company offers plumbing, HVAC and other professional plumbing products through wholesale plumbing distributors Apex Supply Company, Inc. and Home Depot Your "other" Warehouse, LLC. The Company also arranges for the provision of flooring installation services to homebuilders through HD Builder Solutions Group, Inc. The consolidated financial statements include the accounts of the Company and its wholly-owned subsidiaries. All significant intercompany transactions have been eliminated in consolidation.

FISCAL YEAR

The Company's fiscal year is a 52 or 53-week period ending on the Sunday nearest to January 31. Fiscal years 2002 and 2000, which ended February 2, 2003, and January 28, 2001, respectively, include 52 weeks. Fiscal year 2001, which ended February 3, 2002, includes 53 weeks.

CASH EQUIVALENTS

The Company considers all highly liquid investments purchased with a maturity of three months or less to be cash equivalents. The Company's cash and cash equivalents are carried at fair market value and consist primarily of high-grade commercial paper, money market funds, U.S. government agency securities and tax-exempt notes and bonds.

ACCOUNTS RECEIVABLE

The Company has an agreement with a third-party service provider who manages the Company's private label credit card program and directly extends credit to customers. The Company's valuation reserve related to accounts receivable was not material as of February 2, 2003 and February 3, 2002.

MERCHANDISE INVENTORIES

The majority of the Company's inventory is stated at the lower of cost (first-in, first-out) or market, as determined by the retail inventory method.

Certain subsidiaries and distribution centers record inventories at lower of cost (first-in, first-out) or market, as determined by the cost method. These inventories represent approximately 7% of total inventory.

INVESTMENTS

The Company's investments, consisting primarily of high-grade debt securities, are recorded at fair value and are classified as available-for-sale.

INCOME TAXES

The Company provides for federal, state and foreign income taxes currently payable, as well as for those deferred due to timing differences between reporting income and expenses for financial statement purposes versus tax purposes. Federal, state and foreign incentive tax credits are recorded as a reduction of income taxes. Deferred tax assets and liabilities are recognized for the future tax consequences attributable to differences between the financial statement carrying amounts of existing assets and liabilities and their respective tax bases. Deferred tax assets and liabilities are measured using enacted income tax rates expected to apply to taxable income in the years in which those temporary differences are expected to be recovered or settled. The effect of a change in tax rates is recognized as income or expense in the period that includes the enactment date.

NOTES TO CONSOLIDATED FINANCIAL STATEMENTS (CONTINUED)

THE HOME DEPOT, INC. AND SUBSIDIARIES

The Company and its eligible subsidiaries file a consolidated U.S. federal income tax return. Non-U.S. subsidiaries, which are consolidated for financial reporting purposes, are not eligible to be included in consolidated U.S. federal income tax returns. Separate provisions for income taxes have been determined for these entities. The Company intends to reinvest the unremitted earnings of its non-U.S. subsidiaries and postpone their remittance indefinitely. Accordingly, no provision for U.S. income taxes for non-U.S. subsidiaries was recorded in the accompanying Consolidated Statements of Earnings.

DEPRECIATION AND AMORTIZATION

The Company's buildings, furniture, fixtures and equipment are depreciated using the straight-line method over the estimated useful lives of the assets. Improvements to leased assets are amortized using the straight-line method over the life of the lease or the useful life of the improvement, whichever is shorter. The Company's property and equipment is depreciated using the following estimated useful lives:

	Life
Buildings	10-45 years
Furniture, fixtures and equipment	5-20 years
Leasehold improvements	5-30 years
Computer equipment and software	3-5 years

REVENUES

The Company recognizes revenue, net of estimated returns, at the time the customer takes possession of merchandise or receives services. When the Company receives payment from customers before the customer has taken possession of the merchandise or the service has been performed, the amount received is recorded in Deferred Revenue in the accompanying Consolidated Balance Sheets.

SERVICE REVENUES

Total revenues include service revenues generated through a variety of installation and home maintenance programs in Home Depot and EXPO stores as well as through the Company's subsidiary, HD Builder Solutions Group, Inc. In these programs, the customer selects and purchases materials for a project and the Company provides or arranges professional installation. When the Company subcontracts the installation of a project and the subcontractor provides material as part of the installation, both the material and labor are included in service revenues. The Company recognizes this revenue when the service for the customer is completed. All payments received prior to the completion of services are recorded in Deferred Revenue in the accompanying Consolidated Balance Sheets. Net service revenues, including the impact of deferred revenue, were $2.0 billion, $1.6 billion and $1.3 billion for the fiscal years 2002, 2001 and 2000, respectively.

SELF INSURANCE

The Company is self-insured for certain losses related to general liability, product liability, workers' compensation and medical claims. The expected ultimate cost for claims incurred as of the balance sheet date is not discounted and is recognized as a liability. The expected ultimate cost of claims is estimated based upon analysis of historical data and actuarial estimates.

ADVERTISING

Television and radio advertising production costs along with media placement costs are expensed when the advertisement first appears. Included in Current Assets in the accompanying Consolidated Balance Sheets are $20 million and $15 million at the end of fiscal years 2002 and 2001, respectively, relating to prepayments of production costs for print and broadcast advertising.

Gross advertising expense is classified as Selling and Store Operating Expenses and was $895 million, $817 million and $722 million, in fiscal years 2002, 2001 and 2000, respectively. Advertising allowances earned from vendors fully offset gross advertising expenses. In fiscal 2002, 2001 and 2000, advertising allowances exceeded gross advertising expense by $30 million, $31 million and $62 million, respectively. These excess amounts were recorded as a reduction in Cost of Merchandise Sold in the accompanying Consolidated Statements of Earnings.

SHIPPING AND HANDLING COSTS

The Company accounts for certain shipping and handling costs related to the shipment of product to customers from vendors as Cost of Merchandise Sold. However, cost of shipping and handling to customers by the Company is classified as Selling and Store Operating Expenses. The cost of shipping and handling, including internal costs and payments to third parties, classified as Selling and Store Operating Expenses was $341 million, $278 million and $226 million in fiscal years 2002, 2001 and 2000, respectively.

COST IN EXCESS OF THE FAIR VALUE OF NET ASSETS ACQUIRED

Goodwill represents the excess of purchase price over fair value of net assets acquired. In accordance with Statement of Financial Accounting Standards ("SFAS") No. 142, "Goodwill and Other Intangible Assets," the Company stopped amortizing goodwill effective February 4, 2002. Amortization expense was $8 million in both fiscal 2001 and fiscal 2000. The Company assesses the recoverability of goodwill at least annually by determining whether the fair value of each reporting entity supports its carrying value. The Company completed its assessment of goodwill for fiscal 2002 and recorded an impairment charge of $1.3 million.

NOTES TO CONSOLIDATED FINANCIAL STATEMENTS (CONTINUED)
THE HOME DEPOT, INC. AND SUBSIDIARIES

IMPAIRMENT OF LONG-LIVED ASSETS

The Company reviews long-lived assets for impairment when circumstances indicate the carrying amount of an asset may not be recoverable. Impairment is recognized to the extent the sum of undiscounted estimated future cash flows expected to result from the use of the asset is less than the carrying value. When the Company commits to relocate or close a location, a charge is recorded to Selling and Store Operating Expenses to write down the related assets to the estimated net recoverable value.

In August 2002, the Company adopted SFAS No. 146, "Accounting for Costs Associated with Exit or Disposal Activities." In accordance with SFAS No. 146, the Company recognizes Selling and Store Operating Expense for the net present value of future lease obligations, less estimated sublease income when the location closes. Prior to the adoption of SFAS No. 146, the Company recognized this Selling and Store Operating Expense when the Company committed to a plan to relocate or close a location.

STOCK-BASED COMPENSATION

During fiscal 2002 and all fiscal years prior, the Company elected to account for its stock-based compensation plans under Accounting Principles Board Opinion No. 25 ("APB 25"), "Accounting for Stock Issued to Employees," which requires the recording of compensation expense for some, but not all, stock-based compensation rather than the alternative accounting permitted by SFAS No. 123, "Accounting for Stock-Based Compensation."

The following table illustrates the effect on net earnings and earnings per share if the Company had applied the fair value recognition provisions of SFAS No. 123 to stock-based compensation (amounts in millions, except per share data):

| | Fiscal Year Ended | | |
	February 2, 2003	February 3, 2002	January 28, 2001
Net Earnings			
As reported	$3,664	$3,044	$2,581
Pro forma	$3,414	$2,800	$2,364
Basic Earnings per Share			
As reported	$ 1.57	$ 1.30	$ 1.11
Pro forma	$ 1.46	$ 1.20	$ 1.02
Diluted Earnings per Share			
As reported	$ 1.56	$ 1.29	$ 1.10
Pro forma	$ 1.46	$ 1.19	$ 1.01

In December 2002, SFAS No. 148, "Accounting for Stock-Based Compensation – Transition and Disclosure," was issued, which provides three alternative methods of transition for a voluntary change to the fair value method of accounting for stock-based compensation in accordance with SFAS No. 123.

Effective February 3, 2003, the Company adopted the fair value method of recording compensation expense related to all stock options granted after February 2, 2003, in accordance with SFAS Nos. 123 and 148. Accordingly, the fair value of stock options as determined on the date of grant using the Black-Scholes option-pricing model will be expensed over the vesting period of the related stock options. The estimated negative impact on diluted earnings per share is approximately $.02 for fiscal 2003. The actual impact may differ from this estimate as the estimate is based upon a number of factors including, but not limited to, the number of stock options granted and the fair value of the stock options on the date of grant.

DERIVATIVES

The Company measures derivatives at fair value and recognizes these assets or liabilities on the Consolidated Balance Sheets. Recognition of changes in the fair value of a derivative in the Consolidated Statements of Earnings or Consolidated Statements of Stockholders' Equity and Comprehensive Income depends on the intended use of the derivative and its designation. The Company designates derivatives based upon criteria established by SFAS Nos. 133 and 138, "Accounting for Derivative Instruments and Hedging Activities." The Company's primary objective for holding derivative instruments is to decrease the volatility of earnings and cash flow associated with fluctuations in interest rates.

COMPREHENSIVE INCOME

Comprehensive income includes net earnings adjusted for certain revenues, expenses, gains and losses that are excluded from net earnings under generally accepted accounting principles. Examples include foreign currency translation adjustments and unrealized gains and losses on certain hedge transactions.

FOREIGN CURRENCY TRANSLATION

The assets and liabilities denominated in a foreign currency are translated into U.S. dollars at the current rate of exchange on the last day of the reporting period. Revenues and expenses are translated at the average monthly exchange rates, and equity transactions are translated using the actual rate on the day of the transaction.

USE OF ESTIMATES

Management of the Company has made a number of estimates and assumptions relating to the reporting of assets and liabilities, the disclosure of contingent assets and liabilities, and reported amounts of revenues and expenses in preparing these financial statements in conformity with generally accepted accounting principles. Actual results could differ from these estimates.

NOTES TO CONSOLIDATED FINANCIAL STATEMENTS (CONTINUED)

THE HOME DEPOT, INC. AND SUBSIDIARIES

RECLASSIFICATIONS

Certain amounts in prior fiscal years have been reclassified to conform with the presentation adopted in the current fiscal year.

2 LONG-TERM DEBT

The Company's long-term debt at the end of fiscal 2002 and fiscal 2001 consisted of the following (amounts in millions):

	February 2, 2003	February 3, 2002
6$^1/_2$% Senior Notes; due September 15, 2004; interest payable semi-annually on March 15 and September 15	$ 500	$ 500
5$^3/_8$% Senior Notes; due April 1, 2006; interest payable semi-annually on April 1 and October 1	500	500
Capital Lease Obligations; payable in varying installments through May 31, 2027	277	232
Other	51	23
Total long-term debt	1,328	1,255
Less current installments	7	5
Long-term debt, excluding current installments	$1,321	$1,250

The Company has a commercial paper program with maximum available borrowings for up to $1 billion. In connection with the program, the Company has a back-up credit facility with a consortium of banks for up to $800 million. The credit facility, which expires in September 2004, contains various restrictive covenants, none of which are expected to materially impact the Company's liquidity or capital resources.

The Company had $500 million of 6$^1/_2$% Senior Notes and $500 million of 5$^3/_8$% Senior Notes outstanding as of February 2, 2003, collectively referred to as "Senior Notes." The Senior Notes may be redeemed by the Company at any time, in whole or in part, at a redemption price plus accrued interest up to the redemption date. The redemption price is equal to the greater of (1) 100% of the principal amount of the Senior Notes to be redeemed, or (2) the sum of the present values of the remaining scheduled payments of principal and interest to maturity. The Senior Notes are not subject to sinking fund requirements.

Interest Expense in the accompanying Consolidated Statements of Earnings is net of interest capitalized of $59 million, $84 million and $73 million in fiscal years 2002, 2001 and 2000, respectively. Maturities of long-term debt are $7 million for fiscal 2003, $507 million for fiscal 2004, $8 million for fiscal 2005, $509 million for fiscal 2006 and $11 million for fiscal 2007.

As of February 2, 2003, the market values of the publicly traded 6$^1/_2$% and 5$^3/_8$% Senior Notes were approximately $537 million and $538 million, respectively. The estimated fair value of all other long-term borrowings, excluding capital lease obligations, approximated the carrying value of $51 million. These fair values were estimated using a discounted cash flow analysis based on the Company's incremental borrowing rate for similar liabilities.

3 INCOME TAXES

The provision for income taxes consisted of the following (in millions):

	Fiscal Year Ended		
	February 2, 2003	February 3, 2002	January 28, 2001
Current:			
Federal	$1,679	$1,594	$1,267
State	239	265	216
Foreign	117	60	45
	2,035	1,919	1,528
Deferred:			
Federal	174	(12)	98
State	1	(1)	9
Foreign	(2)	7	1
	173	(6)	108
Total	$2,208	$1,913	$1,636

The Company's combined federal, state and foreign effective tax rates for fiscal years 2002, 2001 and 2000, net of offsets generated by federal, state and foreign tax incentive credits, were approximately 37.6%, 38.6% and 38.8%, respectively.

NOTES TO CONSOLIDATED FINANCIAL STATEMENTS (CONTINUED)
THE HOME DEPOT, INC. AND SUBSIDIARIES

A reconciliation of income tax expense at the federal statutory rate of 35% to actual tax expense for the applicable fiscal years is as follows (in millions):

| | Fiscal Year Ended | | |
	February 2, 2003	February 3, 2002	January 28, 2001
Income taxes at federal statutory rate	$2,055	$1,735	$1,476
State income taxes, net of federal income tax benefit	156	172	146
Foreign rate differences	(1)	4	5
Other, net	(2)	2	9
Total	$2,208	$1,913	$1,636

The tax effects of temporary differences that give rise to significant portions of the deferred tax assets and deferred tax liabilities as of February 2, 2003, and February 3, 2002, were as follows (in millions):

	February 2, 2003	February 3, 2002
Deferred Tax Assets:		
Accrued self-insurance liabilities	$ 305	$ 220
Other accrued liabilities	92	138
Net loss on disposition of business	31	31
Total gross deferred tax assets	428	389
Valuation allowance	(31)	(31)
Deferred tax assets, net of valuation allowance	397	358
Deferred Tax Liabilities:		
Accelerated depreciation	(571)	(492)
Accelerated inventory deduction	(149)	–
Other	(39)	(55)
Total gross deferred tax liabilities	(759)	(547)
Net deferred tax liability	$(362)	$(189)

A valuation allowance existed as of February 2, 2003, and February 3, 2002, due to the uncertainty of capital loss utilization. Management believes the existing net deductible temporary differences comprising the deferred tax assets will reverse during periods in which the Company generates net taxable income.

4 EMPLOYEE STOCK PLANS

The 1997 Omnibus Stock Incentive Plan ("1997 Plan") provides that incentive stock options, non-qualified stock options, stock appreciation rights, restricted shares, performance shares, performance units and deferred shares may be issued to selected associates, officers and directors of the Company. The maximum number of shares of the Company's common stock authorized for issuance under the 1997 Plan includes the number of shares carried over from prior plans and the number of shares authorized but unissued in the prior year, plus one-half percent of the total number of outstanding shares as of the first day of each fiscal year. As of February 2, 2003, there were 108 million shares available for future grants under the 1997 Plan.

Under the 1997 Plan, as of February 2, 2003, the Company had granted incentive and non-qualified stock options for 167 million shares, net of cancellations (of which 86 million had been exercised). Incentive stock options and non-qualified options typically vest at the rate of 25% per year commencing on the first anniversary date of the grant and expire on the tenth anniversary date of the grant.

Under the 1997 Plan, as of February 2, 2003, 2 million shares of restricted stock had been issued net of cancellations (the restrictions on 4,600 shares have lapsed). Generally, the restrictions on 25% of the restricted shares lapse upon the third and sixth year anniversaries of the date of issuance with the remaining 50% of the restricted shares lapsing upon the associate's attainment of age 62. The fair value of the restricted shares is expensed over the period during which the restrictions lapse. The Company recorded compensation expense related to restricted stock of $3 million in both fiscal 2002 and 2001 and $455,000 in fiscal 2000.

As of February 2, 2003, there were 2.5 million non-qualified stock options and 1.4 million deferred stock units outstanding under non-qualified stock option and deferred stock unit plans that are not part of the 1997 Plan. The 2.5 million non-qualified stock options have an exercise price of $40.75 per share and were granted in fiscal 2000. During fiscal years 2002, 2001 and 2000, the Company granted 0, 629,000 and 750,000 deferred stock units, respectively, to several key officers vesting at various dates. Each deferred stock unit entitles the officer to one share of common stock to be received up to five years after the vesting date of the deferred stock unit, subject to certain deferral rights of the officer. The fair value of the deferred stock units on the grant dates was $27 million and $31 million for deferred units granted in fiscal 2001 and 2000, respectively. These amounts are being amortized over the vesting periods.

NOTES TO CONSOLIDATED FINANCIAL STATEMENTS (CONTINUED)

THE HOME DEPOT, INC. AND SUBSIDIARIES

The Company recorded stock compensation expense related to deferred stock units of $12 million, $16 million and $6 million in fiscal 2002, 2001 and 2000, respectively.

The per share weighted average fair value of stock options granted during fiscal years 2002, 2001 and 2000 was $17.34, $20.51 and $31.96, respectively. The fair value of these options was determined at the date of grant using the Black-Scholes option-pricing model with the following assumptions:

	Fiscal Year Ended		
	February 2, 2003	February 3, 2002	January 28, 2001
Risk-free interest rate	4.0%	5.1%	6.4%
Assumed volatility	44.3%	48.1%	54.6%
Assumed dividend yield	0.5%	0.4%	0.3%
Assumed lives of options	5 years	6 years	7 years

The Company applies APB 25 in accounting for its stock-based compensation plans and, accordingly, no compensation expense has been recognized in the Company's financial statements for incentive or non-qualified stock options granted. If, under SFAS No. 123, the Company determined compensation expense based on the fair value at the grant date for its stock options, as computed and disclosed above, net earnings and earnings per share would have been reduced to the pro forma amounts below (in millions, except per share data):

	Fiscal Year Ended		
	February 2, 2003	February 3, 2002	January 28, 2001
Net earnings, as reported	$3,664	$3,044	$2,581
Add: Stock-based compensation expense included in reported net earnings, net of related tax effects	10	13	4
Deduct: Total stock-based compensation expense determined under fair value based method for all awards, net of related tax effects	(260)	(257)	(221)
Pro forma net earnings	$3,414	$2,800	$2,364
Earnings per share:			
Basic – as reported	$ 1.57	$ 1.30	$ 1.11
Basic – pro forma	$ 1.46	$ 1.20	$ 1.02
Diluted – as reported	$ 1.56	$ 1.29	$ 1.10
Diluted – pro forma	$ 1.46	$ 1.19	$ 1.01

The following table summarizes stock options outstanding at February 2, 2003, February 3, 2002 and January 28, 2001, and changes during the fiscal years ended on these dates (shares in thousands):

	Number of Shares	Weighted Average Option Price
Outstanding at January 30, 2000	68,419	$18.79
Granted	14,869	49.78
Exercised	(14,689)	13.15
Canceled	(2,798)	30.51
Outstanding at January 28, 2001	65,801	$26.46
Granted	25,330	40.33
Exercised	(16,614)	15.03
Canceled	(5,069)	39.20
Outstanding at February 3, 2002	69,448	$33.33
Granted	31,656	40.86
Exercised	(9,908)	18.27
Canceled	(8,030)	42.74
Outstanding at February 2, 2003	83,166	$37.09
Exercisable	29,431	$29.48

The following table summarizes information regarding stock options outstanding at February 2, 2003 (shares in thousands):

Range of Exercise Prices	Options Outstanding	Weighted Average Remaining Life (Yrs)	Weighted Average Outstanding Option Price	Options Exercisable	Weighted Average Exercisable Option Price
$ 6.00 to 12.00	7,090	3.5	$10.24	7,090	$10.24
12.01 to 20.00	1,191	4.7	17.21	1,191	17.21
20.01 to 30.00	7,438	5.6	22.19	6,090	21.78
30.01 to 42.00	41,745	8.4	37.67	11,161	39.12
42.01 to 54.00	25,702	8.5	48.80	3,899	52.48
	83,166	7.7	$37.09	29,431	$29.48

The Company maintains two employee stock purchase plans (U.S. and non-U.S. plans). The plan for U.S. associates is a tax-qualified plan under Section 423 of the Internal Revenue Code. The non-U.S. plan is not a Section 423 plan. The Company had 43 million shares available for issuance under the Employee Stock Purchase Plans ("ESPPs") at February 2, 2003. The ESPPs allow associates to purchase up to 152 million shares of common stock, of which 109 million shares have been purchased from inception of the plan, at a price equal to the lower of 85% of the stock's fair market value on the first day or the last day of the purchase period. These shares were included in the pro forma calculation of stock-based compensation expense.

During fiscal 2002, 5.2 million shares were purchased under the ESPPs at an average price of $30.89 per share. At February 2, 2003, there were 2.3 million shares outstanding, net of cancellations, at an average price of $34.09 per share.

NOTES TO CONSOLIDATED FINANCIAL STATEMENTS (CONTINUED)
THE HOME DEPOT, INC. AND SUBSIDIARIES

5 LEASES

The Company leases certain retail locations, office space, warehouse and distribution space, equipment and vehicles. While the majority of the leases are operating leases, certain retail locations are leased under capital leases. As leases expire, it can be expected that, in the normal course of business, certain leases will be renewed or replaced.

The Company has two off-balance sheet lease agreements under which the Company leases assets totaling $882 million comprised of an initial lease agreement of $600 million and a subsequent agreement of $282 million. These two leases were created under structured financing arrangements and involve a special purpose entity which meets the criteria for non-consolidation established by generally accepted accounting principles and is not owned by or affiliated with the Company, its management or officers. The Company financed a portion of its new stores opened in fiscal years 1997 through 2002, as well as a distribution center and office buildings, under these lease agreements. Under both agreements, the lessor purchases the properties, pays for the construction costs and subsequently leases the facilities to the Company. The lease term for the $600 million agreement expires in fiscal 2006 and has three two-year renewal options. The lease term for the $282 million agreement expires in 2008 with no renewal option. Both lease agreements provide for substantial residual value guarantees and include purchase options at original cost of each property. Events or circumstances that would require the Company to perform under the guarantees include 1) initial default on the leases with the assets sold for less than book value, or 2) the Company's decision not to purchase the assets at the end of the leases and the sale of the assets results in proceeds less than the initial book value of the assets. The Company's guarantees are limited to 82% of the initial book value of the assets.

The Company also leases an import distribution facility, including its related equipment, under an off-balance sheet lease created as part of a structured financing arrangement totaling $85 million. The lease for the import distribution facility expires in fiscal 2005 and has four 5-year renewal options. The lease agreement provides for substantial residual value guarantees and includes purchase options at the higher of the cost or fair market value of the assets.

The maximum amount of the residual value guarantees relative to the assets under the three off-balance sheet lease agreements described above is estimated to be $799 million. As the leased assets are placed into service, the Company estimates its liability under the residual value guarantees and records additional rent expense on a straight-line basis over the remaining lease terms.

Total rent expense, net of minor sublease income for the fiscal years ended February 2, 2003, February 3, 2002 and January 28, 2001, was $533 million, $522 million and $479 million, respectively. Real estate taxes, insurance, maintenance and operating expenses applicable to the leased property are obligations of the Company under the lease agreements. Certain store leases provide for contingent rent payments based on percentages of sales in excess of specified minimums. Contingent rent expense for the fiscal years ended February 2, 2003, February 3, 2002 and January 28, 2001, was approximately $8 million, $10 million and $9 million, respectively.

The approximate future minimum lease payments under capital and all other leases, including off-balance sheet leases, at February 2, 2003, were as follows (in millions):

Fiscal Year	Capital Leases	Operating Leases
2003	$ 44	$ 541
2004	45	512
2005	44	476
2006	46	440
2007	47	424
Thereafter through 2033	608	4,915
	834	$7,308
Less imputed interest	557	
Net present value of capital lease obligations	277	
Less current installments	5	
Long-term capital lease obligations, excluding current installments	$272	

Short-term and long-term obligations for capital leases are included in the accompanying Consolidated Balance Sheets in Other Accrued Expenses and Long-Term Debt, respectively. The assets under capital leases recorded in Property and Equipment, net of amortization, totaled $235 million and $199 million at February 2, 2003 and February 3, 2002, respectively.

NOTES TO CONSOLIDATED FINANCIAL STATEMENTS (CONTINUED)

THE HOME DEPOT, INC. AND SUBSIDIARIES

6 EMPLOYEE BENEFIT PLANS

The Company maintains three active defined contribution retirement plans (the "Plans"). All associates satisfying certain service requirements are eligible to participate in the Plans. The Company makes cash contributions each payroll period to purchase shares of the Company's common stock, up to specified percentages of associates' contributions as approved by the Board of Directors.

The Company's contributions to the Plans were $99 million, $97 million and $84 million for fiscal years 2002, 2001 and 2000, respectively. At February 2, 2003, the Plans held a total of 33 million shares of the Company's common stock in trust for plan participants.

The Company also maintains a restoration plan to provide certain associates deferred compensation that they would have received under the Plans as a matching contribution if not for the maximum compensation limits under the Internal Revenue Code. The Company funds the restoration plan through contributions made to a grantor trust, which are then used to purchase shares of the Company's common stock in the open market. Compensation expense related to this plan for fiscal years 2002, 2001 and 2000 was not material.

7 BASIC AND DILUTED WEIGHTED AVERAGE COMMON SHARES

The reconciliation of basic to diluted weighted average common shares for fiscal years 2002, 2001 and 2000 was as follows (amounts in millions):

	Fiscal Year Ended		
	February 2, 2003	February 3, 2002	January 28, 2001
Weighted average common shares	2,336	2,335	2,315
Effect of potentially dilutive securities:			
Stock Plans	8	18	37
Diluted weighted average common shares	2,344	2,353	2,352

Stock plans include shares granted under the Company's employee stock purchase plans and stock incentive plans, as well as shares issued for deferred compensation stock plans. Options to purchase 72.1 million, 11.2 million and 10.9 million shares of common stock at February 2, 2003, February 3, 2002 and January 28, 2001, respectively, were excluded from the computation of diluted earnings per share because their effect would have been anti-dilutive.

8 COMMITMENTS AND CONTINGENCIES

At February 2, 2003, the Company was contingently liable for approximately $930 million under outstanding letters of credit issued for certain business transactions, including insurance programs, import inventory purchases and construction contracts. The Company's letters of credit are primarily performance-based and are not based on changes in variable components, a liability or an equity security of the other party.

The Company is involved in litigation arising from the normal course of business. In management's opinion, this litigation is not expected to materially impact the Company's consolidated results of operations or financial condition.

9 ACQUISITIONS AND DISPOSITIONS

In October 2002, the Company acquired substantially all of the assets of FloorWorks, Inc. and Arvada Hardwood Floor Company, and common stock of Floors, Inc., three flooring installation companies primarily servicing the new home builder industry. These acquisitions were accounted for under the purchase method of accounting.

In June 2002, the Company acquired the assets of Maderería Del Norte, S.A. de C.V., a four-store chain of home improvement stores in Juarez, Mexico. The acquisition was accounted for under the purchase method of accounting.

In fiscal 2001, the Company acquired Your "other" Warehouse and Soluciones Para Las Casas de Mexico, S. de R.L. de C.V. These acquisitions were accounted for under the purchase method of accounting.

Pro forma results of operations for fiscal years 2002, 2001 and 2000 would not be materially different as a result of the acquisitions discussed above and therefore are not presented.

In February 2002, the Company sold all of the assets of The Home Depot Argentina S.R.L. In connection with the sale, the Company received proceeds comprised of cash and notes. An impairment charge of $45 million was recorded in Selling and Store Operating Expenses in the accompanying Consolidated Statements of Earnings in fiscal 2001 to write down the net assets of The Home Depot Argentina S.R.L. to fair value.

In October 2001, the Company sold all of the assets of The Home Depot Chile S.A., resulting in a gain of $31 million included in Selling and Store Operating Expenses in the accompanying Consolidated Statements of Earnings.

NOTES TO CONSOLIDATED FINANCIAL STATEMENTS (CONTINUED)

THE HOME DEPOT, INC. AND SUBSIDIARIES

10 QUARTERLY FINANCIAL DATA (UNAUDITED)

The following is a summary of the quarterly consolidated results of operations for the fiscal years ended February 2, 2003 and February 3, 2002 (dollars in millions, except per share data):

	Net Sales	Increase (Decrease) In Comparable Store Sales	Gross Profit	Net Earnings	Basic Earnings Per Share	Diluted Earnings Per Share
Fiscal year ended February 2, 2003:[1]						
First quarter	$14,282	5%	$ 4,360	$ 856	$0.36	$0.36
Second quarter	16,277	1%	4,946	1,182	0.50	0.50
Third quarter	14,475	(2%)	4,580	940	0.40	0.40
Fourth quarter	13,213	(6%)	4,222	686	0.30	0.30
Fiscal year	$58,247	0%	$18,108	$3,664	$ 1.57	$ 1.56
Fiscal year ended February 3, 2002:[1]						
First quarter	$12,200	(3%)	$ 3,655	$ 632	$0.27	$0.27
Second quarter	14,576	1%	4,326	924	0.40	0.39
Third quarter	13,289	0%	4,010	778	0.33	0.33
Fourth quarter	13,488	5%	4,156	710	0.30	0.30
Fiscal year	$53,553	0%	$16,147	$3,044	$ 1.30	$ 1.29

[1]Fiscal year ended February 2, 2003 includes 52 weeks and fiscal year ended February 3, 2002 includes 53 weeks.

Note: The quarterly data may not sum to fiscal year totals due to rounding.

MANAGEMENT'S RESPONSIBILITY FOR FINANCIAL STATEMENTS

The financial statements presented in this Annual Report have been prepared with integrity and objectivity and are the responsibility of the management of The Home Depot, Inc. These financial statements have been prepared in conformity with accounting principles generally accepted in the United States of America and properly reflect certain estimates and judgments based upon the best available information.

The Company maintains a system of internal accounting controls, which is supported by an internal audit program and is designed to provide reasonable assurance, at an appropriate cost, that the Company's assets are safeguarded and transactions are properly recorded. This system is continually reviewed and modified in response to changing business conditions and operations and as a result of recommendations by the external and internal auditors. In addition, the Company has distributed to associates its policies for conducting business affairs in a lawful and ethical manner.

The financial statements of the Company have been audited by KPMG LLP, independent auditors. Their accompanying report is based upon an audit conducted in accordance with auditing standards generally accepted in the United States of America, including the related review of internal accounting controls and financial reporting matters.

The Audit Committee of the Board of Directors, consisting solely of outside directors, meets five times a year with the independent auditors, the internal auditors and representatives of management to discuss auditing and financial reporting matters. In addition, a telephonic meeting is held prior to each quarterly earnings release. The Audit Committee retains the independent auditors and regularly reviews the internal accounting controls, the activities of the outside auditors and internal auditors and the financial condition of the Company. Both the Company's independent auditors and the internal auditors have free access to the Audit Committee.

Carol B. Tomé
Executive Vice President and
Chief Financial Officer

INDEPENDENT AUDITORS' REPORT

The Board of Directors and Stockholders
The Home Depot, Inc.:

We have audited the accompanying consolidated balance sheets of The Home Depot, Inc. and subsidiaries as of February 2, 2003 and February 3, 2002 and the related consolidated statements of earnings, stockholders' equity and comprehensive income, and cash flows for each of the years in the three-year period ended February 2, 2003. These consolidated financial statements are the responsibility of the Company's management. Our responsibility is to express an opinion on these consolidated financial statements based on our audits.

We conducted our audits in accordance with auditing standards generally accepted in the United States of America. Those standards require that we plan and perform the audit to obtain reasonable assurance about whether the financial statements are free of material misstatement. An audit includes examining, on a test basis, evidence supporting the amounts and disclosures in the financial statements. An audit also includes assessing the accounting principles used and significant estimates made by management, as well as evaluating the overall financial statement presentation. We believe that our audits provide a reasonable basis for our opinion.

In our opinion, the consolidated financial statements referred to above present fairly, in all material respects, the financial position of The Home Depot, Inc. and subsidiaries as of February 2, 2003 and February 3, 2002, and the results of their operations and their cash flows for each of the years in the three-year period ended February 2, 2003, in conformity with accounting principles generally accepted in the United States of America.

KPMG LLP

Atlanta, Georgia
February 24, 2003

glossary

absorption costing A product costing approach that assigns all fixed and variable manufacturing costs to the units produced. (788)

accelerated depreciation method A depreciation method that provides for a higher depreciation amount in the first year of the asset's use, followed by a gradually declining amount of depreciation. (362)

account An accounting form that is used to record the increases and decreases in each financial statement item. (48)

account form The form of balance sheet that resembles the basic format of the accounting equation, with assets on the left side and the liabilities and owner's equity sections on the right side. (21, 195)

account payable The liability created by a purchase on account. (15)

account receivable A claim against the customer. (16)

accounting An information system that provides reports to stakeholders about the economic activities and condition of a business. (8)

accounting cycle The process that begins with analyzing and journalizing transactions and ends with the post-closing trial balance. (140)

accounting equation Assets = Liabilities + Owner's Equity (13)

accounting period concept The accounting concept that assumes that the economic life of the business can be divided into time periods. (102)

accounting system The methods and procedures used by a business to collect, classify, summarize, and report financial data for use by management and external users. (238)

accounts receivable A receivable created by selling merchandise or services on credit. (280)

accounts receivable turnover Measures how frequently during the year the accounts receivable are being converted to cash; the relationship between net sales and accounts receivable, computed by dividing the net sales by the average net accounts receivable. (293, 620)

accrual basis Under this basis of accounting, revenues and expenses are reported in the income statement in the period in which they are earned or incurred. (102)

accruals A revenue or expense that has not been recorded. (103)

accrued assets *See* accrued revenues. (104)

accrued expenses Expenses that have been incurred *but not recorded* in the accounts. (103)

accrued liabilities *See* accrued expenses. (103)

accrued revenues Revenues that have been earned *but not recorded* in the accounts. (104)

accumulated depreciation The contra asset account credited when recording the depreciation of a fixed asset. (112)

accumulated other comprehensive income The cumulative effects of other comprehensive income items reported separately in the stockholders' equity section of the balance sheet. (490)

activity analysis The study of employee effort and other business records to determine the cost of activities. (1083)

activity base (drivers) A measure of activity that is related to changes in cost. Used in analyzing and classifying cost behavior. Activity bases are also used in the denominator in calculating the predetermined factory overhead rate to assign overhead costs to cost objects. (667, 746, 1035)

activity cost pools Cost accumulations that are associated with a given activity, such as machine usage, inspections, moving, and production setups. (1034)

activity rate The cost of an activity per unit of activity base, determined by dividing the activity cost pool by the activity base. (1035)

activity-base usage quantity The amount of activity used by a particular product measured in activity-base terms. (1036)

activity-based costing (ABC) method An accounting framework based on determining the cost of activities and allocating these costs to products, customers, or other cost objects, using activity rates. (668, 969, 1034)

adjusted trial balance The trial balance prepared after all the adjusting entries have been posted. (113)

adjusting entries The journal entries that bring the accounts up to date at the end of the accounting period. (103)

adjusting process An analysis and updating of the accounts when financial statements are prepared. (103)

administrative expenses (general expenses) Expenses incurred in the administration or general operations of the business. (194)

aging the receivables The process of analyzing the accounts receivable and classifying them according to various age groupings, with the due date being the base point for determining age. (286)

allowance method The method of accounting for uncollectible accounts that provides an expense for uncollectible receivables in advance of their write-off. (283)

amortization The periodic transfer of the cost of an intangible asset to expense. (373)

annuity A series of equal cash flows at fixed intervals. (526, 999)

appraisal costs Costs to detect, measure, evaluate, and audit products and processes to ensure that they conform to customer requirements and performance standards. (1083)

assets Resources that are owned by the business. (13, 48)

available-for-sale securities Securities that management expects to sell in the future but which are not actively traded for profit. (491)

average cost method The method of inventory costing that is based upon the assumption that costs should be charged against revenue by using the weighted average unit cost of the items sold. (321)

average rate of return A method of evaluating capital investment proposals that focuses on the expected profitability of the investment. (995)

backflush accounting Simplification of the accounting system by eliminating accumulation and transfer of costs as products move through production. (1079)

balance of the account The amount of the difference between the debits and the credits that have been entered into an account. (50)

balance sheet A list of the assets, liabilities, and owner's equity *as of a specific date*, usually at the close of the last day of a month or a year. (19)

balanced scorecard A performance evaluation approach that incorporates multiple performance dimensions by combining financial and nonfinancial measures. (928)

bank reconciliation The analysis that details the items responsible for the difference between the cash balance reported in the bank statement and the balance of the cash account in the ledger. (253)

bond A form of an interest-bearing note used by corporations to borrow on a long-term basis. (522)

bond indenture The contract between a corporation issuing bonds and the bondholders. (523)

book value The cost of a fixed asset minus accumulated depreciation on the asset. (361)

book value of the asset The difference between the cost of a fixed asset and its accumulated depreciation. (112)

boot The amount a buyer owes a seller when a fixed asset is traded in on a similar asset. (368)

bottleneck A condition that occurs when product demand exceeds production capacity. (971)

break-even point The level of business operations at which revenues and expired costs are equal. (754)

budget An accounting device used to plan and control resources of operational departments and divisions. (834)

budget performance report A report comparing actual results with budget figures. (883)

budgetary slack Excess resources set within a budget to provide for uncertain events. (836)

business An organization in which basic resources (inputs), such as materials and labor, are assembled and processed to provide goods or services (outputs) to customers. (2)

business entity concept A concept of accounting that limits the economic data in the accounting system to data related directly to the activities of the business. (13)

business stakeholder A person or entity who has an interest in the economic performance of a business. (6)

business strategy An integrated set of plans and actions designed to enable the business to gain an advantage over its competitors and, in so doing, to maximize its profits. (4)

business transaction An economic event or condition that directly changes an entity's financial condition or directly affects its results of operations. (14)

capital expenditures The costs of acquiring fixed assets, adding to a fixed asset, improving a fixed asset, or extending a fixed asset's useful life. (364)

capital expenditures budget The budget summarizing future plans for acquiring plant facilities and equipment. (852)

capital investment analysis The process by which management plans, evaluates, and controls long-term capital investments involving property, plant, and equipment. (994)

capital leases Leases that include one or more provisions that result in treating the leased assets as purchased assets in the accounts. (370)

capital rationing The process by which management plans, evaluates, and controls long-term capital investments involving fixed assets. (1007)

capital stock The portion of a corporation's owners' equity contributed by investors (owners) in exchange for shares of stock. (15)

carrying amount The balance of the bonds payable account (face amount of the bonds) less any unamortized discount or plus any unamortized premium. (533)

cash Coins, currency (paper money), checks, money orders, and money on deposit that is available for unrestricted withdrawal from banks and other financial institutions. (245)

cash basis Under this basis of accounting, revenues and expenses are reported in the income statement in the period in which cash is received or paid. (102)

cash budget A budget of estimated cash receipts and payments. (849)

cash dividend A cash distribution of earnings by a corporation to its shareholders. (454)

cash equivalents Highly liquid investments that are usually reported with cash on the balance sheet. (257)

cash flows from financing activities The section of the statement of cash flows that reports cash flows from transactions affecting the equity and debt of the business. (561)

cash flows from investing activities The section of the statement of cash flows that reports cash flows from transactions affecting investments in noncurrent assets. (561)

cash flows from operating activities The section of the statement of cash flows that reports the cash transactions affecting the determination of net income. (561)

cash payback period The expected period of time that will elapse between the date of a capital expenditure and the complete recovery in cash (or equivalent) of the amount invested. (996)

cash short and over account An account which has recorded errors in cash sales or errors in making change causing the amount of actual cash on hand to differ from the beginning amount of cash plus the cash sales for the day. (245)

Certified Public Accountant (CPA) Public accountants who have met a state's education, experience, and examination requirements. (11)

chart of accounts A list of the accounts in the ledger. (48)

clearing account Another name for the Income Summary account because it has the effect of clearing the revenue and expense accounts of their balances. (151)

closing entries The entries that transfer the balances of the revenue, expense, and drawing accounts to the owner's capital account. (150)

closing process The transfer process of converting temporary account balances to zero by transferring the revenue and expense account balances to Income Summary, transferring the Income Summary account balance to the owner's capital account, and transferring the owner's drawing account to the owner's capital account. (150)

combination strategy A business strategy that includes elements of both the low-cost and differentiation strategies. (5)

common stock The stock outstanding when a corporation has issued only one class of stock. (448)

common-size statement A financial statement in which all items are expressed only in relative terms. (616)

component A tangible portion of a fixed asset that can be separately identified as an asset and depreciated over its own separate expected useful life. (365)

comprehensive income All changes in stockholders' equity during a period, except those resulting from dividends and stockholders' investments. (490)

consolidated financial statements Financial statements resulting from combining parent and subsidiary statements. (496)

consolidation The creation of a new corporation by the transfer of assets and liabilities of two or more existing corporations, which are then dissolved. (496)

continuous budgeting A method of budgeting that provides for maintaining a twelve-month projection into the future. (837)

contra account An account offset against another account. (112)

contra asset An account that affects an asset account, such as the allowance for uncollectible accounts receivable or accumulated depreciation. (283)

contract rate The periodic interest to be paid on the bonds that is identified in the bond indenture; expressed as a percentage of the face amount of the bond. (524)

contribution margin analysis The systematic examination of the differences between planned and actual contribution margins. (801)

contribution margin Sales less variable costs and variable selling and administrative expenses. (751, 789)

contribution margin ratio The percentage of each sales dollar that is available to cover the fixed costs and provide an operating income. (752)

controllable cost Cost that can be influenced (increased, decreased, or eliminated) by someone such as a manager or factory worker. (796)

controllable expenses Costs that can be influenced by the decisions of a manager. (919)

controllable variance The difference between the actual amount of variable factory overhead cost incurred and the amount of variable factory overhead budgeted for the standard product. (889)

controller The chief management accountant of a division or other segment of a business. (659)

controlling account The account in the general ledger that summarizes the balances of the accounts in a subsidiary ledger. (190)

conversion costs The combination of direct labor and factory overhead costs. (662)

copyright An exclusive right to publish and sell a literary, artistic, or musical composition. (373)

corporation A business organized under state or federal statutes as a separate legal entity. (3)

cost A payment of cash (or a commitment to pay cash in the future) for the purpose of generating revenues. (660)

cost accounting system A branch of managerial accounting concerned with accumulating manufacturing costs for financial reporting and decision-making purposes. (662)

cost allocation The process of assigning indirect cost to a cost object, such as a job. (667)

cost behavior The manner in which a cost changes in relation to its activity base (driver). (746)

cost center A decentralized unit in which the department or division manager has responsibility for the control of costs incurred and the authority to make decisions that affect these costs. (917)

cost of goods sold The cost of the manufactured product sold. (663)

cost of goods sold budget A budget of the estimated direct materials, direct labor, and factory overhead consumed by sold products. (846)

cost of merchandise sold The cost that is reported as an expense when merchandise is sold. (189)

cost of production report A report prepared periodically by a processing department, summarizing (1) the units for which the department is accountable and the disposition of those units and (2) the costs incurred by the department and the allocation of those costs between completed and incomplete production. (714)

cost of quality report A report summarizing the costs, percent of total, and percent of sales by appraisal, prevention, internal failure, and external failure cost of quality categories. (1085)

cost per equivalent unit The rate used to allocate costs between completed and partially completed production. (712)

cost price approach An approach to transfer pricing that uses cost as the basis for setting the transfer price. (931)

cost variance The difference between actual cost and the flexible budget at actual volumes. (880)

costs of quality The cost associated with controlling quality (prevention and appraisal) and failing to control quality (internal and external failure). (1083)

cost-volume-profit analysis The systematic examination of the relationships among selling prices, volume of sales and production, costs, expenses, and profits. (751)

cost-volume-profit chart A chart used to assist management in understanding the relationships among costs, expenses, sales, and operating profit or loss. (758)

credit memorandum A form used by a seller to inform the buyer of the amount the seller proposes to credit to the account receivable due from the buyer. (199)

credits Amounts entered on the right side of an account. (50)

cumulative preferred stock A class of preferred stock that has a right to receive regular dividends that have been passed (not declared) before any common stock dividends are paid. (449)

currency exchange rate The rate at which currency in another country can be exchanged for local currency. (1006)

current assets Cash and other assets that are expected to be converted to cash or sold or used up, usually within one year or less, through the normal operations of the business. (149)

current liabilities Liabilities that will be due within a short time (usually one year or less) and that are to be paid out of current assets. (149)

current ratio A financial ratio that is computed by dividing current assets by current liabilities. (160, 618)

currently attainable standards Standards that represent levels of operation that can be attained with reasonable effort. (881)

debit memorandum A form used by a buyer to inform the seller of the amount the buyer proposes to debit to the account payable due the seller. (201)

debits Amounts entered on the left side of an account. (49)

decentralization The separation of a business into more manageable operating units. (916)

declining-balance method A method of depreciation that provides periodic depreciation expense based on the declining book value of a fixed asset over its estimated life. (361)

deferrals Deferrals are created by recording a transaction in a way that delays or defers the recognition of an expense or revenue. (103)

deferred expenses Items that have been initially recorded as assets but are expected to become expenses over time or through the normal operations of the business. (103)

deferred revenues Items that have been initially recorded as liabilities but are expected to become revenues over time or through the normal operations of the business. (103)

defined benefit plan A pension plan that promises employees a fixed annual pension benefit at retirement, based on years of service and compensation levels. (416)

defined contribution plan A pension plan that requires a fixed amount of money to be invested for the employee's behalf during the employee's working years. (416)

depletion The process of transferring the cost of natural resources to an expense account. (372)

depreciation The decrease in the ability of a fixed asset to provide useful services; the systematic periodic transfer of the cost of a fixed asset to an expense account during its expected useful life. (112, 357)

depreciation expense The portion of the cost of a fixed asset that is recorded as an expense each year of its useful life. (112)

differential analysis The area of accounting concerned with the effect of alternative courses of action on revenues and costs. (957)

differential cost The amount of increase or decrease in cost expected from a particular course of action compared with an alternative. (957)

differential revenue The amount of increase or decrease in revenue expected from a particular course of action as compared with an alternative. (956)

differentiation strategy A business strategy in which a business designs and produces products or services that possess unique attributes or characteristics for which customers are willing to pay a premium price. (4)

direct labor cost The wages of factory workers who are directly involved in converting materials into a finished product. (661)

direct labor rate variance The cost associated with the difference between the standard rate and the actual rate paid for direct labor used in producing a commodity. (886)

direct labor time variance The cost associated with the difference between the standard hours and the actual hours of direct labor spent producing a commodity. (887)

direct materials cost The cost of materials that are an integral part of the finished product. (660)

direct materials price variance The cost associated with the difference between the standard price and the actual price of direct materials used in producing a commodity. (885)

direct materials purchases budget A budget that uses the production budget as a starting point to budget materials purchases. (844)

direct materials quantity variance The cost associated with the difference between the standard quantity and the actual quantity of direct materials used in producing a commodity. (885)

direct method A method of reporting the cash flows from operating activities as the difference between the operating cash receipts and the operating cash payments. (562)

direct write-off method The method of accounting for uncollectible accounts that recognizes the expense only when accounts are judged to be worthless. (283)

discontinued operations Operations of a major line of business or component for a company, such as a division, a department, or a certain class of customer, that have been disposed of. (487)

discount The excess of the face amount of bonds over their issue price; the excess of the par value of a stock over its issue price; the interest deducted from the maturity value of a note or the excess of the face amount of bonds over their issue price. (399, 450, 524)

discount rate The rate used in computing the interest to be deducted from the maturity value of a note. (399)

dishonored note receivable A note that the maker fails to pay on the due date. (291)

dividend yield A ratio, computed by dividing the annual dividends paid per share of common stock by the market price per share at a specific date, that indicates the rate of return to stockholders in terms of cash dividend distributions. (459, 628)

dividends Distributions to the owners (stockholders) of a corporation. (17, 49)

division A decentralized unit that is structured around a common function, product, customer, or geographical territory. (916)

doomsday ratio The ratio of cash and cash equivalents to current liabilities. (258)

double-entry accounting A system of accounting for recording transactions, based on recording increases and decreases in accounts so that debits equal credits. (53)

DuPont formula An expanded expression of return on investment determined by multiplying the profit margin by the investment turnover. (924)

earnings per common share (EPS) Net income per share of common stock outstanding during a period. (488)

earnings per share (EPS) on common stock The profitability ratio of net income available to common shareholders to the number of common shares outstanding. (626)

effective interest rate method The method of amortizing discounts and premiums that provides for a constant

rate of interest on the carrying amount of the bonds at the beginning of each period; often called simply the "interest method." (530)

effective rate of interest The market rate of interest at the time bonds are issued. (524)

electronic data interchange (EDI) An information technology that allows different business organizations to use computers to communicate orders, relay information, and make or receive payments. (1076)

electronic funds transfer (EFT) A system in which computers rather than paper (money, checks, etc.) are used to effect cash transactions. (249)

elements of internal control The control environment, risk assessment, control activities, information and communication, and monitoring. (240)

employee fraud The intentional act of deceiving an employer for personal gain. (239)

employee involvement A philosophy that grants employees the responsibility and authority to make their own decisions about their operations. (1074)

employee's earnings record A detailed record of each employee's earnings. (410)

engineering change order (ECO) A document that initiates a change in the specification or a product or process. (1035)

equity method A method of accounting for an investment in common stock by which the investment account is adjusted for the investor's share of periodic net income and cash dividends of the investee. (493)

equity securities The common and preferred stock of a firm. (491)

equivalent units of production The number of production units that could have been completed within a given accounting period, given the resources consumed. (710)

ethics Moral principles that guide the conduct of individuals. (9)

expenses Assets used up or services consumed in the process of generating revenues. (16, 49)

external failure costs The costs incurred after defective units or services have been delivered to consumers. (1083)

extraordinary items Events and transactions that (1) are significantly different (unusual) from the typical or the normal operating activities of a business and (2) occur infrequently. (487)

factory overhead cost All of the costs of producing a product except for direct materials and direct labor. (662)

FICA tax Federal Insurance Contributions Act tax used to finance federal programs for old-age and disability benefits (social security) and health insurance for the aged (Medicare). (405)

financial accounting The branch of accounting that is concerned with recording transactions using generally accepted accounting principles (GAAP) for a business or other economic unit and with a periodic preparation of various statements from such records. (12, 658)

Financial Accounting Standards Board (FASB) The authoritative body that has the primary responsibility for developing accounting principles. (12)

financial statements Financial reports that summarize the effects of events on a business. (19)

finished goods inventory The direct materials costs, direct labor costs, and factory overhead costs that of finished products that have not been sold. (663)

finished goods ledger The subsidiary ledger that contains the individual accounts for each kind of commodity or product produced. (671)

first-in, first-out (fifo) method A method of inventory costing that assumes the unit product costs should be determined separately for each period in the order in which the costs were incurred. (321, 708)

fiscal year The annual accounting period adopted by a business. (159)

fixed asset impairment A condition when the fair value of a fixed asset falls below its book value and is not expected to recover. (484)

fixed assets Long-term or relatively permanent tangible assets that are used in the normal business operations. (112, 355)

fixed (plant) assets Assets that depreciate over time, such as equipment, machinery, and buildings. (149)

fixed costs Costs that tend to remain the same in amount, regardless of variations in the level of activity. (748)

flexible budget A budget that adjusts for varying rates of activity. (839)

FOB (free on board) destination Freight terms in which the seller pays the transportation costs from the shipping point to the final destination. (203)

FOB (free on board) shipping point Freight terms in which the buyer pays the transportation costs from the shipping point to the final destination. (203)

free cash flow The amount of operating cash flow remaining after replacing current productive capacity and maintaining current dividends. (578)

fringe benefits Benefits provided to employees in addition to wages and salaries. (415)

future value The estimated worth in the future of an amount of cash on hand today invested at a fixed rate of interest. (525)

general ledger The primary ledger, when used in conjunction with subsidiary ledgers, that contains all of the balance sheet and income statement accounts. (190)

generally accepted accounting principles (GAAP) Generally accepted guidelines for the preparation of financial statements. (12)

goal conflict A condition that occurs when individual objectives conflict with organizational objectives. (837)

goodwill An intangible asset that is created from such favorable factors as location, product quality, reputation, and managerial skill. (374)

gross pay The total earnings of an employee for an employee for a payroll period. (403)

gross profit Sales minus the cost of merchandise sold. (189)

gross profit method A method of estimating inventory cost that is based on the relationship of gross profit to sales. (333)

held-to-maturity securities Investments in bonds or other debt securities that management intends to hold to their maturity. (538)

high-low method A technique that uses the highest and lowest total costs as a basis for estimating the variable cost per unit and the fixed cost component of a mixed cost. (748)

horizontal analysis Financial analysis that compares an item in a current statement with the same item in prior statements; the percentage of increases and decreases in corresponding items in comparative financial statements. (71, 612)

ideal standards Standards that can be achieved only under perfect operating conditions, such as no idle time, no machine breakdowns, and no materials spoilage; also called *theoretical standards*. (881)

income from operations (operating income) The excess of gross profit over total operating expenses; revenues less operating expenses and service department charges for a profit or investment center. (193, 922)

income statement A summary of the revenue and expenses *for a specific period of time*, such as a month or a year. (19)

Income Summary An account to which the revenue and expense account balances are transferred at the end of a period. (150)

indirect method A method of reporting the cash flows from operating activities as the net income from operations adjusted for all deferrals of past cash receipts and payments and all accruals of expected future cash receipts and payments. (562)

inflation A period when prices in general are rising and the purchasing power of money is declining. (1006)

intangible assets Long-term assets that are useful in the operations of a business, are not held for sale, and are without physical qualities. (372)

internal controls The detailed policies and procedures used to direct operations, ensure accurate reports, and ensure compliance with laws and regulations. (239)

internal failure costs The costs associated with defects that are discovered by the organization before the product or service is delivered to the consumer. (1083)

internal rate of return method A method of analysis of proposed capital investments that uses present value concepts to compute the rate of return from the net cash flows expected from the investment. (1001)

inventory shrinkage The amount by which the merchandise for sale, as indicated by the balance of the merchandise inventory account, is larger than the total amount of merchandise counted during the physical inventory. (208)

inventory turnover A ratio that measures the relationship between the volume of goods (merchandise) sold and the amount of inventory carried during the period. (334, 621)

investment center A decentralized unit in which the manager has the responsibility and authority to make decisions that affect not only costs and revenues but also the fixed assets available to the center. (923)

investment turnover A component of the rate of return on investment, computed as the ratio of sales to invested assets. (924)

investments The balance sheet caption used to report long-term investments in stocks not intended as a source of cash in the normal operations of the business. (493)

invoice The bill that the seller sends to the buyer. (197)

job cost sheet An account in the work in process subsidiary ledger in which the costs charged to a particular job order are recorded. (665)

job order cost system A type of cost accounting system that provides for a separate record of the cost of each particular quantity of product that passes through the factory. (662)

journal The initial record in which the effects of a transaction are recorded. (51)

journal entry The form of recording a transaction in a journal. (51)

journalizing The process of recording a transaction in the journal. (51)

just-in-time (JIT) manufacturing A business philosophy that focuses on eliminating time, cost, and poor quality within manufacturing processes. (1070)

just-in-time (JIT) processing A processing approach that focuses on eliminating time, cost, and poor quality within manufacturing and nonmanufacturing processes. (718)

last-in, first-out (lifo) method A method of inventory costing based on the assumption that the most recent merchandise inventory costs should be charged against revenue. (321)

lead time The elapsed time between starting a unit of product into the beginning of a process and its completion. (1070)

ledger A group of accounts for a business. (48)

leverage The amount of debt used by a firm to finance its assets; causes the rate earned on stockholders' equity to vary from the rate earned on total assets because the amount earned on assets acquired through the use of funds provided by creditors varies from the interest paid to these creditors. (625)

liabilities The rights of creditors that represent debts of the business. (13, 48)

limited liability corporation A form of corporation that combines attributes of a partnership and a corporation in that it is organized as a corporation, but it can elect to be taxed as a partnership. (4)

long-term liabilities Liabilities that usually will not be due for more than one year. (149)

low-cost strategy A strategy wherein a business designs and produces products or services of acceptable quality at a cost lower than that of its competitors. (4)

lower-of-cost-or-market (LCM) method A method of valuing inventory that reports the inventory at the lower of its cost or current market value (replacement cost). (329)

Management Discussion and Analysis (MDA) An annual report disclosure that provides management's analysis of the results of operations and financial condition. (630)

managerial accounting The branch of accounting that uses both historical and estimated data in providing information that management uses in conducting daily operations, in planning future operations, and in developing overall business strategies. (12, 658)

manufacturing business A type of business that changes basic inputs into products that are sold to individual customers. (2)

manufacturing cells A grouping of processes where employees are cross-trained to perform more than one function. (718)

manufacturing margin The variable cost of goods sold deducted from sales. (789)

margin of safety The difference between current sales revenue and the sales at the break-even point. (766)

market price approach An approach to transfer pricing that uses the price at which the product or service transferred could be sold to outside buyers as the transfer price. (930)

market segment A portion of business that can be assigned to a manager for profit responsibility. (797)

markup An amount that is added to a "cost" amount to determine product price. (965)

master budget The comprehensive budget plan linking all the individual budgets related to sales, cost of goods sold, operating expenses, projects, capital expenditures, and cash. (841)

matching concept A concept of accounting in which expenses are matched with the revenue generated during a period by those expenses. (19, 102)

materiality concept A concept of accounting that implies that an error may be treated in the easiest possible way. (69)

materials inventory The cost of materials that have not yet entered into the manufacturing process. (663)

materials ledger The subsidiary ledger containing the individual accounts for each type of material. (664)

materials requisitions The form or electronic transmission used by a manufacturing department to authorize materials issuances from the storeroom. (664)

maturity value The amount that is due at the maturity or due date of a note. (290)

merchandise inventory Merchandise on hand (not sold) at the end of an accounting period. (189)

merchandising businesses Businesses that purchase products from other businesses and sell them to customers. (3)

merger The joining of two corporations in which one company acquires all the assets and liabilities of another corporation, which is then dissolved. (495)

minority interest The portion of a subsidiary corporation's stock owned by outsiders. (496)

mixed cost A cost with both variable and fixed characteristics, sometimes called a semivariable or semifixed cost. (748)

multiple production department factory overhead rate method A method that allocated factory overhead to product by using factory overhead rates for each production department. (1031)

multiple-step income statement A form of income statement that contains several sections, subsections, and subtotals. (191)

natural business year A fiscal year that ends when business activities have reached the lowest point in an annual operating cycle. (159)

negotiated price approach An approach to transfer pricing that allows managers of decentralized units to agree (negotiate) among themselves as to the transfer price. (931)

net income The amount by which revenues exceed expenses. (19)

net loss The amount by which expenses exceed revenues. (19)

net pay Gross pay less payroll deductions; the amount the employer is obligated to pay the employee. (403)

net present value method A method of analysis of proposed capital investments that focuses on the present value of the cash flows expected from the investments. (999)

net realizable value The estimated selling price of an item of inventory less any direct costs of disposal, such as sales commissions. (330)

noncontrollable costs Costs that cannot be influenced (increased, decreased, or eliminated) by someone such as a manager or factory worker. (796)

nonfinancial measure A performance measure that has not been stated in dollar terms. (1080)

nonparticipating preferred stock A class of preferred stock whose dividend rights are usually limited to a certain amount. (448)

nonvalue-added activities The cost of activities that are perceived as unnecessary from the customer's perspective and are thus candidates for elimination. (1086)

nonvalue-added lead time The time that units wait in inventories, move unnecessarily, and wait during machine breakdowns. (1071)

notes receivable A customer's written promise to pay an amount and possibly interest at an agreed-upon rate, amounts customers owe, for which a formal, written instrument of credit has been issued. (149, 280)

number of days' sales in inventory The relationship between the volume of sales and inventory, computed by dividing the inventory at the end of the year by the average daily cost of goods sold. (334, 621)

number of days' sales in receivables The relationship between sales and accounts receivable, computed by dividing the net accounts receivable at the end of the year by the average daily sales. (293, 620)

number of times interest charges are earned A ratio that measures creditor margin of safety for interest payments, calculated as income before interest and taxes divided by interest expense. (538, 622)

operating leases Leases that do not meet the criteria for capital leases and thus are accounted for as operating expenses. (370)

operating leverage A measure of the relative mix of a business's variable costs and fixed costs, computed as contribution margin divided by operating income. (764)

opportunity cost The amount of income forgone from an alternative to a proposed use of cash or its equivalent. (962)

other comprehensive income items Specified items that are reported separately from net income, including foreign currency items, pension liability adjustments, and unrealized gains and losses on investments. (490)

other expense Expenses that cannot be traced directly to operations. (194)

other income Revenue from sources other than the primary operating activity of a business. (194)

outstanding stock The stock in the hands of stockholders. (446)

overapplied factory overhead The amount of factory overhead applied in excess of the actual factory overhead costs incurred for production during a period. (669)

owner's equity The owner's right to the assets of the business. (13, 48)

par The monetary amount printed on a stock certificate. (446)

parent company The corporation owning all or a majority of the voting stock of the other corporation. (496)

Pareto chart A bar chart that shows the totals of a particular attribute for a number of categories, ranked left to right from the largest to smallest totals. (1084)

partnership A business owned by two or more individuals. (3)

patents Exclusive rights to produce and sell goods with one or more unique features. (373)

payroll The total amount paid to employees for a certain period. (401)

payroll register A multicolumn report used to assemble and summarize payroll data at the end of each payroll period. (408)

period costs Those costs that are used up in generating revenue during the current period and that are not involved in manufacturing a product, such as selling, general, and administratvie expenses. (672)

periodic method The inventory system in which the inventory records do not show the amount available for sale or sold during the period. (192)

permanent differences Differences between taxable and income (before taxes) reported on the income statement that may arise because certain revenues are exempt from tax and certain expenses are not deductible in determining taxable income. (483)

perpetual method The inventory system in which each purchase and sale of merchandise is recorded in an inventory account. (192)

petty cash fund A special cash fund to pay relatively small amounts. (255)

physical inventory A detailed listing of merchandise on hand. (318)

post-closing trial balance The trial balance prepared after the closing entries have been posted. (158)

posting The process of transferring the debits and credits from the journal entries to the accounts. (55)

predetermined factory overhead rate The rate used to apply factory overhead costs to the goods manufactured. The rate is determined by dividing the budgeted overhead cost by the estimated activity usage at the beginning of the fiscal period. (667)

preferred stock A class of stock with preferential rights over common stock. (448)

premium The excess of the issue price of a stock over its par value. (450, 524)

prepaid expenses Items such as supplies that will be used in the business in the future. (15, 103)

present value The estimated worth today of an amount of cash to be received (or paid) in the future. (525)

present value concept Cash to be received (or paid) in the future is not the equivalent of the same amount of money received at an earlier date. (997)

present value index An index computed by dividing the total present value of the net cash flow to be received from a proposed capital investment by the amount to be invested. (1001)

present value of an annuity The sum of the present values of a series of equal cash flows to be received at fixed intervals. (526, 999)

prevention costs Costs incurred to prevent defects from occurring during the design and delivery of products or services. (1083)

price factor The effect of a difference in unit sales price or unit cost on the number of units sold. (802)

price-earnings (P/E) ratio The ratio computed by dividing a corporation's stock market price per share at a specific date by the company's annual earnings per share. (498, 627)

prior period adjustments Corrections of material errors related to a prior period or periods, excluded from the determination of net income. (459)

private accounting The field of accounting where accountants and their staff provide services on a fee basis. (10)

proceeds The net amount available from discounting a note payable. (399)

process A sequence of activities linked together for performing a particular task. (896, 1087)

process cost system A type of cost accounting system that accumulates costs for each of the various departments or processes within a manufacturing facility. (662, 704)

process manufacturers Manufacturers that use large machines to process a continuous flow of raw materials through various stages of completion into a finished state. (704)

process-oriented layout Organizing work in a plant or administrative function around processes (tasks). (1074)

product cost concept A concept used in applying the cost-plus approach to product pricing in which only the costs of manufacturing the product, termed the product cost, are included in the cost amount to which the markup is added. (967)

product costing Determining the cost of a product. (1028)

product costs The three components of manufacturing cost: direct materials, direct labor, and factory overhead costs. (662)

production budget A budget of estimated unit production. (843)

product-oriented layout Organizing work in a plant or administrative function around products; sometimes referred to as product cells. (1074)

profit center A decentralized unit in which the manager has the responsibility and the authority to make decisions that affect both costs and revenues (and thus profits). (919)

profit margin A component of the rate of return on investment, computed as the ratio of income from operations to sales. (924)

profitability The ability of a firm to earn income. (617)

profit-volume chart A chart used to assist management in understanding the relationship between profit and volume. (760)

promissory note A written promise to pay a sum of money on demand or at a definite time. (288)

property, plant, and equipment The section of the balance sheet that includes equipment, machinery, buildings, and land. (149)

proprietorship A business owned by one individual. (3)

public accounting The field of accounting whereby accountants are employed by a business firm or a not-for-profit organization. (10)

pull manufacturing A just-in-time method wherein customer orders trigger the release of finished goods, which trigger production, which trigger release of materials from suppliers. (1074)

purchase method The accounting method used when a corporation acquires the controlling share of the voting common stock of another corporation by paying cash, exchanging other assets, issuing debt, or some combination of these methods. (496)

purchase return or allowance From the buyer's perspective, returned merchandise or an adjustment for defective merchandise. (192)

purchases discounts Discounts taken by the buyer for early payment of an invoice. (192)

push manufacturing Materials are released into production and work in process is released into finished goods in anticipation of future sales. (1075)

quantity factor The effect of a difference in the number of units sold, assuming no change in unit sales price or unit cost. (802)

quick assets Cash and other current assets that can be quickly converted to cash, such as marketable securities and receivables. (418, 619)

quick ratio A financial ratio that measures the ability to pay current liabilities with quick assets (cash, marketable securities, accounts receivable). (418, 619)

rate earned on common stockholders' equity A measure of profitability computed by dividing net income, reduced by preferred dividend requirements, by common stockholders' equity. (626)

rate earned on stockholders' equity A measure of profitability computed by dividing net income by total stockholders' equity. (625)

rate earned on total assets A measure of the profitability of assets, without regard to the equity of creditors and stockholders in the assets. (624)

rate of return on investment (ROI) A measure of managerial efficiency in the use of investments in assets, computed as income from operations divided by invested assets. (923)

ratio of fixed assets to long-term liabilities A leverage ratio that measures the margin of safety of long-term creditors, calculated as the net fixed assets divided by the long-term liabilities. (376, 621)

ratio of liabilities to stockholders' equity A comprehensive leverage ratio that measures the relationship of the claims of creditors to that stockholders' equity. (622)

Raw and In Process Inventory The capitalized cost of direct materials purchases, labor, and overhead charged to the production cell. (1078)

real accounts Term for balance sheet accounts because they are relatively permanent and carried forward from year to year. (150)

receivables All money claims against other entities, including people, business firms, and other organizations. (280)

receiving report The form or electronic transmission used by the receiving personnel to indicate that materials have been received and inspected. (663)

relevant range The range of activity over which changes in cost are of interest to management. (746)

report form The form of balance sheet in which assets, liabilities, and owner's equity are reported in a downward sequence. (21, 195)

residual income The excess of divisional income from operations over a "minimum" acceptable income from operations. (927)

residual value The estimated value of a fixed asset at the end of its useful life. (359)

responsibility accounting The process of measuring and reporting operating data by areas of responsibility. (917)

responsibility center An organizational unit for which a manager is assigned responsibility over costs, revenues, or assets. (835)

restrictions Amounts of retained earnings that have been limited for use as dividends. (458)

restructuring charge The costs associated with involuntarily terminating employees, terminating contracts, consolidating facilities, or relocating employees. (486)

retail inventory method A method of estimating inventory cost that is based on the relationship of gross profit to sales. (332)

retained earnings Net income retained in a corporation. (16)

retained earnings statement A summary of the changes in the retained earnings in a corporation for a specific period of time, such as a month or a year. (19, 458)

revenue The amount a business earns by selling goods or services to its customers. (16)

revenue expenditures Costs that benefit only the current period or costs incurred for normal maintenance and repairs of fixed assets. (364)

revenue recognition concept The accounting concept that supports reporting revenues when the services are provided to customers. (102)

revenues Increases in owner's equity as a result of selling services or products to customers. (49)

reversing entry An entry, exactly opposite of the adjusting entry to which it relates, that may be used to simplify the analysis and recording of the first payroll entry in a period. (161)

sales The total amount charged customers for merchandise sold, including cash sales and sales on account. (191)

sales budget One of the major elements of the income statement budget that indicates the quantity of estimated sales and the expected unit selling price. (842)

sales discounts From the seller's perspective, discounts that a seller may offer the buyer for early payment. (192)

sales mix The relative distribution of sales among the various products available for sale. (762, 799)

sales returns and allowances From the seller's perspective, returned merchandise or an adjustment for defective merchandise. (191)

selling expenses Expenses that are incurred directly in the selling of merchandise. (194)

service businesses Businesses that provide services rather than products to customers. (3)

service department charges The costs of services provided by an internal service department and transferred to a responsibility center. (920)

setup Changing the characteristics of a machine to produce a different product. (1035)

single plantwide factory overhead rate method A method that allocates all factory overhead to products by using a single factory overhead rate. (1029)

single-step income statement A form of income statement in which the total of all expenses is deducted from the total of all revenues. (194)

sinking fund A fund in which cash or assets are set aside for the purpose of paying the face amount of the bonds at maturity. (532)

slide An error in which the entire number is moved one or more spaces to the right or the left, such as writing $542.00 as $54.20 or $5,420.00. (70)

solvency The ability of a firm to pay its debts as they come due. (160, 617)

standard cost A detailed estimate of what a product should cost. (880)

standard cost systems Accounting systems that use standards for each element of manufacturing cost entering into the finished product. (880)

stated value A value, similar to par value, approved by the board of directors of a corporation for no-par stock. (446)

statement of cash flows A summary of the cash receipts and cash payments *for a specific period of time*, such as a month or a year. (19, 561)

statement of stockholders' equity A summary of the changes in the stockholders' equity of a corporation that have occurred during a specific period of time. (457)

static budget A budget that does not adjust to changes in activity levels. (838)

stock Shares of ownership of a corporation. (444)

stock dividend A distribution of shares of stock to its stockholders. (455)

stock split A reduction in the par or stated value of a common stock and the issuance of a proportionate number of additional shares. (453)

stockholders The owners of a corporation. (444)

stockholders' equity The owners' equity in a corporation. (48)

straight-line method A method of depreciation that provides for equal periodic depreciation expense over the estimated life of a fixed asset. (360)

subsidiary company The corporation that is controlled by a parent company. (496)

subsidiary ledger A ledger containing individual accounts with a common characteristic. (190)

sunk cost A cost that is not affected by subsequent decisions. (956)

supplier partnering A just-in-time method that views suppliers as a valuable contributor to the overall success of the business. (1075)

T account The simplest form of an account. (49)

target costing The target cost is determined by subtracting a desired profit from a market method determined price. The resulting target cost is used to motivate cost improvements in design and manufacture. (969)

taxable income The income according to the tax laws that is used as a base for determining the amount of taxes owed. (481)

temporary (nominal) accounts Accounts that report amounts for only one period. (150)

temporary differences Differences between taxable income and income before income taxes, created because items are recognized in one period for tax purposes and in another period for income statement purposes. Such differences reverse or turn around in later years. (481)

temporary investments The balances sheet caption used to report investments in income-yielding securities that can be quickly sold and converted to cash as needed. (491)

theory of constraints (TOC) A manufacturing strategy that attempts to remove the influence of bottlenecks (constraints) on a process. (971)

time tickets The form on which the amount of time spent by each employee and the labor cost incurred for each individual job, or for factory overhead, are recorded. (665)

time value of money concept The concept that an amount of money invested today will earn income. (995)

total cost concept A concept used in applying the cost-plus approach to product pricing in which all the costs of manufacturing the product plus the selling and administrative expenses are included in the cost amount to which the markup is added. (965)

trade discounts Discounts from the list prices in published catalogs or special discounts offered to certain classes of buyers. (205)

trade-in allowance The amount a seller allows a buyer for a fixed asset that is traded in for a similar asset. (368)

trademark A name, term, or symbol used to identify a business and its products. (373)

trading securities Securities that management intends to actively trade for profit. (491)

transfer price The price charged one decentralized unit by another for the goods or services provided. (929)

transposition An error in which the order of the digits is changed, such as writing $542 as $452 or $524. (70)

treasury stock Stock that a corporation has once issued and then reacquires. (452)

trial balance A summary listing of the titles and balances of accounts in the ledger. (68)

two-column journal An all-purpose journal. (55)

uncollectible accounts expense The operating expense incurred because of the failure to collect receivables. (282)

underapplied factory overhead The amount of actual factory overhead in excess of the factory overhead applied to production during a period. (669)

unearned revenue The liability created by receiving revenue in advance. (58, 103)

unit contribution margin The dollars available from each unit of sales to cover fixed costs and provide operating profits. (753)

unit of measure concept A concept of accounting requiring that economic data be recorded in dollars. (13)

units-of-production method A method of depreciation that provides for depreciation expense based on the expected productive capacity of a fixed asset. (361)

unrealized holding gain or loss The difference between the fair market value of the securities and their cost. (492)

value chain The way a business adds value for its customers by processing inputs into a product or service. (6)

value-added activities The cost of activities that are needed to meet customer requirements. (1086)

value-added lead time The time required to manufacture a unit of product or other output. (1071)

value-added ratio The ratio of the value-added lead time to the total lead time. (1071)

variable cost concept A concept used in applying the cost-plus approach to product pricing in which only the variable costs are included in the cost amount to which the markup is added. (968)

variable costing The concept that considers the cost of products manufactured to be composed only of those manufacturing costs that increase or decrease as the volume of production rises or falls (direct materials, direct labor, and variable factory overhead). (751, 788)

variable costs Costs that vary in total dollar amount as the level of activity changes. (746)

vertical analysis An analysis that compares each item in a current statement with a total amount within the same statement; the percentage analysis of component parts in relation to the total of the parts in a single financial statement. (117, 614)

volume variance The difference between the budgeted fixed overhead at 100% of normal capacity and the standard fixed overhead for the actual production achieved during the period. (890)

voucher A special form for recording relevant data about a liability and the details of its payment. (247)

voucher system A set of procedures for authorizing and recording liabilities and cash payments. (247)

work in process inventory The direct materials costs, the direct labor costs, and the applied factory overhead costs that have entered into the manufacturing process but are associated with products that have not been finished. (663)

work sheet A working paper that accountants may use to summarize adjusting entries and the account balances for the financial statements. (140)

working capital The excess of the current assets of a business over its current liabilities. (160)

yield A measure of materials usage efficiency. (717)

zero-based budgeting A concept of budgeting that requires all levels of management to start from zero and estimate budget data as if there had been no previous activities in their units. (838)

Abbreviations and Acronyms Commonly Used in Business and Accounting

AAA	American Accounting Association
ABC	Activity-based costing
AICPA	American Institute of Certified Public Accountants
CIA	Certified Internal Auditor
CIM	Computer-integrated manufacturing
CMA	Certified Management Accountant
CPA	Certified Public Accountant
Cr.	Credit
Dr.	Debit
EFT	Electronic funds transfer
EPS	Earnings per share
FAF	Financial Accounting Foundation
FASB	Financial Accounting Standards Board
FEI	Financial Executives International
FICA tax	Federal Insurance Contributions Act tax
FIFO	First-in, first-out
FOB	Free on board
GAAP	Generally accepted accounting principles
GASB	Governmental Accounting Standards Board
GNP	Gross National Product
IMA	Institute of Management Accountants
IRC	Internal Revenue Code
IRS	Internal Revenue Service
JIT	Just-in-time
LIFO	Last-in, first-out
Lower of C or M	Lower of cost or market
MACRS	Modified Accelerated Cost Recovery System
n/30	Net 30
n/eom	Net, end-of-month
P/E Ratio	Price-earnings ratio
POS	Point of sale
ROI	Return on investment
SEC	Securities and Exchange Commission
TQC	Total quality control

Classification of Accounts

Account Title	Account Classification	Normal Balance	Financial Statement
Accounts Payable	Current liability	Credit	Balance sheet
Accounts Receivable	Current asset	Debit	Balance sheet
Accumulated Depreciation	Contra fixed asset	Credit	Balance sheet
Accumulated Depletion	Contra fixed asset	Credit	Balance sheet
Advertising Expense	Operating expense	Debit	Income statement
Allowance for Doubtful Accounts	Contra current asset	Credit	Balance sheet
Amortization Expense	Operating expense	Debit	Income statement
Bonds Payable	Long-term liability	Credit	Balance sheet
Building	Fixed asset	Debit	Balance sheet
_____ Capital	Owners' equity	Credit	Statement of owner's equity/ Balance sheet
Capital Stock	Stockholders' equity	Credit	Balance sheet
Cash	Current asset	Debit	Balance sheet
Cash Dividends	Stockholders' equity	Debit	Retained earnings statement
Cash Dividends Payable	Current liability	Credit	Balance sheet
Common Stock	Stockholders' equity	Credit	Balance sheet
Cost of Merchandise (Goods) Sold	Cost of merchandise (goods sold)	Debit	Income statement
Deferred Income Tax Payable	Current liability/Long-term liability	Credit	Balance sheet
Depletion Expense	Operating expense	Debit	Income statement
Discount on Bonds Payable	Long-term liability	Debit	Balance sheet
Dividend Revenue	Other income	Credit	Income statement
Dividends	Stockholders' equity	Debit	Retained earnings statement
Employees Federal Income Tax Payable	Current liability	Credit	Balance sheet
Equipment	Fixed asset	Debit	Balance sheet
Exchange Gain	Other income	Credit	Income statement
Exchange Loss	Other expense	Debit	Income statement
Factory Overhead (Overapplied)	Deferred credit	Credit	Balance sheet (interim)
Factory Overhead (Underapplied)	Deferred debit	Debit	Balance sheet (interim)
Federal Income Tax Payable	Current liability	Credit	Balance sheet
Federal Unemployment Tax Payable	Current liability	Credit	Balance sheet
Finished Goods	Current asset	Debit	Balance sheet
Gain on Disposal of Fixed Assets	Other income	Credit	Income statement
Gain on Redemption of Bonds	Other income	Credit	Income statement
Gain on Sale of Investments	Other income	Credit	Income statement
Goodwill	Intangible asset	Debit	Balance sheet
Income Tax Expense	Income tax	Debit	Income statement
Income Tax Payable	Current liability	Credit	Balance sheet
Insurance Expense	Operating expense	Debit	Income statement
Interest Expense	Other expense	Debit	Income statement
Interest Receivable	Current asset	Debit	Balance sheet
Interest Revenue	Other income	Credit	Income statement
Investment in Bonds	Investment	Debit	Balance sheet
Investment in Stocks	Investment	Debit	Balance sheet
Investment in Subsidiary	Investment	Debit	Balance sheet
Land	Fixed asset	Debit	Balance sheet
Loss on Disposal of Fixed Assets	Other expense	Debit	Income statement
Loss on Redemption of Bonds	Other expense	Debit	Income statement
Loss on Sale of Investments	Other expense	Debit	Income statement
Marketable Securities	Current asset	Debit	Balance sheet
Materials	Current asset	Debit	Balance sheet